BRITISH ATHLETICS 2003

Compiled by the
National Union of Track Statisticians

Editors: Rob Whittingham & Peter Matthews

Assistant Editors: Tony Miller, Ian Hodge and Martin Rix

Published by: Umbra Athletics Limited,
Unit 1 Bredbury Business Park,
Bredbury Park Way, Bredbury, Stockport, SK6 2SN
Tel: 0161 406 6320   Fax: 0161 406 6732

ISBN 0 9540390 3 3

Front Cover: Paula Radcliffe - An incredible year

Photos: All photographs provided by Mark Shearman,
22, Grovelands Road, Purley, Surrey, CR8 4LA
Tel: 020 8660 0156   Fax: 020 8660 3437
His help is greatly appreciated

Distributed by: Umbra Athletics Limited,
Unit 1 Bredbury Business Park,
Bredbury Park Way, Bredbury, Stockport, SK6 2SN
Tel: 0161 406 6320   Fax: 0161 406 6732

Printed in
Great Britain by: Clowes Group,
Beccles, Suffolk, NR34 9QE

CONTENTS

NATIONAL UNION OF TRACK STATISTICIANS AND COMPILERS

ABBREVIATIONS & NOTES

A - mark set at altitude over 1000m	q - quarter final
a - automatic timing only known to one tenth of a second	r - race number
	s - semi final
D - performance made in a Decathlon	t - track
dh - downhill	u - unofficial time
e - estimated time	un - unconfirmed performance
et - extra trial	w - wind assisted (> 2.0 m/sec)
ex - exhibition	W - wind assisted (over 4m/sec in decathlon/heptathlon)
h - heat	
H - performance made in a Heptathlon	x - relay team may include outside age-group members
hc - handicap race	
i - indoor	+ - intermediate time
jo - jump off	* - legal performance where best is wind assisted
m - position in race when intermediate time taken	
	" - photo electric cell time
mx- performance in mixed race	# - Unratified (may not be ratifiable)
O -performance made in an Octathlon	& - as yet unratified
o - over age	§ - now competes for another nation
P - performance made in a Pentathlon	¶ - drugs ban (as per IAAF)
Q - qualifying round	

AGE GROUP DESIGNATIONS

U13 - Under 13   (born 1.9.89 or later)   U15 - Under 15   (born 1.9.87 to 31.8.89)
U17 - Under 17   (born 1.9.85 to 31.8.87)   U20 - Under 20   (born 1.1.83 to 31.8.85)
Vxx - Veteran   (age 40 or over Men)   Vxx - Veteran   (age 35 or over Women)

Care must be taken with very young age groups for athletes with an unknown date of birth
from Northern Ireland since their age groups differ slightly.

Italics indicates the athlete competes for a British club but is not eligible to represent Britain.

MULTI - EVENTS

Pentathlon, Heptathlon and Decathlon lists show the complete breakdown of individual
performances in the following order:

Pentathlon (women) - 100mH, SP, HJ, LJ, 800m; Junior: LJ, SP, 75mH, HJ, 800m
Heptathlon (women) - 100mH, HJ, SP, 200m (1st day); LJ, JT, 800m (2nd day) (80mH - Inters)
Decathlon (men)   - 100m, LJ, SP, HJ, 400m (1st day); 110mH, DT, PV, JT, 1500m (2nd day)

Totals which include performances made with following winds in excess of 4 m/s are
denoted by W. The date shown is the second day of competition.

RANKING LISTS:

These show the best performances in each event recorded during the 2002 season.
For each performance the following details are shown:

Performance; wind reading (where appropriate);   name (with, where appropriate, age-group category);
date of birth (DDMMYY);   position in competition;   venue;   date.

The following numbers are used, although strength of performance or lack of information may vary
the guidelines -

50 perfomances   100 athletes for each standard event

Age Groups - 40 Under 20, 30 Under 17, 20 Under 15, 10 Under 13

In the junior men, athletes are shown in older age groups if their performances merit this,
e.g. an U15 can appear in the U17 list etc. For junior women, athletes are shown in their age group as
per womens rules, although juniors of any age will be shown in the main list on merit.

INDEX

Club details and previous personal bests, where better than those recorded in 2002, are shown in the
index for all athletes in the main lists.

VENUES

Tim Grose has done major research on all British Tracks and a full list was shown in the 2000
annual; this list will be repeated in some subsequent annuals - full details at www.runtrackdir.com
  (London tracks for clarification)

LONDON (B)   Barn Elms Sports Ground, Rocks Lane, Barnes (6L, 8S)
LONDON (BP)   Millenium Arena, Battersea Park
LONDON (Cat)   Ladywell Arena, Silvermere Road, Catford (6L, 8S)
LONDON (Col)   Metropolitan Police (Hendon) Track, Hendon Police Training Coll, Colindale (7L, 7S)
LONDON (CP)   Crystal Palace National Sports Centre, Ledrington Road
LONDON (Cr)   Croydon Sports Arena, Albert Road
LONDON (DC)   Dulwich College, College Road, Dulwich (300m, 6L, 6S)
LONDON (Elt)   Sutcliffe Park, Eltham Road (6L, 8S)
LONDON (FP)   Finsbury Park, Endymion Road (6L, 10S)
LONDON (Ha)   New River Sports Centre, White Hart Lane, Wood Green, Haringey
LONDON (He)   Barnet Copthall Stadium, Great North Way, Hendon
LONDON (ME)   Mile End Stadium, Rhodeswell Road
LONDON (Nh)   Terence McMillan Stadium, Newham Leisure Centre, Plaistow
LONDON (Pa)   Paddington Recreation Ground, Randolph Avenue (6L, 6S)
LONDON (PH)   Parliament Hill Fields, Highgate Road, Hampstead
LONDON (SP)   Southwark Park, Hawkstone Road, Surrey Quays (7L, 7S)
LONDON (TB)   Tooting Bec Athletics Track, Tooting Bec Road
LONDON (WF)   Waltham Forest Track, Chingford Road, Walthamstow
LONDON (Wil)   Willesden Sports Stadium, Donnington Road (6L, 8S)
LONDON (WL)   Linford Christie Stadium, Du Cane Road, West London
LONDON (WP)   Wimbledon Park, Home Park Road (6L, 8S)

INTRODUCTION - by Rob Whittingham

Last year in my introduction, I was upbeat about British performances despite a poor showing in the World Championships. This year I am a little more cautious despite a good medal haul in both Commonwealth Games and European Championships. The Commonwealth Games were magnificent and everyone associated with the Manchester games should stand proud. However the medal successes at these championships can flatter; only two weeks later some champions could not qualify for the finals in Munich. The greatest worry is that Britain performed very badly in the World Junior Championships and, with several of our senior stars close to retirement, there will be gaps in our team for some time to come.

Regular readers will know that I do not generally comment on individual athletes in the introduction, but 2002 has been a special year for one British athlete. Paula Radcliffe has had such an exceptional year that it should be brought to all readers' attention. Both Peter Matthews and I feel that Paula's performances last year may represent the best year ever for a British competitor. Such is Paula's prominence that she now ranks fifth amongst the British male marathon runners ! It is hoped that Paula can continue at this level, or better, in 2003. I would like to see her compete more often on the track, although I am aware of the rigours imposed on an athlete running world class marathons as well.

I must, as ever, thank all the people who contribute to the Annual. Peter Matthews makes an enormous contribution in both time and accuracy to keep the Annual at a high standard. Tony Miller continues to improve the standard of the women's lists and as always Ian Hodge contributes in many areas. The new junior compilers are now producing excellent lists and all the stalwarts maintain their standards year on year.

Julie Fletcher from Umbra has taken over even more areas of the book helping to reduce my workload. Marty still encourages me in this venture, this being my twelfth year as editor, and helps to finalise the book each year.

A small change has been made to the book this year. I have corrected an anomoly which has existed for many years with Manchester venues. They are now shown in the same way as London venues with an identification in brackets.
Manchester (Wy) - Wythenshawe, Manchester (Str) - Stretford and the stadium that was used for the Commonwealth Games - Manchester (C) - City of Manchester Stadium.

Peter Matthews and I have started a new website www.britishathletics.info which I hope you find of interest.

This year the book is being supported by AAA of England for which I am grateful.

As usual any corrections are always welcome.

Rob Whittingham
March 2003

7 Birch Green   Glossop   SK13 8PR
e-mail rob@umbra.co.uk

UK ATHLETICS AND OTHER ADDRESSES

UK Athletics
Athletics House
10 Harborne Road
Edgbaston
Birmingham   B15 3AA
Tel: 0121 456 5098

AAA of England
Edgbaston House
3 Duchess Place
Hagley Road
Birmingham B16 8NM
Tel: 0121 452 1500

SCOTLAND
Scotland A.F.
Caledonia House
Reheughs Rigg, South Gyle
Edinburgh EH12 9DQ
Tel: 0131 317 7320

WALES
A.A. of Wales
Catash Road
Catash
Newport NP18 1WA
Tel: 01633 423833

NORTHERN IRELAND
Northern Ireland A.A.F.
Honorary Secretary: J.Allen
Athletics House
Old Coach Road
Belfast BT9 5PR
Tel: 02890 602707

Midland Counties A.A.
11th Floor Edgbaston House
3 Duchess Place
Hagley Road
Birmingham
B16 8NM
Tel: 0121 456 1896

North of England A.A.
Studio 106, EMCO House
5/7 New York Road
Leeds LS2 7PJ
Tel: 01532 461835

South of England A.A.
23 Mitcham Lane
Streatham
London SW16 6LQ
Tel: 0208 664 7244

Commonwealth Games Councils:
England
General Secretary: Miss A.Hogbin
Tavistock House South, Tavistock Square
London WC1H 9JZ
Tel: 0207 388 6643

Northern Ireland
Honorary Secretary: R.J.McColgan MBE
22 Mountcoole Park, Cave Hill
Belfast BT14 8JR
Tel: 01232 716558

Scotland
Honorary Secretary: G.A.Hunter OBE
139 Old Dalkeith Road
Little France
Edinburgh EH16 4SZ
Tel: 0131 664 1070

Wales
Honorary Secretary: M.John MBE
Pennant
Blaenau, Ammanford
Dyfed SA18 3BZ
Tel: 0269 850390

British Athletics League
Honorary Secretary: D. Jeacock
16 Church Street
Wotton Bassett
Wilts SN4 7BQ

National Young Athletes' League
Honorary Secretary: N. Bailey
15 Chaseley Avenue
Cannock
Staffs WS11 1JG
Tel: 01543 574624

Supporters Club - British Athletics Club
Honorary Secretary: Mrs M.Pieri
11 Railway Road
Newbury, Berks RG14 7PE
Tel: 01635 33400

Sports Council
The Sports Council
16 Upper Woburn Place
London WC1H OQP
Tel: 0171 388 1277

Athletics Weekly
Editor: Jason Henderson
Descartes Publishing Limited
83 Park Road, Peterborough PE1 2TN
Tel: 01733 898440

National Union of Track Statisticians
Secretary: Dr. S. Hitchcock
54 Woodbury Avenue
Petersfield GU32 2EB
Tel: 01730 260278

MAJOR OUTDOOR FIXTURES IN 2003

MAY

3-5	British Universities Championships	Gateshead
10-11	County Championships	Various
10-11	Scottish District Championships	Various
25-26	CAU Inter Counties Championships	Bedford

JUNE

1	Bedford International Games	Bedford
7	Northern Ireland Championships	Belfast
12	LAT v Eng v Wal v Others	Riga, LAT
14	LAT v Eng v Wal v Others	Ventspils, LAT
14	English County Schools Championships	Various
14-15	AAA Combined Events Championships	Stoke
20-21	Scottish Championships	Scotstoun, Glasgow
21-22	Welsh Championships	Cwmbran
21-22	Area Championships	Various
21-22	SPAR European Cup Super League	Florence, ITA
28-29	Norwich Union AAA U23 & U20 Champs	Bedford
29	Norwich Union Challenge GBR v USA v RUS	Scotstoun, Glasgow

JULY

5	ITA v GBR v POL U20	Naples, ITA
5	HUN v Eng v Others U23	Debrecen, HUN
5-6	European Cup Combined Events	Tallinn, EST
9-13	IAAF World Youth Championships	Sherbrooke, CAN
11-12	English Schools Championships	Sheffield
17-20	European U23 Championships	Bydgoszcz, POL
19-20	FRA v GBR v Others U23 & U20 Combined Events	FRA
24-27	European Junior Championships	Tampere, FIN
25-27	Norwich Union World Trials & AAA Championships	Birmingham

AUGUST

2	GBR v FRA U23	Ashford
8	Norwich Union London Grand Prix	Crystal Palace, London
16-17	AAA U17 & U15 Championships	Sheffield
23-29	World Student Games	Daegu, KOR
23-31	IAAF World Championships	Paris, FRA

SEPTEMBER

12-13	1st IAAF World Athletics Final	Monte Carlo, MON
21	BUPA Great North Run	Tyneside

OCTOBER

4	IAAF World Half Marathon Championships	Vilamoura, POR

DECEMBER

14	European Cross Country Championships	Edinburgh

RECORDS - MEN
as at 31 December 2002

W = World, E = European, C = Commonwealth, A = UK All-Comers, N = UK, J = Junior

Event	Cat	Mark		Name	Nat	Date			Place
100m	W	9.78		Tim Montgomery	USA	14	Sep	02	Paris (C)
	E,N	9.87		Linford Christie		15	Aug	93	Stuttgart
		9.87		Dwain Chambers		14	Sep	02	Paris (C)
	C	9.84		Donovan Bailey	CAN	27	Jul	96	Atlanta
		9.84		Bruny Surin	CAN	22	Aug	99	Seville
	A	9.97		Maurice Greene	USA	7	Aug	99	London (CP)
	WJ	10.05	#	Davidson Ezinwa	NGR	4	Jan	90	Bauchi
	WJ,EJ,NJ	10.06		Dwain Chambers		25	Jul	97	Ljubljana
200m	W	19.32		Michael Johnson	USA	1	Aug	96	Atlanta
	E	19.72	A	Pietro Mennea	ITA	12	Sep	79	Mexico City
	C	19.68		Frank Fredericks	NAM	1	Aug	96	Atlanta
	A	19.85		Michael Johnson	USA	6	Jul	90	Edinburgh
	N	19.87	A#	John Regis		31	Jul	94	Sestriere
		19.94		John Regis		20	Aug	93	Stuttgart
	WJ	20.07	#	Lorenzo Daniel	USA	18	May	85	Starkville
		20.13		Roy Martin	USA	16	Jun	85	Indianapolis
	EJ,NJ	20.29		Christian Malcolm		19	Sep	98	Kuala Lumpur
300m	W	30.85	A	Michael Johnson	USA	24	Mar	00	Pretoria
	E,C,A,N	31.56		Doug Walker	Sco	19	Jul	98	Gateshead
	WJ	32.08	+	Steve Lewis	USA	28	Sep	88	Seoul
	EJ,NJ	32.53		Mark Richardson		14	Jul	91	London (Ha)
400m	W	43.18		Michael Johnson	USA	26	Aug	99	Seville
	E	44.33		Thomas Schönlebe	GER	3	Sep	87	Rome
	C	44.17		Innocent Egbunike	NGR	19	Aug	87	Zürich
	A	43.98		Michael Johnson	USA	10	Jul	92	London (CP)
	N	44.36		Iwan Thomas		13	Jul	97	Birmingham
	WJ	43.87		Steve Lewis	USA	28	Sep	88	Seoul
	EJ	45.01		Thomas Schönlebe	GER	15	Jul	84	Berlin
	NJ	45.36		Roger Black		24	Aug	85	Cottbus
600m	W	1:12.81		Johnny Gray	USA	24	May	86	Santa Monica
	E	1:14.41		Andrea Longo	ITA	30	Aug	00	Roverto
	C	1:13.2		John Kipkurgat	KEN	23	Mar	74	Pointe-à-Pierre
	A,N	1:14.95		Steve Heard		14	Jul	91	London (Ha)
	WJ	1:14.8	A	Mark Winzenreid	USA	31	Aug	68	Echo Summit
	NJ	1:16.79		Andrew Lill		24	Jul	90	Mansfield
800m	W,E	1:41.11		Wilson Kipketer	DEN	24	Aug	97	Cologne
	C,N	1:41.73	"	Sebastian Coe	Eng	10	Jun	81	Florence
	A	1:43.22		Steve Cram		31	Jul	86	Edinburgh
	WJ	1:43.64		Japheth Kimutai	KEN	13	Aug	97	Zürich
	EJ	1:44.33		Yuriy Borzakovskiy	RUS	25	Sep	00	Sydney
	NJ	1:45.64		David Sharpe		5	Sep	86	Brussels
1000m	W,C	2:11.96		Noah Ngeny	KEN	17	Jul	99	Nice
	E,N	2:12.18		Sebastian Coe		11	Jul	81	Oslo
	A	2:12.88		Steve Cram		9	Aug	85	Gateshead
	WJ	2:15.00		Benjamin Kipkurui	KEN	17	Jul	99	Nice
	EJ	2:17.40		Yuriy Borzakovskiy	RUS	8	Jul	00	Nice
	NJ	2:18.98		David Sharpe		19	Aug	86	Birmingham
1500m	W	3:26.00		Hicham El Guerrouj	MAR	14	Jul	98	Rome
	E	3:28.95		Fermín Cacho	ESP	13	Aug	97	Zürich
	C	3:26.34		Bernard Lagat	KEN	24	Aug	01	Brussels
	A	3:30.2		Hicham El Guerrouj	MAR	5	Aug	00	London (CP)
	N	3:29.67		Steve Cram		16	Jul	85	Nice

1500m	WJ	3:30.24		Cornelius Chirchir	KEN	19 Jul 02	Monaco
	EJ	3:35.51		Reyes Estévez	SPA	16 Aug 95	Zürich
	NJ	3:36.6		Graham Williamson		17 Jul 79	Oslo
1 Mile	W	3:43.13		Hicham El Guerrouj	MAR	7 Jul 99	Rome
	E,N	3:46.32		Steve Cram	Eng	27 Jul 85	Oslo
	C	3:43.40		Noah Ngeny	KEN	7 Jul 99	Rome
	A	3:45.96		Hicham El Guerrouj	MAR	5 Aug 00	London (CP)
	WJ	3:50.41		Noah Ngeny	KEN	16 Jul 97	Nice
	EJ,NJ	3:53.15		Graham Williamson		17 Jul 79	Oslo
2000m	W	4:44.79		Hicham El Guerrouj	MAR	7 Sep 99	Berlin
	E,N	4:51.39		Steve Cram		4 Aug 85	Budapest
	C	4:48.74		John Kibowen	KEN	1 Aug 98	Hechtel
	A	4:48.36		Hicham El Guerrouj	MAR	19 Jul 98	Gateshead
	WJ	4:59.14		Ali Saïdi-Sief	ALG	29 Jun 97	Villeneuve d'Ascq
	EJ	5:04.4		Harald Hudak	GER	30 Jun 76	Oslo
	NJ	5:06.56		Jon Richards		7 Jul 82	Oslo
3000m	W,C	7:20.67		Daniel Komen	KEN	1 Sep 96	Rieti
	E	7:26.62		Mohammed Mourit	BEL	18 Aug 00	Monaco
	A	7:29.69		Haile Gebrselassie	ETH	7 Aug 99	London (CP)
	N	7:32.79		Dave Moorcroft		17 Jul 82	London (CP)
	WJ	7:30.67		Kenenisa Bekele	KEN	24 Aug 01	Brussels
	EJ	7:43.20		Ari Paunonen	FIN	22 Jun 77	Cologne
	NJ	7:48.28		Jon Richards		9 Jul 83	Oslo
2 Miles	W,C	7:58.61		Daniel Komen	KEN	19 Jul 97	Hechtel
	E	8:13.2	i#	Emiel Puttemans	BEL	18 Feb 73	Berlin
	E,N	8:13.51		Steve Ovett		15 Sep 78	London (CP)
	A	8:01.72		Haile Gebrselassie	ETH	7 Aug 99	London (CP)
	WJ	8:13.47		Richard Limo	KEN	30 May 99	Hengelo
	EJ,NJ	8:28.31		Steve Binns		31 Aug 79	London (CP)
5000m	W	12:39.36		Haile Gebreselassie	ETH	13 Jun 98	Helsinki
	E	12:49.71		Mohammed Mourit	BEL	25 Aug 00	Brussels
	C	12:39.74		Daniel Komen	KEN	22 Aug 97	Brussels
	A	12:50.38	i#	Haile Gebrselassie	ETH	14 Feb 99	Birmingham
		13:06.23		Haile Gebrselassie	ETH	5 Aug 00	London (CP)
	N	13:00.41		Dave Moorcroft		7 Jul 82	Oslo
	WJ	12:53.72		Philip Mosima	KEN	5 Jun 96	Rome
	EJ,NJ	13:27.04		Steve Binns		14 Sep 79	London (CP)
10000m	W	26:22.75		Haile Gebreselassie	ETH	1 Jun 98	Hengelo
	E	26:52.30		Mohammed Mourhit	BEL	3 Sep 99	Brussels
	C	26:27.85		Paul Tergat	KEN	22 Aug 97	Brussels
	A	27:20.38		Aloÿs Nizigama	BUR	7 Jul 95	London (CP)
	N	27:18.14	#	Jon Brown		28 Aug 98	Brussels
		27:23.06		Eamonn Martin		2 Jul 88	Oslo
	WJ	27:11.18		Richard Chelimo	KEN	25 Jun 91	Hengelo
	EJ	28:22.48		Christian Leuprecht	ITA	4 Sep 90	Koblenz
	NJ	29:21.9		Jon Brown		21 Apr 90	Walnut
20000m	W	56:55.6		Arturo Barrios	MEX	30 Mar 91	La Flèche
	E	57:18.4		Dionisio Castro	POR	31 Mar 90	La Flèche
	C,N	57:28.7		Carl Thackery	Eng	31 Mar 90	La Flèche
	A	58:39.0		Ron Hill		9 Nov 68	Leicester
1 Hour	W	21,101 m		Arturo Barrios	MEX	30 Mar 91	La Flèche
	E	20,944 m		Jos Hermens	HOL	1 May 76	Papendal
	C,N	20,855 m		Carl Thackery	Eng	31 Mar 90	La Flèche
	A	20,472 m		Ron Hill		9 Nov 68	Leicester
	NJ	18,221 m		Eddie Twohig		16 Jun 81	Leamington

25000m	W	1:13:55.8	Toshihiko Seko	JAP	22	Mar	81	Christchurch, NZL
	E	1:13:57.6	Stéphane Franke	GER	30	Mar	99	Walnut
	C,A,N	1:15:22.6	Ron Hill	Eng	21	Jul	65	Bolton
30000m	W	1:29:18.78	Toshihiko Seko	JAP	22	Mar	81	Christchurch, NZL
	E,C,A,N	1:31:30.4	Jim Alder	Sco	5	Sep	70	London (CP)
Half	W,C	59:06	Paul Tergat	KEN	26	Mar	00	Lisbon
Marathon	E	59:43	António Pinto	POR	15	Mar	98	Lisbon
	A	59:58	Paul Kosgei	KEN	6	Oct	02	South Shields
	N	60:09 #	Paul Evans		15	Jan	95	Marrakech
		60:59	Steve Jones		8	Jun	86	South Shields
	WJ	59:37	Faustin Baha	TAN	26	Mar	00	Lisbon
	NJ	66:41	Stuart Jones		12	Jun	88	Weaverham
Marathon	W,A	2:05:38	Khalid Khannouchi	USA	14	Apr	02	London
	E	2:06:36	António Pinto	POR	16	Apr	00	London
	C	2:05:48	Paul Tergat	KEN	14	Apr	02	London
	N	2:07:13	Steve Jones		20	Oct	85	Chicago
	WJ	2:10:46	Li Zhuhong	CHN	14	Oct	01	Beijing
	NJ	2:23:28	Eddie Twohig		28	Mar	82	Wolverhampton
2000m SC	W,C	5:14.43	Julius Kariuki	KEN	21	Aug	90	Rovereto
	E	5:15.96	Bouabdallah Tahri	FRA	19	Jun	02	Tomblaine
	A	5:19.68	Samson Obwocha	KEN	19	Jul	86	Birmingham
	N	5:19.86	Mark Rowland		28	Aug	88	London (CP)
	WJ,EJ	5:25.01	Arsenios Tsiminos	GRE	2	Oct	80	Athens
	NJ	5:29.61	Colin Reitz		18	Aug	79	Bydgoszcz
3000m SC	W	7:55.28	Brahim Boulami ¶	MAR	24	Aug	01	Brussels, BEL
	(W	7:53.17 #	Brahim Boulami ¶	MAR	16	Aug	02	Zurich)
	E	8:06.91	Simon Vroemen	NED	19	Jul	02	Monaco
	C	7:55.72	Bernard Barmasai	KEN	24	Aug	97	Cologne
	A	8:08.11	Patrick Sang	KEN	7	Jul	95	London (CP)
	N	8:07.96	Mark Rowland		30	Sep	88	Seoul
	WJ	7:58.66	Stephen Cherono	KEN	24	Aug	01	Brussels, BEL
	EJ	8:29.50	Ralf Pönitzsch	GER	19	Aug	76	Warsaw
	NJ	8:29.85	Paul Davies-Hale		31	Aug	81	London (CP)
110m H	W,E,C,N	12.91	Colin Jackson	Wal	20	Aug	93	Stuttgart
	A	13.03	Colin Jackson		4	Sep	94	Sheffield
	WJ	13.12	Liu Xiang	CHN	2	Jul	02	Lausanne
	EJ,NJ	13.44	Colin Jackson		19	Jul	86	Athens
200m H	W,E	22.55	Laurant Ottoz	ITA	31	May	95	Milan
	C	22.59	Darryl Wohlsen	AUS	14	Mar	96	Brisbane
	A,N	22.63	Colin Jackson		1	Jun	91	Cardiff
	NJ	24.02	Paul Gray		13	Sep	87	London (CP)
400m H	W	46.78	Kevin Young	USA	6	Aug	92	Barcelona
	E	47.37	Stéphane Diagana	FRA	5	Jul	95	Lausanne
	C	47.10	Samuel Matete	ZAM	7	Aug	91	Zürich
	A	47.67	Kevin Young	USA	14	Aug	92	Sheffield
	N	47.82	Kriss Akabusi		6	Aug	92	Barcelona
	WJ	48.02	Danny Harris	USA	17	Jun	84	Los Angeles
	EJ	48.74	Vladimir Budko	RUS	18	Aug	84	Moscow
	NJ	50.22	Martin Briggs		28	Aug	83	Schwechat
High	W	2.45	Javier Sotomayor	CUB	27	Jul	93	Salamanca
Jump	E	2.42	Patrik Sjöberg	SWE	30	Jun	87	Stockholm
		2.42 i#	Carlo Thränhardt	GER	26	Feb	88	Berlin
	C,N	2.38 i#	Steve Smith	Eng	4	Feb	94	Wuppertal
	C	2.38	Troy Kemp	BAH	12	Jul	95	Nice
	A	2.41	Javier Sotomayor	CUB	15	Jul	94	London (CP)

Event	Cat	Mark		Name	Country	Date	Location
High	N,WJ,EJ,NJ	2.37		Steve Smith		20 Sep 92	Seoul
Jump	N	2.37		Steve Smith		22 Aug 93	Stuttgart
	WJ,EJ	2.37		Dragutin Topic	YUG	12 Aug 90	Plovdiv
Pole	W,E	6.15	i#	Sergey Bubka	UKR	21 Feb 93	Donetsk
Vault		6.14	A	Sergey Bubka	UKR	31 Jul 94	Sestriere
	C	6.05		Dmitriy Markov	AUS	9 Aug 01	Edmonton
	A	6.05		Sergey Bubka	UKR	10 Sep 93	London (CP)
	N	5.81	i#	Nick Buckfield		8 Feb 02	Bad Segeberg
	N	5.80		Nick Buckfield		27 May 98	Hania
	WJ,EJ	5.80		Maksim Tarasov	RUS	14 Jul 89	Bryansk
	NJ	5.50		Neil Winter		9 Aug 92	San GiulianoTerme
Long	W	8.95		Mike Powell	USA	30 Aug 91	Tokyo
Jump	E	8.86	A	Robert Emmiyan	ARM	22 May 87	Tsakhkadzor
	C	8.62		James Beckford	JAM	5 Apr 97	Orlando
	A	8.54		Mike Powell	USA	10 Sep 93	London (CP)
	N	8.27		Chris Tomlinson		13 Apr 02	Tallahassee
	WJ	8.34		Randy Williams	USA	8 Sep 72	Munich
	EJ	8.24		Vladimir Ochkan	UKR	21 Jun 87	St. Petersburg
	NJ	8.03		Jonathan Moore		18 May 02	Loughborough
Triple	W,E,C,N	18.29		Jonathan Edwards	Eng	7 Aug 95	Gothenburg
Jump	A	18.00		Jonathan Edwards		27 Aug 95	London (CP)
	WJ,EJ	17.50		Volker Mai	GER	23 Jun 85	Erfurt
	NJ	16.58		Tosi Fasinro		15 Jun 91	Espoo
Shot	W	23.12		Randy Barnes	USA	20 May 90	Los Angeles (Ww)
	E	23.06		Ulf Timmermann	GER	22 May 88	Hania
	C	21.97		Janus Robberts	RSA	2 Jun 01	Eugene
	N	21.68		Geoff Capes		18 May 80	Cwmbrân
	A	22.28	#	Brian Oldfield	USA	18 Jun 75	Edinburgh
		21.75		John Godina	USA	17 Aug 97	London (CP)
	WJ	21.05	i#	Terry Albritton	USA	22 Feb 74	New York
		20.65	#	Mike Carter	USA	4 Jul 79	Boston
		20.39	A	Janus Robberts	RSA	7 Mar 98	Germiston
	EJ	20.20		Udo Beyer	GER	6 Jul 74	Leipzig
	NJ	19.46		Carl Myerscough		6 Sep 98	Blackpool
6kg	WJ,EJ	21.96		Edis Elkasevic	CRO	29 Jun 02	Zagreb, CRO
Discus	W,E	74.08		Jürgen Schult	GER	6 Jun 86	Neubrandenburg
	C	70.32		Frantz Kruger	RSA	26 May 02	Salon-de-Provence
	A	68.32		John Powell	USA	30 Aug 82	London (CP)
	N	66.64		Perriss Wilkins		6 Jun 98	Birmingham (Un)
	WJ	65.62	#	Werner Reiterer	AUS	15 Dec 87	Melbourne
	WJ,EJ	63.64		Werner Hartmann	GER	25 Jun 78	Strasbourg
	NJ	60.97		Emeka Udechuku		5 Jul 98	Bedford
1.75 kg	WJ	64.51		Wu Tao	CHN	18 Jul 02	Kingston, JAM
Hammer	W,E	86.74		Yuriy Sedykh	UKR/RUS	30 Aug 86	Stuttgart
	C	80.19		Chris Harmse	RSA	12 Apr 02	Pretoria
	A	85.60		Yuriy Sedykh	UKR/RUS	13 Jul 84	London (CP)
	N	77.54		Martin Girvan		12 May 84	Wolverhampton
	WJ,EJ	78.33		Olli-Pekka Karjalainen	FIN	5 Aug 99	Seinäjoki
	NJ	67.48		Paul Head		16 Sep 84	Karlovac
Javelin	W,E	98.48		Jan Zelezny	CZE	25 May 96	Jena
	C,N	91.46		Steve Backley	Eng	25 Jan 92	Auckland (NS)
	A	95.66		Jan Zelezny	CZE	29 Aug 93	Sheffield
	WJ,EJ	83.87		Andreas Thorkildsen	NOR	7 Jun 01	Fana
	NJ	79.50		Steve Backley		5 Jun 88	Derby
Pent.	W,A	4282		Bill Toomey	USA	16 Aug 69	London (CP)
	E	4273		Rein Aun	EST	18 Jul 68	Tartu
	C,N	3841		Barry King	Eng	20 May 70	Santa Barbara
	NJ	3112		Wayne Dubose		21 Jul 74	London (VP)

12

Dec.	W,E	9026	Roman Sebrle	CZE	27	May	01	Götzis
	C,N	8847	Daley Thompson	Eng	9	Aug	84	Los Angeles
	A	8663	Daley Thompson		28	Jul	86	Edinburgh
	WJ,EJ	8397	Torsten Voss	GER	7	Jul	82	Erfurt
	NJ	8082	Daley Thompson		31	Jul	77	Sittard
(with 1986 Javelin)								
	C,N	8811 #	Daley Thompson	Eng	28	Aug	86	Stuttgart
	WJ,EJ	8114 #	Michael Kohnle	GER	25	Aug	89	Varazdin
	NJ	7488 #	David Bigham		9	Aug	90	Plovdiv
4x100m	W	37.40	United States		8	Aug	92	Barcelona
		37.40	United States		21	Aug	93	Stuttgart
	E,N	37.73	UK National Team		29	Aug	99	Seville
	C	37.69	Canada		3	Aug	96	Atlanta
	A	37.95	United States		28	Aug	00	Gateshead
		37.93 #	Hudson Smith International	USA/TRI	22	Jul	01	London (CP)
	WJ	38.92	United States		21	Jul	02	Kingston, JAM
	EJ,NJ	39.05	UK National Team		22	Oct	00	Santiago
4x200m	W	1:18.68	Santa Monica T.C.	USA	17	Apr	94	Walnut
	E	1:21.10	Italy		29	Sep	83	Cagliari
	C	1:20.79	Jamaica		24	Apr	88	Walnut
	A,N	1:21.29	UK National Team		23	Jun	89	Birmingham
	NJ	1:25.40 i#	UK National Team		2	Mar	96	Liévin
		1:27.6	Borough of Enfield Harriers		13	Jun	82	London (He)
4x400m	W	2:54.20	United States		22	Jul	98	Uniondale
	E,N	2:56.60	UK National Team		3	Aug	96	Atlanta
	C	2:56.75	Jamaica		10	Aug	97	Athens
	A	2:59.85	UK National Team		19	Aug	96	Gateshead
	WJ	3:01.90	United States		20	Jul	86	Athens
	(EJ),NJ	3:03.80	UK National Team		12	Aug	90	Plovdiv
	EJ	3:04.58	East Germany		23	Aug	81	Utrecht
4x800m	WECAN	7:03.89	UK National Team	Eng	30	Aug	82	London (CP)
	NJ	7:26.2	BMC Junior Squad		2	Sep	95	Oxford
4x1500m	W,E	14:38.8	West Germany		16	Aug	77	Cologne
	C	14:40.4	New Zealand		22	Aug	73	Oslo
	A	15:04.7	Italy		5	Jun	92	Sheffield
	N	14:56.8 a#	BMC National Squad		23	Jun	79	Bourges
		15:04.6	UK National Team		5	May	76	Athens (NF)
	NJ	15:52.0	BMC Junior Squad		30	Apr	97	Watford
4x1Mile	W,E	15:49.08	Irish Republic		17	Aug	85	Dublin (B)
	C	15:59.57	New Zealand		1	Mar	83	Auckland
	A	16:21.1	BMC National Squad		10	Jul	93	Oxford
	N	16:17.4	Bristol A.C./Western Kentucky U		25	Apr	75	Des Moines
	NJ	16:56.8	BMC Junior Squad		10	Jul	93	Oxford

Track Walking

1500m	W,E	5:12.0	Algis Grigaliunas	LIT	12	May	90	Vilnius
	C	5:19.1	Dave Smith	AUS	7	Feb	83	Melbourne
	A,N	5:46.2 a	Roger Mills		29	Aug	75	London (CP)
	N	5:19.22 i#	Tim Berrett §		9	Feb	90	East Rutherford
1 Mile	W	5:33.53 i#	Tim Lewis	USA	5	Feb	88	New York
	W,E	5:36.9	Algis Grigaliunas	LIT	12	May	90	Vilnius
	C	5:54.6 i#	Marcel Jobin	CAN	16	Feb	80	Houston
	C,A,N	5:58.9 mx	Andy Penn	Eng	13	Aug	97	Rugby
	N	5:56.39 i#	Tim Berrett §		2	Feb	90	New York
	NJ	6:09.2	Phil Vesty		23	Jun	82	Leicester

Event	Cat	Time		Name	Nat	Date	Venue
3000m	W,E	10:47.11		Giovanni DeBenedictis	ITA	19 May 90	S. G. Valdarno
	C	10:56.22		Andrew Jachno	AUS	7 Feb 91	Melbourne
	A	11:10.02	imx#	Robert Heffernan	IRL	2 Feb 02	Cardiff
		11:19.9		Tim Berrett	CAN	20 Apr 92	Tonbridge
	N	11:24.4		Mark Easton		10 May 89	Tonbridge
	WJ,EJ	11:13.2		Jozef Pribilinec	SVK	28 Mar 79	Banská Bystrica
	NJ	11:54.23		Tim Berrett §		23 Jun 84	London (CP)
5000m	W	18:05.49		Hatem Ghoula	TUN	1 May 97	Tunis
	E	18:07.08	i#	Mikhail Shchennikov	RUS	14 Feb 95	Moscow
		18:17.22		Robert Korzeniowski	POL	3 Jul 92	Reims
	C	18:47.56	i#	Tim Berrett	CAN	20 Feb 93	Winnipeg
		18:51.39		Nick A'Hern	AUS	21 Feb 98	Auckland (NS)
	A	18:56.27	i#	Axel Noack	GER	23 Feb 90	Glasgow
	A,N	19:35.0		Darrell Stone		16 May 89	Brighton
	WJ,EJ	19:19.3		Mikhail Shchennikov	RUS	9 Aug 86	Chemnitz
	NJ	20:16.40		Philip King		26 Jun 93	Lübeck
10000m	W,E	38:02.60		Jozef Pribilinec	SVK	30 Aug 85	Banská Bystrica
	C	38:06.6		Dave Smith	AUS	25 Sep 86	Sydney
	A	39:26.02		Guillaume Leblanc	CAN	29 Jun 90	Gateshead
	N	40:06.65		Ian McCombie		4 Jun 89	Jarrow
	WJ,EJ	38:46.4		Viktor Burayev	RUS	20 May 00	Moscow
	NJ	41:52.13		Darrell Stone		7 Aug 87	Birmingham
(Road)	W,E	37:11		Roman Rasskazov	RUS	28 May 00	Saransk
	NJ	41:47		Darrell Stone		26 Sep 87	Paris
1 Hour	W	15,577 m		Bernardo Segura	MEX	7 May 94	Fana
	E	15,447 m		Jozef Pribilinec	SVK	6 Sep 86	Hildesheim
	C	15,300 m		Dave Smith	AUS	6 Sep 86	Hildesheim
	A	14,383 m		Anatoliy Solomin	UKR	26 Aug 77	Edinburgh
	N	14,324 m	#	Ian McCombie		7 Jul 85	London (SP)
		14,158 m		Mark Easton		12 Sep 87	Woodford
	NJ	13,487 m		Darrell Stone		12 Sep 87	Woodford
20000m	W	1:17:25.6		Bernardo Segura	MEX	7 May 94	Fana
	E	1:18:35.2		Stefan Johansson	SWE	15 May 92	Fana
	C	1:19:48.1		Nathan Deakes	AUS	4 Sep 01	Brisbane
	A	1:24:07.6	#	Phil Vesty		1 Dec 84	Leicester
		1:24:22.0		José Marín	ESP	28 Jun 81	Brighton
	N	1:23:26.5		Ian McCombie		26 May 90	Fana
	WJ,EJ	1:21:29.2	#	Viktor Burayev	RUS	4 Sep 01	Brisbane
	WJ	1:22:16.0		Li Mingcai	CHN	3 Mar 90	Donetsk
	EJ	1:22:42		Andrey Perlov	RUS	6 Sep 80	Hefei
	NJ	1:31:34.4		Gordon Vale		28 Jun 81	Brighton
2 Hours	W,E	29,572 m		Maurizio Damilano	ITA	4 Oct 92	Cuneo
	C	28,800 m	#	Guillaume Leblanc	CAN	16 Jun 90	Sept Îles
		27,720 m		Craig Barratt	NZL	19 Jul 98	Auckland
	A,N	27,262 m	#	Chris Maddocks		31 Dec 89	Plymouth
	A	26,265 m		Jorge Llopart	ESP	28 Jun 81	Brighton
	N	26,037 m		Ron Wallwork		31 Jul 71	Blackburn
30000m	W,E	2:01:44.1		Maurizio Damilano	ITA	4 Oct 92	Cuneo
	C	2:04:55.7		Guillaume Leblanc	CAN	16 Jun 90	Sept Îles
	A,N	2:11:54	#	Chris Maddocks		31 Dec 89	Plymouth
	A	2:17:26.4		Jorge Llopart	ESP	28 Jun 81	Brighton
	N	2:19:18		Chris Maddocks		22 Sep 84	Birmingham
50000m	W,E	3:40:57.9		Thierry Toutain	FRA	29 Sep 96	Héricourt
	C	3:43:50.0		Simon Baker	AUS	9 Sep 90	Melbourne
	A	4:03:52		Gerhard Weidner	GER	1 Jun 75	Woodford
	N	4:05:44.6		Paul Blagg		26 May 90	Fana

Race Walking - Fastest Recorded Times

20km	W,E	1:17:22	Francisco Fernandez	ESP	28 Apr 02	Turku
	C	1:18:14	Nathan Deakes	AUS	16 Jun 01	Dublin
	A	1:20:18	Francisco Fernández	ESP	23 Apr 00	Leamington
	N	1:22:03	Ian McCombie		23 Sep 88	Seoul
	WJ,EJ	1:18:06	Viktor Burayev	RUS	4 Mar 01	Adler
	NJ	1:26:13	Tim Berrett §		25 Feb 84	Dartford
30km	W,E	2:01:44.1 t	Maurizio Damilano	ITA	4 Oct 92	Cuneo
	C	2:04:55.7 t	Guillaume Leblanc	CAN	16 Jun 90	Sept Îles
	A	2:07:47	Simon Baker	AUS	31 Jul 86	Edinburgh
	N	2:07:56	Ian McCombie		27 Apr 86	Edinburgh
	WJ,EJ	2:10:19.4 t	Ralf Kowalsky	GER	29 Mar 81	Berlin (E)
	NJ	2:30:46	Phil Vesty		31 Jul 82	London (VP)
50km	W,E	3:36:39	Robert Korzeniowski	POL	8 Aug 02	Munich
	C	3:43:13	Simon Baker	AUS	28 May 89	L'Hospitalet
	A	3:47:31	Hartwig Gauder	GER	28 Sep 85	St. John's, IoM
	N	3:51:37	Chris Maddocks		28 Oct 90	Burrator
	WJ	4:00:04	Hao Huanquan	CHN	10 Apr 94	Beijing
	EJ	4:07:23	Aleksandr Volgin	RUS	27 Sep 86	Zhytomyr
	NJ	4:18:18	Gordon Vale		24 Oct 81	Lassing

RECORDS set in 2002

100m	W		9.78		Tim Montgomery	USA	14 Sep 02	Paris (C)
	E,N		9.87		Dwain Chambers		14 Sep 02	Paris (C)
1500m	WJ		3:30.24		Cornelius Chirchir	KEN	19 Jul 02	Monaco
H. Mar	A		59:58		Paul Kosgei	KEN	6 Oct 02	South Shields
Marathon	W,A		2:05:38		Khalid Khannouchi	MAR	14 Apr 02	London
	C		2:05:48		Paul Tergat	KEN	14 Apr 02	London
2000SC	E		5:15.96		Boubdallah Tahri	FRA	19 Jun 02	Tomblaine
3000SC	E		8:06.91		Simon Vroemen	NED	19 Jul 02	Monaco
	(W		7:53.17	#	Brahim Boulami ¶	MAR	16 Aug 02	Zurich)
110H	WJ		13.12		Liu Xiang	CHN	2 Jul 02	Lausanne
PV	N		5.81	i#	Nick Buckfield		8 Feb 02	Bad Segeberg
LJ	N		8.27		Chris Tomlinson		13 Apr 02	Tallahassee
	NJ		8.03		Jonathan Moore		18 May 02	Loughborough
SP (6kg)	WJ,EJ		21.96		Edis Elkasevic	CRO	29 Jun 02	Zagreb, CRO
DT	C		70.32		Frantz Kruger	RSA	26 May 02	Salon-de-Provence
(1.75 kg)	WJ		64.51		Wu Tao	CHN	18 Jul 02	Kingston, JAM
HT	C		80.19		Chris Harmse	RSA	12 Apr 02	Pretoria
4x100	WJ		38.92		United States		21 Jul 02	Kingston, JAM

Track Walking

3000m	A	11:10.02	imx#	Robert Heffernan	IRL	2 Feb 02	Cardiff

Race Walking

20kWR	W,E	1:17:22	Francisco Fernandez	ESP	28 Apr 02	Turku
50kWR	W,E	3:36:39	Robert Korziowski	POL	8 Aug 02	Munich

RECORDS - WOMEN

as at 31 December 2002

100m	W	10.49		Florence Griffith Joyner	USA	16 Jul 88	Indianapolis
	E	10.73		Christine Arron	FRA	19 Aug 98	Budapest
	C	10.74		Merlene Ottey	JAM	7 Sep 96	Milan
	A	10.78		Marion Jones	USA	5 Aug 00	London (CP)
	N	11.10		Kathy Smallwood/Cook		5 Sep 81	Rome
	WJ,EJ	10.88		Marlies Oelsner/Göhr	GER	1 Jul 77	Dresden
	NJ	11.27	A	Kathy Smallwood/Cook		9 Sep 79	Mexico City

Event	Cat	Time	Athlete	Country	Date			Place
200m	W	21.34	Florence Griffith Joyner	USA	29	Sep	88	Seoul
	E	21.71	Marita Koch	GER	10	Jun	79	Chemnitz
		21.71 #	Marita Koch	GER	21	Jul	84	Potsdam
		21.71	Heike Drechsler	GER	29	Jun	86	Jena
		21.71 #	Heike Drechsler	GER	29	Aug	86	Stuttgart
	C	21.64	Merlene Ottey	JAM	13	Sep	91	Brussels
	A	22.20	Debbie Ferguson	BAH	29	Jul	02	Manchester (C)
	N	22.10	Kathy Cook		9	Aug	84	Los Angeles
	WJ,EJ	22.19	Natalya Bochina	RUS	30	Jul	80	Moscow
	NJ	22.70 A	Kathy Smallwood/Cook		12	Sep	79	Mexico City
300m	W,E	35.00 +	Marie-José Pérec	FRA	27	Aug	91	Tokyo
		34.1 +	Marita Koch	GER	6	Oct	85	Canberra
	C,A,N	35.46	Kathy Cook	Eng	18	Aug	84	London (CP)
	A	35.46	Chandra Cheeseborough	USA	18	Aug	84	London (CP)
	WJ,EJ	36.24 +	Grit Breuer	GER	29	Aug	90	Split
		35.4 +	Christina Brehmer/Lathan	GER	29	Jul	76	Montréal
	NJ	36.46	Linsey Macdonald		13	Jul	80	London (CP)
		36.2	Donna Murray/Hartley		7	Aug	74	London (CP)
400m	W,E	47.60	Marita Koch	GER	6	Oct	85	Canberra
	C	48.63	Cathy Freeman	AUS	29	Jul	96	Atlanta
	A	49.33	Tatána Kocembová	CZE	20	Aug	83	London (CP)
	N	49.43	Kathy Cook		6	Aug	84	Los Angeles
	WJ,EJ	49.42	Grit Breuer	GER	27	Aug	91	Tokyo
	NJ	51.16	Linsey Macdonald		15	Jun	80	London (CP)
600m	W	1:22.63	Ana Fidelia Quirot	CUB	25	Jul	97	Guadalajara
	E	1:23.5	Doina Melinte	ROM	27	Jul	86	Poiana Brasov
	C	1:22.87	Maria Lurdes Mutola	MOZ	27	Aug	02	Naimette-Xhovemont
	A	1:25.90	Delisa Walton-Floyd	USA	28	Aug	88	London (CP)
	N	1:26.0	Kelly Holmes	Eng	13	Aug	95	Gothenburg
	WJ,EJ	1:25.2	Vera Nikolic	YUG		Jun	67	Belgrade
	NJ	1:27.33	Lorraine Baker		13	Jul	80	London (CP)
800m	W,E	1:53.28	Jarmila Kratochvílová	CZE	26	Jul	83	Munich
	C	1:55.29	Maria Lurdes Mutola	MOZ	24	Aug	97	Cologne
	A	1:57.14	Jarmila Kratochvílová	CZE	24	Jun	85	Belfast
	N	1:56.21	Kelly Holmes		9	Sep	95	Monaco
	WJ	1:57.18	Wang Yuan	CHN	8	Sep	93	Beijing
	EJ	1:57.45 #	Hildegard Ullrich	GER	31	Aug	78	Prague
		1:59.17	Birte Bruhns	GER	20	Jul	88	Berlin
	NJ	1:59.75	Charlotte Moore		29	Jul	02	Manchester (C)
1000m	W,E	2:28.98	Svetlana Masterkova	RUS	23	Aug	96	Brussels
	C	2:29.66	Maria Lurdes Mutola	MOZ	23	Aug	96	Brussels
	A	2:32.08 i#	Maria Lurdes Mutola	MOZ	10	Feb	96	Birmingham
	A,N	2:32.55	Kelly Holmes		15	Jun	97	Leeds
	WJ,EJ	2:35.4 a	Irina Nikitina	RUS	5	Aug	79	Podolsk
		2:35.4	Kathrin Wühn	GER	12	Jul	84	Potsadam
	NJ	2:38.58	Jo White		9	Sep	77	London (CP)
1500m	W	3:50.46	Qu Yunxia	CHN	11	Sep	93	Beijing
	E	3:52.47	Tatyana Kazankina	RUS	13	Aug	80	Zürich
	C	3:57.41	Jackline Maranga	KEN	8	Aug	98	Monaco
	A,N	3:58.07	Kelly Holmes		29	Jun	97	Sheffield
	WJ	3:51.34	Lang Yinglai	CHN	18	Oct	97	Shanghai
	(EJ,)NJ	3:59.96	Zola Budd/Pieterse		30	Aug	85	Brussels
	EJ	4:03.45	Anita Weyermann	SUI	3	Jul	96	Lausanne
1 Mile	W,E	4:12.56	Svetlana Masterkova	RUS	14	Aug	96	Zürich
	C,N,WJ,EJ,NJ	4:17.57	Zola Budd/Pieterse	Eng	21	Aug	85	Zürich
	A	4:19.59	Mary Slaney	USA	2	Aug	85	London (CP)
2000m	W,E,A	5:25.36	Sonia O'Sullivan	IRL	8	Jul	94	Edinburgh
	C,N	5:26.93	Yvonne Murray	Sco	8	Jul	94	Edinburgh
	WJ,EJ,NJ	5:33.15	Zola Budd/Pieterse		13	Jul	84	London (CP)

Event		Time	Name	Nat	Date			Place
3000m	W	8:06.11	Wang Junxia	CHN	13	Sep	93	Beijing
	E	8:21.42	Gabriela Szabo	ROM	19	Jul	02	Monaco
	A	8:21.64	Sonia O'Sullivan	IRL	15	Jul	94	London (CP)
	C,N	8:22.20	Paula Radcliffe	Eng	19	Jul	02	Monaco
	WJ,EJ,NJ	8:28.83	Zola Budd/Pieterse		7	Sep	85	Rome
2 Miles	W	9:11.97 mx	Regina Jacobs	USA	12	Aug	99	Los Gatos
	W,E	9:19.56	Sonia O'Sullivan	IRL	27	Jun	98	Cork
	C	9:27.18	Kathy Butler	CAN	27	Jun	98	Cork
	A	9:27.6 +e	Paula Radcliffe		22	Jul	01	London (CP)
	A,N	9:32.07	Paula Radcliffe		23	May	99	Loughborough
	N	9:27.5 +e	Paula Radcliffe		22	Aug	97	Brussels
	NJ	9:29.6	Zola Budd/Peiterse		26	Aug	85	London (CP)
		10:35.10	Jane Potter		23	May	99	Loughborough
5000m	W	14:28.09	Jiang Bo	CHN	23	Oct	97	Shanghai
	E	14:29.32	Olga Yegorova	RUS	31	Aug	01	Berlin
	C,A,N	14:31.42	Paula Radcliffe	Eng	28	Jul	02	Manchester (C)
	WJ	14:39.96 #	Yin Lili	CHN	23	Oct	97	Shanghai
		14:45.90	Jiang Bo	CHN	24	Oct	95	Nanjing
	(EJ,)NJ	14:48.07	Zola Budd/Pieterse		26	Aug	85	London (CP)
	EJ	14:56.22	Annemari Sandell	FIN	8	Jul	96	Stockholm
10000m	W	29:31.78	Wang Junxia	CHN	8	Sep	93	Beijing
	E,C,N	30:01.09	Paula Radcliffe	Eng	6	Aug	02	Munich
	A	30:52.51	Elana Meyer	RSA	10	Sep	94	London (CP)
	WJ	30:39.41	Lan Lixin	CHN	19	Oct	97	Shanghai
	EJ	31:40.42	Annemari Sandell	FIN	27	Jul	96	Atlanta
	NJ	33:10.6 #	Charlotte Dale		20	Apr	02	Manchester (Str)
1 Hour	W,C	18,393 m #	Tegla Loroupe	KEN	3	Sep	00	Borgholzhausen
	W,C	18,340 m	Tegla Loroupe	KEN	7	Aug	98	Borgholzhausen
	E	18,084 m	Silvana Cruciata	ITA	4	May	81	Rome
	A,N	16,460 m i#	Bronwen Cardy-Wise		8	Mar	92	Birmingham
	N	16,495 m #	Michaela McCallum		2	Apr	00	Asti
	A,N	16,364 m	Alison Fletcher		3	Sep	97	Bromley
	NJ	14,580 m	Paula Simpson		20	Oct	93	Bebington
20000m	W,C	1:05:26.6	Tegla Loroupe	KEN	3	Sep	00	Borgholzhausen
	W	1:06:48.8	Izumi Maki	JPN	19	Sep	93	Amagasaki
	E	1:06:55.5 #	Rosa Mota	POR	14	May	83	Lisbon
	A,N	1:15:46	Caroline Hunter-Rowe	Eng	6	Mar	94	Barry
25000m	W,C	1:27:05.84	Tegla Loroupe	KEN	21	Sep	02	Mengerskirchen
	E	1:29:29.2	Karolina Szabó	HUN	22	Apr	88	Budapest
	A,N	1:35:16	Caroline Hunter-Rowe	Eng	6	Mar	94	Barry
30000m	W,E	1:47:05.6	Karolina Szabó	HUN	22	Apr	88	Budapest
	C,A,N	1:55:03	Caroline Hunter-Rowe	Eng	6	Mar	94	Barry
Half	W,C	65:44 #	Susan Chepkemei	KEN	1	Apr	01	Lisbon
Marathon	W	66:43	Masako Chiba	JAP	19	Jan	97	Tokyo
	E	66:40 #	Ingrid Kristiansen	NOR	5	Apr	87	Sandnes
	E,A,N	66:47	Paula Radcliffe		7	Oct	01	Bristol
	C	66:44	Elana Meyer	RSA	15	Jan	99	Tokyo
	WJ	69:05	Delillah Asiago	KEN	5	May	91	Exeter
	NJ	77:52	Kathy Williams		28	Mar	82	Barry
Marathon	W,E,C,N	2:17:18	Paula Radcliffe	Eng	13	Oct	02	Chicago
	A	2:18:56	Paula Radcliffe		14	Apr	02	London
	WJ	2:23:37	Liu Min	CHN	14	Oct	01	Beijing
	NJ	2:50:09	Siobhan Quenby		16	Oct	83	Milan
2000m SC	W,E	6:11.84	Marina Pluzhnikova	RUS	25	Jul	94	St. Petersburg
	C,A	6:19.00	Irene Limika	KEN	20	May	01	Loughborough
	N	6:29.79	Tara Krzywicki		20	May	01	Loughborough
	WJ	6:25.77	Melissa Rollison	AUS	1	May	00	Sydney
	EJ	6:31.31	Yelena Sayko	UKR	13	Jul	97	Kiev
	NJ	6:55.04	Jo Ankier		22	Jul	01	Grosseto

3000m SC	W,E	9:16.51		Aleysa Turova	BLR	27 Jul 02	Gdansk
	C,WJ	9:30.70		Melissa Rollison	AUS	4 Sep 01	Brisbane
	A	9:48.72		Elizabeth Jackson	USA	1 Jul 01	Glasgow (S)
	N	9:52.71		Tara Krzywicki	Eng	1 Jul 01	Glasgow (S)
	EJ	10:02.42		Galina Yegorova	RUS	11 Jul 02	Cheboksary
	NJ	12:11.1		Lindsey Oliver		22 Aug 93	Horsham
100m H	W,E	12.21		Yordanka Donkova	BUL	20 Aug 88	Stara Zagora
	C	12.44		Glory Alozie	NGR	28 Aug 99	Seville
	A	12.51		Ginka Zagorcheva	BUL	12 Sep 86	London (CP)
	N	12.80		Angie Thorp		31 Jul 96	Atlanta
	WJ	12.76	#	Liu Jing	CHN	18 Oct 97	Shanghai
		12.84		Aliuska López	CUB	16 Jul 87	Zagreb
	EJ	12.88		Yelena Ovcharova	UKR	25 Jun 95	Villeneuve d'Ascq
	NJ	13.25		Diane Allahgreen		21 Jul 94	Lisbon
400m H	W	52.61		Kim Batten	USA	11 Aug 95	Gothenburg
	E,C,N	52.74		Sally Gunnell	Eng	19 Aug 93	Stuttgart
	A	53.69		Sandra Farmer-Patrick	USA	10 Sep 93	London (CP)
	WJ	54.70		Lashinda Demus	USA	19 Jul 02	Kingston, JAM
	EJ	55.26		Ionela Tîrlea	ROM	12 Jul 95	Nice
	NJ	57.27		Vicki Jamison		28 Jul 96	Bedford
High Jump	W,E	2.09		Stefka Kostadinova	BUL	30 Aug 87	Rome
	C	2.04		Hestrie Cloete	RSA	4 Aug 99	Monaco
	A	2.03		Ulrike Meyfarth	GER	21 Aug 83	London (CP)
		2.03		Tamara Bykova	RUS	21 Aug 83	London (CP)
	N	1.95		Diana Elliott/Davies		26 Jun 82	Oslo
		1.95	i#	Debbie Marti		23 Feb 97	Birmingham
		1.95		Susan Jones		24 Jun 01	Bremen
	WJ,EJ	2.01	#	Olga Turchak KZK/UKR		7 Jul 86	Moscow
		2.01		Heike Balck	GER	18 Jun 89	Chemnitz
	NJ	1.91		Lea Haggett		2 Jun 91	Hania
		1.91		Susan Jones		31 Aug 97	Catania
Pole Vault	W	4.81		Stacy Dragila	USA	9 Jun 01	Palo Alto
	E	4.78		Svetlana Feofanova	RUS	16 Jul 02	Stockholm
	C	4.60		Emma George	AUS	20 Feb 99	Sydney
	A	4.72		Stacy Dragila	USA	22 Jul 01	London (CP)
	N	4.41	i#	Janine Whitlock ¶		17 Feb 02	Birmingham
	N	4.40		Janine Whitlock ¶		14 Jul 01	Birmingham
	WJ,EJ	4.46	#	Yelena Isinbayeva	RUS	31 Aug 01	Berlin
		4.40		Yelena Isinbayeva	RUS	24 Jul 00	Tula
	NJ	4.00		Kate Dennison		18 Jul 02	Kingston, JAM
		4.00		Zoe Brown		28 Jul 02	Manchester (C)
Long Jump	W,E	7.52		Galina Chistyakova	RUS	11 Jun 88	St. Petersburg
	C	7.00		Bronwyn Thompson	AUS	7 Mar 02	Melbourne
	N,NJ	6.90		Beverly Kinch	Eng	14 Aug 83	Helsinki
	A	7.14		Galina Chistyakova	RUS	24 Jun 89	Birmingham
	WJ,EJ	7.14	#	Heike Daute/Drechsler	GER	4 Jun 83	Bratislava
Triple Jump	W,E	15.50		Inessa Kravets	UKR	10 Aug 95	Gothenburg
	C,N	15.16	i#	Ashia Hansen	Eng	28 Feb 98	Valencia
		15.15		Ashia Hansen	Eng	13 Sep 97	Fukuoka
	A	14.98		Tatyana Lebedyeva	RUS	16 Jul 00	Gateshead
	WJ,EJ	14.62		Tereza Marinova	BUL	25 Aug 96	Sydney
	NJ	13.05		Michelle Griffith		16 Jun 90	London (CP)
Shot	W,E	22.63		Natalya Lisovskaya	RUS	7 Jun 87	Moscow
	C	19.74		Gael Mulhall/Martin	AUS	14 Jul 84	Berkeley
	A	21.95		Natalya Lisovskaya	RUS	29 Jul 88	Edinburgh
	N	19.36		Judy Oakes		14 Aug 88	Gateshead
	WJ,EJ	20.54		Astrid Kumbernuss	GER	1 Jul 89	Orimattila
	NJ	17.10		Myrtle Augee		16 Jun 84	London (CP)

18

Discus	W,E	76.80	Gabriele Reinsch	GER	9	Jul	88	Neubrandenburg
	C	68.72	Daniela Costian	AUS	22	Jan	94	Auckland
	A	73.04	Ilke Wyludda	GER	5	Aug	89	Gateshead
	N	67.48	Meg Ritchie		26	Apr	81	Walnut
	WJ,EJ	74.40	Ilke Wyludda	GER	13	Sep	88	Berlin
	NJ	55.03	Claire Smithson		30	Jul	02	Manchester (C)
Hammer	W,E	76.07	Mihaela Melinte	ROM	29	Aug	99	Rüdingen
	C	70.19 #	Bronwyn Eagles	AUS	30	Jul	01	Calgary
		69.65	Bronwyn Eagles	AUS	23	Mar	02	Adelaide
		69.65	Bronwyn Eagles	AUS	14	Apr	02	Brisbane
	A	71.73	Olga Kuzenkova	RUS	18	Aug	02	Glasgow (S)
	N	68.15	Lorraine Shaw		17	Mar	01	Nice/Boulouris
	WJ,EJ	71.71	Kamila Skolimowska	POL	9	Sep	01	Melbourne
	NJ	57.97	Rachael Beverley		25	Jul	98	Birmingham
Javelin	W	71.54	Osleidys Menéndez	CUB	1	Jul	01	Rethymno
	E	69.48	Trine Hattestad	NOR	28	Jul	00	Oslo
	C	66.80	Louise Currey	AUS	5	Aug	00	Gold Coast (RB)
	A,N	64.87	Kelly Morgan		14	Jul	02	Birmingham
	WJ	61.99	Wang Yaning	CHN	14	Oct	99	Huizhou
	EJ	61.79 #	Nikolett Szabó	HUN	23	May	99	Schwechat
	EJ	61.52	Nikolett Szabó	HUN	8	Aug	99	Riga
	NJ	54.61	Kelly Morgan		4	Sep	99	Exeter
Hept.	W	7291	Jackie Joyner-Kersee	USA	24	Sep	88	Seoul
	E	7007	Larisa Nikitina	RUS	11	Jun	89	Bryansk
	C,N	6831	Denise Lewis	Eng	30	Jul	00	Talence
	A	6419	Birgit Clarius	GER	21	Jul	91	Sheffield
	WJ,EJ	6542	Carolina Kluft	SWE	10	Aug	02	Munich
	NJ	5833	Joanne Mulliner		11	Aug	85	Lons-le-Saunier
(with 1999 Javelin)								
	W,E	6861	Eunice Barber	FRA	22	Aug	99	Seville
	A	5719	Barbora Potáková	CZE	21	May	00	Hexham
	NJ	5283	Chloe Cozens		23	May	99	Alhama de Murcia
4x100m	W,E	41.37	East Germany		6	Oct	85	Canberra
	C	41.92	Bahamas		29	Aug	99	Seville
	A	41.87	East Germany		5	Aug	89	Gateshead
	N	42.43	UK National Team		1	Aug	80	Moscow
	WJ,EJ	43.33 #	East Germany		20	Jul	88	Berlin
	WJ	43.38	United States		11	Jul	99	Tampa
	EJ	43.48	East Germany		31	Jul	88	Sudbury
	NJ	44.16	UK National Team		12	Aug	90	Plovdiv
4x200m	W	1:27.46	United States		29	Apr	00	Philadelphia
	E	1:28.15	East Germany		9	Aug	80	Jena
	C	1:30.23	Jamaica		28	Apr	01	Philadelphia
	N	1:31.57	UK National Team		20	Aug	77	London (CP)
	A	1:31.49	Russia		5	Jun	93	Portsmouth
	NJ	1:38.34 i#	UK National Team		2	Mar	96	Liévin
		1:42.2	London Olympiades AC		19	Aug	72	Bracknell
4x400m	W,E	3:15.17	U.S.S.R.		1	Oct	88	Seoul
	C	3:20.65	Jamaica		12	Aug	01	Edmonton
	A	3:20.79	Czechoslovakia		21	Aug	83	London (CP)
	N	3:22.01	UK National Team		1	Sep	91	Tokyo
	WJ,EJ	3:28.39	East Germany		31	Jul	88	Sudbury
	NJ	3:30.46	UK National Team		21	Jul	02	Kingston, JAM
4x800m	W,E	7:50.17	U.S.S.R.		5	Aug	84	Moscow
	C	8:20.73	UK National Team	Eng	5	Jun	93	Portsmouth
	A	7:57.08	Russia		5	Jun	93	Portsmouth
	N	8:19.9	UK National Team		5	Jun	92	Sheffield
	NJ	8:39.6	BMC Junior Squad		17	Jul	96	Watford
4x1500m	W,C,A	17:09.75	Australia		25	Jun	00	London (BP)

4x1500m	E	17:19.09		Irish Republic		25 Jun 00	London (BP)
	N	17:41.0		BMC National Squad	Eng	30 Apr 97	Watford
	NJ	18:38.0		BMC Junior Squad		30 Apr 97	Watford
4x1Mile	W	18:39.58		University of Oregon		3 May 85	Eugene
	ECAN	19:17.3		BMC National Squad	Eng	10 Jul 93	Oxford
	NJ	20:16.2		BMC Junior Squad		11 Jun 97	Watford

Track Walking

1500m	W,E	5:47.03	#	Kjersti Tysee Platzer	NOR	1 Sep 02	Knarvik, NOR
	W,C	5:50.41		Kerry Saxby-Junna	AUS	20 Jan 91	Sydney
	E	5:53.0		Sada Eidikyte	LIT	12 May 90	Vilnius
	A	6:04.5	i#	Beate Anders/Gummelt	GER	4 Mar 90	Glasgow
	A,NJ	6:58.5		Carol Tyson		5 Sep 76	Gateshead
	N	6:32.16		Niobe Menendez		13 Aug 00	Tullamore
1 Mile	W,E	6:16.45	#	Kjersti Plätzer	NOR	2 Sep 01	Knarvik
		6:19.31		Ileana Salvador	ITA	15 Jun 91	Siderno
	C	6:35.47	i#	Ann Peel	CAN	15 Feb 87	Fairfax
		6:47.9		Sue Cook	AUS	14 Mar 81	Canberra
	A	6:30.7	i#	Beate Anders/Gummelt	GER	4 Mar 90	Glasgow
	N	7:08.9	mx#	Catherine Charnock		22 Aug 00	Rugby
	A,N	7:14.3		Carol Tyson		17 Sep 77	London (PH)
	NJ	7:31.6		Kate Horwill		22 Aug 93	Solihull
3000m	W,E	11:40.33	i#	Claudia Iovan	ROM	30 Jan 99	Bucharest
		11:48.24		Ileana Salvador	ITA	29 Aug 93	Padua
	C	11:51.26		Kerry Saxby-Junna	AUS	7 Feb 91	Melbourne
	A	12:32.37		Yelena Nikolayeva	RUS	19 Jun 88	Portsmouth
	N	12:49.16		Betty Sworowski		28 Jul 90	Wrexham
	WJ,EJ	12:21.7	i#	Susana Feitór	POR	19 Feb 94	Braga
		12:24.47		Claudia Iovan	ROM	24 Jul 97	Ljubljana
	NJ	13:03.4		Vicky Lupton/White		18 May 91	Sheffield
5000m	W,E	20:02.60		Gillian O'Sullivan	IRL	13 Jul 02	Dublin (S)
	A	21:08.65		Yelena Nikolayeva	RUS	19 Jun 88	Portsmouth
	N	21:42.51		Lisa Kehler		13 Jul 02	Birmingham
	WJ,EJ	20:31.4		Irina Stankina	RUS	10 Feb 96	Adler
	NJ	22:36.81		Vicky Lupton/White		15 Jun 91	Espoo
5k(Road)	WJ,EJ	20:24		Lyudmila Yefimkina	RUS	28 May 00	Saransk
	N	21:36		Vicky Lupton/White		18 Jul 92	Sheffield
10000m	W,E	41:56.23		Nadezhda Ryashkina	RUS	24 Jul 90	Seattle
	C	41:57.22		Kerry Saxby-Junna	AUS	24 Jul 90	Seattle
	A,N	45:09.57		Lisa Kehler		13 Aug 00	Birmingham
	WJ	42:49.7		Gao Hongmiao	CHN	15 Mar 92	Jinan
	EJ	43:35.2		Lyudmila Yefimkina	RUS	20 May 00	Moscow
	NJ	47:04		Vicky Lupton		30 Mar 91	Sheffield (W)
1 Hour	W	13,194 m		Victoria Herazo	USA	5 Dec 92	Santa Monica
	E	12,913 m		Valentina Sachuk	UKR	24 Jun 99	Belaya Tserkov
	C	12,805 m		Wendy Muldoon	AUS	25 Jun 94	Melbourne
	A,N,NJ	11,590 m		Lisa Langford/Kehler		13 Sep 86	Woodford
20000m	W,E	1:26:52.3		Olimpiada Ivanova	RUS	6 Sep 01	Brisbane
	C	1:33:40.2		Kerry Saxby-Junna	AUS	6 Sep 01	Brisbane
	A,N	1:56:59.7		Cath Reader		21 Oct 95	Loughborough
	WJ	1:37:33.9		Gao Kelian	CHN	18 Sep 99	Xian
	EJ	1:39:20.5		Vera Santos	POR	4 Aug 00	Almada
2 Hours	W,C	22,747 m		Carolyn Vanstan	AUS	20 Jun 92	Melbourne
	E	22,239 m		Jana Zárubová	CZE	12 Oct 85	Prague
	A,N	20,502 m		Cath Reader		21 Oct 95	Loughborough
30000m	W,E	2:56:36.0		Cinzia Chianda	ITA	18 Oct 86	Limbiate
50000m	W,E	4:55:19.4		Svetlana Bychenkova	RUS	27 Jun 98	St. Petersburg
	C,N	5:26:59		Sandra Brown	Eng	27 Oct 90	Étréchy

Road Walking - Fastest Recorded Times

10km	W,E	41:04		Yelena Nikolayeva	RUS	20 Apr 96	Sochi
	C	41:30		Kerry Saxby-Junna	AUS	27 Aug 88	Canberra
	A	43:39		Kjersti Tysse Plätzer	NOR	14 Sep 02	Leamington
	N	45:03		Lisa Kehler		19 Sep 98	Kuala Lumpur
	WJ,EJ	41:55		Irina Stankina	RUS	11 Feb 95	Adler
	NJ	47:04 t		Vicky Lupton/White		30 Mar 91	Sheffield (W)
20km	W,E	1:24:50		Olimpiada Ivanova	RUS	4 Mar 01	Adler
	C	1:28:56		Jane Saville	AUS	6 May 00	Vallensbæk
	A	1:28:40		Liu Hongyu	CHN	23 Apr 00	Leamington
	N	1:33:57		Lisa Kehler		17 Jun 00	Eisenhüttenstadt
	WJ,EJ	1:27:35		Natalya Fedoskina	RUS	2 May 99	Mézidon-Canon
	NJ	1:52:03		Vicky Lupton/White		13 Oct 91	Sheffield
50km	W,E	4:34:16		Yelena Ginko	BLR	29 Oct 01	Scanzorosciate
	C,A,N	4:50:51		Sandra Brown	Eng	13 Jul 91	Basildon
	WJ,EJ	4:54:10		Nadyezhda Putilova	RUS	8 Sep 02	St. Petersburg

RECORDS set in 2002

200m	A	22.20		Debbie Ferguson	BAH	29 Jul 02	Manchester (C)
600m	C	1:22.87		Maria Lurdes Mutola	MOZ	27 Aug 02	Naimette-Xhovemont
800m	NJ	2:00.95		Charlotte Moore		28 Jul 02	Manchester (C)
	NJ	1:59.75		Charlotte Moore		29 Jul 02	Manchester (C)
3000m	E	8:21.42		Gabriela Szabo	ROM	19 Jul 02	Monaco
	C,N	8:22.20		Paula Radcliffe	Eng	19 Jul 02	Monaco
5000m	C,A,N	14:31.42		Paula Radcliffe	Eng	28 Jul 02	Manchester (C)
10000m	NJ	33:10.6 #		Charlotte Dale		20 Apr 02	Manchester (Str)
25000m	W,C	1:27:05.84		Tegla Loroupe	KEN	21 Sep 02	Mengerskirchen
Marathon	A	2:18:56		Paula Radcliffe		14 Apr 02	London
	W,E,C,N	2:17:18		Paula Radcliffe	Eng	13 Oct 02	Chicago
3000SC	W,E	9:22.29		Justyna Bak	POL	5 Jun 02	Milan
	W,E	9:21.72		Aleysa Turova	BLR	12 Jun 02	Ostrava
	EJ	10:02.42		Galina Yegorova	RUS	11 Jul 02	Cheboksary
	W,E	9:16.51		Aleysa Turova	BLR	27 Jul 02	Gdansk
400H	WJ	54.85		Lashinda Demus	USA	31 May 02	Baton Rouge
	WJ	54.70		Lashinda Demus	USA	19 Jul 02	Kingston, JAM
PV	N	4.44 i#		Janine Whitlock		17 Feb 02	Birmingham
	NJ	3.91 i#		Kate Denison		23 Feb 02	Birmingham
	E=	4.75 i#		Svetlana Feofanova	RUS	3 Mar 02	Vienna
	E	4.76		Svetlana Feofanova	RUS	16 Jun 02	Villeneuve d, Ascq
	NJ	3.95		Kate Denison		29 Jun 02	Bedford
	E	4.77		Annika Becker	GER	7 Jul 02	Bochum
	E	4.78		Svetlana Feofanova	RUS	16 Jul 02	Stockholm
	NJ	4.00		Kate Dennison		18 Jul 02	Kingston, JAM
	NJ	4.00		Zoe Brown		28 Jul 02	Manchester (C)
LJ	C	6.91 i#		Elva Goulbourne	JAM	23 Feb 02	Fayetteville
	C	7.00		Bronwyn Thompson	AUS	7 Mar 02	Melbourne
DT	NJ	54.90		Claire Smithson		4 Jun 02	Bedford
	NJ	55.03		Claire Smithson		30 Jul 02	Manchester (C)
HT	C	69.38		Bronwyn Eagles	AUS	10 Feb 02	Campbelltown
	C	69.65		Bronwyn Eagles	AUS	23 Mar 02	Adelaide
	C	69.65		Bronwyn Eagles	AUS	14 Apr 02	Brisbane
	A	71.73		Olga Kuzenkova	RUS	18 Aug 02	Glasgow (S)
JT	N	63.03		Kelly Morgan		15 Jun 02	Manchester (C)
	A,N	63.87		Kelly Morgan		14 Jul 02	Birmingham
	A,N	64.87		Kelly Morgan		14 Jul 02	Birmingham
Hept.	WJ,EJ	6470		Carolina Kluft	SWE	20 Jul 02	Kingston, JAM
	WJ,EJ	6542		Carolina Kluft	SWE	10 Aug 02	Munich
4x400	NJ	3:30.46		UK National Team		21 Jul 02	Kingston, JAM
1500WT	W,E	5:47.03 #		Kjersti Tysee Platzer	NOR	1 Sep 02	Knarvik, NOR
5000WT	N	21:42.51		Lisa Kehler		13 Jul 02	Birmingham
	W,E	20:02.60		Gillian O'Sullivan	IRL	13 Jul 02	Dublin (S)
10kWR	A	43:39		Kjersti Tysse Plätzer	NOR	14 Sep 02	Leamington
50kWR	WJ,EJ	4:54:10		Nadyezhda Putilova	RUS	8 Sep 02	St. Petersburg

21

NATIONAL RECORDS OF THE UK - MEN
as at 31 December 2002

These are the best authentic performances for the four home countries of the U.K.
E = England S = Scotland W = Wales NI = Northern Ireland

100m	E	9.87		Linford Christie	15	Aug 93	Stuttgart, GER
		9.87		Dwain Chambers	14	Sep 02	Paris (C), FRA
	S	10.11		Allan Wells	24	Jul 80	Moscow, RUS
	W	10.11		Christian Malcolm	5	Aug 01	Edmonton, CAN
	NI	10.46		Mark Forsythe	17	Jun 89	Tel Aviv, ISR
200m	E	19.87	A#	John Regis	31	Jul 94	Sestriere, ITA
		19.94		John Regis	20	Aug 93	Stuttgart, GER
	W	20.08		Christian Malcolm	8	Aug 01	Edmonton, CAN
	S	20.21		Allan Wells	28	Jul 80	Moscow, RUS
	NI	20.81		Paul McBurney	24	Aug 94	Victoria, CAN
300m	S	31.56		Dougie Walker	19	Jul 98	Gateshead
	E	31.67		John Regis	17	Jul 92	Gateshead
	W	32.06		Jamie Baulch	31	May 97	Cardiff
	NI	33.77		Simon Baird	24	Jun 85	Belfast
400m	W	44.36		Iwan Thomas	13	Jul 97	Birmingham
	E	44.37		Roger Black	3	Jul 96	Lausanne, SUI
		44.37		Mark Richardson	9	Jul 98	Oslo, NOR
		44.37		Mark Richardson	8	Aug 98	Monaco, MON
	S	44.93		David Jenkins	21	Jun 75	Eugene, USA
	NI	45.85		Paul McBurney	13	Jul 97	Birmingham
		45.58		Paul McKee (IRL per IAAF)	14	Jul 02	Dublin (S), IRL
600m	E	1:14.95		Steve Heard	14	Jul 91	London (Ha)
	S	1:15.4		Tom McKean	21	Jul 91	Grangemouth
	W	1:17.8	i	Bob Adams	20	Dec 80	Cosford
		1:18.02		Glen Grant	2	Aug 78	Edmonton, CAN
	NI	1:18.3	i	Joe Chivers	14	Dec 74	Cosford
		1:20.1		Kenneth Thompson	24	May 80	Belfast
800m	E	1:41.73	"	Sebastian Coe	10	Jun 81	Florence, ITA
	S	1:43.88		Tom McKean	28	Jul 89	London (CP)
	W	1:45.44		Neil Horsfield	28	Jul 90	Wrexham
	NI	1:45.52		James McIlroy	28	Aug 02	Roverto, ITA
		1:45.32		while representing IRL	16	Jul 98	Nice
1000m	E	2:12.18		Sebastian Coe	11	Jul 81	Oslo, NOR
	S	2:16.82		Graham Williamson	17	Jul 84	Edinburgh
	W	2:17.36		Neil Horsfield	9	Aug 91	Gateshead
	NI	2:19.05		Mark Kirk	5	Aug 87	Oslo, NOR
		2:15.57		James McIlroy (IRL perIAAF)	5	Sep 99	Rieti, ITA
1500m	E	3:29.67		Steve Cram	16	Jul 85	Nice, FRA
	S	3:33.83		John Robson	4	Sep 79	Brussels, BEL
	NI	3:34.76		Gary Lough	9	Sep 95	Monaco, MON
	W	3:35.08		Neil Horsfield	10	Aug 90	Brussels, BEL
1 Mile	E	3:46.32		Steve Cram	27	Jul 85	Oslo, NOR
	S	3:50.64		Graham Williamson	13	Jul 82	Cork, IRL
	W	3:54.39		Neil Horsfield	8	Jul 86	Cork, IRL
	NI	3:55.0		Jim McGuinness	11	Jul 77	Dublin (B), IRL
2000m	E	4:51.39		Steve Cram	4	Aug 85	Budapest, HUN
	S	4:58.38		Graham Williamson	29	Aug 83	London (CP)
	NI	5:02.61		Steve Martin	9	Jun 84	Belfast
	W	5:05.32		Tony Simmons	4	Jul 75	London (CP)

22

3000m	E	7:32.79	Dave Moorcroft	17 Jul 82	London (CP)
	S	7:45.81	John Robson	13 Jul 84	London (CP)
	W	7:46.40	Ian Hamer	20 Jan 90	Auckland, NZL
	NI	7:49.1	Paul Lawther	27 Jun 78	Oslo, NOR
2 Miles	E	8:13.51	Steve Ovett	15 Sep 78	London (CP)
	S	8:19.37	Nat Muir	27 Jun 80	London (CP)
	W	8:20.28	David James	27 Jun 80	London (CP)
	NI	8:30.6	Paul Lawther	28 May 77	Belfast
5000m	E	13:00.41	Dave Moorcroft	7 Jul 82	Oslo, NOR
	W	13:09.80	Ian Hamer	9 Jun 92	Rome, ITA
	S	13:17.9	Nat Muir	15 Jul 80	Oslo, NOR
	NI	13:27.63	Dermot Donnelly	1 Aug 98	Hechtel, BEL
10000m	E	27:18.14 #	Jon Brown	28 Aug 98	Brussels, BEL
		27:23.06	Eamonn Martin	2 Jul 88	Oslo, NOR
	W	27:39.14	Steve Jones	9 Jul 83	Oslo, NOR
	S	27:43.03	Ian Stewart	9 Sep 77	London (CP)
	NI	28:38.56	Dermot Donnelly	29 Jun 97	Sheffield
20000m	E	57:28.7	Carl Thackery	31 Mar 90	La Flèche, FRA
	S	59:24.0	Jim Alder	9 Nov 68	Leicester
	W	69:37.0	Mick McGeoch	4 Mar 90	Barry
	NI	77:16.0	Ian Anderson	5 Mar 00	Barry
1 Hour	E	20,855 m	Carl Thackery	31 Mar 90	La Flèche, FRA
	S	20,201 m	Jim Alder	9 Nov 68	Leicester
	W	18,898 m	Mike Rowland	7 Aug 73	Stockholm, SWE
	NI	18,354 m	Dave Smyth	19 Sep 65	Bristol (?)
25000m	E	1:15:22.6	Ron Hill	21 Jul 65	Bolton
	S	1:15:34.4	Jim Alder	5 Sep 70	London (CP)
	W	1:27:01.0 e	Mick McGeoch	4 Mar 90	Barry
	NI	1:37:18.0 e	Ian Anderson	5 Mar 00	Barry
30000m	S	1:31:30.4	Jim Alder	5 Sep 70	London (CP)
	E	1:31:56.4	Tim Johnston	5 Sep 70	London (CP)
	W	1:33:49.0	Bernie Plain	1 Dec 73	Bristol
	NI	1:57:30.0	Ian Anderson	5 Mar 00	Barry
Half Marathon	E	60:09 #	Paul Evans	15 Jan 95	Marrakesh, MAR
		61:03	Nick Rose	15 Sep 85	Philadelphia, USA
	W	60:59	Steve Jones	8 Jun 86	South Shields
	S	61:34 #	Paul Evans	15 Mar 92	Lisbon, POR
		62:28	Allister Hutton	21 Jun 87	South Shields
	NI	62:16	Jim Haughey	20 Sep 87	Philadelphia, USA
Marathon	W	2:07:13	Steve Jones	20 Oct 85	Chicago, USA
	E	2:08:33	Charlie Spedding	21 Apr 85	London
	S	2:09:16	Allister Hutton	21 Apr 85	London
	NI	2:13:06	Greg Hannon	13 May 79	Coventry
2000m SC	E	5:19.86	Mark Rowland	28 Aug 88	London (CP)
	S	5:21.77	Tom Hanlon	11 Jun 92	Caserta, ITA
	W	5:23.6	Roger Hackney	10 Jun 82	Birmingham
	NI	5:31.09	Peter McColgan	5 Aug 86	Gateshead
3000m SC	E	8:07.96	Mark Rowland	30 Sep 88	Seoul, SKO
	S	8:12.58	Tom Hanlon	3 Aug 91	Monaco, MON
	W	8:18.91	Roger Hackney	30 Jul 88	Hechtel, BEL
	NI	8:27.93	Peter McColgan	25 Jun 91	Hengelo, HOL

110m H	W	12.91	Colin Jackson	20 Aug 93	Stuttgart, GER
	E	13.00	Tony Jarrett	20 Aug 93	Stuttgart, GER
	S	13.66	Ross Baillie	20 Feb 99	Sydney, AUS
	NI	14.19	C.J. Kirkpatrick	16 Jun 73	Edinburgh
200m H	W	22.63	Colin Jackson	1 Jun 91	Cardiff
	E	22.79	John Regis	1 Jun 91	Cardiff
	S	23.76	Angus McKenzie	22 Aug 81	Edinburgh
	NI	24.81	Terry Price	31 Aug 92	Belfast
400m H	E	47.82	Kriss Akabusi	6 Aug 92	Barcelona, ESP
	W	49.11	Matt Elias	28 Jul 02	Manchester (C)
	NI	49.60	Phil Beattie	28 Jul 86	Edinburgh
	S	50.24	Charles Robertson-Adams	4 Jul 01	Loughborough
High	E	2.38 i	Steve Smith	4 Feb 94	Wuppertal, GER
Jump		2.37	Steve Smith	20 Sep 92	Seoul, SKO
		2.37	Steve Smith	22 Aug 93	Stuttgart, GER
	S	2.31	Geoff Parsons	26 Aug 94	Victoria, CAN
	W	2.25	Robert Mitchell	28 Jul 01	Bedford
	NI	2.20	Floyd Manderson	14 Jul 85	London (CP)
		2.20	Floyd Manderson	21 Jun 86	London (CP)
		2.20	Floyd Manderson	16 Aug 86	Leiden, HOL
Pole	E	5.81 i	Nick Buckfield	8 Feb 02	Bad Segeberg, GER
Vault		5.80	Nick Buckfield	27 May 98	Hania, GRE
	W	5.60	Neil Winter	19 Aug 95	Enfield
	NI	5.25	Mike Bull	22 Sep 73	London (CP)
	S	5.21	Graham Eggleton	10 Jul 82	Grangemouth
Long	E	8.27	Chris Tomlinson	13 Apr 02	Tallahasse, USA
Jump	W	8.23	Lynn Davies	30 Jun 68	Berne, SUI
	NI	8.14	Mark Forsythe	7 Jul 91	Rhede, GER
	S	7.93	Darren Ritchie	13 Jul 02	Birmingham
Triple	E	18.29	Jonathan Edwards	7 Aug 95	Gothenburg, SWE
Jump	W	16.41	Steven Shalders	15 Jun 02	Manchester (C)
	S	16.17	John Mackenzie	17 Sep 94	Bedford
	NI	15.78	Michael McDonald	31 Jul 94	Corby
Shot	E	21.68	Geoff Capes	18 May 80	Cwmbrân
	W	20.45	Shaun Pickering	17 Aug 97	London (CP)
	S	18.93	Paul Buxton	13 May 77	Los Angeles(Ww), USA
	NI	17.61	Iain McMullan	13 Jul 02	Dublin (S), IRL
Discus	E	66.64	Perriss Wilkins	6 Jun 98	Birmingham (Un)
	W	60.43	Lee Newman	12 Aug 98	Enfield
	S	59.84 #	Colin Sutherland ¶	10 Jun 78	San Jose, USA
		58.58	Darrin Morris	22 Jun 91	Enfield
	NI	51.76	John Moreland	1 Jul 95	Antrim
Hammer	NI	77.54	Martin Girvan	12 May 84	Wolverhampton
	E	77.30	David Smith	13 Jul 85	London (CP)
	S	75.40	Chris Black	23 Jul 83	London (CP)
	W	68.64	Shaun Pickering	7 Apr 84	Stanford, USA
Javelin	E	91.46	Steve Backley	25 Jan 92	Auckland(NS), NZL
	W	81.70	Nigel Bevan	28 Jun 92	Birmingham
	NI	75.43	Michael Allen	11 May 02	Belfast
	S	69.20	Roddy James	28 Apr 89	Des Moines, USA

Dec.	E	8847	Daley Thompson	9 Aug 84	Los Angeles, USA
	S	7885 #h	Brad McStravick	6 May 84	Birmingham
		7856 #	Brad McStravick	28 May 84	Cwmbrân
	NI	7874	Colin Boreham	23 May 82	Götzis, AUT
	W	7308 h	Clive Longe	29 Jun 69	Kassel, GER
		7268	Paul Edwards ¶	14 Aug 83	Bonn, GER

(with 1986 Javelin)

	E	8811 #	Daley Thompson	28 Aug 86	Stuttgart, GER
	S	7739	Jamie Quarry	30 May 99	Arles, FRA
	W	7071 #	Paul Jones	4 Jun 00	Arles, FRA
	NI	7076	Brendan McConville	25 Aug 02	Antrim

4x100m	E	37.73	J. Gardener, D.Campbell (UK)		
			M.Devonish, D.Chambers	29 Aug 99	Seville, ESP
	W	38.73	K. Williams, D. Turner,		
			C. Malcolm, J. Henthorn	21 Sep 98	Kuala Lumpur, MAS
	S	39.24	D. Jenkins, A. Wells,		
			C. Sharp, A. McMaster	12 Aug 78	Edmonton, CAN
	NI	40.71	J. McAdorey, I. Craig,		
			P. Brizzell, M. Allen	22 Jun 96	Belfast

4x400m	E	2:57.53	R. Black, D. Redmond, (UK)		
			J. Regis, K. Akabusi	1 Sep 91	Tokyo, JAP
	W	3:00.41	T. Benjamin, I. Thomas,		
			J. Baulch, M. Elias	31 Jul 02	Manchester (C)
	S	3:04.68	M. Davidson, T. McKean,		
			D. Strang, B. Whittle	3 Feb 90	Auckland, NZL
	NI	3:07.27	B. Forbes, M. Douglas,		
			E. King, P. McBurney	21 Sep 98	Kuala Lumpur, MAS

Track Walking

3000m	E	11:24.4	Mark Easton	10 May 89	Tonbridge
	W	11:45.77	Steve Johnson	20 Jun 87	Cwmbrân
	S	11:53.3 #	Martin Bell	9 Aug 95	Birmingham
		11:59.47	Martin Bell	25 May 98	Bedford
	NI	13:15.0	David Smyth	5 Sep 70	Plymouth

5000m	E	19:22.29 i	Martin Rush	8 Feb 92	Birmingham
		19:35.0	Darrell Stone	16 May 89	Brighton
	W	20:08.04 i	Steve Barry	5 Mar 83	Budapest, HUN
		20:22.0	Steve Barry	20 Mar 82	London (WL)
	S	20:13.0	Martin Bell	2 May 92	Enfield
	NI	23:50.0	Jimmy Todd	28 Aug 68	Ballyclare

10000m	E	40:06.65	Ian McCombie	4 Jun 89	Jarrow
	W	41:13.62	Steve Barry	19 Jun 82	London (CP)
	S	41:13.65	Martin Bell	22 Jul 95	Cardiff
	NI	47:37.6	David Smyth	26 Apr 70	Bournemouth

1 Hour	E	14,324 m #	Ian McCombie	7 Jul 85	London (SP)
		14,158 m	Mark Easton	12 Sep 87	Woodford
	W	13,987 m	Steve Barry	28 Jun 81	Brighton
	S	13,393 m	Bill Sutherland	27 Sep 69	London (He)
	NI	12,690 m #	David Smyth	26 Apr 70	Bournemouth
		12,646 m	David Smyth	23 Sep 67	London (PH)

20000m	E	1:23:26.5	Ian McCombie	26 May 90	Fana, NOR
	W	1:26:22.0	Steve Barry	28 Jun 81	Brighton
	S	1:38:53.6	Alan Buchanan	6 Jul 75	Brighton

2 Hours	E	27,262 m #	Chris Maddocks	31 Dec 89	Plymouth
		26,037 m	Ron Wallwork	31 Jul 71	Blackburn

Road Walking

10km	E	40:17		Chris Maddocks	30	Apr 89	Burrator
	W	40:35		Steve Barry	14	May 83	Southport
	S	41:28		Martin Bell	24	Apr 99	Sheffield
	NI	44:49	#	David Smyth	20	Jun 70	Clevedon
		51:53		Arthur Agnew	6	Aug 80	Helsinki, FIN
		51:53		G. Smyth	6	Aug 80	Helsinki, FIN
20km	E	1:22:03		Ian McCombie	23	Sep 88	Seoul, SKO
	W	1:22:51		Steve Barry	26	Feb 83	Douglas, I of M
	S	1:25:42		Martin Bell	9	May 92	Lancaster
	NI	1:39:01		David Smyth		Jul 67	Cardiff
30km	E	2:07:56		Ian McCombie	27	Apr 86	Edinburgh
	W	2:10:16		Steve Barry	7	Oct 82	Brisbane, AUS
	S	2:22:21		Martin Bell	8	May 94	Cardiff
	NI	2:41:15		David Smyth	26	Apr 69	Winterbourne
50km	E	3:51:37		Chris Maddocks	28	Oct 90	Burrator
	W	4:11:59		Bob Dobson	22	Oct 81	Lassing, AUT
	S	4:13:18		Graham White	27	Jun 98	Stockport
	NI	4:45:48		David Smyth	3	May 69	Bristol

NATIONAL RECORDS OF THE UK - WOMEN
as at 31 December 2002

100m	E	11.10		Kathy Smallwood/Cook	5	Sep 81	Rome, ITA
	W	11.39		Sallyanne Short	12	Jul 92	Cwmbrân
	S	11.40		Helen Golden/Hogarth	20	Jul 74	London (CP)
	NI	11.91	#	Joan Atkinson	1	Sep 61	Sofia, BUL
		11.93		Vicki Jamison	2	Aug 97	Belfast
200m	E	22.10		Kathy Cook	9	Aug 84	Los Angeles, USA
	W	22.80		Michelle Scutt	12	Jun 82	Antrim
	S	22.98		Sandra Whittaker	8	Aug 84	Los Angeles, USA
	NI	23.62		Linda McCurry	8	Aug 78	Edmonton, CAN
300m	E	35.46		Kathy Cook	18	Aug 84	London (CP)
	W	36.01		Michelle Probert/Scutt	13	Jul 80	London (CP)
	S	36.46		Linsey Macdonald	13	Jul 80	London (CP)
	NI	38.20		Linda McCurry	2	Aug 78	Edmonton, CAN
400m	E	49.43		Kathy Cook	6	Aug 84	Los Angeles, USA
	W	50.63		Michelle Scutt	31	May 82	Cwmbrân
	S	50.71		Allison Curbishley	18	Sep 98	Kuala Lumpur, MAS
	NI	52.54		Stephanie Llewellyn	9	Jul 95	Cwmbrân
		52.4		Stephanie Llewellyn	1	Jul 95	London (He)
600m	E	1:26.0		Kelly Holmes	13	Aug 95	Gothenburg, SWE
	W	1:26.5		Kirsty McDermott/Wade	21	Aug 85	Zürich, SWZ
	S	1:27.4	i	Linsey Macdonald	12	Dec 81	Cosford
		1:29.88		Anne Clarkson/Purvis	25	Sep 82	Brisbane, AUS
	NI	1:29.46		Jo Latimer	19	May 93	Birmingham
800m	E	1:56.21		Kelly Holmes	9	Sep 95	Monaco, MON
	W	1:57.42		Kirsty McDermott/Wade	24	Jun 85	Belfast
	S	1:59.30		Susan Scott	29	Jul 02	Manchester (C)
	NI	2:01.83		Amanda Crowe	18	Sep 98	Kuala Lumpur, MAS
1000m	E	2:32.55		Kelly Holmes	15	Jun 97	Leeds
	W	2:33.70		Kirsty McDermott/Wade	9	Aug 85	Gateshead
	S	2:37.05		Christine Whittingham	27	Jun 86	Gateshead
	NI	2:48.59		Jane Ewing	26	Jun 90	Antrim

1500m	E	3:58.07	Kelly Holmes	29 Jun 97	Sheffield
	W	4:00.73	Kirsty Wade	26 Jul 87	Gateshead
	S	4:01.20	Yvonne Murray	4 Jul 87	Oslo, NOR
	NI	4:10.68	Amanda Crowe	21 Sep 98	Kuala Lumpur, MAS
1 Mile	E	4:17.57	Zola Budd	21 Aug 85	Zürich, SUI
	W	4:19.41	Kirsty McDermott/Wade	27 Jul 85	Oslo, NOR
	S	4:22.64	Yvonne Murray	22 Jul 94	Oslo, NOR
	NI	4:32.99	Amanda Crowe	30 Aug 98	Glasgow (S)
2000m	S	5:26.93	Yvonne Murray	8 Jul 94	Edinburgh
	E	5:30.19	Zola Budd	11 Jul 86	London (CP)
	W	5:45.81 i	Kirsty Wade	13 Mar 87	Cosford
		5:50.17	Susan Tooby/Wightman	13 Jul 84	London (CP)
	NI	5:57.24	Ursula McKee/McGloin	25 Jun 90	Antrim
3000m	E	8:22.20	Paula Radcliffe	19 Jul 02	Monaco, MON
	S	8:29.02	Yvonne Murray	25 Sep 88	Seoul, SKO
	W	8:47.59	Hayley Tullett	15 Jul 00	Gateshead
	NI	9:16.25	Ursula McKee/McGloin	7 Jun 90	Helsinki, FIN
2 Miles	E	9:27.5 e	Paula Radcliffe	22 Aug 97	Brussels, BEL
		9:32.07	Paula Radcliffe	23 May 99	Loughborough
	S	9:36.85 i	Yvonne Murray	15 Mar 87	Cosford
		9:51.38	Hayley Haining	23 May 99	Loughborough
	W	9:49.73	Hayley Tullett	23 May 99	Loughborough
5000m	E	14:31.42	Paula Radcliffe	28 Jul 02	Manchester (C)
	S	14:56.94	Yvonne Murray	7 Jul 95	London (CP)
	W	15:13.22	Angela Tooby/Tooby-Smith	5 Aug 87	Oslo, NOR
	NI	16:18.71	Sharon Hatch	15 Jun 02	Manchester (C)
10000m	E	30:01.09	Paula Radcliffe	6 Aug 02	Munich, GER
	S	30:57.07	Liz McColgan	25 Jun 91	Hengelo, HOL
	W	31:55.30	Angela Tooby/Tooby-Smith	4 Sep 87	Rome, ITA
	NI	36:19.98 #	Teresa Kidd	25 Aug 85	Dublin (S), IRL
1 Hour	E	16,495 m #	Michaela McCallum	2 Apr 00	Asti
		16,364 m	Alison Fletcher	3 Sep 97	Bromley
	W	16,460 m i#	Bronwen Cardy-Wise	8 Mar 92	Birmingham
		14,400 m	Ann Franklin	5 Mar 89	Barry
	S	12,800 m	Leslie Watson	12 Mar 83	London (He)
20000m	E	1:15:46	Carolyn Hunter-Rowe	6 Mar 94	Barry
	W	1:23:56	Ann Franklin	9 Mar 86	Barry
25000m	E	1:35:16 e	Carolyn Hunter-Rowe	6 Mar 94	Barry
	W	1:44:58 e	Ann Franklin	9 Mar 86	Barry
	S	1:54:55	Leslie Watson	12 Mar 83	London (He)
30000m	E	1:55:03	Carolyn Hunter-Rowe	6 Mar 94	Barry
	W	2:05:59	Ann Franklin	9 Mar 86	Barry
	S	2:16:44	Leslie Watson	12 Mar 83	London (He)
Half Marathon	E	66:47	Paula Radcliffe	7 Oct 01	Bristol
	S	67:11	Liz McColgan	26 Jan 92	Tokyo, JPN
	W	69:56	Susan Tooby/Wightman	24 Jul 88	South Shields
	NI	75:57 #	Moira O'Boyle/O'Neill	23 Mar 86	Cavan, IRL
		76:23	Moira O'Neill	24 Sep 88	Londonderry
Marathon	E	2:17:18	Paula Radcliffe	13 Oct 02	Chicago, USA
	S	2:26:52	Liz McColgan	13 Apr 97	London
	W	2:31:33	Susan Tooby/Wightman	23 Sep 88	Seoul, SKO
	NI	2:37:06	Moira O'Neill	31 Oct 88	Dublin, IRL

2000mSC	E	6:29.79	Tara Krzywicki	20	May 01	Loughborough
	S	7:01.74	Allison Higgins	18	Jul 01	Glasgow (S)
	W	7:34.66	Claire Martin	2	May 98	Bath
	NI	8:01.8	Gemma Turley	30	Jun 01	Bangor (NI)
3000mSC	E	9:52.71	Tara Krzywicki	1	Jul 01	Glasgow (S)
	S	10:55.70	Allison Higgins	11	Aug 01	Glasgow (S)
	W	12:35.60	Sian Davies	5	Jul 01	Stretford
100m H	E	12.80	Angie Thorp	31	Jul 96	Atlanta, USA
	W	12.91	Kay Morley-Brown	2	Feb 90	Auckland, NZL
	NI	13.29	Mary Peters	2	Sep 72	Munich, GER
	S	13.35	Pat Rollo	30	Jul 83	London (CP)
400m H	E	52.74	Sally Gunnell	19	Aug 93	Stuttgart, GER
	S	55.24	Sinead Dudgeon	24	Jul 99	Birmingham
	NI	55.91	Elaine McLaughlin	26	Sep 88	Seoul, SKO
	W	56.43	Alyson Layzell	16	Jun 96	Birmingham
High	E	1.95	Diana Elliott/Davies	26	Jun 82	Oslo, NOR
Jump		1.95 i	Debbie Marti	23	Feb 97	Birmingham
		1.95	Susan Jones	24	Jun 01	Bremen, GER
	NI	1.92	Janet Boyle	29	Sep 88	Seoul, SKO
	S	1.91	Jayne Barnetson	7	Jul 89	Edinburgh
	W	1.88	Rebecca Jones	1	Jun 02	Arles, FRA
Pole	E	4.44 i	Janine Whitlock	17	Feb 02	Birmingham
Vault		4.40	Janine Whitlock	14	Jul 01	Birmingham
	W	4.15	Rhian Clarke	7	Apr 00	Austin, USA
	W	4.15	Rhian Clarke	19	Apr 02	Baton Rouge, USA
	NI	4.00	Zoe Brown	28	Jul 02	Manchester (C)
	S	3.95 A&	Alison Jessee	25	Jun 99	El Paso, USA
		3.95 A&	Alison Jessee	11	Jul 99	Albuquerque, USA
		3.90	Gillian Cooke	2	Jun 02	Glasgow (S)
Long	E	6.90	Bev Kinch	14	Aug 83	Helsinki, FIN
Jump	W	6.52	Gillian Regan	28	Aug 82	Swansea
	S	6.43 #	Moira Walls/Maguire	18	Sep 70	Bucharest, ROM
		6.43	Myra Nimmo	27	May 73	Edinburgh
	NI	6.11	Thelma Hopkins	29	Sep 56	Budapest, HUN
		6.11	Michelle Rea	11	Aug 90	Maia, POR
Triple	E	15.16 i	Ashia Hansen	28	Feb 98	Valencia, SPA
Jump		15.15	Ashia Hansen	13	Sep 97	Fukuoka, JAP
	S	12.89	Karen Hambrook/Skeggs	17	May 92	London (CP)
	W	12.14	Jayne Ludlow	21	May 94	Istanbul, TUR
	NI	12.08	Mary Devlin	8	Jun 02	Belfast
Shot	E	19.36	Judy Oakes	14	Aug 88	Gateshead
	S	18.99	Meg Ritchie	7	May 83	Tucson, USA
	W	19.06 i	Venissa Head	7	Apr 84	St. Athan
		18.93	Venissa Head	13	May 84	Haverfordwest
	NI	16.40 i	Mary Peters	28	Feb 70	Bucharest, ROM
		16.31	Mary Peters	1	Jun 66	Belfast (PP)
Discus	S	67.48	Meg Ritchie	26	Apr 81	Walnut, USA
	W	64.68	Venissa Head	18	Jul 83	Athens, GRE
	E	60.82	Shelley Drew	25	Jul 98	Birmingham
	NI	60.72	Jackie McKernan	18	Jul 93	Buffalo, USA
Hammer	E	68.15	Lorraine Shaw	17	Mar 01	Nice/Boulouris, FRA
	S	59.95	Shirley Webb (SCO?)	8	Sep 02	Manchester (Str)
		58.47	Mhairi Walters	12	May 02	Edinburgh
	W	57.47	Lesley Brannan	28	May 02	Manchester (Str)
	NI	48.90	Julie Kirkpatrick	15	Jun 96	Dublin (S), IRL

Javelin	E	64.87	Kelly Morgan	14	Jul 02	Birmingham
	S	57.19	Lorna Jackson	9	Jul 00	Peterborough
	NI	47.72	Alison Moffitt	21	Aug 99	Belfast
	W	46.89	Caroline White	19	Jun 99	Colwyn Bay
Hept.	E	6831	Denise Lewis	30	Jul 00	Talence, FRA
	S	5803	Jayne Barnetson	20	Aug 89	Kiyev, UKR
	W	5642	Sarah Rowe	23	Aug 81	Utrecht, HOL
	NI	5065 h	Catherine Scott	13	Sep 87	Tullamore, IRL
		4564	Wendy Phillips	18	Jul 82	Birmingham
(with 1999 Javelin)						
	S	5257	Chloe Cozens	24	Sep 00	Watford
	W	5254	Rebecca Jones	2	Jun 02	Arles, FRA
4x100m	E	42.43	H. Oakes, K. Cook, (UK)			
			B. Callender, S. Lannaman	1	Aug 80	Moscow, RUS
	S	45.37	J. Booth, K. Hogg,			
			J. Neilson, S. Whittaker	8	Jun 86	Lloret de Mar,ESP
		45.2	A. MacRitchie, S. Pringle, (ESH)			
			H. Hogarth, E. Sutherland	27	Jun 70	London (CP)
	W	45.37	H. Miles, S. Lewis,			
			S. Short, C. Smart	2	Aug 86	Edinburgh
	NI	46.36	K. Graham, H. Gourlay,			
			J. Robinson, R. Gaylor	31	Aug 85	Tel Aviv, ISR
4x400m	E	3:22.01	L. Hanson, P. Smith, (UK)			
			S. Gunnell, L. Staines	1	Sep 91	Tokyo, JPN
	S	3:31.50	C. Easton, S. Dudgeon,			
			S. Burnside, L. McConnell	31	Jul 22	Manchester (C)
	W	3:35.60	C. Smart, K. Wade,			
			D. Fryar, M. Scutt	4	Jul 82	Dublin (S), IRL
	NI	3:40.12	Z. Arnold, V. Jamison,			
			J. Latimer, S. Llewellyn	22	Jun 96	Belfast

Track Walking

3000m	E	12:49.16	Betty Sworowski	28	Jul 90	Wrexham
	S	13:16.23	Verity Snook	27	May 96	Bedford
	W	14:28.2	Karen Dunster	18	May 91	Portsmouth
5000m	E	21:42.51	Lisa Kehler	13	Jul 02	Birmingham
	S	23:22.52	Verity Snook	19	Jun 94	Horsham
	W	24:32.92	Karen Nipper	21	Jul 84	Lyngby, DEN
10000m	E	45:09.57	Lisa Kehler	13	Aug 00	Birmingham
	S	47:10.07	Verity Larby/Snook	19	Jun 93	Horsham
	W	50:25.0 mx	Lisa Simpson	1	Apr 87	Hornchurch
		51:00.0	Karen Nipper	21	Feb 81	Leicester
1 Hour	E	11,590 m	Lisa Langford/Kehler	13	Sep 86	Woodford
20000m	E	1:56:59.7	Cath Reader	21	Oct 95	Loughborough
2 Hours	E	20,502 m	Cath Reader	21	Oct 95	Loughborough

Road Walking

5km	E	21:36	Vicky Lupton/White	18	Jul 92	Sheffield
	S	22:45	Verity Snook	25	Aug 94	Victoria, CAN
	W	23:35	Lisa Simpson	31	Oct 87	Cardiff
10km	E	45:03	Lisa Kehler	19	Sep 98	Kuala Lumpur, MAS
	S	46:06	Verity Snook	25	Aug 94	Victoria, CAN
	W	49:33	Lisa Simpson	14	Mar 87	Ham
20km	E	1:33:57	Lisa Kehler	17	Jun 00	Eisenhüttenstadt, GER
	S	1:36:40	Sara Cattermole	4	Mar 00	Perth, AUS
50km	E	4:50:51	Sandra Brown	13	Jul 91	Basildon

UK INDOOR RECORDS
as at 20 Mar 2003

MEN

50m	5.61 +	Jason Gardener	16	Feb 00	Madrid, ESP
60m	6.46	Jason Gardener	7	Mar 99	Maebashi, JPN
200m	20.25	Linford Christie	19	Feb 95	Liévin, FRA
300m	32.90	Ade Mafe	31	Jan 92	Karlsruhe, GER
400m	45.39	Jamie Baulch	9	Feb 97	Birmingham
800m	1:44.91	Sebastian Coe	12	Mar 83	Cosford
1000m	2:17.86	Matthew Yates	22	Feb 92	Birmingham
1500m	3:34.20	Peter Elliott	27	Feb 90	Seville, ESP
1 Mile	3:52.02	Peter Elliott	9	Feb 90	East Rutherford, USA
2000m	4:57.09	John Mayock	25	Feb 01	Liévin, FRA
3000m	7:41.09	John Mayock	6	Feb 02	Stockholm, SWE
5000m	13:21.27	Nick Rose	12	Feb 82	New York, USA
50m Hurdles	6.40	Colin Jackson	5	Feb 99	Budapest, HUN
60m Hurdles	7.30	Colin Jackson	6	Mar 94	Sindelfingen, GER
High Jump	2.38	Steve Smith	4	Feb 94	Wuppertal, GER
Pole Vault	5.81	Nick Buckfield	8	Feb 02	Bad Segeberg, GER
Long Jump	8.05	Barrington Williams	11	Feb 89	Cosford
	8.05 #	Stewart Faulkner	27	Feb 90	Seville, ESP
Triple Jump	17.64	Jonathan Edwards	15	Feb 98	Birmingham
Shot	21.47	Carl Myerscough	15	Mar 03	Fayetteville, USA
Heptathlon	5978	Alex Kruger	12	Mar 95	Barcelona, ESP

(7.16, 7.23, 14.79, 2.16, 8.36, 4.90, 2:48.66)

5000m Walk	19:22.29	Martin Rush	8	Feb 92	Birmingham
4 x 200m Relay	1:22.11	UK National Team	3	Mar 91	Glasgow

(Linford Christie, Darren Braithwaite, Ade Mafe, John Regis)

4 x 400m Relay	3:03.20	UK National Team	7	Mar 99	Maebashi, JPN

(Allyn Condon, Solomon Wariso, Adrian Patrick, Jamie Baulch)

WOMEN

50m	6.21	Wendy Hoyte	22	Feb 81	Grenoble, FRA
60m	7.13	Bev Kinch	23	Feb 86	Madrid, SPA
200m	22.83	Katharine Merry	14	Feb 99	Birmingham
300m	37.46 A	Sharon Colyear/Danville	14	Mar 81	Pocatello, USA
400m	50.53	Katharine Merry	18	Feb 01	Birmingham
800m	1:59.21	Kelly Holmes	9	Feb 03	Ghent, BEL
1000m	2:38.45	Jo Fenn	21	Feb 03	Birmingham
1500m	4:02.66	Kelly Holmes	16	Mar 03	Birmingham
1 Mile	4:23.86	Kirsty Wade	5	Feb 88	New York, USA
2000m	5:40.86	Yvonne Murray	20	Feb 93	Birmingham
3000m	8:34.80	Liz McColgan	4	Mar 89	Budapest, HUN
5000m	15:03.17	Liz McColgan	22	Feb 92	Birmingham
50m Hurdles	7.03	Yvette Wray/Luker	21	Feb 81	Grenoble, FRA
60m Hurdles	7.99	Diane Allahgreen	26	Feb 00	Ghent, BEL
High Jump	1.95	Debbie Marti	23	Feb 97	Birmingham
Pole Vault	4.44	Janine Whitlock	17	Feb 02	Birmingham
Long Jump	6.70	Sue Hearnshaw/Telfer	3	Mar 84	Gothenburg, SWE (r3)
	6.70	Sue Hearnshaw/Telfer	3	Mar 84	Gothenburg, SWE (r6)
	6.70	Jo Wise	9	Mar 97	Paris (B), FRA
Triple Jump	15.16	Ashia Hansen	28	Feb 98	Valencia, SPA
Shot	19.06	Venissa Head	7	Apr 84	St. Athan
Pentathlon	4392	Julie Hollman	28	Jan 01	Prague, CZE

(8.78, 1.81, 12.98, 6.13, 2:19.57)

3000m Walk	13:08.64	Niobe Menendez	2	Feb 02	Cardiff
4 x 200m Relay	1:33.96	UK National Team	23	Feb 90	Glasgow

(Paula Thomas, Jenni Stoute, Linda Staines, Sally Gunnell)

4 x 400m Relay	3:32.18	UK National Team	16	Mar 03	Birmingham

(Jenny Meadows, Danielle Halsall, Amy Spencer, Catharine Murphy)

UK ALL TIME LISTS - MEN
as at 31 December 2001

100 Metres

Time	Name	Date
9.87	Linford Christie ¶	15 Aug 93
9.87	Dwain Chambers	14 Sep 02
9.91	Christie	23 Aug 94
9.92	Christie	25 Aug 91
9.94	Chambers	16 Aug 02
9.96	Christie	1 Aug 92
9.96	Chambers	7 Aug 02
9.97	Christie	24 Sep 88
9.97	Christie	15 Aug 93
9.97 A	Christie	23 Sep 95
9.97	Chambers	22 Aug 99
9.98	Jason Gardener	2 Jul 99
10.04	Darren Campbell	19 Aug 98
10.04	Mark Lewis-Francis	5 Jul 02
10.09	Jason Livingston ¶	13 Jun 92
10.11	Allan Wells	24 Jul 80
10.11	Christian Malcolm	5 Aug 01
10.12	Darren Braithwaite	15 Jul 95
10.13	Marlon Devonish	17 Sep 98
10.15	Michael Rosswess	15 Sep 91
10.15	John Regis	29 May 93
10.17	Ian Mackie	25 Aug 96
10.20	Cameron Sharp	24 Aug 83
10.20	Elliot Bunney	14 Jun 86
10.21 A	Ainsley Bennett	8 Sep 79
10.21	Jamie Henderson	6 Aug 87
10.21	Allyn Condon	14 Aug 99
10.22	Mike McFarlane	20 Jun 86
10.23	Marcus Adam	26 Jul 91
10.23	Jason John	15 Jul 94
10.23	Terry Williams	22 Aug 94
10.24	Chris Lambert	14 Jul 01
10.26	Daley Thompson	27 Aug 86
10.26	Ernest Obeng	1 Aug 87
10.28	Julian Golding	22 Jul 97
10.28	Jon Barbour	17 Jun 00
10.28	Tyrone Edgar	20 Apr 02
10.29	Peter Radford (10.31?)	13 Sep 58
10.29	Colin Jackson	28 Jul 90
10.30	Clarence Callender	26 Jul 91
10.30 A	Doug Bignall	6 Jul 00
10.30		22 Apr 01
10.31	Doug Walker ¶	11 Jun 97
10.31	Owusu Dako	16 Apr 00
10.32	Buster Watson	1 Jul 83
10.32	Donovan Reid	4 Aug 84
10.32	Lincoln Asquith	11 Aug 86
10.32	Lenny Paul	29 May 93
10.32	Toby Box	28 Jun 95
10.32	Daniel Money	28 Aug 97
10.33	Brian Green	15 Jul 72
10.33	Solomon Wariso	19 Jun 94
10.33	Daniel Plummer	13 Jul 02
10.34	Drew McMaster	9 Jul 83
10.34	Barrington Williams	5 Aug 88
10.34	Kevin Williams	11 Jun 97
10.35 A	Barrie Kelly	13 Oct 68
10.35	Brian Taylor	29 May 93
10.35	Mark Richardson ¶	2 May 98
10.35 A	Akinola Lashore	10 Apr 99
10.35	Mark Findlay ¶	19 Jun 99

wind assisted

Time	Name	Date
9.90	Christie	24 Aug 91
9.91	Christie	11 Jun 94
9.93	Christie	28 Jan 90
9.95	Christie	22 Jun 90
9.95	Chambers	30 Jun 02
9.97 †	Mark Lewis-Francis	4 Aug 01
10.00	Ian Mackie	18 Jul 98
10.01	Doug Walker ¶	18 Jul 98
10.02	Allan Wells	4 Oct 82
10.07	Cameron Sharp	4 Oct 82
10.07	John Regis	28 Aug 90
10.07	Toby Box	11 Jun 94
10.07	Michael Rosswess	11 Jun 94
10.08	Mike McFarlane	27 May 84
10.08	Jason John	11 Jun 94
10.09 †	Christian Malcolm	4 Aug 01
10.10	Donovan Reid	26 Jun 83
10.11	Drew McMaster	26 Jun 83
10.12	Buster Watson	27 May 84
10.13	Jon Barbour	30 Jun 01
10.14	Ernest Obeng	20 Jun 87
10.14	Marcus Adam	28 Jan 90
10.16	Daniel Money	21 Jun 97
10.17	Terry Williams	23 Aug 94
10.17	Owusu Dako	5 Jul 98
10.17	Tyrone Edgar	30 Jun 01
10.19	Chris Lambert	12 May 02
10.20	Lincoln Asquith	6 Jul 85
10.22	Jamie Henthorn	29 Aug 97
10.22	Danny Joyce	30 Aug 97
10.22	Dwayne Grant	30 Jun 01
10.25	Lenny Paul	14 Jul 91
10.26	Peter Little	21 May 80
10.26	Doug Turner	13 Jul 96
10.27	Barrington Williams	2 Jul 88
10.27	Clarence Callender	22 Jun 91
10.27 A	Doug Bignall	4 Jul 00
10.29		13 Jul 01
10.28	Du'aine (Thorne-)Ladejo	23 May 98
10.29	Trevor Cameron	11 Jun 94

† wind gauge faulty - probably windy

hand timing

Time	Name	Date
10.1	David Jenkins	20 May 72
10.1	Brian Green	3 Jun 72

hand timing - wind assisted

Time	Name	Date
10.0	Allan Wells	16 Jun 79
10.0	Drew McMaster	1 Jun 80
10.1	Dave Roberts	17 Jul 82

200 Metres

19.87 A	John Regis	31 Jul	94
19.94	Regis	20 Aug	93
20.01	Regis	2 Aug	94
20.08	Christian Malcolm	8 Aug	01
20.09	Regis	5 Aug	92
20.09	Linford Christie ¶	28 Sep	88
20.09	Malcolm	24 Aug	01
20.11	Regis	30 Aug	90
20.11	Christie	25 Jun	95
20.12	Regis	10 Jul	91
20.13	Darren Campbell	27 Sep	00
20.18	Julian Golding	19 Sep	98
20.19	Marlon Devonish	29 Jul	02
20.21	Allan Wells	28 Jul	80
20.27	Dwain Chambers	10 Jun	02
20.35	Doug Walker ¶	26 Jul	98
20.36 [10]	Todd Bennett	28 May	84
20.37	Chris Lambert	16 Jun	02
20.41	Marcus Adam	13 Jun	92
20.42 A	Ainsley Bennett	12 Sep	79
20.84		31 Aug	80
20.43	Mike McFarlane	7 Oct	82
20.43	Doug Turner	9 Jun	96
20.47	Cameron Sharp	9 Sep	82
20.47	Darren Braithwaite	13 May	95
20.50	Terry Williams	24 Aug	94
20.50	Tony Jarrett	16 Jul	95
20.50 [20]	Solomon Wariso	16 Jul	95
20.51	Michael Rosswess	28 Sep	88
20.53 i	Allyn Condon	8 Feb	98
20.63		19 Jul	97
20.54	Ade Mafe	25 Aug	85
20.56	Roger Black	4 May	96
20.57	Owusu Dako	16 Jul	95
20.62	Buster Watson	5 Jun	83
20.62	Donovan Reid	28 May	84
20.62	Mark Richardson ¶	24 Aug	97
20.62 i	Daniel Caines	1 Mar	02
20.64 [30]	Dwayne Grant	16 Jun	01
20.65	Jason Gardener	11 Jul	99
20.66 A	Dick Steane	15 Oct	68
20.66	David Jenkins	27 Aug	73
20.67	Tim Benjamin	17 Jun	01
20.70	Chris Monk	20 Aug	73
20.72	Toby Box	24 Aug	94
20.73 A	Ralph Banthorpe	15 Oct	68
20.75	Dave Clark	20 Jan	90
20.76	Andy Carrott	5 Jul	88
20.76 [40]	Clarence Callender	24 Jun	91
20.76	Graham Beasley	16 Jun	02
20.77	Drew McMaster	9 Jul	83
20.79	Phil Goedluck	6 Aug	94
20.79	Paul White	27 May	96
20.79	Jon Barbour	9 Sep	00
20.81	Mike St. Louis	21 Jun	86
20.81	Paul McBurney	24 Aug	94
20.83	Martin Reynolds	22 Jul	70
20.83	Claude Moseley	23 Aug	81
20.83 [50]	John Stewart	9 Sep	00

wind assisted (* 220 yards time less 0.12)

20.08	Regis	2 Jul	93
20.10	Marcus Adam	1 Feb	90
20.11	Allan Wells	20 Jun	80
20.26	Ade Mafe	1 Feb	90
20.36	Doug Turner	27 Jul	97
20.48	Michael Rosswess	9 Sep	90
20.51	Jason John	2 Jul	93
20.55	Buster Watson	10 Aug	85
20.59	Allyn Condon	25 Jul	99
20.60	Tim Benjamin	7 Aug	99
20.60	Dwayne Grant	7 Aug	99 [10]
20.61	Martin Reynolds	22 Jul	70
20.61	Ed White	11 Jul	99
20.62	Adrian Patrick	10 Jun	95
20.64	Drew McMaster	23 Aug	80
20.68	Ian Mackie	29 May	00
20.70 *	Dave Jones	20 May	61
20.70	Trevor Hoyte	14 Sep	79
20.73	Phil Goedluck	23 Apr	95
20.75	Daniel Money	26 May	97
20.76	Paul McBurney	26 May	97 [20]
20.80	Ben Lewis	11 Jul	99

hand timing (* 220 yards time less 0.1)

20.3	David Jenkins	19 Aug	72
20.4 *	Peter Radford	28 May	60
20.6	Donovan Reid	1 Jul	84
20.7 *	Menzies Campbell	10 Jun	67
20.7	Martin Reynolds	2 Aug	70
20.7	Brian Green	3 Jun	72
20.7	Drew McMaster	16 Aug	80
20.7	Claude Moseley	28 Aug	81

hand timing - wind assisted

20.4	Buster Watson	11 Aug	85
20.4	Dwayne Grant	1 Jul	01
20.5	Roger Black	6 Jul	96
20.6	Ainsley Bennett	22 Jun	74
20.6	Mark Richardson ¶	6 Jul	96

300 Metres

31.56	Doug Walker ¶	19 Jul	98
31.67	John Regis	17 Jul	92
31.87	Mark Richardson ¶	19 Jul	98
31.98	Regis	19 Jun	93
31.99	Regis	21 Jun	91
32.06	Jamie Baulch	31 May	97
32.08	Roger Black	8 Aug	86
32.14	Todd Bennett	18 Aug	84
32.23	Solomon Wariso	19 Jul	98
32.26	Mark Hylton	19 Jul	98
32.32	Derek Redmond	16 Jul	88
32.36	Iwan Thomas	19 Jul	98 [10]
32.44	David Jenkins	4 Jul	75
32.45	David Grindley	19 Jun	93

during 400m

32.06 +	Roger Black	29 Aug	91
32.08 +	Iwan Thomas	5 Aug	97
32.26 +	Derek Redmond	1 Sep	87
32.35 +	David Grindley	26 Jun	93

400 Metres

44.36	Iwan Thomas	13	Jul	97
44.37	Roger Black	3	Jul	96
44.37	Mark Richardson ¶	9	Jul	98
44.37	Richardson	8	Aug	98
44.38	Thomas	8	Aug	98
44.39	Black	16	Jun	96
44.41	Black	29	Jul	96
44.46	Thomas	2	Jul	97
44.47	David Grindley	3	Aug	92
44.47	Richardson	5	Aug	97
44.47	Richardson	24	Aug	99
44.50	Derek Redmond	1	Sep	87
44.57	Jamie Baulch	3	Jul	96
44.66	Du'aine Ladejo	16	Jun	96
44.68	Solomon Wariso	26	Jul	98
44.93	David Jenkins	21	Jun	75
44.93	Kriss Akabusi	7	Aug	88
44.98	Daniel Caines	27	Jul	02
45.20	Sean Baldock	12	Aug	00
45.22	Brian Whittle	25	Sep	88
45.24	Mark Hylton	12	Aug	98
45.26	Phil Brown	26	May	85
45.27	Todd Bennett	7	Aug	88
45.30	Ade Mafe	23	Jul	93
45.33	Paul Sanders	15	Jun	91
45.47	David McKenzie	12	Jun	94
45.48	John Regis	17	Apr	93
45.49	Glen Cohen	21	May	78
45.57	Jared Deacon	16	Jun	02
45.63	Adrian Patrick	5	Jul	95
45.64	Paul Harmsworth	7	Aug	88
45.65	Alan Bell	14	Jun	80
45.67	Roger Hunter	19	May	85
45.73	Tim Benjamin	14	Jul	02
45.74	Steve Heard	26	May	85
45.75	Robbie Brightwell	19	Oct	64
45.76	Guy Bullock	16	Jun	96
45.81	Terry Whitehead	14	Jun	80
45.83	Geoff Dearman	29	Jul	00
45.84	Richard Knowles	18	May	97
45.85	Paul McBurney	13	Jul	97
45.88	Wayne McDonald	17	Aug	91
45.91 A	Martin Winbolt-Lewis	17	Oct	68
45.92	Mark Thomas	27	Jun	87
45.94	Paul Slythe	26	Jul	98
45.97	Steve Scutt	14	Sep	79
46.03	Peter Crampton	8	Aug	87
46.03	Chris Rawlinson	25	May	02
46.04	Alan Slack	27	Jun	85
46.08	Tim Graham	19	Oct	64
46.08	Rod Milne	15	Jun	80
46.10	Peter Gabbett	7	Sep	72
46.11	Martin Reynolds	4	Sep	72
46.15	Ainsley Bennett	29	Aug	75
46.16	Gary Armstrong	15	Jul	72
46.16	Claude Moseley	1	Jul	83
46.18	Garry Cook	14	Jun	80
46.19	Roy Dickens	28	May	84
46.20	Dave Nolan	9	Jun	96

hand timing (* 440 yards time less 0.3)

45.6 *	Robbie Brightwell	14	Jul	62
45.7	Adrian Metcalfe	2	Sep	61
45.9	Colin Campbell	2	Jul	68
46.0	Garry Cook	20	May	81

600 Metres

1:14.95	Steve Heard	14	Jul	91
1:15.0 +	Sebastian Coe	10	Jun	81
1:15.4	Garry Cook	30	Jul	84
1:15.4	Tom McKean	21	Jul	91
1:15.6	David Jenkins	3	Aug	74
1:15.94	Brian Whittle	28	Jul	92

800 Metres (* 880 yards time less 0.60)

1:41.73"	Sebastian Coe	10	Jun	81
1:42.33	Coe	5	Jul	79
1:42.88	Steve Cram	21	Aug	85
1:42.97	Peter Elliott	30	May	90
1:43.07	Coe	25	Aug	85
1:43.19	Cram	7	Sep	86
1:43.22	Cram	31	Jul	86
1:43.38	Coe	29	Aug	89
1:43.41	Elliott	1	Sep	87
1:43.42	Cram	17	Aug	88
1:43.84	Martin Steele	10	Jul	93
1:43.88	Tom McKean	28	Jul	89
1:43.98	David Sharpe	19	Aug	92
1:44.09	Steve Ovett	31	Aug	78
1:44.55	Garry Cook	29	Aug	84
1:44.59	Tony Morrell	2	Jul	88
1:44.65	Ikem Billy	21	Jul	84
1:44.65	Steve Heard	26	Aug	92
1:44.92	Curtis Robb	15	Jul	93
1:45.05	Matthew Yates	26	Aug	92
1:45.12	Andy Carter	14	Jul	73
1:45.14	Chris McGeorge	28	Jun	83
1:45.14	John Gladwin	22	Jul	86
1:45.31	Rob Harrison	21	Jul	84
1:45.32	James McIlroy (IRE)	16	Jul	98
1:45.35	Kevin McKay	16	Aug	92
1:45.44	Neil Horsfield	28	Jul	90
1:45.47	Brian Whittle	20	Jul	90
1:45.6	Graham Williamson	12	Jun	83
1:45.64	Paul Herbert	5	Jun	88
1:45.66	Paul Forbes	8	Jun	83
1:45.68	Mark Sesay	7	Aug	99
1:45.69	Steve Crabb	17	Aug	88
1:45.69	Craig Winrow	21	Jun	96
1:45.71	Andy Hart	19	Sep	98
1:45.76	Frank Clement	10	Jul	76
1:45.81	David Strang	12	Jul	96
1:45.81	Anthony Whiteman	5	Aug	00
1:45.82	Jason Lobo	7	Aug	99
1:46.10	Gary Marlow	10	Jul	87
1:46.1	Colin Campbell	26	Jul	72
1:46.16	Gareth Brown	2	Jul	84
1:46.20	David Warren	29	Jun	80
1:46.21	Pete Browne	14	Jul	73
1:46.26	Phil Lewis	27	Jan	74

	1:46.3 a	Chris Carter	4	Sep	66		3:33.79	Dave Moorcroft	27	Jul	82
40	1:46.37	Andrew Lill	28	Jun	92		3:33.83	John Robson	4	Sep	79
	1:46.4	Paul Walker	22	Jul	97		3:34.00	Matthew Yates	13	Sep	91 10
	1:46.51	John Boulter	18	Jun	66		3:34.01	Graham Williamson	28	Jun	83
	1:46.6	Derek Johnson	9	Aug	57		3:34.1 +	Tony Morrell	14	Jul	90
	1:46.63	Peter Hoffmann	11	Jun	78		3:34.50	Adrian Passey	4	Jul	87
	1:46.64	Dave Moorcroft	25	Jul	82		3:34.53	Mark Rowland	27	Jul	88
	1:46.65	Steve Caldwell	31	May	82		3:34.59	Kevin McKay	24	Aug	97
	1:46.72	Mal Edwards	13	Sep	87		3:34.76	Gary Lough	9	Sep	95
	1:46.72	Matt Shone	19	Apr	02		3:35.08	Neil Horsfield	10	Aug	90
	1:46.80 *	John Davies I	3	Jun	68		3:35.26	John Gladwin	5	Sep	86
50	1:46.8	Bob Adams	9	Aug	69		3:35.28	Jack Buckner	1	Jul	86
	1:46.8	Dave Cropper	1	Jul	73		3:35.53	Andrew Graffin	6	Sep	02 20
	1:46.8	Dave McMeekin	6	Jun	74		3:35.66	Frank Clement	12	Aug	78
							3:35.74	Rob Harrison	26	May	86
	1000 Metres						3:35.94	Paul Larkins	10	Jul	87
	2:12.18	Sebastian Coe	11	Jul	81		3:36.53	David Strang	15	Jul	94
	2:12.88	Steve Cram	9	Aug	85		3:36.81	Mike Kearns	26	Jul	77
	2:13.40	Coe	1	Jul	80		3:37.35	Michael East	31	Jul	02
	2:14.90	Coe	16	Jul	86		3:37.55	Colin Reitz	27	Jun	85
	2:15.57	James McIlroy	5	Sep	99		3:37.64	Brendan Foster	2	Feb	74
	2:15.91	Steve Ovett	6	Sep	79		3:37.75	Jon McCallum	1	Aug	00
	2:16.30	Peter Elliott	17	Jan	90		3:37.88	Jason Dullforce	17	Jul	92 30
	2:16.34	Matthew Yates	6	Jul	90		3:37.97	Rod Finch	30	Jul	93
	2:16.82	Graham Williamson	17	Jul	84		3:37.99	Rob Denmark	5	Jun	95
	2:16.99	Tony Morrell	28	Aug	88		3:38.05	Glen Grant	12	Aug	78
	2:17.14	John Gladwin	6	Jul	90		3:38.06	Tim Hutchings	31	Aug	84
10	2:17.20	Rob Harrison	18	Aug	84		3:38.08	Tom Hanlon	28	Jun	92
	2:17.36	Neil Horsfield	9	Aug	91		3:38.1	Jim McGuinness	1	Aug	77
	2:17.43	Gareth Brown	18	Aug	84		3:38.2 a	James Espir	11	Jul	80
	2:17.45	Chris McGeorge	20	Aug	84		3:38.22	Peter Stewart	15	Jul	72
	2:17.63	Kevin McKay	14	Jul	89		3:38.31	Matt Barnes	23	Jul	93
	2:17.75	Steve Crabb	5	Aug	87		3:38.33 +	Tom Mayo	22	Jul	01 40
	2:17.79	David Sharpe	31	Aug	92		3:38.34		19	Aug	01
	2:17.95	Mark Scruton	17	Jul	84		3:38.52	Ray Smedley	15	Jul	72
	2:17.96	Ikem Billy	14	Jul	89		3:38.56	Curtis Robb	26	Jun	93
	2:18.18	Mal Edwards	11	Jul	86		3:38.64	Simon Fairbrother	17	Jun	92
20	2:18.2	John Boulter	6	Sep	69		3:38.65	Ian Stewart II	8	Aug	81
	2:18.28	Garry Cook	23	Aug	81		3:38.66	Glen Stewart	26	May	96
	2:18.31 i	David Strang	30	Jan	93		3:38.68	John Kirkbride	15	Jul	72
	2:18.33	Gary Marlow	5	Aug	87		3:38.7	Jim Douglas	27	Jun	72
	2:18.35	Paul Larkins	27	Jun	86		3:38.78	Mark Scruton	17	Jun	84
	2:18.48	John Mayock	11	Aug	96		3:38.8	Paul Lawther	12	Jun	77
							3:38.9	Ian Hamer	5	Aug	89 50
	1500 Metres (+ during 1 mile)						3:38.93	Brian Treacy	28	Aug	94
	3:29.67	Steve Cram	16	Jul	85		3:39.0	David Lewis	9	Aug	83
	3:29.77	Sebastian Coe	7	Sep	86						
	3:30.15	Cram	5	Sep	86		**1 Mile**				
	3:30.77	Steve Ovett	4	Sep	83		3:46.32	Steve Cram	27	Jul	85
	3:30.95	Cram	19	Aug	88		3:47.33	Sebastian Coe	28	Aug	81
	3:31.34	Cram	27	Jun	85		3:48.31	Cram	5	Jul	86
	3:31.36	Ovett	27	Aug	80		3:48.40	Steve Ovett	26	Aug	81
	3:31.43	Cram	19	Aug	87		3:48.53	Coe	19	Aug	81
	3:31.57	Ovett	29	Jul	81		3:48.8	Ovett	1	Jul	80
	3:31.66	Cram	26	Aug	83		3:48.85	Cram	2	Jul	88
	3:31.86	John Mayock	22	Aug	97		3:48.95	Coe	17	Jul	79
	3:31.95	Coe	7	Jul	81		3:49.20	Peter Elliott	2	Jul	88
	3:31.95	Ovett	8	Jul	81		3:49.22	Coe	27	Jul	85
	3:32.34	Anthony Whiteman	16	Aug	97		3:49.25	Ovett	11	Jul	81
	3:32.69	Peter Elliott	16	Sep	90		3:49.34	Dave Moorcroft	26	Jun	82
	3:33.34	Steve Crabb	4	Jul	87						

	Time	Name	Date	
	3:49.46	Elliott	6 Jul 91	
	3:49.49	Cram	12 Sep 86	
	3:49.57	Ovett	31 Aug 79	
	3:49.65	Cram	29 Aug 84	
	3:49.66	Ovett	14 Jul 81	
	3:49.76	Elliott	14 Jul 90	
	3:49.90	Cram	13 Jul 82	
	3:49.95	Cram	19 Aug 81	
	3:50.32	John Mayock	5 Jul 96	
	3:50.64	Graham Williamson	13 Jul 82	
	3:51.02	John Gladwin	19 Aug 87	
	3:51.31	Tony Morrell	14 Jul 90	
10	3:51.57	Jack Buckner	29 Aug 84	
	3:51.76hc	Steve Crabb	14 Aug 87	
	3:52.20		1 Jul 89	
	3:51.90	Anthony Whiteman	16 Jul 98	
	3:52.44	John Robson	11 Jul 81	
	3:52.75	Matthew Yates	10 Jul 93	
	3:52.99	Mark Rowland	10 Sep 86	
	3:53.20	Ian Stewart II	25 Aug 82	
	3:53.64	Kevin McKay	22 Jul 94	
	3:53.82	Gary Staines	12 Aug 90	
	3:53.85	Rob Harrison	15 Jul 86	
20	3:54.2	Frank Clement	27 Jun 78	
	3:54.30	David Strang	22 Jul 94	
	3:54.39	Neil Horsfield	8 Jul 86	
	3:54.53	Tim Hutchings	31 Jul 82	
	3:54.70	Andrew Graffin	23 Aug 02	
	3:54.9	Adrian Passey	20 Aug 89	
	3:55.0	Jim McGuinness	11 Jul 77	
	3:55.3	Peter Stewart	10 Jun 72	
	3:55.38	Rob Denmark	12 Aug 90	
	3:55.41	Colin Reitz	31 Jul 82	
30	3:55.57	Tom Mayo	22 Jul 01	
	3:55.68	Alan Simpson	30 Aug 65	
	3:55.8	Geoff Smith	15 Aug 81	
	3:55.84	Neil Caddy	25 Aug 96	
	3:55.9	Brendan Foster	10 Jun 72	
	3:55.91	Gary Lough	27 Aug 95	
	3:55.96	David Lewis	23 Aug 83	
	3:56.0	Jim Douglas	10 Jun 72	
	3:56.04	Mike Downes	25 Aug 82	
	3:56.1	Neill Duggan	11 Jun 66	
40	3:56.19	Ian Hamer	5 Jul 91	
	3:56.29 i	Andy Keith	22 Jan 94	
	3:56.36	Steve Martin	5 Aug 86	
	3:56.38	Mike McLeod	31 Aug 79	
	3:56.5	John Kirkbride	10 Jun 72	
	3:56.5	Paul Davies-Hale	20 Aug 89	
	3:56.6	Walter Wilkinson	31 May 71	
	3:56.65	Paul Larkins	17 Jul 87	
	3:56.7	James Espir	15 Aug 81	
	3:56.71	Chris McGeorge	5 Jul 88	
50	3:56.8	Ian McCafferty	11 Jun 69	
	3:56.83	Simon Fairbrother	17 Aug 90	
	3:56.9 a	Ron Speirs	30 Apr 77	
	3:56.95	Sean Cahill	31 Aug 79	
	3:56.95	Dave Clarke	17 Jul 82	
	3:56.90	Alan Salter	9 Jul 85	
	3:57.07	Neil Ovington	11 Jul 86	

2000 Metres

	Time	Name	Date	
	4:51.39	Steve Cram	4 Aug 85	
	4:52.82	Peter Elliott	15 Sep 87	
	4:53.06	Jack Buckner	15 Sep 87	
	4:53.69	Gary Staines	15 Sep 87	
	4:55.20	Cram	28 Aug 88	
	4:55.72	Elliott	28 Aug 88	
	4:56.75	John Mayock	30 Jul 99	
	4:57.71	Steve Ovett	7 Jul 82	
	4:57.82	Ovett	3 Jun 78	
	4:58.38	Graham Williamson	29 Aug 83	
	4:58.57	Mayock	7 Sep 99	
	4:58.84	Sebastian Coe	5 Jun 82	
	4:59.57	Nick Rose	3 Jun 78	
	5:00.37	Tim Hutchings	29 Aug 83	10
	5:01.09	Eamonn Martin	19 Jun 84	
	5:01.28	Andrew Graffin	25 Jun 00	
	5:01.48	Paul Larkins	5 Jun 88	
	5:02.35	Sean Cahill	4 Aug 85	
	5:02.61	Steve Martin	19 Jun 84	
	5:02.8 a	Frank Clement	10 Sep 78	
	5:02.86	David Moorcroft	19 Jul 86	
	5:02.90	Allen Graffin	25 Jun 00	
	5:02.93	Brendan Foster	4 Jul 75	
	5:02.98	Ian Stewart I	4 Jul 75	20
	5:02.98	Gary Lough	11 Aug 96	
	5:02.99	Neil Caddy	11 Aug 96	
	5:03.16	Dave Bedford	8 Jul 72	
	5:03.8	Lawrie Spence	26 May 78	
	5:04.11	Rob Denmark	11 Aug 96	

3000 Metres (+ during 2 Miles)

	Time	Name	Date	
	7:32.79	Dave Moorcroft	17 Jul 82	
	7:35.1	Brendan Foster	3 Aug 74	
	7:36.40	John Nuttall	10 Jul 96	
	7:39.55	Rob Denmark	1 Aug 93	
	7:39.72	Denmark	15 Jul 92	
	7:40.4	Nick Rose	27 Jun 78	
	7:40.43	Jack Buckner	5 Jul 86	
	7:40.94	Eamonn Martin	9 Jul 83	
	7:41.09 i	John Mayock	6 Feb 02	
	7:47.28		23 Jul 95	
	7:41.3	Steve Ovett	23 Sep 77	
	7:41.79	Gary Staines	14 Jul 90	10
	7:42.26	Graeme Fell	9 Jul 83	
	7:42.47	David Lewis	9 Jul 83	
	7:42.77	Billy Dee	18 Jul 92	
	7:43.03	Tim Hutchings	14 Jul 89	
	7:43.1 +	Steve Cram	29 Aug 83	
	7:43.61	Anthony Whiteman	27 Jun 98	
	7:43.90	Ian Stewart II	26 Jun 82	
	7:44.40	Colin Reitz	9 Jul 83	
	7:44.76	Paul Davies-Hale	20 Jul 85	
	7:45.2 +	Geoff Turnbull	12 Sep 86	20
	7:45.29	Dennis Coates	9 Sep 77	
	7:45.41	Jon Brown	1 Aug 98	
	7:45.81	John Robson	13 Jul 84	
	7:46.22 i	Mark Rowland	27 Feb 90	
	7:49.82		28 Jul 89	
	7:46.39	Adrian Royle	28 Jun 83	

	7:46.40	Ian Hamer	20 Jan 90	
	7:46.4	David Bedford	21 Jun 72	
	7:46.6 +	Dave Black	14 Sep 73	
	7:46.83	Ian Stewart I	26 May 76	
30	7:46.85 i	Ricky Wilde	15 Mar 70	
	7:46.95	David James	26 May 80	
	7:47.12	Simon Mugglestone	27 Jun 88	
	7:47.54	Paul Larkins	14 Jul 89	
	7:47.56	Dick Callan	15 Jul 83	
	7:47.6	Dick Taylor	6 Sep 69	
	7:48.00	Richard Nerurkar	15 Jul 92	
	7:48.09	Adrian Passey	28 Jul 89	
	7:48.18	Mike McLeod	9 Jul 78	
	7:48.28	Jon Richards	9 Jul 83	
40	7:48.28	Ian Gillespie	25 May 97	
	7:48.6 +	Nat Muir	27 Jun 80	
	7:48.66	Julian Goater	26 May 80	
	7:48.76	Neil Caddy	2 Aug 98	
	7:48.81	Tim Redman	18 Aug 84	
	7:49.1	Paul Lawther	27 Jun 78	
	7:49.45	Gary Lough	30 May 95	
	7:49.47	Roger Hackney	13 Jul 84	
	7:49.64	Barry Smith	26 Jul 81	
	7:49.72	Ray Smedley	9 Jul 78	
50	7:49.80	Steve Jones	13 Jul 84	
	7:49.83 i	Andy Keith	6 Feb 94	
	7:50.04	Karl Keska	2 Aug 98	
	7:50.20	Jon Solly	8 Aug 86	

2 Miles

	8:13.51	Steve Ovett	15 Sep 78	
	8:13.68	Brendan Foster	27 Aug 73	
	8:14.93	Steve Cram	29 Aug 83	
	8:15.53	Tim Hutchings	12 Sep 86	
	8:15.98	Geoff Turnbull	12 Sep 86	
	8:16.75	Dave Moorcroft	20 Aug 82	
	8:16.94	Foster	17 Jul 79	
	8:17.12	Jack Buckner	12 Sep 86	
	8:17.79	Cram	16 Jul 88	
	8:18.4 i	Nick Rose	17 Feb 78	
	8:22.41		15 Sep 78	
	8:18.57	Moorcroft	27 Jun 80	
	8:18.98	Eamonn Martin	16 Jul 88	
10	8:19.37	Nat Muir	27 Jun 80	
	8:20.28	David James	27 Jun 80	
	8:20.66	David Lewis	7 Sep 84	
	8:21.09	Barry Smith	27 Jun 80	
	8:21.86	David Black	14 Sep 73	
	8:21.97	Rob Denmark	9 Aug 91	
	8:22.0	Ian Stewart I	14 Aug 72	
	8:22.65	Ian Hamer	17 Jul 92	
	8:22.7 i	Graeme Fell	19 Feb 82	
	8:22.98	Geoff Smith	27 Jun 80	
20	8:23.16	Gary Staines	9 Aug 91	
	8:23.80	Billy Dee	9 Aug 91	
	8:23.92	Ray Smedley	6 Aug 76	
	8:24.58	Adrian Royle	16 May 82	
	8:24.82	Eddie Wedderburn	16 Jul 88	
	8:25.02	Tony Simmons	6 Aug 76	
	8:25.52	Colin Reitz	19 Aug 86	

5000 Metres

13:00.41	Dave Moorcroft	7 Jul 82	
13:09.80	Ian Hamer	9 Jun 92	
13:10.15	Jack Buckner	31 Aug 86	
13:10.24	Rob Denmark	9 Jun 92	
13:10.47	Buckner	9 Jun 92	
13:10.48	Buckner	19 Aug 87	
13:11.50	Tim Hutchings	11 Aug 84	
13:12.88	Hutchings	31 Aug 86	
13:13.01	Denmark	17 Jul 91	
13:13.77	Denmark	15 Jun 95	
13:14.28	Gary Staines	15 Aug 90	
13:14.6 a	Brendan Foster	29 Jan 74	
13:15.59	Julian Goater	11 Sep 81	
13:16.70	John Nuttall	8 Jun 95	
13:17.21	Dave Bedford	14 Jul 72	10
13:17.21	Keith Cullen	19 Jul 97	
13:17.84	Eamonn Martin	14 Jul 89	
13:17.9	Nat Muir	15 Jul 80	
13:18.06	Ian Gillespie	19 Jul 97	
13:18.6	Steve Jones	10 Jun 82	
13:18.91	Nick Rose	28 Jun 84	
13:19.03	Jon Brown	5 Aug 98	
13:19.43	John Mayock	31 Jul 02	
13:19.45	Sam Haughian	31 Jul 02	
13:19.66	Ian McCafferty	14 Jul 72	20
13:20.06	Steve Ovett	30 Jun 86	
13:20.09	Adrian Passey	19 Jul 97	
13:20.30	Karl Keska	20 Jul 02	
13:21.13	David Lewis	4 Jul 85	
13:21.14	Barry Smith	7 Jun 81	
13:21.2	Tony Simmons	23 May 76	
13:21.60	Paul Davies-Hale	8 Jul 88	
13:21.73	Geoff Turnbull	5 Sep 86	
13:21.83	Mark Rowland	1 Jun 88	
13:22.17 i	Geoff Smith	12 Feb 82	30
13:26.33		8 Aug 81	
13:22.39	Jon Solly	7 Jul 86	
13:22.54	Dave Clarke	28 Jun 83	
13:22.8 a	Ian Stewart I	25 Jul 70	
13:23.26	Mike McLeod	24 Jun 80	
13:23.36	Richard Nerurkar	10 Aug 90	
13:23.48	John Doherty	1 Jun 85	
13:23.52	Dave Black	29 Jan 74	
13:23.71	Steve Binns	1 Jun 88	
13:24.44	Mike Openshaw	14 Jul 01	
13:25.38	Paul Evans	28 Jun 95	40
13:26.0	Bernie Ford	30 Jul 77	
13:26.19	Adrian Royle	4 Jul 83	
13:26.2	Dick Taylor	13 Jun 70	
13:26.74	Craig Mochrie	25 Aug 89	
13:27.14	Dick Callan	25 Aug 82	
13:27.41	Billy Dee	10 Jul 92	
13:27.63	Dermot Donnelly	1 Aug 98	
13:27.75	Rod Finch	1 Aug 98	
13:28.15	Malcolm Prince	14 Sep 79	
13:28.22	Kris Bowditch	25 Jun 00	50
13:28.29	Simon Mugglestone	8 Jul 88	
13:28.58	Steve Cram	3 Jun 89	
13:28.7 a	Charlie Spedding	13 Aug 78	

10000 Metres

27:18.14	Jon Brown	28	Aug	98
27:23.06	Eamonn Martin	2	Jul	88
27:27.47	Brown	31	May	97
27:30.3	Brendan Foster	23	Jun	78
27:30.80	Dave Bedford	13	Jul	73
27:31.19	Nick Rose	9	Jul	83
27:32.65	Foster	29	Aug	78
27:34.58	Julian Goater	26	Jun	82
27:36.27	David Black	29	Aug	78
27:36.62	Foster	9	Sep	77
27:39.14	Steve Jones	9	Jul	83
27:39.76	Mike McLeod	4	Sep	79
10 27:40.03	Richard Nerurkar	10	Jul	93
27:43.03	Ian Stewart I	9	Sep	77
27:43.59	Tony Simmons	30	Jun	77
27:43.74	Bernie Ford	9	Sep	77
27:43.76	Geoff Smith	13	Jun	81
27:44.09	Karl Keska	25	Sep	00
27:47.16	Adrian Royle	10	Apr	82
27:47.79	Paul Evans	5	Jul	93
27:48.73	Gary Staines	6	Jul	91
27:50.33	Keith Cullen	10	Apr	99
20 27:51.76	Jon Solly	20	Jun	86
27:55.66	Steve Binns	9	Jul	83
27:55.77	Dave Clarke	25	May	82
27:57.77	Ian Hamer	13	Sep	91
27:59.12	Allister Hutton	30	May	86
27:59.24	Carl Thackery	16	Jul	87
27:59.33	Steve Harris	22	Jul	86
28:00.50	Andres Jones	22	Jul	00
28:00.62	Jim Brown	1	Aug	75
28:00.64	Billy Dee	13	Sep	91
30 28:03.31	Rob Denmark	22	Jul	00
28:04.04	Andy Bristow	17	Aug	90
28:04.2	Ian Robinson	20	Apr	96
28:04.48	Mark Steinle	22	Jul	00
28:05.2	Dave Murphy	10	Apr	81
28:06.13	Barry Smith	7	Aug	81
28:06.6	Dick Taylor	22	Jun	69
28:07.43	John Nuttall	25	Aug	95
28:07.57	Tim Hutchings	7	Jul	90
28:08.12	Charlie Spedding	23	Jul	83
40 28:08.44	David Lewis	5	Jun	88
28:09.39	Mark Dalloway	5	Jun	88
28:11.07	Karl Harrison	20	Jun	86
28:11.71	Lachie Stewart	18	Jul	70
28:11.85	Lawrie Spence	29	May	83
28:13.04	Gerry Helme	29	May	83
28:13.13	Colin Moore	29	Jun	90
28:13.36	Jack Buckner	13	Sep	91
28:14.08	Jon Richards	20	Jun	86
28:14.65	Mike Tagg	10	Aug	71
50 28:14.89	Bernie Plain	1	Aug	75
28:15.58	Martin McLoughlin	20	Jun	86
28:16.0	Mike Baxter	23	May	74
28:16.73	Neil Coupland	11	Jun	77
28:17.00	Justin Hobbs	29	Jun	94
28:18.6	John Davies II	11	Apr	79
28:18.68	Terry Thornton	17	Aug	90

10 Kilometres Road

27:34	Nick Rose	1	Apr	84	
27:53	Mike O'Reilly	19	Oct	86	
27:55	Mark Scrutton	5	Mar	84	
27:56	Steve Harris	4	Dec	83	
27:56	John Doherty	4	Jul	86	
27:59	Steve Jones	28	Apr	84	
28:00	Roger Hackney	4	Dec	83	
28:01	Barry Smith	4	Dec	83	
28:02	Steve Binns	15	Apr	89	
28:03	Jon Solly	5	Apr	86	10
28:03	Jack Buckner	28	Feb	87	
28:05	Jon Brown	17	Oct	93	
28:06	Geoff Smith	2	Mar	85	
28:07	Colin Reitz	28	Apr	84	
28:07	Peter Whitehead	4	Jul	96	
28:09	Dave Moorcroft	16	May	82	
28:10	Adrian Leek	10	Mar	84	
28:10	Dave Clarke	5	May	85	
28:11	Jon Richards	5	May	85	
28:12	Dave Murphy	19	May	85	20
28:13	Allister Hutton	28	Apr	84	
28:13	Paul Evans	8	Jan	95	
28:14	Karl Harrison	5	May	85	
28:14	David Lewis	5	Apr	86	
28:14	Eamonn Martin	30	Apr	89	
28:16	Steve Ovett	4	Dec	83	
28:17	Paul Davies-Hale	21	Apr	85	
28:17	Colin Moore	5	May	85	
28:18	Steve Kenyon	15	Sep	85	
28:19	Peter Tootell	28	Apr	84	30
28:19	Nigel Gates	5	May	85	
28:19	Terry Greene	4	Apr	87	

course measurement uncertain

28:01	Steve Kenyon	21	Sep	86
28:04	Dave Bedford	27	Mar	77
28:08	Kevin Forster	15	Jul	84
28:08	Dave Clarke	15	Jul	84

downhill

27:20	Jon Brown	24	Sep	95
27:57	Malcolm East	25	Sep	82

short (50m)

27:50	Mark Scrutton	6	Dec	81

10 Miles Road

46:02	Richard Nerurkar	17	Oct	93	
46:11	Gary Staines	10	Oct	93	
46:19	Nerurkar	23	Jul	95	
46:25	Carl Thackery	7	Apr	91	
46:35	Paul Evans	21	Sep	97	
46:41	Roger Hackney	6	Apr	86	
46:42	Dave Murphy	28	Apr	84	
46:43	Nick Rose	25	Apr	87	
46:48	Geoff Smith	2	May	82	
46:49	Steve Jones	2	Apr	89	
47:00	Paul Davies-Hale	10	Oct	93	
47:02	Martin McLoughlin	10	Oct	93	10
47:07	Geoff Smith	1	May	83	
47:10	Colin Moore	6	Nov	88	
47:10	Jack Buckner	11	Oct	92	

intermediate times

46:10 +	Paul Evans	14	Sep	97
46:21 +	Nigel Adams	15	Sep	91
46:21 +	Carl Thackery	15	Sep	91
46:23 +	Allister Hutton	1	Jan	85

estimated times

46:02 +	Steve Jones	8	Jun	86

course measurement uncertain

45:13	Ian Stewart I	8	May	77
45:37	Barry Smith	22	Mar	81
45:44	Mike McLeod	9	Apr	78
46:03	Colin Moore	29	Aug	83
46:08	Nick Rose	26	Apr	81
46:11	Steve Kenyon	20	Jun	81
46:14	Charlie Spedding	12	Oct	86
46:17	Brendan Foster	9	Apr	78

downhill

46:05	Allister Hutton	3	Apr	82

Half Marathon

1:00:59	Steve Jones	8	Jun	86
1:01:03	Nick Rose	15	Sep	85
1:01:04	Carl Thackery	12	Apr	87
1:01:06	Richard Nerurkar	14	Apr	96
1:01:13	Thackery	3	Oct	93
1:01:14	Jones	11	Aug	85
1:01:17	David Lewis	20	Sep	92
1:01:18	Paul Evans	14	Sep	97
1:01:28	Steve Brooks	23	Mar	97
1:01:31	Steve Kenyon	8	Jun	86
1:01:39	Geoff Smith	25	Sep	83
1:01:39	Paul Davies-Hale	15	Sep	91
1:01:49	Jon Brown	14	Sep	97
1:01:53	Nigel Adams	15	Sep	91
1:01:56	Mark Flint	22	Aug	93
1:01:57	Gary Staines	14	Sep	97
1:02:07	Kevin Forster	5	Apr	87
1:02:07	Martyn Brewer	20	Sep	87
1:02:07	Andrew Pearson	14	Sep	97
1:02:08	Steve Harris	20	Oct	85
1:02:11	Dave Clarke	5	Apr	92
1:02:11	Keith Cullen	20	Aug	00
1:02:15	Dave Murphy	16	Sep	84
1:02:16	Jim Haughey	20	Sep	87
1:02:19	Dave Long I	11	Dec	81
1:02:22	Colin Moore	26	May	85
1:02:23	Mark Steinle	10	Oct	99
1:02:24	Jimmy Ashworth	8	Jun	86
1:02:25	Barry Royden	18	Sep	94
1:02:28	Terry Greene	12	Apr	86
1:02:28	Allister Hutton	21	Jun	87
1:02:28	Andy Coleman	22	Oct	00

course measurement uncertain

1:00:09	Paul Evans	15	Jan	95
1:01:47	Dave Long II	17	Mar	91
1:02:08	Ray Smedly	28	Mar	82
1:02:09	Steve Anders	25	Sep	88
1:02:19	Mike Carroll	3	Jun	90
1:02:23	Charlie Spedding	15	Mar	87

Marathon

2:07:13	Steve Jones	20	Oct	85
2:08:05	Jones	21	Oct	84
2:08:16	Jones	21	Apr	85
2:08:20	Jones	6	Nov	88
2:08:33	Charlie Spedding	21	Apr	85
2:08:36	Richard Nerurkar	13	Apr	97
2:08:52	Paul Evans	20	Oct	96
2:09:08	Geoff Smith	23	Oct	83
2:09:12	Ian Thompson	31	Jan	74
2:09:16	Allister Hutton	21	Apr	85
2:09:17	Mark Steinle	14	Apr	02
2:09:24	Hugh Jones	9	May	82
2:09:28	Ron Hill	23	Jul	70
2:09:28	John Graham	23	May	81
2:09:43	Mike Gratton	17	Apr	83
2:09:44	Jon Brown	18	Apr	99
2:09:54	Tony Milovsorov	23	Apr	89
2:10:12	Gerry Helme	17	Apr	83
2:10:30	Dave Long II	21	Apr	91
2:10:35	Steve Brace	21	Jan	96
2:10:39	Mike O'Reilly	5	Dec	93
2:10:48	Bill Adcocks	8	Dec	68
2:10:50	Eamonn Martin	18	Apr	93
2:10:51	Bernie Ford	2	Dec	79
2:10:52	Kevin Forster	17	Apr	88
2:10:55	Chris Bunyan	18	Apr	83
2:11:06	Dave Buzza	31	Oct	93
2:11:18	Dave Murphy	12	Jun	83
2:11:22	Dave Cannon	6	Sep	80
2:11:25	Paul Davies-Hale	29	Oct	89
2:11:25	Gary Staines	20	Oct	96
2:11:35	Malcolm East	20	Apr	81
2:11:36	Kenny Stuart	15	Jan	89
2:11:40	Steve Kenyon	13	Jun	82
2:11:43	Jimmy Ashworth	29	Sep	85
2:11:44	Jim Dingwall	17	Apr	83
2:11:50	Fraser Clyne	2	Dec	84
2:11:54	Martin McCarthy	17	Apr	83
2:11:58	Mark Hudspith	2	Apr	95
2:12:04	Jim Alder	23	Jul	70
2:12:07	Jon Solly	14	Oct	90
2:12:07	Mark Flint	17	Apr	94
2:12:12	Dennis Fowles	13	May	84
2:12:12	Andy Green	25	Apr	93
2:12:13	John Wheway	17	Apr	88
2:12:17	Dave Long I	16	Jan	82
2:12:19	Don Faircloth	23	Jul	70
2:12:23	Peter Whitehead	2	Apr	95
2:12:32	Trevor Wright	3	Dec	78
2:12:33	Tony Simmons	7	May	78
2:12:37	Carl Thackery	25	Oct	92
2:12:41	Derek Stevens	16	Jun	84
2:12:50	Jeff Norman	7	May	78
2:13:06	Greg Hannon	13	May	79
2:13:12	Chris Stewart	8	Dec	74
2:13:15	Ray Crabb	17	Apr	83
2:13:16	Norman Wilson	20	Apr	81
2:13:17	Mike Hurd	26	Sep	82
2:13:17	Geoff Wightman	29	Sep	91

2000 Metres Steeplechase

5:19.86	Mark Rowland	28 Aug	88
5:20.56	Rowland	17 Aug	90
5:21.77	Tom Hanlon	11 Jun	92
5:22.37	Rowland	16 Sep	90
5:22.96	Hanlon	16 Sep	90
5:23.56	Tom Buckner	17 Jul	92
5:23.6	Roger Hackney	10 Jun	82
5:23.71	Colin Walker	28 Aug	88
5:23.87	Colin Reitz	28 Jun	84
5:24.91	Eddie Wedderburn	19 Aug	86
5:26.24	Paul Davies-Hale	26 Aug	85
5:26.64	Nick Peach	19 Aug	86
10 5:26.82 "	David Lewis	12 Jun	83
5:30.6	Dennis Coates	23 Apr	78
5:30.86	Tony Staynings	26 May	76
5:31.04	John Hartigan	17 Aug	90
5:31.09	Peter McColgan	5 Aug	86
5:31.43	John Bicourt	26 May	76
5:31.59	Mick Hawkins	20 Jan	90
5:32.45	Neil Smart	17 Aug	90
5:33.09	Spencer Duval	17 Jul	92
5:33.59	Mark Sinclair	19 Aug	86
20 5:33.76	Graeme Fell	9 Sep	79

3000 Metres Steeplechase

8:07.96	Mark Rowland	30 Sep	88	
8:12.11	Colin Reitz	5 Sep	86	
8:12.58	Tom Hanlon	3 Aug	91	
8:13.27	Rowland	30 Aug	90	
8:13.50	Reitz	4 Aug	85	
8:13.65	Hanlon	4 Jul	92	
8:13.78	Reitz	21 Jul	84	
8:14.73	Hanlon	15 Jul	92	
8:14.95	Reitz	27 Jul	85	
8:15.16	Graeme Fell	17 Aug	83	
8:18.32	Eddie Wedderburn	5 Jul	88	
8:18.91	Roger Hackney	30 Jul	88	
8:18.95	Dennis Coates	25 Jul	76	
8:20.83	Paul Davies-Hale	10 Jun	84	
8:22.48	John Davies II	13 Sep	74	
10 8:22.82	John Bicourt	8 Jun	76	
8:23.90	Justin Chaston	18 Jul	94	
8:24.64	Spencer Duval	16 Jul	95	
8:25.15	Colin Walker	28 Jun	92	
8:25.37	Christian Stephenson	19 Aug	00	
8:25.50	Tom Buckner	28 Aug	92	
8:26.05	Keith Cullen	21 Aug	95	
8:26.33	Rob Hough	6 Jul	96	
8:26.4	Andy Holden	15 Sep	72	
8:26.45	Stuart Stokes	27 Ju1	02	
20 8:26.6	Gordon Rimmer	4 Jun	80	
8:27.21	Tony Staynings	15 Jun	80	
8:27.8	Steve Hollings	5 Aug	73	
8:27.93	Peter McColgan	25 Jun	91	
8:28.6	Dave Bedford	10 Sep	71	
8:29.46	Julian Marsay	14 Jul	79	
8:29.72	David Lewis	29 May	83	
8:30.6 a	Peter Griffiths	17 Jul	77	
8:30.8	Gerry Stevens	1 Sep	69	
8:31.09	Ian Gilmour	16 Jul	78	
8:31.22	Dave Lee	19 Jun	92	30
8:32.00	Steve Jones	8 Aug	80	
8:32.06	David Camp	10 Aug	74	
8:32.13	Barry Knight	25 Jul	82	
8:32.4 a	Maurice Herriott	17 Oct	64	
8:32.68	Ben Whitby	15 Jul	01	
8:33.0	John Jackson	13 Aug	69	
8:33.8 a	Gareth Bryan-Jones	23 Jul	70	
8:33.8	Peter Morris	4 Aug	73	
8:33.83	Richard Charleston	24 May	80	
8:33.89	Nick Peach	21 Jun	86	40
8:33.97	John Hartigan	20 Jul	90	
8:34.67	Craig Wheeler	9 Jun	99	
8:34.77	Kevin Capper	18 Aug	85	
8:34.83	Ken Baker	1 Jul	84	
8:35.49	Micky Morris	14 Aug	76	
8:35.52	Neil Smart	28 Aug	89	
8:35.6	Ron McAndrew	9 Jul	71	
8:35.8	John Wild	3 Aug	77	
8:36.2 a	Bernie Hayward	26 Jan	74	
8:36.55	Mick Hawkins	16 Jul	95	50

110 Metres Hurdles

12.91	Colin Jackson	20 Aug	93	
12.97 A	Jackson	28 Jul	93	
12.98	Jackson	15 Sep	94	
12.99	Jackson	3 Sep	93	
12.99	Jackson	6 Sep	94	
13.00	Tony Jarrett	20 Aug	93	
13.02	Jackson	30 Aug	94	
13.02	Jackson	22 Aug	98	
13.03	Jackson	4 Sep	94	
13.04	Jackson	16 Aug	92	
13.04	Jackson	12 Aug	94	
13.04	Jarrett	12 Aug	95	
13.04	Jackson	25 Aug	99	
13.29	Jon Ridgeon	15 Jul	87	
13.42	David Nelson	27 Aug	91	
13.43	Mark Holtom	4 Oct	82	
13.44	Hugh Teape	14 Aug	92	
13.49	Andy Tulloch	30 Jun	99	
13.51	Nigel Walker	3 Aug	90	
13.53	Paul Gray	22 Aug	94	
13.54	Damien Greaves	13 Jul	02	10
13.60	Wilbert Greaves	21 Aug	85	
13.60	Neil Owen	28 Jun	95	
13.66	Ross Baillie	20 Feb	99	
13.69	Berwyn Price	18 Aug	73	
13.72	David Hemery	1 Aug	70	
13.75	Lloyd Cowan	17 Jul	94	
13.79	Alan Pascoe	17 Jun	72	
13.82	Mensah Elliott	30 Jul	00	
13.82	Chris Baillie	7 Jul	01	
13.83	Dominic Bradley	14 Jul	01	20
13.86	Ken Campbell	23 Aug	94	
13.90	Andy Turner	3 Aug	02	
13.92	Robert Newton	18 May	02	
13.95	Dominic Girdler	15 Jun	02	
13.96	Steve Buckeridge	31 May	86	

14.00	Matt Douglas	23 May	99
14.02	Mark Lambeth	9 Jul	95
14.03	Brett St Louis	27 Jun	87
14.03	Brian Taylor	19 May	96
30 14.04	Daley Thompson	28 Aug	86
14.04	Mike Robbins	1 May	99
14.05	Liam Collins	4 Jun	00
14.05	Allan Scott	15 Jun	02
14.05	Mohammed Sillah-Freckleton	17 Jul	02
14.06	Natham Palmer	20 Jul	01
14.08	Paul Brice	26 Aug	83
14.09	Colin Hamplett	11 Aug	90
14.09	Tristan Anthony	15 Jun	02
14.10	Graham Gower	15 Jul	72
40 14.10	Bob Danville	4 Jul	76
14.10	Jamie Quarry	25 Jun	94
14.10	Duncan Malins	1 Jul	00
14.10 A	Tim Reetz	4 May	02
14.18		10 May	02
14.11	Neil Fraser	11 Jul	87
14.11	Ererton Harrison	31 Jul	91
14.12	Matthew Clements	17 May	98
14.13	Mark Stern	22 Jun	96
14.14	Mike Hogan	5 Sep	63
14.14	Max Robertson	7 Jun	86
50 14.14	Martin Nicholson	12 Jun	94
14.16 A	Mike Parker	16 Oct	68
14.16	Martyn Hendry	25 Aug	97
14.17	Colin Bovell	23 Jul	94
14.18	Chris Breen	13 Jul	75
14.18	James Archampong	21 Jul	94
14.19	C. J. Kirkpatrick	16 Jun	73
14.20 A	Stuart Storey	16 Oct	68
14.20	Kevin Lumsden	16 Jul	94
14.21	David Wilson	15 Jul	72
14.21	Alan Cronin	13 Jul	75
14.21	Mark Whitby	14 Jun	85

wind assisted

12.94 A	Jackson	31 Jul	94
12.95	Jackson	10 Sep	89
12.99	Jackson	23 Jun	89
13.01	Jackson	2 Jul	93
13.49	Nigel Walker	3 Jun	89
13.65	Berwyn Price	25 Aug	75
13.66	David Hemery	18 Jul	70
13.69	Mensah Elliott	19 Aug	00
13.70	Chris Baillie	1 Jul	01
10 13.91 A	Tim Reetz	3 May	02
13.93		24 May	02
13.93	Robert Newton	7 Aug	99
13.96	Mike Robbins	28 Mar	98
13.97	Brett St Louis	30 Jul	88
13.99	Bob Danville	14 Aug	76
14.06	Tony James	22 Aug	81
14.08	David Wilson	15 Jul	72
14.08	Duncan Malins	18 Jun	00
14.11	Mark Stern	20 Jun	93
20 14.14	James Archampong	25 May	96
14.16	Mark Hatton	14 Jul	79
14.17	C. J. Kirkpatrick	13 Jul	74

14.19	Alan Cronin	25 Aug	75
14.19	Norman Ashman	15 Aug	92
14.22	Phil Barthropp	1 Jul	84
14.22	Dave Sweetman	24 May	98
14.22	Tony Gill	14 Aug	99

hand timing

13.5	Berwyn Price	1 Jul	73
13.6	David Hemery	5 Jul	69
13.7	Alan Pascoe	5 Jul	69
13.7	C. J. Kirkpatrick	29 Jun	74
13.7	Mensah Elliott	2 Sep	00
13.8	Martin Nicholson	25 Jun	94
13.9	Mike Parker	2 Oct	63
13.9	David Wilson	29 Jun	74
13.9	Brian Taylor	8 May	93
14.1	Stuart Storey	2 Aug	67 10
14.1	Colin Bovell	17 Jul	94
14.1	Tim Reetz	12 Jun	02

hand timing - wind assisted

12.8	Colin Jackson	10 Jan	90
13.0	Jarrett	2 Jun	96
13.4	Berwyn Price	7 Jul	76
13.5	Neil Owen	2 Jun	96
13.7	Lloyd Cowan	27 Apr	95
14.0	Laurie Taitt	13 Sep	62
14.0 y	Bob Birrell	9 Sep	61

400 Metres Hurdles

47.82	Kriss Akabusi	6 Aug	92
47.86	Akabusi	27 Aug	91
47.91	Akabusi	26 Aug	91
47.92	Akabusi	29 Aug	90
48.01	Akabusi	5 Aug	92
48.12 A	David Hemery	15 Oct	68
48.52		2 Sep	72
48.14	Chris Rawlinson	11 Aug	99
48.21	Rawlinson	2 Jul	02
48.22	Rawlinson	7 Jun	00
48.22	Rawlinson	5 Jul	00
48.59	Alan Pascoe	30 Jun	75
48.73	Jon Ridgeon	6 Sep	92
48.90	Anthony Borsumato	14 Jul	02
49.03 A	John Sherwood	15 Oct	68
49.88		13 Aug	69
49.07	Gary Cadogan	22 Jul	94
49.11	Gary Oakes	26 Jul	80
49.11	Matt Elias	28 Jul	01 10
49.16	Paul Gray	18 Aug	98
49.25	Max Robertson	28 Aug	90
49.26	Peter Crampton	8 Aug	94
49.26	Matt Douglas	30 Aug	00
49.29	Du'aine Thorne-Ladejo	9 Jun	01
49.49	Mark Holtom	20 Jul	85
49.60	Phil Beattie	28 Jul	86
49.65	Bill Hartley	2 Aug	75
49.82	Martin Gillingham	14 Aug	87
49.82	Gary Jennings	27 Jun	95 20
49.86	Martin Briggs	6 Jun	84
49.95	Steve Sole	24 Jul	83

400H

Time	Name	Date
49.96	Tony Williams	24 Jul 99
50.01	Phil Harries	5 Jun 88
50.05	Lawrence Lynch	15 Jun 96
50.1 a	John Cooper	16 Oct 64
50.16	Paul Thompson	17 May 96
50.16	Steve Surety	16 Jun 02
50.19	Steve Coupland	12 Jun 94
50.24	Charles Robertson-Adams	4 Jul 01
50.30	Liam Collins	14 Jul 02
50.37	Bob Danville	27 Jul 82
50.38	Andy Todd	18 Sep 69
50.40	James Hillier	1 Jul 01
50.49	Eddie Betts	13 Jul 97
50.52	Paul Hibbert	30 Jun 96
50.58	Colin O'Neill	29 Jan 74
50.58	Mike Whittingham	7 Aug 82
50.68	Peter Warden	18 Jun 66
50.68	Jared Deacon	12 May 02
50.70	Noel Levy	8 Jul 94
50.70	Richard McDonald	17 Aug 01
50.71	Steve Hawkins	4 Jun 89
50.79	Mark Davidson	17 Jun 89
50.79	Lloyd Cowan	3 Jun 95
50.82 "	Paul Atherton	12 Jun 83
50.91		6 Jun 84
50.84	Mark Whitby	6 Jun 84
50.86	Wilbert Greaves	18 May 80
50.88	Greg Dunson	7 Jun 92
50.91	Brian Whittle	5 Jun 93
50.94	Trevor Burton	17 Jul 87
50.96	Steven Green	6 Jul 02
50.97	Dave Savage	15 Jun 96
50.98	Tom Farrell	15 Jun 60
50.98	Stan Devine	14 Jul 82

hand timing

Time	Name	Date
49.9	Andy Todd	9 Oct 69
50.5	Wilbert Greaves	12 Feb 80
50.7	Steve Black	20 Aug 74
50.7	Stewart McCallum	21 Mar 76
50.8	Dave Schärer	26 Jun 71

High Jump

Height	Name	Date
2.38 i	Steve Smith	4 Feb 94
2.37		20 Sep 92
2.37 i	Smith	14 Mar 93
2.37	Smith	22 Aug 93
2.37 i	Dalton Grant	13 Mar 94
2.36		1 Sep 91
2.36 i	Smith	5 Feb 93
2.36 i	Smith	24 Feb 94
2.36 i	Smith	10 Feb 96
2.36 i	Smith	8 Feb 98
2.36	Smith	27 Jun 99
2.32 i	Brendan Reilly	24 Feb 94
2.31		17 Jul 92
2.31	Geoff Parsons	26 Aug 94
2.30	Ben Challenger	13 Jul 99
2.28 i	John Holman	28 Jan 89
2.24		27 May 89
2.26	James Brierley	3 Aug 96
2.25	Floyd Manderson	20 Aug 88
2.25	Robert Mitchell	28 Jul 01
2.24	Mark Naylor	28 Jun 80
2.24	John Hill	23 Aug 85
2.24	Phil McDonnell	26 Aug 85
2.23	Mark Lakey	29 Aug 82
2.23 i	David Abrahams	12 Mar 83
2.19		7 Oct 82
2.22	Danny Graham	20 May 00
2.21	Fayyaz Ahmed	29 Jun 86
2.21	Steve Chapman	30 Jul 89
2.21	Martyn Bernard	6 Jul 02
2.20	Brian Burgess	11 Jun 78
2.20	Trevor Llewelyn	15 Jul 83
2.20	Byron Morrison	14 Jul 84
2.20 i	Henderson Pierre	10 Jan 87
2.18		16 Aug 86
2.20	Alex Kruger	18 Jun 88
2.20	Ossie Cham	21 May 89
2.20 i	Warren Caswell	10 Mar 90
2.18		2 Sep 90
2.20	Colin Bent	16 Jun 96
2.20 i	Stuart Ohrland	1 Feb 97
2.18		28 Aug 99
2.20	Stuart Smith	13 Apr 97
2.20	David Barnetson	3 Aug 97
2.20 i	Samson Oni †	28 Jan 01
2.18 †		30 Jun 01
2.15		12 Jul 01
2.20	Dan Turner	28 May 01
2.19 i	Mike Robbins	3 Feb 96
2.17		5 Aug 95
2.19	Jamie Russell	18 May 02
2.18	Tim Foulger	23 Sep 79
2.18	Rupert Charles	25 Jul 82
2.18	Steve Ritchie	15 Jul 89
2.18	Hopeton Lindo	23 Jul 89
2.18	Andrew Lynch	9 Jul 95
2.18 i	Tony Gilhooly	9 Mar 97
2.18		12 Sep 99
2.18	Chuka Enih-Snell	21 Apr 01
2.17 i	Richard Aspden	11 Feb 99
2.16		7 Jul 95
2.16 i	Mike Butterfield	23 Jan 76
2.16 i	Claude Moseley	13 Apr 80
2.16		19 Jul 81
2.16 i	David Watson	13 Mar 82
2.16	Andy Hutchinson	2 Sep 84
2.16	Mike Powell	3 Sep 88
2.16	John Wallace	29 Jul 90
2.16	Rob Brocklebank	7 Jul 95
2.16	Ian Holliday	8 Aug 98
2.16 i	Jason McDade	24 Jan 99
2.16 i	Andrew Penk	20 Feb 00
2.16	Mark Crowley	18 Aug 02

† Note   Oni not eligible for Britain until July 2001

Pole Vault

5.81 i	Nick Buckfield	8	Feb	01
5.80		27	May	98
5.75	Buckfield	7	Sep	97
5.75 A	Buckfield	14	Apr	01
5.71	Buckfield	16	Jun	96
5.70	Buckfield	23	Jul	95
5.70	Buckfield	8	Aug	97
5.70	Buckfield	10	Aug	97
5.65	Keith Stock	7	Jul	81
5.65	Buckfield	26	May	96
5.61	Kevin Hughes	28	Jul	99
5.60	Neil Winter	19	Aug	95
5.59	Brian Hooper	6	Sep	80
5.55	Paul Williamson	13	May	00
5.52	Mike Edwards	13	May	93
5.45 i	Andy Ashurst	16	Feb	92
5.40		19	Jun	88
5.45	Mike Barber	27	Jul	97
10 5.40 A	Jeff Gutteridge ¶	23	Apr	80
5.40		5	Jun	83
5.40 i	Matt Belsham	10	Feb	96
5.35		26	Jun	93
5.40	Tim Thomas	2	Aug	97
5.40	Ben Flint	25	Jul	99
5.35	Ian Tullett	26	Jul	98
5.31 i	Scott Simpson	23	Feb	02
5.20		1	Jul	01
5.30	Dean Mellor	17	Jun	95
5.30	Christian North	25	Jul	99
5.30	Ashley Swain	20	Jul	02
5.26	Mark Johnson	31	Aug	91
20 5.25	Mike Bull	22	Sep	73
5.25	Allan Williams	29	Aug	77
5.25	Daley Thompson	15	Jun	86
5.25	Tom Richards	8	Aug	99
5.25	Mark Beharrell	17	Aug	02
5.21	Graham Eggleton	10	Jul	82
5.21 i	Christian Linskey	20	Feb	99
5.20		24	May	98
5.20	Billy Davey	5	Jun	83
5.20	Warren Siley	4	Aug	90
5.20	Mark Hodgkinson	24	Aug	96
30 5.20	Neil Young	2	Aug	97
5.20	Mark Davis	25	Jul	99
5.18	Steve Chappell	15	Jun	78
5.11	Andrew Gayle	10	Aug	91
5.11	Mark Grant	2	Sep	01
5.10	Darren Wright	12	Jun	88
5.10	Paul Phelps	9	Jul	89
5.02	Bob Kingman	29	Aug	94
5.02 i	Craig Guite	11	Jan	97
5.01	Paul Hoad	16	Aug	86
40 5.01	Andrew Penk	31	Aug	01
5.00	Richard Gammage	19	Aug	84
5.00	Brian Taylor	5	May	91
5.00	Dan Gilby	20	Jul	91
5.00	Paul Wray	26	Jul	91
5.00	Alex Greig	31	May	92
5.00	Barry Thomas	23	Aug	92
5.00	Ian Wilding	1	Jun	96
5.00	Andrew Weston	29	Jul	98
5.00	Matt Weaver	25	Jul	99

Long Jump

8.27	Chris Tomlinson	13	Apr	02
8.23	Lynn Davies	30	Jun	68
8.18 A	Davies	9	Apr	66
8.17	Tomlinson	18	May	02
8.17	Tomlinson	22	Jun	02
8.15	Stewart Faulkner	16	Jul	90
8.14	Davies	18	Jun	69
8.14	Faulkner	25	Aug	89
8.14	Mark Forsythe	7	Jul	91
8.11	Nathan Morgan	24	Jul	98
8.10	Fred Salle	9	Sep	94
8.08	Roy Mitchell	27	Sep	80
8.05 i	Barrington Williams	11	Feb	89
8.01		17	Jun	89
8.03	Steve Phillips	5	Aug	98
8.03	Jonathan Moore	18	May	02 10
8.01	Daley Thompson	8	Aug	84
8.00	Derrick Brown	7	Aug	85
7.98	Alan Lerwill	29	Jun	74
7.94 i	Paul Johnson	10	Mar	89
7.85		3	Jun	89
7.93	Darren Ritchie	13	Jul	02
7.91	John King	26	Sep	87
7.90	Ian Simpson	3	Jun	89
7.90	Chris Davidson	19	Jun	99
7.89	George Audu	12	Aug	00
7.87	Keith Fleming	7	Jun	87 20
7.84	Wayne Griffith	25	Aug	89
7.83	Phil Idowu	25	Jul	00
7.79	John Morbey	11	Jul	64
7.79	Geoff Hignett	31	May	71
7.79	Don Porter	13	Jul	75
7.77	Len Tyson	25	Jul	82
7.77	Dean Macey	27	Sep	00
7.76	Carl Howard	31	Jul	93
7.75	Ken Cocks	2	Jul	78
7.75	Trevor Hoyte	6	May	84 30
7.75	Michael Morgan	30	Jul	94
7.74	Fred Alsop	6	Jun	64
7.74 i	Phil Scott	17	Feb	73
7.68		27	May	73
7.74 i	Aston Moore	10	Jan	81
7.74	John Herbert	14	Jul	85
7.74	David Burgess	4	Jul	87
7.73	Jason Canning	20	Apr	88
7.72	Femi Abejide	20	Jun	86
7.71	Billie Kirkpatrick	2	Jun	78
7.71 i	Keith Connor	20	Feb	81 40
7.70	Kevin Liddington	27	Aug	88
7.70	Julian Flynn	19	Jun	99
7.70	Mark Awanah	16	Jun	02
7.68	Garry Slade	1	Aug	92
7.67	Dave Walker	14	Sep	68
7.67	Oni Onuorah	15	Jun	96
7.66	Tony Henry	12	Jun	77
7.66	Barry Nevison	7	Jul	85
7.66	John Shepherd	18	Jun	88
7.65 i	John Munroe	11	Feb	95 50
7.64		24	Jun	95

wind assisted

	Mark	Name	Date
	8.19	Tomlinson	11 Aug 01
	8.17	Mark Forsythe	11 Jun 89
	8.17	Nathan Morgan	31 May 02
	8.16	Roy Mitchell	26 Jun 76
	8.15	Alan Lerwill	29 May 72
	8.15	Lerwill	15 Jul 72
	8.12	Derrick Brown	14 Jun 86
	8.11	Daley Thompson	7 Aug 78
	8.07	Steve Phillips	11 Jul 99
	8.04	Ian Simpson	3 Jun 89
	7.96	Colin Jackson	17 May 86
10	7.94	John Herbert	25 Jul 82
	7.94	John King	20 Jun 86
	7.94	Chris Davidson	21 Jun 97
	7.93	David Burgess	15 Jun 86
	7.91	Steve Ingram	18 Jun 94
	7.89	John Shepherd	20 Jun 86
	7.87	Paul Johnson	15 May 88
	7.84	Darren Thompson	16 Jun 01
	7.82	Peter Reed	20 Jul 68
	7.82	Femi Abejide	20 Jun 86
20	7.82	Kevin Liddington	25 Jun 89
	7.81	Enyinna Chukukere	9 Apr 94
	7.81	Oni Onuorah	21 Aug 95
	7.76	Aston Moore	7 Aug 77
	7.76	Julian Flynn	19 Jun 99
	7.72	Ken McKay	21 Jun 85
	7.72	Nick Riley	18 Jun 88
	7.70	Derek Cole	29 May 72

Triple Jump

	Mark	Name	Date
	18.29	Jonathan Edwards	7 Aug 95
	18.01	Edwards	9 Jul 98
	18.00	Edwards	27 Aug 95
	17.99	Edwards	23 Aug 98
	17.98	Edwards	18 Jul 95
	17.92	Edwards	6 Aug 01
	17.88	Edwards	27 Jul 96
	17.86	Edwards	28 Jul 02
	17.82	Edwards	25 Jun 96
	17.79	Edwards	14 Aug 96
	17.68	Phillips Idowu	28 Jul 02
	17.57 A	Keith Connor	5 Jun 82
	17.31 i		13 Mar 81
	17.30		9 Jun 82
	17.41	John Herbert	2 Sep 85
	17.30	Larry Achike	23 Sep 00
	17.21	Tosi Fasinro	27 Jul 93
	17.18	Francis Agyepong	7 Jul 95
	17.06	Julian Golley	10 Sep 94
	17.01	Eric McCalla	3 Aug 84
10	16.87	Mike Makin	2 Aug 86
	16.86	Aston Moore	16 Aug 81
	16.75	Vernon Samuels	7 Aug 88
	16.65	Tosin Oke	28 Jul 02
	16.63 A	Femi Akinsanya	10 Apr 99
	16.58		15 Jun 96
	16.46	Fred Alsop	16 Oct 64
	16.43	Jonathan Moore	22 Jul 01
	16.41	Steven Shalders	15 Jun 02
	16.32	Tayo Erogbogbo	21 Aug 95
	16.30	Nick Thomas	22 Jul 00
20	16.30	Femi Abejide	27 Jun 85
	16.29 i	David Johnson	1 Mar 78
	16.18		22 Jun 75
	16.26	Joe Sweeney	3 Aug 91
	16.22	Derek Boosey	15 Jun 68
	16.20	Rez Cameron	5 Jun 88
	16.18	Tony Wadhams	6 Jul 69
	16.17	John Mackenzie	17 Sep 94
	16.16	Conroy Brown	19 Sep 81
	16.15	Wayne Green	10 Jul 88
	16.15	Michael Brown	23 Jul 89
30	16.13	Steven Anderson	11 Jun 83
	16.10	Alan Lerwill	28 Aug 71
	16.09	Courtney Charles	17 Jun 90
	16.08	Craig Duncan	21 Jun 86
	16.02	Peter Akwaboah	15 Jun 89
	15.98	Frank Attoh	5 Sep 80
	15.97	Mike Ralph	23 Jul 64
	15.97	Carl Howard	6 May 95
	15.95	Derek Browne	12 Jun 93
	15.94	Phil Ferdinand	17 Aug 02
40	15.92	John Slaney	15 Oct 77
	15.92	Lawrence Lynch	13 Jul 85
	15.91 i	Akin Oyediran	3 Mar 84
	15.91	Dave Emanuel	31 Aug 91
	15.90	David Wood	16 Sep 84
	15.88	John Phillips	14 May 78
	15.87	Chris Colman	15 Jul 78
	15.87	Stewart Faulkner	22 Aug 87
	15.86 i	Donovan Perkins	23 Jan 81
	15.86	Joe Allison	24 Aug 85
50	15.82	Graham Hamlyn	12 Jul 68
	15.82 i	Charles Madeira-Cole	15 Mar 98
	15.82	Jon Wallace	11 Jul 98

wind assisted

	Mark	Name	Date
	18.43	Jonathan Edwards	25 Jun 95
	18.08	Edwards	23 Jul 95
	18.03	Edwards	2 Jul 95
	17.81	Keith Connor	9 Oct 82
	17.31	Larry Achike	15 Jul 00
	17.30	Tosi Fasinro	12 Jun 93
	17.29 A	Francis Agyepong	29 Jul 95
	17.24		2 Jul 95
	17.02	Aston Moore	14 Jun 81
	16.82	Vernon Samuels	24 Jun 89
	16.65	Fred Alsop	13 Aug 65
	16.49	Tony Wadhams	16 Sep 69
10	16.44	Tayo Erogbogbo	31 May 97
	16.38	Femi Abejide	10 Jun 89
	16.38	Courtney Charles	22 Jul 90
	16.33	David Johnson	28 May 78
	16.32	Craig Duncan	20 Jun 87
	16.32	Rez Cameron	21 May 89
	16.21	Alan Lerwill	28 Aug 71
	16.17	Chris Colman	15 Jul 78
	16.13	Nathan Douglas	30 Jun 02
	16.12	Donovan Perkins	21 Sep 80

Shot

	Mark	Name	Date		
	21.68	Geoff Capes	18 May 80		
	21.55	Capes	28 May 76		
	21.50	Capes	24 May 80		
	21.37	Capes	10 Aug 74		
	21.36	Capes	19 Jun 76		
	21.35	Capes	5 Jun 80		
	21.30	Capes	3 Jul 77		
	21.26 i	Carl Myerscough ¶	8 Mar 02		
	20.72		4 May 02		
	21.20	Capes	22 Aug 76		
	21.18	Capes	8 May 76		
	20.85 i	Mark Proctor	25 Jan 98		
	20.40		7 Jul 99		
	20.45	Shaun Pickering	17 Aug 97		
	20.43	Mike Winch	22 May 74		
	20.33	Paul Edwards ¶	9 Jul 91		
	19.72	Mark Edwards	16 Aug 00		
	19.56	Arthur Rowe	7 Aug 61		
	19.49	Matt Simson	28 Aug 94		
10	19.44 i	Simon Williams	28 Jan 89		
	19.17		18 May 91		
	19.43	Bill Tancred	18 May 74		
	19.18	Jeff Teale ¶	7 Aug 68		
	19.01	Billy Cole	21 Jun 86		
	18.94	Bob Dale	12 Jun 76		
	18.93	Paul Buxton	13 May 77		
	18.85	Lee Newman	2 Jun 96		
	18.79	Steph Hayward	6 Sep 00		
	18.69	Emeka Udechuku	24 Aug 02		
	18.62	Martyn Lucking	2 Oct 62		
20	18.59 i	Alan Carter	11 Apr 65		
	18.26		1 May 65		
	18.50	Mike Lindsay	2 Jul 63		
	18.46	Roger Kennedy	22 May 77		
	18.46 i	Simon Rodhouse	20 Feb 82		
	18.20		25 Jul 82		
	18.35	Peter Tancred	9 Jul 74		
	18.34	Richard Slaney	3 Jul 83		
	18.14 i	Neal Brunning ¶	26 Jan 92		
	17.45		17 Aug 91		
	18.05	John Watts	19 Aug 72		
	18.04	Andy Vince	30 Apr 83		
	17.96	Nigel Spratley	28 Aug 94		
30	17.95	Graham Savory	4 Jun 88		
	17.92	Nick Tabor	9 Apr 83		
	17.87	Bill Fuller	15 Jul 72		
	17.87 i	Ian Lindley	15 Mar 81		
	17.58		25 May 81		
	17.87 i	Antony Zaidman	22 Jan 83		
	17.22		4 Jul 81		
	17.85	Gary Sollitt	4 Jun 82		
	17.79	John Alderson	31 Jul 74		
	17.78	Steve Whyte	11 Feb 89		
	17.69 i	David Readle	24 Feb 01		
	17.50		25 Mar 00		
	17.62	Neil Gray	7 Jun 89		
40	17.61	Iain McMullan	13 Jul 02		
	17.56	Scott Rider	12 May 02		
	17.55	David Callaway	1 Aug 93		
	17.54	Eric Irvine	16 Aug 86		
	17.47	Carl Jennings	13 Sep 87		
	17.45	Abi Ekoku	3 Feb 90		
	17.44	Hamish Davidson	3 Jun 78		
	17.41	Lee Wiltshire	1 May 94		
	17.41	Jamie Cockburn	12 May 96		
	17.40	Barry King	11 Apr 70		
	17.40	Allan Seatory	27 Apr 75	50	

Discus

	Mark	Name	Date	
	66.64	Perris Wilkins ¶	6 Jun 98	
	65.22	Wilkins	30 Aug 97	
	65.16	Richard Slaney	1 Jul 85	
	65.11	Glen Smith	18 Jul 99	
	65.08	Robert Weir	19 Aug 00	
	64.94	Bill Tancred	21 Jul 74	
	64.87	Wilkins	12 Jun 99	
	64.68	Slaney	6 Jul 84	
	64.65	Wilkins	22 Jul 00	
	64.64	Slaney	30 Apr 82	
	63.14	Carl Myerscough ¶	4 May 01	
	62.36	Peter Tancred	8 May 80	
	62.07	Emeka Udechuku	19 Aug 00	
	61.86	Paul Mardle	13 Jun 84	
	61.62	Peter Gordon	15 Jun 91	10
	61.14	Simon Williams	18 Apr 92	
	61.10	Kevin Brown	30 Aug 97	
	61.00	Allan Seatory	6 Oct 74	
	60.92	Graham Savory	10 May 86	
	60.48	Lee Newman	10 May 97	
	60.42	Mike Cushion	16 Aug 75	
	60.08	Abi Ekoku	16 May 90	
	59.84	Colin Sutherland ¶	10 Jun 78	
	59.76	John Hillier	27 Jul 74	
	59.70	John Watts	14 Jul 72	20
	58.64	Steve Casey	19 May 91	
	58.58	Darrin Morris	22 Jun 91	
	58.36	Paul Reed	11 Jul 99	
	58.34	Geoff Capes	29 Sep 73	
	58.08	Mike Winch	7 Sep 75	
	57.58	Arthur McKenzie	17 Aug 69	
	57.14	Mark Proctor	24 Jun 00	
	57.12	Paul Edwards ¶	10 Aug 88	
	57.10	Dennis Roscoe	3 May 80	
	57.00	Gerry Carr	17 Jul 65	30
	56.71	Roy Hollingsworth	14 Sep 63	
	56.66	Gary Herrington	15 Jun 96	
	56.42	Paul Buxton	6 Aug 76	
	56.40	Guy Dirkin	1 Aug 75	
	55.68	Neville Thompson	12 Jun 93	
	55.68	Leith Marar	24 Jul 96	
	55.60	Jeff Clare	25 Jul 88	
	55.52	Jamie Murphy	29 Jul 95	
	55.42	Geoff Tyler	3 May 80	
	55.34	Nick Woolcott	27 Jul 88	40
	55.32	Mike Lindsay	4 May 60	
	55.04	Denzil McDonald	28 Aug 95	
	54.78	Colin Bastien	29 Mar 87	
	54.53	Matthew Twigg	21 Jul 02	
	54.38	Shaun Pickering	26 Aug 89	
	54.36	Matt Symonds	24 Jun 95	
	54.27	Mark Pharoah	27 Nov 56	
	54.25	Bruce Robb	17 Jun 01	
	54.16	Scott Hayes	23 Mar 97	
	54.01	Eric Cleaver	21 Oct 62	50

Hammer					Javelin				
77.54	Martin Girvan	12	May	84	91.46	Steve Backley	25	Jan	92
77.30	Dave Smith I	13	Jul	85	90.81	Backley	22	Jul	01
77.16	Girvan	13	Jul	84	89.89	Backley	19	Jul	98
77.04	Smith I	25	May	85	89.85	Backley	23	Sep	00
77.02	Matt Mileham	11	May	84	89.72	Backley	23	Aug	98
76.92	Girvan	5	May	84	89.58	Backley	2	Jul	90
76.60	Smith I	6	Sep	86	89.22	Backley	11	Jun	98
76.43	Mick Jones	2	Jun	01	89.02	Backley	30	May	97
76.38	Girvan	25	Apr	84	88.80	Backley	2	Aug	98
76.36	Smith I	5	May	85	88.71 A	Backley	13	Sep	98
76.36	Smith I	29	Jun	85	86.94	Mick Hill	13	Jun	93
75.40	Chris Black	23	Jul	83	85.67	Mark Roberson	19	Jul	98
75.10	Dave Smith II	27	May	96	85.09	Nick Nieland	13	Aug	00
75.08	Robert Weir	3	Oct	82	83.84	Roald Bradstock	2	May	87
74.02	Paul Head	30	Aug	90	82.38	Colin Mackenzie	7	Aug	93
73.86	Barry Williams	1	Jul	76	81.70	Nigel Bevan	28	Jun	92
10 73.80	Jason Byrne	19	Sep	92	80.98	Dave Ottley	24	Sep	88
73.20	Paul Dickenson	22	May	76	78.54	Gary Jenson	17	Sep	89
72.63	Bill Beauchamp	25	Jul	99	78.33 A	David Parker	24	Mar	01 10
71.60	Shane Peacock	24	Jun	90	77.84	Peter Yates	21	Feb	87
71.28	Peter Vivian	25	Jun	95	76.66 i	Stuart Faben	3	Mar	96
71.00	Ian Chipchase	17	Aug	74		76.17	30	Mar	02
70.88	Howard Payne	29	Jun	74	76.10	Keith Beard	18	May	91
70.33	John Pearson	30	Jul	00	75.52	Marcus Humphries	25	Jul	87
70.30	Stewart Rogerson	14	Aug	88	75.43	Michael Allen	11	May	02
70.28	Paul Buxton	19	May	79	75.32	Steve Harrison	9	Jul	95
20 69.52	Jim Whitehead	23	Sep	79	75.28	Nigel Stainton	5	Aug	89
69.38	Mike Floyd	18	Jun	00	74.90	Daryl Brand	27	Jun	86
68.64	Shaun Pickering	7	Apr	84	74.72	Chris Crutchley	13	Jul	86
68.18	Ron James	2	Jun	82	74.70	Myles Cottrell	16	May	92 20
67.82	Steve Whyte	15	Apr	89	73.56	Dan Carter	16	Sep	00
67.45	Steve Pearson	27	Jun	98	73.26	David Messom	25	Apr	87
67.32	Gareth Cook	1	Jun	91	72.92	Stefan Baldwin	8	May	93
66.97	Chris Howe	6	Jun	98	71.86	Tony Hatton	3	May	93
66.77	Simon Bown	15	Jun	02	71.79	Phill Sharpe	27	Aug	00
66.53	Russell Devine	15	Feb	01	71.00	Mike Tarran	30	Jun	02
30 66.19	Iain Park	17	Mar	02	70.90	Shane Lewis	6	Jun	98
65.30	Karl Andrews	2	Jul	94	70.30	Tim Newenham	11	Jun	89
65.01	Andy Frost	5	May	02	70.12	Paul Morgan	12	Sep	87
64.95	Mike Ellis	4	Jun	59	70.10	Richard Hooper	21	May	89 30
64.80	Bruce Fraser	30	Sep	73	70.00	Paul Bushnell	22	Jul	90
64.54	Michael Petra	30	May	79	70.00	Phil Parry	2	Jul	94
64.39	Craig Ellams	19	Aug	00	69.90	Ken Hayford	5	Jul	87
64.36	Andrew Tolputt	27	Jun	87	69.90	Tony Smith	6	Jul	96
64.16	Matthew Bell	28	May	02	69.20	Roddy James	28	Apr	89
63.74	Mark Sterling	18	Jul	84	69.02	Kevin Murch	2	Sep	89
40 63.71	David Allen	26	Jun	99	68.91	Stuart Loughran	26	Jul	98
63.20	Peter Gordon	17	Sep	82	68.87	Ton Dobbing	15	Jun	02
63.16	Graham Callow	29	May	89	68.85	Alex van der Merwe	30	Jun	02
62.88	Anthony Swain	13	Apr	97	68.84	James Hurrion	12	Jul	91 40
62.70	Paul Barnard	19	Jul	95	68.78	Neil McLellan	23	Jun	01
62.60	Peter Weir	2	Aug	87	68.74	Jon Clarke	14	Jun	86
62.60	Rob Earle	1	Aug	95	68.74	Tony Norman	23	May	87
62.56	Adrian Palmer	6	Aug	94	68.70	Robert Mullen	2	Jul	96
62.54	Tony Elvin	25	May	70	68.38	James Drennen	12	Jul	91
62.42	Malcolm Fenton	16	May	82	68.30	Mark Lawrence	31	Jul	88
50 62.40	Lawrie Nisbet	5	Jul	86	68.10	Paul Edgington	12	Oct	86
62.32	Peter Aston	6	Sep	75	68.08	Tim Kitney	13	Sep	98
62.28	Lawrie Bryce	13	Oct	73	68.02	Mark Francis	12	Jul	97
					67.62	Alan Holloway	25	Jun	89 50

Decathlon (1985 Tables)

8847	Daley Thompson	9 Aug	84
8811	Thompson	28 Aug	86
8774	Thompson	8 Sep	82
8730	Thompson	23 May	82
8714	Thompson	13 Aug	83
8667	Thompson	18 May	86
8663	Thompson	28 Jul	86
8648	Thompson	18 May	80
8603	Dean Macey	7 Aug	01
8567	Macey	28 Sep	00
8131	Alex Kruger	2 Jul	95
7980	Simon Shirley	24 Aug	94
7922 w	Brad McStravick	28 May	84
7885		6 May	84
7904	David Bigham	28 Jun	92
7901	Peter Gabbett	22 May	72
7889	Eugene Gilkes	18 May	86
7874	Colin Boreham	23 May	82
7861	Anthony Brannen	30 Apr	95
7787	Brian Taylor	30 May	93
7766	Barry Thomas	2 Sep	95
7748	Eric Hollingsworth	30 May	93
7740	Greg Richards	7 Jun	87
7739	Jamie Quarry	30 May	99
7713	James Stevenson	5 Jun	93
7708	Fidelis Obikwu	28 May	84
7663	Rafer Joseph	24 Aug	94
7643 w	Tom Leeson	8 Sep	85
7565		11 Aug	85
7635 w	Du'aine (Thorne-)Ladejo	24 May	98
7633		18 Sep	98
7596	Mike Corden	27 Jun	76
7594	Mark Bishop	3 Sep	89
7579	Mark Luscombe	8 May	88
7571	Alexis Sharp	17 Apr	98
7535	Duncan Mathieson	24 Jun	90
7515	Ken Hayford	9 Jun	85
7500	Barry King	22 May	72
7500	Pan Zeniou	2 Aug	81
7439	Kevan Lobb	19 Aug	84
7431	Alan Drayton	8 Aug	78
7425	Anthony Southward	16 Jun	96
7425 w	Paul Field	21 May	95
7295		2 Jul	95
7411	John Heanley	2 Jul	02
7377	Anthony Sawyer	16 Jun	02
7367	John Garner	8 May	88
7363	Mike Bull	27 Jan	74
7363	Nick Phipps	27 Jun	76
7335	Stewart McCallum	19 Aug	73
7308	Clive Longe	29 Jun	69
7295	Stephen Rogers	4 Jun	95
7275	Buster Watson	18 Jun	78
7268	Paul Edwards ¶	14 Aug	83
7240	Paul Allan	25 Aug	91
7221	Andy Lewis	19 Jun	94
7198	Robert Betts	7 Aug	83
7172	Dave Kidner	20 Aug	72
7159	Roger Hunter	20 Jul	97

7147	Justin Whitfield	12 May	85
7146	Steve Bonnett	30 May	99
7136	Billy Jewers	3 Sep	89

3000 Metres Track Walk

11:24.4	Mark Easton	10 May	89
11:28.4	Phil Vesty	9 May	84
11:29.6 i	Tim Berrett	21 Jan	90
11:54.23		23 Jun	84
11:31.0	Andi Drake	22 Jul	90
11:32.2	Ian McCombie	20 Jul	88
11:33.4	Steve Partington	12 Jul	95
11:35.5	Andy Penn	10 May	97
11:39.0 i+	Martin Rush	8 Feb	92
11:49.48		1 Jul	84
11:44.68	Roger Mills	7 Aug	81
11:45.1	Chris Maddocks	9 Aug	87
11:45.77	Steve Johnson	20 Jun	87
11:47.12 i	Philip King	26 Feb	95
11:49.64		29 May	95
11:49.0	Darrell Stone	10 Jul	90
11:51.1	Paul Nihill	5 Jun	71
11:52.51	Sean Martindale	28 Jul	90
11:53.3	Martin Bell	9 Aug	95
11:53.46	Steve Barry	21 Aug	82
11:54.7	Mike Parker	20 Apr	82
11:55.0	Phil Embleton	24 May	71

10000 Metres Track Walk

40:06.65	Ian McCombie	4 Jun	89
40:39.77	McCombie	5 Jun	88
40:42.53	McCombie	28 Aug	89
40:45.87	McCombie	25 May	87
40:47.5 +	McCombie	26 May	90
40:53.60	Phil Vesty	28 May	84
40:55.6	Martin Rush	14 Sep	91
41:06.57	Chris Maddocks	20 Jun	87
41:10.11	Darrell Stone	16 Jul	95
41:13.62	Steve Barry	19 Jun	82
41:13.65	Martin Bell	22 Jul	95
41:14.3	Mark Easton	5 Feb	89
41:14.61	Steve Partington	16 Jul	95
41:18.64	Andi Drake	5 Jun	88
41:49.06	Sean Martindale	26 Jun	90
41:55.5	Phil Embleton	14 Apr	71
41:59.10	Andy Penn	27 Jul	91
42:06.35	Gordon Vale	2 Aug	81
42:08.57	Paul Blagg	28 Aug	89
42:17.1	Dom King	4 May	02
42:23.0	Mike Parker	2 Feb	86
42:28.0	Philip King	17 May	95
42:34.6	Paul Nihill	28 May	72
42:35.6	Ken Matthews	1 Aug	60
42:40.0	Brian Adams	29 Mar	75
42:41.6	Mick Greasley	25 May	80
42:42.18	Steve Johnson	5 Jun	88
42:44.0	George Nibre	2 Apr	80
42:45.0	Tim Berrett	22 Jul	88

track short

40:54.7	Steve Barry	19 Mar	83

20 Kilometres Road Walk

Time	Name	Date	
1:22:03	Ian McCombie	23 Sep	88
1:22:12	Chris Maddocks	3 May	92
1:22:35	Maddocks	27 May	89
1:22:37	McCombie	11 May	85
1:22:51	Steve Barry	26 Feb	83
1:22:58	McCombie	27 May	89
1:23:15	Barry	14 May	83
1:23:24	McCombie	24 May	86
1:23:26	McCombie	28 Feb	87
1:23:26.5t	McCombie	26 May	90
1:23:34	Andy Penn	29 Feb	92
1:23:34	Martin Rush	29 Feb	92
1:23:58	Darrell Stone	24 Feb	96
1:24:04	Mark Easton	25 Feb	89
1:24:04.0t	Andi Drake	26 May	90
1:24:07.6t	Phil Vesty	1 Dec	84
1:24:09	Steve Partington	24 Sep	94
1:24:25	Tim Berrett	21 Apr	90
1:24:50	Paul Nihill	30 Jul	72
1:25:42	Martin Bell	9 May	92
1:25:53.6t	Sean Martindale	28 Apr	89
1:26:53	Chris Cheeseman	21 Mar	99
1:27:00	Roger Mills	30 Jun	80
1:27:16	Les Morton	25 Feb	89
1:27:35	Olly Flynn	3 Oct	76
1:27:46	Brian Adams	11 Oct	75
1:27:59	Phil Embleton	3 Apr	71
1:28:02	Paul Blagg	27 Feb	82
1:28:15	Ken Matthews	23 Jul	60
1:28:26	Chris Harvey	29 Sep	79
1:28:30	Allan King	11 May	85
1:28:34	Chris Smith	11 May	85
1:28:34	Steve Hollier	19 Jun	99
1:28:37	Dave Jarman	30 Jun	80
1:28:40	Matt Hales	21 Apr	01
1:28:46	Jimmy Ball	4 Apr	87
1:28:46	Steve Taylor	20 Dec	92
1:28:46	Jamie O'Rawe	21 Mar	99
1:28:50	Amos Seddon	3 Aug	74
1:29:07	Philip King	20 Aug	95
1:29:19	Stuart Phillips	31 May	92
1:29:24	George Nibre	6 Apr	80
1:29:27	Graham White	19 Apr	97
1:29:29 +	Steve Johnson	16 Apr	89
1:29:37	John Warhurst	28 Jul	73
1:29:42	Dennis Jackson	10 May	86
1:29:48	Mike Parker	8 May	82
1:29:48	Martin Young	31 Mar	96
1:29:48	Dom King	15 Jun	02
1:29:49	Peter Marlow	3 Aug	74
1:29:53	Don Bearman	11 May	02
1:30:00	John Webb	18 May	68
1:30:02	Bob Dobson	3 Aug	74
1:30:15	Gareth Brown	13 May	89
1:30:16	Roy Thorpe	28 Jul	73
1:30:22	Roy Sheppard	26 Apr	80
1:30:27.38t	Steve Gower	10 Jun	78

no judges

Time	Name	Date	
1:27:04.0t	Steve Hollier	9 Jan	00

50 Kilometres Road Walk

Time	Name	Date	
3:51:37	Chris Maddocks	28 Oct	90
3:53:14	Maddocks	25 Nov	95
3:57:10	Maddocks	12 Mar	00
3:57:48	Les Morton	30 Apr	89
3:58:25	Morton	20 Mar	88
3:58:36	Morton	11 Oct	92
3:59:30	Morton	30 Sep	88
3:59:55	Paul Blagg	5 Sep	87
4:00:02	Maddocks	11 Oct	92
4:00:07	Blagg	30 Sep	88
4:03:08	Dennis Jackson	16 Mar	86
4:03:53	Mark Easton	25 Apr	98
4:06:14	Barry Graham	20 Apr	85
4:07:18	Steve Hollier	18 Jun	00
4:07:23	Bob Dobson	21 Oct	79
4:07:49	Chris Cheesman	2 May	99
4:07:57	Ian Richards	20 Apr	80
4:08:41	Adrian James	12 Apr	80
4:09:15un	Don Thompson	10 Oct	65
4:12:19		20 Jun	59
4:09:22	Mike Smith	27 Mar	89
4:10:23	Darrell Stone	6 May	90
4:10:42	Amos Seddon	9 Mar	80
4:11:32	Paul Nihill	18 Oct	64
4:12:00	Sean Martindale	16 Oct	93
4:12:02	Martin Rush	28 Jul	91
4:12:37	John Warhurst	27 May	72
4:12:50	Darren Thorn	6 May	90
4:13:18	Graham White	27 Jun	98
4:13:25	Allan King	16 Apr	83
4:14:03	Tom Misson	20 Jun	59
4:14:25	Dave Cotton	15 Jul	78
4:15:14	Shaun Lightman	13 Oct	73
4:15:22	Brian Adams	17 Sep	78
4:15:52	Ray Middleton	27 May	72
4:16:30	Karl Atton	20 Apr	97
4:16:45	Gareth Brown	21 Apr	02
4:16:47	George Nibre	9 Mar	80
4:17:24	Andi Drake	18 Oct	87
4:17:34	Gordon Vale	9 Oct	83
4:17:52	Stuart Elms	17 Apr	76
4:18:30	Peter Ryan	10 Apr	82
4:19:00	Carl Lawton	17 Jul	71
4:19:13	Bryan Eley	19 Jul	69
4:19:26	Roger Mills	9 Apr	83
4:19:55	Mick Holmes	4 Aug	73
4:19:57	Barry Ingarfield	21 Oct	79
4:20:05	George Chaplin	27 May	72
4:20:43	Tim Watt	8 Oct	95
4:20:48	Andrew Trigg	1 May	88
4:20:51	Murray Lambden	18 Jul	82
4:21:02	Ron Wallwork	17 Jul	71
4:22:05	Mel McCann	14 Sep	86
4:22:41.0t	Charley Fogg	1 Jun	75
4:23:12	Peter Hodkinson	21 Jul	79
4:23:22	Chris Berwick	12 Jul	86
4:23:32	John Lees	19 Mar	78
4:23:43	Roy Thorpe	17 Jul	76
4:23:50	Paul Jarman	18 Jul	81

4 x 100 Metres Relay

37.73 Great Britain & NI 29 Aug 99
Gardener, Campbell, Devonish,Chambers
37.77 Great Britain & NI 22 Aug 93
Jackson, Jarrett, Regis, Christie ¶
37.98 Great Britain & NI 1 Sep 90
Braithwaite, Regis, Adam, Christie ¶
38.05 Great Britain & NI 21 Aug 93
John, Jarrett, Braithwaite, Christie ¶
38.08 Great Britain & NI 8 Aug 92
Adam, Jarrett, Regis, Christie ¶
38.09 Great Britain & NI 1 Sep 91
Jarrett, Regis, Braithwaite, Christie ¶
38.09 A Great Britain & NI 12 Sep 98
Condon, Devonish, Golding, Chambers
38.14 Great Britain & NI 10 Aug 97
Braithwaite, Campbell, Walker, Golding
38.16 Great Britain & NI 19 Jun 99
Gardener, Campbell, Devonish, Golding
10 38.17 Great Britain & NI 'A' 7 Aug 99
Gardener, Campbell, Devonish,Golding
38.19 Great Britain & NI 11 Aug 02
Malcolm, Campbell, Devonish, Chambers
38.20 England 21 Sep 98
Chambers, Devonish, Golding, Campbell
38.25 Great Britain & NI 9 Aug 97
Chambers, Campbell, Braithwaite, Golding
38.28 Great Britain & NI 1 Oct 88
Bunney, Regis, McFarlane, Christie ¶
38.31 Great Britain & NI 28 Aug 99
Gardener, Campbell, Condon, Chambers
38.34 Great Britain & NI 9 Sep 89
Callender, Regis, Adam, Christie ¶
38.35 Great Britain & NI 28 Aug 00
Chambers, Campbell, Devonish, Gardener
38.36 Great Britain & NI 31 Aug 91
Jarrett, Regis, Braithwaite, Christie ¶
38.39 Great Britain & NI 5 Aug 89
Jarrett, Regis, Adam, Christie ¶
20 38.41 Great Britain & NI 15 Jul 00
Malcolm, Campbell, Devonish, Chambers
38.46 Great Britain & NI 10 Sep 94
Braithwaite, Jarrett, Regis, Christie ¶
38.47 Great Britain & NI 9 Aug 97
Campbell, Devonish, Braithwaite, Golding
38.47 Great Britain & NI 22 Aug 98
Condon, Campbell, Devonish, Chambers
38.52 Great Britain & NI 1 Oct 88
Bunney, Regis, McFarlane, Christie ¶
38.52 Great Britain & NI 22 Aug 98
Condon, Campbell, Walker, Golding
38.52 Great Britain & NI 22 Jul 01
Chambers, Devonish, Malcolm, Barbour
38.53 Great Britain & NI 26 Jun 93
John, Jarrett, Regis, Christie ¶
38.55 Great Britain & NI 10 Aug 02
Malcolm, Campbell, Devonish, Chambers
38.56 Great Britain & NI 27 Jun 98
Condon, Campbell, Walker, Golding
30 38.58 Great Britain & NI 'B' 7 Aug 99
Condon, Mackie, Regis, Chambers

4 x 400 Metres Relay

2:56.60 Great Britain & NI 3 Aug 96
Thomas, Baulch, Richardson ¶, Black
2:56.65 Great Britain & NI 10 Aug 97
Thomas, Black, Baulch, Richardson ¶
2:57.53 Great Britain & NI 1 Sep 91
Black, Redmond, Regis, Akabusi
2:58.22 Great Britain & NI 1 Sep 90
Sanders, Akabusi, Regis, Black
2:58.68 Great Britain & NI 23 Aug 98
Hylton, Baulch, Thomas, Richardson ¶
2:58.86 Great Britain & NI 6 Sep 87
Redmond, Akabusi, Black, Brown
2:59.13 Great Britain & NI 11 Aug 84
Akabusi, Cook, Bennett, Brown
2:59.13 Great Britain & NI 14 Aug 94
McKenzie, Whittle, Black, Ladejo
2:59.46 Great Britain & NI 22 Jun 97
Black, Baulch, Thomas, Richardson ¶
2:59.49 Great Britain & NI 31 Aug 91 10
Mafe, Redmond, Richardson ¶, Akabusi
2:59.71 A Great Britain & NI 13 Sep 98
Hylton, Baulch, Baldock, Thomas
2:59.73 Great Britain & NI 8 Aug 92
Black, Grindley, Akabusi, Regis
2:59.84 Great Britain & NI 31 Aug 86
Redmond, Akabusi, Whittle, Black
2:59.85 Great Britain & NI 19 Aug 96
Baulch, Hylton, Richardson ¶, Black
3:00.19 Great Britain & NI 9 Aug 97
Hylton, Black, Baulch, Thomas
3:00.25 Great Britain & NI 27 Jun 93
Ladejo, Akabusi, Regis, Grindley
3:00.34 Great Britain & NI 25 Jun 95
Thomas, Patrick, Richardson ¶, Black
3:00.40 England 31 Jul 02
Deacon, Baldock, Rawlinson, Caines
3:00.41 Wales 31 Jul 02
Benjamin, Thomas, Baulch, Elias
3:00.46 Great Britain & NI 10 Sep 72 20
Reynolds, Pascoe, Hemery, Jenkins
3:00.57 England 23 Jun 02
Deacon, Benjamin, Baulch, Caines
3:00.58 Great Britain & NI 30 Jun 91
Sanders, Akabusi, Whittle, Black
3:00.61 Great Britain & NI 20 Jun 99
Hylton, Baulch, Wariso, Richardson ¶
3:00.68 Great Britain & NI 11 Sep 82
Jenkins, Cook, Bennett, Brown
3:00.82 England 21 Sep 98
Slythe, Wariso, Hylton, Richardson ¶
3:00.93 Great Britain & NI 19 Jun 92
Redmond, Akabusi, Ladejo, Black
3:00.95 Great Britain & NI 28 Jun 98
Black, Baulch, Thomas, Richardson ¶
3:00.96 Great Britain & NI 11 Aug 01
Hylton, Thomas, Benjamin, Richardson ¶
3:01.03 Great Britain & NI U2319 Jul 92
McKenzie, Grindley, Richardson ¶, Ladejo
3:01.12 Great Britain & NI 28 Jun 87 30
Harmsworth, Whittle, Bennett, Black

UNDER 23

100 Metres

9.97	Dwain Chambers	22	Aug	99
10.04	Mark Lewis-Francis	5	Jul	02
10.09	Jason Livingston ¶	13	Jun	92
10.11	Christian Malcolm	5	Aug	01
10.13	Marlon Devonish	17	Sep	98
10.17	Ian Mackie	25	Aug	96
10.20	Elliot Bunney	14	Jun	86
10.24	Chris Lambert	14	Jul	01

wind assisted

9.97	Mark Lewis-Francis	30	Jun	02
10.07	Toby Box	11	Jun	94
10.09 †	Christian Malcolm	4	Aug	01
10.10	Donovan Reid	26	Jun	83
10.11	Mike McFarlane	4	Oct	82
10.12	Jason John	29	Aug	93
10.13	Jon Barbour	30	Jun	01
10.14	Marcus Adam	28	Jan	90
10.16	Daniel Money	21	Jun	97

hand timing

10.1	David Jenkins	20	May	72
10.2	Derek Redmond	2	May	87

wind assisted

10.1	Drew McMaster	16	Jun	79

200 Metres

20.08	Christian Malcolm	8	Aug	01
20.18	John Regis	3	Sep	87
20.36	Todd Bennett	28	May	84
20.37	Chris Lambert	16	Jun	02
20.38	Julian Golding	24	Aug	97
20.43	Mike McFarlane	7	Oct	82
20.57	Owusu Dako	16	Jul	95
20.62	Donovan Reid	28	May	84
20.63	Roger Black	12	Sep	86
20.63	Marcus Adam	4	Aug	90

wind assisted

20.10	Marcus Adam	1	Feb	90
20.51	Jason John	2	Jul	93
20.53	Dougie Walker ¶	8	May	95
20.55	Darren Campbell	2	Jul	93

hand timing

20.3	David Jenkins	19	Aug	72

400 Metres

44.47	David Grindley	3	Aug	92
44.50	Derek Redmond	1	Sep	87
44.59	Roger Black	29	Aug	86
44.66 A	Iwan Thomas	14	Apr	96
44.69		16	Jun	96
45.09	Mark Richardson ¶	10	Jul	92
45.14	Jamie Baulch	23	Aug	95
45.18	David Jenkins	16	Aug	74
45.24	Mark Hylton	12	Aug	98
45.25	Du'aine Ladejo	3	Jun	92
45.37	Daniel Caines	23	Sep	00

800 Metres

1:43.97	Sebastian Coe	15	Sep	78
1:43.98	Peter Elliott	23	Aug	83
1:44.45	Steve Cram	17	Jul	82
1:44.65	Ikem Billy	21	Jul	84
1:44.92	Curtis Robb	15	Aug	93
1:45.14	Chris McGeorge	28	Jun	83
1:45.32	James McIlroy (IRL)	16	Jul	98
1:45.44	Steve Ovett	25	Jul	76
1:45.64	Paul Herbert	5	Jun	88
1:45.70	David Sharpe	2	Jul	88

1000 Metres

2:15.12	Steve Cram	17	Sep	82
2:16.34	Matthew Yates	6	Jul	90

1500 Metres

3:33.66	Steve Cram	18	Aug	82
3:33.83	John Robson	4	Sep	79
3:34.00	Matthew Yates	13	Sep	91
3:34.45	Steve Ovett	3	Sep	77
3:35.16	Steve Crabb	28	Jun	84
3:35.72	Graham Williamson	15	Jul	80
3:36.70	Kevin McKay	20	Jul	90
3:36.97	Peter Elliott	1	Jul	84
3:37.25	Jack Buckner	31	Aug	83
3:37.38	Frank Clement	30	Jul	74

1 Mile

3:49.90	Steve Cram	13	Jul	82
3:50.64	Graham Williamson	13	Jul	82
3:52.74	John Robson	17	Jul	79
3:53.20	Ian Stewart II	25	Aug	82
3:53.44	Jack Buckner	13	Jul	82
3:54.36	Steve Crabb	21	Jul	84
3:54.39	Neil Horsfield	8	Jul	86
3:54.69	Steve Ovett	26	Jun	77
3:55.38	Rob Denmark	12	Aug	90
3:55.41	Colin Reitz	31	Jul	82

2000 Metres

5:01.90	Jack Buckner	29	Aug	83
5:02.67	Gary Staines	4	Aug	85
5:02.99	Neil Caddy	11	Aug	96

3000 Metres

7:41.3	Steve Ovett	23	Sep	77
7:42.47	David Lewis	9	Jul	83
7:43.90	Ian Stewart II	26	Jun	82
7:45.45	Paul Davies-Hale	13	Jul	84
7:46.6+	David Black	14	Sep	73
7:47.12	Simon Mugglestone	27	Jun	88
7:47.82	Steve Cram	26	Jul	81
7:48.6+	Nat Muir	27	Jun	80
7:48.47 i	John Mayock	1	Mar	92
7:49.45	Paul Lawther	9	Sep	77

2 Miles

8:19.37	Nat Muir	27	Jun	80
8:21.86	David Black	14	Sep	73

5000 Metres

13:17.9	Nat Muir	15	Jul	80
13:19.78	Jon Brown	2	Jul	93
13:22.2	Dave Bedford	12	Jun	71
13:22.85	Ian Stewart I	25	Jul	70
13:23.52	David Black	29	Jan	74
13:24.59	Paul Davies-Hale	1	Jun	84
13:25.0	Steve Ovett	30	Jul	77
13:26.97	John Mayock	9	Jun	92
13:28.29	Simon Mugglestone	8	Jul	88
13:29.28 i	Steve Binns	12	Feb	82

10000 Metres

27:47.0	Dave Bedford	10	Jul	71
27:48.49	David Black	25	Jan	74
28:09.95	Bernie Ford	6	Oct	73
28:12.42	Dave Murphy	13	Jul	79
28:14.08	Jon Richards	20	Jun	86
28:18.8	Nicky Lees	7	May	79
28:19.6	Jon Brown	17	Apr	92
28:20.71	Jim Brown	12	Jul	74
28:20.76	Steve Binns	27	Aug	82
28:24.01	Jack Lane	10	Aug	71

Marathon

2:12:19	Don Faircloth	23	Jul	70
2:16:04	Ian Ray	27	Oct	79
2:16:21	Norman Wilson	10	Sep	77
2:16:47	Ieuan Ellis	19	Sep	82
2:17:13	Brent Jones	13	May	84

3000 Metres Steeplechase

8:16.52	Tom Hanlon	23	Aug	89
8:18.80	Colin Reitz	6	Jul	82
8:20.83	Paul Davies-Hale	10	Jun	84
8:22.48	John Davies	13	Sep	74
8:28.6	Dave Bedford	10	Sep	71
8:29.72	David Lewis	29	May	83
8:29.86	Tony Staynings	2	Aug	75
8:30.64	Dennis Coates	2	Aug	75
8:31.72	Keith Cullen	28	Jun	92
8:31.80	Graeme Fell	8	Aug	81

110 Metres Hurdles

13.11 A	Colin Jackson	11	Aug	88
	13.11	14	Jul	89
13.21	Tony Jarrett	31	Aug	90
13.29	Jon Ridgeon	15	Jul	87
13.57	David Nelson	11	Aug	89
13.60	Neil Owen	28	Jun	95
13.66	Ross Baillie	20	Feb	99
13.69	Berwyn Price	18	Aug	73
13.71	Mark Holtom	6	Sep	80
13.78	Nigel Walker	24	Jun	84
13.82	Damien Greaves	21	Jun	97
13.82	Chris Baillie	7	Jul	01

wind assisted

12.95	Colin Jackson	10	Sep	89

hand timing

13.5	Berwyn Price	1	Jul	73

400 Metres Hurdles

49.11	Gary Oakes	26	Jul	80
49.57	Matt Elias	14	Jul	01
49.75	Max Robertson	30	Aug	85
49.86	Martin Briggs	6	Jun	84
50.01	Phil Harries	5	Jun	88
50.16	Steve Surety	16	Jun	02
50.20	Matt Douglas	17	Sep	98
50.24	Martin Gillingham	24	Jun	84
50.38	Andy Todd	18	Sep	69

hand timing

49.9	Andy Todd	9	Oct	69
50.2	John Sherwood	2	Sep	67

High Jump

2.38 i	Steve Smith	4	Feb	94
	2.37	22	Aug	93
2.32 i	Brendan Reilly	24	Feb	94
	2.31	17	Jul	92
2.31	Dalton Grant	25	Sep	88
2.30 i	Geoff Parsons	25	Jan	86
	2.28	18	May	86
2.30	Ben Challenger	13	Jul	99
2.28 i	John Holman	28	Jan	89
	2.24	27	May	89
2.25	Robert Mitchell	28	Jul	01
2.23	Phil McDonnell	29	Jul	84
2.22 i	Mark Naylor	3	Feb	79
2.22	Danny Graham	20	May	00

Pole Vault

5.70	Nick Buckfield	23	Jul	95
5.60	Neil Winter	19	Aug	95
5.50	Paul Williamson	6	Jul	96
5.42	Mike Barber	26	Aug	95
5.40	Ben Flint	25	Jul	99
5.35	Andy Ashurst	29	Jun	85
5.35	Matt Belsham	26	Jun	93
5.31	Mike Edwards	10	Jun	90
5.30 i	Kevin Hughes	25	Feb	95
	5.30	28	Aug	95
5.30	Ashley Swain	20	Jul	02

Long Jump

8.27	Chris Tomlinson	13	Apr	02
8.15	Stewart Faulkner	16	Jul	90
8.11	Nathan Morgan	24	Jul	98
8.07	Lynn Davies	18	Oct	64
8.04	Roy Mitchell	25	Jun	77
8.00	Daley Thompson	25	Jul	80
8.00	Derrick Brown	7	Aug	85
7.97	Fred Salle	13	Jul	86
7.94 i	Paul Johnson	10	Mar	89
7.89	John King	26	Jul	85

wind assisted

8.16	Roy Mitchell	26	Jun	76
8.11	Daley Thompson	7	Aug	78
7.94	John Herbert	25	Jul	82
7.94	Chris Davidson	21	Jun	97

Triple Jump

17.21	Tosi Fasinro	27	Jul	93
17.12	Phil Idowu	23	Sep	00
17.05	John Herbert	8	Jul	83
16.95	Julian Golley	10	Jul	92
16.76	Keith Connor	12	Aug	78
16.74	Jonathan Edwards	23	Jul	88
16.71	Vernon Samuels	18	May	86
16.69	Aston Moore	12	Aug	78
16.65	Tosin Oke	28	Jul	02
16.54	Eric McCalla	17	Sep	82
16.47	Mike Makin	1	Jul	84

wind assisted

17.30	Tosi Fasinro	12	Jun	93
17.21	Keith Connor	12	Aug	78
16.76	Aston Moore	25	Sep	78
16.44	Tayo Erogbogbo	31	May	97

Shot

19.48	Geoff Capes	21	Aug	71
19.44 i	Simon Williams	28	Jan	89
18.93		23	Jul	89
19.23	Matt Simson	23	May	91
19.01	Billy Cole	21	Jun	86
18.97	Carl Myerscough ¶	25	Jul	99
18.93	Paul Buxton	13	May	77
18.59 i	Alan Carter	11	Apr	65
18.26		1	May	65
18.46	Lee Newman	9	Jul	95
18.40	Steph Hayward	9	Jun	96
18.29 i	Emeka Udechuku	14	Jan	01
18.23		5	Jul	01

Discus

62.07	Emeka Udechuku	19	Aug	00
61.86	Paul Mardle	13	Jun	84
60.48	Robert Weir	13	May	83
59.78	Glen Smith	5	Jun	94
58.99	Carl Myerscough ¶	2	Jul	99
58.52	Colin Sutherland ¶	1	May	77
58.34	Lee Newman	9	Jun	94
58.08	Simon Williams	11	Jun	89
57.04	Richard Slaney	23	Jul	77
56.42	Paul Buxton	6	Aug	76
55.90	Peter Tancred	13	Aug	69

downhill

57.56	Peter Tancred	26	Jul	69

Hammer

75.10	Dave Smith II	27	May	96
75.08	Robert Weir	3	Oct	82
74.62	David Smith I	15	Jul	84
74.18	Martin Girvan	31	May	82
73.80	Jason Byrne	19	Sep	92
71.08	Paul Head	1	Sep	85
71.00	Ian Chipchase	17	Aug	74
69.34	Paul Buxton	26	Aug	77
68.30	Mick Jones	1	Jul	84
67.60	Ron James	19	Sep	81
67.32	Gareth Cook	1	Jun	91

Javelin (1986 Model)

89.58	Steve Backley	2	Jul	90
80.92	Mark Roberson	12	Jun	88
79.70	Nigel Bevan	3	Feb	90
78.56	Mick Hill	2	Aug	86
78.54	Gary Jenson	17	Sep	89
78.33 A	David Parker	24	Mar	01
76.66 i	Stuart Faben	3	Mar	96
74.24		29	Jul	95
76.28	Nick Nieland	9	Jul	94
75.43	Michael Allen	11	May	02
74.70	Myles Cottrell	16	May	92
73.56	Dan Carter	16	Sep	00
71.94	Steve Harrison	9	Jul	94

Decathlon (1985 Tables)

8648	Daley Thompson	18	May	80
8556	Dean Macey	25	Aug	99
7904	David Bigham	28	Jun	92
7723 w	Eugene Gilkes	8	Jul	84
7660		8	Jul	84
7713	Jim Stevenson	5	Jun	93
7668	Fidelis Obikwu	5	Oct	82
7643 w	Tom Leeson	8	Sep	85
7565		11	Aug	85
7616	Barry Thomas	23	Aug	92
7610	Jamie Quarry	24	Aug	94
7594	Mark Bishop	3	Sep	89
7567	Brian Taylor	8	Jul	90
7535	Duncan Mathieson	24	Jun	90

3000 Metres Track Walk

11:28.4	Phil Vesty	9	May	84

10000 Metres Track Walk

40:53.60	Phil Vesty	28	May	84
41:24.7	Martin Rush	6	Jul	86
41:51.55	Andi Drake	25	May	87
41:55.6	Darrell Stone	7	Feb	88
42:24.61	Ian McCombie	29	May	83
42:28.0	Philip King	17	May	95
43:00.67	Sean Martindale	5	Jun	88
43:10.4	Gareth Holloway	2	May	92
43:12.85	Matt Hales	12	Aug	00
43:26.2	Gordon Vale	20	Mar	82

20 Kilometres Road Walk

1:24:07.6t	Phil Vesty	1	Dec	84
1:24:53	Andi Drake	27	Jun	87
1:26:14	Darrell Stone	27	Mar	89
1:26:21	Ian McCombie	8	Aug	82
1:26:32	Martin Rush	25	Feb	84
1:28:02	Paul Blagg	27	Feb	82
1:28:15	Mark Easton	11	May	85
1:28:17	Andy Penn	21	May	88
1:28:40	Matt Hales	21	Apr	01
1:29:01	Steve Partington	11	May	85

50 Kilometres Road Walk

4:10:23	Darrell Stone		6 May	90

UNDER 20

100 Metres

10.06	Dwain Chambers	25	Jul	97
10.10	Mark Lewis-Francis	5	Aug	00
10.12	Christian Malcolm	29	Jul	98
10.21	Jamie Henderson	6	Aug	87
10.25	Jason Livingston ¶	9	Aug	90
10.25	Jason Gardener	21	Jul	94
10.29	Peter Radford (10.31?)	13	Sep	58
10.31	Chris Lambert	21	Aug	99
10.32	Mike McFarlane	6	Aug	78
10 10.34	Lincoln Asquith	25	Aug	83
10.37	Darren Campbell	26	Jul	91
10.38	Elliot Bunney	22	Aug	85
10.39	Jason John	28	Jul	90
10.39	Tyrone Edgar	7	Oct	00
10.41	Jamie Henthorn	28	Jul	95
10.43	Julian Golding	20	Jul	94
10.44	Steve Gookey	3	Aug	90
10.44	Jason Fergus	16	Sep	92
10.45	Luke Davis	21	Jul	97
20 10.46	Marcus Adam	6	Aug	87

wind assisted

9.97 †	Mark Lewis-Francis	4	Aug	01
10.10	Christian Malcolm	18	Jul	98
10.17	Tyrone Edgar	30	Jun	01
10.22	Lincoln Asquith	26	Jun	83
10.22	Dwayne Grant	30	Jun	01
10.28	Darren Campbell	26	Jul	91
10.29	Mike McFarlane	7	Aug	78
10.29	Elliot Bunney	27	May	84
10.29	Trevor Cameron	11	Jun	94
10.31	Aidan Syers	30	Jun	01
10.34	Darren Braithwaite	25	Jun	88
10.34	Julian Golding	17	Sep	94

hand timing

10.3	Martin Reynolds	29	Jun	68

200 Metres

20.29	Christian Malcolm	19	Sep	98
20.54	Ade Mafe	25	Aug	85
20.63	Chris Lambert	21	Aug	99
20.64	Dwayne Grant	16	Jun	01
20.67	David Jenkins	4	Sep	71
20.67	Tim Benjamin	17	Jun	01
20.73 A	Ralph Banthorpe	15	Oct	68
20.78	John Regis	29	Sep	85
20.80	Mike McFarlane	1	Jul	79
10 20.85	Richard Ashby	25	Aug	85
20.86	Lincoln Asquith	28	Aug	83
20.86	Roger Hunter	5	May	84
20.87	Donovan Reid	7	Oct	82
20.87	Mark Smith	28	Jul	90
20.87	Darren Campbell	19	Sep	92
20.91	Jamie Baulch	18	Sep	92
20.91	Ian Mackie	23	Jul	94
20.92	Marcus Adam	8	Aug	87
20.94	Marlon Devonish	6	Aug	95
20 20.95	Allyn Condon	26	Jun	93

wind assisted

20.60	Tim Benjamin	7	Aug	99
20.61	Darren Campbell	11	Aug	91
20.73	Julian Golding	17	Sep	94
20.80	Ben Lewis	11	Jul	99
20.85	Mark Smith	1	Jul	90

hand timing

20.6	David Jenkins	19	Sep	71

hand timing - wind assisted

20.4	Dwayne Grant	1	Jul	01
20.7	Lincoln Asquith	2	Jul	83

300 Metres

32.53	Mark Richardson ¶	14	Jul	91

400 Metres

45.36	Roger Black	24	Aug	85
45.41	David Grindley	10	Aug	91
45.45	David Jenkins	13	Aug	71
45.53	Mark Richardson ¶	10	Aug	91
45.83	Mark Hylton	16	Jul	95
46.03	Peter Crampton	8	Aug	87
46.10	Tim Benjamin	25	Aug	01
46.13	Guy Bullock	31	Jul	93
46.22	Wayne McDonald	17	Jun	89
46.32	Derek Redmond	9	Sep	84	10
46.46	Adrian Metcalfe	19	Sep	61
46.48	Roger Hunter	20	May	84
46.53	Mark Thomas	15	Sep	84
46.54	Michael Parper	7	Jun	97
46.56	Roy Dickens	6	Sep	80
46.59	Carl Southam	17	Sep	92
46.63	Melvin Fowell	18	Aug	79
46.64	Alloy Wilson	31	Jul	98
46.65	Darren Bernard	20	May	88
46.66	Du'aine Ladejo	9	Aug	90	20

hand timing

45.7	Adrian Metcalfe	2	Sep	61

800 Metres (* 880 yards time less 0.60)

1:45.64	David Sharpe	5	Sep	86
1:45.77	Steve Ovett	4	Sep	74
1:46.46	John Gladwin	7	Jul	82
1:46.63	Curtis Robb	6	Jul	91
1:46.80*	John Davies I	3	Jun	68
1:47.0	Ikem Billy	12	Jun	83
1:47.02	Chris McGeorge	8	Aug	81
1:47.18	Rick Soos	14	Aug	02
1:47.22	Kevin McKay	5	Jun	88
1:47.27	Tom Lerwill	22	Aug	96	10
1:47.35	Peter Elliott	23	Aug	81
1:47.53	Graham Williamson	1	Aug	79
1:47.6	Julian Spooner	24	Apr	79
1:47.69	Simon Lees	5	Sep	98
1:47.70	Darryl Taylor	13	Jul	84
1:47.71	Dane Joseph	15	Sep	78
1:47.73	Colin Szwed	9	Sep	77
1:47.75	Garry Cook	3	Jul	77
1:47.79	Craig Winrow	20	Jul	90
1:47.85	Steve Crabb	17	Sep	82	20

1000 Metres

2:18.98	David Sharpe	19	Aug	86
2:19.92	Graham Williamson	8	Jul	79
2:20.0	Steve Ovett	17	Aug	73
2:20.02	Darryl Taylor	18	Aug	84
2:20.37	Johan Boakes	17	Jun	84
2:21.17	Curtis Robb	16	Sep	90
2:21.41	Stuart Paton	17	Sep	82
2:21.7 A	David Strang (GBR?)	26	Jan	87
2:21.71	Kevin Glastonbury	18	Jun	77

1500 Metres

3:36.6 +	Graham Williamson	17	Jul	79	
3:40.09	Steve Cram	27	Aug	78	
3:40.68	Brian Treacy	24	Jul	90	
3:40.72	Gary Taylor	8	Jul	81	
3:40.90	David Robertson	28	Jul	92	
3:41.59	Chris Sly	22	Jul	77	
3:42.2	Paul Wynn	9	Aug	83	
3:42.5	Colin Reitz	8	Aug	79	
3:42.67	Matthew Hibberd	28	Jul	92	
3:42.7	David Sharpe	17	Oct	85	10
3:42.86	Stuart Paton	29	Aug	82	
3:42.89	Alistair Currie	17	Jul	84	
3:43.1 a	Paul Lawther	31	Jan	74	
3:43.24	Nick Hopkins	15	Jun	85	
3:43.37	Davey Wilson	4	Jul	87	
3:43.39	Johan Boakes	30	May	87	
3:43.4	Tom Mayo	5	Jun	96	
3:43.5	Matt Dixon	7	Aug	97	
3:43.69	Jon Richards	1	Jul	83	
3:43.8	John Nuttall	24	Jun	86	20

1 Mile

3:53.15	Graham Williamson	17	Jul	79
3:57.03	Steve Cram	14	Sep	79
3:58.68	Steve Flint	26	May	80
3:59.4	Steve Ovett	17	Jul	74
4:00.31	Johan Boakes	5	Aug	86
4:00.6	Simon Mugglestone	16	Sep	87
4:00.67	Brian Treacy	22	Aug	90
4:01.0	David Sharpe	3	May	86

2000 Metres

5:06.56	Jon Richards	7	Jul	82

3000 Metres

7:48.28	Jon Richards	9	Jul	83	
7:51.84	Steve Binns	8	Sep	79	
7:56.28	John Doherty	13	Jul	80	
7:59.55	Paul Davies-Hale	8	Aug	81	
8:00.1 a	Micky Morton	11	Jul	78	
8:00.7	Graham Williamson	29	Jul	78	
8:00.73	David Black	24	Jul	71	
8:00.8	Steve Anders	1	Aug	78	
8:00.88	Paul Taylor	12	Jun	85	
8:01.2	Ian Stewart I	7	Sep	68	10
8:01.26	Darius Burrows	21	Aug	94	
8:01.43	Nat Muir	28	Aug	77	
8:01.44	Colin Reitz	16	May	79	

5000 Metres

13:27.04	Steve Binns	14	Sep	79	
13:35.95	Paul Davies-Hale	11	Sep	81	
13:37.4	David Black	10	Sep	71	
13:43.82	Simon Mugglestone	24	May	87	
13:44.64	Julian Goater	14	Jul	72	
13:48.74	Jon Richards	28	May	83	
13:48.84	John Doherty	8	Aug	80	
13:49.1 a	Nat Muir	21	Aug	77	
13:53.30	Ian Stewart I	3	Aug	68	
13:53.3 a	Nicky Lees	21	Aug	77	10
13:54.2	Mick Morton	1	Jul	78	
13:54.52	Keith Cullen	8	Jun	91	
13:56.31	Mohamed Farah	23	Jun	01	
14:00.7	Peter Tootell	19	Jun	82	
14:00.7	Mike Chorlton	19	Jun	82	
14:00.85	Paul Taylor	15	Sep	84	
14:03.0	Steve Anders	1	Jul	78	
14:03.09	Jon Brown	11	Aug	90	
14:03.4	Jim Brown	26	Jun	71	
14:05.0	Paul Bannon	24	Jun	72	20

10000 Metres

29:21.9	Jon Brown	21	Apr	90
29:38.6	Ray Crabb	18	Apr	73
29:44.0	Richard Green	27	Sep	75
29:44.8	Jack Lane	23	Sep	69
29:45.8	Dave Murphy	17	Jul	76

2000 Metres Steeplechase

5:29.61	Colin Reitz	18	Aug	79	
5:31.12	Paul Davies-Hale	22	Aug	81	
5:32.84	Tom Hanlon	20	Jul	86	
5:34.8 a	Micky Morris	24	Aug	75	
5:38.01	Ken Baker	1	Aug	82	
5:38.2	Spencer Duval	8	Jul	89	
5:39.3 a	Graeme Fell	11	Jul	78	
5:39.93	Eddie Wedderburn	9	Sep	79	
5:40.2	Paul Campbell	31	Jul	77	
5:40.2	John Hartigan	27	Jun	84	10

3000 Metres Steeplechase

8:29.85	Paul Davies-Hale	31	Aug	81	
8:42.75	Colin Reitz	6	Jun	79	
8:43.21	Kevin Nash	2	Jun	96	
8:44.68	Alastair O'Connor	12	Aug	90	
8:44.91	Ken Baker	30	May	82	
8:45.65	Spencer Duval	17	Jun	89	
8:47.49	Tom Hanlon	8	Jun	86	
8:47.8	Stephen Murphy	16	Jun	02	
8:48.43	Graeme Fell	16	Jul	78	
8:50.14	Dave Long I	13	Jul	73	10
8:51.02	Tony Staynings	14	Jul	72	
8:54.15	Stuart Kefford	18	Sep	92	
8:54.6	Micky Morris	7	Sep	75	
8:54.92	Mark Wortley	4	Jun	88	
8:56.0	John Davies	13	Jun	71	
8:56.0	Eddie Wedderburn	3	Jun	79	
8:56.36	Dave Robertson	15	Jun	91	
8:57.4	Keith Cullen	8	May	91	
8:57.83	Iain Murdoch	3	May	99	
8:59.09	Ben Whitby	27	Jul	96	20

110 Metres Hurdles (3'3")

13.57	Chris Baillie	21	Aug	99
13.77	Kevin Lumsdon	8	Aug	92
13.90	Robert Newton	10	Jul	99
13.97	Dominic Girdler	2	Sep	01
14.01	Jamie Quarry	13	Jul	91
14.06	Neil Owen	4	Jul	92
14.07	Leo Barker	12	Jul	97
14.08	Liam Collins	12	Jul	97
14.11	Nathan Palmer	22	Aug	99
10 14.13	Derek Wilson	25	Jun	83

wind assisted

13.92	Matthew Clements	27	Aug	94
13.96	Dominic Girdler	8	Jul	00

hand timing

13.8	Jon Ridgeon	13	Jul	84
13.8	Paul Gray	16	Jul	88

hand timing - wind assisted

13.6	Mark Holtom	9	Jul	77
13.8	Paul Brice	9	Jul	83
13.8	Colin Jackson	15	Jul	84
13.8	Brett St Louis	11	Jul	87

110 Metres Hurdles (3'6")

13.44	Colin Jackson	19	Jul	86
13.46	Jon Ridgeon	23	Aug	85
13.72	Tony Jarrett	24	May	87
13.84	Chris Baillie	27	Aug	00
13.91	David Nelson	21	Jun	86
13.95	Robert Newton	4	Sep	00
13.97	Paul Gray	30	Jul	88
14.01	Ross Baillie	25	Aug	96
14.03	Brett St Louis	27	Jun	87
10 14.04	Damien Greaves	25	Aug	96
14.06	Mark Holtom	7	Aug	77
14.06	Nathan Palmer	20	Jul	01
14.08	Paul Brice	26	Aug	83
14.14	Neil Owen	17	Sep	92
14.16	Dominic Girdler	21	Jul	01
14.18	James Archampong	21	Jul	94
14.21	Berwyn Price	12	Sep	70
14.24	Nigel Walker	17	Sep	82
14.25	Ben Warmington	31	Jul	98
20 14.26	Alan Scott	24	Jun	01

wind assisted

13.42	Colin Jackson	27	Jul	86
13.82	David Nelson	5	Jul	86
13.93	Robert Newton	7	Aug	99
14.07	Dominic Girdler	20	Jul	01

400 Metres Hurdles

50.22	Martin Briggs	28	Aug	83
50.70	Noel Levy	8	Jul	94
50.96	Steven Green	6	Jul	02
51.07	Philip Beattie	20	Aug	82
51.15 A	Andy Todd	18	Oct	67
51.70		23	Sep	67
51.31	Gary Oakes	9	Sep	77
51.39	Richard McDonald	19	Jun	99
51.48	Bob Brown	19	Jun	88

51.51	Max Robertson	24	Jul	82
51.55	Mark Whitby	26	Aug	83 10
51.63	Mark Rowlands	21	Jun	97
51.66	Paul Goacher	2	Aug	80
51.68	Rhys Williams	17	Jul	02
51.71	Matthew Elias	7	Jun	97
51.73	Matt Douglas	29	Jul	95
51.91	Peter Campbell	19	Jun	88
51.97	Bel Blik	17	Aug	85
52.24	Andrew Abrahams	11	Aug	84
52.25	Jeffrey Christie	16	Jun	01
52.26	Gary Jennings	30	Jun	91 20

hand timing

51.0	Richard McDonald	24	Jul	99
51.5	Max Robertson	10	Jul	82
51.5	Matthew Elias	6	Jun	98
51.8	Jeffrey Christie	1	Jul	01

High Jump

2.37	Steve Smith	20	Sep	92
2.27	Brendan Reilly	27	May	90
2.26	James Brierley	3	Aug	96
2.25	Geoff Parsons	9	Jul	83
2.24	John Hill	23	Aug	85
2.23	Mark Lakey (U17)	29	Aug	82
2.23 i	Ben Challenger	1	Mar	97
2.21		24	Aug	96
2.22	Dalton Grant	3	Jul	85
2.21	Martyn Bernard	6	Jul	02
2.20	Byron Morrison	14	Jul	84 10
2.18	Ossie Cham	14	Jun	80
2.18	Alex Kruger	26	Jun	82
2.18	Steve Ritchie	15	Jul	89
2.18	Hopeton Lindo	23	Jul	89
2.18	Chuka Enih-Snell	21	Apr	01
2.17	Stuart Ohrland	27	Aug	94
2.17	Mike Robbins	5	Aug	95
2.16 i	Claude Moseley	13	Apr	80
2.16	Andy Hutchison	2	Sep	84
2.16	John Holman	4	Jul	87 20
2.16	Andrew Lynch	18	Sep	93
2.16	Richard Aspden	7	Jul	95
2.16	Rob Brocklebank	7	Jul	95
2.16 i	Jason McDade	24	Jan	99

Pole Vault

5.50	Neil Winter	9	Aug	92
5.30	Matt Belsham	16	Sep	90
5.21	Andy Ashurst	2	Sep	84
5.21 i	Christian Linskey	20	Feb	99
5.20		24	May	98
5.20	Billy Davey	5	Jun	83
5.20	Warren Siley	4	Aug	90
5.20	Nick Buckfield	31	May	92
5.20	Ben Flint	2	Aug	97
5.10	Brian Hooper	1	Oct	72
5.10	Mike Edwards	20	Jun	87 10
5.10	Mark Davis	9	Jun	96
5.05	Ian Tullett	22	Aug	87
5.05	Dean Mellor	7	Jul	90
5.02	Paul Williamson	29	May	93

5.00	Keith Stock	3 Jul	76
5.00	Bob Kingman	2 May	92
5.00	Tim Thomas	17 Jun	92
5.00	Mike Barber	1 Jul	92
5.00 sq	Ian Wilding	16 Jul	94
20 5.00	Neil Young	18 May	96

Long Jump

8.03	Jonathan Moore	18 May	02
7.98	Stewart Faulkner	6 Aug	88
7.91	Steve Phillips	10 Aug	91
7.90	Nathan Morgan	25 Jul	97
7.84	Wayne Griffith	25 Aug	89
7.76	Carl Howard	31 Jul	93
7.73	Jason Canning	20 Apr	88
7.72	Daley Thompson	21 May	77
7.70	Kevin Liddington	27 Aug	88
10 7.66	Barry Nevison	7 Jul	85
7.62	Colin Mitchell	11 Jul	78
7.62	Chris Tomlinson	21 Oct	00
7.61	Darren Gomersall	19 Jul	87
7.58	Fred Salle	11 Jun	83
7.56	John Herbert	11 Jul	81
7.56	Colin Jackson	31 Aug	85
7.56	Stuart Wells	12 Jul	97
7.56	Darren Thompson	30 May	98
7.54	Derrick Brown	26 Jun	82

wind assisted

8.04	Stewart Faulkner	20 Aug	88
7.97	Nathan Morgan	13 Jul	96
7.96	Colin Jackson	17 May	86
7.82	Kevin Liddington	25 Jun	89
7.72	John Herbert	15 Jun	80
7.66	Mark Awanah	30 Jun	01
7.60	Brian Robinson (U17)	21 Jul	97
7.58	Gus Udo	8 Jul	78
7.58	Garry Slade	6 Jun	87
7.56	Eddie Starrs	22 Jul	79

Triple Jump

16.58	Tosi Fasinro	15 Jun	91
16.57	Tosin Oke	8 Aug	99
16.53	Larry Achike	24 Jul	94
16.43	Jonathan Moore	22 Jul	01
16.24	Aston Moore	11 Jun	75
16.22	Mike Makin	17 May	81
16.13	Steven Anderson	11 Jun	83
16.03	John Herbert	23 Jun	81
15.99	Steven Shalders	20 Oct	00
10 15.95	Keith Connor	30 Aug	76
15.94	Vernon Samuels	27 Jun	82
15.93	Tayo Erogbogbo	17 Sep	94
15.92	Lawrence Lynch	13 Jul	85
15.88	Julian Golley	28 Jul	90
15.87	Stewart Faulkner	22 Aug	87
15.86	Phillips Idowu	5 Jul	97
15.84	Francis Agyepong	29 Sep	84
15.82	Jon Wallace	11 Jul	98
15.80	David Johnson	14 Jul	72
20 15.79	Paul Johnson	27 Jun	87

wind assisted

16.81	Tosi Fasinro	15 Jun	91
16.67	Larry Achike	24 Jul	94
16.43	Mike Makin	14 Jun	81
16.34	Phillips Idowu	27 Jul	97
16.31	Aston Moore	9 Aug	75
16.07	Vernon Samuels	14 Aug	82
16.01	Julian Golley	22 Jul	90
15.96	Paul Johnson	27 Jun	87
15.95	Lawrence Lynch	26 May	86
15.81	Junior Campbell	28 May	89

Shot (7.26kg)

19.46	Carl Myerscough ¶	6 Sep	98
18.21 i	Matt Simson	3 Feb	89
	18.11	27 Aug	89
17.78 i	Billy Cole	10 Mar	84
	17.72	2 Jun	84
17.36 i	Chris Ellis	8 Dec	84
	17.10	7 Jul	85
17.26 i	Geoff Capes	16 Nov	68
	16.80	30 Jul	68
17.25	Emeka Udechuku	20 Sep	97
17.22	Antony Zaidman	4 Jul	81
16.69	Gregg Beard	30 Sep	00
16.61	Simon Williams	10 Aug	86
16.60	Alan Carter	11 May	63 10
16.48	Martyn Lucking	24 Aug	57
16.47	Paul Buxton	25 May	75
16.23 i	David Readle	30 Jan	99
	16.15	3 Jul	99
16.21	Mike Lindsay	29 Jul	57
16.20 i	Nigel Spratley	19 Mar	89
	16.04	20 May	89
16.18	Tony Satchwell	23 Apr	72
16.10	Martin Fletcher	19 Jun	88
16.03	Jon Wood	26 Sep	70
15.94	Andy Vince	5 May	78
15.94	Mitchell Smith	23 Mar	85 20

Shot (6.25kg)

21.03	Carl Myerscough ¶	13 May	98
19.47	Matt Simson	20 May	89
19.15	Billy Cole	19 May	84
18.66 i	Simon Williams	15 Nov	86
	18.52	11 Jul	86
18.20 i	Chris Ellis	16 Feb	85
	18.13	14 Jul	84
18.06	Greg Beard	2 Sep	01
17.81	Antony Zaidman	16 May	81
17.74	Emeka Udechuku	9 Aug	98
17.67	David Readle	22 Aug	99
17.58	Nigel Spratley	28 May	89 10
17.32	Andy Vince	15 May	77
17.31	Mitchell Smith	11 Jun	85
17.31	Lyndon Woodward	10 Jul	99
17.30	Jamie Cockburn	20 Sep	92
17.26	Neil Gray	19 May	84
17.26 i	Neal Brunning ¶	9 Dec	89
17.22	Richard Slaney	22 Jul	75

Discus (2kg)
60.97	Emeka Udechuku	5	Jul	98
60.19	Carl Myerscough ¶	8	Aug	98
55.10	Glen Smith	31	Aug	91
53.42	Paul Mardle	25	Jul	81
53.40	Robert Weir	10	Aug	80
53.32	Paul Buxton	9	Aug	75
53.02	Simon Williams	16	Aug	86
52.94	Lee Newman	29	Aug	92
52.84	Jamie Murphy	14	Jun	92
10 52.14	Robert Russell	4	Jul	93
51.70	Richard Slaney	27	Jul	75
51.66	Neal Brunning ¶	30	Jul	89
51.28	Adam Major	10	Sep	00
51.10	Mike Lindsay	29	May	57
51.08	Peter Weir	1	Aug	82
51.05	Luke Rosenberg	4	Jul	99
50.74	Tony Satchwell	21	Aug	72
50.64	Colin Bastien	9	Jun	85
50.46	Neil Boyton	16	Jul	83
20 50.07	Scot Thompson	27	Aug	00

Discus (1.75kg)
64.35	Emeka Udechuku	21	Jun	98
61.81	Carl Myerscough ¶	18	Aug	98
60.76	Glen Smith	26	May	91
56.64	Jamie Murphy	19	May	90
56.10	Lee Newman	4	Jul	92
56.00	Simon Williams	17	May	86
55.94	Mark Davies	19	Aug	90
55.44	Neal Brunning ¶	8	Jul	89
55.16	Adam Major	10	Sep	00
10 55.00	Robert Russell	16	May	93

Hammer (7.26kg)
67.48	Paul Head	16	Sep	84
67.10	Jason Byrne	6	Aug	89
66.14	Martin Girvan	21	Jul	79
65.86	Robert Weir	6	Sep	80
65.30	Karl Andrews	2	Jul	94
64.14	Ian Chipchase	25	Sep	71
63.84	Andrew Tolputt	7	Sep	86
63.72	Gareth Cook	10	Jul	88
62.82	Mick Jones	29	Aug	82
10 62.02	Peter Vivian	1	Jul	89
61.34	Ron James	22	Apr	78
61.22	Malcolm Croad	25	Aug	92
61.10	Vaughan Cooper	5	May	84
60.86	David Smith I	2	Aug	81
60.34	Tony Kenneally	1	Aug	82
60.24	Paul Buxton	17	Jun	75
60.04	Eric Berry	16	Jun	73
59.98	David Smith II	3	Jul	93
59.80	Matthew Bell	7	Jun	97
20 59.12	Andrew Grierson	18	Jul	98

Hammer (6.25kg)
74.92	Jason Byrne	17	Dec	89
73.28	Robert Weir	14	Sep	80
72.66	Paul Head	2	Sep	84

71.84	Gareth Cook	28	May	88	
70.36	Andrew Tolputt	21	Sep	86	
69.10	Karl Andrews	3	Aug	94	
67.80	Martin Girvan	7	Jul	79	
67.52	Vaughan Cooper	19	May	84	
67.48	Mick Jones	2	Jun	82	
66.38	Tony Kenneally	10	Jul	82	10

Javelin
79.50	Steve Backley	5	Jun	88	
77.48	David Parker	14	Aug	99	
74.54	Gary Jenson	19	Sep	86	
74.24	Mark Roberson	18	Jul	86	
73.76	Nigel Bevan	29	Aug	87	
71.79	Phill Sharpe	27	Aug	00	
71.74	Myles Cottrell	29	Jul	89	
71.14	Dan Carter	11	Jul	98	
69.62	Stefan Baldwin	8	Jul	89	
68.85	Alex van der Merwe	30	Jun	02	10
68.84	James Hurrion	12	Jul	91	
68.74	Jon Clarke	14	Jun	86	
68.38	James Drennen	12	Jul	91	
68.30	Mark Lawrence	31	Jul	88	
68.08	Tim Kitney	13	Sep	98	
67.22	Richard Atkinson	14	Aug	93	
66.95	Andrew Gallagher	18	Aug	01	
66.74	Stuart Faben	22	Jul	94	
66.62	Mark Francis	13	Jul	96	
66.21	Clifton Green	4	May	98	20

Decathlon (1985 Tables)
8082	Daley Thompson	31	Jul	77	
7488	David Bigham	9	Aug	90	
7480	Dean Macey	22	Aug	96	
7299	Eugene Gilkes	24	May	81	
7274	Jim Stevenson	24	Jun	90	
7247	Brian Taylor	7	May	89	
7169	Barry Thomas	5	Aug	90	
7126	Fidelis Obikwu	16	Sep	79	
7112	Gavin Sunshine	30	Jul	93	
7018	Jamie Quarry	30	Jun	91	10
6958	Roy Mitchell	29	Sep	74	
6936	Anthony Brannen	24	May	87	
6925	Roger Hunter	4	Jun	95	
6843	Ed Coats	30	May	99	
6839	Mark Bushell	30	Apr	95	
6812	Nigel Skinner	19	Aug	84	
6809	Rafer Joseph	26	Jul	87	
6801 w	Kevan Lobb	18	Jun	78	
6774	Jason McDade	30	May	99	
6788	Adrian Hemery	10	Jun	01	20

IAAF Junior
6989	Edward Dunford	4	Aug	02

Junior Implements
7134	Dean Macey	17	Sep	95
7050	Edward Dunford	22	Sep	02
6958 w	Roger Hunter	18	Sep	94
6789	Jamie Quarry	16	Sep	90
6762	Fyn Corcoran	22	Sep	96
6678	Darren Hatton	21	Sep	97

3000 Metres Track Walk

11:54.23	Tim Berrett	23	Jun	84
12:01.89 i	Philip King	21	Feb	93
12:02.0		12	May	92
12:02.04	Phil Vesty	24	Jul	82
12:16.5	David Hucks	5	Aug	84
12:19.8	Gordon Vale	11	Mar	81

5000 Metres Track Walk

20:16.40	Philip King	26	Jun	93
20:33.4 +	Darrell Stone	7	Aug	87
20:47.23	Lloyd Finch	14	Jul	01
20:48.1 +	Dom King	4	May	02
20:55.4	Tim Berrett	9	Jun	84

10000 Metres Track Walk

41:52.13	Darrell Stone	7	Aug	87
42:06.35	Gordon Vale	2	Aug	81
42:17.1	Dom King	4	May	02
42:46.3	Phil Vesty	20	Mar	82
42:47.7	Philip King	2	May	92
43:04.09	Tim Berrett	25	Aug	83
43:09.82	Lloyd Finch	18	May	02
43:42.75	Martin Rush	29	May	83
43:54.25	Gareth Brown	7	Aug	87
44:06.6	Dan King	4	May	02
44:22.12	Gareth Holloway	5	Jun	88
44:22.4	Jon Vincent	1	Apr	89
44:30.0	Andy Penn	15	Mar	86
44:38.0	Ian McCombie	29	Mar	80
44:53.0	Michael Kemp	4	Apr	98
45:04.28	Andi Drake	1	Jul	84
45:04.37	Ian Ashforth	3	Aug	85
45:06.19	Jon Bott	25	May	87
45:13.50	Kirk Taylor	23	Aug	87
45:17.0	Bob Chaplain	28	Jun	75

10k Road - where superior to track time

41:47	Darrell Stone	26	Sep	87
42:29	Steve Hollier	10	Dec	95
42:39	Martin Rush	7	May	83
42:40	Tim Berrett	18	Feb	84
43:18	Richard Dorman	18	Oct	80
43:35	Gareth Brown	12	Apr	87
43:50	Kirk Taylor	12	Apr	87
43:53	Michael Kemp	25	Apr	98
44:08	Nathan Kavanagh	5	May	85
44:08	Gareth Holloway	8	Jul	89
44:09	Jimmy Ball	16	Oct	82

20 Kilometres Road Walk

1:26:13	Tim Berrett	25	Feb	84
1:29:49	Dom King	15	Jun	02
1:29:10	Phil Vesty	18	Jul	82
1:31:34.4t	Gordon Vale	28	Jun	81
1:32:46	Graham Morris	26	Feb	77
1:33:03	Darrell Stone	10	May	86

50 Kilometres Road Walk

4:18:18	Gordon Vale	24	Oct	81

UNDER 17

100 Metres

10.31	Mark Lewis-Francis	21	Aug	99
10.56	Rikki Fifton	29	Jul	01
10.60	Tyrone Edgar	16	Aug	98
10.64	Jon Barbour	12	Jul	97
10.66	Ben Lewis	7	Sep	97
10.67	Michael Nartey	28	Sep	91
10.69	Mike McFarlane	13	Aug	76
10.69	James Ellington	10	Aug	02
10.70	Steve Green	15	Jul	72
10.70	Karl Forde	3	Jul	99
10.70	Craig Pickering	10	Aug	02
10.71	Luke Davis	12	Jul	96
10.71	Tim Benjamin	16	Aug	98
10.72	Peter Little	6	Aug	77
10.72	Trevor Cameron	7	Aug	93

wind assisted

10.26	Mark Lewis-Francis	5	Aug	99
10.38	Kevin Mark	3	Jul	93
10.44	Luke Davis	13	Jul	96
10.51	Tim Benjamin	4	Jul	98
10.56	Dwain Chambers	8	Jul	94
10.57	Trevor Cameron	3	Jul	93
10.58	Tyrone Edgar	16	Aug	98
10.60	Matthew Ouche	7	Jul	01
10.62	Elliot Bunney	25	Jun	83
10.62	Jamie Nixon	7	Jul	85

hand timing

10.5	Michael Powell	17	Sep	78

200 Metres

20.92	Ade Mafe	27	Aug	83
21.19	Tim Benjamin	31	Jul	98
21.24	Peter Little	21	Aug	77
21.25	Mark Richardson ¶	24	Jul	88
21.44	Roger Hunter	2	Aug	81
21.45	Monu Miah	29	Jul	00
21.46	Simon Farenden	7	Jul	01
21.51	Darren Campbell	15	Sep	90
21.51	Ben Lewis	19	Jul	97
21.53	Steve Eden	2	Aug	81
21.56	Trevor Cameron	8	Aug	93
21.58	Christian Malcolm	9	Jul	95
21.62	Tyrone Edgar	24	May	98
21.63	Richard Ashby	7	Aug	83
21.64	Elliot Bunney	7	Aug	83
21.64	Adam Rogers	14	Aug	99

wind assisted

20.98	Tim Benjamin	18	Jul	98
21.17	Mark Richardson	20	Aug	88
21.25	Trevor Cameron	25	Sep	93
21.31	Monu Miah	15	Jul	00
21.32	Graham Beasley	9	Jul	94
21.38	Elliot Bunney	13	Aug	83
21.38	Ben Lewis	12	Jul	97
21.39	Laurence Oboh	15	Jul	00

hand timing - wind assisted

21.0	Peter Little	30	Jul	77

400 Metres

46.43	Mark Richardson ¶	28	Jul	88
46.74	Guy Bullock	17	Sep	92
47.29	Richard Davenport	8	Jun	02
47.81	Mark Hylton	17	Jul	93
47.86	Kris Stewart	13	Jul	96
48.05	David Naismith	10	Aug	96
48.11	Gary Thomas	18	Sep	82
48.22	Robert Tobin	8	Jul	00
48.25	Adrian Patrick	2	Sep	89
10 48.34	Richard McNabb	27	Aug	95
48.35	James Hilston	6	Aug	95
48.36	David Simpson	29	May	89
48.41	Mark Tyler	11	Aug	84
48.46	Phil Harvey	24	Jun	79
48.46	Simon Tunnicliffe	29	May	99

hand timing

47.6	Kris Stewart	3	Aug	96
48.2	David Simpson	8	Jul	89
48.3	David McKenzie	21	Sep	86
48.4	Steve Ovett	20	Aug	72
48.4	Chris Thompson	1	Aug	81
48.4	Martin Bradbury	31	Jul	99

800 Metres

1:49.9	Mark Sesay	18	Jul	89
1:50.55	Michael Rimmer	6	Aug	02
1:50.7	Peter Elliott	16	Sep	79
1:50.90	Craig Winrow	21	Aug	88
1:51.0	Chris McGeorge	1	Jul	78
1:51.05	Mal Edwards	20	Sep	74
1:51.3	Julian Spooner	3	Aug	77
1:51.4	Kevin McKay	19	Aug	85
1:51.6	Neil Horsfield	31	Aug	83
10 1:51.6	David Gerard	21	Jul	84
1:51.8	Paul Burgess	14	Jul	87
1:51.9 +	Johan Boakes	17	Jun	84
1:52.0	Paul Causey	21	Jul	84
1:52.14	Lee Bowron	14	Aug	02
1:52.21	Malcolm Hassan	21	Aug	99

1000 Metres

2:20.37	Johan Boakes	17	Jun	84

1500 Metres

3:47.7	Steve Cram	14	May	77
3:48.49	Johan Boakes	28	Jun	84
3:49.40	Anthony Moran	23	Jul	02
3:49.9	Kelvin Newton	20	Jun	79
3:51.1	Jason Lobo	30	Aug	86
3:51.4	Darren Mead	26	Jul	85
3:51.7	Martin Forder	19	Sep	86
3:51.8	Mark Sesay	22	Aug	89
3:52.0	Stuart Poore	6	Sep	89
10 3:52.24	Lee Bowran	28	Aug	02
3:52.47	Simon Young	4	Aug	90
3:52.6	Glen Stewart	19	Sep	87
3:52.78	Clifton Bradeley	2	Aug	81
3:52.9	Steve Johnson	8	Jul	89
3:53.0	Mark Bateman	31	Aug	74

1 Mile

4:06.7	Barrie Williams	22	Apr	72

2000 Metres

5:28.2 +	Kevin Steere	10	Jul	71

3000 Metres

8:13.42	Barrie Moss	15	Jul	72
8:15.34	Kevin Steere	30	Aug	71
8:16.18	Mohammed Farah	21	Aug	99
8:19.08	Darren Mead	26	Aug	85
8:19.38	Johan Boakes	24	Jun	84
8:24.2	Simon Goodwin	16	Jul	80
8:24.2	Jason Lobo	13	Aug	86
8:25.2	Colin Clarkson	3	Aug	77
8:26.3	Paul Williams	10	Aug	83
8:26.6	Jon Dennis	23	Apr	86 10
8:26.92	Jon Richards	5	Sep	80
8:27.70	Anthony Moran	6	Aug	02
8:29.09	Steve Fury	18	Aug	84
8:29.4	Darrell Smith	16	Jul	83
8:30.4	Nicky Lees	15	Jul	74
8:30.4	David Lewis	13	Aug	78

5000 Metres

14:41.8	Nicky Lees	24	Aug	74

1500 Metres Steeplechase

4:11.2	Steve Evans	15	Jul	74
4:12.3	Chris Sly	15	Jul	74
4:13.1	John Crowley	15	Jul	74
4:13.2	David Lewis	1	Jul	78
4:13.7	Danny Fleming	31	Jul	77
4:13.9	Eddie Wedderburn	31	Jul	77
4:14.0	Dave Robertson	8	Jul	89
4:14.4	Stephen Arnold	7	Sep	85
4:15.0	David Caton	9	Jun	84
4:15.0	Spencer Duval	12	Jul	86 10
4:15.2	Garrie Richardson	8	Jul	89
4:15.3	John Wilson	26	Jul	75
4:16.6	Adrian Green	9	Jun	84
4:17.4	Spencer Newport	9	Jul	83
4:17.7	Kevin Capper	8	Aug	76
4:17.7	Stuart Kefford	8	Jul	89

2000 Metres Steeplechase

5:55.0	David Lewis	20	Aug	78

3000 Metres Steeplechase

9:16.6	Colin Reitz	19	Sep	76

100 Metres Hurdles (3'0")

12.60	Tristan Anthony	14	Aug	99
12.68	Matthew Clements	8	Aug	93
12.90	Steve Markham	17	Aug	91
12.91	Allan Scott	14	Aug	99
12.97	Jon Snade	8	Aug	93
12.97	Andy Turner	16	Aug	97
12.98	Robert Newton	16	Aug	97
12.99	Dominic Girdler	11	Jul	98

13.01	Hugh Teape	3 Aug	80
13.05	Brett St Louis	4 Aug	85
13.07	Jon Ridgeon	7 Aug	83
13.07	David O'Leary	3 Aug	96
13.09	Damien Greaves	8 Jul	94
13.09	Chris Baillie	16 Aug	97
13.10	Ricky Glover	17 Aug	91

(row 2 marked with a marginal "10")

wind assisted

12.47	Matthew Clements	9 Jul	94
12.70	Damien Greaves	9 Jul	94
12.88	Nick Csemiczky	13 Jul	91
12.90	Ricky Glover	13 Jul	91
12.90	Ben Warmington	8 Jul	95
12.96	Nathan Palmer	15 Aug	98
12.96	Dominic Girdler	15 Aug	98
12.99	Neil Owen	1 Jul	90

hand timing

12.8	Brett St Louis	28 Jul	85
12.8	Richard Dunn	29 Jun	91
12.9	Hugh Teape	31 Aug	80

hand timing - wind assisted

12.6	Brett St Louis	20 Jul	85
12.9	Jon Ridgeon	9 Jul	83
12.9	Dominic Girdler	13 Sep	98

110 Metres Hurdles (3'0")

13.71	Matthew Clements	19 May	94
14.16	Ben Warmington	12 Jul	95
14.19	Ross Baillie	19 May	94

hand timing

13.6	Jon Ridgeon	16 Jul	83

110 Metres Hurdles (3'3")

15.07	Edward Dunford	10 Sep	00

wind assisted

13.92	Matthew Clements	27 Aug	94

hand timing

14.5	Kieran Moore	30 Aug	80

110 Metres Hurdles (3'6")

14.89	Tristan Anthony	4 Jul	99

400 Metres Hurdles (2'9")

52.20	Tristan Anthony	18 Jul	99
52.69	Jeffrey Christie	18 Jul	99
52.81	Richard McDonald	10 Aug	96
53.08	Richard Davenport	11 Aug	02
53.14	Martin Briggs	2 Aug	80
53.26	Nange Ursell	11 Jul	98
53.30	Mark Rowlands	31 Jul	94
53.55	Charles Robertson-Adams	31 Jul	94
53.58	Noel Levy	13 Jul	91
53.64	Dean Park	17 May	94
53.69	Max Robertson	2 Aug	80
53.69	Bob Brown	9 Aug	86
53.71	Andrew Bargh	11 Jul	92
53.82	Robert Taylor	9 Aug	86

(row "53.64 Dean Park" marked with a marginal "10")

hand timing

53.2	Phil Beattie	24 May	80
53.8	Carl McMullen	20 Jul	96

400 Metres Hurdles (3'0")

53.06	Phil Beattie	2 Aug	80
53.31	Richard McDonald	28 Jul	96

High Jump

2.23	Mark Lakey	29 Aug	82
2.15	Ossie Cham	14 Jul	79
2.15	Brendan Reilly	7 May	89
2.15	Stanley Osuide	1 Sep	91
2.15	Chuka Enih-Snell	10 Sep	00
2.12	Femi Abejide	11 Jul	81
2.11	Leroy Lucas	6 Aug	83
2.11 i	Ken McKeown	12 Jul	98
2.11		18 Jul	98
2.10	Dalton Grant	18 Sep	82
2.10	Tim Blakeway	29 Aug	87
2.10	James Brierley	16 May	93
2.10	Martin Lloyd	28 Sep	96
2.10	Martin Aram	23 Jul	00
2.09	Steve Smith	10 Sep	89
2.09	Sam Hood	27 Aug	00

(row "2.10 Tim Blakeway" marked with a marginal "10")

Pole Vault

5.20	Neil Winter	2 Sep	90
5.15	Christian Linskey	23 Aug	96
4.90	Warren Siley	8 Sep	89
4.80	Billy Davey	14 Sep	80
4.80	Keith Higham	25 May	02
4.76	Nick Buckfield	11 Jun	89
4.72	Ian Lewis	24 Aug	85
4.71	Chris Tremayne	27 Aug	01
4.70	Richard Smith	7 Jun	97
4.70	Mark Christie	25 Aug	01
4.66	Mike Edwards	24 Aug	85
4.65	Steven Lewis	22 Jun	02
4.60	Ben Flint	10 Jun	95
4.53	Keith Stock	5 Sep	73
4.50	Christian North	26 Aug	90
4.50	Mike Barber	15 Sep	90
4.50	Neil Young	5 Jun	93
4.50	Chris Type	4 Jul	98
4.50	Cameron Johnston	15 Aug	99
4.50	Paul Stevens	8 Jul	00

(row "4.70 Mark Christie" marked with a marginal "10")

Long Jump

7.53	Brian Robinson	21 Jul	97
7.47	Bernard Yeboah	13 Jul	02
7.46	Jonathan Moore	30 Jul	00
7.46	Onen Eyong	9 Sep	01
7.32	Kevin Liddington	16 May	87
7.25	Alan Slack	12 Jun	76
7.21	Hugh Teape	17 May	80
7.21	Jordan Lau	8 Jul	00
7.20	Hugh Davidson	21 Jun	80
7.19	Oni Onuorah	8 Jul	89
7.19	Jermaine Bernard	21 Jul	01
7.18	Barry Nevison	1 May	83
7.17	Hugh Whyte	15 Jul	79
7.17	Mark Awanah	4 Jul	99
7.15	Matthew John	29 Jun	86

(row "7.19 Oni Onuorah" marked with a marginal "10")

wind assisted				
7.60	Brian Robinson	21	Jul	97
7.47	Onen Eyong	2	Sep	01
7.40	Matthew John	10	May	86
7.27	David Mountford	25	Jul	98
7.25	Nathan Morgan	27	Aug	94
7.25	Mark Awanah	25	Jul	98
7.23	Oni Onuorah	26	May	90
7.23	Andy Turner	20	Sep	97

Triple Jump

16.02	Jonathan Moore	13	Aug	00
15.65	Vernon Samuels	18	Jul	81
15.50	Junior Campbell	18	May	86
15.45	Steven Anderson	2	Aug	81
15.28	Larry Achike	22	Jun	91

note resident but not British citizen at this time

15.14	Marvin Bramble	8	Aug	93
15.14	Steven Shalders	18	Jul	98
14.94	Hugh Teape	17	May	80
14.93	Mark Whitehead	26	Aug	85
14.90	Lawrence Lynch	21	Jul	84
14.84	Peter Vaughan	2	May	83
14.83	Malwyn Gordon	10	Jul	98
14.82	Philip Ferdinand	5	Sep	99
14.77	Carl Howard	13	Jul	90
14.76	Delroy Ricketts	13	Jul	90
14.76	Jon Wallace	3	Sep	95

wind assisted				
15.40	Steven Shalders	18	Jul	98
15.25	Marvin Bramble	3	Jul	93
15.08	Lawrence Lynch	29	Apr	84
15.06	Craig Duncan	7	Aug	82
15.01	Malwyn Gordon	15	Aug	98
14.93	Chris Tomlinson	18	Jul	98
14.88	Carl Howard	13	Jul	90
14.87	Darren Gomersall	3	Aug	85
14.84	Nick Leech	8	Jul	78

Shot (7.26kg)

17.30	Carl Myerscough ¶	3	Aug	96

Shot (6.25kg)

16.88	Gregg Beard	29	Aug	99

Shot (5kg)

21.20	Carl Myerscough ¶	22	Sep	96
19.22	Chris Ellis	4	Jun	82
18.91	Gregg Beard	19	Sep	99
18.90	Neal Brunning ¶	6	Sep	87
18.44	Matt Simson	27	Jul	86
18.43	Emeka Udechuku	28	May	95
18.25	Billy Cole	1	Aug	81
17.91	Antony Zaidman	28	May	78
17.76	George Brocklebank	22	Jul	79
17.61	Derrick Squire	15	Jul	00
17.40	Osita Iwenjiora	20	Sep	89
17.36	Piers Selby	10	Jul	92
17.34	Carl Saggers	30	Jul	00
17.30	Jason Mulcahy	7	Jul	89
17.24	Mark Edwards	20	Aug	91

Discus (2kg)

50.60	Carl Myerscough ¶	28	Jul	96
48.96	Emeka Udechuku	19	Aug	95

Discus (1.75kg)

54.70	Emeka Udechuku	18	Jun	95
52.50	Paul Mardle	7	Jul	79

Discus (1.5kg)

62.22	Emeka Udechuku	10	Jul	95
58.14	Carl Myerscough ¶	12	May	96
56.14	Chris Symonds	6	Sep	87
55.94	Simon Williams I	9	Sep	84
55.90	Guy Litherland	14	Sep	85
55.72	Keith Homer	27	Jun	82
55.52	Glen Smith	14	May	88
55.36	Neal Brunning ¶	7	Jun	87
55.17	Gregg Beard	30	May	99
54.18	Matt Symonds	21	Jul	84
53.98	Felice Miele	10	Jul	98
53.80	Paul Mardle	19	May	79
53.69	Carl Saggers	17	Sep	00
52.84	Simon Williams II	31	Aug	97
52.84	Andrew Thomas	11	Aug	02
52.76	Julian Willett	17	Jun	89
52.76	James South	1	Sep	91
52.62	Ashley Knott	22	Sep	91

Hammer (7.26kg)

59.94	Andrew Tolputt	30	Sep	84
57.04	Peter Vivian	27	Jun	87

Hammer (6.25kg)

66.70	Andrew Tolputt	2	Sep	84
64.00	Matthew Sutton	22	Aug	98

Hammer (5kg)

76.28	Andrew Tolputt	11	Aug	84
73.90	Paul Head	29	Aug	81
73.76	Matthew Sutton	14	Jun	98
73.00	Nick Steinmetz	17	Jul	93
71.34	Tony Kenneally	7	Sep	80
70.82	Jason Byrne	20	Jun	87
68.62	Peter Vivian	16	May	87
68.27	Carl Saggers	17	Jun	00
67.64	Gareth Cook	22	Sep	85
67.48	Chris Howe	24	Jun	84
67.21	Ross Thompson	22	Aug	98
66.92	Paul Murden	8	May	85
66.30	Malcolm Croad	21	Jul	90
65.70	Ross Kidner	26	May	97
65.29	Simon Bissell	14	Jul	02
64.82	Vaughan Cooper	13	May	82
64.40	Jonathan Bond	14	May	89
64.32	Neil Homer	18	Aug	84
64.18	Charles Beresford	1	May	89

Javelin (800g -1986 model)

68.26	David Parker	19	May	96
61.00	Phill Sharpe	6	Jul	97

Javelin (800g Original model)

72.78	Gary Jenson	10	Sep	83
69.84	Colin Mackenzie	12	May	79
66.14	David Messom	14	May	81
65.32	Marcus Humphries	26	Aug	78
64.80	Paul Bushnell	1	Sep	85
64.34	Steve Backley	1	Sep	85
63.44	Michael Williams	16	Sep	79

Javelin (700g)

73.56	David Parker	20	Jul	96	
72.48	Gary Jenson	3	Jul	83	
70.30	Colin Mackenzie	6	Jul	79	
68.88	Phill Sharpe	19	Jul	97	
68.26	Ian Marsh	30	Jul	77	
68.18	James Hurrion	3	Jun	90	
67.31	Lee Doran	21	Jul	01	
66.88	David Messom	4	Jul	81	
66.86	Michael Williams	16	Jul	79	
66.52	Marcus Humphries	17	Sep	78	10
66.00	Dan Carter	1	Sep	96	
65.92	Tim Kitney	10	Aug	96	
65.68	Tim Eldridge	18	Aug	91	
65.16	Mark Wells	31	May	77	
64.92	Jason Beaumont	11	Jun	83	
64.92	Paul Bushnell	20	Sep	85	
64.80	Justin Rubio	1	Sep	85	
64.68	Paul Godwin	19	May	90	

Decathlon (Senior Implements)

6484	David Bigham	27	Sep	87
6299	Tom Leeson	21	Sep	80

Decathlon (Junior Implements)

6554	Jim Stevenson	25	Sep	88
6093	Robert Hughes	28	May	89

Decathlon (U17 Implements)

6858	Edward Dunford	2	Sep	01
6706	David Bigham	28	Jun	87
6501	Louis Moore	29	Sep	02

Octathlon

5741	Edward Dunford	17	Jun	01
5550	Dominic Girdler	20	Sep	98
5426	John Holtby	20	Sep	98
5425	Andrae Davis	22	Sep	02
5423	Leo Barker	17	Sep	95
5378	Matthew Lewis	20	Sep	92
5311	Dean Macey	18	Sep	94
5238	Neil Scrivener	21	Sep	97
5208	Fyn Corcoran	18	Sep	94
5158	Ed Coats	25	Aug	96
5149	Paul Hourihan	19	Sep	93
5144	Marc Newton	17	Sep	95
5136	Jamie Russell	20	Sep	98
5121	Chris Hindley	20	Sep	92
5102	Matt Douglas	22	Aug	93
5093	Robert Hollinger	21	Sep	97
5059	Mark Bushell	19	Sep	93

with 100m

5531	Jim Stevenson	18	Sep	88
5304	Tom Leeson	28	Sep	80
5194	Bryan Long	26	Sep	76
5106	Jeremy Lay	29	Sep	85
5096	Onochie Onuorah	17	Sep	89
5090	David Vidgen	22	Sep	91

3000 Metres Track Walk

12:04.9	Philip King	18	May	91
12:29.90	Andy Parker	2	Jul	00
12:30.14	Luke Finch	1	Sep	02
12:34.98	Lloyd Finch	17	Jul	99
12:35.94	David Hucks	30	Aug	82
12:50.9	Jon Vincent	8	Jul	87
12:50.67 i	Stuart Monk	18	Feb	95
12:52.9		12	Jul	95
13:03.5	Ian Ashforth	16	Sep	84
13:05.18	Cameron Smith	3	Sep	00

5000 Metres Track Walk

20:46.5	Philip King	29	Sep	91	
21:52.7	Stuart Monk	22	Jul	95	
21:58.8	Luke Finch	22	Sep	01	
22:17.5	Russell Hutchings	27	Sep	86	
22:19.11	Lloyd Finch	18	Sep	99	
22:32.5	Gareth Holloway	27	Sep	86	
22:35.0	Ian Ashforth	6	Jun	84	
22:37.0	Jon Bott	27	Sep	86	
22:42.0	Martin Young	20	Aug	88	
22:42.19	Jon Vincent	6	Jun	86	10
22:48.91	Andy Parker	30	Jul	00	
22:50.51	Dom King	18	Sep	99	
22:53.7	Tim Berrett	28	Jun	81	
22:53.8	David Hucks	10	Mar	82	
22:57.7	Michael Kemp	31	Aug	96	
23:01.0	Karl Atton	19	Apr	88	
23:16.1	Thomas Taylor	31	May	97	

5k Road - where superior to track time

21:33	Jon Vincent	1	Nov	86
21:47	Lloyd Finch	20	Jun	99
22:04	Gareth Holloway	14	Sep	86
22:05	Karl Atton	19	Mar	88
22:30	Gordon Vale	15	Oct	77
22:31	Jon Bott	3	May	86
22:39	Matthew Hales	23	Jun	96
22:41	Thomas Taylor	26	Apr	97

10000 Metres Track Walk

43:56.5	Philip King	2	Feb	91
45:47.0	Ian Ashforth	12	Sep	84
45:52.39	Lloyd Finch	4	Jul	99
46:11.0	Jon Vincent	20	May	87

10k Road - where superior to track time

43:38 hc	Lloyd Finch	20	Nov	99
	44:21	13	Nov	99
43:49	Philip King	29	Jun	91
45:19	Luke Finch	31	Aug	02

UNDER 15

100 Metres

10.93	Mark Lewis-Francis	12	Jul	97
10.99	Andrew Watkins	20	Jul	02
11.05	Jamie Nixon	21	Jul	84
11.11	Tristan Anthony	17	Aug	97
11.12	Craig Pickering	11	Aug	01
11.17	Jamahl Alert-Khan	11	Aug	01
11.17	Chris Julien	10	Aug	02
11.17	Alex Nelson	1	Sep	02
11.20	Jamie McNiel	29	May	99
11.21	Kevin Mark	13	Jul	91
11.22	Chris Blake	7	Aug	93

wind assisted

11.00	Steve Wiggans	9	Jul	94
11.00	Craig Pickering	11	Aug	01
11.04	Joe Brown	13	Jul	96
11.05	Ray Burke	11	Aug	84
11.06	Duncan Game	5	Jul	86
11.06	Paul Chantler	9	Jul	94
11.07	Wade Bennett-Jackson	7	Jul	01
11.09	Nedum Onuoha	7	Jul	01
11.09	Frank N'Goran	7	Jul	01
11.09	Julian Thomas	7	Jul	01

hand timing

11.0	Norman Ellis	23	Jul	89

hand timing - wind assisted

11.0	Malcolm James	24	Jun	77
11.0	Ian Strange	24	Jun	77
11.0	John Burt	6	Sep	80
11.0	Hilton Thompson	6	Aug	89
11.0	Jeffrey Anderson	6	Aug	89
11.0	Matthew Clements	15	Sep	91

200 Metres

22.13	Andrew Watkins	6	Jul	02
22.30	Jamie Nixon	29	Sep	84
22.31	Mike Williams II	10	Aug	86
22.35	Tristan Anthony	12	Jul	97
22.40	Ben Lewis	8	Jul	95
22.54	Matthew Clements	16	Aug	92
22.58	Jamahl Alert-Khan	12	Aug	01
22.64	Martin Blencowe	8	Jul	00
22.65	Daniel Angus	12	Jul	96
22.65	Simon Farenden	25	Jun	00
22.69	Chris Blake	8	Aug	93
22.74	Laurence Oboh	11	Jul	98
22.76	Julian Thomas	12	Aug	01

wind assisted

22.03	Julian Thomas	7	Jul	01
22.26	Steven Daly	9	Jul	94
22.26	Simon Farenden	8	Jul	00
22.28	Jamahl Alert-Khan	7	Jul	01
22.39	André Duffus	9	Jul	94
22.40	Tom Hyde	15	Aug	98
22.43	Martin Blencoe	8	Jul	00

hand timing

22.2	Mike Williams II	12	Jul	86
22.3	Tony Cairns	12	Jul	86

hand timing - wind assisted

21.9	Tony Cairns	21	Jun	86

300 Metres

37.45	Matthew Petty	5	Jul	97

hand timing

35.9	Richard Davenport	26	Jul	00

during 400m

35.7 +	Richard Davenport	23	Aug	00

400 Metres

49.74	Richard Davenport	23	Aug	00
49.96	Craig Erskine	18	Jul	98
49.97	David McKenzie	23	Jun	85
49.98	Ryan Preddy	11	Jul	98
50.65	Ian Lowthian	29	Jul	95
50.67	Fola Onibije	10	Jul	99
50.72	Craig Glanville	7	Jul	01
50.78	Mike Snow	12	Jul	97
50.88	Aaron Evans	17	Aug	96
50.97	Lewis Robson	13	Jul	02
50.99	Cephas Howard	13	Jul	91
51.00	Paul Roberts	22	Jul	84

hand timing

49.8	Mark Tyler	25	Aug	82
49.9	David McKenzie	11	Aug	85
50.0	Simon Heaton	7	Jul	79
50.1	Ade Mafe	6	Sep	81
50.3	Malcolm James	29	Aug	77
50.7	Cephas Howard	19	May	91
50.9	Alan Leonard	30	Aug	78
50.9	Noel Goode	7	Jul	79

600 Metres

1:23.6	Chris Davies	26	Jul	00

800 Metres

1:55.56	Michael Rimmer	25	Jul	00
1:56.1	Craig Winrow	12	Jul	86
1:56.6	Paul Burgess	13	Jul	85
1:57.1	Delroy Smith	12	Jul	86
1:57.12	Michael Combe	14	Aug	93
1:57.24	Tony Jarman	15	Sep	78
1:57.5	Noel Goode	11	Jul	79
1:57.5	Ryan Preddy	7	Jun	98
1:57.7	Eric Kimani	15	Sep	81
1:57.7	Mark Sesay	11	Aug	87
1:57.87	Austin Finn	7	Jul	91
1:58.1	Piers Counsell	12	Jul	86

1000 Metres

2:35.4	Alex Felce	25	Jul	01

1500 Metres

4:03.0	Glen Stewart	28	Aug	85
4:03.0	Scott West	28	Aug	90
4:03.52	Mike Isherwood	17	Sep	82
4:03.56	Richard Youngs	17	Sep	82
4:03.6	Doug Stones	7	Jul	79
4:03.7	David Gerard	31	Jul	83

4:04.52	Chris Reynolds	10	Jul	99
4:04.63	Lee Bowron	29	Jul	00
4:04.86	Adam Hickey	13	Jul	02
4:05.48	Alex Felce	31	Jul	01
4:05.7	Ben Mabon	1	Sep	85
4:05.8	Graham Green	19	Jun	79

1 Mile

4:21.9	Glen Stewart	11	Sep	85

2000 Metres

5:45.8	Richard Slater	16	Jun	74

3000 Metres

8:47.0	Ben Mabon	16	Jul	85
8:47.48	Mohammed Farah	5	Jul	97
8:48.8	Dale Smith	14	Aug	85
8:51.1	Mark Slowikowski	4	Jun	80
8:53.66	Tom Snow	7	Jun	00
8:54.6	Gary Taylor	14	Sep	77
8:54.6	David Bean	22	Jul	79
8:56.0	Paul Ryder	29	Aug	79
8:56.4	Stuart Bond	10	Sep	91
8:57.0	Philip Hennessy	28	Jul	82
8:57.6	Chris Taylor	16	Jul	69
8:58.4	James Clarke	30	Sep	81

80 Metres Hurdles (2'9")

10.71	Matthew Clements	15	Aug	92
10.75	Daniel Davies	13	Jul	02
10.82	Richard Alexis-Smith	12	Aug	01
10.87	Daniel Maynard	13	Jul	02
10.95	Chris Musa	7	Jul	01
10.99	Edward Dunford	14	Aug	99
11.04	Leon McRae	8	Jul	95
11.07	Robert Hollinger	8	Jul	95
11.10	Seb Bastow	13	Jul	96
11.10	Chris Tye-Walker	12	Jul	97

wind assisted

10.68	Richard Alexis-Smith	12	Aug	01
10.73	Chris Musa	7	Jul	01
10.99	Tom Stimson	7	Jul	01
11.00	Tom Benn	9	Jul	94
11.02	Nick Dowsett	10	Jul	93

hand timing

11.0	Austin Drysdale	22	Jun	75

hand timing - wind assisted

11.0	Tim Greenwood	29	Jun	97

100 Metres Hurdles (3'0")

13.3	Matthew Clements	23	Aug	92

400 Metres Hurdles (2'6")

60.1	Jonathan Gorrie	17	Jun	78

High Jump

2.04	Ross Hepburn	22	Aug	76
2.01	Ken McKeown	10	Aug	96
1.97	Andrew Lynch	29	Aug	88
1.97	Wayne Gray	3	Sep	95

1.96	Chuka Enih-Snell	29	Aug	98
1.95	Mark Lakey	14	Sep	80
1.95	Mark Bidwell	26	Sep	99
1.94	Brian Hall	16	Aug	97
1.93	Ewan Gittins	21	Jul	84
1.91	Mark Smith	15	Jul	89
1.91	Ed Willers	9	Jul	94
1.91	Matthew Brereton	9	Jul	94
1.91	Jamie Russell	21	Sep	96

Pole Vault

4.31	Richard Smith	28	Aug	95
4.30	Neil Winter	2	Jul	88
4.30	Christian Linskey	18	Jun	94
4.18	Ian Lewis	24	May	83
4.00	Jimmy Lewis	9	Sep	79
3.90	Peter Eyre	2	Jul	89
3.90	Martin Parley	6	Jun	92
3.90	Steve Francis	12	Sep	93
3.90	Andrew Corey	17	Aug	96
3.85	Steven Brown	2	Jun	96

Long Jump

6.79	Oni Onuorah	17	Sep	88
6.77	Barry Nevison	30	Aug	81
6.74	Kevin Hibbins	17	Jun	95
6.71	Mark Awanah	17	Aug	97
6.68	Onew Eyong	9	Jul	99
6.67	Gary Wilson	27	Aug	00
6.65	Edward Dunford	25	Sep	99
6.65	Bernard Yeboah	27	Aug	00
6.62	Martin Giraud	25	May	92
6.59	Danny Smith	29	Aug	87
6.58	Tony Allen	8	Aug	82
6.55	Jonathan Moore	17	May	98
6.54	Jordon Lau	11	Jul	98

wind assisted

7.12	Oni Onuorah	17	Sep	88
6.72	David Gilkes	6	Apr	92
6.72	Onew Eyong	15	Aug	99
6.68	Jordon Lau	16	Aug	98
6.63	Ian Strange			77

downhill

6.77	Eric Wood	25	Aug	58

Triple Jump

13.86	Jamie Quarry	10	Jul	87
13.79	Paul Dundas	11	Jun	88
13.77	Eugene Hechevarria	16	Sep	78
13.71	Larry Achike	10	Jun	89

note resident but not British citizen at this time

13.69	Vernon Samuels	25	Aug	79
13.60	Steven Anderson	9	Jun	79
13.60	Steve Folkard	11	Jul	80
13.57	Errol Burrows	11	Jul	80
13.56	Delroy Ricketts	18	Jun	88
13.55	Darren Yeo	15	Jul	89
13.55	Michael Duberry	14	Jul	90
13.43	Michael Powell	12	Sep	76
13.43	Marvin Bramble	8	Sep	91

wind assisted

13.92	Eugene Hechevarria	7	Jul	78
13.87	Vernon Samuels	20	Sep	79
13.83	Chris Tomlinson	12	Jul	96
13.73	Donovan Fraser	6	Jul	79
13.69	Kevin O'Shaughnessy	7	Jul	78
13.60	Dean Taylor	12	Jul	96
13.58	Daniel Puddick	26	May	93

Shot (5kg)

15.62	Chris Ellis	18	Jun	80

Shot (4kg)

18.71	Chris Ellis	14	Jun	80
16.54	Geoff Hodgson	7	Jul	72
16.50	Carl Saggers	14	Jul	98
16.39	Pete Waterman	2	Jul	94
16.39	Gregg Beard	25	Aug	97
16.29	Neal Brunning ¶	11	Sep	85
16.14	Chris Gearing	12	May	01
16.12	Daniel Hepplewhite	26	Aug	01
16.11	Billy Cole	6	Jul	79
16.11	Andrae Davis	29	Jul	00
16.05	John Nicholls	29	Jun	80
16.04	Brendan Hall	1	Sep	02

Discus (1.5kg)

44.20	Matt Symonds	18	Sep	82

Discus (1.25kg)

53.08	Emeka Udechuku	5	Sep	93
52.43	Sam Herrington	1	Sep	01
50.85	Shane Birch	12	Jul	02
50.80	Paul Mardle	3	Sep	77
50.32	Chris Symonds	23	Jul	85
50.04	Keith Homer	11	Jul	80
49.36	James Muirhead	12	May	85
49.32	Lucan Douglas	16	Sep	79
49.22	Spencer English	1	Jun	86
49.10	Simon Bissell	27	Aug	00
48.84	Witold Leonowicz	23	Aug	80

Hammer (5kg)

60.10	Andrew Tolputt	5	Sep	82

Hammer (4kg)

70.78	Andrew Tolputt	9	Jul	82
67.24	Peter Vivian	22	Sep	85
65.42	Matthew Sutton	29	Sep	96
64.28	Jason Byrne	22	Sep	85
63.68	Paul Binley	29	Sep	85
63.60	Richard Fedder	26	Aug	79
63.16	Tony Kenneally	29	May	78
62.06	Nick Steinmetz	4	Aug	91
61.32	John Barnes	8	Jun	96
61.08	Neil Curtis	11	Sep	88
64.70	Matt Lambley	3	Jul	02

Javelin (700g)

58.76	Dan Carter	29	Aug	94

Javelin (600g 1999 Model)

58.27	Mark Lindsay	30	Aug	99
54.11	Thomas Rees	5	Aug	00
54.64	Adam Akehurst	1	Sep	02
54.27	Stuart harvey	15	Jun	02

Javelin (600g pre 1999 Model)

62.70	Paul Godwin	21	May	89
60.56	David Messom	6	Jul	79
60.56	Clifton Green	3	Jul	94
60.34	Richard Lainson	18	Aug	96
59.88	James Hurrion	17	Sep	88
59.52	Paul Brice	19	Aug	79
58.94	Dan Carter	7	Aug	94
58.74	Philips Olweny	6	Aug	95
58.58	Justin Rubio	11	Jun	83
58.58	Rhys Williams	10	Aug	96

Decathlon (Under 15 implements)

5341	Jamie Quarry	28	Jun	87

Octathlon (Under 15 implements)

3933	Aidan Turnbull	1	Oct	95

Pentathlon (80H,SP,LJ,HJ,800)

3403	Edward Dunford	22	Aug	99
3281	Andrae Davis	16	Sep	00
3272	Chris Dack	20	Sep	97
3187	Marc Newton	27	Aug	94
3163	Kevin Drury	27	Aug	94
3129	Mark Awanah	24	Aug	97
3129	Lewis Robson	28	Sep	02
3081	Oliver Mc Neillis	28	Sep	02
3071	Neil Crossley	28	Sep	02
3039	Chuka Enih-Snell	23	Aug	98
3024	Tom Benn	17	Sep	94

(100,SP,LJ,HJ,800)

3199	Onochie Onuorah	17	Sep	88
3085 w	Cephas Howard	21	Sep	91

3000 Metres Track Walk

12:44.64	Lloyd Finch	24	May	98
13:19.57	Philip King	29	May	89
13:35.0	Russell Hutchings	7	Sep	85
13:45.0	John Murphy	14	May	95
13:51.0	Robert Mecham	12	May	92
13:57.06	James Davis	29	Aug	99
13:58.0	Jon Vincent	7	Sep	85
14:03.0	Neil Simpson	1	Apr	89
14:03.5	Nathan Kavanagh	20	Sep	81
14:09.93	Luke Finch	30	Jul	00

3k Road - where superior to track time

13:20	Jonathan Deakin	18	Sep	88
13:29	Robert Mecham	20	Apr	92
13:32	Russell Hutchings	10	Nov	84
13:39	Neil Simpson	6	May	89
13:34	Nick Ball	30	Jun	02

5000 Metres Track Walk

22:54.0	Lloyd Finch	15	Jul	98

UNDER 13

75 Metres

9.6	Josh Baxter	11	Jul	01

80 Metres

10.17	Ricky Jasper	12	Aug	95

hand timing

10.0	Adam Rogers	15	Jul	95

100 Metres

11.86	Chris Julien	3	Sep	00
12.14	Mark Lewis-Francis	3	Sep	95
12.19	Yusuf Alli	30	Aug	02
12.29	Paul Moore	28	Aug	99

wind assisted

12.25	Leon Cameron	8	Sep	96

hand timing

11.8	Cephas Howard	2	Jul	89
11.9	Stephen Buttler	26	Sep	87
11.9	Tristan Anthony	30	Jul	95

hand timing - wind assisted

11.6	Tristan Anthony	28	Aug	95
11.9	Michael Tietz	3	Jun	90

150 Metres

18.5	Tom Rayner	5	Jul	00

200 Metres

24.79	Leon Cameron	8	Sep	96
25.36	Mark Lewis-Francis	3	Sep	95

wind assisted

24.28	Chris Julien	3	Sep	00
24.86	Tom Rayner	3	Sep	00

hand timing

24.0	Stephen Buttler	26	Jul	87
24.1	Tristan Anthony	30	Jul	95
24.4	Cephas Howard	3	Sep	89
24.8	Michael Brown	8	Sep	85
24.8	Paul Twidale	16	May	99
24.9	Joelle Powell	4	Jun	00
25.0	Tyrone Keating	4	Sep	94
25.0	Jamaal Dixon	16	Aug	98
25.0	Chris Julien	2	Jul	00

300 Metres

41.8	Dominic Jones	5	Jul	97

400 Metres

58.06	Sam Allen	25	May	91

hand timing

55.1	Cephas Howard	2	Jul	89
56.5	Craig Erskine	22	Sep	96
57.1	Wayne McDonald	17	Aug	83
57.3	E. Francis	18	May	74
57.4	David Tucker			78
57.6	Frank Adesoyan	27	Aug	90

600 Metres

1:34.7+	Eric Kimani	9	Sep	79

800 Metres

2:04.1	Ben Mabon	8	Jul	83
2:06.4	Eric Kimani	11	Aug	79
2:11.0	Brendan Waters	17	Jun	89
2:11.2	Chris Perrington	6	Aug	78
2:11.2	Gerry Maley	7	Jul	82
2:11.3	Ahmed Ali	10	May	98

1000 Metres

2:54.1	Stephen Holmes	1	Aug	93

1500 Metres

4:18.4	Eric Kimani	26	Sep	79
4:20.5	Ben Mabon	18	Jun	83
4:22.3	David Gerard	12	Aug	81
4:23.9	Mark Slowikowski	12	Jul	78
4:28.0	Ciaran Murphy	16	Jun	84
4:29.3	Dylan Gregory	21	Aug	83
4:29.7	Adam Hickey	28	Aug	00

1 Mile

4:52.0	Tom Quinn	20	Jul	69

3000 Metres

9:31.4	Ben Mabon	24	Jul	83
9:41.4	Mark Slowikowski	21	May	78
9:47.99	Robert Pickering	25	Jun	00
9:49.5	John Tilley	9	Jul	86
9:50.45	Adam Hickey	30	Aug	00
9:50.7	Jacob McCulloch	31	May	00
9:51.1	Sam Hall	23	Sep	98

70 Metres Hurdles (2'3")

11.2	Brendan Kennedy	12	Jun	99
11.2	Elliot Donaldson	17	Jun	99

75 Metres Hurdles (2'3")

11.7	Stephen Cotterill	16	Jul	78
11.7	Sean Ashton	12	Sep	98
11.8	Edward Dunford	28	Sep	97

75 Metres Hurdles (2'6")
wind assisted

11.98	Chris Douglas	2	Sep	00

80 Metres Hurdles (2'6")

12.74	Jermaine Bernard	14	Sep	97

hand timing

11.9	Matthew Clements	27	Aug	90
12.1	Sean Ashton	27	May	98
12.4	Jon Crawshaw	14	Aug	94
12.5	Leo Cotterell	26	Sep	87
12.5	Tristan Anthony	9	Jul	95
12.6	James Dunford	2	Aug	98

80 Metres Hurdles (2'9")

12.92	Sam Allen	18	Aug	91

hand timing

12.6	James Dunford	27	Sep	98
12.7	James Shipp	9	Jun	90

High Jump

1.70	Adrian Pettigrew	22	Jun	99
1.68	Sam Allen	22	Sep	91
1.68	James Dunford	29	Sep	98
1.67	Glen Carpenter	3	Jul	83
1.67	Jamie Dalton	28	Jun	92
1.66	Shane Smith	11	May	86
1.66	Tim Greenwood			95

Pole Vault

3.40	Neil Winter	27	Jul	86
3.20	Ian Lewis	8	Sep	81
3.00	Luke Cutts	14	May	00

Long Jump

5.65	Sam Allen	14	Sep	91
5.64	Kevin Hibbins	18	Jul	93
5.62	Paul Twidale	31	Jul	99
5.61	Robert Creese	23	Jun	90
5.58	Edward Dunford	27	Sep	97
5.58	Matthew Hislop	5	Sep	99
5.55	Jason Davis	9	Jul	95
5.53	Jermaine Bernard	21	Sep	97

wind assisted

5.76	Seamas Cassidy	5	Sep	99
5.74	Edward Dunford	21	Sep	97

Triple Jump

12.57	Rigsby Agoreyo	9	Aug	69
11.78	Edward Dunford	27	Sep	97
11.75	Alain Kacon	15	Sep	01

Shot (4kg)

12.65	Matthew Evans	12	Aug	01

Shot (3.25kg)

14.47	Matthew Evans	22	Jul	01
13.36	Chris Hughes	21	Aug	91
13.11	Tony Quinn	28	Aug	93
12.60	Carl Saggers	7	Jul	96
12.58	Daniel Hepplewhite	15	Aug	99
12.58	Sam Herrington	5	Sep	99
12.46	Paul Beard	31	Aug	86
12.42	Edward Dunford	28	Sep	97

Shot (2.72kg)

13.49	Martin Wilson	13	Sep	92

Discus (1.25kg)

36.98	Sam Herrington	5	Sep	99

Discus (1kg)

42.50	Sam Herrington	12	Sep	99
42.38	Ben Barnes	1	Sep	91
38.92	Chris Hughes	28	Jul	91
38.58	Carl Saggers	15	Sep	96
38.30	Liam Walsh	13	Aug	94
35.50	Edward Dunford	20	Sep	97
35.35	Matthew Evans	28	Jul	01
34.46	Simon Bulley	6	Sep	97

Discus (750g)

43.70	Sam Herrington	8	Jul	99

Hammer (4kg)

38.72	Adrian Johnson	30	Sep	84
38.64	Ross Thompson	14	Aug	94

Hammer (3.25kg)

44.38	Ross Thompson	4	Sep	94
36.96	Edward Dunford	24	Sep	97
35.22	Sean Lewis	29	Sep	00

Javelin (600g Pre 1999 Model)

39.62	P. Shearing	23	May	76

Javelin (400g)

43.02	Max Shale	8	Aug	93
42.29	Edward Dunford	27	Sep	97
41.86	James Dunford	29	Sep	98
41.32	A. Westergren	5	Jul	80
41.20	S. Ahma	2	Jul	92
40.91	Adam Akehurst	30	Jul	00
40.60	Philip Mann	13	Sep	98

Pentathlon (80H,SP,LJ,HJ,800 U15)

2444	James Dunford	27	Sep	98

Pentathlon (75H,SP,LJ,HJ,800)

2562	Edward Dunford	28	Sep	97

1000 Metres Track Walk

4:46.0	Luke Finch	15	Jul	98
4:48.0	Dan King	21	Sep	95
4:48.0	Dom King	21	Sep	95

1k Road - where superior to track time

4:34	Luke Finch	27	Sep	97
4:42	Dom King	23	Sep	95
4:44	Nick Ball	16	Jul	00

2000 Metres Track Walk

9:40.0	Luke Finch	12	Nov	97
9:40.3	Thomas Taylor	19	Jun	93
9:51.0	Lloyd Finch	11	Aug	96
9:57.0	Jamie Nunn	7	Feb	88
10:06.0	Grant Ringshaw	23	Jul	78
10:10.0hc	Dom King	23	Mar	95
10:11.0	John Griffiths	1	Jul	84
10:11.0	Philip King	30	Jun	87

2k Road - where superior to track time

9:16	Lloyd Finch	28	Sep	96
9:38	Luke Finch	12	Sep	98
9:55 hc	Nick Ball	5	Sep	00
9:56	Grant Ringshaw	27	Oct	79
10:01	Gareth Brown	27	Oct	79
10:01	Paul Miles	28	Sep	96

3000 Metres Track Walk

15:02.62	Lloyd Finch	21	Sep	96

3k Road - where superior to track time

14:44	Martin Young	22	Sep	84

UK ALL TIME LISTS - WOMEN

100 Metres

Time	Name	Date
11.10	Kathy Cook	5 Sep 81
11.13	Cook	29 Aug 83
11.15	Paula Thomas	23 Aug 94
11.16	Andrea Lynch	11 Jun 75
11.20	Sonia Lannaman	25 Jul 80
11.20	Heather Oakes	26 Sep 80
11.22	Lynch	21 Aug 76
11.22	Lannaman	13 Aug 77
11.22	Lynch	20 Aug 77
11.22 A	Bev Callender	8 Sep 79
11.35		22 Jul 81
11.22	Oakes	27 Jul 86
11.24	Joice Maduaka	19 Jun 99
11.27	Stephi Douglas	26 Jul 91
11.29	Bev Kinch	6 Jul 90
11.29	Abi Oyepitan	1 Jul 01
11.31	Wendy Hoyte	4 Oct 82
11.31	Shirley Thomas	3 Jul 83
11.31	Simmone Jacobs	24 Sep 88
11.32	Joan Baptiste	24 Aug 83
11.32	Christine Bloomfield	3 Jul 99
11.34	Katharine Merry	25 Jun 94
11.34	Shani Anderson	26 Aug 00
11.34	Amanda Forrester	27 Jul 02
11.35	Sharon Danville	20 Aug 77
11.35	Marcia Richardson	4 Jun 00
11.36 A	Della Pascoe	14 Oct 68
11.39 A	Val Peat	14 Oct 68
11.39	Sallyanne Short	12 Jul 92
11.40	Helen Hogarth	20 Jul 74
11.40	Vernicha James	11 Jun 02
11.41	Jayne Andrews	27 May 84
11.43	Donita Benjamin	11 Aug 00
11.44	Sam Davies	11 Aug 00
11.44	Sarah Wilhelmy	6 May 01
11.44	Diana Allahgreen	13 Jul 02
11.45	Helen Burkart	26 Aug 83
11.46 A	Donna Hartley	22 Mar 75
11.46	Eleanor Cohen	30 Jul 82
11.47	Mary Agyepong	20 Jun 87
11.48	Carmen Smart	26 Aug 89
11.48	Geraldine McLeod	26 May 96
11.48	Andrea Coore	1 Jun 97
11.48	Catherine Murphy	22 Apr 01
11.49	Sophia Smith	25 Aug 96
11.50	Sandra Whittaker	14 Jun 86
11.50	Helen Miles	5 Aug 88
11.51	Kaye Scott	28 May 83
11.51	Sarah Reilly	21 Jun 97
11.52	Pippa Windle	6 Jun 86
11.53	Sharon Williams	31 Aug 95
11.54	Dorothy Hyman	15 Oct 64
11.54	Janis Neilson	24 May 87
11.54	Aileen McGillivary	27 Jun 92
11.55	Anita Neil	1 Sep 72
11.56	Janine Whitlock	14 Aug 99

wind assisted

Time	Name	Date
10.93	Sonia Lannaman	17 Jul 77
11.01	Heather Oakes	21 May 80
11.06	Lannaman	21 May 80
11.08	Oakes	27 May 84
11.08	Kathy Cook	24 Aug 83
11.10	Cook	13 Sep 80
11.11	Lannaman	5 Jun 80
11.11	Cook	26 Jun 83
11.13	Bev Kinch	6 Jul 83
11.13	Shirley Thomas	27 May 84
11.13	Paula Thomas	20 Aug 88
11.17	Abi Oyepitan	30 Jun 01
11.18	Wendy Hoyte	4 Oct 82
11.18	Simmone Jacobs	11 Jun 97
11.19	Bev Callender	21 May 80
11.23	Joan Baptiste	24 Aug 83
11.23	Jayne Andrews	17 Jul 84
11.24	Sarah Wilhelmy	9 Jun 01
11.27	Katharine Merry	11 Jun 94
11.29	Marcia Richardson	29 May 00
11.32	Donna Fraser	25 Apr 97
11.32	Shani Anderson	6 Jul 02
11.34	Sandra Whittaker	22 May 83
11.36	Sallyanne Short	26 Aug 89
11.37	Val Peat	17 Jul 70
11.37	Kaye Scott	22 May 83
11.37	Helen Burkart	11 Sep 83
11.38	Diana Allahgreen	28 May 01
11.39	Pippa Windle	24 Jul 87
11.39	Vernicha James	29 Jun 02
11.40	Phylis Smith	3 Jun 90
11.41	Helen Miles	20 Aug 88
11.43	Dorothy Hyman	2 Sep 60
11.43	Aileen McGillivary	10 Jul 93
11.43	Clova Court	26 May 97
11.45	Michelle Scutt	12 Jun 82
11.45	Rebecca White	4 Jul 98
11.46	Geraldine McLeod	9 Jul 93
11.48	Jakki Harman	23 Jul 88
11.48	Angie Thorp	7 Jul 96
11.49	Ellena Ruddock	29 May 00

hand timing

Time	Name	Date
10.9	Andrea Lynch	28 May 77
11.1	Sonia Lannaman	29 Jun 80
11.1	Heather Oakes	29 Jun 80
11.1	Joan Baptiste	16 Jul 85
11.2	Helen Golden	29 Jun 74
11.2	Sharon Danville	25 Jun 77
11.2	Bev Kinch	14 Jul 84
11.2	Geraldine McLeod	21 May 94

hand timing - wind assisted

Time	Name	Date
10.8	Sonia Lannaman	22 May 76
11.1	Sharon Danville	22 May 76
11.1	Bev Kinch	9 May 87
11.2	Margaret Williams	15 May 76
11.2	Donna Fraser	31 Jan 98

200 Metres

22.10	Kathy Cook	9	Aug	84	
22.13	Cook	9	Sep	82	
22.21	Cook	20	Aug	84	
22.25	Cook	22	Aug	84	
22.26	Cook	24	Aug	83	
22.31	Cook	8	Aug	80	
22.37	Cook	14	Aug	83	
22.38	Cook	9	Aug	84	
22.53	Cook	25	Aug	82	
22.57	Cook	13	Aug	83	
22.58	Sonia Lannaman	18	May	80	
22.69	Paula Thomas	26	Aug	94	
22.72	Bev Callender	30	Jul	80	
22.73	Jenni Stoute	3	Aug	92	
22.75	Donna Hartley	17	Jun	78	
22.76	Katharine Merry	25	Jul	00	
22.80	Michelle Scutt	12	Jun	82	
22.83	Joice Maduaka	25	Jul	99	
22.85	Christine Bloomfield	25	Jul	99	10
22.86	Joan Baptiste	9	Aug	84	
22.92	Heather Oakes	28	Aug	86	
22.93	Vernicha James	21	Jul	01	
22.95	Simmone Jacobs	25	Apr	96	
22.96 i	Donna Fraser	23	Feb	97	
23.08		22	Jul	00	
22.96	Shani Anderson	6	Jul	02	
22.98	Sandra Whittaker	8	Aug	84	
23.06	Sam Davies	28	Aug	00	
23.10	Diane Smith	11	Aug	90	
23.14	Helen Hogarth	7	Sep	73	20
23.14	Helen Burkart	17	Jul	82	
23.15	Andrea Lynch	25	Aug	75	
23.17	Stephi Douglas	12	Jun	94	
23.18	Joslyn Hoyte-Smith	9	Jun	82	
23.20	Sarah Reilly	21	Jun	97	
23.23	Sarah Wilhelmy	13	Jun	98	
23.24	Sallyanne Short	28	Jun	92	
23.28	Catherine Murphy	25	Jul	99	
23.29	Verona Elder	17	Jun	78	
23.29	Aileen McGillivary	25	Jul	93	30
23.30	Sally Gunnell	13	Jun	93	
23.30	Janine Whitlock	25	Jul	99	
23.33	Linsey Macdonald	9	Jun	82	
23.33	Allison Curbishley	8	Jun	98	
23.34	Val Peat	19	Sep	69	
23.35	Melanie Neef	2	Jul	95	
23.36	Shirley Thomas	10	Jun	84	
23.36	Louise Stuart	4	Aug	90	
23.40	Dorothy Hyman	18	Aug	62	
23.40	Sharon Danville	9	Sep	77	40
23.40	Phylis Smith	6	Jun	92	
23.42 A	Lillian Board	17	Oct	68	
23.42	Debbie Bunn	17	Jun	78	
23.43	Sue Hearnshaw	16	Jun	84	
23.43	Emily Freeman	16	Jun	02	
23.45	Amy Spencer	15	Jul	01	
23.46	Janine MacGregor	22	Aug	81	
23.47 A	Angela Baxter	10	May	86	
23.47	Geraldine McLeod	24	Aug	94	

23.48	Wendy Hoyte	7	Jun	75	50
23.48	Denise Ramsden	21	Aug	76	
23.48	Margaret Williams	21	Aug	76	
wind assisted					
22.21	Cook	7	Oct	82	
22.48	Michelle Scutt	4	Jul	82	
22.69	Bev Callender	24	Jun	81	
22.84	Sarah Wilhelmy	10	Jun	01	
22.90	Andrea Lynch	11	Jun	75	
22.90	Donna Fraser	25	Apr	97	
22.90	Allison Curbishley	17	Jul	98	
22.97	Helen Golden	26	Jul	74	
23.00	Joslyn Hoyte-Smith	13	Jun	82	
23.11	Linsey Macdonald	5	Jul	80	10
23.14	Shirley Thomas	28	May	84	
23.15	Margaret Williams	22	Jul	70	
23.19	Sallyanne Short	29	Jan	90	
23.23	Sinead Dudgeon	29	Jul	00	
23.32	Louise Stuart	4	Jun	89	
23.36	Lorna Boothe	30	Mar	80	
23.39 A	Angela Baxter	12	Apr	86	
23.41	Louise Fraser	16	Jun	91	
23.41	Emily Freeman	18	May	02	
23.41	Ellena Ruddock	14	Jul	02	20
hand timing					
22.9	Heather Oakes	3	May	80	
22.9	Helen Barnett	6	Aug	83	
23.0	Helen Golden	30	Jun	74	
23.1	Andrea Lynch	21	May	77	
23.1	Linda Keough	5	Jul	89	
23.2	Dorothy Hyman	3	Oct	63	
23.2	Margaret Williams	2	Aug	70	
23.3	Sharon Danville	30	Jun	74	
23.3	Linsey Macdonald	8	May	82	
23.3	Louise Stuart	25	Aug	91	
hand timing - wind assisted					
23.1	Margaret Williams	14	Jul	74	
23.1	Sharon Danville	17	Sep	77	
23.1	Linda McCurry	2	Jul	78	
23.2	Debbie Bunn	2	Jul	78	
23.2	Sybil Joseph	1	Jun	85	

300 Metres

35.46	Kathy Cook	18	Aug	84	
35.51	Cook	9	Sep	83	
35.71	Donna Fraser	28	Aug	00	
36.00	Katharine Merry	28	Aug	00	
36.01	Michelle Scutt	13	Jul	80	
36.44	Sally Gunnell	30	Jul	93	
36.45	Joslyn Hoyte-Smith	5	Jul	80	
36.46	Linsey Macdonald	13	Jul	80	
36.65	Joan Baptiste	18	Aug	84	
36.69	Helen Burkart	9	Sep	83	
36.92	Phylis Smith	11	Aug	96	10
36.95	Jenni Stoute	21	Jul	91	
36.97	Donna Hartley	4	Jul	75	
37.30	Verona Elder	26	May	76	
37.33	Melanie Neef	8	Jul	94	
hand timing					
36.2	Donna Hartley	7	Aug	74	
37.0	Linda Keough	22	Jul	89	

68

400 Metres

49.43	Kathy Cook	6	Aug	84
49.59	Katharine Merry	11	Jun	01
49.72	Merry	25	Sep	00
49.79	Donna Fraser	25	Sep	00
50.05	Merry	8	Jul	00
50.21	Merry	24	Aug	99
50.21	Fraser	24	Sep	00
50.28	Merry	25	Jun	00
50.32	Merry	24	Sep	00
50.40	Phylis Smith	3	Aug	92
50.63	Michelle Scutt	31	May	82
50.71	Allison Curbishley	18	Sep	98
50.75	Joslyn Hoyte-Smith	18	Jun	82
50.82	Lee McConnell	20	Sep	02
50.93	Lorraine Hanson	26	Aug	91
10 50.98	Linda Staines	26	Aug	91
51.04	Sally Gunnell	20	Jul	94
51.16	Linsey Macdonald	15	Jun	80
51.18	Melanie Neef	6	Aug	95
51.28	Donna Hartley	12	Jul	75
51.36	Catherine Murphy	27	Jul	02
51.41	Sandra Douglas	2	Aug	92
51.53	Jenni Stoute	12	Aug	89
51.70	Verona Elder	10	Jun	78
51.93	Janine MacGregor	28	Aug	81
20 51.97	Linda Forsyth	31	May	82
51.97	Helen Karagounis	27	Jul	02
52.05	Sinead Dudgeon	3	Jul	99
52.12 A	Lillian Board	16	Oct	68
53.00		2	Sep	68
52.13	Helen Burkart	28	Jun	84
52.15 i	Lesley Owusu	9	Mar	01
52.27		15	Jul	01
52.20	Ann Packer	17	Oct	64
52.26	Pat Beckford	14	Aug	88
52.40	Helen Frost	17	Sep	00
52.43	Gladys Taylor	2	Sep	84
30 52.47	Michelle Thomas	3	Jul	99
52.48	Georgina Oladapo	16	Jun	96
52.52	Sybil Joseph	14	Sep	85
52.54	Stephanie Llewellyn	9	Jul	95
52.57 A	Janet Simpson	16	Oct	68
52.65	Jane Parry	11	Jun	83
52.67	Tracey Lawton	8	Jul	84
52.71	Loreen Hall	18	Jun	88
52.75	Sandra Leigh	12	Jul	91
52.77	Michelle Pierre	29	Jul	97
40 52.79	Angela Piggford	2	Jul	89
52.80	Sian Lewis	18	Jun	83
52.83	Ruth Patten	10	Jul	79
52.85	Jannette Roscoe	3	Sep	74
52.89	Janet Smith	6	Aug	88
52.91	Carey Easton	15	Jun	02
52.97	Vicki Jamison	1	Aug	98
52.98	Karen Ford	6	Aug	78
52.98	Dyanna Clarke	28	Jul	79
52.99	Angela Baxter	24	Jul	82
50 52.99	Melanie Purkiss	6	Jul	02
53.01 i	Marilyn Neufville	14	Mar	70

hand timing

51.2	Donna Hartley	28	Jul	78
51.4	Verona Elder	22	May	76
52.2	Liz Barnes	22	May	76
52.4	Stephanie Llewellyn	1	Jul	95
52.6	Marilyn Neufville	20	Jun	70

600 Metres

1:26.0 +	Kelly Holmes	13	Aug	95
1:26.18	Diane Modahl	22	Aug	87
1:26.5 +	Kirsty Wade	21	Aug	85

800 Metres

1:56.21	Kelly Holmes	9	Sep	95
1:56.80	Holmes	25	Sep	00
1:56.95	Holmes	13	Aug	95
1:57.14	Holmes	7	Jul	97
1:57.42	Kirsty Wade	24	Jun	85
1:57.45	Wade	21	Aug	85
1:57.48	Wade	17	Aug	85
1:57.56	Holmes	16	Jul	95
1:57.84	Holmes	15	Jun	96
1:57.88	Wade	9	Jul	85
1:57.88	Holmes	17	Aug	01
1:58.65	Diane Modahl	14	Jul	90
1:58.97	Shireen Bailey	15	Sep	87
1:59.05	Christina Cahill	4	Aug	79
1:59.30	Susan Scott	29	Jul	02
1:59.67	Lorraine Baker	15	Aug	86
1:59.75	Charlotte Moore	29	Jul	02
1:59.76	Paula Fryer	17	Jul	91
1:59.81	Ann Griffiths	10	Aug	94	10
1:59.86	Jo Fenn	29	Jul	02
2:00.10	Tanya Blake	31	May	98
2:00.15	Rosemary Wright	3	Sep	72
2:00.20	Anne Purvis	7	Jul	82
2:00.30	Cherry Hanson	25	Jul	81
2:00.39	Bev Nicholson	28	Aug	88
2:00.55mx	Zola Budd	21	Jun	86
2:00.6 a	Jane Finch	9	Jul	77
2:00.80	Yvonne Murray	10	Jul	87
2:01.1 a	Ann Packer	20	Oct	64	20
2:01.11	Lynne MacDougall	18	Aug	84
2:01.2	Joan Allison	1	Jul	73
2:01.2	Christine Whittingham	26	Aug	78
2:01.24	Chris Benning	28	Jul	79
2:01.25	Hayley Tullett	22	Jul	00
2:01.35	Liz Barnes	10	Jul	76
2:01.36	Gillian Dainty	31	Aug	83
2:01.40	Janet Bell	10	Jul	87
2:01.48	Lesley Kiernan	11	Jun	77
2:01.50	Lillian Board	18	Sep	69	30
2:01.65	Teena Colebrook	21	Jul	84
2:01.66	Pat Cropper	12	Aug	71
2:01.67	Sonya Bowyer	24	Jun	95
2:01.7	Ann Middle	28	Aug	91
2:01.82	Linda Keough	1	Aug	93
2:01.83	Amanda Crowe	18	Sep	98
2:01.86	Helen Daniel	10	Jul	87
2:01.87	Dawn Gandy	19	Jun	88

	2:01.93	Sue Bevan	19	Jul	91	4:07.59	Ann Griffiths	9	Jun	92
40	2:02.0	Margaret Coomber	1	Jul	73	4:07.69	Teena Colebrook	19	Aug	90

800

	2:01.93	Sue Bevan	19 Jul 91
40	2:02.0	Margaret Coomber	1 Jul 73
	2:02.0	Jo White	13 Aug 77
	2:02.0	Lynne Robinson	26 Jul 89
	2:02.34	Lynn Gibson	14 Aug 92
	2:02.39	Emma Davies	17 Sep 98
	2:02.45	Rebecca Lyne	16 Jun 02
	2:02.47	Abigail Hunte	16 Jul 95
	2:02.6	Evelyn McMeekin	20 Aug 78
	2:02.69	Natalie Tait	16 Jul 95
	2:02.70	Janet Marlow	15 Jun 80
50	2:02.79	Sue Morley	27 Jul 85

1000 Metres

	2:32.55	Kelly Holmes	15 Jun 97
	2:32.82	Holmes	23 Jul 95
	2:33.18	Holmes	25 Aug 95
	2:33.70	Kirsty Wade	9 Aug 85
	2:34.92	Christina Cahill	9 Aug 85
	2:35.32	Shireen Bailey	19 Jul 86
	2:35.51	Lorraine Baker	19 Jul 86
	2:35.86	Diane Modahl	29 Aug 93
	2:37.05	Christine Whittingham	27 Jun 86
	2:37.29	Yvonne Murray	14 Jul 89
	2:37.61	Bev Hartigan	14 Jul 89
10	2:37.82	Gillian Dainty	11 Sep 81
	2:38.44	Evelyn McMeekin	23 Aug 78
	2:38.58	Jo White	9 Sep 77
	2:38.67	Lynne MacDougall	19 Jul 86
	2:38.83	Lynn Gibson	29 Aug 93
	2:39.23	Teena Colebrook	24 Jul 90
	2:39.29	Ann Griffiths	16 Sep 90
	2:39.42	Mary Cotton	26 May 76
	2:39.78	Liz Barnes	26 May 76

1500 Metres

	3:58.07	Kelly Holmes	29 Jun 97
	3:59.96	Zola Budd	30 Aug 85
	4:00.57	Christina Cahill	6 Jul 84
	4:00.64	Cahill	1 Oct 88
	4:00.73	Kirsty Wade	26 Jul 87
	4:00.79 +	Budd	21 Aug 85
	4:01.10	Helen Pattinson	19 Jul 02
	4:01.13	Holmes	5 Jul 96
	4:01.20	Yvonne Murray	4 Jul 87
	4:01.23	Hayley Tullett	28 Jul 00
	4:01.38	Liz McColgan	4 Jul 87
	4:01.53	Chris Benning	15 Aug 79
10	4:02.32	Shireen Bailey	1 Oct 88
	4:03.17	Alison Wyeth	7 Aug 93
	4:04.14	Wendy Sly	14 Aug 83
	4:04.81	Sheila Carey	9 Sep 72
	4:05.37	Paula Radcliffe	1 Ju1 01
	4:05.66	Bev Hartigan	20 Jul 90
	4:05.75	Lynn Gibson	20 Jul 94
	4:05.96	Lynne MacDougall	20 Aug 84
	4:06.0	Mary Cotton	24 Jun 78
	4:06.24	Christine Whittingham	5 Jul 86
20	4:07.11	Janet Marlow	18 Aug 82
	4:07.28	Joanne Pavey	29 Jun 97

	4:07.59	Ann Griffiths	9 Jun 92
	4:07.69	Teena Colebrook	19 Aug 90
	4:07.90	Gillian Dainty	16 Jun 84
	4:09.26	Lisa York	13 Jun 92
	4:09.29	Angela Newport	20 Jul 94
	4:09.37	Joyce Smith	7 Sep 72
	4:09.46	Karen Hargrave	4 Sep 89
	4:09.5	Penny Forse	6 Aug 80
	4:09.79	Susan Scott	16 Jun 02	30
	4:10.07	Maxine Baker	28 Jun 92
	4:10.10	Cherry Hanson	30 Aug 81
	4:10.21	Kathy Carter	31 Jul 82
	4:10.22	Kelly Caffel	20 Aug 00
	4:10.32	Lynne Robinson	30 Jul 94
	4:10.41	Jo White	10 Jun 84
	4:10.66	Joan Allison	2 Feb 74
	4:10.68	Amanda Crowe	21 Sep 98
	4:10.7 mx	Sonya Bowyer	16 Jul 96
	4:10.75	Sonia McGeorge	20 Jul 90	40
	4:10.76	Ruth Partridge	16 Jun 84
	4:11.00	Sue Morley	6 Jul 85
	4:11.12	Bridget Smyth	26 May 85
	4:11.23	Paula Fudge	31 Jul 81
	4:11.24 i	Nicky Morris	7 Jan 89
	4:11.24	Rachel Newcombe	3 Jul 02
	4:11.46	Ursula McGloin	20 Jan 90
	4:11.51	Jane Shields	4 Sep 83
	4:11.57	Sue Lamb	18 Jun 96
	4:11.75	Debbie Peel	31 Jul 82	50
	4:11.8	Kerry Gillibrand	3 Jul 02

1 Mile

	4:17.57	Zola Budd	21 Aug 85
	4:19.41	Kirsty Wade	27 Jul 85
	4:21.61	Wade	5 Sep 86
	4:22.64	Christina Cahill	7 Sep 84
	4:22.64	Yvonne Murray	22 Jul 94
	4:24.57	Chris Benning	7 Sep 84
	4:24.87	Alison Wyeth	6 Jul 91
	4:24.94	Paula Radcliffe	14 Aug 96
	4:26.11	Liz McColgan	10 Jul 87
	4:26.16	Teena Colebrook	14 Jul 90
10	4:26.50 i	Hayley Tullett	6 Feb 00
	4:26.52	Bev Hartigan	14 Aug 92
	4:27.80	Lisa York	14 Jul 92
	4:28.04	Kelly Holmes	30 Aug 98
	4:28.07	Wendy Sly	18 Aug 84
	4:28.8	Karen Hargrave	20 Aug 89
	4:29.15	Sue Morley	18 Aug 84
	4:30.08	Lynne MacDougall	7 Sep 84
	4:30.29	Jane Shields	9 Sep 83
	4:30.77	Joanne Pavey	30 Aug 97
20	4:30.89	Ruth Partridge	18 Aug 84
	4:31.17	Lynn Gibson	1 Jul 94
	4:31.24 i	Jo White	5 Feb 83
	4:31.45	Shireen Bailey	17 Sep 89
	4:31.65	Gillian Dainty	26 Jun 82
	4:31.83	Angela Davies	1 Jul 94
	4:32.00	Carole Bradford	18 Aug 84
	4:32.32	Debbie Gunning	5 Jul 91

2000 Metres

5:26.93	Yvonne Murray	8	Jul	94
5:29.58	Murray	11	Jul	86
5:30.19	Zola Budd	11	Jul	86
5:33.85	Christina Cahill	13	Jul	84
5:37.00	Chris Benning	13	Jul	84
5:37.01 +	Paula Radcliffe	19	Jul	02
5:38.50	Alison Wyeth	29	Aug	93
5:40.24	Liz McColgan	22	Aug	87
5:42.15	Wendy Sly	17	Sep	82
5:42.5 +	Joanne Pavey	30	Aug	02
10 5:43.24	Sue Morley	13	Jul	84

3000 Metres

8:22.20	Paula Radcliffe	19	Jul	02
8:26.97	Radcliffe	29	Jun	01
8:27.40	Radcliffe	11	Aug	99
8:28.07	Radcliffe	17	Aug	01
8:28.83	Zola Budd	7	Sep	85
8:28.85	Radcliffe	11	Aug	00
8:29.02	Yvonne Murray	25	Sep	88
8:29.60	Murray	15	Jul	94
8:30.30	Murray	10	Jul	93
8:31.27	Joanne Pavey	30	Aug	02
8:34.80 i	Liz McColgan	4	Mar	89
8:38.23		15	Jul	91
8:37.06	Wendy Sly	10	Aug	83
8:38.42	Alison Wyeth	16	Aug	93
8:40.97	Kathy Butler	24	Aug	01
8:44.46	Chris Benning	22	Aug	84
10 8:45.39	Hayley Tullett	15	Jul	00
8:45.69	Jane Shields	10	Aug	83
8:47.36	Jill Boltz	17	Aug	88
8:47.59	Angela Tooby-Smith	5	Jul	88
8:47.7	Kirsty Wade	5	Aug	87
8:47.71	Lisa York	31	Jul	92
8:48.72	Karen Hargrave	28	Jan	90
8:48.74	Paula Fudge	29	Aug	78
8:49.89	Christina Cahill	20	Jul	85
8:50.52	Debbie Peel	7	Aug	82
20 8:51.33	Sonia McGeorge	29	Aug	90
8:51.40	Ruth Partridge	7	Aug	82
8:52.79	Ann Ford	28	Aug	77
8:53.52 i	Nicky Morris	4	Mar	89
8:59.46		24	Jun	89
8:55.53	Joyce Smith	19	Jul	74
8:56.09	Andrea Wallace	10	Jul	92
8:56.39	Sue Morley	21	Jul	84
8:57.17	Susan Wightman	6	Jun	84
8:57.2	Kathy Carter	7	Apr	84
8:57.3 mx	Liz Yelling	25	Jul	01
30 8:57.75 mx	Sarah Wilkinson	27	Jun	00
8:58.33	Helen Pattinson	30	Jun	02
8:58.44	Kath Binns	26	May	80
8:58.59	Andrea Whitcombe	26	Jul	91
8:58.98	Hayley Yelling	4	Jul	01
8:59.39	Regina Joyce	8	May	81
8:59.45	Jo Dering	11	Aug	90
8:59.65	Gillian Dainty	20	Jul	83
9:00.21	Carole Bradford	9	Jul	85

9:00.3	Bridget Smyth	20	Apr	91
9:00.68	Alison Wright	23	Jun	81 [40]

5000 Metres

14:31.42	Paula Radcliffe	28	Jul	02
14:32.44	Radcliffe	31	Aug	01
14:43.54	Radcliffe	7	Aug	99
14:44.21	Radcliffe	22	Jul	01
14:44.36	Radcliffe	5	Aug	00
14:45.51	Radcliffe	22	Aug	97
14:46.76	Radcliffe	16	Aug	96
14:48.07	Zola Budd	26	Aug	85
14:48.66	Joanne Pavey	6	Sep	02
14:48.79	Radcliffe	20	Jun	99
14:56.94	Yvonne Murray	7	Jul	95
14:59.56	Liz McColgan	22	Jul	95
15:00.37	Alison Wyeth	7	Jul	95
15:09.98	Jill Boltz	18	Jul	92
15:13.22	Angela Tooby-Smith	5	Aug	87
15:14.51	Paula Fudge	13	Sep	81
15:14.62	Kathy Butler	12	May	01 [10]
15:19.12	Hayley Yelling	22	Jul	01
15:21.45	Wendy Sly	5	Aug	87
15:28.63	Andrea Wallace	2	Jul	92
15:29.04	Sonia McGeorge	27	May	96
15:31.23	Catherine Berry	23	Aug	02
15:31.78	Julie Holland	18	Jul	90
15:32.19	Susan Wightman	26	May	85
15:32.34	Jane Shields	5	Jun	88
15:32.62	Andrea Whitcombe	25	Jun	00
15:34.16	Jill Harrison	26	May	85 [20]
15:34.40	Lucy Elliott	2	Jun	97
15:36.35	Birhan Dagne	5	Aug	00
15:38.84	Ann Ford	5	Jun	82
15:40.14	Helen Titterington	17	Jul	89
15:40.85	Sarah Wilkinson	11	Jul	00
15:41.11	Angie Hulley	18	Jul	90
15:41.68	Debbie Peel	27	Jun	85
15:43.99	Angela Newport	9	Jun	99
15:45.03	Lynne MacDougall	29	Jun	97
15:45.08	Liz Yelling	15	Jun	02 [30]
15:46.05	Hayley Haining	7	Aug	99
15:48.1 mx	Tara Krzywicki	5	Aug	98
15:53.28		25	Jul	98
15:49.6	Kath Binns	5	Apr	80
15:50.16	Helen Pattinson	19	Apr	02
15:51.62	Carol Greenwood	26	May	85
15:52.2	Ruth Partridge	23	Aug	89
15:53.84	Heather Knight	6	Jul	96
15:53.86	Sarah Bentley	22	Jul	95
15:53.96	Gillian Palmer	3	Jun	02
15:54.9	Amanda Parkinson	23	Jun	01 [40]
15:55.64	Katie Skorupska	9	Jun	99
15:56.0	Lucy Taylor	15	May	90
15:56.04	Vikki McPherson	25	Jul	98
15:56.4+	Sue Crehan	4	Jul	87
15:56.58	Gillian Palmer	13	Aug	00
15:56.83	Suzanne Rigg	30	Jul	94
15:57.06	Louise Watson	24	Jun	95
15:57.4	Juliet Potter	23	Jun	01

10000 Metres

30:01.09	Paula Radcliffe	6	Aug	02
30:26.97	Radcliffe	30	Sep	00
30:27.13	Radcliffe	26	Aug	99
30:40.70	Radcliffe	10	Apr	99
30:48.58	Radcliffe	4	Apr	98
30:55.80	Radcliffe	7	Apr	01
30:57.07	Liz McColgan	25	Jun	91
31:06.99	McColgan	2	Jul	88
31:07.88	Jill Hunter	30	Jun	91
31:08.44	McColgan	30	Sep	88
31:53.36	Wendy Sly	8	Oct	88
31:55.30	Angela Tooby-Smith	4	Sep	87
31:56.97	Yvonne Murray	24	Aug	94
31:58.39	Liz Yelling	30	Jul	02
31:59.27	Kathy Butler	20	Apr	01
32:20.95	Susan Wightman	2	Jul	88
32:21.61	Andrea Wallace	6	Jun	92
32:24.63	Sue Crehan	4	Jul	87
32:29.73	Hayley Yelling	30	Jul	02
32:30.4	Birhan Dagne	22	Jul	00
32:32.42	Vikki McPherson	15	Jul	93
32:34.7	Sarah Wilkinson	22	Jul	00
32:36.09	Helen Titterington	29	Aug	89
32:41.29	Jenny Clague	20	Jun	93
32:42.0	Jane Shields	24	Aug	88
32:42.84	Angie Hulley	6	Aug	89
32:44.06	Suzanne Rigg	27	Jun	93
32:47.78	Julie Holland	31	Aug	90
32:57.17	Kath Binns	15	Aug	80
32:58.2	Claire Lavers	20	Apr	91
33:04.55	Tara Krzywicki	10	Apr	99
33:05.43	Elspeth Turner	1	Jun	88
33:09.70	Gillian Palmer	16	Jun	02
33:10.25	Shireen Barbour	5	Jul	86
33:10.6	Charlotte Dale	20	Apr	02
33:10.94	Marina Stedman	28	Jul	86
33:12.8	Lucy Elliott	5	Jun	99
33:17.88	Karen Macleod	1	Jul	89
33:19.19	Bernadette Madigan	27	Apr	85
33:19.48	Heather Knight	6	Jun	92
33:21.1	Allison Higgins	20	Apr	02
33:21.46	Louise Watson	14	Jun	96
33:23.25	Zahara Hyde-Peters	12	Jun	94
33:25.74	Penny Thackery	9	Jun	01
33:26.79	Amanda Allen	6	Jun	92
33:27.69	Jill Harrison	22	Jun	86
33:29.27	Bev Jenkins	9	Jun	01
33:30.0	Annette Bell	10	Aug	91
33:30.27	Angie Joiner	4	Apr	98
33:34.03	Lynn Everington	26	May	86
33:34.7	Priscilla Welch	2	Jun	84
33:34.77	Debbie Peel	22	Jun	86
33:34.96	Carol Greenwood	12	Jun	94
33:36.60	Jo Wilkinson	30	Jul	02
33:36.8	Sharon Morris	20	Apr	02
33:38.36	Jo Thompson	29	Jun	97
33:39.0	Veronique Marot	5	Apr	86
33:40.3	Sandra Branney	3	Sep	89
33:40.6	Andrea Paolillo	5	Apr	86

10 Kilometres Road

30:38	Paula Radcliffe	22	Sep	02
30:39	Liz McColgan	11	Mar	89
30:43	Radcliffe	17	Feb	02
30:47	Radcliffe	9	Jun	01
30:59	McColgan	6	Feb	88
31:29	Wendy Sly	27	Mar	83
31:42	Jill Hunter	21	Jan	89
31:56	Andrea Wallace	4	Aug	91
32:14	Priscilla Welch	23	Mar	85
32:15	Angela Tooby-Smith	31	Mar	84
32:20	Zola Budd	2	Mar	85
32:24	Yvonne Murray	2	Nov	97
32:27	Ruth Partridge	11	Mar	89
32:31	Heather Knight	6	Nov	94
32:35	Suzanne Rigg	15	Aug	92
32:38	Jane Shields	23	Mar	85
32:38	Marian Sutton	28	Sep	97
32:41	Jill Harrison	21	Feb	87
32:43	Teresa Dyer	1	Jan	93
32:44	Carole Bradford	14	Oct	85
32:44	Paula Fudge	13	Mar	88
32:45	Sarah Wilkinson	4	Dec	99
32:46	Kirsty Wade	28	Feb	87
32:47	Chris Benning	15	Mar	87
32:52	Susan Wightman	29	Oct	89
32:55	Hayley Yelling	4	Jun	00
32:56	Alison Wyeth	20	Mar	94
33:00	Sheila Catford	24	Aug	88
33:02	Bev Hartigan	8	Apr	95
33:02	Lucy Elliott	19	Apr	98
33:03	Cathy Newman	6	Feb	88
33:04	Glynis Penny	1	Jan	86
33:04	Gillian Stacey	24	Jan	93

course measurement uncertain

31:43	Zola Budd	6	May	84
31:58	Sandra Branney	10	May	89
32:03	Paula Fudge	29	Aug	82
32:29	Yvonne Danson	13	Nov	94
32:36	Mary Cotton	5	Aug	84
32:41	Susan Wightman	4	Mar	84
32:42	Veronique Marot	30	Sep	84
32:46	Amanda Allen	25	Feb	96
32:47	Debbie Peel	15	Apr	84
32:54	Shireen Barbour	3	Aug	86
32:59	Sharon Astley	20	Sep	87

10 Miles Road

51:41	Jill Hunter	20	Apr	91
51:57	Hunter	7	Apr	91
51:51	Angie Hulley	18	Nov	89
52:00	Liz McColgan	5	Oct	97
52:15	Marian Sutton	5	Oct	97
53:42	Suzanne Rigg	10	Oct	93
53:44	Paula Fudge	21	Sep	85
53:44	Andrea Wallace	7	Mar	93
53:49	Véronique Marot	25	Aug	85
53:50	Yvonne Murray	6	Oct	96
53:51	Priscilla Welch	5	Apr	87
54:12	Alison Gooderham	6	Nov	88

intermediate times
51:41 + Paula Radcliffe 22 Oct 00
53:00 + Andrea Wallace 5 May 91
course measurement uncertain
53:17 Joyce Smith 12 Oct 80
53:44 Sarah Rowell 10 Mar 84
downhill
53:42 Karen Macleod 11 Apr 93

Half Marathon
1:07:07 Paula Radcliffe 22 Oct 00
1:07:07 Radcliffe 22 Oct 00
1:07:11 Liz McColgan 26 Jan 92
1:08:42 McColgan 11 Oct 92
1:08:53 McColgan 20 Sep 92
1:09:39 Andrea Wallace 21 Mar 93
1:09:41 Marian Sutton 14 Sep 97
1:09:56 Susan Wightman 24 Jul 88
1:10:54 Alison Wyeth 29 Mar 98
1:11:17 Veronique Marot 21 Jun 87
1:11:29 Liz Yelling 22 Oct 00
1:11:33 Vikki McPherson 14 Sep 97
10 1:11:36 Ann Ford 30 Jun 85
1:11:37 Paula Fudge 24 Jul 88
1:11:38 Sally Ellis 20 Mar 88
1:11:44 Jill Harrison 29 Mar 87
1:11:44 Lorna Irving 6 Sep 87
1:12:06 Sarah Rowell 11 Nov 84
1:12:07 Suzanne Rigg 3 Oct 93
1:12:22 Sandra Branney 4 May 86
1:12:24 Jill Boltz 15 Sep 91
1:12:25 Angie Hulley 1 Apr 90
20 1:12:25 Yvonne Murray 15 Sep 96
1:12:29 Cathy Newman 25 Aug 90
1:12:43 Amanda Allen 16 Sep 01
1:12:49 Sheila Catford 11 Sep 88
1:12:53 Birhan Dagne 22 Aug 99
intermediate times
1:11:44 + Sally-Ann Hales 21 Apr 85
1:11:59 + Angie Hulley 1 Jan 89
1:12:17 + Priscilla Welch 1 Nov 87
estimated time
1:11:57 + Priscilla Welch 10 May 87
course measurement uncertain
1:11:44 Karen Macleod 15 Jan 95
1:12:23 Lynn Everington 6 Sep 87
1:12:32 Yvonne Danson 31 Jul 94

Marathon
2:17:18 Paula Radcliffe 13 Oct 02
2:18:56 Radcliffe 14 Apr 02
2:25:56 Véronique Marot 23 Apr 89
2:26:51 Priscilla Welch 10 May 87
2:26:52 Liz McColgan 13 Apr 97
2:26:54 McColgan 26 Apr 98
2:27:32 McColgan 3 Nov 91
2:27:38 McColgan 15 Nov 92
2:27:54 McColgan 21 Apr 96
2:28:04 Marot 20 Oct 85
2:28:06 Sarah Rowell 21 Apr 85

2:28:38 Sally-Ann Hales 21 Apr 85
2:28:42 Marian Sutton 24 Oct 99
2:29:29 Sally Eastall 8 Dec 91
2:29:43 Joyce Smith 9 May 82
2:29:47 Paula Fudge 30 Oct 88 10
2:30:38 Ann Ford 17 Apr 88
2:30:51 Angie Hulley 23 Sep 88
2:30:53 Yvonne Danson 17 Apr 95
2:31:33 Susan Wightman 23 Sep 88
2:31:33 Andrea Wallace 12 Apr 92
2:31:45 Lynn Harding 23 Apr 89
2:32:53 Gillian Castka 2 Dec 84
2:33:04 Sheila Catford 23 Apr 89
2:33:07 Nicky McCracken 22 Apr 90
2:33:16 Karen Macleod 27 Aug 94 20
2:33:22 Carolyn Naisby 6 Dec 87
2:33:24 Sally Ellis 23 Apr 89
2:33:38 Lynda Bain 21 Apr 85
2:33:41 Sue Reinsford 16 Apr 00
2:34:11 Sally Goldsmith 3 Mar 96
2:34:17 Jo Lodge 29 Sep 02
2:34:19 Jill Harrison 23 Apr 89
2:34:21 Suzanne Rigg 24 Sep 95
2:34:26 Heather MacDuff 16 Oct 88
2:34:43 Beth Allott 2 Dec 01 30
2:35:03 Sandra Branney 23 Apr 89
2:35:10 Sue Crehan 17 Apr 88
2:35:18 Karen Holdsworth 29 Sep 85
2:35:18 Debbie Noy 13 Oct 91
2:35:32 Rose Ellis 23 Apr 89
2:35:39 Hayley Nash 27 Aug 94
2:35:40 Debbie Robinson 29 Oct 01
2:35:53 Julie Coleby 13 May 84
2:36:02 Bev Hartigan 30 Sep 01
2:36:06 Margaret Lockley 13 May 84 40
2:36:12 Kath Binns 12 Jun 82
2:36:21 Glynis Penny 17 Apr 83
2:36:29 Danielle Sanderson 7 Aug 94
2:36:29 Lynne MacDougall 24 Feb 02
2:36:31 Julia Cornford 20 Apr 86
2:36:32 Marina Stedman 23 Apr 89
2:36:34 Lorna Irving 1 Aug 86
2:36:40 Teresa Dyer 17 Apr 94
2:36:52 Gillian Horovitz 20 Jun 92
2:37:06 Moira O'Neill 31 Oct 88 50
course measurement uncertain
2:35:05 Carol Gould 26 Oct 80

2000 Metres Steeplechase (2'6")
6:29.79 Tara Krzywicki 20 May 01
6:36.02 Jayne Knowles 8 Aug 00
6:52.94 Ursula Counsell 11 Aug 02
6:53.02 Clare Martin 20 May 01

3000 Metres Steeplechase (2'6")
9:52.71 Tara Krzywicki 1 Jul 01
10:21.21 Lois Joslin 20 Apr 01
10:44.69 Clare Martin 5 Jun 01
10:47.62 Ursula Counsell 3 Aug 02
10:49.39 Jayne Knowles 3 Jul 01

100 Metres Hurdles

Time	Name	Date		wind assisted	Name	Date		
12.80	Angie Thorp	31 Jul 96		12.78	Shirley Strong	8 Oct 82	
12.82	Sally Gunnell	17 Aug 88		12.78	Strong	13 Aug 83	
12.87	Shirley Strong	24 Aug 83		12.80	Sally Gunnell	29 Jul 88	
12.88	Strong	10 Aug 84		12.83	Strong	13 Sep 81	
12.90	Jacqui Agyepong	25 Jun 95		12.84 A	Kay Morley-Brown	8 Aug 90	
12.91	Strong	12 Aug 83		12.86	Strong	9 Aug 84	
12.91	Kay Morley-Brown	2 Feb 90		12.86	Gunnell	5 Jun 88	
12.92	Diane Allahgreen	29 Jul 02		12.90	Lorna Boothe	8 Oct 82	
12.92	Allahgreen	9 Aug 02		12.98	Diane Allahgreen	1 Jul 01	
12.93	Agyepong	6 Jul 94		13.01	Lesley-Ann Skeete	1 Feb 90	
12.93	Agyepong	8 Jul 94		13.06	Sharon Danville	14 Jul 84	
12.93	Thorp	29 Jul 96		13.08	Michelle Campbell	26 May 95	
12.95	Keri Maddox	25 Aug 99		13.08	Melani Wilkins	1 Jul 01	
13.03	Lesley-Ann Skeete	3 Aug 90		13.12	Pat Rollo	27 May 84	10
13.04	Clova Court	9 Aug 94		13.19	Natasha Danvers	22 Apr 00	
10 13.05	Judy Simpson	29 Aug 86		13.22	Heather Ross	27 May 84	
13.07	Lorna Boothe	7 Oct 82		13.28	Sarah Claxton	5 Jul 98	
13.08	Sam Farquharson	4 Jul 94		13.28	Julie Pratt	23 May 99	
13.08	Julie Pratt	29 Jul 02		13.36	Judith Robinson	11 Jul 87	
13.11	Sharon Danville	22 Jun 76		13.39	Debbie Brennan	29 Jul 88	
13.12	Melani Wilkins	4 Jun 02		13.39	Lauraine Cameron	1 Jul 90	
13.13	Denise Lewis	29 Jul 00		13.44	Yvette Wray-Luker	21 May 80	
13.16	Wendy Jeal	27 Aug 86		13.44	Kerry Robin-Millerchip	27 May 84	
13.19	Rachel King	4 Jun 02		13.44	Rachel King	28 May 98	20
13.20	Natasha Danvers	2 May 98		13.46	Helen Worsey	18 May 02	
20 13.24	Kim Hagger	31 Aug 87		13.48	Elaine McMaster	12 Jun 82	
13.26	Michelle Campbell	3 Aug 90		13.48	Joanne Mulliner	25 Jul 87	
13.29	Mary Peters	2 Sep 72		13.54	Jill Kirk	7 Jun 86	
13.32	Sam Baker	29 Aug 93		13.56	Ann Girvan	15 Jul 84	
13.34	Judy Vernon	7 Sep 73		13.57	Katy Sketchley	14 Jun 98	
13.35	Pat Rollo	30 Jul 83		13.61	Clare Milborrow	28 May 00	
13.36	Louise Fraser	17 Aug 91		13.62	Yinka Idowu	17 Sep 94	
13.36	Sarah Claxton	27 May 01		13.63	Heather Platt	1 Jul 84	
13.44	Judith Robinson	1 Jul 89		13.64	Gemma Fergusson	30 Jun 02	30
13.45	Lorna Drysdale	20 Jul 74		13.66	Maureen Prendergast	14 Apr 84	
30 13.46	Tessa Sanderson	25 Jul 81					
13.46	Nathalie Byer	26 Aug 83		**hand timing**			
13.47	Heather Ross	16 Jun 84		13.0	Judy Vernon	29 Jun 74	
13.49	Blondelle Caines	17 Jul 77		13.0	Blondelle Caines	29 Jun 74	
13.49	Liz Fairs	30 Jul 00		13.1	Melanie Wilkins	2 Jul 95	
13.50 A	Yvette Wray-Luker	8 Sep 79		13.2	Pat Rollo	11 Jun 83	
	13.57	15 Jul 79		13.3	Ann Simmonds	29 Jul 72	
13.52	Bianca Liston	30 Jul 00		13.3	Debbie Brennan	16 Jul 89	
13.52	Tamsin Stephens	15 Jun 02		13.4	Christine Bell	2 Aug 70	
13.53	Ann Simmonds	4 Sep 72		13.4	Bianca Liston	15 Jul 00	
13.53	Lynne Green	27 Jun 88		13.5	Pat Pryce	26 Jul 72	
40 13.54	Debbie Brennan	7 Aug 88		13.5	Liz Sutherland	29 Mar 76	
13.57	Bethan Edwards	29 Aug 92		13.5	Sue Longden	26 Jun 76	
13.58	Lauraine Cameron	19 Jun 90		13.5	Yvette Wray-Luker	7 Jun 80	
13.59	Jane Hale	19 May 96		13.5	Jill Kirk	7 Aug 83	
13.60	Elaine McMaster	7 Oct 82		**hand timing - wind assisted**			
13.60	Joanne Mulliner	25 Jul 87		12.7	Kay Morley-Brown	10 Jan 90	
13.60	Katharine Livesey	17 May 02		12.8	Natasha Danvers	3 Apr 99	
13.62	Gillian Evans	1 Jul 83		12.9	Judy Vernon	18 May 74	
13.62	Jill Kirk	3 Jul 83		13.1	Mary Peters	19 Aug 72	
13.62	Danielle Freeman	3 Jun 00		13.2	Ann Simmonds	19 Aug 72	
50 13.62	Helen Worsey	15 Jun 02		13.2	Liz Sutherland	8 May 76	
13.68	Heather Platt	7 Jul 85		13.3	Kerry Robin-Millerchip	9 May 87	
13.70	Yinka Idowu	14 Jun 92		13.5	Myra Nimmo	24 Jul 74	

400 Metres Hurdles

52.74	Sally Gunnell	19	Aug	93
53.16	Gunnell	29	Aug	91
53.23	Gunnell	5	Aug	92
53.33	Gunnell	12	Aug	94
53.51	Gunnell	24	Jul	94
53.52	Gunnell	4	Aug	93
53.62	Gunnell	7	Aug	91
53.73	Gunnell	26	Jun	93
53.78	Gunnell	3	Aug	91
53.78	Gunnell	3	Aug	92
54.63	Gowry Retchakan	3	Aug	92
54.94	Natasha Danvers	31	Aug	01
55.22	Keri Maddox	12	Aug	00
55.24	Sinead Dudgeon	24	Jul	99
55.91	Elaine McLaughlin	26	Sep	88
56.04	Sue Chick	10	Aug	83
56.05	Wendy Cearns	13	Aug	89
56.06	Christine Warden	28	Jul	79
56.15	Jacqui Parker	27	Jul	91
56.26	Louise Fraser	7	Jun	92
56.42	Vicki Jamison	20	Jun	98
56.43	Alyson Layzell	16	Jun	96
56.46	Yvette Wray-Luker	11	Jul	81
56.53	Tracey Duncan	16	Jun	02
56.61	Louise Brunning	16	Jun	96
56.70	Lorraine Hanson	13	Aug	89
56.72	Gladys Taylor	6	Aug	84
57.00	Simone Gandy	6	Aug	88
57.07	Verona Elder	15	Jul	83
57.38	Sarah Dean	27	Jul	91
57.41	Jennie Matthews	6	Aug	88
57.43	Liz Sutherland	6	Jul	78
57.49	Maureen Prendergast	16	Jun	84
57.52	Clare Sugden	3	Jun	90
57.55	Sharon Danville	8	May	81
57.69	Katie Jones	27	Jul	02
57.76	Aileen Mills	5	Aug	86
57.79	Susan Cluney	15	Jun	80
57.81	Margaret Southerden	10	Jul	82
57.86	Teresa Hoyle	29	Jul	83
58.02	Vyv Rhodes	28	Jun	92
58.04	Clare Bleasdale	16	Jul	94
58.09	Stephanie McCann	12	Jun	94
58.16	Diane Fryar	9	Jul	83
58.19	Sara Elson	4	Jul	92
58.28	Carol Dawkins	14	Sep	85
58.30	Kelly Sotherton	1	Sep	02
58.31	Jannette Roscoe	19	Jul	75
58.31	Fiona Laing	18	Sep	81
58.35	Debbie Skerritt	11	Jul	81
58.41	Lynn Edwards	19	Jun	88
58.43	Jane Low	24	Aug	94
58.44	Maggie Still	19	Jun	88
58.48	Liz Fairs	16	Jun	02
58.50	Nicola Sutton	23	May	99
58.51	Julie Vine	17	Jun	90
58.55	Jackie Stokoe	19	Jul	75
58.62	Sharon Allen	3	May	97
58.68	Kay Simpson	15	Jul	83

58.68	Vicky Lee	5	Aug	86

hand timing

57.5	Vicky Lee	28	Jun	86
57.8	Teresa Hoyle	26	Jul	86
58.0	Fiona Laing	28	Aug	81
58.2	Debbie Skerritt	6	Jun	81

High Jump

1.95	Diana Davies	26	Jun	82
1.95 i	Debbie Marti	23	Feb	97
1.94		9	Jun	96
1.95	Susan Jones	24	Jun	01
1.94	Louise Gittens	25	May	80
1.94 i	Davies	7	Mar	82
1.94 i	Marti	3	Feb	91
1.94 i	Jo Jennings	13	Mar	93
1.91		20	Sep	98
1.94	Marti	9	Jun	96
1.94	Marti	15	Jun	96
1.93	Michelle Dunkley	2	Sep	00
1.92	Barbara Simmonds	31	Jul	82
1.92	Judy Simpson	8	Aug	83
1.92	Janet Boyle	29	Sep	88
1.92 i	Julia Bennett	10	Mar	90
1.89		11	Jun	94
1.92	Lea Goodman	15	Jun	96
1.91	Ann-Marie Cording	19	Sep	81
1.91	Gillian Evans	30	Apr	83
1.91	Jayne Barnetson	7	Jul	89
1.90	Kim Hagger	17	May	86
1.90	Sharon Hutchings	1	Aug	86
1.88 i	Debbie McDowell	17	Jan	88
1.82		7	May	88
1.88 i	Kerry Roberts	16	Feb	92
1.86		6	Jun	92
1.88 i	Kelly Thirkle	16	Feb	92
1.85		10	Aug	91
1.88	Lee McConnell	19	Aug	00
1.88	Rebecca Jones	1	Jun	02
1.87	Barbara Lawton	22	Sep	73
1.87	Moira Maguire	11	May	80
1.87	Louise Manning	6	May	84
1.87	Rachael Forrest	7	Jul	95
1.87	Denise Lewis	21	Aug	99
1.87	Aileen Wilson	15	Jul	01
1.86	Claire Summerfield	7	Aug	82
1.86	Jennifer Farrell	11	May	86
1.86	Catherine Scott	8	May	87
1.86	Michele Marsella	31	May	87
1.85	Brenda Flowers	20	Aug	77
1.85	Gillian Cadman	3	Jun	78
1.85	Julie Peacock	8	Jul	94
1.85	Hazel Melvin	3	Aug	97
1.85 i	Julie Crane	13	Feb	00
1.83		30	May	98
1.85	Julie Hollman	1	Jun	02
1.85	Stephanie Higham	16	Jun	02
1.84	Sarah Rowe	22	Aug	81
1.84	Ursula Fay	6	Aug	83
1.84	Tonia Schofield	20	Aug	83

1.83	Linda Hedmark	4	Jul	71
1.83	Val Rutter	19	Jun	74
1.83 i	Ros Few	25	Feb	75
1.83	Denise Hinton	8	Aug	80
1.83	Joanne Brand	4	Jun	83
1.83	Rhona Scobie	4	Aug	85
1.83	Marion Hughes	19	Jul	86
1.83	Tracey Clarke	2	Aug	87
50 1.83	Kay Fletcher	17	Jun	89
1.83	Gillian Black	25	Jul	99

Pole Vault

4.44 i	Janine Whitlock ¶	17	Feb	02
4.40	Whitlock ¶	14	Jul	01
4.36	Whitlock	1	Jul	01
4.35	Whitlock	5	Jun	00
4.35	Whitlock	27	Jul	01
4.35	Whitlock	4	Aug	01
4.35	Whitlock	6	Aug	01
4.34	Whitlock	23	Jun	01
4.33 i	Whitlock	10	Feb	02
4.31 i	Whitlock	30	May	98
4.31 i	Whitlock	20	Feb	00
4.31	Whitlock	7	Jul	01
4.20	Irie Hill	6	Aug	00
4.20 i	Rhian Clarke	10	Mar	01
4.15		7	Apr	00
4.16	Liz Hughes	6	Jul	02
4.05	Tracey Bloomfield	13	Jul	02
4.04	Lucy Webber	15	Jul	00
4.00	Alison Davies	12	Aug	00
4.00 i	Sonia Lawrence	20	Jan	02
3.90		14	Jul	01
4.00	Kate Dennison	18	Jul	02
10 4.00	Zoe Brown	28	Jul	02
3.95 A	Allie Jessee	25	Jun	99
3.60		4	Aug	98
3.91	Emma Hornby	27	Jun	98
3.90	Kate Staples	26	May	96
3.90	Ellie Spain	6	May	00
3.90	Gillian Cooke	2	Jun	02
3.83	Hilary Smith	10	Jun	01
3.80	Paula Wilson	25	Jul	98
3.80 i	Gael Davies	27	Jan	02
3.75		4	Jul	01
3.80	Hannah Olson	8	Jun	02
20 3.76 A	Krissy Owen	1	May	99
3.55		16	Apr	99
3.75	Louise Schramm	19	Jul	98
3.75	Natalie Olson	16	Jun	02
3.72	Linda Stanton	11	Jun	95
3.71 i	Kirsty Maguire	23	Feb	02
3.60		18	Jul	01
3.70	Clare Ridgley	26	Jun	02
3.66 i	Lindsay Hodges	24	Feb	01
3.55		14	Aug	99
3.60	Fiona Harrison	25	May	98
3.60 i	Larissa Lowe	4	Feb	01
3.60		21	Jul	01
3.60 i	Laura Patterson	18	Feb	01
3.60		12	May	01

3.60 i	Rebecca Lumb	7	Jul	01	30
3.60		4	Aug	01	
3.60	Catherine MacRae	11	Aug	01	
3.60	Rebekah Telford	26	Mar	02	
3.55	Kim Rothman	17	Jun	98	
3.51	Becky Ridgley	18	May	02	
3.50	Noelle Bradshaw	25	Jul	98	
3.50	Helen Roscoe	9	Sep	00	
3.50 i	Louise Gauld	27	Jan	01	
3.41		2	Aug	00	
3.50	Caroline Nutt	19	Aug	01	
3.50 i	Kim Skinner	22	Dec	01	
3.40		11	Aug	01	
3.50 i	Anna Leyshon	24	Feb	02	40
3.50		4	May	02	
3.50	Jennifer Graham	5	Jun	02	
3.45	Ruth Anness	24	Jun	01	
3.40 i	Claire Adams	26	Feb	95	
3.40	Maria Newton	10	May	98	
3.40	Danielle Codd	4	Jul	98	
3.40	Nicole Green	24	Jun	00	
3.40	Kath Callaghan	19	May	01	
3.40	Clare Neve	28	Jul	02	
3.40 mx	Jemma Harding	3	Aug	02	
3.35 i		14	Apr	02	
3.35		7	Jul	02	
3.35	Kathryn Dowsett	24	Apr	99	50

Long Jump

6.90	Bev Kinch	14	Aug	83	
6.88	Fiona May	18	Jul	90	
6.86	May	6	Jul	90	
6.86 A	May	28	Jul	93	
6.85	May	12	Jul	90	
6.83	Sue Hearnshaw	6	May	84	
6.82	May	30	Jul	88	
6.82	May	29	Jun	90	
6.80	May	6	Aug	89	
6.80	Hearnshaw	26	Jun	84	
6.76	Mary Rand	14	Oct	64	
6.76	Jo Wise	2	Aug	99	
6.75	Joyce Hepher	14	Sep	85	
6.73	Sheila Sherwood	23	Jul	70	
6.73	Yinka Idowu	7	Aug	93	
6.73	Jade Johnson	7	Aug	02	
6.70	Kim Hagger	30	Aug	86	10
6.69	Sue Reeve	10	Jun	79	
6.69	Denise Lewis	30	Jul	00	
6.63	Mary Agyepong	17	Jun	89	
6.56	Sarah Claxton	23	May	99	
6.55	Ann Simmonds	22	Jul	70	
6.52	Gill Regan	29	Aug	82	
6.52	Georgina Oladapo	16	Jun	84	
6.51 i	Ruth Howell	23	Feb	74	
6.49		16	Jun	72	
6.51	Julie Hollman	3	Sep	00	
6.47 A	Ashia Hansen	26	Jan	96	20
6.27		26	Jun	94	
6.45	Carol Zeniou	12	May	82	
6.45	Margaret Cheetham	18	Aug	84	

6.44	Sharon Danville	15 Jun	77
6.44	Barbara Clarke	13 Sep	81
6.43	Myra Nimmo	27 May	73
6.40	Judy Simpson	26 Aug	84
6.40	Sharon Bowie	28 Jun	86
6.39	Moira Maguire	22 Jul	70
6.39	Maureen Chitty	28 Jun	72
30 6.39	Sue Longden	12 Sep	76
6.39	Tracy Joseph	27 Jun	98
6.38	Ann Danson	16 Jun	02
6.37	Kelly Wenlock	24 Apr	82
6.36	Andrea Coore	19 Jul	98
6.34 i	Barbara-Anne Barrett	20 Feb	71
6.31		14 Aug	71
6.33 i	Barbara Lawton	21 Nov	70
6.33	Glenys Morton	19 Jul	81
6.33	Joanne Mulliner	13 Sep	86
6.33	Jo Dear	19 May	93
40 6.33	Ruth Irving	2 Jun	01
6.32	Helen Garrett	7 Jun	87
6.32	Jo Willoughby	28 May	89
6.31	Lorraine Campbell	19 May	85
6.28	Janet Robson	4 May	77
6.28	Vikki Schofield	16 Jul	95
6.27	Alix Stevenson	13 Jun	70
6.27	Anita Neil	29 Aug	70
6.27	Sandra Green	14 Jun	80
6.27	Allison Manley	16 Aug	80
50 6.27	Liz Ghojefa	23 Jul	95

wind unconfirmed

6.43	Moira Maguire	18 Sep	70

wind assisted

7.00	Sue Hearnshaw	27 May	84
6.98	Fiona May	4 Jun	89
6.93	Bev Kinch	14 Aug	83
6.84	Sue Reeve	25 Jun	77
6.80	Joyce Hepher	22 Jun	85
6.77	Denise Lewis	1 Jun	97
6.65	Mary Agyepong	4 Jun	89
6.57	Ann Simmonds	22 Aug	70
6.56	Judy Simpson	30 Aug	86
10 6.54	Ruth Howell	16 Jun	72
6.54	Myra Nimmo	19 Jun	76
6.49	Margaret Cheetham	4 Sep	83
6.48	Moira Maguire	17 May	70
6.45	Donita Benjamin	23 Jul	00
6.44	Tracy Joseph	21 Jun	97
6.41	Allison Manley	28 Jul	79
6.40	Barbara-Anne Barrett	17 Jul	71
6.39	Alix Stevenson	6 Jun	70
6.39	Carolyn Ross	19 Apr	87
20 6.38	Joanne Mulliner	1 Jun	85
6.38	Jo Willoughby	6 Aug	89
6.36	Karen Murray	9 Jul	77
6.34	Janet Frank-Lynch	8 Jul	78
6.34	Jill Moreton	8 Jul	78
6.32	Diana Davies	22 May	88
6.32	Liz Ghojefa	16 Jul	94
6.29	Evette Finikin	1 May	89
6.29	Karen Skeggs	17 Jun	89
6.29	Sarah Wellstead	18 May	02

Triple Jump

15.16 i	Ashia Hansen	28 Feb	98
15.15		13 Sep	97
15.02 i	Hansen	7 Mar	99
14.96	Hansen	11 Sep	99
14.94	Hansen	29 Jun	97
14.86	Hansen	31 Jul	02
14.85 i	Hansen	15 Feb	98
14.81 i	Hansen	21 Feb	99
14.78	Hansen	25 Aug	96
14.77	Hansen	2 Aug	97
14.08	Michelle Griffith	11 Jun	94
13.95	Connie Henry	27 Jun	98
13.64	Rachel Kirby	7 Aug	94
13.56	Mary Agyepong	5 Jun	92
13.46	Evette Finikin	26 Jul	91
13.11	Jade Johnson	19 Aug	01
13.03	Shani Anderson	4 May	96
13.03	Kate Evans	26 Apr	97
12.98	Danielle Freeman	13 Jul	02 10
12.97	Debbie Rowe	22 Jul	00
12.97	Rebecca White	3 Aug	02
12.94	Lorna Turner	9 Jul	94
12.92	Liz Patrick	5 Aug	00
12.89	Karen Skeggs	17 May	92
12.84	Anna-Maria Thorpe	23 May	99
12.67	Caroline Stead	1 Jun	96
12.64	Liz Ghojefa	4 Sep	93
12.64	Jodie Hurst	23 Jul	00
12.61	Kerensa Denham	14 Jun	98 20
12.55	Pamela Anderson	29 Jun	96
12.52	Leandra Polius	1 Jul	00
12.52	Emily Parker	13 Jul	02
12.50	Julia Johnson	21 Jun	98
12.45	Lea Goodman	11 Nov	95
12.43	Charmaine Turner	20 Jul	02
12.42	Liz Gibbens	2 Jul	95
12.41 i	Judy Kotey	28 Feb	98
12.33		17 May	98
12.40	Hazel Carwardine	29 Jun	02
12.35	Angela Williams	19 May	01 30
12.34	Azaria Francis	12 May	02
12.32	Rachel Peacock	8 Jun	02
12.30	Stephanie Aneto	18 Aug	02
12.22	Mary Rand	18 Jun	59
12.22	Allison Forbes	9 Sep	89
12.22	Nikki Barr	16 Aug	92
12.20	Stephanie Morgan	18 Aug	02
12.18	Justina Cruickshank	26 May	96
12.17	Katherine Streatfield	26 May	01
12.16	Carly Robson	29 Jun	02 40
12.15 i	Fiona Davidson	22 Jan	95
12.15	Michala Gee	15 Sep	02
12.14	Jayne Ludlow	21 May	94
12.13 i	Maggie Still	21 Jan	96
12.03		2 Jun	96
12.11 i	Caroline Warden	21 Jan	96
12.06		1 May	94
12.11	Marcia Walker	11 Aug	96
12.10	Jane Falconer	30 Aug	93

	12.10	Rachel Brenton	21 Jul 01		15.48	Mary Anderson	8 Sep 85		
	12.10	Linsi Robinson	25 May 02		15.46	Vanessa Redford	14 Jun 80		
50	12.08	Mary Devlin	8 Jun 02		15.45	Susan King	27 Mar 83		
	wind assisted				15.44	Vickie Foster	14 May 00		
	15.00	Hansen	10 Aug 02		15.41	Fatima Whitbread	29 Apr 84		
	14.78 A	Hansen	1 Feb 97		15.32 i	Helen Hounsell	13 Feb 82		
	14.14	Michelle Griffith	25 Jul 00			14.91	22 May 82		
	13.15	Rebecca White	20 Jul 02		15.23	Judy Simpson	18 Jun 88		
	13.14	Debbie Rowe	22 Jul 00		15.21	Uju Efobi	23 Apr 94	30	
	13.04	Kate Evans	23 Jul 00		15.18	Suzanne Allday	18 May 64		
	12.93	Karen Skeggs	13 Jun 92		15.18 i	Lana Newton	Jan 79		
	12.61	Judy Kotey	5 Jul 98			15.09	6 Sep 78		
	12.55	Lauraine Cameron	30 Aug 93		15.09	Jayne Berry	22 Jul 93		
	12.44	Charmaine Turner	29 Jun 02		15.09	Nicola Gautier	1 Jul 00		
	12.42	Nikki Barr	28 Jun 97		15.08	Janet Kane	3 Jun 79		
10	12.39	Karlene Turner	7 Sep 02		15.08	Susan Tudor	30 May 82		
	12.37	Jane Falconer	30 Aug 93		14.98 i	Sandra Smith	21 Dec 85		
	12.35	Rachel Peacock	29 Jun 02			14.95	18 Aug 85		
	12.31	Caroline Warden	23 Jul 94		14.88 i	Jenny Kelly	10 Mar 90		
	12.27	Rachel Brenton	21 Jul 01			14.73	18 May 91		
	12.21	Justina Cruickshank	19 May 96		14.88	Debbie Callaway	15 May 93		
	12.20	Rachel Atkinson	28 Jul 96		14.77	Gay Porter	11 Apr 70	40	
	12.18	Michelle Rea	29 Jun 91		14.76 i	Carol Parker	14 Dec 91		
						14.71	1 Sep 90		
	Shot				14.75 i	Cynthia Gregory	12 Dec 81		
	19.36	Judy Oakes	14 Aug 88			14.70	29 Aug 81		
	19.33	Oakes	3 Sep 88		14.68	Eleanor Gatrell	18 Jul 98		
	19.26	Oakes	29 Jul 88		14.68	Claire Smithson	26 May 01		
	19.13	Oakes	20 Aug 88		14.67	Rosemary Payne	23 Apr 74		
	19.06 i	Venissa Head	7 Apr 84		14.66 i	Terri Salt	7 Jan 84		
		18.93	13 May 84		14.62	Kathryn Farr	7 Jun 92		
	19.05	Oakes	16 Jul 88		14.59	Dawn Grazette	19 May 91		
	19.03	Myrtle Augee	2 Jun 90		14.53	Emma Beales	12 Sep 92		
	19.01	Oakes	17 Sep 88		14.51	Pauline Richards	4 Jul 98	50	
	19.01	Oakes	11 Jun 89						
	19.01	Oakes	11 May 96		**Discus**				
	18.99	Meg Ritchie	7 May 83		67.48	Meg Ritchie	26 Apr 81		
	17.53	Angela Littlewood	24 Jul 80		67.44	Ritchie	14 Jul 83		
	17.45	Yvonne Hanson-Nortey	28 Jul 89		66.04	Ritchie	15 May 82		
	17.08	Jo Duncan	19 Aug 01		65.96	Ritchie	19 Jul 80		
	16.57	Maggie Lynes	20 Jul 94		65.78	Ritchie	17 Jul 81		
	16.40 i	Mary Peters	28 Feb 70		65.34	Ritchie	24 Apr 83		
		16.31	1 Jun 66		65.18	Ritchie	17 May 81		
10	16.40	Julie Dunkley	12 Aug 00		65.08	Ritchie	26 Apr 80		
	16.29	Brenda Bedford	26 May 76		65.02	Ritchie	5 May 84		
	16.12	Denise Lewis	21 Aug 99		65.00	Ritchie	24 Apr 82		
	16.05	Janis Kerr	15 May 76		64.68	Venissa Head	18 Jul 83		
	15.95 i	Philippa Roles	6 Feb 99		60.82	Shelley Drew	25 Jul 98		
		15.19	5 Jul 01		60.72	Jackie McKernan	18 Jul 93		
	15.85 i	Alison Grey	12 Feb 94		60.00	Philippa Roles	9 May 99		
		15.69	11 Jun 94		58.56	Debbie Callaway	19 May 96		
	15.81	Tracy Axten	19 Jul 98		58.18	Tracy Axten	31 May 97		
	15.80	Sharon Andrews	30 Jul 93		58.02	Rosemary Payne	3 Jun 72		
	15.75 i	Caroline Savory	23 Feb 83		57.75	Emma Merry	9 Aug 99		
		15.50	19 Jun 83		57.32	Lynda Wright	16 Jun 84	10	
	15.60 i	Justine Buttle	27 Feb 88		56.63	Emma Carpenter	16 Jun 02		
		15.45	25 Aug 88		56.24	Sharon Andrews	12 Jun 94		
20	15.57	Eva Massey	8 Jun 02		56.06	Kathryn Farr	27 Jun 87		
	15.55	Christina Bennett	13 Jun 99		55.52	Jane Aucott	17 Jan 90		
	15.50	Ade Oshinowo	19 Apr 02		55.42	Lesley Bryant	12 Sep 80		

	Mark	Name	Date		Mark	Name	Date
	55.06	Janet Kane	17 Jun 78		56.76	Esther Augee	15 May 93
	55.04	Lorraine Shaw	14 May 94		55.60	Ann Gardner	9 May 98
	54.81	Claire Smithson	1 Jul 01		55.42	Vicci Scott	23 Jul 01
	54.72	Karen Pugh	27 Jul 86		55.22	Laura Douglas	18 May 02
20	54.68	Emma Beales	10 Jun 95		55.09	Philippa Roles	9 May 99
	54.46	Ellen Mulvihill	14 May 86		54.72	Helen Arnold	26 Jul 97
	54.46	Janette Picton	17 Aug 90		54.15	Sarah Harrison	4 Jul 99
	54.24	Nicola Talbot	15 May 93		54.12	Carys Parry	29 Apr 01 20
	53.96	Julia Avis	27 Apr 86		54.03	Catherine Garden	25 Apr 99
	53.66	Rosanne Lister	22 Jun 91		53.74	Christina Bennett	20 Aug 00
	53.44	Judy Oakes	20 Aug 88		53.13	Katy Lamb	14 Jul 01
	53.16	Sarah Winckless	18 Jun 94		52.31	Andrea Jenkins	1 Jun 02
	52.52	Alison Grey	18 Jun 94		52.28	Samantha Burns-Salmond	3 May 97
	52.46	Vanessa Redford	4 Jul 82		52.15	Lucy Marshall	1 Sep 02
30	52.31	Lauren Keightley	18 Jul 98		51.62	Fiona Whitehead	24 Apr 93
	52.05	Navdeep Dhaliwal	12 Jun 02		51.62	Julie Lavender	15 May 94
	51.82	Catherine Bradley	20 Jul 85		51.37	Ade Oshinowo	30 Mar 02
	51.79	Rebecca Roles	31 May 99		51.34	Helen Taylor	12 Aug 01 30
	51.60	Dorothy Chipchase	20 Jul 73		51.04	Jo Holloway	4 Aug 01
	51.18	Angela Sellars	12 Aug 90		50.62	Janet Smith	16 Aug 97
	51.12	Joanne Brand	26 May 86		50.39	Joanne John	1 Jun 02
	50.98	Sarah Henton	30 Aug 97		50.38	Irene Duffin	31 May 97
	50.57	Brenda Bedford	24 Aug 68		50.34	Jean Clark	27 Jul 97
	50.06	Joanne Jackson	7 May 89		50.27	Helen Wilding	17 Jun 01
40	50.04	Morag Bremner	27 Apr 86		49.93	Sheena Parry	1 Jun 02
	49.92	Fiona Condon	10 Apr 82		49.68	Sue Last	12 Aug 00
	49.89	Kara Nwidobie	30 Jun 02		49.10	Lindsey Jones	25 Aug 97
	49.84	Janis Kerr	15 May 77		48.94	Francis Miller	12 Jul 01 40
	49.84	Denise Sturman	12 Apr 81		48.90	Julie Kirkpatrick	15 Jun 96
	49.66	Gay Porter	19 Aug 70		48.66	Karen Chambers	8 Apr 00
	49.58	Jackie Wright	2 Aug 75		48.32	Helen McCreadie	9 Jun 96
	49.48	Gwen Bird	20 Jul 91		47.70	Angela Bonner	11 May 96
	49.44	Myrtle Augee	14 May 95		47.52	Vicki Clark	1 Aug 98
	49.30	Amanda Barnes	18 Jun 88		47.38	Belinda Heil	2 Jul 00
50	49.25	Vickie Foster	20 May 00		47.06	Caroline Manning	22 Jul 95
	downhill				46.86	Leanne Taylor	12 Jun 97
	51.04	Fiona Condon	7 Jul 79		46.64	Myrtle Augee	5 Jul 95
					46.59	Susan McKelvie	21 Apr 02 50

Hammer

Javelin (1999 Model)

	Mark	Name	Date		Mark	Name	Date
	68.15	Lorraine Shaw	17 Mar 01		64.87	Kelly Morgan	14 Jul 02
	67.98	Shaw	24 Jun 01		63.03	Morgan	15 Jun 02
	67.94	Shaw	2 Jun 01		59.50	Karen Martin	14 Jul 99
	67.68	Shaw	3 Jul 01		58.58	Morgan	8 Jun 02
	67.62	Shaw	27 Feb 01		58.54	Martin	5 Jul 00
	67.44	Shaw	15 Jul 00		58.45	Morgan	12 Aug 00
	67.43	Shaw	19 May 01		58.20	Goldie Sayers	29 Jun 02
	67.14	Shaw	15 Jun 01		58.07	Martin	4 Jun 00
	67.10	Shaw	9 Aug 99		57.99	Morgan	5 Aug 00
	66.97	Shaw	15 Jul 01		57.86	Sayers	7 Jul 02
	63.96	Lyn Sprules	20 Aug 00		57.19	Lorna Jackson	9 Jul 00
	63.61	Liz Pidgeon	27 May 00		55.91	Kirsty Morrison	23 May 99
	62.27	Zoe Derham	16 Jun 02		54.18	Shelley Holroyd	15 Jun 02
	60.88	Rachael Beverley	23 May 99		52.86	Linda Gray	10 Jun 01
	60.38	Suzanne Roberts	18 May 02		52.76	Jenny Kemp	23 Jun 01
	59.95	Shirley Webb	8 Sep 02		51.79	Chloe Cozens	3 Sep 00
	58.97	Diana Holden	4 Jun 02		51.13	Denise Lewis	19 Aug 00 10
	58.47	Mhairi Walters	12 May 02		50.85	Sharon Gibson	18 Jul 99
10	57.63	Nicola Dudman	16 Jun 02		49.25	Nicola Gautier	1 Jul 01
	57.47	Lesley Brannan	28 May 02		48.39	Katie Amos	1 Jun 02
	57.40	Sarah Moore	29 Apr 01				

48.24	Tammie Francis	29 Apr	00
47.74	Joanne Bruce	7 Sep	02
47.73	Helen Mounteney	12 Jul	02
47.72	Alison Moffitt	21 Aug	99
47.66	Samantha Redd	29 Jun	02
47.57	Amy Harvey	7 Oct	00
47.33	Katy Watts	1 Jun	02
46.94	Louise Watton	12 Jul	02
46.89	Caroline White	19 Jun	99
46.81	Noelle Bradshaw	19 Aug	00
46.57	Louise Matthews	28 Apr	02
46.02	Clova Court	12 Aug	00
45.84	Suzanne Finnis	24 Jun	00
45.81	Jennifer West	27 May	01
45.37	Katherine Evans	3 Jul	99
45.29	Lucy Stevenson	30 Aug	99
44.59	Becky Bartlett	12 Jul	02
44.51	Melanie Burrows	12 May	02
44.22	Jenny Grimstone	31 Aug	02
44.11	Rachel Dunn	7 Jul	01
43.81	Hayley Thomas	12 Jul	02
43.79	Jo Chapman	27 Jul	02
43.75	Paula Collis	28 Jul	01
43.74	Sylveen Monaghan	27 May	01
43.70	Chrissie Head	13 Aug	00

Javelin (pre 1999)

77.44	Fatima Whitbread	28 Aug	86
76.64	Whitbread	6 Sep	87
76.34	Whitbread	4 Jul	87
76.32	Whitbread	29 Aug	86
75.62	Whitbread	25 May	87
74.74	Whitbread	26 Aug	87
73.58	Tessa Sanderson	26 Jun	83
73.32	Whitbread	20 Jun	87
62.32	Sharon Gibson	16 May	87
62.22	Diane Royle	18 May	85
60.12	Shelley Holroyd	16 Jun	96
60.00	Julie Abel	24 May	87
59.40	Karen Hough	28 Aug	86
59.36	Kirsty Morrison	4 Sep	93
58.60	Jeanette Rose	30 May	82
58.39	Lorna Jackson	6 Jun	98
57.90	Anna Heaver	1 Jul	87
57.84	Mandy Liverton	3 Jun	90
57.82	Karen Martin	19 Sep	98
56.96	Nicky Emblem	1 Feb	90
56.50	Caroline White	8 Jun	91
56.50	Denise Lewis	11 Aug	96
55.70	Lynn Hayhoe	31 May	92
55.60	Sue Platt	15 Jun	68
55.38	Catherine Garside	19 May	84
55.36	Jackie Zaslona	30 Aug	80
55.30	Clova Court	27 Aug	91
55.04	Joanne Harding	24 May	87
54.50	Karen Costello	11 Jun	94
54.19	Rosemary Morgan	25 Apr	64
54.02	Janeen Williams	29 Mar	80
53.88	Sharon Avann	21 Jul	73
53.32	Maxine Jervis	27 Aug	78
53.04	Kelly Morgan	17 May	98

Heptathlon (1985 Tables)

6831	Denise Lewis	30 Jul	00
6736	Lewis	1 Jun	97
6724	Lewis	22 Aug	99
6654	Lewis	4 Aug	97
6645	Lewis	26 May	96
6623	Judy Simpson	30 Aug	86
6584	Lewis	24 Sep	00
6559	Lewis	22 Aug	98
6513	Lewis	17 Sep	98
6347	Simpson	11 Sep	83
6259	Kim Hagger	18 May	86
6135	Julie Hollman	2 Jun	02
6125	Tessa Sanderson	12 Jul	81
6094	Joanne Mulliner	7 Jun	87
6022	Clova Court	27 Aug	91
6005 w	Kerry Jury	24 May	98
5908		1 Aug	99
5826	Jenny Kelly	3 Jul	94
5803	Jayne Barnetson	20 Aug	89
5794	Kelly Sotherton	30 Jun	02
5784	Nicola Gautier	1 Jul	01
5776	Kathy Warren	12 Jul	81
5747 w	Julia Bennett	5 May	96
5538		4 Jun	00
5702	Yinka Idowu	21 May	95
5700	Vikki Schofield	5 May	96
5691 w	Pauline Richards	24 May	98
5563		5 Jul	98
5644	Danielle Freeman	4 Jun	00
5642	Sarah Rowe	23 Aug	81
5633	Marcia Marriott	18 May	86
5632	Emma Beales	1 Aug	93
5618 w	Sarah Damm	5 May	96
5392		30 Apr	95
5594	Gillian Evans	22 May	83
5577	Katherine Livesey	18 May	02
5555 w	Diana Bennett	24 May	98
5550		1 Jun	97
5548	Val Walsh	18 May	86
5517	Shona Urquhart	21 Aug	88
5495	Charmaine Johnson	24 May	92
5493	Sally Gunnell	28 May	84
5455	Claire Phythian	19 May	95
5446	Manndy Laing	7 Aug	83
5434 w	Debbie Woolgar	8 Jul	90
5380		18 Jun	89
5424	Lisa Gibbs	1 Aug	93
5409	Uju Efobi	19 Jun	94
5391 w	Jackie Kinsella	22 Jun	86
5331		19 Jul	86
5389	Sarah Owen	15 Aug	82
5384	Sue Longden	8 May	82
5358 w	Chloe Cozens	24 May	98
5283		23 May	99
5353	Emma Lindsay	23 Aug	94
5351	Wendy Laing	1 Aug	93
5339	Tracy Joseph	4 Aug	96
5297	Kim Crowther	24 Aug	86
5294	Roz Gonse	2 Jun	02

5279	Fiona Harrison	21	Oct	00
5273 w	Debbie Marti	11	Aug	85
5216		7	Jul	85
5259 w	Anne Hollman	8	Aug	99
5258		26	May	96
5254	Rebecca Jones	2	Jun	02
5244	Val Lemoignan	19	Apr	84
5242	Allison Manley	28	Mar	81
50 5229	Kate Brewington	11	Aug	02

3000 Metres Track Walk

12:49.16	Betty Sworowski	28	Jul	90
12:50.61	Lisa Kehler	29	Jul	00
12:59.3	Vicky Lupton	13	May	95
13:12.01 i	Julie Drake	12	Mar	93
13:16.0		11	Dec	90
13:13.3	Cal Partington	12	Jul	95
13:14.73	Niobe Menendez	11	Aug	01
13:16.23	Verity Snook	27	May	96
13:21.5	Catherine Charnock	8	May	99
13:25.2	Carol Tyson	6	Jul	79
10 13:28.0	Helen Elleker	22	Jul	90

5000 Metres Track Walk

21:42.51	Lisa Kehler	13	Jul	02
21:52.4	Vicky Lupton	9	Aug	95
21:57.68	Kehler	25	Jun	90
22:01.53	Kehler	26	Jul	98
22:02.06	Betty Sworowski	28	Aug	89
22:37.47	Julie Drake	17	Jul	93
22:41.19	Cal Partington	16	Jul	95
22:51.23	Helen Elleker	25	Jun	90
23:11.2	Carol Tyson	30	Jun	79
23:11.7	Catherine Charnock	19	Jun	99
23:15.04	Bev Allen	25	May	87
10 23:19.2	Marion Fawkes	30	Jun	79
23:20.00	Ginney Birch	25	May	85
23:22.52	Verity Snook	19	Jun	94
23:34.43	Sylvia Black	5	Jul	92
23:35.54	Nicky Jackson	25	May	87
23:38.3	Irene Bateman	28	Jun	81
23:46.30	Niobe Menendez	14	Jul	01
23:46.7	Lillian Millen	28	Jun	81
23:47.6	Melanie Wright	29	May	94
23:51.1	Jill Barrett	5	May	84
20 23:55.27	Susan Ashforth	25	May	85

5k Road - where superior to track time

21:36	Vicky Lupton	18	Jul	92
21:50	Betty Sworowski	6	May	90
22:45 +	Verity Snook	25	Aug	94
22:51	Marion Fawkes	29	Sep	79
22:59	Carol Tyson	29	Sep	79
23:00 +	Bev Allen	1	Sep	87
23:09	Catherine Charnock	5	Jun	99
23:13	Sylvia Black	13	Feb	93
23:24	Melanie Wright	9	Apr	95
10 23:25	Irene Bateman	29	Sep	79
23:32 +	Sara-Jane Cattermole	23	Jul	00
23:35	Lisa Simpson	31	Oct	87

10000 Metres Track Walk

45:09.57	Lisa Kehler	13	Aug	00	
45:18.8	Vicky Lupton	2	Sep	95	
45:53.9	Julie Drake	26	May	90	
46:23.08	Betty Sworowski	4	Aug	91	
46:25.2	Helen Elleker	26	May	90	
47:10.07	Verity Snook	19	Jun	93	
47:56.3	Ginney Birch	15	Jun	85	
47:58.3	Bev Allen	21	Jun	86	
48:11.4	Marion Fawkes	8	Jul	79	
48:20.0	Cal Partington	7	May	94	10
48:34.5	Carol Tyson	22	Aug	81	
48:35.8	Melanie Wright	2	Sep	95	
48:56.5	Sarah Brown	18	Apr	91	
48:57.6	Irene Bateman	20	Mar	82	
49:27.0	Sylvia Black	22	Apr	95	
49:39.0	Karen Ratcliffe	22	May	91	
49:41.0	Elaine Callanin	22	Apr	95	
49:51.6	Sara-Jane Cattermole	7	Feb	01	
49:52.1	Niobe Menendez	29	Sep	01	
50:10.2	Brenda Lupton	17	Mar	84	20

track short

48:52.5	Irene Bateman	19	Mar	83

10k Road - where superior to track time

45:03	Lisa Kehler	19	Sep	98	
45:59	Betty Sworowski	24	Aug	91	
46:06	Verity Snook	25	Aug	94	
46:26	Cal Partington	1	Jul	95	
46:38	Niobe Menendez	15	Jun	02	
47:05	Sara-Jane Cattermole	15	Jul	01	
47:51	Catherine Charnock	5	Sep	99	
47:58	Nicky Jackson	27	Jun	87	
47:59	Sylvia Black	29	Mar	92	
48:18	Melanie Wright	9	May	92	10
48:30	Karen Ratcliffe	16	Apr	94	
48:36	Kim Braznell	25	Apr	98	

20 Kilometres Road Walk

1:33:57	Lisa Kehler	17	Jun	00	
1:36:40	Sara Cattermole	4	Mar	00	
1:37:44	Vicky Lupton	27	Jun	99	
1:38:29	Catherine Charnock	11	Sep	99	
1:39:59	Niobe Menendez	21	Apr	02	
1:40:45	Irene Bateman	9	Apr	83	
1:42:02 hc	Lillian Millen	9	Apr	83	
1:44:42		2	Apr	83	
1:43:29	Sharon Tonks	3	Mar	02	
1:43:50	Betty Sworowski	22	Feb	88	
1:43:52	Sylvia Black	14	Jun	97	10
1:44:29	Kim Braznell	21	Mar	99	
1:44:54	Cal Partington	23	Mar	02	
1:45:11	Elaine Callanin	16	Oct	93	
1:46:35	Karen Ratcliffe	21	Apr	02	
1:46:48	Lisa Crump	27	Jun	99	
1:47:10	Liz Corran	29	Jun	96	
1:47:21	Debbie Wallen	17	Apr	99	

50 Kilometres Road Walk

4:50:51	Sandra Brown	13	Jul	91
5:01:52	Lillian Millen	16	Apr	83

4 x 100 Metres Relay

42.43　　Great Britain & NI　　1 Aug 80
Oakes, Cook, Callender, Lannaman
42.60　　Great Britain & NI　　11 Aug 01
Richardson, Wilhelmy, James, Oyepitan
42.66　　Great Britain & NI　　11 Sep 82
Hoyte, Cook, Callender, S.Thomas
42.71　　Great Britain & NI　　10 Aug 83
Baptiste, Cook, Callender, S.Thomas
42.72　　Great Britain & NI　　3 Sep 78
Callender, Cook, Danville, Lannaman
42.84　　England　　31 Jul 02
Maduaka, Anderson, James, Oyepitan
43.02　　Great Britain & NI　　26 Sep 80
Oakes, Cook, Callender, Scutt
43.03　　Great Britain & NI　　15 Aug 81
Hoyte, Cook, Callender, S.Thomas
43.06　　Great Britain & NI　　10 Aug 83
Baptiste, Cook, Callender, S.Thomas
10　43.08　　Great Britain & NI　　11 Aug 01
Richardson, Wilhelmy, James, Oyepitan
43.11　　Great Britain & NI　　11 Aug 84
Jacobs, Cook, Callender, Oakes
43.15　　England　　9 Oct 82
Hoyte, Cook, Callender, Lannaman
43.18　　Great Britain & NI　　4 Aug 79
Barnett, Hoyte, Cook, Oakes
43.18　　Great Britain & NI　　20 Aug 83
Baptiste, Cook, Callender, S.Thomas
43.19　　Great Britain & NI　　20 Sep 80
Oakes, Cook, Callender, Scutt
43.19　　Great Britain & N.I.　　29 Sep 00
Maduaka, Richardson, Davies, Anderson
43.21　　Great Britain & NI　　18 Aug 82
Hoyte, Cook, Callender, S.Thomas
43.26 A　Great Britain & NI Students 13 Sep 79
Wray, Cook, Patten, Callender
43.26　　Great Britain & N.I.　　29 Sep 00
Maduaka, Richardson, Wilhelmy, Anderson
20　43.30　　Great Britain & NI　　30 Aug 86
P.Thomas, Cook, Baptiste, Hoyte
43.3　　Great Britain & NI　　1 Jul 80
Oakes, Cook, Callender, Lannaman
43.31　　Great Britain & NI　　28 Aug 99
Richardson, Anderson, Bloomfield, Maduaka
43.32　　Great Britain & NI　　5 Jun 80
Oakes, Cook, Callender, Lannaman
43.32　　Great Britain & NI　　1 Sep 90
Douglas, Kinch, Jacobs, P.Thomas
43.35　　Great Britain & NI　　17 Aug 85
Andrews, Baptiste, Joseph, Oakes
43.36　　Great Britain & NI'A'　13 Jul 80
Oakes, Cook, Callender, Lannaman
43.36　　Great Britain & NI　　23 Jun 81
Hoyte, Cook, Callender, S.Thomas
43.37　　Great Britain & NI'A'　30 Aug 82
Hoyte, Cook, Callender, S.Thomas
43.38　　Great Britain & NI　　8 Aug 86
P.Thomas, Cook, Baptiste, Oakes
30　43.39　　England　　2 Aug 86
P.Thomas, Cook, Baptiste, Oakes

4 x 400 Metres Relay

3:22.01　　Great Britain & NI　　1 Sep 91
Hanson, Smith, Gunnell, Keough
3:23.41　　Great Britain & NI　　22 Aug 93
Keough, Smith, Joseph, Gunnell
3:23.89　　Great Britain & NI　　31 Aug 91
Smith, Hanson, Keough, Gunnell
3:24.14　　Great Britain & NI　　14 Aug 94
Neef, Keough, Smith, Gunnell
3:24.23　　Great Britain & NI　　8 Aug 92
Smith, Douglas, Stoute, Gunnell
3:24.25　　Great Britain & NI　　30 Jun 91
Gunnell, Hanson, Stoute, Keough
3:24.36　　Great Britain & NI　　5 Jun 93
Smith, Joseph, Stoute, Gunnell
3:24.78　　Great Britain & NI　　1 Sep 90
Gunnell, Stoute, Beckford, Keough
3:25.20　　Great Britain & NI　　7 Aug 92
Douglas, Smith, Stoute, Gunnell
3:25.28　　Great Britain & N.I.　　29 Sep 00　10
Frost, D.Fraser, Curbishley, Merry
3:25.50　　Great Britain & NI　　12 Aug 95
Neef, Llewellyn, Hanson, Oladapo
3:25.51　　Great Britain & NI　　11 Aug 84
Scutt, Barnett, Taylor, Hoyte-Smith
3:25.66　　Great Britain & NI　　23 Aug 98
Fraser, Jamison, Merry, Curbishley
3:25.67　　Great Britain & N.I.　　30 Sep 00
(Danvers, D.Fraser, Curbishley, Merry)
3:25.78　　Great Britain & NI　　9 Aug 97
Curbishley, Pierre, Thomas, Fraser
3:25.82　　Great Britain & NI　　11 Sep 82
Cook, Macdonald, Taylor, Hoyte-Smith
3:25.87　　Great Britain & NI　　19 Jun 82
Forsyth, Hoyte-Smith, Elder, Scutt
3:26.27　　Great Britain & NI　　10 Aug 97
Curbishley, Pierre, Thomas, Fraser
3:26.48　　Great Britain & NI　　22 Jun 97
Curbishley, Fraser, Thomas, Gunnell
3:26.54　　Great Britain & NI　　6 Aug 89　20
Keough, Stoute, Piggford, Gunnell
3:26.6 a　　Great Britain & NI　　17 Aug 75
Roscoe, Taylor, Elder, Hartley
3:26.65　　Great Britain & NI　　11 Aug 02
Karagounis, Frost, Purkiss, McConnell
3:26.73　　Great Britain & NI　　31 Jul 02
Frost, Karagounis, Purkiss, Miller
3:26.89　　Great Britain & NI　　1 Oct 88
Keough, Stoute, Piggford, Gunnell
3:26.89　　Great Britain & NI　　13 Aug 95
Neef, Llewellyn, Hanson, Oladapo
3:26.94　　Great Britain & NI　　12 Aug 01
McConnell, Frost, Danvers, Murphy
3:27.04　　Great Britain & NI　　21 Aug 93
Keough, Smith, Joseph, Gunnell
3:27.06　　England　　28 Aug 94
Smith, Joseph, Keough, Gunnell
3:27.09　　Great Britain & NI　　30 Jul 76
Barnes, Taylor, Elder, Hartley
3:27.17　　Great Britain & NI　　3 Sep 78　30
Williams, Hoyte-Smith, Elder, Hartley

UNDER 23

100 Metres

11.10	Kathy Smallwood	5	Sep	81
11.20	Heather Hunte	26	Sep	80
11.22	Sonia Lannaman	13	Aug	77
11.25	Paula Dunn	27	Aug	86
11.27	Andrea Lynch	20	Jul	74
11.27	Stephi Douglas	26	Jul	91
11.27	Abi Oyepitan	1	Jul	01
11.31	Shirley Thomas	3	Jul	83
11.31	Simmone Jacobs	24	Sep	88
11.34	Katharine Merry	25	Jun	94

wind assisted

10.93	Sonia Lannaman	17	Jul	77
11.01	Heather Hunte	21	May	80
11.13	Shirley Thomas	27	May	84
11.14	Paula Dunn	27	Jul	86
11.17	Abi Oyepitan	30	Jun	01
11.23	Jayne Andrews	17	Jul	84
11.24	Sarah Wilhelmy	9	Jun	01
11.25	Andrea Lynch	27	Jul	74
11.27	Katharine Merry	11	Jun	94
11.30	Bev Goddard	15	Jul	78

hand timing

11.1	Andrea Lynch	29	Jun	74
11.1	Heather Hunte	29	Jun	80

hand timing - wind assisted

10.8	Sonia Lannaman	22	May	76
10.9	Andrea Lynch	18	May	74
11.1	Sharon Colyear	22	May	76

200 Metres

22.13	Kathy Smallwood	9	Sep	82
22.80	Michelle Scutt	12	Jun	82
22.81	Sonia Lannaman	2	May	76
22.85	Katharine Merry	12	Jun	94
22.98	Sandra Whittaker	8	Aug	84
23.06	Heather Hunte	15	Jun	80
23.06	Sam Davies	28	Aug	00
23.11	Bev Goddard	17	Jun	78
23.14	Helen Golden	7	Sep	73
23.18	Andrea Lynch	26	May	74

wind assisted

22.48	Michelle Scutt	4	Jul	82
22.69	Sonia Lannaman	10	Jul	77
22.84	Sarah Wilhelmy	10	Jun	01
22.90	Allison Curbishley	17	Jul	98
22.95	Bev Goddard	10	Aug	78
22.97	Helen Golden	26	Jul	74
23.14	Shirley Thomas	28	May	84

hand timing

22.9	Heather Hunte	3	May	80

hand timing - wind assisted

22.6	Sonia Lannaman	23	May	76

300 Metres

36.01	Michelle Probert	13	Jul	80

during 400m

35.8+	Kathy Smallwood	17	Sep	82

400 Metres

50.46	Kathy Smallwood	17	Sep	82
50.63	Michelle Scutt	31	May	82
50.71	Allison Curbishley	18	Sep	98
51.28	Donna Murray	12	Jul	75
51.77 i	Sally Gunnell	6	Mar	88
51.93	Janine MacGregor	28	Aug	81
51.94	Verona Bernard	26	Jan	74
51.97	Linda Forsyth	31	May	82
51.97	Helen Karagounis	27	Jul	02
52.12A	Lillian Board	16	Oct	68

600 Metres

1:26.18	Diane Edwards	22	Aug	87

800 Metres

1:59.05	Christina Boxer	4	Aug	79
1:59.30	Diane Edwards	4	Jul	87
1:59.67	Lorraine Baker	15	Aug	86
1:59.76	Paula Fryer	17	Jul	91
2:00.39	Bev Nicholson	28	Aug	88
2:00.55 mx	Zola Budd	21	Jun	86
2:00.56	Kirsty McDermott	17	Sep	82
2:00.6a	Jane Colebrook	9	Jul	77
2:01.1a	Ann Packer	20	Oct	64
2:01.2	Christine McMeekin	26	Aug	78

1000 Metres

2:35.51	Lorraine Baker	19	Jul	86

1500 Metres

4:01.93	Zola Budd	7	Jun	86
4:05.76	Yvonne Murray	5	Jul	86
4:06.0	Mary Stewart	24	Jun	78
4:06.84	Paula Radcliffe	2	Jul	95
4:07.06	Christina Boxer	15	Aug	79
4:07.98	Bev Nicholson	7	Jul	89
4:08.92	Janet Marlow	12	Jul	80
4:09.26	Lisa York	13	Jun	92
4:09.7a	Chris Benning	23	Aug	77
4:10.07	Maxine Newman	28	Jun	92

1 Mile

4:23.08	Yvonne Murray	5	Sep	86

2000 Metres

5:29.58	Yvonne Murray	11	Jul	86
5:30.19	Zola Budd	11	Jul	86

3000 Metres

8:34.43	Zola Budd	30	Jun	86
8:37.15	Yvonne Murray	28	Aug	86
8:40.40	Paula Radcliffe	16	Aug	93
8:46.53	Liz Lynch	18	Jul	86
8:47.36	Jill Hunter	17	Aug	88
8:47.71	Lisa York	31	Jul	92
8:51.40	Ruth Smeeth	7	Aug	82
8:53.78	Wendy Smith	26	May	80
8:53.98	Jane Furniss	30	May	82
8:58.44	Kath Binns	26	May	80

5000 Metres

14:49.27	Paula Radcliffe	7	Jul	95
15:17.77	Jill Hunter	26	Aug	88
15:34.92	Jane Furniss	26	Jun	82
15:36.35	Birhan Dagne	5	Aug	00
15:40.14	Helen Titterington	17	Jul	89
15:41.58+	Liz Lynch	30	Aug	86
15:49.6	Kath Binns	5	Apr	80
15:50.54	Yvonne Murray	28	May	84
15:53.96	Gillian Palmer	3	Jun	02
15:55.64	Katie Skorupska	9	Jun	99

10000 Metres

31:41.42	Liz Lynch	28	Jul	86
32:30.4	Birhan Dagne	22	Jul	00
32:32.42	Vikki McPherson	15	Jul	93
32:36.09	Helen Titterington	29	Aug	89
32:41.29	Jenny Clague	20	Jun	93
32:57.17	Kath Binns	15	Aug	80
33:09.70	Gillian Palmer	16	Jun	02
33:40.6	Andrea Everett	5	Apr	86
33:43.80	Yvonne Murray	27	Jul	85
33:59.67	Vicky Gill	29	Mar	02

2000 Metres Steeplechase

6:52.94	Ursula Counsell	11	Aug	02

3000 Metres Steeplechase

10:21.21	Lois Juslin	20	Apr	01

100 Metres Hurdles

12.82	Sally Gunnell	17	Aug	88
13.03	Diane Allahgreen	11	Jul	97
13.06	Shirley Strong	11	Jul	80
13.07	Lesley-Ann Skeete	14	Aug	87
13.11	Sharon Colyear	22	Jun	76
13.17	Jacqui Agyepong	3	Aug	90
13.20	Natasha Danvers	2	May	98
13.22	Judy Livermore	3	Oct	82
13.24	Keri Maddox	12	Jun	93
13.26	Michelle Edwards	3	Aug	90

wind assisted

12.80	Sally Gunnell	29	Jul	88
13.20	Keri Maddox	2	Jul	93
13.22	Heather Ross	27	May	84

hand timing

13.0	Blondelle Thompson	29	Jun	74

hand timing - wind assisted

12.8	Natasha Danvers	3	Apr	99

400 Metres Hurdles

54.03	Sally Gunnell	28	Sep	88
55.69	Natasha Danvers	19	Jul	98
56.26	Louise Fraser	7	Jun	92
56.42	Vicki Jamison	20	Jun	98
57.03	Sue Morley	12	Jun	82
57.45	Jacqui Parker	5	Aug	88
57.56	Simone Gandy	14	Jun	86
57.79	Susan Dalgoutte	15	Jun	80
57.81	Wendy Griffiths	7	Aug	82
57.86	Teresa Hoyle	29	Jul	83

hand timing

57.5	Vicky Lee	28	Jun	86
57.5	Simone Gandy	28	Jun	86

High Jump

1.95	Diana Elliott	26	Jun	82
1.94	Louise Miller	25	May	80
1.93	Susan Jones	2	Sep	00
1.93	Michelle Dunkley	2	Sep	00
1.92	Barbara Simmonds	31	Jul	82
1.92 i	Julia Bennett	10	Mar	90
1.91	Ann-Marie Cording	19	Sep	81
1.91	Jayne Barnetson	7	Jul	89
1.90 i	Lea Haggett	3	Jan	92
1.89		6	May	92
1.89	Judy Livermore	9	Sep	82

Pole Vault

4.00 i	Sonia Lawrence	20	Jan	02
3.90		14	Jul	01
3.90 i	Rhian Clarke	8	Mar	97
3.90		31	May	97
3.90	Tracey Bloomfield	4	Jun	00
3.90	Gillian Cooke	2	Jun	02
3.85	Ellie Spain	29	Jun	02
3.75	Gael Davies	4	Jul	01
3.72	Linda Stanton	11	Jun	95
3.60 i	Janine Whitlock ¶	30	Dec	95
3.60	Clare Ridgley	25	May	98
3.60 i	Laura Patterson	18	Feb	01
3.60		12	May	01
3.60	Catherine MacRae	11	Aug	01

Long Jump

6.88	Fiona May	18	Jul	90
6.79	Bev Kinch	7	Jul	84
6.75	Joyce Oladapo	14	Sep	85
6.73	Yinka Idowu	7	Aug	93
6.73	Jade Johnson	7	Aug	02
6.58	Mary Berkeley	14	Sep	85
6.57	Jo Wise	25	May	92
6.56	Denise Lewis	12	Jun	94
6.56	Sarah Claxton	23	May	99
6.55	Ann Wilson	22	Jul	70

wind assisted

6.98	Fiona May	4	Jun	89
6.80	Joyce Oladapo	22	Jun	85
6.59	Jo Wise	2	Jul	93

Triple Jump

13.75	Michelle Griffith	18	Jul	93
13.48 i	Ashia Hansen	13	Feb	93
13.31		18	Jul	92
13.31	Connie Henry	9	Jul	94
13.16	Rachel Kirby	26	Jul	91
13.11	Jade Johnson	19	Aug	01
13.03	Shani Anderson	4	May	96
12.98	Danielle Freeman	13	Jul	02
12.97	Rebecca White	3	Aug	02
12.94	Lorna Turner	9	Jul	94
12.81	Karen Hambrook	15	Jun	91

wind assisted

13.93	Michelle Griffith	2	Jul	93
13.55	Ashia Hansen	2	Jul	93
13.09	Rebecca White	30	Jun	01

Shot

18.19	Myrtle Augee	14	Aug	87
17.20	Judy Oakes	8	Aug	80
16.55	Yvonne Hanson-Nortey	15	Jun	86
16.40	Julie Dunkley	12	Aug	00
15.95 i	Philippa Roles	6	Feb	99
15.85 i	Alison Grey	12	Feb	94
15.69		11	Jun	94
15.72	Venissa Head	12	Jun	77
15.57	Eva Massey	8	Jun	02
15.55	Christina Bennett	13	Jun	99
15.50	Ade Oshinowo	19	Apr	02

Discus

60.00	Philippa Roles	9	May	99
57.32	Lynda Whiteley	16	Jun	84
56.63	Emma Carpenter	16	Jun	02
56.06	Kathryn Farr	27	Jun	87
55.70	Shelley Drew	25	Jun	95
55.52	Jane Aucott	17	Jan	90
54.72	Karen Pugh	27	Jul	86
54.46	Ellen Mulvihill	14	May	86
54.24	Nicola Talbot	15	May	93
54.16	Janet Thompson	15	May	76

Hammer

62.27	Zoe Derham	16	Jun	02
61.70	Lyn Sprules	12	Jul	97
60.88	Rachael Beverley	23	May	99
60.37	Liz Pidgeon	31	Jul	99
59.95	Shirley Webb	8	Sep	02
58.83	Suzanne Roberts	9	Sep	00
58.47	Mhairi Walters	12	May	02
55.86	Diana Holden	21	Jun	97
55.42	Vicci Scott	23	Jun	01
55.09	Philippa Roles	9	May	99

Javelin (1999 Model)

64.87	Kelly Morgan	14	Jul	02
58.20	Goldie Sayers	29	Jun	02
52.76	Jenny Kemp	23	Jun	01
51.79	Chloe Cozens	3	Sep	00
48.24	Tammie Francis	29	Apr	00
47.33	Katy Watts	1	Jun	02
47.26	Joanne Bruce	18	Jul	99
46.75	Katie Amos	19	Jun	99
45.81	Jennifer West	27	May	01
45.37	Katherine Evans	3	Jul	99

Javelin (pre 1999 Model)

69.54	Fatima Whitbread	3	Jul	83
67.20	Tessa Sanderson	17	Jul	77
60.10	Shelley Holroyd	16	Jul	93
60.00	Julie Abel	24	May	87
59.88	Sharon Gibson	3	Jul	83
58.20	Lorna Jackson	16	Jun	96
57.82	Mandy Liverton	21	Jun	92
56.28	Anna Lockton	20	Jul	85
55.42	Kirsty Morrison	14	Jun	97
55.34	Caroline White	20	Jan	90

Heptathlon (1985 Tables)

6325	Denise Lewis	23	Aug	94
6259	Judy Livermore	10	Sep	82
6094	Joanne Mulliner	7	Jun	87
5816 w	Julie Hollman	24	May	98
5803	Jayne Barnetson	20	Aug	89
5765	Kim Hagger	17	Jul	83
5765	Jenny Kelly	5	Aug	90
5760	Nicola Gautier	23	May	99
5671	Vikki Schofield	3	Jul	94
5644	Danielle Freeman	4	Jun	00

3000 Metres Track Walk

13:15.16+	Vicky Lupton	28	Jun	92

5000 Metres Track Walk

22:12.21	Vicky Lupton	28	Jun	92
22:19.04	Lisa Langford	25	May	87
22:40.0	Julie Drake	21	May	91

5k Road - where superior to track time

21:36	Vicky Lupton	18	Jul	92
22:09	Lisa Langford	8	Apr	89

10000 Metres Track Walk

45:53.9	Julie Drake	26	May	90
46:30.0	Vicky Lupton	14	Sep	94
49:59.0	Carol Tyson	25	Mar	78

10k Road - where superior to track time

45:42	Lisa Langford	3	May	87
45:48	Vicky Lupton	25	Aug	94

20 Kilometres Road Walk

1:38:25	Sara Cattermole	31	Oct	99
1:44:48	Vicky Lupton	3	Sep	94
1:47:21	Debbie Wallen	17	Apr	99
1:49:12	Nikki Huckerby	26	Sep	99
1:49:18	Helen Sharratt	16	Oct	93
1:52:37	Sally Warren	23	Apr	00
1:59:33	Melanie Brookes	9	Aug	86
2:00:26	Elaine Allen	4	Sep	83
2:08:23	Suzanne Ford-Dunn	16	Oct	93
2:09:23	Diane Wood	4	Sep	83

UNDER 20

100 Metres

11.27A	Kathy Smallwood	9	Sep	79
11.42		11	Aug	79
11.30	Bev Kinch	5	Jul	83
11.36A	Della James	14	Oct	68
11.40	Vernicha James	11	Jun	02
11.43	Shirley Thomas	7	Aug	82
11.45	Sonia Lannaman (U17)	1	Sep	72
11.45	Simmone Jacobs	6	Jul	84
11.52	Katharine Merry	16	Sep	92
11.53	Marcia Richardson	21	Jul	91
11.54	Wendy Clarke	8	Jun	75
11.59	Heather Hunte	9	Sep	77
11.59	Stephi Douglas	23	Jul	88
11.59	Rebecca Drummond	8	Jul	95
11.61	Diane Smith (U17)	9	Aug	90
11.61	Donna Hoggarth	16	Sep	92
11.62	Helen Miles	22	Aug	85
11.63	Jane Parry	29	May	82
11.63	Sallyanne Short	23	Aug	87
11.63	Tatum Nelson	25	Jul	97
11.64	Helen Barnett	21	Aug	76
11.64	Georgina Oladapo	22	Aug	85

wind assisted

11.13	Bev Kinch	6	Jul	83
11.25	Shirley Thomas	20	Aug	81
11.26	Simmone Jacobs	27	May	84
11.39	Vernicha James	29	Jun	02
11.40	Katharine Merry	3	Jul	93
11.43	Dorothy Hyman	2	Sep	60
11.45	Stephi Douglas	25	Jun	88
11.45	Rebecca White	4	Jul	98
11.45	Abi Oyepitan	4	Jul	98
11.47	Helen Golden	17	Jul	70
11.50	Rebecca Drummond (U17)	9	Jul	94
11.50	Sam Davies	18	Jul	98
11.51	Amy Spencer (U17)	29	Jun	02
11.53	Wendy Clarke	22	Aug	75
11.53	Sharon Dolby	16	Aug	86

hand timing

11.3	Sonia Lannaman	9	Jun	74
11.3	Heather Hunte	15	Jul	78
11.4	Della James	2	Aug	67

hand timing - wind assisted

11.2	Wendy Clarke	22	May	76
11.3	Helen Golden	30	May	70
11.3	Linsey Macdonald (U17)	3	May	80
11.4	Anita Neil	30	Jun	68
11.4	Helen Barnett	16	May	76
11.4	Jane Parry (U17)	5	Jul	80

downhill

11.3 w	Denise Ramsden	28	Jun	69

200 Metres

22.70 A	Kathy Smallwood	12	Sep	79
22.84		5	Aug	79
22.93	Vernicha James	21	Jul	01
23.10	Diane Smith (U17)	11	Aug	90
23.20	Katharine Merry	13	Jun	93
23.23	Sonia Lannaman	25	Aug	75
23.23	Sarah Wilhelmy	13	Jun	98
23.24	Sandra Whittaker	12	Jun	82
23.28	Simmone Jacobs (U17)	28	Aug	83
23.33	Linsey Macdonald	9	Jun	82
23.35	Donna Murray	26	May	74
23.42	Debbie Bunn (U17)	17	Jun	78
23.45	Amy Spencer (U17)	15	Jul	01
23.46	Shirley Thomas	31	May	82
23.48	Wendy Clarke	7	Jun	75
23.51	Sharon Colyear	26	May	74
23.54	Jane Parry	30	Jul	83
23.57	Sophia Smith	30	Jul	93
23.59	Eleanor Thomas	17	Jul	77
23.60	Michelle Probert (U17)	12	Sep	76
23.61	Danielle Norville	16	Jun	01

wind assisted

23.01	Simmone Jacobs	28	May	84
23.11	Linsey Macdonald (U17)	5	Jul	80
23.16	Donna Murray	27	Jul	74
23.20	Sarah Wilhelmy	18	Jul	98
23.42	Helen Golden	22	Jul	70
23.54	Janine MacGregor	17	Jun	78
23.55	Sallyanne Short	25	Jul	87

hand timing

23.1	Sonia Lannaman	7	Jun	75
23.3	Donna Murray	9	Jun	74
23.3	Sharon Colyear	30	Jun	74
23.3	Linsey Macdonald	8	May	82
23.4	Helen Barnett	17	Jul	76

hand timing - wind assisted

22.9	Donna Murray	14	Jul	74
23.2	Debbie Bunn (U17)	2	Jul	78
23.3	Angela Bridgeman	15	Aug	82
23.3	Amy Spencer (U17)	1	Jul	01

300 Metres

36.46	Linsey Macdonald (U17)	13	Jul	80

400 Metres

51.16	Linsey Macdonald (U17)	15	Jun	80
51.77	Donna Murray	30	Jul	74
52.54	Donna Fraser	10	Aug	91
52.65	Jane Parry	11	Jun	83
52.80	Sian Morris	18	Jun	83
52.98	Karen Williams	6	Aug	78
52.99	Angela Bridgeman	24	Jul	82
53.01 i	Marilyn Neufville	14	Mar	70
53.08	Loreen Hall	29	Jul	84
53.14	Michelle Probert	28	Jul	79
53.18	Lisa Miller	16	Jun	02
53.20	Verona Bernard	8	Jul	72
53.48	Lillian Board	22	Sep	67
53.52	Ruth Kennedy	25	Sep	74
53.52	Kim Wall	20	Jul	01
53.59	Janine MacGregor	11	Jul	78
53.73	Paulette McLean	24	Aug	89
53.75	Linda Keough (U17)	8	Aug	80
53.84	Jenny Meadows	12	Aug	00
53.84	Vernicha James	4	Jun	02

hand timing

52.6	Marilyn Neufville	20	Jun	70
52.8	Lillian Board	9	Jul	67
52.9	Verona Bernard	15	Sep	72
53.3	Tracey Burges	5	Sep	81
53.5	Ruth Kennedy	30	Jun	74
53.7	Linda Keough (U17)	2	Aug	80
53.8	Alison Reid	28	May	81

600 Metres

1:27.33	Lorraine Baker (U17)	13	Jul	80

800 Metres (*880yds less 0.7)

1:59.75	Charlotte Moore	29	Jul	02
2:01.11	Lynne MacDougall	18	Aug	84
2:01.66	Lorraine Baker	26	Jun	82
2:02.00	Diane Edwards	14	Sep	85
2:02.0	Jo White (U17)	13	Aug	77
2:02.18	Lynne Robinson	18	Jul	86
2:02.8 a	Lesley Kiernan	2	Sep	74
2:02.88 i	Kirsty McDermott	22	Feb	81
2:04.01		29	Jul	81
2:03.11	Janet Prictoe	19	Aug	78
2:03.18	Paula Newnham	17	Jun	78
2:03.53	Christine McMeekin	25	Aug	75
2:03.86	Lisa Dobriskey	14	Aug	02
2:04.11	Jemma Simpson	19	Jul	02
2:04.30	Bridget Smyth	19	Aug	86
2:04.6	Janet Lawrence	26	Jul	77
2:04.7*	Rosemary Stirling	13	Aug	66
2:04.85	Louise Parker	28	Jul	79
2:04.95	Denise Kiernan	3	Jun	78
2:05.0 i	Jane Colebrook	11	Dec	76
2:05.05	Rebecca Lyne	31	Jul	01

1000 Metres

2:38.58	Jo White (U17)	9	Sep	77

1500 Metres

3:59.96	Zola Budd	30	Aug	85
4:05.96	Lynne MacDougall	20	Aug	84
4:11.12	Bridget Smyth	26	May	85
4:13.38	Emma Ward	7	May	01
4:13.40	Wendy Smith	19	Aug	78
4:13.94	Charlotte Moore	14	Aug	02
4:14.40	Janet Lawrence	20	Aug	77
4:14.50	Wendy Wright	20	Jun	87
4:14.56	Andrea Whitcombe	22	Aug	90
4:14.58	Ruth Smeeth	16	Jul	78
4:14.58	Lisa Dobriskey	22	Jun	02
4:14.73	Mary Stewart	2	Feb	74
4:15.1	Yvonne Murray	18	Jul	82
4:15.39	Lisa York	26	Aug	89
4:15.55	Sandra Arthurton (U17)	29	Jul	78
4:16.10	Katie Fairbrass	29	May	83
4:16.12	Elise Lyon	3	Jul	83
4:16.13	Bernadette Madigan	12	Aug	79
4:16.2 i	Jo White	28	Jan	78
4:16.4	Julie Holland	15	May	84
4:16.51	Maxine Newman	26	Aug	89

1 Mile

4:17.57	Zola Budd	21	Aug	85

2000 Metres

5:33.15	Zola Budd	13	Jul	84

3000 Metres

8:28.83	Zola Budd	7	Sep	85	
8:51.78	Paula Radcliffe	20	Sep	92	
9:03.35	Philippa Mason	19	Jul	86	
9:04.14	Yvonne Murray	28	May	83	
9:06.16	Helen Titterington	19	Jun	88	
9:07.02	Carol Haigh	24	Jun	85	
9:09.14	Lisa York	19	Jul	89	
9:10.9	Julie Holland	7	Apr	84	
9:12.28	Hayley Haining	20	Jul	91	
9:12.97	Bernadette Madigan	30	Jun	79	10
9:13.4 mx	Caroline Walsh	30	Jun	99	
9:20.38		7	Aug	99	
9:13.81	Andrea Whitcombe	12	Aug	90	
9:14.10	Maxine Newman	19	Jul	89	
9:15.82	Ruth Smeeth	17	Jun	78	
9:17.61 mx	Charlotte Dale	10	Jul	02	
9:17.70 i	Alice Braham	3	Dec	94	
9:18.07	Heidi Moulder	1	Aug	93	
9:20.0	Judith Shepherd	13	Aug	77	
9:20.2	Katrina Wootton	28	Aug	02	
9:20.9	Wendy Wright	26	Apr	86	20

5000 Metres

14:48.07	Zola Budd	26	Aug	85	
15:51.62	Carol Haigh	26	May	85	
15:52.55	Yvonne Murray	29	May	83	
16:11.61 i	Jenny Clague	22	Feb	92	
16:15.36	Louise Kelly	31	Jul	98	
16:16.39	Collette Fagan	20	Jul	01	
16:16.55	Charlotte Dale	3	Jun	02	
16:16.77 i	Paula Radcliffe	22	Feb	92	
16:35.56	Gillian Stacey	22	Aug	90	
16:37.18	Henrietta Freeman	19	Aug	00	10
16:41.9	Katie Skorupska	22	Jun	96	
16:47.4	Sally James	7	Sep	83	
16:48.44	Claire Forbes	21	Apr	90	
16:49.2	Sam Baines	6	Jun	87	
16:50.4	Amanda Tremble	9	Aug	95	
16:50.84	Fiona Truman	30	Apr	88	
16:55.59	Louise Damen	16	Jun	01	
16:58.87	Tanya Povey	23	Apr	98	
17:09.8	Karen Fletcher	23	Aug	98	
17:09.97	Alison Hollington	30	Jul	82	20

10000 Metres

33:10.6	Charlotte Dale	20	Apr	02

2000 Metres Steeplechase

6:55.04	Jo Ankier	22	Jul	01
6:55.83	Bryony Frost	18	May	02
7:01.2	Kathryn Frost	20	Jun	01

3000 Metres Steeplechase

12:11.1	Lindsey Oliver	22	Aug	93

100 Metres Hurdles

13.25	Diane Allahgreen	21	Jul	94
13.30	Sally Gunnell	16	Jun	84
13.32	Keri Maddox	21	Jul	91
13.45	Natasha Danvers	6	Aug	95
13.46	Nathalie Byer	26	Aug	83
13.47	Sam Baker	30	Jun	91
13.49	Angie Thorp	30	Jun	91
13.50	Lesley-Ann Skeete	6	Jun	86
13.52	Julie Pratt	5	Jul	98
10 13.56	Wendy McDonnell	3	Jun	79
13.57	Bethan Edwards	29	Aug	92
13.58	Lauraine Cameron	19	Jun	90
13.62	Sarah Claxton	18	Jul	98
13.66	Helen Worsey	20	Jul	01
13.68	Jacqui Agyepong	7	Aug	87
13.72	Judy Livermore	15	Jul	79
13.73	Ann Girvan (U17)	7	Aug	82
13.73	Yinka Idowu	10	Aug	91
13.75	Sue Scott	21	Jul	70
20 13.76	Shirley Strong	20	Aug	77

wind assisted

13.24	Lesley-Ann Skeete	7	Jun	86
13.28	Sarah Claxton	5	Jul	98
13.39	Lauraine Cameron	1	Jul	90
13.45	Louise Fraser	30	Jul	89
13.45	Sam Baker	30	Jun	91
13.46	Wendy McDonnell	30	Jun	79
13.48	Julie Pratt	5	Jul	98
13.55	Shirley Strong	10	Jul	77
13.56	Ann Girvan	15	Jul	84
10 13.64	Gemma Fergusson	30	Jun	02

hand timing

13.5	Christine Perera	19	Jul	68

hand timing - wind assisted

13.1	Sally Gunnell	7	Jul	84
13.3	Keri Maddox	14	Jul	90
13.4	Judy Livermore	27	May	79
13.4	Sam Baker	14	Jul	90

400 Metres Hurdles

57.27	Vicki Jamison	28	Jul	96
58.02	Vyv Rhodes	28	Jun	92
58.37	Alyson Evans	1	Sep	85
58.68	Kay Simpson	15	Jul	83
58.76	Simone Gandy	28	May	84
58.91	Rachael Kay	6	Aug	99
58.96	Nicola Sanders	17	Jul	99
59.00	Diane Heath	19	Jul	75
59.01	Sara Elson	24	Aug	89
10 59.04	Allison Curbishley	31	Jul	93
59.12	Tracy Allen	29	Jul	89
59.13	Sue Morley	12	Aug	79
59.39	Tracey Duncan	29	Jul	98
59.52	Debbie Church	25	Jul	81
59.56	Lucy Elliott	26	Jul	85
59.65	Debbie Duncan	7	Aug	87
60.06	Faye Harding (U17)	13	Jul	01
60.07	Michelle Cooney	6	Jul	85
60.07	Gemma Dooney	18	Aug	01
20 60.15	Kate Norman	2	Jul	95

hand timing

58.3	Simone Gandy	14	Jul	84
58.7	Sara Elson	18	Jun	89
59.0	Tracy Allen	9	Jul	88
59.3	Michelle Cooney	13	Jul	85
59.4	Diane Wade	21	Jul	79
59.5	Samantha Flynn	12	Jul	86
59.7	Keri Maddox (U17)	9	Jul	88
59.9	Denise Kiernan	6	Sep	78
60.0	Jacqui Parker	13	Jul	85

High Jump

1.91	Lea Haggett	2	Jun	91	
1.91	Susan Jones	31	Aug	97	
1.90	Jo Jennings	29	Sep	88	
1.89	Debbie Marti (U17)	2	Jun	84	
1.89 i	Michelle Dunkley	16	Feb	97	
1.87		7	Jul	95	
1.88	Jayne Barnetson	3	Aug	85	
1.88	Rebecca Jones	1	Jun	02	
1.87	Louise Manning	6	May	84	
1.87	Rachael Forrest	7	Jul	95	
1.87	Aileen Wilson	15	Jul	01	10
1.86	Barbara Simmonds	9	Sep	79	
1.86	Claire Summerfield	7	Aug	82	
1.86	Michele Wheeler	31	May	87	
1.85	Gillian Hitchen	3	Jun	78	
1.85	Sharon McPeake	22	Sep	81	
1.85	Julia Bennett	15	Apr	89	
1.85	Stephanie Higham	16	Jun	02	
1.84	Louise Miller	12	May	79	
1.84	Sarah Rowe	22	Aug	81	
1.84	Ursula Fay (U17)	6	Aug	83	20

Pole Vault

4.00	Kate Dennison	18	Jul	02	
4.00	Zoe Brown	28	Jul	02	
3.90	Ellie Spain	6	May	00	
3.80	Hannah Olson (U15)	8	Jun	02	
3.75	Tracey Bloomfield	9	Aug	98	
3.75	Natalie Olson (U17)	16	Jun	02	
3.71 i	Kirsty Maguire	23	Feb	02	
3.60		18	Jul	01	
3.70	Rhian Clarke	10	Aug	96	
3.66 i	Lindsay Hodges	24	Feb	01	
3.55 (U17)		14	Aug	99	
3.60	Fiona Harrison (U17)	25	May	98	10
3.51 i	Clare Ridgley	17	Feb	96	
3.50		6	May	96	
3.50	Becky Ridgley	23	May	99	
3.50	Caroline Nutt	19	Aug	01	
3.50 i	Kim Skinner (U15)	22	Dec	01	
3.40		11	Aug	01	
3.50	Jennifer Graham	5	Jun	02	
3.45	Laura Patterson	4	Sep	99	
3.40	Danielle Codd	4	Jul	98	
3.40	Gillian Cooke	5	May	01	
3.40	Clare Neve	28	Jul	02	
3.30	Louise Gauld	23	May	99	
3.30	Claire Holmes	25	May	02	
3.30	Eilidh Dorrian	20	Jul	02	

Long Jump

6.90	Bev Kinch	14	Aug	83
6.82	Fiona May	30	Jul	88
6.68	Sue Hearnshaw	22	Sep	79
6.63	Yinka Idowu	21	May	89
6.55	Joyce Oladapo	30	Jul	83
6.52	Georgina Oladapo	16	Jun	84
6.52	Sarah Claxton	31	Jul	98
6.52	Jade Johnson	23	May	99
6.47	Jo Wise	30	Jul	88
10 6.45	Margaret Cheetham (U17)	18	Aug	84
6.43	Myra Nimmo	27	May	73
6.39	Moira Walls	22	Jul	70
6.35	Sharon Bowie	1	Jun	85
6.34	Ann Wilson	3	Aug	68
6.33	Jo Dear	19	May	93
6.31	Joanne Mulliner	1	Jun	85
6.27	Sheila Parkin	3	Aug	64
6.26	Maria Smallwood	14	Jun	80
6.25	Lisa Armstrong	15	Jul	92
20 6.24	Karen Murray	16	Jul	77

wind unconfirmed

6.43	Moira Walls	18	Sep	70

wind assisted

6.93	Bev Kinch	14	Aug	83
6.88	Fiona May	30	Jul	88
6.71	Yinka Idowu	15	Jun	91
6.69	Jo Wise	30	Jul	88
6.53	Sarah Claxton	12	Jul	97
6.49	Margaret Cheetham (U17)	4	Sep	83
6.48	Moira Walls	17	May	70
6.41	Ann Wilson	30	Jun	68

Triple Jump

13.05	Michelle Griffith	16	Jun	90
12.52	Emily Parker	13	Jul	02
12.50	Julia Johnson	21	Jun	98
12.43	Shani Anderson	26	Jun	93
12.42	Liz Gibbens	2	Jul	95
12.41 i	Judy Kotey	28	Feb	98
12.33		17	May	98
12.34	Azaria Francis	12	May	02
12.27	Lorna Turner	26	May	91
12.22	Mary Bignal	18	Jun	59
10 12.22	Angela Williams	16	Sep	00
12.20	Jodie Hurst	8	Jun	96
12.18	Justina Cruickshank	26	May	96
12.17	Katharine Streatfield	26	May	01
12.16	Carly Robson	29	Jun	02
12.14	Jayne Ludlow (U17)	21	May	94
12.10	Jane Falconer	30	Aug	93
12.10	Pamela Anderson	2	Jul	95
12.10	Rachel Brenton (U17)	21	Jul	01
12.10	Linsi Robinson	25	May	02
20 12.04	Rachel Peacock	26	Aug	01
11.96	Linsi Robinson	30	Jun	01

wind assisted

12.61	Judy Kotey	5	Jul	98
12.48	Lorna Turner	30	Jun	91
12.44	Shani Anderson	9	Jul	94
12.39	Karlene Turner	7	Sep	02

Shot

17.10	Myrtle Augee	16	Jun	84
16.24 i	Judy Oakes	26	Feb	77
16.05		26	Aug	77
15.72 i	Alison Grey	29	Feb	92
15.26		13	Jul	91
15.60 i	Justine Buttle	27	Feb	88
15.45		25	Aug	88
15.48	Mary Anderson	8	Sep	85
15.45	Susan King	27	Mar	83
15.27	Julie Dunkley	21	Jun	98
14.75 i	Cynthia Gregory	12	Dec	81
14.70		29	Aug	81
14.71 i	Nicola Gautier	26	Jan	97
14.37		12	Jul	97
14.68	Claire Smithson	26	May	01 10
14.66 i	Terri Salt	7	Jan	84
14.60	Philippa Roles	4	Sep	96
14.59	Dawn Grazette	19	May	91
14.59 i	Christina Bennett	16	Mar	97
14.54	Carol Cooksley	9	Jul	88
14.54 i	Jayne Berry	18	Mar	89
14.45		17	Jun	88
14.49	Eva Massey	9	Aug	99
14.36	Venissa Head	4	Jul	75
14.34	Rebecca Peake	18	Aug	89
14.33	Jenny Kelly	27	May	01 20

Discus

55.03	Claire Smithson	30	Jul	02
54.78	Lynda Whiteley	4	Oct	82
53.12	Emma Carpenter	1	Sep	01
53.10	Kathryn Farr	19	Jul	86
52.58	Emma Merry	22	Aug	93
52.31	Lauren Keightley	18	Jul	98
51.82	Catherine Bradley	20	Jul	85
51.60	Philippa Roles	24	Jul	97
51.24	Jane Aucott	11	Jun	86
51.12	Janette Picton	6	Jun	82 10
50.44	Karen Pugh	8	Jul	83
50.34	Angela Sellars	27	Jul	86
50.30	Julia Avis	19	Sep	82
49.74	Shelley Drew	10	May	92
49.60	Fiona Condon	3	Jun	79
49.56	Sarah Winckless	2	May	92
49.42	Rosanne Lister	29	Aug	88
49.30	Amanda Barnes	18	Jun	88
49.24	Lesley Mallin	31	May	75
49.00	Tracey Whincup	26	Jun	84 20

Hammer

57.97	Rachael Beverley	25	Jul	98
57.63	Nicola Dudman	16	Jun	02
55.22	Laura Douglas	18	May	02
55.10	Mhairi Walters	27	May	00
54.72	Helen Arnold	26	Jul	97
54.48	Lyn Sprules	2	Jul	94
53.80	Carys Parry	17	Oct	00
53.34	Diana Holden	13	Aug	94
53.13	Katy Lamb	14	Jul	01
52.33	Zoe Derham	13	Jun	99 10

51.62	Julie Lavender	15 May	94
51.54	Lucy Marshall	3 Sep	00
51.34	Helen Taylor	12 Aug	01
50.66	Vicci Scott	12 Sep	99
50.52	Catherine Garden	3 Aug	97
50.50	Sarah Harrison	2 Aug	97
49.48	Samantha Burns-Salmond	13 Aug	95
48.98	Liz Pidgeon	21 Sep	96
48.98	Francis Miller (U17)	21 Sep	96
20 48.18	Suzanne Roberts	1 Jun	97

Javelin (1999 Model)

55.40	Goldie Sayers	22 Jul	01
54.61	Kelly Morgan	4 Sep	99
52.54	Jenny Kemp	3 Jul	99
48.15	Chloe Cozens	19 Jun	99
47.73	Helen Mounteney	12 Jul	02
47.66	Samantha Redd	29 Jun	02
47.57	Amy Harvey	7 Oct	00
46.94	Louise Watton	12 Jul	02
46.57	Louise Matthews	28 Apr	02
10 45.84	Suzanne Finnis	24 Jun	00

Javelin (pre 1999 Model)

60.14	Fatima Whitbread	7 May	80
59.40	Karen Hough	28 Aug	86
59.36	Kirsty Morrison	4 Sep	93
57.84	Mandy Liverton	3 Jun	90
57.82	Shelley Holroyd	9 Aug	92
57.80	Julie Abel	5 Jun	83
56.96	Nicky Emblem	1 Feb	90
55.72	Karen Martin	25 Jul	92
55.38	Catherine Garside	19 May	84
10 55.04	Tessa Sanderson	26 Sep	74

Heptathlon (1985 Tables)

5833	Joanne Mulliner	11 Aug	85
5642	Sarah Rowe	23 Aug	81
5496	Yinka Idowu	3 Sep	89
5493	Sally Gunnell	28 May	84
5484	Denise Lewis	30 Jun	91
5459	Jenny Kelly	30 Jul	88
5391 w	Jackie Kinsella	22 Jun	86
5331		19 Jul	86
5377	Uju Efobi	18 Jul	93
5358 w	Chloe Cozens	24 May	98
5283		23 May	99
10 5311	Nicola Gautier	21 Sep	97
5299	Emma Beales	26 Aug	90
5279	Fiona Harrison	21 Oct	00
5273 w	Debbie Marti	11 Aug	85
5216		7 Jul	85
5258 w	Danielle Freeman	23 May	99
5237		19 Jul	98
5254	Rebecca Jones	2 Jun	02
5246	Val Walsh	7 Aug	83
5215	Katherine Livesey	1 Jun	97
5208	Michelle Stone (U17)	30 Sep	84
5208	Mary Anderson	24 Aug	86
20 5194	Jessica Ennis (U17)	4 Aug	02

3000 Metres Track Walk

13:03.4	Vicky Lupton	18 May	91
13:47.0	Julie Drake	5 Jul	88
13:53.0 e+	Lisa Langford	23 Aug	85
14:01.0		17 Aug	85
14:04.1	Susan Ashforth (U17)	19 May	85
14:09.81	Amy Hales (U17)	19 Sep	98

5000 Metres Track Walk

22:36.81	Vicky Lupton	15 Jun	91
23:31.67	Lisa Langford	23 Aug	85
23:55.27	Susan Ashforth (U17)	25 May	85
23:56.9	Julie Drake	24 May	88
24:02.15	Nicky Jackson	27 May	84
24:08.4	Jill Barrett	28 May	83
24:19.0	Vicky Lawrence	13 Jun	87
24:19.06	Sophie Hales	20 Jul	02
24:24.31	Andrea Crofts	4 Jun	89
24:27.73	Carolyn Brown	29 Aug	92 10
24:28.60	Debbie Wallen	26 Jul	98
24:34.6	Tracy Devlin	17 Sep	89

5k Road - where superior to track time

23:05	Lisa Langford	2 Nov	85
23:18	Julie Drake	27 Feb	88
23:35	Lisa Simpson	31 Oct	87
23:44	Nicky Jackson	12 May	84
23:46	Jill Barrett	14 May	83
23:54	Vicky Lawrence	26 Sep	87

10000 Metres Track Walk

47:04.0	Vicky Lupton	30 Mar	91
48:34.0mx	Lisa Langford	15 Mar	86
49:07.8		21 Jun	86
49:48.7	Julie Drake	7 Feb	88
50:25.0mx	Lisa Simpson	1 Apr	87
51:54.5		27 Sep	86
51:00.0	Karen Nipper (U17)	21 Feb	81
51:31.2	Helen Ringshaw	17 Mar	84
52:09.0	Elaine Cox	8 Apr	78
52:10.4	Sarah Brown	20 Mar	82
52:48.5	Kate Horwill	22 Aug	92
53:11.4	Jill Barrett	28 Mar	81 10
53:36.0mx	Suzie Pratt	15 Mar	86
53:39.0	Karen Eden	22 Mar	80

short

50:11.2	Jill Barrett	19 Mar	83

10k Road - where superior to track time

49:10	Vicky Lawrence	14 Mar	87
49:14	Carolyn Brown	29 Mar	92
49:26	Julie Drake	21 May	88
49:33	Lisa Simpson	14 Mar	87
49:47	Jill Barrett	24 Sep	83
51:15	Nicky Jackson	18 Nov	84
51:36	Nicola Phillips	23 Apr	00
51:49	Katie Stones	14 Sep	02
51:51	Elaine Cox	2 Sep	79

Note: LJ, Hep. Although Idowu competed for UK Juniors, she was a Nigerian citizen at the time.

UNDER 17

100 Metres

11.45	Sonia Lannaman	1	Sep	72
11.59	Simmone Jacobs	25	Aug	83
11.60	Katharine Merry	28	Jul	90
11.61	Diane Smith	9	Aug	90
11.66	Amy Spencer	16	Jun	01
11.69	Jane Parry	6	Jun	81
11.70	Linsey Macdonald	24	May	80
11.73	Etta Kessebeh	20	Aug	81
11.77	Hayley Clements	26	Jul	85
10 11.77	Montell Douglas	10	Aug	02
11.78	Tatum Nelson	16	May	94
11.79	Janet Smith	26	Jul	85
11.80	Sharon Dolby	26	Jul	85
11.81	Lisa Goreeph	6	Jun	82

wind assisted

11.47	Katharine Merry (U15)	17	Jun	89
11.50	Rebecca Drummond	9	Jul	94
11.51	Amy Spencer	29	Jun	02
11.61	Linsey Macdonald	16	Jun	79
11.62	Kathleen Lithgow	25	Jun	88
11.62	Donna Maylor	4	Jul	98
11.63	Sharon Dolby	10	Aug	85

hand timing

11.6	Denise Ramsden	19	Jul	68
11.6	Linsey Macdonald	25	May	80
11.6	Jane Parry	2	Aug	80

hand timing - wind assisted

11.3	Linsey Macdonald	3	May	80
11.4	Sonia Lannaman	3	Jun	72
11.4	Jane Parry	5	Jul	80
11.5	Sharon Dolby	20	Jul	85

200 Metres

23.10	Diane Smith	11	Aug	90
23.28	Simmone Jacobs	28	Aug	83
23.42	Debbie Bunn	17	Jun	78
23.43	Linsey Macdonald	20	Aug	80
23.45	Amy Spencer	15	Jul	01
23.49 i	Vernicha James	30	Jan	00
23.62		8	Jul	00
23.50	Katharine Merry	20	Jul	91
23.60	Michelle Probert	12	Sep	76
23.66	Jane Parry	15	Jun	80
10 23.69	Donna Fraser	1	Jul	89
23.79	Sharon Colyear	5	Sep	71
23.90	Angela Bridgeman	20	Aug	80
23.95	Helen Golden	30	Aug	69
23.97	Lisa Goreeph	31	Jul	82
24.06	Fay Nixon	4	Jun	76

wind assisted

23.11	Linsey Macdonald	5	Jul	80
23.41	Katharine Merry	15	Jun	91
23.48	Vernicha James	21	Aug	99
23.64	Jane Parry	5	Jul	80
23.70	Sonia Lannaman	16	Jun	72
23.85	Helen Golden	1	Sep	69
23.96	Sarah Wilhelmy	13	Jul	96

hand timing (* 220 yards less 0.1)

23.8 *	Marilyn Neufville	27	Jul	68
23.8	Janis Walsh (U15)	23	Jun	74
23.8	Janet Smith	1	Jun	85
23.9	Fay Nixon	24	Jul	76
23.9	Hayley Clements	1	Jun	85

hand timing - wind assisted

23.2	Debbie Bunn	2	Jul	78
23.3	Amy Spencer	1	Jul	01

300 Metres

36.46	Linsey Macdonald	13	Jul	80
38.19	Eleanor Caney	22	Jul	00
38.21	Lesley Owusu	27	Aug	95
38.49	Kim Wall	24	May	98
38.49	Gemma Nicol	3	Aug	02
38.60	Karlene Palmer	12	Jul	97
38.75	Gabi Howell	24	May	98
38.90	Liza Parry	15	Jul	00
38.95	Maria Bolsover	8	Jul	95
39.03	Laura Finucane	11	Aug	02 10
39.04	Heather McKay	19	Jun	98
39.07	Nicola Sanders	24	May	98
39.19	Tara Bird	13	Jul	02
39.20	Jenny Christie	13	Jul	02
39.21	Lisa Miller	10	Jul	99

hand timing

38.2	Marilyn Neufville	6	Sep	69
38.4	Kim Wall	10	May	98
38.6	Fay Nixon	10	Sep	77
38.7	Katharine Merry	1	Sep	91

400 Metres

51.16	Linsey Macdonald	15	Jun	80
53.08	Loreen Hall	29	Jul	84
53.75	Linda Keough	8	Aug	80
54.01	Angela Bridgeman	16	Aug	80
54.25	Emma Langston	19	Jun	88
54.57	Lesley Owusu	9	Sep	95

hand timing

53.7	Linda Keough	2	Aug	80

600 Metres

1:27.33	Lorraine Baker	13	Jul	80

800 Metres

2:02.0	Jo White	13	Aug	77
2:03.66	Lesley Kiernan	26	Aug	73
2:03.72	Lorraine Baker	15	Jun	80
2:04.85	Louise Parker	28	Jul	79
2:05.86	Charlotte Moore	31	Jul	01
2:06.5	Rachel Hughes (U15)	19	Jul	82
2:06.5	Emma Langston	10	Aug	88
2:06.51	Danielle Barnes	15	Jul	01
2:06.53	Lynne Robinson	6	Jul	85
2:06.72	Jemma Simpson	19	Aug	00 10
2:06.8	Jayne Heathcote	31	May	87
2:06.82	Rachael Thompson	3	Jun	02
2:07.0	Bridget Smyth	27	Jun	84
2:07.25	Morag MacLarty	21	Jul	01
2:07.3	Amanda Alford	7	May	80

1000 Metres

2:38.58	Jo White	9	Sep	77

1500 Metres

4:15.20	Bridget Smyth	29	Jul	84
4:15.55	Sandra Arthurton	29	Jul	78
4:16.8	Jo White	30	Jul	77
4:19.93	Katrina Wootton	15	Jun	02
4:21.88	Jeina Mitchell	20	Jul	91
4:22.25	Karen Hughes	24	May	81
4:22.25	Clare Keller	7	Jul	85
4:22.51	Elise Lyon	31	Jul	82
4:23.07	Charlotte Moore	22	Aug	01
10 4:23.11	Gillian Stacey	2	Sep	89
4:23.25	Denise Kiernan	20	Aug	77
4:23.37	Dawn Hargan	14	Jun	87
4:23.45	Isabel Linaker (U15)	7	Jul	90
4:23.6	Janette Howes	5	Sep	81
4:23.75	Lynne MacDougall	24	May	81

1 Mile

4:46.0	Sandra Arthurton	13	May	78

3000 Metres

9:20.2 mx	Katrina Wootton	28	Aug	02
9:37.00		2	Jun	02
9:24.38 mx	Rachel Nathan	20	Aug	02
9:31.69		18	Aug	01
9:24.40 mx	Danni Barnes	6	May	02
9:35.46+		23	May	01
9:28.9	Bridget Smyth	21	Apr	84
9:30.0	Yvonne Murray	4	Jul	81
9:32.20	Nikki Slater	28	Aug	93
9:33.1	Alison Hollington	6	Jun	81
9:33.7	Elaine Renouf	23	Jun	02
9:34.5	Louise Watson	28	Aug	88
10 9:34.79	Helen Titterington	28	Jun	86
9:34.9 mx	Charlotte Dale	16	Jul	00
9:35.25		19	Aug	00
9:35.52	Courtney Birch	15	Jul	00

5000 Metres

17:45.2	Kathy Williams	10	May	80

80 Metres Hurdles (2'6")

11.02	Helen Worsey	15	Aug	98
11.07	Amanda Parker	7	Jun	86
11.12	Sam Farquharson	7	Jun	86
11.13	Claire St. John	2	Jun	79
11.16	Ann Girvan	4	Jul	81
11.16	Stephi Douglas	27	Jul	85
11.17	Sara McGreavy	14	Aug	99
11.20	Ann Wilson	11	Aug	66
11.20	Louise Brunning	25	Jul	87
10 11.20	Symone Belle	30	Jul	00
11.22	Sharon Davidge	18	Jul	98
11.23	Rachel Rigby	25	Jul	87
11.25	Louise Fraser	25	Jul	87
11.26	Liz Fairs	17	Jul	93
11.29	Nina Thompson	7	Aug	88

wind assisted

10.96	Helen Worsey	11	Jul	98
11.00	Sharon Davidge	11	Jul	98
11.03	Wendy McDonnell	20	Aug	77

hand timing

11.0	Wendy McDonnell	2	Jul	77

hand timing - wind assisted

10.9	Ann Wilson	16	Jul	66
10.9	Wendy McDonnell	9	Jul	77
10.9	Sam Farquharson	20	Jul	85

100 Metres Hurdles (2'6")

13.66	Ann Girvan	25	Jul	81

100 Metres Hurdles (2'9")

13.73	Ann Girvan	7	Aug	82
13.88	Natasha Danvers	28	Aug	93
13.94	Phyllis Agbo	30	Jun	02
13.98	Claire St. John	11	Aug	79
14.01	Jessica Ennis	30	Jun	02
14.04	Lauraine Cameron	7	Aug	88
14.24	Pam St. Ange	2	Oct	82
14.24	Angie Thorp	9	Jul	89

wind assisted

13.67	Ann Girvan	4	Jul	82
13.76	Natasha Danvers	27	Aug	94
14.10	Sue Mapstone	25	Aug	73
14.27	Heather Ross	27	Aug	78

hand timing

13.7	Ann Girvan	29	Aug	81
14.1	Pam St Ange	7	Aug	83

hand timing - wind assisted

13.7	Nathalie Byer	4	Sep	82
13.9	Angie Thorp	9	Sep	89

300 Metres Hurdles

41.98	Rachael Kay	3	Aug	97	
41.99	Natasha Danvers	10	Jul	93	
42.21	Eilidh Child	20	Jul	02	
42.50	Justine Roach	21	Jul	01	
42.58	Syreeta Williams	12	Jul	97	
42.67	Vicki Jamison	17	Jul	93	
42.68	Gemma Dooney	15	Jul	00	
42.87	Nusrat Ceesay	12	Jul	97	
42.91	Allison Curbishley	18	Aug	91	
43.03	Val Theobalds	13	Aug	89	10
43.03	Wendy Davidson	15	Aug	99	
43.06	Claire Griffiths	18	Aug	91	
43.08	Yewande Ige	13	Jul	96	
43.12	Keri Maddox	6	Aug	88	
43.12	Sian Scott	30	Jul	00	

hand timing

41.8	Rachael Kay	17	Aug	97
42.4	Keri Maddox	8	May	88
42.4	Syreeta Williams	17	Aug	97
42.5	Louise Brunning	8	May	88
42.6	Sian Scott	10	Jun	00
42.8	Rachel Stafford	8	Jul	89
42.8	Vyv Rhodes	8	Jul	89
42.9	Val Theobalds	17	Jun	89

400 Metres Hurdles
60.06	Faye Harding	13	Jul	01
60.87	Karin Hendrickse	31	Jul	82
60.93	Rachael Kay	21	Jul	97
61.02	Claire Edwards	8	Sep	91
61.04	Allison Curbishley	26	Jul	92

hand timing
59.7	Keri Maddox	9	Jul	88
60.8	Jayne Puckeridge	9	Jul	88

High Jump
1.89	Debbie Marti	2	Jun	84
1.85	Louise Manning	11	Sep	82
1.85	Jayne Barnetson	21	Jul	84
1.84	Ursula Fay	6	Aug	83
1.83	Jo Jennings	26	Jul	85
1.83	Tracey Clarke	2	Aug	87
1.83	Aileen Wilson	8	Jul	00
1.82	Elaine Hickey	9	Aug	80
1.82	Kerry Roberts	16	Jul	83
10 1.82	Susan Jones	20	May	94
1.81	Barbara Simmonds	22	Jul	78
1.81	Lea Haggett (U15)	6	Jun	86

Pole Vault
3.80	Hannah Olson (U15)	8	Jun	02
3.75	Natalie Olson	16	Jun	02
3.60	Fiona Harrison	25	May	98
3.55	Lindsay Hodges	14	Aug	99
3.50 i	Kim Skinner (U15)	22	Dec	01
3.40		12	Aug	01
3.44	Clare Ridgley	10	Sep	94
3.40	Clare Neve	28	Jul	02
3.30	Rhian Clarke	4	Jul	93
3.30	Eilidh Dorrian	20	Jul	02
10 3.20	Rebecca Roles	31	Aug	96
3.20	Ellie Spain	13	Sep	98
3.20 i	Kirsty Maguire	20	Feb	99
3.20	Kate Dennison	15	Jul	00
3.20 i	Sunny Brar	4	Feb	01
3.20	Rachel Gibbens	12	May	01
3.20	Claire Holmes	23	Sep	01
3.20	Kimberley Smith	18	Aug	02

Long Jump
6.45	Margaret Cheetham	18	Aug	84
6.32	Georgina Oladapo	23	Jul	83
6.30	Fiona May (U15)	7	Jul	84
6.27		14	Jun	86
6.26	Jo Wise	31	May	87
6.25	Sue Hearnshaw	9	Jul	77
6.24	Sarah Claxton	15	Jun	96
6.23	Sue Scott	27	Jul	68
6.22	Ann Wilson	18	Sep	66
6.22	Michelle Stone	28	Apr	84
10 6.18	Sheila Parkin	4	Aug	62
6.15	Zainab Ceesay	20	Aug	00
6.14	Bev Kinch	26	Jul	80
6.13	Sonya Henry	7	Jul	85
6.13	Jade Johnson	28	May	95
6.12	Karen Glen	10	Aug	80

wind assisted
6.49	Margaret Cheetham (U15)	4	Sep	83
6.49		23	Sep	84
6.47	Fiona May	28	Jun	86
6.41	Sue Hearnshaw	9	Jul	77
6.34	Sarah Claxton	12	Jul	96
6.33	Sue Scott	27	Aug	68
6.28	Bev Kinch	6	Sep	80
6.24	Jade Johnson	28	May	95
6.15	Sue Mapstone	27	May	72
6.15	Karen Glen	5	Jul	80

Triple Jump
12.14	Jayne Ludlow	21	May	94
12.10	Rachel Brenton	21	Jul	01
12.01 i	Emily Parker	25	Feb	01
11.98		14	Jul	01
11.93	Sandra Alaneme	20	Jul	02
11.87	Angela Barratt	21	Jul	01
11.83	Carly Robson	7	Jul	00
11.82	Julia Johnson	30	Jun	96
11.77	Sally Peake	11	Aug	02
11.76	Allison McAllister	26	May	01
11.76	Kosnatu Abdulai	27	May	01 10
11.71	Hayley Warrilow	30	Jun	96
11.68 i	Syreeta Williams	16	Feb	97
11.64	Rachel Peacock	19	Jul	97
11.61	Aisha Myton	30	Jul	00
11.60	Imogen Miles	12	Jul	02

wind assisted
12.27	Rachel Brenton	21	Jul	01
12.07	Rachel Peacock	18	Jul	98
12.05	Emily Parker	2	Sep	01
12.03	Angela Barratt	17	Jun	01
11.89	Sally Peake	11	Aug	02
11.75	Michelle Doherty	21	Jul	01
11.69	Claire Quigg	18	Jul	98
11.68	Rachel Hogg	18	Jul	98
11.60	Lara Richards	15	Aug	99

Shot
15.08	Justine Buttle	16	Aug	86
14.40	Susan King	17	May	81
14.04	Mary Anderson	6	May	84
14.03 i	Terri Salt	19	Mar	83
13.77		17	Sep	83
13.94	Jenny Bloss	13	May	67
13.89 i	Alison Grey	11	Feb	89
13.83		20	May	89
13.68 i	Philippa Roles	26	Feb	94
13.65		6	Aug	94
13.64	Cynthia Gregory	20	Aug	80
13.58 i	Natalie Hart	19	Mar	88
13.32		28	Aug	88
13.49	Lana Newton	11	Jul	75 10
13.46	Julie Dunkley	22	Jun	96
13.35	Carol Cooksley	6	Sep	86
13.35	Claire Smithson	4	Jul	99
13.24	Myrtle Augee	2	Aug	81
13.20	Jayne Thornton	9	Jul	86

Discus

51.60	Emma Merry	27	Jun	90
49.56	Jane Aucott	3	Aug	85
49.36	Claire Smithson	10	Jul	99
48.88	Philippa Roles	13	Aug	94
48.84	Karen Pugh	7	Aug	82
47.58	Catherine Bradley	14	Jul	84
47.54	Lauren Keightley	12	Jul	95
47.50	Sarah Symonds	16	May	90
47.24	Amanda Barnes	3	Aug	85
10 46.76	Fiona Condon	6	Aug	77
46.55	Emma Carpenter	5	Sep	98
46.34	Janette Picton	25	Mar	79
45.93	Joanne Street	3	Jul	99
45.72	Sarah Winckless	1	Jul	90
45.52	Jayne Thornton	12	May	86

Hammer

48.94	Frances Miller	12	Jul	01
48.66	Zoe Derham	16	Aug	97
47.68	Diana Holden	31	Jul	91
47.62	Nicola Dudman	11	Jun	00
46.98	Helen Arnold	29	Jul	95
46.82	Carys Parry	30	Aug	97
45.70	Laura Chalmers	15	Sep	02
45.58	Julie Lavender	13	Sep	92
45.54	Laura Douglas	26	Jun	99
10 45.15	Angela Lockley	12	Aug	01
44.70	Rachael Beverley	15	Jul	95
44.01	Anna Johnson (U15)	10	Aug	02
43.64	Catherine Garden	30	Apr	95
43.36	Vicki Clark	16	Aug	97
43.10	Lucy Marshall	15	Aug	98

Javelin (1999 Model)

46.94	Louise Watton	12	Jul	02
45.24	Samantha Redd	27	May	00
43.81	Hayley Thomas	12	Jul	02
43.11	Charlotte Rees	28	Aug	00
42.82	Becky Bartlett	8	Sep	01
42.37	Jo Chapman	26	May	01
41.99	Sarah Ellis	27	May	00
41.37	Debbie Collinson	21	Apr	02
41.35	Lauren Therin	6	Jul	00
10 41.11	Alison Siggery	5	Aug	00
41.04	Jo Blair	12	Jul	02
41.01	Rosie Semenytsh	19	Jun	02

Javelin (pre 1999 Model)

56.02	Mandy Liverton	11	Jun	89
53.42	Karen Hough	15	Jul	84
53.22	Kirsty Morrison	15	Aug	92
51.92	Goldie Sayers	17	May	98
51.50	Shelley Holroyd	22	Jul	89
50.82	Nicky Emblem	19	Jun	87
50.04	Kim Lisbon	19	Feb	84
50.02	Angelique Pullen	31	Aug	85
49.24	Jacqui Barclay	7	Aug	82
10 49.00	Kelly Morgan	27	Apr	96
48.34	Fatima Whitbread	29	Aug	77

Heptathlon (1985 Tables) Senior

5208	Michelle Stone	30	Sep	84
5194	Jessica Ennis	4	Aug	02
5184	Claire Phythian	20	Aug	89
4901	Phyllis Agbo	28	Apr	02
4815 w	Julie Hollman	2	May	93
4807		30	May	93

Heptathlon (1985 Tables) with 80mH

5037	Michelle Stone	1	Jul	84
5031	Yinka Idowu	18	Sep	88
4945	Phyllis Agbo	24	Jun	01
4915	Denise Lewis	24	Jul	88
4861	Clover Wynter-Pink	26	Jun	94
4841	Rebecca Lewis	18	Sep	94
4839	Jackie Kinsella	21	Jul	85
4830 w	Katherine Livesey	22	Sep	96
4790		28	Jul	96
4794	Claire Phythian	22	May	88
4780	Danielle Freeman	23	Jun	96 10
4746	Chloe Cozens	22	Sep	96
4742	Julie Hollman	26	Sep	93
4673	Denise Bolton	19	Sep	93
4666	Tina Thirwell	20	Sep	98
4657	Rebecca Jones	4	Jul	99

with 100mH

5071	Debbie Marti	5	Jun	83
4661	Suzanne Sherratt	23	Aug	81

3000 Metres Track Walk

14:04.1	Susan Ashforth	19	May	85
14:09.81	Amy Hales	19	Sep	98
14:17.96 i	Katie Ford	28	Feb	98
14:20.70	Sophie Hales	15	Sep	01
14:21.0	Julie Drake	25	Jun	85
14:21.90	Katie Stones	15	Sep	01

5000 Metres Track Walk

23:55.27	Susan Ashforth	25	May	85
24:22.3	Vicky Lawrence	21	Jun	86
24:34.6	Tracy Devlin	17	Sep	89
24:45.4	Karen Eden	9	Jul	78
24:57.5	Angela Hodd	24	Jun	86
25:11.46	Nicola Phillips	21	Aug	99
25:13.8	Carla Jarvis	2	Jun	91
25:15.3	Vicky Lupton	3	Sep	88
25:18.5	Jill Barrett	16	Aug	80
25:20.0	Katie Ford	10	Sep	97 10
25:25.02	Nina Howley	31	Jul	94
25:25.80	Kim Macadam	25	May	85
25:26.41	Becky Tisshaw	6	Jul	97
25:31.14	Zena Lindley	4	Jun	89
25:31.5	Sophie Hales	29	Sep	01

5k Road - where superior to track time

23:57	Sarah Brown	6	Dec	80
24:20	Karen Eden	3	Dec	78

10000 Metres Track Walk

51:00.0	Karen Nipper	21	Feb	81
53:34.1	Vicky Lupton	5	Sep	87

UNDER 15

100 Metres

11.67	Katharine Merry	13	May	89
11.86	Hayley Clements	2	Jul	83
11.89	Joanne Gardner	20	Aug	77
11.92	Jane Parry (U13)	20	Aug	77
11.95	Tatum Nelson	7	Aug	93
12.00	Diane Smith	15	Sep	89
12.02	Renate Chinyou	28	Aug	88
12.02	Sarah Wilhelmy	28	May	94
12.02	Amy Spencer	29	Jul	00
12.07	Margaret Cheetham	29	Jul	83
12.08	Carley Wenham	13	Jul	02
12.09	Libby Alder	8	Jul	95

wind assisted

11.47	Katharine Merry	17	Jun	89
11.67	Tatum Nelson	10	Jul	93
11.78	Jane Parry	8	Aug	78
11.84	Janis Walsh	26	May	74
11.88	Sarah Claxton	9	Jul	94
11.92	Sinead Johnson	11	Aug	01

hand timing

11.8	Janis Walsh	7	Jul	74
11.8	Joanne Gardner	2	Jul	77
11.9	Sonia Lannaman	9	Aug	69
11.9	Linsey Macdonald	26	Aug	78
11.9	Jane Perry	22	Apr	79
11.9	Etta Kessebeh	11	Jul	80

hand timing - wind assisted

11.7	Diane Smith	30	Jul	89
11.8	Sonia Lannaman	30	May	70
11.8	Debbie Bunn (U13)	28	Jun	75
11.8	Delmena Doyley	6	Jul	79

200 Metres

23.72	Katharine Merry	17	Jun	89
23.90	Diane Smith	3	Sep	89
24.05	Jane Parry	16	Jul	78
24.31	Amy Spencer	8	Jul	00
24.39	Hayley Clements	3	Jul	83
24.44	Rachael Kay	8	Jul	95
24.51	Tatum Nelson	8	Aug	93
24.54	Sarah Wilhelmy	31	Jul	94
24.58	Simmone Jacobs	25	Jul	81
24.58	Donna Fraser	22	Aug	87
24.59	Janet Smith	30	Jul	83

wind assisted

23.54	Katharine Merry	30	Jul	89
23.99	Sarah Wilhelmy	9	Jul	94
24.24	Amy Spencer	8	Jul	00
24.25	Vernicha James	11	Jul	98
24.35	Tatum Nelson	27	Jun	93
24.41	Lesley Owusu	9	Jul	93

hand timing

23.8	Janis Walsh	23	Jun	74
24.1	Sonia Lannaman	29	Aug	70

hand timing - wind assisted

23.6	Jane Parry (U13)	9	Jul	77
23.8	Diane Smith	9	Sep	89

300 Metres

41.1	Maria Bolsover	10	Apr	94

400 Metres

56.7	Jane Colebrook	25	Jun	72

800 Metres

2:06.5	Rachel Hughes	19	Jul	82
2:08.7	Emma Langston	12	Jul	86
2:09.58	Sally Ludlam	8	Jun	75
2:09.6	Isabel Linaker	1	Aug	90
2:09.77	Lorraine Baker	19	Aug	78
2:09.80	Hannah Curnock	15	Aug	92
2:10.1	Lesley Kiernan	9	Jul	71
2:10.3	Carol Pannell	9	Jul	71
2:10.6	Christina Boxer	10	Jul	71
2:10.6	Natalie Tait	12	Jul	86
2:10.66	Amanda Pritchard	15	Jul	94
2:10.76	Carolyn Wells	19	Aug	78

1000 Metres

2:51.4	Hayley Haining	20	Aug	86

1500 Metres

4:23.45	Isabel Linaker	7	Jul	90
4:27.9	Joanne Davis	9	Jul	88
4:29.0	Claire Allen	8	Jul	89
4:29.6	Lynne MacDougall	16	Jul	79
4:29.9	Heidi Hosking	9	Jul	88
4:30.12	Charlotte Browning	3	Jul	02
4:30.4	Claire Nicholson	18	Jun	87
4:30.45	Nikki Hamblin	13	Jul	02
4:31.12	Karen Hughes	31	Aug	79
4:31.45	Amanda Alford	22	Jul	78
4:31.6	Michelle Lavercombe	13	Jun	81
4:31.70	Jennifer Mockler	4	Aug	96

1 Mile

4:54.7	Hannah Curnock	9	Sep	92

3000 Metres

9:44.39	mx	Emily Pidgeon	6	May	02

75 Metres Hurdles (2'6")

10.86	Heather Jones	17	Jun	01
10.93	Rachel Halstead-Peel	27	Jul	85
11.00	Louise Fraser	27	Jul	85
11.00	Danielle Selley	20	Jun	98
11.01	Nathalie Byer	16	Aug	80
11.06	Jessica Ennis	30	Jul	00
11.06	Phyllis Agbo	17	Sep	00
11.07	Symone Belle	10	Jul	99
11.08	Nicola Hall	29	May	94
11.08	Sara McGreavy	12	Jul	97
11.09	Catherine Murphy	6	Aug	88
11.09	Orla Bermingham	25	Aug	90

wind assisted

10.95	Symone Belle	9	Jul	99
11.00	Leah McGuire	7	Jul	01
11.01	Naomi Hodge-Dallaway	8	Jul	95

hand timing
10.8	Symone Belle	29	Aug	99

hand timing - wind assisted
10.7	Orla Bermingham	14	Jul	90
10.8	Nathalie Byer	12	Jul	80
10.8	Ann Girvan	12	Jul	80

80 Metres Hurdles (2'6") U17
11.44	Catherine Crawford	4	Jul	99

High Jump
1.83	Ursula Fay	5	Jun	82
1.81	Debbie Marti	18	Sep	82
1.81	Lea Haggett	6	Jun	86
1.80	Jo Jennings	12	Aug	84
1.79 i	Julia Charlton	24	Feb	80
1.78		13	Jul	80
1.79	Aileen Wilson	4	Jul	98
1.78	Claire Summerfield	28	Jul	79
1.78	Dominique Blaize	30	Jun	02
1.75	Anne Gilson	2	Jun	73
1.75	Claire Smith	8	Aug	82
1.75	Jane Falconer	10	Jun	89
1.75	Stephanie Pywell	6	Jul	01

Pole Vault
3.80	Hannah Olson	8	Jun	02
3.50	Fiona Harrison	24	Aug	96
3.50 i	Kim Skinner	22	Dec	01
3.40		12	Aug	01
3.20	Natalie Olson	9	Sep	00
3.10	Cariann Cutts	14	Aug	99
2.90	Becky Lilley	30	Jul	02
2.85	Zoe Holland	25	Jul	99

Long Jump
6.34	Margaret Cheetham	14	Aug	83
6.30	Fiona May	7	Jul	84
6.07	Georgina Oladapo	21	Jun	81
5.98	Sandy French	22	Jul	78
5.93	Jackie Harris	10	Jul	87
5.91	Symone Belle	29	Aug	99
5.88	Sue Scott	11	Aug	66
5.86	Tammy McCammon	18	Aug	91
5.86	Rebekah Passley	12	Aug	01
5.85	Kim Hagger	20	Aug	76
5.81	Yvonne Hallett	24	Aug	86
5.80	Monique Parris	23	May	98

wind assisted
6.49	Margaret Cheetham	4	Sep	83
6.05	Katharine Merry	18	Sep	88
6.02	Michelle Stone	10	Jul	82
5.99	Sandy French	8	Jul	78
5.86	Donna Maylor	13	Jul	96
5.85	Karen Glen	8	Jul	78

Triple Jump
11.47	Ruth Hatch	23	Sep	01

wind assisted
11.48	Ruth Hatch	23	Sep	01

Shot (4kg)
12.16	Susan King	8	Sep	79

Shot (3.25kg)
14.27	Susan King	19	May	79
13.88 i	Chloe Edwards	21	Apr	01
13.69	Gloria Achille	21	Jun	80
13.61	Justine Buttle	4	Aug	84
13.22	Emily Steele	23	Jul	89
13.11	Amy Wilson	2	Sep	95
13.08	Ashley Morris	11	Aug	84
13.05	Tracy Page	21	Jun	86
13.04	Navdeep Dhaliwal	17	May	92
12.97	Alison Grey	23	Aug	87
12.96	April Kalu	23	Jun	96
12.95	Cynthia Gregory	7	Jul	78

Discus
44.12	Philippa Roles	30	Aug	92
41.92	Catherine Garden	12	Sep	93
40.92	Sandra McDonald	24	Jun	78
40.84	Natalie Kerr	24	Jul	94
40.54	Claire Smithson	25	May	97
40.44	Catherine MacIntyre	12	Sep	82
40.34	Natalie Hart	23	Mar	86
40.22	Emma Merry	27	Aug	88
40.18	Kelly Mellis	17	Sep	94
40.14	Clare Tank	29	Aug	88
39.76	Alix Gallagher	6	Jun	87
39.38	Charladee Clarke	1	Sep	85
39.38	Alex Hajipavlis	13	Aug	95

Hammer (4kg)
44.01	Anna Johnson	10	Aug	02

Hammer (3.25kg)
45.15	Anna Johnson	14	Sep	02
42.18	Laura Chalmers	22	Aug	00
40.70	Catherine Marvin	9	Sep	01
39.75	Shaeleen Bruce	9	Jul	00
39.35	Kirsty Walters	8	May	99
38.32	Sarah Holt	15	Jul	00

Hammer (3kg)
51.00	Anna Johnson	3	Sep	02

Javelin (1999 Model)
41.44	Louise Watton	8	Sep	01
40.78	Hayley Thomas	11	Aug	01
38.01	Lauren Therin	15	Aug	99
37.40	Rebecca Pyne	20	Jun	99
37.22	Kylie Clarke	26	Aug	02
36.37	Melissa O'Neill	1	Sep	01
36.03	Kelly-Jane Berry	28	Aug	00
35.98	Debbie Collinson	24	Jun	00

Javelin (pre 1999 Model)
48.40	Mandy Liverton	31	Aug	87
46.98	Kirsty Morrison	30	Jun	90
43.16	Shelley Holroyd	27	Jun	87
43.08	Karen Hough	4	Sep	82
42.70	Emily Steele	23	Sep	89
41.56	Goldie Sayers	12	Jul	96

Pentathlon (with 800m & 75m hdls)

3518	Katharine Merry	18	Sep	88
3509	Aileen Wilson	20	Sep	98
3333	Jackie Harris	27	Jun	87
3296	Claire Everett	19	Sep	93
3273	Dominique Blaize	30	Jun	02
3236	Emma Perkins	10	Sep	00
3225	Amy Nuttell	26	Jun	94
3216	Sally Gunnell	23	Aug	80
3213	Julie Hollman	22	Sep	91
3207	Louise Hazel	17	Sep	00
3202	Emily Bonnett	22	Sep	02
3195	Julia Charlton	10	May	80
3193	Sam Foster	26	Jun	94

with 80mH

3444	Jane Shepherd	16	Jul	83
3350	Claire Smith	3	Jul	82
3295	Paula Khouri	16	Jul	83
3283	Jackie Kinsella	16	Jul	83
3260	Debbie Marti	14	Aug	82

2000 Metres Track Walk

9:35.0	Karen Eden	17	Jun	77

2500 Metres Track Walk

11:50.0	Susan Ashforth	12	Sep	84

3000 Metres Track Walk

14:44.39	Rebecca Mersh	21	Sep	02
14:56.4	Sarah Bennett	26	Sep	93
15:00.0	Susan Ashforth	19	Jun	84
15:00.6	Sally Wish	16	Sep	72
15:06.69	Kelly Mann	30	May	98
15:10.28	Jenny Gagg	21	Sep	02
15:14.6	Amy Hales	31	Aug	96
15:16.4	Natalie Watson	31	Aug	96
15:18.3	Vicky Lawrence	17	Jul	83
15:19.0	Tracy Devlin	28	Mar	87
15:25.06	Sophie Hales	18	Sep	99
15:26.63	Nicola Phillips	20	Sep	97
15:28.0	Kim Macadam	3	Sep	83

short track

15:18.7	Sharon Tonks	19	Mar	83

3k Road - where superior to track time

14:47	Amy Hales	23	Jun	96
14:48	Nikola Ellis	16	Sep	84
14:55	Lisa Langford	6	Dec	80
14:58	Carolyn Brown	19	Aug	87
14:59	Julie Snead	16	Sep	84
15:07	Stephanie Cooper	10	Dec	83
15:09	Angela Hodd	29	Jul	84
15:10	Vicky Lawrence	15	Apr	84

5000 Metres Track Walk

26:47.0hc	Amy Hales	15	Dec	96
26:52.0	Nina Howley	14	Sep	92
27:13.8	Rebecca Mersh	29	Sep	02

5k Road - where superior to track time

26:20	Tracy Devlin	14	Feb	87
26:59	Joanne Clarke	9	Jun	83

UNDER 13

75 Metres

9.83	Amy Spencer	6	Sep	98
9.98	Jenny Igbokwe	3	Sep	00
10.01	Jane Chadwick	3	Sep	00
10.02	Charlene Lashley	6	Sep	98
10.04	Natasha White	1	Sep	02

wind unconfirmed

9.95	Megan Beesley	26	Aug	02

wind assisted

9.96	Joanne Wainwright	8	Sep	96

hand timing

9.7	Carley Wenham	12	Jul	00
9.8	Amy Spencer	19	Jul	98
9.8	Rachel Follos	18	Jul	99
9.8	Felicity James	1	Jul	01
9.9	Cherie Pierre	21	Jul	96
9.9	Charlene Lashley	17	May	98
9.9	Nicola Gossman	2	May	99
9.9	Sinead Johnson	18	Jul	99
9.9	Leah McGuire	30	Aug	99

wind unconfirmed

9.8	Jasmine Rowe	21	Jul	02

80 Metres

10.2	Jane Riley	1	Jun	85
10.2	Helen Seery	20	May	89

100 Metres

11.92	Jane Parry	20	Aug	77
12.32	Katharine Merry	24	Jul	87
12.65	Sarah Claxton	4	Jul	92

hand timing

12.1	Katharine Merry	26	Sep	87
12.3	Joanne Gardner	24	Aug	75
12.3	Debbie Bunn	30	Aug	75

hand timing - wind assisted

11.8	Debbie Bunn	28	Jun	75

150 Metres

19.47	Amy Spencer	6	Sep	98
19.69	Louise Dickson	4	Sep	99
19.78	Rebecca Smith	3	Sep	95
19.78	Jane Chadwick	3	Sep	00

hand timing

19.1	Emma Ania	7	Sep	91
19.1	Emma Heath	18	Jul	99
19.2	Helen Seery	19	Feb	89
19.2	Amy Spencer	28	Jun	98
19.2	Rachel Follos	18	Jul	99
19.2	Stacey Simpson	21	May	00
19.2	Laura Cox	21	May	00
19.3	Alanna Wain	29	Jun	97
19.3	Natalie Pearson	21	May	00

200 Metres

24.49	Jane Parry	20	Aug	77
25.87	Amy Spencer	2	Aug	98
25.88	Myra McShannon	4	Sep	88
25.95	Myra McShannon	20	Aug	76

hand timing

24.2	Jane Parry	28 May	77
25.4	Katharine Merry	21 Jun	87
25.4	Myra McShannon	8 May	88
25.6	Debbie Bunn	5 Jul	75
25.6	Joanne Gardner	24 Aug	75
25.6	Jane Riley	30 Jun	85

wind assisted

23.6	Jane Parry	9 Jul	77

600 Metres

1:37.3	Lisa Lanini	19 Mar	00
1:37.5	Hannah Wood	17 Jul	94
1:38.5	Jenny Meadows	4 Apr	93
1:38.9	Emma Ward	17 Jul	94

800 Metres

2:14.8	Janet Lawrence	10 Jul	71
2:15.05	Rachel Hughes	11 Sep	81
2:16.1	Lisa Lanini	5 Aug	00
2:16.8	Angela Davies	25 Jul	83
2:17.20	Emma Langston	7 Sep	84
2:17.6	Michelle Wilkinson	22 Jun	85
2:17.9	Melissa Rooney	20 Jun	81

1000 Metres

3:00.1	Charlotte Moore	25 Aug	97
3:05.9	Natalie Yates	27 May	01
3:06.4	Charlotte Browning	6 Aug	00
3:07.5	Rebecca Taylor	16 Jun	02
3:08.1	Cheryl Hammond	4 Jul	99

1200 Metres

3:46.4	Lisa Lanini	18 Jul	99
3:49.1	Megan Foley	2 Jul	00
3:49.6	Non Stanford	22 Jul	01
3:50.4	Lynsey Jepson	1 Aug	99
3:50.9	Charlotte Browning	4 Jul	00
3:51.1	Natalie Yates	1 Jul	01
3:51.3	Stephanie Bloor	2 Jul	00
3:52.5	Emily Pidgeon	20 May	01
3:52.9	Emma Hunt	17 May	98
3:53.1	Sara Luck	11 Jul	99

1500 Metres

4:36.9	Rachel Hughes	20 Jul	81
4:39.3	Charlotte Moore	2 Aug	97
4:42.1	Stacey Washington	18 Jul	84

1 Mile

5:22.2	Emily Pidgeon	26 Aug	01

70 Metres Hurdles (2'3")

11.17	Anne-Marie Massey	3 Sep	95
11.24	Alana Watson	8 Sep	96
11.35	Nafalya Francis	27 Aug	01
11.46	Sandra Gunn	13 Aug	88
11.51	Kelly Marshall	11 Jul	98
11.55	Anna Salter	14 Sep	97
11.55	Jade Bee	28 Jul	02

wind unconfirmed

11.37	Vicky Fleetwood	26 Aug	02

wind assisted

11.02	Nafalya Francis	27 Aug	01
11.21	Sandra Gunn	4 Sep	88
11.26	Catriona Burr	4 Sep	88
11.32	Joanne Baker	3 Sep	00

hand timing

11.0	Katharine Merry	20 Sep	87
11.0	Justine Roach	13 Sep	97
11.1	Sarah Claxton	14 Jun	92
11.1	Emma Makin	26 May	98
11.1	Leah McGuire	9 May	99
11.1	Nafalya Francis	1 Jul	01
11.2	Clare Stuart	19 Jun	88

75 Metres Hurdles (2'6")

11.78	Caroline Pearce	7 Aug	93

hand timing

11.3	Katharine Merry	26 Sep	87

High Jump

1.69	Katharine Merry	26 Sep	87
1.68	Julia Charlton	6 Aug	78
1.65	Debbie Marti	20 Sep	80
1.65	Jane Falconer	20 Sep	87
1.63	Lindsey Marriott	11 Aug	79
1.63	Paula Davidge	13 Sep	81
1.60	Denise Wilkinson	17 Jul	76
1.59	Julie O'Dell	28 Jul	74
1.59	Julia Cockram	18 May	80
1.59	Bev Green	30 Aug	86

Pole Vault

3.10	Hannah Olson	9 Sep	00
2.80	Kim Skinner	24 May	00
2.40	Jasmin Hicks	15 Sep	02

Long Jump

5.71	Sandy French	20 Aug	76
5.45	Sarah Wilhelmy	31 Aug	92
5.43	Margaret Cheetham	19 Sep	81
5.42	Katharine Merry	7 Jun	87
5.40	Kerry Gray	1 Sep	84
5.38	Toyin Campbell	6 Aug	77
5.35	Debbie Bunn	7 Sep	75
5.34	Fiona May	12 Jun	82
5.33	Kathryn Dowsett	7 Sep	91
5.32	Ann Flannery	18 Sep	82

wind assisted

5.55	Katharine Merry	10 Jul	87

Triple Jump

9.55	Fiona Ferbrache	14 Jul	94

Shot (3.25kg)

12.20	Susan King	3 Sep	77
10.84	Eden Francis	16 Sep	01
10.77	Michele Morgan	19 Jun	82
10.54	Claire Burnett	1 Sep	85

Shot (2.72kg)

12.07	Becki Hall	14	Aug	01
11.59	Eden Francis	8	Sep	01
11.53	Finesse Thompson	10	Jun	02
11.50	Nimi Iniekio	5	Sep	99
11.42	Candee Rhule	29	Jul	00
11.04	Amy Wilson	12	Sep	93
10.91	Catherine Garden	8	Sep	91
10.83	Nicola Stevenson	27	Aug	01
10.72	Kayleigh Southgate	3	Sep	00
10.60	Lucy Rann	29	Aug	93

Discus (1kg)

34.22	Catherine Garden	25	Aug	91
31.34	Sandra Biddlecombe	9	Sep	90
30.54	Fiona Condon	15	Sep	73

Discus (750g)

39.44	Catherine Garden	8	Sep	91
37.64	Sandra Biddlecombe	4	Jul	90
34.80	Rebecca Saunders	28	Aug	00
34.61	Becki Hall	27	Aug	01
32.70	Claire Smithson	26	Aug	95
32.52	Candace Schofield	7	Sep	97
32.16	Christina Carding	25	Jul	99
31.52	Finesse Thompson	1	Sep	02
31.46	Sian Howe	21	Sep	96
30.54	Eleanor Garden	10	Sep	89

Hammer (4kg)

19.40	Ruth Hay	3	Sep	00

Hammer (3.25kg)

22.76	Ruth Hay	7	Sep	00

Javelin (600g 1999 model)

31.16	Laura Carr	1	Sep	01

Javelin (600g original model)

32.02	Claire Lacey	20	Sep	87
31.60	Emma Langston	2	Sep	84
31.44	Alison Moffitt	6	Jul	82
31.28	Eve Russell	2	Sep	95

Javelin (400g)

38.07	Louise Watton	12	Sep	99
36.06	Samantha Redd	1	Sep	96
34.27	Laura Carr	29	Jul	01
33.90	Lauren Therin	6	Sep	98
33.46	Emma Claydon	26	Jul	92
33.32	Melanie Vaggers	27	Sep	94
32.60	Candace Schofield	10	Aug	97
32.38	Eve Russell	30	Jul	95
31.87	Georgina Field	31	Aug	98
31.74	Josie Jamieson	28	Aug	99

Pentathlon (Under 15 implements)

2607	Jane Shepherd	6	Jun	81
2604	Alison Kerboas	19	Sep	93
2541 ?	Jane Falconer	23	Aug	87

Pentathlon

2811	Katharine Merry	20	Sep	87
2551	Sarah Wilhelmy	2	Aug	92
2519	Naida Bromley	30	Aug	99
2505	Caroline Pearce	26	Sep	93
2451	Seonaid Ferry	17	Jul	94
2419	Donna Medlock	7	Aug	94

1000 Metres Track Walk

4:53.4	Fiona McGorum	9	Sep	01
5:01.9	Rebecca Mersh	12	Jul	01
5:11.1	Amy Hales	4	Sep	94
5:12.9	Laura Gimson	6	Jul	02
5:14.6	Natasha Fox	31	Aug	98
5:17.0	Elizabeth Ryan	10	Jun	79
5:18.0	Margaret O'Rawe	28	Sep	80
5:19.3	Jemma Black	15	Oct	95
5:21.0	Sarah Bennett	30	Sep	90
5:22.6	Carley Tomlin	29	May	00

1k Road - where superior to track time

4:42	Kelly Mann	23	Sep	95
4:43	Natalie Watson	23	Sep	95
4:50	Sarah Bennett	23	Sep	90

2000 Metres Track Walk

10:09.0	Kelly Mann	10	Sep	95
10:17.0	Sarah Bennett	27	Sep	92
10:19.0	Joanne Ashforth	7	Sep	85
10:19.8	Fiona McGorum	29	Sep	01
10:31.0	Claire Walker	7	Sep	85
10:31.0	Jo Pickett	25	Apr	92
10:32.0	Karen Eden	25	Aug	75
10:37.0	Karen Bowers	29	Sep	79
10:38.1	Rebecca Mersh	29	Sep	01
10:41.0	Amy Hales	7	May	94

2k Road - where superior to track time

10:03	Kelly Mann	23	Jun	96
10:15	Fiona McGorum	5	May	01
10:33	Rebecca Mersh	5	May	01
10:36	Yvette Eden	24	Jan	76
10:38	Hayley Hutchings	28	Sep	96
10:39	Laura Fryer	23	Jun	96
10:42	Natalie Evans	28	Sep	96

2500 Metres Track Walk

12:48.9	Claire Walker	20	Jul	85
12:50.5	Vicky Lawrence	4	Jul	82

2.5k Road - where superior to track time

12:39	Amy Hales	16	Oct	93
12:41	Stephanie Cooper	1	May	82

3000 Metres Track Walk

15:41.0	Kelly Mann	30	Jul	95

3k Road - where superior to track time

15:25	Nicola Greenfield	21	Mar	87
15:44	Sarah Bennett	1	Mar	92

UK CLUB RECORDS

MEN

Seniors

4 x 100m	39.49	Haringey	1 Jun	91
4 x 200m	1:23.5	Team Solent	19 Jul	87
4 x 400m	3:04.48	Team Solent	29 Jun	90
1600m Medley	3:20.8	Wolverhampton & Bilston	1 Jun	75
4 x 800m	7:24.4*	North Staffs and Stone	27 Jul	65
4 x 1500m	15:12.6	Bristol	5 Aug	75

* = 4 x 880y time less 2.8sec

Under 20

4 x 100m	41.30	Victoria Park	14 Aug	76
4 x 200m	1:27.6	Enfield	13 Jun	82
4 x 400m	3:15.3	Enfield	5 Sep	82
1600m Medley	3:31.6	Cardiff	14 Aug	71
4 x 800m	7:35.3	Liverpool H	14 Aug	90
4 x 1500m	16:04.3	Blackburn	15 Sep	79
4 x 110H	1:04.8	Oundle Sch	19 May	79

Under 17

4 x 100m	42.22	Thames V H	24 Jun	89
4 x 200m	1:31.2	Herc Wimb	12 Jul	78
4 x 400m	3:23.1 o	Enfield	1 Oct	80
	3:23.2	Haringey	26 Jul	88
1600m Medley	3:36.1	Thurrock	13 Jun	84
4 x 800m	7:52.1	Clydebank	29 Aug	87
4 x 1500m	16:27.0	Liverpool H	14 Sep	88

Under 15

4 x 100m	44.62	Sale	29 Aug	93
4 x 200m	1:36.9	Belgrave	19 Sep	93
4 x 400m	3:31.5o?	Ayr Seaforth	5 Sep	82
	3:31.6	Shaftesbury B	26 Jul	88
1600m Medley	3:48.4	Blackheath	28 Sep	86
4 x 800m	8:13.28o?	Clydebank	2 Sep	89
	8:16.8	Shaftesbury B	14 Sep	88
4 x 1500m	17:52.4 o	Stretford	22 Oct	85
	18:18.4	Tonbridge	6 Jul	80

Under 13

4 x 100m	50.32	Shaftesbury B	5 Sep	99
4 x 200m	1:49.7	Braintree	29 Aug	94
4 x 400m	4:04.5	Blackheath	12 Sep	93
1600m Medley	4:13.7	Blackheath	28 Sep	86
4 x 800m	9:29.8	Sale	28 Jun	88

WOMEN

Seniors

4 x 100m	43.79	Hounslow	18 Sep	82
4 x 200m	1:35.15	Stretford	14 Jul	91
4 x 400m	3:31.62	Essex Ladies	31 May	92
1600m Medley	3:50.6	Coventry Godiva	5 May	84
3 x 800m	6:32.4	Cambridge H	29 Jun	74
4 x 800m	8:41.0	Cambridge H	26 May	75

Under 20

4 x 100m	46.80	Birchfield	26 Sep	98
4 x 200m	1:46.4	Millfield School	11 May	00
4 x 400m	3:50.71	Liverpool H	8 Sep	02
3 x 800m	7:33.2	Essex Ladies	12 Jun	94

Under 17

4 x 100m	47.52o	Hounslow	2 Oct	82
	47.8	B of Enfield	20 Jul	75
	47.8	Croydon	15 Sep	82
	48.08	Wigan & D	6 Sep	92
4 x 200m	1:42.2	London Oly.	19 Aug	72
4 x 400m	3:52.1	City of Hull	3 Jul	82
1600m Medley	4:07.8	Warrington	14 Aug	75
3 x 800m	6:46.5	Haslemere	15 Sep	79
	6:46.5	Bromley L	1 Jul	84
4 x 800m	8:53.1	Havering	24 May	80

Under 15

4 x 100m	48.5	Haringey	15 Sep	79
	49.08	Radley L	16 Jul	83
4 x 200m	1:44.0	Bristol	15 Sep	79
3 x 800m	6:39.8	Havering	13 Sep	78
4 x 800m	9:21.4	Sale	5 Aug	78

Under 13

4 x 100m	53.09	Wigan	5 Sep	99
4 x 200m	1:52.5	Mitcham	24 Jul	82
3 x 800m	7:18.0	Mid Hants	14 Sep	83
4 x 800m	10:02.4	Warrington	16 Sep	75

o overage by current rules

AAA INDOOR CHAMPIONSHIPS & NORWICH UNION INDOOR TRIALS
Cardiff 2 - 3 February 2002

A thrilling 60 metres final saw Jason Gardener just beat Mark Lewis-Francis by one hundreth of a second. Amy Spencer was the star in the women's sprints and Niobe Menendez set a new British record in the 3,000 metres walk.

MEN

60 Metres (3 Feb)
1. Jason Gardener — 6.52
2. Mark Lewis-Francis — 6.53
3. Christian Malcolm — 6.67
4. Doug Turner — 6.69
5. Akinola Lashore — 6.70
6. Marlon Dickson — 6.71

200 Metres (2 Feb)
1. Doug Turner — 21.24
2. Gary Ryan IRL — 21.45
3. Brendon Ghent — 22.10

400 Metres (3 Feb)
1. Robert Daly IRL — 47.58
2. Tim Benjamin — 47.60
3. James Chatt — 48.62

800 Metres (3 Feb)
1. James McIlroy — 1:51.10
2. Dominic Hall — 1:51.79
3. Terry Feasey — 1:51.95
4. Robert Watkinson — 1:52.12
5. Gary Vickers — 1:52.20

1500 Metres (3 Feb)
1. Tony Whiteman — 3:52.44
2. Angus Maclean — 3:52.67
3. Matthew Shone — 3:52.70
4. Gregg Taylor — 3:53.78
5. James Thie — 3:54.07
6. Steve Sharp — 3:54.09

WOMEN

60 Metres (3 Feb)
1. Joice Maduaka — 7.33
2. Abi Oyepitan — 7.41
3. Susan Burnside — 7.42
4. Donita Benjamin — 7.47
5. Sarah Reilly IRL — 7.47
6. Amanda Forrester — 7.48

200 Metres (2 Feb)
1. Amy Spencer — 23.74
2. Sarah Reilly IRL — 23.97
3. Emily Freeman — 24.13

400 Metres (3 Feb)
1. Catherine Murphy — 52.54
2. Karen Gear — 54.36
3. Susan Williams — 55.84

800 Metres (3 Feb)
1. Jenny Meadows — 2:05.07
2. Emma Davies — 2:05.80
3. Jemma Simpson — 2:07.45

3000 Metres (3 Feb)
1. Michael East — 8:18.41
2. David Anderson — 8:18.88
3. Ian Grime — 8:18.89
4. Phil Tedd — 8:29.01
5. Kevin Nash — 8:29.32
6. James Fewtrell — 8:35.17

60 Metres Hurdles (3 Feb)
1. Colin Jackson — 7.60
2. Damien Greaves — 7.75
3. Robert Newton — 7.87
4. Tristan Anthony — 8.02
5. Nathan Palmer — 8.02
6= Mensah Elliott — 8.05
6= Andrew Turner — 8.05

High Jump (3 Feb)
1. Ben Challenger — 2.17
2. Ian Holliday — 2.14
3. Mark Mandy IRL — 2.09
4. Darryl Stone — 2.09
5. Richard Aspden — 2.09
6. Luke Crawley — 2.09

Pole Vault (2 Feb)
1. Nick Buckfield — 5.50
2. Tim Thomas — 5.30
3. Paul Williamson — 5.20
4. Scott Simpson — 5.20
5= Mark Beharrell — 4.90
5= Christian Linskey — 4.90

1500 Metres (3 Feb)
1. Natalie Lewis — 4:25.49
2. Julie Mitchell — 4:26.00
3. Alex Carter — 4:28.66
4. Maria Lynch IRL — 4:29.31
5. Claire Martin — 4:32.36
6. Maria Sharp — 4:35.13

60 Metres Hurdles (3 Feb)
1. Diane Allahgreen — 8.01
2. Rachel King — 8.17
3. Melani Wilkins — 8.20
4. Clare Milborrow — 8.40
5. Sarah Claxton — 8.44
6. Helen Worsey — 8.44

High Jump (2 Feb)
1. Susan Jones — 1.90
2. Julia Bennett — 1.84
3. Deidre Ryan IRL — 1.84
4. Dalia Mikneviciute — 1.78
5= Stephanie Higham — 1.73
5= Debbie Marti — 1.73

Long Jump (3 Feb)
1. Gable Garenamotse BOT — 8.01
2. Andre Fernandez — 7.22
3. Dominique Richards — 7.10
4. Mark Lawrence — 6.92
5. Anthony Malcolm — 6.74
6. Simon Roper — 6.74

Triple Jump (2 Feb)
1. Tosin Oke — 15.95
2. Julian Golley — 15.54
3. Martin Rossiter — 15.11

Shot (2 Feb)
1. Erik van Vreumingen NED — 17.38
2. Gary Sollitt — 16.66
3. Iain McMullan — 16.51
4. David Condon — 16.34
5. Bill Fuller — 16.03
6. Nicholas Owen — 16.01

3000 Metres Walk (2 Feb)
1. Robert Heffernan IRL — 11:10.02
2. Colin Griffin IRL — 11:46.03
3. Andi Drake — 11:58.49
4. Dominic King — 12:00.99
5. Cameron Smith — 12:51.12

Heptathlon (Cardiff 9/10 Mar)
1. Barry Thomas — 5403
2. Paul Tohill — 5074
3. James Lowery — 4991
4. Darren Hatton — 4957

Pole Vault (3 Feb)
1. Janine Whitlock — 4.20
2. Sandra van de Geer NED — 4.00
3= Laura Ballotta ITA — 3.90
3= Lucy Webber — 3.90
5. Kate Dennison — 3.80
6= Zoe Brown — 3.70
6= Gael Davies — 3.70

Long Jump (2 Feb)
1. Kelly Sotherton — 6.22
2. Sarah Claxton — 6.20
3. Donita Benjamin — 6.12
4. Julie Hollman — 5.99
5. Kimberley Rothman — 5.94
6. Sarah Wellstead — 5.94

Triple Jump (3 Feb)
1. Ashia Hansen — 13.53
2. Taniesha Scanlon IRL — 13.00
3. Rebecca White — 12.64
4. Nicoleta Chirita ROM — 12.41
5. Katie Evans — 11.88
6. Anna-Maria Thorpe — 11.78

Shot (2 Feb)
1. Helena Engman   SWE   16.27
2. Joanne Duncan   16.01
3. Philippa Roles   15.88
4. Vicki Foster   14.68
5. Maggie Lynes   14.53
6. Eva Massey   14.26

3000 Metres Walk (2 Feb)
1. Gillian O`Sullivan   IRL   12:17.56
2. Niobe Menendez   13:08.64
3. Sharon Tonks   13:57.87

Pentathlon (Cardiff 9/10 Mar)
1. Kelly Sotherton   4166
2. Kate Brewington   3659
3. Ros Gonse   3604
4. Charmaine Johnson   3314
5. Maureen Knight   3209
6. Tina Thirwell   3130

ESP v GB & NI v CZE v FRA v NED Combined Events Indoors
Zaragoza, ESP 26 - 27 January 2002

MEN – Heptathlon
1. Jan Podebradsky   CZE   5764
2. Francisco Caro   ESP   5669
3. Agustin Capella   ESP   5575
4. **Jamie Quarrie**   **5515**
10. **Barry Thomas**   **5367**
13. **John Heanley**   **5295**
14. **Stephen Bonnett**   **5195**

MEN - Team Score
1. Czech Republic   16630
2. Spain   16563
3. France   16340
4. **Great Britain & NI**   **16177**

WOMEN - Team Score
1. France   12188
2. Netherlands   12104
3. **Great Britain & NI**   **11941**

WOMEN – Pentathlon
1. Karin Ruckstuhl   NED   4298
2. Michaela Hejnova   CZE   4212
3. **Kelly Sotherton**   **4188**
4. **Julia Bennett**   **4130**
14. **Laura Redmond**   **3623**
    Julie Hollman   **dnf**

REEBOK UK INTER-COUNTIES CHAMPIONSHIPS & WORLD TRIALS
Wollaton Park, Nottingham 9 February 2002

MEN 12k
1. Sam Haughian   37:04
2. Matt O`Dowd   37:15
3. Ian Hudspith   37:22
4. Matt Smith   37:24
5. Glynn Tromans   37:26
6. Chris Thompson   37:31

JUNIOR MEN 8k
1. Mohammed Farah   25:13
2. Tom Sharland   25:33
3. Steve Ablitt   25:50
4. Matt Bowser   26:01
5. Matt Lole   26:11
6. Chris Watson   26:24

WOMEN 8k
1. Liz Yelling   27:44
2. Helen Pattinson   27:55
3. Jenny Brown   28:04
4. Angela Mudge   28:10
5. Sharon Morris   28:19
6. Lucy Wright   28:22

JUNIOR WOMEN 6k
1. Charlotte Dale   22:11
2. Faye Fullerton   23:13
3. Henrietta Freeman   23:30
4. Freya Murray   23:34
5. Jessica Nugent   23:37
6. Lisa Dobriskey   23:40

UKA WORLD XC SHORT COURSE TRIALS
Newport 4 March 2002

MEN 4k
1. Rob Whalley   11:18
2. Ben Whitby   11:19
3. Phil Mowbray   11:19
4. Spencer Barden   11:20
5. Ben Noad   11:20
6. Steve Vernon   11:28

WOMEN 4k
1. Helen Pattinson   12:45
2. Charlotte Dale   13:10
3. Amanda Wright-Allen   13:11
4. Sonia Thomas   13:17
5. Lucy Elliott   13:18
6. Hayley Yelling   13:20

ENGLISH NATIONAL CROSS COUNTRY CHAMPIONSHIPS
Bristol 23 February 2002

MEN
1. Sam Haughian   39:26
2. Allen Graffin   39:51
3. Emile de Jonge RSA   40:02
4. Matt Smith   40:12

WOMEN
1. Liz Yelling   27:36
2. Amanda Allen   28:39
3. Lucy Elliott   29:04

JUNIOR MEN
1. Lee McCash   30:49
2. Adam Bowden   30:59
3. Andrew Sherman   31:07

JUNIOR WOMEN
1. Jane Potter   17:47
2. Emma Ward   17:51
3. Kate Reed   17:53

U17 MEN
1. Tom Humphries   19:29

U17 WOMEN
1. Katrina Wootton   18:09

U15 WOMEN
1. Charlotte Browning   16:38

U13 WOMEN
1. Emily Pidgeon   12:54

REGIONAL CROSS COUNTRY CHAMPIONSHIPS

Scotland		Wales		Northern Ireland	
Falkirk 23 February 2002		St. Asaph 23 February 2002		Coleraine 16 February 2002	
MEN		**MEN**		**MEN**	
1. Glen Stewart	39:23	1. Ian Mitchell	43:14	1. Gary McClernon	37:38
WOMEN		**WOMEN**		**WOMEN**	
1. Gillian Palmer	30:07	1. Catherine Dugdale	24:13	1. Ann Paul	21:04

NORWICH UNION AAA INDOOR JUNIOR CHAMPIONSHIPS
Birmingham 23 - 24 February 2002

Yet again these championships were a showcase for the future of British ahletics. In the U20 men Edward Dunford, moving up an age group, repeated last year's double of winning the hurdles and the muti-event. Robert Tobin does not even show below, but ran a very fast 46.80 in the U20 400 for second place. In the U17 men James Ellington took the sprint double with a great time in the 200. However, even this was eclipsed in the U15 age group where Andrew Watkins broke the Britsh best 3 times in the 60 metres and twice in the 200 metres on the way to his sprint double. The women were no less impressive - Amy Spencer's time in the 300 metres has only been beaten by 2 senior British athletes. Emily Pidgeon, only 12 won the U17 1500, the day after winning the English Cross County title (p103). Several other athletes completed double wins, but Dominque Blaize beat them all by adding the pentathlon in March to the high jump, long jump double here.

MEN	Under 20			Under 17			Under 15		
60	Andrew Matthews		6.88	James Ellington		6.93	Andrew Watkins		7.06
200	Paul Hession	IRL	21.61	James Ellington		21.80	Andrew Watkins		22.57
400	David McCarthy	IRL	46.66	Richard Davenport		48.58	Lewis Robson		52.67
800	Gareth Balch		1:55.27	Rhian Hastey		2:01.31	Martyn Gibbons		2:04.40
1500	Ian Carter		4:04.20	Colin Costello	IRL	4:07.97			
3000	Paul Moores		8:37.79	Tom Snow		9:08.44			
60H	Edward Dunford		8.38	Tom Stimson		8.27	Daniel Davis		8.20
HJ	Martin Aram		2.10	Jamie Thomas		1.95	Andrew Allan		1.78
PV	Richard Hurren		4.90	Keith Higham		4.60	Luke Cutts		3.30
LJ	Jason Comissiong		7.07	John Fletcher		6.57	Oliver McNeillis		5.89
TJ	Kevin Thompson		14.93	Graham Jackson		13.53			
SP	Sam Westlake-Cann		14.57	Andrae Davis		16.40	Shane Birch		14.98
3kW	Dominic King		12:24.78						
Hept	Edward Dunford		4758	Andrae Davis (Pent)		3670	Lewis Robson (Pent)		2950

WOMEN	Under 20			Under 17			Under 15		
60	Jeanette Kwakye		7.52	Montell Douglas		7.59	Nimneh Hyde		7.94
200	Claire Bergin	IRL	24.38	Phyllis Agbo		25.06	Nimneh Hyde		25.53
400	Lindsey Singer		55.81	Amy Spencer (300)		37.72			
800	Nisha Desai		2:16.33	Hayley Beard		2:07.98	Laura Crowe	IRL	2:16.43
1500	Zoe Jelbert		4:34.40	Emily Pidgeon		4:49.06			
60H	Symone Belle		8.58	Phyllis Agbo		8.74	Joanna Kirby		9.27
HJ	Stephanie Higham		1.75	Shani Rainford		1.66	Dominique Blaize		1.68
PV	Kate Dennison		3.91	Kim Skinner		3.50			
LJ	Symone Belle		5.94	Rebekah Passley		5.86	Dominique Blaize		5.49
TJ	Linsi Robinson		11.84	Angela Barratt		11.85			
SP	Charlotte Spelzini		13.59	Sally Hinds		11.57	Kayleigh Southgate		11.26
3kW	Sophie Hales		14:34.11						
Pent	Jenny Pacey		3195	Faye Harding		3386	Dominique Blaize		3208

Hept & Pent Cardiff 9/10 Mar

FRA v GB & NI v ESP U23 & U20 Combined Events Indoors
Eaubonne, FRA 23 - 24 February 2002

MEN U23 – Heptathlon

1.	John Heanley	5383
3.	Anthony Sawyer	5322
8.	Paul Tohill	5045
9.	Adrian Hemery	4937
n/s	James Wright	4627

MEN U20 – Heptathlon

1.	Angel Barreda	ESP	5370
8.	Ryan Westaway		4819
9.	Robin Smith		4756
10.	Dave Hughes		4676
12.	John Dickenson		4491

Team Result - Men

1.	France	30951
2.	Spain	30485
3.	Great Britain & NI	30001

WOMEN U23 – Pentathlon

1.	Eva Gerard	FRA	3955
3.	Caroline Pearce		3857
6.	Laura Redmond		3709
7.	Ros Gonse		3697
9.	Kate Brewington		3488

WOMEN U20 – Pentathlon

1.	Aileen Wilson	3955
2.	Rebecca Jones	3905
4.	Paula Hendriks	3677
5.	Jessica Ennis	3654

Team Result - Women

1.	Great Britain & NI	22800
2.	France	22696
3.	Spain	20437

Match Result - Overall

1.	France	53647
2.	Great Britain & NI	52801
3.	Spain	50922

EUROPEAN INDOOR CHAMPIONSHIPS
Vienna, AUT 1 - 3 March 2002

2 Golds, 3 Silvers and 2 Bronzes was a reasonable medal haul. It was mainly the well known names like Jackson, Hansen and Mayock, but Michael East showed a glimpse of what was to come. Jason Gardener won the 60 metres in a very fast time but this unfortunately did not continue through to a good outdoor season.

MEN

60 Metres (3 Mar)

1.	**Jason Gardener**		**6.49**
	(1h1 6.61, 1s2 6.55)		
2.	**Mark Lewis-Francis**		**6.55**
	(1h5 6.57, 1s1 6.60)		
3.	Anatoliy Dovgal	UKR	6.62
4.	Bogelemba Bongelo	BEL	6.67
5.	Francesco Scuderi	ITA	6.69
6.	Patrik Lovgren	SWE	6.70
6s1	Akinola Lashore		6.76
	(3h3 6.72)		

200 Metres (2 Mar)

1.	Marcin Urbas	POL	20.64
2.	**Christian Malcolm**		**20.65**
	(1h6 20.83, 1s3 20.65)		
3.	Robert Mackowiak	POL	20.77
4.	**Daniel Caines**		**21.14**
	(1h5 20.67, 2s1 20.62)		
5.	Radek Zachoval	CZE	21.15
6.	Marcin Jedrusinski	POL	21.78
3s2	Doug Turner		20.84
	(1h3 20.86)		

400 Metres (3 Mar)

1.	Marek Plawgo	POL	45.39
2.	Jimisola Laursen	SWE	45.59
3.	Ioan Vieru	ROM	46.17
4.	Piotr Rysiukiewicz	POL	46.32
5.	Jiri Muzik	CZE	46.36
6.	Marc Foucan	FRA	47.40

800 Metres (3 Mar)

1.	Pawel Czapiewski	POL	1:44.78
2.	Andre Bucher	SUI	1:44.93
3.	Antonio Reina	ESP	1:45.25
4.	Dmitriy Bogdanov	RUS	1:45.84
5.	Sergey Kozhevnikov	RUS	1:46.13
6.	David Fiegen	LUX	1:47.44

1500 Metres (2 Mar)

1.	Rui Silva	POR	3:49.93
2.	Juan Higuero	ESP	3:50.08
3.	**Michael East**		**3:50.52**
	(1h1 3:40.52)		
4.	Branko Zorgo	CRO	3:50.66
5.	Michal Sneberger	CZE	3:50.70
6.	James Nolan	IRL	3:50.84
5h2	Angus Maclean		3:44.30

3000 Metres (2 Mar)

1.	Alberto Garcia	ESP	7:43.89
2.	Antonio Jimenez	ESP	7:46.49
3=	Jesus Espana	ESP	7:48.08
3=	**John Mayock**		**7:48.08**
5.	Michael Buchleitner	AUT	7:54.39
6.	Mohammed Mourhit	BEL	7:59.79

60 Metres Hurdles (2 Mar)

1.	**Colin Jackson**		**7.40**
	(1h4 7.55, 1s1 7.55)		
2.	Elmar Lichtenegger	AUT	7.44
3.	Stanislavs Olijar	LAT	7.51
4.	Florian Schwarthoff	GER	7.59
5.	Robert Kronberg	SWE	7.67
drg	Yevgeniy Pechonkin	RUS	(7.50)
3h3	Damien Greaves		7.82

High Jump (3 Mar)

1.	Staffan Strand	SWE	2.34
2.	Stefan Holm	SWE	2.30
3.	Yaroslav Rybakov	RUS	2.30
4.	Andrey Sokolovskiy	UKR	2.27
5.	Joan Charmant	FRA	2.24
6.	Tomas Janku	CZE	2.24

Pole Vault (2 Mar)

1.	Tim Lobinger	GER	5.75
2.	Patrik Kristiansson	SWE	5.75
3.	Lars Borgeling	GER	5.75
4.	Adam Kolasa	POL	5.70
5.	Thibaut Duval	BEL	5.70
6.	Pavel Gerasimov	RUS	5.60
14=Q	**Nick Buckfield**		**5.40**

Long Jump (2 Mar)

1.	Raul Fernandez	ESP	8.22
2.	Yago Lamela	ESP	8.17
3.	Petar Datchev	BUL	8.17
4.	Aleksey Lukashevich	UKR	8.11
5.	Kirill Sosunov	RUS	8.02
6.	Vladimir Zyuskov	UKR	7.97

Triple Jump (3 Mar)

1.	Christian Olsson	SWE	17.54
2.	Marian Oprea	ROM	17.22
3.	Alexandr Glavatskiy	BLR	17.05
4.	Fabrizio Donato	ITA	16.90
5.	Rotislav Dimitrov	BUL	16.79
6.	Aleksandr Sergeyev	RUS	16.56

International & Championship Results

Shot (2 Mar)
1. Manuel Martinez ESP 21.26
2. Joachim Olsen DEN 21.23
3. Pavel Chumachenko RUS 20.30
4. Ville Tiisanoja FIN 20.19
5. Petr Stehlik CZE 19.86
6. Pavel Lyzhin BLR 19.79
drg Mikulas Konopka SVK (20.87)

WOMEN
60 Metres (3 Mar)
1. Kim Gevaert BEL 7.16
2. Marina Kislova RUS 7.18
3. Georgia Kokloni GRE 7.22
4. Karin Mayr AUT 7.22
5. Marion Wagner GER 7.23
6. Larisa Kruglova RUS 7.25
5s1 Joice Maduaka 7.27
(1h3 7.29)

200 Metres (2 Mar)
1. Muriel Hurtis FRA 22.52
2. Karin Mayr AUT 22.70
3. Gabriele Rockmeier GER 23.05
4. Nora Ivanova-Guner TUR 23.08
5. Sylviane Felix FRA 23.87
6. Ekaterina Tosheva BUL 23.99

400 Metres (3 Mar)
1. Natalya Antyukh RUS 51.65
2. Claudia Marx GER 52.15
3. Karen Shinkins IRL 52.17
4. Natalya Ivanova RUS 52.23
5. Yuliya Pechonkina RUS 52.91
6. Catherine Murphy 52.98
(2h2 51.95)

800 Metres (3 Mar)
1. Jolanda Ceplak SLO 1:55.82
2. Stephanie Graf AUT 1:55.85
3. Elisabeth Grousselle FRA 2:01.46
4. Mayte Martinez ESP 2:01.50
5. Svetlana Cherkasova RUS 2:02.80
6. Sandra Stals BEL 2:07.33
h3 Jennifer Meadows dnf

Heptathlon (1/2 Mar)
1. Roman Sebrle CZE 6280
2. Tomas Dvorak CZE 6165
3. Erki Nool EST 6084
4. Jon Arnar Magnusson ISL 5996
5. Attila Zsivoczky HUN 5957
6. Zsolt Kurtosi HUN 5950

1500 Metres (3 Mar)
1. Yekaterina Puzanova RUS 4:06.30
2. Elena Iagar ROM 4:06.90
3. Alesya Turova BLR 4:07.69
4. Yuliya Kosenkova RUS 4:08.63
5. Daniela Yordanova BUL 4:10.47
6. Olga Komyagina RUS 4:11.97
9. Hayley Tullett 4:17.14
(3h1 4:13.58)

3000 Metres (3 Mar)
1. Marta Dominguez ESP 8:53.87
2. Carla Sacramento POR 8:53.96
3. Yelena Zadorozhnaya RUS 8:58.36
4. Susanne Pumper AUT 8:59.93
5. Liliya Volkova RUS 9:02.48
6. Cristina Grosu ROM 9:02.99

60 Metres Hurdles (2 Mar)
1. Linda Ferga FRA 7.96
2. Kirsten Bolm GER 7.97
3. Patricia Girard FRA 7.98
4. Nicole Ramalalanirina FRA 8.01
5. Flora Redoumi GRE 8.02
6. Diane Allahgreen 8.06
(3h3 8.04)
dsqGlory Alozie ESP (7.84)
not eligible to compete for Spain

High Jump (2 Mar)
1. Marina Kuptsova RUS 2.03
2= Kajsa Bergqvist SWE 1.95
2= Dora Gyorffy HUN 1.95
4. Kathryn Holinski GER 1.93
5= Susan Jones 1.90
1.92Q
5= Anna Ksok POL 1.90
5= Yelena Sivushenko RUS 1.90

4 x 400 Metres (3 Mar)
1. Belarus 3:32.24
2. Poland 3:32.45
3. Italy 3:36.49
4. Austria 3:42.24

4 x 400 Metres (3 Mar)
1. Poland 3:05.50
2. France 3:06.42
3. Spain 3:06.60
4. Russia 3:08.02
5. Austria 3:13.81

Pole Vault (3 Mar)
1. Svetlana Feofanova RUS 4.75
2. Yvonne Buschbaum GER 4.65
3. Monika Pyrek POL 4.60
4. Annika Becker GER 4.55
5. Christine Adams GER 4.50
6. Pavla Hamackova CZE 4.35
15=QJanine Whitlock 4.20

Long Jump (3 Mar)
1. Niki Xanthou GRE 6.74
2. Olga Rublyova RUS 6.74
3. Lyudmila Galkina RUS 6.68
4. Irina Simagina RUS 6.64
5. Styliani Pilatou GRE 6.57
6. Zita Ajkler HUN 6.48

Triple Jump (2 Mar)
1. Tereza Marinova BUL 14.81
2. Ashia Hansen 14.71
3. Yelena Oleynikova RUS 14.30
4. Nadezhda Bazhenova RUS 14.20
5. Cristina Nicolau ROM 14.11
6. Marija Martinovic YUG 14.00

Shot (2 Mar)
1. Vita Pavlysh UKR 19.76
2. Assunta Legnante ITA 18.60
3. Lieja Koeman NED 18.53
4. Valentina Fedyuschina AUT 18.23
5. Lyudmila Sechko RUS 18.14
6. Elena Hila ROM 17.52

Pentathlon (1 Mar)
1. Yelena Prokhorova RUS 4622
2. Naide Gomes POR 4595
3. Carolina Kluft SWE 4535
4. Anzhela Atroshchenko TUR 4503
5. Sonja Kesselschlager GER 4402
6. Magdalena Szczepanska POL 4382

AAA & UK HALF MARATHON CHAMPIONSHIPS
Bath 17 March 2002

MEN
1. William Musyoki KEN 64:14
2. Mark Hudspith 1-AAA 64:17
3. Carl Thackery 2-AAA 64:28
4. Nick Wetheridge 3-AAA 64:30

WOMEN
1. Jo Lodge 74:01
2. Sharon Dixon 75:14
3. Alison Fletcher 76:07

Norwich Union International
GB & NI v RUS v GER v GER v All Stars
Glasgow 9 March 2002

MEN

60 Metres
1. Jason Gardener   6.53

200 Metres
1. Johan Wissman   SWE   20.85
2. Doug Turner   20.94

400 Metres
1. Daniel Caines   46.45

800 Metres
1. Dmitriy Bogdanov   RUS   1:51.84
2. Matt Shone   AS   1:52.98
3. James McIlroy   1:53.08

1500 Metres
1. Michael East   AS   3:43.70
3. John Mayock   3:44.85

60 Metres Hurdles
1. Colin Jackson   7.50

Shot
1. Pavel Chumachenko   RUS   20.59
5. Gary Sollitt   16.57

4 x 400 Metres
1. Russia   3:09.76
3. Great Britain & NI   3:10.10
(Tobin, Caines, Baird, Chatt)

WOMEN

60 Metres
1. Marina Kislova   RUS   7.20
2. Joice Maduaka   7.28

200 Metres
1. Juliet Campbell   AS/JAM   22.88
4. Catherine Murphy   23.71

400 Metres
1. Catherine Murphy   52.49

800 Metres
1. Nicole Teter   AS/USA   2:02.39
3. Jo Fenn   2:04.85

1500 Metres
1. Jolanda Ceplak   AS/SLO   4:05.44
3. Julie Mitchell   4:23.17

60 Metres Hurdles
1. Kirsten Bolm   GER   7.89
3. Diane Allahgreen   8.14

High Jump
1= Dora Gyorffy   AS/HUN   1.96
1= Marina Kuptsova   RUS   1.96
4. Susan Jones   1.89

Pole Vault
1. Svetlana Feofanova   RUS   4.66
3= Janine Whitlock   4.01

Triple Jump
1. Ashia Hansen   14.34

4 x 400 Metres
1. Russia   3:30.27
3. Great Britain & NI   3:37.80
(Clarkson, Meadows, Purkiss, Murphy)

Match Result
1. Russia   66.5
2. Great Britain & NI   61.5
3. All Stars   56.5
4. Germany   42
5. Sweden   39.5

IAAF WORLD CROSS COUNTRY CHAMPIONSHIPS
Dublin, IRL 23 - 24 March 2002

Again, Paula Radcliffe was the only British athlete who made her mark on these championships with a brilliant defence of her long course title. The only other highlight was Charlotte Dale who led for the first lap, cramped up, but was still first Britain home in the junior women.

MEN 4.27k (23 Mar)
1. Kenenisa Bekele   ETH   12:11
2. Luke Kipkosgei   KEN   12:18
3. Hailu Mekonnen   ETH   12:20
4. Sammy Kipketer   KEN   12:26
5. Craig Mottram   AUS   12:27
6. Julius Nyamu   KEN   12:30
23. John Mayock   12:44
30. Philip Mowbray   12:50
39. Spencer Barden   12:53
42. Ben Noad   12:54
72. Robert Whalley   13:10
79. Ben Whitby   13:13

Team
1. Kenya   20
2. Ethiopia   32
3. Spain   57
7. Great Britain & NI   120

MEN 12.07k (24 Mar)
1. Kenenisa Bekele   ETH   34:52
2. John Yuda   TAN   34:58
3. Wilberforce Talel   KEN   35:20
4. Richard Limo   KEN   35:26
5. Charles Kamathi   KEN   35:29
6. Albert Chepkurui   KEN   35:32
43. Sam Haughian   36:53
50. Allen Graffin   37:10
61. Matthew Smith   37:32
69. Ian Hudspith   37:38
70. Glynn Tromans   37:40
103. Matt O`Dowd   38:41

Team
1. Kenya   18
2. Ethiopia   43
3. Morocco   58
10. Great Britain & NI   173

JUNIOR MEN 7.87k (24 Mar)
1. Gebre Gebremariam   ETH   23:18
2. Abel Cheruiyot   KEN   23:19
3. Boniface Kiprop   UGA   23:28
4. Thomas Kiplitan   KEN   23:33
5. Eliud Kipchoge   KEN   23:39
6. Sileshi Sihine   ETH   23:42
31. Tom Sharland   25:15
68. Matthew Lole   26:05
82. Steven Ablitt   26:27
84. Matthew Bowser   26:29
95. David Jones   26:50
105. Chris Watson   27:26

Team
1. Kenya   18
2. Ethiopia   24
3. Uganda   37
11. Great Britain & NI   176

WOMEN 4.27k (24 Mar)

1.	Edith Masai	KEN	13:30
2.	Werknesh Kidane	ETH	13:36
3.	Isabella Ochichi	KEN	13:39
4.	Benita Johnson	AUS	13:42
5.	Suzy Favor-Hamilton	USA	13:47
6.	Abebech Negussie	ETH	13:53
22.	**Helen Pattinson**		**14:18**
35.	**Lucy Elliott**		**14:28**
60.	**Amanda Wright-Allen**		**14:48**
75.	**Sonia Thomas**		**15:01**
78.	**Emma Ward**		**15:04**
80.	**Jane Potter**		**15:10**

Team

1.	Ethiopia	32
2.	Kenya	34
3.	Ireland	85
11.	**Great Britain & NI**	**160**

WOMEN 7.87k (23 Mar)

1.	**Paula Radcliffe**		**26:55**
2.	Deena Drossin	USA	27:04
3.	Colleen de Reuck	USA	27:17
4.	Miwako Yamanaka	JPN	27:19
5.	Eyerusalem Kuma	ETH	27:19
6.	Merima Denboba	ETH	27:21
18.	**Liz Yelling**		**28:07**
20.	**Kathy Butler**		**28:12**
42.	**Hayley Yelling**		**29:00**
46.	**Angela Mudge**		**29:07**
59.	**Jenny Brown**		**29:52**

Team

1.	Ethiopia	28
2.	United States	38
3.	Kenya	41
5.	**Great Britain & NI**	**69**

JUNIOR WOMEN 6.07k (23 Mar)

1.	Viola Kibiwot	KEN	20:13
2.	Tirunesh Dibaba	ETH	20:14
3.	Vivian Cheruiyot	KEN	20:22
4.	Fridah Domongole	KEN	20:23
5.	Peninah Chepchumba	KEN	20:24
6.	Bezunesh Bekele	ETH	20:34
31.	**Charlotte Dale**		**22:01**
45.	**Henrietta Freeman**		**22:15**
46.	**Faye Fullerton**		**22:16**
53.	**Jessica Nugent**		**22:27**
63.	**Freya Murray**		**23:01**
68.	**Lisa Dobriskey**		**23:10**

Team

1.	Kenya	13
2.	Ethiopia	24
3.	Japan	63
8.	**Great Britain & NI**	**130**

EAA EUROPEAN CHALLENGE 10000 Metres
Camaiore, ITA 6 April 2002

Liz Yelling ran well in the 'A' race to achieve a qualifying time for the European Championships and her sister-in-law Hayley won the 'B' race in a personal best.

MEN (Race A)

1.	Dieter Baumann	GER	27:38.51
2.	Jose Rios	ESP	27:38.82
3.	Marco Mazza	ITA	27:44.05
12.	**Sam Haughian**		**28:25.87**
18.	**Matt Smith**		**29:13.60**

MEN (Race B)

1.	Alexander Lubina	GER	28:29.15
2.	Guy Fays	BEL	28:32.54
3.	Dmitriy Semenov	RUS	28:45.35
5.	**Ian Hudspith**		**28:56.41**

Team Result - Men

1.	Italy	1:24:25.40
2.	Spain	1:24:27.20
3.	Germany	1:24:35.38
6.	**Great Britain & NI**	**1:26:35:88**

WOMEN (Race A)

1.	Mihaela Botezan	ROM	31:19.74
2.	Fernanda Ribeiro	POR	31:40.80
3.	Luisa Larraga	ESP	31:45.85
7.	**Liz Yelling**		**32:26.53**

WOMEN (Race B)

1.	**Hayley Yelling**		**32:48.50**
2.	Irma Heere	NED	33:01.55
3.	Rosita Gelpi	ITA	33:08.34

Team Result - Women

1.	Portugal	1:36:29.94
2.	Spain	1:38:01.57
3.	Italy	1:38:31.51

WORLD UNIVERSITIES CROSS COUNTRY CHAMPIONSHIP
Santiago de Compostela, ESP 7 April 2002

MEN 11.63k

1.	Abdellah Bay	MAR	35:01
2.	Aziz Driouch	MAR	35:03
3.	Gunther Weidlinger	AUT	35:09
7.	**Mark Miles**		**35:27**
21.	**Oliver Laws**		**36:24**
22.	**Nicholas Talbot**		**36:32**
28.	**Steven Vernon**		**36:57**
39.	**Ben Tickner**		**37:32**

Team

1.	Spain	32
2.	Morocco	41
3.	**Great Britain & NI**	**78**

WOMEN 6k

1.	Denisa Cotescu	ROM	20:06
2.	Rene Kalmer	RSA	20:08
3.	Ines Monteiro	POR	20:13
13.	**Louise Damen**		**20:53**
15.	**Gillian Palmer**		**21:02**
27.	**Gemma Phillips**		**21:31**
28.	**Collette Fagan**		**21:34**
56.	**Sara Stevenson**		**23:41**

Team

1.	South Africa	23
2.	Spain	25
3.	Romania	29
4.	**Great Britain & NI**	**55**

LONDON MARATHON 14 April 2002
(including AAA Championships)

Khannouchi sets a world best, Tergat runs 2:05 for second, an injured Gebrselassie finishes third in 2:06 and this still is not the main story. Paula Radcliffe running her first marathon exceeds all expectations to smash the British record and set a women only best (what more was to come?). Mark Steinle's 2:09:17 for eighth place on the British all time list was very much lost in all the praise for Paula.

MEN

1.	Khalid Khannouchi	USA	2:05:38
2.	Paul Tergat	KEN	2:05:48
3.	Haile Gebrselassie	ETH	2:06:35
4.	Abdelkader El Mouaziz	MAR	2:06:52
5.	Ian Syster	RSA	2:07:06
6.	Stefano Baldini	ITA	2:07:29
7.	Antonio Pinto	POR	2:09:10
8.	**Mark Steinle (1-AAA)**		**2:09:17**
9.	Tesfaye Jifar	ETH	2:09:50
10.	Mohammed El Hattab	MAR	2:11:50
14.	**Billy Burns (2-AAA)**		**2:17:36**
15.	**Daniel Robinson (3-AAA)**		**2:17:51**
17.	**Nick Wetheridge**		**2:19:41**
20.	**Chris Cariss**		**2:20:46**
21.	**Martin Hilton**		**2:20:54**
22.	**Dave Norman**		**2:21:01**
23.	**Mark Croasdale**		**2:21:10**

WOMEN

1.	**Paula Radcliffe (1-AAA)**		**2:18:56**
2.	Svetlana Zakharova	RUS	2:22:31
3.	Lyudmila Petrova	RUS	2:22:33
4.	Reiko Tosa	JPN	2:22:46
5.	Susan Chepkemei	KEN	2:23:19
6.	Joyce Chepchumba	KEN	2:26:53
7.	Silvia Skvortsova	RUS	2:27:07
8.	Zinaida Semyonova	RUS	2:27:45
9.	Derartu Tulu	ETH	2:28:37
10.	Shitaye Gemechu	ETH	2:28:58
12.	**Jo Lodge (2-AAA)**		**2:38:25**
14.	**Bev Jenkins (3-AAA)**		**2:44:32**
15.	**Alison Fletcher**		**2:44:42**
16.	**Sharon Dixon**		**2:45:05**
17.	**Ruth Pickvance**		**2:45:34**
19.	**Clare Pauzers**		**2:49:26**
20.	**Elizabeth Mycroft**		**2:49:38**

UK ATHLETICS
100k CHAMPIONSHIPS
Moreton-in-Marsh
8 April 2002

MEN

1.	Dennis Walmsley	7:07:39
2.	Chris Finill	7:23:57
3.	Alan Reid	7:36:09

WOMEN

1.	Sharon Gayter	8:53:17
2.	Ramona Thevenet-Smith	9:55:18
3.	Pam Storey	11:49:50

IAAF WORLD HALF MARATHON CHAMPIONSHIPS
Brussels, BEL 5 May 2002

After the euphoria of London, this is probably the low point of British (non) participation in a World Championship.

MEN

1.	Paul Kossgei	KEN	60:39
2.	Gharib Jouad	MAR	60:42
3.	John Yuda	TAN	60:57
4.	Yonas Kifle	ERI	61:05
5.	Tesfaye Jifar	ETH	61:11
6.	Shadrack Hoff	RSA	61:23

Team

1.	Kenya	3:04:42
2.	Japan	3:07:12
3.	Ethiopia	3:07:25

WOMEN

1.	Berhane Adere	ETH	69:06
2.	Susan Chepkemei	KEN	69:13
3.	Jelena Prokopcuka	LAT	69:15
4.	Mihaela Botezan	ROM	69:24
5.	Pamela Chepchumba	KEN	69:30
6.	Olivera Jevtic	YUG	69:33
47.	**Amanda Wright-Allen**		**74:53**

Team

1.	Kenya	3:28:22
2.	Russia	3:30:05
3.	Ethiopia	3:30:58

IAU WORLD CUP
100k CHALLENGE
Torhout, BEL
21 June 2002

MEN

1.	Mario Fattore	ITA	6:34:23
2.	Igor Tyazhkorob	RUS	6:39:33
3.	Fermin Martinez	ESP	6:39:57
33.	**Ian Anderson**		**7:34:46**
40.	**Chris Finill**		**7:42:47**
58.	**Dennis Walmsley**		**8:13:33**

WOMEN

1.	Tatyana Zhyrkova	RUS	7:37:06
2.	Akiko Sekiya	JPN	7:38:03
3.	Monica Cassiraghi	ITA	7:40:00
29.	**Hilary Walker**		**9:04:40**

AQUA-PURA ENGLISH COMMONWEALTH TRIALS
Manchester 15 - 16 June 2002

In a competition which some felt was a trial too many, two British records were set. Kelly Morgan broke Karen Martin's javelin by more than 3 metres and Janine Whitlock again improved her pole vault record but then came news that she had failed a drugs test and she received a two-year ban.

MEN

100 Metres wind 0.3 (15 Jun)		**200 Metres** wind 0.5 (16 Jun)		**400 Metres** (16 Jun)	
1. Dwain Chambers	10.03	1. Marlon Devonish	20.36	1. Daniel Caines	45.32
2. Mark Lewis-Francis	10.07	2. Chris Lambert	20.41	2. Jared Deacon	45.57
3. Chris Lambert	10.28	3. Graham Beasley	20.76	3. Sean Baldock	46.47

800 Metres (16 Jun)
1. Simon Lees — 1:47.89
2. Neil Speaight — 1:48.48
3. Chris Robb — 1:48.50

1500 Metres (16 Jun)
1. Michael East — 3:46.89
2. Anthony Whiteman — 3:47.28
3. Tom Mayo — 3:47.56

5000 Metres (16 Jun)
1. Sam Haughian — 13:42.80
2. Michael Power — AUS — 13:44.32
3. Matt O'Dowd — 13:46.24

10000 Metres (15 Jun) **AAA Champs.**
1. Rob Denmark — 28:43.42
2. John Wild — 28:43.82
3. Andres Jones — 28:43.93
4. Ian Hudspith — 28:46.40
5. Glen Stewart — 28:47.52
6. Matthew Smith — 29:18.93
7. David Taylor — 29:20.02
8. Paul Evans — 29:25.55

3000 Metres Steeplechase (16 Jun)
1. Stuart Stokes — 8:35.6
2. Ben Whitby — 8:38.0
3. Don Naylor — 8:39.0

110 Metres Hurdles wind -1.2 (15 Jun)
1. Damien Greaves — 13.73
2. Mensah Elliott — 13.95
3. Dominic Girdler — 13.95

400 Metres Hurdles (16 Jun)
1. Matt Elias — 49.46
2. Tony Borsumato — 49.52
3. Matt Douglas — 49.76

High Jump (15 Jun)
1. Ben Challenger — 2.23
2. Richard Aspden — 2.14
3. Luke Crawley — 2.14

Pole Vault (15 Jun)
1. Viktor Christiakov — AUS — 5.60
2. Tim Thomas — 5.20
3. Paul Williamson — 5.20

Long Jump (16 Jun)
1. Chris Tomlinson — 7.98
2. Darren Ritchie — 7.76
3. Mark Awanah — 7.70

Triple Jump (15 Jun)
1. Steven Shalders — 16.41
2. Tosin Oke — 16.33
3. Larry Achike — 16.32

Shot (16 Jun)
1. Carl Myerscough — 19.82
2. Mark Proctor — 17.75
3. Emeka Udechuku — 17.48

Discus (16 Jun)
1. Carl Myerscough — 61.22
2. Glen Smith — 58.32
3. Emeka Udechuku — 57.97

Hammer (15 Jun)
1. Mick Jones — 72.16
2. Paul Head — 69.61
3. Mike Floyd — 67.74

Javelin (15 Jun)
1. Nick Nieland — 80.05
2. Mark Roberson — 78.80
3. Mick Hill — 78.15

WOMEN

100 Metres wind 0.1 (15 Jun)
1. Debbie Ferguson — BAH — 11.25
2. Shani Anderson — 11.51
3. Amanda Forrester — 11.57

200 Metres wind -0.5 (16 Jun)
1. Vernicha James — 22.95
2. Shani Anderson — 23.32
3. Emily Freeman — 23.43

400 Metres (16 Jun)
1. Maria Mutola — MOZ — 52.03
2. Helen Karagounis — 52.17
3. Carey Easton — 53.11

800 Metres (16 Jun)
1. Jo Fenn — 2:00.24
2. Agnes Samaria — NAM — 2:00.26
3. Tamsyn Lewis — AUS — 2:00.73

1500 Metres (16 Jun)
1. Helen Pattinson — 4:08.66
2. Susan Scott — 4:09.79
3. Sarah Jamieson — AUS — 4:09.89

5000 Metres (15 Jun)
1. Catherine Berry — 15:32.32
2. Natalie Harvey — AUS — 15:38.25
3. Hayley Yelling — 15:38.30

10000 Metres (16 Jun) **AAA Champs.**
1. Sonia O`Sullivan — IRL — 31:33.19
2. Sabrina Mockenhaupt — GER — 32:27.63
3. Elana Meyer — RSA — 32:36.15
4. Hayley Yelling — 33:07.52
5. Gillian Palmer — 33:09.70
6. Allison Higgins — 33:32.07
7. Jo Wilkinson — 33:40.57
8. Sharon Morris — 34:20.64

100 Metres Hurdles wind 0.7 (15 Jun)
1. Diane Allahgreen — 13.07
2. Natasha Danvers — 13.20
3. Julie Pratt — 13.33

400 Metres Hurdles (16 Jun)
1. Natasha Danvers — 56.44
2. Tracey Duncan — 56.53
3. Katie Jones — 57.71

High Jump (16 Jun)
1. Susan Jones — 1.88
2. Stephanie Higham — 1.85
3. Debbie Marti — 1.82

Pole Vault (16 Jun)
1. Tatiana Grigorieva — AUS — 4.25
2. Irie Hill — 4.15
3. Rhian Clarke — 4.05
drg Janine Whitlock — (4.41)

Long Jump (16 Jun)
1. Jade Johnson — 6.45
2. Ann Danson — 6.38
3. Kelly Sotherton — 6.21

Triple Jump (15 Jun)
1. Ashia Hansen — 14.03
2. Michelle Griffith — 12.99
3. Taneisha Scanlon — IRL — 12.69

Shot (15 Jun)
1. Julie Dunkley — 16.37
2. Myrtle Augee — 15.87
3. Jo Duncan — 15.85

Discus (16 Jun)
1. Shelley Newman — 57.99
2. Emma Carpenter — 56.63
3. Philippa Roles — 56.52

Hammer (16 Jun)
1. Lorraine Shaw — 65.34
2. Zoe Derham — 62.27
3. Suzanne Roberts — 59.75

Javelin (15 Jun)
1. Kelly Morgan — 63.03
2. Karen Martin — 55.02
3. Goldie Sayers — 54.59

SPAR EUROPEAN CUP SUPER LEAGUE
Annecy, FRA 22 - 23 June 2002

The British men bounced back from the disappointment of last year to reclaim the title. Six individual wins plus both relays helped in this good performance. The women had a much harder fight and it was only some last day heroics which saved them from relegation.

MEN

100 Metres wind 0.2 (22 Jun)
1. Dwain Chambers — 10.04
2. Aime Nthepe — FRA — 10.27
3. Konstantin Rurak — UKR — 10.31
4. Francesco Scuderi — ITA — 10.35
5. Marcin Urbas — POL — 10.42
6. Marc Blume — GER — 10.44
7. Markus Poyhonen — FIN — 10.46
8. Andrey Yepishin — RUS — 10.49

200 Metres wind −0.4 (23 Jun)
1. Marlon Devonish — 20.27
2. Marcin Urbas — POL — 20.45
3. Marco Torrieri — ITA — 20.65
4. Konstantin Rurak — UKR — 20.75
5. Ronald Pognon — FRA — 20.79
6. Oleg Sergeyev — RUS — 20.98
7. Steffen Otto — GER — 21.06
8. Stefan Koivikko — FIN — 21.13

400 Metres (22 Jun)
1. Daniel Caines — 45.14
2. Ingo Schultz — GER — 45.33
3. Marek Plawgo — POL — 45.35
4. Marc Raquil — FRA — 45.39
5. Alessandro Attene — ITA — 45.91
6. Vladimir Demchenko — UKR — 46.11
7. Oleg Mishukov — RUS — 46.61
8. Ari Kauppinen — FIN — 47.69

800 Metres (23 Jun)
1. Yuriy Borzakovskiy — RUS — 1:46.58
2. Nils Schumann — GER — 1:46.99
3. Pawel Czapiewski — POL — 1:47.92
4. Nicolas Aissat — FRA — 1:48.01
5. Simon Lees — 1:48.43
6. Wilson Kirwa — FIN — 1:48.52
7. Christian Neunhauserer — ITA — 1:48.61
8. Ivan Geshko — UKR — 1:49.68

1500 Metres (22 Jun)
1. Mehdi Baala — FRA — 3:47.21
2. Michael East — 3:48.26
3. Pawel Czapiewski — POL — 3:48.77
4. Franek Haschke — GER — 3:48.81
5. Ivan Geshko — UKR — 3:48.91
6. Vyacheslav Shabunin — RUS — 3:48.97
7. Christian Obrist — ITA — 3:50.22
8. Juha Kukkamo — FIN — 3:50.41

3000 Metres (23 Jun)
1. Driss Maazouzi — FRA — 7:53.41
2. Mikhail Yeginov — RUS — 7:54.05
3. Jan Fitschen — GER — 7:54.92
4. Anthony Whiteman — 8:00.31

5. Simone Zanon — ITA — 8:03.28
6. Zbigniew Graczyk — POL — 8:16.68
7. Nikolay Novitskiy — UKR — 8:17.38
8. Tuomo Lehtinen — FIN — 8:42.15

5000 Metres (22 Jun)
1. Dmitriy Maksimov — RUS — 14:09.92
2. Sam Haughian — 14:11.60
3. Ismail Sghyr — FRA — 14:14.00
4. Marco Mazza — ITA — 14:14.72
5. Samuli Vasala — FIN — 14:16.63
6. Mario Krockert — GER — 14:22.60
7. Dmitriy Baranovskiy — UKR — 14:43.27
8. Dariusz Kruczkowski — POL — 15:02.78

3000 Metres Steeplechase (23 Jun)
1. Bouabdellah Tahri — FRA — 8:30.22
2. Damian Kallabis — GER — 8:32.04
3. Roman Usov — RUS — 8:34.10
4. Kim Bergdahl — FIN — 8:35.31
5. Angelo Iannelli — ITA — 8:36.47
6. Rafal Wojcik — POL — 8:44.86
7. Stuart Stokes — 8:48.69
8. Sergey Redko — UKR — 9:02.19

110 Metres Hurdles wind 0.7 (23 Jun)
1. Colin Jackson — 13.15
2. Mike Fenner — GER — 13.33
3. Andrea Giaconi — ITA — 13.35
4. Artur Kohutek — POL — 13.53
5. Cedric Lavanne — FRA — 13.64
6. Matti Niemi — FIN — 13.72
7. Andrey Kislykh — RUS — 13.77
8. Sergey Smolenskiy — UKR — 14.04

400 Metres Hurdles (22 Jun)
1. Fabrizio Mori — ITA — 48.41
2. Stephane Diagana — FRA — 48.45
3. Chris Rawlinson — 48.87
4. Pawel Januszewski — POL — 49.20
5. Boris Gorban — RUS — 49.22
6. Henning Hackelbusch — GER — 50.60
7. Gennadiy Gorbenko — UKR — 51.16
8. Jussi Heikkila — FIN — 51.49

High Jump (22 Jun)
1. Gregory Gabella — FRA — 2.30
2. Yaroslav Rybakov — RUS — 2.28
3. Grzegorz Sposob — POL — 2.25
4. Andrey Sokolovskiy — UKR — 2.25
5. Toni Huikuri — FIN — 2.25
6. Giullio Ciotti — ITA — 2.25
7. Martin Buss — GER — 2.22
8. Ben Challenger — 2.19

Pole Vault (23 Jun)
1. Tim Lobinger — GER — 5.75
2= Denis Yurchenko — UKR — 5.65
2= Giuseppe Gibilisco — ITA — 5.65
4. Vasiliy Gorshkov — RUS — 5.55
5. Vesa Rantanen — FIN — 5.40
6. Tim Thomas — 5.05
7. Przemyslaw Czerwinski — POL — 4.85
nh Jean Galfione — FRA

Long Jump (22 Jun)
1. Chris Tomlinson — 8.17
2. Nicola Trentin — ITA — 8.15
3. Salim Sdiri — FRA — 8.03
4. Danila Burkenya — RUS — 7.94
5. Schahriat Bigdeli — GER — 7.82
6. Kenneth Kastren — FIN — 7.77
7. Grzegorz Marciniszyn — POL — 7.53
nm Vladimir Zyuskov — UKR

Triple Jump (23 Jun)
1. Jonathan Edwards — 17.19
2. Fabrizio Donato — ITA — 17.17
3. Charles Friedek — GER — 17.11
4. Julien Kapek — FRA — 17.04
5. Igor Spasovkhodskiy — RUS — 17.01
6. Jacek Kazmierowski — POL — 16.67
7. Andrey Trots — UKR — 16.49
8. Johan Meriluoto — FIN — 16.16

Shot (22 Jun)
1. Yuriy Belonog — UKR — 20.55
2. Ville Tiisanoja — FIN — 20.29
3. Paolo Dal Soglio — ITA — 19.87
4. Ralf Bartels — GER — 19.85
5. Yves Niare — FRA — 19.48
6. Carl Myerscough — 19.41
7. Pavel Chumachenko — RUS — 19.37
8. Leszek Sliwa — POL — 18.73

Discus (23 Jun)
1. Michael Mollenbeck — GER — 66.82
2. Dmitriy Shevchenko — RUS — 62.03
3. Olgierd Stanski — POL — 60.88
4. Timo Tompuri — FIN — 59.79
5. Jean-Claude Retel — FRA — 59.05
6. Cristiano Andrei — ITA — 59.00
7. Kiril Chuprinin — UKR — 58.43
8. Glen Smith — 54.77

Hammer (22 Jun)
1. Olli-Pekka Karjalainen — FIN — 79.25
2. Andrey Skvaruk — UKR — 79.04
3. Maciej Palyszko — POL — 78.25
4. Nicolas Figere — FRA — 77.75

5. Karsten Kobs GER 77.63
6. Vadim Khersontsev RUS 77.10
7. Nicola Vizzoni ITA 73.84
8. **Mick Jones** **70.08**

Javelin (23 Jun)
1. Sergey Makarov RUS 88.24
2. **Steve Backley** **85.03**
3. Boris Henry GER 83.90
4. Harri Haatainen FIN 83.25
5. Dariusz Trafas POL 80.13
6. Oleg Statsenko UKR 69.73
7. Dominique Pause FRA 68.25
8. Alberto Desiderio ITA 67.06

WOMEN
100 Metres wind 0.4 (22 Jun)
1. Muriel Hurtis FRA 10.96
2. Manuela Levorato ITA 11.20
3. Yuliya Tabakova RUS 11.24
4. Sina Schielke GER 11.25
5. Anzhela Kravchenko UKR 11.31
6. **Shani Anderson** **11.38**
7. Beata Szkudlarz POL 11.44
8. Evelina Lisenco ROM 11.58

200 Metres wind 0.6 (23 Jun)
1. Muriel Hurtis FRA 22.51
2. Manuela Levorato ITA 22.76
3. Sina Schielke GER 22.91
4. **Vernicha James** **22.94**
5. Ionela Tirlea ROM 23.04
6. Yuliya Tabakova RUS 23.11
7. Anzhela Kravchenko UKR 23.32
8. Beata Szkudlarz POL 23.83

400 Metres (22 Jun)
1. Antonina Yefremova UKR 50.70
2. Grazyna Prokopek POL 51.34
3. Francine Landre FRA 51.78
4. Otilia Ruicu ROM 51.79
5. Danielle Perpoli ITA 51.85
6. **Helen Karagounis** **52.03**
7. Anna Tkach RUS 52.09
8. Claudia Marx GER 52.45

800 Metres (22 Jun)
1. Irina Mistyukevich RUS 1:59.76
2. Elisabeth Grousselle FRA 1:59.95
3. Ivonne Teichmann GER 2:00.07
4. **Kelly Holmes** **2:00.33**
5. Elena Iagar ROM 2:01.67
6. Yuliya Gurtovenko UKR 2:02.04
7. Anna Jakubczak POL 2:04.25
8. Claudia Salvarani ITA 2:06.65

1500 Metres (23 Jun)
1. Maria Cioncan ROM 4:03.74
2. Lidia Chojecka POL 4:04.84
3. Tatyana Tomashova RUS 4:05.14

4 x 100 Metres (22 Jun)
1. **Great Britain & NI** **38.65**
(Devonish, Lewis-Francis, Malcolm, Condon)
2. Germany 38.88
3. Italy 38.89
4. Poland 39.08
5. Russia 39.10
6. France 39.10
dnf Finland
dq Ukraine

4 x 400 Metres (23 Jun)
1. **Great Britain & NI** **3:00.57**
(Deacon, Benjamin, Baulch, Caines)
2. Germany 3:00.80
3. France 3:00.92

4. **Helen Pattinson** **4:05.20**
5. Irina Lishchinskaya UKR 4:10.95
6. Maria Martins FRA 4:15.04
7. Sara Palmas ITA 4:18.44
8. Kathleen Friedrich GER 4:20.73

3000 Metres (22 June)
1. Gabriela Szabo ROM 8:38.03
2. Yelena Zadorozhnaya RUS 8:39.84
3. Lidia Chojecka POL 8:49.95
4. Kristina da Fonseca-W GER 9:07.40
5. **Kathy Butler** **9:09.36**
6. Gloria Marconi ITA 9:11.37
7. Marina Dubrova UKR 9:23.53
8. Yamna Belkacem FRA 9:52.60

5000 Metres (23 Jun)
1. Olga Yegorova RUS 16:04.26
2. **Jo Pavey** **16:06.65**
3. Fatima Yvelain FRA 16:08.21
4. Sabrina Mockenhaupt GER 16:09.55
5. Maura Viceconte ITA 16:12.24
6. Mihaela Botezan ROM 16:19.39
7. Marzena Michalska POL 16:46.91
8. Marina Dubrova UKR 16:56.35

3000 Metres Steeplechase (23 Jun)
1. Justyna Bak POL 9:43.38
2. Cristina Casandra ROM 9:49.51
3. Melanie Schulz GER 9:49.79
4. **Tara Krzywicki** **10:23.21**
5. Pierangela Baronchelli ITA 10:24.49
6. Yuliya Ignatova UKR 10:26.24
7. Yekaterina Volkova RUS 10:37.78
dnf Laurence Duquenoy FRA

100 Metres Hurdles wind -0.2 (23 Jun)
1. Patricia Girard FRA 12.64
2. Kirsten Bolm GER 12.85
3. Mariya Koroteyeva RUS 12.94
4. **Diane Allahgreen** **13.11**
5. Yelena Krasovskaya UKR 13.12
6. Aurelia Trywianska POL 13.12
7. Carmen Zamfir ROM 13.24
8. Margaret Macchiut ITA 13.24

4. Russia 3:00.93
5. Poland 3:01.99
6. Ukraine 3:05.97
7. Italy 3:06.01
8. Finland 3:07.16

Match Result
1. **Great Britain & NI** **111**
2. Germany 107
3. France 105
4. Russia 94
5. Italy 89.5
6. Poland 85
7. Ukraine 63.5
8. Finland 60

400 Metres Hurdles (22 Jun)
1. Yuliya Pechonkina RUS 53.38
2. Anna Olichwierczuk POL 55.11
3. **Natasha Danvers** **55.68**
4. Sylvanie Morandais FRA 55.75
5. Ulrike Urbansky GER 56.20
6. Tatyana Debelaya UKR 56.33
7. Monika Niederstatter ITA 56.60
8. Medina-Elena Tudor ROM 60.05

High Jump (23 Jun)
1. Irina Mikhalchenko UKR 1.95
2. Oana Pentelimon ROM 1.93
3. Kathryn Holinski GER 1.93
4= Marina Kuptsova RUS 1.90
4= **Susan Jones** **1.90**
6. Lucie Finez FRA 1.90
7= Anna Ksok POL 1.87
7= Antonietta Di Martino ITA 1.87

Pole Vault (22 Jun)
1. Svetlana Feofanova RUS 4.70
2. Yvonne Buschbaum GER 4.60
3. Vanessa Boslak FRA 4.45
4. Monika Pyrek POL 4.20
6= Natalya Kushch UKR 4.10
6= Francesca Dolcini ITA 4.10
drg **Janine Whitlock** **(5)** **(4.10)**

Long Jump (23 Jun)
1. Tatyana Kotova RUS 7.42
2. Cristina Nicolau ROM 6.65
3. Bianca Kappler GER 6.64
4. Silvia Favre ITA 6.45
5. **Jade Johnson** **6.42**
6. Katarzyna Klisowska POL 6.41
7. Haydy Aron FRA 6.38
8. Yelena Shekhovtsova UKR 6.11

Triple Jump (22 Jun)
1. Anna Pyatykh RUS 14.67
2. **Ashia Hansen** **14.62**
3. Magdelin Martinez ITA 14.54
4. Yelena Govorova UKR 14.37
5. Cristina Nicolau ROM 14.33
6. Liliana Zagacka POL 13.77

7.	Roselise Retel	FRA	13.63	4. Ester Balassini ITA	65.49	**4 x 400 Metres** (23 Jun)
8.	Nicole Herschmann	GER	13.30	5. Susanne Keil GER	65.13	**1. Great Britain & NI 3:27.87**

Shot (23 Jun)

1.	Svetlana Krivelyova	RUS	19.63
2.	Astrid Kumbernuss	GER	19.61
3.	Krystyna Zakowicz	POL	18.52
4.	Elena Hila	ROM	17.93
5.	Assunta Legnante	ITA	17.89
6.	Laurence Manfredi	FRA	16.52
7.	Yelena Dementiy	UKR	16.16
8.	**Julie Dunkley**		**15.85**

Discus (22 Jun)

1.	Natalya Sadova	RUS	65.91
2.	Nicoleta Grasu	ROM	63.05
3.	Franka Dietzsch	GER	59.30
4.	Viktoriya Boyko	UKR	58.20
5.	Joanna Wisniewska	POL	58.06
6.	**Shelley Newman**		**57.89**
7.	Agnes Maffeis	ITA	57.39
8.	Melina Robert-Michon	FRA	53.94

Hammer (23 Jun)

1.	Olga Kuzenkova	RUS	73.07
2.	Manuela Montebrun	FRA	68.53
3.	Irina Sekachova	UKR	66.88

6.	Kamila Skolimowska	POL	64.39
7.	**Lorraine Shaw**		**63.09**
8.	Cristina Buzau	ROM	59.82

Javelin (22 Jun)

1.	Tatyana Shikolenko	RUS	64.61
2.	Felicia Moldovan	ROM	61.59
3.	Steffi Nerius	GER	59.98
4.	Sarah Walter	FRA	58.78
5.	Tatyana Lyakhovich	UKR	57.22
6.	**Kelly Morgan**		**56.55**
7.	Ewa Rybak	POL	55.67
8.	Claudia Coslovich	ITA	54.98

4 x 100 Metres (22 Jun)

1.	France	42.41
2.	Germany	42.49
3.	Russia	43.11
4.	Ukraine	43.51
5.	Italy	44.24
6.	Poland	44.54
7.	Romania	45.22
dnf Great Britain & NI		
(Maduaka, Anderson, Forrester, James)		

(Murphy, Frost, Karagouinis, McConnell)

2.	Germany	3:28.72
3.	Italy	3:29.14
4.	Romania	3:29.97
dsq France		
dsq Poland		
dsq Russia		
dsq Ukraine		

Match Result

1.	Russia	122.5
2.	Germany	103
3.	France	89
4.	Romania	88
5.	**Great Britain & NI**	**80.5**
6.	Poland	75.5
7.	Ukraine	73.5
8.	Italy	73

EUROPEAN CUP FOR COMBINED EVENTS

Maribor, SLO
29 -30 June 2002

MEN (League 2)

1.	Madis Kallas	EST	7529
2.	Jndrek Kaseorg	EST	7397
3.	**Anthony Sawyer**		**7271**
13.	**Brendan McConville**		**6996**
15.	**Alex Gibson**		**6887**
26.	**Steve Bonnett**		**6220**

Team Result

1.	Estonia	22178
2.	**Great Britain & NI**	**21154**
3.	Norway	20996

Bydgoszcz, POL
29 -30 June 2002

WOMEN (Super League)

1.	Karin Ertl	GER	6017
2.	Sabine Krieger	GER	5973
3.	Sonja Kesselschlager	GER	5950
12.	**Kelly Sotherton**		**5794**
23.	**Nicola Gautier**		**5307**
25.	**Roz Gonse**		**5275**
27.	**Laura Redmond**		**5098**

Team Result

1.	Germany	17940
2.	Russia	17449
3.	Ukraine	17381
8.	**Great Britain & NI**	**16376**

ITA v GB & NI v ESP (U20)
Gorizia, ITA 6 July 2002

MEN

100 Metres wind -1.3

1.	Alessandro Rocco ITA	10.68
2.	**Karl Forde**	**10.74**
5.	**Andrew Matthews**	**10.98**

200 Metres wind 0.5

1.	Borreguero Garcia ESP	21.32
2.	**Leon Baptiste**	**21.41**
5.	**Karl Forde**	**22.00**

400 Metres

1.	Alonso Testa ESP	47.67
4.	**Ryan Palmer**	**48.68**
6.	**Adam Charlton**	**50.22**

800 Metres

1.	Romera Crespo ESP	1:52.95
2.	**Michael Rimmer**	**1:53.85**
5.	**Gareth Balch**	**1:55.60**

1500 Metres

1.	Gonzalez Lorento ESP	3:48.71
4.	**Matt Bowser**	**3:51.84**
6.	**Derek Watson**	**3:54.88**

3000 Metres

1.	Stefano Scaini ITA	8:24.67
2.	**Ed Prickett**	**8:25.33**
3.	**Tom Sharland**	**8:27.54**

3000 Metres Steeplechase
1.	Marco Carbonetti	ITA	9:05.90
2.	Frank Tickner		9:08.24
4.	Daniel Lewis		9:24.39

110 Metres Hurdles wind -0.8
1.	Serra Lopez	ESP	14.33
5.	David Hughes		14.84
6.	Kris Jones		15.21

400 Metres Hurdles
1.	Steve Green	50.96
2.	Rhys Williams	52.46

High Jump
1.	Martyn Bernard	2.21
2.	Mark Crowley	2.15

Pole Vault
1.	Emanuele Formichetti	ITA	4.90
3.	Matthew Dorian		4.70
nh	Richard Hurren		

WOMEN
100 Metres wind -0.8
1.	Vicenza Cali	ITA	11.56
2.	Amy Spencer		11.75
3.	Jade Lucas-Read		12.01

200 Metres wind 0.5
1.	Giulia Arcioni	ITA	24.28
2.	Danielle Norville		24.35
4.	Katherine Jones		24.98

400 Metres
1.	Kim Wall	54.35
3.	Gemma Nicol	55.23

800 Metres
1.	Donna Riding	2:08.6
3.	Morag MacLarty	2:08.9

1500 Metres
1.	Charlotte Moore	4:20.14
6.	Freya Murray	4:38.99

3000 Metres
1.	Rachael Nathan	9:41.75
3.	Danielle Barnes	9:51.52

100 Metres Hurdles wind -0.7
1.	Gemma Fergusson	14.05
4.	Phyllis Agbo	14.29

Long Jump
1.	Louis Burgess	7.44
2.	Marlon Lewis	7.43

Triple Jump
1.	Minguez Ferrer	ESP	15.26
2.	Kevin Thompson		15.25
5.	Matthew Thurgood		14.69

Shot
1.	Dave Dawson	16.64
3.	Sam Westlake-Cann	16.44

Discus
1.	Fernandez Cuesta	ESP	55.73
3.	Sam Westlake-Cann		49.65
4.	Roger Bate		49.02

Hammer
1.	Massimo Marussi	ITA	71.14
3.	Carl Saggers		65.89
6.	Roger Bate		61.41

400 Metres Hurdles
1.	Elisa Scardanzan	ITA	60.65
2.	Sian Scott		60.78
4.	Justine Roach		62.49

High Jump
1.	Raffaella Lamera	ITA	1.84
2.	Rebecca Jones		1.84
3.	Stephanie Higham		1.82

Pole Vault
1.	Pi Pages	ESP	3.80
3.	Zoe Brown		3.60
5.	Natalie Olson		3.50

Long Jump
1.	Karlene Turner	5.86
5.	Elaine Smith	5.75

Triple Jump
1.	Simona La Mantia	ITA	13.33
4.	Emily Parker		11.91
6.	Azaria Francis		11.63

Shot
1.	Chiara Rosa	ITA	16.72
3.	Rebecca Peake		13.96
5.	Charlotte Spelzini		13.58

Javelin
1.	Alex van der Merwe	64.45
2.	Andrew Gallagher	62.26

5k Walk
1.	Daniele Paris	ITA	20:29.15
4.	Daniel King		21:46.29
dnf	Andrew Parker		

4 x 100 Metres
1.	Italy	40.27
3.	Great Britain & NI	41.49
	(Matthews, Fifton, Baptiste, Fowles)	

4 x 400 Metres
1.	Great Britain & NI	3:12.93
	(Williams, Burgess, Palmer, Green)	

Match Result - Men
1.	Great Britain & NI	143.5
2.	Spain	140.5
3.	Italy	138

Discus
1.	Biserka Cesar	ITA	48.15
3.	Ellisha Dee		44.45
6.	Emma Forrester		41.50

Hammer
1.	Franco Castells	ESP	60.96
3.	Laura Douglas		54.88
4.	Nicola Dudman		52.40

Javelin
1.	Silvia Carli	ITA	48.79
3.	Samantha Redd		45.49
5.	Louise Mathews		40.11

5k Walk
1.	Sibilla Di Vincenzo	ITA	22:38.80
5.	Sophie Hales		24:35.56
6.	Katie Stones		27:34.98

4 x 100 Metres
1.	Great Britain & NI	45.36
	(Kwakye, Douglas, Spencer, Lucas-Read)	

4 x 400 Metres
1.	Great Britain & NI	3:39.14
	(Nicol, Thompson, Griffiths, Wall)	

Match Result - Women
1.	Italy	160
2.	Great Britain & NI	145
3.	Spain	99

Match Result - Combined
1.	Italy	298
2.	Great Britain & NI	288.5
3.	Spain	239.5

AAA CHAMPIONSHIPS Birmingham 12 - 14 July 2002
Including Norwich Union European Trials

As last year, the championships contained a mix of excellent performances together with a worrying lack of competitors in some events. Kelly Morgan broke the javelin record twice and Lisa Kehler set a best for the 5000 metres Walk. Susan Jones also came close to the high jump record. For the men, all the sprint races were close with excellent times all round. A sour note for the championships was the positive drugs tests for Janine Whitlock and Perriss Wlikins becoming known.

MEN

100 Metres wind 1.9 (13 Jul)
1. Mark Lewis-Francis — 10.06
2. Darren Campbell — 10.11
3. Jason Gardener — 10.13
4. Christian Malcolm — 10.29
5. Allyn Condon — 10.32
6. Daniel Plummer — 10.33
7. Curtis Browne — 10.47

200 Metres wind 2.2 (14 Jul)
1. Marlon Devonish — 20.18w
2. Darren Campbell — 20.26w
3. Christian Malcolm — 20.29w
4. Dwayne Grant — 20.60w
5. Julian Golding — 20.62w
6. Graham Beasley — 20.90w
7. Dwain Chambers — 23.81w
dsq Doug Turner

400 Metres (14 Jul)
1. Tim Benjamin — 45.73
2. Sean Baldock — 45.84
3. Jared Deacon — 45.89
4. Du`aine Ladejo — 46.23
5. Jamie Baulch — 46.42
6. Mark Hylton — 46.49
7. Cori Henry — 46.56
8. Graham Hedman — 46.61

800 Metres (14 Jul)
1. James McIlroy — 1:50.09
2. Neil Speaight — 1:50.71
3. Alasdair Donaldson — 1:50.80
4. Dominic Hall — 1:50.86
5. Sam Ellis — 1:51.31
6. James Mayo — 1:52.76
7. Tim Alexander — 1:52.86
8. Terry Feasey — 1:53.01

1500 Metres (14 Jul)
1. Tony Whiteman — 3:38.24
2. John Mayock — 3:38.97
3. Michael East — 3:39.18
4. Andrew Graffin — 3:40.24
5. Gregg Taylor — 3:40.70
6. Angus Maclean — 3:42.19
7. Adam Zawadski — 3:44.17
8. Chris Bolt — 3:44.23

5000 Metres (14 Jul)
1. John Wild — 13:52.59
2. Rob Denmark — 13:53.18
3. Matthew Smith — 13:53.47
4. Karl Keska — 13:54.34
5. Mark Miles — 13:54.94
6. Glen Stewart — 13:59.39
7. Spencer Barden — 14:01.54
8. Andres Jones — 14:03.56

10000 Metres (see Manchester 15 Jun)

3000 Metres Steeplechase (14 Jul)
1. Ben Whitby — 8:40.12
2. Christian Stephenson — 8:44.31
3. Patrick Davoren — 8:47.92
4. Jermaine Mays — 8:49.14
5. Mark Warmby — 8:49.33
6. Craig Wheeler — 8:52.79
7. Nick Talbot — 8:52.88
8. Andrew Robinson — 8:54.85

110 Metres Hurdles wind 0.3 (13 Jul)
1. Colin Jackson — 13.40
2. Tony Jarrett — 13.52
3. Damien Greaves — 13.54
4. Mensah Elliott — 13.85
5. Dominic Girdler — 13.95
6. Paul Gray — 14.00
7. Andrew Turner — 14.26
8. Chris Baillie — 14.30

400 Metres Hurdles (14 Jul)
1. Chris Rawlinson — 48.68
2. Anthony Borsumato — 48.90
3. Matt Elias — 49.79
4. Matthew Douglas — 50.12
5. Liam Collins — 50.30
6. Richard Smith — 51.36
7. Charles Robertson-Adams — 51.95
8. Steve Surety — 53.88

High Jump (13 Jul)
1. Dalton Grant — 2.20
2. Ben Challenger — 2.20
3. Mark Landy — IRL — 2.10
4. Luke Crawley — 2.10
5. Martin Lloyd — 2.10
6= Brian Hall — 2.05
6= Darryl Stone — 2.05
8= Robert Brocklebank — 2.05
8= Stanley Osuide — 2.05

Pole Vault (14 Jul)
1. Nick Buckfield — 5.35
2. Mark Davis — 5.20
3. Christian North — 5.20
4= Ian Tullett — 5.00
4= Paul Williamson — 5.00
6. Tim Thomas — 5.00
7= Mark Beharrell — 5.00
7= Kevin Hughes — 5.00
7= Ashley Swain — 5.00

Long Jump (13 Jul)
1. Darren Ritchie — 7.93
2. Chris Tomlinson — 7.82
3. Mark Awanah — 7.46
4. Steve Phillips — 7.24w
5. Levi Edwards — 7.03
6. Mark Lawrence — 6.65
7. Julian Flynn — 6.58

Triple Jump (14 Jul)
1. Phillips Idowu — 17.02
2. Tosin Oke — 16.60
3. Steven Shalders — 16.09
4. Julian Golley — 15.25
5. Martin Rossiter — 15.00
6. Mike McKernan — 14.96
7. John Hilton — 14.62

Shot (14 Jul)
1. Mark Proctor — 18.54
2. Emeka Udechuku — 17.19
3. Scott Rider — 17.19
4. David Readle — 16.80
5. Iain McMullen — 16.48
6. Lyndon Woodward — 16.42
7. Greg Beard — 16.24
8. Bryan Kelly — 16.08

Discus (14 Jul)
1. Bob Weir — 58.22
2. Glen Smith — 56.38
3. Emeka Udechuku — 56.28
4. Kevin Brown — JAM — 53.90
5. Lee Newman — 52.85
6. Matthew Twigg — 51.26
7. Bruce Robb — 51.18
8. Neville Thompson — 50.54

Hammer (13 Jul)
1. Mick Jones — 72.26
2. Paul Head — 67.61
3. Mike Floyd — 66.33
4. Bill Beauchamp — 65.20
5. Simon Bown — 64.73
6. Iain Park — 64.03
7. Andy Frost — 62.80
8. Shane Peacock — 61.96

Javelin (13 Jul)

1.	Mick Hill	77.86
2.	Mark Roberson	74.23
3.	Nick Nieland	73.20
4.	Stuart Faben	70.03
5.	Phillip Sharpe	66.38
6.	Tom Dobbing	64.77
7.	Neil McLellan	64.24
8.	Peter Yates	63.22

WOMEN

100 Metres wind 1.6 (13 Jul)

1.	Joice Maduaka	11.31
2.	Abi Oyepitan	11.42
3.	Diane Allahgreen	11.44
4.	Amanda Forrester	11.54
5.	Sabrina Scott	11.58
6.	Emily Freeman	11.67
7.	Marcia Richardson	11.69
8.	Susan Burnside	11.75

200 Metres wind 3.1 (14 Jul)

1.	Shani Anderson	23.03w
2.	Joice Maduaka	23.21w
3.	Ellena Ruddock	23.41w
4.	Emily Freeman	23.41w
5.	Sabrina Scott	24.01w
6.	Danielle Halsall	24.12w
7.	Susan Williams	24.18w
8.	Kelly Sotherton	24.23w

400 Metres (13 Jul)

1.	Lee McConnell	51.59
2.	Catherine Murphy	52.10
3.	Helen Karagounis	52.45
4.	Melanie Purkiss	53.03
5.	Helen Frost	53.27
6.	Carey Easton	53.73
7.	Jenny Meadows	53.99
8.	Lesley Owusu	54.08

800 Metres (13 Jul)

1.	Susan Scott	2:03.89
2.	Jo Fenn	2:04.12
3.	Emma Davies	2:05.52
4.	Hayley Ovens	2:06.62
5.	Rebecca Lyne	2:06.68
6.	Jennifer Ward	2:07.53
7.	Jeina Mitchell	2:08.10
8.	Lucy Vaughan	2:09.15

1500 Metres (14 Jul)

1.	Kelly Holmes	4:06.02
2.	Helen Pattinson	4:06.98
3.	Hayley Tullett	4:08.23
4.	Joanne Pavey	4:11.16
5.	Rachel Newcombe	4:11.81
6.	Sarah Bull	4:12.21
7.	Kerry Gillibrand	4:17.53
8.	Tina Brown	4:22.59

5000 Metres Walk (13 Jul)

1.	Steve Hollier	20:41.29
2.	Don Bearman	21:55.07
3.	Nathan Adams	23:11.68

5000 Metres (14 Jul)

1.	Hayley Yelling	16:11.23
2.	Catherine Dugdale	16:25.14
3.	Debbie Sullivan	16:28.37
4.	Collette Fagan	16:33.31
5.	Jane Potter	17:05.24

10000 Metres (see Manchester 16 Jun)

2000 Metres Steeplechase (13 Jul)

1.	Tara Krzywicki	6:31.77
2.	Claire Entwistle	6:54.92
3.	Ursula Counsell	7:04.94
4.	Jane Pidgeon	7:11.67
5.	Joanne King	7:20.16

100 Metres Hurdles wind 1.6 (14 Jul)

1.	Diane Allahgreen	13.00
2.	Julie Pratt	13.27
3.	Rachel King	13.34
4.	Bianca Liston	13.78
5.	Liz Fairs	13.81
6.	Kate Brewington	13.85
7.	Kerry Jury	13.86
8.	Stefanie Pullinger	14.16

400 Metres Hurdles (13 Jul)

1.	Natasha Danvers	56.14
2.	Sinead Dudgeon	56.88
3.	Tracey Duncan	57.51
4.	Katie Jones	57.97
5.	Hannah Wood	60.13
6.	Liz Fairs	60.87
7.	Jennifer Culley	60.87
8.	Hannah Stares	63.80

High Jump (14 Jul)

1.	Susan Jones	1.92
2.	Debbi Marti	1.75
3.	Julie Crane	1.75
4=	Natalie Clark	1.70
4=	Aileen Wilson	1.70

Pole Vault (13 Jul)

1.	Irie Hill	4.15
2=	Tracey Bloomfield	4.05
2=	Rhian Clarke	4.05
4=	Liz Hughes	3.90
4=	Lucy Webber	3.90
6.	Zoe Brown	3.70
7.	Laura Ballotta	ITA	3.70
drg	Janine Whitlock	(4.35)

Decathlon (Wrexham 22-23 Jun)

1.	Adrian Hemery	6620
2.	James Lowery	6460
3.	Paul Tohill	6395
4.	James Wright	6220
5.	Andrew East	6092
6.	Carl Marchment	5924
7.	Daniel Brandwood	5822
8.	Brian Hughes	5578

Long Jump (14 Jul)

1.	Jade Johnson	6.52
2.	Sarah Claxton	6.17
3.	Donita Benjamin	6.08
4.	Sarah Wellstead	6.03
5.	Natasha May	6.01
6.	Caroline Pearce	5.79
7.	Rebecca White	5.78
8.	Elaine Smith	5.75

Triple Jump (13 Jul)

1.	Ashia Hansen		14.50
2.	Yamile Aldama	CUB	14.40
3.	Michelle Griffith		13.18
4.	Danielle Freeman		12.98
5.	Taneisha Scanlon	IRL	12.75
6.	Rebecca White		12.65
7.	Leandra Polius		12.45
8.	Deborah Rowe		12.37

Shot (13 Jul)

1.	Myrtle Augee	16.16
2.	Julie Dunkley	15.89
3.	Joanne Duncan	15.71
4.	Maggie Lynes	14.79
5.	Philippa Roles	14.52
6.	Eva Massey	14.15
7.	Kara Nwidobie	13.99
8.	Rebecca Peake	13.28

Discus (13 Jul)

1.	Philippa Roles	56.32
2.	Shelley Newman	54.08
3.	Emma Carpenter	53.28
4.	Kara Nwidobie	47.10
5.	Rebecca Roles	46.13
6.	Vav Dhaliwal	44.40
7.	Elaine Cank	44.21
8.	Joanna Bradley	43.40

Hammer (14 Jul)

1.	Lorraine Shaw	64.97
2	Liz Pidgeon	62.08
3.	Zoe Derham	59.89
4.	Suzanne Roberts	58.93
5.	Diana Holden	57.23
6.	Shirley Webb	56.40
7.	Lesley Brannan	55.71
8.	Sarah Moore	54.96

Javelin (14 Jul)
1. Kelly Morgan 64.87
2. Goldie Sayers 56.96
3. Karen Martin 56.34
4. Kirsty Morrison 48.44
5. Katy Watts 41.01

5000 Metres Walk (13 Jul)
1. Lisa Kehler 21:42.51
2. Sharon Tonks 24:05.49
3. Estle Viljoen RSA 24:26.11

Heptathlon (Wrexham 22-23 Jun)
1. Caroline Pearce 5108
2. Kate Brewington 4971
3. Maureen Knight 4593
4. Kirsty Roger 4426
5. Victoria Consterdine 4162
6. Amanda Wale 3848

IAAF WORLD JUNIOR CHAMPIONSHIPS
Kingston, JAM 16 - 21 July 2002

A very disappointing championship with one outstanding exception. Vernicha James managed a complete set of medals with an individual gold in the 200 metres and bronze and silver in the two relays. These were the only medals won.

MEN

100 Metres wind -0.6 (17 Jul)
1. Darrel Brown TRI 10.09
2. Marc Burns TRI 10.18
3. Willie Hordge USA 10.36

200 Metres wind 0.9 (19 Jul)
1. Usain Bolt JAM 20.61
2. Brendan Christian ANT 20.74
3. Wes Felix USA 20.82

400 Metres (18 Jul)
1. Darold Williamson USA 45.37
2. Jonathan Fortenberry USA 45.73
3. Jermaine Gonzales JAM 45.84
h4 Robert Tobin dnf

800 Metres (19 Jul)
1. Alex Kipchirchir KEN 1:46.59
2. Salem Amer Al-Badri QAT 1:46.63
3. David Fiegen LUX 1:46.66
5s2 Ricky Soos 1:50.17
(2h2 1:48.82)

1500 Metres (21 Jul)
1. Yassine Bensghir MAR 3:40.72
2. Abdulrahman Suleiman QAT 3:41.72
3. Samwel Mwera TAN 3:41.75

5000 Metres (16 Jul)
1. Hillary Chenonge KEN 13:28.30
2. Markos Geneti ETH 13:28.83
3. Gebre Gebremariam ETH 13:29.13

10000 Metres (20 Jul)
1. Gebre Gebremariam ETH 29:02.71
2. Sileshi Sihine ETH 29:03.74
3. Solomon Bushendich KEN 29:05.96

3000 Metres Steeplechase (20 Jul)
1. Michael Kipyego KEN 8:29.54
2. David Kirwa KEN 8:31.44

WOMEN

100 Metres wind -0.2 (17 Jul)
1. Lauryn Williams USA 11.33
2. Simone Facey JAM 11.43
3. Marshevet Hooker USA 11.48
3s1 Jeanette Kwakye 11.75
(5h3 11.76)

3. Ali Abubaker Kamal QAT 8:33.67
12. Stephen Murphy 9:05.80
(5h2 8:56.85)

110 Metres Hurdles wind 2.6 (21 Jul)
1. Antwon Hicks USA 13.42w
2. Shi Dongpeng CHN 13.58w
3. Shamar Sands BAH 13.67w

400 Metres Hurdles (19 Jul)
1. Louis van Zyl RSA 48.89
2. Kenneth Ferguson USA 49.38
3. Bershawn Jackson USA 50.00
4. Steven Green 51.14
(1h5 51.68, 2s1 51.12)
3s2 Rhys Williams 51.68
(3h4 51.71)

High Jump (18 Jul)
1. Andra Manson USA 2.31
2. Zhu Wannan CHN 2.23
3. Jermaine Mason JAM 2.21
10. Martyn Bernard 2.14
(Q 2.18)
23=Q Mark Crowley 2.12

Pole Vault (21 Jul)
1. Maksym Mazuryk UKR 5.55
2. Vladyslav Revenko UKR 5.55
3. Vincent Favretto FRA 5.40

Long Jump (18 Jul)
1. Ibrahim Al-Waleed QAT 7.99
2. Fabrice Lapierre AUS 7.74
3. Trevell Quinley USA 7.71

Triple Jump (20 Jul)
1. David Giralt CUB 16.68
2. Li Yanxi CHN 16.66
3. Aleksandr Sergeyev RUS 16.55

200 Metres wind -0.2 (19 Jul)
1. Vernicha James 22.93
(1h3 23.14, 1s2 23.07)
2. Anneisha McLaughlin JAM 22.94
3. Sanya Richards USA 23.09
7. Amy Spencer 23.76
(2h5 23.46, 3s3 23.65)

Shot 6kg (16 Jul)
1. Edis Elkasevic CRO 21.47
2. Sean Shields USA 20.54
3. Mika Vasara FIN 20.50

Discus 1.75kg (18 Jul)
1. Wu Tao CHN 64.51
2. Dmitriy Sivakov BLR 62.00
3. Michal Hodun POL 61.74

Hammer 6kg (17 Jul)
1. Werner Smit RSA 76.43
2. Ali Mohamed Al-Zinkawi KUW 73.69
3. Aliaksandr Kazulka BLR 72.72

Javelin (21 Jul)
1. Igor Janik POL 74.16
2. Vladislav Shkurlatov RUS 74.09
3. Jung Sang-Jin KOR 73.99
24Q Alex van der Merwe 59.89

Decathlon (16/17 Jul)
1. Leonid Andreyev UZB 7693
2. Nadir El Fassi FRA 7677
3. Mikko Halvari FIN 7587

10000 Metres Walk (17 Jul)
1. Vladimir Kanaykin RUS 41:41.40
2. Xu Xingde CHN 41:44.00
3. Lu Ronghua CHN 41:46.07
dsq Dominic King

4 x 100 Metres (21 Jul)
1. United States 38.92
2. Jamaica 39.15
3. Trinidad & Tobago 39.17

4 x 400 Metres (21 Jul)
1. United States 3:03.71
2. Jamaica 3:04.06
3. Japan 3:05.80

400 Metres (18 Jul)
1. Monique Henderson USA 51.10
2. Sanya Richards USA 51.49
3. Sheryl Morgan JAM 52.61
5. Lisa Miller 53.20
(2h4 54.39, 3s1 53.28)
5s2 Kim Wall 54.05
(3h1 54.18)

116

800 Metres (19 Jul)
1. Janeth Jepkosgei KEN 2:00.80
2. Lucia Klocova SVK 2:01.73
3. Juliana de Azevedo BRA 2:03.81
4. **Jemma Simpson** 2:04.11
   (3h2 2:05.60)

1500 Metres (21 Jul)
1. Viola Kibiwot KEN 4:12.57
2. Berhane Herpassa ETH 4:13.59
3. Olesya Syreva RUS 4:14.32
4. **Lisa Dobriskey** 4:14.72
   (1h2 4:19.83)
7h1 Katrina Wootton 4:24.04

3000 Metres (16 Jul)
1. Meseret Defar ETH 9:12.61
2. Mariem Al Aoui Selsouli MAR 9:16.28
3. Olesya Syreva RUS 9:16.58

5000 Metres (21 Jul)
1. Meseret Defar ETH 15:54.94
2. Tirunesh Dibaba ETH 15:55.99
3. Vivian Cheruiyot KEN 15:56.04

100 Metres Hurdles wind 3.4 (21 Jul)
1. Anay Tejeda CUB 12.81w
2. Agnieszka Frankowska POL 13.16w
3. Tina Klein GER 13.23w
3h3 Gemma Fergusson 13.81

400 Metres Hurdles (19 Jul)
1. Lashinda Demus USA 54.70
2. Melanie Walker JAM 56.03
3. Camille Robinson JAM 56.14

High Jump (20 Jul)
1. Blanka Vlasic CRO 1.96
2. Anna Ksok POL 1.87
3. Petrina Price AUS 1.87
14Q Rebecca Jones 1.80
17Q Stephanie Higham 1.75

Pole Vault (18 Jul)
1. Floe Kuhnert GER 4.40
2. Yuliya Golubchikova RUS 4.30
3. Nataliya Belinskaya RUS 4.20
7. **Kate Dennison** 4.00

Long Jump (19 Jul)
1. Adina Anton ROM 6.46
2. Wang Lina CHN 6.36
3. Esther Aghatise NGR 6.34

Triple Jump (17 Jul)
1. Mabel Gay CUB 14.09
2. Arianna Martinez CUB 13.74
3. Costa Keila da Silva BRA 13.70

Shot (20 Jul)
1. Valerie Adams NZL 17.73
2. Zhang Ying CHN 16.76
3. Laura Gerraughty USA 16.62

Discus (19 Jul)
1. Ma Xuejun CHN 58.85
2. Xu Shaoyang CHN 57.87
3. Seema Antil CHN 55.83
9. **Claire Smithson** 50.85

Hammer (20 Jul)
1. Ivana Brkljacic CRO 65.39
2. Martina Danisova SVK 63.91
3. Yuliya Rozenfeld RUS 60.83
18Q Laura Douglas 52.65
19Q Nicola Dudman 52.56

Javelin (17 Jul)
1. Linda Brivule LAT 55.35
2. Ilze Gribule LAT 54.16
3. Urszula Jasinska POL 54.06

Heptathlon (19/20 Jul)
1. Carolina Kluft SWE 6470
2. Olga Alekseyeva KAZ 5727
3. Olga Levenkova RUS 5712

10000 Metres Walk (18 Jul)
1. Fumi Mitsumura JPN 46:01.51
2. Liu Siqi CHN 46:07.15
3. Maryna Tsikhanava BLR 46:14.67

4 x 100 Metres (21 Jul)
1. Jamaica 43.40
2. United States 43.66
3. **Great Britain & NI** 44.22
(Lucas-Read, Kwakye, Spencer, James)
   (2h1 44.49 Norville for Kwakye)

4 x 400 Metres (21 Jul)
1. United States 3:29.95
2. **Great Britain & NI** 3:30.46
   (Wall, Spencer, James, Miller)
(2h2 3:38.49
   Wall, Thompson, Griffiths, Miller)
3. Russia 3:30.72

GB & NI v GER (U23) Newport 20 July 2002

MEN

100 Metres wind 2.9
1. **Daniel Plummer** 10.48w
dsq Tim Abeyie

200 Metres wind
1. Rasgawa Pinnock GER 21.52
2. **Dominic Papura** 21.61
4. **Finlay Wright** 22.37

400 Metres
1. **Ian Lowthian** 48.08
3. **Alloy Wilson** 48.21

800 Metres
1. **Angus Maclean** 1:48.82
3. **Sam Ellis** 1:49.98

1500 Metres
1. **Chris Bolt** 4:10.09
2. **Tom Carter** 4:10.73

3000 Metres
1. **Chris Thompson** 8:15.12
3. **James Fewtrell** 8:19.06

3000 Metres Steeplechase
1. Raphael Schafer GER 8:52.99
3. **Jermaine Mays** 9:31.79
dnf Adam Bowden

110 Metres Hurdles wind 2.3
1. Thomas Blaschek GER 13.96w
2. **Robert Newton** 14.09w
3. **Dominic Girdler** 14.15w

400 Metres Hurdles
1. **Steve Surety** 50.58
3. **Richard Smith** 51.93

High Jump
1. **Robert Mitchell** 2.15
3. **Martin Lloyd** 2.05

Pole Vault
1. Marvin Osei-Tutu GER 5.50
2. **Ashley Swain** 5.30
3. **Mark Beharrell** 5.00

Long Jump
1. Andreas Pohle GER 8.11w
3. **Chris Tomlinson** 7.74
4. **Andre Fernandez** 7.38w

Triple jump
1. **Phil Ferdinand** 15.92
2. **Nathan Douglas** 15.90w

Shot
1. Sven-Erik Hahn GER 17.72
3. **David Readle** 16.20
4. **Nicholas Owen** 15.84

Discus
1. Karsten Friedrich GER 52.20
3. **Scott Thompson** 50.79
4. **Luke Rosenberg** 48.51

Hammer
1. Markus Esser GER 74.49
3. **Andy Frost** 61.20
4. **Graeme Allan** 56.82

Javelin
1. Stefan Wenk   GER   79.15
3. Michael Tarran   61.89
4. Rhys Williams   61.41

10000 Metres Walk
1. Frank Werner   GER 43:37.35
2. Daniel King   45:33.82
4. Nathan Adams   47:47.50

WOMEN
100 Metres wind 3.1
1. Katherine Endacott   11.58w
4. Laura Turner   11.99w

200 Metres wind 3.0
1. Katchi Habel   GER   24.53w
2. Katherine Endacott   24.66w
3. Lisa Trotman   24.79w

400 Metres
1. Jenny Meadows   53.77
2. Danielle Halsall   53.91

800 Metres
1. Juliane Becker   GER   2:08.64
3. Catherine Riley   2:09.36
4. Suzanne Hasler   2:09.91

1500 Metres
1. Natalie Lewis   4:27.17
2. Susan Cripsey   4:29.30

3000 Metres
1. Louise Damen   9:39.64
3. Jane Potter   9:43.14

100 Metres Hurdles wind 1.6
1. Kathrin van Buhren   GER   13.71
2. Kate Brewington   13.90
4. Lynne Fairweather   17.93

4 x 100 Metres
1. Great Britain & NI   40.89
(Plummer, Wright, Abeyie, Papura)
dnf Germany

4 x 400 Metres
1. Germany   3:13.71
2. Great Britain & NI   3:13.83
(Bayley, Ellis, Smith, Wilson)

400 Metres Hurdles
1. Tina Kron   GER   59.16
2. Hannah Wood   59.20
3. Samantha Adamson   61.32

High Jump
1. Katja Schotz   GER   1.86
3. Natalie Clark   1.75
4. Judith Payne   1.65

Pole Vault
1. Gillian Cooke   3.80
2. Ellie Spain   3.80

Long Jump
1. Jade Johnson   6.69
4. Natasha May   6.02

Triple Jump
1. Rebecca White   13.15w
3. Danielle Freeman   12.50w

Shot
1. Aline Schaffel   GER   16.43
3. Kara Nwidobie   14.28
4. Joanna Bennett   12.06

Discus
1. Jana Tucholke   GER   58.30
3. Claire Moore   45.94
4. Kara Nwidobie   45.27

Match result – Men
1. Germany   99
2. Great Britain & NI   89

Hammer
1. Bianca Achilles   GER   58.32
2. Shirley Webb   57.53
3. Mhairi Walters   56.25

Javelin
1. Jana Ladewig   GER   54.33
3. Goldie Sayers   50.57
4. Claire Moore   0.39

5000 Metres Walk
1. Stephanie Panzig   GER 24:02.79
2. Sophie Hales   24:19.06

4 x 100 Metres
1. Germany   45.65
2. Great Britain & NI   46.51
(Brewington, Trotman, Turner, Endacott)

4 x 400 Metres
1. Great Britain & NI   3:39.92
(Halsall, Wood, Clarkson, Meadows)
2. Germany   3:40.98

Match Result – Women
1. Germany   94
2. Great Britain & NI   86

Match Result – Combined
1. Germany   193
2. Great Britain & NI   175

XVII COMMONWEALTH GAMES
Manchester 26 - 31 July 2002

The Commonwealth Games always provide English athletes with a chance to shine and in front of capacity crowds on every day, they won 12 gold, 6 silver and 11 bronze. Wales won 4 silver and a very small Scotland team won just 1 silver and 1 bronze. As usual the standard was very mixed, but Paula Radclifffe continued her great season with a first major track gold medal in a fast time. Some medallists were to find their performances here would not qualify for the final in Munich 2 weeks later.

MEN
100 Metres wind 0.2 (27 Jul)
1. Kim Collins   STK   9.98
2. Uchenna Emedolu   NGR   10.11
3. Pierre Brown   CAN   10.12
4= Deji Aliu   NGR   10.15
4= Dwight Thomas   JAM   10.15
6. Jason Gardener   Eng   10.22
(2h6 10.34, 4q3 10.33, 4s2 10.21)
7. Mark Lewis-Francis Eng   10.54
(1h1 10.25, 1q2 10.13, 2s1 10.15)
8. Dwain Chambers   Eng   11.19
(1h5 10.19, 1q1 10.17, 1s2 10.06)

7q1 Kevin Williams   Wal   10.65
(4h5 10.63)
7q2 Jamie Henthorn   Wal   10.74
(5h2 10.81)

200 Metres wind 1.4 (29 Jul)
1. Frankie Fredericks   NAM   20.06
2. Marlon Devonish   Eng   20.19
(1h1 20.61, 1q4 20.63, 2s1 20.55)
3. Darren Campbell   Eng   20.21
(1h5 20.87, 2q2 20.70, 4s1 20.58)

4. Dominic Demeritte   BAH   20.21
5. Abdul Aziz Zakari   GHA   20.29
6. Morne Nagel   RSA   20.35
7. Joseph Batangdon   CMR   20.36
8. Christian Malcolm   Wal   20.39
(2h1 21.01, 3q1 20.61, 3s2 20.55)
6s2 Chris Lambert   Eng   21.02
(1h2 20.77, 2q3 20.90)
7s1 Doug Turner   Wal   21.11
(3h5 21.18, 4q4 21.24)
6q3 Jamie Henthorn   Wal   21.58
(4h2 21.35)

400 Metres (28 Jul)
1. Michael Blackwood JAM 45.07
2. Shane Niemi CAN 45.09
3. Avard Moncur BAH 45.12
4. **Daniel Caines** Eng **45.13**
   (1h5 47.37, 2q4 46.11, 1s2 44.98)
5. Alleyne Francique GRN 45.47
6. Eric Milazar MRI 45.64
7. Chris Brown BAH 45.67
8. Clinton Hill AUS 46.00
6s1 **Sean Baldock** Eng **45.71**
   (3h1 46.02, 3q3 46.26)
7s2 **Tim Benjamin** Wal **45.89**
   (3h3 46.89, 4q4 46.54)
7s1 **Paul McKee** NIr **45.91**
   (4h3 47.02, 4q3 46.47)
8s1 **Jared Deacon** Eng **46.07**
   (2h2 46.52, 3q2 46.66)

800 Metres (29 Jul)
1. Mbulaeni Mulaudzi RSA 1:46.32
2. Joseph Mutua KEN 1:46.57
3. Kris McCarthy AUS 1:46.79
4. Otukile Lekote BOT 1:47.04
5. Japheth Kimutai KEN 1:47.46
6. **James McIlroy** NIr **1:47.77**
   (2h4 1:49.21, 3s1 1:46.93)
7. Paskar Owor UGA 1:48.96
8. Glody Dube BOT 2:17.40
5s2 **Neil Speaight** Eng **1:47.22**
   (3h2 1:49.67)
6s1 **Joel Kidger** Eng **1:48.12**
   (3h4 1:49.47)
7s1 **Matt Shone** Wal **1:49.08**
   (4h4 1:49.67)
4h3 **Curtis Robb** Eng **1:50.34**

1500 Metres (31 Jul)
1. **Michael East** Eng **3:37.35**
   (3h1 3:46.90)
2. William Chirchir KEN 3:37.70
3. Youcef Abdi AUS 3:37.77
4. **Anthony Whiteman** Eng **3:38.04**
   (1h2 3:43.25)
5. Graham Hood CAN 3:38.08
6. Julius Achon UGA 3:38.33
7. Kevin Sullivan CAN 3:40.95
8. **Tom Mayo** Eng **3:41.70**
   (5h2 3:45.56)
11. **Jonathan McCallum** Sco **3:48.02**
   (5h1 3:47.37)
12. **Colm McLean** NIr **3:51.90**
   (6h2 3:45.72)
8h2 **Lee Merrien** Gue **3:47.68**
6h1 **Matt Shone** Wal **3:47.83**

5000 Metres (31 Jul)
1. Sammy Kipketer KEN 13:13.51
2. Benjamin Limo KEN 13:13.57
3. Willy Kiptoo Kirui KEN 13:18.02
4. **John Mayock** Eng **13:19.43**
5. **Sam Haughian** Eng **13:19.45**

6. Craig Mottram AUS 13:25.21
7. Sean Kaley CAN 13:26.28
8. Mike Power AUS 13:34.04
11. **Matt O`Dowd** Eng **13:43.33**
14. **Glen Stewart** Sco **13:49.70**
15. **Donald Naylor** Wal **14:09.38**

10000 Metres (26 Jul)
1. Wilberforce Talel KEN 27:45.39
2. Paul Kosgei KEN 27:45.46
3. John Yuda TAN 27:45.78
4. John Ch. Korir KEN 27:45.83
5. Martin Sulle TAN 28:15.60
6. Jeff Schiebler CAN 28:29.22
7. Sean Kaley CAN 28:31.99
8. Michael Aish NZL 28:35.27
11. **Glen Stewart** Sco **29:04.03**
12. **Rob Denmark** Eng **29:08.59**
14. **Andres Jones** Wal **29:15.44**
15. **Jon Wild** Eng **29:18.17**
19. **Ian Hudspith** Eng **29:33.43**

Marathon (28 Jul)
1. Francis Robert Naali TAN 2:11:58
2. Joshua Chelanga KEN 2:12:44
3. Andrew Letherby AUS 2:13:23
4. Eric Wainaina KEN 2:13:27
5. Luketz Swartbooi NAM 2:13:40
6. Jonathan Wyatt NZL 2:14:20
7. Lee Troop AUS 2:16:44
8. Josiaah Bembe RSA 2:18:16
10. **Dominic Bannister** Eng **2:19:31**
12. **Stuart Hall** Eng **2:19:53**
16. **Simon Pride** Sco **2:23:56**
dnf **Mark Hudspith** Eng

3000 Metres Steeplechase (27 Jul)
1. Stephen Cherono KEN 8:19.41
2. Ezekiel Kemboi KEN 8:19.78
3. Abraham Cherono KEN 8:19.85
4. **Stuart Stokes** Eng **8:26.45**
5. Joel Bourgeois CAN 8:33.98
6. **Donald Naylor** Wal **8:38.68**
7. **Ben Whitby** Eng **8:40.87**
8. **Christian Stephenson** Wal **8:41.32**
9. **Pat Davoren** Eng **8:44.43**

110 Metres Hurdles wind 0.4 (30 Jul)
1. Shaun Bownes RSA 13.35
2. **Colin Jackson** Wal **13.39**
   (1h3 13.34)
3. Maurice Wignall JAM 13.62
4. **Tony Jarrett** Eng **13.70**
   (2h2 13.65)
5. Charles Allen CAN 13.71
6. Ricardo Melbourne JAM 13.94
7. **Chris Baillie** Sco **14.73**
   (3h2 13.95)
dnf **Damien Greaves** Eng
   (2h3 13.78)
5h2 **Paul Gray** Wal **14.11**
3h1 **Mensah Elliott** Eng **14.27**

400 Metres Hurdles (29 Jul)
1. **Chris Rawlinson** Eng **49.14**
   (1h2 49.66)
2. **Matt Elias** Wal **49.28**
   (1h1 49.11)
3. Ian Weakley JAM 49.69
4. **Anthony Borsumato** Eng **49.72**
   (2h1 49.26)
5. Dinsdale Morgan JAM 50.14
6. Willie Smith NAM 50.14
7. Ashoka Jayasundra SRI 50.63
8. **Matt Douglas** Eng **51.01**
   (4h1 49.38)
6h1 **Richard McDonald** Sco **51.46**
7h2 **James Hillier** Wal **51.54**

High Jump (29 Jul)
1. Mark Boswell CAN 2.28
2. Kwaku Boateng CAN 2.25
3. **Ben Challenger** Eng **2.25**
   (2.15Q)
4. Nick Moroney AUS 2.20
5. Germaine Mason JAM 2.20
6. **Dalton Grant** Eng **2.15**
   (2.15Q)
7= Damon Thompson BAR 2.15
7= Craig Norman JAM 2.15
10. **Robert Mitchell** Wal **2.15**
   (2.15Q)
11. **Richard Aspden** Eng **2.10**
   (2.10Q)
nh **Martin Aram** IoM
   (2.10Q)

Pole Vault (30 Jul)
1. Okkert Brits RSA 5.75
2. Paul Burgess AUS 5.70
3. Dominic Johnson LCA 5.60
4= Viktor Chistiakov AUS 5.50
4= **Nick Buckfield** Eng **5.50**
4= Dmitri Markov AUS 5.50
7. **Tim Thomas** Wal **5.20**
8. **Kevin Hughes** Eng **5.05**
nh **Paul Williamson** Eng

Long Jump (30 Jul)
1. **Nathan Morgan** Eng **8.02**
   (7.77Q)
2. Gable Garenamotse BOT 7.91
3. Kareem Str-Thompson CAY 7.89
4. **Darren Ritchie** Sco **7.88**
   (7.77Q)
5. Osbourne Moxey BAH 7.87
6. **Chris Tomlinson** Eng **7.79**
   (7.97Q)
7. Arnaud Casquette MRI 7.64
8. Randy Lewis GRN 7.63
Q **Mark Awanah** Eng nm

119

Triple Jump (28 Jul)
1. Jonathan Edwards Eng 17.86
2. Phillips Idowu Eng 17.68
3. Leevan Sands BAH 17.26
4. Andrew Owusu GHA 16.84
5. Tosin Oke Eng 16.65
6. Steven Shalders Wal 16.37
7. Andrew Murphy AUS 16.37
8. Brian Wellman BER 15.84

Shot (31 Jul)
1. Justin Anlezark AUS 20.91
2. Janus Robberts RSA 19.97
3. Carl Myerscough Eng 19.91
   (18.36Q)
4. Brad Snyder CAN 19.63
5. Chima Ugwu NGR 18.46
6. Clay Cross AUS 18.10
7. Mark Proctor Eng 18.08
   (17.61Q)
8. Dave Stoute TRI 17.60
9. Emeka Udechuku Eng 17.54
   (17.92Q)
11. Lee Newman Wal 16.59
    (16.69Q)

Discus (27 Jul)
1. Frantz Kruger RSA 66.39
2. Jason Tunks CAN 62.61
3. Bob Weir Eng 59.24
   (59.14Q)
4. Chima Ugwu NGR 59.19
5. Glen Smith Eng 57.52
   (59.30Q)
6. Emeka Udechuku Eng 57.33
   (55.72Q)
7. Janus Robberts RSA 57.02
8. Lee Newman Wal 53.81
   (52.88Q)

WOMEN
100 Metres wind 1.5 (27 Jul)
1. Debbie Ferguson BAH 10.91
2. Veronica Campbell JAM 11.00
3. Sevatheda Fynes BAH 11.07
4. Susanthika Jayansinghe SRI 11.08
5. Amanda Forrester Eng 11.34
   (2h1 11.44, 3s2 11.37)
6. Shani Anderson Eng 11.36
   (3h2 11.50, 4s2 11.39)
7. Abi Oyepitan Eng 11.37
   (3h3 11.37, 4s1 11.36)
8. Natasha Mayers VIN 11.38

200 Metres wind 0.0 (29 Jul)
1. Debbie Ferguson BAH 22.20
2. Juliet Campbell JAM 22.54
3. Lauren Hewitt AUS 22.69
4. Natasha Mayers VIN 22.84
5. Cydonie Mothersille CAY 22.95
6. Joice Maduaka Eng 23.04
   (2h1 23.00, 4s2 23.25)

Hammer (28 Jul)
1. Mick Jones Eng 72.55
2. Philip Jensen NZL 69.48
3. Paul Head Eng 68.60
4. Stuart Rendell AUS 67.51
5. Iain Park Sco 65.51
6. Bill Beauchamp Eng 64.96
7. Petros Mitsides CYP 53.34
8. Nicolas Li Yun Fong MRI 53.13

Javelin (31 Jul)
1. Steve Backley Eng 86.81
2. Scott Russell CAN 78.98
3. Nick Nieland Eng 78.63
4. William Hamlyn-Harris AUS 77.31
5. Andrew Currey AUS 76.98
6. Mark Roberson Eng 74.52
7. Michael Allen Nir 67.07
8. James Goulding FIJ 64.43

Decathlon (27/28 Jul)
1. Claston Bernard JAM 7830
2. Matt McEwen AUS 7685
3. Jamie Quarry Sco 7630
4. Barry Thomas Eng 7546
5. Georgios Andreou CYP 7503
6. Mike Nolan CAN 7499
7. Anthony Sawyer Eng 7204
8. John Heanley Eng 7162
9. Dale Garland Gue 6919

20k Walk (28 Jul)
1. Nathan Deakes AUS 1:25:35
2. Luke Adams AUS 1:26:03
3. David Rotich Kimutai KEN 1:28:20
4. Andy Penn Eng 1:29:15
5. Don Bearman Eng 1:37:29
dsq Dominic King Eng
dsq Steve Partington IoM

7. Sharon Cripps AUS 23.04
dns Beverly McDonald JAM
6s1 Shani Anderson Eng 23.60
   (2h4 23.38)
7s1 Emily Freeman Eng 23.79
   (3h3 23.64)

400 Metres (28 Jul)
1. Aliann Pompey GUY 51.53
2. Lee McConnell Sco 51.68
   (4h1 55.62, 2q3 52.15, 1s2 51.29)
3. Sandie Richards JAM 51.79
4. Allison Beckford JAM 51.81
5. Heide Seyerling RSA 52.87
6. Catherine Murphy Wal 52.91
   (1h3 53.09, 2q152.15, 3s2 51.36)
7. Clementine Bewouda CMR 53.00
8. Christine Amertil BAH 53.45
6s2 Helen Karagounis Eng 51.97
   (3h1 54.47, 4q1 52.69)
6s1 Helen Frost Eng 52.71
   (2h4 53.78, 4q3 52.67)

50k Walk (30 Jul)
1. Nathan Deakes AUS 3:52:40
2. Craig Barrett NZL 3:56:42
3. Tim Berrett CAN 4:04:25
4. Duane Cousins AUS 4:09:59
5. Tony Sargisson NZL 4:13:19
6. Steve Hollier Eng 4:16:46
7. Gareth Brown Eng 4:40:07
dsq Mark Easton Eng

4 x 100 Metres (31 Jul)
1. England 38.62
   (Gardener, Devonish, Condon, Campbell)
   (2h1 39.06)
2. Jamaica 38.62
3. Australia 38.87
4. Canada 38.94
5. Trinidad & Tobago 38.97
6. Nigeria 39.01
7. Cameroon 39.52
8. Wales 39.73
   (Williams, Turner, Malcolm, Shalders)
   (4h2 39.62
Williams, Turner, Henthorn, Malcolm)

4 x 400 Metres (31 Jul)
1. England 3:00.40
   (Deacon, Baldock, Rawlinson, Caines)
   (1h2 3:04.01
   Hylton, Henry, Deacon, Baldock)
2. Wales 3:00.41
   (Benjamin, Thomas, Baulch, Elias)
   (2h2 3:04.18)
3. Bahamas 3:01.35
4. South Africa 3:01.83
5. Australia 3:02.22
6. Nigeria 3:11.16
dsq Jamaica
dsq Sri Lanka

8s1 Melanie Purkiss Eng 53.32
   (4h3 54.14, 6q2 53.08)
8q2 Carey Easton Sco 54.10
   (5h4 54.97)

800 Metres (28 Jul)
1. Maria Mutola MOZ 1:57.35
2. Diane Cummins CAN 1:58.82
3. Agnes Samaria NAM 1:59.15
4. Susan Scott Sco 1:59.30
   (2h2 2:02.82, 4s1 2:01.03)
5. Tamsyn Lewis AUS 1:59.73
6. Charlotte Moore Eng 1:59.75
   (2h5 2:03.38, 3s1 2:00.95)
7. Jo Fenn Eng 1:59.86
   (2h4 2:04.17, 3s2 2:03.04)
8. Michelle Ballentine JAM 2:03.75
6s2 Emma Davies Wal 2:03.93
   (4h2 2:04.02)
3h3 Rebecca Lyne Eng 2:05.26
6h4 Kelly McNeice Nir 2:06.68

1500 Metres (31 Jul)
1. Kelly Holmes — Eng — 4:05.99
   (1h2 4:11.27)
2. Hayley Tullett — Wal — 4:07.52
   (2h1 4:17.36)
3. Helen Pattinson — Eng — 4:07.62
   (3h1 4:17.39)
4. Jackline Maranga — KEN — 4:08.47
5. Sarah Jamieson — AUS — 4:09.38
6. Mardrea Hyman — JAM — 4:10.47
7. Naomi Mugo — KEN — 4:11.47
8. Rachel Newcombe — Wal — 4:13.56
   (6h2 4:15.18)
10. Kerry Gillibrand — Eng — 4:15.54
   (4h1 4:18.29)
11. Kelly McNeice — NIr — 4:16.46
   (8h2 4:18.45)
12. Hayley Ovens — Sco — 4:16.95
   (7h2 4:15.39)
6h1 Natalie Lewis — Wal — 4:23.45

5000 Metres (28 Jul)
1. Paula Radcliffe — Eng — 14:31.42
2. Edith Masai — KEN — 14:53.76
3. Iness Chenonge — KEN — 15:06.06
4. Dorcus Inzikuru — UGA — 15:18.01
5. Jo Pavey — Eng — 15:19.91
6. Benita Johnson — AUS — 15:26.55
7. Restituta Joseph — TAN — 15:33.07
8. Courtney Babcock — CAN — 15:42.83
10. Catherine Berry — Eng — 15:44.87
14. Gillian Palmer — Sco — 16:29.63
15. Catherine Dugdale — Wal — 16:43.49

10000 Metres (30 Jul)
1. Salina Kosgei — KEN — 31:27.83
2. Susan Chepkemei — KEN — 31:32.04
3. Susie Power — AUS — 31:32.20
4. Liz Yelling — Eng — 31:58.39
5. Hayley Yelling — Eng — 32:29.73
6. Jo Wilkinson — Eng — 33:36.60
7. Allison Higgins — Sco — 33:58.69
8. Gillian Palmer — Sco — 34:25.50

Marathon (28 Jul)
1. Kerryn McCann — AUS — 2:30:05
2. Krishna Stanton — AUS — 2:34:52
3. Jackie Gallagher — AUS — 2:36:37
4. Debbie Robinson — Eng — 2:39:42
5. Teresa McCluskey — NIr — 2:40:29
6. Bev Hartigan — Eng — 2:41:27
7. Carol Galea — MLT — 2:45:48
8. Marian Sutton — Eng — 2:45:55
12. Penny Buckingham — Gue — 2:58:40

100 Metres Hurdles wind 0.6 (31 Jul)
1. Lacena Golding-Clark — JAM — 12.77
2. Vonette Dixon — JAM — 12.83
3. Angela Atede — NGR — 12.98
4. Diane Allahgreen — Eng — 13.01
   (1h2 12.92)
5. Angela Whyte — CAN — 13.17

6. Julie Pratt — Eng — 13.26
   (4h1 13.08)
7. Jacquie Munro — AUS — 13.31
dns Bridgette Foster — JAM
5h1 Melani Wilkins — Eng — 13.29
6h2 Rachael King — Wal — 13.58
7h2 Tamsin Stephens — NIr — 13.59

400 Metres Hurdles (28 Jul)
1. Jana Pittman — AUS — 54.40
2. Debbie-Ann Parris — JAM — 55.24
3. Karlene Haughton — CAN — 56.13
4. Melanie Walker — JAM — 57.10
5. Sonia Brito — AUS — 57.79
6. Sinead Dudgeon — Sco — 58.68
   (4h2 57.11)
7. Natasha Danvers — Eng — 87:12
   (3h1 56.12)
dns Deon Hemmings — JAM
5h2 Tracey Duncan — Eng — 57.45
5h1 Katie Jones — Eng — 57.69

High Jump (30 Jul)
1. Hestrie Cloete — RSA — 1.96
2. Susan Jones — Eng — 1.90
3. Nicole Forrester — CAN — 1.87
4. Bobby Aloysius — IND — 1.87
5. Karen Beautle — JAM — 1.84
6= Maresa Cadienhead — CAN — 1.79
6= Stephanie Higham — Eng — 1.79
6= Petrina Price — AUS — 1.79
6= Debbie Marti — Eng — 1.79
10= Julie Crane — Wal — 1.79
10= Becky Jones — Wal — 1.79

Pole Vault (29 Jul)
1. Tatiana Grigorieva — AUS — 4.35
2. Kym Howe — AUS — 4.15
3= Bridgid Isworth — AUS — 4.10
3= Stephanie McCann — CAN — 4.10
3= Irie Hill — Eng — 4.10
   (4.00Q)
6. Dana Ellis — CAN — 4.00
7. Zoe Brown — NIr — 3.90
   (4.00Q)
8. Lucy Webber — Eng — 3.90
   (4.00Q)
10. Tracey Bloomfield — Eng — 3.90
   (4.00Q)
11= Rhian Clarke — Wal — 3.80
   (3.90Q)
13Q Sonia Lawrence — Wal — 3.90
15Q Gillian Cooke — Sco — 3.60

Long Jump (29 Jul)
1. Elva Goulbourne — JAM — 6.70
2. Jade Johnson — Eng — 6.58
   (6.65Q)
3. Anju Bobby George — IND — 6.49
4. Chinedu Odozor — NGR — 6.39
5. Chantal Brunner — NZL — 6.39
6. Bronwyn Thompson — AUS — 6.38

7. Jackie Edwards — BAH — 6.19
8. Esther Aghatise — NGR — 6.01
9. Ruth Irving — Sco — 5.98
   (6.20Q)
11. Ann Danson — Eng — 5.88
   (6.09Q)
12. Sarah Claxton — Eng — 5.77
   (6.08Q)
14Q Kimberley Goodall — Gue — 5.54

Triple Jump (31 Jul)
1. Ashia Hansen — Eng — 14.86
2. Francoise Mbango — CMR — 14.82
3. Trecia Smith — JAM — 14.32
4. Suzette Lee — JAM — 13.54
5. Althea Williams — CAN — 13.25
6. Nicole Mladenis — AUS — 13.04
7. Tan. Robinson-Scanlon — Eng — 12.98
8. Michelle Griffith — Eng — 12.90

Shot (28 Jul)
1. Vivian Chukwuemeka — NGR — 17.53
2. Valerie Adams — NZL — 17.45
3. Veronica Abrahamse — RSA — 16.77
4. Cleopatra Borel — TRI — 16.27
5. Myrtle Augee — Eng — 16.05
   (16.32Q)
6. Joanne Duncan — Eng — 15.99
   (16.00Q)
7. Julie Dunkley — Eng — 15.81
   (15.80Q)
8. Candice Scott — TRI — 15.33
15Q Eva Massey — NIr — 14.27

Discus (30 Jul)
1. Beatrice Faumuina — NZL — 60.83
2. Neelam Jaswant Singh — IND — 58.49
3. Shelley Newman — Eng — 58.13
4. Philippa Roles — Wal — 57.65
5. Alison Lever — AUS — 57.25
6. Elizna Naude — RSA — 55.41
7. Claire Smithson — Eng — 55.03
8. Monique Nacsa — AUS — 54.46
10. Jacqui McKernan — NIr — 50.45
nm Emma Carpenter — Eng

Hammer (26 Jul)
1. Lorraine Shaw — Eng — 66.83
   (66.10Q)
2. Bronwyn Eagles — AUS — 65.24
3. Karyne DiMarco — AUS — 63.40
4. Brooke Krueger — AUS — 63.13
5. Candice Scott — TRI — 60.93
6. Tasha Williams — NZL — 60.43
7. Jennifer Joyce — CAN — 60.39
8. Zoe Derham — Eng — 59.57
9. Suzanne Roberts — Eng — 58.66
   (58.85Q)
12. Mhairi Walters — Sco — 54.09
   (56.03Q)

14Q	**Lesley Brannan**	Wal	**55.90**	6.	Nicole Haynes	CAN	5753	4.	Australia	43.72

14Q **Lesley Brannan** Wal **55.90**
16Q **Shirley Webb** Sco **55.58**
18Q **Sarah Moore** Wal **51.43**
19Q **Laura Douglas** Wal **50.12**

6. Nicole Haynes CAN 5753
7. **Kelly Sotherton** Eng **5728**
8. **Kerry Jury** Eng **5554**
10. **Kimberley Goodall** Gue **4784**

4. Australia 43.72
5. Nigeria 44.10
6. Sri Lanka 44.25
7. Fiji 47.02
8. Sierra Leone 47.45

Javelin (29 Jul)
1. Laverne Eve BAH 58.46
2. Cecilia McIntosh AUS 57.42
3. **Kelly Morgan** Eng **57.09**
4. Sorochkwu Ihuefo NGR 52.24
5. Jeska Kabasindi UGA 51.33
6. **Goldie Sayers** Eng **51.32**
7. **Karen Martin** Eng **50.28**
8. Bernadette Ravina MRI 49.58

20k Walk (28 Jul)
1. Jane Saville AUS 1:36:34
2. **Lisa Kehler** Eng **1:36:45**
3. Yuan Yufang MAS 1:40:00
4. Natalie Saville AUS 1:42:38
5. Simone Wolowiec AUS 1:43:10
6. Gabrielle Gorst NZL 1:44:48
7. **Niobe Menendez** Eng **1:46:16**
8. **Sharon Tonks** Eng **1:49:21**
9. Sara-Jane Cattermole Sco 1:50:29
dnf Cal Partington IoM

4 x 400 Metres (31 Jul)
1. Australia 3:25.63
2. **England** **3:26.73**
(Frost, Karagounis, Purkiss, Miller)
(1h2 3:30.63 Meadows for Purkiss)
3. Nigeria 3:29.16
4. **Scotland** **3:31.50**
(Easton, Dudgeon, Burnside, McConnell)
(4h2 3:36.41
Nicol, Burnside, Easton, Dudgeon)
5. Canada 3:32.24
6. Cameroon 3:32.74
7. Trinidad & Tobago 3:39.14
dnf Jamaica

Heptathlon (26/27 Jul)
1. Jane Jamieson AUS 6059
2. Kylie Wheeler AUS 5962
3. Margaret Simpson GHA 5906
4. Clare Thompson AUS 5867
5. **Julie Hollman** Eng **5825**

4 x 100 Metres (31 Jul)
1. Bahamas 42.44
2. Jamaica 42.73
3. **England** **42.84**
(Maduaka, Anderson, James, Oyepitan)

FRA v GB & NI v ESP (U23) Niort, FRA 3 August 2002

MEN

100 Metres wind −0.5
1. Yannick Urbino FRA 10.56
4. **Darren Chin** **10.74**
6. **Tim Abeyie** **10.84**

200 Metres wind −1.1
1. **Dwain Grant** **21.02**
6. **Kris Stewart** **21.80**

400 Metres
1. Castejon Rodriguez ESP 46.92
2. **Ian Lowthian** **47.78**
6. **Tim Bayley** **48.48**

800 Metres
1. **Joel Kidger** **1:52.77**
2. **Sam Ellis** **1:52.92**

1500 Metres
1. Cerezo Fernandez ESP 3:42.62
2. **Angus Maclean** **3:43.90**
5. **Chris Bolt** **3:45.42**

3000 Metres
1. **Chris Thompson** **8:11.76**
5. **James Fewtrell** **8:19.90**

3000 Metres Steeplechase
1. Dandrieux Zouaoui FRA 8:39.30
5. **Adam Bowden** **9:19.37**

110 Metres Hurdles wind −1.2
1. Ruiz Vivancos ESP 13.83
2. **Andy Turner** **13.90**
dnf Rob Newton

400 Metres Hurdles
1. Videgain Romero ESP 50.11
3. **Steve Surety** **50.29**
5. **Richard Smith** **51.14**

High Jump
1. Koma Fatty ESP 2.12
4. **Brian Hall** **2.00**
6. **Chris Giblin** **2.00**

Pole Vault
1. Carillo Hinojo ESP 5.30
4. **Mark Beharrell** **5.05**
5. **Ashley Swain** **5.05**

Long Jump
1. Frederic Erin FRA 7.59
2. **Andre Fernandez** **7.54**
3. **Alex Hall** **7.46**

Triple Jump
1. Rodrique Los Angeles ESP 15.75
3. **Nathan Douglas** **15.59**
nm Andre Fernandez

Shot
1. Aukusitino Hoatau FRA 17.98
3. **Dave Readle** **16.54**
5. **Lyndon Woodward** **15.67**

Discus
1. Aukusitino Hoatau FRA 53.43
4. **Luke Rosenberg** **48.45**
5. **Scot Thompson** **47.57**

Hammer
1. **Andy Frost** **64.46**
6. **David Little** **56.31**

Javelin
1. Fernandez Peralta ESP 71.14
3. **Phil Sharpe** **68.25**
6. **Luke Rosenberg** **48.86**

5k Walk
1. Guimera Dominguez ESP 21:14.92
5. **Dan King** **22:43.37**
6. **Luke Finch** **23:33.94**

4 x 100 Metres
1. France 39.87
2. **Great Britain & NI** **39.93**
(Chin, Grant, Abeyie, Stewart)

4 x 400 Metres
1. Spain 3:10.07
2. **Great Britain & NI** **3:11.84**
(Lowthian, Bayley, Wilson, Surety)

Match Result – Men
1. Spain 152
2. France 150
3. **Great Britain & NI** **116**

WOMEN

100 Metres wind –0.4
1.	Gwladys Belliard	FRA	11.82
2.	**Emily Freeman**		**11.91**
4.	**Susan Burnside**		**11.99**

200 Metres wind –0.8
1.	**Emily Freeman**	**24.28**
2.	**Katherine Endacott**	**24.41**

400 Metres
1.	**Danielle Halsall**	**54.40**
dnf	Lesley Clarkson	

800 Metres
1.	Ponce Desviat	ESP	2:03.97
2.	**Rebecca Lyne**		**2:05.22**
6.	**Catherine Riley**		**2:12.59**

1500 Metres
1.	Garcia Alfonso	ESP	4:20.78
4.	**Natalie Lewis**		**4:25.05**
5.	**Susan Crispey**		**4:26.85**

3000 Metres
1.	**Louise Damen**	**9:29.28**

3000 Metres Steeplechase
1.	Yamina Bouchaouante	FRA	10:13.31
3.	**Ursula Counsell**		**10:47.62**

100 Metres Hurdles wind –0.3
1.	Ulgade Loureiro	ESP	13.56
2.	**Tamsin Stephens**		**13.75**
4.	**Lynne Fairweather**		**13.98**

400 Metres Hurdles
1.	Francine Lenfant	FRA	58.58
3.	**Nicola Sanders**		**59.18**
5.	**Hannah Wood**		**60.45**

High Jump
1.	Gaelle Niare	FRA	1.85
2.	**Samantha Adamson**		**1.74**
6.	**Natalie Clark**		**1.60**

Pole Vault
1.	Emilie Becot	FRA	4.05
5.	**Sonia Lawrence**		**3.70**
6.	**Ellie Spain**		**3.70**

Long Jump
1.	**Natasha May**	**6.26**
2.	**Rebecca White**	**6.01**

Triple Jump
1.	Helena Innocent	FRA	13.26
3.	**Rebecca White**		**12.98**
4.	**Danielle Freeman**		**12.72w**

Shot
1.	Ursula Ruiz Perez	ESP	14.70
3.	**Kara Nwidobie**		**14.27**
5.	**Joan Macpherson**		**12.46**

Discus
1.	Amelie Perrin	FRA	52.59
2.	**Kara Nwidobie**		**47.00**
4.	**Joan Macpherson**		**42.62**

Hammer
1.	Berta Castells Franco	ESP	60.65
3.	**Zoe Derham**		**57.85**
4.	**Shirley Webb**		**57.17**

Javelin
1.	Celine Mateo	FRA	49.11
2.	**Chloe Cozens**		**47.61**
6.	**Katie Watts**		**41.94**

3k Walk
1.	Carmen Bone Lopez	ESP	13:51.23
5.	**Claire Reeves**		**15:12.76**
6.	**Nicola Phillips**		**15:21.67**

4 x 100 Metres
1.	**Great Britain & NI**	**45.63**

(Fairweather, Freeman, Burnside, Endacott)

4 x 400 Metres
1.	**Great Britain & NI**	**3:43.13**

(Wood, Sanders, Lyne, Halsall)

Match Result – Women
1.	France	159.5
2.	**Great Britain & NI**	**135**
3.	Spain	124.5

Match Result - Combined
1.	France	309.5
2.	Spain	276.5
3.	**Great Britain & NI**	**251**

SUI v GB & NI v FRA v GER (Combined Events)   Pratteln, SUI 3 - 4 August 2002

Men U23 Decathlon
1.	Xaver Weibel	SUI	7316
4.	**Gerard Plunkett**		**7112**
7.	**Adrian Hemery**		**6924**
12.	**James Lowery**		**6688**
13.	**Paul Tohill**		**6678**

Men U20 Decathlon
1.	**Edward Dunford**	**6989**
8.	**David Hughes**	**6413**

dnf **Robin Smith**
dnf **John Dickenson**

Women U23 Heptathlon
1.	Katja Keller	GER	5734
6.	**Ros Gonse**		**5273**
10.	**Laura Redmond**		**5050**
12.	**Caroline Pearce**		**5017**
dnf	Gillian Stewart		

Women U20 Heptathlon
1.	Patricia Polifka	GER	5219
2.	**Jessica Ennis**		**5194**
8.	**Louise Hazel**		**4693**
dnf	Phyllis Agbo		
dnf	Rebecca Jones		

18th EUROPEAN CHAMPIONSHIPS   Munich, GER 6 - 11 August 2002

The European Championships saw a good medal total with 7 golds, 1 silver and 6 bronze and many of the golds were excellent performances. Paula Radcliffe's medal and time in the 10,000 metres was magnificent, while Colin Jackson and Steve Backley secured their fourth consecutive titles. Dwain Chambers bounced back well from his Commonwealth disappointment.

MEN

100 Metres wind –0.3 (7 Aug)
1.	**Dwain Chambers**		**9.96**
	(1h1 10.23, 1q4 10.08, 1s1 10.12)		
2.	Francis Obikwelu	POR	10.06
3.	**Darren Campbell**		**10.15**
	(2h3 10.36, 1q3 10.29, 3s2 10.30)		
4.	Roland Nemeth	HUN	10.27
5.	Markus Poyhonen	FIN	10.31
6.	Aime-Issa Nthepe	FRA	10.32
7.	Aristotelis Gavelas	GRE	10.36
dsq	Yeoryios Theodoridis	GRE	
6s1	Jason Gardener		10.36
	(2h5 10.29, 2q1 10.28)		

200 Metres wind –0.5 (9 Aug)
1.	Konstadinos Kenteris	GRE	19.85
2.	Francis Obikwelu	POR	20.21
3.	**Marlon Devonish**		**20.24**
	(1h3 20.81, 2q2 20.41, 2s2 20.23)		
4.	**Christian Malcolm**		**20.30**
	(2h1 20.82, 3q3 20.66, 3s1 20.54)		
5.	Marcin Jedrusinski	POL	20.31
6.	Marco Torrieri	ITA	20.68
7.	Troy Douglas	NED	20.73
dnf	Marcin Urbas	POL	
q1	**Darren Campbell**		**dsq**
	(1h2 20.66)		

400 Metres (8 Aug)
1. Ingo Schulz GER 45.14
2. David Canal ESP 45.24
3. **Daniel Caines** **45.28**
   (2h5 46.06, 1s1 45.35)
4. Marek Plawgo POL 45.40
5. Zsolt Szeglet HUN 45.74
6. Cedric Van Branteghem BEL 45.95
7. Karel Blaha CZE 46.21
dnsTim Benjamin
   (3h2 46.15, 3s2 46.07)
4h3Sean Baldock **46.62**

800 Metres (11 Aug)
1. Wilson Kipketer DEN 1:47.25
2. Andre Bucher SUI 1:47.43
3. Nils Schumann GER 1:47.60
4. Pawel Czapiewski POL 1:47.92
5. Arnoud Okken NED 1:48.39
6. Bram Som NED 1:48.56
7. Rene Herms GER 1:48.86
8. Nicolas Aissat FRA 1:49.16
5s1 James McIlroy **1:49.15**
   (4h3 1:47.67)
7h4Anthony Whiteman **1:50.60**

1500 Metres (8 Aug)
1. Mehdi Balla FRA 3:45.25
2. Reyes Estevez ESP 3:45.25
3. Rui Silva POR 3:45.43
4. Fouad Chouki FRA 3:45.46
5. Juan Higuero ESP 3:45.81
6. **Michael East** **3:46.30**
   (5h2 3:41.82)
7. Christian Obrist ITA 3:46.57
8. Marko Koers NED 3:46.68
9. **Anthony Whiteman** **3:47.10**
   (4h1 3:47.40)
12. **John Mayock** **3:48.41**
    (6h2 3:42.63)

5000 Metres (11 Aug)
1. Alberto Garcia ESP 13:38.18
2. Ismail Sghyr FRA 13:39.81
3. Sergey Lebed UKR 13:40.00
4. Roberto Garcia ESP 13:40.85
5. Kamiel Maase NED 13:41.42
6. Mark Carroll IRL 13:42.87
7. Balazs Csillag HUN 13:49.03
8. Salvatore Vincenti ITA 13:50.53
9. **Sam Haughian** **13:50.75**

10000 Metres (7 Aug)
1. Jose Martinez ESP 27:47.65
2. Dieter Baumann GER 27:47.87
3. Jose Rios ESP 27:48.29
4. Stefano Baldini ITA 27:50.98
5. **Karl Keska** **28:01.72**
6. Hassan Lahssini FRA 28:05.13
7. Marco Mazza ITA 28:05.94
8. Dmitriy Maksimov RUS 28:19.20

Marathon (11 Aug)
1. Janne Holmen FIN 2:12:14
2. Pavel Loskutov EST 2:13:18
3. Julio Rey ESP 2:13:21
4. Daniele Caimmi ITA 2:13:30
5. Alberto Juzdado ESP 2:13:35
6. Alejandro Gomez ESP 2:13:40
7. Kamal Ziani ESP 2:13:51
8. Karl Rasmussen NOR 2:14.00

Team Result
1. Spain 8:54:27
2. Italy 9:00:17
3. Portugal 9:38:54

3000 Metres Steeplechase (10 Aug)
1. Antonio Jimenez ESP 8:24.34
2. Simon Vroemen NED 8:24.45
3. Luis Martin ESP 8:24.72
4. Bob Tahri FRA 8:26.86
5. Eliseo Martin ESP 8:28.63
6. Vadym Slobodenyuk UKR 8:30.16
7. Martin Proll AUT 8:33.24
8. Rafal Wojcik POL 8:35.41

110 Metres Hurdles wind 0.4 (10 Aug)
1. **Colin Jackson** **13.11**
   (1h1 13.41, 1s2 13.21)
2. Stanislav Olijars LAT 13.22
3. Artur Kohutek POL 13.32
4. Florian Schwarthoff GER 13.37
5. Mike Fenner GER 13.39
6. Devis Favaro ITA 13.59
7. Robert Kronberg SWE 13.63
8. Zhivko Videnov BUL 13.67
s1 **Tony Jarrett** **dq**
   (2h4 13.63)
4h2Damien Greaves **13.90**

400 Metres Hurdles (9 Aug)
1 Stephane Diagana FRA 47.58
2. Jiri Muzik CZE 48.43
3. Pawel Januszewski POL 48.46
4. Fabrizio Mori ITA 49.05
5. Periklis Iakovakis GRE 49.07
6. Stepan Tesarik CZE 49.41
7. Ruslan Mashchenko RUS 50.02
dnf Chris Rawlinson
   (2h4 49.73, 2s2 49.48)
5s1 **Anthony Borsumato** **49.37**
   (2h2 49.93)
4h3Matt Elias **50.18**

High Jump (8 Aug)
1. Yaroslav Rybakov RUS 2.31
2. Stefan Holm SWE 2.29
3. Staffan Strand SWE 2.27
3. Alessandro Talotti ITA 2.27
5. Tomas Janku CZE 2.25
6. Svatoslav Ton CZE 2.25
7. Martin Buss GER 2.25
8. Jan Janku CZE 2.22

18=QBen Challenger 2.15
Q Dalton Grant nh

Pole Vault (10 Aug)
1. Alex Averbukh ISR 5.85
2. Lars Borgeling GER 5.80
3. Tim Lobinger GER 5.80
4. Patrik Kristiansson SWE 5.80
5. Stepan Janacek CZE 5.75
6= Denis Yurchenko UKR 5.70
6= Adam Ptacek CZE 5.70
8. Vasiliy Gorshkov RUS 5.70

Long Jump (11 Aug)
1. Aleksey Lukashevich UKR 8.08
2. Sinisa Ergotic CRO 8.00
3. Yego Lamela ESP 7.99w
4. Roman Shchurenko UKR 7.96
5. Danila Burkenya RUS 7.90
6. **Chris Tomlinson** **7.78**
   (7.81Q)
7. Salim Sdiri FRA 7.78
8. Vladimir Malyavin RUS 7.73

Triple Jump (8 Aug)
1. Christian Olsson SWE 17.53
2. Charles Friedek GER 17.33
3. **Jonathan Edwards** **17.32**
   (16.99Q)
4. Fabrizio Donato ITA 17.15
5. **Phillips Idowu** **16.92**
   (17.54Q)
6. Aleksandr Glavatskiy BLR 16.86
7. Julien Kapek FRA 16.66
8. Kostas Zalaggitis GRE 16.62
nm **Tosin Oke**
   (16.48Q)

Shot (6 Aug)
1. Yuriy Bilonog UKR 21.37
2. Joachim Olsen DEN 21.16
3. Ralf Bartels GER 20.58
4. Arsi Harju FIN 20.47
5. Manuel Martinez ESP 20.45
6. Ville Tiisanoja FIN 20.20
7. Gheorghe Guset ROM 20.05
8. Rutger Smith NED 19.73

Discus (11 Aug)
1. Robert Fazekas HUN 68.83
2. Virgilijus Alekna LTU 66.62
3. Michael Mollenbeck GER 66.37
4. Mario Pestano ESP 64.69
5. Aleksander Tammert EST 64.55
6. Dmitriy Shevchenko RUS 63.97
7. Zoltan Kovago HUN 63.63
8. Leonid Cherevko BLR 61.72
21Q **Bob Weir** **58.37**

Hammer (7 Aug)
1. Adrian Annus HUN 81.17
2. Vladislav Piskunov UKR 80.39
3. Alex Papadimitriou GRE 80.21

4. Balazs Kiss HUN 80.17
5. Andrey Skvaruk UKR 80.15
6. Tibor Gecsek HUN 79.25
7. Libor Charfreitag SVK 79.20
8. Olli-Pekka Karjalainen FIN 78.57

Javelin (9 Aug)
1. **Steve Backley** **88.54**
   (85.76Q)
2. Sergey Makarov RUS 88.05
3. Boris Henry GER 85.33
4. Eriks Rags LAT 84.07
5. Raymond Hecht GER 83.95
6. Aleksandr Ivanov RUS 82.66
7. Dariusz Trafas POL 80.37
8. Aki Parviainen FIN 78.92
10. **Mick Hill** **76.12**
    (79.38Q)
25Q Nick Nieland **71.92**

Decathlon (7/8 Aug)
1. Roman Sebrle CZE 8800
2. Erki Nool EST 8438
3. Lev Lobodin RUS 8390
4. Jon Arnar Magnusson ISL 8238

WOMEN
100 Metres wind –0.7 (7 Aug)
1. Ekaterini Thanou GRE 11.10
2. Kim Gevaert BEL 11.22
3. Manuela Levorato ITA 11.23
4. Glory Alozie ESP 11.32
5. Melanie Paschke GER 11.37
6. **Abi Oyepitan** **11.41**
   (2h4 11.40, 3s1 11.33)
7. Odiah Sidibe FRA 11.57
8. Alenka Bikar SLO 11.63
6h2 Joice Maduaka **11.60**

200 Metres wind –0.3 (9 Aug)
1. Muriel Hurtis FRA 22.43
2. Kim Gevaert BEL 22.53
3. Manuela Levorato ITA 22.75
4. Sylviane Felix FRA 22.89
5. Gabi Rockmeier GER 23.00
6. Karin Mayr AUT 23.06
7. Jacqueline Poelman NED 23.31
8. Alenka Bikar SLO 23.37
8s1 **Shani Anderson** **23.60**
    (4h1 23.42)

400 Metres (8 Aug)
1. Olesya Zykina RUS 50.45
2. Grit Breuer GER 50.70
3. **Lee McConnell** **51.02**
   (2h3 51.24)
4. Grazyna Prokopek POL 51.53
5. Anastasia Kapachinskaya RUS 51.69
6. Antonina Yefremova UKR 52.02
7. Svetlana Usovich BLR 52.10
8. Birgit Rockmeier GER 52.91
h1 **Catherine Murphy** **dnf**

5. Jaakko Ojaniemi FIN 8192
6. Mike Maczey GER 8158
7. Laurent Hernu FRA 8051
8. Aleksandr Pogorelov RUS 8016

20 Kilometres Walk (6 Aug)
1. Francisco Fernandez ESP 1:18:37
2. Vladimir Andreyev RUS 1:19:56
3. Juan Molina ESP 1:20:36
4. Viktor Burayev RUS 1:20:36
5. Ivan Trotskiy BLR 1:20:52
6. Yevgeniy Misyulya BLR 1:20:56
7. Alessandro Gandellini ITA 1:21:03
8. Robert Heffernan IRL 1:21:10
dsq Andi Drake

50 Kilometres Walk (8 Aug)
1. Robert Korzeniowski POL 3:36:39
2. Aleksey Voyevodin RUS 3:40:16
3. Jesus Angel Garcia ESP 3:44:33
4. German Skurygin RUS 3:48:58
5. Trond Nymark NOR 3:50:16
6. Denis Langlois FRA 3:50:47
7. Aleksandar Rakovic YUG 3:51:47
8. Francesco Galdenzi ITA 3:52:17

800 Metres (8 Aug)
1. Jolanda Ceplak SLO 1:57.65
2. Mayte Martinez ESP 1:58.86
3. **Kelly Holmes** **1:59.83**
   (1h1 2:03.18, 1s2 2:00.66)
4. Ludmila Formanova CZE 2:00.23
5. Claudia Gesell GER 2:00.51
6. Nedia Semedo POR 2:00.54
7. Ivonne Teichmann GER 2:00.87
8. Natalya Dedkova BLR 2:04.24
6s1 **Jo Fenn** **2:02.99**
    (2h3 2:02.91)

1500 Metres (11 Aug)
1. Sureyya Ayhan TUR 3:58.79
2. Gabriela Szabo ROM 3:58.81
3. Tatyana Tomashova RUS 4:01.28
4. Judit Varga HUN 4:02.37
5. Daniela Yordanova BUL 4:03.03
6. Natalia Rodriguez ESP 4:06.15
7. Alesya Turova BLR 4:06.64
8. Nuria Fernandez ESP 4:07.11
4h1 **Kelly Holmes** **4:08.11**
5h2 **Helen Pattinson** **4:09.66**
7h3 **Hayley Tullett** **4:10.68**

5000 Metres (10 Aug)
1. Marta Dominguez ESP 15:14.76
2. Sonia O`Sullivan IRL 15:14.85
3. Yelena Zadorozhnaya RUS 15:15.22
4. Olga Yegorova RUS 15:16.65
5. **Jo Pavey** **15:18.70**
6. Mihaela Botezan ROM 15:19.12
7. Elvan Abeylegesse TUR 15:24.41
8. Gunhild Haugen NOR 15:30.19
18. **Hayley Yelling** **16:26.41**

4 x 100 Metres (11 Aug)
1. **Great Britain & NI** **38.19**
   (Malcolm, Campbell, Devonish, Chambers)
   (1h1 38.55)
2. Ukraine 38.53
3. Poland 38.71
4. Germany 38.88
5. France 38.97
6. Spain 39.07
7. Russia 39.12
dnf Italy

4 x 400 Metres (11 Aug)
1. **Great Britain & NI** **3:01.25**
   (Deacon, Elias, Baulch, Caines)
   (1h1 3:02.97
   Deacon, Baldock, Baulch, Elias)
2. Russia 3:01.34
3. France 3:02.76
4. Czech Republic 3:03.82
5. Ireland 3:04.13
6. Greece 3:04.26
7. Germany 3:08.56
dsq Poland

10000 Metres (6 Aug)
1. **Paula Radcliffe** **30:01.09**
2. Sonia O`Sullivan IRL 30:47.59
3. Lyudmila Biktasheva RUS 31:04.00
4. Mihaela Botezan ROM 31:13.96
5. Jelena Prokopcuka LAT 31:17.72
6. Olivera Jevtic YUG 31:47.82
7. Constantina Tomescu ROM 31:53.61
8. Gunhild Haugen NOR 31:57.02
20. **Liz Yelling** **32:44.44**

Marathon (10 Aug)
1. Maria Guida ITA 2:26:05
2. Luminita Zaituc GER 2:26:58
3. Sonja Oberem GER 2:28:45
4. Jane Salumae EST 2:33:46
5. Rosaria Console ITA 2:35:23
6. Nadezhda Wijenberg NED 2:36:06
7. Marie Soderstrom SWE 2:36:13
8. Ulrike Maisch GER 2:36:41

Marathon Team
1. Germany 10:17:20
2. Russia 10:55:29

100 Metres Hurdles wind –0.7 (9 Aug)
1. Glory Alozie ESP 12.73
2. Yelena Krasovska UKR 12.88
3. Yana Kasova BUL 12.91
4. Patricia Girard FRA 13.03
5= Haydy Aron FRA 13.07
5= **Diane Allahgreen** **13.07**
   (3h1 13.10, 3s1 12.92)
7. Susanna Kallur SWE 13.09
8. Svetla Dimitrova BUL 13.75

400 Metres Hurdles (8 Aug)

1.	Ionela Tirlea	ROM	54.95
2.	Heike Meissner	GER	55.89
3.	Anna Olichwierczuk	POL	56.18
4.	Monika Niederstatter	ITA	56.34
5.	Yekaterina Bakhvalova	RUS	56.39
6.	Malgorzata Pskit	POL	56.78
7.	**Natasha Danvers**		**56.93**
	(4h1 56.55)		
8.	**Sinead Dudgeon**		**59.39**
	(2h2 56.91)		
5h3	Tracey Duncan		57.54

High Jump (11 Aug)

1.	Kajsa Bergqvist	SWE	1.98
2.	Marina Kuptsova	RUS	1.92
3.	Olga Kaliturina	RUS	1.89
4.	Oana Pantelimon	ROM	1.89
5=	Anna Ksok	POL	1.89
5=	Blanka Vlasic	CRO	1.89
7=	Susan Jones		1.89
	(1.90Q)		
7=	Kathryn Holinski	GER	1.89

Pole Vault (9 Aug)

1.	Svetlana Feofanova	RUS	4.60
2.	Yelena Isinbayeva	RUS	4.55
3.	Yvonne Buschbaum	GER	4.50
4.	Yelena Belyakova	RUS	4.50
5.	Annika Becker	GER	4.50
6.	Monique de Wilt	NED	4.40
7=	Anna Rogowska	POL	4.30
7=	Krizstina Molnar	HUN	4.30

Long Jump (7 Aug)

1.	Tatyana Kotova	RUS	6.85
2.	**Jade Johnson**		**6.73**
	6.60Q		
3.	Tunde Vaszi	HUN	6.73
4.	Concepcion Montaner	ESP	6.67
5.	Heike Drechsler	GER	6.64
6.	Stiliani Pilatou	GRE	6.58
7.	Olga Rublyova	RUS	6.58
8.	Sofia Schulte	GER	6.43

Triple Jump (10 Aug)

1.	**Ashia Hansen**		**15.00w**
	14.22Q		
2.	Heli Koivula	FIN	14.83w
3.	Yelena Oleynikova	RUS	14.54
4.	Mihaela Gindila	ROM	14.43
5.	Cristina Nicolau	ROM	14.39
6.	Magdelin Martinez	ITA	14.27w
7.	Hrissopiyi Devetzi	GRE	14.15
8.	Anna Pyatykh	RUS	14.08

Shot (10 Aug)

1.	Irina Korzhanenko	RUS	20.64
2.	Vita Pavlysh	UKR	20.02
3.	Svetlana Krivelyova	RUS	19.56
4.	Astrid Kumbernuss	GER	19.22
5.	Nadezhda Ostapchuk	BLR	19.07
6.	Nadine Kleinert	GER	18.68
7.	Krystyna Zabawska	POL	18.63
8.	Assunta Legnante	ITA	18.23

Discus (7 Aug)

1.	Ekaterini Vogoli	GRE	64.31
2.	Natalya Sadova	RUS	64.12
3.	Anastasia Kelesidou	GRE	63.92
4.	Vera Pospisilova	CZE	62.31
5.	Marzena Wysocka	POL	62.20
6.	Areti Abatzi	GRE	61.49
7.	Teresa Machado	POR	60.41
8.	Vladimira Rackova	CZE	59.28
10.	**Shelley Newman**		**57.38**
	56.57Q		

Hammer (9 Aug)

1.	Olga Kuzenkova	RUS	72.94
2.	Kamila Skolimowska	POL	72.46
3.	Manuela Montebrun	FRA	72.04
4.	Florence Ezeh	FRA	68.03
5.	Sini Poyry	FIN	67.47
6.	Ester Balassini	ITA	67.27
7.	Alexandra Papayeoryiou	GRE	66.49
8.	Clarissa Claretti	ITA	66.25
20Q	**Lorraine Shaw**		**61.50**

Javelin (8 Aug)

1.	Mirela Manjani	GRE	67.47
2.	Steffi Nerius	GER	64.09
3.	Mikaela Ingberg	FIN	63.50
4.	Tatyana Shikolenko	RUS	63.24
5.	Aggeliki Tsiolakoudi	GRE	63.14
6.	Elisabetta Marin	ITA	60.12
7.	Taina Kolkkala	FIN	59.81
8.	Nikolett Szabo	HUN	59.28
12.	**Kelly Morgan**		**53.89**
	(56.90Q)		

Heptathlon (9/10 Aug)

1.	Carolina Kluft	SWE	6542
2.	Sabine Braun	GER	6434
3.	Natalya Sazanovich	BLR	6341
4.	Austra Skujyte	LTU	6275
5.	Svetlana Sokolova	RUS	6150
6.	Kathleen Gutjahr	GER	6106
7.	Michaela Hejnova	CZE	6032
8.	Liga Klavina	LAT	5996
dnf	**Julie Hollman**		

20 Kilometres Walk (7 Aug)

1.	Olimpiada Ivanova	RUS	1:26:42
2.	Yelena Nikolayeva	RUS	1:28:20
3.	Erica Alfridi	ITA	1:28:33
4.	Gillian O'Sullivan	IRL	1:28:46
5.	Claudia Iovan	ROM	1:29:57
6.	Elisabetta Perrone	ITA	1:30:25
7.	Kristina Saltanovic	LTU	1:30:44
8.	Annarita Sidoti	ITA	1:31:19

4 x 100 Metres (11 Aug)

1.	France	42.46
2.	Germany	42.54
3.	Russia	43.11
4.	Belgium	43.22
5.	Ukraine	43.38
6.	Italy	43.46
7.	Poland	43.96
8.	Belarus	44.34
5h1	**Great Britain & NI**	**44.45**
	(Maduaka, Anderson, Forrester, Oyepitan)	

4 x 400 Metres (11 Aug)

1.	Germany	3:25.10
2.	Russia	3:25.59
3.	Poland	3:26.15
4.	**Great Britain & NI**	**3:26.65**
	(Karagounis, Frost, Purkiss, McConnell)	
	(2h2 3:33.88)	
5.	France	3:31.71
6.	Belarus	3:32.46
7.	Sweden	3:32.65
8.	Greece	3:37.38

IAU EUROPEAN
24 HOUR TRIAL
Gravigny FRA, 7/8 Sep 2002

MEN			kilometres
1.	Jens Lukas	GRE	267.294
2.	Alain Prual	FRA	264.796
3.	Jean-Pierre Guyomarc'h	FRA	255.726
38.	**Stuart Buchan**		**176.688**

WOMEN			
1.	Edit Berces	HUN	232.284
2.	Irina Reoutovitch	RUS	226.825
3.	Irina Koval	RUS	225.036
17.	**Sharon Gayter**		**158.016**

Norwich Union Challenge GB & NI v USA v RUS Glasgow 18 August 2002

MEN

100 Metres wind 1.2
1.	Dwain Chembers	10.28
4.	Jason Gardener	10.34

200 Metres wind 1.6
1.	Darvis Patton	USA	20.16
2.	Marlon Devonish		20.60
4.	Christian Malcolm		20.82

400 Metres
1.	Antonio Pettigrew	USA	46.13
3.	Jared Deacon		46.46
4.	Du`aine Thorne-Ladejo		46.70

1500 Metres
1.	Michael East	3:55.15
5.	Anthony Whiteman	3:57.21

110 Metres Hurdles wind 2.2
1.	Larry Wade	USA	13.24w
2.	Colin Jackson		13.32w
dnf Tony Jarrett			

400 Metres Hurdles
1.	Joey Woody	USA	49.14
3.	Matt Elias		49.46
5.	Anthony Borsumato		49.72

Long Jump
1.	Savante Stringfellow	USA	8.20
5.	Chris Tomlinson		7.57
6.	Darren Ritchie		7.54

Triple Jump
1.	Jonathan Edwards	17.54
3.	Phillips Idowu	17.28

Javelin
1.	Sergey Makarov	RUS	87.99
2.	Steve Backley		83.06
4.	Mick Hill		75.86

4 x 100 Metres
1.	Great Britain & NI	39.48

(Plummer, Devonish, Grant, Chambers)

WOMEN

100 Metres wind 1.9
1.	Chryste Gaines	USA	11.12
4.	Abi Oyepitan		11.56
6.	Amanda Forrester		11.77

200 Metres wind 1.5
1.	Joice Maduaka	23.37
2.	Shani Anderson	23.59

400 Metres
1.	Jearl Miles-Clark	USA	51.65
3.	Lee McConnell		52.16
6.	Melanie Purkiss		54.00

1500 Metres
1.	Tatyana Tomashova	RUS	4:09.64
2.	Kelly Holmes		4:10.38
5.	Susan Scott		4:12.90

100 Metres Hurdles wind 0.6
1.	Gail Devers	USA	12.79
4.	Julie Pratt		13.25
6.	Diane Allahgreen		13.42

Pole Vault
1.	Svetlana Feofanova	RUS	4.62
5.	Irie Hill		3.75
6.	Kate Dennison		3.60

Match Result
1.	United States	144
2.	Great Britain & NI	117
3.	Russia	116

Triple Jump
1.	Ashia Hansen	13.96
5.	Michelle Griffith	13.44

Hammer
1.	Olga Kuzenkova	RUS	71.73
3.	Lorraine Shaw		63.62
6.	Zoe Derham		55.23

4 x 100 Metres
1.	Russia	43.99
dnf Great Britain & NI		

(Allahgreen, Maduaka, Anderson, Oyepitan)

Catalonia v GB & NI 'A' v CUB v YUG Barcelona, ESP 6 September 2002

MEN

100 Metres wind -0.6
1.	Daniel Plummer	10.64
3.	Darren Chin	10.77

400 Metres
1.	Tim Benjamin	46.39
4.	Graham Hedman	47.48

800 Metres
1.	Miguel Quesada	CAT	1:49.24
3.	Chris Moss		1:50.28
6.	Joel Kidger		1:52.99

1500 Metres
1.	Reyes Estevez	CAT	3:43.37
2.	James Thie		3:43.99
4.	Gregg Taylor		3:46.05

3000 Metres
1.	Jose Rios	CAT	8:05.81
5.	Stephen Hepples		8:18.28
6.	Chris Thompson		8:22.23

110 Metres Hurdles wind -0.2
1.	Yoel Hernandez	CUB	13.89
2.	Chris Baillie		14.13
3.	Andrew Turner		14.21

High Jump
1.	Raul Touset	CUB	2.15
2.	Mark Crowley		2.15
4.	Martyn Bernard		2.12

Long Jump
1.	Luis Melis	CUB	8.00
4.	Andre Fernandez		7.51
nm Mark Awanah			

Shot
1.	Alexis Paumier	CUB	17.60
3.	Emeka Udechuku		16.81
5.	Greg Beard		15.86

Javelin
1.	Emeterio Gonzalez	CUB	81.95
5.	Alex van der Merwe		64.44
8.	Emeka Udechuku		49.53

Medley Relay (400x300x200x100)
1.	Great Britain & NI	1:50.22

(Fernandez, Beasley, Chin, Plummer)

WOMEN

100 Metres wind -0.6
1.	Amanda Forrester	11.55
3.	Eleanor Ruddock	12.00

400 Metres
1.	Melanie Purkiss	54.52
3.	Kim Wall	55.32

800 Metres
1.	Susan Scott	2:02.93
2.	Lucy Vaughan	2:04.12

3000 Metres
1. Sonja Stolic YUG 9:00.13
2. Diane Henaghan 9:14.27
4. Sarah Bull 9:18.11

100 Metres Hurdles wind 1.4
1. Anay Tejada CUB 13.26
2. Symone Belle 14.18
5. Stefanie Pullinger 15.13

Pole Vault
gst Dana Cervantes ESP 4.22
1. Tracey Bloomfield 3.92
2. Zoe Brown 3.72

Triple Jump

1. Biljana Mitrovic YUG 13.67
3. Danielle Freeman 12.72
5. Emily Parker 11.89

Shot
1. Yumileidi Cumba CUB 18.88
3. Julie Dunkley 16.03
6. Kara Nwidobie 13.42

Javelin
1. Sonia Bicet CUB 63.27
3. Goldie Sayers 47.43
6. Samantha Redd 39.38

Medley Relay (400x300x200x100)

1. Great Britain & NI 2:08.67
(Purkiss, Wall, Ruddock, Forrester)

Match Result
1. Great Britain & NI 221
2. Yugoslavia 165
3. Cuba 154
4. Catalonia 144

AAA & INTER-COUNTIES 10k Road
Bradford 8 September 2002

MEN
1. Julius Kimtai KEN 29:32
2. Julius Kibet KEN 29:34
3. Allen Graffin 29:45

Team
1. Tipton Harriers 19

WOMEN
1. Miriam Wangari KEN 33:48
2. Sharon Morris 33:50
3. Dorothea Lee 35:08

Team
1. Headington RR 29

IAU EUROPEAN 100k CHAMPIONSHIP
Winschoten,NED 15 Sep 2002

MEN
1. Pascal Fetozon FRA 6:34:16
2. Denis Zhalybin RUS 6:36:19
3. Oleg Kharitonov RUS 6:41:16
35. William Sichel 7:51:11
41. Ian Anderson 8:08:34

WOMEN
1. Elvira Kolpakova RUS 7:24:52
2. Monica Casiraghi ITA 7:33:14
3. Danielle Sanderson 7:47:29
18. Hilary Walker 8:54:41

9th IAAF WORLD CUP IN ATHLETICS
Madrid, ESP 20 - 21 September 2002

This was a championship too many for most of Britain's top athletes with only Jonathan Edwards managing a win. Europe included four representatives from Britain in the women's match.

MEN

100 Metres wind −0.3 (20 Sep)
1. Uchenna Emedolu AFR 10.06
2. Kim Collins AME 10.06
3. Francis Obikwelu EUR 10.09
4. Jon Drummond USA 10.10
5. Dwain Chambers 10.16
6. Jamal Al-Saffar ASI 10.38
7. Marc Blume GER 10.46
8. Patrick Johnson OCE 10.58
9. Angel Rodriguez ESP 10.78

200 Metres wind −0.6 (21 Sep)
1. Francis Obikwelu EUR 20.18
2. Frank Fredericks AFR 20.20
3. Marlon Devonish 20.32
4. Ramon Clay USA 20.32
5. Dominic Demeritte AME 20.47
6. Gennadiy Chernovol ASI 20.73
7. Julian Martinez ESP 21.23
8. Oliver Konig GER 21.32
9. Dallas Roberts OCE 21.61

400 Metres (20 Sep)
1. Michael Blackwood AME 44.60
2. Ingo Schulz GER 44.86
3. Fawzi Al-Shammari ASI 45.14
4. Eric Milazar AFR 45.41
5. Alvin Harrison USA 45.46
6. Clinton Hill OCE 45.74
7. Tim Benjamin 45.80
8. David Canal ESP 46.21
9. Zsolt Szeglet EUR 46.26

800 Metres (21 Sep)
1. Antonio Reina ESP 1:43.83
2. Djabir Said-Guerni AFR 1:44.03
3. David Krummenacker USA 1:45.14
4. Andre Bucher EUR 1:45.31
5. Nils Schumann GER 1:45.34
6. Oscar dos Santos AME 1:46.01
7. Mihail Kolganov ASI 1:47.45
8. James McIlroy 1:48.43
dnf Kris McCarthy OCE

1500 Metres (20 Sep)
1. Bernard Lagat AFR 3:31.20
2. Reyes Estevez ESP 3:33.67
3. Mehdi Baala EUR 3:38.04
4. Youcef Abdi OCE 3:41.01
5. Franek Haschke GER 3:41.58
6. Michael East 3:41.88
7. Abdulrahman Suleiman ASI 3:42.27
8. Hudson de Souza AME 3:42.58
9. Seneca Lassiter USA 4:05.82

3000 Metres (21 Sep)
1. Craig Mottram OCE 7:41.37
2. David Galvan AME 7:47.43
3. Roberto Garcia ESP 7:53.96
4. Paul Bitok AFR 7:56.31
5. Anthony Whiteman 8:03.33
6. Ahmed Ibrahim Warsama ASI 8:08.31
7. Sergey Lebed EUR 8:08.65
8. Bolota Asmerom USA 8:10.66
9. Raphael Schafer GER 8:33.89

5000 Metres (20 Sep)

1.	Alberto Garcia	ESP	13:30.04
2.	Paul Kosgei	AFR	13:31.71
3.	Ismail Sghyr	EUR	13:32.82
4.	Mebrahtom Keflezighi	USA	13:33.44
5.	**John Mayock**		**13:38.63**
6.	Michael May	GER	13:39.73
7.	Abdulhak Zakaria	ASI	13:54.68
8.	Michael Power	OCE	13:58.07
9.	Sean Kaley	AME	14:33.57

3000 Metres Steeplechase (21 Sep)

1.	Wilson Boit Kipketer	AFR	8:25.34
2.	Luis Miguel Martin	ESP	8:26.35
3.	Khamis Saifeldin	ASI	8:30.66
4.	Anthony Famiglietti	USA	8:32.72
5.	Simon Vroeman	EUR	8:36.06
6.	Peter Nowill	OCE	8:39.22
7.	Filmon Ghirmai	GER	8:42.29
8.	**Stuart Stokes**		**8:43.38**
9.	Joel Bourgeois	AME	8:56.13

110 Metres Hurdles wind -2.2 (21 Sep)

1.	Anier Garcia	AME	13.10
2.	Allen Johnson	USA	13.45
3.	Stanislav Olijar	EUR	13.58
4.	Shaun Bownes	AFR	13.67
5.	Felipev Vivancos	ESP	13.79
6.	Florian Schwarthoff	GER	13.79
7.	Tim Ewen	OCE	14.10
dsq	**Colin Jackson**		
dnf	Liu Xiang	ASI	

400 Metres Hurdles (20 Sep)

1.	James Carter	USA	48.27
2.	Mubarak Al-Nubi	ASI	48.96
3.	**Chris Rawlinson**		**49.18**
4.	Jiri Muzik	EUR	49.28
5.	Ian Weakley	AME	49.62
6.	Jose Romera	ESP	49.68
7.	Llewellyn Herbert	AFR	50.52
8.	Christian Duma	GER	50.57
9.	Mowen Boino	OCE	51.66

High Jump (20 Sep)

1.	Yaroslav Rybakov	EUR	2.31
2.	Mark Boswell	AME	2.29
3.	**Ben Challenger**		**2.20**
4.	Abderrahmane Hammad	AFR	2.15
5=	Martin Buss	GER	2.15
5=	Ignacio Perez	ESP	2.15
7.	Nathan Leeper	USA	2.10
8.	Cui Kai	ASI	2.10
nh	Nick Moroney	OCE	

Pole Vault (21 Sep)

1.	Okkert Brits	AFR	5.75
2.	Jeff Hartwig	USA	5.70
3.	Lars Borgeling	GER	5.40
4.	Dominic Johnson	AME	5.20
5=	Paul Burgess	OCE	5.20
5=	Andres Hinojo	ESP	5.20
7.	**Tim Thomas**		**5.00**
nh	Aleksandr Averbukh	EUR	
nh	Daichi Sawano	ASI	

Long Jump (20 Sep)

1.	Savante Stringfellow	USA	8.21
2.	Ivan Pedroso	AME	8.19
3.	Yago Lamela	ESP	8.11
4.	Hussein Al-Sabee	ASI	7.92
5.	Younes Moudrik	AFR	7.90
6.	**Chris Tomlinson**		**7.85**
7.	Aleksey Lukashevich	EUR	7.83
8.	Tim Parravicini	OCE	7.69
9.	Andreas Pohle	GER	7.26

Triple Jump (21 Sep)

1.	**Jonathan Edwards**		**17.34**
2.	Walter Davis	USA	17.23w
3.	Christian Olsson	EUR	17.05
4.	Charles Friedek	GER	16.91w
5.	Jadel Gregorio	AME	16.61w
6.	Kazuyoshi Ishikawa	ASI	16.50
7.	Olivier Sanou	AFR	16.30
8.	Raul Chapado	ESP	15.91
9.	Viktor Chistiakov	OCE	14.96

Shot (20 Sep)

1.	Adam Nelson	USA	20.80
2.	Justin Anlezark	OCE	20.77
3.	Ralf Bartels	GER	20.67
4.	Janus Robberts	AFR	20.00
5.	Yuriy Bilonog	EUR	19.88
6.	Manuel Martinez	ESP	19.76
7.	**Carl Myerscough**		**19.13**
8.	Bradley Snyder	AME	18.99
9.	Li Rongxiang	ASI	10.09

Discus (21 Sep)

1.	Robert Fazekas	EUR	71.25
2.	Frantz Kruger	AFR	66.78
3.	Mario Pestano	ESP	64.64
4.	Michael Mollenbeck	GER	64.57
5.	Jason Tunks	AME	62.89
6.	Adam Setliff	USA	61.52
7.	**Bob Weir**		**58.91**
8.	Peter Elvy	OCE	56.60
9.	Koji Murofushi	ASI	41.93

Hammer (20 Sep)

1.	Adrian Annus	EUR	80.93
2.	Koji Murofushi	ASI	80.08
3.	Karsten Kobs	GER	78.44
4.	Chris Harmse	AFR	77.16
5.	Moises Campeny	ESP	73.21
6.	John McEwen	USA	71.03
7.	Phillip Jensen	OCE	67.09
8.	Mick Jones		66.92
9.	Yosvany Suarez	AME	66.33

Javelin (21 Sep)

1.	Sergey Makarov	EUR	86.44
2.	Boris Henry	GER	81.60
3.	Emeterio Gonzalez	AME	79.77
4.	**Steve Backley**		**79.39**
5.	Gerhardus Pienaar	AFR	78.91
6.	Li Rongxiang	ASI	78.12
7.	William Hamlyn-Harris	OCE	74.48
8.	Gustavo Dacal	ESP	68.26
9.	Chris Clever	USA	65.73

4 x 100 Metres (20 Sep)

1.	United States		37.95
2.	Americas		38.32
3.	Africa		38.63
4.	Europe		38.86
5.	Asia		38.91
6.	**Great Britain & NI**		**39.23**
	(Barbour, Devonish, Malcolm, Plummer)		
7.	Oceania		39.58
8.	Spain		39.64
dsq	Germany		

4 x 400 Metres (21 Sep)

1.	Americas		2:59.19
2.	United States		2:59.21
3.	Africa		3:01.69
4.	Asia		3:03.02
5.	**Great Britain & NI**		**3:03.34**
	(Deacon, Baulch, Benjamin, Elias)		
6.	Oceania		3:03.65
7.	Germany		3:05.31
dsq	Europe		
dsq	Spain		

Match Result

1.	Africa	134
2.	United States	119
3.	Europe	115
4.	Americas	111
5.	Spain	94
6.	Germany	86.5
7.	**Great Britain & NI**	**86**
8.	Asia	80
9.	Oceania	62.5

WOMEN

400 Metres (20 Sep)

1.	Ana Guevara	AME	49.56
2.	Jearl Miles Clark	USA	50.27
3.	Olesya Zykina	RUS	50.67
4.	**Lee McConnell**	**EUR**	**50.82**
5.	Kaltouma Nadjina	AFR	51.11
6.	Claudia Marx	GER	52.30
7.	Tatyana Roslanova	ASI	52.44
8.	Rosemary Hayward	OCE	52.76
9.	Miriam Bravo	ESP	53.79

5000 Metres (21 Sep)

1.	Olga Yegorova	RUS	15:18.15
2.	Marta Dominguez	ESP	15:19.73
3.	**Jo Pavey**	**EUR**	**15:20.10**
4.	Benita Johnson	OCE	15:20.83
5.	Susan Chepkemei	AFR	15:27.04
6.	Akiko Kawashima	ASI	15:41.95
7.	Sabrina Mockenhaupt	GER	15:42.22
8.	Nora Rocha	AME	15:45.48
9.	Collette Liss	USA	15:59.44

Long Jump (21 Sep)

1.	Tatyana Kotova	RUS	6.85
2.	Maurren Maggi	AME	6.81
3.	Concepcion Montaner	ESP	6.68
4.	**Jade Johnson**	**EUR**	**6.41**
5.	Chantal Brunner	OCE	6.35
6.	Yelena Kashcheyeva	ASI	6.32
7.	Sofia Schulte	GER	6.16
8.	Francoise Mbango	AFR	6.06
9.	Brianna Glenn	USA	5.91

Triple Jump (20 Sep)

1.	Francoise Mbango	AFR	14.37
2.	**Ashia Hansen**	**EUR**	**14.32**
3.	Carlota Castrejana	ESP	14.13
4.	Trecia Smith	AME	13.82
5.	Yuliana Perez	USA	13.79
6.	Yelena Oleynikova	RUS	13.79
7.	Wu Lingmei	ASI	13.60
8.	Sofia Schulte	GER	12.73
9.	Michelle Apostolou	OCE	12.12

4 x 400 Metres (21 Sep)

1.	Americas	3:23.53
2.	United States	3:24.67
3.	Russia	3:26.59
4.	Africa	3:26.84
5.	**Europe**	**3:29.21**
	(McConnell last leg)	
6.	Germany	3:31.09
7.	Oceania	3:31.32
8.	Spain	3:36.50
9.	Asia	3:37.18

Match Result

1.	Russia	126
2.	Europe	123
3.	Americas	110

20th IAAF WORLD RACE WALKING CUP
Turin, ITA 12 - 13 October 2002

MEN

20k (12 Oct)

1.	Jefferson Perez	ECU	1:21:26
2.	Vladimir Andreyev	RUS	1:21:50
3.	Alejandro Lopez	MEX	1:22:01
46.	**Steve Partington**		**1:31:41**
63.	**Steve Hollier**		**1:35:18**
66.	**Andi Drake**		**1:36:06**
68.	**Dominic King**		**1:37:40**

Team Result

1.	Russia	24
2.	Belarus	28
3.	Italy	34
15.	**Great Britain & NI**	**175**

50k (13 Oct)

1.	Aleksey Voyevodin	RUS	3:40:59
2.	German Skurygin	RUS	3:42:08
3.	Tomasz Lipiec	POL	3:45:37

Team Result

1.	Russia	7
2.	France	59
3.	People's Republic of China	78

WOMEN

20k (12 Oct)

1.	Erica Alfridi	ITA	1:28:55
2.	Olimpiada Ivanova	RUS	1:28:57
3.	Natalya Fedoskina	RUS	1:28:59
71.	**Sharon Tonks**		**1:48:33**
75.	**Sara-Jane Cattermole**		**1:52:44**
dsq	Lisa Kehler		

Team Result

1.	Russia	9
2.	Italy	26
3.	Romania	42
dnf	**Great Britain & NI**	

RWA NATIONAL WALK CHAMPIONSHIPS

MEN

20k East Moseley (3 Mar)

1.	Andi Drake	1:24:43
2.	Andy Penn	1:26:04
3.	Don Bearman	1:30:09
4.	Gareth Brown	1:32:08
5.	Chris Cheeseman	1:34:06

Team Result

1.	Steyning	285

35k Sutton Coldfield (6 Jul)

1.	Martin Young	3:04:39
2.	Nathan Adams	3:09:44
3.	Mike Smith	3:11:56
4.	Chris Berwick	3:18:24
5.	Steve Arnold	3:22:23

Team Result

1.	Coventry Godiva

50k Colchester (8 Sep)

1.	Mike Smith	4:42:48
2.	Chris Berwick	4:56:13
3.	Steve Arnold	5:09:50
4.	Bob Dobson	5:24:57
5.	Dave Ratcliffe	5:25:57

Team Result

1.	Coventry Godiva	293

WOMEN

20k East Moseley (3 Mar)

1.	Lisa Kehler	1:43:08
2.	Sharon Tonks	1:43:29
3.	Kim Braznell	1:49:44
4.	Karen Ratcliffe	1:51:23
5.	Katherine Horwill	1:56:27

Team Result

1.	Dudley and Stourbridge	254

5k Sutton Coldfield (6 Jul)

1.	Lisa Kehler	22:20
2.	Sharon Tonks	23:53
3.	Karen Ratcliffe	25:27
4.	Jo Hesketh	26:11
5.	Ann Wheeler	28:28

Team Result

1.	Nuneaton

10k Leicester (31 Aug)

1.	Estle Viljoen	RSA	49:06
2.	Sharon Tonks		52:07
3.	Kim Braznell		53:18
4.	Sophie Hales		53:59
5.	Katherine Horwill		54:01

Team Result

1.	Steyning	17

EKIDEN RELAY
Chiba, JPN
23 November 2002

MEN (10k, 5k, 10k, 5k, 12.195k)

1.	Ethiopia	1:57:53
2.	Kenya	2:00:16
3.	Japan	2:00:19
15.	**Great Britain & NI**	**2:05:06**
	Mark Miles	**28:42**
	Chris Davies	**14:17**
	Ian Hudspith	**29:55**
	Rob Birchall	**14:18**
	Neil Wilkinson	**37:54**

WOMEN (10k, 5k, 10k, 5k, 4.767k, 7.428k)

1.	Ethiopia	2:14:07
2.	Japan	2:14:42
3.	Romania	2:16:37
8.	**Great Britain & NI**	**2:21:55**
	Andrea Green	**34:01**
	Kate Reed	**16:05**
	Debbie Robinson	**33:40**
	Lisa Heyes	**16:27**
	Morag McDonnell	**16:37**
	Susan Partridge	**25:05**

SPAR EUROPEAN CROSS COUNTRY CHAMPIONSHIPS
Medulin, CRO 8 December 2002

Both the men's teams were disappointing, but the junior women were magnificent and the senior women won a medal by packing in the lower places. Charlotte Dale is a real prospect.

SENIOR MEN (9830m)

1.	Sergey Lebed	UKR	28:58
2.	Mustapha Essaid	FRA	29:03
3.	Fabian Roncero	ESP	29:03
4.	Enrique Henriques	POR	29:05
5.	Helder Ornelas	POR	29:08
6.	Juan de la Ossa	ESP	29:10
19.	**Allen Graffin**		**29:40**
21.	**Jon Brown**		**29:41**
23.	**Glynn Tromans**		**29:45**
30.	**Spencer Barden**		**29:53**
63.	**Ben Noad**		**31:18**
71.	**Dominic Bannister**		**31:44**

Team

1.	Spain	31
2.	France	43
3.	Portugal	57
4.	**Great Britain & NI**	**93**

JUNIOR MEN (6170m)

1.	Yevgeniy Rybakov	RUS	18:16
2.	Anatoliy Rybakov	RUS	18:17
3.	Halil Akkas	TUR	18:23
19.	**Luke Beevor**		**19:12**
25.	**Edward Prickett**		**19:19**
30.	**Mohamed Farah**		**19:25**
45.	**Tom Humphries**		**19:41**
46.	**Jonathan Blackledge**		**19:41**
dnf	**Tom Sharland**		

Team

1.	Russia	37
2.	France	57
3.	Italy	92
7.	**Great Britain & NI**	**119**

SENIOR WOMEN (6170m)

1.	Helena Javornik	SLO	20:16
2.	Galina Bogomolova	RUS	20:18
3.	Elvan Abeylegesse	TUR	20:19
4.	Aniko Kalovics	HUN	20:21
5.	**Hayley Tullett**		**20:25**
6.	Sonja Stolic	YUG	20:27
14.	**Hayley Yelling**		**20:49**
20.	**Liz Yelling**		**21:00**
41.	**Sharon Morris**		**21:34**
51.	**Louise Damen**		**21:53**
56.	**Dianne Henaghan**		**22:02**

Team

1.	Russia	48
2.	Portugal	54
3.	**Great Britain & NI**	**80**

JUNIOR WOMEN (3730m)

1.	**Charlotte Dale**		**12:26**
2.	Elina Lindgren	FIN	12:27
3.	Galina Yegorova	RUS	12:28
7.	**Freya Murray**		**12:40**
8.	**Danielle Barnes**		**12:40**
11.	**Rachael Nathan**		**12:44**
12.	**Lisa Dobriskey**		**12:45**
26.	**Katrina Wootton**		**13:00**

Team

1.	**Great Britain & NI**	**27**
2.	Russia	35
3.	Belgium	105

REGIONAL CHAMPIONSHIPS

SCOTLAND
Scotstoun, Glasgow 8-9 June

MEN

Event	Athlete		Mark
100	Nick Smith		10.50
200	Dallas Roberts	NZL	21.08
400	Allan Stuart		47.27
800	Ally Donaldson		1:49.72
1500	Jon McCallum		3:49.45
5000	Glen Stewart		14:11.67
10000	Jamie Reid		31:14.31
3kSt	Andrew Lemoncello		9:23.00
110H	Chris Baillie		14.12
400H	Charles Robertson-Adams		51.19
HJ	Andrew Macfarlane		2.00
PV	Matthew Dorrian		4.60
LJ	Chris Tomlinson		7.98w
TJ	David Watson		14.24w
SP	Ian McMullan		16.77
DT	Kevin Brown	JAM	55.27
HT	Paul Head		68.35
JT	Tom Dobbing		67.08
Dec	Martin Taylor		6174
Pen	Jamie Quarry		3354

Dec   Grangemouth 24/25 Aug
Pen   Glasgow 7 Jul

WOMEN

Event	Athlete	Mark
100	Susan Burnside	11.81
200	Lee McConnell	23.79
400	Carey Easton	54.24
800	Susan Scott	2:02.64
1500	Kathy Butler	4:18.42
5000	Gillian Palmer	16:10.26
100H	Lynne Fairweather	13.98
400H	Sinead Dudgeon	58.47
HJ	Hazel Melvin	1.65
PV	Gillian Cooke	3.80
LJ	Ruth Irving	6.12w
TJ	Julia Straker	11.44w
SP	Mhairi Walters	13.05
DT	Navdeep Dhaliwal	44.15
HT	Shirley Webb	56.57
JT	Lorna Jackson	44.14
Hept	Shona McKinnon	2600
Pen	Wendy Davidson	3498

Hept   Grangemouth 24/25 Aug
Pen   Glasgow 7 Jul

WALES
Newport 8 – 9 June

MEN

Event	Athlete	Mark
100	Christian Malcolm	10.71
200	Tim Benjamin	21.73
400	Matt Elias	46.59
800	Lea Farmer	1:56.87
1500	Matt Shone	3:53.09
5000	Andres Jones	14:55.6
10000	not contested	
3kSt	David Jones	10:03.12
110H	Colin Jackson	13.8
400H	James Hillier	51.75
HJ	Robert Mitchell	2.10
PV	not contested	
LJ	Kris Davies	7.23w
TJ	Charles Madeira-Cole	15.10
SP	Andy Turner	14.26
DT	Lee Newman	53.02
HT	Graham Holder	58.52
JT	Derek Hermann	60.89
Dec	Neil Edwards	4410
3kW	Mark Williams	13:37.28

Dec   Wrexham 22/23 June

WOMEN

Event	Athlete	Mark
100	Catherine Murphy	12.34
200	Angharad James	25.65
400	Faye Harding	55.55
800	Hayley Tullett	2:07.77
1500	Rachel Newcombe	4:19.86
3000	Sam Gray	10:13.36
100H	Rachel King	13.9
400H	Faye Harding	63.60
HJ	Alisa Wallace	1.65
PV	Rhian Clarke	4.00
LJ	Aimee Cutler	5.60w
TJ	Helen Baker	11.57
SP	Liz Edwards	10.69
DT	Philippa Roles	54.45
HT	Sarah Moore	55.77
JT	Charlotte Rees	42.40
Hept	Victoria Consterdine	4162
3kW	not contested	

Hept   Wrexham 22/23 June

NORTHERN IRELAND
Belfast 8 June

MEN

Event	Athlete		Mark
100	John McAdorey	IRL	10.34w
200	Paul McKee	IRL	20.85w
400	Robert Daly	IRL	46.71
800	Ciaran O`Connell	IRL	1:55.31
1500	Conor Sweeney	IRL	3:48.87
5000	Kevin Seward		15:17.39
10000	David Brady		32:19.34
3kSt	Steven Cairns		9:03.10
110H	Paul Conroy	IRL	14.68w
400H	Stephen McDonnell	IRL	52.04
HJ	Paul Tohill		1.90
PV	Ruairi O`Brien	IRL	4.20
LJ	Gareth Devlin	IRL	7.26w
TJ	Patrick Shannon	IRL	15.11w
SP	Iain McMullen		16.70
DT	John Moreland		45.12
HT	Mark Hanily	IRL	55.68
JT	Michael Allen		69.84
Dec	Brendan McConville		7076
3kW	Bobby King	IRL	14:56.9

10k   Antrim 7 July
Dec   Antrim 24/25 Aug

WOMEN

Event	Athlete		Mark
100	Anna Boyle		11.89w
200	Ciara Sheehy	IRL	23.40w
400	Vicki Jamison		54.07
800	Adrienne McIvor	AUS	2:03.24
1500	Geraldine Hendricken	IRL	4:09.56
5000	Sharon Hatch		16:26.77
100H	Jane Hale		13.84w
400H	Fiona Harwood	IRL	59.88
HJ	Deidre Ryan	IRL	1.80
PV	Zoe Brown		3.80
LJ	Antoinette Furlong	IRL	6.07w
TJ	Sharon Foley-Gallen	IRL	12.39w
SP	Eva Massey		15.57
DT	Jackie McKernan		49.92
HT	Eva Massey		32.46
JT	Alison Moffitt	IRL	43.31
	Bronagh McAuley		3026
3kW	Gesilda Penrose	IRL	20:57.2
10000	Suzanne McCormick		38:05.85
2kSt	Cathy McCourt		8:38.76

10k   Antrim 7 July
Hept   Antrim 24/25 Aug

132

AREA CHAMPIONSHIPS

	SOUTH			MIDLAND			NORTH	
	Watford 1 - 2 June			Birmingham 1 - 2 June			Jarrow 1 June	

MEN

	SOUTH			MIDLAND			NORTH	
100	Daniel Plummer	10.7		Brendon Ghent	10.87		Michael Tietz	10.83
200	Graham Hedman	21.24		Brendon Ghent	21.43		Craig Telford	22.07
400	Sean Baldock	46.51		Cori Henry	46.46		Ian Lowthian	47.48
800	Andrew Knight	1:52.73		Martin Flook	1:54.84		Rob Watkinson	1:51.75
1500	Michael Skinner	3:50.15		Paul Richardson	3:56.11		Darren Middleton	3:57.15
5000	Nick Anderson	14:59.97	3000	Gordon Lee	8:44.6	5000	Andy Caine	14:32.54
10k	Michael Coleman	30:31.2	5000	Anthony Graham	15:15.72	10k	Paul Freary	31:06.94
3kSt	Pat Davoren	8:55.56		Kevin Hope	9:30.1		not contested	
110H	Duncan Malins	14.39		Ed Grey	15.6		Peter Monaghan	15.41
400H	Steven Green	51.1		Jeff Christie	52.05		Richard Smith	51.94
HJ	Mark Crowley	2.10		Tom Parsons	2.10		Danny Graham	2.10
PV	Ashley Swain	4.90		Scott Simpson	5.00		Mark Beharrell	5.10
LJ	Darren Thompson	7.34		Julian Flynn	7.32w		Simon Roper	7.18w
TJ	Tosin Oke	15.76		Mike McKernan	14.27w		Dave Sanderson	14.53
SP	Emeka Udechuku	17.50		Lyndon Woodward	16.21		Bryan Kelly	16.62
DT	Emeka Udechuku	55.16		Glen Smith	57.25		Bryan Kelly	53.72
HT	Simon Bown	65.68		Matthew Bell	62.94		Mike Floyd	64.02
JT	Dan Carter	69.56		Mike Tarran	59.82		Matthew Allison	63.91
Dec	Alex Gibson	7028		Sam Bishop	5857		Gerard Plunkett	6787
10kW	Richard Emsley	53:18.0		Steven Arnold	51:38.14			

10k	Brighton 14 Aug		10k	Manchester (Str) 14 May
Dec	London (He) 10/11 Aug		Dec	Hexham 15/16 June
10kW	London (He) 11 Aug			

WOMEN

	SOUTH			MIDLAND			NORTH	
100	Sabrina Scott	11.74=		Amanda Forrester	11.89		Emily Freeman	11.88
	Kelly Thomas	11.74=						
200	Sabrina Scott	23.73		Amanda Forrester	24.02		Emily Freeman	23.71
400	Karen Gear	54.12		Lindsey Singer	56.82		Danielle Halsall	54.39
800	Jeina Mitchell	2:07.25		Sally Evans	2:11.2		Vickie Lawrence	2:06.58
1500	Jo Wilkinson	4:21.15		Kate Reed	4:26.38		Claire Entwistle	4:28.47
5000	Sharon Morris	16:52.1		Kath Scales	17:31.99		Pauline Powell	17:00.37
						3kSt	not contested	
100H	Melani Wilkins	13.3		Sara McGreavy	14.53		Gemma Fergusson	14.14
400H	Hannah Stares	59.7		Hannah Wood	59.3		Liz Fairs	59.05
HJ	Natalia Norford	1.60		Julie Crane	1.75		Stephanie Higham	1.80
PV	Tracey Bloomfield	4.00		Emma Hornby	3.75		Linda Stanton	3.20
LJ	Lucy Atunumuo	5.90		Jacqui Spargo	5.94w		Natasha May	6.04w
TJ	Michelle Griffith	12.66		Debbie Rowe	12.71w		Hazel Carwardine	12.38w
SP	Julie Dunkley	16.19		not contested			Kara Nwidobie	13.90
DT	Emma Carpenter	52.71		Nicola Talbot	47.39		Kara Nwidobie	47.99
HT	Liz Pidgeon	61.42		Lorraine Shaw	64.38		Shirley Webb	55.29
JT	Kirsty Morrison	55.74		Sharon Gibson	43.21		Stacey Mohamed	38.45
Hept	Kate Brewington	5229		Isha Al-Sadek	3402		Danielle Parkinson	4221
10kW	Claire Reeves	54:47.0	5kW	Ann Wheeler	28:07.19			

Hept	London (He) 10/11 Aug		Hept	Hexham 15/16 Jun
10kW	London (He) 11 Aug			

AGE CHAMPIONSHIPS

U23
Bedford 29 - 30 June

MEN
100	Tyrone Edgar	10.31w
200	Dominic Papura	21.15
400	Ian Lowthian	49.01
800	Sam Ellis	1:53.17
1500	Chris Bolt	3:53.19
3000		
5000	James Fewtrell	14:26.58
3kSt	Adam Bowden	9:12.76
110H	Dominic Girdler	14.0
400H	Steven Surety	51.8
HJ	Robert Mitchell	2.13
PV	Ashley Swain	5.15
LJ	Mark Awanah	7.60w
TJ	Tosin Oke	16.27w
SP	David Readle	16.91
DT	Luke Rosenberg	50.48
HT	Andy Frost	63.05
JT	Phill Sharpe	71.09
10kW	Nathan Adams	46:22.2

WOMEN
100	Susan Burnside	11.61w
200	Emily Freeman	23.51w
400	Jennifer Meadows	54.13
800	Joanna Ross	2:10.88
1500	Natalie Lewis	4:25.82
3000		
5000	Gillian Palmer	16:13.87
100H	Tamsin Stephens	13.67
400H	Michelle Carey IRL	58.7
HJ	Natalie Clark	1.69
PV	Ellie Spain	3.85
LJ	Natasha May	6.17w
TJ	Rebecca White	12.90
SP	Eva Massey	15.49
DT	Emma Carpenter	53.56
HT	Zoe Derham	60.57
JT	Goldie Sayers	58.20

MEN
100	Andrew Watkins	11.07
200	Andrew Watkins	22.41
400	Kris Robertson	52.06
800	Grant Prendergast	1:58.79
1500	Adam Hickey	4:08.03

WOMEN
100	Carley Wenham	12.08
200	Joey Duck	25.49
800	Laura Crowe IRL	2:10.37
1500	Charlotte Browning	4:38.53

U20
Bedford 29 - 30 June

MEN
100	Karl Forde	10.6w
200	Leon Baptiste	21.41w
400	Adam Charlton	48.95
800	Ricky Soos	1:50.21
1500	Derek Watson	3:58.73
3000	Matthew Bowser	8:20.38
5000	Thomas Sharland	14:32.2
3kSt	Mohd Al-Banai KSA	9:16.98
110H	David Hughes	14.68w
400H	Steven Green	51.6
HJ	Mark Crowley	2.15
PV	Richard Hurren	4.60
LJ	Jonathan Moore	7.57w
TJ	Kevin Thompson	15.07
SP	Samuel Westlake-Cann	16.42
DT	Roger Bate	49.99
HT	Carl Saggers	64.81
JT	Alex van der Merwe	68.85
Dec	Edward Dunford	6583
10kW	Dominic King	42:49.8
3000	Manchester 15/16 June	
Dec	Wrexham 22/23 June	

WOMEN
100	Vernicha James	11.45w
200	Amy Spencer	23.58w
400	Kim Wall	54.63
800	Jemma Simpson	2:09.65
1500	Lisa Dobriskey	4:23.22
3000	Sally Oldfield	9:33.51
5000	Kathryn Frost	17:17.92
100H	Gemma Fergusson	13.76
400H	Sian Scott	61.06
HJ	Rebecca Jones	1.83
PV	Kate Dennison	3.95
LJ	Elaine Smith	5.97w
TJ	Emily Parker	12.19w
SP	Charlotte Spelzini	13.72
DT	Claire Smithson	53.91
HT	Nicola Dudman	54.22
JT	Samantha Redd	47.66
Hept	Phyllis Agbo	4868
5kW	Sophie Hales	25:18.56
3000	Manchester 15/16 June	
Hept	Wrexham 22/23 June	

U15 Birmingham 10 - 11 August

MEN
80H	Daniel Maynard	10.87
HJ	David Shields	1.90
PV	James Hoad	3.60
LJ	Darryl Thomas	6.48
TJ	Ryhan Thomas	12.04
SP	Shane Birch	14.99

WOMEN
75H	Clare Cooper	11.17
HJ	Dominique Blaize	1.65
LJ	Amy Harris	5.59w
SP	Tolani Agoro	11.83
DT	Ruth Hay	34.40

U17
Birmingham 10 - 11 August

MEN
100	James Ellington	10.69
200	Julian Thomas	22.10
400	Simon Toye	48.42
800	Michael Rimmer	1:53.81
1500	Lee Bowron	3:58.19
3000	Craig Ivemy	8:38.43
1500St	Chris Hart	4:20.72
100H	Tom Stimson	13.48
	Richard Davenport	53.08
	Oliver Sweeney	1.91
	Keith Higham	4.50
	Bernard Yeboah	7.32w
	Graham Jackson	14.29w
	Chris Gearing	17.05
	Andrew Thomas	52.84
	Simon Bissell	63.18
	Sam Kelvey	60.66
Dec	Louis Moore	6501
5kW	Luke Finch	23:56.41
Dec	Stoke 28/29 Sep	

WOMEN
	Montell Douglas	11.77
	Montell Douglas	24.33
300	Gemma Nicol	38.49
	Rachael Thompson	2:11.32
	Rachel Jones	4:33.74
	Rachael Nathan	9:55.38
80H	Heather Jones	11.56
300H	Eilidh Child	42.49
	Shani Rainford	1.71
	Hannah Olson	3.80
	Catherine Holdsworth	5.83w
	Sally Peake	11.89w
	Sally Hinds	12.10
	Lucy Sutton	37.00
	Laura Chalmers	45.23
	Louise Watton	43.39
	Nadia Bromley	4574
	Katie Stones	25:57.11
Hept	Stoke 28/29 Sep	

DT	Shane Birch	45.85
HT	Matt Lambley	62.18
JT	Adam Akehurst	48.24
Pent	Lewis Robson	3129
3kW	Nick Ball	14:43.39
Pent	Stoke 28 Sep	
JT	Lucy Boggis	32.09
Pent	Jade Surman	3126
3kW	Rebecca Mersh	15:26.01
Pent	Stoke 29 Sep	

UK MERIT RANKINGS 2002 by Peter Matthews

This is the 35th successive year that I have compiled annual merit rankings of British athletes – an assessment of form during the outdoor season. The major factors by which the rankings are determined are win-loss record, performances in the major meetings, and sequence of marks. While indoor marks are excluded from the main rankings, I have also assessed overall form including these, and have appended any changes at the end of appropriate events.

I endeavour to be as objective as possible, but form can often provide conflicting evidence, or perhaps an athlete may not have shown good enough results against leading rivals, or in very important competition, to justify a ranking which his or her ability might otherwise warrant. I can only rank athletes on what they have actually achieved. Much depends on having appropriate opportunities and perhaps getting invitations for the prestige meetings. Difficulties also arise when athletes reach peak form at different parts of the season or, through injury, miss significant competition. Also, increasingly, many of our top athletes are competing overseas instead of in domestic meetings, which makes comparisons of form difficult. It is often difficult to compare juniors with seniors and many top U23 and U20 athletes missed events such as the AAAs through clashes of fixtures.

Once again it should be pointed out that the rankings are by no means necessarily the order in which I think the athletes would have finished in an idealised contest, but simply my attempt to assess what has actually happened in 2002.

I hope that I have not missed many performances, but I would be very pleased to receive any missing results at 10 Madgeways Close, Great Amwell, Herts SG12 9RU.

For each event the top 12 are ranked. On the first line is shown the athlete's name, then their date of birth followed, in brackets, by the number of years ranked in the top 12 (including 2002), their ranking last year (2001), in italics their IAAF world ranking, their best mark prior to 2002, and finally their best performances of the year (generally six), followed for completeness, by significant indoor marks indicated by 'i'. Then follow placings at major meetings, providing a summary of the athlete's year at the event. *(Note: IAAF rankings include indoor performances)*

Abbreviations include

AAA-23	AAA Under-23 Championships
AAA-J	AAA Under-20 Championships
BrGP	British Grand Prix at Crystal Palace
BIG	Bedford International
BL	British League/UK Womens' League
B.Univs	British Universities at Bedford
CAU	Inter-Counties at Bedford
CG	Commonwealth Games Manchester
CGT	Commonwealth Games Trials at Manchester
Cup	BAL Cup Final at Bedford (also major clashes in semis – sf)
Derby	U20/U23 Inter-Regional 11/8
EC	European Championships at Munich
E.Chall	European Challenge (Throws and 10,000m)
E.Clubs	European Clubs Cup
ECp	European Cup
E.Sch	English Schools
GPF	Grand Prix Final
IA	Inter-Area at Watford
IS	Inter-Services
JIvIt,Sp	Junior International v Italy and Spain at Gorizia
JLF	Junior League Final
Jnr IA	Junior Inter-Area
LI	Loughborough International
Lough	Loughborough Development Meeting (17 Jul)
Sheffield	NU Classic at Sheffield
WCp	World Cup at Madrid (Walks at Turin)
WG	Welsh Games at Cardiff
WJ	World Junior Championships at Kingston, Jamaica
3nU23	Under 23 International v France and Spain at Niort
v USA	UK v USA and Russia at Glasgow

100 METRES

1. **Dwain Chambers** 5.4.78 (7y, 1) *IAAF 3* 9.97 '99   9.87, 9.94, 9.95w, 9.96, 9.98, 10.02
   2 Walnut, 2 Modesto, 3 Athens, 1 CGT, 1 ECp, 1 Oslo, 1 Sheffield , 8 CG, 1 EC, 3 Zürich, 1 v USA,
   1 BrGP, 1 Berlin, 2 GPF, 5 WCp
2. **Mark Lewis-Francis** 4.9.82 (4y, 2) *IAAF 10* 10.10 '00, 9.97w? '01   9.97w, 10.04, 10.06, 10.07, 10.08, 10.10
   1 Tallahassee, 1 LI, 2 CGT, 2 Sheffield, 3 Paris, 1 AAA, 7 CG, 7 BrGP, 5 Brussels, 3 Rieti
3. **Darren Campbell** 12.9.73 (11y, 7) *IAAF 25* 10.04 '98   10.11, 10.15, 10.19, 10.27, 10.28, 10.29
   3 AUS Ch, 6 Doha, 1B BL2 (1), 4 Milan, 5 CGT, 2 Funchal. 3 Zagreb, 2 AAA, 3 EC, 7h1 Zürich, 3 Poznan
4. **Jason Gardener** 18.9.75 (8y, 12) *IAAF 14* 9.98 '99   10.11w, 10.13, 10.17, 10.21, 10.22, 10.22w
   5 Athens, 4 CGT, 3 Sheffield, 7 Lausanne, 3 AAA, 1 Heusden, 6 CG, 6s1 EC, 4 v USA, 8h2 BrGP
5. **Chris Lambert** 6.4.81 (3y, 5) *IAAF 89* 10.24 '01   10.19w, 10.28, 10.30w, 10.30w, 10.32, 10.36
   1 Heps, 1 Riga, 3 CGT, dns AAA-23
6. **Christian Malcolm** 3.6.79 (6y, 3) *IAAF 65* 10.11, 10.09w? '01   10.29, 10.36, 10.39, 10.44, 10.52, 10.63
   1 Welsh, 7 Lille, 1 BL3 (2), 2 WG, 4 AAA
7. **Daniel Plummer** 4.1.81 (1y, -) 10.74, 10.7 '01, 10.67w '96   10.33, 10.35w, 10.36w, 10.38, 10.39, 10.41
   2 LI, dns CAU, 1 South, 6 CGT, 3B Sheff, 6 AAA, 1 U23 v Ger, 5B Glas, 6=h2 BrGP, 1B BL2 (4), 1 Barc
8. **Marlon Devonish** 1.6.76 (6y, 8) 10.13 '98   10.30w, 10.32, 10.38, 10.42w, 10.43, 10.50
   3 LI, 3 Rehlingen, 1 CAU, 2 Bydgsozcz, 3 Bratislava
9. **Allyn Condon** 24.8.74 (6y, -) 10.21 '99   10.26w, 10.32, 10.44, 10.47, 10.51w, 10.54
   1B LI, 5s1 CAU, 5 AAA, 2B Dublin
10. **Tyrone Edga**r 29.3.82 (2y, 11) 10.39 '00, 10.17w '01   10.20w, 10.28, 10.29, 10.31w, 10.36w, 10.40
    3 Kiev, 2 Cottbus, 2h4 CGT, 1 AAA-23, 1 BL1 (2), 5s1 AAA
11. **Doug Bignal**l 20.10.74 (3y, 6) 10.30 '01, 10.27Aw '00   10.29w, 10.30w, 10.32, 10.34, 10.39, 10.53
12. **Dwayne Grant** 17.7.82 (1y, -) 10.47, 10.22w '01   10.48w, 10.49w, 10.52, 10.56w, 10.58, 10.59
    2 CAU, 3 Riga, 8 CGT

Chambers, whose great season was marred only by his pulling up at the Commonwealth Games, is ranked top for the fourth successive year and he challenged hard for the world top ranking, taking second to Tim Montgomery after his defeat in the Grand Prix Final, where Chambers equalled Linford Christie's European record 9.87. Lewis-Francis ran a series of good times, but was unfortunate to pull a muscle when close to a medal in Manchester, and Campbell was third after returning to top form at the right time. Plummer is the top newcomer. While sprint standards remain excellent, the 10th best 'legal' time at 10.33 is the worst since 1996.

200 METRES

1. **Marlon Devonish** 1.6.76 (7y, 2) *IAAF 6* 20.25 '99   20.18w, 20.19, 20.23, 20.24, 20.27, 20.32
   1 LI, 1 CAU, 2 Bydgoszcz, 1 CGT, 1 ECp, 5 Sheffield, 5 Lausanne, 1 AAA, 2 CG, 3 EC, 2 v USA, 3 BrGP,
   6 Brussels, 3 Rieti, 3 WCp
2. **Darren Campbell** 12.9.73 (8y, 12) *IAAF 24* 20.13 '00   20.21, 20.26w, 20.52, 20.58, 20.62, 20.66
   3 AUS Ch, 1B BL2 (1), 1 Funchal, 2 Zagreb, 2 AAA, 3 CG, dq EC qf, 2 Poznan
3. **Christian Malcolm** 3.6.79 (6y, 1) *IAAF 6* 20.08 '02
   20.29w, 20.30, 20.39, 20.53, 20.54, 20.55
   5 Milan, 2 Hengelo, 6 Sheffield, 2 WG, 3 AAA, 8 CG, 4 EC, 4 v USA, 4 BrGP
4. **Chris Lambert** 6.4.81 (3y, 9) *IAAF 45* 20.63 '99
   20.37, 20.41, 20.48w, 20.68w, 20.76w, 20.77
   1 Heps, 1 Riga, 2 CGT, 6s2 CG
5. **Dwain Chambers** 5.4.78 (4y, 3) *IAAF 26* 20.31 '01   20.27, 20.38, 20.55, 20.64, 21.22
   1 Bydgoszcz, 2 Athens, 2 Sheffield, 7 AAA
6. **Dwayne Grant** 17.7.82 (2y, 5) *IAAF 61* 20.64, 20.4w '01
   20.60w, 20.79, 20.82, 20.83w, 20.85, 20.88
   4 Kiev, 3 Tartu, 4 CGT, 2 AAA-23, 4 AAA, 2 Dublin, 4 Bangor, 1 3nU23, 5 BrGP
7. **Doug Turner** 2.12.66 (8y, 4) *IAAF 32* 20.43 '96, 20.36w '97   20.75, 20.76, 21.11, 21.18, 21.24; 21.2;
   20.59i, 20.84i, 20.86i, 20.92i   2 Welsh, 3 Lisbon, fs AAA, 1 Cup sf Eton, 7s1 CG, BL3: -,1,-,2
8. **Julian Golding** 17.2.75 (9y, 6) 20.18 '98   20.62w, 21.02, 21.04, 21.09, 21.57; 21.1
   2 Celle L, 3B WG, 3 BL1 (2), 5 AAA, dq B Dublin, 1 BL2 (3), 7 Poznan
9. **Graham Beasley** 24.10.77 (1y, -) 21.03 '99, 20.83w '01   20.76, 20.78, 20.90, 20.90w, 21.07, 21.16w;
   21.1w?   2B LI, 3 CGT, 3 Celle L, 6 AAA, 1 Cup, BL1: 1,1,1,1
10. **Allyn Condon** 24.8.74 (7y, -) 20.63 '97, 20.53i '98, 20.59w '99   20.86w, 20.90, 21.28, 21.57; (21.06 dq)
    2 BL2 (1), 1B LI, 4 Hengelo, dq (5) CGT, dnf h2 AAA
11. **Cori Henry** 9.12.76 (1y, -) 21.34 '96, 20.9 '99, 20.8w '96   20.98, 21.11; 21.5, 21.6, 21.6
    5 CGT, BL2: -,1,2,-
12. **Dominic Papura** 12.2.81 (1y, -) 21.67, 21.61w, 21.5w '01   21.15, 21.29, 21.32w, 21.61; 21.3, 21.4
    2 B.Univs, 4 LI, 1 AAA-23, 2 U23 v Ger
– **Mark Lewis-Francis** 4.9.82 (1y, -) 21.82 '99, 21.8 '98   20.94; 1 Tallahassee
– **Daniel Caines** 15.5.79 (0y, -) 21.05 '01   20.62i, 20.67i, 20.83+i, 21.12i, 21.14i, 21.43i

nr **Paul Brizzel** IRL 3.10.76 20.54A, 20.65 '00   20.59w, 20.72, 20.82w, 20.89, 20.96, 20.99w
   dns CAU, 2 NI, dnf CGT, 1 ECp 1A, 1 Irish, 2 Bangor, 6h3 EC
nr **Paul McKee** IRL 15.10.77 21.20, 20.87w '00   20.81, 20.85w, 21.16w, 21.21, 21.42, 21.79
   2 CAU, 1 NI, 1B Bangor
Including Indoors: 6. Turner, 7. Grant ...10. Caines, 11. Condon, 12. Henry
Devonish is top ranked after 2nd, 3rd and 2nd in the last three years and he made the world top ten for the first time. He and Campbell took silver and bronze medals at the Commonwealth Games, as Malcolm slips from first to third, although making the finals in both Manchester and Munich. Lambert moved up to fourth, but was injured after looking most impressive at the Trials. Beasley, after several years just outside the top 12, is the top newcomer. As in the 100m many sprinters had thin or ragged seasons, with odd races all over Europe. Similarly to the 100, the 10th best 'legal' time at 20.90 is the worst since 1994, but still good.

400 METRES

1. **Daniel Caines** 15.5.79 (3y, 3) *IAAF 10*   45.37 '00
   44.98, 45.13, 45.14, 45.28, 45.30, 45.32
   2 Seville, 1 CGT, 1 ECp, 1 Sheffield, 4 CG, 3 EC, 4 BrGP
2. **Tim Benjamin** 2.5.82 (2y, 6) *IAAF 49*   46.10 '01
   45.73, 45.80, 45.89, 46.07, 46.15, 46.28, (45.65dq)
   2 LI, 2 Rehlingen, 5 Bratislava, dq CGT, 1 AAA, 7s2 CG, dns EC, 1 Barcelona, 7 WCp
3. **Sean Baldock** 3.12.76 (6y, 7 *IAAF 81*   45.20 '00
   45.71, 45.84, 45.92, 45.96, 46.02, 46.03
   2r2 E.Clubs, 1 South, 3 CGT, 1 BL1 (2), 2 AAA, 6s1 CG, 4h3 EC
4. **Jared Deacon** 15.10.75 (8y, 8) *IAAF 61*   45.69 '00
   45.57, 45.84, 45.89, 45.96, 46.05, 46.07
   2 Riga, 2 Tartu, 2 CGT, 3 AAA, 8s1 CG, 3 v USA
5. **Du'aine Thorne-Ladejo** 14.2.71 (8y, -) 44.66 '96
   46.05, 46.23, 46.37A, 46.46, 46.49, 46.53
   1 Veszprém, 3 WG, 4 AAA, 3 Bangor, 2B Dublin, 1 Cup, 4 v USA
6. **Jamie Baulch** 3.5.73 (9y, 5) *IAAF 89*   44.57 '96
   46.01, 46.36, 46.42, 46.47, 46.63, 46.94
   dns CGT, 4 Hamburg, 5 Funchal, 5 AAA, 3C Dublin
7. **Chris Rawlinson** 19.5.72 (1y, -) 47.18 '99
   46.03, 46.13, 46.16; 48.06i, 48.11i
   1 Athens, 1 LI, 1 E.Clubs B
8. **Mark Hylton** 24.9.76 (9y, 4) *IAAF 95*   45.24 '98
   46.18, 46.35, 46.42, 46.49, 46.55, 47.1
   1 CAU, 2A BIG, 6 Sheffield, 4 BL1 (2), 6 AAA, 1 Cup sf Eton
9. **Cori Henry** 9.12.76 (1y, -) 46.50 '96
   46.46, 46.50, 46.56, 46.65, 47.1, 47.3, (46.39dq)
   1 BL2 (1), 2 CAU, 1 Mid, dq h1 CGT, 7 AAA
10. **Graham Hedman** 6.2.79 (1y, -) 47.63 '01
    46.37, 46.39, 46.61, 46.61, 46.65, 46.71
    1B BIG, 4 CGT, 8 AAA, 4 Barcelona, BL1: -,2,3,-
11. **Mark Brown** 3.11.76 (2y, -) 46.37 '99
    46.86, 46.93, 46.95, 47.3
    5 CGT, 5 BL1 (2), 1 Cup sf He
12. **Iwan Thomas** 5.1.74 (8y, 2) 44.36 '97
    46.48, 47.00, 47.07, 47.07, 47,17, 47.2
    7 AUS Ch, 3 BL1 (2), 6 WG, 5s2 AAA, 7 Dublin
– **Matt Elias** 25.4.79 (1y, -) 46.9, 46.88i '01
    46.59, 47.01, 48.55; 47.39i
    1C LI, 1 Welsh
– **Robert Tobin** 20.12.83 (1y, 12) 47.10 '01
    46.80, 46.91, 47.42; 46.80i, 47.78i
    3 LI, 1 Sth-J, 2h4 CGT, dnf h3 WJ
nr **Paul McKee** IRL 15.10.77 45.92 '00
    45.58, 45.62, 45.91, 45.92, 46.03, 46.03
    1 BL1 (1), 1 Riga, 1 Tartu, 1 ECp 2A, 2 Haniá, 1 Irish, 7s1 CG, 5s1 EC
Caines takes his first top ranking after two years ranked third, and Benjamin continues his progress. Baldock and Deacon achieved their highest ever rankings, the latter also continuing to excel on relay first legs. Mark Richardson, top ranked each year 1999-2001, was unable to run at all in 2002. Although better than 2001 (46.56), the tenth best of 46.46 is worse than in any of the great British years for this event, 1993-2000.

800 METRES
1. **James McIlroy** 30.12.76 (4y, 3) *IAAF 43* 1:45.32 '98 1:45.52, 1:46.40, 1:46.88, 1:46.93, 1:47.35, 1:47.67
   2 BL2 (1), 5 Kalamata, 4 Lisbon, 1 Eton, 1 Cork, 1 AAA, 6 CG, 5s1 EC, 7 BrGP, 2 Rovereto, 8 WCp
2. **Simon Lees** 19.11.79 (3y, 1) *IAAF 78* 1:47.35 '01 1:47.60, 1:47.62, 1:47.83, 1:47.89, 1:48.43, 1:49.47
   1B Walnut, 1 LI, 5 ECp, 1 Wyth, 1 CGT
3. **Neil Speaight** 9.9.78 (4y, 2) *IAAF 75* 1:47.16 '01 1:46.92, 1:47.22, 1:47.35, 1:47.37A, 1:47.61, 1:48.25
   5/5/10 in RSA, 2 E.Clubs, 2 CGT, 1 Sheff, 2 Eton, 2 AAA, 2 Dublin, 2 Bangor, 5s2 CG, 4 Watf, 9 BrGP, 1 BL1 (4)
4. **Ricky Soos** 28.6.83 (2y, 6) 1:48.43 '01 1:47.18, 1:47.22, 1:48.04, 1:48.10, 1:48.17, 1:48.44
   2 LI, 5 CGT, 2 Solihull, 1 AAA-J, 5s1 WJ, 3 Watford, 10 BrGP
5. **Joel Kidger** 16.3.80 (1y, -) 1:50.9 '01 1:47.82, 1:48.12, 1:48.16, 1:48.25, 1;48.40, 1:48.69
   2 B.Univs, 5 LI, 3 Wyth, 4 CGT, 4 Sheffield, 1 Cup sf Eton, 6s1 CG, 1 3nU23, 5 Watford, 6 Barcelona
6. **Alasdair Donaldson** 21.6.77 (5y, 9) 1:47.32 '00 1:48.09, 1:48.13, 1:49.69, 1:49.72, 1:49.90, 1:50.17
   3 LI, 1 Scot, 2 Wyth, dns CGT, 3 AAA, 1 Edinburgh, 1 Cup sf He
7. **Matthew Shone** 10.7.75 (4y, 5) 1:47.99 '99 1:46.72, 1:49.08, 1:49.24, 1:49.67, 1:49.82, 1:50.11;
   1:49.66i 4 Cape Town, 6 LI, 7 Bratislava, 5 Sheffield, 4 WG, 7s1 CG, 3 BL1 (3)
8. **Anthony Whiteman** 13.11.71 (5y, -) *IAAF 75* 1:45.81 '00 1:46.23A, 1:47.7, 1:48.81, 1:50.60
   2 Pretoria, 9 Cape Town, 7h4 EC
9. **Curtis Robb** 7.6.72 (8y, -) 1:44.92 '93 1:48.50, 1:48.57, 1:50.34, 1:52.1, 1:52.11
   1B BL4 (1), 3 CGT, 6 Sheffield, dnf h2 AAA, 4h3 CG
10. **Chris Moss** 17.6.79 (4y, 8) 1:47.75 '00 1:48.01, 1:49.32, 1:50.28, 1:51.18, 1:51.85
    1 Cup, 6 Watford, 3 Barcelona, BL1: -,-,1,1B
11. **Angus Maclean** 20.9.80 (1y, -) 1:49.39 '01 1:48.82, 1:49.51, 1:49.64, 1:50.17, 1:50.50, 1:51.11
    6 CGT, 3 Sheffield, 2 U23 v Ger; BL2: 4,1,-,-
12. **Dominic Hall** 21.2.71 (1y, -) 1:49.1 '98 1:49.47, 1:49.50, 1:49.97, 1:50.3, 1:50.46, 1:50.50
    1B Wyth, 3h1 CGT, 3 Solihull, 2 Sheffield, 4 AAA, 11 Watford, 1 Ashford
– **Tom Mayo** 2.5.77 (0y, -) 1:49.1 '99 1:48.17, 1:50.44, 1:51.3 2 CAU, 7 Watford
– **Michael East** 20.1.78 (0y, -) 1:48.66 '01 1:48.30; 4 LI
– **Chris Mulvaney** 25.5.81 (0y, -) 1:49.69i '01, 1:49.86 '00 1:48.56, 1:50.43, 1:51.21;
    1:48.14i, 1:48.45i, 1:49.78i 7 SEC (11th rank including indoors).

McIlroy returned to top ranking and Lees was unfortunate to be injured after a good start to the season; he just edges Speaight whom he beat conclusively at the Commonwealth Trials. Soos is the highest ranked junior since Chris McGeorge was also 4th in 1981. Kidger, who improved by three seconds and is coached by McGeorge, is the top newcomer. Tenth best, 1:48.14, is a big improvement on 2001's 1:48.85, but a far cry from the record of 1:46.13 in 1988.

1500 METRES – 1 MILE
1. **Michael East** 20.1.78 (3y, 5) *IAAF 31* 3:38.94/3:59.61M '01
   3:37.35, 3:39.18, 3:58.40M (3:41.9), 3:41.74, 3:41.82, 3:41.88; 3:40.52i
   2 Dessau, 1 CGT, 2 ECp, 14 Sheffield, 3 AAA, 1 CG, 6 EC, 1 v USA, 11 BrGP, 6 WCp
2. **Anthony Whiteman** 13.11.71 (8y, 2) *IAAF 20* 3:32.34 '97, 3:51.90M '98 3:32.43, 3:53.21M, 3:38.04,
   3:38.24, 3:57.54M, 3:42.21 2 CGT, 6 Oslo, 4 Sheffield, 1 AAA, 7 Monaco, 4 CG, 9 EC, 5 v USA, 9 BrGP
3. **John Mayock** 26.10.70 (11y, 1) *IAAF 19* 3:31.86 '97, 3:50.32M '96 3:34.89, 3:36.28, 3:37.94, 3:55.85M (3:39.7),
   3:38.84, 3:38.97; 3:38.90i 10 Seville, 2 Cork, 2 AAA, 3 Heusden, 12 EC, 8 BrGP, 8 Berlin, 9 Rieti
4. **Andrew Graffin** 20.12.77 (4y, 4) *IAAF 33* 3:35.97/3:55.42M '01 3:35.53, 3:36.69, 3:37.33, 3:54.70M (3:38.2),
   3:37.70, 3:38.01 2 BL1 (1), 6 E.Clubs, 3 Kalamata, 5 Seville, 4 CGT, 3 Sheffield, 4 AAA, 1 Bangor,
   2 Malmö, 7 BrGP, 10 Berlin, 11 Rieti, 4 S.Francisco
5. **Tom Mayo** 2.5.77 (4y, 3) *IAAF 84* 3:38.3/3:55.57M '01 3:40.25, 3:41.66, 3:41.70, 3:41.72, 3:42.69,
   3:43.27 1 LI, 1B Seville, 3 CGT, 10 Sheffield, 15 Lausanne, 8 CG, 13 BrGP
6. **Gregg Taylor** 1.8.77 (2y, 12) *IAAF 86* 3:42.73 '01 3:40.70, 3:41.10, 3:42.35, 3:42.68, 3:42.77, 3:43.18
   3 LI, 4 Wyth, 11 CGT, 5 AAA, 2 BL1 (3), 2 Watford, 4 Barcelona
7. **James Thie** 27.6.78 (3y, 8) *IAAF 90* 3:42.85/4:01.7M '00 3:58.24M, 3:41.06, 3:42.94, 3:43.85, 3:43.99, 3:44.07
   7 LI, 2 CAU, 1 Wyth, 9h2 CGT, 7h3 AAA, 1 Edinburgh, 1 Watford, 2 BL3 (4), 2 Barcelona, 6 S.Francisco
8. **Angus Maclean** 20.9.80 (3y, 6) *IAAF 86* 3:39.88 '01 3:41.61, 3:41.67, 3:42.19, 3:42.93, 3:43.48,
   3:43.90; 3:43.47i 8 LI, 6h1 CGT, 1 Eton, 1 BL2 (2), 6 AAA, 2 3nU23, 4 Watford
9. **Chris Mulvaney** 25.5.81 (1y, -) 3:46.84 '99, 4:02.95Mi '01 3:41.89, 3:42.34, 3:42.46, 3:42.91, 3:43.03,
   3:45.32; 4:01.63iM 3r5 Walnut, 1 SEC, 2 NCAA, 5 CGT
10. **Adam Zawadski** 19.12.74 (1y, -) 3:42.90 '01 3:42.32, 3:44.17, 3:44.81, 3:45.39, 3:45.94, 3:46.01
    4 LI, 2 Wyth, 8 CGT, 1 Solihull, 7 AAA, 14 Watford, 1 Cup
11. **Jonathan McCallum** 19.11.75 (3y, -) 3:37.75 '00 3:39.57, 3:45.90, 3:46.29, 3:47.37, 3:48.02, 3:49.45
    5 LI, 5 Kalamata, 1 Scot, 5h1 AAA, 11 CG
12. **Chris Bolt** 21.9.80 (1y, -) 3:42.36 '00 3:42.92, 3:44.23, 3:44.60, 3:45.39, 3:45.42, 3:46.44
    1B Wyth, 5h1 CGT, 3 Solihull, 1 AAA-23, 8 AAA, 1 U23 v Ger, 5 3nU23, 3 BL1 (4), 10 Watf, 4 Watf 28/8
– **Matthew Shone** 10.7.75 (0y, -) 3:46.19 '01 3:42.08, 3:42.5, 3:47.83, 3:53.09; 3:45.73i, 3:49.28i
    1 BL1 (1), 1 Wyth, 1 Welsh, 6h1 CG
nr **Gareth Turnbull** IRL 14.5.79 3:38.28 '01, 3:57.89M '00 3:57.61M; 1 Philadelphia

138

nr **Conor Sweeney** IRL 28.12.81 3:43.85 '01 3:41.30, 3:42.79, 3:43.36, 4:01.58M, 3:44.22, 3:44.31
4 Philadelphia, 1 B.Univs, 2 LI, 5 Wyth, 1 NI, 12 CG, 7 Cork, 2 Edinburgh, 18 Watford
M = 1 mile time (1500m times in brackets).
After Mayock had been top for seven years, East took over in 2002, a year in which he made a great breakthrough
from his European Indoor bronze to his Commonwealth gold, although he did not run as fast as the next three men.
Whiteman, who won his first AAA titles, both indoors and out, is second for the seventh successive year, and Mayock
is third after his seven years at the top. Graffin had an excellent series of times and was unfortunate to miss the major
championships with 4th in both trial races after pushing the pace.

5000 METRES
1. **Sam Haughian** 9.7.79 (2y, 9) *IAAF 73* 13:46.35 '01 13:19.45, 13:25.56, 13:38.52, 13:42.80, 13:46.04,
13:50.75 2 LI, 1 Wyth, 1 CGT, 2 ECp, 14 Rome, 5 CG, 9 EC
2. **John Mayock** 26.10.70 (5y, -) *IAAF 21* 13:26.97 '92 13:19.43, 13:38.63. 13:39.49
8 Eugene, 4 CG, 5 WCp
3. **Karl Keska** 7.5.72 (6y, 3) 13:23.07 '99 13:20.30, 13:54.34, 13:59.5+ 4 AAA, 5 Heusden
4. **Matt O'Dowd** 15.4.76 (3y, 2) 13:30.56 '01 13:43.33, 13:46.24, 14:09.49 11 LI, 3 CGT, 11 CG
5. **Allen Graffin** 20.12.77 (3y, 6) 13:40.07 '01 13:45.77, 13:46.36, 13:47.03, 14:10.90
3 LI, 13 Milan, 4 CGT, 8 Cork
6. **Rob Denmark** 23.11.68 (11y, 4) 13:10.24 '92 13:46.63, 13:53.18 2 Wyth, 2 AAA
7. **Ian Hudspith** 23.9.70 (3y, -) 13:52.8 '97 13:46.90, 13:47.88 4 LI, 5 Wyth
8. **Jon Wild** 30.8.73 (2y, 7) 13:45.1 '96 13:52.39, 13:54.92; 8 Wyth, 1 AAA
9. **Glen Stewart** 7.12.70 (3y, 5) 13:37.17 '01 13:47.10, 13:49.70, 13:53.03, 13:59.39, 14:11.67, 14:13.1
7 LI, 4 Wyth, 1 Scot, 6 AAA, 14 CG, 6 Watford
10. **Spencer Barden** 31.3.73 (4y, -) 13:43.84 '97 13:48.03, 13:49.24, 14:01.54, 14:08.11, 14:09.19
5 LI, 5 E.Clubs, 5 CGT, dnf Solihull, 7 AAA, 6 Ninove
11. **Matt Smith** 26.12.74 (1y, -) 14:01.53 '99 13:53.30, 13:53.47, 13:55.84, 14:18e+ 8 LI, 11 Cork, 3 AAA
12. **Mark Miles** 24.3.77 (2y,12) 13:53.74 '01 13:48.60, 13:54.94, 14:23.0
1 B.Univs, dnf LI, 7 Wyth, dnf CGT, 5 AAA
Haughian, who sliced big chunks off his pb four times, takes top ranking through greater depth of performance than
Mayock, who beat him at the Commonwealth Games and who ranks for the first time at this event since 1994. There
was little clear evidence to separate most of those ranked from 4th onwards. Denmark's 11 years in the rankings
ties the event record set by Julian Goater and Nick Rose. Last year's number one, Mike Openshaw, did not race at
5000m in 2002.

10,000 METRES
1. **Karl Keska** 7.5.72 (4y, 1) 27:44.09 '00 5 EC 28:01.72, 15 Brussels 28:11.20
2. **Jon Brown** 27.2.71 (7y, -) 27:18.14 '98 6 Stanford 27:53.42
3. **Sam Haughian** 9.7.79 (2y, 10) 29:10.5 '01 12 E.Chall 28:25.87
4. **Rob Denmark** 23.11.68 (7y, 7) 28:03.31 '00 1 AAA 28:43.42, 12 CG 29:08.59
5. **Andres Jones** 3.2.77 (3y, -) 28:00.50 '00 3 AAA 28:43.93, 14 CG 29:15.44, 1 CAU 30:26.8
6. **Jon Wild** 30.8.73 (2y, 3) 28:39.33 '01 2 AAA 28:43.82, 15 CG 29:18.17
7. **Ian Hudspith** 23.9.70 (4y, 5) 28:35.11 '97 4 AAA 28:46.40, 5B E.Chall 28:56.41, 19 CG 29:33.43
8. **Glen Stewart** 7.12.70 (2y, 4) 28:40.14 5 AAA 28:47.52, 11 CG 29:04.03
9. **Adam Sutton** 22.3.81 (2y, 9) 29:10.98 '01 7 Walnut 28:40.32, dnf AAA
10. **Matt Smith** 26.12.74 (2y, 6) 28:43.45 '01 18 E.Chall 29:13.60, 6 AAA 29:18.93
11. **Christian Nicolson** 19.9.73 (1y, -) 29:40.17 '00 4B Stanford 28:52.36, dnf AAA
12. **David Taylor** 9.1.64 (5y, 11) 29:00.04 '99 7 AAA 29:20.02
Keska is top for the third successive year and Brown returns with his first 10,000 track race since his three years
at the top 1996-8. The AAA race was crucial in determining many ranking positions, with the Commonwealth Games
10k, which was particularly disappointing for the British contingent. A plus point, however, was that the tenth best
of 28:52.36 was the best since 1992 (and the first sub-29 since 1994); still, of course well short of the standards of
the 1970s and the 1980s (record 28:11.07 in 1986).

HALF MARATHON (First ranked 1999)
1. **Jon Brown** 27.2.71 (1y, -) 61:49 '97 1 Victoria, CAN 62:32, in NY Marathon 63:51
2. **Mark Steinle** 22.11.74 (3y, -) 62:23 '99 London Mar 62:47+, 1 Murcia 63:02, 4 Pretoria 67:11A
3. **Nick Jones** 10.7.74 (4y, 3) 63:12 '00 4 Wilmslow 63:25, 2 Helsby 64:37, 1 Wrexham 64:38
4. **David Taylor** 9.1.64 (2y, -) 63:24 '97 5 Wilmslow 63:47
5. **Allen Graffin** 20.12.77 (1y, -) 7 GNR 64:09
6. **Mark Hudspith** 19.1.69 (2y, -) 63:19 '97, 62:50dh '95 2 Bath (1 AAA) 64:17
7. **Ben Noad** 6.5.76 (1y, -) 0 9 GNR 64:18
8. **Carl Thackery** 14.10.62 (2y, -) 61:04 '87 3 Bath (2 AAA) 64:28
9. **Nick Wetheridge** 11.10.72 (3y, 6) 64:03 '01 4 Bath (3 AAA) 64:30, 13 GNR 65:55
10. **Kassa Tadesse** 21.8.74 (2y, -) 62:51 '97 6 Wilmslow 64:43, 6 Bath 65:19
nr **John Mutai** KEN 26.5.66 60:52 '99 5 GNR 63:30, 2 Reading 64:08

MARATHON
1. **Mark Steinle** 22.11.74 (3y, 1) 2:10:46 '01   8 London (1 AAA) 2:09:17
2. **Matt O'Dowd** 15.4.76 (1y, -) 0   8 New York 2:12:20
3. **Dominic Bannister** 1.4.68 (2y, -) 2:14:39 '00   1 Ferrara 2:16:18, 11 CG 2:19:36
4. **Stuart Hall** 21.12.64 (2y, 9) 2:18:46 '01   2 Seville 2:16:23, 12 CG 2:19:53, dnf Singapore
5. **Billy Burns** 13.12.69 (4y, 7) 2:15:42 '00   14 London (2 AAA) 2:17:36, 19 Dublin 2:30:14
6. **Daniel Robinson** 13.1.75 (2y, 5) 2:16:51   15 London (3 AAA) 2:17:51
7. **Simon Pride** 20.7.67 (2y, 4) 2:16:27 '01   1 Belfast 2:22:21, 16 CG 2:23:56
8. **Chris Birchall** 8.3.79 (1y, -) 2:43:17 '98   23 Chicago 2:18:57
9. **Nick Wetheridge** 11.10.72 (1y, -)   17 London 2:19:41
10. **Chris Cariss** 1.3.75 (1y, -) 2:25:23 '01   20 London 2:20:46
11. **Martin Hilton** 9.5.75 (1y, -)   21 London 2:20:54
12. **David Norman** 4.11.78 (1y, -)   22 London 2:21:01
nr **John Mutai** KEN 26.5.66 2:13:20 '00   5 Dubai 2:13:56, 14 Amsterdam 2:16:23

Steinle retains his top ranking from his fine run in London but was unable to run thereafter. Just seven under 2:20 is the worst since the 1960s and a damning indictment of the collapse in British distance running depth. Jon Brown dropped out when well placed in New York.

3000 METRES STEEPLECHASE
1. **Stuart Stokes** 5.12.76 (6y, 2) *IAAF 39* 8:33.15 '01   8:26.45, 8:35.6, 8:38.80, 8:39.90, 8:40.02, 8:43.38
   2 LI, 1 Wyth, 1 CGT, 7 ECp, 4 CG, 8 Linz, 8 WCp
2. **Donald Naylor** 5.9.71 (4y, 5) *IAAF 82* 8:39.2 '01   8:38.68, 8:39.0, 8:45.20, 8:47.79, 8:53.3, 8:56.17
   3 LI, 3 Wyth, 3 CGT, dnf AAA, 6 CG, BL3: -,-,1,1
3. **Benedict Whitby** 6.1.77 (5y, 1) *IAAF 69* 8:32.68 '01   8:38.0, 8:40.12, 8:40.87, 8:49.75, 8:51.03, 8:57.66
   4 LI, 2 CGT, 1 AAA, 7 CG
4. **Christian Stephenson** 22.7.74 (5y, 3) *IAAF 84* 8:25.37 '00   8:41.32, 8:42.7, 8:44.31, 8:54.72, 9:01.12
   5 CGT, 2 AAA, 8 CG
5. **Pat Davoren** 13.3.72 (1y, -) *IAAF 97* 8:55.95 '99   8:41.3, 8:44.43, 8:47.92, 8:50.21, 8:55.56, 9:01.29
   1 South, 4 CGT, 3 AAA, 9 CG
6. **Charlie Low** 9.10.74 (5y, 4) 8:37.63 '00   8:44.4, 8:46.06, 8:52.84, 8:54.57, 8:58.66, 9:01.38
   6 LI, 2 Wyth, 6 CGT, 2 Cup sf He, 1 Cup, BL1: -,3,2,3
7. **Stephen Murphy** 6.1.83 (1y, -) 9:22.94 '00   8:47.8, 8:54.52, 8:56.85, 9:03.89, 9:05.80   8 LI, 7 CGT, 12 WJ
8. **Jermaine Mays** 23.12.82 (1y, -) 9:10.8 '01   8:46.48, 8:49.14, 9:02.0, 9:02.99, 9:09.08, 9:19.76
   2 South, 10 CGT, 3 AAA-23, 4 AAA, 3 U23 v Ger
9. **Mark Warmby** 12.12.78 (1y, -) 9:08.38 '00   8:49.33, 8:49.94, 8:56.30, 8:56.5, 8:57.37, 9:01.58
   2 BL1 (1), 6 Wyth, dnf CGT, 5 AAA
10. **Nick Talbot** 14.12.77 (1y, -) 8:55.59 '99   8:49.2, 8:52.02, 8:52.88, 8:59.66, 9:02.64, 9:02.8
   4 B.Univs, 4 Wyth, 8 CGT, 7 AAA, 1 BL2 (4)
11. **Craig Wheeler** 14.6.76 (4y, -) 8:34.67 '99   8:52.79, 8:55.80, 9:00.07, 9:01.35, 9:10.12, 9:14.6
   8 Wyth, dnf CGT, 6 AAA, BL1: 3,7,3,5
12. **Andrew Robinson** 20.4.78 (1y, -) 8:58.58 '99   8:53.39, 8:53.73, 8:54.85, 8:58.40, 8:58.78, 9:02.2
   7 LI, 7h1 CGT, 2 BL1 (2), 8 AAA, 1 Cup sf He, 2 Watford
– **Steve Cairns** 3.11.67 (0y, -) 8:55.2 '99   8:51.06, 8:59.80, 9:01.20, 9:02.57, 9:03.10, 9:14.06
   5 LI, 1 CAU, 1 NI, 7 Eur. Police, BL1: -,4,4,-

Stokes, who had a splendid run at the Commonwealth Games, makes it to the top after ranking 11-8-5-3-2 in the previous five years. Taking over 14 seconds off his pb, Davoren is the highest ranked of six newcomers, with the 19 year-olds Murphy and Mays making notable progress.

110 METRES HURDLES
1. **Colin Jackson** 18.2.67 (19y, 1) *IAAF 3* 12.91 '93, 12.8w '90   13.11, 13.15, 13.18, 13.21, 13.23, 13.24
   1 AUS Ch, 1 Welsh, 1 Dortmund, 3 Ostrava, 2 Prague, 1 ECp, 3 Sheffield, 4 Lausanne, 4 Paris, 4 Zagreb,
   1 AAA, 2 CG, 1 EC, 1 Helsinki, 2 v USA, 1 Linz, 3 BrGP, 1 Rovereto, 3 Yokohama, dq WCp
2. **Anthony Jarrett** 13.8.68 (17y, 2) *IAAF 22* 13.00 '93   13.40, 13.52, 13.58, 13.63, 13.65, 13.68
   5 Turin, 1 BL1 (2), 2 WG, 2 AAA, 1 Bangor, 4 CG, dq s1 EC, dnf v USA, 4 Helsinki
3. **Damien Greaves** 19.9.77 (8y, 3) *IAAF 55* 13.62 '00   13.54, 13.73, 13.74, 13.75, 13.78, 13.78w
   1 LI, 1A BIG, 1 CGT, 2 C.Ligure, 7 Sheffield, 3 AAA, dnf CG, 4h2 EC, BL1: 1,2,-,-
4. **Mensah Elliott** 29.8.76 (4y, 6) 13.82, 13.7, 13.69w '00   13.85, 13.87, 13.95, 13.98, 13.99, 14.01;
   (13.89 & 13.96dq)   1 Bath, 5 LI, dq (1) CAU, dq (1) South, 2A BIG, 2 CGT, 5 BL1 (2), 4 AAA,
   1m1 Cup sf He, 3h1 CG, BL2: 1,1,1,1
5. **Paul Gray** 25.5.69 (13y, 4) 13.53 '94   13.85, 13.91, 13.93, 13.96, 14.00, 14.05
   2 LI, 1 CAU, 2 Welsh, 6A BIG, 5 CGT, 4 WG, 6 AAA, 4 Dublin, 5h2 CG
6. **Dominic Girdler** 6.3.82 (2y, 10) 14.16, 14.07w '01   13.95, 13.95, 14.01, 14.04, 14.05, 14.05; 14.0
   3 B.Un, 3 Bath, 3B LI, 2 CAU, 7A BIG, 3 CGT, 1 AAA-23, 1 Lough, 5 AAA, 5 U23 v Ger, 1 Der, 4 Merksem, BL1: 1B,7,-,-

7.	**Neil Owen** 18.10.73 (9y, 8) 13.60 '95, 13.5w '96 13.90, 13.90w, 13.91, 13.96, 14.00, 14.01
	4 Bath, 5r2 E.Clubs, dq (2) South, 4A BIG, 4 CGT, 2 Lough, 3h2 AAA, 1m2 Cup sf He, BL1: 2,4,1,-
8.	**Chris Baillie** 21.4.81 (4y, 5) 13.82, 13.70w '01 13.95, 13.95, 13.96, 13.97, 14.01, 14.04
	4 LI, 3 CAU, 1 Scot, 8 CGT, 3 C.Lig, 8 AAA, 1 Cup sf Stoke, 7 CG, 2 BL1 (3), 2 Der, 1 Cup, 1 Namur, 3 Barc
9.	**Andrew Turner** 19.9.80 (1y, -) 14.29, 14.22w '01
	13.90, 13.97w, 14.01, 14.10, 14.10, 14.14; (14.09dq)
	7 LI, 5 CAU, 5A BIG, 5h3 CGT, dq h2 AAA-23, 6 BL1 (2), 7 AAA, 3g U23 v Ger, 2 3nU23, 3 Merksem, 4 Barcelona, BL2: 3,2,-,2
10.	**Robert Newton** 10.5.81 (4y, 9) 13.95 '00, 13.93w '99 13.92, 13.92, 14.05, 14.09w, 14.19, 14.20; 14.1
	2 Bath, 3 LI, dnf CAU, 2 Scot, 3A BIG, 9 CGT, 2 AAA-23, 1B BL1 (2), 4h4 AAA, 4 U23 v Ger, dnf 3nU23, 5 Merksem, BL2: 2,5,-,5
11.	**Allan Scott** 27.12.82 (1y, -) 14.26 '01 14.05, 14.10, 14.29, 14.31, 14.32, 14.38
	1 B.Univs, 6 LI, 4 BL1 (1), 4 CAU, 3 Scot, 7 CGT
12.	**Tristan Anthony** 16.12.82 (1y, -) 14.81, 14.64w '01, 14.8 '99 14.09, 14.14, 14.26, 14.33, 14.51; 14.3, 14.4
	5 B.Univs, 1B Bath, 4B LI, 2B BIG, 6 CGT, 3 AAA-23, 4h1 AAA, BL2: 4,-,2,3

Jackson bows out having ranked as UK No. 1 for 15 years (a record for any event), the last 11 in succession and he has now ranked in the world's top ten for 17 successive seasons. Jarrett is number two for the 14th time (he was top in 1991). Greaves is third for the third successive year. Elliott, after falling foul of judges in a couple of races, matched his best year of 2000 to rank fourth ahead of a closely bunched group to tenth, of whom Girdler and Turner made most progress. The 10th best of 13.95 is easily a new record, the previous best being 14.05 in 1999 and 2000.

400 METRES HURDLES
1.	**Chris Rawlinson** 19.5.72 (8y, 1) *IAAF 8* 48.14 '99 48.21, 48.26, 48.49, 48.68, 48,87, 49.14
	1 Walnut, 1 E.Clubs B, 4 Athens, dq h1 CGT, 3 ECp, 1 Lausanne, 2 Paris, 1 AAA, 8 Monaco, 1 CG, dnf EC, 6 Zürich, 7 BrGP, 8 Berlin, 8 GPF, 3 WCp
2.	**Matt Elias** 25.4.79 (5y, 4) *IAAF 25* 49.57 '01 49.11, 49.18, 49.28, 49.46, 49.46, 49.59
	2 AUS Ch, 1 CGT, 3 Funchal, 2 WG, 3 AAA, 2 CG, 4h3 EC, 2B Zürich, 3 v USA, 6 BrGP
3.	**Anthony Borsumato** 13.12.73 (6y, 2) *IAAF 22* 49.30 '01 48.90, 49.19, 49.20, 49.26, 49.37, 49.42
	1 Dortmd, 5 Prague, 2 CGT, 5 Zagb, 2 AAA, 4 CG, 5s1 EC, 3B Zürich, 5 v USA, 4 Linz, 2 Rovert, 5 Padua
4.	**Matthew Douglas** 26.11.76 (8y, 5) *IAAF 44* 49.26 '00 49.38, 49.49, 49.63, 49.66, 49.76, 49.79
	5 Walnut, 2 B.Univs, 4 E.Clubs, 2 Riga, 1 Tartu, 1 Meilen, 3 CGT, 1 Dublin, 2A Lough, 4 AAA, 1 Cup sf He, 8 CG, 1 Cup, 2 La Laguna, BL1: 1,2,-,-
5.	**Steve Surety** 18.2.80 (2y, 9) *IAAF 82* 51.8/51.82 '01 50.16, 50.29, 50.36, 50.48, 50.5, 50.58
	1 B.Univ, 1 LI, 1 CAU, 1 Riga, 2 Tartu, 4 CGT, 1 AAA-23, 8 AAA, 1 U23 v Ger, 1 Namur, 3 3nU23, 1 Derby
6.	**Liam Collins** 23.10.78 (1y, 0) 0 50.30, 50.70, 50.76, 50.99, 51.16, 51.28
	dns B.Univs, 2 N.East, 2 CAU, 5 Scot, 5 CGT, 3 C.Lig, 1r3 Annecy, 2r2 Tarare, 2 BL2 (2), 1B Lough, 5 AAA
7.	**Jared Deacon** 15.10.75 (1y, 0) 53.67 '01 50.68, 51.0, 51.08, 51.08, 51.73, 53.13
	1 N.East, 2 CAU, 5r4 Annecy, 3r1 Tarare, BL1: 2,-,-,2
8.	**Richard McDonald** 11.1.80 (4y, 8) 50.70 '01 50.83, 50.9, 51.10, 51.46, 51.48, 51.57
	2r4 Walnut, 4 LI, 3h1 CGT, 1 C.Ligure, 6r3 Annecy, 3r2 Tarare, dq B Lough, 3h1 AAA, 4h1 CG, 2 Derby
9.	**Charles Robertson-Adams** 5.12.77 (3y, 9) 50.24 '01 50.97, 51.05, 51.08, 51.1, 51.19, 51.30
	1 West, dq LI, dns CAU, 1 Scot, dq CGT, 4 B'ham U, 7 AAA, BL1: 3.4,2,2B
10.	**Steve Green** 15.1.83 (1y, -) 52.29 '01 50.96, 51.05, 51.1, 51.12, 51.14, 51.6
	4 B.Univs, 1 Ox v C, 1 Sth-J, 1 South, 7 CGT, 1 AAA-J, 1 JI v It,Sp, 4 WJ, 1 Jnr IC, 1 IA
11.	**Noel Levy** 22.6.75 (6y, -) 50.70 '94 51.04, 51.21, 51.29, 51.32, 51.55, 51.63
	1B LI, 3 BIG, 6 CGT, 2B Lough, 4h3 AAA, BL1: -,5,3,-
12.	**James Hillier** 3.4.78 (4y, 6) 50.40 '01 51.02, 51.21, 51.37, 51.42, 51.52, 51.54
	2 DrakeR, 1 Welsh, 4 BIG, 4 Geneva, 2 B'Ham U, dnf WG, 6h2 AAA, 1 Cup sf Stoke, 7h2 CG, BL1: -,3,5,-

Rawlinson is top for the fifth time. Elias and Borsumato had excellent years, with Elias 4-1 ahead on win-loss, and Collins and Deacon are the top newcomers to the event. The tenth best of 50.97 equalled the record set in 1996.

HIGH JUMP
1.	**Ben Challenger** 7.3.78 (6y, 1) *IAAF 35* 2.30 '99 2.26, 2.25, 2.23, 2.20, 2.20, 2.20
	4= LI, 3 E.Cl, 1 BIG, 2 Meilen, 1 CGT, 8 ECp, 5 Funch,1 BL1 (2), 2 AAA, 1 Lough, 3 CG, dnq 18= EC, 3 Som, 3 WCp
2.	**Dalton Grant** 8.4.66 (18y, 2) *IAAF 67* 2.37i '94, 2.36 '91 2.26, 2.20, 2.20, 2.15, 2.15, 2,15; 2.20i
	1 LI, nh Brat, 1 Veszprém, 1 AAA, 4 WG, nh Lough, 3 Bangor, 6 CG, dnq nh EC, 5= Rovereto, BL1: 1,-,-,1
3.	**Martyn Bernard** 15.12.84 (1y, -) 2.06 '01 2.21, 2.18, 2.15, 2.15, 2.15, 2.14
	2 LI, 3 CAU, 11= CGT, 2 AAA-J, 1 JI v It,Sp, 10 WJ, 1J= Derby, 1 BL3 (4), 4 Barcelona
4.	**Mark Crowley** 15.11.83 (1y, -) 2.05 '01 2.16, 2.15, 2.15, 2.15, 2.15, 2.15
	3 LI, 2 CAU, 1 South, 2 BIG, 4= CGT, 1 AAA-J, 2 JI v It,Sp, dnq 22= WJ, 2 Der, 1 JLF, 2 Barc, BL2: 1,-,2,1
5.	**Robert Mitchell** 14.9.80 (4y, 3) 2.25 '01 2.15, 2.15, 2.15, 2.13, 2.10, 2.10
	1 Welsh, 6 CGT, 1 AAA-23, 1 U23 v Ger, 10 CG, 2 BL1 (3), 1= Cup
6.	**Richard Aspden** 15.10.76 (3y, -) 2.17i '99, 2.16 '95 2.14, 2.10, 2.10, 2.10, 2.05, 2.05; 2.10i, 2.09i
	5= CAU, 2 South, 7= BIG, 2 CGT, 11 CG, 3 Cup, BL1: 5,8,4,-

7. **Luke Crawley** 5.9.81 (2y, -) 2.15 '00   2.14, 2.10, 2.10, 2.10, 2.06, 2.00; 2.09i
    1 B.Univs, 4= LI, 4= BIG, 3 CGT, 3 AAA-23 ,4 AAA
8. **Jamie Russell** 1.10.81 (3y, 8) 2.15, 2.16i "01   2.19, 2.14, 2.13, 1.95; 2.18i, 2.13i, 2.10i
    4= CGT, 1 BL3 (2)
9. **Martin Aram** 2.12.83 (2y, 11) 2.10 '00   2.12, 2.11, 2.10, 2.10, 2,10, 2.05; 2.10i
    1 Nth-J, 3 AAA-J, 1 E.Sch, nh CAU, 2 JnrIA, BL4: 1,2,1,1
10. **Martin Lloyd** 18.6.80 (3y, -) 2.15 '98   2.10, 2.10, 2.10, 2.10, 2.10, 2.10
    10 BIG, 2 AAA-23, 3g BL1 (2), 5 AAA, 3 U23 v Ger, 3 Derby, 1 Ashford, 1 IA
11. **Danny Graham** 3.8.79 (6y, 4) 2.22 '00   2.13, 2.10, 2.08, 2.04, 2.00, 2.00
    1 North, 3 BIG, 11= CGT, 3 IA, BL4: 2=,-,-,3
12. **Tom Parsons** 5.5.84 (1y, -) 2.01 '01   2.10, 2.07, 2.05, 2.05, 2.05, 2.04; 2.08i
    1 Mid-J, 1 Mid, 4 AAA-J, 2 E.Sch, 2 Lough, 1 Jnr IA
–   **Ian Holliday** 9.12.73 (5y, 9) 2.16 '98   2.05, 2.05, 2.04, 2.00i, 2.00i; 2.14i, 2.05i
    2 BL2 (1), 5= CAU, 2 North, 7= CGT
nr **Mark Mandy** IRL 19.11.72 2.26i '97, 2.25 '95   2.10, 2.10, 2.10, 2.10, 2.10, 2.10; 2.15i, 2.13i
    1 CAU, 4= BIG, 3 AAA, 1 Cup sf Stoke, 1= Cup, BL1: 2,4,1,2

Including Indoors: 6, Russell, 7, Aspden, 8, Crawley, 9, Aram, 10, Lloyd, 11, Holliday, 12, Graham
Challenger was top for the third successive year, and although not back to his best 2.30 form, did well to take the Commonwealth bronze medal. He was 3-2 v Grant, who increased his event record to 18 years ranked. 10th best of 2.13 matched that of 2001 as the lowest since 1987, and standards were generally depressing, but encouragement came from the juniors Bernard and Crowley. Bernard is the highest ranked debutant since Geoff Parsons and Mark Lakey came in at 1st and 3rd in 1982. Aspden is ranked for the first time since 1996. Russell had the fourth best but only competed a couple of times on his return from the USA.

POLE VAULT

1. **Nick Buckfield** 5.6.73 (11y, 1) *IAAF 35*   5.80 '98   5.50, 5.35, 5.35; 5.81i, 5.62i, 5.60i, 5.50i, 5.40i
    nh Modesto, 9 Sheffield, 1 AAA, 4= CG
2. **Tim Thomas** 18.11.73 (8y, 2) 5.40 '97   5.25, 5.20, 5.20, 5.05, 5.05, 5.00; 5.30i, 5.10i
    8 BIG, 2 CGT, 6 ECp, 3 Cork, 1 WG, 6 AAA, 7 CG, 1= Gateshead, 7 WCp
3. **Paul Williamson** 16.6.74 (10y, 3) 5.55 '00   5.20, 5.18, 5.15, 5.15, 5.10, 5.00; 5.20i
    nh Modesto, 4= E.Clubs, nh South, 3 CGT, 4= AAA, 3 Cup sf He, nh CG, 3 BL1 (3), 2 Cup
4. **Ashley Swain** 3.10.80 (3y, 15) 5.20 '01   5.30, 5.20, 5.15, 5.10, 5.10, 5.05   2 B.Univs, 1 Stoke 12/5, 3 LI,
    nh CAU, 1 Sth, 1= BIG, 8= CGT, 1 AAA-23, 2 U23 v Ger, 1 BL1 (2), 2 BL2 (2), 7= AAA, 5 3nU23, 1 Der, 3 Cup
5. **Mark Beharrel** 10.1.81 (1y, -) 4.91 '99   5.25, 5.20, 5.10, 5.10, 5.05, 5.01   3 B.Univs, 2 Stoke 12/5, 1 LI,
    1 North, 7 BIG, 5 CGT, 2 AAA-23, 3 U23 v Ger, 7= AAA, 4 3nU23, 1 Cup, BL2: -,1,-,1
6. **Christian North** 2.2.74 (3y, 12) 5.30 '99   5.20, 5.20, 5.10, 5.10, 5.00, 4.90; 5.15 street
    2 Mid, 8= CGT, 3 AAA, 2 Cup sf He, BL1: 6,2,1,2
7. **Mark Davis** 1.3.77 (4y, -) 5.20 '99   5.20, 5.00, 5.00, 4.95, 4.80, 4.80; 4.90i
    3 Mid, 5 BIG, 12= CGT, 2 AAA, 4 Cup, BL1: -,3,4,5
8. **Kevin Hughes** 30.4.73 (10y, 6) 5.61 '99   5.20, 5.10, 5.05, 5.00, 5.00, 5.00
    3= BIG, 4 CGT, 7= AAA, 1 Cup sf He, 8 CG, BL1: 1,5,6,7
9. **Ben Flint** 16.9.78 (6y, 10) 5.40 '99   5.10, 5.00, 5.00, 5.00, 5.00, 5.00,
    1 B.Univs, 2 Yorks, nh LI, 2 North, 10 CGT, 10= AAA, 1= Gateshead, BL1: 2,6,2,1
10. **Scott Simpson** 21.7.79 (3y, 7) 5.20 '01   5.00, 5.00, 5.00, 5.00, 4.90, 4.80; 5.30i, 5.20i
    5 LI, 1 Mid, 11 CGT, 10= AAA, 1 Cup sf Stoke, BL1: -,4,5,3
11. **Ian Tullett** 15.8.69 (14y, 4) 5.35 '98   5.00, 5.00, 4.95, 4.81, 4.80, 4.70; 4.95i, 4.90i, 4.90i
    2 LI, 4 South, 3= BIG, 6= CGT, 4= AAA
12. **Christian Linskey** 14.6.80 (5y, 8) 5.21i '99, 5.20 '98   5.00, 5.00, 5.00, 4.80, 4.80, 4.70; 4.90i
    1 Yorks, nh LI, nh CAU, 3 North, 6= CGT, 10= AAA, 5 Cup, BL1: 3,-,-,4
–   **Matt Belsham** 11.10.71 (10y, -) 5.35 '93, 5.40i '96   5.10; 1= BIG

Including Indoors: 4. Beharrel, 5. Swain, 6. North, 7. Simpson, 8. Davis, 9. Hughes, 10. Flint
Buckfield is top for the sixth time, but only competed four times outdoors after taking the UK indoor record to 5.81. Thomas and Williamson stay in 2nd and 3rd places but with lesser marks this year. Swain was 5-5 against the only newcomer Beharrel, and they were the only men ranked to improve their bests.

LONG JUMP

1. **Chris Tomlinson** 15.9.81 (4y, 2) *IAAF 17*   7.87, 8.19w '01   8.27, 8.17, 8.17, 7.98, 7.98w, 7.97
    1 T'hassee, 1 LI, 1 Scot, 1 CGT, 1 ECp, 2 AAA, 3 U23 v Ger, 6 CG, 6 EC, 5 v USA, 6 WCp, BL1; 1,2,-,-
2. **Nathan Morgan** 30.6.78 (7y, 1) *IAAF 34*   8.11 '98   8.17w/8.06, 8.11w/7.86, 8,.02, 7.77, 7.69
    2 LI, 1 Riga, 4 CGT, 1 CG
3. **Darren Ritchie** 14.2.75 (6y, 8) *IAAF 61*   7.90 '00, 7.92w '99   7.93, 7.88, 7.83, 7.79, 7.78, 7.77
    1 CAU, 2 Scot, 2 BIG, 2 CGT, 1 BL1 (2), 1 AAA, 2 Cup sf Derby, 4 CG, 2 Brasscht, 6 v USA, BL2: 1,-,-,1
4. **Jonathan Moore** 31.5.84 (3y, 3) 7.98 '01   8.03, 7.57w/7.23, 7.36   3 LI, 6 CGT, 1 AAA-J
5. **Phillips Idowu** 30.12.78 (2y, -) 7.83 '00   7.79w/7.59, 7.68   1 BIG, 5 CGT

6. **Mark Awanah** 23.9.82 (2y, 12) 7.37 '00, 7.66w '01   7.70, 7.60w/7.58, 7.46, 7.25, 7.08
     3 CGT, 1 AAA-23, 3 AAA, dnq nj CG, nj Barcelona, BL2: 16,1,-,3
7. **Andre Fernandez** 2.3.80 (1y, -) 7.31 '00, 7.34w '01   7.54, 7.51, 7.38w, 7.36, 7.36, 7.33
     2 CAU, 4 South, 8 CGT, 2 AAA-23, 3 BL1 (2), 4 U23 v Ger, 2 3nU23, 2 Ashf, 2 Derby, 4 Barc, BL2: 2,2,-,2
8. **Louis Burgess** 21.3.83 (1y, -) 6.85 '01   7.44, 7.42w, 7.40, 7.32, 7.25, 7.23
     1 Sth-J, 3 AAA-J, 1 JI v It.Sp, 2 Cup sf Eton, 1 Derby, 3 Ashford, 1 IA, 1 JLF
9. **Marlon Lewis** 7.9.83 (1y, -) 6.99, 7.02w '00   7.47w, 7.43, 7.39, 7.30, 7.29, 7.28
     1 Mid-J, 2 AAA-J, 2 JI v It, Sp, 1 E.Sch, 3 Derby
10. **Alex Hall** 2.2.82 (1y, -) 7.29 '99   7.46, 7.43, 7.26w, 7.25, 7.17, 7.14
     2 South, 5 AAA-23, 3 Cup sf He, 3 3nU23
11. **Steve Phillips** 17.3.72 (12y, 5) 8.03 '98, 8.07w '99   7.44, 7.40, 7.35, 7.24w, 7.12w, 7.10
     2/2/2 in Spain, 4 AAA, 2 Cup sf Stoke, BL4: 1,1,1,1
12. **Bernard Yeboah** 7.1.86 (1y, -) 7.03, 7.10w '01   7.47, 7.32w, 7.14, 7.09, 7.09w
     5 AAA-J, 1 E.Sch-I, 1 AAA-17
– **Darren Thompson** 6.11.79 (4y, 4) 7.56 '98, 7.84w '01   7.34, 7.23w; 8 E.Clubs, 1 South
nr **Gable Garenamtose** BOT 28.2.77 7.99, 8.26w '01   7.91, 7.80w, 7.78, 7.74, 7.57, 7.48; 8.01i, 7.86i, 7.86i
     1 B.Univs, 1 Gavá, 1 Izegem, 1 WG, 2 CG, 1 African Ch

The season started wonderfully well, as in April Tomlinson took the 36 year-old British record of Lynn Davies and a record three men went over 8 metres in the first major outdoor clash of the domestic season: Tomlinson, Morgan and Moore finishing in that order at Loughborough. Tragically Moore's season was ended just over a month later by a serious injury. Tomlinson again jumped 8.17 for a splendid European Cup victory, but he was not over 8m thereafter, and indeed was 2-3 against Ritchie, who made an excellent return from injury. Morgan only competed four times, but was over 8m three times and triumphed at the Commonwealth Games; his season was just too thin to give him top ranking over Tomlinson, who beat him 2-1. Apart from the potential showed by Idowu in his two LJ competitions and the very inconsistent talent of Awanah, there was a huge gap after the top four, but there are four juniors in the top 12.

TRIPLE JUMP

1. **Jonathan Edwards** 10.5.66 (16y, 1) *IAAF 1* 18.29/18.43w '95 17.86, 17.78, 17.75, 17.67w, 17.63, 17.59
     1 Milan, 1 Turin, 1 ECp, 1 Oslo, 2 Sheffield, 1 Paris, 2 Rome, 1 Stockholm, 2 Monaco, 1 CG, 3 Eur,
     1 Zürich, 1 v USA, 3 BrGP, 7 Brussels, 2 GPF, 1 WCp
2. **Phillips Idowu** 30.12.78 (6y, 3) *IAAF 5* 17.33, 17.38w '01 17.68, 17.54, 17.34w, 17.29, 17.28, 17.28
     2 E.Clubs, 1 C;Ligure, 1 Sheff, 12 Paris, 1 AAA, 2 CG, 5 EC, 3 v USA, 2 BrGP, 4 Bruss, 2 Berlin, 7 GPF
3. **Tosin Oke** 1.10.80 (4y, 9) *IAAF 52* 16.57 '99 16.65, 16.60, 16.48, 16.38, 16.33, 16.27w
     1 South, 2 CGT, 1 AAA-23, 2 AAA, 5 CG, nj EC, 10 BrGP
4. **Larry Achike** 31.1.75 (11y, 2) *IAAF 26* 17.30/17.31w '00 16.71, 16.69, 16.45, 16.42w, 16.34, 16.32
     6 Kalamata, 4 Hamburg, 3 CGT, 11 Oslo, 8 Sheffield, 11 Lausanne, 1 Cup, 5 BrGP, 7 Berlin, BL1: 1,-,1,-
5. **Steven Shalders** 24.12.81 (4y, 5) *IAAF 61* 16.28 '01 16.41, 16.37, 16.37, 16.35, 16.21, 16.09
     1 B.Univs, 1 LI, 1 CGT, 1 Kortrijk, 3 AAA, 6 CG
6. **Nicholas Thomas** 4.4.79 (5y, 12) 16.31 '00 16.17, 15.83, 15.65, 15.48, 15.44, 14.83
     2 CAU, 2 BL1 (1), 1 BIG, 4 CGT
7. **Nathan Douglas** 4.12.82 (2y, 11) 15.50 '01 16.13w, 15.90w, 15.69, 15.66, 15.60, 15.59
     2 LI, 5 CGT, 2 AAA-23, 8 C.Ligure, 3 U23 v Ger, 3 3nU23, 1 Derby
8. **Philip Ferdinand** 18.11.82 (1y, -) 14.98 '00, 15.34w '01 15.94, 15.92, 15.42w, 15.40, 15.30w, 14.99w;
     15.35i 2 B.Univs, 5 LI, 2 U23 v Ger, 1 Cup sf Stoke, 2 Cup, 1 IA, BL1: 6,2,-1
9. **Julian Golley** 12.9.71 (13y, 5) 17.06 '94 15.77w/15.66, 15.46, 15.29, 15.25, 15.20, 15.17; 15.54i, 15.28i
     1 CAU, 3 South, 10 Milan, 7 CGT, 4 AAA, 2 Cup sf He, 1 Ashford, BL2: -,1,1,-
10. **Femi Akinsanya** 29.11.69 (10y, 7) 16.63A '99, 16.58 '96 15.66, 15.58, 15.52, 15.45, 14.81; 15.59i
     BL3: 2,1,-,1
11. **Martin Rossiter** 4.9.69 (1y, -) 15.20 '97, 15.53w '99 15.43, 15.36, 15.36w/15.12, 15.35, 15.27w, 15.00;
     15.11i 3 CAU, 6 CGT, 5 AAA, 1 Cup sf He, BL3: 1,2,-,2
12. **Charles Madeira-Cole** 29.11.77 (5y, 10) 15.82i/15.79 '98, 15.86w '01 15.43w/15.22, 15.20, 15.10, 14.33
     1 Welsh, 2 BIG, BL1: 5,1,-,-
– **Michael McKernan** 28.11.78 (1y, 10) 15.49 '01
     16.01w?, 15.12, 14.96, 14.96, 14.87, 14.71
     5 CAU, 1 Mid, 4 BIG, 8 CGT, 6 AAA, 2 Cup sf Stoke, 2 IA

Edwards is UK no.1 for the 13th time and 12th year in succession (a new record for any event). He won 10 of his 17 competitions and was over 17m in all but one. For the third successive year Edwards was world number one and Idowu moved up to fifth in the world; he was over 17m in 10 of his 12 competitions. Achike lost form in mid-season and Oke took the chance to compete in the championships; they were 1-1 on win-loss. Shalders had an excellent year with four Welsh records. Again standards in depth do not match those at the top and the 10th best of 15.66 was only a little better than in 2001.

SHOT

1. **Carl Myerscough** 21.10.79 (3y, -) *IAAF 20* 19.46 '98, 19.71i dq '00 20.72, 20.59, 20.30, 20.07, 19.91, 19.82; 21.26, 21.08i 4 Walnut, 3 Drake R, 8 NCAA, 1 CGT, 6 ECp, 3 CG, 7 WCp
2. **Mark Proctor** 15.1.63 (12y, 1) *IAAF 79* 20.40 '99, 20.85i '98 19.13, 18.91, 18.54, 18.46, 18.08, 18.07 1 LI, 3 BIG, 2 CGT, 1 AAA, 1 IS, 4 Cup sf He, 7 CG, BL1: 1,1,-,-
3. **Emeka Udechuku** 10.7.79 (6y, 2) 18.23, 18.29i '01 18.69, 18.25, 17.92, 17.62, 17.54, 17.50 2 B.Univs, 3 CAU, 1 South, 3 CGT, 2 AAA, 1 Cup sf He, 9 CG, 1 IA, 3 Barcelona, BL1: 3,3,1,1
4. **Scott Rider** 22.9.77 (3y, 6) 17.04 '00 17.56, 17.44, 17.38, 17.38, 17.34, 17.26 2 LI, 2 CAU, 3 Riga, 6 Tartu, 4 CGT, 3 AAA, 1 Cup sf Eton, BL1: 2,-2,2,-
5. **Iain McMullen** 15.6.78 (3y, 9) 16.56 '01 17.61, 17.43, 17.26, 17.15, 17.07, 16.78 3 LI, 1 CAU, 1 Scot, 4 BIG, 1 NI, 6 CGT, 1 Irish, 5 AAA, 3 Bangor, BL1: 4,2,3,2
6. **David Readle** 10.2.80 (3y, -) 17.69i '01, 17.50 '00 16.95, 16.91, 16.90, 16.80, 16.69, 16.54; 17.28i 3 North, 5 CGT, 1 AAA-23, 6 BL1 (2), 4 AAA, 3 U23 v Ger, 3 3nU23, 1 Derby, 2 Cup
7. **Mark Edwards** 2.12.74 (7y, 4) 19.72 '00 18.41, 17.53, 16.58 nt CAU, 7 CGT
8. **Lee Newman** 1.5.73 (10y, 3) 18.85 '96 16.94, 16.69, 16.59, 16.44 4 BL1 (3), 11 CG
9. **Gary Sollitt** 13.1.72 (9y, 11) 17.29i '99, 17.14 '97 17.85, 16.49, 16.22, 15.93, 15.92, 15.86; 16.66i, 16.57i, 16.54i 5 CAU, 2 BIG, 9 CGT, 5 Cup, BL2: 2,1,-,2
10. **Bryan Kelly** 29.12.73 (1y, -) 16,18 '01 16.80, 16.62, 16.36, 16.36, 16.35, 16.26 4 E.Clubs B, 1 North, 10 CGT, 8 AAA, 1 Cup, BL1: 5,4,nt,-
11. **Greg Beard** 10.9.82 (3y, 12) 16.69 '00 16.80, 16.54, 16.28, 16.26, 16.24, 16.23 8 E.Cl, 3 Sth, 5 BIG, 8 CGT, 4 AAA-23, 7 AAA, 2 Lough, 3 Cup sf He, 2 Der, 1 Ashf, 5 Barc; BL1: 10,5,5,-
12. **Lyndon Woodward** 22.11.80 (2y, 10) 16.48 '01 16.52, 16.42, 16.22, 16.21, 15.88, 15,67; 16.33i, 16.06i 1 Mid, 11 CGT, 3 AAA-23, 6 AAA, 2 Cup sf Stoke, 5 3nU23
– **Nick Owen** 17.7.80 (0y, -) 15.59 '00 16.29, 16.26, 16.17, 16.07, 16.05, 16.03 1 B.Univs, 2 Surrey, 4 LI, 9 CAU, 2 AAA-23, 4 U23 v Ger, 4 Bangor, 2 Ashford

Including Indoors: 7. Sollitt, 8. Edwards, 9. Newman, 10. Kelly, 11. Woodward, 12. Beard
Myerscough returned from his two-year ban to take top ranking, although held back by injury from his form indoors when he took Geoff Capes' 26 year-old UK indoor record with 21.08 and then improved to 21.26. Proctor moves down a place after five top rankings. Moving up are Rider and McMullen, who set three N.Irish records. The three U23 athletes were very close for positions 11-12. The tenth best of 16.80 is the best since 1997.

DISCUS

1. **Carl Myerscough** 21.10.79 (3y, -) *IAAF 40* 60.19 '98 63.14, 62.17, 62.00, 61.76, 61.22, 60.23 5 Walnut, 2 NCAA, 1 CGT
2. **Robert Weir** 4.2.61 (15y, 1) *IAAF 44* 65.08 '00 62.46, 60.72, 59.24, 59.14, 59.11, 59.07 6 Modesto, 4 CGT, 1 AAA, 1 Lough, 1 Cup sf Stoke, 3 CG, dnq 21 EC, 7 WCp, BL1: -,1,1,-
3. **Glen Smith** 21.5.72 (12y, 2) *IAAF 62* 65.11 '99 63.10, 61.87, 59.30, 59.15, 58.96, 58.32 13 Halle, 1 Mid, 3 Lough 5/6, 2 CGT, 8 ECp, 2 AAA, 2 Lough, 2 Cup sf Stoke, 5 CG, 1 Cup, BL1: 2,2,2,2
4. **Emeka Udechuku** 10.7.79 (6y, 3) *IAAF 91* 62.07 '00 58.64, 58.39, 58.21, 58.15, 57.97, 57.86 1 B.Univs, 11 Halle, 1 LI, 1 Lough 22/5, 2 CAU, 1 South, 1 Lough 5/6, 3 CGT, 3 AAA, 3 Lough, 1 Cup sf He, 6 CG, 1 IA, BL1: 1,3,3,1
5. **Lee Newman** 1.5.73 (10y, 6) 60.48 '97 56.28, 55.58, 55.10, 55.04, 54.54, 54.44 2 LI, 3 CAU, 5 Riga, 1 Welsh, 5 CGT, 5 AAA, 8 CG, 2 Cup, BL1: 4,5,5,-
6. **Matthew Twigg** 18.7.69 (1y, -) 51.63 '01 54.53, 51.89, 51.84, 51.51, 51.26, 51.25 4 CAU, 3 Mid, 4 Lough 5/6, 7 CGT, 6 AAA, 3 Cup sf Stoke, 2 IA, BL4: 1,1,-,2
7. **Bruce Robb** 27.7.77 (3y, 6) 54.25 '01 52.22, 51.61, 51.45, 51.18, 51.18, 51.13 4 LI, 9 CAU, 3 Scot, 6 CGT, 1 BL3 (2), 7 AAA, 1 Cup sf Derby, 3 Cup
8. **Bryan Kelly** 29.12.73 (1y, -) 50.95 '01 53.72, 52.76, 52.09, 50.79, 50.54, 50.41 2 E.Clubs B, 1 North, 12 AAA, 5 Cup, BL1: 5,8,7,-
9. **Paul Reed** 2.6.62 (12y, 10) 58.36 '99 53.86, 53.22, 52.84, 51.08, 50.40, 49.71 2 Lough 22/5, 3 LI, 1 Police, 2 Cup sf Derby, 4 Eur Police, BL1: 8,-,8,4
10. **Neville Thompson** 28.3.55 (20y, -) 55.68 '93 50.71, 50.54, 50.37, 50.29, 49.04, 47.11 8 AAA, 3 Cup sf He, 4 Cup, BL1: 9,10,6,5
11. **Mark Wiseman** 9.2.69 (1y, -) 51.07 '01 53.57, 51.69, 51.60, 50.71, 50.25, 49.48 3 Lough 22/5, 2 South, 8 CGT, 10 AAA, 1 IS, 6 Cup, BL2: 3,1,3,1
12. **Luke Rosenberg** 29.6.80 (2y, 11) 52.81 '01 50.48, 49.61, 49.38, 49.33, 49.32, 48.56 4 B.Univs, 4 Lough 22/5, 6 CAU, 9 CGT, 1 AAA-23, 9 AAA, 7 U23 v Ger, 4 3nU23, BL1: 11,6,-,6
– **Scot Thompson** 10.8.81 (0y, -) 51.42 '01 52.97, 52.34, 51.66, 51.36, 51.29, 51.25 B.Univs, 5 LI, 10 CAU, 2 Scot, 2 AAA-23, 11 AAA, 5 U23 v Ger, 5 3nU23, 1 Derby, 7 BL1 (4)
nr **Kevin Brown** JAM 10.9.64 (17y, 7) 62.10 '00 60.54, 57.44, 57.40, 57.20, 56.70, 56.63 6 E.Clubs, 2 Mid, 2 Lough 5/6, 1 Scot, 1 JAM Ch, 4 AAA, 4 Lough, 2 Cup sf He, 9 CG, BL1: 3,4,4,9

Drugs dq: **Perriss Wilkins** 12.12.67 (6y, 4) 66.64 '98 64.34, 57.08, 56.86, 55.40 1 BL2 (1), 1 CAU
Myerscough becomes the first man to top shot and discus rankings simultaneously and the next three each move down a place. Weir is second after nine successive years at number one and Smith makes the top three for the seventh successive year. Unusually for this event there were three newcomers, two of them aged 33 – Twigg and Wiseman. Neville Thompson is ranked for an event record 21st time. Although with worse marks, Rosenberg beat S Thompson 5-2.

HAMMER

1. **Michael Jones** 23.7.63 (21y, 1) *IAAF 34*   76.43 '01   73.99, 73.33, 73.25, 73.21, 72.55, 72.26
    10 Halle, 1 LI, 1 BL1 (1), 5 E.Clubs, 1 CGT, 8 ECp, 1 AAA, 1 Lough, 1 Cup sf He, 1 CG, 1 Cup, 8 WCp
2. **Paul Head** 1.7.65 (20y, 3) *IAAF 78*   74.02 '90   69.61, 69.19, 68.60, 68.35, 67.98, 67.74
    1 Essex, 1 CAU, 1 Scot, 2 CGT, 2 AAA, 2 Cup sf He, 3 CG, 1 Ashford, BL1: 2,2,2,2
3= **Bill Beauchamp** 9.9.70 (8y, 4) *IAAF 94*   72.63 '99   68.78, 68.09, 67.75, 67.69, 67.07, 66.09
    2 LI, 2 CAU, 4 CGT, 6 Varazdin, 4 AAA, 6 CG
3= **Michael Floyd** 26.9.76 (5y, 5) 69.38 '00   67.74, 66.33, 66.33, 65.98, 65.97, 64.92
    3 LI, 3 CAU, 1 North, 3 CGT, 3 AAA, 2 Lough, 1 Cup sf Stoke, 3 Cup, BL2: 1,1,1,1; 3g BL1 (2)
5. **Simon Bown** 21.11.74 (5y, 6) 65.32 '99   66.77, 65.68, 65.05, 64.93, 64.85, 64.73
    2 Essex, 5 CAU, 1 South, 5 CGT, 5 AAA, 1 IA, BL1: 4,4,3,3
6. **Iain Park** 16.7.74 (3y, -) 64.64 '98   69.29, 67.64, 66.19, 66.13, 65.91, 65.71
    4 LI, 4 CAU, 2 Scot, 6 CGT, 6 AAA, 1 Cup sf Eton, 5 CG, 1/1/1 HC, BL1: 5,-,5,-
7. **Andrew Frost** 17.4.81 (1y, -) 61.30 '01   65.01, 64.46, 64.02, 63.86, 63.22, 63.14
    1 B.Univs. 1 Hants, 5 LI, 2 South, 9 CGT, 1 AAA-23, 7 AAA, 3 U23 v Ger, 1 3nU23, 1 Derby, 2 Ashford
8. **Matthew Bell** 2.6.78 (2y, 11) 63.83 '02   64.16, 63.85, 63.84, 63.73, 63.17, 62.94
    6 CAU, 1 Mid, 8 CGT, 9 AAA
9. **John Pearson** 30.4.66 (14y, 9) 70.33 '00   64.42, 64.39, 63.99, 63.21, 62.84, 62.83   6 LI
10. **Shane Peacock** 5.3.63 (17y, 7) 71.60 '90   63.83, 61.96, 61.41, 61.22, 60.96, 60.54
    11 CGT, 8 AAA, 2 Cup sf Stoke, BL1: 9,5,4,4
11. **Chris Howe** 17.11.67 (13y, 10) 66.97 '98   63.58, 62.94, 62.81, 61.70, 61.38, 60.89
    3 South, 3 Scot, 7 CGT, 11 AAA, 3 Cup sf He, 3 Ashford, BL1: 6,6,6,-
12. **Dave Smith** 21.6.62 (12y, -) 77.30 '85   63.40, 62.35, 60.33, 59.89, 59.87, 59.24 2 Nth, 1 Cup sf Der, 2/3/2 HC

Jones was top (and AAA champion) for the fifth successive year – and again by a wide margin – although his marks were down. He achieved a thoroughly deserved Commonwealth gold medal, after 4th in 1986 and 1994 and 2nd in 1998. This was his 21st successive year in the top ten (an event record) with the last 17 in the top four. Last year's No.2 David Smith (the younger), did not compete in 2002, and the next four each move up a place. Head, Commonwealth bronze medallist, moves back to second and has been in the top five for 16 years in succession and has 20 years in all in the rankings. Beauchamp and Floyd were 2-2 and close in all those contests, but Beauchamp edges ahead on better marks. Park started the year with a pb and maintained good form before a splendid further pb in October to return to the rankings at no. 6 and Frost is the highest newcomer. Also ranking for the first time since 1996 is Dave Smith, British No. 1 1985-8, who at the age of 40, had better marks than other contenders for the final spot. Chris Black, six times the British number one but last ranked in 1986, was not far away from a return to the lists – at the age of 52 he set world over-50 records at 60.52 and 60.97 with the senior hammer.

JAVELIN

1. **Steve Backley** 12.2.69 (16y, 1) *IAAF 3*   91.46 '92   88.54, 87.29, 86.81, 85.76, 85.54, 85.03
    2/2 in RSA,1 Florø, 2 vECp, 3 Sheffield, 6 Stockholm, 1 Bangor, 1 CG, 1 EC, 2 v USA, 6 BrGP, 4 WCp
2. **Mick Hill** 22.10.64 (19y, 2) *IAAF 22*   86.94 '93   82.90, 82.33, 79.59, 79.38, 78.70, 78.56A   7/8 in RSA,
    2 LI, 1 CAU, 1 BIG, 3 CGT, 5 Sheffield, 1 Varazdin, 1 AAA, 1 Dublin, 5 Bangor, 10 EC, 4 v USA, 10 BrGP
3. **Nick Nieland** 31.1.72 (11y, 3) *IAAF 36*   85.09 '00   80.05, 78.63, 77.11, 76.89, 76.72, 75.87
    6 Halle, 1 LI, 2 BIG, 1 CGT, 11 Sheffield, 1 BL1 (2), 3 AAA, 4 Bangor, 3 CG, dnq 25 EC
4. **Mark Roberson** 13.3.67 (17y, 4) *IAAF 57*   85.67 '98   78.80, 74.52, 74.23, 73.78, 73.77, 73.68
    10 Halle, 3 LI, 5 BIG, 2 CGT, 12 Sheffield, 2 AAA, 6 CG, BL1: 2,-,1,1
5. **David Parker** 28.2.80 (7y, 5) 78.33A '01, 78.24 '00   74.80, 74.22, 72.99, 72.75, 72.41, 69.74
    10A E.Chall, 1 Loigh 27/4, 1 B.Univs, 16 Halle, 4 LI, 4 BL1 (1), 3 CAU, 3 BIG, 4 CGT
6. **Stuart Faben** 28.2.75 (8y, 7) 75.37 '00, 76.66i '96   76.17, 75.18, 73.97, 73.03, 72.50, 71.78
    1 Alfaz, 2 Lough 27/4, 6 E.Clubs, 4 BIG, 5 CGT, 4 AAA, 2 Cup sf He, 3 Gent, 1 Cup, BL1: 1,3,2,2
7. **Michael Allen** 7.3.80 (2y, -) 68.34 '00   75.43, 73.19, 69.84, 67.07   1 Belfast, 2 CAU, 1 NI, 7 CG
8. **Ben Haughton** 6.8.80 (2y, -) 64.34 '97   71.85, 70.03, 69.33, 69.03, 68.68, 68.58
    4 CAU, 6 Riga, 8 Tartu, 3 NI, 7 CGT, 5 Dublin, 8 Bangor, 2 Derby, 2 Cup, 1 Namur, BL2: 1,-,2,-
9. **Phill Sharpe** 6.3.81 (4y, 9) 71.79 '00   71.09, 69.70, 69.30, 68.25, 68.17, 67.96
    7 CAU, 6 BIG, 8 CGT, 1 AAA-23, 5 AAA, 1 Cup sf Derby, 3 3nU23, 1 Derby, BL1: 3,2,-,3
10. **Alex van der Merwe** 5.1.84 (1y, -) 64.04 '01   68.85, 68.73, 67.54, 65.46, 64.45, 64.41
    5 LI, 1 Sth-J, 8 BIG, 1 AAA-J, 1 v It,Sp-J, dnq 24 WJ, 1 Jnr IA, 7 Barcelona
11. **Tom Dobbing** 5.2.73 (2y, 11) 65.22 '93   68.87, 67.08, 66.94, 65.58, 64.85, 64.77
    8 BL1 (1), 5 CAU, 3 South, 9 BIG, 1 Scot, 6 CGT, 6 AAA, 1 IS
12. **Dan Carter** 15.4.80 (5y, 6) 73.56 '00   69.56, 65.48, 64.13, 62.28   1 Sth, 7 BIG, 11 CGT, 4 BL1 (2), 10 AAA
–   **Mike Tarran** 10.12.80 (0y, -) 64.25 '00   71.00, 63.80, 61.89, 59.82, 59.52
    1 Mid, 2 AAA-23, 3 U23 v Ger, BL1: -,8,-,4

Backley is number one for a record 13th time and he excelled to win a third Commonwealth title and a record fourth European title. Although he missed the Commonwealth Games, Hill came back to win the AAA title and ranks in the top three for the 17th consecutive year and as No.2 for the 12th time. The next three keep their places, but all the top five were below their previous level of marks.

DECATHLON

1. **Jamie Quarry** 15.11.72 (10y, 2) 7739 '99   3 CG 7630, dnf Desenzano
2. **Barry Thomas** 28.4.72 (12y, 3) *IAAF 64*   7766 '95   4 CG 7546, 5 Azusa 7505, dnf Desenzano
3. **Anthony Sawyer** 29.4.80 (3y, 8) *IAAF 96*   6983 '01   3 Hexham 7377, 3 ECp2 7271, 7 CG 7204, 1 Mid 7197, 1 Woodford 7182
4. **John Heanley** 25.9.80 (2y, 6) 7129 '01   9 Arles 7411, 8 CG 7162, 1 Perpignan 7057w, 2 Issoudrun 7017
5. **Brendan McConville** 3.1.79 (3y, 9) 6911 '01   1 NI 7076, 2 Mid 7007, 13 ECp2 6996
6. **Gerard Plunkett** 30.6.80 (2y, -) 6587 '99   4 U23 Pratteln 7112, 5 Hexham 6787
7. **Alex Gibson** 3.11.77 (1y, -) 6360 '01   1 South 7028, 15 ECp2 6887, 3 Mid 6857, 5 Woodford 6594
8. **Adrian Hemery** 6.8.82 (2y, 11) 6788 '01   7 U23 Pratteln 6924, 1 AAA 6620, 1 Watford 6519
9. **Dale Garland** 13.10.80 (1y, -) 6294 '01   9 CG 6919
10. **Stephen Bonnett** 13.7.78 (3y, -) 7146 '99   2 Woodford 6805, 4 Mid 6562, 26 ECp2 6220
11. **James Lowery** 17.10.80 (1y, -) 6070 '01   12 U23 Pratteln 6688, 2 AAA 6460
12. **Paul Tohill** 9.10.82 (1y, -) 6250 '01   13 U23 Pratteln 6678, 6 Woodford 6472, 5 Mid 6432, 3 AAA 6395
–   **Darren Hatton** 21.3.79 (3y, 7) 7020 '01   3 Woodford 6803, dnf (6178) Mid, dnf Hexham

Dean Macey missed the season through injury and Quarry is top for the second time (first equal in 1998) due to his fine showing at the Commonwealth Games, where he was a place ahead of Thomas. Sawyer, who had five decathlons at 7182 or better compared to his pre-season best of 6983, takes third.

20 KILOMETRES WALK

1. **Andrew Penn** 31.3.67 (12y, 1) 1:23:34 '92
   1 Manx 1:26:29, 2 RWA 1:26:04, 2 CGT 1:27:06, 4 CG 1:29:15
2. **Steve Partington** 17.9.65 (16y, 4) 1:24:18 '90
   3 Manx 1:28:48, 9 CGT 1:33:23, 1 Manx 9/5 1:32:26, 13 Dublin 1:31:10, dq CG, 46 WCp 1:31:41
3. **Andi Drake** 6.2.65 (10y, 1) 1:24:04.0t '90
   2 Manx 1:27:48, 1 RWA 1:24:43, dq CGT, Dublin & EC; 66 WCp 1:36:06
4. **Dominic King** 30.5.83 (1y, -) 0
   dq RWA (1:32:41), 7 CGT 1:32:23, 11 Dublin 1:29:48; dq CG, 68 WCp 1:37:40
5. **Don Bearman** 16.4.66 (3y, 8) 1:29:56 '01
   3 RWA 1:30:09, 10 CGT 1:35:13, 1 Basildon 1:29:53, dnf Dublin, 5 CG 1:37:29
6. **Mark Easton** 24.5.63 (13y, 5) 1:24:04 '89
   4 Manx 1:30:10, 12 Dublin 1:31:06
7. **Steve Hollier** 27.2.76 (5y, 2) 1:28:34 '99, 1:27:04ut '00
   27 Eisenhüttenstadt 1:33:09, 63 WCp 1:35:18, 1:31:09t in 25,441m 2Hr Nuneaton
8. **Gareth Brown** 10.5.68 (5y, -) 1:30:15 '89
   4 RWA 1:32:08
9. **Chris Cheeseman** 11.12.58 (8y, 6) 1:26:53 '99
   5 Manx 1:34:00, 5 RWA 1:34:06, 2 Basildon 1:31:47, dnf Dublin
10. **Matthew Hales** 6.10.79 (4y, 3) 1:28:40 '01
    8 CGT 1:33:11, 28 Eisenhüttenstadt 1:34:51

Penn retains the top ranking with a consistent series of performances, followed by Partington, the first British finisher in a very poor showing at the World Cup. Drake matches his best ranking of third (fourth time, first in 1990) and King is the first junior to be ranked at this event since Tim Berrett (now CAN) in 1984. The 10th best time of 1:33:11 is much better than that of 2001 (1:35:10), but worse than any other year since 1979.

50 KILOMETRES WALK

1. **Mark Easton** 24.5.63 (6y, -) 4:04:53 '98
   1 St-Oedenrode 4:11:29, 2 CCG 4:11:36, dq CG
2. **Steve Hollier** 27.2.76 (5y, 1) 4:07:18 '00
   1 Manx 4:17:35, 3 CGT 4:14:33, 6 CG 4:16:46
3. **Gareth Brown** 10.5.68 (4y, -) 4:27:22 '96
   4 CGT 4:16:45, 7 CG 4:40:07
4. **Chris Cheeseman** 11.12.58 (7y, 2) 4:07:49 '99
   5 CGT 4:18:49
5. **Karl Atton** 14.9.71 (5y, 3) 4:16:30 '97
   6 CGT 4:23:05
6. **Peter Kaneen** 12.7.61 (3y, 6) 4:40:00 '01
   7 CGT 4:35:31
7. **Michael Smith** 20.4.63 (10y, 5) 4:09.22 '89
   dnf CGT, 3 Dublin 4:44:56, 1 RWA 4:42:58

Easton regains the top ranking he held in 1998 and Hillier is second, his fifth successive year in the top three. Hollier is the only man aged under 30 ranked and there are no newcomers.

WOMEN

100 METRES
1. **Joice Maduaka** 30.9.73 (6y, 4) *IAAF 40*   11.24 '99   11.29w, 11.31, 11.39, 11.43w, 11.47, 11.50; 11.4w
    3 AUS Ch, 1 LI, 5 Hengelo, 2A BIG, 4 CGT, 4r1 Annecy, 1 Funch, 1 AAA, 1m2 Cup sf He, 6h2 EC, 7 BrGP
2. **Abi Oyepitan** 30.12.79 (5y, 2) *IAAF 44*   11.29/11.17w '01   11.33r, 11.36, 11.37, 11.37, 11.38, 11.40
    2 LI, 1 CAU, 2 AAA, 2 Dublin, 1m1 Cup sf He, 7 CG, 6 EC, 4 v USA, 8 BrGP
3. **Shani Anderson** 7.8.75 (6y, 6) *IAAF 52*   11.34/11.3w '00   11.32w, 11.36, 11.38, 11.39, 11.44, 11.48w
    5 Dessau, 3A BIG, 2 CGT, 6 ECp, 6 Sheffield, 1 Cork, 6 CG
4. **Amanda Forrester** 29.9.78 *IAAF 81*   (3y, 3) 11.37 '01   11.34, 11.37, 11.44, 11.54, 11.55, 11.57
    3 LI, 4 CAU, 1 Mid, 5A BIG, 3 CGT, 5r1 Annecy, 4 AAA, 1 Lough, 5 CG, 6 v USA, 1 Barcelona
5. **Diane Allahgreen** 21.2.75 (3y, 7) *IAAF 60*   11.50, 11.38w '01   11.44, 11.48, 11.50, 11.50w, 11.55, 11.60
    1B LI, 2 CAU, 4A BIG, 2 Cork, 3 AAA, 1 Cup sf Derby
6. **Vernicha James** 6.6.84 (2y, 12) *IAAF 90*   11.85 '00, 11.43w '01   11.39w, 11.40, 11.45w, 11.53, 11.53,
    11.54w   4 AUS Ch, 1 Bratislava, 3h2 CGT, 1 AAA-J
7. **Sabrina Scott** 2.6.79 (2y, 10) 11.68, 11.50w '01   11.58, 11.63, 11.64, 11.65, 11.71, 11.71
    3 CAU, 1= South, 6 CGT, 5 AAA, 3 Lough, BL2: 2,2,-
8. **Emily Freeman** 24.11.80 (1y, -) 11.83 '99, 11.66w '01   11.58, 11.60w, 11.66, 11.67, 11.67, 11.68
    1 B.Univs, 4 LI, 5 CAU, 1 North, 5 CGT, 6r1 Annecy, 6 AAA, 2 3nU23, 2 Derby, BL2: 1,1,-
9. **Amy Spencer** 19.9.85 (1y, -) 11.66 '01   11.51w, 11.55w, 11.60w, 11.68, 11.74, 11.75; 11.7
    5 LI, 2 AAA-J, 2 JI v It.Sp
10. **Marcia Richardson** 10.2.72 (12y, 5) 11.35/11.29w '00   11.67, 11.69, 11.73, 11.73, 11.74, 11.78
    2B LI, 5s1 CAU, 3 South, 7 CGT, 7 AAA, 1 Cup sf Eton, BL1: 1,1,-
11. **Susan Burnside** 3.2.80 (1y, -) 11.74, 11.61w '01   11.61w, 11.66, 11.66w, 11.75, 11.75, 11.75w
    6 LI, 6 CAU, 1 Scot, 9 CGT, 1 AAA-23, 8 AAA, 4 3nU23, 1 Derby
12. **Sarah Wilhelmy** 2.2.80 (2y, 2) 11.44, 11.24w '01   11.63w, 11.72, 11.75, 11.81
    6 Modesto, 6A BIG, 5 Bydgoszcz, 7 Cork
–   **Katherine Endacott** 29.1.80 (0y, -) 11.89 '99, 11.76w '01   11.58w, 11.73w, 11.81w, 11.87, 12.02, 12.04;
    11.9, 11.9   4 South, 5h1 CGT, 2 AAA-23, 2 v U23 v Ger, 1 IA
–   **Emma Ania** 7.2.79 (0y, -) 12.05, 11.97w '96   11.50w, 11.63w, 11.64, 11.84, 11.85, 11.89w; 11.80i 1 ISL Ch
Maduaka returns to the top ranking she had in 1998-9. She was, just, the fastest UK sprinter in 2002 and she beat
Oyepitan 3-0, but top ranking is not quite as clear-cut as that, because Oyepitan made the finals of both the major
championships. Forrester peaked perfectly, running her three fastest times of the year at the Commonwealth
Games, where she was the first British finisher, just ahead of Oyepitan and Anderson, but the latter had a better set
of performances.

200 METRES
1. **Vernicha James** 6.6.84 (3y, 1) *IAAF 28*   22.93 '01   22.93, 22.94, 22.95, 23.02, 23.07, 23.13
    2 AUS Ch, 4 LI, 1 CGT, 4 ECp, 1 WJ
2. **Joice Maduaka** 30.9.73 (7y, 2) *IAAF 43*   22.83 '99   23.00, 23.04, 23.21w, 23.25, 23.25w, 23.26
    1 LI, 2A BIG, 4 CGT, 2 AAA, 1 Cup sf He, 6 CG, 1 v USA
3. **Shani Anderson** 7.8.75 (4y, 5) *IAAF 51*   23.20 '00, 23.12w '01   22.96, 23.03w, 23.32, 23.35, 23.38, 23.41
    4 F-de-Fra, 1 BL1 (1), 4 Dess, 6 Cottb, 5A BIG, 2 CGT, 4 Sheff, 1 Cork, 1 AAA, 6s1 CG, 8s1 EC, 2 v USA
4. **Emily Freeman** 24.11.80 (2y,12) *IAAF 80*   23.72, 23.67i '01   23.41w, 23.41w, 23.43, 23.51w, 23.53, 23.53
    1 B.Univs, 2 LI, 2 CAU, 1 North, 3 CGT, 1 AAA-23, 4 AAA, 7s1 CG, 1 3nU23, 1 Derby, BL2: 1,1,-
5. **Amy Spencer** 19.9.85 (2y, 6) *IAAF 65*   23.45, 23.3w '01   23.46, 23.47, 23.58w, 23.60, 23.64, 23.65;
    23.44i   1 CAU, 4A BIG, 5 CGT, 1 AAA-J, 7 WJ, 2 Cup
6. **Ellena Ruddock** 23.2.76 (2y, -) 23.71 '97   23.41w, 23.78, 23.87, 23.90, 23.99, 24.14; 24.1w; 23.91i
    2B LI, 6 CGT, 3 AAA, 1m1 Cup sf Stoke, 1 IA, BL1: 2,6,2
7. **Sabrina Scott** 2.6.79 (1y, -) 24.37 '00, 24.1 '01   23.73, 23.83, 23.90, 23.92, 24.01w, 24.02
    4 CAU, 1 South, 7 CGT, 2 BL2 (2), 5 AAA
8. **Lee McConnell** 9.10.78 (2y, 9) 23.66 '01   23.48w, 23.79, 23.93, 24.26   3 LI, 1 Scot
9. **Abi Oyepitan** 30.12.79 (2y, 11) 23.71 '01   23.52, 24.26; 1B LI
10. **Melanie Purkiss** 11.3.79 (3y, -) 23.80, 23.64w '99
    23.81, 24.19; 24.0; 1 BL1 (3), 1 Cup sf Eton, 1 Cup
11. **Catherine Murphy** 21.9.75 (9y, 7) *IAAF 28*   23.28 '99   23.84, 23.92; 23.42i, 23.58i, 23.71i, 23.78+i
    3h2 AUS Ch, 1 BL1 (3)
12. **Kelly Sotherton** 13.11.76 (1y, -) 24.03 '97, 24.01w '01   23.83, 23.93, 23.93, 23.99, 24.12, 24.23w; 23.9;
    24.11i   8 AAA
–   **Sinead Dudgeon** 9.7.76 (2y, -) 23.59 '99, 23.23w '00   23.93, 23.96; 1 B'ham U, 2 BL1 (2)
–   **Emma Ania** 7.2.79 (0y, -) 24.32 '95, 23.83w '00   23.64w, 23.70w, 23.73; 1/1/1 in Iceland
nr **Sarah Reilly** IRL 3.7.73 (2y, -) 23.02 '01   23.90, 24.03, 24.34; 24.1w; 23.30i, 23.51i, 23.66i, 23.72i,
    23.90i   6 Sheffield, 3 BL1 (2), 2 Irish, 1m2 Cup sf Stoke, 6h3 EC
Inc indoors: 4. Spencer, 5. Freeman, 6. Murphy, 7. Ruddock, 8. Scott, 9. McConnell, 10. Oyepitan, 11. Sotherton, 12. Purkiss

Still with a year to go as a junior, James retains her top ranking and 16 year-old Spencer moves up a place to 5th. Maduaka and Anderson were 2-2, with the former retaining her second ranking with slightly better times and a Commonwealth Games final place. Freeman made the biggest improvement, from 12th to 4th. Most of those in the bottom half of the rankings had thin seasons at this event, but showed decent form in their few races.

400 METRES
1. **Lee McConnell** 9.10.78 (2y, 3) *IAAF 12*   52.05 '01   50.82, 51.02, 51.24, 51.29, 51.29, 51.59
   1 Basel, 1 Florø, 7 Sheffield, 1 AAA, 2 CG, 3 EC, 6 Zürich, 3 v USA, 4 WCp
2. **Catherine Murphy** 21.9.75 (3y, 4) *IAAF 20*   51.84 '01   51.36, 51.50, 52.10, 52.10, 52.14, 52.15; 51.79i, 51.95i   1 AUS Ch, 4 Belém, 7 Doha, 7 Athens, 6 Sheffield, 2 AAA, 6 CG, dnf h1 EC
3. **Helen Karagounis** 28.9.81 (2y, 8) *IAAF 54*   52.75 '01   51.97, 52.03, 52.17, 52.45, 52.49, 52.69
   1 B.Univs, 1 LI, 2 CGT, 6 ECp, 8 Sheffield, 3 AAA, 6s2 CG
4. **Helen Frost** 12.3.74 (6y, 7) *IAAF 90*   52.40 '00   52.67, 52.71, 52.85, 53.09, 53.14, 53.24
   4/1 in RSA, 3 Kiev, 4 Cottbus, 6 CGT, 2 BL1 (2), 5 AAA, 6s1 CG, 2 Cup
5. **Lisa Miller** 13.1.83 (2y, 10) 53.14 '01   53.18, 53.20, 53.28, 53.89, 54.34, 54.39
   3 Atlanta, 2 CAU, 4 CGT, 5 WJ
6. **Melanie Purkiss** 11.3.79 (1y, -) 54.38 '01   52.99, 53.03, 53.08, 53.32, 53.56, 53.65
   7 CAU, 5 Riga, 5 Tartu, 7 CGT, 1 BL1 (2), 4 AAA, 8s1 CG, 6 v USA, 1 Barcelona
7. **Lesley Owusu** 21.12.78 (4y, 6) *IAAF 58*   52.27, 52.15i '01   52.39, 52.55, 53.43, 53.52, 53.73, 53.79; 52.93i, 53.42i   2 DrakeR, 3 Big12, 3h2 NCAA, dq (8) CGT, 8 AAA, 1 Cup sf Eton
8. **Carey Easton** 16.11.79 (1y, -) 54.28 '98   52.91, 53.11, 53.62, 53.73, 53.88, 54.10
   2 Basel, 4 Riga, 1 Scot, 3 CGT, 6 AAA, 8q2 CG
9. **Jennifer Meadows** 17.4.81 (3y, 11) 53.32 '01   53.67, 53.7, 53.77, 53.77, 53.99, 54.06; 53.25i, 53.47i   2 LI, 1 AAA-23, 7 AAA, 1 U23 v Ger, 1 BL:3 (3), 1 Nth IC
10. **Danielle Halsall** 27.6.81 (1y, -) 56.27 '01   53.91, 54.24, 54.27, 54.39, 54.40, 54.48
   3 B.Univs, 1 North, 4h2 CGT, 2 AAA-23, 2 U23 v Ger, 1 3nU23, 1 Derby, 1 Cup, BL1: 1,3,-
11. **Karen Gear** 30.9.79 (3y, 9) 53.31 '01   54.12, 54.20, 54.41, 54.54, 54.7, 54.71; 54.30i, 54.36i, 54.39i   1 CAU, 1 South, 4h1 CGT, 3h2 AAA, 1 IA
12. **Kim Wall** 21.4.83 (2y, 12) 53.52 '01   54.05, 54.18, 54.33, 54.35, 54.44, 54.5
   4 B.Univs, 3 LI, 3 South, 6 Bratislava, 5h1 CGT, 1 AAA-J, 1 JI v It,Sp, 5s2 WJ, 1J Derby, 1 Jnr IA, 3 Barc
– **Venicha James** 6.6.84 (0y, -) 0   53.84; 1 BIG
– **Sinead Dudgeon** 9.7.76 (2y, -) 52.05 '99   53.95; 3 Lough

Merry and Fraser, the top two for the two previous years, and Curbishley, top ranked in 1998, were unable to run at all, but there was again good depth of talent at this event. McConnell had a magnificent breakthrough to world class, improving her pb six times, including at AAAs, Commonwealth Games, European Champs and World Cup. Murphy beat Karagounis 3-0 to ensure second ranking, although the latter was admirably consistent in major events. Miller finished her junior career with 5th at the World Juniors and there are three newcomers to the rankings: Purkiss, Easton (now Marshall) and Halsall, who improved her best by 2.36 sec.

800 METRES
1. **Kelly Holmes** 19.4.70 (10y, 1) *IAAF 10*   1:56.21 '95   1:59.83, 2:00.17, 2:00.33, 2:00.46, 2:00.66, 2:02.11   1 Dessau, 1 Seville, 4 ECp, 4 Sheffield, 3 EC
2. **Susan Scott** 26.9.77 (2y, 6) *IAAF 34*   2:03.96 '01   1:59.30, 2:01.03, 2:01.47, 2:02.64, 2:02.82, 2:02.93   1 Gavá, 1 Scot, 1 AAA, 4 CG, 6 BrGP, 1 Barcelona
3. **Joanne Fenn** 19.10.74 (5y, 4) *IAAF 27*   2:02.81 '01   1:59.86, 2:00.24, 2:01.49, 2:02.11, 2:02.24, 2:02.91   4 AUS Ch, 3 LI, 1 BIG, 3 Bratislava, 1 CGT, 2 AAA, 7 CG, 6s1 EC, 2 Malmö, 7 BrGP
4. **Charlotte Moore** 4.1.85 (1y, -) *IAAF 63*   2:05.86 '01   1:59.75, 2:00.95, 2:02.39, 2:03.38, 2:03.88, 2:04.95mp   6 LI, 4 CGT, 1 Edinburgh, 6 CG
5. **Rebecca Lyne** 4.7.82 (2y, 11) 2:05.05 '01   2:02.45, 2:04.36, 2:04.89, 2:05.22, 2:05.26, 2:06.42   1 Lough 27/4, 1 B.Univs, 1 Stret 14/5, 2 Wyth, 5 CGT, 10 Sheffield, 5 AAA, 3h3 CG, 2 3nU23
6. **Jemma Simpson** 10.2.84 (1y, -) 2:06.62 '01   2:04.11, 2:05.15, 2:05.34, 2:05.60, 2:06.4mx, 2:06.53   4 LI, 3 Wyth, 8 CGT, 1 AAA-J, 4 WJ
7. **Emma Davies** 9.10.78 (5y, 8) *IAAF 85*   2:02.39 '98   2:03.93, 2:04.02, 2:05.33, 2:05.52, 2:05.87, 2:06.22; 2:04.67i, 2:04.87i   2 Stret 14/5, 5 LI, 3 CAU, 2 Welsh, 4 Wyth, 3 AAA, 6s2 CG, 1 Cup
8. **Lucy Vaughan** 20.4.69 (2y, 12) 2:03.9 '01   2:03.70, 2:04.12, 2:04.4mx, 2:04.66, 2:04.7, 2:05.17   1 BL2 (1), 6 Riga, 7 Tartu, 9 CGT, 3 Eton, 8 AAA, 1 Ashford, 1 Watford, 2 Barcelona
9. **Lisa Dobriskey** 23.12.83 (1y, -) 2:08.4 '01   2:03.86, 2:04.8, 2:05.02, 2:05.23, 2:06.7, 2:06.9   1 Sth-J, 2 BIG, 1J Derby, 2 Ashford, 2 Watford, BL2: 2,-,1
10. **Alex Carter** 1.4.80 (3y, 7) 2:03.78mp '00   2:04.72, 2:04.99, 2:05.94, 2:07.20, 2:07.42, 2:08.6   2 Lough 27/4, 1 LI, 1 Wyth, 7 CGT, 12 Sheffield, dnf h2 AAA
11. **Jenny Meadows** 17.4.81 (1y, -) *IAAF 75*   2:05.8 '01   2:04.46, 2:05.39, 2:06.55; 2:03.35i, 2:04.34i, 2:05.07i, 2:05.83i   2 Riga, 6 Tartu, 5h3 CGT
12. **Hayley Ovens** 5.12.75 (1y, -) 2:07.69mx '01   2:06.06, 2:06.62, 2:07.03, 2:07.66   2 Edinburgh, 4 AAA

- **Helen Pattinson** 2.1.74 (1y, -) 2:03.75 '00   2:03.20mx, 2:06.63mx
- **Rachel Newcombe** 25.2.67 (4y, 9) 2:03.28 '98   2:04.69, 2:05.38mx, 2:09.1, 2:09.60
  4 CAU, 3 Watford, BL2: 1,-,1
- **Hayley Tullett** 17.2.73 (6y, 5) 2:01.25 '00   2:06.39, 2:07.77; 2:03.76i   2 Solihull, 1 Welsh
nr **Kelly McNeice** IRL 17.6.78 2:08.58 '98   2:04.55, 2:04.61, 2:06.04, 2:06.07, 2:06.56, 2:06.68
  3 Riga, 4 Tartu, 2 NI, 3h2 CGT, 2 ECp 2B, 2 Irish, 6h4 CG
Including indoors: 5. Davies, 6. Lyne, 7. Simpson, 8. Vaughan, 9. Meadows, 10. Dobriskey, 11. Carter.
Holmes is top ranked for the eighth time at 800m, a new record for the event, although she did not run as fast as Scott, who improved her best by 4.66 sec., and the amazing 17 year-old Moore, who improved by 6.19 sec. and set British junior records in semi-final and final at the Commonwealth Games. Scott and Moore were joined by Fenn in breaking 2 minutes in the CG final. This was an encouraging year, with two more juniors, Simpson and Dobriskey joining Moore in the top ten, and progress from other youngsters in Lyne and Meadows, who was at her best indoors. The 10th best of 2:04.11 is the best since 1994. Tanya Blake, 2nd in 2001, opted to run for Malta and did not run in Britain in 2002, so she is not ranked.
mp = male pacemaker, mx = mixed race

1500 METRES

1. **Kelly Holmes** 19.4.70 (8y, -) *IAAF 11*   3:58.07 '97   4:01.91, 4:03.93, 4:05.99, 4:06.02, 4:06.15, 4:08.11
   1 Hengelo, 3 Paris, 3 Rome, 1 AAA, 1 CG, 4h1 EC, 2 v USA, 12 Berlin, dnf Rieti, 3 S.Francisco
2. **Helen Pattinson** 2.1.74 (5y, 2) *IAAF 20*   4:04.82 '00   4:01.10, 4:05.20, 4:06.27, 4:06.32, 4:06.98, 4:07.62
   4 Hengelo, 1 Izegem, 1 CGT, 4 ECp, 2 AAA, 3 Monaco, 3 CG, 5h2 EC, 10 Berlin
3. **Hayley Tullett** 17.2.73 (6y, 2) *IAAF 24*   4:01.23 '00   4:07.52, 4:07.76, 4:08.23, 4:10.63, 4:10.68,
   4:17.36; 4:08.88i   13 Oslo, 3 AAA, 13 Monaco, 2 CG, 7h3 EC
4. **Susan Scott** 26.9.77 (3y, -) *IAAF 87*   4:16.16 '99   4:09.79, 4:12.90, 4:14.49, 4:16.25, 4:19.62
   1 LI, 2 CGT, 5 v USA
5. **Rachel Newcombe** 25.2.67 (2y, 7) *IAAF 64*   4:14.01 '01   4:11.24, 4:11.81, 4:13.56, 4:13.64, 4:15.18,
   4:16.43   5 LI, 2 Wyth, 1 Welsh, 5 CGT, 3 Eton, 5 AAA, 8 CG, 1 BL3 (3)
6. **Kerry Gillibrand** 13.9.76 (3y, 6) 4:13.02 '01   4:11.8, 4:14.53, 4:15.54, 4:16.14, 4:17.53, 4:18.29
   1 BL1 (1), 6 LI, 1 E.Clubs B, 1 Wyth, 6 CGT, 4 Eton, 7 AAA, 10 CG
7. **Hayley Ovens** 5.12.75 (1y, -) 4:19.87 '01   4:12.47, 4:15.39, 4:16.95, 4:17.03, 4:18.53, 4:19.30
   3 LI, 4 Wyth, 2 Scot, 4 CGT, 12 CG
8. **Charlotte Moore** 4.1.85 (1y, -) 4:23.07 '01   4:13.94, 4:16.53, 4:20.14   3 Wyth, 1 Jl v IT.Sp, 1 Watford
9. **Sarah Bull** 4.6.75 (2y, 9) *IAAF 91*   4:13.68 '01   4:12.21, 4:12.97, 4:14.67, 4:14.79, 4:17.90, 4:18.79
   7 LI, 5 Wyth, 7 CGT, 9 Cork, 6 AAA, 2 Watford
10. **Jo Pavey** 20.9.73 (2y, -) 4:07.28 '97   4:11.16; 4 AAA
11. **Lisa Dobriskey** 23.12.83 (1y, -) 4:25.85 '01   4:14.58, 4:14.72, 4:19.83, 4:19.95, 4:22.6, 4:23.22
    4 LI, 3 Solihull, 1 AAA-J, 4 WJ
12. **Catherine Berry** 8.10.75 (1y, -) 4:21.40/4:38.28M '01   4:15.65, 4:16.25, 4:20.51, 4:41.95M, 4:23.73;
    4:45.46Mi   9 Madrid, 12 Cork, 3 Heusden, 5 S.Francisco
- **Paula Radcliffe** 17.12.73 (8y, 3) 4:05.37 '01, 4:24.94M '96   c.4:12-4:13 in 3000m at Monaco
nr **Kelly McNeice** IRL 17.6.78   4:16.46, 4:18.45, 4:20.40mx, 4:22.45, 4:23.87   10 LI, 11 CG
Holmes ranks top for the seventh time (an event record) in nine years from Pattinson and Tullett, all three winning medals at the Commonwealth Games. Scott is a clear fourth and Newcombe beat Gillibrand 5-1. Pavey is hard to rank, she was fifth fastest but only had one race; that however was an important one, 4th at the AAAs. There was further improvement in the tenth best standard: whereas in 2000 this at 4:17.45 was the second worst in 23 years, the 2001 mark was 4:14.14 and this year not worse than 4:13.0 (conservative estimate for Paula Radcliffe's 1500m time during her 3000m), the best since 1992.

3000 METRES (not ranked in 2001)

1. **Paula Radcliffe** 17.12.73 8:26.97 '01   8:22.20, 8:48.04+, 8:56.84+; 2 Monaco
2. **Jo Pavey** 20.9.73 8:36.58 '01   8:31.27, 8:52.6+, 8:54.2+, 8:54.79, 8:57.71, c.9:04+   1 LI, 4 Bruss, 5 GPF
3. **Kathy Butler** 22.10.73 8:40.97 '01   9:04.51, 9:09.36; 8 Eugene, 5 ECp
4. **Catherine Berry** 8.10.75 9:09.61mx/9:21.89 '01   9:02.79, 9:09.76, 9:19.59, 9:20.5+; 9:12.09i
   1 Knoxville, 10 Eugene, 7 Linz
5. **Helen Pattinson** 2.1.74 9:03.71 '01   8:58.33; 9 Sheffield
6. **Hayley Tullett** 17.2.73 8:45.39 '00, 8:45.36i '01   9:07.98; 2 LI
7. **Gillian Palmer** 30.12.80 9:16.12 '00   9:12.47, 9:13.78; 3 LI, 1 Eton
8. **Dianne Henaghan** 6.8.65 9:22.68 '00   9:14.27, 9:14.58; 1 Edinburgh, 4 Barcelona
9. **Liz Yelling** 5.12.74 8:57.3mx '01, 9:15.25 '98   9:19.43, 9:20.1e+; 4 LI
10. **Charlotte Dale** 23.3.84 9:34.9mx/9:35.25 '00   9:17.61mx, 9:25.04; 5 LI
11. **Sarah Bull** 4.6.75 9:21.77 '01   9:18.11, 9:43.05; 6 Barcelona
12. **Hayley Yelling** 3.1.74 8:58.98mx '01   9:19.50+, 9:28.3, 9:30.14, 9:37.4+, 9:38.38+   6 LI, 1 Cup sf Eton
+ during longer race
Radcliffe broke her British and Commonwealth record by 4.77 sec. at Monaco and Pavey took 5.31 sec off her best.

5000 METRES (Previously ranked 1982-90, 1992, 1995-2001)
1. **Paula Radcliffe** 17.12.73 (7y, 1) *IAAF 1*   14:32.44 '01   14:31.42, 14:57.65+; 1 CG
2. **Jo Pavey** 20.9.73 (3y, 2) *IAAF 12*   14:58.27 '00   14:48.66, 15:06.34, 15:09.99, 15:18.70, 15:19.91, 15:20.10   5 Hengelo, 2 ECp, 8 Oslo, 11 Rome, 5 CG, 5 EC, 4 Berlin, 3 WCp
3. **Catherine Berry** 8.10.75 (3y, 6) *IAAF 82*   15:57.61 '01   15:31.23, 15:32.32, 15:44.87   1 CGT, 10 CG, 11 BrGP
4. **Kathy Butler** 22.10.73 (3y, 3) 15:10.69 '98   15:17.59; 2 Walnut, dnf Oslo
5. **Hayley Yelling** 3.1.74 (3y, 4) *IAAF 69*   15:19.12 '01   15:38.30, 15:54.8e+, 16:11.23, 16:15.5+, 16:21.0+, 16:26.41   3 CGT, 1 AAA, 18 EC
6. **Liz Yelling** 5.12.74 (4y, -) *IAAF 61*   15:50.85 '98   15:45.08, 15:53.8+, 15:59e+; 4 CGT
7. **Helen Pattinson** 2.1.74 (1y, -) 0   15:50.16; 10 Walnut
8. **Gillian Palmer** 30.12.80 (3y, 8) 15:56.58 '00   15:53.96, 16:10.26, 16:13.87, 16:22e+, 16:29.63   2 Wyth, 1 Scot, 1 AAA-23, 14 CG
9. **Jo Wilkinson** 2.5.73 (1y, -) 17:08.62 '00   15:59.54, 16:10.07, 16:38e+, 16:39.2+   1 CAU, 1 Solihull
10. **Charlotte Dale** 23.3.84 (1y, -) 0   15:58.8mx, 16:16.55, 16:17.47   1 Kent, 5 Wyth, 1 Watford
11. **Lucy Wright** 17.11.69 (3y, -) 15:59.51 '98   16:10.32; 3 Wyth
12. **Allison Higgins** 8.4.72 (1y, -)   16:47.10 '01   16:09.0, 16:29.6+, 16:39e+, 16:39.95   1 Ayr, 2 CAU
–   **Jo Lodge** 6.1.68 (0y, -) 16:24.55 '01   16:05.23; 1 BL1 (2)
Radcliffe won her first track gold medal in Manchester in a new Commonwealth record and is ranked top for the eighth time in eight years at this event. Pavey, second for the third successive year, was also in the world top ten.

10,000 METRES
1. **Paula Radcliffe** 17.12.73 (5y, 1) 30:26.97 '00   1 EC 30:01.09
2. **Liz Yelling** 5.12.74 (3y, 5) 33:07.9 '00   4 CG 31:58.39, 7A E.Chall 32:26.53, 20 EC 32:44.44
3. **Hayley Yelling** 3.1.74 (2y, -) 32:52.5 '00   5 CG 32:29.73, 1B E.Chall 32:48.50, 4 AAA 33:07.52
4. **Gillian Palmer** 30.12.80 (1y, -) 0   5 AAA 33:09.70, 2 Stretford 33:16.0, 8 CG 34:25.50
5. **Allison Higgins** 8.4.72 (2y, 9) 34:29.3mx '01   3 Stretford 33:21.1, 6 AAA 33:32.07, 7 CG 33:58.69
6. **Jo Wilkinson** 2.5.73 (1y, -) 0   6 CG 33:36.60, 7 AAA 33:40.57
7. **Charlotte Dale** 23.3.84 (1y, -) 0   1 Stretford 33:10.6, dnf AAA
8. **Sharon Morris** 5.7.68 (1y, -) 0   4 Stretford 33:36.8, 8 AAA 34:20.64
9. **Vicky Gill** 21.8.80 (1y, -) 0   11 Stanford 33:59.67, 14 AAA 35:13.58
10. **Louise Damen** 12.10.82 (1y, -) 0   1 Poole 34:05.1
Radcliffe is top for the fifth year at this event and world number one with her European record in Munich. The tenth mark at 34:05.1 was the best since 1994.

HALF MARATHON (First ranked 1999)
1. **Paula Radcliffe** 17.12.73 (4y, 1) 66:47 '01   71:04/67:52 London, 69:01/68:17 Chicago
2. **Liz Yelling** 5.12.74 (3y, 2) 71:29 '01   8 GNR 71:42
3. **Marian Sutton** 7.10.63 (2y, -) 69:41 '97   1 Helsby 73:08, 76:02+
4. **Jo Lodge** 6.1.68 (2y, -) 75:21 '99   1 Bath (AAA) 74:01, 1 Wolverhampton 74:12
5. **Susan Harrison** 6.8.71 (1y, -) 76:47 '01   10 GNR 73:43
6. **Sharon Morris** 5.7.68 (2y, 8) 74:04 '01   11 GNR 74:24
7. **Amanda Wright/Allen** 14.7.68 (2y, 4) 72:43 '01   47 World 74:53
8. **Sharon Dixon** 22.4.68 (1y, -) 76:01 '01   2 Bath (AAA) 75:14
9. **Alison Fletcher** 8.6.61 (1y, -) 76:49 '93   3 Bath (AAA) 76:07, 1 Paddock Wood 75:22, 14 GNR 75:49
10. **Vicky Pincombe** 19.6.73 (3y, 11) 74:59 '01   2 Exeter 75:52, 1 Stroud 75:28
11. **Andrea Green** 14.12.68 (3y, 6) 73:28 '00   1 Reading 76:36, 2 Paddock Wood 77:47, 1 Dartford 75:53
Radcliffe is top ranked for the fourth time, although she did not actually run a half marathon in 2002 – but each of her components in her marathons were well ahead of any rival! Liz Yelling is second for the third successive year.

MARATHON
1. **Paula Radcliffe** 17.12.73 (1y, -) 0   1 London (1 AAA) 2:18:56, 1 Chicago 2:17:18
2. **Marian Sutton** 7.10.63 (11y, -) 2:28:42 '99   1 Austin 2:31:44dh, 8 CG 2:45:55
3. **Jo Lodge** 6.1.68 (3y, -) 2:40:51 '00   12 London (2 AAA) 2:38:25, 7 Berlin 2:34:17
4. **Lynne MacDougall** 18.2.65 (3y, 4) 2:37:20 '01   2 Seville 2:36:29
5. **Debbie Robinson** 31.1.68 (2y, 2) 2:35:40 '01   4 CG 2:39:42
6. **Susan Harrison** 6.8.71 (1y, -) 2:48:53 '01   5 Dublin 2:38:52
7. **Bev Hartigan** 10.6.67 (2y, 1) 2:36:02 '01   6 CG 2:41:27
8. **Shona Crombie-Hicks** 1.6.71 (3y, 11) 2:42:44 '00   6 Dublin 2:40:53
9. **Trudi Thomson** 18.1.59 (7y, 5) 2:38:23 '95   5 Seville 2:46:30, 1 Belfast 2:49:39, 8 Stockholm 2:48:15, 7 Dublin 2:42:30
10. **Michaela McCallum** 2.6.66 (3y, -) 2:38:28 '99   12 Paris 2:41:41
11. **Angela Mudge** 8.7.70 (1y, -) 0   15 Paris 2:43:05

12. **Amy Stiles** 6.2.75 (2y, 7) 2:45:02 '01
2 Florence 2:44:11
– **Bev Jenkins** 6.2.70 (1y, -) 0
14 London (3 AAA) 2:44:32
– **Alison Fletcher** 8.6.61 (1y, -) 2:49:18 '01
15 London 2:44:42
nr **Teresa McCluskey** 6.7.69 IRL 2:35:27 '01
2 Belfast 2:50:33, 5 CG 2:40:29

Radcliffe's season at events from 3000m to marathon was one of the greatest by any athlete in the history of the sport, with her extraordinary marathons at the top of the list. Sutton suffered at the Commonwealth Games, but had a good win in Austin, and Lodge was desperately unfortunate not to be selected for the European Championships, but had some recompense with a fine run in Berlin. The tenth mark of 2:42:30 is the best since 1995.

2000/3000 METRES STEEPLECHASE (First ranked 2001)

1. **Tara Krzywicki** 9.3.74 (2y, 1) 9:52.71 '01, 6:29.79 '01
4 ECp 10:23.21, 6 Walnut 10:24.6, 2000m: 1 AAA 6:31.77, 1 LI 6:35.29
2. **Ursula Counsell** 7.12.82 (1y, -) 0   3 3nU23 10:47.62, 2 Merksem 10:51.70, 1 CAU 10:55.91;
2000m: 1 Derby 6:52.94, 2 LI 6:53.27, 3 AAA 7:04.94
3. **Claire Entwistle** 9.12.76 (1y, -) 0   2000m: 2 AAA 6:54.92, 1 Stretford 7:05.03
4. **Bryony Frost** 21.2.84 (1y, -) 7:11.2 '01   2000m: 3 LI 6:55.83, 2 Derby 7:11.09
5. **Tina Brown** 22.8.76 (1y, -)   3 Merksem 10:56.22; 2000m: 1 IA 7:00.09

Still not much action at this new event. Krzywicki remains a class apart.

100 METRES HURDLES

1. **Diane Allahgreen** 21.2.75 (9y, 1) *IAAF 18*   12.99 '99, 12.98w '01   12.92, 12.92, 13.00, 13.01, 13.07,
13.07   1 LI, 1 CAU, 2A BIG, 4 Istanbul, 1 CGT, 4 ECp, 4 Haniá, 3 Cork, 1 AAA, 4 CG, 5= EC, 6 v USA
2. **Julie Pratt** 20.3.79 (6y, 5) *IAAF 59*   13.40/13.28w '99 & 00   13.08, 13.25, 13.26, 13.27, 13.29, 13.30
1/1 Bath, 4 LI, 3 CAU, 1 Riga, 5 Tartu, 4A BIG, 3 CGT, 1 Sheff, 2 WG, 2 AAA, 6 CG, 8 BrGP, 4 v USA, BL2: 1,-,1
3. **Melani Wilkins** 18.1.73 (9y, 2) *IAAF 67*   13.17 '00, 13.1 '95, 13.08w '01   13.12, 13.27w, 13.29, 13.34,
13.38, 13.67; 13.3   3 LI, 2 CAU, 1 South, 1A BIG, 1 Cup sf Eton, 5h1 CG, 5 Brasschaat, 2 Cup, BL1: 3,-,1
4. **Rachel King** 11.5.76 (6y, 6) *IAAF 65*   13.46 '99, 13.44w '98   13.19, 13.22w, 13.31, 13.32, 13.34, 13.43
2 LI, dnf CAU, 1 Welsh, 3A BIG, 4 CGT, 2 C.Ligure, 2 Sheffield, 3 WG, 3 AAA, 6h2 CG
5. **Natasha Danvers** 19.9.77 (8y, -) 13.20 '98, 13.19w '00, 12.8w '99   13.20, 13.30; 2 CGT
6. **Helen Worsey** 29.8.82 (3y, 10) 13.66 '01   13.46w, 13.62, 13.63, 13.70, 13.80w; 13.6
1 B.Univs, 2/2 Bath, 5 LI, dns CAU, 2B BIG, 5 CGT, 3 AAA-23
7. **Tamsin Stephens** 2.8.80 (1y, -) 13.93 '00, 13.78w '01   13.52, 13.57, 13.59, 13.60, 13.61, 13.66
2 B.Univs, 3/3 Bath, 1B LI, 4 CAU, 1B BIG, 6 CGT, 1 AAA-23, 6 Bangor, 7h2 CG, 2 3nU23, 1 Cup
8. **Gemma Fergusson** 20.8.84 (1y, -) 14.14, 14.07w '01   13.64w, 13,76, 13.81, 13.83, 13.87, 13.88
4/4 Bath, 3B LI, 2 Nth-J, 1 North, 3B BIG, 7 CGT, 1 AAA-J, 1 JI v It,Sp, 3h2 WJ
9. **Lynne Fairweather** 15.1.80 (1y, -) 0   13.73w, 13.76, 13.81, 13.90, 13.92, 13.98; 13.9
2B LI, 2 BL1 (1), 2h2 CAU, 1 Scot, 4h1 CGT, 2 AAA-23, 6 (fell) U23 v Ger, 4 3nU23, 1 Derby
10. **Liz Fairs** 1.12.77 (4y, 9) 13.49 '00   13.72, 13.76, 13.81, 13.89, 13.91, 14.10
5 CAU, 5 AAA, 1 Cup sf Derby, BL1: 1.1.2
11. **Kelly Sotherton** 13.11.76 (1y, -) 14.15 '00, 14.08w '01   13.71, 13.82, 13.89, 13.90, 13.94, 13.96; 13.98
3h2 CAU, 8 CGT, 2 IA
12. **Bianca Liston** 28.5.78 (3y, -) 13.52, 13.4 '00   13.78, 13.91, 13.91, 13.95, 13.95, 13.96; 13.9
4B LI, 5h2 CAU, 2 South, 5A BIG, 3h2 CGT, 2 BL1 (2), 4 AAA
– **Katherine Livesey** 15.12.79 (0y, -) 14.15 '00, 13.80w '01   13.60, 13.77w, 13.84w, 14.13, 14.30A
– **Kate Brewington** 15.10.81 (0y, -) 14.20, 14.1w '01   13.85, 13.89, 13.90, 13.94, 13.95, 14.02w
9 CGT, 4 AAA-23, 6 AAA, 2 U23 v Ger, 3 Lough, BL4: 1,-,1

Allahgreen retains her top ranking and ran her pb of 12.92 in preliminary rounds of both Commonwealth Games and Europeans. Wilkins was unfortunate to be injured at a crucial stage of the season and yields second place to Pratt, who made good progress after four years at number five. Danvers was an excellent 2nd at the CG Trials, but that was the only time she ran at 100mh. Worsey beat Stephens 4-2.

400 METRES HURDLES

1. **Natasha Danvers** 19.9.77 (6y, 1) *IAAF 12*   54.94 '01   55.68, 56.12, 56.14, 56.39, 56.44, 56.55
1 Walnut, 1 CGT, 3 ECp, 4 Sheffield, 1 AAA, 7 CG, 7 EC, 3 Poznan, 4 Yokohama
2. **Sinead Dudgeon** 9.7.76 (6y, 2) *IAAF 41*   55.24 '99   56.88, 56.91, 57.10, 57.11, 57.26, 57.51;
56.70 – 1 hurdle missing   1 Scot, 2 Lisbon, 1 Annecy, 1 Tarare, 2 AAA, 6 CG, 8 EC, 1 Chaux de Fonds
3. **Tracey Duncan** 16.5.79 (4y, 4) *IAAF 29*   57.92 '00   56.53, 56.76, 57.04, 57.45, 57.51, 57.52
3 AUS Ch, 1 LI, 4 Hengelo, 7 Bratislava, 2 CGT, 8 Sheffield, 3 AAA, 5h2 CG, 5h3 EC, 1 IA

4. **Katie Jones** 4.1.77 (2y, -) *IAAF 64*   58.75 '00   57.69, 57.71, 57.93, 57.97, 58.49, 58.61
    1B LI, 1 BL1 (1), 1 Riga, 1 Tartu, 3 CGT, 4 Annecy, 4 Tarare, 4 AAA, 5h1 CG
5. **Liz Fairs** 1.12.77 (1y, -) 61.50 '01   58.48, 58.6, 59.05, 59.26, 59.29, 59.30
    1 CAU, 1 North, 1A BIG, 4 CGT, 3 Annecy, 2 Tarare, 6 AAA, 1 BL1 (3)
6. **Kelly Sotherton** 13.11.76 (1y, -) 61.8 '97   58.30, 58.72   1 Cup, 2 IA
7. **Hannah Wood** 17.11.81 (3y, 15) 59.55 '01   58.8, 59.0, 59.06, 59.20, 59.3, 59.69
    2 B.Univs, 3 LI, 1 Mid, 2A BIG, 5 CGT, 2B C.Lig, 2 AAA-23, 5 AAA, 3 U23 v Ger, 1B Lough, 5 3nU23, 1 Der, 5 IA
8. **Nicola Sanders** 23.6.82 (3y, -) 58.96 '99   58.72, 59.18, 59.93, 60.00, 61.0, 61.72
    1C Lough, 3 3nU23, 4 Chaux de Fonds, 1 Namur
9. **Hannah Stares** 13.11.78 (2y, 7) 60.28 '01   59.7, 59.8, 60.45, 60.77, 60.82, 61.2
    3 B.Univs, 3 Bath, 5B LI, 6 CAU, 1 South, 6A BIG, 6h2 CGT, 8 AAA, 5B Lough, 7 IA
10. **Jennifer Culley** 4.3.75 (1y, -) 61.8 '01   60.3, 60.34, 60.87, 61.09, 61.18, 61.25
    3B LI, 2 CAU, 3 South, 7h1 CGT, 7 AAA, 3B Lough, 2 Ashford
11. **Samantha Adamson** 27.3.82 (1y, -) 60.53 '01   60.0, 60.1, 60.2, 60.21, 60.28, 60.3
    4 Bath, 4B LI, 4 South, 1B BIG, 6 CGT, 3 AAA-23, 3h3 AAA, 4 U23 v Ger, 3 Derby, 1 Ashford
12. **Susan Williams** 2.6.77 (1y, -) 60.84 '01   59.89, 60.1, 60.4, 60.50, 61.5, 61.61
    4 CAU, 2 South, 7A BIG, dq h2 CGT, 4C Lough, 2 Plate, 3 IA
–   **Sian Scott** 20.3.84 (1y, 10) 60.50 '01   60.48, 60.49, 60.78, 61.05, 61.06, 61.40
    1 Sth-J, 5 LI, 3h4 South, 3h2 CGT, 1 AAA-J, 1 E.Sch, 1 JI v It, Sp, 1 BL4 (3)
–   **Gowry Retchakan** 21.6.60 (11y, -) 54.63 '92   59.6, 60.4, 60.5; 1 Cup sf He
nr **Maiteland Marks** USA 19.9.76 57.81 '01   58.10, 58.41, 58.85, 59.11, 59.12, 59.13
    1 B.Univs, 2 LI, 3A BIG, 4A C.Ligure, 3 Lough, 2 Cup sf He
nr **Michelle Carey** IRL 20.2.81 59.64 '01   59.57, 58.67, 58.7, 59.11, 59.37, 59.79
    dq B.Univs, 1 Bath, 3 Riga, 2 Tartu, 2 ECp2B, 1 AAA-23, 1 Irish, 5 Lough, 2 Derby, 3 Cup

Danvers is top ranked for the third year running, but was not as fast as in 2000-01, and Dudgeon, who like Danvers made both major finals, was again second.

HIGH JUMP

1. **Susan Jones** 8.6.78 (8y, 1) *IAAF 17*   1.95 '01   1.92, 1.91, 1.90, 1.90, 1.90, 1.89; 1.92i
    1 LI, 1 BL1 (1), 1 CAU, 1 CGT, 4= ECp, 1 Sheff, 12= Laus, 1 WG, 1 AAA, 2 CG, 7= EC, 1 Cup, 7= BrGP
2. **Rebecca Jones** 17.1.83 (4y, 8) *IAAF 85*   1.83 '00   1.88, 1.84, 1.83, 1.80, 1.80, 1.79; 1.86i, 1.83i
    2 LI, 1 AAA-J, 2 JI v It, Sp, dnq 15 WJ, 10= CG
3. **Stephanie Higham** 26.12.83 (2y, 4) 1.83 '01   1.85, 1.83, 1.82, 1.80, 1.80, 1.79; 1.80i
    4 LI, 1 Nth-J, 1 North, 3 BIG, 2 CGT, 2 AAA-J, 3 JI v It, Sp, dnq 16= WJ, 6= CG
4. **Debbie Marti** 14.5.68 (17y, 10) 1.94 '96, 1.95i '97   1.85, 1.82, 1.82, 1.81, 1.80, 1.80
    2 CAU, 2 BIG, 3 CGT, 2 Sheffield, 2 AAA, 6= CG
5. **Julie Crane** 26.9.76 (6y, -) 1.83 '98, 1.85i '00   1.83, 1.82, 1.80, 1.80, 1.80, 1.79
    3 LI, 3 E.Clubs B, 1 Mid, 4 BIG, 4 CGT, 3 AAA, 1 Cup sf Stoke, 10= CG, 2 Cup, BL1: 2,nh,1
6. **Julia Bennett** 26.3.70 (15y, 5) 1.89 '94, 1.92i '90   1.83, 1.80, 1.80, 1.79, 1.76, 1.75; 1.84i, 1.81i
    5 CGT, 3 Sheffield, 7 Cork, 1 Cup sf Eton, 3 Cup
7. **Julie Hollman** 16.2.77 (3y, 7) 1.83 '01   1.85, 1.82, 1.82, 1.77, 1.71, 1.70
    1 Tallahassee, 4= Cup
8= **Jessica Ennis** 28.1.86 (1y, -) 1.75 '01   1.80, 1.77, 1.75, 1.74, 1.74, 1.70; 1.80i, 1.76i
    7 CGT, 4 AAA-J, 1 E.Sch-I
8= **Emma Perkins** 4.9.85 (2y, 12) 1.78 '01   1.80, 1.75, 1.75, 1.75, 1.75, 1.70; 1.72i
    1 Sth-17, 5 BIG, 6 CGT, 2 E.Sch-I, 1 Sch.Int, 1 Jnr IC
10. **Natalie Clark** 4.9.82 (1, -) 1.76 '99   1.78, 1.77, 1.75, 1.75, 1.75, 1.73; 1.78i, 1.77i
    1 B.UNivs, 5 LI, 2 North, 8 CGT, 1 AAA-23, 1 BL3 (2), 4= AAA, 4 U23 v Ger, 6 3nU23, 1 Derby
11. **Lindsey-Ann McDonnell** 13.8.79 (2y, 6) 1.80 '00   1.80, 1.78, 1.75, 1.75, 1.75, 1.75; in AUS
12. **Kerry Jury** 19.11.68 (5y, -) 1.81 '97   1.77, 1.76, 1.76, 1.70, 1.70; 1.70i
    3= CAU, 9 CGT, 3 Lough
–   **Aileen Wilson** 30.3.84 (4y, 3) 1.87 '01   1.75, 1.75, 1.75, 1,74, 1.70; 1.83i, 1.80i
    3 AAA-J, 2 BL3 (2), 1 E.Sch, 2 Lough, 4= AAA
–   **Jo Jennings** 20.9.69 (13y, 9) 1.94i '93, 1.91 '98   1.70. 1.65; 1.81i 2 BL1 (3), 2 IA

Including indoors: 8. Wilson, 9. Ennis, 10. Perkins; rest down one place

Jones was top for the third successive year and unbeaten by a British jumper, but unfortunately her main rival in recent years, Michelle Dunkley, was unable to compete at all and Aileen Wilson was restricted by injury and standards in depth remain depressed. There was little between those ranked 2nd to 5th, who all cleared 1.79 at the Commonwealth Games, the two juniors, Jones and Higham being marginally preferred.

POLE VAULT

1. **Irie Hill** 16.1.69 (4y, 2) *IAAF 66* 4.20 '00 4.15, 4.15, 4.10, 4.10, 4.05, 4.05
   6 AUS Ch, 2 CGT, 3 WG, 1 AAA, 1 Cup sf Eton, 3= CG, 5 v USA, 12= BrGP, 1 World Masters, BL1: -,1,nh
2. **Rhian Clarke** 19.4.77 (10y, 3) *IAAF 76* 4.15 '00, 4.20i '01 4.15, 4.09, 4.05, 4.05, 4.05, 4.00; 4.02i
   5 NCAA, 1 Welsh, 3 CGT, 4 WG, 2= AAA, 1 Cup sf He, 5 Lough, 11= CG
3. **Tracey Bloomfield** 13.9.79 (5y, 5) 3.90 '00 4.05, 4.00, 4.00, 3.95, 3.92, 3.90
   1 South, 3 BIG, 6 CGT, 2= AAA, 6 Lough, 10 CG, 2 Ashford, 1 IA, 2 Barcelona
4. **Lucy Webber** 5.2.72 (5y, 4) 4.04 '00 4.00, 4.00, 3.95, 3.95, 3.95, 3.90
   4 Irvine, 1B Modesto, 3 South, 2 BIG, 4 CGT, 4= AAA, 2 Cup sf He, 8 CG, 1 Cup, 1 Ashford, 4 IA
5. **Elizabeth Hughes** 9.6.77 (2y, -) 3.75 '01 4.16, 4.10, 4.05, 3.95, 3.92, 3.90
   1 LI, 2 South, 5 BIG, 7= CGT, 4= AAA, 4 Lough, 3=g U23 v Ger, 3 Ashford
6. **Kate Dennison** 7.5.84 (2y, 9) 3.80 '01 4.00, 3.95, 3.85, 3.85, 3.80, 3.80; 3.91i, 3.85i
   5 LI, 1 Mid-J, 6 BIG, 5 CGT, 1 AAA-J, 7 WJ, 6 v USA, BL4: 1,-,1
7. **Zoe Brown** 15.9.83 (2y, 10) 3.81 '01 4.00, 3.90, 3.90, 3.85, 3.82, 3.80
   1 NI, 13= CGT, 2 AAA-J, 3 JI v It,Sp, 6 AAA, 1 Bangor, 7 Lough, 7 CG, 1 JLF, 3 Barcelona
8. **Gillian Cooke** 3.10.82 (1y, -) 3.40 '01 3.90, 3.80, 3.80, 3.80, 3.80, 3.80
   1 B.Univs, 4 LI, 1 BL1 (1), 1 Scot, 9 CGT, 8 AAA, 5 U23 v Ger, 15 CG, 1 Derby
9. **Ellie Spain** 23.8.82 (2y, -) 3.90 '00 3.85, 3.80, 3.80, 3.75, 3.70, 3.70
   9 BIG, 7= CGT, 1 AAA-23, 9 AAA, 6 U23 v Ger, 6 3nU23, 2 Derby, BL1: 3,2,-
10. **Sonia Lawrence** 19.1.80 (2y, 6) 3.90 '01 3.90, 3.70, 3.70, 3.65; 4.00i, 3.90i
    5 WG, 8g U23 v Ger, 13 CG, 5 3nU23
11. **Emma Hornby** 12.12.73 (6y, 7) 3.91 '98 3.75, 3.75, 3.72, 3.65, 3.60, 3.60
    1 Mid, 7 BIG, 13= CGT, 12 AAA, 1 Cup sf Stoke, BL1: 2,7=,-
12. **Hannah Olson** 29.1.88 (1y, -) 3.51 '01 3.80, 3.80, 3.70, 3.70, 3.65, 3.60
    3 LI, 1 Sth-15, 8 BIG, 1 Ashford 8/6, nh CGT, 1 AAA-17, 1 U15IA
− **Natalie Olson** 9.5.86 (1y, -) 3.50 '01 3.75, 3.70, 3.65, 3.60, 3.60, 3.60
    7 LI, 1 Sth-17, 2 Ashford 8/6, 10 CGT, 3 AAA-J, 5 JI v It,Sp, 1 Sch.Int, 2 AAA-17, 4 Ashford, 1 Jnr IA
nr **Janine Whitlock** 11.8.73 (6y, 1) 4.40 '01 4.25, 3.92, (4.41, 4.35, 4.10 dq); 4.44i, 4.33i, 4.20i, 4.20i
    2 LI; 1 BIG, (dq: 1 CGT, 5 ECp, 1 AAA)

Including indoors: 2. Webber, 4. Bloomfield,... 8. Lawrence, 9. Cooke...
Whitlock's sad drugs ban meant that our best ever female vaulter (top for the last five years) was not ranked and Hill takes over after three years at second. Clarke retains her unique record of ranking every year since this event was first included in 1993. Bloomfield and Webber were very closely matched and they were 5-1 and 3-1 v Hughes. Dennison and Brown both set UK junior records. Hannah Olson comes into the rankings at the age of 14, just ahead of her 16 year-old sister Natalie. Standards continue to progress, with 10th best over the past six years being successively 3.40, 3.60, 3.60, 3.70, 3.75 and now 3.90.

LONG JUMP

1. **Jade Johnson** 7.6.80 (6y, 1) *IAAF 7* 6.59, 6.68w '01 6.73, 6.69, 6.65, 6.64, 6.60, 6.60
   1 CAU, 1 Bydgoszcz, 1 CGT, 5 ECp, 1 WG, 1 AAA, 1 U23 v Ger, 2 CG, 2 EC, 4 Zürich, 3 BrGP, 3 Berlin, 4 WCp
2. **Sarah Claxton** 23.9.79 (7y, 2) *IAAF 99* 6.56 '99 6.30, 6.28, 6.25, 6.23, 6.22, 6.17; 6.20i
   1 LI, 10 CAU, 1 BIG, 5 CGT, 2 AAA, 1 Cup sf He, 12 CG, 1 Brasschaat, 1 Cup, 1 IA
3. **Ann Danson** 4.5.71 (9y, 3) 6.21 '00, 6.38w '94 6.38, 6.31w, 6.25, 6.18, 6.17w/6.13, 6.11
   2 Tallahassee, 3 LI, 2 BL1 (1), 2 BIG, 2 CGT, 11 CG, 2 Cup, 2 IA
4. **Julie Hollman** 16.2.77 (6y, 4) 6.51 '00 6.42, 6.24, 6.21, 6.03; 5.99i 1H Götzis, 3H CG
5. **Kelly Sotherton** 13.11.76 (4y, 6) 6.23, 6.28w '01 6.22, 6.21, 6.20, 6.18, 6.17, 6.11; 6.22i
   2 CAU, 3 CGT, 2H CG, 1 Rugby, 1 Sandown
6. **Ruth Irving** 20.7.74 (9y, 8) 6.33 '01 6.25, 6.20, 6.20, 6.20, 6.15, 6.12w, 6.06
   1 Tallahassee, 2 LI, 1 Scot, 6 CGT, 10 AAA, 9 CG, BL1: -,2,1
7. **Donita Benjamin** 7.3.72 (4y, 7) 6.26/6.45w '00 6.17w, 6.10, 6.08, 6.04, 6.04w, 6.03; 6.12i
   7 CAU, 3 BIG, 1 Izegem, 7 CGT, 3 AAA, 1 IS, BL1: 1,1,-
8. **Natasha May** 21.2.80 (1y, -) 5.90 '01 6.26, 6.22, 6.17w, 6.12, 6.04w, 6.02
   2 Izegem, 1 AAA-23, 4 BL1 (2), 5 AAA, 5 U23 v Ger, 1 3nU23, 2 Brasschaat
9. **Sarah Wellstead** 22.10.79 (2y, 9) 6.10, 6.14w '01
   6.29w, 6.14, 6.12, 6.04, 6.03, 6.00
   1 Surrey, 4 CAU, 3 Riga, 7 Tartu, 8 CGT, 4 AAA, 1 Lough, 1 Ashford, 3 IA
10. **Ashia Hansen** 5.12.71 (6y, -) 6.47A '96, 6.27 '94 6.18, 5.93 4 CGT, 3 BL1 (2)
11. **Kim Rothman** 6.9.64 (2y, -) 6.19 '00 6.08w?, 6.01, 6.00, 5.99w, 5.97, 5.97w; 6.13i, 6.03i
    4 Surrey, 5 CAU, 2 Scot, 4 BIG, 9 CGT, 3 Cup, BL1: 3,5,2
12. **Jacqueline Spargo** 12.1.71 (6y, -) 6.08 '96, 6.11w '95 6.07w, 6.02, 5.98, 5.94w, 5.91, 5.87
    1 Mid, 10 CGT, 1 Cup sf Stoke, 2 Rugby, 4 IA, BL2: 1.2.1

Johnson retains the top ranking and moved into the world top ten with splendid silver medals at both Commonwealth Games and European Championships. There was a big gap after her, with Claxton having just the best overall record over a closely matched group. Natasha May is the one newcomer, following in the footsteps of elder sister Fiona (UK No.1 1987-93 before her switch to Italy).

TRIPLE JUMP

1. **Ashia Hansen** 5.12.71 (12y, 1) *IAAF 1* 15.15 '97, 15.16i '98 15.00w/14.60, 14.86, 14.62, 14.50, 14.36w/ 14.25, 14.32; 14.71i, 14.62i 1 CGT, 2 ECp, 4 Rome, 3 Sheff, 1 AAA, 1 CG, 1 EC, 1 v USA, 2 WCp
2. **Michelle Griffith** 6.10.71 (12y, -) 14.08 '94, 14.14w '00 13.44, 13.18, 13.13w, 13.09, 13.07, 13.07 1 CAU, 1 South, 2 BIG, 2 CGT, 6 C.Ligure, 6 Sheffield, 3 AAA, 1 Cup sf Eton, 8 CG, 2 BL1 (3), 5 v USA
3. **Rebecca White** 5.6.80 (3y, 3) 12.85, 13.09w '01 13.15w, 12.97, 12.90, 12.74, 12.70w, 12.65 1 B.Un, 1 West, 2 E.Clubs B, 5 CGT, 1 AAA-23, 2 BL1 (2), 6 AAA, 1 U23 v Ger, 1 Cup sf Stoke, 3 3nU23, 2 Cup
4. **Danielle Freeman** 11.2.80 (1y, -) 0 12.98, 12.87, 12.72, 12.72w, 12.50w/12.18, 12.04 2 North, 2 AAA-23, 4 AAA, 3 U23 v Ger, 4 3nU23, 3 Barcelona
5. **Debbie Rowe** 8.9.72 (9y, 2) 12.97, 13.14w '00 12.84, 12.71w, 12.58, 12.57w, 12.55, 12.51 2 Tallahassee, 1 LI, 1 BL1 (1), 3 CAU, 1 Mid, 8 AAA, 2 Cup sf Stoke, 3 Cup
6. **Charmaine Turner** 5.12.81 (1y, -) 12.05 '01 12.44w/12.34, 12.43, 12.26w, 12.25, 12.19, 12.09 2 B.Un, 3 LI, 5 CAU, 3 South, 6 BIG, 9 CGT, 3 AAA-23, 9 AAA, 3 Cup sf Eton, 4g U23 v Ger, 2 Der, 1 IA, BL1: 3,3,4
7. **Rachel Peacock** 18.5.82 (2y, 12) 12.04, 12.10w '01 12.35w/12.20, 12.32, 12.28, 12.22w, 12.17, 12.08 3 B.Univs, 4 CAU, 4 South, 1 Budapest, 7 CGT, 5 AAA-23, 11 AAA, 2 Cup sf Eton, BL4: 1,1,-
8. **Leandra Polius** 14.5.80 (3y, 9) 12.52 '00 12.45, 12.34, 12.25w 9 CAU, 4 CGT, 6 AAA-23, 7 AAA
9. **Emily Parker** 7.11.84 (1y, -) 12.01i, 11.98, 12.05w '01 12.52, 12.30, 12.19w, 12.14, 12.00, 11.96 2 Sth-J, 2 Budapest, 11 CGT, 1 AAA-J, 4 JI v It,Sp, 1 E.Sch, 1 JIC, 6 Cup, 1J IA, 5 Barcelona
10. **Hazel Carwardine** 6.11.80 (1y, -) 12.10 '01 12.40, 12.38w/12.17, 12.18, 12.14, 12.02, 11.92; 12.17i, 12.08i 1 North, 12 CGT, 4 AAA-23, 12 AAA, 1 Cup sf Derby
11. **Azaria Francis** 12.4.83 (1y, -) 11.80, 12.04w '01 12.34, 12.16, 12.13, 12.09, 12.06, 12.03 4 B.Univs, 2 LI, 1 Sth-J, 4 BIG, 15 CGT, 3 AAA-J, 6 JI v It,Sp, 2J IA
12. **Katie Evans** 4.2.74 (8y, 6) 13.03 '97, 13.04w '00 12.33, 12.06, 12.02, 12.01, 11.91w, 11.88 5 BIG, 8 CGT, 3 Cup sf Stoke, BL1: 4,4,5
nr **Yamilé Aldama** CUB 14.8.72 14.77 '99 14.54w/14.35, 14.50w, 14.40, 14.16, 13.91, 13.49 2 Sheffield, 2 AAA, 1 Cup sf He, BL1: -,1,1
nr **Taneisha Robinson-Scanlon** IRL 19.11.77 12.72 '01 12.98, 12.81, 12.80, 12.75, 12.72, 12.69; 13.00i 2 CAU, 2 South, 3 BIG, 3 CGT, 3 ECp 2A, 2 WG, 5 AAA, 7 CG, 1 Cup, BL1: 2.-,3

Hansen was not only UK number one for the eighth time, but also world number one. Griffith returns to second place but was a long way short of her best. Freeman made a most encouraging start at the event to come straight in at number four. Yamilé Aldama, the Cuban who won the World silver medal in 1999 and was 4th in the Olympics, is married to a Scotsman and is seeking a British passport. Also unranked is Jamaican born Robinson-Scanlon, Irish for international competition, who competed for England at the Commonwealth Games.

SHOT

1. **Myrtle Augee** 4.2.65 (20y, -11) *IAAF 83* 19.03 '90 16.54, 16.32, 16.16, 16.11, 16.05, 15.94 1 Kent, 2 South, 2 CGT, 3 Varazdin, 1 AAA, 5 CG
2. **Joanne Duncan** 27.12.66 (9y, 2) *IAAF 80* 17.08 '01 16.73, 16.21, 16.18, 16.17, 16.00, 15.99; 16.06i, 16.01i 4B E.Chall, 8 Halle, 1 CAU, 1 BIG, 3 CGT, 1 Lough, 1 BL2 (2), 3 AAA, 1 Cup sf He, 6 CG, 1 Ashf, 1 IA, BL2: 1,1,3
3. **Julie Dunkley** 11.9.79 (6y, 2) *IAAF 87* 16.40 '00 16.37, 16.29, 16.19, 16.03, 15.92, 15.89 2 Kent, 1 LI, 1 South, 1 CGT, 8 ECp, 2 AAA, 7 CG, 1 Cup, 2 Ashford, 2 IA, 3 Barcelona, BL1: 1,1,-
4. **Eva Massey** 22.12.80 (4y, 3) 15.32 '01 15.57, 15.49, 15.34, 15.33, 15.33, 15.32 1 B.Univs, 2 LI, 2 CAU, 1 NI, 5 CGT, 1 AAA-23, 6 AAA, dnq 15 CG
5. **Maggie Lynes** 19.2.63 (15y, 4) 16.57 '94 15.38, 15.33, 15.28, 14.79, 14.69, 14.67; 14.71i 3 Kent, 1 BL2 (1), 3 CAU, 3 South, 4 CGT, 4 AAA
6. **Ade Oshinowo** 12.2.80 (1y, -) 14.84 '01 15.50, 15.02, 14.69, 14.45, 13.93, 13.91; 14.75i, 14.62i 2 AAA-23
7. **Philippa Roles** 1.3.78 (7y, 5) 15.95i '99, 15.19 '01 14.91, 14.66, 14.52, 14.42, 14.32, 14.25; 15.88i, 15.84i, 15.06i 3 LI, 1 E.Clubs B, 5 AAA, 1 Cup sf Stoke, 2 Cup, BL1: 2,2,2
8. **Christina Bennett** 27.2.78 (6y, 7) 15.55 '99 15.12, 14.94, 14.74, 14.14, 14.13, 13.96 1 Surrey, 4 CAU, 6 CGT, 3 Cup sf Eton, 3 Cup
9. **Vickie Foster** 1.4.71 (7y, 6) 15.44 '00 14.39, 14.36, 14.18, 14.15, 14.06, 14.02; 14.68i 1 West, 6 CAU, 4 South, 1 Cup sf Eton, 4 Cup, BL1: 3,3,1
10. **Kara Nwidobie** 13.4.81 (1y, -) 13.38 '00 14.28, 14.27, 13.99, 13.97, 13.91, 13.90 7 CAU, 1 North, 3 AAA-23, 4 U23 v Ger, 7 AAA, 2 Cup sf Derby, 3 3nU23, 1 Derby, 6 Barcelona
11. **Nicola Gautier** 21.3.78 (3y, 9) 15.09 '00 14.07, 14.07, 13.76, 13.29, 13.09 8 CAU, 7 CGT, 1 Cup sf Derby
12. **Rebecca Peake** 22.6.83 (2y, 12) 14.34 '01 14.23, 14.10, 14.03, 13.98, 13.96, 13.74; 14.11i 2 B.Univs, 5 LI, 9 CAU, 3 BIG, 8 CGT, 2 AAA-J, 3 JI v It,Sp, 8 AAA, 2 Bangor, 1 Jnr IA
-   **Claire Smithson** 3.8.83 (0y, -) 14.68 '01 14.16, 14.06, 14.04, 13.91, 13.32, 13.22 1 Sth-J, 4 LI, 5 South, 2 BIG, 3 AAA-J, 4 Ashford

Including Indoors: 5. Roles, 6. Lynes, 7. Oshinowo
Augee returned to the top ranking she held in 1990 and 1992-3, as she beat Duncan 3-0 and Dunkley 3-2. The next four all slip one place from 2001, although Roles would be higher with indoor marks included. Duncan beat Dunkley 3-2. A 'new' thrower was discovered this year in Oshinowo, who was born in London but who has lived in the USA for a while. The 10th best of 14.28 is well down on 2001's 14.66 and is the worst since 1993.

DISCUS
1. **Shelley Newman** 8.8.73 (11y, 1) *IAAF 30*   60.82 '98   60.29, 59.62, 58.39, 58.34, 58.13, 58.10
    7 E.Chall, 16 Halle, 2 LI, 1 CAU, 1 Florø, 1 BIG, 1 CGT, 6 ECp, 5 Sheffield, 1 Varazdin, 2 AAA,
    1 Cup sf He, 2 Lough, 3 CG, 10 EC, 1 Cup
2. **Philippa Roles** 1.3.78 (8y, 2) *IAAF 44*   60.00 '99   58.26, 57.65, 56.82, 56.75, 56.52, 56.32
    15 E.Chall, 6 Halle, 1 LI, 1 E.Clubs B, 1 Welsh, 3 CGT, 10 Sheffield, 1 WG, 1 AAA, 1 Cup sf Stoke,
    1 Lough, 4 CG, 2 Cup, BL1: 1,1,1
3. **Claire Smithson** 3.8.83 (4y, 3) *IAAF 83*   54.81 '01   55.03, 54.90, 54.34, 53.91, 53.61, 52.57
    5 LI, 1 Sth-J, 2 South, 2 BIG, 4 CGT, 1 AAA-J, 9 Varazdin, 9 WJ, 7 CG, 1 Ashford
4. **Emma Carpenter** 16.5.82 (3y, 4) *IAAF 83*   53.12 '01   56.63, 53.88, 53.67, 53.56, 53.28, 52.71
    6 LI, 2 CAU, 1 South, 3 BIG, 2 CGT, 1 AAA-23, 2 WG, 3 AAA, nt CG, 3 Cup
5. **Emma Merry** 2.7.74 (13y, 5) 57.75 '99   54.01, 53.38, 51.70, 51.66, 50.38, 50.30
    3 LI, 2 BL1 (1), 5 CGT
6. **Jackie McKernan** 1.7.65 (18y, -) 60.72 '93   53.84, 50.71, 50.45, 49.92, 49.52   3 CAU, 1 NI, 10 CG
7. **Rebecca Roles** 14.12.79 (3y, 6) 51.79 '99   51.16, 50.46, 50.02, 49.67, 49.48, 48.64
    4 LI, 4 CAU, 4 BIG, 6 CGT, 3 WG, 5 AAA, 2 Cup sf Stoke, BL1: 3,2,2
8. **Kara Nwidobie** 13.4.81 (1y, -) 45.51 '01   49.89, 49.03, 47.97, 47.53, 47.26, 47.19
    7 CAU, 1 North, 7 CGT, 2 AAA-23, 6 U23 v Ger, 4 AAA, 1 Cup sf Derby, 2 3nU23, 1 Derby
9. **Navdeep Dhaliwal** 30.11.77 (1y, -) 44.58 '01   52.05, 51.20, 47.22, 46.44, 45.35, 45.06
    5 CAU, 3 Mid, 6 BIG, 1 Scot, 9 CGT, 6 AAA, 2 Cup sf He, 6 Cup, BL1: 5,6,3
10. **Elaine Cank** 5.12.79 (1y, -) 46.40 '99   47.02, 46.86, 46.53, 46.35, 46.10, 46.06
    6 CAU, 2 Mid, 8 CGT, 7 AAA, 2 Cup sf Derby, 4 Cup, 1 IA, BL1: 6,-,5
11. **Vickie Foster** 1.4.71 (5y, 8) 49.25 '00   47.73, 46.88, 46.76, 46.23, 46.05, 45.79
    1 West, 11 CAU, 3 South, 1 Cup sf Eton, 5 Cup, 2 IA, BL1: 4,5,4
12. **Joanna Bradley** 23.8.79 (1y, -) 49.10 '00   46.74, 45.58, 45.54, 45.46, 44.64, 44.51
    4 South, 10 CGT, 8 AAA, 2 Ashford, 3 IA, BL2: 3,1,3
–   **Sue Backhouse** 6.12.78 (1y, -) 45.29 '00   47.31, 46.94, 46.00, 45.98, 45.36, 44.76
    1 B.Univs, 7 LI, 8 CAU, 2 North, 5 BIG, 11 CGT, 9 AAA, 3 Cup sf Derby, 3 Lough, BL2: 1,3,4
–   **Ade Oshinowo** 12.2.80 (0y, -) 47.98 '01   49.14, 46.77, 46.31A, 46.13, 44.56, 41.66   6 AAA-23
The top five are the same as in 2001. Drew ranks first for the sixth successive year and Roles second for the fourth successive year; they were 3rd and 4th at the Commonwealth Games. Smithson, who set two UK junior records, and Carpenter continued their progress. McKernan returned after two years of retirement, won her 13th NI discus title and equalled both Debbie Callaway's record 18 years in the discus rankings and Lesley Mallin's 19-year span.

HAMMER
1. **Lorraine Shaw** 2.4.68 (9y, 1) *IAAF 17*   68.15 '01   66.83, 66.10, 65.43, 65.34, 64.97, 64.81
    3 E.Chall, 1 Peri, 1 Mid, 1 CGT, 7 ECp, 1 BL1 (2), 1 AAA, 1 Lough, 1 Cup sf Stoke, 1 CG, dnq 20 EC, 3 v USA, 1 Cup
2. **Zoe Derham** 24.11.80 (5y, 4) *IAAF 73*   60.35 '01   62.27, 61.70, 61.43, 60.65, 60.57, 60.50
    2 Perivale, 13 E.Chall, 7 Halle, 3 LI, 2 BL1 (1), 2 Mid, 3 BIG, 2 CGT, 1 AAA-23, 11 Varazdin, 3 AAA,
    2 Lough, 3 3nU23, 8 CG, 6 v USA, 1 Derby, 2 Cup
3. **Elizabeth Pidgeon** 27.4.77 (7y, 3) *IAAF 68*   63.61 '00   62.08, 61.42, 61.39, 60.79, 60.26, 60.21
    1 Lough 27/4, 8 Halle, 2 CAU, 1 South, 1 BIG, 4 CGT, 2 AAA, 4 Lough, 1 Cup sf He, 1 Ashf, 1 IA, BL2: -,1,1
4. **Lyn Sprules** 11.9.75 (10y, 2) *IAAF 78*   63.96 '00   61.11, 60.94, 60.52, 60.39, 60.12, 59.41
    1 Middx, 1 LI, 1 CAU, 2 South, 2 BIG, 5 CGT, 3 Cup, BL1: 1,-,1
5. **Suzanne Roberts** 19.12.78 (3y, 6) *IAAF 93*   58.83 '00   60.38, 59.75, 59.72, 59.38, 59.16, 58.93
    3 Peri, 2 Lough 27/4, 2 B.Un, 2 LI, 1 BL2 (1), 3 CAU, 5 BIG, 3 CGT, 12 Varaz, 4 AAA, 3 Lough, 9 CG, 2 Nth IC
6. **Shirley Webb** 28.9.81 (1y, -) 54.37 '01   59.95, 59.88, 59.71, 59.03, 58.83, 58.08
    1 B.Univs, 1 Scot E-S, 4 LI, 1 Scot, 1 North, 6 CGT, 2 AAA-23, 6 AAA, 3 U23 v Ger, 4 3nU23, dnq 16 CG,
    7g v USA, 2 Derby, 2 IA, 1 Nth IC
7. **Diana Holden** 12.2.75 (12y, 8) 57.95 '98   58.97, 58.17, 57.94, 57.84, 57.71, 57.52
    4 Perivale, 2 Middx, 3 South, 4 BIG, 7 CGT, 5 AAA, 2 Cup sf He, 4 Cup
8. **Mhairi Walters** 19.6.81 (3y, 7) 58.31 '01   58.47, 57.36, 56.43, 56.25, 56.03, 54.47
    2 Scot E-S, 5 LI, 2 Scot, 10 CGT, 4 U23 v Ger, 12 CG
9. **Lesley Brannan** 13.9.76 (2y, 9) 56.62 '01   57.47, 57.21, 57.10, 56.64, 56.58, 55.90
    6 LI, 3 Welsh, 9 CGT, 1 WG, 7 AAA, dnq 14 CG, BL1: 3,2,2
10. **Sarah Moore** 15.3.73 (11y, 5) 57.40 '01   56.18, 55.78, 55.77, 55.14, 55.11, 54.98
    1 West, 4 CAU, 6 BIG, 1 Welsh, 2 WG, 8 AAA, dnq 18 CG, BL4: 1,1, -

11. **Laura Douglas** 4.1.83 (1y, -) 52.00 '00   55.22, 54.88, 54.87, 54.60, 54.23, 54.08
    7 LI, 1 E.Clubs B, 2 & 1J Welsh, 4 WG, 2 AAA-J, 3 JI v It.Sp, dnq 18 WJ, dnq 19 CG, 3 Der, 1 JLF, BL1: 5,-,3
12. **Nicola Dudman** 5.10.83 (2y, 12) 54.54 '01   57.63, 54.22, 52.92, 52.86, 52.56, 52.44
    6 Perivale, 1 Sth-J, 6 South, 7 BIG, 8 CGT, 1 AAA-J, 4 JI v It,Sp, dnq 19 WJ, 4 Derby, 2 Ashford, 1 Jnr IA

Shaw was a little below her best for most of the year, but was in top form to win Commonwealth gold and ranks top for the ninth time; she was over 61m in all 17 competitions. Derham moves up to 2nd and Pidgeon, who beat Sprules 3-2 and Roberts 4-2, is third for the third successive year. The biggest improvement was made by Webb, who ranks for the first time at 6th, just ahead of former British record holder Holden, who improved her pb by a metre. The tenth best at 57.47 again improved the record level (1999 – 53.60, 2000 – 54.68, 2001- 56.06). Two juniors complete the rankings.

JAVELIN

1. **Kelly Morgan** 17.6.80 (5y, 3) *IAAF 20* 58.45 '00   64.87, 63.03, 58.58, 57.09, 56.90, 56.55
   1 CGT, 6 ECp, 1 AAA, 3 CG, 12 EC
2. **Goldie Sayers** 16.7.82 (5y, 2) *IAAF 45* 55.40 '01   58.20, 57.86, 56.96, 56.85, 54.59, 53.63
   1 B.Univs, 1 CAU, 2 Riga, 5 Tartu, 3 CGT, 1 AAA-23, 4 Pihtip, 2 AAA, 3 U23 v Ger, 6 CG,1 Cup, 3 Barc
3. **Karen Martin** 24.11.74 (11y, 1) *IAAF 60* 59.50 '00   56.34, 55.59, 55.02, 50.91, 50.28, 49.19
   1 LI, 2 CGT, 1 IS, 3 AAA, 3 Varazdin, 7 CG
4. **Shelley Holroyd** 17.5.73 (13y, -) 53.06 '00, 60.12# '96   54.18, 52.08, 51.25, 50.63, 48.89
   2 LI, 4 CGT, 1 BL1 (2), 1 Cup sf Stoke
5. **Kirsty Morrison** 28.10.75 (10y, 4) *IAAF 80* 55.91 '99, 59.36# '93   55.74, 55.01, 54.38, 52.81A, 51.55, 51.15
   3 LI, 1 South, 5 CGT, 4 AAA, 1 Cup sf He, 2 Cup, 1 Ashford, 1 IA, BL1: 1,2,-
6. **Lorna Jackson** 9.1.74 (10y, 6) 57.19 '00, 58.39# '98   48.54, 48.24, 48.14, 48.01, 45.07, 44.81
   4 LI, 5 CAU, 1 Scot, 8 CGT, BL1: -,3,1
7. **Katie Amos** 13.11.78 (4y, 10) 47.55 '01, 50.34# '98   48.39, 46.76, 46.47, 45.50, 45.40, 44.37
   1 Essex, 2 CAU, 2 South, 10 CGT, 2 IA, BL2: 1,2,2
8. **Chloe Cozens** 9.4.80 (4y, 8) 51.79 '00   47.61, 46.66, 45.92, 45.84, 44.84, 43.47
   2 B.Univs, 5 LI, 3 BL1 (1), 2 E.Clubs B, 2 Scot, 6 CGT, 4 AAA-23, 2 3nU23, 3 Derby
9. **Sharon Gibson** 31.12.61 (23y, 9) 50.85 '99, 62.32# '87   48.73, 46.59, 46.38, 44.51, 44.03, 43.84
   3 CAU, 1 Mid, 7 CGT
10. **Samantha Redd** 16.2.84 (2y, 12) 47.13 '01   47.66, 47.48, 47.46, 45.49, 44.53, 44.25
    6 LI, 1 Sth-J, 5 South, 12 CGT, 1 AAA-J, 3 JI v It.Sp, 2 E.Sch, 1 Der, 3 Ashf, 2 Jnr IC, 2 IA-J, 6 Barcelona
11. **Katy Watts** 25.3.81 (2y, 11) 46.29 '01   47.33, 46.03, 44.86, 44.52, 44.13, 43.70
    4 CAU, 3 South, 11 CGT, 2 AAA-23, 5 AAA, 6 3nU23, BL3: 1,1,-
12. **Louise Watton** 30.10.86 (1y, -) 41.44 '01   46.94, 46.28, 45.17, 45.16, 44.86, 44.14
    1 Sth-U17, 1 E.Sch-I, 1 Sch.Int, 1 AAA-17, 1 Jnr IC
–   **Joanne Bruce** 26.10.78 (1y, -) 47.26 '99   47.74, 47.66, 44.93, 43.75, 43.65, 42.90
    2 Surrey, 4 South, 1 Cup sf Eton, 3 Cup, 1 Yeovil

= old specification

Although she lost form, perhaps due to her shoulder problem, Morgan threw wondrously well when she took the UK record from 59.50 to 63.03 with her first throw at the Commonwealth Trials and then to 63.87 and 64.87 at the AAAs. Sayers continued to improve and remains second while Martin drops to third. Gibson is ranked for the 23rd year to equal the women's record for any event shared by Tessa Sanderson (javelin) and Judy Oakes (shot); Gibson the only one to do so in successive years. The standard in depth continues to be weak. There is little to choose between those at the foot of the rankings and three more just outside.

HEPTATHLON

1. **Julie Hollman** 16.2.77 (6y, 1) *IAAF 13* 5933 '01   5 Götzis 6135, 1 Desenzano 6093, 5 CG 5825, dnf EC
2. **Kelly Sotherton** 13.11.76 (4y, 6) *IAAF 43* 5585 '97
   12 ECp 5794, 12 Arles 5772, 8 Talence 5742, 9 Desenzano 5734, 7 CG 5728
3. **Kerry Jury** 19.11.68 (13y, 3) *IAAF 66* 6005w '98, 5908 '99
   15 Arles 5657, 10 Desenzano 5631, 8 CG 5554; and 6145 decathlon
4. **Katherine Livesey** 15.12.79 (6y, 5) *IAAF 74* 5554 '01   1 Big 12 5577, 3 Coll.Station 5574, dnf NCAA
5. **Nicola Gautier** 21.3.78 (7y, 2) 5784 '01   23 ECp 5307, dnf Arles
6. **Rosalyn Gonse** 1.3.82 (2y, 9) 5053 '01   1g Mid 5294, 25 ECp 5275, 6 U23 Pratteln 5273
7. **Rebecca Jones** 17.1.83 (2y, 11) 5186 '00   24 Arles 5254, 1 Woodford 5140, dnf JI
8. **Laura Redmond** 19.4.81 (2y, 7) 5114 '01   4 Hexham 5176, 27 ECp 5098, 10 U23 Pratteln 5050
9. **Caroline Pearce** 1.9.80 (1y, -) 4795 '01   1 AAA 5108, 12 U23 Pratteln 5017
10. **Kate Brewington** 15.10.81 (2y, 10) 4969 '01   1 South 5229, 2 AAA 4971, 2g Mid 4824
11. **Jessica Ennis** 28.1.86 (1y, -) 4801 '01   2 JI Pratteln 5194, 2 AAA-J 4837
12. **Gillian Stewart** 21.1.80 (1y, -) 4806 '97   5 Hexham 5043, dnf g U23 Pratteln

Hollman retained top ranking and set personal bests in her first two heptathlons of the year, and Sotherton was splendidly consistent in second place, with all five heptathlons well in excess of her pre-season best. Jury retired after 13 years in the rankings, the last seven either 2nd or 3rd.

WALKS

Priority is given to form at the standard international distance of 20 kilometres, although performances at other distances are also taken into account. 3000m and 5000m performances are on the track, unless indicated by R for road marks (+ indicates intermediate time). All distances from 10k up are on the road unless shown by t. Previous bests are shown for track 5000m and road or track 10km and 20km. (B) indicates an event not held under full IAAF definition of walking.

1. **Lisa Kehler** 15.3.67 (17y, 1) 21:57.68 '90, 45:03 '98, 1:33:57 '00   3000m: 13:03.76+
   5km: 21:42:51, 22:34.1; 22:20R, 23:54+R; 1 RWA, 1 AAA, 1 IA
   10km: 45:53, 48:16+, 48:22+, 48:29+; 1 Dublin
   20km: 1 RWA 1:43:08, 3 CGT 1:39:13, 2 CG 1:36:45, dnf WCp
2. **Niobe Menendez** 1.9.66 (5y, 1) 23:46.30 '01, 48:08 '01, 1:40:12 '99   3000m: 13:08.64i
   5km: 25:26.84; 1 E.Vets
   10km: 46:38, 47:18, 48:22+, 49:19+, 49:26 (B); 1 W.Vets, 1 Dublin, 1 E.Vets
   20km: 1 Manx 1:40:05, 4 CGT 1:39:59, 15 Naumburg 1:41:23, 7 CG 1:46:16
3. **Sharon Tonks** 18.4.70 (5y, 2) 24:20.07 '98, 49:46 '00, 1:46:15 '01
   3000m: 13:53.8, 14:17+; 13:57.87i
   5km: 24:05.49; 23:53R; 2 RWA, 2 AAA
   10km: 48:40, 50:29, 50:51+, 52:07, 52:44+; 2 RWA, 4 Leamington
   20km: 2 RWA 1:43:29, 6 CGT 1:45:21, 8 CG 1:49:21, 71 WCp 1:48:33
4. **Sara-Jane Cattermole** 29.1.77 (4y, 3) 24:43.9 '01, 47:05 '01, 1:36:40 '00
   3000m: 13:52.6, 14:00.8, 14:20.31mx, 14:29.6
   5000m: 24:44.3; 23:44R
   10km: 47:48, 47:57, 50:19, 51:37+, 52:46+
   20km: 1 Camb, WA 1:41:51, 7 CGT 1:46:04, 9 CG 1:50:29, 75 WCp 1:52:44
5. **Kim Braznell** 28.2.56 (9y, -) 24:16.4 '95, 48:36 '98, 1:44:29 '99   5000m: 26:22.83
   10km: 52:25+, 53:18; 3 RWA
   20km: 3 RWA 1:49:44, 9 CGT 1:46:53, 1 Mid 1:45:07
6. **Karen Ratcliffe** 1.6.61 (7y, 8) 24:12.11 '93, 48:30 '94, 1:59:45 '89   3000m: 14:38.8
   5000m: 25:27R, 25:36R; 1 Mid, 3 RWA   10km: 52:16+
   20km: 3 RWA 1:51:23, 8 CGT 1:46:35, dnf Dublin
7. **Cal Partington** 27.6.66 (7y, -) 22:41.19 '95, 46:26 '95, 1:48:46 '97
   20km: 1 York 1:44:54, dnf CG
8. **Sophie Hales** 30.3.85 (1y, -) 25:31.5 '01, 53:18 '01
   3000m: 15:03.31; 14:34.11i
   5000m: 24:19.06, 24:35.56, 25:00.7, 25:18.56, 25:28.5, 25:31.24; 23:53R short; 1 AAA-J, 5 JI v It.Sp, 3 U23 v Ger, 1 ESch, 1 Jnr IA
   10km: 52:05, 52:24, 53:20, 53:21, 53:50, 53:59; 1 AAA-J, 2J Dublin, 4 RWA, 4J Leamington
9. **Kate Horwill** 26.1.75 (3y, -) 25:08.24 '99, 49:38 '99, 1:51:38 '99   3000m: 14:58.5
   5000m: 25:42R, 25:58R
   10km: 52:42, 54:06; 5 RWA, 5 Leamington
   20km: 5 RWA 1:56:27, 10 CGT 1:49:54
10. **Jo Hesketh** 16.6.69 (2y, 7) 53:08 '01, 1:50:35 '01
   3000m: 15:08.9, 15:16.39
   5km: 26:00.4, 26:26.5, 25:22R short
   10km: 52:58, 53:31, 54:40, 54:54; 3 Dublin, 6 RWA, 6 Leamington
   20km: 11 CGT 1:50:45
11. **Katie Stones** 22.11.85 (1y, -) 26:47.3 '01, 54:40 '01
   3000m: 14:25.66, 14:28.81, 14:33.1; 1 Nth-J, 1 ES-I   5000m: 25:57.11; 6 JI v It,Sp
   10km: 51:49, 52:56; 3J Dublin, 3J Leamington
12. **Jane Gibson** (Kennaugh) 26.1.73 (4y, 4) 25:16.2 '01, 51:34 '99, 1:47:39 '01
   5km: 25:11R   10km: 52:28
   20km: 2 Manx 1:51:12, dq RWA, dq CGT, 1 Manx 9/5 1:52:37
nr **Estle Viljoen** RSA 8.7.70 24:53.02 '01, 51:41 '01, 1:47:18 '01
   3000m: 13:51.73, 14:09.99, 14:14.7, 14:21e+; 1 CAU, 1 IA
   5km: 24:26.11; 23:28R, 25:10R; 3 AAA
   10km: 48:50, 49:06, 50:16.7t, 50:52+; 1 RWA, 3 Leamington
   20km: 2 S.Af Ch 1:49:23.4t, 5 CGT 1:44:16, 13 Eisenhüttenstadt 1:46:37, 17 Dublin 1:48:22
Kehler is top for a record eighth time and is ranked for a record 17th time.

With thanks to Tony Miller, Alan Lindop, Ian Tempest, John Powell, Julie Fletcher and Rob Whittingham for their comments.

2002 LISTS - MEN

50 Metres - Indoors

5.73+	Mark Lewis-Francis	U23	4.09.82	2mh2	Lievin, FRA	24	Feb
5.81+	Christian Malcolm		3.06.79	5mh1	Lievin, FRA	24	Feb

60 Metres - Indoors

6.49	Jason Gardener		18.09.75	1	Vienna, AUT	3	Mar
	6.52			1	Cardiff	3	Feb
	6.53			1h1	Birmingham	17	Feb
	6.53			1	Glasgow	9	Mar
	6.54			1s2	Cardiff	3	Feb
	6.54			3	Birmingham	17	Feb
	6.55			1s2	Vienna, AUT	3	Mar
	6.57			4	Ghent, BEL	10	Feb
	6.58			1h2	Ghent, BEL	10	Feb
	6.61			1h1	Vienna, AUT	2	Mar
	6.62			1h2	Cardiff	3	Feb
6.53	Mark Lewis-Francis	U23	4.09.82	2	Cardiff	3	Feb
	6.53			2	Birmingham	17	Feb
	6.54			2h2	Birmingham	17	Feb
	6.55			1s3	Cardiff	3	Feb
	6.55			2	Vienna, AUT	3	Mar
	6.56			1	Birmingham	27	Jan
	6.57			1h6	Cardiff	3	Feb
	6.57			1h5	Vienna, AUT	2	Mar
	6.60			1s2	Vienna, AUT	3	Mar
	6.62			2h2	Lievin, FRA	24	Feb
	6.63			4	Stockholm, SWE	6	Feb
	6.65			1	Birmingham	20	Jan
	6.66			1h2	Stockholm, SWE	6	Feb
	6.66			4h1	Ghent, BEL	10	Feb
	6.67			1s1	Birmingham	12	Jan
	6.69			1h1	Birmingham	12	Jan
	6.70			8	Ghent, BEL	10	Feb
	6.75			1h1	Birmingham	20	Jan
	6.75			6	Lievin, FRA	24	Feb
6.65	Akinola Lashore		28.03.73	1s3	Birmingham	12	Jan
	6.70			5	Cardiff	3	Feb
	6.71			6h2	Birmingham	17	Feb
	6.72			3h3	Vienna, AUT	2	Mar
	6.73			3s3	Cardiff	3	Feb
	6.74			1	Birmingham	12	Jan
6.67	Christian Malcolm		3.06.79	3	Cardiff	3	Feb
	6.68			1s1	Cardiff	3	Feb
	6.69			1h3	Cardiff	3	Feb
	6.72			5h1	Lievin, FRA	24	Feb
6.69	Doug Turner		2.12.66	4	Cardiff	3	Feb
	6.74			2s2	Cardiff	3	Feb
6.71	Marlon Dickson		17.11.78	6	Cardiff	3	Feb
	6.71			2s1	Cardiff	3	Feb
	6.71			7h2	Birmingham	17	Feb
6.72	Darren Chin	U23	30.06.81	2s3	Cardiff	3	Feb
	6.75			7	Cardiff	3	Feb
6.73	Dan Donovan		8.10.70	3s1	Cardiff	3	Feb
6.73	Chris Lambert	U23	6.04.81	1	Allston, USA	9	Feb
	6.73			1	Ithaca, USA	24	Feb
	6.74			1s2	Ithaca, USA	24	Feb
6.74	Daniel Money		17.10.76	2	Birmingham	12	Jan

6.75	Brian Doyle		12.03.77	1	Glasgow	20	Jan
	53 performances to 6.75 by 11 athletes						
6.76	Kevin Ellis		18.06.76	2s3	Birmingham	12	Jan
6.76	Nick Smith	U23	6.12.82	1r3	Edinburgh	10	Feb
6.77	Allyn Condon		24.08.74	1	Sheffield	20	Jan
6.77	Daniel Plummer	U23	4.01.81	3s2	Cardiff	3	Feb
6.78	Brendon Ghent		7.09.76	5s1	Cardiff	3	Feb
6.78	Steven Shalders	U23	24.12.81	1	Glasgow	23	Feb
6.83	Gavin Neblett		27.12.79	3h6	Cardiff	3	Feb
6.84	Nick Thomas		4.04.79	2s2	Birmingham	12	Jan
6.84	Nathan Morgan		30.06.78	4	Birmingham	27	Jan
	(20)						
6.85	Terence Stamp		18.02.70	1s1	Glasgow	20	Jan
6.85	Gavin Eastman	U23	28.06.80	7s1	Cardiff	3	Feb
6.85	Colin Wilson		30.10.77	4h6	Cardiff	3	Feb
6.85	Laurence Oboh	U20	14.05.84	1s3	Birmingham	23	Feb
6.87	Mark Hanson	U23	13.05.81	2	Glasgow	23	Feb
6.88	Daniel Caines		15.05.79	3	Birmingham	20	Jan
6.88	Andrew Matthews	U20	26.10.84	1	Birmingham	23	Feb
6.90	Tyrone Edgar	U23	29.03.82	1h6	Birmingham	12	Jan
6.90	Dominique Richards		12.09.79	4h5	Cardiff	3	Feb
6.91	Gary Jones		6.01.72	6h3	Cardiff	3	Feb
	(30)						
6.93	David Samuyiwa		4.08.72	4s3	Birmingham	12	Jan
6.93	Richard Rubenis		10.11.73	2r2	Birmingham	27	Jan
6.93	Simon Farenden	U17	6.10.85	2r4	Cardiff	16	Feb
6.93	James Ellington	U17	6.09.85	1s2	Birmingham	23	Feb
6.93	Jonathon Oparka	U23	29.01.80	2	Glasgow	28	Dec
6.94	Henry Richards	U23	15.05.81	3s2	Birmingham	12	Jan
6.94	Paul Nwaolise		31.05.73	3	Sheffield	20	Jan
6.94	Allan Stuart	U23	14.08.81	2r8	Edinburgh	10	Feb
6.94	Tim Abeyie	U23	7.11.82	1r3	Cardiff	16	Feb
6.94	Owusu Dako		23.05.73	1s2	Glasgow	23	Feb
	(40)						
6.94	Jason Comissiong	U20	7.09.83	3	Birmingham	23	Feb
6.95	Curtis Browne		11.09.75	5s1	Birmingham	12	Jan
6.95	Mensah Elliott		29.08.76	5s3	Birmingham	12	Jan
6.95	Matthew Thomas		27.04.76	3h1	Cardiff	3	Feb
6.95	Rikki Fifton	U20	17.06.85	2r1	Cardiff	16	Feb
6.95	Craig Pickering	U17	16.10.86	3	Birmingham	23	Feb
6.96	Phil Kerry	U20	19.03.83	2s1	Birmingham	23	Feb
6.96	Edwin Grey	U23	23.03.81	2h8	Glasgow	23	Mar
6.96	Ian Clarke		6.11.72	2	Eton	8	Dec
6.96	Aaron Hamilton	U23	7.08.82	2	Manchester	28	Dec
	(50)						
6.98	Leroy Slue	U23	11.12.81	4s2	Birmingham	12	Jan
6.98	Fabian Collymore	U20	19.10.84	2s3	Birmingham	23	Feb
6.99	Graeme Welsh		8.10.75	6	Glasgow	19	Jan

hand timing

6.7	Lashore		(6.65)	1	Eton	6	Jan
6.8	D. Housden			2	Eton	6	Jan
6.8	Nick Thomas		(6.84)	3	Eton	6	Jan
6.8	Craig Telford		1.06.79	1	Jarrow	6	Jan
6.9	David Samuyiwa		(6.93)	1q1	Bedford	19	Jan
6.9	Jason Comissiong	U20	(6.94)	1s1	Bedford	19	Jan
6.9	Rikki Fifton	U20	(6.95)	1s2	Bedford	19	Jan
6.9	Cleophuis Joseph		11.09.79	1	Birmingham	22	Jan
6.9	Ugochi Anomelechi	U20	29.10.83	1r3	London (CP)	6	Feb
6.9	Nathan Douglas	U23	4.12.82	1r2	Eton	1	Dec
6.9	Craig Pickering	U17	(6.95i)	1r3	Eton	1	Dec

Foreign

6.78		*Aiah Yambasu (SLE)*		*10.11.73*	*2h6*	*Cardiff*	*3 Feb*
6.80		*Gilbert Opiyo (KEN)*	*U23*	*19.12.81*	*1*	*Cardiff*	*16 Feb*
6.87		*Henry Audu (NGR)*		*5.03.79*	*1*	*Eton*	*8 Dec*
6.99		*Paul Brizzel (IRL)*		*3.10.76*	*6s1*	*Birmingham*	*12 Jan*

Outdoors

6.89	0.8	Darren Campbell		12.09.73	1	Gold Coast (RB), AUS	15 Mar

75 Metres - Under 13

9.9		Richard Kilty	2.09.89	1	Manchester (Wy)	26 Aug
10.1		Chris Bennett-Grant		1	Lewes	21 May
10.1		Anthony Shurman	27.11.89	1	Horsham	18 Aug

100 Metres

9.87	2.0	Dwain Chambers		5.04.78	2	Paris, FRA	14 Sep
	9.94	1.6			2h2	Zurich, SUI	16 Aug
	9.96	-0.3			1	Munich, GER	7 Aug
	9.98	0.5			1	London (CP)	23 Aug
	10.02	0.3			1	Berlin, GER	6 Sep
	10.03	0.3			1	Manchester (C)	15 Jun
	10.04	0.2			1	Annecy, FRA	22 Jun
	10.05	-0.1			1	Oslo, NOR	28 Jun
	10.05	-1.3			3	Zurich, SUI	16 Aug
	10.06	0.8			1s2	Manchester (C)	27 Jul
	10.08	1.8			2	Walnut CA, USA	21 Apr
	10.08	-0.2			3	Athens, GRE	10 Jun
	10.08	0.1			1q4	Munich, GER	6 Aug
	10.12	0.0			1s1	Munich, GER	7 Aug
	10.12	-1.1			1h2	London (CP)	23 Aug
	10.14	1.4			2	Modesto CA, USA	11 May
	10.16	1.6			1	Bydgoszcz, POL	8 Jun
	10.16	-0.3			5	Madrid, ESP	20 Sep
	10.17	0.7			1q1	Manchester (C)	26 Jul
	10.19	0.3			1h5	Manchester (C)	26 Jul
	10.23	0.3			1h1	Manchester (C)	15 Jun
	10.23	0.2			1h1	Munich, GER	6 Aug
	10.28	1.2			1	Glasgow (S)	18 Aug
	10.31				1r2	Philadelphia PA, USA	27 Apr
10.04	0.4	Mark Lewis-Francis	U23	4.09.82	3	Saint-Denis, FRA	5 Jul
	10.06	1.9			1	Birmingham	13 Jul
	10.07	0.3			2	Manchester (C)	15 Jun
	10.08	0.3			5	Brussels, BEL	30 Aug
	10.10	2.0			1	Loughborough	18 May
	10.13	0.7			1q2	Manchester (C)	26 Jul
	10.13	-0.6			2h1	London (CP)	23 Aug
	10.14	1.0			1	Tallahassee FL, USA	13 Apr
	10.14	1.5			1s2	Birmingham	13 Jul
	10.15	0.2			2s1	Manchester (C)	27 Jul
	10.18	0.7			3	Rieti, ITA	8 Sep
	10.25	-0.2			1h1	Manchester (C)	26 Jul
	10.25	0.5			7	London (CP)	23 Aug
	10.30	0.1			1h2	Manchester (C)	15 Jun
	10.32	-0.9			1h2	Birmingham	13 Jul
10.11	1.9	Darren Campbell		12.09.73	2	Birmingham	13 Jul
	10.15	-0.3			3	Munich, GER	7 Aug
	10.19	0.3			7h1	Zurich, SUI	16 Aug
	10.27	0.0			3	Zagreb, CRO	8 Jul
	10.28	1.5			2s2	Birmingham	13 Jul

(Campbell)		10.29	-0.1		2	Funchal, POR	29 Jun
		10.29	-0.6		1q3	Munich, GER	6 Aug
		10.30	0.1		3s2	Munich, GER	7 Aug
		10.32	-1.0		4	Milan, ITA	5 Jun
		10.32	0.8		1h1	Birmingham	13 Jul
		10.34	0.0		6	Doha, QAT	15 May
		10.36	0.4		2h3	Munich, GER	6 Aug
		10.38	-0.3		3	Brisbane, AUS	12 Apr
		10.40	0.6		1h4	Manchester (C)	15 Jun
10.13	1.9	Jason Gardener		18.09.75	3	Birmingham	13 Jul
		10.17	-0.2		5	Athens, GRE	10 Jun
		10.21	0.8		4s2	Manchester (C)	27 Jul
		10.22	0.2		6	Manchester (C)	27 Jul
		10.23	-0.1		1h3	Manchester (C)	15 Jun
		10.25	-0.4		1s1	Birmingham	13 Jul
		10.25	1.8		1	Heusden, BEL	20 Jul
		10.28	-0.1		2q1	Munich, GER	6 Aug
		10.29	1.0		2h5	Munich, GER	6 Aug
		10.30	-0.3		7r1	Lausanne, SUI	2 Jul
		10.31	0.3		4	Manchester (C)	15 Jun
		10.33	0.7		4q3	Manchester (C)	26 Jul
		10.34	0.1		2h6	Manchester (C)	26 Jul
		10.34	1.2		4	Glasgow (S)	18 Aug
		10.36	0.0		6s1	Munich, GER	7 Aug
10.28	0.9	Tyrone Edgar	U23	29.03.82	2	Auburn, USA	20 Apr
		10.29			1h1	Cottbus, GER	1 Jun
		10.40	0.7		2	Cottbus, GER	1 Jun
10.28	0.3	Chris Lambert	U23	6.04.81	3	Manchester (C)	15 Jun
		10.32	-0.1		2h3	Manchester (C)	15 Jun
		10.36	0.9		1s2	Annapolis, USA	11 May
		10.37	1.9		1h2	Bedford	29 Jun
10.29	1.9	Christian Malcolm		3.06.79	4	Birmingham	13 Jul
		10.36	1.6		1h3	Birmingham	13 Jul
		10.39	-0.3		2	Cardiff	8 Jul
10.32	1.6	Marlon Devonish		1.06.76	2	Bydgoszcz, POL	8 Jun
		10.38	2.0		3	Loughborough	18 May
10.32	1.3	Doug Bignall		20.10.74	1	Long Beach CA, USA	8 Jun
		10.34	1.4		1r2	Norwalk, USA	6 Apr
		10.39 A	-0.6		1	Xalapa, MEX	29 Jun
10.32	1.9	Allyn Condon		24.08.74	5	Birmingham	13 Jul
	(10)						
10.33	1.9	Daniel Plummer	U23	4.01.81	6	Birmingham	13 Jul
		10.38	2.0		2	Loughborough	18 May
		10.39	1.0		2	Tallahassee FL, USA	13 Apr
10.37	1.9	Kevin Ellis		18.06.76	1r1	Norwalk, USA	6 Apr
10.38	2.0	Ian Mackie		27.02.75	4	Loughborough	18 May
		89 performances to 10.40 by 13 athletes					
10.46	-0.4	Curtis Browne		11.09.75	4s1	Birmingham	13 Jul
10.46	-0.6	Jon Barbour	U23	3.11.80	8h1	London (CP)	23 Aug
10.46	1.5	Darren Chin	U23	30.06.81	3	Fribourg, SUI	24 Aug
10.49	0.3	Nick Smith	U23	6.12.82	4h1	Manchester (C)	15 Jun
10.49	1.5	Dan Donovan		8.10.70	5s2	Birmingham	13 Jul
10.52	0.1	Dwayne Grant	U23	17.07.82	2h2	Manchester (C)	15 Jun
10.54	-1.8	Uvie Ugono		8.03.78	2	Watford	19 May
	(20)						
10.55	-1.8	Marlon Dickson		17.11.78	3	Watford	19 May
10.55	1.1	Nathan Morgan		30.06.78	2	Loughborough	17 Jul
10.60	1.5	Michael Tietz		14.09.77	2r4	Fribourg, SUI	24 Aug
10.62	1.5	Kevin Williams		15.12.71	8s2	Birmingham	13 Jul
10.63	1.8	Graham Beasley		24.10.77	4	Celle Ligure, ITA	26 Jun

10.64	0.1	Jamie Henthorn		20.02.77	3h2	Manchester (C)	15	Jun
10.65	0.8	Jamie Baulch		3.05.73	1	Gold Coast (RB), AUS	15	Mar
10.65	-0.1	Terence Stamp		18.02.70	3h3	Manchester (C)	15	Jun
10.65		Matthew Thomas		27.04.76	1	London (FP)	11	Aug
10.66	2.0	Brendon Ghent		7.09.76	1h2	Alfaz del Pi, ESP	30	Mar
	(30)							
10.66	1.8	Kris Stewart	U23	11.04.80	1	Edinburgh	11	May
10.69	0.7	Chris Tomlinson	U23	15.09.81	1r2	Tallahassee FL, USA	13	Apr
10.69	1.9	Gavin Eastman	U23	28.06.80	3h2	Bedford	29	Jun
10.69	1.1	James Ellington	U17	6.09.85	1	Birmingham	10	Aug
10.70	1.7	Leon McRae	U23	3.11.80	1r2	Nashville, USA	20	Apr
10.70	-0.7	Akinola Lashore		28.03.73	2s3	Watford	1	Jun
10.70	1.1	Craig Pickering	U17	16.10.86	2	Birmingham	10	Aug
10.71	2.0	Mark Hanson	U23	13.05.81	5	Loughborough	18	May
10.71	-1.8	Brian Doyle		12.03.77	6	Watford	19	May
10.71	0.7	Julian Golding		17.02.75	1h2	Imperia, ITA	27	Jun
	(40)							
10.72	-0.7	Colin Wilson		30.10.77	3s3	Watford	1	Jun
10.72	1.9	Leon Baptiste	U20	23.05.85	1	Derby	8	Sep
10.73	1.9	Tim Ward	U23	27.05.82	6	Norwalk, USA	6	Apr
10.73	-0.3	Steven Shalders	U23	24.12.81	1rB	Cardiff	8	Jul
10.74	1.8	Matt Elias		25.04.79	1	Gold Coast (RB), AUS	23	Apr
10.74	-1.3	Karl Forde	U20	15.04.83	2	Gorizia, ITA	6	Jul
10.74	-1.2	Rikki Fifton	U20	17.06.85	1	Watford	1	Sep
10.75	2.0	Clive Turner	U20	24.11.84	6	Loughborough	18	May
10.75	1.9	Chris Stobart	U23	27.03.82	4h2	Bedford	29	Jun
10.75		Gary Jones		6.01.72	3	London (FP)	11	Aug
	(50)							
10.77	1.0	Nathan Honour		15.11.77	3	Kingston	12	May
10.77	1.3	Christopher Hamilton		14.11.78	4h2	Bedford	25	May
10.77	1.9	Adam Charlton	U20	11.05.84	2	Derby	8	Sep
10.78	0.6	Daniel Money		17.10.76	7	Bedford	25	May
10.78	1.0	Aidan Syers	U20	29.06.83	1	London (BP)	12	Jun
10.79	-0.9	Akeem Ogunyemi		4.06.74	5h2	Birmingham	13	Jul
10.79	0.0	Jonathon Oparka	U23	29.01.80	1	Glasgow (S)	14	Jul
10.80	0.6	Nick Thomas		4.04.79	5h4	Manchester (C)	15	Jun
10.81	-1.4	Lawrence Baird		14.12.77	5rB	Watford	19	May
10.82	1.0	Tyrone Swaray		7.11.77	3	London (BP)	12	Jun
	(60)							
10.82	1.0	Warren Prince	U20	18.03.85	2rB	Edinburgh	6	Jul
10.84	?	Chris Page	U23	13.11.80	3	Concordia, USA	27	Apr
10.84	-1.0	Graham Hedman		6.02.79	2h5	Watford	1	Jun
10.84	-2.9	Doug Turner		2.12.66	1h2	Newport	8	Jun
10.84		Andy Hughes		10.07.67	1	Cosford	30	Jun
10.84	0.5	Tim Abeyie	U23	7.11.82	6	Niort, FRA	3	Aug
10.84	0.3	Darren Scott		7.03.69	3rB	London (He)	3	Aug
10.85	-0.8	Dominic Papura	U23	12.02.81	3	Bedford	4	May
10.85	1.6	William Pobie		6.12.78	6h3	Birmingham	13	Jul
10.85	1.8	Ian Kennedy	U20	1.10.83	1rC	Namur, BEL	31	Aug
	(70)							
10.86	1.0	Solomon Wariso		11.11.66	1rB	London (BP)	12	Jun
10.86	0.7	Ryan Moseley	U23	8.10.82	3rC	Birmingham	6	Jul
10.87	1.1	Julian Thomas	U17	28.12.86	3	Birmingham	10	Aug
10.88	1.6	Andrew Mensah		30.11.71	7h3	Birmingham	13	Jul
10.90	-2.6	Edwin Grey	U23	23.03.81	2s2	Bedford	4	May
10.91	0.5	Tony Waddington		30.06.75	2	Edinburgh	6	Jul
10.92	1.9	Darren Wall	U23	6.04.80	5h2	Bedford	29	Jun
10.92	0.6	Jamie McNiel	U20	23.11.84	1	Nottingham	13	Jul
10.92	0.5	Wade Bennett-Jackson	U17	27.02.87	1s2	Birmingham	10	Aug
10.93	0.0	Laurence Oboh	U20	14.05.84	5r2	Bedford	4	Jun
	(80)							

10.94		Richard Rubenis		10.11.73	2	Cosford	27	Apr
10.94	-1.4	Alastair Gordon		16.04.78	6rB	Watford	19	May
10.95	-0.8	Marcus Adam		28.02.68	4	Bedford	4	May
10.95	1.0	Leroy Slue	U23	11.12.81	4	Kingston	12	May
10.95	-0.7	Joshua Wood		19.04.74	5s3	Watford	1	Jun
10.95	1.8	Adebowale Ademuyewo	U20	14.05.83	1ro	Bedford	29	Jun
10.95	1.8	Dominic Girdler	U23	6.03.82	1rB	Loughborough	17	Jul
10.95		Mark Holloway	U20	6.10.83	2	Watford	24	Jul
10.95	1.0	Ryan Scott	U17	20.02.87	1h3	Birmingham	10	Aug
10.96	1.8	Iwan Thomas		5.01.74	3	Gold Coast (RB), AUS	23	Apr
	(90)							
10.96		Allan Stuart	U23	14.08.81	1	Edinburgh	22	May
10.96		Brett Rund		27.07.77	2	Edinburgh	22	May
10.96	0.0	Gary Carr	U23	24.09.82	5	Glasgow (S)	8	Jun
10.97	0.1	Steven Fowles	U20	16.05.85	1	Watford	26	May
10.98	0.1	Andrew Matthews	U20	26.10.84	2	Watford	26	May
10.98	1.6	Ben Lewis	U23	6.03.81	6	London (He)	3	Aug
10.98		Alex Hall	U23	2.02.82	3	Ashford	18	Aug
10.99	0.0	Andrew Watkins	U15	8.12.87	2	Glasgow (S)	20	Jul
10.99	0.2	Carlos Holder	U17	28.03.86	4	Manchester (Str)	6	Aug
10.99	1.9	Alex Animashaun	U20	23.07.85	3	Derby	8	Sep

wind assisted

9.95	2.7	Chambers		(9.87)	1	Sheffield	30	Jun
9.97	2.7	Mark Lewis-Francis	U23	(10.04)	2	Sheffield	30	Jun
10.11	2.7	Jason Gardener		(10.13)	3	Sheffield	30	Jun
		10.22	3.3		1h4	Birmingham	13	Jul
10.19	2.9	Chris Lambert	U23	(10.28)	1	Annapolis, USA	12	May
		10.30	2.3		1	Riga, LAT	31	May
		10.30	3.5		1s2	Bedford	29	Jun
10.20	3.1	Tyrone Edgar	U23	(10.28)	1s1	Bedford	29	Jun
		10.31	2.2		1	Bedford	29	Jun
		10.36	3.7		1h1	Bedford	29	Jun
10.26	4.3	Allyn Condon		(10.32)	1rB	Loughborough	18	May
10.29	2.8	Doug Bignall		(10.32)	2	Sacramento CA, USA	1	Jun
		10.30			1	Whittier CA, USA	18	May
10.30	2.1	Marlon Devonish		(10.32)	3	Bratislava, SVK	11	Jun
10.35	3.3	Plummer	U23	(10.33)	1	Basildon	11	May
		10.36	2.5		3rB	Sheffield	30	Jun
		16 performances to 10.40 by 9 athletes						
10.47	2.5	Jamie Henthorn		(10.64)	5rB	Sheffield	30	Jun
10.47	3.3	Dan Donovan		(10.49)	2h4	Birmingham	13	Jul
10.48	2.5	Dwayne Grant	U23	(10.52)	1h1	Bedford	25	May
10.48	4.3	Tim Abeyie	U23	(10.84)	2h3	Bedford	29	Jun
10.49	3.4	Daniel Money		(10.78)	3s1	Bedford	25	May
10.50	3.4	Uvie Ugono		(10.54)	4s1	Bedford	25	May
10.50	4.7	Marlon Dickson		(10.55)	2r1	Lisbon, POR	25	May
10.52	2.4	Brendon Ghent		(10.66)	1h5	Bedford	25	May
10.52	3.5	Aidan Syers	U20	(10.78)	1h1	Bedford	29	Jun
10.53	3.3	Kevin Williams		(10.62)	5h4	Birmingham	13	Jul
10.56	3.3	Graham Hedman		(10.84)	2	Basildon	11	May
10.57	4.3	Gary Carr	U23	(10.96)	3h3	Bedford	29	Jun
10.58	5.2	Leon McRae	U23	(10.70)	1	Knoxville TN, USA	28	Apr
10.58	3.3	Nick Thomas		(10.80)	3	Basildon	11	May
10.62	3.1	Finlay Wright	U23	7.02.81	4s1	Bedford	29	Jun
10.63	2.4	Karl Forde	U20	(10.74)	1h2	Bedford	29	Jun
10.64	2.2	Leon Baptiste	U20	(10.72)	1	London (He)	25	Aug
10.65	3.1	Gavin Eastman	U23	(10.69)	5s1	Bedford	29	Jun
10.67	3.7	Jonathon Oparka	U23	(10.79)	2h1	Bedford	29	Jun

10.72	3.7	Leroy Slue	U23	(10.95)	5h1	Bedford	29	Jun
10.75	3.5	Mark Holloway	U20	(10.95)	2h1	Bedford	29	Jun
10.76	2.3	Nathan Honour		(10.77)	2h2	Kingston	12	May
10.76	2.2	Vincent Bruce	U20	15.04.83	2	London (He)	25	Aug
10.78	4.0	Jason Fergus		11.10.73	2h1	Basildon	11	May
10.78	2.4	Tony Waddington		(10.91)	4h5	Bedford	25	May
10.80	3.7	Roddy Pitt	U23	4.03.81	6h1	Bedford	29	Jun
10.80	2.1	Wade Bennett-Jackson	U17	(10.92)	1	Crawley	26	Aug
10.81	4.2	Jamie McNiel	U20	(10.92)	2h4	Bedford	29	Jun
10.81	4.1	Ryan Scott	U17	(10.95)	2s1	Birmingham	10	Aug
10.82	2.4	Andrew Matthews	U20	(10.98)	2h2	Bedford	29	Jun
10.82	4.2	Jamahl Alert-Khan	U17	12.09.86	3h4	Bedford	29	Jun
10.83	3.5	Ian Kennedy	U20	(10.85)	4h1	Bedford	29	Jun
10.83	4.2	Steven Fowles	U20	(10.97)	4h4	Bedford	29	Jun
10.85	4.0	Paul Nwaolise		31.05.73	2	Cudworth	25	Aug
10.86	2.2	Julian Thomas	U17	(10.87)	1	Birmingham	31	Aug
10.87	3.3	Patrick Osborne		5.06.74	5r1	Long Beach CA, USA	20	Apr
10.87	3.3	Gavin Neblett		27.12.79	6	Basildon	11	May
10.90	2.4	Phil Kerry	U20	19.03.83	3h2	Bedford	29	Jun
10.90		Steven Cavanagh	U20	9.07.85	1	Tullamore, IRL	28	Jul
10.91	4.2	James Bridge	U20	28.11.83	5h4	Bedford	29	Jun
10.91	2.2	Ross O'Donovan	U17	12.03.86	1h6	Birmingham	10	Aug
10.92	3.0	Adebowale Ademuyewo	U20	(10.95)	2h3	Bedford	29	Jun
10.93	3.5	Jason Comissiong	U20	7.09.83	5h1	Bedford	29	Jun
10.93	4.2	Jahmaine Merchant	U20	3.08.83	6h4	Bedford	29	Jun
10.94	4.0	Michael Smith		3.06.79	3	Cudworth	25	Aug
10.95	4.1	Jamie Gill	U17	29.10.85	3s1	Birmingham	10	Aug
10.96	3.3	Matthew Russell	U23	20.01.81	7	Basildon	11	May
10.96	5.9	David Pugh	U17	15.08.86	5	Belfast	8	Jun
10.96	4.0	Craig Yates	U20	9.02.83	1	Cudworth	25	Aug
10.97	5.0	John Heanley	U23	25.09.80	1D	Perpignan, FRA	20	Apr
10.97	3.5	Nathan Martin	U20	10.05.84	6h1	Bedford	29	Jun
10.97	3.0	Ugochi Anomelechi	U20	29.10.83	3h3	Bedford	29	Jun
10.98	3.5	Alex Animashaun	U20	(10.99)	7h1	Bedford	29	Jun
10.99	2.4	Ian Clarke		6.11.72	8h5	Bedford	25	May

hand timing

10.4 w		Nick Smith	U23	(10.49)	1	Coatbridge	21	Apr
10.4 w		Graham Beasley		(10.63)	1rB	Wigan	31	Aug
	10.6	1.2			1s1	Watford	1	Jun
		2 performances to 10.4 by 2 athletes						
10.5 w	3.1	Aidan Syers	U20	(10.78)	1s1	Bedford	29	Jun
10.5 w		Dominic Papura	U23	(10.85)	1	Gloucester	27	Jul
	10.7	1.5			1	Loughborough	27	Apr
10.5 w		Du'aine Thorne-Ladejo		14.02.71	2rB	Wigan	31	Aug
10.6	-1.9	Brendon Ghent		(10.66)	1h2	Torrevieja, ESP	3	Apr
10.6	1.2	Matthew Thomas		(10.65)	2s1	Watford	1	Jun
10.6		Leon Baptiste	U20	(10.72)	1	London (Cr)	28	Jul
10.6 w	2.9	Steve Surety	U23	18.02.80	2	Loughborough	22	May
10.6 w	2.2	Karl Forde	U20	(10.74)	1	Bedford	29	Jun
	10.7	2.0			1s2	Bedford	29	Jun
10.6 w		Nathan Douglas	U23	4.12.82	1	Portsmouth	13	Jul
	10.7				1	London (Ha)		
10.6 w		William Pobie		(10.85)	3rB	Wigan	31	Aug
10.6 w		Richard Rubenis		(10.94)	1	Telford	7	Sep

10.7	2.0	Colin Wilson		(10.72)	1s1	London (ME)	11	May
10.7		Andy Turner	U23	19.09.80	1	Nottingham	11	May
10.7		Adrian Patrick		15.06.73	1	Bracknell	11	May
10.7	1.7	Mark Hanson	U23	(10.71)	1	London (ME)	11	May
10.7		Scott Herbert		12.02.74	1	Par	18	May
10.7	1.2	Graham Hedman		(10.84)	3s1	Watford	1	Jun
10.7	1.9	Tim Abeyie	U23	(10.84)	5r3	Bedford	4	Jun
10.7		Andrew Mensah		(10.88)	1	Perivale	22	Jun
10.7		Nathan Honour		(10.77)	1	Ashford	3	Aug
10.7		Gary Carr	U23	(10.96)	2	Ashford	3	Aug
10.7		Michael Champion		3.01.75	1	Bromley	24	Aug
10.7 w		Tony Cunningham	U20	20.02.83	2	Coatbridge	21	Apr
10.7 w		Ryan Scott	U17	(10.95)	1	Yate	21	Apr
10.7 w	4.0	Christopher Hamilton		(10.77)	1	Cudworth	11	May
10.7 w	2.9	Gavin Stephens		12.09.77	3	Loughborough	22	May
10.7 w		Alex Hall	U23	(10.98)	1	Bournemouth	8	Jun
10.7 w	3.1	Mark Holloway	U20	(10.95)	2s1	Bedford	29	Jun
10.9					1	Bracknell	22	Jun
10.7 w		Derek Morgan		4.04.69	2	Gloucester	22	Jun
10.7 w		Jason Harding	U23	24.09.82	1	Telford	6	Jul
10.7 w		Louis Burgess	U20	21.03.83	1	Basildon	13	Jul
10.8					1	Hilversum, NED	30	Mar
10.7 w		Philip Ellershaw		9.02.76	1	Liverpool	14	Jul
10.7 w	3.2	Akeem Ogunyemi		(10.79)	1	London (He)	21	Jul
10.7 w		Neil Mitchell	U20	25.09.84	1	Nuneaton	28	Jul
10.7 w		Darren Scott		(10.84)	4rB	Wigan	31	Aug
10.7 w		Henry Richards	U23	15.05.81	2	Telford	7	Sep
10.8		Laurence Oboh	U20	(10.93)	1	London (He)	28	Apr
10.8		Alex Riley	U20	17.09.83	1	Loughborough	11	May
10.8		Warren Prince	U20	(10.82)	1	Luton	11	May
10.8		Cori Henry		9.12.76	2	Nottingham	11	May
10.8		Alwin John		7.01.79	1	Burton	19	May
10.8		Brett Rund		(10.96)	1	Coatbridge	2	Jun
10.8		Nathan Martin	U20	(10.97w)	1	London (TB)	22	Jun
10.8		Jamie McNiel	U20	(10.92)	1	Birmingham	22	Jun
10.8		Ian Kennedy	U20	(10.85)	2	Eton	23	Jun
10.8		Peter Vickers	U20	11.06.84	1	Scunthorpe	25	Jun
10.8	2.0	Andrew Matthews	U20	(10.98)	2s2	Bedford	29	Jun
10.8		Tim Barton		3.10.70	2	Telford	6	Jul
10.8		Daniel May		27.06.71	1rB	Basildon	13	Jul
10.8		Philip Taylor	U20	20.03.85	2	Liverpool	14	Jul
10.8		Phil Kerry	U20	(10.90w)	2	Nuneaton	28	Jul
10.8		Michael Smith		(10.94w)	1	Blackpool	3	Aug
10.8		Ben Ellis	U23	16.11.81	1	Bournemouth	3	Aug
10.8 w		Danny Whittaker	U17	10.01.86	1	Burnley	5	May
10.8 w		Louis Moore	U17	8.09.85	1	Worcester	5	May
10.8 w	3.2	Ben Lewis	U23	(10.98)	1	Cannock	11	May
10.8 w		Jamie Gill	U17	(10.95w)	1	Sutton Coldfield	19	May
11.0					1h3	Birmingham	25	May
10.8 w		Stuart Wenden	U20	21.01.84	1h2	London (Cat)	28	May
10.8 w	3.1	Adebowale Ademuyewo	U20	(10.95)	5s1	Bedford	29	Jun
10.8 w	3.1	Jamahl Alert-Khan	U17	(10.82w)	6s1	Bedford	29	Jun
10.8 w		Adam Potter	U23	12.04.80	2	Gloucester	27	Jul
10.8 w		Alloy Wilson	U23	25.01.80	2	London (FP)	25	Aug

Additional Juniors

10.9		Daniel Topliss	U17	8.12.85	2rB	Nottingham	7 Apr
10.9		Robert Tobin		20.12.83	1	Basingstoke	28 Apr
10.9		Alex Animashaun		(10.99)	1	Watford	15 Jun
10.9		Jahmaine Merchant		(10.93w)	1rB	Scunthorpe	25 Jun
10.9	2.0	Vincent Bruce		(10.76w)	5s2	Bedford	29 Jun
10.9 w		Alex Nelson	U15	21.03.88	1	Worcester	5 May
10.9 w		David Aguirreburualde	U17	29.11.85	1	Blackburn	11 May
10.9 w		Robert Henry		31.05.85	1	Hull	11 May
10.9 w		Richard Davenport	U17	12.09.85	1	Yate	18 May
10.9 w	3.1	Ugochi Anomelechi		(10.97w)	7s1	Bedford	29 Jun
10.9 w		Dwayne Bovell	U17	2.12.85	1	Bromley	24 Aug

Additional Under 17 (1 - 18 above)

11.0		Ben Hamblin		2.11.85	1	Great Yarmouth	12 May
		11.04 w 3.4			2h3	Watford	25 May
11.0		Jamie Gill		(10.95w)	1h3	Birmingham	25 May
		11.03 -0.5			1	Birmingham	25 May
11.0 w		Matthew Woolley		6.05.86	1rB	Worcester	5 May
	(20)						
11.0 w		Alan Selby		2.07.86	1	Cudworth	5 May
11.0 w	5.6	Louis Moisey		9.08.86	1	Sutton Coldfield	19 May
		11.02 w 2.6			1h7	Birmingham	10 Aug
		11.12 -0.1			1	Birmingham	1 Sep
11.0 w		R. Derrick			2h1	Bournemouth	22 May
11.0 w		Simon Williamson		16.01.86	3	London (FP)	25 Aug
		11.1			1	London (Elt)	
11.02	0.5	Ross O'Donovan		(10.91w)	2s2	Birmingham	10 Aug
11.04		Richard Davenport		(10.9w)	1h1	Tamworth	26 Aug
11.06 w 3.1		Dwayne Bovell		(10.9w)	3s3	Birmingham	10 Aug
		11.10 1.0			1rB	Derby	8 Sep
11.05	0.5	Daniel Topliss		(10.9)	1	Manchester (C)	26 May
11.06 w		Alistair McKenzie		15.04.86	3h1	Glasgow (S)	1 Jun
11.08	0.1	Calvin McLaggon		13.11.85	1	Tullamore, IRL	3 Aug
11.08 w 4.1		Tony Barnett			4s1	Birmingham	10 Aug
11.09	-0.4	Paul Judson		20.06.86	1h2	Birmingham	10 Aug
11.10	1.8	Sam Huggins		30.11.85	1	Basildon	11 May
11.10	1.0	Jamahl Alert-Khan		(10.82w)	2rB	Derby	8 Sep
11.1		Michael Coupland		5.01.86	1	Sheffield	27 Apr
	(30)						
11.1		Victor Barzey		10.01.86	1	Erith	4 May
11.1		Chinedum Onuoha		12.11.86	2	Stockport	5 May
		11.12 -0.9			1s2	Nottingham	12 Jul
11.1		Stephen Thompson		5.09.86	1	Tullamore, IRL	22 Jun
11.1		Ben Higgins		27.09.86	1	Chelmsford	21 Jul
11.1		Christian Lee		19.02.87	1	Peterborough	24 Aug
11.1 w		David Thomas	U15	13.02.88	1	Grimsby	7 Sep
		11.25 w 3.0			1	Cudworth	14 Sep
		11.5			1	Grimsby	29 Sep
		11.55 0.6			4h2	Birmingham	10 Aug
11.11 w 4.1		Gary Atkinson		7.01.87	5s1	Birmingham	10 Aug
11.15 w 4.1		Ben Samuels			6s1	Birmingham	10 Aug

Additional Under 15 (1 - 3 above)

11.17	0.7	Chris Julien		14.09.87	2	Birmingham	10 Aug
11.17	0.4	Alex Nelson		(10.9w)	1	Birmingham	1 Sep
11.30	0.9	Paul Crawford		4.10.87	1s2	Birmingham	10 Aug
11.3		Gavin Comber		28.05.88	1	London (B)	8 Sep
		11.41 0.7			4	Birmingham	10 Aug
11.32	1.6	Emlyn Akoto-Dwemoh		15.09.87	1	London (He)	25 Aug

11.38	0.4	James Sinclair	22.10.87	2	Birmingham	1 Sep
11.39 w	2.4	David Hurst	25.10.87	2s1	Birmingham	10 Aug
11.48	0.6			2h2	Birmingham	10 Aug
11.4 w		David Pitt	1.09.88	2	Worcester	5 May
11.5				1rB	Oxford	8 Sep
	(10)					
11.4 w		Jay Brown	27.10.87	1	Kettering	1 Sep
11.48		Daniel Maynard	4.12.87	1	Tamworth	26 Aug
11.5		Daniel Davis	12.12.87	1	London (CP)	7 Apr
11.5		Harry Akines-Aryeety	29.08.88	1	London (TB)	19 May
				2	Kingston	11 May
11.5		Miles Marshall	20.02.88	2	London (TB)	19 May
		11.59 0.4		3	Kingston	11 May
11.5		Danny Mulholand	11.01.88	1	Tullamore, IRL	1 Jun
11.5		Adryan Viera	4.11.87	1	Bath	15 Jun
11.5		Nick Wilding	11.11.87	1	Cannock	15 Jun
		11.59 -0.7		3s1	Nottingham	12 Jul
11.5		Seyi Akande	21.12.87	1	Chelmsford	21 Jul
11.5		Tasham Christian	6.10.87	1	Ware	4 Aug
		11.54		1	Basildon	11 May
	(20)					
11.5 w		Joelle Powell	2.03.88	1rB	Worcester	5 May
11.5 w		Kyle Cashin	11.10.87	1	Sutton Coldfield	19 May
11.5 w		Ricardo Francis	26.11.88	1	Mandale	21 Jul
11.51	0.6	Kie Barker	1.11.87	3h2	Birmingham	10 Aug
11.53	1.2	Darryl Thomas	23.11.87	1h4	Birmingham	10 Aug
11.60		Tom Rayner	26.01.88	1	Manchester (Str)	12 May
11.60	-0.1	Fabien Alexander	26.04.88	2h3	Nottingham	12 Jul
11.60	0.9	Sam Kavanagh	1.11.87	5s2	Birmingham	10 Aug

Under 13

12.1		James Pilkington	21.10.89	3	Amiens, FRA	14 Sep
12.19 w	2.1	Yusuf Aliu	10.01.90	1	Birmingham	31 Aug
12.2	-1.2	Precious Ojighoro	27.12.89	1rB	Kingston	28 Jul
12.3		Juan De Leon-Padmore	1.04.90	1	Telford	21 Jul
12.3		Michael Weekes	17.11.89	1	Watford	8 Sep
12.4		Jamie Jones	16.10.89	1	Barry	9 Jul
12.4		Sam Boxall	5.12.89	1	Chelmsford	21 Jul
12.5		Luke Smith	7.11.89	1	Salisbury	15 Jun
12.6		Ben Riekstins	11.09.90	2	Telford	21 Jul
12.68		Mark Atkinson		1	Bangor	21 Jul
	(10)					
12.7		Gavin Hoyte		1	Tonbridge	30 Jun
12.73		William McCleery		2	Bangor	21 Jul
12.77	-1.2	James Alaka	8.09.89	1	Kingston	28 Jul

Foreign

10.2 w		Gilbert Opiyo (MLT) U23	19.12.81	1	Gloucester	22 Jun
		10.56 1.9		2h2	Bedford	29 Jun
10.32 w	3.4	Paul Brizzel (IRL)	3.10.76	5	Cork, IRL	6 Jul
		10.59 A 0.4		3rB	Germiston, RSA	5 Apr
		10.63 1.5		10	Cape Town, RSA	19 Apr
10.34 w	5.9	John McAdorey (IRL)	16.09.74	1	Belfast	8 Jun
		10.45 1.3		1s	Dublin, IRL	13 Jul
10.38 w	5.9	Jonathan Carleton (IRL)	4.11.79	2	Belfast	8 Jun
		10.65 1.2		s	Dublin, IRL	14 Jul
10.40	1.5	Joselyn Thomas (SLE)	11.07.71	3s2	Birmingham	13 Jul
10.48 w	3.3	Henry Audu (NGR)	5.03.79	3h4	Birmingham	13 Jul
		10.70 -0.4		7s1	Birmingham	13 Jul
10.6 w	2.9	Josephus Thomas ¶(SLE)	11.07.71	1	Loughborough	22 May
		10.90 w 2.4		6h5	Bedford	25 May

150 Metres

17.33		Alisdair MacKenzie	U17	1	Glasgow (S)	24 Apr

200 Metres

20.19	1.4	Marlon Devonish		1.06.76	2	Manchester (C)	29 Jul
20.23	0.2				2s2	Munich, GER	9 Aug
20.24	-0.5				3	Munich, GER	9 Aug
20.27	-0.4				1	Annecy, FRA	23 Jun
20.32	-0.6				3	Madrid, ESP	21 Sep
20.36	0.5				1	Manchester (C)	16 Jun
20.36	0.5				6	Brussels, BEL	30 Aug
20.38	0.4				3	Rieti, ITA	8 Sep
20.41	-0.8				2q2	Munich, GER	8 Aug
20.43	-0.5				3	London (CP)	23 Aug
20.46	0.3				1h1	Manchester (C)	16 Jun
20.55	0.2				5	Lausanne, SUI	2 Jul
20.55	0.4				2s1	Manchester (C)	29 Jul
20.60	1.6				2	Glasgow (S)	18 Aug
20.61	0.5				1h1	Manchester (C)	28 Jul
20.63	-0.4				1q4	Manchester (C)	28 Jul
20.64	1.6				2	Bydgoszcz, POL	8 Jun
20.81	1.9				5	Sheffield	30 Jun
20.81	0.1				1h3	Munich, GER	8 Aug
20.21	1.4	Darren Campbell		12.09.73	3	Manchester (C)	29 Jul
20.52	0.3				2	Zagreb, CRO	8 Jul
20.58	0.4				4s1	Manchester (C)	29 Jul
20.62	0.0				2	Poznan, POL	18 Aug
20.66	-0.2				1h2	Munich, GER	8 Aug
20.70	0.5				2q2	Manchester (C)	28 Jul
20.81	-0.8				1	Funchal, POR	29 Jun
20.84	-1.8				1	Meilen, SUI	9 Jun
20.87	1.0				3	Brisbane, AUS	13 Apr
20.87	0.7				1h5	Manchester (C)	28 Jul
20.27	1.3	Dwain Chambers		5.04.78	2	Athens, GRE	10 Jun
20.38	1.9				2	Sheffield	30 Jun
20.55	1.6				1	Bydgoszcz, POL	8 Jun
20.64	1.9				2h1	Birmingham	14 Jul
20.30	-0.5	Christian Malcolm		3.06.79	4	Munich, GER	9 Aug
20.39	1.4				8	Manchester (C)	29 Jul
20.53	1.9				1h1	Birmingham	14 Jul
20.54	-0.5				3s1	Munich, GER	9 Aug
20.55	0.4				3s2	Manchester (C)	29 Jul
20.58 i					2	Birmingham	17 Feb
20.61	0.8				3q1	Manchester (C)	28 Jul
20.65 i					1s3	Vienna, AUT	1 Mar
20.65 i					2	Vienna, AUT	2 Mar
20.66	-0.3				3q3	Munich, GER	8 Aug
20.71 i					1	Lievin, FRA	24 Feb
20.77	-0.5				4	London (CP)	23 Aug
20.81	1.9				6	Sheffield	30 Jun
20.82	0.8				2h1	Munich, GER	8 Aug
20.82	1.6				4	Glasgow (S)	18 Aug
20.83 i					1h6	Vienna, AUT	1 Mar
21.00	-3.1				2	Hengelo, NED	2 Jun
20.37	-0.1	Chris Lambert	U23	6.04.81	1h3	Manchester (C)	16 Jun
20.41	0.5				2	Manchester (C)	16 Jun
20.77	1.3				1h2	Manchester (C)	28 Jul
20.82	1.2				1	New Haven, USA	20 Apr
20.90	1.3				2q3	Manchester (C)	28 Jul

20.59 i		Doug Turner		2.12.66	3	Birmingham	17	Feb
20.75	1.9				3h1	Birmingham	14	Jul
20.76	-3.7				3	Lisbon, POR	15	Jun
20.84 i					3s2	Vienna, AUT	1	Mar
20.86 i					1h3	Vienna, AUT	1	Mar
20.92 i					1	Cardiff	10	Feb
20.94 i					2	Glasgow	9	Mar
20.62 i		Daniel Caines		15.05.79	2s1	Vienna, AUT	1	Mar
20.67 i					1h5	Vienna, AUT	1	Mar
20.83 i+				1m		Birmingham	17	Feb
20.76	0.5	Graham Beasley		24.10.77	3	Manchester (C)	16	Jun
20.78	0.3				2h1	Manchester (C)	16	Jun
20.90	1.9				4h1	Birmingham	14	Jul
20.79	-0.5	Dwayne Grant	U23	17.07.82	5	London (CP)	23	Aug
20.82	0.5				4	Manchester (C)	16	Jun
20.85	0.5				1h2	Manchester (C)	16	Jun
20.88	0.3				4	Bangor, NI	21	Jul
20.99	-0.6				3	Tartu, EST	2	Jun
20.90	-0.1	Allyn Condon		24.08.74	2h3	Manchester (C)	16	Jun
	(10)							
20.94	-0.3	Mark Lewis-Francis	U23	4.09.82	1	Tallahassee FL, USA	13	Apr
20.98	-0.1	Cori Henry		9.12.76	3h3	Manchester (C)	16	Jun
		76 performances to 21.00 by 12 athletes including 13 indoors						
21.02	0.5	Julian Golding		17.02.75	2	Celle Ligure, ITA	26	Jun
21.03	0.3	Jamie Henthorn		20.02.77	3h1	Manchester (C)	16	Jun
21.04	-0.1	Tyrone Edgar	U23	29.03.82	4h3	Manchester (C)	16	Jun
21.15	2.0	Dominic Papura	U23	12.02.81	1	Bedford	30	Jun
21.21 !	1.2	Chris Rawlinson		19.05.72	1h6	Bedford	5	May
21.24	-0.4	Kris Stewart	U23	11.04.80	1	Bedford	6	May
21.24	-0.3	Graham Hedman		6.02.79	1	Watford	2	Jun
21.30	0.3	Jared Deacon		15.10.75	2	Glasgow (S)	9	Jun
	(20)							
21.31	0.3	Adrian Patrick		15.06.73	4h1	Manchester (C)	16	Jun
21.32	-0.1	Brett Rund		27.07.77	5h3	Manchester (C)	16	Jun
21.33	1.7	Robert Tobin	U20	20.12.83	1h1	Portsmouth	11	May
21.34	0.4	Leon Baptiste	U20	23.05.85	1	Nottingham	13	Jul
21.35	0.5	Brian Doyle		12.03.77	3h2	Manchester (C)	16	Jun
21.38	-0.9	Darren Chin	U23	30.06.81	2		24	Aug
21.40 !	1.1	Tim Benjamin	U23	2.05.82	1h3	Bedford	26	May
21.40	0.5	Brendon Ghent		7.09.76	4h2	Manchester (C)	16	Jun
21.41	-0.9	Jon Barbour	U23	3.11.80	1r1	Hayward, USA	6	Apr
21.41	1.9	Dan Donovan		8.10.70	7h1	Birmingham	14	Jul
	(30)							
21.41	0.3	Uvie Ugono		8.03.78	1	London (BP)	14	Aug
21.44	0.0	Adam Charlton	U20	11.05.84	1h1	London (He)	25	Aug
21.46	0.2	Matt Elias		25.04.79	2	Gold Coast (RB), AUS	15	Mar
21.46	1.3	Tim Abeyie	U23	7.11.82	2	Leiden, NED	8	Jun
21.53	-1.5	Rikki Fifton	U20	17.06.85	2	Watford	1	Sep
21.54	-1.6	Chris Stobart	U23	27.03.82	1	Derby	11	Aug
21.55	-0.8	Laurence Oboh	U20	14.05.84	1h4	Watford	2	Jun
21.62	-0.3	Finlay Wright	U23	7.02.81	5	Watford	2	Jun
21.62	0.6	Darren Scott		7.03.69	1	Manchester (Str)	9	Jul
21.63 i		Ben Lewis	U23	6.03.81	2	Birmingham	19	Jan
	(40)							
21.63	1.0	Allan Stuart	U23	14.08.81	3	Namur, BEL	31	Aug
21.64	0.0	Matt Douglas		26.11.76	1	Watford	28	Aug
21.65	-0.3	Solomon Wariso		11.11.66	4	Bedford	4	Jun
21.65	-0.7	Neil Mitchell	U20	25.09.84	1h1	Nottingham	12	Jul
21.65	-0.5	Julian Thomas	U17	28.12.86	1	Nottingham	13	Jul
21.66	0.6	Lawrence Baird		14.12.77	2	Manchester (Str)	9	Jul
21.67 i		Daniel Plummer	U23	4.01.81	2r1	Birmingham	27	Jan

21.72	-1.5	Karl Forde	U20	15.04.83	1	Derby	11	Aug
21.73	-1.1	Chris Tomlinson	U23	15.09.81	1rC	Birmingham	6	Jul
21.73	0.6	Jonathon Oparka	U23	29.01.80	1	Glasgow (S)	14	Jul
	(50)							
21.74	-1.1	Curtis Browne		11.09.75	2rC	Birmingham	6	Jul
21.76	0.8	Darren Wall	U23	6.04.80	1	Portsmouth	11	May
21.77	-0.5	Jamahl Alert-Khan	U17	12.09.86	2	Nottingham	13	Jul
21.77	0.0	Nathan Honour		15.11.77	1	Watford	1	Sep
21.78 i		Paul Whitehouse	U20	10.03.83	2	Birmingham	24	Feb
21.80 i		James Ellington	U17	6.09.85	1	Birmingham	24	Feb
	22.25	-1.4			2s1	Birmingham	11	Aug
21.80	-0.4	Kevin Williams		15.12.71	4r2	Bedford	4	Jun
21.81	0.3	Colin Wilson		30.10.77	2	London (BP)	4	Aug
21.83		Richard Davenport	U17	12.09.85	1	Tamworth	26	Aug
21.85	2.0	Gary Carr	U23	24.09.82	6	Bedford	30	Jun
	(60)							
21.87	0.3	Matthew Thomas		27.04.76	3	London (BP)	14	Aug
21.88	-1.2	Alastair Gordon		16.04.78	4rB	Birmingham	6	Jul
21.89	0.6	Iwan Thomas		5.01.74	4	Gold Coast, AUS	8	Apr
21.89	-1.8	Nick Smith	U23	6.12.82	2	Edinburgh	12	May
21.89	1.6	Adam Rogers	U20	10.04.83	3h1	Bedford	30	Jun
21.90	-0.7	Nick Budden		17.11.75	4	Merksem, BEL	17	Aug
21.93	0.6	Roddy Pitt	U23	4.03.81	2	Glasgow (S)	14	Jul
21.95 i		Steve Surety	U23	18.02.80	3r1	Birmingham	27	Jan
21.95	0.3	Tony Waddington		30.06.75	3	Edinburgh	6	Jul
21.95	0.4	David Riley	U20	25.10.84	3	Nottingham	13	Jul
	(70)							
21.97		Jason Rogers	U20	19.07.84	1	Edinburgh	28	Jul
21.98	-0.3	James Marshall	U23	6.02.81	2	Birmingham	2	Jun
21.99		Peter Vickers	U20	11.06.84	1	Gateshead	25	Aug
21.99	-0.5	Mark McNeill	U23	19.10.82	2	Beveren, BEL	7	Sep
22.00	0.0	Ryan Moseley	U23	8.10.82	1	Watford	24	Jul
22.01	0.8	Dale Garland	U23	13.10.80	2	Portsmouth	11	May
22.03 i		Aaron Aplin	U20	25.11.83	1	Birmingham	19	Jan
	22.15	1.6			4h1	Bedford	30	Jun
22.04	-0.3	Leighton Green		10.01.78	6	Watford	2	Jun
22.05	-0.3	William Pobie		6.12.78	7	Watford	2	Jun
22.05	-0.5	Alex Williams	U17	7.11.85	3	Nottingham	13	Jul
	(80)							
22.06	0.8	Chris Bennett	U23	18.10.80	3	Portsmouth	11	May
22.07 i		Gavin Stephens		12.09.77	1s1	Glasgow	23	Feb
	22.20				1h7	Bedford	5	May
22.07	-0.4	Rob Harle		1.06.79	5	Bedford	6	May
22.07	0.7	Craig Telford		1.06.79	1	Jarrow	1	Jun
22.09		Dwayne Stoddart	U23	29.12.80	2	Watford	24	Aug
22.11 i		James Chatt	U23	11.02.80	2	Glasgow	23	Feb
22.13 i		David Brackstone	U23	13.03.82	3	Glasgow	23	Feb
22.13	1.2	Andrew Watkins	U15	8.12.87	1	Brecon	6	Jul
22.13	-1.0	Ben Hamblin	U17	2.11.85	2h3	Nottingham	12	Jul
22.13	0.4	James Bridge	U20	28.11.83	4	Nottingham	13	Jul
	(90)							
22.13	-1.8	Craig Pickering	U17	16.10.86	2	Birmingham	11	Aug
22.14	-0.5	John Kelley	U20	6.08.84	1	Manchester (C)	26	May
22.15	-0.4	Geoff Dearman		4.08.77	6	Bedford	6	May
22.15	-0.3	Carlos Holder	U17	28.03.86	1	Manchester (C)	25	May
22.16 i		Fabian Collymore	U20	19.10.84	1	Birmingham	13	Jan
22.16	0.2	Warren Prince	U20	18.03.85	1r1	Bedford	4	Jun
22.16	0.6	Richard Workman		31.05.71	3	Manchester (Str)	9	Jul
22.17 i		Richard Rubenis		10.11.73	1r2	Birmingham	27	Jan
22.17	0.2	Nick Thomas		4.04.79	2r1	Bedford	4	Jun
22.17	-0.5	Ryan Scott	U17	20.02.87	4	Nottingham	13	Jul

22.18	0.3	Leon McRae	U23	3.11.80	7	Los Angeles CA, USA	17	Mar
22.18	-2.3	Andy Hughes		10.07.67	1h1	Watford	2	Jun
22.19	2.0	Vincent Bruce	U20	15.04.83	1h2	London (He)	25	Aug
22.20 i		Monu Miah	U20	10.01.84	2h1	Birmingham	13	Jan
22.20		Michael Burslem	U23	1.12.80	3h6	Bedford	5	May
22.20	-0.3	Grenville Field		17.11.77	4	Birmingham	2	Jun

wind assisted

20.18	2.2	Marlon Devonish		(20.19)	1	Birmingham	14	Jul
20.41	2.9				1h2	Birmingham	14	Jul
20.90	3.4				1	Loughborough	18	May
20.26	2.2	Campbell		(20.21)	2	Birmingham	14	Jul
20.73	2.9				2h2	Birmingham	14	Jul
20.29	2.2	Christian Malcolm		(20.30)	3	Birmingham	14	Jul
20.48	2.4	Lambert	U23	(20.37)	1	Riga, LAT	31	May
20.68	2.8				1	Annapolis, USA	12	May
20.76	2.5				1s2	Annapolis, USA	11	May
20.83	2.3				1h3	Annapolis, USA	11	May
20.60	2.2	Dwayne Grant	U23	(20.79)	4	Birmingham	14	Jul
20.83	2.9				3h2	Birmingham	14	Jul
20.98	4.4				1	Kilkenny, IRL	19	May
21.00	2.4				2	Riga, LAT	31	May
20.62	2.2	Julian Golding		(21.02)	5	Birmingham	14	Jul
20.86	4.5	Allyn Condon		(20.90)	1rB	Loughborough	18	May
20.90	2.2	Beasley		(20.76)	6	Birmingham	14	Jul

17 performances to 21.00 by 8 athletes

21.06	3.6	Leon Baptiste	U20	(21.34)	1	Derby	8	Sep
21.06	3.6	Adam Charlton	U20	(21.44)	2	Derby	8	Sep
21.15	3.4	Laurence Oboh	U20	(21.55)	2	Loughborough	18	May
21.17	3.4	Kris Stewart	U23	(21.24)	3	Loughborough	18	May
21.20	4.5	Graham Hedman		(21.24)	3rB	Loughborough	18	May
21.29	4.5	Adrian Patrick		(21.31)	5rB	Loughborough	18	May
21.40	2.9	Alastair Gordon		(21.88)	4h2	Birmingham	14	Jul
21.46	2.1	Leon McRae	U23	(22.18)	2r2	Knoxville TN, USA	28	Apr
21.78	4.3	James Bridge	U20	(22.13)	2	London (He)	25	Aug
21.82	2.3	Craig Pickering	U17	(22.13)	1	Watford	26	May
21.87	3.6	Aaron Aplin	U20	(22.15)	3	Derby	8	Sep
21.92	2.1	Peter Brend		2.02.77	1h1	Portsmouth	11	May
21.92	3.6	Jahmaine Merchant	U20	3.08.83	4	Derby	8	Sep
21.94	3.6	Adebowale Ademuyewo	U20	14.05.83	5	Derby	8	Sep
21.98	3.6	Alex Animashaun	U20	23.07.85	6	Derby	8	Sep
22.04	2.4	Craig Yates	U20	9.02.83	1	Cudworth	25	Aug
22.07	2.7	Daniel Roberts	U20	29.11.84	2	Watford	25	May
22.07	2.8	Martin Davolls	U20	2.09.83	2rB	Derby	8	Sep
22.08	2.7	Vincent Bruce	U20	(22.19)	3	Watford	25	May
22.08	3.5	Michael Smith		3.06.79	2	Cudworth	25	Aug
22.08	4.3	James Nicol	U20	3.06.85	3	London (He)	25	Aug
22.08		Wade Bennett-Jackson	U17	27.02.87	1	Crawley	26	Aug
22.12	2.3	James Ellington	U17	(21.80i)	3	Watford	26	May
22.14	3.5	Martin Bradbury	U23	20.10.82	3	Cudworth	25	Aug
22.18	2.7	Neil Simpson	U20	11.09.83	4	Watford	25	May

hand timing

21.1		Brian Doyle		(21.35)	1	Stellenbosch, RSA	16	Feb
21.3	-0.7	Daniel Plummer	U23	(21.67i)	1	Basildon	12	May
21.3 w	4.1	Brendon Ghent		(21.40)	1	Stoke-on-Trent	21	Jul
21.3 w?		Du'aine Thorne-Ladejo		14.02.71	2	Wigan	31	Aug
21.5	-0.5	Mark Hylton		24.09.76	2	Wigan	7	Jul

21.5		David Brackstone	U23	(22.13i)	1	Sheffield (W)	31 Aug
21.5 w	2.3	Nick Smith	U23	(21.89)	2	London (He)	21 Jul
21.6	1.4				2rB	Watford	19 May
21.5 w?		Neil Mitchell	U20	(21.65)	1	Nuneaton	28 Jul
21.5 w?		Darren Scott		(21.62)	3	Wigan	31 Aug
21.6		Ian Mackie		27.02.75	1	Grangemouth	28 Apr
21.6		Alex Hall	U23	2.02.82	1	Bournemouth	8 Jun
21.6		Gary Carr	U23	(21.85)	1	Ashford	3 Aug
21.6		Michael Smith		(22.08w)	1	Blackpool	3 Aug
21.6		Gavin Eastman	U23	28.06.80	1rB	Derby	4 Aug
21.6 w?		Colin Wilson		(21.81)	4	Wigan	31 Aug
21.7	1.1	Daniel Money		17.10.76	3h3	Bedford	26 May
21.7		Matthew Thomas		(21.87)	1	London (FP)	25 Aug
21.7 w	2.3	Mark Brown		3.11.76	3	London (He)	21 Jul
22.0					3rB	Wigan	31 Aug
21.7 w	4.7	Andy Wilkinson		4.01.79	1	Stoke-on-Trent	21 Jul
21.8		Clive Turner	U20	24.11.84	1	London (ME)	11 May
21.8		Peter Brend		(21.92w)	2	Derby	4 Aug
21.8		Gary Jones		6.01.72	2	London (FP)	25 Aug
21.8		Kevin Ellis		18.06.76	2rB	Wigan	31 Aug
21.8 w		Richard Davenport	U17	(21.83)	1	Bournemouth	22 Jun
21.9		Mike Groves	U20	21.03.84	1	Aberdare	28 Apr
21.9		Sean Baldock		3.12.76	1	Crawley	1 May
21.9		Warren Prince	U20	(22.16)	1	Luton	12 May
21.9		Brian Darby		14.10.72	1	Sutton Coldfield	12 May
21.9		John Kelley	U20	(22.14)	1	Banbury	19 May
21.9		Andrew Whitmore	U20	8.02.85	1	Luton	8 Jun
21.9		Rob Harle		(22.07)	1	London (TB)	22 Jun
21.9	0.5	Andy Hughes		(22.18)	1	Watford	3 Jul
21.9		Nic Andrews	U23	3.10.81	2	Street	4 Aug
21.9		Adam Potter	U23	12.04.80	1	Street	4 Aug
22.0		Louis Burgess	U20	21.03.83	1	Hilversum, NED	30 Mar
22.0		Matthew Russell	U23	20.01.81	1	Chelmsford	1 Apr
22.0		Alex Riley	U20	17.09.83	1	Loughborough	2 May
22.0	1.1	Geoff Dearman		(22.15)	2h5	Bedford	5 May
22.0		Nick Thomas		(22.17)	1	London (Nh)	5 May
22.0		Tim Ward	U23	27.05.82	2h6	Bedford	5 May
22.0	0.3	Philip Octave		12.06.78	3	London (ME)	11 May
22.0		David Naismith		15.12.79	1	Nottingham	12 May
22.0		Scott Herbert		12.02.74	1	Par	19 May
22.0		Craig Telford		(22.07)	1	Gateshead	8 Jun
22.0		Aaron Aplin	U20	(22.15)	1	Scunthorpe	23 Jun
22.0		Andrew Matthews	U20	26.10.84	1	Eton	28 Jul
22.0		Daniel Cossins	U20	22.12.84	1	London (WP)	3 Aug
22.0		Conrad Williams	U23	20.03.82		London (Cat)	24 Aug
22.0		Ian Horsburgh		10.01.78	2rB	Sheffield (W)	31 Aug
22.0		Dwayne Stoddart	U23	(22.09)	1rB	Watford	31 Aug
22.0		James Bridge	U20	(22.13)	1	London (Ha)	15 Sep
22.0 w		Wade Bennett-Jackson	U17	(22.08w)	1	Sandown IOW	18 Sep

Additional Under 17 (1 - 10 above)

22.05	-0.5	Alex Williams		7.11.85	3	Nottingham	13 Jul
22.08 w		Wade Bennett-Jackson		(22.0w)	1	Crawley	26 Aug
22.32	-0.4				1	Kingston	4 Aug
22.13	-1.8	Craig Pickering		(21.82w)	2	Birmingham	11 Aug
22.1		Simon Toye		24.09.85	1	Southend	6 May

22.1		Simon Farenden		6.10.85	1	Hull	8 Jun
22.1		Ryan Scott		20.02.87	1	Yate	23 Jun
22.17	-0.5				4	Nottingham	13 Jul
22.1	1.1	Paul Judson		20.06.86	1rB	Watford	31 Aug
22.31 w 2.8					3rB	Derby	8 Sep
22.34	0.0				2	Birmingham	1 Sep
22.13	1.2	Andrew Watkins	U15	8.12.87	1	Brecon	6 Jul
22.13	-1.0	Ben Hamblin		2.11.85	2h3	Nottingham	12 Jul
22.15	-0.3	Carlos Holder		28.03.86	1	Manchester (C)	25 May
22.21	1.0	Jamie Gill		29.10.85	2	Birmingham	26 May
22.22	-0.5	Ben Higgins		27.09.86	6	Nottingham	13 Jul
(20)							
22.24	-0.3	Dean Daniel		12.04.87	2	Manchester (C)	25 May
22.25	1.1	Calvin McLaggon		13.11.85	1	Brecon	6 Jul
22.25	-1.4	James Ellington		(21.80i)	2s1	Birmingham	11 Aug
22.28	-0.3	Danny Whittaker		10.01.86	3	Manchester (C)	25 May
22.3		Nick Leavey		27.08.86	1	Ashford	28 Jul
22.35	-0.3	Michael Coupland		5.01.86	4	Manchester (C)	25 May
22.4		Victor Barzey		10.01.86	1	London (CP)	7 Apr
22.4		Kevin Fry		28.12.85	2	Bournemouth	22 Jun
22.4		Ben Samuels			2	Hoo	18 Aug
22.44 w 3.9		Dwayne Bovell		2.12.85		Crawley	26 Aug
22.48	-1.3	Alan Selby		2.07.86	3h2	Nottingham	12 Jul
(30)							
22.5		Daniel Topliss		8.10.85	1	Nottingham	7 Apr
22.5		Sam Huggins		30.11.85	2	Southend	6 May
22.5		Richard Abrahams		14.09.85	1	London (PH)	2 Jun
22.5		Nathan Stevens		7.08.86	3	St. Peter Port, Gue	15 Sep
22.5		Setonsi Osho		28.09.86	2	Sandown IOW	18 Sep

Additional Under 15 (1 above)

22.8 w		Alex Nelson		21.03.88	1	Worcester	5 May
23.07	0.8				2	Birmingham	1 Sep
22.93	0.4	David Hurst		25.10.87	1s3	Nottingham	13 Jul
22.99	-1.4	James Sinclair		22.10.87	2	Nottingham	13 Jul
23.0		Chris Julien		14.09.87	1	London (ME)	11 May
23.10	0.8				3	Birmingham	1 Sep
23.0		Tasham Christian		6.10.87	1	Ware	4 Aug
23.18	0.8				2	Birmingham	11 Aug
23.11	0.4	Joshua Butterworth		21.04.88	2s3	Nottingham	13 Jul
23.15	-0.8	Sam Kavanagh		1.11.87	1rB	Birmingham	1 Sep
23.17		Lewis Robson		9.01.88	2	Gateshead	24 Aug
23.30		Tom Rayner		26.01.88	2	Manchester (C)	25 May
(10)							
23.3		Daniel Davis		12.12.87	2	London (CP)	7 Apr
23.45	1.6				1h1	Kingston	12 May
23.3		Miles Marshall		20.02.88	2	London (CP)	7 Apr
23.32	0.9				1	Kingston	12 May
23.3		Gavin Comber		28.05.88	1	Tonbridge	6 Aug
23.3 w		Stephen Prosser		24.10.87	1	Crawley	31 Mar
23.34	0.8	Paul Crawford		4.10.87	4	Birmingham	1 Sep
23.4		Harry Akines-Aryeety		29.08.88	2	London (TB)	19 May
23.4		Joelle Powell		2.03.88	1	Abingdon	8 Sep
23.4		Adam Daish		27.10.87	1	Bedford	15 Sep
23.45	1.3				2	London (He)	25 Aug
23.42	0.8	Dom Parsons		8.09.87	4	Birmingham	11 Aug
23.44	0.4	Jeli Ogunbowale		8.01.88	3s3	Nottingham	13 Jul
(20)							
23.45	0.2	Ricky Harris		8.02.88	4s1	Nottingham	13 Jul
23.5		Nick Wilding		11.11.87	1rB	Sutton Coldfield	19 May
23.52		Daniel Maynard		4.12.87	1	Tamworth	26 Aug

23.52	-0.8	Kyle Cashin		11.10.87	2rB	Birmingham	1	Sep
23.55	0.4	Des Bowden		13.01.88	4s3	Nottingham	13	Jul
23.59	-1.4	Nick Kanonik		24.10.87	1h3	Nottingham	12	Jul
23.59	0.4	Ricardo Francis		26.11.88	5s3	Nottingham	13	Jul

Under 13

24.8 w?		Precious Ojighoro		27.12.89	1	Kingston	28	Jul
25.0		Juan De Leon-Padmore		1.04.90	1	Telford	21	Jul
25.18 w	2.3	Yusuf Aliu		10.01.90	1	Birmingham	31	Aug
25.7					1	Mandale	21	Jul
25.6		James Pilkington		21.10.89	1	Bury St. Edmunds	22	Sep
25.7		Chris Clarke		25.01.90	1	Bedford	15	Sep
25.7		Sam Boxall		5.12.89	2	Bury St. Edmunds	22	Sep
25.9		Edward Chan			1	Birmingham	1	Sep
26.0		Joshua Fogg		13.10.89	1	Barnsley	21	Jul
26.0		Michael Weekes		17.11.89	1	Bedford	18	Aug
26.1		Luke Smith		7.11.89	1	Hereford	2	Jun
	(10)							
26.3	1.2	Tony Corrigan		24.09.90	2	Birmingham	1	Sep
26.4		Christian Booker		29.06.90	1	Sutton Coldfield	19	May
26.4		Daryl Mccarthey		6.09.89	1	Chelmsford	15	Jun
26.4		James Alaka		8.09.89	1	Ashton-U-Lyne	21	Jul
26.4		James Farmer		10.02.90	2	Kingston	28	Jul
26.4		David Paar		28.09.89	3	Bedford	15	Sep

Foreign

20.59 w	2.1	*Paul Brizzel (IRL)*		*3.10.76*	*1*	*Dublin (S), IRL*	*13*	*Jul*
20.72	*0.3*				*2*	*Bangor, NI*	*21*	*Jul*
20.81	*0.2*	*Paul McKee (IRL)*		*15.10.77*	*1rB*	*Bangor, NI*	*21*	*Jul*
21.34 w		*John McAdorey (IRL)*		*16.09.74*	*1rC*	*Kilkenny, IRL*	*19*	*May*
21.5 w		*Gilbert Opiyo (KEN)*	*U23*	*19.12.81*	*1*	*Gloucester*	*22*	*Jun*
21.70	*2.0*				*4*	*Bedford*	*30*	*Jun*
21.81 w	*3.5*	*Jonathan Carleton (IRL)*		*4.11.79*	*2h1*	*Belfast*	*8*	*Jun*
21.9	*1.2*	*Joselyn Thomas (SLE)*		*11.07.71*	*1rB*	*Loughborough*	*22*	*May*
22.11					*1*	*Aldershot*	*10*	*Jul*
21.92 w	*4.1*	*Liam McDermid (IRL)*	*U20*	*23.11.84*	*3rB*	*Kilkenny, IRL*	*19*	*May*
22.08 i					*2s2*	*Glasgow*	*19*	*Jan*
22.0	*0.3*	*Matthew Marraud*	*U23*	*15.01.82*	*1*	*London (ME)*	*11*	*May*

300 Metres

32.5	Chris Rawlinson		19.05.72	1	Azusa, USA	13	Apr
32.61	Tim Benjamin	U23	2.05.82	1	Gothenburg, SWE	27	Aug
33.13	Matt Elias		25.04.79	1	Gold Coast (S), AUS	23	Apr
33.7	Jared Deacon		15.10.75	1	Gateshead	18	Apr
33.77	Iwan Thomas		5.01.74	2	Gold Coast, AUS	23	Apr
34.14	Nick Budden		17.11.75	1	Loughborough	17	Jul
34.45	Conrad Williams	U23	20.03.82	1	Kingston	17	Mar
34.5	Adam Charlton	U20	11.05.84	1	Peterborough	7	Apr
34.58 i	Steve Surety	U23	18.02.80	2r1	Birmingham	22	Jan
34.69 i	Simon Plaskett		9.04.79	1r2	Birmingham	22	Jan
	(10)						
34.7	Andrew Steele	U20	19.09.84	1	Manchester (Str)	27	Mar
34.7	Robert Lewis		2.09.78	1	Southampton	8	Sep

intermediate time

32.7 i+	Daniel Caines		15.05.79	1m	Birmingham	17	Feb

Foreign

34.5	*Paul McKee (IRL)*		*15.10.77*	*1*	*Bangor, NI*	*20*	*Apr*

400 Metres

44.98	Daniel Caines		15.05.79	1s2	Manchester (C)	27	Jul
	45.13			4	Manchester (C)	28	Jul
	45.14			1	Annecy, FRA	22	Jun
	45.28			3	Munich, GER	8	Aug
	45.30			1h3	Manchester (C)	15	Jun
	45.32			1	Manchester (C)	16	Jun
	45.35			1s1	Munich, GER	7	Aug
	45.39			2	Seville, ESP	8	Jun
	45.60			4	London (CP)	23	Aug
	45.67			1	Sheffield	30	Jun
	46.06 i			1	Birmingham	17	Feb
	46.06			2h4	Munich, GER	6	Aug
	46.11			2q4	Manchester (C)	26	Jul
	46.35 i			1	Stockholm, SWE	6	Feb
	46.45 i			1	Glasgow	9	Mar
	46.50 i			2	Lievin, FRA	24	Feb
45.57	Jared Deacon		15.10.75	2	Manchester (C)	16	Jun
	45.84			1h2	Manchester (C)	15	Jun
	45.89			3	Birmingham	14	Jul
	45.96			2	Tartu, EST	2	Jun
	46.05			1s1	Birmingham	13	Jul
	46.07			8s1	Manchester (C)	27	Jul
	46.13			2	Riga, LAT	31	May
	46.38			1	Gateshead	11	May
	46.46			3	Glasgow (S)	18	Aug
45.71	Sean Baldock		3.12.76	6s1	Manchester (C)	27	Jul
	45.84			2	Birmingham	14	Jul
	45.92			1	Birmingham	6	Jul
	45.96			1s2	Birmingham	13	Jul
	46.02			3h1	Manchester (C)	26	Jul
	46.03			1h1	Manchester (C)	15	Jun
	46.26			3q3	Manchester (C)	26	Jul
	46.47			3	Manchester (C)	16	Jun
	46.5			1	Azusa, USA	13	Apr
45.73	Tim Benjamin	U23	2.05.82	1	Birmingham	14	Jul
	45.80			7	Madrid, ESP	20	Sep
	45.89			7s2	Manchester (C)	27	Jul
	46.07			3s2	Munich, GER	7	Aug
	46.15			3h2	Munich, GER	6	Aug
	46.28			2s2	Birmingham	13	Jul
	46.30			2	Rehlingen, GER	20	May
	46.39			1	Barcelona, ESP	6	Sep
46.01	Jamie Baulch		3.05.73	4	Hamburg, GER	12	Jun
	46.36			4s1	Birmingham	13	Jul
	46.42			5	Birmingham	14	Jul
	46.47			1h4	Manchester (C)	15	Jun
46.03	Chris Rawlinson		19.05.72	1	Lisbon, POR	25	May
	46.13			1	Loughborough	18	May
	46.16			1	Athens, GRE	11	May
46.05	Du'aine Thorne-Ladejo		14.02.71	2s1	Birmingham	13	Jul
	46.23			4	Birmingham	14	Jul
	46.37 A			2rB	Pretoria, RSA	12	Apr
	46.46			3	Bangor, NI	21	Jul
	46.49			1	Bedford	17	Aug
46.18	Mark Hylton		24.09.76	3s1	Birmingham	13	Jul
	46.35			2	Bedford	4	Jun
	46.42			1	Bedford	25	May
	46.49			6	Birmingham	14	Jul

46.37	Graham Hedman		6.02.79	2	Birmingham	6	Jul
46.39				2h3	Manchester (C)	15	Jun
46.46	Cori Henry		9.12.76	1	Birmingham	1	Jun
46.50				2	Bedford	25	May
(10)							
46.48	Iwan Thomas		5.01.74	3	Birmingham	6	Jul
63 performances to 46.5 by 11 athletes including 4 indoors							
46.59	Matt Elias		25.04.79	1	Newport	8	Jun
46.80 i	Robert Tobin	U20	20.12.83	2	Birmingham	24	Feb
46.80				2h4	Manchester (C)	15	Jun
46.86	Mark Brown		3.11.76	5	Birmingham	6	Jul
46.9	Peter Brend		2.02.77	1	Derby	4	Aug
46.94				3	Bedford	25	May
47.12	David Naismith		15.12.79	2h1	Manchester (C)	15	Jun
47.13 A	Ruben Tabares		22.10.78	5rB	Pretoria, RSA	12	Apr
48.02				4	Loughborough	18	May
47.13	Simon Plaskett		9.04.79	4h3	Manchester (C)	15	Jun
47.19	Allan Stuart	U23	14.08.81	5h3	Manchester (C)	15	Jun
47.21	Paul Slythe		5.09.74	1	London (He)	3	Aug
(20)							
47.24	Adam Charlton	U20	11.05.84	1	Belgrade, YUG	21	Sep
47.29	Richard Davenport	U17	12.09.85	1	Birmingham	25	May
47.3	Andre Fernandez	U23	2.03.80	2	Wigan	7	Jul
47.65				2	Ashford	18	Aug
47.35	Ian Lowthian	U23	10.10.80	3h2	Manchester (C)	15	Jun
47.36	Andrew Steele	U20	19.09.84	1	Manchester (C)	25	May
47.38	Jonathan Edwards		6.11.78	1	Bedford	6	May
47.4	Matt Douglas		26.11.76	1	Watford	4	Sep
47.41	Geoff Dearman		4.08.77	6s2	Birmingham	13	Jul
47.46	Alastair Gordon		16.04.78	1	Crawley	12	May
47.48	Conrad Williams	U23	20.03.82	1	Ashford	18	Aug
(30)							
47.52	Steve Surety	U23	18.02.80	1	Watford	31	Jul
47.61	Sam Ellis	U23	23.06.82	2	Bedford	6	May
47.61	Adrian Patrick		15.06.73	3	Watford	2	Jun
47.65 i	James Chatt	U23	11.02.80	1	Birmingham	27	Jan
47.92				4h2	Manchester (C)	15	Jun
47.68	Craig Yates	U20	9.02.83	2	Manchester (C)	25	May
47.69	Andy Wilkinson		4.01.79	7s2	Birmingham	13	Jul
47.72	Richard Workman		31.05.71	2	Jarrow	1	Jun
47.76	Tim Bayley	U23	4.10.81	1h4	Watford	1	Jun
47.80	Dale Garland	U23	13.10.80	1D1	Manchester (C)	27	Jul
47.85	Louis Burgess	U20	21.03.83	3	Ashford	18	Aug
(40)							
47.90	Bradley Yiend	U23	25.10.80	3	Bedford	6	May
47.9	Liam Collins		23.10.78	1	Loughborough	27	Apr
47.9	Martyn Morant		26.06.78	1	Bath	12	May
48.67				5	Watford	19	May
48.0	Russell Nicholls	U20	8.03.83	2rB	Bedford	4	Jun
48.06				2	Watford	26	May
48.0	Alloy Wilson	U23	25.01.80	2	Derby	11	Aug
48.21				3	Newport	20	Jul
48.01	Ryan Palmer	U20	21.06.83	3	Manchester (C)	25	May
48.10	Sandy Scott		1.09.76	4	Bedford	6	May
48.1	Nic Andrews	U23	3.10.81	1	Bournemouth	28	Apr
48.1	Wayne Martin		12.08.76	3rB	Watford	19	May
48.48				2h3	Watford	1	Jun
48.1	David Brackstone	U23	13.03.82	1	Luton	3	Aug
(50)							
48.1	Richard Smith	U23	12.10.82	1	Gateshead	25	Aug
48.13	Simon Toye	U17	24.09.85	1	Nottingham	13	Jul

48.14 i	Lawrence Baird		14.12.77	2	Birmingham	13	Jan
48.25				1rB	Birmingham	6	Jul
48.30	Ian Deeth		25.06.79	2h4	Watford	1	Jun
48.3	Rhys Williams	U20	27.02.84	1	Cheltenham	6	May
49.22				1	Newport	8	Jun
48.3	Simon Lees		19.11.79	1	Sutton Coldfield	11	May
48.3	Tom Nimmo		9.05.71	1rB	Cardiff	19	May
48.3	Darren Eldin	U23	10.04.82	2	Manchester (Str)	25	Jun
48.52				2h2	Bedford	29	Jun
48.31	Gavin Dublin	U20	5.10.83	2	Nottingham	13	Jul
48.32	Steve Green	U20	15.01.83	1	Oxford	18	May
(60)							
48.33	Andrew Bennett	U23	30.09.82	2rB	London (He)	3	Aug
48.35 i	Nick Budden		17.11.75	1	Birmingham	20	Jan
48.53				3h4	Birmingham	12	Jul
48.35	James McIlroy		30.12.76	4rB	Bangor, NI	21	Jul
48.37	Philip Taylor	U20	20.03.85	4	Manchester (C)	25	May
48.38	Oliver Teasel	U20	24.04.84	2h1	Manchester (C)	25	May
48.39	Adam Potter	U23	12.04.80	1	Beveren, BEL	7	Sep
48.50	Neil Jennings		18.09.77	4	Watford	19	May
48.5	James Davies	U23	5.12.82	1	Wakefield	21	Apr
48.5	Tony Draper		23.04.74	1	London (CP)	11	May
48.5	Adam Rogers	U20	10.04.83	1	Hexham	6	Jul
(70)							
48.5	Richard Rubenis		10.11.73	1	Telford	6	Jul
48.5	Ricky Soos	U20	28.06.83	1	Grantham	18	Aug
48.68				2	Birmingham	25	May
48.54 i	Tony Borsumato		13.12.73	4r1	Erfurt,GER	1	Feb
48.55	Brian Darby		14.10.72	5h1	Birmingham	12	Jul
48.57	Richard McDonald	U23	11.01.80	1r1	Stanford, USA	29	Mar
48.7	Scott McDiarmid	U23	15.11.80	1	Glasgow	3	Sep
48.73	Noel Levy		22.06.75	5	Bedford	17	Aug
48.74	Darrell Maynard	V40	21.08.61	2	Potsdam, GER	21	Aug
48.8	Mark O'Neill	U23		2	Yate	8	Jun
48.93				3h2	Bedford	29	Jun
48.81	Darryn Campbell	U23	14.07.82	1	Portsmouth	11	May
(80)							
48.86 i	Leon McRae	U23	3.11.80	1r7	Blacksburg, USA	19	Jan
48.87	Dedan Simmons	U20	9.04.83	2h1	Bedford	29	Jun
48.9	Stuart Marshall	U23	2.12.80	2	Telford	6	Jul
48.9	Michael Rimmer	U17	3.02.86	1	Derby	3	Aug
48.9	Martin Bradbury	U23	20.10.82	1	Sheffield (W)	31	Aug
48.91 i	Eddie Williams		1.10.70	4	Birmingham	12	Jan
48.95	Victor Barzey	U17	10.01.86	3	Nottingham	13	Jul
48.96	Nick Leavey	U17	27.08.86	2	Birmingham	11	Aug
49.00	Matt Menlove		20.12.79	1	Basildon	11	May
49.0	Michael Parper		20.05.78	2	Kingston	12	May
(90)							
49.0	Chris Bennett	U23	18.10.80	3	Bedford	19	May
49.0	Lee Notman		14.10.75	1	Coatbridge	2	Jun
49.0	Curtis Robb		7.06.72	2	Chelmsford	6	Jul
49.0	David Pratt		23.11.75	5	Wigan	7	Jul
49.09				2	Newport	8	Jun
49.01	Chris Page	U23	13.11.80	1		29	Mar
49.01	David Creak	U20	30.08.83	3h4	Watford	1	Jun
49.04 i	Adam Buckley	U23	6.12.80	6	Birmingham	12	Jan
49.05	Carl McEwan	U23	9.04.81	7	Bedford	6	May
49.10	Grenville Field		17.11.77	1	Edinburgh	6	Jul
49.1	Ian Palmer	U23	22.11.81	1	Bournemouth	11	May
(100)							
49.1	James Nasrat	U20	10.01.83	1	Newport	12	May

49.1	Lea Farmer	U23	22.01.80	2	Cardiff	18 May
49.1	Ahmed Al-Kowarri		30.11.78	1	Aberdeen	4 Aug
49.14 i	Hugh Kerr		4.01.76	1	Glasgow	23 Jan
49.15	Jason Rogers	U20	19.07.84	1	Grangemouth	25 May
49.17	Daniel Brandwood	U23	1.10.82	D	London (He)	10 Aug
49.17	Richard Buck	U17	14.11.86	3	Birmingham	11 Aug
49.18	Stephen Murphy	U23	10.02.82	1	Edinburgh	22 May

Additional Under 20 (1 - 18 above)

49.20	Robert Smith		3.03.85	4	Nottingham	13 Jul
49.2	Darren St.Clair		6.04.85	1	London (ME)	11 May
	49.25			2	London (He)	25 Aug
	(20)					
49.3	Stuart Wenden		21.01.84	1	London (CP)	12 May
	49.35			5	Nottingham	13 Jul
49.36	Richard Sheeran	U17	27.11.85	5	Derby	8 Sep
49.39	Kassim Riley		9.08.84	1rB	Derby	8 Sep
49.41	Dan Bray		6.09.83	2	Derby	8 Sep

Additional Under 17 (1 - 7 above)

49.51	Richard Parry		23.05.86	4	Birmingham	11 Aug
49.70	David Proctor		22.10.85	2	Manchester (C)	26 May
49.70	Ryan Thomas		21.03.87	3	Kingston	4 Aug
	(10)					
49.75	Richard Yates		26.01.86	1h2	Nottingham	12 Jul
49.84	Robert Lightfoot		7.09.85		Glasgow (S)	20 Jul
49.90	Tom Chapman		29.12.85	4s3	Nottingham	12 Jul
49.9	Andrae Davis		27.09.85	1	London (WF)	2 Jun
	50.18			2	Basildon	11 May
49.94	Craig Stewart		24.11.85	1	Edinburgh	12 May
49.95	Craig Glanville		21.09.86	1h4	Nottingham	12 Jul
50.07	Lee Waters		1.06.86	2h4	Nottingham	12 Jul
50.09	Neil Gray		16.03.86	1	Glasgow	20 Jul
50.21	Peter Warke		22.05.86	2h1	Birmingham	10 Aug
50.27	Richard Strachan		18.11.86	5	Manchester (Str)	23 Jul
	(20)					
50.44	Wayne Booth		12.10.85	3h4	Nottingham	12 Jul
50.5	Nathan Stevens		7.08.86	2	St. Peter Port, Gue	15 Sep
	50.94			3h5	Nottingham	12 Jul
50.6	Ricki Glover		2.11.85	2	Corby	12 May
50.6	Moyo Sankofa		12.12.86	4	Watford	14 Sep
	50.86			8	Birmingham	11 Aug
50.61	Chris Campbell		13.04.86	1	Gateshead	11 May
50.67	Paul Judson		20.06.86	3rB	Derby	8 Sep
50.85	Thomas Franks		8.11.85	4	Birmingham	25 May
50.89	Michael Prosser		11.10.86	5h4	Nottingham	12 Jul
50.9	Steven Gregg		27.06.87	2	Hull	8 Jun
	51.08			2h1	Nottingham	12 Jul
50.9	Richard Gadd		30.07.86	1	Bury St. Edmunds	4 Aug
	(30)					
50.95	Ashley Bayliss		14.01.86	1	Newport	8 Jun
50.97	Lewis Robson	U15	9.01.88	1	Nottingham	13 Jul
50.98	David Vass		31.12.85	5s2	Nottingham	12 Jul
51.0	Ben Green		14.08.86	1	Bury	21 Jul
51.0	Sean Foster		10.11.86	2	Ipswich	28 Jul

Additional Under 15 (1 above)

51.94	Andrew Kelly		15.11.87	2	Nottingham	13 Jul
52.06	Kris Robertson		9.09.87	1	Birmingham	10 Aug
52.1	Andrew Watkins		8.12.87	1	Barry	12 May
52.20	Arran Topham		25.06.88	1h1	Nottingham	12 Jul
52.21	Sam Kavanagh		1.11.87	3	Birmingham	1 Sep

52.3	Andrew Walcott		6.01.88	1	Sutton Coldfield	19	May
53.18				4h3	Nottingham	12	Jul
52.3	Dom Parsons		8.09.87	1	Woodford	21	Jul
52.46				4s1	Nottingham	12	Jul
52.43	Ben Beasley		25.02.88	3s1	Nottingham	12	Jul
52.49	David Nelson		18.09.87	1h3	Nottingham	12	Jul
(10)							
52.49	Thomas Hockedy		20.11.87	5s1	Nottingham	12	Jul
52.51	Bruce Tasker		2.09.87	1	Newport	8	Jun
52.52	Wayne Taylor		17.10.87	1s2	Nottingham	12	Jul
52.56	Martyn Gibbons		7.09.87	1	Birmingham	25	May
52.90	Sean Brindley		1.01.88	3h3	Nottingham	12	Jul
53.08	Sean McQueen		28.02.88	2h1	Birmingham	10	Aug
53.2	Neil Crossley		15.04.88	1	Bournemouth	22	Jun
53.36				4s2	Nottingham	12	Jul
53.32	Daniel Spuffard		6.09.87	3h2	Nottingham	12	Jul
53.4	Sam Kissi		16.02.88	1	Brighton	21	Jul
53.50	Scott Partyka		19.03.88	4h1	Birmingham	10	Aug
(20)							
53.50	Stephen Tidy		14.10.87	2	London (He)	25	Aug
53.52	Kelvin Wilson		7.05.88	4	Birmingham	1	Sep
53.6	Robert Bates		29.10.87	2	Birmingham	15	Jun
53.67	Ross Owen		16.11.87	1h2	London (He)	25	Aug
53.7	Chris Larner		20.01.88	1	Bath	18	Aug

Under 13

60.1	Issac Harland		9.11.89	1	Hoo	2	Jun
60.7	Nathan Woodward		17.10.89	1	Loughborough	10	Jul
60.8	Tom Nightingale		23.12.89	1	Bury St. Edmunds	4	Aug
61.2	Matthew Lumm			1	Bedford	15	Sep
61.2	Douglas Hunt		3.12.89	1rB	Watford	18	Sep
61.6	Declan Murray		13.07.90	1	Macclesfield	17	Jul
61.63	Alexander Blair		23.11.89	1	Grangemouth	1	May
62.0	Mike Cole		1.12.89	2	Braunton	7	Jul
62.3	James Alaka		8.09.89	2	Bromley	9	Jun
62.4	O. Short			1	Leicester	15	Jun

Foreign

45.58	*Paul McKee (IRL)*		*15.10.77*	*1*	*Dublin, IRL*	*14*	*Jul*
47.28	*Oliver Jean-Theodore (FRA)*		*13.11.74*	*6*	*Birmingham*	*6*	*Jul*
47.99 i	*Kemel Thompson (JAM)*		*25.09.74*	*1*	*Glasgow*	*24*	*Feb*
48.1				*1*	*Wigan*	*31*	*Aug*
49.38	*Liam McDermid (IRL)*	*U20*	*23.11.84*	*1*	*Edinburgh*	*11*	*May*

600 Metres

1:18.42	Richard Davenport	U17	12.09.85	1	Watford	28	Aug
1:36.8	Lewis Denton	U13	17.10.89	1	Crawley	23	Jul

800 Metres

1:45.52	James McIlroy		30.12.76	2	Rovereto, ITA	28	Aug
1:46.40				7	London (CP)	23	Aug
1:46.88				1	Cork, IRL	6	Jul
1:46.93				3s1	Manchester (C)	28	Jul
1:47.35				5	Kalamata, GRE	1	Jun
1:47.67				4h3	Munich, GER	9	Aug
1:47.69				1	Eton	3	Jul
1:47.77				6	Manchester (C)	29	Jul
1:48.11				4	Lisbon, POR	15	Jun
1:48.43				8	Madrid, ESP	21	Sep
1:46.23 A	Anthony Whiteman		13.11.71	2	Pretoria, RSA	12	Apr
1:47.7				1	London (He)	8	Jun
1:48.81				9	Cape Town, RSA	19	Apr

1:46.72	Matt Shone		10.07.75	4	Cape Town, RSA	19	Apr
1:46.92	Neil Speaight		9.09.78	2	Dublin (S), IRL	19	Jul
	1:47.22			5s2	Manchester (C)	28	Jul
	1:47.35			9	London (CP)	23	Aug
	1:47.37 A			5	Pretoria, RSA	12	Apr
	1:47.61			4	Watford	14	Aug
	1:48.25			2	Lisbon, POR	26	May
	1:48.48			2	Manchester (C)	16	Jun
	1:48.57			1=h3	Manchester (C)	15	Jun
	1:48.91 A			5	Germiston, RSA	5	Apr
1:47.18	Ricky Soos	U20	28.06.83	3	Watford	14	Aug
	1:47.22			2	Watford	31	Jul
	1:48.04			10	London (CP)	23	Aug
	1:48.10			2	Loughborough	18	May
	1:48.17			2	Solihull	22	Jun
	1:48.44			1	Manchester (Str)	6	Aug
	1:48.72			5	Manchester (C)	16	Jun
	1:48.82			2h2	Kingston, JAM	16	Jul
1:47.60	Simon Lees		19.11.79	1	Loughborough	18	May
	1:47.62			1rB	Walnut CA, USA	21	Apr
	1:47.83			1	Manchester (Wy)	3	Jun
	1:47.89			1	Manchester (C)	16	Jun
	1:48.43			5	Annecy, FRA	23	Jun
1:47.82	Joe Kidger	U23	16.03.80	5	Watford	14	Aug
	1:48.12			6s1	Manchester (C)	28	Jul
	1:48.16			3	Manchester (Wy)	3	Jun
	1:48.25			2	Bedford	6	May
	1:48.40			5	Loughborough	18	May
	1:48.69			4	Manchester (C)	16	Jun
1:48.01	Chris Moss		17.06.79	6	Watford	14	Aug
1:48.09	Alasdair Donaldson		21.06.77	2	Manchester (Wy)	3	Jun
	1:48.13			3	Loughborough	18	May
1:48.14 i	Chris Mulvaney	U23	25.05.81	2	Fayetteville AR, USA	24	Feb
	1:48.45 i			1	Fayetteville AR, USA	18	Jan
	1:48.56			1h3	Starkville MS, USA	10	May
(10)							
1:48.17	Tom Mayo		2.05.77	7	Watford	14	Aug
1:48.30	Mike East		20.01.78	4	Loughborough	18	May
1:48.50	Curtis Robb		7.06.72	3	Manchester (C)	16	Jun
	1:48.57			1=h3	Manchester (C)	15	Jun
1:48.82	Angus Maclean	U23	20.09.80	2	Newport	20	Jul
1:48.83	Sam Ellis	U23	23.06.82	8	Watford	14	Aug
1:48.85	Chris Bolt	U23	21.09.80	4	Watford	31	Jul
1:48.91	Raymond Adams	U23	5.11.81	4	Manchester (Wy)	3	Jun
1:48.93	Gregg Taylor		1.08.77	5	Watford	31	Jul
	57 performances to 1:49.00 by 18 athletes including 2 indoors						
1:49.01	Nic Andrews	U23	3.10.81	1	Street	6	May
1:49.03	Andrew Graffin		20.12.77	1	Birmingham	6	Jul
(20)							
1:49.47	Dominic Hall		21.02.71	3	Solihull	22	Jun
1:49.50	James Mayo		24.02.75	6	Tartu, EST	2	Jun
1:49.6	Tony Draper		23.04.74	1	Bedford	19	May
1:49.63	James Nasrat	U20	10.01.83	3	Eton	3	Jul
1:49.68	Gary Vickers		26.02.71	9	Watford	14	Aug
1:49.89	Neil Dougal	U23	7.03.80	5	Eton	3	Jul
1:49.90	Jon McCallum		19.11.75	3h3	Manchester (C)	15	Jun
1:50.00	Michael Skinner		21.11.79	6	Watford	31	Jul
1:50.00	James Thie		27.06.78	1	Manchester (Str)	20	Aug
1:50.06	Kevin Sheppard		27.01.79	2	Manchester (Str)	20	Aug
(30)							
1:50.18	Chris Reynolds	U20	23.01.85	1	Nottingham	13	Jul

1:50.2	Mohamed Farah	U20	23.03.83	1	Derby	4	Aug
1:50.27	Terry Feasey		5.08.77	3h3	Birmingham	12	Jul
1:50.35	Tim Alexander		6.09.79	7	Watford	31	Jul
1:50.44	Richard Girvan		26.07.76	5r2	Stanford, USA	3	May
1:50.46	Tom Carter	U23	20.08.82	3	Manchester (Str)	20	Aug
1:50.5	Jermaine Mays	U23	23.12.82	1	Blackpool	3	Aug
1:50.51	Andrew Brown		17.06.77	2rB	Manchester (Wy)	3	Jun
1:50.54	Adam Zawadzki		19.12.74	5	Birmingham	6	Jul
1:50.55	Michael Rimmer	U17	3.02.86	2	Manchester (Str)	6	Aug
(40)							
1:50.56	Oliver Teasel	U20	24.04.84	2	Nottingham	13	Jul
1:50.57	Stuart Bailey		6.08.78	1rB	Watford	14	Aug
1:50.62	Tom Ranger		20.11.77	4	Manchester (Str)	20	Aug
1:50.63	Tom Nimmo		9.05.71	2	Edinburgh	20	Jul
1:50.70	Rob Watkinson		10.03.74	5	Manchester (Str)	20	Aug
1:50.7	Rob Hooton		5.05.73	2rB	Solihull	22	Jun
1:50.7	Andrew Fulford	U23	23.06.82	2	Blackpool	3	Aug
1:50.73	David Gow		9.02.79	3	Manchester (Str)	14	May
1:50.74	Steve Rees-Jones		24.12.74	4	Manchester (Str)	6	Aug
1:50.75	Steve Turvill		17.02.75	9	Watford	31	Jul
(50)							
1:50.76	Vince Wilson		1.04.73	1rC	Manchester (Wy)	3	Jun
1:50.92	Peter Walsh	U23	5.05.80	1	Manchester (Str)	30	Apr
1:50.94	Matt Thomson	U23	20.09.81	8r1	Stanford, USA	3	May
1:50.97	Jason Lobo		18.09.69	7	Manchester (Wy)	3	Jun
1:51.12	Phil Winfield	U20	10.02.84	10	Watford	31	Jul
1:51.18	Ben Wiffen	U20	30.10.84	3	Nottingham	13	Jul
1:51.20	Andi Knight		26.10.68	8	Eton	3	Jul
1:51.26	Brad Donkin		6.12.71	3rB	Manchester (Wy)	3	Jun
1:51.27	Andrew Baddeley	U23	20.06.82	1rB	Manchester (Str)	20	Aug
1:51.31	Ian Munro	U20	5.09.83	3	Bedford	6	May
(60)							
1:51.32	Gavin Massingham	U23	4.10.82	6	Manchester (Str)	6	Aug
1:51.35	Neil Kirk		14.09.78	1	Mount Pleasant, USA	4	May
1:51.40	Colin McCourt	U20	11.12.84	2rC	Watford	14	Aug
1:51.4	Eddie Williams		1.10.70	3	Derby	4	Aug
1:51.47	Richard Ashe		5.10.74	6	Solihull	22	Jun
1:51.5	Ric Sumner	U23	20.09.80	4rB	Solihull	22	Jun
1:51.51	Nick McCormick	U23	11.09.81	1	Manchester (Str)	23	Jul
1:51.6	Damien Moss	U23	2.09.82	1	Corby	12	May
1:51.6	Gavin Maley		19.05.78	3	Blackpool	3	Aug
1:51.63	David Moulton	U23	7.09.81	3rC	Watford	14	Aug
(70)							
1:51.79	Michael Coltherd	U23	28.12.82	3	Manchester (Str)	30	Apr
1:51.8	Sean Kelly		8.11.72	5	Watford	22	May
1:51.86	Paul Laslett	U23	12.05.80	5rC	Watford	14	Aug
1:51.9	Andrew Brown		20.12.77	1rC	Watford	31	Jul
1:51.96	Robert Whittle	U23	14.06.81	2rB	Eton	3	Jul
1:51.99	Gareth Balch	U20	18.05.83	3rC	Manchester (Wy)	3	Jun
1:52.0	Allen Graffin		20.12.77	2	Watford	8	May
1:52.09	Andrew Dean	U20	25.09.83	7rC	Watford	14	Aug
1:52.14	Ian Salisbury		22.11.70	3rB	London (He)	3	Aug
1:52.14	Lee Bowron	U17	2.10.85	1rD	Watford	14	Aug
(80)							
1:52.15	Alasdair Mclean-Foreman	U23	10.11.81	5h4	Manchester (C)	15	Jun
1:52.2	Tom Lancashire	U20	2.07.85	2	Chelmsford	6	Jul
1:52.25	James Parker		28.10.79	10rC	Watford	14	Aug
1:52.26	John Rogers		30.07.73	3	Manchester (Str)	28	May
1:52.3	Richard Davenport	U17	12.09.85	6	Watford	22	May
1:52.38	Tom Holden	U20	2.02.84	5	Nottingham	13	Jul
1:52.4	Matthew Bowser	U20	3.07.83	2	Derby	4	Aug

1:52.43	James Bowler		2.09.79	4rB	Eton	3	Jul
1:52.46	Ian Davey	U23	25.10.82	1rD	Manchester (Wy)	3	Jun
1:52.54	Lea Farmer	U23	22.01.80	2rD	Watford	14	Aug
(90)							
1:52.63	Chris Clement	U20	19.07.83	1rC	Watford	28	Aug
1:52.69	Chris Stoves	U20	20.02.84	3rB	Manchester (Str)	14	May
1:52.70	Darrell Maynard	V40	21.08.61	1	Potsdam, GER	24	Aug
1:52.7	Ian Tinsley	U23	23.01.81	4	Blackpool	3	Aug
1:52.71	Jon Stewart	U23	22.05.80	5	Manchester (Str)	28	May
1:52.72	Adrian McGarva		17.12.74	3rD	Watford	14	Aug
1:52.73	Alex Tanner		29.12.78	4rD	Watford	14	Aug
1:52.78	Richard Dowse	U20	3.01.85	8	Birmingham	6	Jul
1:52.81	Nathan Dosanjh		13.02.79	5r3	Athens GA, USA	12	Apr
1:52.9	James Fewtrell	U23	22.12.80	3rB	Wigan	7	Jul
(100)							
1:52.91	Mark Sanford		19.04.78	11rC	Watford	14	Aug
1:52.92	Gareth Hill		24.05.79	7	Dublin, IRL	19	Jul
1:52.92	Dean Clark		20.12.73	1rE	Watford	14	Aug
1:52.94 i	Hugh Kerr		4.01.76	1	Glasgow	9	Jan

Additional Under 20 (1 - 17 above)

1:53.1	Chris Warburton		23.08.83	5	Derby	4	Aug
1:53.12	Shugri Omar		20.12.84	5rD	Watford	14	Aug
1:53.15	Adam Vandenberg		2.06.84	4	Street	6	May
(20)							
1:53.78	Alan Wales		7.08.85	3	Glasgow (S)	14	Jul
1:53.86	Oliver Barrett		25.12.84	9rD	Watford	14	Aug
1:53.88	Darren St.Clair		6.04.85	1	Watford	26	May
1:53.9	Scott Overall		9.02.83	4	London (ME)	11	May
1:54.03	Steven Evison		29.01.83	6rB	Manchester (Str)	20	Aug
1:54.03	Graeme Oudney		11.04.85	3	Manchester (Str)	3	Sep
1:54.08	Stephen Davies		16.02.84	5	Street	6	May
1:54.1	Adam Watt		29.10.84	2	Ayr	11	Aug
1:54.19	Thomas Gayle		16.06.83	1rB	Manchester (Str)	6	Aug
1:54.24	David Proctor	U17	22.10.85	1	Manchester (Str)	17	Sep
(30)							
1:54.27	Matt Warley		1.08.85	6	Street	6	May
1:54.29	Joseph Maynard		25.07.85	8	Street	6	May
1:54.3	Ed Prickett		28.01.83	5	Luton	3	Aug
1:54.34	Drew Graham		14.11.84	2h2	Nottingham	12	Jul
1:54.57	Tom Snow	U17	7.09.85	4rF	Watford	14	Aug
1:54.6	Richard Clayton		12.11.84	1rB	London (Elt)	7	Aug

Additional Under 17 (1 - 5 above)

1:54.68	Ben Harding		12.12.86	2	Nottingham	13	Jul
1:55.61	Jamie Buckley		3.02.86	5rE	Eton	3	Jul
1:55.7	Ahmed Ali		31.03.86	10rC	Watford	31	Jul
1:55.74	Matthew Armstrong		13.12.85	4	Nottingham	13	Jul
1:55.76	Ben Green		14.08.86	3rC	Manchester (Str)	23	Jul
(10)							
1:56.01	Steven Fennell		4.04.86	5	Nottingham	13	Jul
1:56.13	Chris Gowell		26.09.85	1rI	Watford	14	Aug
1:56.3	Paul Lipman		2.09.85	2	Watford	18	Sep
1:56.46	Richard Yates		26.01.86	3rC	Manchester (Str)	6	Aug
1:56.66	Stuart Morland		16.05.86	1h2	Nottingham	12	Jul
1:56.69	Michael Sawrey		30.05.86	6rC	Manchester (Str)	20	Aug
1:56.70	Andrew Donaldson		23.01.86	1h3	Manchester (C)	25	May
1:56.88	Anthony Moran		8.01.86	5rD	Manchester (Str)	14	May
1:56.93	Matt Wood		14.12.86	2h3	Manchester (C)	25	May
1:57.06	Tom Settle		25.07.86	5rC	Manchester (Str)	6	Aug
(20)							
1:57.1	Ricki Glover		2.11.85	1	Corby	22	Jun

1:57.2	Darren Froggatt		1	Birmingham	1	Sep
1:57.24	Adam Mitchell	12.06.86	3h3	Manchester (C)	25	May
1:57.4	Chris Smith	4.12.85	3	Nuneaton	28	Jul
1:57.50	Rhian Hastey	5.08.86	1	Cudworth	14	Sep
1:57.7	Alex Felce	11.09.86	4	Solihull	10	Jul
1:57.7	Robert Lightfoot	7.09.85	1	Wrexham	13	Jul
1:57.9	Andre Depovre		1	Cleckheaton	3	Aug
1:57.9	Richard Hill	12.02.86	3	Birmingham	1	Sep
1:58.1	Tim Haughian	29.11.86	1	Eton	15	May
	(30)					
1:58.13	Alistair Hay	7.09.85	1	Edinburgh	12	May
1:58.29	Jason Atkinson	28.10.85	5rB	Street	6	May
1:58.3	Chris Knights	17.10.85	7	Sheffield (W)	31	Aug
1:58.32	Kirk Wilson	21.12.85	2	Gateshead	12	May
1:58.44	Craig Bravington	9.12.86	2rE	Watford	28	Aug

Under 15

1:58.79	Grant Prendergast	8.09.87	1	Birmingham	11	Aug
1:59.07	Martyn Gibbons	7.09.87	2	Birmingham	11	Aug
1:59.50	Abdi Igi	15.12.87	5rB	Manchester (Str)	3	Sep
1:59.8	Leon Danile	28.07.88	1	Peterborough	26	Aug
1:59.81	Lewis Robson	9.01.88	3	Birmingham	11	Aug
1:59.9	Mark Burgess	13.11.87	5	Watford	18	Sep
2:00.51	Mark Mitchell	23.05.88	4	Birmingham	11	Aug
2:00.77	Steven Rusling	21.02.88	5	Birmingham	11	Aug
2:02.00	James Brewer	18.06.88	1s1	Nottingham	12	Jul
2:02.23	Jordan West	4.11.88	3s1	Nottingham	12	Jul
	(10)					
2:02.4	Jake McCulloch	21.12.87	1	Bracknell	12	May
2:02.70	Sam Bradley	2.12.87	9rC	Watford	4	Sep
2:03.08	Bobby Whittaker	28.02.88	1	Birmingham	1	Sep
2:03.69	Ben Rusius	26.01.88	8	Manchester (Str)	3	Sep
2:03.87	Sam Brasier	5.11.87	3h1	Nottingham	12	Jul
2:03.88	Robert Hodges	5.12.87	4h1	Nottingham	12	Jul
2:04.09	Ollie Ralph	21.02.88	1h2	Nottingham	12	Jul
2:04.14	Jonathan Taylor	10.10.87	1	Gateshead	24	Aug
2:04.28	George Glancy	3.09.87	5rl	Eton	3	Jul
2:04.4	Robert Bates	29.10.87	2	Nuneaton	14	Jul
	(20)					
2:04.5	Ross Finlayson	26.09.87	2h2	Glasgow	29	Aug
2:05.1	Ian Whitefield	22.12.87	1	Cheltenham	17	Jul
2:05.4	Steven Smith	3.09.87	1	Bedford	15	Sep
2:05.42	Nathan Elliott	4.03.88	5h1	Nottingham	12	Jul
2:05.58	Edward Aston	10.08.88	1h3	Nottingham	12	Jul

Under 13

2:13.1	Christian Booker	29.06.90	1	Yate	21	Jul
2:14.3	Nathan Woodward	17.10.89	1	Solihull	8	Jul
2:14.63	David Fitzsimons	8.09.89	1	Grangemouth	24	Aug
2:14.8	Lewis Denton	17.10.89	1	Kingston	28	Jul
2:16.3	Mike Cole	1.12.89	3rE	Exeter	25	Jun
2:16.7	Daniel Price	31.10.89	2	Kingston	28	Jul
2:17.6	Paige Haines	28.06.90	3	Kingston	28	Jul
2:18.0	Chris Mcgarrity	7.09.89	4h3	Shettleston	29	Aug
2:18.3	Adam Green		1	Warrington	2	Jun
2:18.4	Peter Humphrey	7.10.89	1	London (TB)	24	Aug

Foreign

1:47.96	Gareth Turnbull (IRL)		14.05.79	1	Bedford	6	May
1:49.79	Conor Sweeney (IRL)	U23	28.12.81	2	Dublin, IRL	14	Jul
1:50.49	Abdel-Karim Ouou (ALG)		18.07.77	1rC	Watford	14	Aug
1:50.54	Des English (IRL)		6.06.67	4	Boston, USA	1	Jun

1000 Metres

2:19.23 i	Anthony Whiteman		13.11.71	2	Piraeus, GRE	20	Feb
3:01.5	Jonathan Hampson	U13	1.10.89	1	Crawley	23	Jul

1500 Metres

3:32.43	Anthony Whiteman		13.11.71	7	Monaco, MON	19	Jul
	3:38.04			4	Manchester (C)	31	Jul
	3:38.24			1	Birmingham	14	Jul
	3:40.3 +			9m	London (CP)	23	Aug
	3:42.21			4	Sheffield	30	Jun
3:34.89	John Mayock		26.10.70	8	Berlin, GER	6	Sep
	3:36.28			9	Rieti, ITA	8	Sep
	3:37.94			3	Heusden, BEL	20	Jul
	3:38.84			2	Cork, IRL	6	Jul
	3:38.90 i			3	Ghent, BEL	10	Feb
	3:38.97			2	Birmingham	14	Jul
	3:39.53 i			6	Lievin, FRA	24	Feb
	3:39.7 +			8m	London (CP)	23	Aug
	3:42.58			10	Seville, ESP	8	Jun
	3:42.63			6h2	Munich, GER	6	Aug
	3:42.72			1h2	Birmingham	12	Jul
3:35.53	Andrew Graffin		20.12.77	10	Berlin, GER	6	Sep
	3:36.69			11	Rieti, ITA	8	Sep
	3:37.33			1	Bangor, NI	21	Jul
	3:37.70			2	Malmo, SWE	13	Aug
	3:38.01			5	Seville, ESP	8	Jun
	3:38.14			3	Kalamata, GRE	1	Jun
	3:38.2 +			7m	London (CP)	23	Aug
	3:40.24			4	Birmingham	14	Jul
	3:41.05			1	Gothenburg, SWE	27	Aug
	3:41.54			3	Sheffield	30	Jun
	3:42.61			2h1	Birmingham	12	Jul
	3:42.8			2	Watford	19	May
3:37.35	Mike East		20.01.78	1	Manchester (C)	31	Jul
	3:39.18			3	Birmingham	14	Jul
	3:40.52 i			1h1	Vienna, AUT	1	Mar
	3:41.74			2	Dessau, GER	29	May
	3:41.82			5h2	Munich, GER	6	Aug
	3:41.88			6	Madrid, ESP	20	Sep
	3:41.9 +			12m	London (CP)	23	Aug
	3:41.93 i			7	Birmingham	17	Feb
3:39.57	Jon McCallum		19.11.75	5	Kalamata, GRE	1	Jun
3:40.25	Tom Mayo		2.05.77	2	Bilbao, ESP	29	May
	3:41.66			15	Lausanne, SUI	2	Jul
	3:41.70			8	Manchester (C)	31	Jul
	3:41.72			1rB	Seville, ESP	8	Jun
	3:42.69			1	Loughborough	18	May
3:40.70	Gregg Taylor		1.08.77	5	Birmingham	14	Jul
	3:41.10			2	Watford	14	Aug
	3:42.35			1h1	Birmingham	12	Jul
	3:42.68			1	Manchester (Str)	23	Jul
	3:42.77			4	Manchester (Wy)	3	Jun
3:41.06	James Thie		27.06.78	1	Watford	14	Aug
	3:42.94			1	Watford	28	Aug
3:41.61	Angus Maclean	U23	20.09.80	4	Watford	14	Aug
	3:41.67			1	Eton	3	Jul
	3:42.19			6	Birmingham	14	Jul
	3:42.93			2	Tullamore, IRL	1	Jun

3:41.89	Chris Mulvaney	U23	25.05.81	4h1	Baton Rouge LA, USA	30	May
	3:42.34			2	Fayetteville AR, USA	13	Apr
	3:42.46			3r5	Walnut CA, USA	20	Apr
	3:42.91			1	Starkville MS, USA	12	May
	(10)						
3:42.08	Matt Shone		10.07.75	1	Manchester (Wy)	3	Jun
	3:42.5			1	Watford	19	May
3:42.32	Adam Zawadzki		19.12.74	2	Manchester (Wy)	3	Jun
3:42.43	Michael Skinner		21.11.79	6	Watford	14	Aug
3:42.73	Nick McCormick	U23	11.09.81	7	Watford	14	Aug
3:42.84	James McIlroy		30.12.76	6	Cape Town, RSA	19	Apr
3:42.85	James Bowler		2.09.79	7	Palo Alto CA, USA	3	May
3:42.92	Chris Bolt	U23	21.09.80	3h1	Birmingham	12	Jul
65 performances to 3:43.00 by 17 athletes including 4 indoors							
3:43.30	Joe Kidger	U23	16.03.80	2	Watford	28	Aug
3:43.3	John Rogers		30.07.73	1	Manchester (Str)	11	Jun
3:43.42	Richard Ashe		5.10.74	8	Watford	14	Aug
	(20)						
3:43.62	Tom Carter	U23	20.08.82	6	Manchester (Wy)	3	Jun
3:43.72	Ben Whitby		6.01.77	3	Eton	3	Jul
3:43.97	Tom Ranger		20.11.77	4h2	Manchester (C)	15	Jun
3:44.18	Rob Hooton		5.05.73	6	Eton	3	Jul
3:44.67	Colin McCourt	U20	11.12.84	8	Eton	3	Jul
3:44.76	Steve Sharp		31.12.75	11	Watford	14	Aug
3:44.89	Neil Speaight		9.09.78	3	Watford	28	Aug
3:44.90	Iain Murdoch	U23	10.07.80	1	Namur, BEL	31	Aug
3:45.00	Spencer Barden		31.03.73	12	Watford	14	Aug
3:45.10	James Fewtrell	U23	22.12.80	6h2	Birmingham	12	Jul
	(30)						
3:45.31	Richard Vint		16.02.79	4r2	Palo Alto CA, USA	30	Mar
3:45.48	Stuart Stokes		5.12.76	13	Watford	14	Aug
3:45.56	Chris Thompson	U23	17.04.81	4h1	Birmingham	12	Jul
3:45.60	Neil Bangs	U23	28.03.80	8h2	Birmingham	12	Jul
3:45.72	Mark Miles		24.03.77	1	Manchester (Str)	25	Jun
3:45.82	David Hibbert		31.01.79	3	Manchester (Str)	14	May
3:45.88	Richard Ward	U23	5.05.82	4	London (He)	3	Aug
3:45.96	Andrew Baddeley	U23	20.06.82	2	Bedford	6	May
3:46.23	Lee Merrien		26.04.79	6h1	Birmingham	12	Jul
3:46.30	Ben Reese		29.03.76	4	Knoxville TN, USA	12	Apr
	(40)						
3:46.58	Chris Livesey	U23	8.08.80	3rB	Manchester (Wy)	3	Jun
3:46.60	Ben Tickner	U23	13.07.81	8h3	Birmingham	12	Jul
3:46.68	Stephen Hepples	U23	6.01.80	1	Manchester (Str)	6	Aug
3:46.85	Kevin Sheppard		27.01.79	2rB	Watford	14	Aug
3:46.93	Derek Watson	U20	22.05.83	4rB	Manchester (Wy)	3	Jun
3:47.01	Steve Body		6.11.75	3rB	Watford	14	Aug
3:47.02	Rod Finch		5.08.67	5	Watford	28	Aug
3:47.09	Oliver Laws	U23	18.03.80	6	Watford	28	Aug
3:47.13	Phil Tedd		7.11.76	1rB	Loughborough	18	May
3:47.53	Alasdair Mclean-Foreman	U23	10.11.81	6rB	Manchester (Wy)	3	Jun
	(50)						
3:47.57	Andrew Sherman	U23	28.09.81	6rB	Watford	14	Aug
3:47.60	Ed Prickett	U20	28.01.83	5	Watford	31	Jul
3:47.78	Mohamed Farah	U20	23.03.83	9	Watford	28	Aug
3:47.96	Robert Whittle	U23	14.06.81	1rB	Solihull	22	Jun
3:48.08	Steven Vernon	U23	17.10.80	7rB	Manchester (Wy)	3	Jun
3:48.12	Matthew Bowser	U20	3.07.83	2	Manchester (Str)	25	Jun
3:48.14	Steve Rees-Jones		24.12.74	9h1	Birmingham	12	Jul
3:48.15	Jermaine Mays	U23	23.12.82	1rC	Watford	14	Aug
3:48.32	Ricky Soos	U20	28.06.83	4	Bedford	6	May
3:48.34	Edward Jackson	U23	4.01.82	8rB	Watford	14	Aug

3:48.43	Adam Bowden	U23	5.08.82	2rC	Watford	14	Aug
3:48.53	Neil Kirk		14.09.78	6	Ann Arbor, USA	10	May
3:48.63	Andy Renfree		18.05.75	6	Manchester (Str)	23	Jul
3:48.72	Scott Overall	U20	9.02.83	10rB	Watford	14	Aug
3:48.91	Tom Lancashire	U20	2.07.85	1	Nottingham	13	Jul
3:49.03 i	Rob Whalley		11.02.68	2	Cardiff	6	Jan
3:49.10	Dave Taylor		9.01.64	3rC	Watford	14	Aug
3:49.1	Ian Grime		29.09.70	1	Loughborough	5	Jun
3:49.14	Stuart Bailey		6.08.78	4	Manchester (Str)	14	May
3:49.22	Chris Parr	U20	13.11.84	8	Edinburgh	20	Jul
	(70)						
3:49.28	Nick Goodliffe	U23	12.05.82	7	Manchester (Str)	23	Jul
3:49.40	Anthony Moran	U17	8.01.86	8	Manchester (Str)	23	Jul
3:49.40	Chris Reynolds	U20	23.01.85	11rB	Watford	14	Aug
3:49.49	Michael Green		12.10.76	1	Tallahassee FL, USA	11	May
3:49.50	David Anderson		2.10.77	6	Solihull	22	Jun
3:49.51	Andy Caine		17.06.77	9	Manchester (Str)	23	Jul
3:49.57	Peter Riley		6.07.79	3	York	13	Apr
3:49.64 i	Joe Mills		9.07.72	3	Cardiff	10	Feb
3:49.64	Steve Neill		11.08.66	11	Watford	28	Aug
3:49.81	Richard Girvan		26.07.76	6	London (He)	3	Aug
	(80)						
3:49.96	Gareth Raven		9.05.74	2	Manchester (Str)	9	Jul
3:49.99	Steve Murphy	U20	6.01.83	8	Watford	31	Jul
3:50.03	Alister Moses		5.07.78	10h3	Birmingham	12	Jul
3:50.03	Michael Openshaw		8.04.72	5	London (He)	3	Aug
3:50.04 i	Kojo Kyereme		23.12.74	4h1	Cardiff	2	Feb
3:50.06	Lee Emanuel	U20	24.01.85	10	Watford	31	Jul
3:50.14	Jason Lobo		18.09.69	5	Manchester (Str)	14	May
3:50.14	Darren Middleton	U23	14.10.80	3	Manchester (Str)	6	Aug
3:50.22	Mark Shankey	U20	19.12.84	5	Duffel, BEL	25	May
3:50.27	Alex Wright	U23	29.06.82	10	Manchester (Str)	23	Jul
	(90)						
3:50.33	Nathan Dosanjh		13.02.79	7r3	Walnut CA, USA	20	Apr
3:50.34	Alan Wales	U20	7.08.85	3	Namur, BEL	31	Aug
3:50.55	Andrew Robinson		20.04.78	8	London (He)	3	Aug
3:50.6	Ian Gillespie		18.05.70	3	Watford	19	May
3:50.86	Rob Scanlon		13.04.74	9rB	Manchester (Wy)	3	Jun
3:50.90	Alex Hodgkinson	U20	1.12.84	3rB	Eton	3	Jul
3:50.9	Andrew Hennessy		24.08.77	2	Derby	4	Aug
3:51.02	Mark Sanford		19.04.78	8rB	Solihull	22	Jun
3:51.06	Tom Penfold	U20	4.05.84	3	Nottingham	13	Jul
3:51.1	Rob Watkinson		10.03.74	1	Wakefield	3	Aug
	(100)						
3:51.14	Mark Draper	U20	28.06.84	14	Watford	28	Aug
3:51.15	Alastair O'Connor		22.06.71	7	Manchester (Str)	14	May
3:51.15	Curtis Robb		7.06.72	12	Manchester (Wy)	3	Jun
3:51.26	Stewart Reid		15.11.73	9	London (He)	3	Aug
3:51.28	Jonathan Burrell		24.11.75	5rB	Eton	3	Jul
3:51.42	Neil Chisholm		26.01.74	6	Berne, SUI	14	Sep

Additional Under 20 (1 - 17 above)

3:52.01	Tom Sharland		5.10.83	13	Watford	31	Jul
3:52.11	Kris Berry		13.11.84	2	Grangemouth	4	Sep
3:52.12	Jamie Atkinson		12.02.84	1rC	Eton	3	Jul
	(20)						
3:52.24	Lee Bowron	U17	2.10.85	1rB	Watford	28	Aug
3:52.66	Shugri Omar		20.12.84	2rB	Watford	28	Aug
3:54.02	Luke Gunn		22.03.85	1rE	Watford	14	Aug
3:54.07	Michael Rimmer	U17	3.02.86	1rD	Solihull	22	Jun

3:54.11	Robert Goodwin	19.04.84	6	Manchester (Str)	20 Aug
3:54.3	Gareth Balch	18.05.83	3	Watford	24 Apr
3:54.61 i	James Nasrat	10.01.83	5	Cardiff	10 Feb
3:54.86	Andrew Toward	29.07.83	4rD	Manchester (Wy)	3 Jun
3:55.56	Thomas Gayle	16.06.83	11rC	Manchester (Wy)	3 Jun
3:55.57	Andrew Murdock	16.02.85	h	Glasgow (S)	8 Jun

Under 17 (1 - 3 above)

3:55.66	Michael Smart	18.11.85	1	Birmingham	1 Sep
3:56.23	James Ellis	6.09.85	5rE	Watford	14 Aug
3:57.14	Chris Hart	23.05.86	10	Manchester (Str)	20 Aug
3:58.81	Paul Erwood	26.03.86	7	Street	6 May
3:59.51	Tom Snow	7.09.85	11rB	Watford	31 Jul
3:59.57	Ahmed Ali	31.03.86	3rD	Eton	3 Jul
3:59.65	Matthew Barnes-Smith	5.10.85	4rC	Watford	31 Jul
	(10)				
3:59.66	Alistair Hay	7.09.85	3	Glasgow (S)	20 Jul
4:00.2	Chris Knights	17.10.85	1	Watford	21 Aug
4:00.42	Richard Newton	10.02.87	3	Nottingham	13 Jul
4:00.82	Ben Green	14.08.86	8rC	Watford	31 Jul
4:01.0	Darsham Singh	26.07.86	2	Watford	26 May
4:01.01	James Horsman	27.09.85	7rG	Solihull	22 Jun
4:01.2	Ben Harding	12.12.86	3rC	Watford	28 Aug
4:01.4	Steven Fennell	4.04.86	3rD	Watford	28 Aug
4:01.5	Richard Bough	12.12.85	1	Burton	21 Jul
4:01.6	Craig Ivemy	28.03.86	5rC	Watford	28 Aug
	(20)				
4:01.64	Tom Russell	3.10.85	4	London (He)	25 Aug
4:01.77	Kirk Wilson	21.12.85	4rB	Edinburgh	20 Jul
4:02.11	Ben Jones	14.01.86	1	Manchester (Str)	11 Jun
4:03.54	Sean Dirrane	17.10.85	2rF	Manchester (Wy)	3 Jun
4:03.7	Tim Haughian	29.11.86	5	Watford	26 May
4:03.9	Simon Mills	30.04.86	2	Bebington	5 May
4:04.69	Matt Wood	14.12.86	9rB	Manchester (Str)	23 Jul
4:04.73	Michael Sawrey	30.05.86	10rB	Manchester (Str)	23 Jul
4:05.14	Ross Toole	8.10.86	5	Grangemouth	4 Sep
4:05.2	Alex Felce	11.09.86	1	Yate	14 Jul
	(30)				
4:05.22	Garry Bristow	3.05.87	4h2	Birmingham	10 Aug
4:05.97	Tom Settle	25.07.86	12rB	Manchester (Str)	23 Jul

Under 15

4:04.86	Adam Hickey	30.05.88	1	Nottingham	13 Jul
4:07.77	Mark Burgess	13.11.87	1rG	Watford	14 Aug
4:08.07	Abdi Igi	15.12.87	2	Birmingham	11 Aug
4:09.56	Laurence Cox	15.03.88	2	Nottingham	13 Jul
4:10.65	Andrew Livingstone	3.05.88	3	Nottingham	13 Jul
4:11.36	Ian Whitfield	22.12.87	5	Nottingham	13 Jul
4:12.79	Jonathan Taylor	10.10.87	6	Nottingham	13 Jul
4:15.35	Ashleigh Pain	16.10.87	3h2	Nottingham	12 Jul
4:15.80	Chris Brown	5.09.87	5	Birmingham	11 Aug
4:16.29	Ben Rusius	26.01.88	6	Birmingham	11 Aug
	(10)				
4:17.21	James Whittington	5.01.88	4h1	Nottingham	12 Jul
4:18.36	Jason Maxfield	28.03.88	5h2	Nottingham	12 Jul
4:19.68	George Glancy	3.09.87	6h2	Nottingham	12 Jul
4:19.76	Mark Mitchell	23.05.88	1	Inverness	19 May
4:20.21	Abdi Wahab	10.02.89	4h1	Birmingham	10 Aug
4:20.25	Kris Gauson	29.01.88	1	Grangemouth	24 Aug

Under 13

4:42.7	Chris McGarrity		7.09.89	5h3	Glasgow	3	Sep
4:44.5	Simon Gallant		7.12.89	1	Kingston	28	Jul
4:44.7	Jake Meeking		15.09.89	3	Street	16	Jul
4:45.1	Declan Murray		13.07.90	1	Macclesfield	17	Jul
4:45.5	Curtis Pearce		1.05.90	1	Warrington	2	Jun
4:46.4	Aidan Reid		26.12.89	1	Coventry	2	Jun
4:47.0	Marcus Ely			1	Birmingham	1	Sep
4:47.4	Alasdair Botfield		11.11.89	1	Yate	21	Jul
4:47.5	Scott Hawkins		24.03.90	1	Linwood	12	Sep
4:47.6	Tom Carpenter		26.03.90	1	Yate	1	Sep

Foreign

3:41.30	*Conor Sweeney (IRL)*	*U23*	*28.12.81*	*7*	*Cork, IRL*	*6*	*Jul*
3:41.79	*Colm McLean (IRL)*	*U23*	*7.06.80*	*8*	*Kassel, GER*	*14*	*Jun*
3:46.28	*Des English (IRL)*		*6.06.67*	*4*	*Boston, USA*	*29*	*Jun*
3:47.04	*Thomas Frazer (IRL)*	*U23*	*10.09.81*	*2*	*Dublin (S), IRL*	*14*	*Jul*
3:49.43	*John Frazer (IRL)*	*U23*	*10.09.81*	*2rC*	*Manchester (Wy)*	*3*	*Jun*
3:49.7	*Abdel-Karim Ouou (ALG)*		*18.07.77*	*1*	*London (Elt)*	*7*	*Aug*

1 Mile

3:53.21	Anthony Whiteman		13.11.71	6	Oslo, NOR	28	Jun
	3:57.54			9	London (CP)	23	Aug
3:54.70	Andrew Graffin		20.12.77	7	London (CP)	23	Aug
	3:57.32			4	San Francisco, USA	15	Sep
	3:57.48 i			1	New York NY, USA	8	Feb
	3:59.19 i			5	Boston, USA	25	Jan
3:55.85	John Mayock		26.10.70	8	London (CP)	23	Aug
3:58.24	James Thie		27.06.78	6	San Francisco, USA	15	Sep
3:58.40	Mike East		20.01.78	11	London (CP)	23	Aug
4:01.63 i	Chris Mulvaney	U23	25.05.81	8	Fayetteville AR, USA	2	Feb
4:03.45 i	Neil Kirk		14.09.78	2	Indianapolis IN, USA	9	Feb
4:03.57	Tom Mayo		2.05.77	13	London (CP)	23	Aug
4:06.06 i	Graeme Reid		14.04.79	1r2	New York NY, USA	3	Feb
4:06.09	James Mayo		24.02.75	1	Bedford	26	May
	(10)						
4:06.44	Matthew Bowser	U20	3.07.83	3	Bedford	26	May
4:06.45 i	James Bowler		2.09.79	1	Lincoln NE, USA	23	Feb
4:06.47 i	Alasdair Mclean-Foreman	U23	10.11.81	4	Notre Dame, USA	2	Feb
4:07.85 i	Richard Vint		16.02.79	5	Notre Dame, USA	2	Feb
4:08.45	Tom Ranger		20.11.77	4	Bedford	26	May
4:08.72	Paul Richardson	U23	11.02.82	5	Bedford	26	May
4:08.82	Ian Gillespie		18.05.70	6	Bedford	26	May
4:09.70	Kevin Sheppard		27.01.79	7	Bedford	26	May

Relay first leg

4:06.9	Peter Riley	6.07.79	Philadelphia PA, USA	27 Apr

Foreign

3:57.61	*Gareth Turnbull (IRL)*		*14.05.79*	*1*	*Philadelphia PA, USA 27 Apr*
4:01.58	*Conor Sweeney (IRL)*	*U23*	*28.12.81*	*4*	*Philadelphia PA, USA 27 Apr*

2000 Metres

5:22.37 i	Andy Renfree	18.05.75	1	Glasgow	23	Jan
5:22.53 i	Don Naylor	5.09.71	2	Glasgow	23	Jan

3000 Metres

7:41.09 i	John Mayock		26.10.70	3	Stockholm, SWE	6	Feb
	7:44.0 i+			2m	Birmingham	17	Feb
	7:48.08 i			3=	Vienna, AUT	2	Mar
	8:00.50			7	Sheffield	30	Jun
7:51.72 i	Ian Gillespie		18.05.70	8	Boston, USA	27	Jan
	8:17.3			1	Exeter	28	May
7:52.62	Anthony Whiteman		13.11.71	7	Hengelo, NED	2	Jun
	5 performances to 8:00.00 by 3 athletes including 4 indoors						
8:00.25	Chris Thompson	U23	17.04.81	1	Eton	3	Jul
8:01.42 i	Glen Stewart		7.12.70	2	Glasgow	20	Jan
	8:03.49			1	Edinburgh	20	Jul
8:01.49	Sam Haughian		9.07.79	8	Sheffield	30	Jun
8:02.20	Allen Graffin		20.12.77	10	Sheffield	30	Jun
8:02.39	Spencer Barden		31.03.73	3	Eton	3	Jul
8:03.17	Don Naylor		5.09.71	4=	Eton	3	Jul
8:03.17	Steve Sharp		31.12.75	4=	Eton	3	Jul
(10)							
8:03.2 i+	Andrew Graffin		20.12.77	6m	Birmingham	17	Feb
8:04.26	James Fewtrell	U23	22.12.80	6	Eton	3	Jul
8:04.36	Angus Maclean	U23	20.09.80	1	Street	6	May
8:05.06	Mark Miles		24.03.77	7	Eton	3	Jul
8:06.3	Tom Mayo		2.05.77	1	Palmerston North, NZL	3	Dec
8:07.64	Ian Hudspith		23.09.70	8	Eton	3	Jul
8:07.91	Ian Grime		29.09.70	9	Eton	3	Jul
8:08.86	Steve Body		6.11.75	10	Eton	3	Jul
8:08.89	Rob Denmark		23.11.68	11	Eton	3	Jul
8:09.01	Nick McCormick	U23	11.09.81	2	Edinburgh	20	Jul
(20)							
8:09.16	James Thie		27.06.78	2	Street	6	May
8:09.89 i	Julian Moorhouse		13.11.71	2	Birmingham	12	Jan
8:09.99	Andy Caine		17.06.77	3	Edinburgh	20	Jul
8:10.30 i	Gavin Thompson	U23	9.04.80	7	Ypsilanti, USA	19	Apr
8:10.67	Michael Green		12.10.76	1	Troy, USA	6	Apr
8:10.91 i	Rob Whalley		11.02.68	3	Birmingham	12	Jan
8:11.26	Tom Sharland	U20	5.10.83	3	Street	6	May
8:11.72	Oliver Laws	U23	18.03.80	13	Eton	3	Jul
8:12.28 i	Gregg Taylor		1.08.77	4	Birmingham	12	Jan
	8:15.37			16	London (CP)	23	Aug
8:12.43	Stephen Hepples	U23	6.01.80	4	Edinburgh	20	Jul
(30)							
8:13.46 i	Peter Riley		6.07.79	1	Boston, USA	3	Mar
8:13.80	Kairn Stone		21.10.76	4	Street	6	May
8:15.13	Glynn Tromans		17.03.69	15	Eton	3	Jul
8:15.27 i	Andrew Norman	U23	19.08.80	16	Ames, USA	9	Feb
8:15.4	Jon Wild		30.08.73	1	Manchester (Str)	11	Jun
8:15.89	Will Levett		6.09.75	16	Eton	3	Jul
8:16.43	Ed Prickett	U20	28.01.83	5	Street	6	May
8:16.5	Andrew Hennessy		24.08.77	1	Street	16	Jul
8:17.25	Adam Sutton	U23	22.03.81	1	Waltham, MA, USA	1	Jun
8:18.08	Alex Haines	U23	27.10.82	6	Street	6	May
(40)							
8:18.19	Ben Tickner	U23	13.07.81	1	Derby	11	Aug
8:18.41 i	Mike East		20.01.78	1	Cardiff	3	Feb
8:18.88 i	David Anderson		2.10.77	2	Cardiff	3	Feb
8:19.0	Neil Bangs	U23	28.03.80	1	Watford	24	Apr
8:19.1	Martyn Cryer	U23	16.10.81	1	Loughborough	27	Apr
8:19.48	Matthew Watson	U23	23.02.80	5	Edinburgh	20	Jul
8:19.52	David Hibbert		31.01.79	1	Manchester (Str)	28	May
8:19.6	Chris Davies		19.10.76	1	Rugby	3	Aug
8:19.69 i#	Chris Birchall		8.03.79	24	Ames, USA	9	Feb

189

8:20.38	Matthew Bowser	U20	3.07.83	1	Manchester (C)	16	Jun
(50)							
8:21.3	Lee Merrien		26.04.79	1	St. Peter Port, Gue	24	Mar
8:21.40	Mark Brown		1.08.79	6	Edinburgh	20	Jul
8:21.67	Iain Murdoch	U23	10.07.80	2	Derby	11	Aug
8:22.20	Mark Shankey	U20	19.12.84	2	Manchester (C)	16	Jun
8:22.35	Craig Wheeler		14.06.76	1	Manchester (Str)	9	Jul
8:22.86 i	Paul Howarth		30.10.77	1r1	Indianapolis IN, USA	26	Jan
8:22.93	Nick Goodliffe	U23	12.05.82	2	Manchester (Str)	9	Jul
8:23.12	Matt Janes	U23	12.12.82	1rB	Eton	3	Jul
8:23.81	Martin Hilton		9.05.75	2rB	Eton	3	Jul
8:24.08	Andres Jones		3.02.77	7	Street	6	May
(60)							
8:24.63	Nathaniel Lane		10.04.76	8	Street	6	May
8:24.86	Chris Bolt	U23	21.09.80	1	Watford	4	Sep

Additional Under 20 (1 - 4 above)

8:26.17	Chris Parr		13.11.84	2	Nottingham	13	Jul
8:27.79	Anthony Moran	U17	8.01.86	4	Manchester (Str)	6	Aug
8:28.36	Colin McCourt		11.12.84	4	Manchester (C)	16	Jun
8:29.26	Luke Beevor		4.03.84	3	Nottingham	13	Jul
8:30.07	Antony Ford		26.05.83	6	Manchester (C)	16	Jun
8:30.07	Phil Banks		8.03.83	7	Manchester (C)	16	Jun
(10)							
8:30.62	Frank Tickner		12.10.83	11	Street	6	May
8:30.7	Jamie Atkinson		12.02.84	3	London (Cat)	25	Jul
8:31.11	Matthew Barnes-Smith	U17	5.10.85	12	Street	6	May
8:33.01	Tom Humphries		24.09.84	9	Manchester (C)	16	Jun
8:33.55	Mark Draper		28.06.84	10	Manchester (C)	16	Jun
8:34.38	Steve Murphy		6.01.83	3	Belgrade, YUG	21	Sep
8:35.1	Steve Ablitt		16.11.83	1	Watford	31	Jul
8:35.42	Paul Hutton		20.12.84	2	Manchester (Str)	20	Aug
8:35.81	Colin Hawkins		23.03.84	3	Manchester (Str)	20	Aug
8:36.12	Sam Jacobs		19.09.84	14	Street	6	May
(20)							
8:36.54	John Millington		7.09.83	5	Nottingham	13	Jul
8:37.04	Edward McGinley		29.01.83	3	Namur, BEL	31	Aug
8:37.18	Ricky Soos		28.06.83	1	Birmingham	25	May
8:37.79 i	Paul Moores		3.08.84	1	Birmingham	23	Feb
8:38.02	Scott Overall		9.02.83	11	Manchester (C)	16	Jun
8:38.43	Craig Ivemy	U17	28.03.86	1	Birmingham	11	Aug
8:38.71	Shugri Omar		20.12.84	3	Watford	4	Sep

Additional Under 17 (1 - 3 above)

8:43.28	Chris Hart		23.05.86	2	Manchester (Str)	3	Sep
8:47.56	James Mitchell		11.10.86	4	Manchester (Str)	20	Aug
8:48.04	Keith Gerrard		24.03.86	3	Nottingham	13	Jul
8:49.84	Chris Knights		17.10.85	3	Birmingham	11	Aug
8:50.05	Lee Bowron		2.10.85	1	Watford	2	Jun
8:53.32	Ben Jones		14.01.86	6	Manchester (Str)	20	Aug
8:54.08	James Horsman		27.09.85	4	Nottingham	13	Jul
(10)							
8:55.5	Alistair Hay		7.09.85	1	Grangemouth	19	May
8:56.05	Sam Clegg		31.12.85	11	Manchester (Str)	23	Jul
8:57.43	James Phillipson		18.03.87	1	Manchester (C)	26	May
8:57.5	Oliver Holden		30.05.86	1	Birmingham	22	Jun
8:59.1	Sam Hall		15.10.85	6	Eton	23	Jun
8:59.6	Gary Taylor		5.07.86	11	Watford	24	Jul

Under 15

8:57.5	Andrew Livingstone		3.05.88	1	Chelmsford	21	Sep
9:04.7	Adam Hickey		30.05.88	1	London (Nh)	30	Jun

9:12.8	Laurence Cox	15.03.88	7	Watford	28 Aug
9:15.33	Robert Pickering	3.11.87	10	Manchester (Str)	20 Aug
9:22.57	Ben Rusius	26.01.88	12	Manchester (Str)	20 Aug
9:26.0	Ben Wilson	1.07.88	1	Woodford	21 Jul
9:28.1	Mark Bailey		3	Chelmsford	21 Sep
9:28.88	Abdi Igi	15.12.87	1	Watford	2 Jun
9:30.6	Craig Peters	4.03.88	1	Bristol	24 Jul
9:31.1	Stephen Blake	29.09.87	1	Watford	21 Aug
	(10)				
9:31.28	Jon Pepper	2.06.88	2	Watford	2 Jun
9:31.5	Ben Tyler	14.03.88	1	Woodford	21 Jul
9:33.0	Robert Hodges	5.12.87	2	Grimsby	29 Sep
9:34.28	George Glancy	3.09.87	3	Watford	2 Jun
9:35.2	Phil McAdams	15.09.87	2	Watford	8 Sep
9:35.42	Abdi Wahab	10.02.89	4	Watford	2 Jun
9:37.2	Jason Maxfield	28.03.88	1	Sheffield	27 Apr
9:39.2	Steven Rusling	21.02.88	1	Grangemouth	17 Aug

Under 13

10:15.82	Simon Gallant	7.12.89	1	Portsmouth	12 May
10:23.7	Nathan White	1.11.89	1	Eton	12 Jun
10:30.08	Duncan Taylor	5.09.89	12	Watford	10 Jul
10:31.2	Tom Nightingale	23.12.89	1	Watford	24 Jul
10:43.9	Grant Tilley	2.07.91	17	Watford	28 Aug
10:53.3	Edwin Cauthron	20.02.90	1	Exeter	24 Sep
10:56.1	Ross Docherty	15.08.90		Watford	24 Jul

Foreign

7:57.90 i	Gareth Turnbull (IRL)		14.05.79	1	Glasgow	24 Feb
8:09.24	Dermot Donnelly (IRL)		23.09.70	12	Eton	3 Jul
8:20.9	Colm McLean (IRL)	U23	7.06.80	2	Dublin (S), IRL	Apr
8:21.8	Abdel-Karim Ouou (ALG)		18.07.77	1	London (Cat)	25 Jul
8:22.2	John Downes (IRL)		21.07.67	2	Watford	24 Apr
8:23.5	Thembelani Zola (RSA)		14.02.75	1	Bury St. Edmunds	16 Jun
8:24.08	Mustaffa Mohamed (SUD)		11.11.78	2	Manchester (Str)	6 Aug

2 Miles

8:17.06 i	John Mayock	26.10.70	2	Birmingham	17 Feb
8:37.94 i	Andrew Graffin	20.12.77	6	Birmingham	17 Feb

5000 Metres

13:19.43	John Mayock	26.10.70	4	Manchester (C)	31 Jul
	13:38.63		5	Madrid, ESP	20 Sep
	13:39.49		8	Eugene OR, USA	26 May
13:19.45	Sam Haughian	9.07.79	5	Manchester (C)	31 Jul
	13:25.56		14	Rome, ITA	12 Jul
	13:38.52		1	Manchester (Wy)	3 Jun
	13:42.80		1	Manchester (C)	16 Jun
	13:46.04		2	Loughborough	18 May
	13:50.75		9	Munich, GER	11 Aug
13:20.30	Karl Keska	7.05.72	5	Heusden, BEL	20 Jul
	13:54.34		4	Birmingham	14 Jul
	13:59.5 +		2m	Munich, GER	7 Aug
13:43.33	Matt O'Dowd	15.04.76	11	Manchester (C)	31 Jul
	13:46.24		3	Manchester (C)	16 Jun
13:45.77	Allen Graffin	20.12.77	8	Cork, IRL	6 Jul
	13:46.36		3	Loughborough	18 May
	13:47.03		4	Manchester (C)	16 Jun
13:46.63	Rob Denmark	23.11.68	2	Manchester (Wy)	3 Jun
	13:53.18		2	Birmingham	14 Jul

13:46.90	Ian Hudspith		23.09.70	4	Loughborough	18	May
13:47.88				5	Manchester (Wy)	3	Jun
13:47.10	Glen Stewart		7.12.70	4	Manchester (Wy)	3	Jun
13:49.70				14	Manchester (C)	31	Jul
13:53.03				7	Loughborough	18	May
13:59.39				6	Birmingham	14	Jul
13:48.03	Spencer Barden		31.03.73	5	Loughborough	18	May
13:49.24				5	Manchester (C)	16	Jun
13:48.60	Mark Miles		24.03.77	7	Manchester (Wy)	3	Jun
13:54.94				5	Birmingham	14	Jul
13:50.8 (10)	Chris Thompson	U23	17.04.81	1	Watford	14	Aug
13:52.59	Jon Wild		30.08.73	1	Birmingham	14	Jul
13:54.92				8	Manchester (Wy)	3	Jun
13:52.64 i	Graeme Reid		14.04.79	1	Boston, USA	9	Feb
14:32.46				4	Glasgow (S)	9	Jun
13:52.81	Peter Riley		6.07.79	2	Philadelphia PA, USA	25	Apr
13:53.30	Matt Smith		26.12.74	11	Cork, IRL	6	Jul
13:53.47				3	Birmingham	14	Jul
13:55.84				8	Loughborough	18	May
13:53.60	Andrew Graffin		20.12.77	7	Bellville, RSA	8	Mar
13:57.44	Glynn Tromans		17.03.69	9	Manchester (Wy)	3	Jun
13:57.5	Rod Finch		5.08.67	2	Watford	14	Aug
13:59.45	Ian Grime		29.09.70	9	Loughborough	18	May
13:59.68	Mark Warmby		12.12.78	4	Chiba, JPN	23	Nov
	42 performances to 14:00.00 by 20 athletes						
14:00.5	Mohamed Farah	U20	23.03.83	3	Watford	14	Aug
14:01.26	Adam Sutton	U23	22.03.81	1r2	Raleigh NC, USA	29	Mar
14:01.81	Mark Steinle		22.11.74	10	Manchester (Wy)	3	Jun
14:02.88	Phil Mowbray		19.03.73	10	Loughborough	18	May
14:03.56	Andres Jones		3.02.77	8	Birmingham	14	Jul
14:06.02	Ian Gillespie		18.05.70	12	Manchester (Wy)	3	Jun
14:06.44	Rob Birchall		14.06.70	14	Manchester (Wy)	3	Jun
14:07.18	David Hibbert		31.01.79	1rB	Manchester (Wy)	3	Jun
14:07.29	Gavin Thompson	U23	9.04.80	6	Hillsdale, USA	8	Jun
14:07.85	Christian Nicolson		19.09.73	9	Ludvika, SWE	27	Jun
14:08.05 (30)	Mark Morgan		19.08.72	15	Manchester (Wy)	3	Jun
14:09.38	Don Naylor		5.09.71	15	Manchester (C)	31	Jul
14:09.5	Stephen Hepples	U23	6.01.80	5	Watford	14	Aug
14:10.06	Kojo Kyereme		23.12.74	8	Manchester (C)	16	Jun
14:12.10	Gareth Raven		9.05.74	2rB	Manchester (Wy)	3	Jun
14:12.73	Steve Sharp		31.12.75	2	London (He)	3	Aug
14:13.11	James Fewtrell	U23	22.12.80	12	Loughborough	18	May
14:13.7	Oliver Laws	U23	18.03.80	7	Watford	14	Aug
14:14.2	Kevin Farrow		8.09.75	1	Watford	14	Sep
14:15.63	Andrew Norman	U23	19.08.80	9	Stanford, USA	10	May
14:16.01 (40)	Tom Sharland	U20	5.10.83	13	Loughborough	18	May
14:16.61	Will Levett		6.09.75	4rB	Manchester (Wy)	3	Jun
14:17.61	Kairn Stone		21.10.76	14	Loughborough	18	May
14:19.54	Malcolm Campbell		3.01.71	5r2	Raleigh NC, USA	29	Mar
14:19.89	Alex Haines	U23	27.10.82	5rB	Manchester (Wy)	3	Jun
14:20.58	Steve Body		6.11.75	1	Bedford	26	May
14:22.58 +	Mark Hudspith		19.01.69	1	Manchester (C)	15	Jun
14:23.08	Bobby Quinn		10.12.65	3	Glasgow (S)	9	Jun
14:25.43	Michael Green		12.10.76	3	Atlanta GA, USA	17	May
14:25.85	Nathaniel Lane		10.04.76	16	Manchester (Wy)	3	Jun
14:26.27 (50)	Mark Brown		1.08.79	8rB	Manchester (Wy)	3	Jun
14:26.7	Andy Caine		17.06.77	10	Watford	14	Aug

14:27.7	Nick Goodliffe	U23	12.05.82	11	Watford	14	Aug
14:28.65	Chris Birchall		8.03.79	1	Charleston, USA	5	Apr
14:28.65	AC Muir		20.06.73	5	Solihull	22	Jun
14:29.0	Ben Tickner	U23	13.07.81	4	Bedford	6	May
14:29.28	Antony Ford	U20	26.05.83	10rB	Manchester (Wy)	3	Jun
14:30.11	Paul Evans	V40	13.04.61	2	Birmingham	6	Jul
14:30.81	Steve Cairns		3.11.67	17	Manchester (Wy)	3	Jun
14:31.3	Martyn Cryer	U23	16.10.81	5	Bedford	6	May
(60)							
14:32.45	Ewen North		13.07.78	7r2	Philadelphia PA, USA	25	Apr
14:33.3	Martin Hilton		9.05.75	1rB	Watford	14	Aug
14:33.59	Robert Gould		16.01.76	3	Birmingham	6	Jul
14:34.00 i	Paul Howarth		30.10.77	12	Indianapolis IN, USA	9	Feb
14:35.43	Jamie Reid		6.07.73	5	Glasgow (S)	9	Jun
14:35.51	Chris Davies		19.10.76	16	Loughborough	18	May
14:35.75	Guy Amos		15.06.63	4	Bedford	26	May
14:36.2	Spencer Newport		5.10.66	1	Wigan	7	Jul
14:36.6	Martin Yelling		7.02.72	2	Bedford	19	May
14:36.81	Dave Norman		4.11.78	1rC	Manchester (Wy)	3	Jun
(70)							
14:39.19	Jerome Brooks		9.08.73	6	Dublin, IRL	13	Jul
14:39.22	Alaster Stewart		5.10.72	1rB	Birmingham	6	Jul
14:39.3	Adrian Mussett		14.04.72	1	Luton	8	Jun
14:39.49	David Ricketts		2.12.79	2rC	Manchester (Wy)	3	Jun
14:40.2	Nick Talbot		14.12.77	2	Wigan	7	Jul
14:40.26	Stewy Bell		29.07.67	1	Gateshead	12	May
14:40.6	Mike Coleman		14.05.78	1	Kingston	3	Aug
14:41.18	Steffan White		21.12.72	10	Manchester (C)	16	Jun
14:41.3	David Anderson		2.10.77	1	London (PH)	8	Jun
14:41.34	Tim Don		14.01.78	13	Cape Town, RSA	19	Apr
(80)							
14:42.0	Matt Janes	U23	12.12.82	3	Wigan	7	Jul
14:42.3	Scott Overall	U20	9.02.83	4	Wigan	7	Jul
14:42.5	Gordon Lee		28.03.67	3rB	Watford	14	Aug
14:42.55	Owain Matthews	U23	4.11.81	19r3	Stanford, USA	29	Mar
14:42.66	Matthew Watson	U23	23.02.80	6	Bedford	29	Jul
14:42.8	Chris Cariss		1.03.75	4rB	Watford	14	Aug
14:42.98	Bashir Hussain		20.12.64	3	Santa Barbara, USA	18	May
14:43.3	Tom Naylor		9.01.79	5rB	Watford	14	Aug
14:43.44	Rick Hayman		11.10.79	12rB	Manchester (Wy)	3	Jun
14:43.47	Paul Freary		3.04.68	3	London (He)	3	Aug
(90)							
14:43.5	Scott Tompsett		21.08.77	1	London (B)	3	Aug
14:43.7	Huw Lobb		29.08.76	6rB	Watford	14	Aug
14:44.0	Matthew Lole	U20	23.01.83	1	Telford	6	Jul
14:44.24	Mohamed El-Sadiki		3.11.74	3rC	Manchester (Wy)	3	Jun
14:45.02	Andy Parker		5.08.75	4rC	Manchester (Wy)	3	Jun
14:45.05	Christopher Winward		25.03.75	2	Jarrow	1	Jun
14:45.1	Andy Morgan-Lee		1.03.69	8rB	Watford	14	Aug
14:45.64	David Webb	U23	17.03.82	9	Bedford	29	Jun
14:45.7	Alastair O'Connor		22.06.71	1	Chelmsford	6	Jul
14:46.13	Andy Renfree		18.05.75	4	Watford	19	May
(100)							
14:47.7	Ian Mitchell		10.03.76	1	Cudworth	12	May
14:48.8	Dave Wardle		1.10.75	9rB	Watford	14	Aug

Additional Under 20 (1 - 5 above)

14:53.7	Andrew Toward		29.07.83	2	Manchester (C)	25	May
14:54.18	Sam Jacobs		19.09.84	2r2	Solihull	22	Jun
14:54.42	Edward McGinley		29.01.83	7rC	Manchester (Wy)	3	Jun
14:54.8	Phil Banks		8.03.83	10	Bedford	6	May

15:02.7	Tom Humphries		24.09.84	4	Bedford	29	Jun
	(10)						
15:08.6	Mark Draper		28.06.84	6	Watford	31	Aug
15:08.65	Darren Malin		19.06.85	1	Edinburgh	11	May
15:15.0	Jonathan Blackledge		15.09.84	4	London (CP)	24	Jul
15:15.62	Luke Northall		30.11.84	1	Grangemouth	26	May
15:19.8	John Millington		7.09.83	2	Burton	19	May
15:21.55	Steve Murphy		6.01.83	10	London (He)	3	Aug
15:23.0	Phil McGlory		2.09.83	3	Manchester (C)	25	May
15:23.8	Colin Hawkins		23.03.84	3	Cleckheaton	4	May
15:26.8	Iain Donnan		21.06.85	3	Ayr	11	Aug
15:28.6	Gavin Smith		15.02.85	3	Eton	21	Jul
	(20)						
15:29.8	James Mason		12.03.83	3	Oxford	18	May

Foreign

14:05.23	*Dermot Donnelly (IRL)*		*23.09.70*	*11*	*Manchester (Wy)*	*3*	*Jun*
14:33.05	*Joe McAllister (IRL)*	*U23*	*23.12.80*	*5*	*Dublin (S), IRL*	*14*	*Jul*
14:38.4	*John Downes (IRL)*		*21.07.67*	*1*	*Welwyn*	*29*	*Mar*
14:42.7	*Mustaffa Mohamed (SUD)*		*11.11.78*	*2*	*Sheffield (W)*	*31*	*Aug*
14:48.3	*Abdel-Karim Ouou (ALG)*		*18.07.77*	*1*	*London (Cat)*	*18*	*Jul*

5 Miles Road

22:49	Chris Davies	19.10.76	1	Wolverhampton	1	Dec
23:19	Allen Graffin	20.12.77	3	Balmoral	30	Mar
23:26	Glynn Tromans	17.03.69	1	Alsager	3	Feb
23:32	Jon Wild	30.08.73	1	Ruislip	3	Mar
23:36	Andy Caine	17.06.77	3	Loughrea, IRL	13	Oct
23:47	Matthew Vaux-Harvey	30.03.76	2	Alsager	3	Feb
23:49	Ian Grime	29.09.70	2	Ruislip	3	Mar
23:51	Dave Taylor	9.01.64	3	Alsager	3	Feb
23:51	Ben Noad	6.05.76	8	Balmoral	30	Mar
23:54	Kris Bowditch	14.01.75	4	Alsager	3	Feb
	(10)					
23:54	Glen Stewart	7.12.70	9	Balmoral	30	Mar
23:57	Neil Wilkinson	12.03.69	3	Ruislip	3	Mar
23:58	Dominic Bannister	1.04.68	6	Loughrea, IRL	13	Oct

10000 Metres

27:53.42	Jon Brown		27.02.71	6	Stanford, USA	3	May
28:01.72	Karl Keska		7.05.72	5	Munich, GER	7	Aug
	28:11.20			15	Brussels, BEL	30	Aug
28:25.87	Sam Haughian		9.07.79	12rA	Camaiore, ITA	6	Apr
28:40.32	Adam Sutton	U23	22.03.81	7	Walnut CA, USA	19	Apr
28:43.42	Rob Denmark		23.11.68	1	Manchester (C)	15	Jun
	29:08.59			12	Manchester (C)	26	Jul
28:43.82	Jon Wild		30.08.73	2	Manchester (C)	15	Jun
	29:18.17			15	Manchester (C)	26	Jul
28:43.93	Andres Jones		3.02.77	3	Manchester (C)	15	Jun
	29:15.44			14	Manchester (C)	26	Jul
28:46.40	Ian Hudspith		23.09.70	4	Manchester (C)	15	Jun
	28:56.41			5rB	Camaiore, ITA	6	Apr
	29:33.43			19	Manchester (C)	26	Jul
28:47.52	Glen Stewart		7.12.70	5	Manchester (C)	15	Jun
	29:04.03			11	Manchester (C)	26	Jul
28:52.36	Christian Nicolson		19.09.73	4rB	Stanford, USA	3	May
	(10)						
29:13.60	Matt Smith		26.12.74	18rA	Camaiore, ITA	6	Apr
	29:18.93			6	Manchester (C)	15	Jun
29:20.02	Dave Taylor		9.01.64	7	Manchester (C)	15	Jun
29:25.55	Paul Evans	V40	13.04.61	8	Manchester (C)	15	Jun

29:26.80	Glynn Tromans		17.03.69	9	Manchester (C)	15	Jun
29:27.05	Peter Riley		6.07.79	2	Princeton, USA	17	May
29:27.07	Andy Caine		17.06.77	10	Manchester (C)	15	Jun
29:45.19				14rB	Stanford, USA	3	May
29:29.85	Chris Birchall		8.03.79	6	Philadelphia PA, USA	25	Apr
29:31.64	Mark Steinle		22.11.74	12	Prague, CZE	17	Jun
29:38.2	Mark Miles		24.03.77	1	Bedford	4	May
29:46.29	Malcolm Campbell		3.01.71	11	Manchester (C)	15	Jun
(20)							
29:51.64	Will Levett		6.09.75	12	Manchester (C)	15	Jun
29:56.44	Rob Birchall		14.06.70	13	Manchester (C)	15	Jun
29:57.6	AC Muir		20.06.73	2	Bedford	4	May
30:07.37	Gavin Thompson	U23	9.04.80	2	Ypsilanti, USA	16	May
30:16.66	Jamie Reid		6.07.73	16	Manchester (C)	15	Jun
30:22.82	Graeme Reid		14.04.79	2	Lawrenceville, USA	4	May
30:31.2	Mike Coleman		14.05.78	1	Brighton	14	Aug
30:32.9	Mohamed El-Sadiki		3.11.74	1	Cudworth	25	Aug
30:33.0	Jason Simpson		14.01.67	1	London (TB)	24	Aug
30:33.2	David Ricketts		2.12.79	3	Bedford	4	May
(30)							
30:39.2	Robert Gould		16.01.76	2	Bedford	25	May
30:39.75	Neil Wilkinson		12.03.69	20	Walnut CA, USA	19	Apr
30:40.80	Andrew Swearman		1.02.74	17	Manchester (C)	15	Jun
30:43.06	Nathaniel Lane		10.04.76	18	Manchester (C)	15	Jun
30:49.5	Nick Anderson		1.10.70	2	Brighton	14	Aug
30:49.77	Dave Norman		4.11.78	20	Manchester (C)	15	Jun
30:52.75	Spencer Barden		31.03.73	2	Bedford	17	Aug
30:58.8	Gareth Williams		16.08.66	3	Brighton	14	Aug
30:59.7	Matthew Watson	U23	23.02.80	3	Bedford	25	May
31:01.84	Bashir Hussain		20.12.64	2	Santa Barbara, USA	17	May
(40)							
31:02.0	Peter Grime		8.11.69	4	Bedford	4	May
31:03.5	Alan Stimpson		25.04.68	1	Cudworth	25	Aug
31:06.94	Paul Freary		3.04.68	1	Manchester (Str)	14	May
31:07.2	Kevin Farrow		8.09.75	1	Oldham	14	Jul
31:15.1	Stewy Bell		29.07.67	1	Darlington	14	Jul
31:15.5	Stuart Major		5.05.70	1	London (He)	21	Jul
31:22.80	Keith Chapman	U23	15.02.81	2	Manchester (Str)	14	May
31:24.3	Andy Parker		5.08.75	1	Derby	21	Jul
31:24.32	Lee Dunn		21.08.70	3	Manchester (Str)	14	May
31:30.6	Barry Royden		15.12.66	4	Brighton	14	Aug
(50)							
31:35.89	Andrew Norman	U23	19.08.80	3	Houston, USA	17	May
31:39.41	Steve Murdoch	V40	16.04.61	4	Manchester (Str)	14	May
31:41.8	David Watson		23.09.70	2	Cudworth	25	Aug
31:44.0	Chris Davies		19.10.76	1	Stoke-on-Trent	21	Jul
31:44.6	Ray Plant		13.05.68	2	Stoke-on-Trent	21	Jul
31:44.8	Patrick Curran		15.12.76	5	Brighton	14	Aug
31:46.4	Gareth Deacon		8.08.66	3	Stoke-on-Trent	21	Jul
31:52.3	Mike Trees		26.09.62	2	London (TB)	24	Aug
31:52.37	Jason Hodgson		21.02.73	5	Manchester (Str)	14	May
31:55.2	Charles Herrington		28.09.71	3	London (TB)	24	Aug
(60)							
31:56.1	Mark Hargreaves	V40	26.08.60	1	Poole	21	Aug

10000 Metres Road

28:40	Jon Brown		27.02.71	4	Richmond	22	Sep
29:09	Mark Steinle		22.11.74	1	London	21	Jul
29:22	Karl Keska		7.05.72	9	Richmond	22	Sep
29:23	Matt O'Dowd		15.04.76	5	Bishop Auckland	25	Aug
29:30	Matt Smith		26.12.74	6	Moreton-in-Marsh	15	Sep

29:34	Neil Wilkinson		12.03.69	1	Manchester	17	Mar
29:37	Stuart Stokes		5.12.76	2	Manchester	17	Mar
29:37	Rob Birchall		14.06.70	1	Silverstone	7	May
29:39	Will Levett		6.09.75	2	Silverstone	7	May
29:40	Ben Noad		6.05.76	6	Swansea	22	Sep
	(10)						
29:42	Ian Hudspith		23.09.70	2	Dewsbury	3	Feb
29:42	Mark Hudspith		19.01.69	3	Dewsbury	3	Feb

Where better than track bests

29:45	Allen Graffin		20.12.77	3	Bradford	8	Sep
29:46	Daniel Robinson		4.08.73	3	London	21	Jul
29:53	Angus Maclean	U23	20.09.80	1	Eastleigh	17	Mar
29:54	Nick Jones		10.07.74	1	Leyland	26	Dec
29:56	Steve Body		6.11.75	2	Eastleigh	17	Mar
29:57	Ian Grime		29.09.70	8	Moreton-in-Marsh	15	Sep
29:58	Mike Trees	V40	26.09.62	3	Katsuda, JPN	11	Feb
29:59	Martin Scaife		18.05.72	9	Moreton-in-Marsh	15	Sep

30:00	Michael Openshaw		8.04.72	1	Leeds	1	Dec
30:04	Alastair O'Connor		22.06.71	3	Manchester	17	Mar
30:05	Dominic Bannister		1.04.68	1	Skipton	7	Jul
30:05	Stewy Bell		29.07.67	11	Moreton-in-Marsh	15	Sep
30:05	Chris Davies		19.10.76	8	Swansea	22	Sep
30:06	Andrew Jones		10.10.78	12	Moreton-in-Marsh	15	Sep
30:08	Jerome Brooks		9.08.73	13	Moreton-in-Marsh	15	Sep
30:08	Lee Rodriguez		30.01.74	2	Edinburgh	22	Sep
30:09	Dave Norman		4.11.78	14	Moreton-in-Marsh	15	Sep
30:10	Gareth Raven		9.05.74	4	Dewsbury	3	Feb
30:10	Stephen Hepples	U23	6.01.80	4	Leeds	1	Dec

Foreign

28:47	*Julius Kimtai (KEN)*			5	*Richmond*	22	*Sep*

10 Miles Road

47:29	Matt O'Dowd		15.04.76	2	Portsmouth	8	Sep
47:33	Jon Brown		27.02.71	5	Washington	7	Apr
47:53 +	Mark Steinle		22.11.74	m	London	14	Apr
48:10	Ben Noad		6.05.76	3	Portsmouth	8	Sep
48:20	Carl Thackery		14.10.62	7	Bruges, BEL	3	Mar
48:35	Michael Openshaw		8.04.72	1	Carlisle	16	Nov
48:53	Kassa Tadesse		21.08.74	4	Portsmouth	8	Sep
48:55	Daniel Robinson		4.08.73	5	Portsmouth	8	Sep
48:59	Dominic Bannister		1.04.68	1	Bramley	24	Feb
49:10	Mike Coleman		14.05.78	1	Canterbury	27	Jan
	(10)						
49:10	Martin Scaife		18.05.72	10	Bruges, BEL	3	Mar
49:22	Stephen Hepples	U23	6.01.80	2	Carlisle	16	Nov
49:35	Allan Adams		11.09.72	3	Carlisle	16	Nov
49:45	Andy Morgan-Lee		1.03.69	7	Portsmouth	8	Sep
49:46	Jamie Reid		6.07.73	1	Motherwell	7	Apr
49:57	Paul Evans	V40	13.04.61	8	Portsmouth	8	Sep

Foreign

49:44	*Richard Nifah (GHA)*		25.08.74	1	*Twickenham*	20	*Oct*
49:45	*John Downes (IRL)*		21.07.67	2	*Twickenham*	20	*Oct*

Half Marathon

62:32	Jon Brown		27.02.71	1	Victoria, CAN	13	Oct
	63:51 +			m	New York NY, USA	3	Nov
62:47 +	Mark Steinle		22.11.74	m	London	14	Apr
	63:02			1	Murcia, ESP	17	Mar

196

63:25	Nick Jones		10.07.74	4	Wilmslow	24	Mar
	64:37			2	Helsby	20	Jan
	64:38			1	Wrexham	24	Feb
63:47	Dave Taylor		9.01.64	5	Wilmslow	24	Mar
64:09	Allen Graffin		20.12.77	7	South Shields	6	Oct
64:17	Mark Hudspith		19.01.69	2	Bath	17	Mar
64:18	Ben Noad		6.05.76	9	South Shields	6	Oct
64:28	Carl Thackery		14.10.62	3	Bath	17	Mar
64:30	Nick Wetheridge		11.10.72	4	Bath	17	Mar
64:36	Carl Warren		28.09.69	1	Helsby	20	Jan
(10)							
64:43	Kassa Tadesse		21.08.74	6	Wilmslow	24	Mar
64:47	Paul Evans	V40	13.04.61	5	Bath	17	Mar
65:06	Matt Smith		26.12.74	10	South Shields	6	Oct
65:10	Daniel Robinson		4.08.73	1	Grove Park	24	Mar
65:24	Dave Norman		4.11.78	8	Wilmslow	24	Mar
65:41	Tim Dickinson		14.10.72	9	Wilmslow	24	Mar
65:52	Neil Wilkinson		12.03.69	12	South Shields	6	Oct
65:53	Mark Dalkins		9.09.71	10	Wilmslow	24	Mar
65:59	Rob Birchall		14.06.70	2	Abu Dhabi, UAE	15	Feb
66:08	Chris Cariss		1.03.75	17	South Shields	6	Oct
(20)							
66:13	Steve Brooks		8.06.70	15	Egmond aan Zee, NED	13	Jan
66:18	Gareth Raven		9.05.74	18	South Shields	6	Oct
66:19	Malcolm Campbell		3.01.71	9	Austin TX, USA	3	Feb
66:25	Glen Stewart		7.12.70	9	Glasgow	8	Sep
66:32	Darren Daniels		2.09.70	11	Wilmslow	24	Mar
66:39	Stuart Stokes		5.12.76	5	Benidorm, ESP	24	Nov
66:43	Dave Mitchinson		4.09.78	8	Bath	17	Mar
66:44	Tommy Murray	V40	18.05.61	1	Stranraer	2	Mar
66:44	Martin Rees	V45	28.02.53	9	Bath	17	Mar
66:45	Stuart Hall		21.12.64	1	Exeter	5	May
(30)							
66:46	Ian Fisher		15.09.70	1	York	27	Jan
66:46	Andy Parker		5.08.75	20	South Shields	6	Oct
66:47	Allan Adams		11.09.72	10	Glasgow	8	Sep
66:48	Martin Hilton		9.05.75	10	Bath	17	Mar
66:48	Andrew Jones		10.10.78	12	Wilmslow	24	Mar
66:49	Richie Gardiner		11.06.73	11	Bath	17	Mar
66:56	Jason Simpson		14.01.67	2	Fleet	17	Mar

Foreign

63:30	*John Mutai (KEN)*		*26.05.66*	*5*	*South Shields*	*6*	*Oct*

Marathon

2:09:17	Mark Steinle	22.11.74	8	London	14	Apr
2:12:20	Matt O'Dowd	15.04.76	8	New York NY, USA	3	Nov
2:16:18	Dominic Bannister	1.04.68	1	Ferrara, ITA	17	Mar
	2:19:36		10	Manchester (C)	28	Jul
2:16:23	Stuart Hall	21.12.64	2	Seville, ESP	24	Feb
	2:19:53		12	Manchester (C)	28	Jul
2:17:36	Billy Burns	13.12.69	14	London	14	Apr
2:17:51	Daniel Robinson	4.08.73	15	London	14	Apr
2:18:57	Chris Birchall	8.03.79	23	Chicago, USA	13	Oct
2:19:41	Nick Wetheridge	11.10.72	17	London	14	Apr
2:20:46	Chris Cariss	1.03.75	20	London	14	Apr
2:20:54	Martin Hilton	9.05.75	21	London	14	Apr
(10)						
2:21:01	Dave Norman	4.11.78	22	London	14	Apr
2:21:10	Mark Croasdale	10.01.65	23	London	14	Apr
2:21:16	Huw Lobb	29.08.76	24	London	14	Apr

197

2:21:24	Darren Bilton		9.03.72	25	London	14	Apr
	2:23:13			3	Las Vegas, USA	3	Feb
2:21:46	Jamie Reid		6.07.73	1	Fort William	28	Apr
2:22:08	Ian Fisher		15.09.70	26	London	14	Apr
2:22:21	Simon Pride		20.07.67	1	Belfast	6	May
	2:23:56			16	Manchester (C)	28	Jul
2:22:27	Nick Francis		29.08.71	27	London	14	Apr
2:22:27	Adrian Mussett		14.04.72	11	Dublin, IRL	28	Oct
2:22:54	Rhodri Jones		14.08.66	28	London	14	Apr
(20)							
2:23:15	Ray Plant		13.05.68	29	London	14	Apr
2:23:21	Richie Gardiner		11.06.73	30	London	14	Apr
2:23:36	Tim Dickinson		14.10.72	31	London	14	Apr
2:23:49 dh	Peter Fleming (137m dh)	V40	5.01.61	12	Austin TX, USA	17	Feb
	28 performances to 2:24:00 by 24 athletes						
2:24:12	Michael Green		12.10.76	7	Hartford, USA	12	Oct
2:24:26	Nick Altmann		19.11.72	27	Berlin, GER	27	Sep
2:24:39	Gareth Williams		16.08.66	33	London	14	Apr
2:25:10	Ian Malone		17.03.64	35	London	14	Apr
2:25:21	Joe Loader		21.07.73	37	London	14	Apr
2:25:32	David Brady		5.07.62	4	Belfast	6	May
(30)							
2:26:20	Andrew Weir		22.08.67	56	Berlin, GER	29	Sep
2:26:26	Mike Smith		1.02.68	1	Abingdon	20	Oct
2:26:48	Bill Speake		24.01.71	39	London	14	Apr
2:27:10	Nick Janvier		9.08.70	40	London	14	Apr
2:27:11	Dave Robertson	V40	11.09.61	41	London	14	Apr
2:28:09	Mike Jubb		20.06.70	42	London	14	Apr
2:28:18	Dennis Walmsley		5.09.62	2	Longford, IRL	25	Aug
2:28:25	Richard Szade		15.02.71		Pyongyang, KOR	7	Apr
2:28:32	Seb Shepley		23.11.67	43	London	14	Apr
2:28:32	Dai Roberts	V40	10.05.61	75	Chicago, USA	13	Oct
(40)							
2:28:48	Robin Bentley		17.02.65	44	London	14	Apr
2:28:52	Dave Cavers		9.04.63	45	London	14	Apr
2:29:00	Derek Brown	V40	23.01.60	47	London	14	Apr
2:29:20	Ieuan Ellis	V40	11.05.60	49	London	14	Apr
2:29:23	Peter Hockin	V40	16.05.61	51	London	14	Apr
2:29:36	Peter Roper		25.07.65	53	London	14	Apr
2:29:42	Ronnie James		14.12.64	1	Kingston	13	Oct
2:29:53	Garry Payne	V45	31.01.57	18	Dublin, IRL	28	Oct
2:29:55	James McGaughey		4.12.73	54	London	14	Apr
2:30:03	Mike Proudlove		26.01.70	1	Stoke-on-Trent	16	Jun
(50)							
2:30:18	Nick Martyn		28.09.63	55	London	14	Apr
2:30:29	Steve Payne	V45	1.12.55	56	London	14	Apr
2:30:45	Martin Roscoe		19.09.64	57	London	14	Apr
2:30:50	David McGregor	V45	12.06.56	58	London	14	Apr
2:31:26	Rob Hand	V40	17.01.62	59	London	14	Apr
2:31:35	Andrew Barber		20.08.74	60	London	14	Apr
2:31:36	Shane Snow		31.10.66	43	New York NY, USA	3	Nov
2:31:40	Andy Farquharson		24.08.65	61	London	14	Apr
2:31:41	Mark Goodridge		13.04.70	62	London	14	Apr
2:31:57	Greg Hull		16.11.65	64	London	14	Apr
(60)							
2:32:04	Dominic Croft			1	Cardiff	1	Sep
2:32:15	Simon Bell		26.12.66	65	London	14	Apr
2:32:39	Greg Dell		20.11.64	66	London	14	Apr
2:32:40	Ronnie Adams		6.06.62	8	Benidorm, ESP	24	Nov
2:32:52	Simon Lund		22.12.65	2	Abingdon	20	Oct
2:32:55	Billy Coyle		3.10.62	67	London	14	Apr
2:33:18	Bill Gristwood	V40	20.03.59	71	London	14	Apr

2:33:18	Darren Hale	V40	2.10.59	29	Athens, GRE	3	Nov
2:33:28	David Symonds		21.10.68	72	London	14	Apr
2:33:32	Matthew Adcock		9.04.68	73	London	14	Apr
(70)							
2:33:43	Tony Cummings	V40	18.11.60	75	London	14	Apr
2:33:53	Mark Hargreaves	V40	26.08.60	1	New Milton	22	Sep
2:33:56	Nick Berrill		6.10.64	77	London	14	Apr
2:33:58	Danny Norton			9	Benidorm, ESP	24	Nov
2:34:03	Toby Lambert		31.08.79	78	London	14	Apr
2:34:05	Neil Cayton		19.03.70	79	London	14	Apr
2:34:11	Brian Hall		24.01.63	80	London	14	Apr
2:34:17	Andrew Pead		18.02.66	82	London	14	Apr
2:34:20	Kassa Tadesse		21.08.74	18	Dubai, UAE	11	Jan
2:34:27	Gary Matthews	V40	9.04.60	2	Manchester	13	Oct
(80)							
2:34:32	Husseyin Ibrahim		13.05.68	83	London	14	Apr
2:34:34	Chris Harvey		1.08.64	1	Lake Vyrnwy	2	Jun
2:34:35	Alan McCullough		9.08.63	8	Belfast	6	May
2:34:49	Lee Martin		21.05.64	84	London	14	Apr
2:34:52	Dave Stone		13.02.70	85	London	14	Apr
2:35:02	Brian Fieldsend			2	Fort William	28	Apr
2:35:08	John Redmond	V45	15.10.57	87	London	14	Apr
2:35:09	Adrian Iszatt		6.03.66	88	London	14	Apr
2:35:19	Scott Brittain		24.08.75	89	London	14	Apr
2:35:23	David Miller		14.05.71	90	London	14	Apr
(90)							
2:35:28	Paul Freary		3.04.68	137	Chicago, USA	13	Oct
2:35:38	Paul Cameron			3	Abingdon	20	Oct
2:35:43	Alan Ruben	V45	9.03.57	60	New York NY, USA	3	Nov
2:35:49	Michael Evans			2	Cardiff	1	Sep
2:35:59	Paul Harwood		19.07.71	93	London	14	Apr
2:36:03	Andrew Thake		16.11.76	94	London	14	Apr
2:36:05	Nigel Payne		27.01.67	95	London	14	Apr
2:36:06	Alasdair Tatham		16.09.72	96	London	14	Apr
2:36:08	Ian Johnston		12.02.68	97	London	14	Apr
2:36:15	Andrew McNeill		2.12.65	98	London	14	Apr
(100)							
2:36:17	James Snodgrass			99	London	14	Apr
2:36:20	Martin Ferguson		17.09.64	3	Fort William	28	Apr
2:36:21	Richard Gay	V50	26.10.50	100	London	14	Apr
2:36:21	Mike McGeoch	V45	15.08.55	101	London	14	Apr
2:36:23	John Worthington		6.02.70	102	London	14	Apr
2:36:24	Paul Prosser			103	London	14	Apr
2:36:24	Chris Olden			2	New Milton	22	Sep

Foreign

2:13:56	John Mutai (KEN)		26.05.66	5	Dubai, UAE	11	Jan
2:18:13	Julius Kimtai (KEN)			16	London	14	Apr
2:25:58	Tomas Abyu (ETH)		5.05.78	1	Manchester	13	Oct
2:29:57	Patrick McKinney (IRL)			7	Belfast	6	May
2:34:13	Laurent Charion (FRA)		24.07.64	81	London	14	Apr

100 Kilometres Road

7:07:39	Dennis Walmsley		5.09.62	1	Moreton-in-Marsh	7	Apr
7:17:06	Chris Finill	V40	31.12.58	1	Cardiff	1	Sep
7:23:57				2	Moreton-in-Marsh	7	Apr
7:42:47				43	Torhout, BEL	22	Jun
7:34:23	Ian Anderson		23.03.71	33	Torhout, BEL	22	Jun
7:36:09	Alan Reid		19.04.66	3	Moreton-in-Marsh	7	Apr
7:42:08	Matt Lynas			2	Cardiff	1	Sep
7:51:11	William Sichel	V45	1.10.53	40	Winschoten, NED	14	Sep
7:54:32	John McLaughlin			3	Cardiff	1	Sep

8:06:28	Andy Cleeve			4	Cardiff	1	Sep

24 Hours Road

230.501 km	Stuart Buchan	V40	20.03.60	1	Hull	7	Jul
217.663 km	Walter Hill	V45	19.06.53	1	Doncaster	2	Jun
211.056 km	Adrian Stott	V45	5.08.54	2	Hull	7	Jul
190.494 km	Garth Peterson			3	Hull	7	Jul
187.594 km	Phil Adams	V40	25.08.61	2	Doncaster	2	Jun

1500 Metres Steeplechase - Under 17

4:19.85	Chris Hart		23.05.86	1	Nottingham	13	Jul
4:21.42	Alex Felce		11.09.86	2	Nottingham	13	Jul
4:23.41	Russell England		18.11.85	3	Nottingham	13	Jul
4:27.32	Daniel Russell		2.04.87	1	Birmingham	1	Sep
4:31.09	Steven Pogue		12.09.85	1	Gateshead	12	May
4:31.62	James Minter		20.08.87	5	Nottingham	13	Jul
4:32.47	Andrew Clark		1.10.85	1	Grangemouth	25	Aug
4:32.74	Stephen Irwin		16.05.86	2	Grangemouth	25	Aug
4:33.5	Adrian Holliday		17.01.87	1	Manchester (C)	25	May
4:33.52	Matthew Butler		25.02.86	6	Nottingham	13	Jul
	(10)						
4:34.86	Sam Hall		15.10.85	1	Watford	25	May
4:35.36	David Marteau		31.12.86	3	Birmingham	11	Aug
4:35.5	William Armstrong		19.11.86	1	London (BP)	21	Jul
4:35.5	Sean Dirrane		17.10.85	1	Middlesbrough	21	Jul
4:36.56	Paul Simner		13.12.85	2	Birmingham	26	May
4:39.7	Carl Dowling		9.09.85	1	London (CP)	12	May
4:39.8	Daniel Quinn		21.12.86	1	Chelmsford	21	Sep
4:40.0	Tom Michaelson		3.01.87	1	Mandale	21	Jul
4:42.1	Enrique Melin		29.06.87	2	Chelmsford	21	Sep

2000 Metres Steeplechase

5:35.73	Pat Davoren		13.03.72	1	Eton	3	Jul
5:41.41	Andrew Robinson		20.04.78	3	Eton	3	Jul
5:41.78	Kevin Sheppard		27.01.79	4	Eton	3	Jul
5:44.21	Tom Bedford	U20	12.12.83	1	Nottingham	13	Jul
5:47.02	Frank Tickner	U20	12.10.83	2	Nottingham	13	Jul
5:47.81	Steve Murphy	U20	6.01.83	1	Watford	25	May
5:48.29	Charlie Low		9.10.74	2	Solihull	22	Jun
5:49.10	Peter Kellie	U20	2.01.84	6	Eton	3	Jul
5:49.85	Andrew Thomas	U23	29.01.81	1	Watford	1	Sep

Additional Under 20 (1 - 4 above)

5:55.03	Luke Gunn		22.03.85	1	Watford	1	Sep
5:55.33	Ian Bowles		6.01.84	1	Manchester (Wy)	3	Jun
5:55.72	Chris Warburton		23.08.83	2	Watford	1	Sep
5:58.44	Daniel Lewis		16.10.83	3	Watford	1	Sep
6:02.47	Alistair Smith		22.02.84	6	Nottingham	13	Jul
6:05.4	Paul Moores		3.08.84	1	Birmingham	22	Jun
	(10)						
6:08.1	Oliver Brewer		14.09.83	1	Cudworth	12	May
6:08.73	Gavin Smith		15.02.85	8	Nottingham	13	Jul
6:09.73	Mark Buckingham		4.05.85	4	Manchester (Wy)	3	Jun
6:11.39	Mark Donoghue		27.09.83	9	Nottingham	13	Jul
6:11.5	William Docherty		2.04.85	3	Eton	23	Jun
6:11.91	Alex Haynes		6.09.84	10	Nottingham	13	Jul
6:12.33	James Henry		31.07.84	2	Manchester (Str)	11	Jun
6:13.1	Thomas Bark		18.10.83	3	Worcester	6	Jul
6:14.49	Daniel Russell	U17	2.04.87	1rB	Derby	8	Sep
6:14.7	Alex Felce	U17	11.09.86	1	London (B)	8	Sep

3000 Metres Steeplechase

Time	Name		DOB	Pos	Venue	Date	
8:26.45	Stuart Stokes		5.12.76	4	Manchester (C)	27	Jul
8:35.6				1	Manchester (C)	16	Jun
8:38.80				1	Manchester (Wy)	3	Jun
8:39.90				8	Linz, AUT	19	Aug
8:40.02				2	Loughborough	18	May
8:43.38				8	Madrid, ESP	21	Sep
8:48.69				7	Annecy, FRA	23	Jun
8:38.0	Ben Whitby		6.01.77	2	Manchester (C)	16	Jun
8:40.12				1	Birmingham	14	Jul
8:40.87				7	Manchester (C)	27	Jul
8:49.75				2h2	Birmingham	12	Jul
8:51.03				4	Loughborough	18	May
8:38.68	Don Naylor		5.09.71	6	Manchester (C)	27	Jul
8:39.0				3	Manchester (C)	16	Jun
8:45.20				3	Loughborough	18	May
8:47.79				3	Manchester (Wy)	3	Jun
8:53.3				1	Luton	3	Aug
8:41.3	Pat Davoren		13.03.72	4	Manchester (C)	16	Jun
8:44.43				9	Manchester (C)	27	Jul
8:47.92				3	Birmingham	14	Jul
8:50.21				4h2	Birmingham	12	Jul
8:41.32	Chris Stephenson		22.07.74	8	Manchester (C)	27	Jul
8:42.7				5	Manchester (C)	16	Jun
8:44.31				2	Birmingham	14	Jul
8:54.72				1h1	Birmingham	12	Jul
8:44.4	Charlie Low		9.10.74	6	Manchester (C)	16	Jun
8:46.06				2	Manchester (Wy)	3	Jun
8:52.84				6	Loughborough	18	May
8:54.57				3	Birmingham	6	Jul
8:46.48	Jermaine Mays	U23	23.12.82	1h2	Birmingham	12	Jul
8:49.14				4	Birmingham	14	Jul
8:47.8	Steve Murphy	U20	6.01.83	7	Manchester (C)	16	Jun
8:54.52				8	Loughborough	18	May
8:49.2	Nick Talbot		14.12.77	8	Manchester (C)	16	Jun
8:52.02				4	Manchester (Wy)	3	Jun
8:52.88				7	Birmingham	14	Jul
8:49.33	Mark Warmby		12.12.78	5	Birmingham	14	Jul
8:49.94				3h2	Birmingham	12	Jul
(10)							
8:50.3	Gary Blackman	U23	24.09.80	1	Bedford	6	May
8:50.50	Paul Farmer		23.11.77	5h2	Birmingham	12	Jul
8:51.06	Steve Cairns		3.11.67	5	Loughborough	18	May
8:52.79	Craig Wheeler		14.06.76	6	Birmingham	14	Jul
8:53.39	Andrew Robinson		20.04.78	7	Loughborough	18	May
8:53.73				2	Birmingham	6	Jul
8:54.85				8	Birmingham	14	Jul
8:54.4	Iain Murdoch	U23	10.07.80	2	Bedford	6	May

46 performances to 8:55.00 by 16 athletes

Time	Name		DOB	Pos	Venue	Date	
8:55.23	Andrew Hennessy		24.08.77	9	Birmingham	14	Jul
8:55.54	Andrew Franklin	U23	13.09.80	2h1	Birmingham	12	Jul
8:56.5	Adam Bowden	U23	5.08.82	9	Manchester (C)	16	Jun
8:57.18	Alastair O'Connor		22.06.71	9	Loughborough	18	May
(20)							
8:58.63	Richard Vint		16.02.79	5	Indianapolis IN, USA	17	May
9:01.92	Andy Morgan-Lee		1.03.69	7	Manchester (Wy)	3	Jun
9:02.65	Owain Matthews	U23	4.11.81	4rB	Stanford, USA	3	May
9:07.51	Delroy Simon		27.11.78	6	Birmingham	6	Jul
9:07.85	Bruce Raeside	U23	2.12.81	6h1	Birmingham	12	Jul
9:08.24	Frank Tickner	U20	12.10.83	2	Gorizia, ITA	6	Jul

9:08.5	Simon Wurr		7.01.77	1	London (TB)	22	Jun
9:10.11	Lee Hurst		29.07.72	9	Lisbon, POR	26	May
9:12.4	Huw Lobb		29.08.76	2	Derby	4	Aug
9:12.5	Andy Fooks		26.04.75	2	Watford	31	Aug
(30)							
9:13.52	Andrew Thomas	U23	29.01.81	3	Watford	1	Jun
9:17.1	Andrew Lemoncello	U23	12.10.82	5	Bedford	6	May
9:17.33	Kevin Nash		6.02.77	5	London (He)	3	Aug
9:17.99	Bashir Hussain		20.12.64	1	Long Beach CA, USA	9	Jun
9:18.0	Martin Roscoe		19.09.64	1	Cleckheaton	4	May
9:19.1	Dave Mitchinson		4.09.78	2	London (Nh)	4	May
9:19.15	Daniel Lewis	U20	16.10.83	6	London (He)	3	Aug
9:20.17	John Brown		2.02.69	10	Manchester (Wy)	3	Jun
9:20.5	Andrew Mitchell	U23	30.07.80	3	Derby	11	Aug
9:21.0	Chris Sampson		30.09.75	2	Cleckheaton	4	May
(40)							
9:21.45	Ewan Malloch		4.08.76	11	Manchester (Wy)	3	Jun
9:21.5	Luke Gunn	U20	22.03.85	1	Derby	11	Aug
9:21.6	Sullivan Smith		16.09.76	2	Sheffield (W)	31	Aug
9:22.6	Ian Bowles	U20	6.01.84	1	Liverpool	18	May
9:23.55	Lee Garland		18.12.74	12	Manchester (Wy)	3	Jun
9:24.0	Peter Kellie	U20	2.01.84	1	Stoke-on-Trent	21	Jul
9:24.2	Kevin Murphy		6.04.74	2	Chelmsford	6	Jul
9:24.2	Richard Harris		16.08.71	1	Cudworth	1	Sep
9:25.2	Jonathon Creak		10.04.74	1	Portsmouth (RN)	17	Jul
9:25.3	Mike Hutchinson		5.10.65	6	Wigan	31	Aug
(50)							
9:25.99	James Fitzsimmons		20.04.74	11h2	Manchester (C)	15	Jun
9:26.6	Mark Griffith	U23	25.11.81	6	Bedford	6	May
9:27.0	Daniel Yates	U23	7.06.81	4	Derby	11	Aug
9:27.7	Alan Wray		6.01.71	8	Wigan	31	Aug
9:27.8	James Williams	U23	17.07.82	2	Eton	21	Jul
9:28.0	Matthew Bell		14.07.76	3	Sheffield	31	Aug
9:28.2	David Swinburn		4.06.78	1	Gateshead	8	Jun
9:28.6	Neil Gamester	U20	15.02.83	2	Bedford	19	May
9:29.4	Tom Payn		18.10.79	3	London (He)	21	Jul
9:29.62	Rob Berry		29.07.69	13	Manchester (Wy)	13	Jun
(60)							
9:30.1	Kevin Hope		18.04.78	1	Birmingham	1	Jun
9:30.2	Tim Woodthorpe		3.01.79	3	Wigan	7	Jul
9:30.4	Ron McWilliam		20.08.68	2	Portsmouth (RN)	17	Jul
9:31.1	Chris Symonds		21.11.73	3	Derby	4	Aug
9:31.37	Tom Tipping		29.04.66	1	Inverness	11	Aug
9:31.5	John Rice	U23	29.08.81	3	Cleckheaton	4	May
9:32.8	Tim Hyde		22.02.72	4	Derby	4	Aug
9:32.82	Martin Graham	U23	25.04.81	2	Glasgow (S)	8	Jun
9:33.3	Alistair Smith	U20	22.02.84	1	Eton	21	Jul
9:33.4	James Bailey	U20	1.06.83	5	Derby	4	Aug
(70)							
9:33.8	Wayne Dashper		19.10.74	3	Portsmouth (RN)	17	Jul
9:34.14	Paul Martin		10.07.78	1rB	Ashford	18	Aug
9:34.2	Barry Stoddart			1	Blandford	17	Jun
9:35.0	Robert Cole		13.10.79	1	Middlesbrough	6	Jul
9:35.1	Steve Millward		29.06.79	8	Bedford	6	May
9:35.1	Shaun O'Grady		24.08.75	1	Middlesbrough	3	Aug
9:35.7	Francis Malone-Lee	U23	3.03.80	9	Bedford	6	May
9:35.9	Gary Collis	U23	3.01.80	1	Yate	9	Jun
9:36.73	Daniel Simons		8.06.76	3	Bedford	25	May
9:37.0	Tim Lawrence	U20	31.03.84	4	Cleckheaton	4	May
(80)							
9:37.1	Mohamed El-Sadiki		3.11.74	4	Sheffield	31	Aug
9:37.5	Stephen Bazell		1.02.74	3	Luton	3	Aug

9:38.1	Louis Hubbard	U20	31.07.85	1	Rugby	31	Aug
9:38.3	Andy Wood	V40	27.03.62	4	Portsmouth (RN)	17	Jul
9:38.70	Alex Felce	U17	11.09.86	5	Watford	14	Aug
9:38.7	Simon Bell		26.12.66	3	London (Elt)	13	Jul
9:39.0	Adrian Whitwam		25.11.75	1	Aldershot	30	May
9:39.4	Jason Ward		15.09.78	1	Rotherham	6	Jul
9:39.9	Chris Shelton		19.10.78	1	Hull	8	Jun
9:39.9	James Henry	U20	31.07.84	1	Cudworth	25	Aug
	(90)						
9:40.1	Andrew Lingard	U23	12.09.81	1	Basildon	13	Jul
9:41.0	David Webb	U23	17.03.82	3	Grimsby	6	Jul
9:41.1	Oliver Brewer	U20	14.09.83	1	Derby	4	May
9:41.2	Mike Hoey		29.04.69	1	Bournemouth	8	Jun
9:41.9	Mark Sanford		19.04.78	1	Southampton	19	May
9:41.94	Mark Bryant		1.01.72	10	Birmingham	6	Jul
9:42.1	James Baker		21.12.76	1	Hastings	3	Aug
9:43.0	Richard Williams	U23	22.10.81	4	London (Elt)	13	Jul
9:43.1	Lee Rodriguez		30.01.74	1	Worthing	13	Jul
9:43.14	Andrew Dunwoody		6.02.76	1	Antrim	18	Jun

Additional Under 20 (1 - 13 above)

9:43.36	Lee Pickering		16.09.83	6	Watford	14	Aug
9:45.2	Paul McCloskey		9.05.85	1	Coatbridge	2	Jun
9:47.9	Gavin Smith		15.02.85	2	Hastings	8	Jun
9:48.3	James Connor		21.03.83	3	Rugby	31	Aug
9:48.6	William Docherty		2.04.85	9	Wigan	31	Aug

Foreign

9:33.30	*Martin Kearns (IRL)*		*6.04.73*	*9*	*Birmingham*	*6*	*Jul*

60 Metres Hurdles - Indoors

7.40	Colin Jackson		18.02.67	1	Vienna, AUT	2	Mar
	7.44			1	Birmingham	17	Feb
	7.48			1	Karlsruhe, GER	25	Jan
	7.49			1	Ghent, BEL	10	Feb
	7.50			1	Glasgow	9	Mar
	7.51			1h2	Karlsruhe, GER	25	Jan
	7.53			1h1	Ghent, BEL	10	Feb
	7.54			1h2	Erfurt,GER	1	Feb
	7.55			1h4	Vienna, AUT	1	Mar
	7.55			1s1	Vienna, AUT	2	Mar
	7.57			2	Dortmund, GER	27	Jan
	7.57			1r1	Sindelfingen, GER	10	Mar
	7.58			1h1	Dortmund, GER	27	Jan
	7.58			2	Erfurt,GER	1	Feb
	7.58			1r2	Sindelfingen, GER	10	Mar
	7.60			1	Cardiff	3	Feb
	7.70			1h1	Cardiff	3	Feb
7.75	Damien Greaves		19.09.77	2	Cardiff	3	Feb
	7.82			3h3	Vienna, AUT	1	Mar
	7.85			1h3	Cardiff	3	Feb
7.84	Robert Newton	U23	10.05.81	1	Birmingham	19	Jan
	7.87			3	Cardiff	3	Feb
	7.88			1	Cardiff	10	Feb
	7.91			1h2	Cardiff	3	Feb
7.87	Allan Scott	U23	27.12.82	1h3	Glasgow	24	Feb
	7.90			1	Glasgow	24	Feb
7.89	Andy Turner	U23	19.09.80	2	Birmingham	19	Jan
	7.92			1h2	Birmingham	19	Jan
	7.92			2h3	Cardiff	3	Feb

7.89	Chris Baillie	U23	21.04.81	1	Glasgow	20	Jan
7.91	Mensah Elliott		29.08.76	2h2	Cardiff	3	Feb
7.92	Tony Jarrett		13.08.68	8	Birmingham	17	Feb
7.92	Dominic Girdler	U23	6.03.82	2	Glasgow	23	Feb
7.92	Tim Reetz	U23	18.11.80	1	Boston, USA	9	Mar
(10)							
7.97	Neil Owen		18.10.73	3	Birmingham	13	Jan
7.98	Nathan Palmer	U23	16.06.82	3h2	Cardiff	3	Feb
7.98	Tristan Anthony	U23	16.12.82	3h3	Cardiff	3	Feb

37 performances to 8.00 by 13 athletes

8.08	Dwayne Stoddart	U23	29.12.80	4	Cardiff	16	Feb
8.12	Richard Sear		21.08.79	1h2	Glasgow	24	Feb
8.16	Jamie Quarry		15.11.72	4P	Warsaw, POL	7	Mar
8.19	Dominic Bradley		22.12.76	1	Sheffield	20	Jan
8.23	Chris Tye-Walker	U23	20.09.82	6	Glasgow	24	Feb
8.34	Paul Tohill	U23	9.10.82	5	Glasgow	20	Jan
8.37	Luke Gittens	U23	4.01.81	4h1	Cardiff	3	Feb
(20)							
8.38	Edward Dunford	U20	15.09.84	1	Birmingham	24	Feb
8.40	Richard Baderin	U20	25.03.83	2	Birmingham	24	Feb
8.41	Francis Smith	U23	2.10.81	1	Glasgow	13	Jun
8.42	John Heanley	U23	25.09.80	4h2	Glasgow	20	Jan
8.43	Alex Zulewski	U23	6.06.82	1H	Cardiff	10	Mar
8.44	David Hughes	U20	31.05.84	3rB	Cardiff	16	Feb
8.46	Edwin Grey	U23	23.03.81	4	Birmingham	19	Jan
8.49	Perry Batchelor		11.12.75	1h1	Birmingham	19	Jan
8.50	James Hillier		3.04.78	5h2	Cedar Falls, USA	22	Feb
8.53	Barry Thomas		28.04.72	H	Cardiff	10	Mar
(30)							
8.54	Kirk Harries		7.08.74	5h1	Cardiff	3	Feb

hand timing

8.1	Mohammed Sillah-Freckleton	U23	11.09.80	1	Eton	6	Jan

Foreign

8.4 i	Richard Alleyne (BAR)	U20	7.05.83	1	Eton	8	Dec
8.43 i	Joe Naughton (IRL)		17.10.74	H	Tallinn, EST	3	Feb
8.49 i	Lee Okoroafor (NGR)		12.09.76	8	Birmingham	13	Jan

75 Metres Hurdles - Under 13

12.0	David Paar	28.09.89	1	Bedford	18	Aug
12.4	Mike Baker	6.04.90	1	Blackheath	22	Jun
12.5	A. Mitchell	5.11.89	1	Chelmsford	15	Jun
12.7	Alexander Law	14.10.89	1	Millfield	4	Aug
12.8	James Mercer	18.11.89	1	Bromley	25	Aug
13.0	Nathan French		1	Chelmsford	14	Jul
13.04	Stuart Price	16.11.89	1	Crawley	26	Aug
13.1	Steven Banks	4.10.89	1	Southend	6	May
13.1	Andrew Smith	15.11.89	P	Dundee	1	Sep

80 Metres Hurdles - Under 13

13.2		Alexander Law	14.10.89	1	Millfield	12	Jun
13.54	-1.5	Mike Baker	6.04.90	1	Kingston	28	Jul
13.7		Stuart Price	16.11.89	1	Kingston	18	Aug
14.0		Marshall Courtney	12.01.90	1	London (TB)	24	Aug
14.11	-1.5	James Green	25.04.90	2	Kingston	28	Jul
14.18	-0.9	Charlie Rowberry	25.02.90	1	Kingston	28	Jul
14.19		Kim Johnson	22.01.90	2	Woking	1	Sep
14.2		Mike Cole	1.12.89	1	Exeter	30	Apr
14.31	-1.0	Andrew Machin		1rB	Kingston	28	Jul
14.34	-2.2	Oliver Crawshaw	20.03.90	1	Kingston	11	May

80 Metres Hurdles - Under 15

10.75	0.9	Daniel Davis	12.12.87	1	Nottingham	13	Jul
10.87	-1.2	Daniel Maynard	4.12.87	1	Birmingham	11	Aug
11.24	-1.2	Jordan Roye	3.11.87	3	Birmingham	11	Aug
11.44	1.3	Miles Jones	17.12.87	2	London (He)	25	Aug
11.48	0.5	Oliver McNeillis	24.11.87	P	Derby	22	Sep
11.51	-1.2	Vito Tomasi	17.01.88	4	Birmingham	11	Aug
11.54	-0.1	Neil Crossley	15.04.88	1P	Stoke-on-Trent	28	Sep
11.59	-0.1	Lewis Robson	9.01.88	2	Stoke-on-Trent	21	Sep
11.59 w	2.7	Michael Johnson	19.09.87	1	Birmingham	1	Sep
12.0				1	London (He)	5	May
11.6		Andrew Hill	3.12.87	1	Cheltenham	2	Jun
11.63	0.9			5	Nottingham	13	Jul
		(10)					
11.6 w		Nick Canty	9.02.88	3	Eton	6	Jul
11.8	-2.5			2h3	Nottingham	12	Jul
11.62	0.9	Guy Stroud	9.08.88	4	Nottingham	13	Jul
11.70	0.5	Stuart Todd	4.09.87	1h	Grangemouth	24	Aug
11.7		Lloyd Gumbs	5.10.87	1	Leicester	15	Jun
11.79	-0.3	Owen Jones	2.09.87	2	Tullamore, IRL	3	Aug
11.79	1.3	Ieuan Lewis	27.11.87	3	London (He)	25	Aug
11.80	2.0	Luke Keteleers	8.01.88	1h2	London (He)	25	Aug
11.8		Alex McCarthy		2	Bournemouth	22	Jun
11.8		Leon Watson	9.07.88	2	Stoke-on-Trent	30	Jun
11.8		Lawrence Scott	17.09.87	3	Stoke-on-Trent	30	Jun
		(20)					
11.90		Shaun Henderson		1	Gateshead	24	Aug
11.9		Tyrone Carter	11.08.88	2	London (WF)	2	Jun
11.9		Wayne Taylor	17.10.87	1	Scunthorpe	26	Aug
11.9		Adam Akehurst	13.09.87	1	Sandown IOW	18	Sep
11.92				1	Woking	1	Sep
12.0		Francis Baker	22.09.87	2	London (He)	5	May
12.0		Bradley Humphries	21.09.88	3	Bournemouth	22	Jun
12.0		Charles Dickson	25.11.88	1	Eton	6	Jul
12.0		Daniel Bacon	5.10.87	1	Bingham	7	Jul
12.0	-2.5	Gianni Frankis	16.04.88	4h3	Nottingham	12	Jul

100 Metres Hurdles - Under 17 (3'0")

13.40	1.2	Tom Stimson		2.09.86	1	Nottingham	13	Jul
13.43	0.2	Richard Alexis-Smith		13.02.87	1h1	Nottingham	12	Jul
13.55	-0.6	Ryan McNamara		17.06.86	2	Birmingham	11	Aug
13.57	1.2	Segun Ogunysheye		9.09.85	2	Nottingham	13	Jul
13.67	1.2	Joe Tenny		9.06.87	5	Nottingham	13	Jul
13.67	-0.6	Jordan Fleary		1.12.85	3	Birmingham	11	Aug
13.69	0.3	Edward Harrison		10.12.86	1h3	Birmingham	11	Aug
13.7 w		Matt Hansford		20.02.86	1	Bournemouth	22	Jun
13.74	1.2				6	Nottingham	13	Jul
13.71	-0.6	Craig France		1.01.87	6	Birmingham	11	Aug
13.71		Daniel Maynard	U15	4.12.87	1	Tamworth	26	Aug
		(10)						
13.75	1.3	Robert James		1.04.87	1	Birmingham	31	Aug
13.78		Darren Lewis		12.04.86	2	Tamworth	26	Aug
13.8		Duncan Hawksworth		23.05.86	1	Bingham	30	Jun
14.10	-1.7				3h2	Nottingham	12	Jul
13.8 w		Chris Baily		1.12.86	1	Pitreavie	12	Jun
14.1					1	Coatbridge	23	Jun
13.8 w		Jack Singleton		17.12.85	3	Bournemouth	22	Jun
13.84	0.0	Barry O'Brien		21.04.86	4	Glasgow (S)	20	Jul
13.84	1.3	Philip Browne		10.11.85	2	Birmingham	31	Aug
13.9		Andrew Holgate		16.08.86	1	Cheltenham	2	Jun
14.16	0.0				6	Glasgow (S)	20	Jul

13.9		Richard Hansard	5.11.86	1	Watford	30	Jun
			14.09 w 2.5		3	Watford	26	May
			14.15	0.5	4h1	Birmingham	11	Aug
13.9 w		Peter Corbett	5.11.85	4	Bournemouth	22	Jun
	(20)						
13.97 w 2.5	Chris Duck	7.06.86	2	Watford	26	May
14.03 w 2.7	Patrick Halcrow	9.01.86	1	Basildon	11	May
14.1		Ryan Shaw		1	Basildon	19	May
14.05	0.3	Maurice Ryan	17.02.86	3h3	Birmingham	11	Aug
14.08	-2.3	Louis Moore	8.09.85	1D	Stoke-on-Trent	29	Sep
14.09	0.2	Ryan Shaw	30.12.86	6h1	Nottingham	12	Jul
14.1		Mark McCluskey	19.07.86	1	Coatbridge	19	May
		14.20	0.5	6h1	Birmingham	11	Aug
14.1		Ben Carne	11.06.86	2	London (Cr)	19	May
14.1		James Dohnal	18.09.85	D	Preston	30	Jun
14.1 w		Glenn Etherington	10.12.86	5	Bournemouth	22	Jun
14.1 w		Richard Reeks	6.12.85	6	Bournemouth	22	Jun
	(30)						
14.12	1.5	Euron Roberts	18.11.85	1	Brecon	6	Jul
14.17	0.5	Nick Pritchard	19.01.87	5h1	Birmingham	11	Aug

110 Metres Hurdles - Under 20 (3'3")

14.29	-0.4	Edward Dunford	15.09.84	1	Watford	1	Sep
14.84	0.8	Richard Baderin	25.03.83	4	Derby	8	Sep
14.51	0.7	Robert Henry	31.05.85	1	Manchester (C)	25	May
14.53	2.0	Steve Green	15.01.83	2	London (He)	25	Aug
14.64	0.8	Andrew Hopkinson	20.09.83	2	Derby	8	Sep
14.67 w		Ross Tressider	8.01.83	1	Basildon	11	May
		14.96	-0.4	4	Watford	1	Sep
14.75 w 2.6	Peter Irving	28.01.83	2h2	Watford	26	May
		14.93	1.0	3	Watford	26	May
14.76 w 2.6	Kenneth Frempong	17.07.84	3h1	Watford	26	May
		14.78	1.0	2	Watford	26	May
14.77 w 2.3	Kris Jones	7.03.83	1	Cardiff	26	Aug
		15.00		1	Newport	12	May
14.81	0.8	Tom Carey	26.02.84	3	Derby	8	Sep
	(10)						
14.88	-0.4	Nick Gayle	4.01.85	3	Watford	1	Sep
14.95	0.7	Suote Nyananyo	3.10.84	3	Manchester (C)	25	May
15.00	1.0	Mark Winship	29.09.83	4	Watford	26	May
15.08	0.8	Adam Draycott	7.11.84	5	Derby	8	Sep
15.09	1.0	Paul McKeown	23.01.83	5	Watford	26	May
15.09	1.0	Richard Fitzgerald	6.06.84	6	Watford	26	May
15.11 w 3.3	David Collard	25.01.85	1	Edinburgh	11	May
		15.19	-0.1	1	Grangemouth	14	Jun
15.13 w 3.3	Calum Laing	21.08.83	2	Edinburgh	11	May
15.16	0.9	Richard Myers	21.12.83	3h1	Manchester (C)	25	May
15.16	1.4	Duncan Rogers	10.10.84	4h1	Watford	26	May
	(20)						
15.25	0.6	Colin Bailey	15.11.83	2h2	Watford	26	May
15.27	2.0	Greg Smith	29.01.84	3	London (He)	25	Aug
15.29	2.0	Richard Aidoo	15.02.85	2	Kingston	11	May
15.39		Ben Hazell	1.10.84	D	Derby	22	Sep
15.44	-0.1	Matthew Thompson	29.12.84	2	Grangemouth	14	Jun
15.48	0.7	Daniel Armstrong	16.11.84	6	Manchester (C)	25	May
15.48	2.0	Simon Wombwell		5	London (He)	25	Aug

hand timing

14.5	1.2	Robin Smith	11.09.83	1	Cannock	15	Jun
14.5		Richard Baderin	(14.84)	1	Scunthorpe	23	Jun
14.6	1.2	Nick Gayle	(14.88)	2	Cannock	15	Jun

14.7		Ross Tressider		(14.67w)	1	Bedford	28	Apr
14.7		Stephen Alexander		6.10.84	1	Macclesfield	15	Jun
14.8		Richard Fitzgerald		(15.09)	1	Eton	23	Jun
14.8 w		Darren Lewis	U17	12.04.86	1	Tipton	18	Aug
14.9		Suote Nyananyo		(14.95)	4	Scunthorpe	23	Jun
14.9		Peter Middleton		27.01.84	3	Wakefield	28	Jul
15.0	-1.3	Daniel Armstrong		(15.48)	5h1	Nottingham	12	Jul
15.0	-1.3	Matt Love		28.12.84	6h1	Nottingham	12	Jul
15.1		David Taylor		21.11.84	1	Bournemouth	22	Jun
15.1	1.7	William Sharman		12.09.84	6	Nottingham	13	Jul
15.1		Michael Dyer		27.09.84	1	Eton	28	Jul
15.2		Colin Bailey		(15.25)	1	Manchester (Str)	26	Aug
15.2		Ben Hazell		(15.39)	1	London (He)	15	Sep
15.4		Andrew Grubb		26.12.83	1	Nottingham	11	May
15.4		L. Edimann			1	Bournemouth	15	Jun
15.4		Tom Reynolds		20.12.84		Bangor	30	Jun
15.4		Craig MacKay		30.10.84	3	Eton	28	Jul
15.4		Calum Laing		(15.13w)	1	Jarrow	18	Aug
15.4		Dan Bray		6.09.83	2	London (He)	15	Sep
15.5		Robert Miller		20.01.84	3	Eton	23	Jun
15.5		Rupert Gardner		9.10.84	1r2	London (He)	15	Sep
15.5		Bertram Nnanyere		26.09.83	2r2	London (He)	15	Sep

doubtful

14.5	-0.6	Simon Wombwell			1	Watford	12	May

110 Metres Hurdles

13.11	0.4	Colin Jackson	18.02.67	1	Munich, GER	10	Aug
	13.15	0.7		1	Annecy, FRA	23	Jun
	13.18	1.1		4	Lausanne, SUI	2	Jul
	13.21	0.8		1s2	Munich, GER	10	Aug
	13.23	-0.8		1	Helsinki, FIN	13	Aug
	13.24	1.0		4	Zagreb, CRO	8	Jul
	13.31	1.9		1	Perth, AUS	16	Mar
	13.34	0.7		1h3	Manchester (C)	29	Jul
	13.36	0.2		1	Naimette, BEL	27	Aug
	13.36	0.0		1	Rovereto, ITA	28	Aug
	13.37	-1.6		3	London (CP)	23	Aug
	13.38	-0.3		1	Linz, AUT	19	Aug
	13.39	0.4		2	Manchester (C)	30	Jul
	13.40	0.4		2	Prague, CZE	17	Jun
	13.40	0.3		1	Birmingham	13	Jul
	13.41	1.1		1	Dortmund, GER	8	Jun
	13.41	-0.9		1h1	Munich, GER	9	Aug
	13.43	1.2		3	Sheffield	30	Jun
	13.43	-0.6		2h2	Zagreb, CRO	8	Jul
	13.44	0.0		4	Saint-Denis, FRA	5	Jul
	13.44	-1.4		3	Yokohama, JPN	16	Sep
	13.46	1.0		1	Adelaide, AUS	23	Mar
	13.46	-1.6		3	Ostrava, CZE	12	Jun
	13.47	0.0		1	Velenje, SLO	14	Jun
	13.48	0.4		1h1	Brisbane, AUS	13	Apr
	13.57	0.0		1h2	Birmingham	13	Jul
	13.71	-1.1		1	Brisbane, AUS	14	Apr
13.40	-0.8	Tony Jarrett	13.08.68	4	Helsinki, FIN	13	Aug
	13.52	0.3		2	Birmingham	13	Jul
	13.58	0.9		1	Bangor, NI	21	Jul
	13.63	-0.1		2h4	Munich, GER	9	Aug
	13.65	0.1		2h2	Manchester (C)	29	Jul

Time	Wind	Name	Cat	DOB	Pos	Venue	Date	
(Jarrett)					1	Birmingham	6	Jul
13.68	-0.5				4	Manchester (C)	30	Jul
13.70	0.4				2	Cardiff	8	Jul
13.71	0.4				2h3	Birmingham	13	Jul
13.75	0.0				1	Veszprem, HUN	29	Jun
13.78	-1.3				1	Dublin, IRL	19	Jul
13.78	-0.5				5	Turin, ITA	7	Jun
13.80	-0.7				1r2	Veszprem, HUN	30	Jun
13.91	-0.6				3	Birmingham	13	Jul
13.54	0.3	Damien Greaves		19.09.77	1	Manchester (C)	15	Jun
13.73	-1.2				1h3	Birmingham	13	Jul
13.74	0.0				1	Loughborough	18	May
13.75	1.3				2h3	Manchester (C)	29	Jul
13.78	0.7				2	Birmingham	6	Jul
13.80	-0.5				1h1	Manchester (C)	15	Jun
13.82	-0.6				1	Bedford	4	Jun
13.87	0.1				4h2	Munich, GER	9	Aug
13.90	0.5				2	Celle Ligure, ITA	26	Jun
13.94	1.1				2	Loughborough	18	May
13.85	1.3	Paul Gray		25.05.69	4	Cardiff	8	Jul
13.91	0.4				1	Bedford	25	May
13.93	1.3				1h1	Birmingham	13	Jul
13.96	0.4				6	Birmingham	13	Jul
14.00	0.3				4	Birmingham	13	Jul
13.85	0.3	Mensah Elliott		29.08.76	2	Bedford	4	Jun
13.87	0.1				2	Manchester (C)	15	Jun
13.95	-1.2				2h1	Birmingham	13	Jul
13.98	0.4				1h3	Manchester (C)	15	Jun
13.99	-0.3				1h2	Manchester (C)	15	Jun
13.90	0.8	Neil Owen		18.10.73	4	Birmingham	6	Jul
13.91	-0.5				4	Manchester (C)	15	Jun
13.96	-1.2				4	Bedford	4	Jun
14.00	0.1				2	Niort, FRA	3	Aug
13.90	-1.2	Andy Turner	U23	19.09.80	3	Loughborough	18	May
13.92	1.3	Robert Newton	U23	10.05.81	3	Bedford	4	Jun
13.92	0.1				2h2	Manchester (C)	15	Jun
13.95	0.8	Chris Baillie	U23	21.04.81	3h2	Manchester (C)	29	Jul
13.95	0.1				3	Celle Ligure, ITA	26	Jun
13.96	1.1				4	Loughborough	18	May
13.97	1.3				3	Manchester (C)	15	Jun
13.95	-1.2	Dominic Girdler	U23	6.03.82	5	Birmingham	13	Jul
13.95	0.3							

73 performances to 14.00 by 10 athletes

Time	Wind	Name	Cat	DOB	Pos	Venue	Date	
14.05	-0.3	Allan Scott	U23	27.12.82	2h3	Manchester (C)	15	Jun
14.05	0.9	Mohammed Sillah-Freckleton	U23	11.09.80	2h1	Loughborough	17	Jul
14.09	0.8	Tristan Anthony	U23	16.12.82	3h2	Manchester (C)	15	Jun
14.10 A	1.8	Tim Reetz	U23	18.11.80	1	Alamosa, USA	4	May
14.18	0.4				1	Stanford, USA	10	May
14.24	0.6	Nathan Palmer	U23	16.06.82	1	Cardiff	26	Aug
14.25	0.3	Duncan Malins		12.06.78	2rB	Loughborough	18	May
14.25	0.9	Liam Collins		23.10.78	4h1	Loughborough	17	Jul
14.39	-0.5	Matt Douglas		26.11.76	2	Bedford	17	Aug
14.45	0.3	Richard Sear		21.08.79	6rB	Loughborough	18	May
14.48	1.6	Dwayne Stoddart	U23	29.12.80	2h2	Loughborough	17	Jul
(20)								
14.62	-0.2	Francis Smith	U23	2.10.81	2r2	Birmingham	6	Jul
14.64	1.5	Lee Tindal	U23	19.02.80	3	Watford	2	Jun
14.75	1.8	Paul Crossley		30.03.79	1	Edinburgh	6	Jul
14.77	1.6	David Hughes	U20	31.05.84	3h2	Loughborough	17	Jul
14.78	1.2	Paul Tohill	U23	9.10.82	3	Namur, BEL	31	Aug
14.80	0.9	Anthony Sawyer	U23	29.04.80	D	Maribor, SLO	30	Jun

14.83	1.9	Jamie Quarry		15.11.72	3D	Hexham	16 Jun
14.91	-1.1	Greg Dunson		2.12.63	1r3	Birmingham	6 Jul
14.92	0.0	John Heanley	U23	25.09.80	1D	Arles, FRA	2 Jun
14.92	1.9	Edward Dunford	U20	15.09.84	D	Pratteln, SUI	4 Aug
	(30)						
14.93	0.4	Nick Cooper		4.02.77	3h1	Watford	2 Jun
15.07	1.5	Charles Akpabio		14.10.79	4	Watford	2 Jun
15.09	0.0	Martyn Hendry		10.04.75	1	Glasgow (S)	14 Jul
15.11	0.6	Barry Thomas		28.04.72	3D1	Manchester (C)	28 Jul
15.16		Noel Levy		22.06.75	2	Ashford	18 Aug
15.17	-1.1	Isaac McCalla	U23	28.03.82	3r3	Birmingham	6 Jul
15.20		James Hillier		3.04.78	3	Des Moines IA, USA	13 Apr
15.21	-0.8	Kris Jones	U20	7.03.83	6	Gorizia, ITA	6 Jul
15.21	-1.0	Richard Baderin	U20	25.03.83	2	Watford	1 Sep
15.22	1.8	James Lowery	U23	17.10.80	D	Pratteln, SUI	4 Aug
	(40)						
15.23	1.4	James Wright	U23	2.04.82	1D	Wrexham	23 Jun
15.25	1.8	Edwin Grey	U23	23.03.81	3	Edinburgh	6 Jul
15.26	-0.1	Stephen Alexander	U20	6.10.84	2r2	London (He)	3 Aug
15.29		Paul Gilding		2.10.75	3	Ashford	18 Aug
15.30	1.3	Colin Roberts	U23	20.01.81	5h2	Bedford	30 Jun
15.32	1.4	Brendan McConville		3.01.79	D	Maribor, SLO	30 Jun
15.33	0.0	Adrian Hemery	U23	6.08.82	D	Pratteln, SUI	4 Aug
15.34	-1.2	Perry Batchelor		11.12.75	6h1	Bedford	25 May
15.38	1.8	Robin Smith	U20	11.09.83	5	Edinburgh	6 Jul
15.39	-1.6	Jason McDade	U23	3.04.80	2D	London (He)	11 Aug
	(50)						
15.44	-0.5	Anthony Southward		31.01.71	5	Bedford	17 Aug
15.47		Gareth Power	U23	5.06.82	2ro	Bedford	6 May
15.47	-2.8	James Quirk		16.03.78	4rB	Bath	12 May
15.48		Andy Lewis		9.03.68	D	Valladolid, ESP	8 Jun
15.50	0.4	Alex Beech		17.04.77	5h1	Watford	2 Jun
15.50	0.6	Dale Garland	U23	13.10.80	6D1	Manchester (C)	28 Jul
15.53	-0.1	Richard McDonald	U23	11.01.80	4rB	London (He)	3 Aug
15.53	-0.1	Richard Scott		14.09.73	5rB	London (He)	3 Aug
15.60	-1.2	James Parker	U23	29.09.80	3	Kingston	11 May
15.60	-0.5	Andrew Bargh		21.08.76	6	Bedford	17 Aug
	(60)						
15.62	-1.5	Paul Gripton		9.11.76	5h3	Bedford	25 May
15.63		Calum Laing	U20	21.08.83	1	Grangemouth	5 Jun
15.63	1.2	Gez Plunkett	U23	30.06.80	D	Pratteln, SUI	4 Aug
15.63		Mark Winship	U20	29.09.83	3rB	Copenhagen, DEN	21 Sep
15.65		Steve Bonnett		13.07.78	D	Woodford	28 Apr
15.67	-1.4	Emile Robinson	U23	26.11.81	2	Jarrow	1 Jun

wind assisted

13.32	2.2	Jackson		(13.11)	2	Glasgow (S)	18 Aug
13.78	2.4	Greaves		(13.54)	1	Watford	19 May
13.90	2.4	Owen		(13.90)	2	Watford	19 May
13.97	2.3	Turner	U23	(13.90)	3	Newport	20 Jul
13.91A	3.0	Tim Reetz	U23	(14.18)	1h1	Alamosa, USA	3 May
	13.93	3.1		(14.18)	2h3	San Angelo TX, USA	24 May
		6 performances to 14.00 by 5 athletes					
14.58	5.0	David Hughes	U20	(14.77)	1h1	Bedford	30 Jun
14.67	2.6	Anthony Sawyer	U23	(14.80)	1	Basildon	11 May
14.82	2.6	Alex Zulewski	U23	1.11.83	2	Basildon	11 May
14.83	3.0	Kris Jones	U20	(15.21)	3	Bedford	30 Jun
15.02	2.1	Richard Baderin	U20	(15.21)	2h2	Bedford	30 Jun
15.06	2.4	Anthony Southward		(15.44)	5	Watford	19 May
15.17	3.0	Peter Irving	U20	28.01.83	5	Bedford	30 Jun
15.18	5.0	Andrew Hopkinson	U20	20.09.83	3h1	Bedford	30 Jun

15.27	5.0	Duncan Rogers	U20	10.10.84	4h1	Bedford	30	Jun
15.38	5.0	Calum Laing	U20	(15.63)	5h1	Bedford	30	Jun
15.49	2.1	Olly Mahony	U20	21.10.83	4h2	Bedford	30	Jun
15.51	2.4	Michael Dyer	U20	27.09.84	D	Wrexham	23	Jun
15.59 ?	2.1	Colin Bailey (15.69?)	U20	15.11.83	3	Cudworth	14	Sep
15.66	2.6	Martin Ohrland		19.11.79	4	Basildon	11	May
15.66	2.6	John Franklin		1.03.66	5	Basildon	11	May

hand timing

13.8		Jackson		(13.11)	1	Newport	9	Jun
14.0	1.6	Girdler	U23	(13.95)	1	Bedford	30	Jun
14.1	1.8	Tim Reetz	U23	(14.18)	1	Loughborough	12	Jun
14.7		Jamie Quarry		(14.83)	1	Basildon	13	Jul
14.7 w?		Edward Dunford	U20	(14.92)	2	Wigan	31	Aug
14.8	-0.6	Colin Roberts	U23	(15.30)	1	Loughborough	27	Apr
14.8 w	2.7	John Heanley	U23	(14.92)		Perpignan, FRA	21	Apr
14.8 w		Richard Baderin	U20	(15.21)	1	Liverpool	14	Jul
14.9		Ken Campbell		30.09.72	1r2	Coatbridge	2	Jun
14.9 w	2.6	Chris Tye-Walker	U23	20.09.82	2	Loughborough	22	May
15.0		Charles Akpabio		(15.07)	1	Bury St. Edmunds	13	Jul
15.0	1.9	Daniel Everett	U23	30.01.81	2	London (He)	21	Jul
15.0 w?		Isaac McCalla	U23	(15.17)	3	Wigan	31	Aug
15.0 w?		Charles Robertson-Adams		5.12.77	4	Wigan	31	Aug
15.1		Paul Gilding		(15.29)	1	Woodford	18	May
15.1	1.5	Alex Zulewski	U23	(14.82w)	6	Bedford	19	May
15.1		Chris Hargrave		27.02.79	1	London (Ha)	22	Jun
15.1 w		Martin Ohrland		(15.66w)	1	Chelmsford	14	Jul
		15.3	0.7		D	Watford	29	Sep
15.2	2.0	Gareth Power	U23	(15.47)	4h2	Bedford	6	May
15.2		Alex Beech		(15.50)	1	Exeter	18	May
15.2		James Parker	U23	(15.60)	1	Bournemouth	8	Jun
15.2		Kris Jones	U20	(15.21)	2	Aberdare	15	Jun
15.2	1.5	Edwin Grey	U23	(15.25)	6h1	Bedford	30	Jun
15.2		Dale Garland	U23	(15.50)	2	St. Peter Port, Gue	14	Sep
15.3		Jason McDade	U23	(15.39)	1	Ipswich	12	May
15.3	-1.4	Perry Batchelor		(15.34)	1	Liverpool	18	May
15.3		Adrian Hemery	U23	(15.33)	1	Loughborough	12	Jun
15.3		Richard Scott		(15.53)	5	Wigan	31	Aug
15.4		Emile Robinson	U23	(15.67)	1	Cudworth	4	May
15.4		Ross Tressider	U20	8.01.83	2	Basildon	4	May
15.4	-4.0	Gary Smith		20.02.71	1r2	Cardiff	18	May
15.4	1.6	Paul Gripton		(15.62)	5r2	Watford	19	May
15.4		William Wyllie		12.07.73	1	Yate	9	Jun
15.4		Chris Fuller	U23	2.02.82	2	Walton	13	Jul
15.5		Peter Irving	U20	(15.17w)	1	Crawley	4	May
15.5		Gary Myles		3.02.63	2	Telford	6	Jul
15.5		Andrew Bargh		(15.60)	6	Derby	4	Aug
15.5		Nick Gayle	U20	4.01.85	1r2	Sheffield	31	Aug
15.6		Livio Salvador-Aylott		18.07.73	D	-, USA	1	Apr
15.6		Andrew Grant	U23	4.10.82	3	Grangemouth	28	Apr
15.6		Michael Dyer	U20	(15.51w)	3	Basildon	4	May
15.6		Joe Appiah		26.10.70	2	London (CP)	11	May
15.6		Nick Foxworthy	U20	20.05.83	2	Exeter	18	May
15.6		Mark Winship	U20	(15.63)	4r2	Bedford	19	May
15.6	-0.4	David Taylor	U20	21.11.84	1	Chelmsford	6	Jul
15.6		Nigel Hayman		25.09.74	2	Bury St. Edmunds	13	Jul
15.6		Gareth Evans		28.05.77	3	Portsmouth (RN)	17	Jul

15.6	Andrew Dean		30.06.78	1r2	Luton	3	Aug
15.6	Dimean Cookey		8.10.79	1	London (Cat)	22	Aug
15.6	Martin Lloyd	U23	18.06.80	D	Erith	22	Sep

Foreign

14.59	0.3	Stephen McDonnell (IRL) U23	24.07.80	2		Dublin (S), IRL	14	Jul
14.59 w	5.0	Richard Alleyne (BAR) U20	7.05.83	2h1		Bedford	30	Jun
		14.70		3		Bridgetown, BAR	10	Mar
14.68		Paul Conroy (IRL)	24.08.71	1		Belfast	8	Jun
14.8		Lee Okoroafor (NGR)	12.09.76	1		Portsmouth (RN)	17	Jul
		15.68		D		Woodford	28	Apr
14.83		Peter Monaghan (IRL) U23	25.05.81	h		Dublin (S), IRL	13	Jul
15.23	0.9	Olau Thomassen (DEN) U23	19.02.80	h		Loughborough	17	Jul
15.3		Joe Naughton (IRL)	17.10.74	1		Walton	8	Jun
15.4		Royden John (RSA)	6.09.72	1		Walton	13	Jul
15.4		Christiaan De Jager (RSA)	23.04.74	1rB		Walton	13	Jul

200 Metres Hurdles

24.54	-1.7	Steve Green	U20	15.01.83	1	Oxford	18 May

300 Metres Hurdles

34.48	Chris Rawlinson		19.05.72	1	Sheffield	30 Jun
35.46	Tony Borsumato		13.12.73	3	Sheffield	30 Jun
35.56	Matt Douglas		26.11.76	4	Sheffield	30 Jun

400 Metres Hurdles

48.21	Chris Rawlinson	19.05.72	1	Lausanne, SUI	2	Jul
	48.26		2	Saint-Denis, FRA	5	Jul
	48.49		1	Walnut CA, USA	21	Apr
	48.68		1	Birmingham	14	Jul
	48.87		3	Annecy, FRA	22	Jun
	49.14		1	Manchester (C)	29	Jul
	49.17		4	Athens, GRE	10	Jun
	49.18		3	Madrid, ESP	20	Sep
	49.48		2s2	Munich, GER	8	Aug
	49.52		8	Paris, FRA	14	Sep
	49.66		1h2	Manchester (C)	28	Jul
	49.73		2h4	Munich, GER	7	Aug
	49.73		7	London (CP)	23	Aug
	49.98		1rB	Lisbon, POR	25	May
	50.55		1h2	Birmingham	13	Jul
	50.86		1	Athens, GRE	12	May
48.90	Tony Borsumato	13.12.73	2	Birmingham	14	Jul
	49.19		4	Linz, AUT	19	Aug
	49.20		5	Zagreb, CRO	8	Jul
	49.26		2h1	Manchester (C)	28	Jul
	49.37		5s1	Munich, GER	8	Aug
	49.42		3rB	Zurich, SUI	16	Aug
	49.46		1h3	Birmingham	13	Jul
	49.52		2	Manchester (C)	16	Jun
	49.72		4	Manchester (C)	29	Jul
	49.72		5	Glasgow (S)	18	Aug
	49.77		2	Rovereto, ITA	28	Aug
	49.90		5	Prague, CZE	17	Jun
	49.93		2h2	Munich, GER	7	Aug
	49.96		5	Padua, ITA	1	Sep
	50.25		1	Dortmund, GER	8	Jun
	50.76		1h4	Manchester (C)	15	Jun

49.11	Matt Elias		25.04.79	1h1	Manchester (C)	28	Jul
49.18				2rB	Zurich, SUI	16	Aug
49.28				2	Manchester (C)	29	Jul
49.46				1	Manchester (C)	16	Jun
49.46				3	Glasgow (S)	18	Aug
49.59				6	London (CP)	23	Aug
49.71				1h1	Birmingham	13	Jul
49.73				1h2	Manchester (C)	15	Jun
49.77				2	Brisbane, AUS	13	Apr
49.79				3	Birmingham	14	Jul
50.00				2	Cardiff	8	Jul
50.18				4h3	Munich, GER	7	Aug
50.48				1h2	Brisbane, AUS	11	Apr
49.38	Matt Douglas		26.11.76	4h1	Manchester (C)	28	Jul
49.49				2	La Laguna, ESP	14	Sep
49.63				1	Meilen, SUI	9	Jun
49.66				1	Dublin (S), IRL	19	Jul
49.76				3	Manchester (C)	16	Jun
49.79				2h2	Manchester (C)	15	Jun
49.82				2	Loughborough	17	Jul
49.87				2h1	Birmingham	13	Jul
50.01				2	Birmingham	6	Jul
50.12				4	Birmingham	14	Jul
50.23				3	Brasschaat, BEL	14	Aug
50.34				1	Tartu, EST	2	Jun
50.7				2	Riga, LAT	31	May
50.71				1	Bedford	17	Aug
50.82				4	Lisbon, POR	25	May
51.0				1	London (He)	21	Jul
50.16	Steve Surety	U23	18.02.80	4	Manchester (C)	16	Jun
50.29				3	Niort, FRA	3	Aug
50.36				1	Namur, BEL	26	Jul
50.48				2	Tartu, EST	2	Jun
50.5				1	Riga, LAT	31	May
50.58				1	Newport	20	Jul
50.77				1	Loughborough	18	May
50.78				2h3	Birmingham	13	Jul
50.8				1	Derby	11	Aug
50.88				2h4	Manchester (C)	15	Jun
50.9				1	Bedford	26	May
50.30	Liam Collins		23.10.78	5	Birmingham	14	Jul
50.70				2h2	Birmingham	13	Jul
50.76				1rB	Loughborough	17	Jul
50.99				5	Manchester (C)	16	Jun
50.68	Jared Deacon		15.10.75	1	Gateshead	12	May
51.0				2	Bedford	25	May
50.83	Richard McDonald	U23	11.01.80	2r4	Walnut CA, USA	21	Apr
50.9				1	Azusa, USA	13	Apr
50.96	Steve Green	U20	15.01.83	1	Gorizia, ITA	6	Jul
50.97	Charles Robertson-Adams		5.12.77	1	Bath	12	May
	82 performances to 51.0 by 10 athletes						
51.02	James Hillier		3.04.78	2r2	Birmingham (Un)	19	Jun
51.04	Noel Levy		22.06.75	2rB	Loughborough	17	Jul
51.14	Richard Smith	U23	12.10.82	5	Niort, FRA	3	Aug
51.33	Jeffrey Christie	U23	24.09.82	4h2	Birmingham	13	Jul
51.5	Nange Ursell	U23	1.10.81	1	Wigan	7	Jul
52.55				4h2	Manchester (C)	15	Jun
51.68	Rhys Williams	U20	27.02.84	3s2	Kingston, JAM	17	Jul
51.73	Leon McRae	U23	3.11.80	1r4	Atlanta GA, USA	18	May
52.0	David Brackstone	U23	13.03.82	1	Sheffield (W)	31	Aug
52.66				5h2	Manchester (C)	15	Jun

52.29	Rupert Gardner	U20	9.10.84	1	Nottingham	13	Jul
52.44	Bradley Yiend	U23	25.10.80	4h1	Birmingham	13	Jul
(20)							
52.6	Andrew Bennett	U23	30.09.82	1rB	Watford	19	May
53.52				1h2	Watford	1	Jun
52.7	Richard Scott		14.09.73	1h3	Watford	1	Jun
52.89				1rC	Birmingham	6	Jul
52.8	Ian Neely		29.12.74	6	Riga, LAT	31	May
53.21				4	Belfast	8	Jun
52.86	Dale Garland	U23	13.10.80	2rB	Birmingham (Un)	19	Jun
53.0	Robert Lewis		2.09.78	1	Southampton	8	Sep
53.12	Chris Sleeman	U23	20.03.80	5h3	Birmingham	13	Jul
53.18	Dan Bray	U20	6.09.83	2	Nottingham	13	Jul
53.28	Joe Lloyd		9.04.73	2rC	Loughborough	17	Jul
53.6	Derek Paisley		1.12.73	1	Coatbridge	2	Jun
53.66				3	Glasgow (S)	9	Jun
53.64	Richard Castillo	U23	3.12.81	3rB	Birmingham (Un)	19	Jun
(30)							
53.70	John Bell		10.09.73	2	Birmingham	1	Jun
53.7	Andrew Bargh		21.08.76	5	Watford	1	Jun
53.72				2h2	Watford	1	Jun
53.81	James Lee		6.02.79	3h2	Bedford	26	May
53.9	James Parker	U23	29.09.80	6	Watford	1	Jun
53.96				3h2	Watford	1	Jun
53.95	Howard Frost	U23	9.12.81	3h3	Manchester (C)	15	Jun
54.0	Ryan Dinham	U20	19.08.85	1	London (He)	28	Apr
55.26				4rB	Loughborough	18	May
54.1	Martin Thomas		21.09.78	1	Chelmsford	6	Jul
54.17	David O'Leary	U23	3.08.80	5rB	Birmingham	6	Jul
54.2	Joel Hopkins		24.11.77	2rB	Derby	4	Aug
54.45				3h1	Watford	1	Jun
54.2	Ross Tressider	U20	8.01.83	1	Basildon	18	Aug
55.31				4	London (He)	25	Aug
(40)							
54.25	Peter Irving	U20	28.01.83	3h2	Bedford	29	Jun
54.27	Lee Wiscombe	U23	12.07.80	5h1	Manchester (C)	15	Jun
54.3	Mark Winship	U20	29.09.83	2	London (He)	28	Apr
54.48				2h2	Nottingham	12	Jul
54.35	Ben Sumner	U20	16.08.83	2	Copenhagen, DEN	21	Sep
54.37	Andy Clements	U23	28.11.82	2	Portsmouth	11	May
54.4	Alex Zulewski	U23	6.06.82	4	Derby	4	Aug
54.5	Jon Goodwin		22.09.76	1	Kingston	20	May
55.65				3h3	Bedford	4	May
54.57	Tom Carey	U20	26.02.84	3	Nottingham	13	Jul
54.60	Ian Monaghan	U23	6.11.81	6	Watford	19	May
54.6	Ben Caldwell	U23	3.03.82	2	Chelmsford	6	Jul
(50)							
54.6	Nick Edwards	U23	22.03.81	1	Portsmouth (RN)	17	Jul
54.6	Alex Beech		17.04.77	3	Eton	21	Jul
55.37				4h1	Watford	1	Jun
54.7	Graeme Lammie	U23	3.10.81	1	Glasgow (S)	14	Jul
55.38				4rB	London (He)	3	Aug
54.7	John McIlwham		29.02.72	2	Blackpool	3	Aug
54.7	Mensah Elliott		29.08.76	3	Watford	31	Aug
54.7	David Taylor	U20	21.11.84	1	Rugby	31	Aug
54.77	Andrew Dean		30.06.78	2	Edinburgh	6	Jul
54.8	Peter Middleton	U20	27.01.84	1	Gateshead	15	Jun
55.41				1	Gateshead	12	May
55.0	Sean Reidy	U23	27.01.81	1	Peterborough	22	Jun
55.93				4h3	Bedford	29	Jun
55.01	Stephen Murphy	U23	10.02.82	3	Edinburgh	6	Jul

55.1	Mark Garner	U20	2.11.83	1	Mansfield	28	Apr
	56.88			6h2	Nottingham	12	Jul
55.1	Austin Ferns	U23	12.01.81	3h3	Watford	1	Jun
55.1	Daniel Everett	U23	30.01.81	4	Blackpool	3	Aug
	55.71			6	Birmingham (Un)	19	Jun
55.1	Darren Robinson	U23	20.06.80	2	London (ME)	3	Aug
55.12	Andrew Grubb	U20	26.12.83	4	Nottingham	13	Jul
55.16	Wilby Williamson	U23	8.08.81	1	Bangor	21	Jul
55.2	Simon Wilson		30.04.74	3	London (CP)	11/12	May
55.2	Dave Savage		13.11.72	5	Bedford	19	May
55.2	Ben Hazell	U20	1.10.84	5	Eton	21	Jul
	55.22			5	Nottingham	13	Jul
55.2	Paul Couldridge		9.05.74	2	Salisbury	3	Aug
	(70)						
55.36	Nick Cooper		4.02.77	1	London (BP)	26	Jun
55.4	Howard Moscrop	V40	16.12.57	5	Blackpool	3	Aug
55.5	Ian Palmer	U23	22.11.81	3h4	Bedford	4	May
55.6	Russell Frost	U23	23.06.80	3	Chelmsford	6	Jul
55.7	Gerald Manville		21.12.78	6	Eton	21	Jul
55.7	Robert Gascoigne		5.10.74	5	Watford	31	Aug
	56.00			4	Jarrow	1	Jun
55.86	Joseph Maynard	U20	25.07.85	1	Newport	9	Jun
55.87	Lee Tindal	U23	19.02.80	3	Portsmouth	11	May
55.89	Guy Dunlop	U20	28.07.83	2	Belfast	11	May
55.9	Ian Purcell	U20	20.12.84	1	Antrim	26	May
	56.34			3	Belfast	11	May
	(80)						
55.97	Andrew Kennard		2.01.66	3	Bedford	17	Aug
56.0	Oliver Teasel	U20	24.04.84	1	Derby	28	Apr
56.0	David Brown		1.03.78	1	Yate	9	Jun

Additional Under 20 (1 - 19 above)

56.1	Adam Fell		20.04.85	1	Cleckheaton	15	Jun
	(20)						
56.3	Alex Court		27.02.84	2	London (CP)	12	May
56.38	Malcolm Hawkins		17.12.83	4h1	Nottingham	12	Jul
56.40	Matthew Williams		31.01.84	2	Newport	9	Jun
56.61	Tim Wallis			5h2	Nottingham	12	Jul
56.7	Michael Dyer		27.09.84	1	Bracknell	12	May
56.7	Adam Draycott		7.11.84	1	Birmingham	18	Aug
56.9	Chris Ball		29.06.83	1	Bebington	28	Jul

Under 17

| 58.4 | Ben Carne | | 11.06.86 | 4 | Eton | 23 | Jun |

Foreign

| 51.45 | *Stephen McDonnell (IRL)* | *U23* | *24.07.80* | *1* | *Dublin (S), IRL* | *14* | *Jul* |
| 52.27 | *Olau Thomassen (DEN)* | *U23* | *19.02.80* | *1* | *Randers, DEN* | *27* | *Aug* |

400 Metres Hurdles - Under 17

53.08	Richard Davenport		12.09.85	1	Birmingham	11	Aug
	51.7 (during a flat 400m race)			1	Gloucester	24	Aug
55.68	Ben Carne		11.06.86	1	Nottingham	13	Jul
56.21	Chris Duck		7.06.86	1	Watford	25	May
56.45	Darren Lewis		12.04.86	1	Glasgow (S)	20	Jul
56.72	Edward Harrison		10.12.86	1	Kingston	4	Aug
57.09	Michael Newton		3.04.86	3	Nottingham	13	Jul
57.2	Kieran Flannery		29.04.87	1	Gateshead	15	Jun
57.27	Stuart Rowan		16.01.87	3	Glasgow (S)	20	Jul
57.32	Ogadima Duru		5.09.86	2	Birmingham	1	Sep
57.38	Richard Gray		20.08.86	3	Tullamore, IRL	3	Aug

57.55	Jon Baty		1.02.87	4	Nottingham	13	Jul
57.99	Gareth Wiltshire		6.09.85	2h2	Birmingham	11	Aug
58.00	James Findlay		18.09.86	2	Grangemouth	25	Aug
58.0	Andrew Johnson		13.05.86	1	London (Cr)	19	May
58.19	Daniel Townson			4	Birmingham	1	Sep
58.25	Andrew Tippet			2h3	Birmingham	11	Aug
58.3	Craig Stewart		24.11.85	2	Grangemouth	17	Aug
58.54	Jonathan Long		4.10.86	1	Basildon	12	May

High Jump

2.26	Ben Challenger		7.03.78	1	Loughborough	17	Jul
2.25				3	Manchester (C)	29	Jul
2.23				1	Manchester (C)	15	Jun
2.20				1	Birmingham	6	Jul
2.20				2	Birmingham	13	Jul
2.20				3	Madrid, ESP	20	Sep
2.19				1	Bedford	4	Jun
2.19				8	Annecy, FRA	22	Jun
2.18 i				6	Wuppertal, GER	1	Feb
2.17 i				1	Cardiff	3	Feb
2.17				3	Somosko, HUN	25	Aug
2.16				3	Lisbon, POR	25	May
2.15				QB	Manchester (C)	28	Jul
2.15				18=B	Munich, GER	6	Aug
2.26	Dalton Grant		8.04.66	3	Bangor	21	Jul
2.20 i				8	Ottenhausen, GER	3	Feb
2.20				1	Veszprem, HUN	30	Jun
2.20				1	Birmingham	13	Jul
2.15				1	Watford	19	May
2.15				QA	Manchester (C)	28	Jul
2.15				6	Manchester (C)	29	Jul
2.15				5=	Rovereto, ITA	28	Aug
2.21	Martyn Bernard	U20	15.12.84	1	Gorizia, ITA	6	Jul
2.18				QA	Kingston, JAM	17	Jul
2.15				1	Cudworth	12	May
2.15				2	Bedford	29	Jun
2.15				1	Derby	11	Aug
2.19	Jamie Russell	U23	1.10.81	1	Odessa TX, USA	18	May
2.18 i				1	Champaign, USA	2	Feb
2.16	Mark Crowley	U20	15.11.83	1	London (WF)	18	Aug
2.15				2	Bedford	4	Jun
2.15				1	Bedford	29	Jun
2.15				2	Gorizia, ITA	6	Jul
2.15				2	Derby	11	Aug
2.15				2	Barcelona, ESP	6	Sep
2.15	Robert Mitchell	U23	14.09.80	1	Newport	20	Jul
2.15				QA	Manchester (C)	28	Jul
2.15				10	Manchester (C)	29	Jul
	38 performances to 2.15 by 6 athletes including			4 indoors			
2.14 i	Ian Holliday		9.12.73	2	Cardiff	3	Feb
2.05				2	Bedford	19	May
2.14	Richard Aspden		15.10.76	2	Manchester (C)	15	Jun
2.14	Luke Crawley	U23	5.09.81	3	Manchester (C)	15	Jun
2.13	Danny Graham		3.08.79	1	Manchester (Str)	11	Jun
	(10)						
2.12 i	Chuka Enih-Snell	U20	2.03.84	1	Cardiff	16	Feb
2.12	Martin Aram	U20	2.12.83	3	Bedford	29	Jun
2.10 i	Martin Lloyd	U23	18.06.80	1=	Bedford	20	Jan
2.10				2	Bedford	29	Jun
2.10	Tom Parsons	U20	5.05.84	1	Birmingham	2	Jun

2.10	Brian Hall	U23	17.11.82	1	Chelmsford	6	Jul
2.10	Rob Brocklebank		12.10.76	7	Cork, IRL	6	Jul
2.10	Chris Binns	U23	7.05.82	1	Manchester (Str)	17	Sep
2.09 i	Darryl Stone	U20	6.06.83	4	Cardiff	3	Feb
2.05				1	Hoo	4	May
2.09 i	Chris Giblin	U23	20.06.81	4	Cardiff	16	Feb
2.08				1	Liverpool	11	May
2.07	Jamie Creighton	U20	15.09.83	1	Wakefield	28	Jul
	(20)						
2.06	Andrew Macfarlane	U20	28.03.83	1	Grimsby	6	Jul
2.06	Adam Gallie	U20	5.11.84	1	Tamworth	26	Aug
2.05 i	Stanley Osuide		30.11.74	3	Birmingham	13	Jan
2.05				3	Watford	2	Jun
2.05 i	Paul Tohill	U23	9.10.82	2=	Glasgow	20	Jan
1.95				6	Watford	19	Jun
2.05	Tony Gilhooly		26.03.76	3	Alfaz del Pi, ESP	30	Mar
2.05	Jason McDade	U23	3.04.80	3	Watford	19	May
2.05	Stuart Livingstone		29.08.79	1	Coatbridge	2	Jun
2.05	Daniel Leonard	U20	3.01.84	1	Milton Keynes	15	Jun
2.05	Dan Turner		27.11.78	3	Derby	4	Aug
2.04	Calvin Hall	U20	15.11.83	5	Bedford	29	Jun
	(30)						
2.03	Julian Harrison		4.08.76	1	Leeds	14	Jul
2.02	Thomas Mill	U17	21.12.85	1	Mansfield	12	Jul
2.01 i	Matthew Ostridge	U20	23.02.83	7	Cardiff	16	Feb
2.01 i	William Sharman	U20	12.09.84	1H	Cardiff	10	Mar
1.95					Kettering	1	Sep
2.01	Martin Ohrland		19.11.79	1	Chelmsford	14	Jul
2.00 i	Samson Oni	U23	25.06.81	4=	Birmingham	13	Jan
2.00 i	James Wild	U23	1.10.82	4=	Birmingham	13	Jan
2.00 i	Chris France	U20	29.01.84	3	Birmingham	27	Jan
1.98				1	Telford	11	May
2.00 i	Robert Paul	U23	12.11.80	1=	Eton	9	Feb
2.00 i	Simon Thomas	U23	4.03.81	1	Glasgow	24	Feb
1.95				Q	Bedford	5	May
	(40)						
2.00 i	Gareth Moir	U23	17.12.80	1=H	Cardiff	10	Mar
1.95				1	Kingston	4	May
2.00	Brendan McConville		3.01.79	1	Belfast	12	May
2.00	Colin McMaster	U23	15.01.80	1	Edinburgh	12	May
2.00	Ricardo Prevost	U17	31.10.85	1	Watford	25	May
2.00	Alex Girdler	U20	13.05.84	2	Birmingham	1	Jun
2.00	Oliver Sweeney	U17	13.07.86	1	London (He)	11	Jun
2.00	Mark Sweeney		26.02.77	1	Aldershot	12	Jun
2.00	Colin Bailey	U20	15.11.83	1	Blackpool	16	Jun
2.00	Jamie Thomas	U17	7.06.86	1	Birmingham	22	Jun
2.00	Matthew Thurgood	U20	29.12.83	2	Southend	22	Jun
	(50)						
2.00	Ben Smith	U23	12.06.82	5	Birmingham	6	Jul
2.00	Andrew Palmer		13.04.77	1	London (BP)	13	Jul
2.00	Colin Bent		12.04.70	1	Portsmouth	17	Jul
2.00	John Heanley	U23	25.09.80	3D	Manchester (C)	27	Jul
2.00	Anthony Sawyer	U23	29.04.80	5D	Manchester (C)	27	Jul
2.00	Andy Scarr	U20	7.05.85	1	London (Cr)	28	Jul
2.00	Daniel MacDonald	U17	12.09.85	1	Yeovil	26	Aug
2.00	Andrew Penk		19.09.78	1	Cardiff	26	Aug
2.00	Tim Maitland	U17	5.12.86	1	Birmingham	1	Sep
2.00	Camara Stewart	U20	11.09.83	1	Derby	8	Sep
	(60)						
1.99	Kevin Sempers	U17	24.11.85	2	Mansfield	12	Jul
1.98	Zico Benjamin	U20	4.12.84	D	Birmingham	1	Jun

1.98	Gareth Haines	U20	21.11.84	1	Neath	14	Jul
1.98	Craig Baker	U20	26.05.85	1D	Crawley	14	Sep
1.97 i	Ryan Westaway	U20	2.03.83	H	Eaubonne, FRA	23	Feb
1.97	Richard Laws		8.10.75	1	Hastings	8	Jun
1.97	Richard Lowe	U23	7.07.81	1	Exeter	7	Jul
1.96	Gavin Fordham		1.02.79	1	Luton	11	May
1.96	Tony Higbee	U20	21.09.83	D	Bournemouth	29	Jun
1.96	Matthew Clay	U20	9.06.84	1	Leeds	14	Jul
	(70)						
1.95 i	Steve Bonnett		13.07.78	8=H	Zaragoza, ESP	26	Jan
	1.95			1D	Woodford	26	Apr
1.95 i	Ian Leitch	U20	12.07.84	1	Glasgow	31	Jan
1.95 i	David Collard	U20	25.01.85	2	Glasgow	31	Jan
1.95 i	Mark Latham	U20	13.05.85	8	Birmingham	24	Feb
1.95	Barry Thomas		28.04.72	7=D	Azusa, USA	18	Apr
1.95	Chris Petts	U23	22.01.80	2	Kingston	4	May
1.95	Stuart Ohrland		6.09.75	3	Basildon	11	May
1.95	Greg Goodrem	U20	14.09.83	2	Basildon	12	May
1.95	Adam Heslop	U17	15.04.86	1	Manchester (C)	25	May
1.95	Sam Bishop		17.08.79	D	Birmingham	1	Jun
	(80)						
1.95	Geoff Parsons		14.08.64	2	Loughborough	5	Jun
1.95	Daniel Burns	U20	6.09.84	2	Gateshead	8	Jun
1.95	Gez Plunkett	U23	30.06.80	D	Hexham	15	Jun
1.95	Yans Skrivanos	U17	10.10.86	1	Bournemouth	15	Jun
1.95	Dale Garland	U23	13.10.80	2	Bracknell	22	Jun
1.95	Paul Gilding		2.10.75	1	Peterborough	22	Jun
1.95	Emeka Maddy	U20	19.12.84	2	London (TB)	22	Jun
1.95	Noel Reid	U23	19.11.81	2	Peterborough	22	Jun
1.95	Mark Bidwell	U20	4.09.84	1	Nottingham	23	Jun
1.95	Michael Whitehouse	U17	6.08.86	1	Aldershot	3	Jul
	(90)						
1.95	James Alix	U23	24.12.81	1	Worcester	6	Jul
1.95	Dan Plank	U23	27.04.82	6	Birmingham	6	Jul
1.95	Edward Dunford	U20	15.09.84	5	Birmingham	18	Aug
1.95	Dominic Girdler	U23	6.03.82	1	Tamworth	26	Aug
1.95	Louis Jones	U20	20.07.83	1	Kettering	1	Sep
1.95	Richard Blair	U20	15.09.84	5	Derby	8	Sep
1.95	Jacob Knox-Hooke	U20	11.04.85	6	Derby	8	Sep
1.95	James Brierley		31.07.77	7	Singapore, SIN	8	Sep
1.95	Simon Phelan	U17	26.02.86	1	St. Peter Port, Gue	14	Sep

Additional Under 17 (1 - 11 above)

1.93	Darren Steadman		26.01.87	1	Chelmsford	15	Jun
1.90	Howard Gale		23.09.85	1	Welwyn	29	Mar
1.90	Louis Moore		8.09.85	1	Worcester	5	May
1.90	David Cole		15.04.87	1	Eton	9	May
1.90	David Robb		25.09.85	1	Tullamore, IRL	1	Jun
1.90	Tim Payne		23.09.86	2	Birmingham	15	Jun
1.90	Daniel Campbell		24.02.86	3	Kingston	15	Jun
1.90	Robert Johnson		10.07.86	1	London (BP)	15	Jun
1.90	Lee Pursglove		14.10.86	1	Blackpool	16	Jun
	(20)						
1.90	Ian Newbury		17.09.86	1	Neath	14	Jul
1.90	David Shields	U15	18.02.88	1	Birmingham	11	Aug
1.90	Scott Keating		24.10.86	1	Chelmsford	18	Aug

Additional Under 15 (1 above)

1.88	Andrew Allan		9.04.88	1	Grangemouth	17	Aug
1.81	Oliver McNeillis		24.11.87	1P	Stoke-on-Trent	28	Sep
1.80	Peter Richardson		14.07.88	1	London (BP)	14	Jul

1.78	James Russell	19.09.87	1	Nottingham	12	Jul
1.78	Peter Nelson	8.10.87	2	Nottingham	12	Jul
1.78	Antoine Allen	20.12.87	3	Birmingham	11	Aug
1.78	Wayne Taylor	17.10.87	1	Scunthorpe	26	Aug
1.77	Stefan Cross	27.01.88	1	Chelmsford	18	Aug
1.76	Mark McCrea	17.09.87	2	Tullamore, IRL	1	Jun
	(10)					
1.76	Kierran Lakeland	10.02.88	1	Basingstoke	22	Jun
1.76	Dan Smith	16.04.88	1	Bournemouth	22	Jun
1.75	Francis Baker	22.09.87	1	Great Yarmouth	12	May
1.75	Clint Herring	3.10.87	1	Peterborough	15	Jun
1.75	Philip Shaw	18.11.87	1	Watford	15	Jun
1.75	Fraser Davies	30.01.88	1P	Jarrow	30	Jun
1.75	Nick Fladgley	23.11.87	1	Southampton	30	Jun
1.75	Richard Clarke	27.09.87	3=	Nottingham	12	Jul
1.75	Adam Henderson	25.09.87	5	Nottingham	12	Jul
1.75	Robbie Grabarz	3.10.87	1	Bedford	18	Aug
	(20)					
1.75	Jack Field	6.11.87	1	Woking	1	Sep

Under 13

1.62	Tom Morgan	2.11.89	1	Erith	14	Jul
1.61	Nathan Woodward	17.10.89	1	Nuneaton	8	Sep
1.59	Freddie Pask	9.11.89	1	Grimsby	7	Sep
1.50	Mike Cole	1.12.89	1		26	May
1.50	Marshall Courtney	12.01.90	1	London (BP)	22	Jun
1.50	Scott Owens	15.06.90	1	Crawley	23	Jul
1.50	Robin Tuck	19.10.89	1	Kingston	28	Jul
1.49	Thomas Graham	10.09.89	1	Chelmsford	15	Jun
1.49	Nat Senior	14.11.89	1	Hemel Hempstead	23	Jun
1.48	Kyle Millesom	18.09.89	1	Bournemouth	15	Jun
	(10)					
1.48	Oliver Snowball		P	Crawley	14	Sep

Foreign

2.15 i	*Mark Mandy (IRL)*	*19.11.72*	*1*	*Birmingham*	*13*	*Jan*
	2.10		*1*	*Cannock*	*11*	*May*
2.05	*Marien Sanchez (CUB)*	*28.05.77*	*1*	*Lancaster*	*6*	*Jul*
2.00	*Wana Mkandwire (MAW) U23*	*4.10.80*	*5*	*Chelmsford*	*6*	*Jul*
1.97	*Nick Stanisavijevic (YUG) U17*	*10.12.86*	*1*	*Eton*	*28*	*Jul*
1.95	*Reg Stasaitis(LTU)*	*6.04.67*	*1*	*Bromley*	*13*	*Jul*

Pole Vault

5.81 i	Nick Buckfield	5.06.73	1	Bad Segeberg, GER	8	Feb
	5.62 i		1	Bedford	19	Jan
	5.60 i		8	Donetsk, RUS	24	Feb
	5.50 i		1	Cardiff	2	Feb
	5.50		4=	Manchester (C)	30	Jul
	5.40 i		14=Q	Vienna, AUT	1	Mar
	5.35		9	Sheffield	30	Jun
	5.35		1	Birmingham	14	Jul
5.31 i	Scott Simpson	21.07.79	1	Glasgow	23	Feb
	5.20 i		4	Cardiff	2	Feb
	5.00		1	Birmingham	1	Jun
5.30 i	Tim Thomas	18.11.73	2	Cardiff	2	Feb
	5.25		1	Cardiff	8	Jul
	5.20		2	Manchester (C)	15	Jun
	5.20		7	Manchester (C)	30	Jul
	5.10 i		1	Birmingham	12	Jan
	5.05		6	Annecy, FRA	23	Jun
	5.05		3	Cork, IRL	6	Jul

5.30	Ashley Swain	U23	3.10.80	2	Newport	20	Jul
	5.20			1	Birmingham	6	Jul
	5.15			1	Bedford	30	Jun
	5.10			1=	Bedford	4	Jun
	5.10			2	Wigan	7	Jul
	5.05			5	Niort, FRA	3	Aug
5.25	Mark Beharrell	U23	10.01.81	1	Bedford	17	Aug
	5.20			1	Wigan	7	Jul
	5.10			1	Jarrow	1	Jun
	5.10			5	Manchester (C)	15	Jun
	5.05			4	Niort, FRA	3	Aug
5.20 i	Paul Williamson		16.06.74	3	Cardiff	2	Feb
	5.20			3	Manchester (C)	15	Jun
	5.18			1	Irvine CA, USA	5	May
	5.15			4=	Lisbon, POR	26	May
	5.15			2	Bedford	17	Aug
	5.10			2	London (He)	21	Jul
5.20	Christian North		2.02.74	2	Birmingham	6	Jul
	5.20			3	Birmingham	14	Jul
	5.10			2	London (He)	21	Jul
	5.10			1	London (He)	3	Aug
	5.15 street			1	Cheltenham	17	Aug
5.20	Mark Davis		1.03.77	2	Birmingham	14	Jul
5.20	Kevin Hughes		30.04.73	1	London (He)	21	Jul
	5.10			4	Manchester (C)	15	Jun
	5.05			8	Manchester (C)	30	Jul
5.10	Matt Belsham		11.10.71	1=	Bedford	4	Jun
	(10)						
5.10	Ben Flint		16.09.78	2	London (He)	3	Aug
5.00 i	Dean Mellor		25.11.71	1	Birmingham	19	Jan
	4.80			12=	Manchester (C)	15	Jun
5.00	Christian Linskey	U23	14.06.80	1	Cudworth	11	May
5.00	Ian Tullett		15.08.69	6=	Manchester (C)	15	Jun
5.00	Mark Grant		17.05.71	4	London (He)	21	Jul
	49 performances to 5.00 by 15 athletes including 11 indoors						
4.90 i	Richard Hurren	U20	24.09.83	1	Birmingham	24	Feb
	4.71			4	Loughborough	18	May
4.85	Chris Tremayne	U20	11.11.84	1	Nottingham	13	Jul
4.81	Chris Mills		12.11.75	1	Worthing	13	Jul
4.80 i	Cameron Johnston	U23	22.10.82	3	Eton	6	Jan
	4.80			1	Watford	19	Jun
4.80 i	Andrew Penk		19.09.78	3=	Birmingham	12	Jan
	4.70			2	Cardiff	8	Jul
	(20)						
4.80 i	Martin Densley	U23	1.05.81	5	Birmingham	27	Jan
	4.20			1	Perivale	22	Jun
4.80	Matt Weaver		14.11.73	4	Loughborough	19	May
4.80	Keith Higham	U17	7.11.85	1	Manchester (C)	25	May
4.80	Leigh Walker		17.08.77	3	Watford	2	Jun
4.80	Tom Richards		13.11.78	2	Oxford	26	Jun
4.80	Egryn Jones		1.11.71	2	Sheffield (W)	31	Aug
4.75	Chris Boundy		25.12.79	1	Jarrow	12	Jun
4.75	Alan Richardson	U23	15.01.81	1	Carlisle	16	Jun
4.75	Barry Thomas		28.04.72	2DB	Manchester (C)	28	Jul
4.70 i	Jamie Quarry		15.11.72	2	Glasgow	20	Jan
	4.65			D	Hexham	16	Jun
	(30)						
4.70 i	Chris Type	U23	5.10.81	5	Glasgow	23	Feb
	4.70			4	Bedford	5	May
4.70	Mark Christie	U20	11.09.84	2	Manchester (C)	25	May
4.70	Paul Stevens	U20	15.11.83	3	Manchester (C)	25	May
	4.80 street			1	Gateshead	17	Aug

4.70	Matthew Dorrian	U20	24.03.84	3=	Gorizia, ITA	6	Jul
4.70	Ian Noble		2.04.77	1	Oldham	14	Jul
4.65	Steven Lewis	U17	20.05.86	1	Birmingham	22	Jun
4.61	John Heanley	U23	25.09.80	11D	Arles, FRA	2	Jun
4.61	Paul Walker	U20	15.08.85	1	Brecon	6	Jul
4.60	Adam Davis		19.11.72	1	Tamworth	18	May
4.60	Rob Thickpenny		17.07.76	1	Loughborough	22	May
	(40)						
4.60	Gavin Showell		29.09.72	1	Worcester	6	Jul
4.56	Tim Holsgrove	U23	11.12.82	1	Rugby	31	Aug
4.55	Brendan McConville		3.01.79	1D	Antrim	25	Aug
4.50	Allan Williams	V45	30.05.53	1	Potsdam, GER	23	Aug
4.45	Olly Mahony	U20	21.10.83	2	Nottingham	13	Jul
4.40	Steve McLennan		17.11.78	2	Southampton	22	Jun
4.40	Paul Miles	U23	14.09.80	1	Birmingham	3	Jul
4.40	Nick Pritchard		5.12.72	1	Cardiff	26	Aug
4.32 i	Darren Hatton		21.03.79	2H	Cardiff	10	Mar
	4.32			1=D	Birmingham	2	Jun
4.32	Zico Benjamin	U20	4.12.84	1D	Birmingham	2	Jun
	(50)						
4.30 i	Glyn Price		12.09.65	6	Cardiff	6	Jan
	4.20			2	Barry	14	Aug
4.30 i	Alasdair Strange	U20	5.04.83	2	Glasgow	23	Jan
4.30 i	Douglas Graham		1.01.77	2	Glasgow	26	Jan
	4.20			1	Glasgow (S)	14	Jul
4.30	Gerald Manville		21.12.78	1	Blandford	17	Jun
4.30	Anthony Sawyer	U23	29.04.80	3	Southampton	22	Jun
4.30	Paul Hoad		29.10.63	1	Norwich	24	Aug
4.30	Karl Russell	U23	3.11.81	3	Bangor	7	Sep
4.30	Matthew Buck		5.04.74	3	Singapore, SIN	8	Sep
4.25	Mark Allen	U20	9.07.85	1D	Wrexham	23	Jun
4.25	Matthew McPherson		1.08.75	2	Grangemouth	3	Jul
	(60)						
4.25	David McFall	U23	15.10.80	1	Brecon	1	Sep
4.22 i	Gavin Fordham		1.02.79	3H	Cardiff	10	Mar
	4.15			2	London (Nh)	4	May
4.22	Livio Salvador-Aylott		18.07.73	1	Ashford	18	May
4.22	Ian Bowley	U23	14.11.81	1	London (Ha)	22	Jun
4.20 i	Gez Plunkett	U23	30.06.80	6	Wakefield	12	Jan
	4.10			D	Pratteln, SUI	4	Aug
4.20	Kevin Tufton	U23	30.04.80	1	Stevenage	4	May
4.20	Chris Wills		18.05.76	1	Sutton Coldfield	12	May
4.20	Mark Harvey	U20	2.07.84	1	Neath	14	May
4.20	Alex Kruger		18.11.63	5	Cardiff	18	May
4.20	Warren Jousiffe		27.05.77	2	Bedford	19	May
	(70)						
4.20	Bob Kingman		21.02.73	10	Watford	19	May
4.20	Anthony Southward		31.01.71	11	Watford	19	May
4.20	Paul Tohill	U23	9.10.82	5	Loughborough	22	May
4.20	Kit Branch	U20	5.06.85	1	Watford	25	May
4.20	Iain Black		18.09.70	2	Glasgow (S)	29	May
4.20	Adrian Hemery	U23	6.08.82	3	Oxford	26	Jun
4.20	Steve Leader		24.11.66	7	London (He)	21	Jul
4.20	James Lowery	U23	17.10.80	D	Pratteln, SUI	4	Aug
4.20	Adam Walker		16.11.79	1	Horsham	18	Aug
4.20	Ian Dodsworth	U20	16.12.84	4	Gateshead	25	Aug
	(80)						
4.18	Paul Jones		11.04.78	D	Woodford	28	Apr
4.12 i	James Wright	U23	2.04.82	4H	Cardiff	10	Mar
4.10 i	Ian McKenzie	U23	3.07.81	3	Glasgow	12	Jan
4.10 i	Jason O'Hara		28.10.76	7	Ledford	19	Jan

4.10 i	Steve Bonnett		13.07.78	14H	Zaragoza, ESP	27	Jan
4.10				6	Cardiff	19	May
4.10	David Ingram	U23	19.01.80	1	Ware	13	Jul
4.10	Warren White	U23	23.08.80	1	Chelmsford	3	Aug
4.10	Mike Finch	U17	11.01.86	1	Hull	8	Sep

Additional Under 17 (1 - 3 above)

4.01	Chris Wilson		23.09.85	1	London (WF)	18	Aug
4.00	Laurence Steele		24.04.86	1	Blackpool	8	Sep
3.95	Stephen Carpenter		30.12.85	4	Nottingham	13	Jul
3.95	Tom Davies		9.11.86	6	Nottingham	13	Jul
3.80	Martin Vincent		12.04.86	1	Rugby	21	Apr
3.80	Nathan Lawton		3.11.86	1	Stoke-on-Trent	12	May
3.80	Jason Rees		17.09.85	1	Cwmbran	16	Jun
	(10)						
3.80	Mike Cox		15.01.86	7	Nottingham	13	Jul
3.80	Michael Johnson		25.09.85	1	Grantham	28	Jul
3.70	Kyle Corrigan		27.09.86	1	Antrim	25	May
3.70	James Hoad	U15	1.02.88	2	Kingston	4	Aug
3.70	Alex Williams	U15	12.01.88	1	Tamworth	26	Aug
3.70	Louis Moore		8.09.85	1D	Stoke-on-Trent	29	Sep
3.60	Craig Springer			1	London (WF)	2	Jun
3.60	Nathan Johnson			3	Birmingham (Un)	12	Jun
3.60	Carl Titman		9.09.86	2	Grantham	15	Jun
3.60	Paul Yeomans		9.10.85	1	Watford	26	Jun
	(20)						
3.60	Gareth Lapsins		5.07.87	2	Grangemouth	25	Aug
3.60	Chris Kirk		6.09.85	2D	Stoke-on-Trent	29	Sep

Additional Under 15 (1 - 2 above)

3.40	Luke Cutts		13.02.88	1	Wakefield	5	May
3.22	Max Eaves		31.05.88	1	Bolton	2	Jun
3.20	Adam Coward		26.03.88	4	Nottingham	12	Jul
3.20	Jordon Briody		17.11.87	5	Nottingham	12	Jul
3.20	James Bayliffe		11.10.87	3	Birmingham	10	Aug
3.20	Isaac Clayton		12.10.87	1	Par	15	Sep
3.10 i	Michael Walker		22.07.88	2	Birmingham	24	Feb
2.80				1	Cardiff	5	May
3.10	Andrew King		19.07.88	1	London (BP)	21	Jul
	(10)						
3.00	Neil Cottrell			4	London (He)	25	Aug
3.00	Sam Horton		2.04.88	2	Tamworth	26	Aug
2.90	Joe Routledge			2	Coventry	2	Jun
2.90	Peter Abernethy		3.09.87	1	Antrim	17	Aug
2.90	Andrew Marsh	U13	26.01.90	1	Stoke-on-Trent	3	Sep
2.85	Connor Driscoll			1	Chelmsford	15	Jun
2.85	A. Phillips			3	Watford	15	Jun
2.85	Scott McKevitt		15.09.87	1	Grantham	22	Jun
2.80	David Cookson		15.02.88	1	Wigan	19	May
2.80	Francis Baker		22.09.87	1	London (WF)	2	Jun
	(20)						
2.80	James Gainey		9.10.87	1	Cardiff	26	Aug

Under 13 (1 above)

2.30	Raymond Davies		11.09.90	1	Telford	11	May
2.12	Matthew Green		18.08.90	2		20	Jul
2.05	Mike Cole		1.12.89	1	Millfield	4	Aug
2.00	Matthew Coleman		6.03.90	3		20	Jul
2.00	Matthew Clark		4.06.90	4		20	Jul

Foreign

4.60	*Matt Pilsborough (USA)*		*10.07.79*	*1*	*Birmingham (Un)*	*31*	*May*

Long Jump

8.27	0.2	Chris Tomlinson	U23	15.09.81	1	Tallahassee FL, USA	13	Apr
	8.17	1.4			1	Loughborough	18	May
	8.17	0.9			1	Annecy, FRA	22	Jun
	7.98	-0.6			1	Manchester (C)	16	Jun
	7.98 w	3.1			1	Glasgow (S)	9	Jun
	7.97	-0.3			QA	Manchester (C)	30	Jul
	7.85	0.7			6	Madrid, ESP	20	Sep
	7.82	1.2			2	Birmingham	13	Jul
	7.81	1.6			*	Glasgow (S)	9	Jun
	7.81	-0.8			QB	Munich, GER	9	Aug
	7.79	1.1			6	Manchester (C)	30	Jul
	7.78	0.4			6	Munich, GER	11	Aug
	7.74	1.7			3	Newport	20	Jul
	7.66	0.9			2	Birmingham	6	Jul
	7.57				5	Glasgow (S)	18	Aug
	7.51	0.3			1	Watford	19	May
8.17 w	2.5	Nathan Morgan		30.06.78	1	Riga, LAT	31	May
	8.11 w	4.1			2	Loughborough	18	May
	8.06	1.6			*	Riga, LAT	31	May
	8.02	1.0			1	Manchester (C)	30	Jul
	7.86	1.4			*	Loughborough	18	May
	7.77	0.3			QB	Manchester (C)	30	Jul
	7.69	-0.8			4	Manchester (C)	16	Jun
8.03	1.3	Jonathan Moore	U20	31.05.84	3	Loughborough	18	May
	7.57 w	2.3			1	Bedford	29	Jun
7.93	1.1	Darren Ritchie		14.02.75	1	Birmingham	13	Jul
	7.88	1.1			4	Manchester (C)	30	Jul
	7.83				2	Cuxhaven, GER	20	Jul
	7.79	-1.4			1	Birmingham	6	Jul
	7.78	0.0			2	Brasschaat, BEL	14	Aug
	7.77	0.1			QA	Manchester (C)	30	Jul
	7.76	-0.9			2	Manchester (C)	16	Jun
	7.73 w	3.9			1	Kortrijk, BEL	29	Jun
	7.62	1.0			2	Bedford	4	Jun
	7.56 w	2.6			2	Glasgow (S)	9	Jun
	7.54				6	Glasgow (S)	18	Aug
	7.54 w	2.7			1	Watford	31	Aug
7.79 w	2.9	Phillips Idowu		30.12.78	1	Bedford	4	Jun
	7.68	-1.5			5	Manchester (C)	16	Jun
	7.59	1.0			*	Bedford	4	Jun
7.70	0.3	Mark Awanah	U23	23.09.82	3	Manchester (C)	16	Jun
	7.60 w	2.2			1	Bedford	29	Jun
	7.58	1.7			*	Bedford	29	Jun
7.54	0.3	Andre Fernandez	U23	2.03.80	2	Niort, FRA	3	Aug
	7.51	-1.0			4	Barcelona, ESP	6	Sep

45 performances to 7.50 by 7 athletes including 9 wind assisted

7.47	1.6	Bernard Yeboah	U17	7.01.86	1	Nottingham	13	Jul
7.47 w	2.7	Marlon Lewis	U20	7.09.83	2	Bedford	30	Jun
	7.43	0.2			2	Gorizia, ITA	6	Jul
7.46	0.4	Alex Hall	U23	2.02.82	3	Niort, FRA	3	Aug
	(10)							
7.44	1.0	Steve Phillips		17.03.72	2	Alicante, ESP	6	Apr
7.44	-0.3	Louis Burgess	U20	21.03.83	1	Gorizia, ITA	6	Jul
7.40		Nathan Douglas	U23	4.12.82	1	Portsmouth	13	Jul
7.37 w		Leigh Smith	U23	24.09.82	1	Stoke-on-Trent	21	Jul
	7.19	1.5			1	Bedford	17	Aug
7.36 w		Philip Greenland	U20	10.10.84	1	Ashford	18	Aug
	7.19				1	Kingston	11	May
7.34	0.3	Darren Thompson		6.11.79	1	Watford	1	Jun

7.32 w	3.7	Julian Flynn		3.07.72	1	Birmingham	1	Jun
		7.20	2.0		*	Birmingham	1	Jun
7.29 w	3.7	Adrian Phillips		29.07.75	1	London (He)	21	Jul
		7.27			1	Watford	3	Jul
7.26		Femi Akinsanya		29.11.69	1	Luton	3	Aug
7.26 w		Matthew Hulyer	U20	20.06.84	1	Ashford	28	Apr
	(20)							
7.23	2.0	Dale Garland	U23	13.10.80	3	Bedford	29	Jun
7.23 w	3.1	Kris Davies	U23	30.10.81	1	Newport	9	Jun
		7.04	1.6		7	Bedford	29	Jun
7.22 w		Martin Rutt	U23	3.08.81	1	Rugby	21	Apr
		6.91			1	Yate	9	Jun
7.21 w	2.7	Barry Thomas		28.04.72	3D	Azusa, USA	18	Apr
		7.17	-0.3		2D	Manchester (C)	27	Jul
7.20 w	2.8	Jamie Quarry		15.11.72	5	Loughborough	18	May
		7.18	1.0		*	Loughborough	18	May
7.19		Simon Roper		20.09.79	1	Derby	21	Jul
7.18 w	3.2	John Heanley	U23	25.09.80	4	Bedford	29	Jun
		7.12	1.7		15D	Arles, FRA	1	Jun
7.17		David Mountford	U23	23.06.82	1	Cannock	11	May
7.16		Michael Nesbeth		1.03.79	1	Kingston	11	May
7.16		Dominic Girdler	U23	6.03.82	1	Tamworth	26	Aug
	(30)							
7.14 i		Jason Comissiong	U20	7.09.83	1	Bedford	20	Jan
		7.05 w	2.4		6	Bedford	29	Jun
		6.84	-1.5		7	Watford	1	Jun
7.14	1.8	Levi Edwards	U23	23.11.80	6	Newport	20	Jul
7.13 w	2.7	Anthony Sawyer	U23	29.04.80	D	Woodford	27	Apr
7.12	1.4	Andy Lewis		9.03.68	D	Hexham	15	Jun
7.11		Jermaine Bernard	U20	1.12.84	1	Bury St. Edmunds	22	Sep
7.10 i		Dominique Richards		12.09.79	3	Cardiff	3	Feb
7.10 w	5.3	Jon Ramos	U23	29.06.80	3	London (He)	21	Jul
		7.05			1	Derby	4	Aug
7.08		Tom Roe	U23	25.06.82	1	Great Yarmouth	11	May
7.08		Stuart Wells		26.07.79	1	Colchester	26	Aug
7.08 w		Jordon Lau	U20	23.09.83	2	London (Ha)	22	Jun
		6.95	1.3		5	Nottingham	13	Jul
	(40)							
7.07	1.3	Martin Taylor	U23	31.01.82	4	Bedford	4	Jun
7.06		Gary Smith		20.02.71	1	Luton	11	May
7.06	-1.1	Onen Eyong	U20	18.02.85	4	Nottingham	13	Jul
7.06 w		Chris Kirk	U17	6.09.85	1	Cudworth	14	Sep
		6.83	0.4		3	Nottingham	13	Jul
7.03		Ioan Hughes		8.10.78	1	Bangor	8	May
7.03	0.5	Paul Ralph		16.12.67	2	Bedford	17	Aug
7.03 w	3.3	Paul Jones		11.04.78	D	Woodford	27	Apr
		6.86			1	Connah's Quay	12	May
7.03 w	4.1	Nick Dowsett		24.11.78	1	Wigan	31	Aug
		7.01			1	Basildon	12	May
7.02	1.7	Richard Blair	U20	15.09.84	1	Grangemouth	25	Aug
7.02	1.1	Leo Barker		26.12.78	2	Rugby	31	Aug
	(50)							
7.00		Stewart Faulkner		19.02.69	1	London (TB)	1	Jun
6.99		Mark Lawrence		26.01.71	1	Nottingham	11	May
6.99		Ryan James	U20	10.05.85	1	Tamworth	26	Aug
6.97 i		Steve Bonnett		13.07.78	10=H	Zaragoza, ESP	26	Jan
		6.96	1.8		D	Woodford	27	Apr
6.97		Stuart Benson	U23	12.02.81	2	Loughborough	5	Jun
6.97		Julian Thomas	U17	28.12.86	1	Coventry	2	Jun
6.97 w		"J.J." Jegede	U17	3.10.85	1	Chelmsford	15	Jun
		6.62	-1.5		1	Basildon	12	May

6.96	0.0	Chris Davidson		4.12.75	4	Watford	19 May
6.96 w	2.6	Paul Tohill	U23	9.10.82	2	Belfast	8 Jun
6.96		Richardo Childs	U20	9.10.84	1	Brecon	6 Jul
	(60)						
6.96	1.7	Matthew Clay	U20	9.06.84	1	Cudworth	25 Aug
6.96	1.7	Louis Moore	U17	8.09.85	1D	Stoke-on-Trent	28 Sep
6.96 w		Mitchell Wilkin	U17	6.12.85	1	Southend	22 Jun
6.88					1	Southend	18 Aug
6.95	1.4	Gareth Brown		2.09.73	4	Rugby	31 Aug
6.94 w		Dwayne Galloway	U17	22.01.86	1	Stoke-on-Trent	30 Jun
6.83	0.4				2	Nottingham	13 Jul
6.93		Jonathan Jones		12.09.74	1	Bournemouth	12 May
6.93 w		Graham Jackson	U17	11.12.85	1	Jarrow	22 Jun
6.70					*	Jarrow	22 Jun
6.93 w	2.8	Jon French		11.12.75	2	Chelmsford	6 Jul
6.93 w	2.2	Suote Nyananyo	U20	3.10.84	2	Grangemouth	25 Aug
6.93 w		Simon Clarke		31.10.78	3	Wigan	31 Aug
6.86					1	Jarrow	4 May
	(70)						
6.92 w		Joey Addai-Poku	U17	28.08.86	1	London (Cr)	19 May
6.76	0.0				2	Birmingham	11 Aug
6.92		Gavin Stephens		12.09.77	2	Loughborough	22 May
6.91	0.6	Alex Gibson		3.11.77	D	London (He)	10 Aug
6.91 w	2.3	James Wright	U23	2.04.82	D	London (He)	10 Aug
6.90		Nick Thomas		4.04.79	1	London (Nh)	4 May
6.90		Edward Dunford	U20	15.09.84	1	Gloucester	24 Aug
6.89 w	3.7	John Dickinson	U20	27.01.83	D	Wrexham	23 Jun
6.88		Darren Hatton		21.03.79	1	Ashford	18 May
6.88	0.5	William Wyllie		12.07.73	2	Watford	14 Sep
6.86		Richard Askew	U20	26.04.84	1	Scunthorpe	23 Jun
	(80)						
6.86 w		Nathan Palmer	U23	16.06.82	1	Cardiff	26 Aug
6.85		Stephen Alexander	U20	6.10.84	1	Cudworth	21 Apr
6.85	0.6	Chris Weitz	U20	28.04.83	1	Manchester (C)	26 May
6.85 w		Keith Bennington	V50	5.05.50	1	Leeds	15 Sep
6.83		John Fletcher	U17	15.07.86	1	Spenborough	15 Jun
6.82		Gavin Fordham		1.02.79	2	London (Nh)	4 May
6.82		Curtis May	U20	28.01.84	2	Kingston	11 May
6.82	1.9	Brendan McConville		3.01.79	D	Birmingham	1 Jun
6.82		Sam Nash		22.10.71	1	London (TB)	21 Jul
6.81 i		Tony Malcolm		15.02.76	1	Cardiff	19 Jan
	(90)						
6.81		Michael Murray		8.12.79	4	Bedford	19 May
6.81 w	2.5	Andrew Thomas		9.02.74	3	Newport	9 Jun
6.81 w	2.3	David Hughes	U20	31.05.84	D	Wrexham	22 Jun
6.80		Mark Holloway	U20	6.10.83	1	Bracknell	11 May
6.80		Daniel Williams	U23	26.03.81	3	Cannock	11 May
6.80		Martin Rossiter		4.09.69	3	Cardiff	19 May

Additional Under 17 (1 - 9 above)

6.78	1.6	Ezekiel Ewulo		29.01.86	1	London (CP)	7 Apr
	(10)						
6.76 w	2.9	Will Fleckney		19.10.85	4	London (He)	25 Aug
6.70					1	Luton	11 May
6.72	0.3	Gary Wilson		18.09.85	4	Nottingham	13 Jul
6.72		Chris Baily		1.12.86	3	Glasgow (S)	20 Jul
6.69 i					1P	Glasgow	14 Dec
6.67		David Hughes		31.10.85	2	Luton	12 May
6.62 w		Nick Filby		17.09.85	3	Chelmsford	15 Jun
6.61		Matt Hansford		20.02.86	O	Exeter	25 May

6.61		Steven Small	6.12.85	1	Bournemouth	22	Jun
6.61	0.9	Uche Oduoza	15.10.86	O	Derby	21	Sep
6.59	-2.1	Kyle Griffiths	19.09.86	7	Nottingham	13	Jul
6.59		James Davies	29.09.86	1	Walton	13	Jul
	(20)						
6.57		David Holborow	27.09.85	2	Bournemouth	22	Jun
6.52 i		Alistair Hinze	25.09.85	2	Bedford	19	Jan

Under 15

6.48		Jack Field	6.11.87	1	Plymouth	1	Jun
6.48	1.9	Darryl Thomas	23.11.87	1	Birmingham	10	Aug
6.43	0.6	Oliver McNeillis	24.11.87	2	Birmingham	10	Aug
6.34		Deonte Green	26.01.88	1	Bury St. Edmunds	22	Sep
6.25		Lewis Robson	9.01.88	1P	Jarrow	1	Jun
6.12		Luke Thomas	27.03.89	1	Tonbridge	30	Jun
6.11	1.9	Dolapo Awoyinka	19.11.87	3	London (He)	25	Aug
6.09	2.0	Martin Ormerod	12.10.87	5	London (He)	25	Jul
6.08		Joseph Skinnard	14.09.87	2	Bournemouth	22	Jun
5.98		James Hoad	1.02.88	1	Ashton-U-Lyne	21	Jul
	(10)						
5.97		Daniel Glymond	15.02.88	1	Cudworth	5	May
5.96		Daniel Bartram	1.02.89	1	Stoke-on-Trent	30	Jun
5.90		Anthony McWilliams	14.12.87	1	Corby	15	Jun
5.90		Adam Akehurst	13.09.87	1	Portsmouth	25	Sep
5.89 w	3.8	James Jackson	20.02.88	2	Birmingham	31	Aug
5.88		Ian Tobin	2.09.89	1	Ware	4	Aug
5.87		Steven Horsburgh	11.11.87	1	Sheffield (W)	5	May

Under 13

5.35		Juan De Leon-Padmore	1.04.90	1	Tamworth	30	Jun
5.22		Ben Riekstins	11.09.90	1	Telford	7	Sep
5.13		J. Ward		1	Grimsby	5	May
5.07		Jamie Jones	16.10.89	1	Cardiff	8	Jul
5.05		Enrico Faucher-Folie	5.01.90	1	London (Elt)	21	Jul
5.04		Daniel Lewis	8.11.89	1	London (Cr)	30	Jun
5.02		James Pilkington	21.10.89	1	King's Lynn	11	Aug
5.01	1.4	Matthew Mammana	20.09.90	1	Kingston	28	Jul
4.99		Jake Meeking	15.09.89	1	Bath	18	Aug
4.96		J. Blundell		1	Cheltenham	19	May
	(10)						
4.95		S. Ellis			Nuneaton	19	May

Unconfirmed

7.07		Julian Clare	13.09.74	1	Warrington		Jun

Foreign

8.01 i		*Gable Garenamotse (BOT)*	*28.02.77*	*1*	*Cardiff*	*3*	*Feb*
		7.91	*1.0*	*2*	*Manchester (C)*	*30*	*Jul*
7.46	*1.9*	*Gareth Devlin (IRL)*	*2.06.76*	*5*	*Tallinn, EST*	*22*	*Jun*
7.19		*Keston Thomas (GRN)* U23	*17.04.81*	*1*	*Ilford*	*13*	*Jul*
7.04		*Lee Okoroafor (NGR)*	*12.09.76*	*1*	*Loughborough*	*22*	*May*
7.02 i		*Joe Naughton (IRL)*	*17.10.74*	*H*	*Tallinn, EST*	*2*	*Feb*
6.94		*Gary Munroe (CAN)*	*12.04.69*	*1*	*Cosford*	*30*	*Jun*
6.91	*0.7*	*Femi Daramola (NGR)*	*19.12.71*	*5*	*Watford*	*19*	*May*
6.91		*Reg Stasaitis (LTU)*	*6.04.67*	*1*	*London (BP)*	*3*	*Aug*

Triple Jump

17.86	0.7	Jonathan Edwards		10.05.66	1	Manchester (C)	28	Jul
	17.78	0.7			1	Stockholm, SWE	16	Jul
	17.75	1.1			1	Saint-Denis, FRA	5	Jul
	17.67 w	3.1			1	Milan, ITA	5	Jun
	17.63	0.3			1	Zurich, SUI	16	Aug
	17.59	1.2			2	Monaco, MON	19	Jul
	17.54	1.3			1	Glasgow (S)	18	Aug
	17.51	-0.1			1	Oslo, NOR	28	Jun
	17.41	1.8			2	Paris, FRA	14	Sep
	17.34	0.3			1	Madrid, ESP	21	Sep
	17.32	0.2			3	Munich, GER	8	Aug
	17.25	0.4			2	Rome, ITA	12	Jul
	17.21	-1.6			3	London (CP)	23	Aug
	17.19	0.9			1	Annecy, FRA	23	Jun
	17.18	1.2			1	Turin, ITA	7	Jun
	17.06	1.5			2	Sheffield	30	Jun
	16.99	0.9			QA	Munich, GER	6	Aug
	16.89	1.0			*	Milan, ITA	5	Jun
	16.75	-0.4			7	Brussels, BEL	30	Aug
17.68	1.2	Phillips Idowu		30.12.78	2	Manchester (C)	28	Jul
	17.54	0.6			QA	Munich, GER	6	Aug
	17.34 w	3.9			1	Sheffield	30	Jun
	17.29	0.0			2	London (CP)	23	Aug
	17.28	-1.5			1	Celle Ligure, ITA	26	Jun
	17.28	1.1			3	Glasgow (S)	18	Aug
	17.23	-0.6			4	Brussels, BEL	30	Aug
	17.23	0.1			2	Berlin, GER	6	Sep
	17.18	0.4			2	Lisbon, POR	26	May
	17.12	1.4			*	Sheffield	30	Jun
	17.02	-1.0			1	Birmingham	14	Jul
	16.92	-1.0			5	Munich, GER	8	Aug
	16.42	-0.5			12	Saint-Denis, FRA	5	Jul
	16.35	1.8			7	Paris, FRA	14	Sep
16.71	0.0	Larry Achike		31.01.75	5	London (CP)	23	Aug
	16.69	0.5			2	Canberra, AUS	16	Mar
	16.45	0.8			6	Kalamata, GRE	1	Jun
	16.42 w	7.0			8	Sheffield	30	Jun
	16.34	0.0			4	Hamburg, GER	12	Jun
	16.32	0.9			3	Manchester (C)	15	Jun
	16.27	-0.6			11	Oslo, NOR	28	Jun
16.65	0.7	Tosin Oke	U23	1.10.80	5	Manchester (C)	28	Jul
	16.60	-1.4			2	Birmingham	14	Jul
	16.48	0.5			QB	Munich, GER	6	Aug
	16.38	0.6			10	London (CP)	23	Aug
	16.33	0.5			2	Manchester (C)	15	Jun
	16.27 w	3.3			1	Bedford	30	Jun
16.41	1.3	Steven Shalders	U23	24.12.81	1	Manchester (C)	15	Jun
	16.37	1.1			1	Kortrijk, BEL	29	Jun
	16.37	-0.6			6	Manchester (C)	28	Jul
	16.35	1.4			1	Loughborough	18	May

50 performances to 16.20 by 5 athletes including 4 wind assisted

16.17		Nick Thomas		4.04.79	1	Basildon	12	May
16.13 w	3.6	Nathan Douglas	U23	4.12.82	2	Bedford	30	Jun
	15.69	-2.6			8	Celle Ligure, ITA	26	Jun
16.01 w?		Mike McKernan		28.11.78	1	Rugby	3	Aug
	15.12	-0.5			8	Manchester (C)	15	Jun
15.94	0.8	Philip Ferdinand	U23	18.11.82	2	Bedford	17	Aug
15.77 w	2.7	Julian Golley		12.09.71	1	Bedford	25	May
	15.66	1.8			*	Bedford	25	May
15.66	0.0	Femi Akinsanya		29.11.69	1	Sheffield (W)	31	Aug

15.43		Martin Rossiter		4.09.69	2	Sheffield (W)	31 Aug
15.43 w 2.2		Charles Madeira-Cole		29.11.77	1	Birmingham	6 Jul
	15.22 0.9				*	Birmingham	6 Jul
15.30 0.7		Kevin Thompson	U20	24.10.83	1	Nottingham	13 Jul
15.10		Jon Hilton		11.01.74	1	Blackburn	4 May
15.06		Paul Ralph		16.12.67	3	Bedford	17 Aug
14.91		Malwyn Gordon	U23	29.04.82	1	Yate	8 Jun
14.86 w		Mark Awanah	U23	23.09.82	2	Bedford	19 May
	14.63 1.9				2	Watford	31 Aug
14.71		Dave Sanderson		6.05.71	3	Bedford	19 May
14.69 0.2 (20)		Matthew Thurgood	U20	29.12.83	5	Gorizia, ITA	6 Jul
14.68 0.8		Jason Comissiong	U20	7.09.83	1	Watford	31 Aug
14.68 w		Alan Saulters	U20	29.01.83	1	Belfast	6 Apr
	14.14 1.2				3	Belfast	8 Jun
14.59 0.7		Keith Newton		12.12.68	4	Watford	19 May
14.57 w		Anthony Nelson	U20	14.09.84	1	London (He)	15 Sep
	14.30				1	Kingston	15 Jun
14.54 1.0		Ademola Oyediran	V40	27.11.59	4	Watford	2 Jun
14.54		Ruddy Farquharson	V40	26.03.61	1	Portsmouth	17 Jul
14.53 w		Lewis Cheung	U20	12.12.83	1	Derby	8 Sep
	14.10				4	Cudworth	25 Aug
14.53 w		Duaine Wilkins	U20	17.07.85	2	Derby	8 Sep
	14.31				1	Birmingham	18 Aug
14.51 w 3.8		Dale Garland	U23	13.10.80	1	Abingdon	23 Jun
	14.36 0.9				3	Bedford	4 May
14.49 (30)		Paul Revell	U23	18.11.80	2	Derby	11 Aug
14.48 -0.3		Gary White	U20	16.06.85	3	Nottingham	13 Jul
14.47		David Wellstead	U23	17.12.82	3	Ashford	18 Aug
14.45		Oladipo Senbanjo	U23	20.03.82	1	Oxford	18 May
14.45 w 3.1		Graham Jackson	U17	11.12.85	1	Cudworth	14 Sep
	14.40				1	Cleckheaton	15 Sep
14.41		John Heanley	U23	25.09.80	5	Bedford	19 May
14.40 i		Curtis May	U20	28.01.84	1	Bedford	20 Jan
	14.36 w 2.7				2	Abingdon	23 Jun
	14.31 0.8				1	Watford	25 May
14.36		Lawrence Harvey	U23	26.08.81	4	Ashford	18 Aug
14.35 w 4.3		Andy Bell	U20	2.09.84	1	London (He)	25 Aug
	14.33 w?				1	Tonbridge	3 Aug
	14.19 1.5				*	London (He)	25 Aug
14.34 1.0		Sayo Ojo	U23	9.05.80	4	Birmingham	6 Jul
14.34 0.5 (40)		Steve Phillips		17.03.72	1	Rugby	31 Aug
14.32 w		Craig Phillips	U17	29.09.85	1	Connah's Quay	1 Jun
	14.08				2	Glasgow (S)	20 Jul
14.27 1.1		Semi Majekodunmi	U20	29.06.83	5	Bedford	30 Jun
14.26 2.0		David Watson	U20	29.06.83	6	Bedford	30 Jun
14.25		David Budd		8.12.79	3	Cudworth	25 Aug
14.21 i		Christian Campbell	U20	10.06.85	2	Birmingham	24 Feb
14.20 2.0		Michael Murray		8.12.79	6	Bedford	17 Aug
14.19 0.1		Jonathan Best	U23	9.11.82	7	Watford	19 May
14.18		Dennis Fennemore	U20	19.06.84	1	London (WF)	18 Aug
14.17		Mark Lawrence		26.01.71	3	Derby	4 Aug
14.17 (50)		Enyioma Anomelechi	U20	10.03.85	2	Kingston	15 Jun
14.16		Paul Weston		6.10.67	2	Gloucester	4 May
14.16 w 2.2		Conrad Williams	U23	20.03.82	1	Chelmsford	6 Jul
	14.02				2	Blackpool	3 Aug
14.11		Stuart Benson	U23	12.02.81	3	Derby	11 Aug
14.06 w		John Wiggans		1.07.71	2	Exeter	4 Jul

14.05 i		Simon Sawhney	U20	10.06.83	2	Glasgow	17 Feb
14.05		Naved Childs	U23	12.05.81	2	Oxford	18 May
14.05		Junior Lewis		19.03.66	2	Southend	22 Jun
14.03 w	2.9	Jeavon Nicely	U17	27.11.86	1	Birmingham	1 Sep
13.76					1	Birmingham	22 Jun
14.02	0.9	Frederick Annan	U17	7.06.86	2	Nottingham	12 Jul
14.00		George Goss		28.07.77	1	London (Ha)	8 Jun
(60)							
13.98 w		Paul Curran		3.04.77	4	Belfast	8 Jun
13.97 i		Matt Barton	U23	22.05.81	3	Glasgow	24 Feb
13.84					1	Guildford	22 Jun
13.97		Tim Medcalf		19.02.79	6	Ashford	18 Aug
13.97	-0.3	Michael Brown	V40	6.05.62	4	Watford	31 Aug
13.96	-0.8	Chris Alexis	U20	29.12.84	2	Watford	25 May
13.96		Mitchell Wilkin	U17	6.12.85	1	Southend	18 Aug
13.94		Rez Cameron	V40	18.05.60	6	Bedford	19 May
13.92		Robert Forbes		13.09.75	1	Glasgow (S)	14 Jul
13.92 w		Bertram Nnanyere	U20	26.09.83	1	London (He)	15 Sep
13.91		Adam Zeller	U23	6.06.81	1	Loughborough	22 May
(70)							
13.91 w	2.8	Jon Ramos	U23	29.06.80	5	London (He)	21 Jul
13.85	0.3	Richard Blair	U20	15.09.84	3	Belgrade, YUG	21 Sep

Additional Under 17 (1 - 5 above)

13.70		Andrew Nicholson		25.03.86	1	Crawley	11 May
13.66	0.7	Chris Jefferson		9.07.87	5	Nottingham	12 Jul
13.65 w	5.2	Bernard Yeboah		7.01.86	2	Birmingham	1 Sep
13.59					1	Ashford	28 Apr
13.58		Hugh Yates		26.01.86	1	Bournemouth	15 Jun
13.49		Andrew Owens		5.11.85	1	Bebington	15 Jun
(10)							
13.49 w	2.1	Anthony Mattis		25.03.86	3	Birmingham	10 Aug
13.46		Adie Saunderson		14.03.86	1	Tullamore, IRL	1 Jul
13.40		Dexter Nicholls		28.05.87	1	Ashford	19 May
13.36		Gary Wilson		18.09.85	1	London (WF)	2 Jun
13.29 w	3.8	Tyrone Carter	U15	11.08.88	1	London (He)	25 Aug
12.88					1	Chelmsford	15 Jun
13.28 w		Daryl Harris	U15	23.11.87	1	Oxford	16 Jun
13.26	1.3	John Stacey		23.11.85	7	Nottingham	12 Jul
13.25 w	3.6	Adam Chandley		4.12.85	5	Birmingham	10 Aug
13.10					1	Liverpool	11 May
13.22		Mike Okoigun		1.02.87	2	London (BP)	21 Jul
13.20		Leon Barnett		30.11.85	2	Bedford	12 Jun
(20)							
13.18		Christopher Fay		1.07.86	1	Cheltenham	19 May
13.18		C. Ingham			1	Basingstoke	22 Jun
13.15	1.5	Wyn Roberts			6	Birmingham	10 Aug
13.14		Dwayne Galloway		22.01.86	1B	Cheltenham	19 May
13.13	1.5	Graeme Matthews		21.06.86	11	Nottingham	12 Jul

Additional Under 15 (1 - 2 above)

12.65	-0.9	Joe Dyson		2.11.87	1	Manchester (C)	25 May
12.60		Dolapo Awoyinka		19.11.87	2	Chelmsford	15 Jun
12.50		Owen Jones		2.09.87	1	Carmarthen	15 Jun
12.49 i		Alain Kacou		25.10.88	1	London (CP)	17 Feb
12.15					1	London (TB)	24 Aug
12.48		Daniel Blackett		4.10.88	1	Hexham	29 Jun
12.44 w	2.9	Matthew Burton		18.12.87	2	Mansfield	12 Jul
12.09					2	London (BP)	15 Jun
12.39		Nick Reddyoff		21.04.88	1	Cleckheaton	15 Jun
12.37 w	3.0	Wolfgang Mwanfe		26.08.88	2	London (He)	25 Aug
12.31					1	London (He)	15 Jun

12.36		Daniel Haque	26.07.88	1	Tonbridge	8	Sep
12.30		Lewis Robson	9.01.88	1	Jarrow	17	Jun
12.21		Stewart Gilson	13.09.87	1	Street	15	Jun
12.14		Isaac Clayton	12.10.87	1	Exeter	7	Jul
12.10		Ben Warnes	2.01.88	1	Grantham	22	Jun
12.10 w 2.4		Joe Steele	13.02.88	3	London (He)	25	Aug
12.07		Gary Cross	26.03.88	1	Birmingham	27	Jun
12.07 w 2.4		Mark Cawthorne	7.09.87	5	Mansfield	12	Jul
12.06		Marcus Faure	15.01.88	1	Kingston	15	Jun
12.04	1.1	Rhyan Thomas	9.02.88	1	Birmingham	11	Aug
	(20)						
12.03		Joshua Butterworth	21.04.88		Nottingham	12	May
12.03 w		M. Pallot		2	Bournemouth	22	Jun
12.02 w		Thomas Hockedy	20.11.87	3	Bournemouth	22	Jun
12.01		Sam Stanislaus	29.04.88	2	Gateshead	24	Aug
12.00		Warren Robinson	17.09.87	1	Jarrow	15	Jun

Under 13

11.57 w?	Matthew Calver	14.09.89	1	Bournemouth	15	Jun
10.67	Marshall Courtney	12.01.90	1	London (TB)	24	Aug
10.36	David Clunie	18.02.90	1	Grangemouth	18	Aug
9.71	D. Simpson		2	Bournemouth	15	Jun
9.65	Mike Cole	1.12.89	3	Millfield	4	Aug
9.56	Alexander Blair	23.11.89	3	Grangemouth	14	Jun
9.52	Luke Stanbury		1	Barry	9	Jul
9.51	Shoaib Gill	14.12.89	2	Bebington	1	Jun
9.43	Jamie Pugh		1	Yate	11	May
9.43	Liam Hill		1	Glasgow (S)	12	Jun
9.40	Steven Sparks	24.04.90	1	Glasgow (S)	12	Mar

Foreign

15.32 i	*Gable Garenamotse (BOT)*	28.02.77	2	*Glasgow*	24	Feb
14.45	*Reg Stasaitis (LTU)*	6.04.67	1	*London (BP)*	3	Aug
14.44 w	*Michael McDonald (IRL)*	24.08.65	1	*Exeter*	4	Jul
	14.10 -1.2		5	*Olsztyn, POL*	19	Aug
14.44 w 3.7	*Femi Daramola (NGR)*	19.12.71	3	*Wigan*	31	Aug
	14.18 -0.5		3	*London (He)*	3	Aug
14.32	*Michael Corrigan (IRL)*	1.12.77	2	*London (ME)*	11	May

Shot

21.26 i	Carl Myerscough ¶	21.10.79	1	Fayetteville AR, USA	8	Mar
	21.08 i		1	Lincoln NE, USA	23	Feb
	20.72		1	Lincoln NE, USA	4	May
	20.59		1	Columbia SC, USA	18	May
	20.30		4	Walnut CA, USA	21	Apr
	20.07		1	Lincoln NE, USA	11	May
	19.91		3	Manchester (C)	31	Jul
	19.82		1	Manchester (C)	16	Jun
	19.78		3	Des Moines IA, USA	27	Apr
	19.41		6	Annecy, FRA	22	Jun
	19.14		8	Baton Rouge LA, USA	1	Jun
	19.13		7	Madrid, ESP	20	Sep
	18.36		QB	Manchester (C)	30	Jul
19.13	Mark Proctor	15.01.63	1	Cosford	30	Jun
	18.91		1	Watford	3	Jul
	18.54		1	Birmingham	14	Jul
	18.46		1	Loughborough	5	Jun
	18.08		7	Manchester (C)	31	Jul
	18.07		1	Loughborough	18	May
	18.02		1	Portsmouth	17	Jul

(Proctor)	17.75			2	Manchester (C)	16	Jun
	17.61			QA	Manchester (C)	30	Jul
	17.59			3	Bedford	4	Jun
	17.58			1	Watford	19	May
	17.55			1	Birmingham	6	Jul
18.69	Emeka Udechuku		10.07.79	1B	London (TB)	24	Aug
	18.25			1	London (TB)	24	Aug
	17.92			QB	Manchester (C)	30	Jul
	17.62			1	London (He)	21	Jul
	17.54			9	Manchester (C)	31	Jul
	17.50			1	Watford	1	Jun
	17.48			3	Manchester (C)	16	Jun
	17.39			1	Watford	1	Sep
	17.31			1	London (He)	3	Aug
	17.19			2	Birmingham	14	Jul
	17.12 i			1	Birmingham	22	Jan
	17.04			1	Wigan	31	Aug
18.41	Mark Edwards		2.12.74	1	Loughborough	11	May
	17.53			1	Manchester (Str)	11	Jun
17.85	Gary Sollitt		13.01.72	2	Bedford	4	Jun
17.61	Iain McMullan		15.06.78	1	Dublin, IRL	13	Jul
	17.43			3	Loughborough	18	May
	17.26			1	Bedford	25	May
	17.15			3	Bangor	21	Jul
	17.07			1	Belfast	11	May
17.56	Scott Rider		22.09.77	1	Watford	12	May
	17.44			2	Loughborough	18	May
	17.38			3	Riga, LAT	31	May
	17.38			4	Manchester (C)	16	Jun
	17.34			2	Watford	19	May
	17.26			2	Tartu, EST	2	Jun
	17.19			3	Birmingham	14	Jul
17.28 i	David Readle	U23	10.02.80	3	Manhattan KS, USA	15	Feb
	16.95			5	Manchester (C)	16	Jun
	53 performances to 17.00 by 8 athletes including 4 indoors						
16.94	Lee Newman		1.05.73	1	Manchester (Str)	23	Jul
16.80	Bryan Kelly		29.12.73	1	Bebington	12	May
	(10)						
16.80	Greg Beard	U23	10.09.82	2	Loughborough	17	Jul
16.52	Lyndon Woodward	U23	22.11.80	1	Cannock	11	May
16.43	Neil Elliott		10.04.71	4	Bedford	25	May
16.34 i	David Condon		11.04.72	4	Cardiff	2	Feb
	16.28			3	Alfaz del Pi, ESP	30	Mar
16.34	Bill Fuller		19.10.76	1	Kingston	20	Apr
16.29	Nick Owen	U23	17.07.80	2	Bedford	29	Jun
16.14	Morris Fox		30.04.63	2	Birmingham	1	Jun
16.00	Bruce Robb		27.07.77	1	Glasgow (S)	24	Apr
15.92	Gregor Edmunds		25.04.77	1	Mihgavie	8	Jun
15.89	Paul Reed	V40	2.06.62	7	Olsztyn, POL	18	Aug
	(20)						
15.84	Guy Marshall ¶		24.09.71	1	Hull	7	Apr
15.76	Scot Thompson	U23	10.08.81	5	Bangor	21	Jul
15.63	Adam Davis		19.11.72	2	Watford	3	Jul
15.53	Bruce Aitken		11.12.70	1	Coatbridge	28	Apr
15.37	Perriss Wilkins ¶		12.12.67	3	Bedford	19	May
15.36	John Nicholls		1.09.65	1	Leeds (South)	14	Jul
15.28	Marcus Gouldbourne	U23	12.06.81	1	Manchester (Str)	28	May
15.22	David Dawson	U20	3.02.84	1	Salisbury	3	Aug
15.16	Sam Westlake-Cann	U20	14.09.83	1	Bath	18	Aug
15.03 i	Lewis Capes		26.05.71	1	Bedford	2	Mar
	14.54			11	Watford	19	May

230

Mark	Name			Pos	Venue	Date
15.03	Scott Hayes		4.01.73	1	Great Yarmouth	3 Aug
14.98	Phil Adams		3.11.71	1	Nuneaton	14 Jul
14.90	Matthew Twigg		18.07.69	1	Corby	11 May
14.79 i	Derrick Squire	U20	7.12.83	2	Birmingham	20 Jan
14.67				1	Rugby	3 Aug
14.77	Andy Turner		29.08.63	1	Bournemouth	12 May
14.75	Jason Young		18.07.69	1	Inverness	13 Jul
14.73 i	Peter Cranfield	U20	26.09.84	2	Birmingham	16 Feb
14.50				1	Warrington	16 Jun
14.68	Jamie Quarry		15.11.72	4D	Manchester (C)	27 Jul
14.64	Willie Falconer		20.12.78	5	Glasgow (S)	9 Jun
14.63	Mark Wiseman		9.02.69	4	Loughborough	22 May
(40)						
14.54	James South		4.01.75	1	London (TB)	4 May
14.46 i	Nick Vince	U23	29.01.82	3	Glasgow	20 Jan
14.45	Peter Maitland		21.01.73	2	Sheffield (W)	31 Aug
14.40	Mark Davies		10.01.71	1	Portsmouth	22 Jun
14.37	Rory Birbeck		24.09.73	1	Warrington	6 Jul
14.32	Craig Rogers		14.02.76	3	Cannock	11 May
14.31	Denzil McDonald		11.10.65	8	Wigan	31 Aug
14.30	Glen Smith		21.05.72	9	London (He)	3 Aug
14.27	Luke Rosenberg	U23	29.06.80	3	Watford	3 Jul
14.27	Andrew Wain		2.06.65	2	Salisbury	3 Aug
(50)						
14.24	Alistair Gunn			2	Nethybridge	10 Aug
14.16 i	Iain Styles		2.10.75	4	Glasgow	24 Feb
13.99				5	Bedford	5 May
14.15	David Lovett		13.09.78	1	Chelmsford	3 Aug
14.10	Graeme Allan	U23	24.09.80	2	Manchester (Str)	6 May
14.04	Andy Frost	U23	17.04.81	1	Woking	14 Aug
14.03	Mike Small	V45	31.03.54	1	London (He)	28 Jul
14.03	Guy Perryman	V40	2.11.58	2	Tonbridge	3 Aug
14.01	Malcolm Fenton	V45	12.02.56	2	London (He)	28 Jul
13.94	Paul Corrigan		19.01.66	1	Jarrow	4 May
13.94	Tony Norman		5.07.63	1	London (TB)	22 Jun
(60)						
13.90 i	Neil Griffin	V50	28.05.48	1	Eton	8 Dec
13.52				2	London (BP)	13 Jul
13.88	Darren Hatton		21.03.79	D	Hexham	15 Jun
13.87	Barry Thomas		28.04.72	D	Desenzano, ITA	12 May
13.86	Ben Roberts	U23	15.01.80	1	Connah's Quay	12 May
13.86	James Coombes	U23	4.10.81	1	Neath	1 Jun
13.84	Brett Marsh		20.01.76	1	Horsham	22 Jun
13.84	Mark Leitch		17.11.68	5	London (He)	21 Jul
13.84	Gordon Martin		16.07.68	3	Nethybridge	10 Aug
13.82	Gez Plunkett	U23	30.06.80	D	Pratteln, SUI	3 Aug
13.80	James Cottrell	U23	19.12.80	2	Watford	14 Sep
(70)						
13.74	Kyle Stevens	U20	3.06.85	1	London (TB)	1 Jun
13.73	Gareth Cook		20.02.69	4	Kingston	11 May
13.72	Simon Bennett		16.10.72	1	Exeter	12 May
13.69 i	Garry Hagan	U20	21.11.84	1	Cardiff	16 Feb
13.68	Justin Bryan		16.08.69	2	Newport	9 Jun
13.67	David Abernethy	V45	5.09.55	1	Lancaster	10 Aug
13.69	Alex Gibson		3.11.77	1	Bury St. Edmunds	16 Jun
13.58 i	Rob Earle	V40	15.09.60	3	Bedford	3 Mar
13.29				1	Chelmsford	1 May
13.58	Simon Armstrong		29.05.62	2	Bournemouth	12 May
13.58	Jason McDade	U23	3.04.80			
(80)						
13.57	Greg Richards	V45	25.04.56	1	Bracknell	18 May

13.54	Andy Lewis		9.03.68	3D	Valladolid, ESP	8	Jun
13.52	Daniel Brunt		23.04.76	1	Rotherham	31	Mar
13.52	Andrew Rollins		20.03.78	6	Wigan	31	Aug
13.50	Matthew Allison		26.02.73	3	Cudworth	25	Aug
13.48	Simon Williams	U23	5.10.80	1	Ashford	3	Aug
13.44 i	Nick Crimmen		15.07.65	4	Wakefield	12	Jan
	13.26			1	Wigan	4	May
13.44	Antony Zaidman	V40	18.03.62	7	Bedford	19	May
13.43 i	John Painter ¶	V40	12.06.58	1	King's Lynn	10	Feb
13.40	Graeme Stark		12.10.63	2	Rotherham	13	Jul
	(90)						
13.38 i	Ian Lindley	V45	3.12.55	3	Glasgow	16	Mar
13.38	Carl Saggers	U20	20.09.83	1	London (BP)	3	Aug
13.34	Alex Kruger		18.11.63	2	Cardiff	18	May

Foreign

16.01	*Tony Soalla-Bell (SLE)*		*3.10.76*	*13Q*	*Manchester (C)*	*30*	*Jul*
13.97	*Joe Naughton (IRL)*		*17.10.74*	*2*	*Chelmsford*	*6*	*Jul*

Shot - Under 20 - 6.25kg

17.12	Derrick Squire		7.12.83	1	Nottingham	13	Jul
16.85	David Dawson		3.02.84	1	Exeter	11	May
16.18	Sam Westlake-Cann		14.09.83	1	London (He)	25	Aug
15.94	Nsa Harrison		27.11.83	1	Malvern	15	Jun
15.72	Peter Cranfield		26.09.84	1	Warrington	10	Mar
15.50	Stuart Millar		9.03.83	1	Abingdon	8	Sep
15.41	Chris Gearing	U17	30.09.86	1	London (WF)	18	Aug
15.33	Carl Saggers		20.09.83	2	London (WF)	18	Aug
15.16	Kyle Stevens		3.06.85	1	Eton	23	Jun
14.78	Edward Dunford		15.09.84	2	Birmingham	18	Aug
	(10)						
14.45	Josh Lamb		14.04.83	1	Crawley	31	Mar
14.45	Andrew Thomas	U17	14.06.86	4	Derby	8	Sep
14.36	Garry Hagan		21.11.84	5	Grangemouth	25	May
14.35	Andrew Shorrock		28.09.84	4	Nottingham	13	Jul
14.32	Brian Doherty		2.06.83	1	Edinburgh	12	May
13.93	Dale Hewitson		11.09.84	1	Gateshead	11	May
13.86	Martin Aram		2.12.83	2	Blackburn	11	May
13.85	Roger Bate		16.01.83	1	Ormskirk	23	Jun
13.82 i	Ndubuisi Monye		10.05.85	1	Eton	27	Jan
13.77	Ben Lawrence	U17	13.04.86	1	Tipton	18	Aug
	(20)						
13.72	James Bergl		23.02.85	1	Leamington	15	Jun
13.71	Tom Bivins		18.11.83	5	Nottingham	13	Jul
13.67	Andrae Davis	U17	27.09.85	1	Basildon	11	May

Shot - Under 20 - 6kg (IAAF Junior)

16.44	Sam Westlake-Cann		14.09.83	3	Gorizia, ITA	6	Jul
16.34	David Dawson		3.02.84	2	Bedford	29	Jun
16.15	Derrick Squire		7.12.83	3	Bedford	29	Jun
15.74	Peter Cranfield		26.09.84	1	Manchester (C)	25	May
15.30	Edward Dunford		15.09.84	3	Watford	1	Sep
15.19	Carl Saggers		20.09.83	5	Bedford	29	Jun
14.82	Kyle Stevens		3.06.85	6	Bedford	29	Jun
14.69	Stuart Millar		9.03.83	7	Bedford	29	Jun
14.67	Glenn Williams		24.03.85	1	Cardiff	26	Aug
14.54	Andrew Shorrock		28.09.84	2	Manchester (C)	25	May
14.49 i	Garry Hagan		21.11.84	2	Glasgow	17	Feb
14.47 i	Brian Doherty		2.06.83	3	Glasgow	17	Feb
13.64	Craig Sturrock		7.01.85	9	Bedford	29	Jun
13.56	Paul Bilenkyj		9.11.84	3	Watford	25	May

Shot - Under 17 - 5kg

17.41	Chris Gearing	30.09.86	1	Hoo	11	Sep
16.40 i	Andrae Davis	27.09.85	1	Birmingham	24	Feb
	16.18		1	Watford	24	Apr
16.00	Andrew Thomas	14.06.86	1	Birmingham	31	Aug
15.93	Kieran Kelly	14.02.86	1	Salisbury	15	Jun
15.93	Jake Babb	7.12.85	1	Birmingham	22	Jun
15.76	Simon Cooke	3.10.85	1	Wimbourne	5	May
15.66	Ben Lawrence	13.04.86	2	Birmingham	11	Aug
15.42	Bill Walter	11.10.85	1	Bournemouth	7	Apr
15.36	Sam Herrington	2.10.86	1	Corby	22	Jun
15.18	Daniel Hepplewhite	2.09.86	6	Nottingham	12	Jul
	(10)					
15.07	Jason Joseph	27.11.85	2	Watford	26	May
15.06	Richard Parker	21.11.86	1	Stoke-on-Trent	30	Jun
15.03	Samuel Clague	26.02.86	8	Nottingham	12	Jul
15.02	Bobby Lockwood	1.02.86	1	London (Ha)	5	May
14.96	Nat Seaman	27.11.85	2	Tamworth	26	Aug
14.75	Simon Bissell	25.12.85	1	Bebington	5	May
14.69 i	Alistair McDiarmid	16.10.85	5	Birmingham	24	Feb
	14.18		1	Birmingham	1	Sep
14.38	William Lowndes	10.10.86	1	Manchester (C)	26	May
14.22	Matthew Corrigan	1.12.85	1	Jarrow	22	Jun
14.14	Chris Harrison	19.09.85	1		16	Jun
	(20)					
14.10	Andrew Bennett	19.12.85	1	Southampton	19	May
14.06	Jake Evans	26.07.86	2	Cheltenham	19	May
14.03	Richard May	10.12.85	1	Cudworth	15	Jun
14.00	Ryan Spencer-Jones	14.10.86	1	Cardiff	26	Aug
13.97	Jamie Pritchard	25.09.85	1	Brecon	6	Jul
13.96	Grant Duller	20.11.85	1	Grantham	15	Jun
13.90	Matthew Woolley	6.05.86	1	Burton	21	Jul
13.85 i	Chris Nutting	12.10.85	2	Birmingham	20	Jan
13.82	Dale Fletcher	4.09.85	2	Grantham	15	Jun
13.81	Iain Smith-Gillespie	5.02.86	1	London (TB)	5	May

Shot - Under 15 - 4kg

16.40	Shane Birch	22.10.87	1	Hoo	11	Sep
16.04	Brendan Hall	5.09.87	1	Woking	1	Sep
15.65	Jay Thomas	5.10.88	1P	Watford	28	Sep
15.63	Matthew Evans	9.09.88	1	Tullamore, IRL	3	Aug
15.35	Adam Akehurst	13.09.87	2	Woking	1	Sep
15.33	Daniel Brunsdon	18.04.88	1	Bournemouth	12	Jun
14.24	Damien Kingwell	6.07.88	2	Birmingham	10	Aug
13.74	Thomas Senior	26.01.88	1	Cudworth	15	Jun
13.70	Rhyan Thomas	9.02.88	3	Nottingham	12	Jul
13.58	Matthew Ansell	23.09.87	1	Crawley	12	May
	(10)					
13.55	Gerraint Baldwin		2	Cardiff	26	Aug
13.45	Edward McSorley		3	Tullamore, IRL	3	Aug
13.40	David Thomas	13.02.88	1	Grimsby	7	Sep
13.28	Neil Crossley	15.04.88	P	Stoke-on-Trent	28	Sep
13.24	Jack Teasdale	14.09.87	7	Birmingham	10	Aug
13.22	Marcus Higgins	3.11.88	6	Nottingham	12	Jul
13.11	Chris Mccabe	25.09.87	7	Nottingham	12	Jul
13.10	Marco Marchetta	6.10.87	8	Birmingham	10	Aug
13.10	Stuart Turner	25.12.87				
13.09	Ben Ash	3.05.88	8	Nottingham	12	Jul
	(20)					
13.02	Sam Allan	16.09.88	1	Rotherham	30	Jun

Shot - Under 13 - 3.25kg

11.96	Kevin Thompson	29.12.89	1	London (TB)	21	Jul
11.51	Ricky Stappleton	8.12.89	1	Kingston	28	Jul
11.50	Juan De Leon-Padmore	1.04.90	1	Nottingham	19	May
11.09	Jordan Woods		1	Birmingham	1	Sep
11.02	Kim Johnson	22.01.90	1	Oxford	18	Aug
10.98	Jonathan Mulonso	22.04.90	1		25	Jun
10.90	Daniel Twiss					
10.85	Murray Brown	2.01.90	1	Grangemouth	8	Sep
10.70	Charlie Yeomans		1	Erith	14	Jul
10.67	Kurt Taylor	1.10.89	1	Aberdare	1	Jun

Discus

64.34	Perriss Wilkins ¶	12.12.67	1	Abingdon	11	May
	56.86		1	Bedford	19	May
	57.08 after drugs dsq		1	Bedford	25	May
63.14	Carl Myerscough ¶	21.10.79	1	Lincoln NE, USA	4	May
	62.17		1	Lincoln NE, USA	29	Mar
	62.00		1	Lincoln NE, USA	11	May
	61.76		2	Baton Rouge LA, USA	31	May
	61.22		1	Manchester (C)	16	Jun
	60.23		1	Columbia SC, USA	19	May
	60.07		5	Walnut CA, USA	21	Apr
	59.48		1	Austin TX, USA	5	Apr
63.10	Glen Smith	21.05.72	5	La Jolla, USA	27	Apr
	61.87		1	Long Beach CA, USA	20	Apr
	59.30		Q	Manchester (C)	26	Jul
	59.15		2	Stoke-on-Trent	21	Jul
	58.96		2	Loughborough	17	Jul
	58.32		2	Manchester (C)	16	Jun
	57.52		5	Manchester (C)	27	Jul
	57.48		13	Halle, GER	12	May
	57.25		1	Birmingham	2	Jun
	57.23		2	Watford	19	May
	56.57		2	London (He)	3	Aug
	56.38		2	Birmingham	14	Jul
62.46	Bob Weir	V40	4.02.61	1	Stoke-on-Trent	21	Jul
	60.72		1	Birmingham (Un)	19	Jun
	59.24		3	Manchester (C)	27	Jul
	59.14		Q	Manchester (C)	26	Jul
	59.11		1	Loughborough	17	Jul
	59.07		2B	Salinas CA, USA	21	May
	58.98		6	Modesto CA, USA	11	May
	58.91		7	Madrid, ESP	21	Sep
	58.77		1	London (He)	3	Aug
	58.37		21Q	Munich, GER	9	Aug
	58.22		1	Birmingham	14	Jul
	57.43		4	Manchester (C)	16	Jun
58.64	Emeka Udechuku	10.07.79	3B	Pula, CRO	10	Mar
	58.39		1	Bedford	4	May
	58.21		3	Loughborough	17	Jul
	58.15		1	Watford	19	May
	57.97		3	Manchester (C)	16	Jun
	57.86		11	Halle, GER	12	May
	57.67		1	Loughborough	18	May
	57.33		6	Manchester (C)	27	Jul
	57.23		1	Manchester (Str)	25	Jun
	56.67		1	Wigan	31	Aug
	56.66		1	Loughborough	5	Jun

(Udechuku)	56.34			Q	Bedford	4	May
	56.28			3	Birmingham	14	Jul
	56.03			2	Bedford	25	May
56.28	Lee Newman		1.05.73	2	Birmingham (Un)	12	Jun
	50 performances to 56.00 by 6 athletes						
54.53	Matthew Twigg		18.07.69	1	Stoke-on-Trent	21	Jul
53.86	Paul Reed	V40	2.06.62	1	Gateshead	24	Aug
53.72	Bryan Kelly		29.12.73	1	Jarrow	1	Jun
53.57	Mark Wiseman		9.02.69	1	Portsmouth (RN)	17	Jul
	(10)						
52.97	Scot Thompson	U23	10.08.81	1	Jarrow	22	Sep
52.22	Bruce Robb		27.07.77	1	Grangemouth	20	Apr
51.18	Gary Herrington	V40	31.03.61	2	Exeter	4	Jul
50.98	Denzil McDonald		11.10.65	1	Ashford	18	Aug
50.71	Neville Thompson	V45	28.03.55	6	London (He)	3	Aug
50.56	Scott Rider		22.09.77	6	Watford	19	May
50.48	Luke Rosenberg	U23	29.06.80	1	Bedford	29	Jun
50.44	Neil Elliott		10.04.71	7	Watford	19	May
49.77	Mark Proctor		15.01.63	2	Portsmouth (RN)	17	Jul
49.53	Marcus Gouldbourne	U23	12.06.81	1	Cleckheaton	1	Sep
	(20)						
49.18	Peter Gordon	V50	2.07.51	2	Jarrow	22	Sep
49.04	James South		4.01.75	1	London (TB)	4	May
48.77	Edward Reid	U23	22.07.81	1	Loughborough	12	Jun
48.47	Niklas Iliffe	U23	6.03.81	1	Southampton	17	Jul
48.00	Andy Turner		29.08.63	1	Bournemouth	7	Apr
47.94	Andrew Brittan		17.01.67	1	Telford	6	Jul
47.56	David Lovett		13.09.78	1	Portsmouth	13	Jul
47.43	Scott Hayes		4.01.73	1	Bury St. Edmunds	13	Aug
47.35	Nick Woolcott	V40	7.04.61	1	Watford	12	May
47.00	John Moreland	V40	13.09.58	2	Loughborough	12	Jun
	(30)						
46.71	Andrew Rollins		20.03.78	1	Manchester (Str)	11	Jun
46.52	Morris Fox		30.04.63	1	Luton	3	Aug
46.35	Andy Kruszewski	V40	7.04.59	2	Wigan	15	Aug
46.22	Mark Davies		10.01.71	1	Basildon	15	May
46.08	Sam Westlake-Cann	U20	14.09.83	1	Yeovil	26	Aug
45.60	Simon Williams	U23	5.10.80	3	Ashford	18	Aug
45.52	David Abernethy	V45	5.09.55	1	Preston	8	Jun
45.49	Michael Jemi-Alade		13.10.64	2	Luton	3	Aug
45.18	Greg Beard	U23	10.09.82	4	Watford	1	Jun
44.91	Daniel Brunt		23.04.76	1	Hull	7	Apr
	(40)						
44.91	Adam Davis		19.11.72	4	Derby	4	Aug
44.84	Matthew Allison		26.02.73	1	Cudworth	25	Aug
44.69	Felice Miele	U23	24.11.81	1	Watford	8	Sep
44.56	James Rumbold	U23	4.11.81	1	Bournemouth	16	Jul
44.20	Nick Owen	U23	17.07.80	1	London (B)	17	Jul
44.19	Neil Griffin	V50	28.05.48	1	London (BP)	13	Jul
44.12	Scott Jenns	U23	13.12.80	1	Burton	18	May
44.11	Nick Vince	U23	29.01.82	6	Bedford	29	Jun
43.91	Mike Small	V45	31.03.54	1	London (He)	11	Aug
43.75	Bill Fuller		19.10.76	1	Kingston	4	May
	(50)						
43.72	Greg Richards	V45	25.04.56	1	Hoo	4	May
43.65	Rob Earle	V40	15.09.60	1	Ware	5	Jun
43.57	Paul Head		1.07.65	3	Basildon	12	May
43.10	Josh Lamb	U20	14.04.83	Q	Bedford	4	May
43.09	Simon Read		24.06.70	2	Watford	14	Sep
43.08	Daniel Greaves	U23	4.10.82	7	Birmingham	2	Jun
43.00	Alexis Sharp		31.10.72	6	London (He)	21	Jul

42.86	Leslie Richards	U20	29.03.85	1	Darlington	14	Jul
42.83	Roger Bate	U20	16.01.83	3	Jarrow	1	Jun
42.83	Ali Morganella		28.05.77	4	Jarrow	1	Jun
(60)							
42.76	Leith Marar		7.11.68	1	London (PH)	13	Jul
42.70	Gareth Cook		20.02.69	2	Eton	4	May
42.63	Peter Cranfield	U20	26.09.84	3	Cudworth	25	Aug
42.46	Rafer Joseph		21.07.68	1	London (He)	8	Jun
42.43	Ian Taylor		2.07.67	2	Telford	6	Jul
42.35	Gareth Bull	U20	3.03.85	2	Derby	11	Aug
42.24	Steven Hale		20.04.77	1	Brierley Hill	3	Aug
42.16	Carl Saggers	U20	20.09.83	8	Loughborough	17	Jul
42.04	Bruce Aitken		11.12.70	2	Coatbridge	28	Apr
42.04	David Readle	U23	10.02.80	2	Manchester (Str)	20	Aug
(70)							
41.87	Ashley Ward		1.08.64	3	Edinburgh	6	Jul
41.86	Barry Thomas		28.04.72	4	Edinburgh	6	Jul
41.85	Graeme Allan	U23	24.09.80	4	Watford	19	May
41.80	Neil Sougrin		14.05.71	1	London (WF)	18	May
41.69	David Bauer		25.03.66	1	Ashford	3	Aug
41.44	Guy Marshall ¶		24.09.71	2	Hull	7	Apr
41.43	David Dawson	U20	3.02.84	1	Exeter	14	Apr
41.41	Willie Falconer		20.12.78	Q	Bedford	4	May
41.38	Alex Kruger		18.11.63	5	Sheffield (W)	3	Aug
41.22	Iain Park		16.07.74	14	London (He)	3	Aug
(80)							
41.15	Jake Louth	U23	20.05.82	1	Lincoln	21	Apr
41.12	Bill Renshaw	V50	7.08.49	1	Derby	11	May
41.04	Gary Parsons		17.05.71	1	Great Yarmouth	16	Jun
40.98	Malcolm Fenton	V45	12.02.56	3	Wigan	15	Aug
40.96	Jan Drzewiecki	V40	29.11.57	1	Bracknell	12	May
40.96	Darren Hatton		21.03.79	3	Ashford	18	May
40.92	Edward Dunford	U20	15.09.84	2	Rugby	8	Jun
40.90	Ben Roberts	U23	15.01.80	1	Connah's Quay	12	May
40.77	Justin Bryan		16.08.69	1	Cardiff	10	Jul
40.74	Roger Hunter		10.03.76	1	Cleckheaton	3	Aug
(90)							
40.61	John Little	V45	14.04.53	1	Carlisle	8	Jun
40.51	Alan Rudkin		5.11.78	6	Luton	3	Aug
40.43	Lyndon Woodward	U23	22.11.80	3	Telford	6	Jul
40.39	Steve Whyte		14.03.64	1	Luton	8	Jun
40.39	Garry Hagan	U20	21.11.84	6	Glasgow (S)	9	Jun
40.33	Alan Porter		21.10.75	7	London (He)	21	Jul
40.13	John Painter ¶	V40	12.06.58	1	Norwich	5	Jun
40.10	Jonathan Ward		25.11.65	3	Worthing	13	Jul
40.08	Iain Styles		2.10.75	7	Bedford	4	May
40.08	Gez Plunkett	U23	30.06.80	7	Watford	31	Aug

Foreign

60.54	Kevin Brown (JAM)		10.09.64	1B	Birmingham (Un)	12	Jun
47.19	Garry Power (IRL)	V40	1.09.62	2	London (TB)	4	May
44.75	Tony Soalla-Bell (SLE)		3.10.76	13Q	Manchester (C)	26	Jul

Discus - Under 20 - 1.75kg

49.99	Roger Bate		16.01.83	1	Bedford	29	Jun
49.65	Sam Westlake-Cann		14.09.83	3	Gorizia, ITA	6	Jul
49.62	Carl Saggers		20.09.83	1	Eton	23	Jun
48.17	Josh Lamb		14.04.83	1	Watford	25	May
47.90	Sam Herrington	U17	2.10.86	1	Derby	8	Sep
47.87	Leslie Richards		29.03.85	1	Nottingham	12	Jul
46.88	Brian Doherty		2.06.83	5	Bedford	29	Jun

46.82	Garry Hagan		21.11.84	6	Bedford	29	Jun
45.87	Robert Jukes		18.09.83	3	Nottingham	12	Jul
45.69	Chris Orr		20.06.83	1	Carlisle	11	May
	(10)						
45.44	Peter Cranfield		26.09.84	1	Liverpool	12	May
45.15	Edward Dunford		15.09.84	D	Derby	22	Sep
45.13	Andrew Thomas	U17	14.06.86	1	Scunthorpe	23	Jun
44.98	Alistair McDiarmid	U17	16.10.85	3	London (Cr)	28	Jul
44.85	Gareth Bull		3.03.85	1	Brecon	6	Jul
44.62	Paris Norriss		27.02.85	4	Nottingham	12	Jul
44.60	Chris Gearing	U17	30.09.86	1	London (WF)	18	Aug
43.42	Mark Wyss		12.07.85	1	Cheltenham	15	Jun
43.21	Glyn Hooson-Owen		22.01.85	5	Nottingham	12	Jul
43.06	Ben Kelsey		23.09.84	1	Eton	28	Jul
	(20)						
42.92	Peter Hughes		12.12.83	2	Brecon	6	Jul
42.81	Simon Bissell	U17	25.12.85	4	Derby	8	Sep
42.39	Steven Marlow		13.12.84	6	Nottingham	12	Jul
42.39	Mervyn Luckwell		27.11.84	1	Basildon	18	Aug
42.06	Stuart Semple		3.11.83	1	Woking	18	Aug
42.00	Felix Hatton		9.10.84	3	Bournemouth	22	Jun
41.81	David Dawson		3.02.84	1	Exeter	26	Mar
41.74	Tony Gallagher		16.10.84	2	Bebington	28	Jul
41.58	Lewis Williamson	U17	7.09.85	2	Cudworth	21	Apr

Discus - Under 17 - 1.5kg

52.84	Andrew Thomas		14.06.86	1	Birmingham	11	Aug
52.48	Sam Herrington		2.10.86	2	Birmingham	11	Aug
51.45	Alistair McDiarmid		16.10.85	3	Birmingham	11	Aug
49.80	Simon Cooke		3.10.85	4	Birmingham	11	Aug
48.61	Simon Bissell		25.12.85	1	Wigan	14	Jul
48.30	Chris Gearing		30.09.86	1	Watford	8	Sep
47.90	Bobby Lockwood		1.02.86	1	London (BP)	15	Jun
47.76	Andrae Davis		27.09.85	1	Southend	6	May
46.36	Jason Joseph		27.11.85	1	Enfield	28	Aug
45.69	Kieran O'Keefe		19.03.86	2	Nottingham	13	Jul
	(10)						
45.04	Nnamdi Efobi		14.09.86	1	London (He)	15	Jun
44.99	Robert Bridgewater		18.04.86	6	Birmingham	11	Aug
44.94	David Coleman		14.02.86	3	Nottingham	13	Jul
44.84	David Price		12.01.87	1	Macclesfield	8	Sep
44.35	David Attwood		5.04.87	6	Nottingham	13	Jul
44.12	Lewis Williamson		7.09.85	1	Cleckheaton	15	Jun
43.57	Samuel Clague		26.02.86	1	Street	12	Jun
42.85	Daniel Hepplewhite		2.09.86	1	Bournemouth	16	Jul
42.82	Gavin Hill		22.12.86	1	Jarrow	22	Jun
42.67	Toby Hunt		28.12.86	1	Ashford	20	Jun
	(20)						
42.52	Chris Horne		17.05.86	1	Exeter	18	Aug
42.05	Dale Fletcher		4.09.85	1	Grantham	12	May
41.91	Greg Nixon		2.09.85	1	Tamworth	26	Aug
41.89	Thomas Toal		23.12.86	1	Leicester	15	Jun
41.82	Damien Hines		6.09.85	1	Blackpool	30	Jun
41.71	Alex Hitchens		12.12.86	4	Bournemouth	24	Jun
41.38	A. Ward			1	Birmingham	22	Jun
41.18	Matthew Corrigan		1.12.85	1	Carlisle	15	Jun
41.03	Barry Roberts		24.09.86	1	Brecon	6	Jul

overage

| 43.64 | John Harper | U20 | 23.08.85 | 3 | Tullamore, IRL | 3 | Aug |

Discus - Under 15 - 1.25kg

50.85	Shane Birch	22.10.87	1	Nottingham	12	Jul
43.77	Kieran McConnell	13.10.87	2	Nottingham	12	Jul
43.34	Nicholas Webb	23.09.87	1	Woking	1	Sep
40.83	Matthew Ansell	23.09.87	2	London (He)	25	Aug
40.80	Adam Akehurst	13.09.87	1	Portsmouth	24	Mar
39.90	Karl Fitzgerald	4.11.87	3	Birmingham	10	Aug
39.42	Matthew Evans	9.09.88	1	Cardiff	26	Aug
39.17	Samuel Johnson	20.06.88	4	Nottingham	12	Jul
38.96	Kieran Mason	26.11.87	2	Bedford	15	Sep
38.52	Iain Crombie	30.09.88	5	Nottingham	12	Jul
	(10)					
38.50	Jon Kingsberry	19.03.88	1	Bangor	5	Sep
37.82	Elliot Betts	13.11.87	1	Birmingham	1	Sep
37.71	Mark Rumble	10.07.88	1	Oxford	22	May
37.33	Lewis Edwards	13.09.87	2	Birmingham	1	Sep
37.26	Ben Graham	15.09.87	1	York	8	Sep
37.24	Ben Wade	9.11.87	7	Nottingham	12	Jul

Discus - Under 13 - 1kg

32.59	Daniel Twiss		1	Eton	14	Jul
29.20	Jamie Stevenson	8.12.89		Guernsey	14	Sep
27.82	Mark Tough	3.03.90	1	Grangemouth	24	Aug
27.81	Tom Wade	16.06.90	1	Bromley	22	Jun
27.42	Ryan Williams	6.09.89	1		25	Jun
27.32	Allan Mackay	25.03.90	2	Grangemouth	24	Aug
27.02	Jonathan Mulonso	22.04.90	1	Kingston	28	Jul
26.90	Nick Cranfield	25.06.90	1	Warrington	7	Apr
25.80	James Callaghan	30.12.89	1	Colwyn Bay	30	Mar
25.58	Murray Brown	2.01.90	3	Grangemouth	24	Aug

Hammer

73.99	Mick Jones	23.07.63	1	Loughborough	17	Jul
	73.33		1	London (He)	21	Jul
	73.25		1	Bedford	17	Aug
	73.21		3	Hobart, AUS	9	Mar
	72.55		1	Manchester (C)	28	Jul
	72.26		1	Birmingham	13	Jul
	72.16		1	Manchester (C)	15	Jun
	71.38		10	Halle, GER	12	May
	71.23		1	Loughborough	18	May
	71.00		3	Melbourne, AUS	7	Mar
	70.73		1	Perivale	17	Mar
	70.08		8	Annecy, FRA	22	Jun
	69.37		1	Watford	19	May
	68.47		1	Sandown IOW	18	Sep
	66.92		8	Madrid, ESP	20	Sep
	66.85		5	Lisbon, POR	25	May
69.61	Paul Head	1.07.65	2	Manchester (C)	15	Jun
	69.19		1	Basildon	11	May
	68.60		3	Manchester (C)	28	Jul
	68.35		1	Glasgow (S)	8	Jun
	67.98		1	Bedford	26	May
	67.74		2	Watford	19	May
	67.61		2	Birmingham	13	Jul
	66.52		1	London (He)	21	Jul
	66.07		2	London (He)	3	Aug
	65.85		2	Birmingham	7	Jul
	65.82		Q	Bedford	26	May

69.29	Iain Park		16.07.74	1	Eton	19	Oct
	67.64			1B	Eton	20	Oct
	66.19			1	Barking	17	Mar
	66.13			2	Glasgow (S)	8	Jun
	65.91			6	Manchester (C)	15	Jun
	65.71			2	Watford	3	Jul
	65.58			1	Eton	21	Jul
	65.57			4	Bedford	26	May
	65.51			5	Manchester (C)	28	Jul
	65.02			1	Manchester (Str)	6	May
68.78	William Beauchamp		9.09.70	1	London (Nh)	4	May
	68.09			1	London (ME)	11	May
	67.75			6	Varazdin, CRO	6	Jul
	67.69			4	Manchester (C)	15	Jun
	67.07			2	Loughborough	18	May
	66.09			1	Watford	3	Jul
	66.01			2	Bedford	26	May
	65.57			Q	Bedford	26	May
	65.20			4	Birmingham	13	Jul
67.74	Mike Floyd		26.09.76	3	Manchester (C)	15	Jun
	66.33			3	Loughborough	18	May
	66.33			3	Birmingham	13	Jul
	65.98			1	Birmingham	7	Jul
	65.97			3	Bedford	26	May
66.77	Simon Bown		21.11.74	5	Manchester (C)	15	Jun
	65.68			1	Watford	2	Jun
	65.05			1	Watford	1	Sep
65.01	Andy Frost	U23	17.04.81	1	Bedford	5	May
	55 performances to 65.00 by 7 athletes						
64.42	John Pearson		30.04.66	1	Loughborough	22	May
64.16	Matthew Bell		2.06.78	1	Corby	28	May
63.83	Shane Peacock		5.03.63	4	London (He)	3	Aug
	(10)						
63.58	Chris Howe		17.11.67	7	Manchester (C)	15	Jun
63.40	Dave Smith	V40	21.06.62	2	Eton	19	Oct
62.13	Malcolm Fenton	V45	12.02.56	1	Ipswich	12	May
61.96	Steve Sammut		3.05.67	1	Enfield	28	Aug
61.30	Graeme Allan	U23	24.09.80	1	Bebington	11	May
60.97	Chris Black	V50	1.01.50	1	Manchester (Str)	6	May
60.97	Graham Holder		16.01.72	7	Loughborough	18	May
60.63	Steve Minnikin		4.01.72	1	Sheffield (W)	31	Aug
60.56	Glen Kerr		27.10.74	10	Birmingham	13	Jul
60.17	Kevin Davies		11.01.78	1	Woodford	18	May
	(20)						
59.58	Rob Careless		7.09.74	1	Nottingham	12	May
59.12	Gareth Cook		20.02.69	1	Kingston	11	May
58.99	Carl Saggers	U20	20.09.83	3	Loughborough	17	Jul
58.89	Rob Earle	V40	15.09.60	6	Watford	2	Jun
58.61	David Allan		17.10.70	5	Glasgow (S)	8	Jun
58.22	Adrian Palmer		10.08.69	2	Aberdare	15	Jun
57.68	Wayne Clarke		24.12.75	1	Peterborough	21	Apr
57.26	David Little	U23	28.02.81	2	Derby	11	Aug
56.54	Bob Weir	V40	4.02.61	5B	Eton	19	Oct
55.93	Tom Dempsey	U20	15.12.83	1	Cannock	18	May
	(30)						
55.80	Ross Thompson	U23	7.12.81	1	Gateshead	8	Jun
55.39	Stuart Thurgood		17.05.76	1	Woodford	17	Jul
54.83	David Robinson		12.01.78	1	Perivale	14	Sep
54.79	Steve Whyte		14.03.64	1	Luton	8	Jun
54.41	Roger Bate	U20	16.01.83	2	Derby	21	Jul
54.35	Derrick Squire	U20	7.12.83	2	Telford	6	Jul

54.05	Chris Walsh		1.10.78	1	Gateshead	12	May
53.87	Bill Fuller		19.10.76	1	Kingston	4	May
53.19	Calum Bruce		28.02.75	1	Dunfermerlin	14	Apr
52.88	Gavin Cook		30.03.70	1	Perivale	22	Jun
	(40)						
52.76	Matthew Sutton	U23	8.09.81	3	Derby	11	Aug
52.22	Peter Fuller		30.04.78	2	Kingston	18	May
52.20	Matthew Frampton	U20	10.04.84	1	Bournemouth	3	Aug
52.01	Andy Turner		29.08.63	2	Exeter	23	Jun
51.88	Alan James	V40	26.03.62	6	Watford	31	Aug
51.78	Damon Cripps		9.10.70	1	Manchester (Str)	1	May
51.39	Mark Gulliver		11.02.72	3	Wakefield	21	Sep
51.21	Steve McEvoy		23.05.63	1	London (Col)	8	Jun
50.83	John Owen		28.10.64	4	Sheffield (W)	31	Aug
50.48	Mark Roberson		21.03.75	7	Watford	31	Aug
	(50)						
50.43	James Hawkins		14.12.79	2	Kingston	3	Aug
50.17	David Readle	U23	10.02.80	1	Lincoln NE, USA	4	May
50.15	Nick Fogg		24.03.78	5	Watford	3	Jul
50.12	Ewart Hulse	V40	21.01.62	1	Wrexham	31	Jul
50.09	Anthony Swain		17.01.75	1	Wakefield	3	Aug
50.05	Daniel Martin	U23	9.03.82	1	Sandown IOW	18	May
49.99	Adam Beauford	U23	24.10.81	3	Bedford	5	May
49.97	Karim Chester	U20	6.11.84	5	Kingston	20	Apr
49.92	Paul Farley	U20	1.12.84	2	Sandown IOW	18	May
49.73	Mark Sheridan		17.06.70	2	Crawley	12	May
	(60)						
49.53	Maurice Hicks		1.01.70	3	Exeter	23	Jun
49.49	Kamran Khan	U20	2.10.83	8	Watford	31	Aug
49.17	Paul Dickenson	V50	4.12.49	2	Oxford	8	Jun
49.09	Bruce Shepherd		20.03.67	1	Aberdeen	30	May
48.52	Peter Cranfield	U20	26.09.84	2	Rugby	31	Aug
48.49	Neil Bulman		7.09.77	3	Rugby	31	Aug
48.32	Russell Payne	V40	11.09.60	3	Worcester	6	Jul
47.99	John Nevis		24.12.69	2	Cleckheaton	4	May
47.69 ?	Mike Small	V45	31.03.54	1	Ewell	19	Jan
46.10				1P	Ewell	23	Feb
47.30	Leslie McIntosh	U23	25.02.81	4	Cudworth	25	Aug
	(70)						
47.29	Michael Madden		13.09.65	1	Walton	8	Jun
47.18	Eric Kerr		9.12.64	6	Cardiff	18	May
47.00	Martin Hayes		31.08.79	1	Cleckheaton	3	Aug
46.97	Bruce Aitken		11.12.70	2	Coatbridge	28	Apr
46.72	Andrew Benn		2.09.77	2	Guildford	18	May
46.36	Brett Marsh		20.01.76	1	Par	18	May
46.34	Oliver Hoad	U23	1.10.81	5	Bedford		May
46.14	Ben Jones	U23	6.11.82	15	Bedford	26	May
45.89	Sam Broadley	U23	17.05.81	2	Cleckheaton	3	Aug
45.60	Jason Joseph	U17	27.11.85	1	Bromley	8	Jun
	(80)						
45.52	Neil Knott		6.02.70	1	Solihull	8	Jun
45.49	Michael Reiss		17.06.63	2	London (PH)	8	Jun
45.44	Mark Proctor		15.01.63	3	Portsmouth	17	Jul
45.33	Andrew Smith	U20	2.10.84	1	Darlington	14	Jul

Foreign

63.11	*Luke Greenfield (NZL)*	*U23*	*6.05.81*	*2*	*London (ME)*	*11*	*May*
61.45	*John Osazuwa (NGR)*	*U23*	*4.05.81*	*7*	*Watford*	*19*	*May*

Hammer - Under 20 - 6.25kg

66.17	Carl Saggers	20.09.83	1	London (Cr)	28	Jul
62.53	Tom Dempsey	15.12.83	1	Birmingham	15	Jun

60.14	Roger Bate		16.01.83	1	Manchester (Str)		
57.82	Simon Bissell	U17	25.12.85	2	Scunthorpe	23	Jun
57.20	Matthew Frampton		10.04.84	1	Bournemouth	11	May
55.26	Derrick Squire		7.12.83	1	Cannock	15	Jun
55.26	Kamran Khan		2.10.83	3	Nottingham	12	Jul
55.16	Karim Chester		6.11.84	1	London (CP)	12	May
54.26	Peter Cranfield		26.09.84	1	Liverpool	11	May
53.97	Jason Joseph	U17	27.11.85	3	London (WF)	18	Aug
	(10)						
53.36	Paul Farley		1.12.84	3	London (He)	25	Aug
52.71	Andrew Smith		2.10.84	5	Nottingham	12	Jul
52.23	James Forde		10.04.85	6	Nottingham	12	Jul
50.78	David Procter		11.11.84	1	Neath	14	Jul
50.77	Paul Nash		13.02.84	1	Stourport	28	Jul
50.17	Kevin Deacon		25.02.84	1	Colchester	25	Aug
49.06	Andrew Thomas	U17	14.06.86	6	Derby	8	Sep
48.85	Fraser Campbell	U17	30.05.86	1	Elgin	10	Sep
48.40	Robert Mungham		1.12.84	1	Guildford	26	May

Hammer - Under 20 - 6kg (IAAF Junior)

66.22	Carl Saggers		20.09.83	1	Watford	19	Jun
62.43	Roger Bate		16.01.83	2	Bedford	29	Jun
60.88	Matthew Frampton		10.04.84	2	Watford	1	Sep
57.89	Karim Chester		6.11.84	4	Bedford	29	Jun
57.83	Kamran Khan		2.10.83	2	Manchester (C)	25	May
57.55	Derrick Squire		7.12.83	5	Bedford	29	Jun
54.80	Peter Cranfield		26.09.84	3	Manchester (C)	25	May
51.17	Glenn Williams		24.03.85	1	Cardiff	26	Aug
49.31	Laurence Harwood		9.03.85	8	Bedford	29	Jun
49.02	James Rees		25.07.83	2	Cardiff	26	Aug
	(10)						
48.83	Matthew Maitland		27.08.83	2	Grangemouth	25	May

Hammer - Under 17 - 5kg

65.26	Simon Bissell		25.12.85	1	Wigan	14	Jul
62.62	Gordon Grierson		12.10.85	1	Perivale	14	Sep
61.08	Jason Joseph		27.11.85	1	London (He)	15	Jun
58.07	Matthew Lambley	U15	18.09.87	1	Manchester (Str)	8	Sep
56.81	Andrew Thomas		14.06.86	1	Birmingham	6	Jul
55.98	Fraser Campbell		30.05.86	3	Glasgow	20	Jul
54.13	Alistair McDiarmid		16.10.85	1	Gateshead	24	Aug
53.32	Mark Covington		3.10.85	1	Portsmouth	19	May
53.11	Charles Hogarth		11.02.86	1	Middlesbrough	15	Jun
52.98	Michael Bomba		10.10.86	1	Rotherham	30	Jun
	(10)						
52.09	James Smith		11.12.86	6	Birmingham	10	Aug
52.04	Robert Dudman		9.06.86	2	Kingston	4	Aug
50.64	Matthew Richards		10.05.86	1	Brecon	22	Jun
50.13	Nnamdi Efobi		14.09.86	2	Tonbridge	30	Jun
50.04	James Earle		18.05.87	1	Braintree	8	Aug
49.47	Chris Gearing		30.09.86	2	Watford	26	May
49.26	John Honey		6.02.86	2	Newport	8	Jun
49.01	Kieran O'Keefe		19.03.86	1	Sutton Coldfield	19	May
48.71	Jamie Pritchard		25.09.85	1	Newport	16	May
48.51	Ben Lawrence		13.04.86	1	Cannock	11	May
	(20)						
47.83	Sean Penny		17.06.86	1	Bournemouth	24	Jun
47.67	Jack Pallister		22.02.87	1	Stoke-on-Trent	15	Jun
47.53	Jamie Gregory		24.12.86	1	Grimsby	30	Jun
47.46	Alex Hitchens		12.12.86	1	Par	22	Sep
47.25	Joe Connor		17.12.86	3	Birmingham	22	Jun
47.13	Sam Herrington		2.10.86	4	Birmingham	31	Aug

Hammer - Under 15 - 4kg

64.70	Matthew Lambley	18.09.87	1	Birmingham	3	Jul
53.64	Sean Lewis	10.09.87	2	Birmingham	10	Aug
50.39	Alex Smith	6.03.88	1	Blackpool	8	Sep
	57.99 overage		1B	Eton	19	Oct
50.01	Luke Shortman	14.10.87	3	Nottingham	13	Jul
47.97	Alistair Tawanaee	31.03.88	3	Birmingham	10	Aug
47.15	Marc Preston	20.09.87	4	Nottingham	13	Jul
45.96	Scott McKevitt	15.09.87	5	Nottingham	13	Jul
45.29	Kyle Wild	28.10.87	7	Nottingham	13	Jul
45.05	Lewis Edwards	13.09.87	8	Nottingham	13	Jul
43.80	Scott Church	17.05.88	1B	Sandown IOW	14	Aug
(10)						
43.19	Chris Scott	21.03.88	1	Sandown IOW	18	Sep
42.60	Karl Fitzgerald	4.11.87	1	Scunthorpe	4	Jun
42.60	Jon Kingsberry	19.03.88	1	Bangor	24	Jun
42.06	Daniel Chapman	14.09.88	1	Eton	6	Jul
41.85	Kieran McConnell	13.10.87	1	London (Cr)	30	Jun
41.59	Kieran Mason	26.11.87	4	London (He)	25	Aug
41.58	Matthew Reilly		1	Exeter	23	Jun
41.11	Matthew Ansell	23.09.87	1	Sandown IOW	27	Jul
40.62	Chris Shorthouse	23.06.88	2	Stoke-on-Trent	30	Jun
40.31	James Popowoski	9.01.88	10	Nottingham	13	Jul
(20)						
40.08	Thomas Higgs	11.12.87	11	Nottingham	13	Jul

overage

41.08	Josh Steele	14.09.87	1	Bedford	5	Oct

Javelin

88.54	Steve Backley	12.02.69	1	Munich, GER	9	Aug
	87.29		1	Floro, NOR	1	Jun
	86.81		1	Manchester (C)	31	Jul
	85.76		QA	Munich, GER	7	Aug
	85.54		1	Bangor, NI	21	Jul
	85.03		2	Annecy, FRA	23	Jun
	84.93		3	Sheffield	30	Jun
	84.45 A		2	Germiston, RSA	5	Apr
	84.03 A		2	Pretoria, RSA	12	Apr
	83.06		2	Glasgow (S)	18	Aug
	82.49		6	London (CP)	23	Aug
	80.55		6	Stockholm, SWE	16	Jul
	79.39		4	Madrid, ESP	21	Sep
	79.07		1	Reduit, MRI	21	Apr
82.90	Mick Hill	22.10.64	5	Sheffield	30	Jun
	82.33		1	Varazdin, CRO	6	Jul
	79.59		1	Dublin, IRL	19	Jul
	79.38		QA	Munich, GER	7	Aug
	78.70		1	Bedford	4	Jun
	78.56 A		7	Germiston, RSA	5	Apr
	78.15		3	Manchester (C)	15	Jun
	77.86		1	Birmingham	13	Jul
	76.49		10	London (CP)	23	Aug
	76.38		1	Bedford	26	May
	76.12		10	Munich, GER	9	Aug
	75.86		4	Glasgow (S)	18	Aug
	73.98		2	Loughborough	18	May
	73.87		1	Bangor, NI	21	Jul
	73.13 A		8	Pretoria, RSA	12	Apr

80.05	Nick Nieland		31.01.72	1	Manchester (C)	15	Jun
	78.63			3	Manchester (C)	31	Jul
	77.11			1	Loughborough	18	May
	76.89			2	Bedford	4	Jun
	76.72			6	Halle, GER	11	May
	75.87			11	Sheffield	30	Jun
	75.53			1	Bangor, NI	21	Jul
78.80	Mark Roberson		13.03.67	2	Manchester (C)	15	Jun
	74.52			6	Manchester (C)	31	Jul
	74.23			2	Birmingham	13	Jul
	73.78			10	Halle, GER	11	May
	73.77			1	Wigan	31	Aug
	73.68			12	Sheffield	30	Jun
	73.09			3	Loughborough	18	May
76.17	Stuart Faben		28.02.75	1	Alfaz del Pi, ESP	30	Mar
	75.18			1	Torrevieja, ESP	3	Apr
	73.97			3	Ghent, BEL	24	Jul
	73.03			4	Bedford	4	Jun
75.43	Michael Allen	U23	7.03.80	1	Belfast	11	May
	73.19			2	Bedford	26	May
74.80	David Parker	U23	28.02.80	3	Bedford	4	Jun
	74.22			4	Manchester (C)	15	Jun
	51 performances to 73.00 by 7 athletes						
71.09	Phill Sharpe	U23	6.03.81	1	Bedford	30	Jun
71.00	Mike Tarran	U23	10.12.80	2	Bedford	30	Jun
69.56	Dan Carter	U23	15.04.80	1	Watford	2	Jun
(10)							
68.87	Tom Dobbing		5.02.73	6	Manchester (C)	15	Jun
68.85	Alex van der Merwe	U20	5.01.84	1	Bedford	30	Jun
67.65	Keith Beard	V40	8.11.61	3	Sittard, NED	6	Jul
67.42	Gez Plunkett	U23	30.06.80	3	Bedford	30	Jun
67.17	Chris Hughff	U23	5.12.81	2	Loughborough	22	May
66.40	David Sketchley		25.02.76	1	Colchester	26	Aug
66.33	Neil McLellan		10.09.78	1	Nantes, FRA	28	Apr
65.71	Jonathan Lundman	U23	7.12.81	4	Bedford	30	Jun
65.11	Simon Carter		5.03.75	1	Watford	14	Sep
64.79	Peter Yates	V45	15.06.57	1	Hemel Hempstead	3	Aug
(20)							
64.09	Simon Bennett		16.10.72	2	Bedford	19	May
64.04	Tony Smith	V40	17.05.58	5	Watford	19	May
63.91	Matthew Allison		26.02.73	1	Jarrow	1	Jun
63.54	Steve Harrison		19.12.72	1	Bromley	8	Jun
63.53	Ian Burns		20.09.77	3	Jarrow	1	Jun
63.44	Andrew Gallagher	U20	15.02.83	6	Bedford	26	May
63.37	Clifton Green		10.10.79	6	Watford	19	May
63.21	Anthony Lovett	U23	20.09.82	2	Watford	31	Aug
62.85	Patrick Boundy		19.02.79	1	Stevenage	4	May
62.56	Trevor Ratcliffe		9.03.64	2	Watford	12	May
(30)							
62.54	Ben Saville		10.11.77	1	Grimsby	12	May
61.81	Nigel Bevan		3.01.68	1	Stoke-on-Trent	21	Jul
61.42	Andy Hayward		26.10.74	2	Gateshead	24	Aug
61.41	Rhys Williams	U23	4.10.81	4	Newport	20	Jul
60.99	Alex Gibson		3.11.77	D	Maribor, SLO	30	Jun
60.89	Derek Hermann		7.04.79	1	Newport	8	Jun
60.85	Paul Howard		19.10.66	3	London (He)	21	Jul
60.79	Stuart Millar	U20	9.03.83	1	Grangemouth	25	Aug
60.70	Jonathan Clarke		20.11.67	2	Cardiff	18	May
60.58	Chris Smith		27.11.75	1	Dundee	15	Sep
(40)							
60.56	David McKay	U23	22.09.80	5	Bedford	30	Jun

60.25	Ken Hayford		10.03.63	1	London (Elt)	13	Jul
60.01	Stewart McMillan		12.09.69	1	Grangemouth	2	Jun
59.66	Sean Carson	U20	13.04.84	1	Edinburgh	11	May
59.45	Jason Hallett	U23	29.03.82	3	Newport	8	Jun
59.33	Steven Cotton		8.02.79	2	Exeter	11	May
59.27	Jim McFarlane		16.06.79	1	Oxford	18	May
59.16	Sam Goddard	U20	4.01.83	1	Erith	4	May
59.15	Felix Hatton	U20	9.10.84	1	Nottingham	12	Jul
58.84	Kevin Murch	V40	11.11.58	1	London (He)	27	Jul
	(50)						
58.74	Phil Parry		4.10.65	10	Birmingham	6	Jul
58.36	Peter Johnson		25.09.75	1	Cudworth	14	Sep
58.35	Eric Workman	U20	2.03.83	1	Portsmouth	11	May
58.34	Matthew Dingley	U20	12.01.83	1	Birmingham	25	May
58.25	David Evans		23.01.76	3	Bedford	6	May
58.25	Wesley Smith		26.02.79	1	London (PH)	8	Jun
58.22	John Powell	V40	4.06.62	5	Potsdam, GER	22	Aug
57.86	Jon Wilkinson	V40	17.02.62	1	Telford	11	May
57.73	David Harding	U23	8.11.80	2	Oxford	26	Jun
57.64	Livon Houslin	V40	2.11.60	1	Perivale	22	Jun
	(60)						
57.58	Darren Hatton		21.03.79	2D	Woodford	28	Apr
57.51	Jim Everard	U23	16.05.81	4	Basildon	11	May
57.44	Alex Simpson	U23	19.01.82	2	Watford	14	Sep
57.17	Lee Doran	U20	5.03.85	1	Carlisle	31	Mar
57.14	Robert Miller	U20	20.01.84	2	London (WF)	18	Aug
57.13	Peter Fraser		28.01.78	2	Bedford	17	Aug
57.08	Barry Thomas		28.04.72	5D	Azusa, USA	19	Apr
57.04	Steve Jamieson		4.02.79	1	Woodford	4	May
56.99	Steve Rogers		1.09.71	3	Singapore, SIN	8	Sep
56.91	Tony Norman		5.07.63	1	Kingston	18	May
	(70)						
56.88	Jonathan Harvey	U20	12.09.83	1	Ipswich	7	Apr
56.85	Jeremy Smyth		11.08.78	2	Edinburgh	11	May
56.82	Martin Travis	U20	10.07.85	1	Bath	18	Aug
56.81	David McKown	U20	27.02.84	1	Blackpool	1	Jun
56.52	Anthony Llewellyn	U20	21.12.83	1	London (BP)	13	Jul
56.17	Greg Markham		28.11.78	1	Rotherham	31	Mar
56.16	Terry Greenwood		22.08.74	1	Douglas IOM	4	May
55.83	Paul Cooper		4.12.76	5	Basildon	11	May
55.78	Stuart Walker		22.09.78	5	Jarrow	1	Jun
55.56	James Deacon-Brown	U20	26.05.84	1	Jarrow	18	Aug
	(80)						
55.30	Robert Eggleton	U20	13.02.84	1	Cannock	11	May
55.23	Steve Greening		15.02.68	5	Birmingham	2	Jun
55.05	Simon Williams	U23	3.01.82	3	Sheffield (W)	31	Aug
55.02	David Turner	U20	4.07.84	2	Derby	8	Sep
54.98	Chris Gasson		28.02.79		Dartford	4	May
54.90	Graham Lay		13.11.75	7	Glasgow (S)	8	Jun
54.68	Mark Lindsay	U20	5.11.84	1	Manchester (C)	25	May
54.24	Andrew Ormesher	U20	29.05.85	4	Nottingham	12	Jul
53.23	Mark Wyss	U20	12.07.85	5	Nottingham	12	Jul

Foreign

71.85	*Ben Houghton (IRL)*	*U23*	*6.08.80*	*1*	*Namur, BEL*	*31*	*Aug*
58.63	*Leon Karagounis (GRE)*		*15.10.75*	*7*	*Merksem, BEL*	*17*	*Aug*
57.73	*Ciaran Doherty (IRL)*		*14.01.75*	*D*	*Navan*	*12*	*May*
57.29	*Wu Yu (CHN)*			*4*	*Bedford*	*6*	*May*
56.03	*Pieter Schoeman (RSA)*		*1.01.79*	*1*	*London (WF)*	*3*	*Aug*

Javelin - Under 17 - 700gm

60.66	Sam Kelvey	12.07.86	1	Birmingham	11 Aug
57.74	Allandre Johnson	8.12.85	1	Kingston	4 Aug
56.74	Tyson Johnson	24.06.87	3	Birmingham	11 Aug
56.51	Philip Mann	25.10.85	1	Nottingham	12 Jul
55.10	Gavin Dudzik	22.02.86	1	Tullamore, IRL	22 Jun
54.89	Thomas Rees	9.03.86	1	Newport	8 Jun
54.50	Peter Hutcheson	18.11.86	1	London (Cr)	19 May
52.32	Luke Millington	7.11.86	5	Birmingham	11 Aug
52.04	Callum McDonald	30.04.86	1	Burton	21 Jul
51.60	James Hopley	28.01.87	2	Abingdon	8 Sep
	(10)				
51.15	Sean Leckenby	26.09.86	1	Middlesbrough	21 Jul
50.91	Roy Chambers	9.02.86	2	Watford	25 May
50.50	Simon Cooke	3.10.85	1	Poole	5 May
50.10	James Evans	7.11.86	2	Brecon	6 Jul

Javelin - Under 15 - 600gm

54.64	Adam Akehurst	13.09.87	1	Woking	1 Sep
54.27	Stuart Harvey	2.09.87	1	Ashford	15 Jun
52.59	James Campbell	1.04.88	1	Glasgow	27 Aug
51.90	Sam Allan	16.09.88	1	Leeds (South)	2 Jul
51.56	Adam Sharp	1.04.88	2	Mansfield	12 Jul
49.92	Philip Gregory	14.02.88	1	Birmingham	1 Sep
49.16	Josh Stannard	15.10.87	5	Mansfield	12 Jul
48.17	Joe Waller	13.11.87	1	Horsham	18 Aug
46.64	Carl Quinlan	8.09.87	7	Mansfield	12 Jul
45.78	Alex McEwan	8.12.87	2	Crawley	15 Jun
	(10)				
45.78	Neil Crossley	15.04.88	3	Abingdon	8 Sep
45.77	Daniel Brunsdon	18.04.88	3	London (He)	25 Aug
45.55	Mark Rumble	10.07.88	1	Oxford	7 Jul
45.52	Josh Turnbull	3.12.88	1	Brecon	6 Jul
45.42	Callum Stewart	13.01.88	8	Mansfield	12 Jul
44.99	Ken Robertson	6.04.88	1	Coatbridge	5 May
44.82	Sheldon Mills	10.02.88	1	London (BP)	15 Jun
44.72	Peter Glasse	1.05.88	1	Bangor	15 May
44.50	Thomas Amphlett	21.10.87	4	Abingdon	8 Sep
43.55	Max Blake		5	London (He)	25 Aug
	(20)				
43.17	James Sinclair	22.10.87	1	Jarrow	12 Jun
43.07	Joel Gebbie	14.09.87	2	Erith	14 Jul

Under 13

28.83	Michael Sturla			Exeter	30 Jul

Javelin - Under 13 - 400gm

38.42	Andrew Marsh	26.01.90	1	Cannock	3 Jul
38.41	B. Byrd		1	Telford	15 Jul
38.41	Charles Conn	9.05.90	1	Crawley	26 Aug
36.79	Alex Howard	28.08.90	1	Isle of Wight	15 Sep
35.87	Matthew Keep	14.07.90	1		1 Sep
35.74	Daniel Twiss		1	Highgate	4 Jun
35.58	Rory Trow	18.02.90	1	Kingston	28 Jul
34.57	Tom Nichol		1	Watford	27 Apr
34.47	Kevin Thompson	29.12.89	1		25 Jun
34.36	Simon Birch	11.09.89	1	Eastbourne	7 Jul
	(10)				
33.20	Darren Foster	14.10.89	1	Carlisle	13 Jul
33.06	Philip Alvey	3.07.90	1	Neath	14 Jul

Decathlon

7630	Jamie Quarry		15.11.72	3	Manchester (C)	28 Jul
	11.12/0.6	7.16/-1.1 14.68 1.94	50.10 14.96/0.6	38.08 4.65 50.69	4:31.94
7546	Barry Thomas		28.04.72	4	Manchester (C)	28 Jul
	11.22/0.6	7.17/-0.3 13.28 1.94	50.99 15.11/0.6	39.11 4.75 54.09	4:35.01
7505				5	Azusa, USA	19 Apr
	11.19/2.0	7.21w/2.7 13.42 1.95	51.65 15.59/-1.4	39.55 4.65 57.08	4:37.19
7411	John Heanley	U23	25.09.80	9	Arles, FRA	2 Jun
	11.45/-3.7	7.12/1.7 10.68 1.99	50.12 14.92/0.0	35.34 4.61 54.06	4:21.00
7162				8	Manchester (C)	28 Jul
	11.36/-0.1	6.85/-0.1 10.01 2.00	49.44 15.09/0.6	34.64 4.25 49.78	4:21.11
7057 w				1	Perpignan, FRA	20 Apr
	10.97W/5.0	7.00w/2.6 10.42 1.98	51.16 14.8w/2.7	29.95 4.30 48.30	4:29.88
7017				2	Issoudun, FRA	29 Sep
	11.57/-0.3	6.79/0.6 9.60 1.98	50.65 15.71/-1.5	34.75 4.50 53.14	4:31.79
7377	Anthony Sawyer	U23	29.04.80	3	Hexham	16 Jun
	11.22w/2.1	7.08w/2.2 12.74 1.95	49.70 14.89/1.9	36.55 4.25 49.62	4:26.73
7271				3	Maribor, SLO	30 Jun
	11.43/-0.8	6.73/-0.6 13.07 1.92	49.57 14.80/0.9	38.87 4.20 50.11	4:31.2
7204				7	Manchester (C)	28 Jul
	11.17/-0.1	6.87/-0.4 12.71 2.00	49.30 15.54/0.6	35.31 4.15 48.11	4:33.34
7197				1	Birmingham	2 Jun
	11.41/-2.6	6.70w/3.6 12.84 1.86	49.47 15.27/-2.8	39.33 4.22 53.94	4:34.6
7182				1	Woodford	28 Apr
	11.19w/2.9	7.13w/2.7 12.08 1.95	49.68 15.13/1.5	38.59 4.08 45.93	4:39.89
7112	Gez Plunkett	U23	30.06.80	4	Pratteln, SUI	4 Aug
	11.61/1.2	6.35/0.0 13.82 1.89	50.43 15.63/1.2	39.15 4.10 61.92	4:42.20
6787				5	Hexham	16 Jun
	11.59w/2.5	6.50w/2.5 12.65 1.95	51.52 16.24w/4.0	37.12 3.85 59.94	4:56.33
7076	Brendan McConville		3.01.79	1	Antrim	25 Aug
	11.61/1.3	6.60/1.4 11.89 1.98	50.63 15.35w/2.9	34.77 4.55 47.15	4:26.76
7007				2	Birmingham	2 Jun
	11.85/-2.6	6.82/1.9 11.80 1.92	49.93 15.45/-2.8	34.44 4.32 50.26	4:27.12
6996				13	Maribor, SLO	30 Jun
	11.64/0.4	6.72/0.6 12.28 1.89	49.93 15.32/1.4	35.27 4.30 46.74	4:28.3
7028	Alex Gibson		3.11.77	1	London (He)	11 Aug
	11.10/1.0	6.91/0.6 13.37 1.85	50.48 16.48/0.0	37.53 3.90 58.30	4:45.25
6887				15	Maribor, SLO	30 Jun
	11.37/0.0	6.50/-0.8 11.87 1.83	49.81 16.05/1.3	36.26 4.00 60.99	4:45.0
6857				3	Birmingham	2 Jun
	11.26/-2.6	6.82/1.7 12.47 1.80	49.79 16.10/-1.7	37.46 3.82 54.68	4:47.26
6594				5	Woodford	28 Apr
	11.73w/2.9	6.35 11.46 1.77	50.82 16.02w/2.8	33.08 3.78 58.64	4:46.86
6924	Adrian Hemery	U23	6.08.82	7	Pratteln, SUI	4 Aug
	11.42/1.9	6.63/0.0 12.27 1.86	51.12 15.33/0.0	38.01 3.90 51.70	4:33.17
6620				1	Wrexham	23 Jun
	11.71/-1.8	6.58W/5.3 11.77 1.89	51.48 15.71/1.4	33.07 3.95 49.20	4:40.24
6519				1	Watford	29 Sep
	11.6/-1.1	6.29/0.0 11.61 1.83	51.30 15.9/0.7	39.58 3.80 47.92	4:36.72
6919	Dale Garland	U23	13.10.80	9	Manchester (C)	28 Jul
	11.01/-0.1	7.16/-0.6 9.66 1.88	47.80 15.50/0.6	30.95 3.55 45.94	4:17.22
6805	Steve Bonnett		13.07.78	2	Woodford	28 Apr
	11.66/-1.5	6.96/1.8 11.98 1.95	50.87 15.65/1.5	36.19 3.98 42.52	4:38.15
6562				4	Birmingham	2 Jun
	11.85/-2.4	6.45/1.3 12.07 1.86	50.11 16.00/-2.8	34.55 4.02 44.36	4:40.38
(10)						
6803	Darren Hatton		21.03.79	3	Woodford	28 Apr
	11.74/-1.5	6.74w/2.2 13.36 1.86	51.42 15.97/1.5	37.11 4.18 57.58	5:07.36
6712	Paul Jones		11.04.78	4	Woodford	28 Apr
	11.76/-1.5	7.03w/3.3 11.74 1.83	51.16 15.85/1.5	35.66 4.18 45.36	4:41.54

246

6688   James Lowery   U23   17.10.80 12   Pratteln, SUI   4 Aug
11.34/1.9 6.54/-0.9 11.14 1.86 50.02 15.22/1.8 35.67 4.20 39.55 4:46.61
6460   2   Wrexham   23 Jun
11.69/-1.8 6.41W/4.8 11.28 1.92 52.27 15.37/1.4 33.94 4.05 45.03 4:58.39

6678   Paul Tohill   U23   9.10.82 13   Pratteln, SUI   4 Aug
11.49/1.2 6.64/0.0 11.23 1.89 50.90 15.27/1.2 31.24 4.00 48.15 4:41.48
6472   6   Woodford   28 Apr
11.75/-1.2 6.67w/3.7 11.39 1.92 50.82 15.52/1.5 31.99 3.98 43.20 4:59.10
6432   5   Birmingham   2 Jun
11.96/-2.4 6.31/1.8 10.76 1.95 50.59 15.68/-2.8 34.64 4.02 43.30 4:52.60

6593   Livio Salvador-Aylott   18.07.73 3   Long Beach CA, USA 9 Jun
11.23w/2.3 6.66w/3.0 11.98 1.75 51.63 16.16w/2.1 34.69 4.00 54.84 4:58.55

6400   James Wright   U23   2.04.82 2   London (He)   11 Aug
11.29/1.0 6.91w/2.3 9.21 1.76 51.56 15.36/-1.6 28.12 4.00 46.40 4:45.16

36 performances to 6400 by 16 athletes

6388   Edward Dunford   U20   15.09.84 1   Hexham   19 May
11.63/0.2 6.40   12.55 1.89 53.7 15.66/0.0 39.64 3.52 50.01 5:12.35

6350   Jason McDade   U23   3.04.80 3   London (He)   11 Aug
11.4/1.0 6.70w/2.5 11.74 2.00 53.07 15.39/-1.6 34.50 3.60 45.56 5:38.40

6184   Leo Barker   26.12.78 4   London (He)   11 Aug
11.51/0.6 6.83/0.6 12.00 1.73 51.62 15.70/1.0 30.45 3.10 44.01 4:49.30

6183   Gavin Fordham   1.02.79 8   Woodford   28 Apr
11.67/-1.5 6.59w/2.8 10.23 1.92 51.13 15.86w/2.8 31.21 3.98 41.54 5:21.50

(20)
6174   Martin Taylor   U23   31.01.82 1   Grangemouth   25 Aug
11.44/1.5 6.82   11.52 1.71 51.41 16.22/-2.1 33.91 3.70 44.89 5:18.08

6130   Daniel Brandwood   U23   1.10.82 5   London (He)   11 Aug
11.11/1.0 6.36w/2.4 10.08 1.64 49.17 16.55/0.0 36.51 4.00 32.34 4:57.51

6119   Jan Schuler   29.10.72 2   Watford   29 Sep
11.9/0.2 6.14/0.0 11.15 1.74 50.40 15.9/0.7 37.63 3.60 42.42 4:48.15

6092   Andrew East   U23   25.07.81 5   Wrexham   23 Jun
11.70/-1.8 6.22W/4.6 9.92 1.80 50.51 16.12/1.4 31.56 3.45 46.55 4:48.79

6026   Paul Gilding   2.10.75 6   London (He)   11 Aug
11.54/1.0 6.61/1.0 10.55 1.94 53.88 15.52/-1.6 30.42 3.20 39.27 5:02.15

6008   Martin Lloyd   U23   18.06.80 1   Erith   22 Sep
11.8 6.39   9.72 2.08 53.6 15.6 35.15 3.60 37.52 5:17.8

5993   Chris Gunn   U23   13.09.82 2   Calgary, CAN   12 May
12.02w/2.4 6.00/0.2 11.27 1.75 52.78 15.89/2.0 32.01 3.90 44.22 4:56.89

5958   Ondrej Choutka   24.11.76 8   Hexham   16 Jun
12.06/0.6 6.40w/3.1 12.27 1.83 53.58 17.98w/3.9 29.58 3.55 46.00 4:36.40

5941   Michael Dyer   U20   27.09.84 1   London (He)   11 Aug
11.65/1.5 6.41w/3.4 10.27 1.82 53.47 15.93/-1.6 28.82 3.20 44.83 4:47.70

5938   Lee Manvell   U23   11.12.80 9   Hexham   9 Jun
11.82/0.6 6.21/1.6 10.71 1.80 52.23 17.37w/3.9 28.82 3.85 40.41 4:37.18

5935   John Dickinson   U20   27.01.83 11   Woodford   28 Apr
11.68/1.1 6.59   9.79 1.77 51.63 17.77w/2.8 32.29 3.68 38.15 4:39.26

5924   Carl Marchment   U23   30.12.82 6   Wrexham   23 Jun
12.18/-2.9 6.39W/6.9 9.93 1.77 51.95 16.91/1.8 35.27 3.85 42.52 4:58.72

5894   Chris Awde   U20   14.02.85 2   London (He)   11 Aug
11.35/1.7 6.58/0.9 9.80 1.82 52.20 17.57/-1.0 34.99 3.00 40.54 4:49.06

5880   Ben Hazell   U20   1.10.84 12   Woodford   28 Apr
11.90/1.1 6.59/-2.4 10.01 1.77 51.95 17.05/1.9 31.46 3.08 43.46 4:37.51

5857   Sam Bishop   17.08.79 7   Birmingham   2 Jun
12.05/-2.4 6.06W/4.3 10.80 1.95 52.51 18.25/-1.7 35.18 3.32 44.34 4:50.97

5817   Robert Miller   U20   20.01.84 3   London (He)   11 Aug
11.61/1.5 6.65/1.8 9.48 1.73 53.23 16.88/0.0 28.13 3.00 54.20 4:55.39

5814   Gerald Manville   21.12.78 2   Aldershot   5 Jul
11.8 6.07   8.83 1.80 52.3 16.9 30.11 4.00 41.81 4:43.57

5772   Chris Oakes   19.10.70 3   Aldershot   5 Jul
11.5 6.17   12.02 1.92 55.5 16.3 34.50 3.20 36.41 5:08.80

5708	Ryan Westaway		U20	2.03.83	14		Woodford			28 Apr
	12.10/1.1	6.59/1.9	8.85	1.86	53.15	15.73w/2.8	27.44	3.68	38.06	5:17.94
5705	Martin Ohrland			19.11.79	4		Watford			29 Sep
	12.0/-1.1	6.18/-0.6	10.07	2.01	53.05	15.3/0.7	26.11	3.10	33.78	4:55.82
(40)										
5699	Mike Bull			6.06.70	8		Birmingham			2 Jun
	11.88/-2.4	6.22w2.7	11.36	1.71	52.20	16.93/-1.7	32.12	3.42	34.72	4:55.26
5683	Stuart Caudery			19.11.66	1		Exeter			29 Sep
	12.4	5.99	10.28	1.87	53.8	16.2	31.80	4.00	37.66	5:05.5
5578	Brian Hughes			6.01.70	8		Wrexham			23 Jun
	12.44/-2.9	6.35w/2.2	9.85	1.77	54.18	17.22/1.8	34.83	3.75	43.18	5:22.43
5537	Nick Foxworthy		U20	20.05.83	4		London (He)			11 Aug
	12.02/0.6	6.16/1.7	10.38	1.88	55.22	15.91/1.0	31.83	3.40	44.75	6:00.34
5515	Mark Bishop			12.02.67	8		London (He)			11 Aug
	12.04/1.7	6.44w/2.4	12.04	1.73	53.56	16.52/0.0	34.67	3.70	49.77	dnf
5398	Tim Howell		U23	6.12.82	10		Wrexham			23 Jun
	12.39/-2.9	6.08w/2.8	9.87	1.77	55.21	16.00/1.8	28.46	3.35	39.04	5:09.06
5301	Robert Sinclair			8.11.77	10		Hexham			16 Jun
	12.00/0.6	5.71/1.8	9.27	1.65	53.29	18.60w/3.9	30.10	3.45	39.46	4:41.12
5169	Matthew Kelly		U23	4.12.80	1		Jarrow			29 Sep
	12.0/-0.2	6.08/-1.7	9.60	1.69	53.1	18.8	31.32	2.45	50.10	5:01.5
5102	David Ingram		U23	19.01.80	2		Crawley			15 Sep
	11.95w/2.8	5.52/1.4	8.51	1.71	55.04	17.6/1.6	24.07	4.00	30.22	4:52.7
5061	Ashley Pritchard			14.07.79	2		Jarrow			29 Sep
	12.5/-0.2	5.65/-1.5	8.44	1.72	58.0	17.5	31.48	3.45	47.94	5:04.4
(50)										
5011	Karl Russell		U23	3.11.81	2		Antrim			25 Aug
	12.25/1.3	5.56	8.16	1.56	55.27	19.35w/2.9	28.22	4.20	34.40	4:45.10
4949	Joe Appiah			26.10.70	2		Erith			22 Sep
	11.6	6.55	8.57	1.73	56.2	15.6	19.63	32.26	5:23.6	
4921	Peter Coates			21.03.68	1		Gateshead			24 Aug
	12.3	5.97	9.49	1.68	55.2	18.9	28.18	3.20	35.68	4:55.1
4919	Matt Ledger		U23	23.11.81	11		Hexham			16 Jun
	12.31/0.6	6.16/1.7	10.13	1.86	60.28	17.87w/3.9	31.03	3.05	48.10	6:22.70

unfinished

5582	Anthony Southward			31.01.71			Birmingham			2 Jun
	11.71/-2.6	6.67w/3.7	11.75	1.80	50.51	15.33w/2.8	38.47	4.02		

Foreign

6670	*Lee Okoroafor (NGR)*			*12.09.76*	*1*		*Lagos, NGR*			*20 Jun*
	10.8	*6.98*	*11.74*	*2.00*	*50.54*	*14.9*	*36.33*	*2.31*	*50.21*	*4:51.60*
5695	*Ciaran Doherty (IRL)*			*14.01.75*	*1*		*Navan*			*12 May*
	11.94/0.4	*6.11/1.7*	*12.21*	*1.82*	*57.32*	*16.40*	*34.74*	*3.20*	*57.72*	*5:52.98*

Decathlon - Under 20 with Under 20 implements

7050	Edward Dunford			15.09.84	1		Derby			22 Sep
	11.25/0.2	6.73/1.0	14.84	1.92	52.77	14.74/-3.9	45.15	3.70	49.34	5:05.82
6654	Ben Hazell			1.10.84	2		Derby			22 Sep
	11.68/0.3	6.53/1.7	12.64	1.83	50.58	15.39/-0.4	34.86	3.80	47.86	4:42.30
6370	David Hughes			31.05.84	2		Hexham			19 May
	11.21/0.2	6.45	12.63	1.77	49.8	15.37(3'6")/0.0	32.64	3.32	43.23	5:00.10
6332	Matthew Walden			30.11.83	3		Derby			22 Sep
	11.75/-0.9	6.52/0.4	12.07	1.86	51.30	15.98/-3.0	35.27	3.40	43.20	4:47.60
6298	Michael Dyer			27.09.84	4		Derby			22 Sep
	11.66/0.3	6.39/-0.1	10.77	1.83	51.35	15.40/-3.9	34.67	3.10	46.57	4:38.49
6005	William Sharman			12.09.84	5		Derby			22 Sep
	12.16/-0.3	5.49/1.3	10.94	1.86	51.40	15.50/-0.4	34.44	3.40	42.69	5:01.79
6005	Robert Henry			31.05.85	6		Derby			22 Sep
	11.32/0.2	5.85/-0.5	12.79	1.65	51.64	15.70/-3.9	33.95	3.60	41.32	5:14.13

5984	Matthew Clay			9.06.84	1	Rotherham				29 Sep
	11.9	6.52	11.41 1.94	52.2	16.7	34.80	3.00	39.90	4:46.6	
5981	Robert Miller			20.01.84	3	Grangemouth				25 Aug
	11.72w/2.1	6.29	11.30 1.74	52.57	16.50/-1.5	29.81	3.00	57.04	4:53.94	
5898	Tony Higbee			21.09.83	1	Bournemouth				30 Jun
	11.4	6.18	10.32 1.96	52.9	16.2	36.72	3.10	38.82	5:09.0	
(10)										
5853	Colin Bailey			15.11.83	3	Hexham				19 May
	12.26/0.2	6.21	9.52 1.92	56.7	15.85/0.0	30.80	3.72	50.63	5:04.16	
5838	David Taylor			21.11.84	7	Derby				22 Sep
	11.42/0.2	6.47/0.4	10.72 1.80	15.70/-3.9		31.47	2.10	38.19	4:48.74	
5837	Tom Reynolds			20.12.84	1	Antrim				25 Aug
	11.91/1.3	6.16	11.41 1.74	53067	15.57w/2.9	32.68	3.60	38.13	5:06.43	
5620	Ross Tressider			8.01.83	1	Watford				29 Sep
	11.9/-0.4	6.34/0.0	10.65 1.73	51.96	14.99/0.3	31.95	2.00	38.28	4:53.32	
5588	Danny Thompson			27.12.84	9	Derby				22 Sep
	11.99/-0.3	5.99/1.4	10.24 1.83	53.63	16.11/-0.4	26.61	3.30	34.82	4:48.74	
5572	Paris Norriss			27.02.85	3	Bournemouth				30 Jun
	12.0	5.66	12.90 1.72	55.9	17.2	44.50	3.20	40.19	5:13.0	
5550	Oliver Bournat			4.12.84	10	Derby				22 Sep
	12.30/-1.7	5.75/-0.8	12.73 1.80	54.41	17.53/-2.0	33.85	2.70	42.50	4:45.18	
5529	Chris Awde			14.02.85	2	Grantham				30 Jun
	11.9	6.22	10.63 1.74	53.1	17.3	38.37	3.30	38.24	5:20.2	
5490	Benjamin McIlroy			2.09.83	2	Antrim				25 Aug
	12.0/1.3	5.75	10.15 1.74	53.82	15.48w/2.9	29.06	3.40	31.84	4:57.74	
5451	Ross Elliott			6.09.83	11	Derby				22 Sep
	11.63/0.2	6.03/1.1	11.67 1.77	53.41	16.78/-3.0	32.50	3.50	25.11	5:25.51	
(20)										
5363	Robert Simmonds			30.08.85	12	Derby				22 Sep
	12.88/-1.7	5.70/1.5	9.59 1.80	55.41	18.68/-2.5	34.28	3.10	48.96	4:26.51	
5352	Andrew Grubb			26.12.83	2	Derby				30 Jun
	11.8	5.62	9.13 1.77	53.1	15.6	31.24	2.80	31.75	4:49.3	
5283	Michael McConkey			5.12.84	3	Antrim				25 Aug
	12.62/1.3	5.47	12.26 1.68	56.10	18.78w/2.9	35.70	3.30	40.55	4:43.61	
5185	Mark Allen			9.07.85	8	Birmingham				2 Jun
	12.28/-3.9	5.46/1.3	11.90 1.56	58.09	16.37/-1.4	34.18	3.72	42.21	5:40.90	
5071	Barrie Prowse			2.03.85	4	Bournemouth				30 Jun
	12.0	5.55	9.10 1.78	54.9	18.1	28.71	2.90	38.96	4:45.9	
5049	Stephen Stapely			19.05.84	4	Hemel Hempstead				30 Jun
	11.9/-0.5	6.11/-0.2	11.60 1.71	59.1	16.4/-0.2	31.97	2.50	45.11	6:06.3	
5034	Liam Wright			26.07.85	4	Grantham				30 Jun
	12.3	5.86	9.46 1.74	57.5	18.8	33.48	3.20	44.78	5:06.6	

Decathlon - Under 20 with IAAF Junior implements

6989	Edward Dunford			15.09.84	1	Pratteln, SUI				4 Aug
	11.28/1.9	6.67/-1.1	14.47 1.92	52.71	14.92/1.5	43.60	3.80	52.03	5:11.81	
6552	David Hughes			31.05.84	2	Wrexham				23 Jun
	11.57/-3.9	6.81w/2.3	12.99 1.80	50.51	14.74w/2.4	33.56	3.45	44.24	4:57.99	
6356	Zico Benjamin			4.12.84	1	Grangemouth				25 Aug
	11.87w/2.1	6.10	10.72 1.92	52.25	15.99/-1.5	32.33	4.30	42.95	4:42.39	
	6288				2	Birmingham				2 Jun
	12.18/-3.1	6.24/2.2	11.14 1.98	52.53	16.41/-1.4	29.67	4.32	42.27	4:42.62	
6351	Robin Smith			11.09.83	3	Wrexham				23 Jun
	11.95/-3.9	6.61W/5.4	11.77 1.80	51.91	15.48w/2.4	36.17	3.75	41.79	4:56.61	
6325	John Dickinson			27.01.83	4	Wrexham				23 Jun
	12.036/-3.9	6.89w/3.7	9.96 1.86	51.25	16.70/1.7	35.42	3.85	41.92	4:36.23	
6218	Ryan Westaway			2.03.85	4	Birmingham				2 Jun
	12.22/-3.9	6.68/1.9	11.70 1.92	52.26	15.97/-1.4	32.61	3.72	40.93	4:54.78	
6069	Ben Hazell			1.10.84	7	Wrexham				23 Jun
	11.92/-3.9	6.37w/3.6	11.39 1.83	51.34	16.22/1.7	26.92	3.35	44.08	4:36.92	

5860	Michael Dyer			27.09.84	8	Wrexham		23	Jun
	12.10/-3.9	5.97w/2.7 11.71	1.77	52.60	15.51w/2.4	32.27	2.85 45.63	4:50.42
5835	Chris Awde			14.02.85	5	Birmingham		2	Jun
	11.68/-3.1	6.36w/3.2 12.66	1.68	50.71	18.38/-1.4	37.01	3.12 37.00	4:49.86
5635	Nick Foxworthy			20.05.83	9	Wrexham		23	Jun
	12.41/-1.9	6.15W/4.1 11.00	1.86	55.54	16.06/1.7	35.20	3.75 46.76	6:01.80
(10)
5412	Mark Allen			9.07.85	10	Wrexham		23	Jun
	12.63/-3.9	5.63W/4.3 12.07	1.71	57.40	17.74/1.7	36.59	4.25 44.87	5:38.81

Decathlon - Under 17 with Under 17 implements

6501	Louis Moore			8.09.85	1	Stoke-on-Trent		29	Sep
	11.17/-0.1	6.96/1.7 12.27	1.83	52.75	14.08/-2.3	35.95	3.70 40.59	5:02.51
6264	Andrae Davis			27.09.85	2	Stoke-on-Trent		29	Sep
	11.63/-0.1	6.14/1.5 15.00	1.74	50.77	14.51/-2.3	38.94	2.80 36.12	4:37.82
5888	Kevin Sempers			24.11.85	3	Stoke-on-Trent		29	Sep
	11.91/-0.1	6.08/0.9 12.57	1.98	54.32	15.13/-2.3	34.76	2.90 42.71	5:08.52
5761	Chris Kirk			6.09.85	4	Stoke-on-Trent		29	Sep
	11.81/-0.1	6.86/-0.1 10.01	1.86	53.13	14.85/-2.1	27.53	3.60 32.42	5:13.35
5404	James Dohnal			18.09.85	5	Stoke-on-Trent		29	Sep
	12.04/-0.1	6.16/-0.1 10.94	1.71	52.19	14.89/-2.3	32.38	2.60 30.13	5:01.45
5394	George Beeken			4.09.86	6	Stoke-on-Trent		29	Sep
	12.11/-0.1	5.80/0.6 10.93	1.74	55.23	14.94/-2.3	37.81	2.50 36.79	5:00.41
5319	Joseph Evling-White			3.12.86	7	Stoke-on-Trent		29	Sep
	12.33/-0.1	5.92/0.4 10.97	1.77	54.82	15.48/-2.1	31.66	2.80 30.64	4:44.12
5238	Stephen Miller			15.12.85	8	Stoke-on-Trent		29	Sep
	12.06/-0.1	5.81/1.1 10.29	1.65	53.93	15.11/-2.3	25.72	2.60 40.12	4:47.33
5204	Ryan Shaw			30.12.86	9	Stoke-on-Trent		29	Sep
	11.96/-0.1	6.30/-0.1 10.83	1.59	53.95	15.02/-2.3	32.98	2.20 41.57	5:29.53
5189	James Dunford			14.01.86	10	Stoke-on-Trent		29	Sep
	12.69/-0.1	5.60/-0.1 11.63	1.71	58.83	15.76/-2.3	36.85	2.60 44.19	4:53.97
(10)
5130	Adam Booth			22.10.85	11	Stoke-on-Trent		29	Sep
	12.34/-0.1	5.42/0.9 10.23	1.77	56.05	15.00/-2.1	29.92	2.80 32.73	4:49.74
5096	Craig Glanville			21.09.86	1	Jarrow		29	Sep
	11.9/-0.9	5.56/-1.5 10.51	1.66	50.9	14.9	23.55	2.25 32.08	4:44.9
4936	Sean Tough			25.12.86	12	Stoke-on-Trent		29	Sep
	11.90/-0.1	5.24/1.5 11.22	1.50	54.28	15.48/-2.1	32.75	2.70 34.08	5:18.70

Octathlon - Under 17

5425	Andrae Davis			27.09.85	1	Derby		22	Sep
	5.89/0.6	41.56	41.00 50.23	14.34/1.0		1.83	15.97 4:46.35 (a)
4975	Louis Moore			8.09.85	1	Birmingham		2	Jun
	13.57/-2.6	6.87w/3.4 38.66	52.66	1.88	32.69	11.96	5:22.53	(b)
4957	Andrew Staniland			21.01.87	1	Rotherham		29	Sep
	14.6	6.18	13.10 54.6	38.95	1.80	47.91	5:08.2	(d)
4897	Kevin Sempers			24.11.85	2	Derby		22	Sep
	6.07/-0.7	31.70	45.74 53.13	14.77/-0.9		1.98	11.46 5:06.99 (a)
4703	James Dunford			14.01.86	3	Derby		22	Sep
	5.62/-0.8	36.10	46.19 57.14	14.96/1.0		1.86	12.39 5:00.07 (a)
4627	Chris Kirk			6.09.85	2	Jarrow		30	Jun
	6.93	24.14	34.38 52.7	14.7	1.84	10.04	4:55.8	(a)
4620	Toby Hunt			28.12.86	1	Derby		30	Jun
	5.87	39.70	48.36 57.3	15.9	1.61	14.28	5:02.9	(a)
4604	James Dohnal			18.09.85	1	Preston		30	Jun
	6.01	31.98	36.90 53.9	14.1	1.79	10.73	4:59.0	(a)
4603	Matthew Woolley			6.05.86	4	Derby		22	Sep
	6.32/-0.7	36.14	49.44 55.18	15.34/-0.7		1.50	13.47 5:20.79 (a)
4573	Roy Chambers			9.02.86	1	Hemel Hempstead		30	Jun
	61.18/-1.0	35.16	44.88 55.6	16.2/-0.4		1.72	12.46 5:05.5 (a)

4538	Matt Hansford				20.02.86	1	Exeter		26 May
	6.61	31.59	34.19	54.8	14.0	1.82	11.89	5:42.3	(a)
4519	Kyle Freeman				12.10.85	5	Derby		22 Sep
	5.63/-0.7	34.03	40.33	56.21	15.58/0.3		1.77	11.26	4:41.01 (a)
4515	John Stacey				23.11.85	6	Derby		22 Sep
	6.01/-0.7	28.64	34.44	53.97	14.81/1.8		1.80	11.00	4:53.92 (a)
4492	Craig Glanville				21.09.86	8	Derby		22 Sep
	5.88/0.7	22.32	27.54	50.18	14.74/1.8		1.68	10.46	4:24.05 (a)
4483	Sam Griffin				18.10.85	9	Derby		22 Sep
	5.72/0.6	29.09	48.15	56.15	15.29/-1.0		1.74	11.08	4:52.04 (a)
4453	Patrick Halcrow				9.01.86	2	Grantham		30 Jun
	5.91	36.10	32.55	57.6	14.4	1.78	13.24	5:20.1	(a)
4443	Jon Baty				1.02.87	11	Derby		22 Sep
	5.64/-0.6	34.72	29.10	52.57	15.11/1.0		1.71	11.91	5:00.81 (a)
4437	Pepi Nanci				7.10.86	12	Derby		22 Sep
	5.63/0.6	35.99	48.14	57.30	16.23/-1.0		1.74	11.62	5:02.26 (a)
4436	Ryan Shaw				30.12.86	13	Derby		22 Sep
	6.08/0.6	33.59	39.28	53.68	14.74/1.0		1.59	11.18	5:14.62 (a)
4435	Benjamin Kerr				1.05.86	1	Grangemouth		25 Aug
	5.64	30.94	35.79	55.04	14.95/-1.2		1.87	10.60	5:00.14 (a)
(20)									
4392	George Beeken				4.09.86	2	Grangemouth		25 Aug
	5.63	33.29	37.55	57.38	14.71/-1.2		1.78	10.61	4:55.53 (a)
4383	Edward Harrison				10.12.86	1	Erith		22 Sep
	5.79	32.17	1.64	52.8	13.8	9.92	35.69	5:11.1	(e)
4377	Jack Singleton				17.12.85	14	Derby		22 Sep
	5.66/1.1	32.61	40.56	53.53	14.59/-0.9		1.62	11.11	5:16.17 (a)
4345	Simon Phelan				26.02.86	1	London (He)		11 Aug
	5.89/1.9	15.15w/2.6	37.89	57.50	1.94		10.06	27.36	5:03.17 (c)
4335	Joseph Evling-White				3.12.86	17	Derby		22 Sep
	5.98/-0.2	32.51	31.29	55.88	15.42/0.3		1.68	11.11	4:48.07 (a)
4335	Richard Reeks				6.12.85	1	Exeter		29 Sep
	5.69	26.50	40.45	55.1	14.6	1.85	10.53	5:13.6	(a)
4327	Stephen Miller				15.12.85	3	Grangemouth		25 Aug
	5.66	26.37	40.73	54.53	14.85/-1.2		1.66	10.57	4:51.66 (a)
4304	Uche Oduoza				15.10.86	18	Derby		22 Sep
	6.61/0.9	27.69	26.66	5..41	16.81/-3.8		1.86	11.96	5:19.77 (a)
4270	Aaron Flood				7.10.85	2	Hemel Hempstead		30 Jun
	5.60/1.4	32.07	37.17	56.1	15.2/-0.4		1.75	10.06	4:59.5 (a)
4269	Robert Rumble				18.10.86	19	Derby		22 Sep
	5.47/-0.3	31.41	34.43	55.45	15.86	1.74	9.93	4:37.17	(a)
(30)									
4261	Lee Pursglove				14.10.86	20	Derby		22 Sep
	5.49/1.0	34.61	38.22	55.36	15.94/-0.7		1.86	10.09	5:17.97 (a)
4241	Chris Record				12.09.86	4	Derby		30 Jun
	5.41	33.90	49.77	57.5	15.0		1.61	10.84	5:14.4 (a)
4225	Mark Fletcher				4.11.86	22	Derby		22 Sep
	6.37/0.9	31.58	19.37	54.19	15.34/1.8		1.71	10.20	5:48.14 (a)
4220	Stephen Carpenter				30.12.85	23	Derby		22 Sep
	5.69/0.5	24.20	37.98	55.67	14.95/-1.0		1.80	9.43	4:55.09 (a)
4216	Daniel Pope				24.12.86	24	Derby		22 Sep
	5.46/0.6	26.80	24.25	53.28	14.89/-0.7		1.71	10.17	4:36.76 (a)
4200	Adam Booth				22.10.85	3	Hexham		19 May
	5.23	29.28	31.36	56.9	14.72/1.0		1.81	10.34	4:49.27 (a)

Order of Events   a)   LJ, DT, JT, 400m, 100mH, HJ, SP, 1500m
                             b)   100mH, LJ, JT, 400m, HJ, DT, SP, 1500m
                             c)   LJ, 100mH, JT, 400m, HJ, SP, DT, 1500m
                             d)   LJ, SP, HJ, 400m, 100mH, DT, JT, 1500m
                             e)   LJ, DT, HJ, 400m, 100mH, SP, JT, 1500m

Pentathlon - Under 15

3129	Lewis Robson			9.01.88	1	Stoke-on-Trent	28 Sep
	11.59/-0.2	12.58	1.66	5.96/0.2	2:07.26	(b)	
3081	Oliver McNeillis			24.11.87	2	Stoke-on-Trent	28 Sep
	11.49/0.2	12.03	1.81	6.09/0.6	2:18.83	(b)	
3071	Neil Crossley			15.04.88	3	Stoke-on-Trent	28 Sep
	11.54/-0.1	13.28	1.69	5.49/0.2	2:09.07	(b)	
2866	Adam Akehurst			13.09.87	4	Stoke-on-Trent	28 Sep
	12.03/0.2	15.01	1.69	5.84/0.8	2:33.15	(b)	
2780	Kris Robertson			9.09.87	1	Grangemouth	22 Jun
	12.80	5.08	23.71	11.15	2:17.62	(d)	
2769	Nic Phillips			12.10.87	2	Bournemouth	29 Jun
	12.4	11.85	5.45	1.56	2:08.3	(a)	
2758	Guy Stroud			9.08.88	3	Bournemouth	29 Jun
	11.8	11.34	5.73	1.65	2:19.6	(a)	
2725	Thomas Higgs			11.12.87	4	Bournemouth	29 Jun
	12.6	10.53	5.74	1.71	2:16.2	(a)	
2717	Jason Briggs			8.10.87	4	Derby	21 Sep
	12.54	11.63	5.52	1.69	2:19.16	(a)	
2707	Jack Field			6.11.87	2	Exeter	28 Sep
	13.2	9.87	6.15	1.72	2:17.2	(a)	
(10)							
2695	Fraser Davies			30.01.88	1	Rotherham	28 Sep
	12.3	5.71	12.01	1.69	2:25.5	(c)	
2666	Wayne Taylor			17.10.87	5	Stoke-on-Trent	28 Sep
	11.88/-0.1	9.18	1.63	5.67/0.0	2:16.27	(b)	
2660	David Jones			5.11.87	1	Antrim	25 Aug
	12.24/0.7	12.41	5.46	1.57	2:21.23	(a)	
2574	James Bayliffe			11.10.87	5	Bournemouth	29 Jun
	12.1	9.87	5.10	1.68	2:16.9	(a)	
2560	Daniel Bacon			5.10.87	2	Derby	29 Jun
	12.9	11.53	5.13	1.54	2:16.6	(a)	
2548	Gregor Simey			25.10.88	6	Stoke-on-Trent	28 Sep
	12.41/0.2	10.33	1.57	5.22/0.8	2:15.62	(b)	
2541	Francis Baker			22.09.87	10	Derby	21 Sep
	12.38/0.5	10.55	5.29/-0.9	1.63	2:21.66	(a)	
2521	Edward Dickson			4.09.87	12	Derby	21 Sep
	12.29/0.4	10.02	5.69/-1.1	1.60	2:25.85	(a)	
2511	Luke Keteleers			8.01.88	13	Derby	21 Sep
	12.02/0.5	10.79	5.53/-1.1	1.57	2:27.99	(a)	
2500	Joseph Skinnard			14.09.87	3	Exeter	28 Sep
	12.07	10.02	5.40	1.51	2:13.4	(a)	

unconfirmed

2501	Joss Hay		6.06.88	1	Dundee	1 Sep

Order of Events   a)   80mH, SP, LJ, HJ, 800m
                   b)   80mH, SP, HJ, LJ, 800m
                   c)   80mH, LJ, SP, HJ, 800m
                   d)   80mH, LJ, 200, SP, 800m

2000 Metres Walk - Track

7:45.84	Andy Penn		31.03.67	1	Tamworth	26 Aug
7:49.30	Steve Hollier		27.02.76	2	Tamworth	26 Aug
11:44.4	Andrew Graham	U13	19.12.89	1	Dartford	29 Sep

3000 Metres Walk - Track

11:55.7	Steve Hollier		27.02.76	1	Sutton Coldfield	12 May
	12:09.45			1	Watford	1 Sep
	12:20.6 +			2m	Birmingham	12 Jul
11:58.4	Steve Partington		17.09.65	1	Douglas IOM	16 Jun

11:58.49 i	Andi Drake		6.02.65	3	Cardiff	2	Feb
	12:20.49 +			1m	Birmingham	12	Jul
12:00.99 i	Dom King	U20	30.05.83	4	Cardiff	2	Feb
	12:10.45 i			1	Birmingham	20	Jan
	12:22.27			1	Southend	6	May
12:20.46	Dan King	U20	30.05.83	1	Bedford	26	May
12:28.63 i	Lloyd Finch	U20	26.10.83	2	Birmingham	20	Jan
	12:40.96			2	Bedford	26	May
12:30.14	Luke Finch	U17	21.09.85	3	Watford	1	Sep
12:35.60 i	Cameron Smith	U20	17.01.84	2	Birmingham	24	Feb
12:38.24	Matthew Hales		6.10.79	1	Crawley	11	May
12:42.2	Peter Kaneen	V40	12.07.61	2	Douglas IOM	16	Jun
(10)							
12:42.34 i	Nathan Adams	U23	14.04.82	2	Cardiff	16	Feb
	12:56.23			3	Bedford	26	May
12:49.02 i	Andrew Parker	U20	10.12.83	4	Birmingham	24	Feb
13:20.37 i	Mark Williams		7.09.64	1	Cardiff	19	Jan
	13:24.7			2	Sutton Coldfield	12	May
13:21.35	Andrew Goudie		4.10.78	4	Bedford	26	May
13:27.5	Steve Arnold			3	Sutton Coldfield	12	May
13:31.10 i	Martin Bell	V40	9.04.61	9	Cardiff	2	Feb

Under 15

14:08.26	Nick Ball	U15	29.04.88	1	Derby	22	Sep

3 Kilometres Walk - Road - Under 15

13.34	Nick Ball		29.04.88	1	Steyning	30	Jun

5000 Metres Walk - Track

20:36.0	Steve Hollier		27.02.76	1	Dartford	29	Sep
20:48.1 +	Dom King	U20	30.05.83	1m	Colchester	4	May
21:06.3	Steve Partington		17.09.65	1	Douglas IOM	3	Jul
21:40.3	Matthew Hales		6.10.79	1	Dartford	16	Mar
21:46.29	Dan King	U20	30.05.83	4	Gorizia, ITA	6	Jul
21:55.07	Don Bearman		16.04.66	2	Birmingham	13	Jul
22:08.5	Nathan Adams	U23	14.04.82	2	Dartford	16	Mar
22:15.9	Martin Young		11.07.72	2	Dartford	29	Sep
22:15.93	Luke Finch	U17	21.09.85	1	Derby	22	Sep
23:11.7	Andrew Parker	U20	10.12.83	2	Dudley	13	Oct
(10)							
23:22.6	Andrew Goudie		4.10.78	3	Dartford	16	Mar
23:34.4	Mark Williams		7.09.64	4	Dartford	16	Mar
23:56.8	Lloyd Finch	U20	26.10.83	2	Dartford	29	Sep
23:58.2	Dave Turner	V40	20.10.57	4	Dartford	29	Sep
24:20.07	Neil Bates	U20	5.04.84	2	Derby	29	Sep

5 Kilometres Walk - Road - Under 17

22:04	Luke Finch	U17	21.09.85	1	Sheffield	27	Apr

10000 Metres Walk - Track

42:17.1	Dom King	U20	30.05.83	1	Colchester	4	May
	42:49.8			1	Bedford	30	Jun
43:09.82	Lloyd Finch	U20	26.10.83	1	Leamington	18	May
44:06.6	Dan King	U20	30.05.83	2	Colchester	4	May
44:52.0 +	Steve Hollier		27.02.76	1m	Nuneaton	27	Oct
45:32.37	Andrew Parker	U20	10.12.83	2	Leamington	18	May
46:10.0	Nathan Adams	U23	14.04.82	3	Leamington	18	May
46:14.61	Mark Williams		7.09.64	1	Birmingham	17	Apr
46:24.0 +	Darrell Stone		2.02.68	2m	Nuneaton	27	Oct
46:55.33	Luke Finch	U17	21.09.85	4	Leamington	18	May

10 Kilometres Walk - Road

42:16 +	Andi Drake		6.02.65	1	East Molesey	3	Mar
43:35				1	Leamington	23	Mar
42:18	Steve Partington		17.09.65	1	Douglas IOM	7	Apr
42:41				1	St. Johns IOM	18	Jul
42:45				1	Douglas IOM	30	Mar
42:57				4	Leamington	14	Sep
43:08				2	Sheffield	27	Apr
42:21	Dom King	U20	30.05.83	1	Sheffield	27	Apr
43:34 +				4	Manchester	21	Apr
43:36				2	Leamington	23	Mar
42:47	Steve Hollier		27.02.76	3	Leamington	14	Sep
42:54				1	Tamworth	1	Dec
42:56				1	Leicester	1	Sep
43:48				1	Birmingham	16	Nov
43:57				1	Tamworth	20	Oct
42:54	Darrell Stone		2.02.68	1	East Molesey	6	Jan
43:02	Luke Finch	U17	21.09.85	2	Tamworth	1	Dec
43:59				2	Birmingham	16	Nov
43:12	Don Bearman		16.04.66	2	East Molesey	6	Jan
43:14	Lloyd Finch	U20	26.10.83	2	Sheffield	27	Apr
43:16	Chris Cheeseman	V40	11.12.58	3	East Molesey	6	Jan
43:20 +	Andy Penn		31.03.67	2	Manchester	21	Apr
43: ?+				2	East Molesey	3	Mar
(10)							
44:23	Martin Young		11.07.72	5	Leamington	14	Sep
44:51	Dan King	U20	30.05.83	4	Sheffield	27	Apr
44:59	Andrew Goudie		4.10.78	4	East Molesey	6	Jan
45:02	Peter Kaneen	V40	12.07.61	2	Douglas IOM	5	May
45:17	Mark Easton		24.05.63	1	London (VP)	1	Jan
45:33	Andrew Parker	U20	10.12.83	5	Sheffield	27	Apr
45:39	Nathan Adams	U23	14.04.82	4	Leamington	23	Mar
45:59	Gareth Brown		10.05.68	11	Leamington	14	Sep
46:15	Karl Atton		14.09.71	5	Leamington	23	Mar
47:08	Martin Rush		25.12.64	12	Leamington	14	Sep
(20)							
47:42	Neil Bates	U20	5.04.84	8	Leamington	14	Sep

20 Kilometres Walk - Road

1:24:43	Andi Drake		6.02.65	1	East Molesey	2	Mar
1:27:48				2	Douglas IOM	16	Feb
1:26:04	Andy Penn		31.03.67	2	East Molesey	2	Mar
1:26:29				1	Douglas IOM	16	Feb
1:27:06				2	Manchester	21	Apr
1:29:15				4	Manchester (C)	28	Jul
1:28:48	Steve Partington		17.09.65	3	Douglas IOM	16	Feb
1:31:10				13	Dublin, IRL	15	Jun
1:31:41				46	Turin, ITA	12	Oct
1:32:26				1	Douglas IOM	9	May
1:33:23				9	Manchester	21	Apr
1:29:48	Dom King	U20	30.05.83	11	Dublin, IRL	15	Jun
1:32:23				7	Manchester	21	Apr
1:29:53	Don Bearman		16.04.66	1	Basildon	11	May
1:30:09				3	East Molesey	3	Mar
1:30:10	Mark Easton		24.05.63	4	Douglas IOM	16	Feb
1:31:06				12	Dublin, IRL	15	Jun
1:31:09 +t	Steve Hollier		27.02.76	1m	Nuneaton	27	Oct
1:33:11				27	Eisenhuttenstadt, GER	2	Jun

1:31:47	Chris Cheeseman	V40	11.12.58	2	Basildon	11	May
1:32:08	Gareth Brown		10.05.68	4	East Molesey	3	Mar
1:33:11	Matthew Hales		6.10.79	8	Manchester	21	Apr
1:35:20 t	(10) Luke Finch	U17	21.09.85	2	Nuneaton	27	Oct
1:35:39	Martin Young		11.07.72	15	Dublin, IRL	15	Jun
1:36:08	Nathan Adams	U23	14.04.82	11	Manchester	21	Apr
1:37:30	Mark Williams		7.09.64	1	Sutton Coldfield	4	May
1:37:50	Dan King	U20	30.05.83	6	East Molesey	3	Mar
1:38:27	Peter Kaneen	V40	12.07.61	2	Douglas IOM	9	May

30 Kilometres Walk - Road

2:26:47	Martin Young		11.07.72	1	Birmingham	3	Aug
2:28:32 +	Steve Hollier		27.02.76	6m	Manchester (C)	30	Jul
2:28:41 +				2m	Manchester	21	Apr
2:30:22 +	Mark Easton		24.05.63	3m	Manchester	21	Apr
2:34:09 +	Chris Cheeseman	V40	11.12.58	4m	Manchester	21	Apr
2:34:16 +	Karl Atton		14.09.71	5m	Manchester	21	Apr
2:34:17 +	Gareth Brown		10.05.68	6m	Manchester	21	Apr
2:36:50 +	Peter Kaneen	V40	12.07.61	7m	Manchester	21	Apr
2:39:14 +	Mike Smith		20.04.63	8m	Manchester	21	Apr

35 Kilometres Walk - Road

2:54:24 +	Steve Hollier		27.02.76	6m	Manchester (C)	30	Jul
3:04:30	Martin Young		11.07.72	1	Sutton Coldfield	9	Jul
3:09:44	Nathan Adams	U23	14.04.82	2	Sutton Coldfield	9	Jul
3:11:55	Mike Smith		20.04.63	3	Sutton Coldfield	9	Jul

50 Kilometres Walk - Road

4:11:29	Mark Easton		24.05.63	1	St. Oedenrode, NED	10	Mar
4:11:36				2	Manchester	21	Apr
4:14:33	Steve Hollier		27.02.76	3	Manchester	21	Apr
4:16:46				6	Manchester (C)	30	Jul
4:17:35				1	Douglas IOM	16	Feb
4:16:45	Gareth Brown		10.05.68	4	Manchester	21	Apr
4:18:49	Chris Cheeseman	V40	11.12.58	5	Manchester	21	Apr
4:23:05	Karl Atton		14.09.71	6	Manchester	21	Apr
4:35:31	Peter Kaneen	V40	12.07.61	7	Manchester	21	Apr
4:42:58	Mike Smith		20.04.63	1	Colchester	8	Sep
4:53:31	Dave Turner	V40	20.10.57	1	Bradford	3	Jun
4:56:13	Chris Berwick	V55	1.05.46	2	Colchester	8	Sep
4:56:55	Peter Ryan	V45	9.04.54	2	Bradford	3	Jun
4:56:55	(10) Martin Fisher	V40	27.09.62	3	Bradford	3	Jun

100 Miles Walk - Track

20:41:17 +	Kevin Perry	V50	7.12.48	2m	Blackpool	11	Aug
21:07:15 +	Ian Statter	V45	11.07.57	3m	Blackpool	11	Aug
21:28:09 +	Martin Fisher		27.09.62	4m	Blackpool	11	Aug
21:39:22 +	Chris Flint	V55	6.12.44	5m	Blackpool	11	Aug

24 Hours Walk - Track

182.591 km	Kevin Perry	V50	7.12.48	2	Blackpool	11	Aug
179.764 km	Ian Statter	V45	11.07.57	3	Blackpool	11	Aug
177.227 km	Martin Fisher		27.09.62	4	Blackpool	11	Aug
171.627 km	Chris Flint	V55	6.12.44	7	Blackpool	11	Aug

4 x 100 METRES

38.19	National Team	1	Munich, GER	11	Aug
	(C.Malcolm, D.Campbell, M.Devonish, D.Chambers)				
38.55	National Team	1h2	Munich, GER	10	Aug
	(C.Malcolm, D.Campbell, M.Devonish, D.Chambers)				
38.62	England	1	Manchester (C)	31	Jul
	(J.Gardener, M.Devonish, A.Condon, D.Campbell)				
38.65	National Team	1	Annecy, FRA	22	Jun
	(C.Lambert, M.Devonish, C.Malcolm, D.Chambers)				
39.06	England	2h1	Manchester (C)	31	Jul
	(J.Gardener, M.Devonish, A.Condon, D.Campbell)				
39.21	National Team	1	Bedford	4	Jun
	(J.Gardener, D.Campbell, C.Malcolm, D.Chambers)				
39.23	National Team	6	Madrid, ESP	20	Sep
	(J.Barbour, M.Devonish, C.Malcolm, D.Plummer)				
39.30	National Under 23 Team	U23 2	Bedford	4	Jun
	(T.Edgar, D.Grant, D.Plummer, M.Lewis-Francis)				
39.48	National Team	1	Glasgow (S)	18	Aug
	(D.Plummer, M.Devonish, D.Grant, D.Chanbers)				
39.62	Wales	4h2	Manchester (C)	30	Jul
	(K.Williams, D.Turner, J.Henthorn, C.Malcolm)				
39.73	Wales (Cardiff AAC)	8	Manchester (C)	31	Jul
	(K.Williams, D.Turner, C.Malcolm, S.Shalders)				
39.93	National Under 23 Team	U23 2	Niort, FRA	3	Aug
	(D.Chin, D.Grant, T.Abeyie, K.Stewart)				
40.15	Wales	3	Newport	20	Jul
	(S.Shalders, J.Henthorne, K.Williams, C.Malcolm)				
40.17	Wales	2	Sheffield	30	Jun
	(K.Williams, D.Turner, J.Henthorn, C.Malcolm)				
40.19	England	2	Leiden, NED	8	Jun
	(D.Grant, T.Edgar, T.Abeyie, D.Chin)				
40.22	England	1	Loughborough	18	May
	(A.Condon, D.Campbell, J.Barbour, D.Chambers)				
40.22	England	3	Sheffield	30	Jun
	(D.Plummer, J.Gardener, M.Devonish, D.Greaves)				
40.32	National Team	1r2	Hayward, USA	6	Apr
40.35	United Kingdom	3	Bedford	4	Jun
40.39	Birchfield Harriers	1	Birmingham	6	Jul
	(C.Brown, Morgan, B.Ghent, M.Lewis-Francis)				
40.52	Scotland	2	Loughborough	18	May
	(K.Stewart, I.Mackie, B.Doyle, N.Smith)				
40.78	Wales	2	Cardiff	8	Jul
	(K.Williams, S.Shalders, J.Henthorn, C.Malcolm)				
40.86	National Junior Team	U20 3	Loughborough	18	May
	(A.Matthews, L.Oboh, J.Ellington, A.Syers)				
40.89	Wales	3	Loughborough	18	May
	(K.Williams, D.Turner, P.Gray, S.Shalders)				
40.89	National Under 23 Team	U23 4	Newport	20	Jul
	(D.Plummer, F.Wright, T.Abeyie, D.Papura)				

Additional National Teams

41.17	Scotland U23 Team	U23 2	Namur, BEL	31	Aug

Additional Club Teams (1 - 2 above)

41.22	Belgrave Harriers	1	Watford	19	May
41.33	Newham & Essex Beagles	1	London (He)	3	Aug
41.45	Woodford Green & Essex Ladies	3	London (He)	3	Aug
41.55	Shaftesbury Barnet Harriers	4	London (He)	3	Aug

DWAIN CHAMBERS. Won the European Championships after Commonwealth disappointment.

DARREN CAMPBELL. Won 2 medals in his hometown Manchester.

MARLON DEVONISH. Medals at both European Championships and Commonwealth Games.

DANIEL CAINES. Slight disappointment individually but 2 relay Gold medals.

MICHAEL EAST. Exceeded all expectations with Commonwealth Gold.

COLIN JACKSON. Wins 4th European title.

CHRIS RAWLINSON. Wins 1st major title at the Commonwealth Games.

CHRIS TOMLINSON. Breaks Lynn Davies' long-standing British record.

JONATHAN EDWARDS. Commonwealth Gold, European Bronze.

PHILLIPS IDOWU. Commonwealth Silver and 5th ranked in the World.

X

MICK JONES. A well deserved Commonwealth Gold medal.

VERNICHA JAMES. Won an individual Gold at the World Junior Championships and was a member of both medal winning relay teams.

KELLY HOLMES. Gold at the Commonwealth Games.

JADE JOHNSON. Exceeded all expectations with Silver at both Commonwealth and European.

XVI

41.6	Sale Harriers Manchester		1	Bedford	19 May
41.6	Blackheath Harriers		1A	London (He)	21 Jul
41.7	Windsor S E & H AC		2	Derby	4 Aug
41.9	Thames Valley Harriers		3	Derby	4 Aug
41.97	Brunel West London University		1	Bedford	6 May
42.0	Harrow AC		1A	Eton	21 Jul
42.01	Bath University		2	Bedford	6 May
42.07	Border Harriers		5	Birmingham	6 Jul
42.1	Notts AC		3	Bedford	19 May
42.19	Trafford AC		6	Birmingham	6 Jul
42.24	Loughborough University		3	Bedford	6 May
42.3	Enfield & Haringey AC		2A	London (He)	21 Jul
42.6	Team Solent		4	Bedford	19 May
42.77	UWIC		4	Bedford	6 May

Additional Under 20 Teams (1 above)

41.49	National Junior Team		3	Gorizia, ITA	6 Jul
	(A.Matthews, R.Fifton, L.Baptiste, S.Fowles)				
41.67	West Midlands Schools	U19	1	Nottingham	13 Jul
41.94	Surrey Schools	U19	2	Nottingham	13 Jul
42.34	Enfield & Haringey AC		1	Derby	8 Sep
42.57	Middlesex Schools	U17	1h2	Nottingham	13 Jul
42.57	Midlands		1	Watford	1 Sep
42.58	Birchfield Harriers		2	Derby	8 Sep
42.64	Shaftesbury Barnet Harriers		3	Belgrade, YUG	21 Sep
42.66	Kent Schools	U19	3	Nottingham	13 Jul
42.66	Blackheath Harriers		3	Derby	8 Sep

Additional Under 20National Teams

43.42	Wales		2	Grangemouth	25 May
43.82	Scotland		3	Grangemouth	25 May
44.53	Northern Ireland	U18	4	Tullamore, IRL	3 Aug

Additional Under 20 Club Teams (1 - 4 above)

42.94	Sale Harriers Manchester		4	Derby	8 Sep
43.0	Croydon Harriers		1	London (He)	15 Sep
43.3	Trinity School, Croydon		1	Oxford	9 May
43.72	Notts AC		6	Derby	8 Sep
43.95	City of Stoke AC	U17	1	Birmingham	1 Sep
44.0	Thames Valley Harriers		1	Eton	28 Jul

Additional Under 17 Teams (1 - 2 above)

42.99	Northumberland Schools		2	Nottingham	13 Jul
43.14	London Schools		3	Nottingham	13 Jul
43.15	England Schools		1	Glasgow (S)	20 Jul
43.17	Kent Schools		2h2	Nottingham	13 Jul
43.33	Essex Schools		4	Nottingham	13 Jul
43.56	Cambridgeshire Schools		5	Nottingham	13 Jul
43.89	Nottinghamshire Schools		3h2	Nottingham	13 Jul
43.91	Scotland Schools		3	Glasgow (S)	20 Jul

Additional Under 17 National Team

44.04	Wales Schools		4	Glasgow (S)	20 Jul

Additional Under 17 Club Teams (1 above)

44.01	Enfield & Haringey AC		2	Birmingham	1 Sep
44.13	Birchfield Harriers		1	Birmingham	31 Aug
44.33	Notts AC		3	Birmingham	1 Sep
44.71	Shaftesbury Barnet Harriers		4	Birmingham	1 Sep
44.74	Liverpool Harriers AC		5	Birmingham	1 Sep

44.95	Sale Harriers Manchester	6	Birmingham	1	Sep
45.0	Woodford Green & Essex Ladies	1	Woodford	21	Jul
45.07	Pitreavie AAC	1	Glasgow (S)	9	Jun
45.3	Belfast High School	1	Antrim	25	May

Under 15 Teams

45.14	London Schools	1	Nottingham	13	Jul
45.76	Enfield & Haringey AC	1	Birmingham	1	Sep
45.9	Chelmsford AC	1	Chelmsford	17	Sep
45.91	Sale Harriers Manchester	2	Birmingham	1	Sep
45.92	Somerset Schools	2	Nottingham	13	Jul
46.00	Staffordshire Schools	3	Nottingham	13	Jul
46.04	Gateshead Harriers & AC	3	Birmingham	1	Sep
46.05	Humberside Schools	4	Nottingham	13	Jul
46.16	Derbyshire Schools	1h3	Nottingham	13	Jul
46.19	Kent Schools	2h2	Nottingham	22	Jun

Additional Under 15 Club Teams (1-4 above)

46.59	Croydon Harriers	1	Birmingham	31	Aug
46.98	City of Edinburgh AC	1	Glasgow (S)	9	Jun
47.1	Halesowen A & CC	1	Yate	21	Jul
47.14	Liverpool Harriers AC	4	Birmingham	1	Sep
47.2	Blackheath Harriers	2	Croydon	19	May
47.21	Notts AC	5	Birmingham	1	Sep

Under 13 Teams

51.25	Surrey AA	1r2	Kingston	28	Jul
52.12	Buckinghamshire AA	1r1	Kingston	28	Jul
52.23	Kent AA	2r2	Kingston	28	Jul
52.71	Enfield & Haringey AC	1	Birmingham	1	Sep
53.03	Liverpool Harriers AC	2	Birmingham	1	Sep
53.8	Shaftesbury Barnet Harriers	1	London (BP)	21	Jul
53.87	Wirral AC	1	Birmingham	31	Aug
53.9	Halesowen A & CC	1	Yate	21	Jul
53.9	Medway & Maidstone AC	1	Tonbridge	15	Sep
53.9	Colchester & Tendring AC	1	Bury St Edmunds	22	Sep

4 x 200 METRES

1:26.29 i	Wales	1	Cardiff	10	Feb
	(K.Williams, D.Papura, D.Turner, C.Malcolm)				
1:28.06 i	Loughborough University	1	Glasgow	24	Feb
1:29.24 i	Bath University	2	Glasgow	24	Feb
1:29.35 i	Brunel WL University	1h2	Glasgow	23	Feb
1:30.25 i	Wales	U20 1	Cardiff	10	Feb
	(G.Llewellyn, I.Hunt, R.Williams, P.Newark)				
1:30.27 i	UWIC	4	Glasgow	24	Feb
1:30.68 i	England	3	Cardiff	10	Feb

Additional Under 20 Teams (1 above)

1:31.77 i	England	2	Cardiff	10	Feb
	(M.Miah, A.Aplin, K.Thompson, R.Tobin)				
1:34.14 i	Kilbarchan AC	1	Glasgow	24	Mar
1:35.05 i	Pitreavie AAC	U17 1	Glasgow	9	Mar
1:35.17 i	Giffnock North AC	2	Glasgow	24	Mar

Additional Under 17 Teams (1 above)

1:36.29 i	Nottinghamshire Schools	1	Birmingham	20	Feb
1:36.32 i	City of Edinburgh AC	2	Glasgow	9	Mar
1:36.6	The King's School, Canterbury	1	Oxford	9	May
1:36.99 i	Staffordshire Schools	2	Birmingham	20	Feb

1:37.27 i	Warwickshire & Gloucestershire Schools	3	Birmingham	20 Feb
1:37.4	Millfield School	2	Oxford	9 May
1:37.53 i	Ayr Seaforth AAC	3	Glasgow	9 Mar
1:37.7	Croydon Harriers	1	Wimbledon	10 Jul

Under 15 Teams

1:41.10 i	Staffordshire Schools	1	Birmingham	20 Feb
1:41.38 i	Nottinghamshire Schools	2	Birmingham	20 Feb
1:42.4	Millfield School	1	Oxford	9 May
1:43.0	Croydon Harriers	1	Kingston	18 Aug
1:42.03 i	Hereford & Worcester Schools	3	Birmingham	20 Feb
1:44.04 i	City of Edinburgh AC	1	Glasgow	24 Mar

Under 13 Teams

1:57.67 i	Giffnock North AC	1h1	Glasgow	6 Feb
2:00.4	Croydon Harriers	1	Walton	23 Jun
2:01.05 i	Falkirk Victoria Harriers	1h1	Glasgow	24 Mar
2:01.85 i	Kirkintilloch Olympians	2	Glasgow	24 Mar

4 x 400 METRES

| 3:00.40 | England | 1 | Manchester (C) | 31 Jul |

(J.Deacon 46.1, S.Baldock 45.4, C.Rawlinson 44.5, D.Caines 44.4)

| 3:00.41 | Wales | 2 | Manchester (C) | 31 Jul |

(T.Benjamin 45.8, I.Thomas 46.0, J.Baulch 44.5, M.Elias 44.2)

| 3:00.57 | National Team | 1 | Annecy, FRA | 23 Jun |

(J.Deacon 45.8, T.Benjamin 45.2, J.Baulch 45.13, D.Caines 44.47)

| 3:01.25 | National Team | 1 | Munich, GER | 11 Aug |

(J.Deacon 45.7, M.Elias 45.4, J.Baulch 45.5, D.Caines 44.67)

| 3:02.97 | National Team | 1h1 | Munich, GER | 10 Aug |

(J.Deacon 46.2, S.Baldock 45.7, J.Baulch 45.71, M.Elias 45.34)

| 3:03.34 | National Team | 5 | Madrid, ESP | 21 Sep |

(J.Deacon 45.6, J.Baulch 46.1, T.Benjamin 45.73, M.Elias 45.96)

| 3:04.01 | England | 1h2 | Manchester (C) | 30 Jul |

(M.Hylton 46.8, C.Henry 46.3, J.Deacon 45.4, S.Baldock 45.6)

| 3:04.18 | Wales | 2h2 | Manchester (C) | 30 Jul |

(T.Benjamin 46.2, I.Thomas 46.4, J.Baulch 45.6, M.Elias 46.0)

| 3:08.07 | Belgrave Harriers | 3r2 | Lisbon, POR | 25 May |

(N.Levy, T.Bayley, M.Douglas, S.Baldock)

| 3:09.71 | England | 1 | Loughborough | 18 May |

(M.Hylton, N.Levy, J.Deacon, A.Gordon)

| 3:09.78 | Newham & Essex Beagles | 1 | Birmingham | 6 Jul |

(M.Brown, P.Slythe, A.Gordon, I.Thomas 46.4)

| 3.10.10 i | National Team | 3 | Glasgow | 9 Mar |

(R.Tobin 48.3, D.Caines 45.96, L.Baird 47.9, J.Chatt 47.9)

| 3:10.39 | Border Harriers | 1 | Watford | 19 May |

(L.Notman, I.Neely, J.Deacon, P.McKee 45.3)

| 3:10.52 | Woodford Green & Essex Ladies | 2 | Birmingham | 6 Jul |

(M.Morant, L.McRae, S.Thompson, G.Hedman)

| 3:10.60 | Belgrave Harriers | 2 | Watford | 19 May |

(Parker, I.Deeth, M.Douglas, T.Bayley)

| 3:10.66 | Trafford AC | 3 | Watford | 19 May |

(R.Workman, L.Baird, S.Plaskitt, N.Jennings)

| 3:11.07 | Belgrave Harriers | 3 | Birmingham | 6 Jul |

(Law, A.Bennett, T.Bayley, S.Baldock)

| 3:11.84 | National Under 23 Team | U23 2 | Niort, FRA | 3 Aug |

(I.Lowthian, T.Bayley, A.Wilson, S.Surety)

3:11.94	South	1	Derby	11 Aug
3:12.03	Brunel West London University	1	Bedford	6 May
3:12.85	Loughborough University	2	Loughborough	18 May

(D.Naismith, J.Chatt, B.Yiend, L.Collins)

Additional National Teams

3:13.83	National Under 23 Team	U23	2	Newport	20	Jul
	(T.Bayley, Ellis, R.Smith, A.Wilson)					
3:16.09	Scotland		6	Loughborough	18	May
	(I.Deeth, R.McDonald, S.Scott, C.Robertson-Adams)					

Additional Club Teams (1 - 7 above)

3:14.4	Thames Valley Harriers		1r2	London (He)	21	Jul
3:14.8	Blackheath Harriers		1r1	London (He)	21	Jul
3:16.0	Kent AC		1	Chelmsford	6	Jul
3:16.2	Team Solent		2	Derby	4	Aug
3:16.6	Windsor S E & H AC		3	Derby	4	Aug
3:16.9	Enfield & Haringey AC		4	Derby	4	Aug
3:18.3	City of Edinburgh AC		1	Sheffield (W)	31	Aug
3:18.4	Notts AC		3	Watford	31	Aug
3:18.5	Basingstoke & Mid Hants AC		2	Eton	21	Jul
3:18.78	Enfield & Haringey AC	U20	1	Derby	8	Sep
3:19.1	Liverpool Harriers AC		2	Chelmsford	6	Jul
3:19.16	Shaftesbury Barnet Harriers	U20	1	Belgrade, YUG	21	Sep
3:20.3	City of Stoke AC		1	Cardiff	21	Jul
3:20.5	Sale Harriers Manchester		5	Bedford	19	May
3:20.7	City of Norwich AC		3	Chelmsford	6	Jul

Additional Under 20 Teams (1 - 2 above)

3:12.93	National Junior Team		1	Gorizia, ITA	6	Jul
	(R.Williams, L.Burgess, R.Palmer, S.Green)					
3:13.38	National Junior Team		3	Loughborough	18	May
	(L.Burgess, R.Williams, R.Nicholls, R.Tobin)					
3:18.77	South		1	Watford	1	Sep
	(R.Alleyne, R.Fifton, M.Holloway, L.Baptiste)					
3:20.90	England Schools	U17	1	Glasgow (S)	20	Jul
3:22.13	Wales		3	Grangemouth	26	May
3:22.85	Wales	U18	1	Tullamore, IRL	3	Aug
3:23.4	Blackheath Harriers		2	Croydon	28	Jul
3:23.58	Birchfield Harriers		3	Derby	8	Sep

Additional Under 20 Club Teams (1 - 4 above)

3:23.89	Sale Harriers Manchester		4	Derby	8	Sep
3:24.6	Derby & County AC		1	Birmingham	18	Aug
3:25.4	Harrow AC		3	Croydon	28	Jul
3:25.54	Sale Harriers Manchester	U17	1	Birmingham	1	Sep
3:26.3	Gateshead Harriers & AC		1	Cleckheaton	15	Sep
3:26.7	Belgrave Harriers		4	Croydon	28	Jul
3:27.6	Havant AC		1	Eton	28	Jul

Additional Under 17 Teams (1 - 2 above)

3:23.67	Wales Schools		2	Glasgow (S)	20	Jul
3:25.29	Scotland Schools		3	Glasgow (S)	20	Jul
3:29.4	Essex AA		1	Kingston	4	Aug
3:30.46	Gateshead Harriers & AC		2	Birmingham	1	Sep
3:30.6	Surrey AA		2	Kingston	4	Aug
3:31.24	Notts AC		3	Birmingham	1	Sep
3:32.2	Medway & Maidstone AC		1	Tonbridge	15	Sep
3:33.1	Cwmbran AC		1	Worcester	5	May

Additional Under 17 Club Teams (1 - 5 above)

3:33.21	Enfield & Haringey AC		4	Birmingham	1	Sep
3:33.6	Ashford AC		1	London (Elt)	21	Jul
3:33.8	Blackheath Harriers		2	Tonbridge	15	Sep
3:33.97	Harrow AC		5	Birmingham	1	Sep
3:34.1	Liverpool Pembroke Sefton		1	Bebington	5	May

Under 15 Teams

3:44.9	Ashford AC	1	Tonbridge	15	Sep
3:48.8	Gateshead Harriers & AC	1	Cudworth	21	Jul
3:50.2	City of Sheffield AC	1r2	(Mandale)	21	Jul
3:50.8	Mandale AC	1r1	(Mandale)	21	Jul
3:50.9	Sale Harriers Manchester	2r1	(Mandale)	21	Jul
3:51.2	Cambridge Harriers	2	Tonbridge	15	Sep
3:51.5	Notts AC	1	Coventry	2	Jun
3:51.7	Mansfield AC	1r1	Stoke-on-Trent	30	Jun
3:51.7	City of Edinburgh AC	1	Grangemouth	17	Aug
3:52.3	Medway & Maidstone AC	3	Tonbridge	15	Sep

Under 13 Teams

4:26.8	Tonbridge AC	1	Erith	14	Jul
4:30.5	Medway & Maidstone AC	1	Tonbridge	26	May
4:38.6	Cambridge Harriers	2	Bromley	9	Jun

3 x 800 METRES

Under 15 Teams

6:47.3	Chelmsford AC	1	Chelmsford	21	Sep
6:52.53	City of Edinburgh AC	1	Grangemouth	26	May
6:56.8	Thurrock Harriers	2	Chelmsford	21	Sep
6:57.01	Kilbarchan AAC	2	Grangemouth	26	May

Under 13 Teams

7:25.00	Giffnock North AC	1	Grangemouth	26	May
7:31.3	Newham & Essex Beagles	1	Chelmsford	21	Sep
7:34.27	Medway & Maidstone AC	1	Tonbridge	15	Sep

4 x 800 METRES

7:54.5	Gosforth Harriers	1	Middlesbrough	23	Jul
7:56.4	Sunderland Harriers	2	Middlesbrough	23	Jul
7:58.1	Morpeth Harriers	3	Middlesbrough	23	Jul

Under 20 Teams

8:39.6	Radley College	U17	1	Oxford	9	May
8:40.7	Haberdasher's Aske School		1	Oxford	9	May
8:42.7	Uppingham School		2	Oxford	9	May

Additional Under 17 Teams (1 above)

9:00.1	Millfield School	2	Oxford	9	May
9:05.6	Campion School	3	Oxford	9	May
9:13.8	Berkhamsted School	4	Oxford	9	May
9:23.3	Haberdasher's Aske School	5	Oxford	9	May

Under 15 Teams

9:25.8	Campion School	1	Oxford	9	May
9:38.9	St Malachy's College	1	Belfast	13	Jun
9:49.4	Millfield School	2	Oxford	9	May
9:50.1	Radley College	3	Oxford	9	May

1600 METRES MEDLEY

3:30.2	Kent AC	1	Tonbridge	15	Sep
3:43.8	Blackheath Harriers	3	Tonbridge	15	Sep

2002 LISTS - WOMEN

60 Metres - Indoors

7.27	Joice Maduaka		30.09.73	5s1	Vienna, AUT	3	Mar
	7.28			1s2	Cardiff	3	Feb
	7.28			2	Glasgow	9	Mar
	7.29			1h3	Vienna, AUT	2	Mar
	7.31			1h2	Cardiff	3	Feb
	7.33			1	Cardiff	3	Feb
	7.33			6h1	Birmingham	17	Feb
	7.39			2	Birmingham	27	Jan
	7.39			4h1	Ghent, BEL	10	Feb
	7.40			1h1	Birmingham	12	Jan
	7.40			6	Ghent, BEL	10	Feb
	7.42			1	Birmingham	12	Jan
	7.47			1s1	Birmingham	12	Jan
7.29	Diane Allahgreen		21.02.75	4h1	Birmingham	17	Feb
	7.30			8	Birmingham	17	Feb
	7.31			1	Birmingham	27	Jan
	7.45			1s2	Birmingham	12	Jan
	7.48			3	Birmingham	12	Jan
7.32	Abi Oyepitan		30.12.79	1s1	Cardiff	3	Feb
	7.41			2	Cardiff	3	Feb
	7.48			6h2	Birmingham	17	Feb
	7.50			1h1	Cardiff	3	Feb
7.37	Susan Burnside	U23	3.02.80	1h3	Cardiff	3	Feb
	7.41			2s1	Cardiff	3	Feb
	7.42			3	Cardiff	3	Feb
	7.43			1	Glasgow	20	Jan
	7.46			1	Glasgow	12	Jan
7.42	Donita Benjamin		7.03.72	7h1	Birmingham	17	Feb
	7.47			4	Cardiff	3	Feb
7.45	Emma Ania		7.02.79	1	Kopavogur, ISL	30	Dec
7.48	Amanda Forrester		29.09.78	2s2	Cardiff	3	Feb
	7.48			6	Cardiff	3	Feb
	7.50			7h2	Birmingham	17	Feb

33 performances to 7.50 by 7 athletes

7.50	Emily Freeman	U23	24.11.80	1s1	Glasgow	23	Feb
7.51	Kelly Thomas	U23	9.01.81	1	Glasgow	23	Feb
7.52	Janine Whitlock ¶		11.08.73	3	Birmingham	27	Jan
	(10)						
7.52	Jeanette Kwakye	U20	20.03.83	1J	Birmingham	23	Feb
7.54	Claire Rooney	U20	23.08.83	1	Glasgow	12	Jan
7.55	Amy Spencer	U17	19.09.85	6	Birmingham	27	Jan
7.55	Katherine Endacott	U23	29.01.80	2h1	Cardiff	3	Feb
7.55	Rachel King		11.05.76	2	Cardiff	10	Feb
7.56	Anyika Onuora	U20	28.10.84	3J	Birmingham	23	Feb
7.58	Sara Whigham	U20	7.10.83	1r14	Edinburgh	10	Feb
7.59	Shani Anderson		7.08.75	5	Blacksburg, USA	9	Feb
7.59	Montell Douglas	U17	24.01.86	1U17	Birmingham	23	Feb
7.60	Christine Harrison-Bloomfield		12.02.68	7	Birmingham	27	Jan
	(20)						
7.60	Danielle Norville	U20	18.01.83	1J	Cardiff	10	Feb
7.60	Seandelle Haley	U20	19.03.84	4J	Birmingham	23	Feb
7.61	Melanie Roberts		2.03.78	1h2	Sheffield	20	Jan
7.61	Malgorzata Wardrop		25.03.77	2	Glasgow	20	Jan
7.61	Angharad James		7.04.79	4h2	Cardiff	3	Feb
7.61	Ashia Hansen		5.12.71	3h3	Cardiff	3	Feb
7.61	Zoe Wilson		28.08.76	2h4	Cardiff	3	Feb

7.62	Gemma Nicol	U17	27.07.86	2r14	Edinburgh	10	Feb
7.63	Ellena Ruddock		23.02.76	2h2	Birmingham	12	Jan
7.63	Susie Williams		2.06.77	4h3	Cardiff	3	Feb
(30)							
7.64	Janette Niccolls		7.09.76	5h3	Cardiff	3	Feb
7.64	Sinead Johnson	U17	24.12.86	2U17	Birmingham	23	Feb
7.65	Laura Turner	U23	12.08.82	3s1	Glasgow	23	Feb
7.65	Jemma Sims	U20	2.05.85	1h1J	Birmingham	23	Feb
7.69	Yvette Henry		8.06.73	1h1	Glasgow	23	Feb
7.69	Emma Bryson	U23	5.04.81	2s2	Glasgow	23	Feb
7.70	Helen Roscoe		4.12.79	2	Birmingham	22	Jan
7.70	Karen Gear		30.09.79	4rB	Birmingham	27	Jan
7.70	Kelly Sotherton		13.11.76	5h2	Cardiff	3	Feb
7.70	Anna Boyle	U20	29.03.83	1s2	Nenagh, IRL	7	Dec
(40)							
7.71	Kerry Jury		19.11.68	2	Sheffield	20	Jan
7.71	Kathryn Evans	U20	1.03.84	2r4	Edinburgh	10	Feb
7.72	Nicola Gossman	U17	4.11.86	3r4	Edinburgh	10	Feb
7.73	Rebecca White	U23	5.06.80	1	Cardiff	6	Jan
7.73	Karen Oughton	U20	26.01.83	7J	Birmingham	23	Feb
7.74	Sharon Davidge	U23	15.09.81	4h1	Cardiff	3	Feb
7.74	Carolyn McKenna	U20	4.05.84	4J	Glasgow	17	Feb
7.74	Kadi-Ann Thomas	U17	10.02.86	1s317	Birmingham	23	Feb
7.75	Natasha May	U23	21.02.80	5s2	Glasgow	23	Feb

Additional Under 17 (1 - 6 above)

7.79	Pamela Paterson	26.10.85	1	Glasgow	12	Jan
7.83	Phyllis Agbo	16.12.85	4rB	Cardiff	16	Feb
7.83	Sarah Holmes	21.11.85	2h3	Birmingham	23	Feb
7.84	Christina Clubley	4.11.85	5rB	Cardiff	6	Feb
(10)						
7.85	Lia Tappin	9.01.87	1	Eton	8	Dec
7.87	Rachel Conway	30.09.87	1	Cardiff	23	Nov
7.88	Jessica Ennis	28.01.86	1	Sheffield	20	Jan
7.88	Nicole MacDermott	15.08.86	6	Birmingham	23	Feb
7.89	Tamara Doherty	15.11.85	4r4	Glasgow	10	Feb
7.90	Emma Strachan	10.04.87	2	Birmingham	20	Feb
7.91	Lauren Dickson	2.04.86	3	Glasgow	31	Jan
7.92	Jessica Tucker	3.06.87	1	Cardiff	10	Feb
7.93	Charlene Lashley	1.09.85	4s3	Birmingham	23	Feb
7.93	Louise Dickinson	5.11.86	2	Cardiff	23	Nov
(20)						
7.94	Kelly Roomes	19.01.87	3h3	Birmingham	23	Feb
7.94	Denae Matthew	3.04.87	1h6	Birmingham	23	Feb
7.96	Anna Conolly	19.04.86	2h2	Birmingham	23	Feb
7.99	Laura Robinson	11.10.85	3	Sheffield	20	Jan

overage

7.85	Louise Bloor	21.09.85	1	Manchester	28	Dec

Under 15

7.83	Kimberly Skinner	21.09.87	1	Glasgow	2	Mar
7.94	Nimneh Hyde	20.09.87	1	Birmingham	23	Feb
7.98	Tanya Hinds	19.05.88	2	Birmingham	23	Feb
8.00	Cherelle Norriston	29.11.88	1h5	Birmingham	23	Feb
8.01	Rachel Conway	30.09.87	3	Birmingham	23	Feb
8.02	Amy Clancy	26.03.88	2	Glasgow	12	Jan
8.02	Natalie Doyle	5.01.89	1	Glasgow	3	Feb
8.05	Amy Godsell	31.03.88	5	Birmingham	23	Feb
8.06	Kelly Fairweather	5.03.88	6	Birmingham	23	Feb
8.08	Joey Duck	14.04.89	3s2	Birmingham	23	Feb

hand timing

7.5	Burnside	U23	(7.37)	1h1	Glasgow	20	Jan
7.6	Malgorzata Wardrop		(7.61)	2h1	Glasgow	20	Jan
7.7	Kadi-Ann Thomas	U17	(7.74)	2U17	Bedford	19	Jan
7.7	Helen Williams		2.06.77	1	Eton	9	Feb
7.8	Amala Onuora	U17	16.03.86	2	Eton	9	Feb

Foreign

7.43	*Sarah Reilly (IRL)*	*3.07.73*	*2*	*Birmingham*	*12*	*Jan*
7.72	*Leanne O'Callaghan (IRL)*	*15.07.74*	*5rB*	*Birmingham*	*27*	*Jan*

75 Metres - Under 13

9.8		Jasmine Rowe	14.09.89	1	Nuneaton	21	Jul
9.9 i		Hannah Francis-Smithson	10.11.89	1	Dortmund, GER	17	Mar
9.9		Amelia Montagnani	10.03.90	1	London (TB)	30	Jun
9.9		Verity Collins	22.01.90	1	Blackpool	21	Jul
9.9		Chinedu Monye	29.12.89	1	Woking	22	Sep
9.9 w		Natasha White	8.12.89	1	London (Ha)	30	Jun
		10.04		1	Birmingham	1	Sep
9.95		Megan Beesley	15.11.89	1	Tamworth	26	Aug
10.0		Shelley Marquis	26.12.89	1	London (TB)	2	Jun
10.0		Abbey Nicol	1.01.90	2	London (TB)	2	Jun
10.0		Shauna Craigen	16.5.91	2	Nuneaton	21	Jul
	(10)						
10.1		Julie Keenleyside	22.12.89	1	Gateshead	21	Apr
10.1		Emily Mitchell	19.12.90	1	Yate	30	Jun
10.1		Philippa Tappin	19.03.91	1rB	London (Ha)	30	Jun
10.1		Kate Taylor	4.05.90	2	London (TB)	30	Jun
10.1		Kelly-Ann Melia	8.01.90	1	Birmingham	21	Jul

100 Metres

11.31	1.6	Joice Maduaka	30.09.73	1	Birmingham	13	Jul
	11.39	0.5		1s2	Birmingham	13	Jul
	11.47	1.2		1h3	Manchester (C)	15	Jun
	11.50	0.9		3	Brisbane, AUS	12	Apr
	11.53	-1.1		1h3	Brisbane, AUS	12	Apr
	11.55	-0.5		7	London (CP)	23	Aug
	11.57	0.7		2	Bedford	4	Jun
	11.57	-1.2		4r1	Annecy, FRA	22	Jun
	11.60	0.7		6h2	Munich, GER	6	Aug
	11.61	0.1		4	Manchester (C)	15	Jun
11.33	0.2	Abi Oyepitan	30.12.79	3s1	Munich, GER	7	Aug
	rolling start, reaction less than 0.100 but performance allowed to stand						
	11.36	0.3		4s1	Manchester (C)	27	Jul
	11.37	-0.3		3h3	Manchester (C)	26	Jul
	11.37	1.5		7	Manchester (C)	27	Jul
	11.38	1.7		1s1	Birmingham	13	Jul
	11.40	1.1		1s1	Bedford	26	May
	11.40	0.3		2h4	Munich, GER	6	Aug
	11.41	-0.7		6	Munich, GER	7	Aug
	11.42	1.6		2	Birmingham	13	Jul
	11.55	1.4		1	Bedford	26	May
	11.56	1.9		4	Glasgow (S)	18	Aug
	11.56	-0.5		8	London (CP)	23	Aug
	11.57	1.2		1h1	Bedford	26	May
	11.57	0.9		1h3	Birmingham	13	Jul
11.34	1.5	Amanda Forrester	29.09.78	5	Manchester (C)	27	Jul
	11.37	0.8		3s2	Manchester (C)	27	Jul
	11.44	-0.5		2h1	Manchester (C)	26	Jul
	11.54	1.6		4	Birmingham	13	Jul

(Forrester)		11.55	-0.6			1	Barcelona, ESP	6 Sep
		11.57	0.1			3	Manchester (C)	15 Jun
		11.58	0.2			2h1	Manchester (C)	15 Jun
		11.63	0.5			2s2	Birmingham	13 Jul
11.36	1.5	Shani Anderson			7.08.75	6	Manchester (C)	27 Jul
		11.38	0.4			6	Annecy, FRA	22 Jun
		11.39	0.8			4s2	Manchester (C)	27 Jul
		11.44	-0.7			6	Sheffield	30 Jun
		11.50	0.5			3h2	Manchester (C)	26 Jul
		11.51	0.1			2	Manchester (C)	15 Jun
		11.58	0.7			3	Bedford	4 Jun
		11.59	-0.2			1h2	Manchester (C)	15 Jun
		11.63	0.9			5	Dessau, GER	29 May
11.40	1.0	Vernicha James	U20	6.06.84		1	Bratislava, SVK	11 Jun
		11.53	1.4			1	Adelaide, AUS	23 Mar
		11.53	0.9			4	Brisbane, AUS	12 Apr
11.44	1.6	Diane Allahgreen			21.02.75	3	Birmingham	13 Jul
		11.48	1.9			1h4	Birmingham	13 Jul
		11.50	1.7			2s1	Birmingham	13 Jul
		11.55	1.1			1rB	Loughborough	18 May
		11.60	1.4			2	Bedford	26 May
		11.60	0.7			4	Bedford	4 Jun
11.58	1.2	Emily Freeman	U23	24.11.80		2h3	Manchester (C)	15 Jun
11.58	1.6	Sabrina Scott			2.06.79	5	Birmingham	13 Jul
		11.63	1.1			2s1	Bedford	26 May
		11.64	1.2			2h1	Bedford	26 May
		11.65	1.7			3s1	Birmingham	13 Jul
11.64	1.2	Emma Ania			7.02.79	1	Kopavogur, ISL	27 Jul
		56 performances to 11.65 by 9 athletes						
11.66	1.2	Susan Burnside	U23	3.02.80		3h3	Manchester (C)	15 Jun
	(10)							
11.67	1.1	Marcia Richardson			10.02.72	2rB	Loughborough	18 May
11.68	1.5	Amy Spencer	U17	19.09.85		1h2	Bedford	29 Jun
11.69	1.9	Melanie Roberts			2.03.78	2h4	Birmingham	13 Jul
11.70	1.1	Jeanette Kwakye	U20	20.03.83		3rB	Loughborough	18 May
11.70	0.2	Christine Harrison-Bloomfield			12.02.68	3h1	Manchester (C)	15 Jun
11.70	1.7	Donita Benjamin			7.03.72	5s1	Birmingham	13 Jul
11.72	1.4	Sarah Wilhelmy	U23	2.02.80		5	Bydgoszcz, POL	8 Jun
11.74	-1.8	Kelly Thomas	U23	9.01.81		1=	Watford	1 Jun
11.75	1.1	Malgorzata Wardrop			25.03.77	4s1	Bedford	26 May
11.77	1.3	Montell Douglas	U17	24.01.86		1	Birmingham	10 Aug
	(20)							
11.79	1.1	Lisa Miller	U20	13.01.83		3	Leiden, NED	8 Jun
11.87	-0.4	Danielle Norville	U20	18.01.83		3rB	Gorizia, ITA	6 Jul
11.87	-1.2	Katherine Endacott	U23	29.01.80		1	Watford	1 Sep
11.88	1.8	Jade Lucas-Read	U20	17.01.84		1rC	Bedford	4 Jun
11.89	1.9	Sinead Johnson	U17	24.12.86		1s1	Birmingham	10 Aug
11.91	1.7	Ellena Ruddock			23.02.76	6s1	Birmingham	13 Jul
11.92	1.9	Kadi-Ann Thomas	U17	10.02.86		2s1	Nottingham	13 Jul
11.94	1.8	Janette Niccolls			7.09.76	2rC	Bedford	4 Jun
11.95		Sara Whigham	U20	7.10.83		1	Edinburgh	28 Apr
11.95	0.9	Kelly Sotherton			13.11.76	4h3	Birmingham	13 Jul
	(30)							
11.97	0.0	Anna Boyle	U20	29.03.83		3rB	Bangor	21 Jul
11.98	-0.8	Catherine Murphy			21.09.75	3	Birmingham	6 Jul
12.00	1.8	Natalie Beattie			30.01.78	3rC	Bedford	4 Jun
12.01	1.9	Amala Onuora	U17	16.03.86		2s1	Birmingham	10 Aug
12.02	1.9	Lanre Atijosan	U17	17.10.86		3s1	Nottingham	13 Jul
12.03		Donna Maylor	U23	20.05.82		1	Birmingham (Un)	19 Jun
12.03	1.7	Keeley Butler			24.03.75	8s1	Birmingham	13 Jul
12.05A	0.3	Lesley Owusu			21.12.78	5rB	El Paso TX, USA	6 Apr

265

12.05	1.7	Louise Hazel	U17	6.10.85	2s2	Nottingham	13	Jul
12.05	-0.6	Anyika Onuora	U20	28.10.84	1	Nottingham	13	Jul
	(40)							
12.06	1.9	Syreena Pinel		13.01.79	4h4	Birmingham	13	Jul
12.07	1.4	Yvette Henry		8.06.73	1	Cudworth	15	Sep
12.08	-0.6	Carley Wenham	U15	14.03.88	1	Nottingham	13	Jul
12.09		Gemma Ryde	U20	23.06.83	1rB	Edinburgh	28	Apr
12.09		Karen Oughton	U20	26.01.83	2	Birmingham (Un)	19	Jun
12.10	-0.6	Helen Taylor	U20	29.01.84	1h2	Nottingham	12	Jul
12.12	1.9	Helen Williams		2.06.77	5h4	Birmingham	13	Jul
12.13		Emma Bryson	U23	5.04.81	2rB	Edinburgh	28	Apr
12.13	0.6	Katy Sketchley		9.07.73	1	Portsmouth	11	May
12.14	-1.4	Zoe Wilson		28.08.76	2h2	Watford	1	Jun
	(50)							
12.15	1.3	Kirsteen McDiarmid	U17	28.04.86	1	Edinburgh	28	Jul
12.16	1.5	Lisa Trotman	U23	6.12.82	2h2	Jarrow	1	Jun
12.16		Rebecca White	U23	5.06.80	3	Birmingham (Un)	19	Jun
12.17	0.0	Felicia Louisy		17.05.74	4rB	Bedford	4	Jun
12.17	0.8	Sharon Wilson		27.10.74	1rB	London (He)	3	Aug
12.18	0.7	Clare Milborrow		10.01.77	1	Crawley	11	May
12.18	-1.4	Michelle Turner		25.12.77	3h2	Watford	1	Jun
12.19	1.3	Claire Rooney	U20	23.08.83	2J	Edinburgh	11	May
12.19	0.9	Laura Turner	U23	12.08.82	5h3	Birmingham	13	Jul
12.20	1.9	Molly Russell	U17	3.08.86	4s1	Nottingham	13	Jul
	(60)							
12.21	1.7	Nicole MacDermott	U17	15.08.86	3s2	Nottingham	13	Jul
12.21	-0.6	Xanine Powell		21.05.79	2	London (BP)	14	Aug
12.23	1.7	Nicola Gossman	U17	4.11.86	1	Edinburgh	11	May
12.23	1.2	Angharad James		7.04.79	5h1	Bedford	26	May
12.25	0.0	Susie Williams		2.06.77	7rB	Bedford	4	Jun
12.25	-0.6	Amy Dowsett	U20	30.12.84	2h2	Nottingham	12	Jul
12.26		Gemma Nicol	U17	27.07.86	2	Edinburgh	28	Apr
12.26	1.3	Liz Williams		2.06.77	4	Loughborough	17	Jul
12.28	mx	Nicola Sanders	U23	23.06.82	1	Watford	28	Aug
12.29	1.2	Sian Robinson	U23	31.03.82	6h1	Bedford	26	May
	(70)							
12.29	0.8	Katie Jones		4.01.77	2rB	London (He)	3	Aug

Additional Under 17 (1 - 12 above)

12.31	1.9	Natalie Jowett		18.09.86	5s1	Nottingham	13	Jul
12.32	1.9	Kelly Birkin		27.04.86	1	Brecon	6	Jul
12.35	1.7	Kelly Roomes		19.01.87	4s2	Nottingham	13	Jul
12.35	1.2	Phyllis Agbo		16.12.85	1h2	London (He)	25	Aug
12.38	1.9	Hayley Robertson		29.10.86	6s1	Nottingham	13	Jul
12.38	1.7	Sally Irwin		12.10.85	5s2	Nottingham	13	Jul
12.39	1.9	Pamela Paterson		26.10.85	5s1	Birmingham	10	Aug
12.44	1.2	Sarah Holmes		21.11.85	4	Watford	26	May
	(20)							
12.45	1.7	Sabina Astarita		15.10.86	2	Edinburgh	11	May
12.47	1.9	Kessia Sherliker		9.11.85	1h2	Portsmouth	11	May
12.47		Tamara Doherty		15.11.85	2	Edinburgh	22	May
12.47	0.9	Louise Dickson		4.09.86	2	Birmingham	1	Sep
12.48	1.2	Michelle Nash-Odei		19.03.87	6	Watford	26	May
12.48	1.9	Danielle Barker		19.01.87	2	Brecon	6	Jul
12.48	1.2	Deandra Smith		3.12.86	2h2	London (He)	25	Aug
12.50		Lisa Ferguson		10.09.86	4	Edinburgh	28	Apr
12.51	mx 0.7	Louise Dickinson		5.11.86	1	Manchester (Str)	23	Jul
12.51	0.9	Denae Matthew		3.04.87	3	Birmingham	1	Sep
	(30)							
12.52	1.9	Louise Morgan		8.09.85	7s1	Nottingham	13	Jul
12.55	-0.9	Jessica Tucker		3.06.87	1h3	Newport	8	Jun
12.56		Leigh Whiteside		6.08.86	1	Belfast	15	Jun

12.56	1.9	Jemma Buttler		17.06.87	7s1	Birmingham	10 Aug
12.56	0.9	Laura Willey		22.10.86	4	Birmingham	1 Sep
12.60	1.8	Louise Bloor		21.09.85	5s2	Birmingham	10 Aug

Additional Under 15 (1 above)

12.37	2.0	Rachel Conway		30.09.87	2	Birmingham	10 Aug
12.39	1.8	Amy Gibbs		30.03.89	2	Watford	26 May
12.39	-0.6	Joscelynn Hopeson		18.05.88	2	Nottingham	13 Jul
12.39	2.0	Tanya Hinds		19.05.88	3	Birmingham	10 Aug
12.40	2.0	Joey Duck		14.04.89	4	Birmingham	10 Aug
12.49	0.4	Lauren Duncan		21.03.88	2s2	Birmingham	10 Aug
12.51	1.6	Dominique Blaize		3.10.87	1	Kingston	12 May
12.51	-0.6	Natalie Pearson		7.06.88	3	Nottingham	13 Jul
12.55		Roisin Willi		29.10.87	1	Gateshead	24 Aug
	(10)						
12.58	1.1	Abbi Tyson		5.07.89	2s1	Birmingham	10 Aug
12.58		Natalie Morrisey		22.08.88	1	Tamworth	26 Aug
12.60	1.8	Kelly Fairweather		5.03.88	4	Watford	26 May
12.60	1.8	Lisa Papura		21.04.88	1	Brecon	6 Jul
12.61	1.8	Cherelle Norriston		29.11.88	5	Watford	26 May
12.61	0.7	Louise Crilly		18.01.88	1	Grangemouth	24 Aug
12.62	-1.6	Nimneh Hyde		20.09.87	1	Birmingham	25 May
12.63	0.7	Amy Clancy		26.03.88	2	Grangemouth	24 Aug
12.67	1.8	Joedy Platt		27.11.87	6	Watford	26 May
12.68	0.4	Annabelle Lewis		20.03.89	4s2	Birmingham	10 Aug

wind assisted

11.29	3.7	Joice Maduaka		(11.31)	1h2	Birmingham	13 Jul
	11.43	3.8			1	Loughborough	18 May
11.32	2.8	Shani Anderson		(11.36)	1	Cork, IRL	6 Jul
	11.48	3.6			4h1	Dessau, GER	29 May
11.39	2.7	Vernicha James	U20	(11.40)	1s1	Bedford	29 Jun
	11.45	3.5			1	Bedford	29 Jun
	11.54	2.6			1h1	Bedford	29 Jun
11.47	3.8	Oyepitan		(11.36)	2	Loughborough	18 May
11.50	2.8	Allahgreen		(11.44)	2	Cork, IRL	6 Jul
11.50	3.4	Emma Ania		(11.64)	1	Reykjavik, ISL	16 Aug
	11.63	3.2			1	Hafnarfirdi, ISL	23 Aug
11.51	3.6	Amy Spencer	U17	(11.68)	1s2	Bedford	29 Jun
	11.55	3.5			2	Bedford	29 Jun
	11.60	3.8			5	Loughborough	18 May
11.57	3.8	Forrester		(11.34)	3	Loughborough	18 May
	11.61	2.7			1h1	Birmingham	13 Jul
11.58	3.1	Katherine Endacott	U23	(11.87)	2	Newport	20 Jul
11.60	3.8	Freeman	U23	(11.58)	4	Loughborough	18 May
11.61	4.3	Susan Burnside	U23	(11.66)	1	Bedford	29 Jun
11.63	2.8	Sarah Wilhelmy	U23	(11.72)	3	Cork, IRL	6 Jul

20 performances to 11.65 by 12 athletes

11.70	2.7	Jade Lucas-Read	U20	(11.88)	2s1	Bedford	29 Jun
11.75	3.8	Montell Douglas	U17	(11.77)	2h4	Bedford	29 Jun
11.75	3.5	Danielle Norville	U20	(11.87)	4	Bedford	29 Jun
11.76	3.7	Ellena Ruddock		(11.91)	3h2	Birmingham	13 Jul
11.78	4.1	Anna Boyle	U20	(11.97)	3	Kilkenny, IRL	19 May
11.82	4.8	Sara Whigham	U20	(11.95)	1h3	Bedford	29 Jun
11.83	2.7	Anyika Onuora	U20	(12.05)	4s1	Bedford	29 Jun
11.84	4.3	Donna Maylor	U23	(12.03)	3	Bedford	29 Jun
11.88	4.3	Lisa Trotman	U23	(12.16)	4	Bedford	29 Jun
11.91	4.3	Laura Turner	U23	(12.19)	5	Bedford	29 Jun
11.92	4.3	Sian Robinson	U23	(12.29)	6	Bedford	29 Jun

11.93	3.7	Lesley Owusu		(12.05A)	1	Emporia, USA	6	Apr
11.98	4.0	Yvette Henry		(12.07)	1	Cudworth	25	Aug
12.00	4.4	Sarah Claxton		23.09.79	2	Basildon	11	May
12.00	3.7	Keeley Butler		(12.03)	5h2	Birmingham	13	Jul
12.03	4.8	Carolyn McKenna	U20	4.05.84	3h3	Bedford	29	Jun
12.05	2.7	Karen Oughton	U20	(12.09)	6s1	Bedford	29	Jun
12.06	3.8	Emma Bailey	U20	25.07.84	3h4	Bedford	29	Jun
12.06	3.1	Carley Wenham	U15	(12.08)	1h1	London (He)	25	Aug
12.07	3.1	Karlene Palmer	U23	23.10.80	3h2	Bedford	29	Jun
12.11	2.7	Xanine Powell		(12.21)	4h1	Birmingham	13	Jul
12.12	2.7	Susie Williams		(12.25)	5h1	Birmingham	13	Jul
12.16	4.6	Gemma Bennett	U20	4.01.84	1	Basildon	11	May
12.16	2.8	Danielle Barker	U17	(12.48)	1	Cardiff	26	Aug
12.18	3.8	Angharad James		(12.23)	8	Loughborough	18	May
12.18	3.8	Louisa Wells	U20	30.12.84	4h4	Bedford	29	Jun
12.19	3.8	Molly Russell	U17	(12.20)	5h4	Bedford	29	Jun
12.21	2.7	Amy Dowsett	U20	(12.25)	7s1	Bedford	29	Jun
12.24	2.3	Rhiannon Burdon	U20	29.10.83	1J	Portsmouth	11	May
12.24	4.8	Cara Roberts	U20	24.05.85	4h3	Bedford	29	Jun
12.26	2.1	Gemma Thompson	U17	17.01.86	3	Tullamore, IRL	1	Jun
12.26	3.1	Rozelle Cavaciuti	U20	21.05.84	1	Cardiff	26	Aug
12.27	4.4	Lisa Allen		7.04.78	3	Basildon	11	May
12.29	3.2	Joey Duck	U15	(12.40)	1s3	Birmingham	10	Aug

Additional Under 17 (1 - 5 above)

12.31	2.4	Kelly Birkin		(12.32)	2h1	Birmingham	10	Aug
12.45		Katie Flaherty		1.10.85	1	Basildon	11	May
12.45	2.1	Michelle Nash-Odei		(12.48)	2h2	Watford	26	May
12.53	2.8	Susan Bagnall		4.08.86	3	Cardiff	26	Aug
12.54		Doyin Akindude		13.09.86	2	Basildon	11	May
12.54	2.4	Laura Willey		(12.56)	3h3	Birmingham	10	Aug
12.56	2.3	Leah Caddick		1.06.86	1	Cudworth	15	Sep

Additional Under 15 (1 - 2 above)

12.32	3.2	Rachel Conway		(12.37)	2s3	Birmingham	10	Aug
12.37	2.7	Tanya Hinds		(12.39)	1h6	Birmingham	10	Aug
12.40	2.4	Natalie Morrisey		(12.58)	1	Cudworth	15	Sep
12.48	2.3	Cherelle Norriston		(12.61)	2h1	Watford	25	May
12.50	3.1	Nicole Sadler		10.11.58)	2h1	London (He)	25	Aug
12.60	2.7	Annabelle Lewis		(12.68)	3h6	Birmingham	10	Aug

hand timing

11.4 w	3.2	Maduaka		(11.31)	1	London (He)	21	Jul

1 performance to 11.6 by 1 athlete including 1 wind assisted

11.7		Susie Williams		(12.25)	1	Alicante, ESP	18	May
11.8		Janette Niccolls		(11.94)	1	Horsham	6	Jul
11.8		Kelly Sotherton		(11.95)	1	Sandown IOW	18	Sep
11.8 w		Helen Williams		(12.12)	1	Portsmouth	18	May
11.9		Ellena Ruddock		(11.91)	1	Coventry	28	Apr
11.9	0.3	Jenny Meadows	U23	17.04.81	1	Scunthorpe	7	Jul
11.9		Melanie Purkiss		11.03.79	1	Southampton	17	Jul
11.9		Carley Wenham	U15	(12.08)	1	Crawley	21	Jul
11.9		Karen Oughton	U20	(12.09)	1	Nuneaton	28	Jul
11.9		Laura Turner	U23	(12.19)	1	Perivale	18	Aug
12.0		Amala Onuora	U17	(12.01)	2	London (CP)	7	Apr
12.0		Michelle Turner		(12.18)	1	Guildford	27	Apr
12.0		Syreena Pinel		(12.06)	1	Loughborough	11	May

12.0		Katherine Jones	U20	21.01.85	1	Cannock	15	Jun
12.0		Sian Robinson	U23	(12.29)	1	Nuneaton	14	Jul
12.0	1.7	Zoe Wilson		(12.14)	1	Stoke-on-Trent	21	Jul
12.0		Nicola Robinson	U17	16.04.86	2	Nuneaton	28	Jul
12.0		Nicole Bowring		27.01.74	2	Milton Keynes	7	Sep
12.0 w	3.0	Symone Belle	U20	12.11.84	1J	London (ME)	11	May
12.0 w	3.1	Danielle Halsall	U23	27.06.81	2	Stoke-on-Trent	21	Jul
12.1	1.3	Karlene Palmer	U23	(12.07w)	2	Loughborough	27	Apr
12.1		Kirsteen McDiarmid	U17	(12.15)	1	Glasgow (S)	5	May
12.1	1.5	Eleanor Caney	U20	28.05.84	1h2	Birmingham	25	May
12.1		Felicia Louisy		(12.17)	1	Bournemouth	8	Jun
12.1		Xanine Powell		(12.21)	1	Perivale	8	Jun
12.1		Molly Russell	U17	(12.20)	1	Basildon	6	Jul
12.1		Cherie Pierre	U20	15.05.84	1	London (Cr)	28	Jul
12.1		Rebecca Britton	U20	3.10.83	3	Nuneaton	28	Jul
12.1		Liz Williams		(12.26)	1	Guildford	10	Aug
12.1 w	5.8	Lindsey-Ann McDonnell		13.08.79	6	Perth, AUS	16	Mar
12.1 w		Kay Reynolds		15.09.67	1	Abingdon	27	Apr
12.1 w	3.3	Helen Pryer		21.01.79	2	Abingdon	23	Jun

Additional Under 17 (1 - 4 above)

12.2		Nicola Gossman		(12.23)	2	Glasgow (S)	5	May
12.2		Nicole MacDermott		(12.21)	2	Milton Keynes	15	Jun
12.2		Kessia Sherliker		(12.47)	1	Portsmouth	6	Jul
12.2		Emma Strachan		10.04.87	1	Dudley	18	Aug
12.2 w		Nicola Bentley		9.10.86	3rB	Scunthorpe	23	Jun
		12.3			1rB	Macclesfield	19	May
12.3		Kelly Birkin		(12.32)	1	Aberdare	28	Apr
12.3		Kimberley Wainwright		18.01.86	1	Leeds	5	May
12.3		Lisa Ferguson		10.09.86	1	Aberdeen	7	Jun
12.3		Louise Morgan		(12.52)	1	Ipswich	15	Jun
12.3		Natalie Jowett		(12.31)	3	London (Ha)	30	Jun
12.3		Rachel Egbuniwe		5.07.86	1	London (ME)	6	Jul
12.3		Phyllis Agbo		(12.35)	2	London (He)	25	Aug
12.3 w		Ashleigh Palmer-Johnson		19.09.86	1	Portsmouth	18	May
12.3 w		Ni-Kysha Ferguson		8.09.86	5	Scunthorpe	23	Jun
		12.4			1	Macclesfield	19	May
12.4		Katie Flaherty		(12.45w)	1	Ipswich	21	Apr
12.4		Charlotte Beckett		4.01.86	1	Milton Keynes	21	Apr
12.4		Gemma Thompson		(12.26w)	1	Antrim	27	Apr
12.4		Louise Dickinson		(12.51m)	1	Sheffield	28	Apr
12.4		Tamara Doherty		(12.47)	3	Glasgow (S)	5	May
12.4		Hayley Allerston		13.04.86	1	Blackpool	5	May
12.4		Deandra Smith		(12.48)	1	Welwyn	6	May
12.4		Faye Harding		7.09.85	1	Connah's Quay	12	May
12.4		Emma Wilson		15.07.87	2	London (TB)	2	Jun
12.4		Natasha Date		18.11.86	1	Bournemouth	22	Jun
12.4		Samantha Clegg		17.03.87	2	Bournemouth	22	Jun
12.4		Michelle Nash-Odei		(12.48)	2	London (TB)	30	Jun
12.4		Lianne George		25.11.86	2	London (ME)	6	Jul

Additional Under 15 (1 above)

12.3		Nimneh Hyde		(12.62)	1	Stafford	19	May
12.3		Kelly Fairweather		(12.60)	1	London (TB)	2	Jun
12.3		Joey Duck		(12.40)	2	London (Ha)	30	Jun
12.3		Lauren Duncan		(12.49)	1r1	Ealing	27	Jul

12.5		Cherelle Norriston	(12.61)	1	London (ME)	11	May
12.5		Dominique Blaize	(12.51)	1	London (TB)	1	Jun
12.5		Lyndsey Fairweather	5.03.88	1r2	London (TB)	2	Jun
12.5		Donna Walker	10.07.88	1	London (BP)	15	Jun
12.5		Fern Parker	20.02.88	1	Portsmouth	15	Jun
12.5		Natalie Morrisey	(12.58)	1	Tamworth	21	Jul
12.5		Nicole Sadler	(12.50w)	1	Watford	4	Aug
12.5		Roisin Willi	(12.55)	1h3	Gateshead	24	Aug
12.6		Hannah Frankson	11.01.89	2	London (TB)	2	Jun
12.6		Cassie Gear	19.04.88	2	Andover	3	Jun
12.6		Kirsty Hollings	4.10.87	3=	London (Ha)	30	Jun
12.6		Kirsty Thomas	2.10.87	1	Gateshead	7	Jul

Under 13

12.8		Torema Dorsett	15.02.90	1	Perivale	12	May
12.8		Jasmine Rowe	14.09.89	1	Nottingham	25	Aug
12.98	1.7	Holly Croxford	6.12.89	1	Portsmouth	11	May
13.0		Amelia Montagnani	10.03.90	1	London (BP)	31	Aug
13.0 w		Mariam Ajayi	13.02.91	1rB	Braunton	6	Jul
		13.8		2	London (He)	8	Jun
13.0 w		Temi Duro-Emmanuel	19.06.90	1rB	Braunton	6	Jul
		13.4		1	London (He)	8	Jun
13.08		Monica Bramwell	24.10.89	1	Hemel Hempstead	1	Jul
13.1		Chinedu Monye	29.12.89	1	Portsmouth	18	May
13.1		Megan Beesley	15.11.89	1	Cosford	31	Aug
13.1		Morgan Brown	24.12.89	1	Colwyn Bay	7	Sep
13.2		Alison Wylie	12.09.89	1	Aberdeen	7	Apr
13.2		Verity Collins	22.01.90	1	Blackpool	8	Sep
13.25		Charlotte Cole	06.91	2	Woking	1	Sep
13.3		Sarah Grewcock	25.06.90	1	Loughborough	11	May
13.3		Aliysa Coddington	20.06.90	1	Braunton	6	Jul
13.3		Natasha White	8.12.89	1	Chelmsford	18	Aug
13.39	-1.7	Megan Edwards	6.01.90	1r2	Kingston	28	Jul
13.39		Kirsty Hunter	16.12.89	1	Grangemouth	24	Aug

Foreign

12.00	0.5	*Sarah Reilly (IRL)*	3.07.73	2	*Gold Coast, AUS*	8	Apr
12.00 w	4.1	*Leanne O'Callaghan (IRL)*	15.07.74	5	*Kilkenny, IRL*	19	May
		12.09 1.8		4rC	*Bedford*	4	Jun

150 Metres - Under 13

19.1		Torema Dorsett	15.02.90	1	Norwich	2	Jun
19.4		Vanessa Nakangu	3.12.89	1	London (TB)	6	Jun
19.6		Megan Beesley	15.11.89	1	Tamworth	26	Aug
19.6 w		Natasha White	8.12.89	1	London (Ha)	30	Jun
19.7		Magali Franka	24.01.90	1	London (TB)	30	Jun
19.7		Verity Collins	22.01.90	1	Blackpool	21	Jul
19.8		Laura Egan	8.09.89	1	Coatbridge	19	May
19.8		Chinedu Monye	29.12.89	1	Bracknell	26	Jun
19.8		Amelia Montagnani	10.03.90	1	Abingdon	21	Jul
19.9		Holly Croxford	6.12.89	1	Bracknell	30	Mar
(10)							
19.9		Stacey Lennon	15.01.90	1	Sheffield	19	May
19.9		Shelley Marquis	26.12.89	2	London (TB)	2	Jun
19.9		Rachel Wallader	1.09.89	2	Carmarthen	21	Jul
20.0		Mariam Ajayi	13.02.91	1	Brighton	30	Jun
20.0		Lyndsey Jones	27.11.89	1rB	Carmarthen	21	Jul
20.0		Natasha Mullen	25.05.90	2	Carmarthen	21	Jul
20.1		Hollie Owen	16.06.90	1	Telford	30	Jun

200 Metres

Time	Wind	Name	Cat	DOB	Pos	Venue	Day	Mon
22.93	-0.2	Vernicha James	U20	6.06.84	1	Kingston, JAM	19	Jul
22.94	0.6				4	Annecy, FRA	23	Jun
22.95	-0.5				1	Manchester (C)	16	Jun
23.02	-0.1				1h2	Manchester (C)	16	Jun
23.07	-0.1				1s2	Kingston, JAM	19	Jul
23.13	1.2				2	Brisbane, AUS	13	Apr
23.14	1.4				1h3	Kingston, JAM	18	Jul
23.51	0.9				2	Adelaide, AUS	23	Mar
23.51	1.5				1h3	Brisbane, AUS	13	Apr
22.96	1.7	Shani Anderson		7.08.75	1	Cork, IRL	6	Jul
23.32	-0.5				2	Manchester (C)	16	Jun
23.35	0.0				2h1	Manchester (C)	16	Jun
23.38	0.4				2h4	Manchester (C)	28	Jul
23.41					1h2	Birmingham	14	Jul
23.42	-1.1				4h1	Munich, GER	8	Aug
23.53	0.0				1	Ludvika, SWE	27	Jun
23.59	1.5				2	Glasgow (S)	18	Aug
23.60	0.2				6s1	Manchester (C)	29	Jul
23.60	1.0				8s1	Munich, GER	9	Aug
23.00	0.2	Joice Maduaka		30.09.73	2h1	Manchester (C)	28	Jul
23.04	0.0				6	Manchester (C)	29	Jul
23.25	-0.2				4s2	Manchester (C)	29	Jul
23.26	0.0				1h1	Manchester (C)	16	Jun
23.37	1.5				1	Glasgow (S)	18	Aug
23.50	-0.5				4	Manchester (C)	16	Jun
23.64	-1.6				2	Bedford	4	Jun
23.42 i		Catherine Murphy		21.09.75	2	Birmingham	13	Jan
23.58 i					1s1	Birmingham	13	Jan
23.71 i					4	Glasgow	9	Mar
23.78 +					1	Vienna, AUT	3	Mar
23.84	-1.2				3h2	Brisbane, AUS	13	Apr
23.43	-0.5	Emily Freeman	U23	24.11.80	3	Manchester (C)	16	Jun
23.53	-0.1				2h2	Manchester (C)	16	Jun
23.53					1	Wakefield	7	Jul
23.64	0.1				3h3	Manchester (C)	28	Jul
23.71	-1.5				1	Jarrow	1	Jun
23.79	0.2				7s1	Manchester (C)	29	Jul
23.44 i		Amy Spencer	U17	19.09.85	1	Birmingham	27	Jan
23.46	1.6				2h5	Kingston, JAM	18	Jul
23.47	0.0				3h1	Manchester (C)	16	Jun
23.60	-0.5				5	Manchester (C)	16	Jun
23.64	1.0				1	Bedford	25	May
23.65	-0.3				3s3	Kingston, JAM	19	Jul
23.74 i					1	Cardiff	2	Feb
23.76 i					2s2	Birmingham	13	Jan
23.76	-0.2				7	Kingston, JAM	19	Jul
23.52	1.8	Abi Oyepitan		30.12.79	1rB	Loughborough	18	May
23.73	1.4	Sabrina Scott		2.06.79	1	Watford	2	Jun
23.73	1.0	Emma Ania		7.02.79	1	Reykjavik, ISL	7	Aug
23.78	-0.5	Ellena Ruddock		23.02.76	6	Manchester (C)	16	Jun
	(10)							
23.79	0.2	Lee McConnell		9.10.78	1	Glasgow (S)	9	Jun

51 performances to 23.79 by 11 athletes including 6 indoors

Time	Wind	Name		DOB	Pos	Venue	Day	Mon
23.81	-0.5	Melanie Purkiss		11.03.79	1	London (He)	3	Aug
23.83	0.7	Kelly Sotherton		13.11.76	1H2	Manchester (C)	26	Jul
23.93	1.8	Helen Frost		12.03.74	3rB	Loughborough	18	May
23.93	-0.4	Sinead Dudgeon		9.07.76	2	Birmingham	6	Jul
23.94	-0.5	Lesley Owusu		21.12.78	1	Lincoln NE, USA	4	May
23.94	1.7	Amanda Forrester		29.09.78	5	Sheffield	30	Jun

23.97	-0.5	Christine Harrison-Bloomfield		12.02.68	8	Manchester (C)	16 Jun
24.04	0.2	Susan Burnside	U23	3.02.80	2	Glasgow (S)	9 Jun
24.05	1.1	Lisa Miller	U20	13.01.83	3	Leiden, NED	8 Jun
	(20)						
24.06	1.6	Sarah Wilhelmy	U23	2.02.80	6	Bydgoszcz, POL	8 Jun
24.29	1.8	Anyika Onuora	U20	28.10.84	1	Derby	8 Sep
24.33	0.4	Montell Douglas	U17	24.01.86	1	Birmingham	11 Aug
24.34	1.4	Susan Williams		2.06.77	2	Watford	2 Jun
24.35	0.5	Danielle Norville	U20	18.01.83	2	Gorizia, ITA	6 Jul
24.36	1.3	Julie Hollman		16.02.77	1H2	Gotzis, AUT	1 Jun
24.40	1.2	Katherine Livesey		15.12.79	2H2	Baton Rouge LA, USA	29 May
24.41	-0.8	Katherine Endacott	U23	29.01.80	2	Niort, FRA	3 Aug
24.44	-1.5	Lisa Trotman	U23	6.12.82	2	Jarrow	1 Jun
24.44	-1.5	Melanie Roberts		2.03.78	3	Jarrow	1 Jun
	(30)						
24.44	-0.7	Kerry Jury		19.11.68	3H7	Arles, FRA	1 Jun
24.45 i		Karen Gear		30.09.79	1rB	Birmingham	27 Jan
	24.84	1.8			4rB	Loughborough	18 May
24.47 i		Emma Bryson	U23	5.04.81	2	Glasgow	24 Feb
	24.51	0.2			3	Glasgow (S)	9 Jun
24.47	1.4	Helen Pryer		21.01.79	3	Watford	2 Jun
24.47	0.0	Rachel Harris	U23	17.07.82	3h1	Birmingham	14 Jul
24.53	-1.4	Malgorzata Wardrop		25.03.77	2	Glasgow (S)	2 Jun
24.55	-0.4	Danielle Halsall	U23	27.06.81	4	Birmingham	6 Jul
24.55		Keeley Butler		24.03.75	3	Wakefield	7 Jul
24.56	1.4	Janette Niccolls		7.09.76	4	Watford	2 Jun
24.59		Gemma Ryde	U20	23.06.83	1rB	Edinburgh	28 Apr
	(40)						
24.61		Liz Williams		2.06.77	4h2	Birmingham	14 Jul
24.64	0.0	Nicole Bowring		27.01.74	4h1	Birmingham	14 Jul
24.67		Zoe Wilson		28.08.76	5h2	Birmingham	14 Jul
24.68		Jennifer Culley		4.03.75	1	Claremont, USA	23 Mar
24.70	-1.2	Natalie Beattie		30.01.78	3rB	Bedford	4 Jun
24.70	0.0	Kim Wall	U20	21.04.83	7h1	Manchester (C)	16 Jun
24.72	1.7	Jessica Ennis	U17	28.01.86	1H	Wrexham	22 Jun
24.72		Sara Todd		3.11.79	1	Gateshead	25 Aug
24.73	-0.3	Katherine Jones	U20	21.01.85	1	Nottingham	13 Jul
24.75 i		Helen Roscoe		4.12.79	4	Birmingham	27 Jan
	25.26	-0.1			6h2	Manchester (C)	16 Jun
	(50)						
24.75	-0.1	Victoria Barr	U23	14.04.82	2h4	Bedford	5 May
24.75	1.5	Karen Oughton	U20	26.01.83	1h2	Bedford	5 May
24.78	1.0	Helen Thieme/Karagounis	U23	28.09.81	6	Bedford	25 May
24.80	1.9	Cherie Pierre	U20	15.05.84	1	Watford	25 May
24.81 i		Jemma Sims	U20	2.05.85	2	Birmingham	24 Feb
	25.09	2.0			2h2	Birmingham	26 May
24.85	0.2	Sara Whigham	U20	7.10.83	4	Glasgow (S)	9 Jun
24.86	1.7	Louise Hazel	U17	6.10.85	2H	Wrexham	22 Jun
24.86		Michelle Thomas		16.10.71	6h2	Birmingham	14 Jul
24.87 i		Kim Goodwin		16.05.70	2rB	Birmingham	27 Jan
	25.28	1.0			8	Bedford	25 May
24.87	0.0	Xanine Powell		21.05.79	6h1	Birmingham	14 Jul
	(60)						
24.89	-1.3	Kelly Thomas	U23	9.01.81	4	Bedford	6 May
24.89	-1.2	Gemma Nicol	U17	27.07.86	1J	Edinburgh	12 May
24.90	-0.3	Bernice Wilson	U20	21.04.84	3	Nottingham	13 Jul
24.93	-0.1	Yvette Henry		8.06.73	3h4	Bedford	5 May
24.93	-1.1	Emma Strachan	U17	10.04.87	1h2	Nottingham	12 Jul
24.94 mx		Nicola Sanders	U23	23.06.82	1	Watford	28 Aug
24.96 i		Amala Onuora	U17	16.03.86	1s1	Birmingham	24 Feb
	24.98	-2.0			1	Crawley	12 May

24.97	-1.6	Felicia Louisy		17.05.74	3h1	Watford	2	Jun
24.97	-0.3	Shereen Charles	U20	27.10.84	4	Nottingham	13	Jul
24.98	0.2	Sharon Wilson		27.10.74	6	Glasgow (S)	9	Jun
	(70)							
25.00	-0.7	Sinead Johnson	U17	24.12.86	1h1	Birmingham	26	May
25.01	-0.9	Donna Walker	U15	10.07.88	1h4	Nottingham	12	Jul
25.02	1.9	Amy Dowsett	U20	30.12.84	2	Watford	25	May
25.02	0.7	Louretta Thorne		6.05.77	2rB	Birmingham	6	Jul
25.05	0.0	Sabina Astarita	U17	15.10.86	1	Glasgow (S)	20	Jul
25.06 i		Phyllis Agbo	U17	16.12.85	1	Birmingham	24	Feb
25.22	1.5				2H2	Pratteln, SUI	3	Aug
25.07	0.7	Liz Fairs		1.12.77	3rB	Birmingham	6	Jul
25.07		Nicole Crosby		23.10.76	1rB	Wakefield	7	Jul
25.09	-0.1	Angharad James		7.04.79	4h4	Bedford	5	May
25.10	1.8	Julie Pratt		20.03.79	1	London (Ha)	20	Apr
	(80)							
25.11	1.5	Sarah Tomlins	U23	5.04.82	3h2	Bedford	5	May
25.11	1.0	Vicky Ward		19.06.72	7	Bedford	25	May
25.12 i		Nicola Gossman	U17	4.11.86	2	Birmingham	24	Feb
25.33	1.7				7s2	Caen, FRA	1	Jun
25.12	1.5	Karlene Palmer	U23	23.10.80	4h2	Bedford	5	May
25.13	1.0	Katie Flaherty	U17	1.10.85	2	Nottingham	13	Jul
25.14	1.0	Kessia Sherliker	U17	9.11.85	3	Nottingham	13	Jul
25.16 mx		Laura Turner	U23	12.08.82	2	Watford	28	Aug
25.17	-1.1	Simone Baugh	U17	25.02.87	2h2	Nottingham	12	Jul
25.17	0.4	Kirsteen McDiarmid	U17	28.04.86	1rB	Edinburgh	28	Jul
25.19	0.7	Michelle Pierre		30.09.73	4rB	Birmingham	6	Jul
	(90)							
25.19	0.4	Roz Gonse	U23	1.03.82	2H1	Pratteln, SUI	3	Aug
25.21	-0.3	Amanda Shaw	U20	28.09.84	5	Nottingham	13	Jul
25.24	-1.2	Jackie Scott	U20	31.01.85	2J	Edinburgh	12	May
25.24	-1.5	Sian Robinson	U23	31.03.82	3	Birmingham	1	Jun
25.25	1.4	Helen Williams		2.06.77	7	Watford	2	Jun
25.27	1.0	Louise Dickinson	U17	5.11.86	5	Nottingham	13	Jul
25.27	0.6	Kelly Birkin	U17	27.04.86	2	Tullamore, IRL	3	Aug
25.28		Ni-Kysha Ferguson	U17	8.09.86	1	Manchester (Str)	11	May
25.28	1.3	Michelle Nash-Odei	U17	19.03.87	1	Kingston	12	May
25.29	-0.8	Lucy Evans	U23	2.10.82	5s2	Bedford	6	May
	(100)							
25.29		Titi Ameobi	U20	20.11.84	1J	Gateshead	11	May
25.29		Joey Duck	U15	14.04.89	2	Nottingham	13	Jul
25.29	-0.9	Kate Brewington	U23	15.10.81	1H1	London (He)	10	Aug

Additional Under 17 (1 - 19 above)

25.30	-0.6	Danielle Barker		19.01.87	2	Tullamore, IRL	3	Aug
	(20)							
25.37	1.6	Kelly Roomes		19.01.87	1h2	London (He)	25	Aug
25.40	-0.2	Nicole MacDermott		15.08.86	1	Birmingham	1	Sep
25.42	0.4	Leah Caddick		1.06.86	6	Birmingham	11	Aug
25.44	-0.8	Charlotte Beckett		4.01.86	2h2	Birmingham	11	Aug
25.46	-0.2	Nicola Bentley		9.10.86	3s1	Birmingham	11	Aug
25.50	0.6	Lauren Candlish		4.04.86	3	Tullamore, IRL	3	Aug
25.54	-1.4	Nicola Robinson		16.04.86	1h2	Birmingham	26	May
25.57 i		Jemma Thake		17.12.85	1	Birmingham	27	Jan
25.57	-0.3	Camilla Harkness		10.01.87	3h4	Nottingham	12	Jul

Additional Under 15 (1 - 2 above)

25.36	-0.6	Natalie Morrisey		22.08.88	1h1	Nottingham	12	Jul
25.53 i		Nimneh Hyde		20.09.87	1	Birmingham	24	Feb
25.67	1.2	Amy Clancy		26.03.88	1	Grangemouth	24	Aug
25.70	1.0	Amy Harris		14.09.87	2s1	Nottingham	13	Jul

25.73	0.8	Amy Gibbs		30.03.89	1h1	Watford	26	May
25.75		Kim Skinner		21.09.87	1	Edinburgh	28	Apr
25.77	1.0	Nicole Sadler		10.11.88	3s1	Nottingham	13	Jul
25.81	-0.8	Carley Wenham		14.03.88	1	Crawley	12	May
	(10)							
25.82 i		Kelly Fairweather		5.03.88	3	Birmingham	24	Feb
25.87	1.2	Louise Crilly		18.01.88	2	Grangemouth	24	Aug
25.95	1.0	Sarah Adams		14.09.88	5s1	Nottingham	13	Jul
25.96	1.4	Lauren Duncan		21.03.88	1	London (He)	25	Aug
25.99	1.9	Laura Scougall		21.01.89	3s2	Nottingham	13	Jul

wind assisted

23.03	3.1	Anderson		(22.96)	1	Birmingham	14	Jul
	23.72	2.7			4	Fort-de-France Mart, FRA	27	Apr
23.21	3.1	Maduaka		(23.00)	2	Birmingham	14	Jul
	23.25	3.8			1	Loughborough	18	May
	23.61	2.8			1h3	Birmingham	14	Jul
23.41	3.8	Emily Freeman	U23	(23.43)	2	Loughborough	18	May
	23.41	3.1			4	Birmingham	14	Jul
	23.51	5.4			1	Bedford	30	Jun
23.41	3.1	Ellena Ruddock		(23.78)	3	Birmingham	14	Jul
23.48	3.8	Lee McConnell		(23.79)	3	Loughborough	18	May
23.58	2.8	Spencer	U17	(23.46)	1	Bedford	30	Jun
23.64	2.9	Emma Ania		(23.73)	1h1	Kopavogur, ISL	28	Jul
	23.70	2.4			1	Reykjavik, ISL	17	Aug
23.70	3.8	James	U20	(22.93)	4	Loughborough	18	May
		14 performances to 23.79 by 8 athletes						
23.89	2.8	Lisa Miller	U20	(24.05)	2J	Bedford	30	Jun
23.90	3.8	Susan Burnside	U23	(24.04)	5	Loughborough	18	May
23.94		Christine Harrison-Bloomfield		(23.97)	1	Long Beach CA, USA	20	Apr
23.99	4.0	Jenny Meadows	U23	(24.0)	1	Cudworth	25	Aug
24.11	3.5	Kim Wall	U20	(24.70)	1	London (He)	25	Aug
24.12	3.1	Danielle Halsall	U23	(24.55)	6	Birmingham	14	Jul
24.13	5.4	Katherine Endacott	U23	(24.41)	2	Bedford	30	Jun
24.18	3.1	Susie Williams		2.06.77	7	Birmingham	14	Jul
24.23	5.4	Lisa Trotman	U23	(24.44)	3	Bedford	30	Jun
24.47	2.3	Malgorzata Wardrop		(24.53)	1	Glasgow (S)	29	May
24.52	2.5	Jessica Ennis	U17	(24.72)	1H1	Pratteln, SUI	3	Aug
24.60	2.4	Sara Whigham	U20	(24.85)	1h1	Bedford	5	May
24.67	2.5	Amala Onuora	U17	(24.98)	1	Watford	25	May
24.82	2.4	Lucy Evans	U23	(25.29)	1h2	Bedford	5	May
24.95		Tamsin Stephens	U23	2.08.80	2h2	Belfast	8	Jun
24.97	2.1	Katie Flaherty	U17	(25.13)	1h2	Watford	25	May
25.00	3.8	Angharad James		(25.09)	6	Loughborough	18	May
25.10	2.7	Jackie Scott	U20	(25.24)	1	Grangemouth	15	Jun
25.14	2.4	Katie Butler	U23	16.05.80	3h1	Bedford	5	May
25.14	3.5	Kelly Roomes	U17	(25.37)	3	London (He)	25	Aug
25.16	2.8	Kelly Birkin	U17	(25.27)	1	Brecon	6	Jul
25.17		Anna Boyle	U20	29.03.83	5	Belfast	8	Jun
25.18	2.5	Michelle Nash-Odei	U17	(25.28)	3	Watford	25	May
25.24		Danielle Barker	U17	(25.30)	1	Cardiff	26	Aug
25.27	2.7	Wendy Davidson	U23	14.10.82	1H2	Hexham	15	Jun

Additional Under 17 (1 - 8 above)

25.37	2.1	Sarah Holmes		21.11.85	3h2	Watford	25	May
25.37	3.5	Jemma Thake		(25.57i)	4	London (He)	25	Aug
25.58	3.5	Ashleigh Palmer-Johnson		19.09.86	5	London (He)	25	Aug

Under 15

25.49	2.3	Amy Gibbs		(25.73)	1	Watford	26 May
25.63	2.6	Lisa Papura		21.04.88	1	Brecon	6 Jul
25.67		Rachel Conway		30.09.87	1	Cardiff	26 Aug
25.84	2.7	Holly Littlejohn		15.02.88	2	Birmingham	26 May

hand timing

23.6 w	2.2	Maduaka		(23.00)	1	London (He)	21 Jul
		1 performance to 23.7 by 1 athlete including 1 wind assisted					
24.0	1.3	Jenny Meadows	U23	(23.99w)	1	Scunthorpe	7 Jul
24.3		Katherine Endacott	U23	(24.41)	1	Exeter	23 Jun
24.4		Helen Thieme/Karagounis	U23	(24.78)	1	Coventry	28 Apr
24.4	-0.1	Karen Gear		(24.84)	2	Exeter	11 May
24.4		Nicole Bowring		(24.64)	1	London (CP)	11 May
24.4	-0.1	Helen Pryer		(24.47)	2h2	Watford	2 Jun
24.4		Janette Niccolls		(24.56)	1	Perivale	27 Jul
24.4 w		Sara Whigham	U20	(24.85)	1	Scunthorpe	23 Jun
24.5		Carley Wenham	U15	(25.81)	1	Crawley	21 Jul
24.6		Liz Fairs		(25.07)	1	Sheffield	27 Apr
24.6		Faye Harding	U17	7.09.85	1	Wrexham	19 May
24.6 w	2.7	Michelle Thomas		(24.86)	2	Stoke-on-Trent	21 Jul
24.7		Amala Onuora	U17	(24.98)	2	London (TB)	7 Apr
24.8		Kelly Thomas	U23	(24.89)	1	Loughborough	27 Apr
24.8		Sarah Tomlins	U23	(25.11)	3	Horsham	6 Jul
24.8	1.3	Kim Goodwin		(25.28)	2	Scunthorpe	7 Jul
24.8	0.7	Gemma Nicol	U17	(24.89)	1	London (WF)	18 Aug
24.8 w		Louretta Thorne		(25.02)	1rB	Milton Keynes	7 Sep
		25.0			1rB	Bournemouth	8 Jun
24.9		Karlene Palmer	U23	(25.12)	2	Loughborough	27 Apr
24.9		Simone Baugh	U17	(25.17)	1	Derby	15 Jun
24.9		Laura Finucane	U17	3.08.86	1	Bolton	4 Aug
24.9 w		Eleanor Caney	U20	28.05.84	3	Scunthorpe	23 Jun
24.9 w		Vicky Griffiths	U20	9.10.84	1rB	Scunthorpe	23 Jun
25.0	1.9	Sabina Astarita	U17	(25.05)	2	Grangemouth	15 Jun
25.0		Claire Brason	U20	16.03.83	3	Wakefield	28 Jul
25.0		Carey Easton/Marshall		16.11.79	1	Coatbridge	11 Aug
25.0		Laura Turner	U23	(25.16)	1	Perivale	18 Aug
25.0 w		Ni-Kysha Ferguson	U17	(25.28)	4	Scunthorpe	23 Jun
25.1		Clare Milborrow		10.01.77	1	Guildford	27 Apr
25.1		Syreena Pinel		13.01.79	1	Loughborough	12 May
25.1		Leah Caddick	U17	(25.42)	2	Wrexham	19 May
25.1	1.7	Vicky Ward		(25.11)	4	Coventry	19 May
25.1		Claire Spurway		4.04.78	1	Gloucester	25 May
25.1	1.9	Nicola Gossman	U17	(25.33)	3	Grangemouth	15 Jun
25.1		Jeanette Kwakye	U20	20.03.83	1	London (WF)	23 Jun
25.1		Helen Williams		(25.25)	1rB	Horsham	6 Jul
25.1	1.9	Michelle Pierre		(25.19)	2	London (He)	21 Jul
25.1		Lucy Parsons		10.02.79	2	Eton	21 Jul
25.1		Nicola Robinson	U17	(25.54)	2	Nuneaton	28 Jul
25.1		Rebecca Britton	U20	3.10.83	3	Nuneaton	28 Jul
25.1 w	2.3	Charlotte Beckett	U17	(25.44)	1h3	Watford	25 May
		25.3			1	Milton Keynes	15 Jun
25.1 w		Sian Adlam/Darby		8.11.70	1rB	Yate	9 Jun

Additional Under 17 (1 - 11 above)

25.2		Gemma Thompson		17.01.86	2	Tullamore, IRL	22 Jun
25.2 w		Rowi Mortimer		4.07.86	1	Yate	19 May

25.2 w		Nicola Bentley		(25.46)	2rB	Scunthorpe	23	Jun
25.3		Tara Bird		22.07.87	1rB	London (WF)	23	Jun
25.4		Kadi-Ann Thomas		10.02.86	1rB	Bedford	18	May
25.4		Rachael Thompson		15.11.85	3	Wrexham	19	May
25.4 ?		Shelley Fielding		10.11.86	1	Street	19	Jun
25.4		Camilla Harkness		(25.57)	1	Portsmouth	6	Jul
25.5		Deandra Smith		3.12.86	1H	Hemel Hempstead	29	Jun
25.5		Molly Russell		3.08.86	3	London (TB)	30	Jun
25.5 w		Laura Robinson		11.10.85	6	Scunthorpe	23	Jun

Additional Under 15 (1 above)

25.3 w	2.7	Natalie Morrisey		(25.36)	1	Cudworth	15	Sep
25.5		Amy Gibbs		(25.73)	1	London (CP)	12	May
25.6		Nicole Sadler		(25.77)	1	Bury St. Edmunds	22	Sep
25.7		Nimneh Hyde		(25.53i)	1	Stafford	19	May
25.7		Lauren Duncan		(25.96)	1r1	Ealing	27	Jul
25.7		Holly Littlejohn		(25.84w)	1	Rugby	25	Aug
25.8		Kara Graham		13.10.87	1	Southend	6	May
25.8		Joedy Platt		27.11.87	1	Exeter	9	Jun
26.0		Kelly Fairweather		(25.82i)	1	London (TB)	2	Jun
26.0		Fern Parker		20.02.88	1	Andover	23	Jun

Under 13

26.3		Monica Bramwell		24.10.89	1	Hemel Hempstead	6	Jul
26.8		Jasmine Rowe		14.09.89	1	Telford	7	Sep
26.9		Megan Beesley		15.11.89	1	Cosford	31	Aug
27.0		Holly Croxford		6.12.89	1	Oxford	18	May
27.0		Verity Collins		22.01.90	1	Nelson	27	Jul
27.2		Torema Dorsett		15.02.90	1	Perivale	12	May
27.29	-1.7	Megan Edwards		6.01.90	1	Kingston	27	Jul
27.30 i		Kirsty Hunter		16.12.89	1	Glasgow	3	Feb
27.45					1	Edinburgh	25	May
27.3		Aliysa Coddington		20.06.90	1rB	Braunton	6	Jul
27.3		Natasha White		8.12.89	1	Chelmsford	18	Aug
	(10)							
27.4		Amelia Montagnani		10.03.90	1rB	London (CP)	7	Apr
27.4		Chinedu Monye		29.12.89	2rB	Eton	27	Apr
27.51		Charlotte Cole		06.91	2	Kingston	28	Jul
27.7		Alison Wylie		12.09.89	1	Aberdeen	15	Sep

Foreign

23.30 i		*Sarah Reilly (IRL)*		*3.07.73*	*1*	*Birmingham*	*13*	*Jan*
23.90	*0.0*				*2*	*Dublin (S), IRL*	*13*	*Jul*
24.52 i		*Maiteland Marks (USA)*		*19.09.76*	*3*	*Glasgow*	*23*	*Feb*
24.8					*1*	*Bromley*	*8*	*Jun*
24.7	*-0.4*	*Michelle Carey (IRL)*	*U23*	*20.02.81*	*2*	*Loughborough*	*5*	*Jun*
24.94	*0.0*	*Leanne O'Callaghan (IRL)*		*15.07.74*	*4*	*Dublin (S), IRL*	*13*	*Jul*

300 Metres

37.1 i+	Catherine Murphy		21.09.75	2m	Birmingham	17	Feb
37.72 i	Amy Spencer	U17	19.09.85	1	Birmingham	24	Feb
38.49	Gemma Nicol	U17	27.07.86	1	Tullamore, IRL	3	Aug
38.86	Carey Easton/Marshall		16.11.79	1rB	Alfaz del Pi, ESP	30	Mar
39.03	Laura Finucane	U17	3.08.86	2	Birmingham	11	Aug
39.09	Liz Williams		2.06.77	1	Loughborough	17	Jul
39.19	Tara Bird	U17	22.07.87	1	Nottingham	13	Jul
39.20	Jenny Christie	U17	28.09.85	2	Nottingham	13	Jul

Additional Under 17 (1 - 5 above)

39.7	Leah Caddick	1.06.86	1	Wrexham	19	May
	39.72		2	Manchester (C)	25	May
39.73	Rowi Mortimer	4.07.86	3	Nottingham	13	Jul
39.75	Faye Harding	7.09.85	1	Brecon	6	Jul
39.8	Eilidh Child	20.02.87	1	Edinburgh	11	May
	40.07		2	Grangemouth	14	Jun
39.8	Rachael Thompson	15.11.85	2	Wrexham	19	May
(10)						
39.90	Lauren Candlish	4.04.86	4	Birmingham	11	Aug
40.16	Ni-Kysha Ferguson	8.09.86	1h3	Manchester (C)	25	May
40.18	Jemma Thake	17.12.85	4	Nottingham	13	Jul
40.21	Nicola Bentley	9.10.86	3	Manchester (C)	25	May
40.24	Lauren Webb	17.11.85	2	Watford	26	May
40.30	Victoria Wester	24.12.85	2h3	Manchester (C)	25	May
40.35	Tamara Doherty	15.11.85	1	Edinburgh	11	May
40.36	Kimberley Wainwright	18.01.86	5	Nottingham	13	Jul
40.41	Holly Barlow	4.10.86	6	Nottingham	13	Jul
40.42	Sarah Shuttleworth	16.08.86	1	Birmingham	1	Sep
(20)						
40.54	Emma-Lisa Carroll	23.03.86	2	Birmingham	1	Sep
40.55	Laura Robinson	11.10.85	5	Manchester (C)	25	May
40.8	Shadina Dodds	16.08.86	1	Telford	11	May
	40.90		2h3	Nottingham	12	Jul
40.85	Sonia Hodgkinson	2.12.86	3	Birmingham	1	Sep
41.06	Lois Brooks	10.01.87	2	Manchester (Str)	11	May
41.07 i	Sabina Astarita	15.10.86	1	Glasgow	31	Jan
41.09	Lianne George	25.11.86	5h1	Nottingham	12	Jul
41.1	Louise Dickinson	5.11.86	1	Sutton Coldfield	24	Aug
	41.29		5s1	Birmingham	10	Aug
41.1	Maria Garavand	30.06.86	1	Bury St. Edmunds	22	Sep
41.17 i	Sarah Rhodes	4.01.86	2s1	Birmingham	23	Feb
(30)						
41.2	Charlotte Beckett	4.01.86	1	High Wycombe	11	May
41.2	Lucy Rodgers	1.07.87	1	Chelmsford	15	Jun
	41.29		4	Watford	26	May
41.2	Danielle Marsh	22.04.86	2	Birmingham	15	Jun
41.2	Kirsteen McDiarmid	28.04.86	1	Grangemouth	30	Jun
41.23	Gemma Brown	22.06.86	3h2	Manchester (C)	25	May
41.29	Kate McGing	12.04.86	4h3	Nottingham	12	Jul

400 Metres

50.82	Lee McConnell	9.10.78	4	Madrid, ESP	20	Sep
	51.02		3	Munich, GER	8	Aug
	51.24		2h3	Munich, GER	7	Aug
	51.29		1s2	Manchester (C)	27	Jul
	51.29		6	Zurich, SUI	16	Aug
	51.59		1	Birmingham	13	Jul
	51.68		2	Manchester (C)	28	Jul
	51.87		1	Basel, SUI	20	May
	52.15		2q3	Manchester (C)	27	Jul
	52.16		3	Glasgow (S)	18	Aug
	52.21		1	Floro, NOR	1	Jun
	52.89		7	Sheffield	30	Jun
	53.58		1h2	Birmingham	12	Jul
51.36	Catherine Murphy	21.09.75	3s2	Manchester (C)	27	Jul
	51.50		4	Belem, BRA	5	May
	51.79 i		2	Birmingham	17	Feb
	51.95 i		2h2	Vienna, AUT	1	Mar
	52.10		1	Santiago, CHI	28	Apr

(Murphy)	52.10			2	Birmingham	13	Jul
	52.14			1	Adelaide, AUS	23	Mar
	52.15			2q1	Manchester (C)	27	Jul
	52.18			1	Brisbane, AUS	12	Apr
	52.49 i			1	Glasgow	9	Mar
	52.54 i			1	Cardiff	3	Feb
	52.86			6	Sheffield	30	Jun
	52.91			6	Manchester (C)	28	Jul
	52.98 i			6	Vienna, AUT	3	Mar
	53.05			7	Doha, QAT	15	May
	53.06 i			1s2	Cardiff	2	Feb
	53.09			1h3	Manchester (C)	26	Jul
	53.35			7	Athens, GRE	10	Jun
	53.43			1h3	Birmingham	12	Jul
	53.44 i			1	Stockholm, SWE	6	Feb
	53.47			1h3	Brisbane, AUS	11	Apr
51.97	Helen Thieme/Karagounis	U23	28.09.81	6s2	Manchester (C)	27	Jul
	52.03			6	Annecy, FRA	22	Jun
	52.17			2	Manchester (C)	16	Jun
	52.45			3	Birmingham	13	Jul
	52.49			1h3	Manchester (C)	15	Jun
	52.69			4q1	Manchester (C)	27	Jul
	52.97			8	Sheffield	30	Jun
	53.35			1h1	Birmingham	12	Jul
	53.62			1	Loughborough	18	May
52.39	Lesley Owusu		21.12.78	1	Lincoln NE, USA	4	May
	52.55			3h2	Baton Rouge LA, USA	30	May
	52.93 i			3	Lincoln NE, USA	9	Feb
	53.42 i			1	Lincoln NE, USA	15	Feb
	53.43			1h2	Columbia SC, USA	18	May
	53.52			3	Columbia SC, USA	19	May
52.67	Helen Frost		12.03.74	4q3	Manchester (C)	27	Jul
	52.71			6s1	Manchester (C)	27	Jul
	52.85			5	Kiev, UKR	25	May
	53.09			1	Durban, RSA	8	Feb
	53.14			2	Birmingham	6	Jul
	53.24			4	Cottbus, GER	1	Jun
	53.27			5	Birmingham	13	Jul
	53.55			6	Manchester (C)	16	Jun
52.91	Carey Easton/Marshall		16.11.79	2h3	Manchester (C)	15	Jun
	53.11			3	Manchester (C)	16	Jun
	53.62			2	Basel, SUI	20	May
52.99	Melanie Purkiss		11.03.79	1	Birmingham	6	Jul
	53.03			4	Birmingham	13	Jul
	53.08			6q2	Manchester (C)	27	Jul
	53.32			8s1	Manchester (C)	27	Jul
	53.56			7	Manchester (C)	16	Jun
	53.65			2h2	Manchester (C)	15	Jun
53.18	Lisa Miller	U20	13.01.83	4	Manchester (C)	16	Jun
	53.20			5	Kingston, JAM	18	Jul
	53.28			3s1	Kingston, JAM	17	Jul
53.25 i	Jenny Meadows	U23	17.04.81	1	Glasgow	20	Jan
	53.47 i			1	Cardiff	10	Feb
	53.67			2	Loughborough	18	May
	53.7			1	Wigan	4	Aug
	75 performances to 53.7 by 9 athletes including 12 indoors						
53.84	Vernicha James (10)	U20	6.06.84	1	Bedford	4	Jun
53.91	Danielle Halsall	U23	27.06.81	2	Newport	20	Jul
53.95	Sinead Dudgeon		9.07.76	3	Loughborough	17	Jul

54.02	Emily Freeman	U23	24.11.80	2	Bedford	4	Jun
54.05	Kim Wall	U20	21.04.83	5s2	Kingston, JAM	17	Jul
54.07	Vicki Jamison		19.05.77	1	Belfast	8	Jun
54.12	Karen Gear		30.09.79	1	Watford	2	Jun
54.25	Nicole Bowring		27.01.74	4h3	Manchester (C)	15	Jun
54.28	Shani Anderson		7.08.75	1h2	Bedford	26	May
54.31	Michelle Pierre		30.09.73	4	Birmingham	6	Jul
54.69	Kim Goodwin		16.05.70	6h3	Manchester (C)	15	Jun
	(20)						
54.76	Liz Williams		2.06.77	5	Watford	2	Jun
54.85	Lesley Clarkson	U23	18.07.82	4	Geneva, SUI	15	Jun
54.85	Susan Burnside	U23	3.02.80	1	Grangemouth	3	Jul
55.00	Gemma Nicol	U17	27.07.86	2	Bedford	30	Jun
55.03	Emma Davies		9.10.78	1	Cardiff	8	Jul
55.04	Hannah Wood	U23	17.11.81	1rB	Imperia, ITA	27	Jun
55.04	Natalie Street	U20	8.11.83	1	Nottingham	13	Jul
55.20	Anita Eagland		29.09.72	2	London (He)	3	Aug
55.28 i	Tracey Duncan		16.05.79	2s1	Cardiff	2	Feb
55.60				3r3	Palafrugell, ESP	11	May
55.30	Jane McKay		22.04.77	1	Edinburgh	11	May
	(30)						
55.3	Jo Fenn		19.10.74	1	Coventry	19	May
55.95 i				3	Birmingham	13	Jan
55.33	Laura Finucane	U17	3.08.86	1	Manchester (Str)	11	Jun
55.39	Jennifer Culley		4.03.75	1	Claremont, USA	23	Mar
55.42 i	Susie Williams		2.06.77	2	Birmingham	27	Jan
55.5	Sarah Tomlins	U23	5.04.82	2	Derby	11	Aug
55.81				6	Watford	2	Jun
55.55	Faye Harding	U17	7.09.85	1	Newport	8	Jun
55.56	Mary McClung		19.12.71	2	Edinburgh	11	May
55.60	Katie Jones		4.01.77	6	Birmingham	6	Jul
55.6	Clare Hill		14.12.76	1rB	Stoke-on-Trent	19	May
56.13				3	Dublin (S), IRL	14	Jul
55.6	Kathryn Sage		27.03.76	1	Aberdare	15	Jun
55.65				2	Cardiff	8	Jul
	(40)						
55.64	Lisa Whigham	U23	14.08.80	1	Wakefield	7	Jul
55.68	Rachael Thompson	U17	15.11.85	2	Manchester (Str)	11	Jun
55.7	Alex Carter	U23	1.04.80	1	Loughborough	22	May
55.71	Vicky Ward		19.06.72	6h2	Manchester (C)	15	Jun
55.72	Vicky Griffiths	U20	9.10.84	1	Manchester (C)	26	May
55.81 i	Lindsey Singer	U20	4.06.83	1	Birmingham	24	Feb
56.82				1	Birmingham	2	Jun
55.89	Liz Fairs		1.12.77	1rB	London (He)	3	Aug
55.9	Lucy Parsons		10.02.79	2	Aberdare	15	Jun
56.42				3	Newport	8	Jun
56.0	Lisa Dobriskey	U20	23.12.83	1	Eton	4	Aug
56.01	Rebecca Sweeney	U20	9.02.85	2h1	Nottingham	12	Jul
	(50)						
56.08	Michelle Thomas		16.10.71	5h3	Birmingham	12	Jul
56.1	Melanie Brown		10.12.70	2	Eton	4	Aug
56.16				2	Wakefield	7	Jul
56.14	Marilyn Okoro	U20	23.09.84	2	Nottingham	13	Jul
56.19	Claire Robinson		18.01.78	1	Birmingham (Un)	19	Jun
56.2	Charlotte Best	U20	7.03.85	1	Crawley	27	Jul
56.23	Catherine Riley	U23	4.06.82	3	Manchester (Str)	11	Jun
56.30	Natalie Plateau	U20	19.10.84	3h1	Nottingham	12	Jul
56.3	Jemma Simpson	U20	10.02.84	1J	Bath	12	May
56.43 i				2	Birmingham	24	Feb
56.3	Amy Freeman	U23	23.08.82	1	Bolton	4	Aug
56.66				7h1	Birmingham	12	Jul

Time	Name	Cat	DOB	Pos	Venue	Date	
56.38 i	Hannah Stares		13.11.78	1rB	Birmingham	27	Jan
	57.2			2	Loughborough	22	May
	(60)						
56.4	Samantha Singer	U23	8.05.82	1	Bromley	8	Jun
	56.52			7	Watford	2	Jun
56.49	Kathryn Evans	U20	1.03.84	2	Glasgow (S)	2	Jun
56.5	Louretta Thorne		6.05.77	1	High Wycombe	11	May
	57.37			6h2	Bedford	26	May
56.5	Rachel Harris	U23	17.07.82	1	Stourport	12	May
	57.32 i			2rB	Birmingham	27	Jan
56.5	Suzanne McGowan		13.04.78	3	Eton	4	Aug
	56.78			4	Glasgow (S)	9	Jun
56.54 i	Olivia Hines	U20	19.10.83	4	Birmingham	24	Feb
56.54	Nicola Sanders	U23	23.06.82	5	Bedford	6	May
56.6	Claire Brason	U20	16.03.83	1rB	Birmingham	18	Aug
	57.37			3h1	Jarrow	1	Jun
56.7	Lois Cresswell	U23	12.01.81	2rB	Rugby	19	May
	57.12			7	Bedford	6	May
56.7	Lauren Candlish	U17	4.04.86	2	Derby	21	Jul
	56.88			1	Edinburgh	28	Jul
	(70)						
56.7	Lucy Vaughan		20.04.69	2	Eton	21	Jul
56.7	Melanie Canning	U20	19.05.85	1	London (He)	21	Jul
56.7	Sophie Douglas	U20	16.01.85	2	Guildford	10	Aug
	56.84			1h3	Nottingham	12	Jul
56.71 i	Rachael Kay	U23	8.09.80	3h2	Cardiff	2	Feb
56.75	Kim Searle	U20	27.12.83	3	Manchester (C)	26	May
56.79 i	Dawn Higgins		10.12.75	3	Cardiff	10	Feb
56.89	Jenny Harris		9.01.79	3	Portsmouth	11	May
56.9	Kirsten Martin		24.04.76	4	Aberdare	15	Jun
	56.91			4	Newport	8	Jun
56.93 mx	Charlotte Moore	U20	4.01.85	1	London (FP)	11	Aug
	57.0			1	Bournemouth	11	May
	57.45			3h1	Bedford	29	Jun
57.0	Nicola Gauld	U23	28.03.82	1	Aberdeen	21	Apr
	57.09			2	Grangemouth	20	Apr
	(80)						
57.0	Alex Cooke	U23	24.06.82	1	Luton	12	May
57.0	Sian Scott	U20	20.03.84	1	Bournemouth	8	Jun
57.08	Angharad James		7.04.79	5	Newport	8	Jun
57.15	Elaine Wells		30.05.78	1	Crawley	11	May
57.2	Ruth Brereton	U23	26.06.81	3	London (TB)	24	Aug
57.30	Rhianna Parker-Simpson	U20	20.07.83	1	Birmingham	25	May
57.3	Nisha Desai	U20	5.08.84	1	Gateshead	15	Jun
	57.57			1	Gateshead	12	May
57.3	Rowi Mortimer	U17	4.07.86	1	Bristol	24	Jul
57.32 i	Celia Brown		22.01.77	3s2	Glasgow	24	Feb
57.33	Alice Butler		27.07.73	3	Wakefield	7	Jul
	(90)						
57.34	Virginia Mitchell	V35	29.01.63	1	Potsdam, GER	21	Aug
57.37	Jenny Christie	U17	28.09.85	3h4	Bedford	29	Jun
57.40	Mhari MacDonald	U20	10.02.83	2J	Edinburgh	11	May
57.4	Vicky Lawrence		9.06.73	1	Blackpool	5	May
57.4	Laura Curtis	U23	2.05.81	3	Wigan	4	Aug
57.4	Rachel Newcombe	V35	25.02.67	1rB	Wigan	4	Aug
57.4	Leri Davies		31.01.79	2rB	Wigan	4	Aug
57.41	Donna Chatting	U20	30.10.83	2h2	Nottingham	12	Jul
57.45	Philippa Aukett	U20	9.09.84	1J	Crawley	11	May
57.48	Hazel Connell	U23	8.01.82	1rB	Edinburgh	28	Apr
57.5	Michele Gillham		8.10.74	1rB	Eton	4	Aug
57.5	Louise Gregory		11.05.74	1	Norwich	24	Aug

280

Additional Under 17 (1 - 7 above)

57.6	Lauren Webb		17.11.85	1	Portsmouth	6 Jul
57.62	Sarah Shuttleworth		16.08.86	2rB	Derby	8 Sep
57.7	Clare Bennett		21.09.86	1	Eton	28 Jul
(10)						
57.9	Shadina Dodds		16.08.86	1	Tipton	18 Aug
58.0	Sophie Mabbett		27.10.86	1rB	Eton	28 Jul
58.2	Eilidh Child		20.02.87	1	Middlesbrough	23 Jun
58.2	Emma-Lisa Carroll		23.03.86	1rB	Wakefield	28 Jul
58.3	Laura Robinson		11.10.85	2rB	Wakefield	28 Jul
58.4	Jenny Bliss		6.07.86	1	Colchester	18 May
58.5	Hayley Beard		2.12.85	1	Welwyn	29 Mar
58.5	Gemma Collier		25.11.85	1	Exeter	23 Jun
58.59 mx	Lois Brooks		10.01.87	1	Manchester (Str)	23 Jul
58.6	Leah Caddick		1.06.86	1	Wigan	18 Aug
(20)						
58.9	Katrina Wootton		2.09.85	2	Bedford	27 Jul
58.99	Victoria Wester		24.12.85	1rB	Edinburgh	28 Jul

Foreign

54.40	Maiteland Marks (USA)		19.09.76	1	Palafrugell, ESP	11 May
54.9	Michelle Carey (IRL)	U23	20.02.81	1	Bath	12 May
	55.25			5	Loughborough	18 May
55.51	Zoe Arnold (IRL)		10.11.76	2	Dublin (S), IRL	14 Jul
57.31	Kelly McNeice (IRL)		17.06.78	1	Antrim	29 Jun

600 Metres

1:28.8 +	Kelly Holmes	19.04.70	2m	Munich, GER	8 Aug

Under 13

1:42.2	Holly Croxford	6.12.89	1	Portsmouth	6 Jul
1:44.4	Katie Knowles	6.06.90	1	Carn Brea	18 Aug
1:44.6	Laura Wright	11.10.89	2	Southampton	6 Jul
1:44.7	Lucy Mcloughlin	17.06.91	1	Manchester (Str)	6 May
1:45.1	Aisha Green	5.10.89	1	Woking	22 Sep
1:45.6	Clare Craddock	20.12.89	1	Manchester (Str)	26 Aug
1:45.7	Stephanie James	27.09.90	1	Blackpool	22 Sep
1:46.3	Emily Wilkins	10.10.89	1	Aldershot	11 Aug
1:47.3	Louise Eley	11.10.89	2	Woking	14 Jul
(10)					
1:47.5	Lisa Butterworth	8.04.90	1	Birmingham (Un)	1 Apr
1:48.2	Samantha Mallon	13.11.90	1	Wavertree	11 May
1:48.3	Leigh Lennon	22.05.91	1	Manchester (Str)	4 May

800 Metres

1:59.30	Susan Scott		26.09.77	4	Manchester (C)	29 Jul
	2:01.03			4s1	Manchester (C)	28 Jul
	2:01.47			6	London (CP)	23 Aug
	2:02.64			1	Glasgow (S)	9 Jun
	2:02.82			2h2	Manchester (C)	27 Jul
	2:02.93			1	Barcelona, ESP	6 Sep
	2:03.89			1	Birmingham	13 Jul
	2:04.80			1	Gava, ESP	26 May
1:59.75	Charlotte Moore	U20	4.01.85	6	Manchester (C)	29 Jul
	2:00.95			3s1	Manchester (C)	28 Jul
	2:02.39			4	Manchester (C)	16 Jun
	2:03.38			2h5	Manchester (C)	27 Jul
	2:03.88			1	Edinburgh	20 Jul
	2:04.95 mp			1	Street	6 May
	2:05.00			4h1	Manchester (C)	15 Jun

1:59.83	Kelly Holmes		19.04.70	3	Munich, GER	8	Aug
	2:00.17			1	Dessau, GER	29	May
	2:00.33			4	Annecy, FRA	22	Jun
	2:00.46			1	Seville, ESP	8	Jun
	2:00.66			1s2	Munich, GER	7	Aug
	2:02.11			4	Sheffield	30	Jun
	2:03.18			1h1	Munich, GER	6	Aug
1:59.86	Jo Fenn		19.10.74	7	Manchester (C)	29	Jul
	2:00.24			1	Manchester (C)	16	Jun
	2:01.49			7	London (CP)	23	Aug
	2:02.11			3	Adelaide, AUS	23	Mar
	2:02.24			2	Malmo, SWE	13	Aug
	2:02.91			2h3	Munich, GER	6	Aug
	2:02.99			6s1	Munich, GER	7	Aug
	2:03.04			3s2	Manchester (C)	28	Jul
	2:03.10			1	La Chaux de Fonds, SUI	18	Aug
	2:03.38			1	Bedford	4	Jun
	2:03.43			3	Gothenburg, SWE	27	Aug
	2:03.70			3	Bratislava, SVK	11	Jun
	2:03.84			2h1	Manchester (C)	15	Jun
	2:04.03			4	Brisbane, AUS	13	Apr
	2:04.12			2	Birmingham	13	Jul
	2:04.17			2h4	Manchester (C)	27	Jul
	2:04.85 i			3	Glasgow	9	Mar
2:02.45	Rebecca Lyne	U23	4.07.82	5	Manchester (C)	16	Jun
	2:04.36			2h3	Manchester (C)	15	Jun
	2:04.89			2	Manchester (Wy)	3	Jun
2:03.20 mx	Helen Pattinson		2.01.74	1	Manchester (Str)	3	Sep
2:03.35 i	Jenny Meadows	U23	17.04.81	5	Birmingham	17	Feb
	2:04.34 i			1h1	Cardiff	2	Feb
	2:04.46			2	Riga, LAT	31	May
2:03.70	Lucy Vaughan		20.04.69	1	Watford	14	Aug
	2:04.12			2	Barcelona, ESP	6	Sep
	2:04.4 mx			1	Watford	18	Sep
	2:04.66			1	Ashford	18	Aug
	2:04.7			1	Coventry	19	May
2:03.76 i	Hayley Tullett		17.02.73	6	Birmingham	17	Feb
	2:06.39			2	Solihull	22	Jun
2:03.86	Lisa Dobriskey	U20	23.12.83	2	Watford	14	Aug
	2:04.8			1	Eton	4	Aug
	(10)						
2:03.93	Emma Davies		9.10.78	6s2	Manchester (C)	28	Jul
	2:04.02			4h2	Manchester (C)	27	Jul
	2:04.67 i			7	Birmingham	17	Feb
	2:04.87 i			2	Cardiff	10	Feb
2:04.11	Jemma Simpson	U20	10.02.84	4	Kingston, JAM	19	Jul
2:04.69	Rachel Newcombe	V35	25.02.67	3	Watford	14	Aug
2:04.72	Alex Carter	U23	1.04.80	1	Manchester (Wy)	3	Jun
	2:04.99			7	Manchester (C)	16	Jun
62 performances to 2:05.0 by 14 athletes including 6 indoors							
2:05.56	Joanna Ross	U23	18.02.81	2	Glasgow (S)	9	Jun
2:05.87	Katrina Wootton	U17	2.09.85	4	Watford	14	Aug
2:06.06	Hayley Ovens		5.12.75	2h2	Birmingham	12	Jul
2:06.14	Catherine Riley	U23	4.06.82	3h3	Manchester (C)	15	Jun
2:06.23	Jennifer Ward		22.09.78	3h3	Birmingham	12	Jul
2:06.58	Vicky Lawrence		9.06.73	1	Jarrow	1	Jun
	(20)						
2:06.60	Mary McClung		19.12.71	3	Bedford	4	Jun
2:06.75	Sarah Bull		4.06.75	1	Manchester (Str)	23	Jul
2:06.77	Jane McKay		22.04.77	4	Eton	3	Jul
2:06.82	Rachael Thompson	U17	15.11.85	6	Manchester (Wy)	3	Jun

2:06.95 mx	Kelly Caffel		10.02.79	1	Manchester (Str)	20	Aug
2:06.97	Donna Riding	U20	28.11.83	6	Watford	14	Aug
2:07.10	Karen Johns	U23	18.08.80	2	Jarrow	1	Jun
2:07.25	Jeina Mitchell		21.01.75	1	Watford	1	Jun
2:07.35	Natalie Lewis	U23	25.05.82	5	Eton	3	Jul
2:07.4 mx	Danielle Barnes	U17	8.10.85	2	Exeter	30	Apr
2:11.27 i				3	Birmingham	17	Feb
(30)							
2:07.44	Laura Finucane	U17	3.08.86	1	Nottingham	13	Jul
2:07.54	Kerry Gillibrand		13.09.76	1	Birmingham	6	Jul
2:07.98 i	Hayley Beard	U17	2.12.85	1	Birmingham	24	Feb
2:08.91				7	Watford	14	Aug
2:08.10	Ruth Little		24.05.84	5	Melbourne, AUS	14	Dec
2:08.35 mx	Karen Hill		6.11.72	3	Manchester (Str)	20	Aug
2:09.78				3	Birmingham	6	Jul
2:08.36	Sally Evans		14.05.75	4h2	Manchester (C)	15	Jun
2:08.36	Sue Evans	U23	19.09.81	4h3	Birmingham	12	Jul
2:08.45 mx	Louise Whittaker	U23	29.11.82	1	Manchester (Str)	23	Jul
2:09.15				1	London (He)	3	Aug
2:08.62	Tina Brown		22.08.76	5h3	Birmingham	12	Jul
2:08.9	Morag MacLarty	U17	10.02.86	3	Gorizia, ITA	6	Jul
2:08.98	Sarah Bouchard		23.10.74	1	Manchester (Str)	20	Aug
(40)							
2:09.00	Faye Fullerton	U20	31.05.84	1J	Basildon	12	May
2:09.16	Charlene Snelgrove	U23	6.05.82	1h1	Jarrow	1	Jun
2:09.17	Sarah Salmon		9.09.74	4	Canberra, AUS	28	Mar
2:09.19 i	Jillian Jones		23.12.69	4h1	Cardiff	2	Feb
2:09.90				6	Eton	3	Jul
2:09.25	Charlotte Best	U20	7.03.85	4	Bedford	4	Jun
2:09.53	Suzanne Hasler	U23	7.04.82	5	Merksem, BEL	17	Aug
2:09.59	Lesley Owusu		21.12.78	2	Stanford, USA	29	Mar
2:09.66	Bev Blakeman		4.04.74	2h1	Jarrow	1	Jun
2:09.74	Anna Simmonds	U17	22.09.86	3	Glasgow (S)	20	Jul
2:10.2	Claire Entwistle		9.12.76	1	Scunthorpe	7	Jul
(50)							
2:10.23	Nisha Desai	U20	5.08.84	2	Watford	1	Sep
2:10.31	Danielle Thornal		9.08.75	3	Waltham, MA, USA	1	Jun
2:10.32	Alice Butler		27.07.73	1rB	Manchester (Wy)	3	Jun
2:10.46	Ellen Leggate		4.02.78	1	Oxford	26	Jun
2:10.65 i	Roseline Addo	U23	7.06.80	3	Chapel Hill NC, USA	27	Feb
2:10.95	Lois Brooks	U17	10.01.87	2rB	Manchester (Wy)	3	Jun
2:11.0	Nina Anderson		26.01.72	1	London (FP)	25	Aug
2:11.10	Adele Bevan	U20	26.03.84	3	Watford	31	Jul
2:11.1	Dorothea Lee		28.07.77	1	London (ME)	12	Jun
2:11.16 mx	Nikki Daniels	U23	25.08.82	1rB	Manchester (Str)	3	Sep
2:12.4				2	Cardiff	4	Aug
(60)							
2:11.23	Kirsty Baird		29.08.71	4	Glasgow (S)	9	Jun
2:11.29	Nikki Hamblin	U15	20.05.88	2	Birmingham	11	Aug
2:11.3	Hannah England	U17	6.03.87	1rB	Solihull	22	Jun
2:11.3	Anouska McConnell		13.04.76	2	Scunthorpe	7	Jul
2:11.38	Lisa Whigham	U23	14.08.80	5	Glasgow (S)	9	Jun
2:11.4	Abby Westley	U17	15.07.87	1	Cudworth	11	May
2:11.5	Emma Brady		3.01.74	1	Aberdare	15	Jun
2:11.53	Nicola Gauld	U23	28.03.82	2	Edinburgh	12	May
2:11.53	Stacey Johnson	U17	15.04.87	4	Nottingham	13	Jul
2:11.68	Katie Brennan	U23	27.04.82	2	Manchester (Str)	6	Aug
(70)							
2:11.7	Kathryn Sage		27.03.76	1	Cardiff	4	Aug
2:11.80	Vicki Jamison		19.05.77	4	London (He)	3	Aug
2:11.83	Danielle Woods	U20	2.10.84	1rB	Birmingham	6	Jul

2:11.9	Sally Oldfield	U20	25.06.84	1J	Corby	11	May
2:11.97	Debbie Jones		6.01.78	1rB	Eton	3	Jul
2:11.98	Claire Gibson	U23	25.12.82	7	Glasgow (S)	9	Jun
2:12.10	Barbara Parker	U23	8.11.82	6h3	Birmingham	12	Jul
2:12.1	Joanne Dawes	U20	4.10.83	1	Birmingham	18	Aug
2:12.13	Karen Montador		14.05.79	3	Edinburgh	12	May
2:12.30	Lizzie McWilliams	U17	2.06.87	2	Tullamore, IRL	3	Aug
	(80)						
2:12.31	Charlotte Browning	U15	8.10.87	4	Watford	31	Jul
2:12.40	Louisa Wood	U23	31.10.80	3rB	Watford	14	Aug
2:12.56	Lucy Pringle		3.08.78	4	Watford	1	Jun
2:12.70	Lynne Gallagher		21.11.74	2rB	Eton	3	Jul
2:12.70	Philippa Aukett	U20	9.09.84	4	Nottingham	13	Jul
2:12.74	Sarah Heath	V40	4.01.62	5rB	Watford	14	Aug
2:12.81	Carolyn Plateau	U15	22.08.88	1	Nottingham	13	Jul
2:12.85	Claire Hiscock/East		10.03.70	6rB	Watford	14	Aug
2:12.87	Eleanor Baker	U20	11.12.83	3	Ashford	18	Aug
2:12.93	Sally Read-Cayton	V35	1.04.65	8rB	Watford	14	Aug
	(90)						
2:12.98	Hollie Smith	U20	9.12.84	2J	Basildon	12	May
2:13.00	Julie Hollman		16.02.77	H	Gotzis, AUT	2	Jun
2:13.0	Hannah Whitmore	U20	24.02.84	3rB	Solihull	22	Jun
2:13.05	Laurie Cossey	U23	24.11.81	6	Watford	1	Jun
2:13.10	Sara Stevenson	U23	12.11.82	4	Bedford	30	Jun
2:13.1	Rachael Nathan	U17	27.04.86	1	Grantham	12	May
2:13.1	Dominique Oughton	U23	2.01.81	3	Derby	11	Aug
2:13.13	Rachel Jones	U17	25.09.85	1	Inverness	1	Sep
2:13.2	Sue Cripsey	U23	8.01.81	1	Great Yarmouth	12	May
2:13.21	Caroline Nelson	U17	1.07.86	1rC	Manchester (Wy)	3	Jun

Additional Under 17 (1 - 13 above)

2:13.6	Laura Kirk		20.02.87	2	Cudworth	11	May
2:14.07	Linzi Snow		8.06.87	1rC	Watford	14	Aug
2:14.53	Sara Luck		18.11.86	1	Watford	26	May
2:14.65 mx	Aimee Simcox		5.07.86	1rC	Manchester (Str)	3	Sep
2:14.79 mx	Katie Harrison		22.10.86	2rC	Manchester (Str)	3	Sep
2:16.0				2	Nuneaton	21	Jul
2:14.8	Suzanne Boyes		26.05.87	3	Cudworth	11	May
2:14.98	Stephanie Reynolds		15.06.86	1h2	Grangemouth	25	Aug
	(20)						
2:15.11	Helen Glover		17.06.86	4	Street	6	May
2:15.2	Isabelle Stoate		16.07.86	2rD	Watford	14	Aug
2:15.3	Vicky Holland		12.01.86	1	Abingdon	8	Sep
2:15.36	Clare Bennett		21.09.86	2	Watford	26	May
2:15.38	Jenna Hill		16.10.85	5rC	Watford	14	Aug
2:15.45	Rosanna Mooney		14.07.86	4	Glasgow (S)	20	Jul
2:15.8	Jo Harper		11.05.87	1	Birmingham	9	Jun
2:15.82	Gemma Turtle		15.05.86	4	Watford	22	May
2:15.84	Lauren Cunningham		22.08.87	3	Watford	26	May
2:15.9	Helen Hudson		10.01.86	3	Wakefield	28	Jul
	(30)						
2:16.02	Josephine Rhodes		22.03.86	3rC	Eton	3	Jul
2:16.07	Georgina Riddiough		28.11.86	4h4	Nottingham	12	Jul
2:16.23	Nicola Maddick		6.08.87	4	Manchester (Wy)	26	May
2:16.5	Sharon Lamont		12.08.86	1	Glasgow (S)	5	May
2:16.57	Claire Wilson		7.11.85	2	Grangemouth	25	Aug
2:16.6	Emma-Lisa Carroll		23.03.86	2	Birmingham	22	Jun
2:16.63	Emma Hopkins		16.09.86	2	Birmingham	1	Sep
2:16.64 i	Leanne Muscroft		2.12.85	6	Birmingham	24	Feb
2:17.00				4h3	Nottingham	12	Jul
2:16.67	Hayley Rule		11.10.86	8rC	Watford	14	Aug

2:16.70	Sarah Paterson	22.06.87	3	Birmingham	1 Sep
2:16.76	Debbie Brett	9.09.85	5h4	Nottingham	12 Jul
2:16.8	Elysia Ridley	3.12.86	1	Cheltenham	6 May
2:16.82	Leonie Smith	20.12.86	1rD	Eton	3 Jul
2:16.9	Kelly Rodmell	26.11.85	1	Gateshead	15 Jun
2:17.0	Elaine Renouf	2.07.87	1rB	Glasgow (S)	5 May

Additional Under 15 (1 - 3 above)

2:13.57	Louise Collier	14.02.88	2	Nottingham	13 Jul
2:13.95	Megan Foley	14.04.88	3	Nottingham	13 Jul
2:15.13 mx	Emma Jackson	7.06.88	2rD	Manchester (Str)	23 Jul
2:16.63			3h2	Nottingham	12 Jul
2:15.6	Lyndsey Barr	19.01.88	1	London (Nh)	2 Jun
2:16.0	Danielle McCann	22.09.87	1	Manchester (C)	25 May
2:16.04	Danielle Christmas	21.12.87	4	Nottingham	13 Jul
2:16.36	Lora Symonds	7.06.88	2h2	Nottingham	12 Jul
(10)					
2:16.4	Emma Macalister-Hall	19.02.89	2	Manchester (C)	25 May
2:17.0	Lucy Bowers	12.01.88	2	Eton	2 Jun
2:17.60 i	Emma Cloggie	10.07.88	2	Birmingham	24 Feb
2:18.51			P	Grangemouth	22 Jun
2:17.7	Laura Warner	8.03.88	1	Watford	12 May
2:17.71	Lauren Baird	21.09.87	1	Grangemouth	14 Jun
2:17.81	Cecilia Savundra	29.12.87	3	Kingston	12 May
2:17.96	Emily Pidgeon	1.06.89	2	Birmingham	25 May
2:18.0	Ellie McLoughlin	9.02.89	3	Manchester (C)	25 May
2:18.0	Justine Kinney	6.04.88	1	Birmingham	15 Jun
2:18.0	Laura Scougall	21.01.89	2	Birmingham	15 Jun
(20)					
2:18.47	Hannah Brooks	25.06.88	3rB	Watford	31 Jul
2:18.5	Sarah Waldron	11.02.88	2	Watford	12 May
2:18.6 mx	Emma Haley	23.02.88	2rC	Watford	18 Sep
2:19.5			1	Colchester	16 Jun
2:18.68	Lucie Howarth	15.12.87	5	Watford	26 May
2:18.8	Thalia Jones	16.09.87	2	Cudworth	11 May

Under 13

2:22.02	Bryony Swanson	18.10.89	1	Glasgow (S)	2 Jun
2:22.3	Rebecca Taylor	17.11.89	1	Bromley	2 Jun
2:24.3	Lisa Butterworth	8.04.90	1	Birmingham	16 Jun
2:25.2	Rebecca Shield	1.10.89	1	Jarrow	7 Jul
2:25.2	Abbie Johnson	29.03.90	1	Cleckheaton	21 Jul
2:25.4	Clare Craddock	20.12.89	1	Cleckheaton	1 Sep
2:25.6	Debby Samuels	8.02.90	1	Horsham	6 Jul
2:25.6	Emily Wilkins	10.10.89	1	Abingdon	21 Jul
2:25.92	Katie Knowles	6.06.90	4	London (He)	25 Aug
2:25.97	Lyndsey Sharp	11.07.90	1	Birmingham	1 Sep
(10)					
2:26.3	Jordan Kinney	15.05.90	3	Birmingham	16 Jun
2:26.68	Abbey Mcghee	2.03.90	2	Glasgow (S)	2 Jun
2:27.0	Hannah Stammas	16.01.90	2	Abingdon	21 Jul
2:27.59	Kirsty Hunter	16.12.89	1P	Grangemouth	22 Jun
2:27.62	Laura Kennedy	10.09.89	1	Grangemouth	24 Aug
2:27.74	Leigh Lennon	22.05.91	1	Manchester (Str)	20 Jul
2:28.0	Laura Evans	22.12.89	1	Bury	
2:28.08	Lucy Mcloughlin	17.06.91	1	Manchester (Str)	11 May

Foreign

| 2:01.92 | *Tanya Blake (MLT)* | *16.01.71* | *4* | *Portland, USA* | *18 May* |
| 2:04.55 | *Kelly McNeice (IRL)* | *17.06.78* | *3* | *Riga, LAT* | *31 May* |

1000 Metres - Under 13

3:07.5	Rebecca Taylor	17.11.89	1	Bromley	16	Jun
3:13.4	Emily Wilkins	10.10.89	1	Bracknell	10	Jul
3:15.5	Sarah Hopkinson	11.08.91	5	Cheltenham	24	Jul
3:15.7	Megan Edwards	11.01.90	1	Ashford	4	Aug

1200 Metres - Under 13

3:53.40	Bryony Swanson	18.10.89	1	Inverness	21	Apr
3:53.7	Lucy Mcloughlin	17.06.91	1	Blackpool	21	Jul
3:56.0	Rebecca Taylor	17.11.89	1	Crawley	21	Jul
3:57.3	Emily Wilkins	10.10.89	1	Eton	2	Jun
3:58.06	Claire Hollis	8.11.89	1	Birmingham	31	Aug
3:59.8	Sarah Hopkinson	11.08.91	1	Swindon	21	Jul
3:59.9	Stephanie James	27.09.90	2	Blackpool	21	Jul
4:00.3	Laura Murphy	10.12.89	1	Birmingham	1	Sep
4:01.0	Laura Evans	22.12.89	1	Preston	9	May
4:01.5	Lisa Butterworth	8.04.90	1	Telford	30	Jun
4:01.5	(10) Kayleigh Brown	24.11.89	1	Carmarthen	21	Jul
4:01.6	Sophie Crumly	6.07.90	1	Oxford	9	Jul
4:01.7	Hayley Luke	3.01.90	2	Oxford	9	Jul

1500 Metres

4:01.10	Helen Pattinson	2.01.74	3	Monaco, MON	19	Jul
	4:05.20		4	Annecy, FRA	23	Jun
	4:06.27		4	Hengelo, NED	2	Jun
	4:06.32		10	Berlin, GER	6	Sep
	4:06.98		2	Birmingham	14	Jul
	4:07.62		3	Manchester (C)	31	Jul
	4:08.66		1	Manchester (C)	16	Jun
	4:09.66		5h2	Munich, GER	9	Aug
	4:10.59		1	Izegem,	8	Jun
	4:17.39		3h1	Manchester (C)	30	Jul
	4:18.66		1h2	Manchester (C)	15	Jun
4:01.91	Kelly Holmes	19.04.70	3	Rome, ITA	12	Jul
	4:03.93		1	Hengelo, NED	2	Jun
	4:05.99		1	Manchester (C)	31	Jul
	4:06.02		1	Birmingham	14	Jul
	4:06.15		3	Saint-Denis, FRA	5	Jul
	4:08.11		4h1	Munich, GER	9	Aug
	4:08.48		12	Berlin, GER	6	Sep
	4:10.38		2	Glasgow (S)	18	Aug
	4:11.27		1h2	Manchester (C)	30	Jul
4:07.52	Hayley Tullett	17.02.73	2	Manchester (C)	31	Jul
	4:07.76		13	Monaco, MON	19	Jul
	4:08.23		3	Birmingham	14	Jul
	4:08.88 i		3	Piraeus, GRE	20	Feb
	4:10.63		13	Oslo, NOR	28	Jun
	4:10.68		7h3	Munich, GER	9	Aug
	4:12.43 i		4	Stockholm, SWE	6	Feb
	4:13.58 i		3h1	Vienna, AUT	2	Mar
	4:17.14 i		9	Vienna, AUT	3	Mar
	4:17.36		2h1	Manchester (C)	30	Jul
4:09.79	Susan Scott	26.09.77	2	Manchester (C)	16	Jun
	4:12.90		5	Glasgow (S)	18	Aug
	4:14.49		1	Loughborough	18	May
	4:16.25		1	Edinburgh	11	May
	4:19.62		1h1	Manchester (C)	15	Jun
4:11.16	Joanne Pavey	20.09.73	4	Birmingham	14	Jul

4:11.24	Rachel Newcombe	V35	25.02.67	3	Eton	3	Jul
4:11.81				5	Birmingham	14	Jul
4:13.56				8	Manchester (C)	31	Jul
4:13.64				5	Manchester (C)	16	Jun
4:15.18				6h2	Manchester (C)	30	Jul
4:16.43				2	Manchester (Wy)	3	Jun
4:19.07				4h2	Manchester (C)	15	Jun
4:19.86				1	Newport	8	Jun
4:11.8	Kerry Gillibrand		13.09.76	4	Eton	3	Jul
4:14.53				6	Manchester (C)	16	Jun
4:15.54				10	Manchester (C)	31	Jul
4:16.14				1	Manchester (Wy)	3	Jun
4:17.53				7	Birmingham	14	Jul
4:18.29				4h1	Manchester (C)	30	Jul
4:18.94				3h2	Manchester (C)	15	Jun
4:12.21	Sarah Bull		4.06.75	6	Birmingham	14	Jul
4:12.97				9	Cork, IRL	6	Jul
4:14.67				7	Manchester (C)	16	Jun
4:14.79				2	Watford	14	Aug
4:17.90				5	Manchester (Wy)	3	Jun
4:18.79				2h2	Manchester (C)	15	Jun
4:12.47	Hayley Ovens		5.12.75	4	Manchester (C)	16	Jun
4:15.39				7h2	Manchester (C)	30	Jul
4:16.95				12	Manchester (C)	31	Jul
4:17.03				4	Manchester (Wy)	3	Jun
4:18.53				3	Loughborough	18	May
4:19.30				1	Grangemouth	1	May
4:12/13 c	Paula Radcliffe		17.12.73	m	Monaco, MON	19	Jul
(10)							
4:13.94	Charlotte Moore	U20	4.01.85	1	Watford	14	Aug
4:16.53				3	Manchester (Wy)	3	Jun
4:14.58	Lisa Dobriskey	U20	23.12.83	3	Solihull	22	Jun
4:14.72				4	Kingston, JAM	21	Jul
4:19.83				1h2	Kingston, JAM	19	Jul
4:19.95				4	Loughborough	18	May
4:15.65	Catherine Berry		8.10.75	12	Cork, IRL	6	Jul
4:16.25				3	Heusden,	20	Jul
4:18.36 i+	Kathy Butler		22.10.73	3m	New York NY, USA	19	Jan
4:18.42				1	Glasgow (S)	9	Jun
4:19.47	Natalie Lewis	U23	25.05.82	5h2	Manchester (C)	15	Jun
4:19.93	Katrina Wootton	U17	2.09.85	6h2	Manchester (C)	15	Jun
4:19.98	Freya Murray	U20	20.09.83	2	Edinburgh	11	May
	77 performances to 4:20.0 by 17 athletes including 5 indoors, 1 estimated						
4:20.21	Sarah Salmon		9.09.74	1	Canberra, AUS	23	Nov
4:20.85 mx	Vicky Lawrence		9.06.73	1	Manchester (Str)	28	May
4:22.85				1	Bedford	26	May
4:21.15	Jo Wilkinson		2.05.73	1	Watford	2	Jun
(20)							
4:21.18	Ellen Leggate		4.02.78	4h1	Manchester (C)	15	Jun
4:21.69	Clare Martin		18.05.76	5h1	Manchester (C)	15	Jun
4:21.76	Julie Mitchell		3.10.74	6h1	Manchester (C)	15	Jun
4:21.92	Debbie Sullivan		13.02.72	2	Watford	2	Jun
4:21.93	Louise Whittaker	U23	29.11.82	3	Watford	14	Aug
4:22.13	Sharon Morris		5.07.68	4	Watford	14	Aug
4:22.25	Tina Brown		22.08.76	5	Watford	14	Aug
4:23.30 mx	Rachael Nathan	U17	27.04.86	1	Watford	28	Aug
4:26.9				1	Grantham	11	May
4:23.56	Jo Fenn		19.10.74	1	Palafrugell, ESP	11	May
4:24.4	Lucy Wright		17.11.69	1rB	Solihull	22	Jun
(30)							
4:24.53	Danielle Barnes	U17	8.10.85	11	Manchester (Wy)	3	Jun

4:24.65	Jo Ankier	U23	5.08.82	7h1	Manchester (C)	15	Jun
4:24.76	Faye Fullerton	U20	31.05.84	11	Loughborough	18	May
4:25.18	Dorothea Lee		28.07.77	12	Loughborough	18	May
4:25.18	Rebecca Lyne	U23	4.07.82	7	Watford	14	Aug
4:25.3	Sally Oldfield	U20	25.06.84	1	Corby	12	May
4:25.88	Gillian Palmer	U23	30.12.80	3	Edinburgh	11	May
4:26.25	Vicky Holland	U17	12.01.86	2	Nottingham	13	Jul
4:26.38	Kate Reed	U23	28.09.82	1	Birmingham	2	Jun
4:26.40	Sally Evans		14.05.75	12	Manchester (Wy)	3	Jun
(40)							
4:26.43	Jemma Simpson	U20	10.02.84	1	Street	6	May
4:26.85	Sue Cripsey	U23	8.01.81	5	Niort, FRA	3	Aug
4:27.11	Maria Skelton	U23	18.05.80	4	Dublin (S), IRL	14	Jul
4:27.54	Claire Entwistle		9.12.76	2rB	Manchester (Wy)	3	Jun
4:27.68 mx	Suzanne Owen		5.05.79	1	Manchester (Str)	6	Aug
4:27.77	Jo Harper	U17	11.05.87	3	Nottingham	13	Jul
4:27.84	Eleanor Baker	U20	11.12.83	8	Watford	14	Aug
4:27.85	Tara Krzywicki		9.03.74	1	Birmingham (Un)	19	Jun
4:28.04	Danielle Thornal		9.08.75	8h1	Manchester (C)	15	Jun
4:28.07	Catherine Dugdale		29.11.74	9	Watford	14	Aug
(50)							
4:28.3	Lauren Deadman	U20	27.03.84	1	Eton	21	Jul
4:28.56	Katie Thomas		20.12.78	10	Watford	14	Aug
4:28.66 i	Alex Carter	U23	1.04.80	3	Cardiff	3	Feb
4:28.78 mx	Liz Proctor		31.10.72	2	Manchester (Str)	6	Aug
4:29.10	Ursula Counsell	U23	7.12.82	3rB	Manchester (Wy)	3	Jun
4:29.1	Claire Smallwood		15.03.77	1	Darlington	4	Aug
4:29.4	Danielle Woods	U20	2.10.84	3rB	Solihull	22	Jun
4:29.5	Louise Damen	U23	12.10.82	1	Kingston	27	Jul
4:29.59	Penny Thackray		18.08.74	2	Jarrow	1	Jun
4:29.66 mx	Gemma Phillips	U23	27.10.80	3	Manchester (Str)	6	Aug
(60)							
4:29.70	Rosanna Iannone		15.06.79	11	Watford	14	Aug
4:29.91	Charlotte Best	U20	7.03.85	1rB	Eton	3	Jul
4:29.91	Karen Hill		6.11.72	3	Birmingham	6	Jul
4:30.00	Morag MacLarty	U17	10.02.86	1	Grangemouth	25	Aug
4:30.12	Charlotte Browning	U15	8.10.87	2rB	Eton	3	Jul
4:30.2	Jane Potter	U23	24.10.81	3	Watford	1	Sep
4:30.35	Sandra Andreou	V35	24.07.62	4	Watford	2	Jun
4:30.45	Nikki Hamblin	U15	20.05.88	1	Nottingham	13	Jul
4:30.6	Hayley Yelling		3.01.74	1	London (ME)	11	May
4:30.66	Rachel Felton		27.06.79	12	Durham NC, USA	6	Apr
(70)							
4:30.7	Meredith Pannett		13.06.71	1	London (DC)	12	Jul
4:30.8	Sonia Thomas		16.05.79	3	Loughborough	5	Jun
4:31.0	Bryony Frost	U20	21.02.84	6rB	Solihull	22	Jun
4:31.05 mx	Sarah Bouchard		23.10.74	4	Manchester (Str)	6	Aug
4:31.17	Charlotte Wickham	U20	21.06.85	1J	Gateshead	12	May
4:31.19	Debbie Jones		6.01.78	5rB	Manchester (Wy)	3	Jun
4:31.30	Rachel Jones	U17	25.09.85	2	Glasgow (S)	20	Jul
4:31.5 mx	Joanna Ross	U23	18.02.81	1	Glasgow	3	Sep
4:31.79	Louisa Wood	U23	31.10.80	7rB	Manchester (Wy)	3	Jun
4:31.89	Kirsty Law	U15	20.01.88	2	Nottingham	13	Jul
(80)							
4:31.94	Zoe Jelbert	U20	21.01.84	8rB	Manchester (Wy)	3	Jun
4:32.19 mx	Donna Riding	U20	28.11.83	2	Manchester (Str)	3	Sep
4:32.86				1	Derby	8	Sep
4:32.2	Vicky Webster	U20	14.08.84	1	London (He)	21	Jul
4:32.22	Bev Blakeman		4.04.74	13	Manchester (Wy)	3	Jun

2002 - W - 1500

4:32.2 mx	Hayley Beard	U17	2.12.85	1	Watford	18	Sep
4:40.3				1	London (Nh)	7	Sep
4:32.32 i	Helen Zenner	U23	15.08.82	1	Cardiff	10	Feb
4:32.58	Emily Pidgeon	U15	1.06.89	3	Nottingham	13	Jul
4:32.60	Jennifer Pereira	U20	8.08.85	2	Ashford	18	Aug
4:32.83 i	Karen Montador		14.05.79	2	Glasgow	20	Jan
4:32.9	Kathryn Frost	U20	21.02.84	8rB	Solihull	22	Jun
(90)							
4:33.05	Hannah England	U17	6.03.87	4	Nottingham	13	Jul
4:33.1	Jilly Ingman		17.08.78	1	Lincoln	7	Jul
4:33.25	Frances Briscoe	U20	12.04.83	3	Watford	26	May
4:33.48	Ruth Proctor	U20	4.05.84	3	Wakefield	7	Jul
4:33.76	Elaine Renouf	U17	2.07.87	2	Edinburgh	11	May
4:33.8	Nikki Daniels	U23	25.08.82	3	Yate	7	Jul
4:33.8 mx	Gemma Turtle	U17	15.05.86	2	Watford	21	Aug
4:34.16	Rachael Ogden		23.07.79	5	Watford	2	Jun
4:35.01	Abby Westley	U17	15.07.87	5	Nottingham	13	Jul
4:35.49	Leonie Smith	U17	20.12.86	6	Street	6	May

Additional Under 17 (1 - 13 above)

4:36.4 mx	Josephine Rhodes		22.03.86	3	Watford	24	Apr
4:37.42				8	Street	6	May
4:37.51	Stephanie Wilson		18.10.86	6	Nottingham	13	Jul
4:37.94	Helen Glover		17.06.86	2	Watford	26	May
4:37.60	Becky Ellis		20.12.86	1rC	Manchester (Wy)	3	Jun
4:37.84 mx	Rachael Thompson		15.11.85	1	Manchester (Str)	17	Sep
4:38.7	Suzanne Boyes		26.05.87	1	Wakefield	21	Apr
4:39.55	Sarah Ponsford		15.05.87	7	Nottingham	13	Jul
(20)							
4:39.83	Susie Hignett		26.02.86	8	Nottingham	13	Jul
4:40.27	Jenna Hill		16.10.85	3	Manchester (Wy)	25	May
4:40.30	Eloise Pittwood		4.12.85	9	Nottingham	13	Jul
4:40.9	Stacey Johnson		15.04.87	1	Nuneaton	21	Jul
4:41.14	Isabelle Stoate		16.07.86	8rB	Eton	3	Jul
4:41.5	Sharon Lamont		12.08.86	1	Derby	21	Jul
4:41.5 mx	Rosanna Mooney		14.07.86	1	Dumfries	28	Jul
4:41.58	Nicola Maddick		6.08.87	4	Manchester (Wy)	25	May
4:42.42	Nicola Sykes		30.06.87	5	Watford	26	May
4:43.65 mx	Helen Hudson		10.01.86	6	Manchester (Str)	6	Aug
4:43.68				2	Manchester (Str)	23	Jul
4:43.98	Emma-Lisa Carroll		23.03.86	2	Birmingham	1	Sep
(30)							
4:45.18 mx	Emma Hunt		25.04.86	2rC	Watford	31	Jul
4:45.2	Louise Durman		23.11.86	1	Abingdon	8	Sep
4:45.5	Victoria Calloway		22.03.86	1	Birmingham	9	Jun
4:45.54 i	Emma Whittaker		31.10.85	2	Cardiff	16	Feb
4:45.73 mx	Linzi Snow		8.06.87	1rE	Watford	31	Jul
4:46.26	Cara Dowden		11.05.87	7	Glasgow (S)	20	Jul
4:46.29	Lucy Ferguson		11.06.87	6h2	Nottingham	12	Jul
4:46.43	Laura Bickerstaff		10.11.85	3	Tullamore, IRL	3	Aug

Additional Under 15 (1 - 4 above)

4:39.20 mx	Non Stanford		8.01.89	1rB	Street	6	May
4:39.58	Laura Dowsing		17.06.89	4	Nottingham	13	Jul
4:40.34	Emma Pallant		4.06.89	6rB	Eton	3	Jul
4:40.9	Danielle Christmas		21.12.87	1	Crawley	21	Jul
4:41.6	Megan Foley		14.04.88	2	Crawley	21	Jul
4:41.74	Hannah Jones		9.06.88	3h1	Nottingham	12	Jul
(10)							

4:42.0	Emma Jackson	7.06.88	1	Nuneaton	21	Jul
4:42.18	Gillian Moss	6.10.88	1	Watford	26	May
4:42.3	Natalie Real	14.11.87	1	Street	19	Jun
4:43.40 mx	Claire Tarplee	22.09.88	5rB	Street	6	May
4:43.60	Catherine Conway	30.03.88	6	Nottingham	13	Jul
4:44.09	Sarah Waldron	11.02.88	2	Watford	26	May
4:44.60	Charlie Gaspar	7.09.87	5h1	Nottingham	12	Jul
4:45.68	Emily Collinge	27.02.88	7h1	Nottingham	12	Jul
4:46.3	Carolyn Plateau	22.08.88	1	Abingdon	11	May
4:46.55	Gemma Curley	13.05.88	2rC	Watford	14	Aug
	(20)					
4:46.88	Laura Quine	16.02.88	1	Manchester (C)	25	May
4:47.47	India Lee	31.05.88	4h2	Nottingham	12	Jul
4:47.82	Lucy Bowers	12.01.88	4	Watford	26	May

Under 13

4:53.78	Sarah Simpson	22.11.89	1	London (BP)	6	Jul
4:59.7	Lucy McLoughlin	17.06.91	1	Wigan	13	Jul
4:59.9	Bryony Swanson	18.10.89	1	Grangemouth	15	Jun
4:59.9	Katie Knowles	6.06.90	8rC	Exeter	30	Jul
5:01.2	Sarah Hopkinson	11.08.91	1	Worcester	13	Aug
5:02.0	Carys Davies	9.05.90	1	Newport	13	Jul
5:02.9	Rebecca Taylor	17.11.89	1	Bromley	1	Sep
5:06.0	Yasmin Smith	19.10.89	1	Kingston	28	Jul
5:07.7	Lucy Gemmell	20.10.89	1	Warrington	18	Sep

Foreign

4:16.46	*Kelly McNeice (IRL)*	*17.06.78*	*11*	*Manchester (C)*	*31*	*Jul*
4:22.98	*Tanya Blake (MLT)*	*16.01.71*	*4*	*Walnut CA, USA*	*21*	*Apr*
4:30.97	*Stephanie Van Graan (RSA)*	*4.02.77*	*4*	*Birmingham*	*6*	*Jul*

1 Mile

4:32.83	Kelly Holmes	19.04.70	3	San Francisco, USA	15	Sep
4:36.70 i	Kathy Butler	22.10.73	3	New York NY, USA	19	Jan
4:41.95	Catherine Berry	8.10.75	5	San Francisco, USA	15	Sep

2000 Metres

5:37.01 +	Paula Radcliffe	17.12.73	1m	Monaco, MON	19	Jul
5:53.56 +			1m	Manchester (C)	28	Jul
5:42.5 +	Joanne Pavey	20.09.73	5m	Brussels, BEL	30	Aug

3000 Metres

8:22.20	Paula Radcliffe	17.12.73	2	Monaco, MON	19	Jul
8:48.04 +			1m	Manchester (C)	28	Jul
8:56.84 +			1m	Munich, GER	6	Aug
8:31.27	Joanne Pavey	20.09.73	4	Brussels, BEL	30	Aug
8:52.6 +			3m	Manchester (C)	28	Jul
8:54.2 +			6m	Berlin, GER	6	Sep
8:54.79			1	Loughborough	18	May
8:57.71			5	Paris, FRA	14	Sep
9:04 +c			m	Rome, ITA	12	Jul
9:14.4 +			4m	Madrid, ESP	21	Sep
8:58.33	Helen Pattinson	2.01.74	9	Sheffield	30	Jun
9:02.79	Catherine Berry	8.10.75	7	Linz, AUT	19	Aug
9:09.76			10	Eugene OR, USA	26	May
9:12.09 i			1	Blacksburg, USA	23	Feb
9:19.59			1	Knoxville TN, USA	11	Apr
9:04.51	Kathy Butler	22.10.73	8	Eugene OR, USA	26	May
9:09.36			5	Annecy, FRA	22	Jun

9:07.98	Hayley Tullett			17.02.73	2	Loughborough	18 May
9:12.47	Gillian Palmer	U23		30.12.80	1	Eton	3 Jul
9:13.78					3	Loughborough	18 May
9:14.27	Dianne Henaghan	V35		6.08.65	4	Barcelona, ESP	6 Sep
9:14.58					1	Edinburgh	20 Jul
9:17.61 mx	Charlotte Dale	U20		23.03.84	1	Watford	10 Jul
9:25.04					5	Loughborough	18 May
9:18.11	Sarah Bull			4.06.75	6	Barcelona, ESP	6 Sep
(10)							
9:19.43	Liz Yelling			5.12.74	4	Loughborough	18 May
9:19.50 +	Hayley Yelling			3.01.74	1m	Manchester (C)	15 Jun
9:28.3					1	Eton	21 Jul

26 performances to 9:20.0 by 12 athletes including 1 indoors

9:20.2 mx	Katrina Wootton	U17		2.09.85	1	Watford	28 Aug
9:37.00					1	Watford	2 Jun
9:22.15	Sharon Morris			5.07.68	1	Watford	1 Sep
9:24.17 mx	Sarah Salmon			9.09.74	1	Canberra, AUS	30 Nov
9:24.38 mx	Rachael Nathan	U17		27.04.86	1	Manchester (Str)	20 Aug
9:31.93					1	Glasgow (S)	20 Jul
9:24.40 mx	Danielle Barnes	U17		8.10.85	1	Street	6 May
9:40.76					9	Loughborough	18 May
9:26.53 mx	Suzanne Owen			5.05.79	2	Manchester (Str)	20 Aug
9:36.7					2	Loughborough	12 Jun
9:26.61	Andrea Green			14.12.68	2	Eton	3 Jul
9:27.00 mx	Vicky Gill	U23		21.08.80	1rB	Manchester (Str)	6 Aug
(20)							
9:27.78 mx	Catherine Dugdale			29.11.74	2	Street	6 May
9:32.52					3	Eton	3 Jul
9:28.45	Hayley Ovens			5.12.75	1	Edinburgh	28 Apr
9:28.49 mx	Sarah Wilkinson			2.01.70	1	Manchester (Str)	14 May
9:28.55 mx	Allison Higgins			8.04.72	1	Grangemouth	5 Jun
9:38.56					5	Edinburgh	20 Jul
9:29.28	Louise Damen	U23		12.10.82	1	Niort, FRA	3 Aug
9:31.12	Sally Oldfield	U20		25.06.84	1	Manchester (Wy)	3 Jun
9:32.5	Lucy Elliott	V35		9.03.66	1	Rugby	19 May
9:33.0	Elaine Renouf	U17		2.07.87	1	Middlesbrough	23 Jun
9:34.0 mx	Sue Cripsey	U23		8.01.81	1	Watford	24 Jun
9:50.3					1	Basildon	7 Sep
9:34.20	Maria Skelton	U23		18.05.80	4	Dublin (S), IRL	24 Apr
(30)							
9:34.88	Kate Reed	U23		28.09.82	4	Eton	3 Jul
9:34.9	Penny Thackray			18.08.74	1	Sheffield	27 Apr
9:35.00 mx	Louise Whittaker	U23		29.11.82	2rB	Manchester (Str)	6 Aug
9:35.04	Claire Smallwood			15.03.77	3	Edinburgh	20 Jul
9:35.39 mx	Ann-Marie Hutchison			21.08.77	3	Street	6 May
9:45.4					1	Cardiff	10 Jul
9:36.03	Collette Fagan	U23		6.06.82	4	Edinburgh	20 Jul
9:36.1	Sonia Thomas			16.05.79	1	Loughborough	12 Jun
9:36.23	Susannah Rutherford			26.02.79	3	Tempe AZ, USA	13 Apr
9:37.9	Jo Lodge			6.01.68	2	Rugby	19 May
9:38.16 mx	Jenny Heath			22.12.77	2	Manchester (Str)	25 Jun
9:45.5					3	Rugby	19 May
(40)							
9:38.7	Jo Wilkinson			2.05.73	1	Southampton	27 Apr
9:39.2	Sharon Hatch	V35		5.09.64	1	Belfast	11 May
9:40.59	Ruth Proctor	U20		4.05.84	1	Nottingham	13 Jul
9:41.77	Katie Thomas			20.12.78	2	Watford	1 Sep
9:42.4	Meredith Pannett			13.06.71	1	Erith	19 Jun
9:43.14	Jane Potter	U23		24.10.81	3	Newport	20 Jul
9:44.39 mx	Emily Pidgeon	U15		1.06.89	4rB	Street	6 May
9:44.89	Vicky Webster	U20		14.08.84	2	Nottingham	13 Jul

9:45.5	Emma Ward	U23	2.01.82	1	Stoke-on-Trent	28	Apr
9:46.09	Kathryn Frost	U20	21.02.84	3	Nottingham	13	Jul
9:46.3	Dorothea Lee		28.07.77	1	Wigan	15	Aug
(50)							
9:46.6	Jennifer Pereira	U20	8.08.85	1	Eton	27	Jul
9:47.32 mx	Sarah Singleton	V35	18.12.65	2	Manchester (Str)	14	May
9:57.6				1	Liverpool	11	May
9:47.53	Bryony Frost	U20	21.02.84	4	Nottingham	13	Jul
9:48.97	Aine Hoban	U20	13.07.84	1	Manchester (Str)	20	Aug
9:49.07	Laura Kenney	U20	27.06.85	5	Nottingham	13	Jul
9:49.6	Tina Brown		22.08.76	1	Rugby	25	Aug
9:49.89 mx	Gemma Turtle	U17	15.05.86	1	Watford	19	Jun
9:51.94				2	Nottingham	13	Jul
9:50.3	Sam Gray		11.01.78	1	Nottingham	25	Aug
9:50.35	Mel Ellis	V35	16.04.64	1	London (He)	3	Aug
9:51.14 i	Clare Martin		18.05.76	1	Cardiff	20	Jan
(60)							
9:52.1	Helen Lawrence		3.12.76	1	Connah's Quay	5	May
9:52.32	Birhan Dagne		8.04.78	1	London (BP)	6	Jul
9:53.11	Kath Scales		28.06.77	1	Birmingham (Un)	19	Jun
9:53.4	Rosalind Lewis		16.02.76	1	London (He)	8	Jun
9:53.83	Dennise Smith	U23	29.10.82	7	Edinburgh	20	Jul
9:54.35	Gemma Phillips	U23	27.10.80	2	Birmingham (Un)	19	Jun
9:54.5	Faye Fullerton	U20	31.05.84	1	London (He)	28	Apr
9:54.93	Jessica Nugent	U20	27.08.84	4	Manchester (C)	16	Jun
9:55.27 mx	Gill Keddie		1.02.69	3	Manchester (Str)	6	Aug
9:55.6	Suzanne Boyes	U17	26.05.87	1	Sheffield (W)	19	May
(70)							
9:56.43 mx	Angela Dickie		6.01.77	4	Manchester (Str)	6	Aug
9:56.5	Freya Murray	U20	20.09.83	1	Derby	28	Apr
9:56.9	Lisa Mawer		22.05.68	2	Cudworth	11	May
9:57.10	Jo Kelsey		20.05.77	1	Kingston	12	May
9:57.28	Shona Hughes		18.02.70	8	Edinburgh	20	Jul
9:57.32	Leonie Smith	U17	20.12.86	3	Nottingham	13	Jul
9:57.5	Vicky Holland	U17	12.01.86	1	Stourport	28	Jul
9:57.56 mx	Sarah Paterson	U23	7.09.80	5	Manchester (Str)	6	Aug
9:58.3	Morag McDonnell		27.08.73	1	Gateshead	8	Aug
9:59.22 mx	Clare Miller		30.06.76	1	Manchester (Str)	28	May

Additional Under 17 (1 - 8 above)

10:08.85	Jo Harper		11.05.87	1	Birmingham	26	May
10:13.89	Becky Ellis		20.12.86	4	Nottingham	13	Jul
(10)							
10:17.54	Josephine Rhodes		22.03.86	2	Watford	2	Jun
10:18.9 mx	Sarah Ponsford		15.05.87	2	Watford	22	May
10:19.93				3	Birmingham	11	Aug
10:19.14 mx	Emma Whittaker		31.10.85	6	Street	6	May
10:34.33				7	Nottingham	13	Jul
10:19.57	Kiera Vogel		31.05.86	2	Birmingham	11	Aug
10:19.82	Jenna Hill		16.10.85	3	Derby	8	Sep
10:20.9	Rachel Jones		25.09.85	2	Grangemouth	15	Jun
10:21.0	Cheryl Hammond		13.07.87	4	London (He)	28	Apr
10:25.3	Helen Glover		17.06.86	1	Exeter	21	Apr
10:25.43 mx	Katherine Humphries		28.11.85	7	Street	6	May
10:40.41				9	Nottingham	13	Jul
10:25.50	Emma Hunt		25.04.86	6	Nottingham	13	Jul
(20)							
10:26.5 mx	Karrie Hewitt		19.03.86	3	Manchester (Str)	6	Aug
10:27.5	Sharon Lamont		12.08.86	3	Grangemouth	15	Jun
10:29.9	Stephanie Wilson		18.10.86	1	Eton	2	Jun
10:35.89	Samantha Crowe		28.09.86	3	Manchester (Wy)	25	May
10:36.8	Cheryl Guiney		24.09.85	2	Tullamore, IRL	22	Jun

10:37.07	Rachel Gibbs		13.10.85	4	Watford	2	Jun
10:37.81	Jolene Ennis		17.03.87	6	Birmingham	11	Aug
10:38.2	Natasha Barnes-Smith		21.04.87	1	Bury St. Edmunds	27	Jul
10:39.5	Eloise Pittwood		4.12.85	2	London (PH)	27	Apr

Additional Under 15 (1 above)

| 10:47.61 | India Lee | | 31.05.88 | 3 | Marsa, MLT | 26 | Jul |
| 11:07.7 | Abbie Lawson | | 1.03.88 | 1 | Exeter | 29 | Sep |

Foreign

| *9:47.70 i* | *Kelley Wilder (USA)* | | *30.07.71* | *1* | *Glasgow* | *23* | *Feb* |
| *9:55.4 mx* | *Stephanie Van Graan (RSA)* | | *4.02.77* | *1rB* | *Watford* | *22* | *May* |

5000 Metres

14:31.42	Paula Radcliffe		17.12.73	1	Manchester (C)	28	Jul
	14:57.65 +			1m	Munich, GER	6	Aug
14:48.66	Joanne Pavey		20.09.73	4	Berlin, GER	6	Sep
	15:06.34			8	Oslo, NOR	28	Jun
	15:09.99			11	Rome, ITA	12	Jul
	15:18.70			5	Munich, GER	10	Aug
	15:19.91			5	Manchester (C)	28	Jul
	15:20.10			3	Madrid, ESP	21	Sep
	15:25.11			5	Hengelo, NED	2	Jun
	16:06.65			2	Annecy, FRA	23	Jun
15:17.59	Kathy Butler		22.10.73	2	Walnut CA, USA	19	Apr
15:31.23	Catherine Berry		8.10.75	11	London (CP)	23	Aug
	15:32.32			1	Manchester (C)	15	Jun
	15:44.87			10	Manchester (C)	28	Jul
15:38.30	Hayley Yelling		3.01.74	3	Manchester (C)	15	Jun
	15:54.8 +e			5m	Manchester (C)	30	Jul
	16:11.23			1	Birmingham	14	Jul
	16:15.5 +			1mrB	Campomarino, ITA	6	Apr
	16:21.0 +			4m	Manchester (C)	16	Jun
	16:26.41			18	Munich, GER	10	Aug
15:45.08	Liz Yelling		5.12.74	4	Manchester (C)	15	Jun
	15:53.8 +			4m	Manchester (C)	30	Jul
	15:59 +e			m	Munich, GER	6	Aug
15:50.16	Helen Pattinson		2.01.74	10	Walnut CA, USA	19	Apr
15:53.96	Gillian Palmer	U23	30.12.80	2	Manchester (Wy)	3	Jun
	16:10.26			1	Glasgow (S)	8	Jun
	16:13.87			1	Bedford	30	Jun
	16:22 +e			5m	Manchester (C)	16	Jun
	16:29.63			14	Manchester (C)	28	Jul
15:58.8 mx	Charlotte Dale	U20	23.03.84	1	London (CP)	3	Jun
	16:16.55			5	Manchester (Wy)	3	Jun
	16:17.47			1	Watford	14	Aug
15:59.54	Jo Wilkinson		2.05.73	1	Solihull	22	Jun
	16:10.07			1	Bedford	25	May
	(10)						
16:05.23	Jo Lodge		6.01.68	1	Birmingham	6	Jul
16:09.0	Allison Higgins		8.04.72	1	Ayr	10	Apr
	16:29.6 +			m	Manchester (C)	16	Jun
16:10.32	Lucy Wright		17.11.69	3	Manchester (Wy)	3	Jun
16:18.71	Sharon Hatch	V35	5.09.64	5	Manchester (C)	15	Jun
	16:26.77			1	Belfast	8	Jun
16:19.62	Catherine Dugdale		29.11.74	6	Manchester (C)	15	Jun
	16:25.14			2	Birmingham	14	Jul
	16:27.61			9	Manchester (Wy)	3	Jun
16:24.13	Louise Damen	U23	12.10.82	7	Manchester (C)	15	Jun
16:25.01	Penny Thackray		18.08.74	6	Manchester (Wy)	3	Jun

16:25.70	Andrea Green		14.12.68	7	Manchester (Wy)	3	Jun
16:26.24	Maria Skelton	U23	18.05.80	8	Manchester (Wy)	3	Jun
16:28.27	Debbie Sullivan		13.02.72	3	Birmingham	14	Jul

48 performances to 16:30.0 by 20 athletes

16:32.31	Susan Partridge	U23	4.01.80	2	Glasgow (S)	8	Jun
16:33.31	Collette Fagan	U23	6.06.82	4	Birmingham	14	Jul
16:35.38	Jenny Heath		22.12.77	8	Manchester (C)	15	Jun
16:38.61	Tara Krzywicki		9.03.74	9	Manchester (C)	15	Jun
16:38.90	Lucy Elliott	V35	9.03.66	2	Birmingham	6	Jul
16:40.67 i	Susie Rutherford		26.02.79	3	Ames, USA	8	Feb
17:13.84				11	Manchester (C)	15	Jun
16:41.72	Jilly Ingman		17.08.78	5	Solihull	22	Jun
16:44.0 mx	Meredith Pannett		13.06.71	2	London (CP)	12	May
16:46.94				2	Watford	14	Aug
16:44.67	Morag McDonnell		27.08.73	1	Gateshead	11	May
16:49.60	Claire Smallwood		15.03.77	6	Solihull	22	Jun

(30)

16:51 +e	Sharon Morris		5.07.68	9m	Manchester (C)	16	Jun
16:52.1				1	Watford		
16:51.94	Christina Radon		12.07.79	4	Bedford	25	May
16:52.1 +	Suzanne Owen		5.05.79	1	Manchester (Str)	20	Apr
16:56.00				5	Glasgow (S)	8	Jun
16:52.83	Sarah Salmon		9.09.74	2	Canberra, AUS	29	Jan
16:53 +e	Bev Hartigan	V35	10.06.67	10m	Manchester (C)	16	Jun
16:57.26	Laura McCreesh		18.12.80	5	Sotteville, FRA	6	Jul
17:00.37	Pauline Powell		17.05.73	1	Jarrow	1	Jun
17:01.14	Henrietta Freeman	U20	12.07.83	7	Bedford	25	May
17:04.43	Vicky Gill	U23	21.08.80	5	Manchester (Str)	10	May
17:05.24	Jane Potter	U23	24.10.81	5	Birmingham	14	Jul

(40)

17:05.52	Ann MacPhail		3.05.70	1	Wakefield	7	Jul
17:05.76	Alison Fletcher	V40	8.06.61	1	Potsdam, GER	21	Aug
17:06.19	Caroline Herbert/Hoyte		30.06.70	3	Watford	14	Aug
17:06.21	Jo Kelsey		20.05.77	1			
17:09.94	Clare Miller		30.06.76	1	Edinburgh	12	May
17:10.38	Sarah Davey		17.11.78	1	Tallahassee FL, USA	11	May
17:10.44	Sue Cripsey	U23	8.01.81	4	Watford	14	Aug
17:11.7	Jenny Clague		6.08.73	1	Scunthorpe	7	Jul
17:12.3	Louise Watson		13.12.71	2	Watford	1	Jun
17:15.82	Rachel Goddard		30.04.73	8	Solihull	22	Jun

(50)

17:17.17	Chris Howard		9.11.70	3	Olsztyn, POL	18	Aug
17:17.89	Kathryn Waugh		20.02.73	3	Gateshead	11	May
17:17.92	Kathryn Frost	U20	21.02.84	1	Bedford	30	Jun
17:18.86	Paula Gowing		31.05.78	26	Philadelphia PA, USA	25	Apr
17:22.10	Bryony Frost	U20	21.02.84	2	Bedford	30	Jun
17:23.32	Sarah Singleton	V35	18.12.65	12	Manchester (Wy)	3	Jun
17:25.6	Sam Gray		11.01.78	1	Yate	7	Jul
17:26.3 mx	Madelaine Clarke-Gay		16.03.69	1	Exeter	14	Apr
17:30.1	Katie Skorupska		3.11.78	1	Oxford	18	May
17:30.3	Ruth Proctor	U20	4.05.84	1	Great Yarmouth	11	May
17:31.10	Gill Keddie		1.02.69	2	Solihull	22	Jun
17:31.99	Kath Scales		28.06.77	1	Birmingham	2	Jun

Foreign

16:46.64	*Kelley Wilder (USA)*		*30.07.71*	*3*	*Glasgow (S)*	*8*	*Jun*

10000 Metres

30:01.09	Paula Radcliffe		17.12.73	1	Munich, GER	6	Aug
31:58.39	Liz Yelling		5.12.74	4	Manchester (C)	30	Jul
32:26.53				7	Campomarino, ITA	6	Apr
32:44.44				20	Munich, GER	6	Aug

32:29.73	Hayley Yelling			3.01.74	5	Manchester (C)	30 Jul
	32:48.50				1rB	Campomarino, ITA	6 Apr
	33:07.52				4	Manchester (C)	16 Jun
33:09.70	Gillian Palmer	U23	30.12.80		5	Manchester (C)	16 Jun
	33:16.0				2	Manchester (Str)	20 Apr
	34:25.50				8	Manchester (C)	30 Jul
33:10.6	Charlotte Dale	U20	23.03.84		1	Manchester (Str)	20 Apr
33:21.1	Allison Higgins		8.04.72		3	Manchester (Str)	20 Apr
	33:32.07				6	Manchester (C)	16 Jun
	33:58.69				7	Manchester (C)	30 Jul
33:36.60	Jo Wilkinson		2.05.73		6	Manchester (C)	30 Jul
	33:40.57				7	Manchester (C)	16 Jun
33:36.8	Sharon Morris		5.07.68		4	Manchester (Str)	20 Apr
	34:20.64				8	Manchester (C)	16 Jun
33:59.67	Vicky Gill	U23	21.08.80		11	Palo Alto CA, USA	29 Mar
34:05.1	Louise Damen	U23	12.10.82		1	Poole	21 Aug
(10)							
34:11.78	Sarah Salmon		9.09.74		4	Melbourne, AUS	14 Dec
34:23.9	Pauline Powell		17.05.73		5	Manchester (Str)	20 Apr
34:30.20	Sarah Davey		13.10.78		12	Philadelphia PA, USA	25 Apr
34:41.30	Bev Hartigan	V35	10.06.67		9	Manchester (C)	16 Jun
34:48.86	Susan Partridge	U23	4.01.80		13	Barakaldo, ESP	13 Jul
34:51.28	Lucy Elliott	V35	9.03.66		10	Manchester (C)	16 Jun
34:55.76	Debbie Sullivan		13.02.72		11	Manchester (C)	16 Jun
35:09.70	Jo Kelsey		20.05.77		13	Manchester (C)	16 Jun
35:10.30	Alison Fletcher	V40	8.06.61		2	Potsdam, GER	16 Aug
35:15.4	Christina Radon		12.07.79		6	Manchester (Str)	20 Apr
(20)							
35:21.57	Lisa Heyes		5.06.71		16	Manchester (C)	16 Jun
35:29.6	Sarah Singleton	V35	18.12.65		7	Manchester (Str)	20 Apr
35:49.98	Penny Thackray		18.08.74		18	Manchester (C)	16 Jun
36:05.9	Alyson Dixon		24.09.78		1	Bedford	4 May
36:17.9	Gemma Phillips	U23	27.10.80		2	Bedford	4 May
36:36.2 mx	Hannah Leach	V35	7.02.66		1	Bromley	31 Jul
36:40.32	Charlotte Sanderson		18.03.79		2	Houston, USA	17 May
36:53.2	Sula Young		2.01.79		3	Bedford	4 May

5 Kilometres Road

15:02 +	Paula Radcliffe		17.12.73		1m	Richmond	22 Sep
	15:17 +				1m	San Juan, PUR	17 Feb
15:36	Kathy Butler		22.10.73		6	Carlsbad, USA	7 Apr
15:41	Amanda Allen		14.07.68		1	Telford	28 Aug
16:02	Catherine Berry		8.10.75		13	Carlsbad, USA	7 Apr
16:03	Birhan Dagne		8.04.78		8	Kassel, GER	11 May
16:04	Louise Damen	U23	12.10.82		1	Yeovil	14 Aug
16:13	Lucy Wright		17.11.69		1	Hereford	18 Apr
16:15	Gillian Palmer	U23	30.12.80		1	Glasgow	24 Mar
16:17	Dianne Henaghan	V35	6.08.65		1	Sunderland	24 Jul
16:21 +	Liz Yelling		5.12.74		14m	New York NY, USA	8 Jun
(10)							
16:21	Bev Hartigan	V35	10.06.67		1	Birmingham	11 Jul
16:23	Debbie Sullivan		13.02.72		11	London (HP)	1 Sep
16:24	Lucy Elliott	V35	9.03.66		1	Southampton	10 Mar
16:29	Jenny Heath		22.12.77		1	Chester	19 May
16:35	Hayley Yelling		3.01.74		12	London (HP)	1 Sep
16:36	Meredith Pannett		13.06.71		1	Yeovilton	11 Sep
16:38	Charlotte Moore	U20	4.01.85		1	Boscombe	13 Dec
16:40	Morag McDonnell		27.08.73		2	Sunderland	24 Jul
16:42	Annie Emmerson		10.05.70		1	London (HP)	25 Jan
16:42 +	Vicky Pincombe		19.06.73		2m	Eastleigh	17 Mar

16:43	Charlotte Dale	U20	23.03.84	13	London (HP)	1	Sep
16:46 +	Andrea Green		14.12.68	3m	Eastleigh	17	Mar
16:47	Lisa Heyes		5.06.71	2	Chester	19	May
16:50	Claire Smallwood		15.03.77	3	Sunderland	24	Jul
16:54	Susan Partridge	U23	4.01.80	1	Shettleston	28	Apr
16:56	Tara Krzywicki		9.03.74	1	Birmingham	20	Oct
16:57	Sarah Wilkinson		2.01.70	1	Manchester	9	Jul

8 Kilometres Road

24:38 +	Paula Radcliffe		17.12.73	1m	San Juan, PUR	17	Feb

5 Miles Road

26:17 +	Paula Radcliffe		17.12.73	1m	Chicago, USA	13	Oct
26:43	Lucy Wright		17.11.69	1	Alsager	3	Feb
26:46	Liz Yelling		5.12.74	8	Balmoral	30	Mar
26:55	Lucy Elliott	V35	9.03.66	2	Manchester	26	May
26:56	Sharon Morris		5.07.68	3	Manchester	26	May
27:01	Amanda Allen		14.07.68	10	Balmoral	30	Mar
27:04	Dianne Henaghan	V35	6.08.65	2	Alsager	3	Feb
27:04	Angie Mudge		8.07.70	1	Cupar	2	Mar
27:07	Bev Hartigan		10.06.67	4	Manchester	26	May
27:23	Kate Burge		15.10.72	1	Wolverhampton	1	Dec
	(10)						
27:27	Debbie Robinson		31.01.68	3	Alsager	3	Feb
27:30	Jenny Heath		22.12.77	1	Manchester	4	Jun
27:31	Susan Partridge	U23	4.01.80	6	Manchester	26	May
27:31	Meredith Pannett		13.06.71	5	Loughrea, IRL	13	Oct
27:35	Vicky Pincombe		19.06.73	1	Exmouth	10	Feb
27:36	Pauline Powell		17.05.73	7	Manchester	26	May
27:36	Emma Phillips		10.06.74	2	Wolverhampton	1	Dec
27:39	Bev Jenkins		6.02.70	14	Balmoral	30	Mar
27:39	Lisa Heyes		5.06.71	8	Manchester	26	May
27:44	Penny Thackray		18.08.74	16	Balmoral	30	Mar
	(20)						
27:49	Jane Livings		13.08.70	1	Weston, USA	17	Jan
27:52	Helen Purdy		5.10.75	2	Exmouth	10	Feb
27:55	Lisa Mawer		22.05.68	9	Manchester	26	May
27:59	Suzanne Owen		5.05.79	10	Manchester	26	May

10 Kilometres Road

30:38	Paula Radcliffe		17.12.73	1	Richmond	22	Sep
	30:43			1	San Juan, PUR	17	Feb
	32:47 +			1m	Chicago, USA	13	Oct
33:05	Charlotte Dale	U20	23.03.84	1	Whitstable	6	May
	33:06			3	London (HP)	21	Jul
	33:37			1	Ashford	13	Oct
33:18	Liz Yelling		5.12.74	14	New York NY, USA	8	Jun
33:24	Catherine Berry		8.10.75	9	Mobile, USA	23	Mar
33:24	Amanda Allen		14.07.68	4	Moreton-in-Marsh	15	Sep
	33:36			2	Laganside	21	Apr
	33:46			2	Swansea	22	Sep
33:37	Rowan Smith		25.10.68	1	Portsmouth	5	Jun
	33:42			1	Wakefield	7	Apr
33:42	Debbie Robinson		31.01.68	1	Sheffield	1	Dec
33:48	Jo Wilkinson		2.05.73	1	Silverstone	7	May
33:50	Marian Sutton	V35	7.10.63	1	Stubbington	12	Jan
	33:57			1	Chichester	3	Feb
33:50	Sharon Morris		5.07.68	2	Bradford	8	Sep
	(10)						
33:50	Andrea Green		14.12.68	5	Moreton-in-Marsh	15	Sep
	33:58			3	Swansea	22	Sep

Time	Name	Cat	DOB	Pos	Venue	Date
33:53	Lucy Elliott	V35	9.03.66	1	Eastleigh	17 Mar
33:56	Lucy Wright		17.11.69	1	Dudley	1 May
33:58	Louise Damen	U23	12.10.82	1	Poole	26 Dec
34:02	Vicky Pincombe		19.06.73	2	Eastleigh	17 Mar
34:02	Jenny Heath		22.12.77	3	Mold	20 Oct
34:14	Kathy Butler		22.10.73	9	San Juan, PUR	17 Feb
34:15	Tara Krzywicki		9.03.74	1	Fradley	24 Mar
34:17	Sheila Fairweather		24.11.77	1	Glasgow	12 Jan
34:19	Lynne MacDougall	V35	18.02.65	1	Paisley	1 Sep
	(20)					
34:19	Susan Partridge	U23	4.01.80	1	Edinburgh	22 Sep
34:21	Kerry Gillibrand		13.09.76	1	Leeds	1 Ded
34:24	Debbie Sullivan		13.02.72	1	Chelmsford	24 Nov
34:31	Lisa Mawer		22.05.68	1	Rothwell	21 Apr
34:32	Tracy Brindley		25.08.72	2	Edinburgh	22 Sep
34:37	Jo Lodge		6.01.68	1	Wolverhampton	14 Jul
34:39	Dianne Henaghan	V35	6.08.65	6	Bishop Auckland	25 Aug
34:43	Amy Stiles		6.02.75	1	Lordshill	30 Jun
34:43	Bev Hartigan	V35	10.06.67	1	Newark	14 Jul
34:44	Karen Sindall	U23	17.01.81	1	Southend	6 Oct
	(30)					
34:47	Jenny Clague		6.08.73	1	Speke	10 Mar
34:49	Penny Thackray		18.08.74	2	Wakefield	7 Apr
34:49	Meredith Pannett		13.06.71	1	Datchet	22 Jun
34:49	Trudi Thomson	V40	18.01.59	3	Edinburgh	22 Sep
34:52	Claire Smallwood		15.03.77	1	Morpeth	6 Aug
34:53	Morag McDonnell		27.08.73	1	Tholthorpe	1 Sep
34:59	Alison Fletcher	V40	8.06.61	1	Cliffe Woods	14 Jul

short course

Time	Name	Cat	DOB	Pos	Venue	Date
33:03	Liz McColgan	V35	24.05.64	1	Arbroath	6 Oct

15 Kilometres Road

Time	Name	Cat	DOB	Pos	Venue	Date
49:05 +	Paula Radcliffe		17.12.73	1m	Chicago, USA	13 Oct
49:06 +				1m	London	14 Apr
54:22	Amanda Proctor		25.07.71	1	Hayling Island	24 Nov

10 Miles Road

Time	Name	Cat	DOB	Pos	Venue	Date
52:40 +	Paula Radcliffe		17.12.73	1m	Chicago, USA	13 Oct
54:26 +				2m	London	14 Apr
54.00 +	Liz Yelling		5.12.74	m	South Shields	6 Oct
54:34				4	Portsmouth	8 Sep
55:51	Jo Lodge		6.01.68	5	Portsmouth	8 Sep
56:13	Andrea Green		14.12.68	6	Portsmouth	8 Sep
56:15	Sue Harrison		6.08.71	7	Portsmouth	8 Sep
56:40	Vicky Gill	U23	21.08.80	1	Manchester	11 Aug
56:44	Alison Fletcher	V40	8.06.61	8	Portsmouth	8 Sep
56:56	Sharon Morris		5.07.68	1	Ware	22 Sep
57:11	Sara Carson		14.09.68	1	Carlisle	16 Nov
57:37	Lisa Heyes		5.06.71	1	Leyland	2 Jun
57:41	Morag McDonnell		27.08.73	9	Portsmouth	8 Sep
	(10)					
57:59	Pauline Powell		17.05.73	2	Manchester	11 Aug
58:03	Jo Kelsey		20.05.77	1	Pocklington	24 Feb
58:07	Kate Burge		15.10.72	1	Llandudno	10 Nov
58:16	Trudi Thomson	V40	18.01.59	1	Motherwell	7 Apr
58:30	Jude Craft		13.08.72	1	Maidenhead	29 Mar
58:40	Ruth Pickvance	V40	29.09.61	1	Lytham St Annes	3 Mar
58:41	Kath Bailey		25.03.68	3	Ostend,	3 Mar
58:43	Amy Stiles		6.02.75	10	Portsmouth	8 Sep
58:47	Alison Crook		19.01.72	1	Leith	11 Sep
58:53	Anna Critchlow		4.12.67	1	Twickenham	20 Oct

Foreign
58:48   Teresa Duffy/McCluskey (IRL)   6.07.69   1   Ballycotton, IRL   10 Mar

Half Marathon

69:01 +	Paula Radcliffe		17.12.73	1m	Chicago, USA	13	Oct
71:04 +				1m	London	14	Apr
71:42	Liz Yelling		5.12.74	8	South Shields	6	Oct
73:08	Marian Sutton	V35	7.10.63	1	Helsby	20	Jan
73:43	Sue Harrison		6.08.71	10	South Shields	6	Oct
74:01	Jo Lodge		6.01.68	1	Bath	17	Mar
74:12				1	Wolverhampton	1	Sep
74:24	Sharon Morris		5.07.68	11	South Shields	6	Oct
74:53	Amanda Allen		14.07.68	47	Brussels, BEL	5	May
75:14	Sharon Dixon		22.04.68	2	Bath	17	Mar
75:22	Alison Fletcher	V40	8.06.61	1	Paddock Wood	24	Mar
75:28	Vicky Pincombe		19.06.73	1	Stroud	27	Oct
(10)							
75:53	Andrea Green		14.12.68	1	Dartford	21	Jul
76:11	Susan Partridge	U23	4.01.80	15	South Shields	6	Oct
76:21	Trudi Thomson	V40	18.01.59	16	South Shields	6	Oct
76:24	Lynne MacDougall	V35	18.02.65	10	Glasgow	8	Sep
76:56	Debbie Robinson		31.01.68	1	Hillingdon	9	Jun
77:02	Jane Livings		13.08.70	1	Watford	3	Feb
77:12	Louise Watson		13.12.71	17	South Shields	6	Oct
77:19	Ruth Pickvance	V40	29.09.61	4	Bath	17	Mar
77:19	Morag McDonnell		27.08.73	18	South Shields	6	Oct
77:35	Melanie Hayward		14.07.71	1	York	27	Jan
(20)							
77:37	Pauline Powell		17.05.73	2	Llanwddyn	15	Sep
77:50	Helen Lawrence		3.12.76	1	Chester	26	May
77:51	Kate Burge		15.10.72	3	Llanwddyn	15	Sep
78:02	Kath Bailey		25.03.68	1	Jersey	19	May
78:05	Bev Jenkins		6.02.70	1	Leyland	10	Mar
78:08	Karen Sindall	U23	17.01.81	1	Roding Valley	3	Mar
78:12	Shona Crombie-Hicks		1.06.71	m	Dublin, IRL	28	Oct
78:18	Sula Young		2.01.79	2	Nottingham	15	Sep
78:25	Allison Higgins		8.04.72	1	Stranraer	2	Mar
78:27	Madelaine Clarke-Gay		16.03.69	2	Bideford	3	Mar
(30)							
78:29	Jude Craft		13.08.72	3	Stroud	27	Oct
78:39	Michaela McCallum	V35	2.06.66	6	Bath	17	Mar
78:39	Ann MacPhail		3.05.70	12	Glasgow	8	Sep
78:43	Channah Patton		22.02.72	3	Wilmslow	24	Mar
78:41	Dorothea Lee		28.07.77	1	Amsterdam, NED	20	Oct
78:44	Penny Thackray		18.08.74	1	Sheffield	28	Apr

Note Paula Radcliffe's second half marathon times of 68:17 (Chicago) and 67:52 (London)

Marathon

2:17:18	Paula Radcliffe		17.12.73	1	Chicago, USA	13	Oct
2:18:56				1	London	14	Apr
2:31:44 dh	Marian Sutton (137m dh)	V35	7.10.63	1	Austin TX, USA	17	Feb
2:45:55				8	Manchester (C)	28	Jul
2:34:17	Jo Lodge		6.01.68	7	Berlin, GER	29	Sep
2:38:25				12	London	14	Apr
2:36:29	Lynne MacDougall	V35	18.02.65	2	Seville, ESP	24	Feb
2:38:52	Sue Harrison		6.08.71	5	Dublin, IRL	28	Oct
2:39:42	Debbie Robinson		31.01.68	4	Manchester (C)	28	Jul
2:40:53	Shona Crombie-Hicks		1.06.71	6	Dublin, IRL	28	Oct
2:41:27	Bev Hartigan	V35	10.06.67	6	Manchester (C)	28	Jul
2:41:41	Michaela McCallum	V35	2.06.66	12	Paris, FRA	7	Apr

2:42:30	Trudi Thomson	V40	18.01.59	7	Dublin, IRL	28	Oct
2:46:30				5	Seville, ESP	24	Feb
2:48:15				8	Stockholm, SWE	8	Jun
2:49:39				1	Belfast	6	May
(10)							
2:43:05	Angie Mudge		8.07.70	15	Paris, FRA	7	Apr
2:44:11	Amy Stiles		6.02.75	2	Florence, ITA	24	Nov
2:44:32	Bev Jenkins		6.02.70	14	London	14	Apr
2:44:42	Alison Fletcher	V40	8.06.61	15	London	14	Apr
2:45:05	Sharon Dixon		22.04.68	16	London	14	Apr
2:45:14	Ruth Pickvance	V40	29.09.61	4	Reggio Emilia	15	Dec
2:45:34				17	London	14	Apr
2:46:13	Vivienne Conneely		4.01.76	21	Chicago, USA	13	Oct
2:46:28	Pauline Powell		17.05.73	1	Manchester	13	Oct
2:49:26	Clare Pauzers	V35	2.08.62	19	London	14	Apr
2:49:38	Helen Cawthorne	V40	9.07.61	21	London	14	Apr
(20)							
2:50:35	Samantha Bretherwick		16.04.69	23	London	14	Apr
2:51:26	Sarah Campbell		31.10.74	25	London	14	Apr
2:52:13	Juliette Clark	V35	22.04.64	26	London	14	Apr
2:53:05	Michelle Lee		11.09.72	27	London	14	Apr
2:53:06	Jacqueline Massey	V35	24.01.64	28	London	14	Apr
2:54:10	Rosalyn Alexander		18.05.73	15	Dublin, IRL	28	Oct
2:54:29	Gillian Horovitz	V45	7.06.55	37	Boston, USA	15	Apr
2:55:07	Gill O'Connor	V40	24.09.61	16	Dublin, IRL	28	Oct
2:55:23	Helen Burrell	V35	1.07.63	1	Sheffield	28	Apr
2:55:35	Jo Dering		7.02.69	31	London	14	Apr
(30)							
2:55:37	Angela Allen		23.09.67	32	London	14	Apr
2:55:59	Lesley Whiley	V40	14.05.60	33	London	14	Apr
2:56:08	Judy Brown	V45	27.10.54	34	London	14	Apr
2:56:35	Sue Dolan	V40	25.01.61	35	London	14	Apr
2:56:44	Anita Mellowdew		1.12.70	36	London	14	Apr
2:57:06	Adele Gerrard	V40	24.11.59	1	Inverness	29	Sep
2:57:23	Lucy Carr			28	Paris, FRA	7	Apr
2:58:25	Alison Vuagniaux	V40	31.05.60	38	London	14	Apr
2:58:33	Susan Spencer-Cusick	V35	8.07.63	39	London	14	Apr
2:58:38	Pat Affleck	V45	13.02.57	40	London	14	Apr
(40)							
2:58:40	Penny Buckingham	V35	26.04.67	12	Manchester (C)	28	Jul
2:58:54	Veronica Iturbe	V40	30.11.61	41	London	14	Apr
2:58:54	Anne Power	V35	20.03.63	42	London	14	Apr
2:59:05	Nicola Aitken		18.12.78	19	Dublin, IRL	28	Oct
2:59:20	Lorraine McCarthy	V35	30.12.63	54	Berlin, GER	29	Sep
2:59:39	Veronique Binglow	V35	11.06.65	43	London	14	Apr
2:59:44	Beverley Wilson	V35	26.03.67	44	London	14	Apr
2:59:48	Beverley Edwards	V35	1.09.65	45	London	14	Apr
3:00:22	Vicki Perry	V40	25.11.57	46	London	14	Apr
3:00:22	Lisa Godding-Feltham		24.11.69	47	London	14	Apr
(50)							
3:00:45	Helen Sly		13.12.67	2	Nottingham	15	Sep
3:00:59	Alison Crook		19.01.72	8	Athens, GRE	3	Nov
3:01:09	Claire Davidson		17.09.68	23	Dublin, IRL	28	Oct
3:01:18	Susanne Carson		2.05.67	49	London	14	Apr
3:01:21	Treena Carney	V40	29.08.61	50	London	14	Apr
3:01:26	Chris Howard		9.11.70	5	Belfast	6	May
3:01:26	Kate Jenkins		26.03.74	1	Elgin	1	Sep
3:01:40	Lisa Arundale-Burns		29.07.72	51	London	14	Apr
3:01:48	Andrea Dennison	V35	22.04.63	52	London	14	Apr
3:01:58	Monique Hollinshead		31.12.67	53	London	14	Apr
(60)							

3:02:03	Andrea Devine		18.05.67	54	London	14	Apr
3:02:09	Zina Marchant	V50	30.09.50	55	London	14	Apr
3:02:11	Amanda Yorwerth		18.05.67	1	Bungay	7	Apr
3:02:24	Susanna Harrison	V35	25.01.63	56	London	14	Apr
3:02:39	Gemma Fiddes		28.03.75	57	London	14	Apr
3:02:44	Tracey Curl	V35	8.07.62	58	London	14	Apr
3:02:59	Helen Fines		11.07.73	2	Manchester	13	Oct
3:03:00	Jeannette Coleman	V45	3.02.57	3	Manchester	13	Oct
3:03:04	Sally Baker		30.11.67	52	New York NY, USA	3	Nov
3:03:08	Sue Cariss	V50	17.11.49	59	London	14	Apr
(70)							
3:03:13	Wendy Davies	V40	13.06.60	103	Chicago, USA	13	Oct
3:03:30	Dorothy Smale	V40	26.05.60	60	London	14	Apr
3:03:41	Patricia Matheson	V45	7.01.54	61	London	14	Apr
3:03:55	Emma Latto		16.01.69	62	London	14	Apr
3:04:29	Anne Kirtley	V35	12.02.66	2	Sheffield	28	Apr
3:04:53	Erica Christie	V45	10.03.56	26	Dublin, IRL	28	Oct
3:05:03	Sharon Gannon	V35	16.01.64	63	London	14	Apr
3:05:24	Mathilde Heaton		2.09.74	64	London	14	Apr
3:05:55	Melissa Arkinstall		15.05.76	66	London	14	Apr
3:06:01	Dawn Kenwright	V45	30.08.55	67	London	14	Apr
(80)							
3:06:13	Gail Burles		14.11.67	68	London	14	Apr
3:06:23	Louise Cooper		25.08.75	69	London	14	Apr
3:06:25	Lucy Townsend		26.03.72	1	Abingdon	20	Oct
3:06:27	Helen Yule	V35	10.09.65	70	London	14	Apr
3:06:31	Pippa Major	V35	23.04.65	72	London	14	Apr
3:06:33	Revis Crowle	V40	26.01.62	73	London	14	Apr
3:06:35	Maddie Horton		7.06.78	1	Cornwall	17	Nov
3:06:38	Amanda Proctor		25.07.71	74	London	14	Apr
3:06:56	Nicola Thompson		10.02.68	75	London	14	Apr
3:07:02	Helen Smethurst	V35	6.10.64	76	London	14	Apr
(90)							
3:07:04	Julia Myatt	V35	3.08.63	77	London	14	Apr
3:07:09	Fiona Shenton	V40	19.04.59	3	Sheffield	28	Apr
3:07:10	Zoe Pike		17.11.71	78	London	14	Apr
3:07:21	Jenny Gray	V40	21.06.60	80	London	14	Apr
3:08:12	Nathalie Christie		28.02.74	119	Chicago, USA	13	Oct
3:08:17	Christina Wellington		18.02.77	82	London	14	Apr
3:08:18	Carol Bould	V50	8.11.51	101	Berlin, GER	29	Sep
3:08:21	Kathy Kaiser	V50	24.08.51	83	London	14	Apr
3:08:36	Alyson Parlett	V35	12.02.64	85	London	14	Apr
3:08:44	Jillian Tait		4.02.76	86	London	14	Apr
(100)							
3:08:46	Angela Sadler	V40	25.07.59	87	London	14	Apr
3:08:52	Vicky Skelton		4.11.67	88	London	14	Apr
3:08:54	Kellie Trollope		28.12.74	89	London	14	Apr
3:08:55	Andrea Banner		5.06.70	90	London	14	Apr
3:08:55	Glennys Disney	V40	11.06.59	91	London	14	Apr

Foreign

2:40:29	*Teresa Duffy/McCluskey (IRL)*		*6.07.69*	*5*	*Manchester*	*28*	*Jul*
2:50:22	*Carin Hume (RSA)*		*25.03.75*	*13*	*Dublin, IRL*	*28*	*Oct*
2:53:24	*Jessica Draskau-Petersson (DEN)*		*8.09.77*	*14*	*Dublin, IRL*	*28*	*Oct*
2:54:32	*Anna McCutcheon (CAN)*		*3.03.68*	*29*	*London*	*14*	*Apr*
3:05:31	*Siri Terjesen (USA)*		*29.06.75*	*1*	*Kingston*	*13*	*Oct*

100 Kilometres - Road

7:47:29	Danielle Sanderson	V35	26.10.62	3	Winschoten, NED	14	Sep
8:53:17	Sharon Gayter	V35	30.10.63	1	Moreton-in-Marsh	7	Apr
8:54:41	Hilary Walker	V45	9.11.53	18	Winschoten, NED	14	Sep

2000 Metres Steeplechase (2'6" barriers)

6:31.77	Tara Krzywicki		9.03.74	1	Birmingham	13	Jul
	6:35.29			1	Loughborough	18	May
6:52.94	Ursula Counsell	U23	7.12.82	1	Derby	11	Aug
6:54.92	Claire Entwistle		9.12.76	2	Birmingham	13	Jul
6:55.83	Bryony Frost	U20	21.02.84	3	Loughborough	18	May
7:00.09	Tina Brown		22.08.76	1	Watford	1	Sep
7:01.32	Kathryn Frost	U20	21.02.84	4	Loughborough	18	May
7:11.67	Jane Pidgeon	V35	23.01.64	4	Birmingham	13	Jul
7:18.51	Joanne King		6.08.69	2	Watford	1	Sep
7:21.84	Ruth Waller	U20	6.03.84	2	Derby	11	Aug
7:29.03	Sarah Beevers		18.11.76	3	Manchester (Str)	25	Jun
(10)							
7:33.03	Fiona Lampkin		4.10.69	3	Watford	1	Sep

Foreign

7:10.94	*Liz Egan (IRL)*	*3.06.79*	*1*	*Watford*	*14*	*Aug*

3000 Metres Steeplechase (2'6" barriers)

10:23.21	Tara Krzywicki		9.03.74	4	Annecy, FRA	23	Jun
	10:24.6			6	Walnut CA, USA	19	Apr
10:47.62	Ursula Counsell	U23	7.12.82	3	Niort, FRA	3	Aug
	10:51.70			2	Merksem, BEL	17	Aug
	10:55.91			1	Bedford	26	May
10:56.22	Tina Brown		22.08.76	3	Merksem, BEL	17	Aug
10:58.13	Paula Gowing	3' barriers	1.05.78	7	Columbia SC, USA	19	May
11:09.64	Louise Brown		6.05.78	5	Gava, ESP	26	May
11:23.69	Jane Pidgeon	V35	23.01.64	2	Bedford	26	May
11:40.24	Joanne King		6.08.69	3	Bedford	26	May

50 Metres Hurdles - Indoors

7.2	Clare Milborrow	10.01.77	1	Horsham	24	Jan

60 Metres Hurdles - Indoors

8.01	Diane Allahgreen	21.02.75	1	Cardiff	3	Feb
	8.04		3h3	Vienna, AUT	2	Mar
	8.06		7	Vienna, AUT	2	Mar
	8.07		1h2	Cardiff	3	Feb
	8.14		3	Glasgow	9	Mar
	8.19		2h2	Eaubonne, FRA	13	Feb
	8.26		5	Eaubonne, FRA	13	Feb
	8.28		1	Birmingham	27	Jan
	8.35		2	Birmingham	13	Jan
8.17	Rachel King	11.05.76	2	Cardiff	3	Feb
	8.23		1	Cardiff	10	Feb
	8.26		1h1	Cardiff	3	Feb
	8.31		5h1	Vienna, AUT	2	Mar
	8.39		2	Birmingham	27	Jan
	8.39		1	Cardiff	16	Feb
	8.41		1rB	Cardiff	16	Feb
	8.46		1	Cardiff	20	Jan
8.20	Melani Wilkins	18.01.73	3	Cardiff	3	Feb
	8.20		1h3	Cardiff	3	Feb
8.34	Sarah Claxton	23.09.79	1	Birmingham	13	Jan
	8.39		2h1	Cardiff	3	Feb
	8.44		5	Cardiff	3	Feb
8.40	Clare Milborrow	10.01.77	4	Cardiff	3	Feb
	8.40		2h2	Cardiff	3	Feb
	8.55		3	Cardiff	10	Feb

8.43	Helen Worsey	U23	29.08.82	1	Glasgow	24	Feb
	8.44			6	Cardiff	3	Feb
	8.45			3h2	Cardiff	3	Feb
	8.49			1h1	Glasgow	24	Feb
	8.55			3	Birmingham	27	Jan
8.47	Liz Fairs		1.12.77	3h1	Cardiff	3	Feb
	8.51			7	Cardiff	3	Feb
8.49	Sara McGreavy	U23	13.12.82	2h3	Cardiff	3	Feb
8.55	Kerry Jury		19.11.68	1	Sheffield	20	Jan
	34 performances to 8.55 by 9 athletes						
8.57	Katherine Livesey		15.12.79	1P	Lincoln NE, USA	22	Feb
	(10)						
8.57	Kelly Sotherton		13.11.76	1P	Cardiff	10	Mar
8.58	Symone Belle	U20	12.11.84	1	Birmingham	24	Feb
8.59	Tamsin Stephens	U23	2.08.80	5	Birmingham	27	Jan
8.62	Kate Brewington	U23	15.10.81	2P	Cardiff	10	Mar
8.65	Claire Pearson		23.09.78	4h2	Cardiff	3	Feb
8.66	Chanelle Garnett	U20	16.08.85	2	Cardiff	10	Feb
8.67	Alyssa Fullelove	U23	16.09.81	1	Glasgow	20	Jan
8.67	Rebecca Jones	U20	17.01.83	1P1	Eaubonne, FRA	24	Feb
8.68	Caroline Pearce	U23	1.09.80	3P1	Eaubonne, FRA	24	Feb
8.72	Lynne Fairweather	U23	15.01.80	2	Glasgow	20	Jan
	(20)						
8.75	Lorna Rogers		10.01.74	4h1	Cardiff	3	Feb
8.75	Vicky Williams	U23	11.04.81	5h3	Cardiff	3	Feb
8.76	Jessica Ennis	U17	28.01.86	1P2	Eaubonne, FRA	24	Feb
8.79	Julie Hollman		16.02.77	P	Zaragoza, ESP	27	Jan
8.80	Clova Court	V40	10.02.60	6	Birmingham	27	Jan
8.81	Aileen Wilson	U20	30.03.84	1P	Glasgow	10	Feb
8.81	Justine Roach	U20	21.12.84	2	Birmingham	24	Feb
8.84	Allison English		4.03.79	5h1	Cardiff	3	Feb
8.84	Julia Bennett		26.03.70	6h1	Cardiff	3	Feb
8.84	Sara Todd		3.11.79	5h2	Glasgow	24	Feb
	(30)						
8.92	Sarah Lane	U23	4.06.81	5h2	Cardiff	3	Feb
8.95	Grace Smith	U23	30.01.82	3rB	Birmingham	27	Jan
8.95	Sharon Davidge	U23	15.09.81	6h3	Cardiff	3	Feb
8.96	Gemma Bennett	U20	4.01.84	4	Birmingham	24	Feb
8.96	Roz Gonse	U23	1.03.82	P	Eaubonne, FRA	24	Feb
8.97	Jenni Molloy	U20	23.09.83	6h2	Cardiff	3	Feb
8.98	Cathy Crawford	U20	17.12.84	3rB	Cardiff	16	Feb
8.98	Claire Lomas	U23	18.04.80	3h1	Glasgow	24	Feb
8.99	Hannah Stares		13.11.78	3P	Bedford	13	Jan

hand timing

8.5	King		(8.17)	1h2	Birmingham	13	Jan
8.7	Julie Hollman		(8.79)	1	Bedford	19	Jan
8.8	Katherine Porter	U23	19.08.82	2	Bedford	19	Jan

60 Metres Hurdles - Indoors - Under 17 (2'6" barriers)

8.74	Phyllis Agbo		16.12.85	1	Birmingham	24	Feb
8.75	Heather Jones		10.09.86	1	Cardiff	23	Nov
8.82	Samantha Britton		12.09.86	1s2	Birmingham	24	Feb
8.85	Stephanie Madgett		22.02.87	4	Birmingham	24	Feb
8.86	Nicola Robinson		16.04.86	1	Birmingham	20	Jan
8.90	Jessica Ennis		28.01.86	1	Sheffield	20	Jan
8.93	Katey Read		20.03.86	5	Birmingham	24	Feb
8.94	Staci Stewart		20.09.85	1	Glasgow	17	Feb
8.95	Christina Waters		4.06.87	6	Birmingham	24	Feb
9.00	Stacy Flint		18.10.85	4s1	Birmingham	24	Feb
	(10)						
9.03	Pamela Paterson		26.10.85	3	Glasgow	31	Jan

302

9.04		Claire Jones	8.11.86	2P	Glasgow	14	Dec
9.07		Lisa McManus	3.01.86	2	Birmingham	20	Jan
9.10		Amy Beighton	6.03.86	5s1	Birmingham	24	Feb
9.1		Catherine Holdsworth	3.01.86	2	Bedford	19	Jan
	9.16			1P	Bedford	13	Jan
9.1		Maria Garavand	30.06.86	1	King's Lynn	10	Feb
9.15		Cheryl Cairney	27.03.87	2h2	Glasgow	17	Feb
9.17		Samantha Day	8.02.86	1	Birmingham	20	Feb
9.18		Faye Harding	7.09.85	1P	Cardiff	10	Mar
9.19		Victoria Garrard	22.11.87	2	Manchester (C)	28	Dec
9.20		Emma Morris	21.02.86	1P	Glasgow	10	Feb
	(20)						
9.2		Louise Massingham	28.02.87	1	London (CP)	16	Feb
9.2		Rachel Peckham	14.02.87	1	Eton	3	Mar
9.2		Chloe Van Vulven	10.09.87	1	Chelmsford	15	Dec

60 Metres Hurdles - Indoors - Under 17 (2'6" barriers)

9.18		Kimberly Skinner	21.09.87	1	Glasgow	3	Feb
9.26		Lucy Boggis	27.01.89	P	Glasgow	14	Dec
9.27		Joanna Kirkby	26.10.87	1	Birmingham	24	Feb
9.29		Natalie Doyle	5.01.89	2	Glasgow	3	Feb
9.29		Faye Richold	24.10.87	1s2	Birmingham	24	Feb

70 Metres Hurdles - Under 13

11.3		Vicky Fleetwood	13.04.90	1	Leicester	15	Jun
11.3		Hannah Francis-Smithson	10.11.89	1	Cleckheaton	21	Jul
11.55	0.7	Jade Bee	30.12.89	1	Kingston	28	Jul
11.58	-0.8	Ashley Helsby	1.07.90	1	Birmingham	1	Sep
11.6		Jennifer Heckford	24.12.89	2	London (TB)	30	Jun
11.6	-0.8	Julie Chadwick	20.05.90	2	Birmingham	1	Sep
11.61		Lyndsey Sharp	11.07.90	1	Glasgow (S)	2	Jun
11.7		Jennifer Taker	16.03.90	1	Wigan	14	Jul
11.73	0.7	Helen Van Kempa	28.10.90	2	Kingston	28	Jul
11.77	-0.8	Natasha Small	9.09.89	3	Birmingham	1	Sep
	(10)						
11.78	0.7	Hayley Comer	26.09.89	3	Kingston	28	Jul
11.79		Rebecca Hughes	4.04.90	2	Tamworth	26	Aug

75 Metres Hurdles - Under 15

11.17	-0.9	Clare Cooper	7.11.87	1	Birmingham	11	Aug
11.2		Kylie Robilliard	11.06.88	1	Guernsey	15	Sep
	11.24	1.2		1	Nottingham	13	Jul
11.26	1.2	Nafalya Francis	21.04.89	2	Nottingham	13	Jul
11.3		Vicky Garrad	22.11.87	1	Bebington	15	Jun
	11.35	1.2		3	Nottingham	13	Jul
11.3		Emily Bonnett	22.09.87	P	Bournemouth	30	Jun
	11.75 w	2.5		4	London (He)	25	Aug
	11.83	-1.5		P	Derby	22	Sep
11.39 w	2.2	Lucy Boggis	27.01.89	1	Watford	26	May
	11.5			1	Bournemouth	8	Jun
	11.52	1.2		6	Nottingham	13	Jul
11.4		Emily Noble	28.04.88	1	Cleckheaton	7	Jul
	11.47	1.2		5	Nottingham	13	Jul
11.41	1.2	Jo Kirby	26.10.87	4	Nottingham	13	Jul
11.43	-0.3	Joanne Baker	15.10.87	1r1	Birmingham	1	Sep
11.5		Faye Richold	24.10.87	1h1	Bedford	18	May
	11.54 w	2.2		2	Watford	26	May
	11.74	2.0		1	London (Ha)	20	Apr
	(10)						
11.5		Harriet Shurley	30.06.88	1r1	Milton Keynes	7	Sep
	11.56	-0.6		3s2	Birmingham	11	Aug

303

11.57	0.5	Natalie Doyle	5.01.89	1h3	Birmingham	11 Aug
11.6		Helen Asher	25.12.88	2	Liverpool	12 May
11.6		Samantha Jones	2.12.87	1	Neath	14 Jul
		11.73 w 2.5		1	Brecon	6 Jul
		11.85 -0.3		2	Tullamore, IRL	3 Aug
11.70 w 2.2		Chloe Van Wulven	10.09.87	3	Watford	26 May
		11.7		1	London (Ha)	30 Jun
11.72	1.0	Yvonne Elms	6.05.88	2	Grangemouth	24 Aug
11.75	1.6	Sally Hughes	17.02.88	1h1	Newport	8 Jun
11.80 w 2.2		Hannah Weekes	14.12.87	4	Watford	26 May
11.8		Alison Bennett	12.04.88	1	Bedford	15 Sep
		11.84 1.1		3h2	London (He)	25 Aug
11.87		Stephanie Peaston	28.10.87	1	Edinburgh	28 Apr
	(20)					
11.87 w 2.5		Lauren Ambrose	26.02.88	6	London (He)	25 Aug
11.90	1.7	Meliha Tas	25.05.89	3h1	London (He)	25 Aug
11.9	1.5	Stehanie Innes	26.12.88	1h2	Grangemouth	19 Jun

80 Metres Hurdles - Under 17

11.33	-1.4	Nicola Robinson	16.04.86	1h1	Birmingham	11 Aug
11.35	0.8	Phyllis Agbo	16.12.85	2	Nottingham	13 Jul
11.39	-1.4	Heather Jones	10.09.86	2h1	Birmingham	11 Aug
11.47	0.8	Catherine Holdsworth	3.01.86	3	Nottingham	13 Jul
11.56	-1.4	Harriet Robinson	21.04.87	3h1	Birmingham	11 Aug
11.61	-0.3	Lisa McManus	3.01.86	1h2	Birmingham	25 May
11.61	0.8	Christina Waters	4.06.87	4	Nottingham	13 Jul
11.61	1.8	Samantha Britton	12.09.86	1	Cudworth	15 Sep
11.62	-2.2	Katey Read	20.03.86	2	Birmingham	11 Aug
11.69		Staci Stewart	20.09.85	1	Grangemouth	14 Jun
	(10)					
11.75	-0.3	Kimberley Brown	1.02.87	2h2	Birmingham	25 May
11.77	1.8	Stacy Flint	18.10.85	2	Cudworth	15 Sep
11.78	1.0	Ciaran Andrews	20.03.86	2	Watford	26 May
11.85	-1.1	Samantha Day	8.02.86	2h1	Birmingham	25 May
11.91	1.0	Stephanie Madgett	22.02.87	3	Watford	26 May
12.01	-0.3	Gemma Werrett	15.03.86	3h2	Birmingham	25 May
12.01	1.0	Natasha Clementis	11.09.86	4	Watford	26 May
12.03	-2.3	Pamela Paterson	26.10.85	5h2	Birmingham	11 Aug
12.08	1.8	Frances Noble	2.05.86	5	Cudworth	15 Sep

wind assisted

11.42	4.1	Catherine Holdsworth	(11.47)	1	Basildon	11 May
11.71	3.2	Stacy Mullan	15.09.86	1	Tullamore, IRL	1 Jun
11.72	2.6	Stacy Flint	(11.77)	1	Birmingham	31 Aug
11.75	2.8	Claire Jones	8.11.86	2	Cardiff	26 Aug
11.78	2.6	Gemma Werrett	(12.01)	2	Birmingham	31 Aug
11.85	2.2	Claire Sargent	11.03.86	1	Birmingham	1 Sep
11.99	2.2	Amy Beighton	6.03.86	2	Birmingham	1 Sep

hand timing

11.2		Nicola Robinson	(11.33)	1	Telford	30 Jun
11.3 w	3.3	Heather Jones	(11.39)	1	Carmarthen	11 May
11.4		Lisa McManus	(11.61)	1	Leicester	15 Jun
11.4		Kimberley Brown	(11.75)	1	Tamworth	21 Jul
11.6		Maria Garavand	30.06.86	1	London (Ha)	30 Jun
11.6		Anna Conolly	19.04.86	2	Telford	7 Sep
11.7		Angie Broadbelt	12.09.85	1	Perivale	27 Jul
11.7		Claire Sargent	(11.85w)	2	Perivale	27 Jul
11.8		Gemma Werrett	(12.01)	1	Coventry	28 Apr
11.8		Samantha Day	(11.85)	1	Tamworth	5 May

11.8		Amy Beighton		(11.99w)	4	Loughborough	11	May
11.8		Stacy Mullan		(11.71w)	1	Antrim	25	May
11.8		Rachel Peckham		14.02.87	1	Guildford	29	Jun
11.8		Marchessa Hollyfield		7.11.85	1	Woking	22	Sep
11.9		Stephanie Madgett		(11.91)	1	Eton	2	Jun
11.9		Ellen Howarth-Brown		26.04.87	1	Sandown IOW	19	Sep
11.9 w		Natasha Clementis		(12.01)	1	Portsmouth	18	May
12.0		Samantha Cook		6.05.87	1	Milton Keynes	21	Apr
12.0		Rachel Gibbens		31.01.86	1	Bedford	18	May
12.0		Emma Giles		26.07.86	1	London (TB)	2	Jun
12.0		Carly Dean		14.10.85	1	Bournemouth	9	Jun
12.0		Jenny Bliss		6.07.86	1	Brighton	6	Jul
12.0		Emily Bonnett	U15	22.09.87	1	Eton	6	Jul
12.0		Claire Jones		(11.75w)	2	Neath	14	Jul
12.0		Eilidh Child		20.02.87	2	Grangemouth	14	Jul

100 Metres Hurdles

12.92	0.8	Diane Allahgreen	21.02.75	1h2	Manchester (C)	29	Jul
	12.92	0.0		3s1	Munich, GER	9	Aug
	13.00	1.6		1	Birmingham	14	Jul
	13.01	0.6		4	Manchester (C)	31	Jul
	13.07	0.7		1	Manchester (C)	15	Jun
	13.07	-0.7		5=	Munich, GER	9	Aug
	13.10	-0.6		1h2	Birmingham	14	Jul
	13.10	0.5		3h1	Munich, GER	8	Aug
	13.11	-0.2		4	Annecy, FRA	23	Jun
	13.12	2.0		2	Bedford	4	Jun
	13.13	0.4		4	Hania, GRE	30	Jun
	13.18	-1.5		1	Bedford	25	May
	13.26	0.0		1h2	Manchester (C)	15	Jun
	13.42	0.6		6	Glasgow (S)	18	Aug
	13.44	-0.5		4	Istanbul, TUR	9	Jun
	13.45	-2.0		1h1	Bedford	25	May
13.08	0.9	Julie Pratt	20.03.79	4h1	Manchester (C)	29	Jul
	13.25	0.6		4	Glasgow (S)	18	Aug
	13.26	0.6		6	Manchester (C)	31	Jul
	13.27	1.6		2	Birmingham	14	Jul
	13.29	0.5		1	Riga, LAT	31	May
	13.30	0.0		1	Sheffield	30	Jun
	13.33	0.7		3	Manchester (C)	15	Jun
	13.34	2.0		4	Bedford	4	Jun
	13.37	0.0		2	Cardiff	8	Jul
	13.37	-0.6		2h2	Birmingham	14	Jul
	13.37	-0.6		8	London (CP)	23	Aug
	13.40	1.3		1h3	Bedford	25	May
	13.43	0.9		1h1	Manchester (C)	15	Jun
	13.52	0.2		1	London (Ha)	20	Apr
	13.61	-1.5		3	Bedford	25	May
13.12	2.0	Melani Wilkins	18.01.73	1	Bedford	4	Jun
	13.29	0.9		5h1	Manchester (C)	29	Jul
	13.34	-1.5		2	Bedford	25	May
	13.38	-0.7		1h1	Watford	2	Jun
13.19	2.0	Rachel King	11.05.76	3	Bedford	4	Jun
	13.31	0.0		2	Sheffield	30	Jun
	13.32	1.6		2rC	Celle Ligure, ITA	26	Jun
	13.34	1.6		3	Birmingham	14	Jul
	13.43	0.7		2h3	Manchester (C)	15	Jun
	13.45	1.7		1h1	Birmingham	14	Jul
	13.54	0.0		3	Cardiff	8	Jul

(King)		13.56	0.7			4	Manchester (C)	15 Jun
		13.58	0.8			6h2	Manchester (C)	29 Jul
		13.59	-1.7			1	Basel, SUI	20 May
		13.61	-0.8			1h1	Basel, SUI	20 May
		13.61	1.7			1h4	Bedford	25 May
13.20	0.7	Natasha Danvers		19.09.77		2	Manchester (C)	15 Jun
		13.30	0.7			1h3	Manchester (C)	15 Jun
13.52	0.7	Tamsin Stephens	U23	2.08.80		3h3	Manchester (C)	15 Jun
		13.57	1.7			1rB	Bedford	4 Jun
		13.59	0.8			7h2	Manchester (C)	29 Jul
		13.60	2.0			6	Bangor	21 Jul
		13.61	-2.0			2h1	Bedford	25 May
13.60	-0.6	Katherine Livesey		15.12.79		1H1	Columbia SC, USA	17 May
13.62	0.7	Helen Worsey	U23	29.08.82		5	Manchester (C)	15 Jun
		13.63	0.0			2h2	Manchester (C)	15 Jun

57 performances to 13.65 by 8 athletes

13.71	0.1	Kelly Sotherton		13.11.76	4H	Talence, FRA	21 Sep
13.72	1.7	Liz Fairs		1.12.77	2h1	Birmingham	14 Jul
	(10)						
13.76	1.8	Gemma Fergusson	U20	20.08.84	1	Bedford	30 Jun
13.76	-2.6	Lynne Fairweather	U23	15.01.80	2	Bedford	30 Jun
13.78	1.6	Bianca Liston		28.05.78	4	Birmingham	14 Jul
13.81		Julie Hollman		16.02.77	1	Tallahassee FL, USA	13 Apr
13.82	0.8	Katy Sketchley		9.07.73	1	Portsmouth	11 May
13.82	-0.2	Kerry Jury		19.11.68	1H1	Manchester (C)	26 Jul
13.85	1.6	Kate Brewington	U23	15.10.81	6	Birmingham	14 Jul
13.92	0.6	Sarah Claxton		23.09.79	1rB	Brasschaat, BEL	14 Aug
13.93	0.7	Alyssa Fullelove	U23	16.09.81	5h3	Manchester (C)	15 Jun
13.94	1.8	Phyllis Agbo	U17	16.12.85	2	Bedford	30 Jun
	(20)						
13.95	1.7	Stefanie Pullinger	U20	3.04.83	4h1	Birmingham	14 Jul
13.96	1.3	Kay Reynolds		15.09.67	3h3	Bedford	25 May
13.96	0.4	Symone Belle	U20	12.11.84	1h2	Watford	2 Jun
13.96	1.7	Sara McGreavy	U23	13.12.82	4rB	Bedford	4 Jun
14.00	-0.7	Jacqui Agyepong		5.01.69	2h1	Watford	2 Jun
14.01	1.8	Jessica Ennis	U17	28.01.86	4	Bedford	30 Jun
14.04	0.8	Jane Hale		4.01.74	2r1	London (BP)	12 Jun
14.05	-1.2	Susan Jones		8.06.78	3	Bedford	17 Aug
14.09	-1.3	Clare Milborrow		10.01.77	1	Alfaz Del Pi, ESP	6 Apr
14.11	1.8	Gemma Bennett	U20	4.01.84	5	Bedford	30 Jun
	(30)						
14.16	0.8	Leyna Hird	U20	4.02.84	2	Nottingham	13 Jul
14.20	0.4	Caroline Pearce	U23	1.09.80	6rB	Loughborough	18 May
14.27	1.4	Chanelle Garnett	U20	16.08.85	2h2	Bedford	30 Jun
14.28	1.7	Roz Gonse	U23	1.03.82	2H2	Pratteln, SUI	3 Aug
14.30	1.7	Clova Court	V40	10.02.60	6h1	Birmingham	14 Jul
14.31	1.4	Cathy Crawford	U20	17.12.84	4h2	Bedford	30 Jun
14.32	1.7	Claire Pearson		23.09.78	7rB	Bedford	4 Jun
14.32	0.8	Hannah Elwiss	U20	8.12.84	4	Nottingham	13 Jul
14.33	0.6	Wendy Davidson	U23	14.10.82	3H2	Hexham	15 Jun
14.33	0.3	Katie Jones		4.01.77	1rB	Birmingham	6 Jul
	(40)						
14.35	0.9	Nicola Gautier		21.03.78	7h1	Manchester (C)	15 Jun
14.36	1.0	Catriona Pennet	U20	10.10.83	1	Derby	8 Sep
14.51	-1.2	Ruth Dales	U23	29.10.80	5h2	Bedford	30 Jun
14.53	1.3	Rebecca Jones	U20	17.01.83	1H2	Woodford	27 Apr
14.55		Aileen Wilson	U20	30.03.84	3	Tallahassee FL, USA	13 Apr
14.55	0.0	Lauren McLoughlin	U23	8.09.82	3	Gold Coast, AUS	23 Apr
14.56	0.0	Vicky Williams	U23	11.04.81	4	Merksem, BEL	17 Aug
14.57		Sara Todd		3.11.79	1	Gateshead	11 May
14.57	0.8	Emma Duck	U23	9.02.81	2	Portsmouth	11 May

14.61	-1.2	Hannah Stares		13.11.78	6	Bedford	6	May
	(50)							
14.62		Lowri Roberts	U23	9.10.81	1	Birmingham (Un)	19	Jun
14.73	-2.4	Joanne Erskine	U20	28.05.85	2	Edinburgh	11	May
14.74	1.0	Maria Garavand	U17	30.06.86	2	Derby	8	Sep
14.75	0.9	Louise Hazel	U17	6.10.85	1H2	Pratteln, SUI	3	Aug
14.78	1.3	Katy Lestrange		17.09.79	6h3	Bedford	25	May
14.79	0.3	Joanne Suddes		27.01.77	2rB	Birmingham	6	Jul
14.79		Katherine Porter	U23	19.08.82	2	Ashford	18	Aug
14.80	1.3	Seemita Gumbs	U23	27.12.81	7h3	Bedford	25	May
14.83	0.4	Laura Turner	U23	12.08.82	4h2	Watford	2	Jun
14.83	0.6	Emma Reid	U23	5.01.81	4	Glasgow (S)	8	Jun
	(60)							
14.85	0.8	Danielle Fawkes	U20	11.08.85	5	Nottingham	13	Jul
14.86	-2.0	Belinda Samuels		29.11.78	6h1	Bedford	25	May
14.89	0.8	Sharon-Louise Walls	U20	9.10.84	6	Nottingham	13	Jul
14.89	1.6	Allison English		4.03.79	2	Cudworth	15	Sep
14.94	0.7	Gillian Stewart	U23	21.01.80	4H3	Pratteln, SUI	3	Aug
14.94		Samantha Day	U17	8.02.86	1	Tamworth	26	Aug
14.96	0.6	Laura Redmond	U23	19.04.81	5H2	Hexham	15	Jun
14.99	-0.4	Wendy Laing	V35	29.12.62	2	Potsdam, GER	24	Aug
15.06		Nusrat Ceesay	U23	18.03.81	3	Birmingham (Un)	19	Jun
15.09	0.5	Maureen Knight		15.11.73	1H2	London (He)	10	Aug
	(70)							
15.11	0.8	Charmaine Johnson	V35	4.06.63	3	Portsmouth	11	May
15.14	0.4	Julia Bennett		26.03.70	6H2	Desenzano, ITA	11	May
15.16		Claire Lomas	U23	18.04.80	3	Edinburgh	28	Apr
15.19	0.8	Claire Lidster	U23	26.10.81	4	Portsmouth	11	May
15.26	1.6	Hannah Longmore	U23	12.11.80	3	Cudworth	15	Sep
15.28	1.8	Anna Clayton	U20	20.03.85	2h2	London (He)	25	Aug
15.29	-1.2	Danielle Parkinson	U23	2.09.81	6	Bedford	17	Aug
15.30	-1.2	Rachael Kay	U23	8.09.80	6h2	Bedford	30	Jun
15.31	-1.2	Susan Potter		11.08.79	7	Bedford	17	Aug
15.32	1.3	Kirsty Roger		24.03.78	2H2	Woodford	27	Apr
	(80)							
15.37	1.2	Rebecca Mitchell	U20	10.12.83	2	Tullamore, IRL	30	Jun
15.38		Sally Hogan		16.11.79	1	Oxford	18	May
15.39	0.6	Amy Teale	U23	30.12.82	6	Glasgow (S)	8	Jun

wind assisted

13.08	4.4	Allahgreen		(12.92)	1	Loughborough	18	May
		13.14 2.2			3	Cork, IRL	6	Jul
13.22	4.4	King		(13.19)	2	Loughborough	18	May
13.27	4.4	Wilkins		(13.12)	3	Loughborough	18	May
13.31	4.4	Pratt		(13.08)	4	Loughborough	18	May
		13.39 3.1			1	Basildon	11	May
13.46	4.4	Helen Worsey	U23	(13.62)	5	Loughborough	18	May
13.64	2.3	Gemma Fergusson	U20	(13.76)	1h1	Bedford	30	Jun
		8 performances to 13.65 by 6 athletes						
13.71	2.5	Clare Milborrow		(14.09)	1	Crawley	11	May
13.73	2.7	Lynne Fairweather	U23	(13.76)	1	Edinburgh	11	May
13.84	3.7	Jane Hale		(14.04)	1	Belfast	8	Jun
13.89	4.4	Alyssa Fullelove	U23	(13.93)	6	Loughborough	18	May
13.99	2.3	Jessica Ennis	U17	(14.01)	2h1	Bedford	30	Jun
14.03	2.3	Gemma Bennett	U20	(14.11)	4h1	Bedford	30	Jun
14.22	2.7	Hannah Stares		(14.61)	4h3	Bedford	5	May
14.36	2.5	Sara Todd		(14.57)	2h1	Bedford	5	May
14.40	2.7	Vicky Williams	U23	(14.56)	5h3	Bedford	5	May
14.41	2.9	Lowri Roberts	U23	(14.62)	3h2	Bedford	5	May
14.58	2.9	Grace Smith	U23	30.01.82	5h2	Bedford	5	May

14.74	2.9	Laura Turner	U23	(14.83)	6h2	Bedford	5	May
14.94	2.5	Sally Hogan		(15.38)	4h1	Bedford	5	May
14.94	2.1	Danielle Parkinson	U23	(15.29)	4H1	London (He)	10	Aug
15.01	2.1	Nicola Plews	U20	15.12.83	1H1	London (He)	10	Aug
15.05	3.7	Rebecca Mitchell	U20	(15.37)	4	Belfast	8	Jun
15.34	2.5	Amy Teale	U23	(15.39)	5h1	Bedford	5	May

hand timing

13.3	-1.3	Wilkins		(13.12)	1	Watford	2	Jun
13.5	0.6	Pratt		(13.08)	1	Eton	4	Aug

2 performances to 13.5 by 2 athletes

13.6	1.9	Helen Worsey	U23	(13.62)	1h1	Bedford	30	Jun
13.9 w		Kay Reynolds	V35	(13.96)	1	Abingdon	27	Apr
13.9 w	2.9	Sarah Claxton		(13.92)	1	London (He)	21	Jul
14.1 w		Leyna Hird	U20	(14.16)	1	Exeter	7	Sep
14.2		Vicky Williams	U23	(14.56)	1	Yate	9	Jun
14.3		Claire Pearson		(14.32)	1	Loughborough	11	May
14.3	1.8	Sara Todd		(14.57)	1	Scunthorpe	7	Jul
14.3 w	4.8	Wendy Davidson	U23	(14.33)	1P	Glasgow (S)	7	Jul
14.3 w	3.3	Ruth Dales	U23	(14.51)	1	Cudworth	25	Aug
14.4					1	Leeds	14	Jul
14.4		Justine Roach	U20	21.12.84	1	Loughborough	11	May
14.4 w		Laura Turner	U23	(14.83)	2	Exeter	7	Sep
14.7					2	Walton	8	Jun
14.5		Emma Duck	U23	(14.57)	2	Exeter	18	May
14.5		Maria Garavand	U17	(14.74)	2	Norwich	24	Aug
14.5 w	2.3	Katherine Porter	U23	(14.79)	2	London (He)	21	Jul
14.6		Donna-Louise Hutt		6.06.72	1	Rugby	25	Aug
14.6 w	2.3	Jenny Kelly		20.06.70	3	London (He)	21	Jul
15.2					1	Bury St. Edmunds	16	Jun
14.7		Katy Lestrange		(14.78)	1	Warrington	11	May
14.7		Samantha Adamson	U23	27.03.82	1	Guernsey	26	May
14.7		Sarah Lane	U23	4.06.81	2	Yate	7	Jul
14.7 w	3.3	Allison English		(14.89)	2	Cudworth	25	Aug
14.8		Natasha Spence		8.11.74	2	Abingdon	11	May
14.8 w	3.3	Sharon-Louise Walls	U20	(14.89)	3	Cudworth	25	Aug
14.9	0.7	Nusrat Ceesay	U23	(15.06)	1	Loughborough	12	Jun
14.9		Wendy Laing	V40	(14.99)	1	Tidworth	21	Jul
14.9 w	4.8	Fiona Harrison	U23	30.11.81	2P	Glasgow (S)	7	Jul
14.9 w	2.9	Angie Broadbelt	U17	12.09.85	2	London (He)	21	Jul
15.0	1.1	Hannah Longmore	U23	(15.26)	3	Cudworth	11	May
15.0	0.5	Alison Keys	U23	11.07.81	2	Cannock	11	May
15.0		Nicola Sanders	U23	23.06.82	1	London (B)	8	Jun
15.0	1.8	Rachael Kay	U23	(15.30)	2	Scunthorpe	7	Jul
15.0		Lyndsay Fitzgerald	U23	31.01.80	4	Derby	11	Aug
15.0		Lorraine Brackstone/Godber		15.02.78	1rB	Rugby	25	Aug
15.0 w	2.7	Emily Parker	U20	7.11.84	2	Abingdon	23	Jun
15.1					3	Bedford	27	Jul
15.0 w	2.9	Leanne Buxton		27.05.78	3	Stoke-on-Trent	21	Jul
15.1		Susan Potter		(15.31)	1rB	Exeter	18	May
15.1		Charmaine Johnson	V35	(15.11)	2	Bournemouth	8	Jun
15.1		Jackie Jenner		25.10.76	1	Horsham	27	Jul
15.1		Sarah Godbeer		10.06.77	1rB	Abingdon	27	Jul
15.2	0.2	Samantha Male		11.04.76	3	Eton	21	Jul
15.2	-0.3	Diana Osagede	U20	18.01.85	2rB	Eton	4	Aug
15.2	1.8	Marchessa Hollyfield	U17	7.11.85	1	London (He)	15	Sep
15.2 w	3.8	Laura Curtis	U23	2.05.81	1rB	Scunthorpe	7	Jul

Additional Under 17 (1 - 3 above)

15.3	Amy Beighton	6.03.86	2	Telford	7	Sep

Foreign

13.97	*1.0*	*Maiteland Marks (USA)*	*19.09.76*	*4*	*Imperia, ITA*	*27 Jun*

300 Metres Hurdles - Under 17

42.21	Eilidh Child	20.02.87	1	Glasgow (S)	20	Jul
43.15	Maria Garavand	30.06.86	1	Nottingham	13	Jul
43.7	Emma Giles	26.07.86	1	Basingstoke	22	Jun
44.22			2	Watford	25	May
44.1	Jenny Bliss	6.07.86	1	Crawley	15	Jun
44.82			1	Crawley	12	May
44.13	Natasha Clementis	11.09.86	1	Watford	25	May
44.2	Ellen Howarth-Brown	26.04.87	1	Hastings	27	Jul
44.21			1	Kingston	4	Aug
44.21	Catherine Holdsworth	3.01.86	1	Basildon	11	May
44.34	Gemma Collier	25.11.85	1h2	Nottingham	12	Jul
44.48	Phyllis Agbo	16.12.85	3	Birmingham	11	Aug
44.69	Faye Harding	7.09.85	1	Brecon	6	Jul
	(10)					
44.71	Marchessa Hollyfield	7.11.85	2h2	Nottingham	12	Jul
44.85	Emma Makin	12.10.85	3	Nottingham	13	Jul
44.90	Carly Dean	14.10.85	4	Birmingham	11	Aug
44.99	Angie Broadbelt	12.09.85	2h1	Nottingham	12	Jul
45.1	Stacy Mullan	15.09.86	1	Tullamore, IRL	22	Jun
45.76			2	Tullamore, IRL	1	Jun
45.1	Amy Forsyth	16.10.85	1	London (TB)	20	Jul
46.11			4h2	Nottingham	12	Jul
45.13	Naida Bromley	27.09.86	3h2	Birmingham	11	Aug
45.26	Amy Beighton	6.03.86	3h1	Birmingham	11	Aug
45.59	Cherri Morrison	27.09.86	3h3	Birmingham	11	Aug
45.7	Kathryn Perry	2.10.85	1	Mansfield	14	Apr
46.43			6h1	Nottingham	12	Jul
	(20)					
45.7	Jessica Case	29.10.85	2	Kingston	12	May
46.11			5h1	Nottingham	12	Jul
45.7	Harriet Robinson	21.04.87	1	Bromley	6	Jul
46.78			5	Watford	25	May
45.79	Rebecca Long	3.10.86	4h1	Nottingham	12	Jul
45.8	Nicola Schofield	13.09.86	2	Kingston	6	Jul
46.90			1rB	Kingston	4	Aug
45.8	Leila Corfield	7.02.86	1	Birmingham	21	Jul
46.66			5h3	Nottingham	12	Jul
46.0	Emma Morris	21.02.86	1	Gateshead	20	Apr
46.71			1	Gateshead	12	May
46.0	Christina Waters	4.06.87	1	Bebington	12	May
46.38			2	Manchester (Wy)	26	May
46.0	Samantha Day	8.02.86	1	Tamworth	2	Jun
46.03			1	Birmingham	26	May
46.27	Emma Smith	14.09.85	4	Watford	25	May
46.29	Patricia Blair	18.03.86	2	Grangemouth	25	Aug
	(30)					
46.3	Natalie Hooper	10.08.86	2	Birmingham	21	Jul
46.34			2	Birmingham	26	May
46.4	Jenny Christie	28.09.85	1	Corby	19	May
46.4	Rachel Peckham	14.02.87	1rB	Kingston	6	Jul
46.5	Rachel Gibbens	31.01.86	2	Kingston	27	Jul
46.6	Jenna Wyatt	3.12.86	1	Woking	14	Jul
46.7	Kathy Clarke	16.10.85	1	Birmingham	15	Jun
46.7	Heather Rodgers	12.09.86	1	Carlisle	30	Jun

46.8	Rachel Culshaw	11.08.86	1	Manchester (Str)	11 May
46.85	Karen Moorcroft	12.12.86	1rB	Birmingham	1 Sep
46.9	Rachel Chadwick	21.09.85	2	Erith	5 May
	(40)				
46.9	Bacardi King	13.05.86	1	Hull	12 May

400 Metres Hurdles

55.68	Natasha Danvers	19.09.77	3	Annecy, FRA	22 Jun
	56.12		3h1	Manchester (C)	27 Jul
	56.14		1	Birmingham	13 Jul
	56.39		4	Sheffield	30 Jun
	56.44		1	Manchester (C)	16 Jun
	56.55		4h1	Munich, GER	7 Aug
	56.60		3	Poznan, POL	18 Aug
	56.76		1	Walnut CA, USA	21 Apr
	56.93		7	Munich, GER	8 Aug
	57.86		1h1	Birmingham	12 Jul
	57.86		4	Yokohama, JPN	16 Sep
	59.03		1h2	Manchester (C)	15 Jun
56.53	Tracey Duncan	16.05.79	2	Manchester (C)	16 Jun
	56.76		3	Brisbane, AUS	13 Apr
	57.04		4	Hengelo, NED	2 Jun
	57.45		5h2	Manchester (C)	27 Jul
	57.51		3	Birmingham	13 Jul
	57.52		1	Watford	1 Sep
	57.54		5h3	Munich, GER	7 Aug
	57.88		2h1	Brisbane, AUS	11 Apr
	57.96		8	Sheffield	30 Jun
	57.98		1h1	Manchester (C)	15 Jun
	58.74		7	Bratislava, SVK	11 Jun
	58.77		1	Melbourne, AUS	5 Apr
	58.82		1	Loughborough	18 May
	58.91		1h3	Birmingham	12 Jul
56.88	Sinead Dudgeon	9.07.76	2	Birmingham	13 Jul
	56.91		2h2	Munich, GER	7 Aug
	57.10		1	La Chaux de Fonds, SUI	18 Aug
	57.11		4h2	Manchester (C)	27 Jul
	57.26		1r4	Annecy, FRA	28 Jun
	57.51		1r1	Tarare, FRA	29 Jun
	58.47		1	Glasgow (S)	9 Jun
	58.68		6	Manchester (C)	28 Jul
	58.88		1h2	Birmingham	12 Jul
	59.39		8	Munich, GER	8 Aug
	56.70 (1 hurdle missing)		2	Lisbon, POR	15 Jun
57.69	Katie Jones	4.01.77	5h1	Manchester (C)	27 Jul
	57.71		3	Manchester (C)	16 Jun
	57.93		1	Tartu, EST	2 Jun
	57.97		4	Birmingham	13 Jul
	58.49		1	Riga, LAT	31 May
	58.61		4r4	Annecy, FRA	28 Jun
	58.68		1h3	Manchester (C)	15 Jun
	59.26		4r1	Tarare, FRA	29 Jun
58.30	Kelly Sotherton	13.11.76	2	Watford	1 Sep
	58.72		1	Bedford	17 Aug
58.48	Liz Fairs	1.12.77	4	Manchester (C)	16 Jun
	58.6		1	Bedford	4 Jun
	59.05		1	Jarrow	1 Jun
	59.26		3r3	Annecy, FRA	28 Jun
	59.29		1	Bedford	26 May
	59.30		1h1	Jarrow	1 Jun

58.72	Nicola Sanders	U23	23.06.82	4	La Chaux de Fonds, SUI	18	Aug
	59.18			3	Niort, FRA	3	Aug
58.8	Hannah Wood	U23	17.11.81	2	Bedford	30	Jun
	59.0			2	Bedford	4	Jun
	59.06			5	Manchester (C)	16	Jun
	59.20			3	Newport	20	Jul
	59.3			1	Birmingham	2	Jun
	58 performances to 59.3 by 8 athletes						
59.6	Gowry Retchakan	V40	21.06.60	1	London (He)	21	Jul
59.7	Hannah Stares		13.11.78	1	Watford	1	Jun
	60.45			3	Bedford	5	May
(10)							
59.89	Susie Williams		2.06.77	1h2	Watford	1	Jun
60.0	Samantha Adamson	U23	27.03.82	3	Bedford	30	Jun
	60.21			6	Manchester (C)	16	Jun
60.05	Ruth Brereton	U23	26.06.81	2h2	Watford	1	Jun
60.30	Justine Roach	U20	21.12.84	2rB	Loughborough	18	May
60.3	Jennifer Culley		4.03.75	3	Watford	1	Jun
	60.34			3rB	Loughborough	18	May
60.31	Celia Brown		22.01.77	1	Manchester (Str)	6	Aug
60.46	Claire Brason	U20	16.03.83	7	Manchester (C)	16	Jun
60.48	Sian Scott	U20	20.03.84	1	Nottingham	13	Jul
60.65	Sara Todd		3.11.79	1	Gateshead	12	May
60.75	Laura Curtis	U23	2.05.81	4	Watford	1	Sep
(20)							
61.18	Louise Aylwin	U23	8.04.80	4h3	Manchester (C)	15	Jun
61.25	Joanne Suddes		27.01.77	2	Glasgow (S)	9	Jun
61.3	Faye Harding	U17	7.09.85	4=	Bedford	4	Jun
	61.32			4	Loughborough	18	May
61.4	Michele Gillham		8.10.74	1	Eton	4	Aug
	62.28			5h1	Birmingham	12	Jul
61.54	Melanie Canning	U20	19.05.85	2h1	Nottingham	12	Jul
61.58	Joanne Oates		21.02.78	3	Amsterdam, NED	26	May
61.8	Gemma Dooney	U20	12.05.84	3	Stoke-on-Trent	19	May
	62.10			2	Manchester (C)	25	May
61.8	Shona MacPherson	U23	31.08.80	1	Coventry	19	May
	61.88			2	Manchester (Str)	6	Aug
61.82	Jane Hale		4.01.74	2	Bath	12	May
62.4	Claire Heafford	U23	9.07.81	2h4	Watford	1	Jun
	63.05			3	Kingston	12	May
(30)							
62.44	Maria Garavand	U17	30.06.86	1	Derby	8	Sep
62.45	Claire Holmes	U20	11.08.85	3	Manchester (C)	25	May
62.53	Emma Reid	U23	5.01.81	3	Glasgow (S)	9	Jun
62.7	Kim Heffernan	V35	20.12.66	1	Wakefield	7	Jul
	64.91			6h2	Birmingham	12	Jul
62.75	Donna Porazinski	U23	28.01.81	5rB	Bath	12	May
62.8	Katherine Porter	U23	19.08.82	1	London (ME)	11	May
	65.74			6h3	Watford	1	Jun
62.8	Niki Pocock		9.05.79	1	Eton	21	Jul
	62.92			4h3	Watford	1	Jun
62.92	Sam Watts	U23	13.10.81	2	Oxford	26	Jun
62.93	Virginia Mitchell	V35	29.01.63	2	Potsdam, GER	17	Aug
62.98	Emily Parker	U20	7.11.84	2	Watford	25	May
(40)							
63.0	Lyndsay Fitzgerald	U23	31.01.80	2	Cheltenham	6	May
	63.07			3	Bath	12	May
63.0	Susan Potter		11.08.79	1	Bournemouth	11	May
	64.78			7	London (He)	3	Aug
63.0	Louise Douglass	U23	8.12.80	4h4	Watford	1	Jun
	63.45			5	Ashford	18	Aug

63.0	Teresa Impey	U23	6.05.81	2	Eton	21	Jul
	64.04			4r2	Bedford	17	Aug
63.19	Leanne Buxton		27.05.78	5	London (He)	3	Aug
63.20	Jessica Cunliffe		25.11.77	3	Birmingham	6	Jul
63.2	Rebecca Wright		20.12.77	2	London (ME)	11	May
63.23	Natalie Kydd	U20	27.06.84	1	Edinburgh	22	May
63.36	Nusrat Ceesay	U23	18.03.81	2	Birmingham (Un)	19	Jun
63.36	Natalie Christmas	U20	9.04.84	4	Nottingham	13	Jul
	(50)						
63.39	Sarah-Jane Pickett	U20	24.10.84	2h2	Nottingham	12	Jul
63.4	Charlotte Randall	U23	10.05.80	2	London (TB)	27	Apr
	64.44			5	Kingston	12	May
63.54	Helen Walker	U23	12.10.80	5h1	Madison, USA	18	May
63.56	Anastasia Hounslow	U23	13.12.82	4	Kingston	12	May
63.7	Faith Cripps	U20	23.09.83	1	Guildford	27	Apr
	64.51			4h2	Watford	1	Jun
63.7	Alyssa Fullelove	U23	16.09.81	1rB	Coventry	19	May
64.0	Katy Taylor	U23	18.06.80	1	Peterborough	11	May
	64.59			2	Oxford	18	May
64.0	Jackie Cooke		20.06.76	1	Nuneaton	9	Jun
64.1	Katy Sketchley		9.07.73	2	Welwyn	29	Mar
64.1	Joanne Erskine	U20	28.05.85	2	Eton	23	Jun
	64.95			1	Edinburgh	12	May
	(60)						
64.14	Gemma Bennett	U20	4.01.84	1h2	Bedford	29	Jun
64.14	Carly Austin	U20	16.05.83	6	Ashford	18	Aug
64.4	Kirsty Baird		29.08.71	2	Grangemouth	14	Jul
64.5	Kate Norman		1.01.76	4=rB	Watford	4	Jun
	64.63			5h2	Watford	1	Jun
64.6	Christine Amede	V35	7.08.63	1rB	Eton	27	Apr
64.61	Claire Acford	V35	17.03.64	3	Potsdam, GER	17	Aug
64.7	Michelle Thomas		16.10.71	1rB	Rugby	25	Aug
64.8	Seonaid Murray	U20	16.03.85	1	Birmingham	22	Jun
	65.51			5	Manchester (C)	25	May
64.8	Sian Davies	U20	16.02.85	1	Yate	23	Jun
	65.06			4h1	Nottingham	12	Jul
65.1	Michelle Debono		1.05.72	4h1	Watford	1	Jun
	(70)						
65.2	Tracey Hilton		9.03.78	4	Wakefield	7	Jul
65.24	Ruth Waller	U20	6.03.84	2rB	Birmingham	6	Jul
65.3	Claire Lidster	U23	26.10.81	1	Southampton	27	Apr
65.3	Naida Bromley	U17	27.09.86	2	Cudworth	25	Aug
65.31	Lucy Aukett	U20	9.09.84	5h1	Nottingham	12	Jul
65.4	Veronica Boden	V40	23.12.58	2	Bournemouth	8	Jun
65.47	Rebecca Reid	U20	9.11.83	4	Manchester (C)	25	May
65.48	Angela Shearer	U20	18.01.85	5h1	Caen, FRA	29	May
65.54	Jenny Christie	U17	28.09.85	4rB	Birmingham	19	Jun
65.6	Claire Bryant	U23	1.02.80	1	Portsmouth	6	Jul
	(80)						
65.70	Judith Owen		20.06.71	6	Kingston	12	May
65.7	Sarah Newman		7.10.79	3	Aberdare	15	Jun
65.71	Gemma Collier	U17	25.11.85	5	Bedford	17	Aug
65.90	Catriona Pennet	U20	10.10.83	4	Derby	8	Sep
65.9	Claire Entwistle		9.12.76	1	Wigan	15	Aug
65.97	Emma Peters	U20	12.01.84	1	Birmingham	26	May
66.0	Emma Giles	U17	26.07.86	1	Hoo	7	Sep
66.09	Cherri Morrison	U17	27.09.86	1rB	Derby	8	Sep
66.2	Elizabeth Waters		19.02.77	1	Corby	11	May
66.2	Sarah Beevers		18.11.76	3rB	Wakefield	7	Jul
	(90)						
66.26	Jayne Mould	U20	7.11.83	3	Birmingham	25	May

66.3	Dana Harvey	U23	7.08.81	1	Reading	8	Jun
66.4	Linda Crocker		2.04.79	1rB	Basingstoke	7	Sep
66.43	Hayley Goodall	U20	20.09.84	3	London (He)	25	Aug

Additional Under 17 (1 - 7 above)

66.7	Marchessa Hollyfield		7.11.85	1	Woking	22	Jun
66.8	Kathryn Perry		2.10.85	1	Cleckheaton	15	Sep
67.0	Emma Makin		12.10.85	2	Manchester (Str)	28	Apr
67.0	Emma Morris		21.02.86	2	Cleckheaton	15	Sep
67.05	Jenni Owens		15.05.87	5	Derby	8	Sep
68.0	Emma Smith		14.09.85	1rB	London (WF)	18	Aug

Foreign

58.10	*Maiteland Marks (USA)*		*19.09.76*	*3*	*Loughborough*	*17*	*Jul*
58.57	*Michelle Carey (IRL)*	*U23*	*20.02.81*	*2*	*Tartu, EST*	*2*	*Jun*
61.16	*Mandy Bloomer (IRL)*		*3.03.74*	*2*	*Belfast*	*8*	*Jun*

High Jump

1.92 i	Susan Jones		8.06.78	Q	Vienna, AUT	1	Mar
	1.92			1	Birmingham	14	Jul
	1.91			1	Cardiff	8	Jul
	1.90 i			1	Cardiff	2	Feb
	1.90 i			6=	Stockholm, SWE	6	Feb
	1.90 i			5=	Vienna, AUT	2	Mar
	1.90			4=	Annecy, FRA	23	Jun
	1.90			2	Manchester (C)	30	Jul
	1.90			QB	Munich, GER	9	Aug
	1.89 i			4	Glasgow	9	Mar
	1.89			7=	Munich, GER	11	Aug
	1.88			1	Manchester (C)	16	Jun
	1.85			1	Sheffield	30	Jun
	1.85			12=	Lausanne, SUI	2	Jul
	1.85			1	Bedford	17	Aug
	1.85			7=	London (CP)	23	Aug
	1.84			1	Loughborough	18	May
	1.84			1	Bedford	25	May
1.88	Rebecca Jones	U20	17.01.83	1H	Arles, FRA	1	Jun
	1.86 i			1	Cardiff	19	Jan
	1.84			2	Gorizia, ITA	6	Jul
	1.83 i			1P	Eaubonne, FRA	24	Feb
	1.83			1	Bedford	30	Jun
1.85	Debbie Marti		14.05.68	1	Kingston	11	May
1.85	Julie Hollman		16.02.77	1H	Gotzis, AUT	1	Jun
1.85	Stephanie Higham	U20	26.12.83	2	Manchester (C)	16	Jun
	1.83			2	Bedford	30	Jun
1.84 i	Julia Bennett		26.03.70	2	Cardiff	2	Feb
	1.83			1	Eton	21	Jul
1.83 i	Aileen Wilson	U20	30.03.84	1P	Glasgow	10	Feb
	1.75			2	Scunthorpe	7	Jul
1.83	Julie Crane		26.09.76	1	London (He)	3	Aug
	31 performances to 1.83 by 8 athletes including 9 indoors						
1.81 i	Jo Jennings		20.09.69	1	Birmingham	12	Jan
	1.70			2	London (He)	3	Aug
1.80	Lindsey-Ann McDonnell		13.08.79	2	Perth, AUS	13	Jan
	(10)						
1.80 i	Jessica Ennis	U17	28.01.86	2	Cardiff	10	Feb
	1.80			1	Nottingham	13	Jul
1.80	Emma Perkins	U17	4.09.85	2	Nottingham	13	Jul

313

1.78 i	Natalie Clark	U23	4.09.82	1	Birmingham	22	Jan
1.78				1	Scunthorpe	7	Jul
1.78 i	Dalia Mikneviciute		5.09.70	4	Cardiff	2	Feb
1.78	Dominique Blaize	U15	3.10.87	1P	Hemel Hempstead	30	Jun
1.77	Shani Rainford	U17	6.07.87	3	Nottingham	13	Jul
1.77	Kerry Jury		19.11.68	4H	Manchester (C)	26	Jul
1.75	Kelly Sotherton		13.11.76	6H	Bydgoszcz, POL	29	Jun
1.75	Samantha Adamson	U23	27.03.82	1	Brighton	6	Jul
1.74	Katherine Livesey		15.12.79	1H	College Station, USA	14	Mar
	(20)						
1.74	Fiona Harrison	U23	30.11.81	1	Derby	11	Aug
1.73 i	Stephanie Pywell	U17	12.06.87	1	Birmingham	13	Jan
1.73				1	Cleckheaton	15	Sep
1.73 i	Liz Sweeney	U17	13.01.86	1	Birmingham	27	Jan
1.65				1	Macclesfield	30	Mar
1.73	Claire Wright	U20	9.09.83	1	Warrington	12	May
1.72	Emma Morris	U17	21.02.86	1H	Jarrow	29	Jun
1.71 i	Caroline Pearce	U23	1.09.80	3P	Eaubonne, FRA	24	Feb
1.71				1H	Wrexham	22	Jun
1.71	Sarah Fielding Smith	U17	19.11.86	1	Crawley	15	Jun
1.71	Laura Pitts	U17	9.01.86	4	Nottingham	13	Jul
1.70 i	Judith Payne	U23	7.07.80	5=	Birmingham	12	Jan
1.70				1	Oxford	26	Jun
1.70 i	Catriona Christie	U20	26.04.85	3	Glasgow	20	Jan
1.65				1	London (He)	28	Apr
	(30)						
1.70 i	Gillian Black		27.10.79	4	Glasgow	20	Jan
1.70				1	Edinburgh	28	Apr
1.70	Carly Sharp	U15	7.09.87	1	Edinburgh	28	Apr
1.70	Ceri Stokoe	U23	19.04.82	1	Carmarthen	11	May
1.70	Hazel Melvin		19.11.73	1	Coventry	19	May
1.70	Rachel Howard	U17	5.08.87	1	Tamworth	2	Jun
1.70	Denise Gayle		11.09.79	1	London (Ha)	8	Jun
1.70	Ailsa Wallace		12.03.77	1	Singapore, SIN	8	Sep
1.70 i	Frances McKirdy	U17	9.07.87	1	Chelmsford	15	Dec
1.68				5	Nottingham	13	Jul
1.69 i	Helen Smith	U20	9.10.84	1	Bedford	20	Jan
1.65				1	Watford	26	May
1.69	Danielle Fidge	U20	19.03.85	1	London (Cr)	23	Jun
	(40)						
1.69	Jennifer Glaysher	U20	3.05.83	5	Bedford	30	Jun
1.68	Sarah-Jane Darrington	U20	25.06.85	1	Luton	12	May
1.68	Nadine Simpson	U17	28.02.86	2	Watford	25	May
1.68	Maureen Knight		15.11.73	2H	Birmingham	1	Jun
1.68	Paula Naylor	U17	13.09.86	1	Cudworth	15	Jun
1.68	Sarah Allison	U17	18.11.86	2	Jarrow	22	Jun
1.68	Rachel Culshaw	U17	11.08.86	1H	Preston	29	Jun
1.68	Natalie Hulse	U23	2.12.82	2	Derby	11	Aug
1.67 i	Natasha Speight	U15	9.09.87	1	Birmingham	27	Jan
1.61				3	Nottingham	12	Jul
1.67	Gillian Stewart	U23	21.01.80	3=H	Hexham	15	Jun
	(50)						
1.67	Danielle Freeman	U23	11.02.80	1	Lincoln	7	Jul
1.67	Vicky Milne	U23	12.07.80	1	Bebington	4	Aug
1.67 i	Phyllis Agbo	U20	16.12.85	3=P	Glasgow	14	Dec
1.65		U17		2H	Wrexham	22	Jun
1.67 i	Lisa Ferguson	U17	10.09.86	3=P	Glasgow	14	Dec
1.65				1	Aberdeen	21	Apr
1.67 i	Catherine Smy	U17	7.04.87	3=P	Glasgow	14	Dec
1.65				1	Edinburgh	11	May

1.66 i	Ayamba Akim			21.06.72	1	Bedford	20 Jan
1.66 i	Claire Huck	U17		11.10.86	2	Birmingham	23 Feb
1.66	Michelle Hammond	U20		26.03.85	1	Par	11 May
1.66	Juliet Fullwood	U20		1.07.85	1	Grantham	15 Jun
1.66	Rebecka Bell	U17		1.12.85	1	Grantham	22 Jun
	(60)						
1.66	Victoria Hawkins	U20		12.06.84	1=	Birmingham	22 Jun
1.66	Wendy Laing	V35		29.12.62	1	Tidworth	21 Sep
1.65 i	Nicole Smallwood			9.10.77	5	Birmingham	12 Jan
1.65					5	Bedford	25 May
1.65 i	Rachel Martin			9.09.78	5=	Sheffield	19 Jan
1.65					1	Birmingham	6 Jul
1.65 i	Jenny Pacey	U20		5.02.83	5=	Sheffield	19 Jan
1.65					1H	Birmingham	1 Jun
1.65 i	Kirsty Roger			24.03.78	2P	Glasgow	10 Feb
1.65					2H	Woodford	27 Apr
1.65 i	Antonia Bemrose			3.09.79	2	Glasgow	24 Feb
1.65					2=	Bedford	4 May
1.65 i	Catriona Forrest	U20		25.08.84	4	Birmingham	24 Feb
1.65 i	Laura Redmond	U23		19.04.81	6P	Eaubonne, FRA	24 Feb
1.65 i	Kate Brewington	U23		15.10.81	2P	Cardiff	10 Mar
1.65					1=H	London (He)	10 Aug
	(70)						
1.65	Katia Lannon	U17		14.09.85	1	Derby	28 Apr
1.65	Susannah Green	U23		5.12.81	4	Bedford	4 May
1.65	Gayle O'Connor			24.08.79	1	Bebington	12 May
1.65	Natalia Norford	U23		29.09.82	1	Luton	12 May
1.65	Wendy Davidson	U23		14.10.82	3H	Birmingham	1 Jun
1.65	Roz Gonse	U23		1.03.82	4H	Birmingham	1 Jun
1.65	Emily Mason	U20		28.04.85	2	Manchester (Str)	4 Jun
1.65	Sarah Wellstead			22.10.79	1	Walton	8 Jun
1.65	Gemma Eastman	U17		1.02.87	2	Bournemouth	22 Jun
1.65	Amy Fuller	U17		24.06.87	1	Ware	23 Jun
	(80)						
1.65	India Hadland	U20		7.01.85	1	Braunton	6 Jul
1.65	Lucy McManus	U17		2.03.87	1	Aldershot	20 Jul
1.65	Jemma Scott	U20		14.03.83	1	Wakefield	28 Jul
1.65	Hayley Goodall	U20		20.09.84	2	Eton	4 Aug
1.65	Lauren Ambrose	U15		26.02.88	1	St. Albans	4 Aug
1.65	Danielle Parkinson	U23		2.09.81	1	Manchester (Str)	6 Aug
1.65	Jenny Brown	V40		21.05.59	1	Potsdam, GER	21 Aug
1.65	Aneska Binks			24.06.77	1=	Nottingham	25 Aug
1.65	Diana Davies	V40		7.05.61	1=	Nottingham	25 Aug
1.65	Amy Woodman	U20		1.11.84	1=	Nottingham	25 Aug
	(90)						
1.65	Becky Mawer	U20		31.01.84	1	Grimsby	1 Sep

Additional Under 17 (1 - 17 above)

1.63	Lucy Howes			27.06.86	1	London (PH)	27 Apr
1.63	Tania Spurling			20.08.87	1	Hemel Hempstead	23 Jun
1.63	Samantha Case			5.01.86	1H	Bournemouth	29 Jun
	(20)						
1.63	Rachel Egbuniwe			5.07.86	1	London (ME)	6 Jul
1.62	Katie O'Sullivan			16.02.87	2	Walton	8 Jun
1.62	Caroline Newton			26.10.85	1	Leicester	15 Jun
1.62	Donna Wilson			1.10.86	3	Bournemouth	22 Jun
1.62	Celia Dupont			23.07.87	15	Nottingham	13 Jul
1.62	Katie Donnelly			12.11.85	1	Tamworth	26 Aug
1.62	Jenny Christie			28.09.85	1=H	Stoke-on-Trent	28 Sep
1.62	Lauren Newman			17.01.87	1=H	Stoke-on-Trent	28 Sep

Additional Under 15 (1 - 4 above)

1.64	Wendy Meadows-Smith	15.07.88	1	Nottingham	12	Jul
1.64	Jessica Horler	9.06.88	2	Nottingham	12	Jul
1.63	Katie Sadler	15.01.88	1	Reading	7	May
1.63	Vikki Hubbard	13.07.89	1	Grantham	14	Jul
1.62	Rachael MacKenzie	23.12.87	1	Inverness	1	Sep
1.62	Amy Grainger	7.08.88	1	Brierley Hill	15	Sep
	(10)					
1.61 i	Ashley Little	19.01.89		Dortmund, GER	17	Mar
	1.60		P	Jarrow	30	Jun
1.61	Isaura Collyer	21.10.87	2	Peterborough	26	Aug
1.60	Amy Pelling	10.12.88	1	Birmingham	26	May
1.60	Lucy Boggis	27.01.89	1	Eton	2	Jun
1.60	Hayley Buchanan	9.11.87	1	Grangemouth	19	Jun
1.60	Caroline Sellars	26.09.87	1	Jarrow	22	Jun
1.60	Juliet Fielden	9.10.88	1	Crawley	26	Jun
1.60	Abigail Atta-Pannin	8.05.88	1	Brighton	30	Jun
1.60	Hannah Weekes	14.12.87	P	Hemel Hempstead	30	Jun
1.60	Odette Regent	27.11.87	1	Ashford	4	Aug
	(20)					
1.60	Eve Carrington	19.04.88	2	Grangemouth	24	Aug
1.60	Erin Leggate	6.02.89	3	Grangemouth	24	Aug
1.60	Chloe Van Wulven	10.09.87	1	Birmingham	1	Sep
1.60	Nimneh Hyde	20.09.87	2	Birmingham	1	Sep
1.60	Erica Bodman		1	Guernsey	15	Sep
1.60	Emily Bonnett	22.09.87	P	Derby	22	Sep

Under 13

1.55	Amelia Montagnani	10.03.90	1	Hemel Hempstead	6	Jul
1.48	Lauren Vickers	11.05.90	2	London (BP)	31	Aug
1.46	Anna Cathro	6.01.90	1	Coatbridge	23	Jun
1.46	Rebecca Ford	19.01.90	1	Grangemouth	24	Aug
1.45	Vicky Wheatland	13.12.89	1	Thurrock	19	Aug
1.45	Rachel Wallader	1.09.89	1	Nuneaton	1	Sep
1.45	Hatty Scaramalga	31.05.90	1	Street	17	Sep
1.44	Kayley Alcorn	22.01.90	1	Crawley	1	Sep
1.44	Jessica Higman	4.06.90	1	Grimsby	7	Sep
1.43	Nadine Hinze	19.12.89	1	Brighton	30	Jun
	(10)					
1.43	Megan Tyler	2.05.90	1	Manchester (Str)	21	Jul

Foreign

1.70	*Niina Masalin (FIN)*	*3.01.77*	*3*	*London (He)*	*3*	*Aug*

Pole Vault

4.44 i	Janine Whitlock ¶	11.08.73	4	Birmingham	17	Feb
	4.33 i		4	Ghent, BEL	10	Feb
	4.25		1	Bedford	4	Jun
	4.20 i		1	Cardiff	3	Feb
	4.20 i		15=	Vienna, AUT	1	Mar
	4.10 i		1	Birmingham	22	Jan
	4.01 i		3=	Glasgow	9	Mar
	4.00 i		15=	Piraeus, GRE	20	Feb
	3.95 i		9	Wuppertal, GER	1	Feb
	3.92		2	Loughborough	18	May
	4.41 drug disqualification		1	Manchester (C)	16	Jun
	4.35 after drug disqualification		1	Birmingham	13	Jul
	4.10 after drug disqualification		5	Annecy, FRA	22	Jun

4.16	Liz Hughes		9.06.77	1	Portsmouth	6	Jul
4.10				1	Chelmsford	27	Jul
4.05				4	Loughborough	17	Jul
3.95				1	London (He)	8	Jun
3.92				1	Loughborough	18	May
3.90				2	Watford	1	Jun
3.90				4=	Birmingham	13	Jul
3.90				3=	Newport	20	Jul
4.15	Rhian Clarke		19.04.77	1	Baton Rouge LA, USA	19	Apr
4.09				1	Houston, USA	27	Apr
4.05				2	Austin TX, USA	23	Mar
4.05				3	Manchester (C)	16	Jun
4.05				2=	Birmingham	13	Jul
4.02 i				1	Bloomington, USA	22	Feb
4.00 A				1	El Paso TX, USA	13	Apr
4.00				5	Baton Rouge LA, USA	29	May
4.00				1	Newport	9	Jun
4.00				1	London (He)	21	Jul
3.95 i				1	Baton Rouge LA, USA	26	Jan
3.95				4	Cardiff	8	Jul
3.90				3	Regensburg, GER	22	Jun
3.90				5	Loughborough	17	Jul
3.90				QA	Manchester (C)	28	Jul
4.15	Irie Hill		16.01.69	2	Manchester (C)	16	Jun
4.15				1	Birmingham	13	Jul
4.10				3=	Manchester (C)	29	Jul
4.10				12=	London (CP)	23	Aug
4.05				3	Cardiff	8	Jul
4.05				2	Brasschaat,	14	Aug
4.00				1	Ballarat, AUS	19	Jan
4.00				6	Adelaide, AUS	23	Mar
4.00				1	Regensburg, GER	22	Jun
4.00				1	Cheltenham	17	Jul
4.00				QA	Manchester (C)	28	Jul
4.00				1	Melbourne, AUS	12	Oct
3.96				1	Nivelles,	16	Aug
3.95				2	Melbourne, AUS	3	Mar
3.90				6	Brisbane, AUS	13	Apr
3.90				2	Meilen, SUI	9	Jun
3.90				3	Berne, SUI	28	Jun
3.90				1	Birmingham	6	Jul
3.90				1	Eton	21	Jul
4.05	Tracey Bloomfield		13.09.79	2=	Birmingham	13	Jul
4.00				1	Guildford	27	Apr
4.00				1	Watford	1	Jun
3.95				3	Bedford	4	Jun
3.92				2	Barcelona, ESP	6	Sep
3.90 i				1	Cardiff	10	Feb
3.90				1	Guildford	18	May
3.90				2	Portsmouth	6	Jul
3.90				6	Loughborough	17	Jul
3.90				QB	Manchester (C)	28	Jul
3.90				10	Manchester (C)	29	Jul
3.90				1	Watford	1	Sep
4.00 i	Sonia Lawrence	U23	19.01.80	1	Cardiff	20	Jan
3.90 i				1	Cardiff	16	Feb
3.90				13QB	Manchester (C)	28	Jul
4.00	Lucy Webber		5.02.72	4	Irvine	5	May
4.00				1	Ashford	18	Aug
3.95				1	Bromley	18	May
3.95				2	Bedford	4	Jun

(Webber)	3.95			1	Bromley	8	Jun
	3.90 i			1	Birmingham	13	Jan
	3.90 i			1	Birmingham	27	Jan
	3.90 i			3=	Cardiff	3	Feb
	3.90			4=	Birmingham	13	Jul
	3.90			QA	Manchester (C)	28	Jul
	3.90			8	Manchester (C)	29	Jul
4.00	Kate Dennison	U20	7.05.84	7	Kingston, JAM	18	Jul
	3.95			1	Bedford	29	Jun
	3.91 i			1	Birmingham	23	Feb
	3.85			1	Birmingham	26	May
	3.85			5	Manchester (C)	16	Jun
4.00	Zoe Brown	U20	15.09.83	QA	Manchester (C)	28	Jul
	3.90			1	Bangor	21	Jul
	3.90			7	Manchester (C)	29	Jul
	3.85			2	Bedford	29	Jun
3.90	Gillian Cooke	U23	3.10.82	1	Glasgow (S)	2	Jun
	(10)						
3.85	Ellie Spain	U23	23.08.82	1	Bedford	29	Jun

89 performances to 3.85 by 11 athletes including 17 indoors

3.80 i	Gael Davies		5.02.79	3	Birmingham	27	Jan
	3.40			5	Amsterdam, NED	26	May
3.80	Hannah Olson	U15	29.01.88	1	Ashford	8	Jun
3.75	Emma Hornby		12.12.73	1	Birmingham	2	Jun
3.75	Natalie Olson	U17	9.05.86	10	Manchester (C)	16	Jun
3.71 i	Kirsty Maguire	U20	5.07.83	2	Birmingham	23	Feb
	3.60			1	Grangemouth	20	Apr
3.70	Clare Ridgley		11.09.77	2	Oxford	26	Jun
3.60	Rebekah Telford		4.11.76	1	Stoke-on-Trent	26	Mar
3.60	Catherine MacRae		1.01.79	12	Manchester (C)	16	Jun
3.54	Larissa Lowe	V35	19.08.63	1	Exeter	7	Sep
	(20)						
3.51	Becky Ridgley	U23	26.02.80	1	Exeter	18	May
3.50 i	Rebecca Lumb		3.09.77	1	Wakefield	12	Jan
3.50 i	Caroline Nutt	U20	17.06.83	3	Wakefield	12	Jan
	3.40			1	Scunthorpe	23	Jun
3.50 i	Helen Roscoe		4.12.79	2	Birmingham	22	Jan
3.50 i	Hilary Smith		28.02.76	11	Cardiff	3	Feb
	3.50			1	Birmingham	3	Jul
3.50 i	Kim Skinner	U15	21.09.87	1	Glasgow	17	Feb
	3.40			1	Grangemouth	7	Aug
3.50 i	Anna Leyshon	U23	19.01.80	1	Glasgow	24	Feb
	3.50			4	Bedford	4	May
3.50	Laura Patterson	U23	31.01.81	1	London (BP)	27	Apr
3.50	Jennifer Graham	U20	1.07.84	1	Grangemouth	5	Jun
3.50	Alison Davies	V40	6.04.61	10=	Birmingham	13	Jul
3.40 i	Lindsay Hodges	U23	21.09.82	2	Cardiff	6	Jan
	(30)						
3.40 i	Linda Stanton		22.06.73	6	Birmingham	27	Jan
	3.40			7	Birmingham	6	Jul
3.40	Kath Callaghan	U23	11.04.80	1	Ashford	18	May
3.40	Clare Neve	U17	11.06.86	1	Wakefield	28	Jul
3.40 mx	Jemma Harding		15.02.79	1	Hastings	3	Aug
	3.35 i			1	Bedford	14	Apr
3.40	Ruth Anness		3.10.78	1	Norwich	26	Aug
3.30	Claire Holmes	U20	11.08.85	2	Manchester (C)	25	May
3.30	Eilidh Dorrian	U17	8.10.85	3	Glasgow (S)	20	Jul
3.20 i	Sundeep Brar	U20	26.02.85	1	Eton	6	Jan
	2.75			3	Watford	8	Sep
3.20 i	Rachel Gibbens	U17	31.01.86	2	Bedford	19	Jan
	3.10			1	London (He)	10	Aug

318

3.20 A	Allie Murray-Jessee	V35	13.01.67	3	Albuquerque NM, USA	27	Apr
	3.20			3	Glasgow (S)	2	Jun
	3.90 A unconfirmed			1	El Paso TX, USA	22	May
	3.75 unconfirmed			2	Albuquerque NM, USA	15	Jun
	(40)						
3.20	Suzanne Woods		29.12.76	1	Loughborough	11	May
3.20	Dawn-Alice Wright		20.01.76	2	Stoke-on-Trent	21	Jul
3.20	Louise Hart	U20	27.05.83	2	Bedford	27	Jul
3.20	Noelle Bradshaw	V35	18.12.63	2	Kingston	27	Jul
3.20	Kimberley Smith	U17	18.01.87	1	Tipton	18	Aug
3.20	Michelle Sharrock	U23	8.09.82	2	Cudworth	25	Aug
3.10	Lindsay Johnson	U23	3.12.81	2	Manchester (Str)	4	Jun
3.10	Amy Rennison	U20	15.06.83	10	Birmingham	6	Jul
3.10	Angie Nichols	U20	22.09.84	1	High Wycombe	1	Sep
3.06	Jocelyn Hird	U20	3.12.83	5	Beveren,	7	Sep
	(50)						
3.00 i	Caroline Smith	U20	31.07.83	1	Bedford	19	Jan
	2.90			1	Abingdon	11	May
3.00	Tracy Morris		25.12.69	1	Sutton Coldfield	11	May
3.00	Melissa Stamp	U23	5.07.81	1	Gateshead	11	May
3.00	Sally Woodcock	U23	14.03.80	2	Jarrow	1	Jun
3.00	Jacqui-Ann Lloyd	U20	16.06.84	1	Neath	1	Jun
3.00	Kate Alexander		28.04.74	2	Bromley	8	Jun
3.00	Jayne Collins	U23	27.03.80	1	Sutton Coldfield	24	Aug
3.00	Sara Nichols	U20	9.06.83	2	Woking	1	Sep
3.00	Maria Newton	V35	22.07.66	1	London (BP)	8	Sep
2.90 i	Anna Watson	U23	30.04.82	1	Glasgow	23	Jan
	2.60			3	Grangemouth	20	Apr
	(60)						
2.90	Hollie Tinn	U23	14.04.81	7	Bedford	4	May
2.90	Catryn Grundy	U17	25.05.86	1	Brecon	6	Jul
2.90	Becky Lilley	U15	4.03.88	1	Exeter	30	Jul
2.90	Gemma Dowsett	U20	3.02.84	1	Hoo	18	Aug
2.90	Helen Webb	U23	14.04.80	3	Nottingham	25	Aug
2.90	Judy Turton	U20	26.05.84	2	High Wycombe	1	Sep
2.90	Jenny Wood	V45	23.02.57	1	Leeds	15	Sep
2.82	Susan Yeomans	V45	16.03.53	1	Stevenage	7	Jul
2.80 i	Amy Teasdale	U17	3.09.86	6	Birmingham	24	Feb
	2.70			2	Wakefield	21	Apr
2.80 i	Carys Holloway	U23	23.07.82	4	Glasgow	24	Feb
	2.80			9=	Bedford	4	May
	(70)						
2.80	Nikki Witton		30.09.72	1	Newport	11	May
2.80	Rachel Fairless	U23	19.03.82	4	Jarrow	1	Jun
2.80	Kirsty Obern	U23	7.03.81	6	Birmingham	2	Jun
2.80	Sophie Dewell	U20	18.09.83	1	Jarrow	19	Jun
2.80	Jo Hughes		7.02.71	6	Eton	4	Aug
2.75	Jenny Cuthbertson	U20	11.06.84	1	Stockport	4	Aug
2.70 i	Janet Lyon	V35	12.03.62	1	Glasgow	10	Feb
	2.70			1	Aberdeen	6	Jun
2.70 i	Helen Croskell		22.11.72	1	London (TB)	16	Feb
	2.65			1	Aberdeen	4	Aug
2.70	Mandy Humble		15.08.79	1	Liverpool	21	Apr
2.70	Emily Morris	U23	30.09.82	4	Stoke-on-Trent	19	May
	(80)						
2.70	Ella Teasdale	U17	8.09.85	2	Bolton	23	Jun
2.70	Rebecca Guthrie	U20	19.03.83	1	Nuneaton	14	Jul
2.70	Amie Everitt		1.11.78	3	Eton	21	Jul
2.70	Helen Leadbetter	U23	24.06.82	1	Worthing	27	Jul
2.70	Sharon Beattie		26.11.72	4	Wigan	4	Aug
2.70	Lorna Bayley	U20	6.07.85	4	Kingston	27	Jul

2.65		Sarah Friday	U23	14.11.82	2	Brecon	1	Sep
2.60 i		Christine James	V45	1.06.55	2	Eton	3	Mar
2.60		Nadine Simpson	U17	28.02.86	3	Eton	27	Apr
2.60		Karen Smith		25.12.78	3	Ashford	18	May
	(90)							
2.60		Kiera Lacey	U17	13.08.86	5	Jarrow	1	Jun
2.60		Nicola Laing	U15	5.05.88	2	Grangemouth	14	Jun
2.60		Elizabeth Harris	U23	19.12.80	2	Horsham	6	Jul
2.60		Samantha Baldwin	U17	29.04.86	1	High Wycombe	6	Jul
2.60		Laura Pangbourne	U17	10.11.85	1	Salisbury	27	Jul
2.60		Ann Wainwright	V45	26.10.54	2	London (He)	27	Jul
2.60		Lucy Howcroft	U23	23.04.82	1	Salisbury	27	Jul
2.60		Caitlin Dutton	U17	15.12.86	8=	Birmingham	10	Aug
2.60		Hannah Abraham	U15	26.01.89	7	Birmingham	10	Aug
2.60		Natasha Brunning		10.03.73	4	Milton Keynes	7	Sep
	(100)							
2.60		Anna Ferguson	U20	30.06.84	1	Luton	7	Sep
2.60		Julia Witrylak	U17	25.08.87	1	Blackpool	8	Sep
2.60		Elizabeth Yarnold	U15	31.10.88	1	Tonbridge	8	Sep
2.60		Judith Kay	U15	29.06.88	1	Southampton	15	Sep
2.60 i		Gillian Kerr	U20	10.11.83	3	Glasgow	8	Dec
2.60 i		Jenny Searle		07.06.76	1	Ewell	9	Dec

Additional Under 15 (1 - 7 above)

2.57	Sarah Murtagh		18.11.88	1	Antwerp, BEL	20	Jul
2.55	Emma Ely		20.01.88	1	Woking	1	Sep
2.40	Jessica Abraham		26.01.89	1	Newport	28	Aug

Under 13

2.40	Jasmin Hicks		1.03.90	1	Par	15	Sep
2.20	Katherine Ogden		25.01.90	1	Lier, BEL	20	Jul
2.00	Emily Holt		10.07.90	2	Lier, BEL	20	Jul

Foreign

3.95		Laura Ballotta (ITA)		17.08.71	4	Bedford	4	Jun
3.70		Erin Kinnear (IRL)	U20	26.10.84	1	Derby	11	Aug
3.50		Juliet Claffey (IRL)		30.04.78	1	Dublin (S), IRL	14	Jul
3.40 ?		Eloise Dubrarid (AUS)		25.06.75	2	Dublin (S), IRL	14	Jul
3.30		Marion Gourio (FRA)	U23	9.02.80	1	Manchester (Str)	11	May
3.20 i		Shirley Austin (IRL)		20.01.73	2	Eton	6	Jan
		3.10			2	Kingston	27	Jul
2.70		Sarolta Kotai (HUN)		22.02.79	1	Dartford	27	Jul

Long Jump

6.73	1.1	Jade Johnson	U23	7.06.80	2	Munich, GER	7	Aug
	6.69	1.7			1	Newport	20	Jul
	6.65	-0.6			QB	Manchester (C)	28	Jul
	6.64	0.8			1	Bydgoszcz, POL	8	Jun
	6.60	-0.5			QB	Munich, GER	6	Aug
	6.60				3	London (CP)	23	Aug
	6.58	-0.4			2	Manchester (C)	29	Jul
	6.52	-0.4			1	Birmingham	14	Jul
	6.48	0.3			4	Zurich, SUI	16	Aug
	6.45	-0.5			1	Manchester (C)	16	Jun
	6.42	-1.5			5	Annecy, FRA	23	Jun
	6.41	0.2			3	Berlin, GER	6	Sep
	6.41	0.4			4	Madrid, ESP	21	Sep
	6.34	1.4			1	Bedford	26	May
	6.22	1.4			1	Cardiff	8	Jul
6.42	1.3	Julie Hollman		16.02.77	1H	Gotzis, AUT	2	Jun
	6.24	-0.5			2H	Desenzano, ITA	12	May
	6.21				1	Eton	27	Apr

6.38	0.7	Ann Danson		4.05.71	2	Manchester (C)	16 Jun
6.31 w	3.5				2	Amsterdam, NED	26 May
6.25					2	Tallahassee FL, USA	13 Apr
6.30	1.0	Sarah Claxton		23.09.79	1	Loughborough	18 May
6.28	1.0				1	Bedford	17 Aug
6.25	-0.2				1	Brasschaat,	14 Aug
6.23	1.5				1	London (He)	21 Jul
6.22	-0.7				1	Bedford	4 Jun
6.20 i					2	Cardiff	2 Feb
6.29 w		Sarah Wellstead		22.10.79	1	Exeter	18 May
6.14					1	London (Nh)	7 Sep
6.26	-0.9	Natasha May	U23	21.02.80	1	Niort, FRA	3 Aug
6.22	0.0				2	Brasschaat,	14 Aug
6.25	0.5	Ruth Irving		20.07.74	1	Tallahassee FL, USA	13 Apr
6.20	1.0				2	Loughborough	18 May
6.20	-0.1				QA	Manchester (C)	28 Jul
6.22 i		Kelly Sotherton		13.11.76	1	Cardiff	2 Feb
6.22					1	Sandown IOW	18 Sep
6.21	-0.1				3	Manchester (C)	16 Jun
6.20					1	Rugby	25 Aug

37 performances to 6.20 by 8 athletes including 2 indoors and 2 wind assisted

6.18	-0.4	Ashia Hansen		5.12.71	4	Manchester (C)	16 Jun
6.17 w	3.8	Donita Benjamin		7.03.72	1	Rugby	19 May
6.12 i					3	Cardiff	2 Feb
6.10	0.1				1	Birmingham	6 Jul
		(10)					
6.14		Kerry Jury		19.11.68	1	Wakefield	7 Jul
6.13 i		Kim Rothman	V35	6.09.64	1	Cardiff	10 Feb
6.08 w?					1	Peterborough	26 Aug
6.01	-0.2				4	Bedford	4 Jun
6.07 w		Jackie Spargo		12.01.71	1	Stoke-on-Trent	21 Jul
6.02					2	Rugby	25 Aug
6.05	1.8	Tracy Joseph		29.11.69	1	Portsmouth	12 May
6.05	1.0	Symone Belle	U20	12.11.84	4	Loughborough	18 May
6.01	1.9	Lara Richards	U20	7.03.83	5	Loughborough	18 May
6.01	1.8	Caroline Pearce	U23	1.09.80	2	Bedford	29 Jun
6.01	-0.9	Rebecca White	U23	5.06.80	1	Niort, FRA	3 Aug
5.98 w		Laura Singleton	U20	6.04.85	1	Birmingham	15 Jun
5.69					2	Cannock	11 May
5.97 w	2.5	Elaine Smith	U20	16.05.83	1	Bedford	30 Jun
5.84					2	Moscow, RUS	21 Sep
		(20)					
5.95		Lucy Atunumuo	U23	4.11.80	1	London (TB)	27 Apr
5.95 w	3.0	Naida Bromley	U17	27.09.86	1	Cudworth	15 Sep
5.67	1.8				*	Cudworth	15 Sep
5.93 w		Rebekah Passley	U17	9.03.87	1	Ashford	18 May
5.86 i					1	Birmingham	23 Feb
5.83					1	Kingston	12 May
5.93 w		Gemma Holt		20.12.72	2	Ashford	18 May
5.58					2	Eton	21 Jul
5.93 w	4.0	Karlene Turner	U20	9.01.85	5	Rugby	19 May
5.90					1	London (WF)	18 Aug
5.90 w		Stephanie Morgan		4.03.75	1	Exeter	4 Jul
5.89					3	Rugby	25 Aug
5.89 w	5.2	Julia Bennett		26.03.70	4	Alicante, ESP	6 Apr
5.83 i					6=P	Zaragoza, ESP	27 Jan
5.70					1	Bedford	27 Jul
5.85 w	3.3	Kimberley Goodall	U20	5.10.83	1 H	Woodford	28 Apr
5.73	1.1				4	Bedford	17 Aug
5.84	0.1	Joanna Trotman	U23	5.10.80	2	Kingston	11 May
5.84		Kate Brewington	U23	15.10.81	1	Colchester	26 Aug

5.83		Lucy Butler	U23	18.11.81	1	Loughborough	12	Jun
5.83 w	2.6	Catherine Holdsworth	U17	3.01.86	1	Birmingham	10	Aug
5.76	1.8				*	Birmingham	10	Aug
5.81	0.6	Katherine Livesey		15.12.79	3H	College Station, USA	15	Mar
5.81		Hazel Carwardine	U23	6.11.80	2	Manchester (Str)	11	May
5.81	1.7	Rebecca Jones	U20	17.01.83	13=H	Arles, FRA	2	Jun
5.80 w		Emily Parker	U20	7.11.84	1	Kingston	25	Jun
5.68					2	Loughborough	17	Jul
5.79		Debbie Harrison		13.11.78	2	Coventry	28	Apr
5.79		Fiona Westwood	U23	27.02.81	1	Wakefield	21	May
5.78 w	3.5	Phyllis Agbo	U17	16.12.85	2H	Woodford	28	Apr
5.67 i					3	Cardiff	10	Feb
5.65	-0.1				2	Watford	26	May
5.76 w	2.8	Sally Peake	U17	8.02.86	2	Birmingham	10	Aug
5.66	1.2				*	Birmingham	10	Aug
(40)								
5.75 i		Mary Devlin		14.09.79	2	Nenagh, IRL	16	Feb
5.76w	4.0				1	Tullamore, IRL	30	Jun
5.73					1	Belfast	6	Apr
5.74 w		Jade Surman	U15	27.03.89	1	Birmingham	16	Jun
5.64					1	Birmingham	22	Jun
5.74 w	3.1	Roz Gonse	U23	1.03.82	1	Abingdon	23	Jun
5.66 i					3P	Eaubonne, FRA	24	Feb
5.60					3	Peterborough	26	Aug
5.73 w	4.2	Sarah Roberts		25.06.78	2	Birmingham	2	Jun
5.65					1	Yate	1	Sep
5.72 i		Amy Woodman	U20	1.11.84	4	Birmingham	23	Feb
5.66	1.3				5	Bedford	30	Jun
5.72		Danielle Humphreys	U20	16.05.84	1	Mansfield	28	Apr
5.72		Emma Perkins	U17	4.09.85	1	Worthing	27	Jul
5.72		Rachel Brenton	U20	18.01.85	2	London (Nh)	7	Sep
5.71		Lanre Atijosan	U17	17.10.86	1	Ilford	21	Jul
5.71 w	2.5	Belinda Samuels		29.11.78	7	Rugby	10	May
5.70					1	Cannock	11	May
(50)								
5.70		Katy Benneworth	U20	5.10.84	1	London (SP)	7	Sep
5.68 i		Aileen Wilson	U20	30.03.84	1P	Glasgow	10	Feb
5.68 i		Emma Hughes	U23	15.09.80	5	Cardiff	16	Feb
5.68 w	3.4	Louise Bloor	U17	21.09.85	3	Birmingham	10	Aug
5.67	1.5				*	Birmingham	10	Aug
5.67		Laura Redmond	U23	19.04.81	1	Glasgow (S)	2	Jun
5.67 w	2.5	Leandra Polius	U23	14.05.80	3	London (He)	21	Jul
5.66		Charmaine Turner	U23	5.12.81	1	Bracknell	11	May
5.65 i		Gillian Cooke	U23	3.10.82	1	Glasgow	12	Jan
5.64					4	Bedford	5	May
5.65		Chanelle Garnett	U20	16.08.85	3	Ashford	18	May
5.65		Rosie Curling	U23	5.09.80	1	Oxford	18	May
(60)								
5.64		Sophie Newington	U17	15.09.85	2	Brecon	6	Jul
5.63	0.0	Jessica Ennis	U17	28.01.86	2H	Pratteln, SUI	4	Aug
5.63 w		Stephanie Madgett	U17	22.02.87	4	Ashford	18	May
5.63 w	2.3	Laura Ridley	U17	20.03.86	2	Cudworth	15	Sep
5.60					1	Glasgow (S)	20	Jul
5.63 w	3.5	Rachel Abbs	U17	21.12.86	3	Cudworth	15	Sep
5.46					1	Jarrow	12	Jun
5.62		Imogen Miles	U17	7.08.86	1	Cannock	14	Sep
5.61	1.7	Rachel Peacock	U23	18.05.82	Q	Bedford	5	May
5.61	0.0	Jackie Jenner		25.10.76	2	Watford	2	Jun
5.61		Aimee Palmer	U17	7.11.86	1	Cannock	15	Jun
5.61	1.9	Zainab Ceesay	U20	27.10.83	6	Bedford	30	Jun
(70)								

5.61		Wendy Davidson	U23	14.10.82	4	Derby	21 Jul
5.60		Aimee Cutler	U23	7.10.81	3	Stoke-on-Trent	19 May
5.59		Frances Harris		1.06.72	4	Stoke-on-Trent	19 May
5.59		Jenny Kelly		20.06.70	1	Wigan	4 Aug
5.59 w		Kate Evans		4.02.74	10	Rugby	19 May
5.59 w		Joanne Nicoll	U20	27.12.84	3	Grangemouth	26 May
5.59 w	5.2	Amy Harris	U15	14.09.87	1	Birmingham	11 Aug
		5.48			1	Birmingham	21 Jul
5.58		Wendy Laing	V35	29.12.62	1	Tidworth	21 Sep
5.57	1.4	Maureen Knight		15.11.73	2H	Birmingham	2 Jun
5.57	0.8	Ellie Darby	U17	20.12.85	1	Mansfield	12 Jul
	(80)						
5.57 w		Nicola Baker		8.10.74	2	Exeter	4 Jul
5.56		Anna Clayton	U20	20.03.85	1	Ipswich	7 Apr
5.56		Rachel Egbuniwe	U17	5.07.86	1	Luton	18 Aug
5.55		Michala Gee		8.12.75	2	Cudworth	11 May
5.55		Cara Roberts	U20	24.05.85	1	Bournemouth	22 Jun
5.55		Fiona Harrison	U23	30.11.81	1	Scunthorpe	4 Aug
5.54		Emma Heath	U17	1.10.86	1	Yate	11 May
5.54		Jenny Pacey	U20	5.02.83	4	Peterborough	26 Aug
5.53		Joy Danby	U20	5.09.84	2	Mansfield	28 Apr
5.53		Cathryn Dale		31.05.77	3	Coventry	28 Apr
	(90)						
5.52		Sarah Still		24.09.75	1	Aberdeen	21 Apr
5.52		Vicky Griffiths	U20	9.10.84	1	Derby	28 Apr
5.52		Henrietta Paxton	U20	19.09.83	2	Bournemouth	22 Jun
5.52		Tara Murphy	U20	16.05.85	3	Bournemouth	22 Jun
5.52		Carly Robson	U20	5.12.83	1	London (Cr)	28 Jul
5.52 w	4.3	Dominique Blaize	U15	3.10.87	2	Birmingham	11 Aug
		5.51 i			1P	Cardiff	10 Mar
		5.49 1.0			1	Kingston	12 May
5.51		Frances Noble	U17	2.05.86	1	Leeds	3 Jul
5.51 i		Rebecca Hampson	U20	14.07.84	1	Cardiff	27 Nov
5.50		Louise Hazel	U17	6.10.85	1	Peterborough	26 Aug
5.50 w	2.6	Natalie Clark	U23	4.09.82	3	Cudworth	25 Aug

Additional Under 17 (1 - 21 above)

5.47		Denae Matthew		3.04.87	1	Loughborough	12 May
5.46		Carly Walker		30.08.87	3	Bournemouth	8 Jun
5.46		Elen Davies		24.04.86	1	Norwich	12 Jun
5.44		Nike Osifodunrin		21.11.86	1	Glasgow (S)	2 Jun
5.43	0.0	Deandra Smith		3.12.86	3	Watford	26 May
5.42		Jade Halket		5.05.86	1H	Grangemouth	25 Aug
5.41		Amanda Fletcher		18.11.86	1	Rugby	21 Apr
5.41		Lisa Ferguson		10.09.86	2	Glasgow (S)	2 Jun
5.40		Angela Barrett		25.12.85	1	Ashford	30 Jun
	(30)						
5.40		Sophie Mabbett		27.10.86	2	Eton	27 Jul
5.38 i		Michelle Nash-Odei		19.03.87	2	London (CP)	16 Feb
5.38		Georgina Shaw		13.03.86	1	Blackpool	21 Jul
5.37		Layla Hawkins		3.09.86	2	London (Cr)	28 Jul
5.36		Lauren Taylor		29.10.86	1	Abingdon	16 Jun
5.34		Rachel Peckham		14.02.87	1	Walton	21 Apr
5.34	0.9	Shelley Revitt		28.11.85	4	Manchester (Wy)	25 May
5.33		Natalie Jowett		18.09.86	2	Kingston	6 Jul
5.32		Sheryl Punter		17.06.87	1	Sheffield	19 May
5.30 i		Cherri Morrison		27.09.86	2	Wakefield	12 Jan
		5.30			1	Manchester (Wy)	24 Apr
	(40)						
5.30		Faye Harding		7.09.85	1	Wrexham	19 May
5.30		Harriet Robinson		21.04.87	1	Bromley	16 Jun

Additional Under 15 (1 -3 above)

5.35		Claire Linskill	12.01.88	1	Bournemouth	28	Apr
5.33		Emily Bonnett	22.09.87	1	Bournemouth	22	Jun
5.31		Hannah Frankson	11.01.89	1	Bury St. Edmunds	27	Jul
5.31 w	2.1	Alice Simpson	26.02.89	1	Cudworth	15	Sep
5.28	1.8			P	Cudworth	15	Sep
5.29 w	3.6	Gemma Weetman	4.10.87	2	Mansfield	12	Jul
5.24				1	Telford	24	Apr
5.21		Saskia Kalmeijer	10.08.88	1	Abingdon	28	Apr
5.20		Emma Bonny	9.09.87	1	Barking	7	Apr
	(10)						
5.19 w	3.8	Alison Bennett	12.04.88	4	Mansfield	12	Jul
5.17				1	Southend	18	Aug
5.17		Kirsty Parr	6.04.88	1	Scunthorpe	4	Aug
5.17		Jade Christie	20.11.87	1	Luton	15	Sep
5.16	0.6	Hannah Weekes	14.12.87	5	Mansfield	12	Jul
5.15		Rachel Conway	30.09.87	1	Brierley Hill	19	May
5.15	1.9	Emily Martin	7.10.88	6	Mansfield	12	Jul
5.14		Jane Hunt	8.09.87	1	Grantham	22	Jun
5.13		Lizzie Berry	15.02.88	2	Cudworth	15	Sep
5.13 w	2.6	Carly Sharp	7.09.87	2	Birmingham	1	Sep
5.12		Ashley Little	19.01.89	1	Manchester (C)	26	May

Under 13

5.24 w	2.6	Chioma Chilaka	2.09.89	4	Birmingham	10	Aug
5.14	1.9			*	Birmingham	10	Aug
5.08		Megan Beesley	15.11.89	1	Banbury	14	Jul
4.95		Faye Roger	21.12.89	1	Liverpool	21	May
4.86		Amelia Montagnani	10.03.90	1	Crawley	15	Sep
4.80		Kerry Steel	13.10.89	1	Grangemouth	24	Aug
4.79		Emma Lewis		1	Bangor	22	Jun
4.78		Eleanor Markendale	9.10.89	1	Blackburn	11	May
4.73		Vicky Fleetwood	13.04.90	1	Nuneaton	14	Jul
4.72		Emily Godley	22.10.89	1	Bromley	22	Jun
4.58		Jennifer Taker	16.03.90	1	Manchester (Str)	26	Aug
	(10)						
4.57		Elizabeth Roach	12.09.90	1	Nelson	27	Jul
4.55		Natalie Betts	26.12.89	1	Portsmouth	11	May
4.54		Nadine Hinze	19.12.89	1	London (Nh)	2	Jun
4.54		Sarah Williams	23.03.91	1	Banbury	14	Jul
4.52		Roxanne Walby	8.02.90	2	Blackburn	11	May
4.52		Kimberley Smith	11.11.89	1	Oxford	12	Jun
4.51		Saranna Blair	4.02.90	1	Kingston	28	Jul

Foreign

5.87	*1.6*	*Taneisha Robinson-Scanlon (IRL)*	*19.11.77*	*6*	*Rugby*	*19*	*May*
5.76	*1.5*	*Margaret Veldman (NED)*	*7.06.74*	*3*	*Jarrow*	*1*	*Jun*
5.71		*Jacqui Stokes (IRL)*	*V35*	*1.04.67*	*1*	*Wigan*	*4 Aug*

Triple Jump

15.00 w	3.1	Ashia Hansen	5.12.71	1	Munich, GER	10	Aug
14.86			-0.4	1	Manchester (C)	31	Jul
14.71 i				2	Vienna, AUT	2	Mar
14.62 i				2	Lievin, FRA	24	Feb
14.62			0.0	2	Annecy, FRA	22	Jun
14.60			1.3	*	Munich, GER	10	Aug
14.50			2.0	1	Birmingham	13	Jul
14.44 i				1	Karlsruhe, GER	25	Jan
14.36 i				2	Birmingham	17	Feb
14.36 w			5.7	3	Sheffield	30	Jun

(Hansen)		14.34 i		1	Glasgow	9	Mar
		14.32	0.1	2	Madrid, ESP	20	Sep
		14.30 i		Q	Vienna, AUT	1	Mar
		14.25	1.4	*	Sheffield	30	Jun
		14.24	0.4	4	Rome, ITA	12	Jul
		14.22	-0.2	QB	Munich, GER	8	Aug
		14.21 i		3	Piraeus, GRE	20	Feb
		14.03	0.6	1	Manchester (C)	15	Jun
		13.96	0.7	1	Glasgow (S)	18	Aug
		13.53 i		1	Cardiff	3	Feb
13.44	1.0	Michelle Griffith	6.10.71	5	Glasgow (S)	18	Aug
		13.18	-1.1	3	Birmingham	13	Jul
		13.13 w	2.1	6	Celle Ligure, ITA	26	Jun
		13.09		1	Eton	21	Jul
		13.07		1	La Jolla, USA	27	Apr
		13.07	1.6	6	Sheffield	30	Jun
		13.06 w	2.2	2	Bedford	4	Jun
		12.99	0.1	2	Manchester (C)	15	Jun
		12.98	1.6	1	Bedford	25	May
		12.93	1.1	*	Celle Ligure, ITA	26	Jun
		12.90	-0.7	8	Manchester (C)	31	Jul
		12.89	-0.4	2	London (He)	3	Aug
		12.66	0.3	1	Watford	1	Jun
13.15 w	5.0	Rebecca White U23	5.06.80	1	Newport	20	Jul
		12.97	1.8	3	Niort, FRA	3	Aug
		12.90	1.4	1	Bedford	29	Jun
		12.74		1	Bath	12	May
		12.65	1.7	6	Birmingham	13	Jul
		12.64 i		3	Cardiff	3	Feb
12.98	1.7	Danielle Freeman U23	11.02.80	4	Birmingham	13	Jul
		12.87	1.6	2	Bedford	29	Jun
		12.50 w	3.1	3	Newport	20	Jul
12.84	0.9	Debbie Rowe	8.09.72	2	Tallahassee FL, USA	13	Apr
		12.71 w	2.5	1	Birmingham	1	Jun
		12.58	0.9	1	Loughborough	18	May
12.64 i		Ruth Irving	20.07.74	1	Jarrow	15	Dec
		12.00		1	Gateshead	25	Aug
12.52	0.2	Emily Parker U20	7.11.84	1	Nottingham	13	Jul

47 performances to 12.50 by 7 athletes including 10 indoors and 7 wind assisted

12.45	1.5	Leandra Polius U23	14.05.80	7	Birmingham	13	Jul
12.44 w	2.8	Charmaine Turner U23	5.12.81	3	Bedford	29	Jun
		12.43	1.6	4	Newport	20	Jul
12.40	2.0	Hazel Carwardine U23	6.11.80	4	Bedford	29	Jun
	(10)						
12.39 w		Karlene Turner U20	9.01.85	1	Milton Keynes	7	Sep
		11.95		1	Derby	8	Sep
12.35 w	2.6	Rachel Peacock U23	18.05.82	5	Bedford	29	Jun
		12.32		1	Bournemouth	8	Jun
12.34		Azaria Francis U20	12.04.83	1	Kingston	12	May
12.33		Kate Evans	4.02.74	1	Birmingham	9	Jun
12.30		Stephanie Aneto	23.08.77	1	Ashford	18	Aug
12.24	-1.1	Caroline Stead	14.09.71	4	Bedford	17	Aug
12.20	0.0	Stephanie Morgan	4.03.75	2	Olsztyn, POL	18	Aug
12.16	1.8	Carly Robson U20	5.12.83	2	Bedford	29	Jun
12.15	2.0	Michala Gee	8.12.75	1	Cudworth	15	Sep
12.10	1.7	Linsi Robinson U20	9.01.84	1	Birmingham	25	May
	(20)						
12.10	-0.1	Marcia Walker	27.05.70	6	Manchester (C)	15	Jun
12.08	1.1	Mary Devlin	14.09.79	2	Belfast	8	Jun
12.06 w	5.2	Liz Patrick	29.08.77	2	Birmingham	1	Jun
		11.83	1.8	6	Birmingham	6	Jul

12.04 w		Alison McAllister	U20	26.02.85	1	Birmingham	16	Jun
11.90	0.2				4	Nottingham	13	Jul
12.03		Rachel Brenton	U20	18.01.85	1	Abingdon	16	Jun
12.02 w		Angela Barrett	U17	25.12.85	1	Exeter	7	Sep
11.85 i					1	Birmingham	24	Feb
11.83	-0.6				1	Watford	26	May
11.95 w		Kelly Sotherton		13.11.76	5	Birmingham	6	Jul
11.88	0.9				*	Birmingham	6	Jul
11.93		Sandra Alaneme	U17	7.01.86	1	Glasgow (S)	20	Jul
11.92 w		Sara Barry	U20	8.06.83	1	Yate	21	Apr
11.74	0.8				*	Bedford	29	Jun
11.89 w 2.6		Sally Peake	U17	8.02.86	1	Birmingham	11	Aug
11.77	0.3				*	Birmingham	11	Aug
(30)								
11.88		Maurine Okwue		13.05.78	2	Perivale	27	Jul
11.84 w 2.1		Kosnatu Abdulai	U20	8.02.85	3	London (He)	25	Aug
11.62	0.0				3	Watford	16	May
11.83		Helen Baker		5.02.79	1	Exeter	23	Jun
11.82 i		Aisha Myton	U20	3.01.84	5	Cardiff	10	Feb
11.71					3	Kingston	12	May
11.82		Natalie Brant	U23	11.12.82	1	Kingston	6	Jul
11.81		Sarah Wellstead		22.10.79	1	Portsmouth	6	Jul
11.70		Jodie Hurst		21.06.77	2	Cannock	11	May
11.69		Julia Straker	U23	25.11.82	1	Gateshead	12	May
11.66		Sarah Roberts		25.06.78	2	Bath	11	Aug
11.66 w		Sian Jones	U20	20.01.83	1	Cardiff	26	Aug
11.46					1	Newport	8	Jun
(40)								
11.63 w 3.1		Michelle Doherty	U20	24.09.84	4	Belfast	8	Jun
11.48					1	Tullamore, IRL	1	Jun
11.62		Kate Kinner	U23	28.05.81	1	Loughborough	22	May
11.60	2.0	Imogen Miles	U17	7.08.86	3	Nottingham	12	Jul
11.60	2.0	Alison Rough	U20	1.06.83	1	Grangemouth	25	Aug
11.59		Emma Wooff	U20	21.05.85	1	Stoke-on-Trent	19	May
11.55		Joanne Stanley		30.03.77	2	Gateshead	12	May
11.54		Vicky Lambert	U20	20.11.84	2	Wakefield	7	Jul
11.50	0.5	Lucy Butler	U23	18.11.81	5	Loughborough	18	May
11.46	1.3	Nia Nwidobie	U17	4.01.86	1	Cudworth	15	Sep
11.42	0.5	Janice Pryce	V40	2.09.59	2	Potsdam, GER	22	Aug
(50)								
11.41		Carly Palmer	U20	21.12.84	1	Milton Keynes	15	Jun
11.41	0.5	Jenny Brown	V40	21.05.59	3	Potsdam, GER	22	Aug
11.39		Nicky Clark		14.04.77	1	Leeds	14	Apr
11.38 w		Julia Bennett		26.03.70	2	London (Ha)	7	Sep
11.36	1.3	Rebekah Passley	U17	9.03.87	8	Bedford	17	Aug
11.36		Jackie Jenner		25.10.76	5	Ashford	18	Aug
11.36 w 2.2		Cathryn Dale		31.05.77	4	Birmingham	1	Jun
11.33					2	Loughborough	5	Jun
11.35		Sarah Claxton		23.09.79	1	Bromley	8	Jun
11.33	1.9	Anna Kelly	U17	18.05.87	4	Nottingham	12	Jul
11.32 w 2.4		Helen Taylor	U20	29.01.84	2	Cudworth	15	Sep
11.09					2	Bebington	28	Jul
(60)								
11.30		Kara Miller	U20	6.04.85	1	Poole	7	Sep
11.29	0.5	Irie Hill		16.01.69	2	Melbourne, AUS	8	Oct
11.26		Ruth Hatch	U17	4.07.87	1	Kingston	4	Aug
11.26 i		Alison Croad	U23	10.06.82	2	Cardiff	23	Nov
11.20					1	Bournemouth	11	May
11.25		Rachel Mawhinny	U17	28.09.86	1	Belfast	15	Jun
11.24		Gemma Holt		20.12.72	1	Ashford	18	May
11.24	1.1	Nicola Martell	U17	20.09.85	5	Nottingham	12	Jul

11.22		Katherine Silto	U20	12.08.83	1	High Wycombe	18 May
11.22		Lara Richards	U20	7.03.83	2	Grangemouth	25 May
11.20		Kerry Saunders		28.03.77	2	Derby	21 Jul
	(70)						
11.19	1.8	Tania Spurling	U17	20.08.87	7	Nottingham	12 Jul
11.17		Laura Betts	U20	6.11.84	1	London (CP)	12 May
11.17		Louise Wood	U20	13.05.83	1	Bury St. Edmunds	16 Jun
11.16 w		Natasha Brunning		10.03.73	3	Milton Keynes	7 Sep
11.14		Jenny Bliss	U17	6.07.86	1	Brighton	6 Jul
11.13	0.1	Sarah Hunter		19.05.78	9	Birmingham	6 Jul
11.13		Diana Osagede	U20	18.01.85	1	London (He)	15 Sep
11.13 w		Catherine Smy	U17	7.04.87	1	Banchory	31 Aug
11.09		Zoe Davidson	U17	17.12.85	3	Glasgow (S)	20 Jul
11.07		Chanelle Garnett	U20	16.08.85	2	Hemel Hempstead	6 Jul
	(80)						
11.07 w	3.2	Gillian Kerr	U20	10.11.83	2	Grangemouth	25 Aug
11.05		Ruth Clements		15.05.74	1	Abingdon	27 Jul
11.04 i		Louise Gauld	U23	24.08.80	1	Glasgow	13 Jan
11.04 i		Sarah Strevens	U23	7.10.81	2	Bedford	20 Jan
11.01					2	Guildford	27 Apr
11.04		Becky Allen	U23	26.11.82	1	Norwich	11 Aug
11.04 w		Susan Bagnall	U17	4.08.86	2	Cardiff	26 Aug
10.98					1	Brecon	1 Sep
11.03		Joanne Reade	U20	28.11.84	1	Nottingham	12 May
11.02 i		Katharine Streatfield	U20	28.07.83	2	Glasgow	17 Feb
11.02		Annie Bowden	U23	5.06.82	2	Oxford	26 Jun
11.01 i		Andrea Hall		28.01.77	3	Bedford	20 Jan
	(90)						
11.01		Ann-Margaret Polius	U17	17.06.86	2	Chelmsford	15 Jun
11.01 w		Samantha Nicholas	U17	3.09.85	3	Cardiff	26 Aug
11.00		Claire Baker	U20	13.08.84	4	Birmingham	25 May
11.00		Lisa Durant	U17	6.10.85	1	Bournemouth	22 Jun
11.00		Sophie Mabbett	U17	27.10.86	1	Portsmouth	6 Jul

Additional Under 17 (1 - 19 above)

10.99		Phoebe Bointon		11.04.87	2	Bournemouth	22 Jun
	(20)						
10.95		Emma Lyons		14.06.87	1	Cleckheaton	15 Sep
10.93		Kirsty Smith		25.04.87	4	Derby	8 Sep
10.88		Elen Davies		24.04.86	2	London (He)	28 Apr
10.86 w		Vicky Lloyd		5.03.86	4	Cardiff	26 Aug
10.84					2	Brecon	6 Jul
10.85		Kamela Monks		6.05.87	1	High Wycombe	6 Jul
10.75		Louise Bloor		21.09.85	1	Cudworth	11 May
10.74		Yasmin Regis		12.12.86	2	Bromley	6 Jul
10.73		Lisa Mulholland		19.12.85	3	Kingston	4 Aug
10.72		Ashia Hibbert		30.03.86	2	Jarrow	4 Aug
10.71 i		Claire Wait		7.11.86	1	Birmingham	20 Jan
	(30)						
10.71		Layla Hawkins		3.09.86	3	Eton	23 Jun
10.71 w		Lyndsey Maund		27.02.86	5	Cardiff	26 Aug
10.70		Ni-Kysha Ferguson		8.09.86	4	Scunthorpe	23 Jun
10.70		Deborah Sephton		9.01.87	1	Wakefield	21 Sep

Foreign

14.54 w	5.5	Yamile Aldama (CUB)		14.08.72	2	Sheffield	30 Jun
14.40	0.6				2	Birmingham	13 Jul
13.00 i		Taneisha Robinson-Scanlon(IRL)		19.11.77	2	Cardiff	3 Feb
12.98	-0.8				7	Manchester (C)	31 Jul
12.14		Anna-Maria Thorpe (BAR)		15.07.71	1	Bedford	18 May
11.48	0.9	Lydia Saka (SWE)		20.01.79	6	Watford	1 Jun
11.11	1.5	Cathriona Hannafin (IRL)		19.09.72	3	Scunthorpe	7 Jul

Shot

16.73	Jo Duncan	V35	27.12.66	8	Halle, GER	11	May
16.21				1	Wakefield	7	Jul
16.18				1	Bedford	26	May
16.17				1	Watford	1	Sep
16.06 i				1	Eton	6	Jan
16.01 i				2	Cardiff	2	Feb
16.00				QB	Manchester (C)	27	Jul
15.99				6	Manchester (C)	28	Jul
15.97				1	Crawley	20	Apr
15.95				1	Loughborough	27	Apr
15.91				1	Bedford	4	Jun
15.85				3	Manchester (C)	15	Jun
15.82				1	Loughborough	17	Jul
15.71				3	Birmingham	13	Jul
15.66				1	Ashford	18	Aug
15.62				4B	Pula, CRO	10	Mar
15.49 i				2	Cardiff	10	Feb
15.40				1	London (He)	21	Jul
15.18 i				1	Bedford	20	Jan
15.18				1	Barking	7	Apr
16.54	Myrtle Augee	V35	4.02.65	1	London (CP)	12	May
16.32				QA	Manchester (C)	27	Jul
16.16				1	Birmingham	13	Jul
16.11				2	Watford	2	Jun
16.05				5	Manchester (C)	28	Jul
15.94				3	Varazdin, CRO	6	Jul
15.87				2	Manchester (C)	15	Jun
16.37	Julie Dunkley		11.09.79	1	Manchester (C)	15	Jun
16.29				2	London (CP)	12	May
16.19				1	Watford	2	Jun
16.03				3	Barcelona, ESP	6	Sep
15.92				2	Watford	1	Sep
15.89				2	Birmingham	13	Jul
15.86				1	Rugby	19	May
15.85				8	Annecy, FRA	23	Jun
15.81				7	Manchester (C)	28	Jul
15.80				QA	Manchester (C)	27	Jul
15.75				1	Loughborough	18	May
15.57				1	Birmingham	6	Jul
15.33				2	Ashford	18	Aug
15.31				1	Bedford	17	Aug
15.88 i	Philippa Roles		1.03.78	3	Cardiff	2	Feb
15.84 i				1	Cardiff	10	Feb
15.06 i				1	Cardiff	19	Jan
14.91				3	Loughborough	18	May
15.57	Eva Massey	U23	22.12.80	1	Belfast	8	Jun
15.49				1	Bedford	30	Jun
15.34				2	Bedford	26	May
15.33				1	Bedford	6	May
15.33				2	Loughborough	18	May
15.32				1	Antrim	18	Jun
15.27				5	Manchester (C)	15	Jun
15.01				1	London (BP)	6	Jul
15.50	Ade Oshinowo	U23	12.02.80	2	Champaign, USA	19	Apr
15.02				1	Champaign, USA	10	May
15.38	Maggie Lynes	V35	19.02.63	3	London (CP)	12	May
15.33				3	Watford	2	Jun
15.28				4	Manchester (C)	15	Jun
15.12	Christina Bennett		27.02.78	1	Kingston	12	May

58 performances to 15.00 by 8 athletes including 7 indoors

14.68 i	Vickie Foster		1.04.71	4	Cardiff	2	Feb
	14.39			4	Watford	2	Jun
14.28	Kara Nwidobie	U23	13.04.81	4	Newport	20	Jul
	(10)						
14.23	Rebecca Peake	U20	22.06.83	1	Cudworth	25	Aug
14.16	Claire Smithson	U20	3.08.83	4	Loughborough	18	May
14.07	Nicola Gautier		21.03.78	7	Manchester (C)	15	Jun
13.94	Carol Parker		22.09.69	1	Coventry	28	Apr
13.77	Eleanor Gatrell		5.10.76	1	Salisbury	6	Jul
13.72	Charlotte Spelzini	U20	7.01.83	1	Bedford	30	Jun
13.28	Debbie Woolgar	V35	10.03.65	2	Crawley	11	May
13.24	Joanna Bennett	U20	6.08.83	1	Kingston	12	May
13.21	Jenny Kelly		20.06.70	1	Wigan	4	Aug
13.15	Alana Smith	U20	18.01.85	1	Scunthorpe	23	Jun
	(20)						
13.13 i	Mhairi Walters	U23	19.06.81	1	Glasgow	13	Jan
	13.05			1	Glasgow (S)	8	Jun
13.09	Lydia Morgan	U20	1.09.83	1	Birmingham	22	Jun
12.99	Emma Merry		2.07.74	2	Coventry	28	Apr
12.93 i	Joan Macpherson	U23	18.09.80	2	Glasgow	23	Feb
	12.71			1	Colchester	18	May
12.90	Charmaine Johnson	V35	4.06.63	1	London (He)	27	Jul
12.87	Claire Everett		25.06.79	3	Coventry	19	May
12.86 i	Alison Rodger	U20	29.10.84	5	Cardiff	16	Feb
	12.58			1	Edinburgh	11	May
12.85 i	Paula Hendriks	U20	25.01.83	1P	Eaubonne, FRA	24	Feb
	12.79			4	Tallahassee FL, USA	13	Apr
12.82	Mary Anderson		2.09.67	2	Glasgow (S)	8	Jun
12.77	Kelly Sotherton		13.11.76	3	Coventry	28	Apr
	(30)						
12.73	Chloe Cozens	U23	9.04.80	2	Loughborough	22	May
12.72	Julie Hollman		16.02.77	2	Eton	27	Apr
12.70	Rebecca Roles		14.12.79	4	Rugby	19	May
12.70	Nicola Dudman	U20	5.10.83	2	Watford	1	Sep
12.65	Elaine Cank		5.12.79	2	Cudworth	25	Aug
12.63 i	Emma Carpenter	U23	16.05.82	6	Cardiff	16	Feb
12.63	Lesley Brannan		13.09.76	1	Connah's Quay	12	May
12.54	Sally Hinds	U17	2.02.86	1	Glasgow (S)	20	Jul
12.50	Natalie Hart		25.05.72	1	Colchester	16	Jun
12.29	Amy Wilson	U23	31.12.80	2	Colchester	16	Jun
	(40)						
12.24	Chloe Edwards	U17	12.05.87	2	Glasgow (S)	20	Jul
12.23	Kate Morris	U20	18.01.83	6	Watford	2	Jun
12.15	Laura Redmond	U23	19.04.81	4H	Pratteln, SUI	3	Aug
12.13	Gillian Stewart	U23	21.01.80	7	Rugby	19	May
12.12	Lucy Sutton	U17	29.08.86	3	Glasgow (S)	20	Jul
12.01 i	Laura Douglas	U20	4.01.83	2	Cardiff	10	Feb
	11.61			1	Connah's Quay	12	May
12.00	Lorraine Shaw		2.04.68	6	Birmingham	6	Jul
12.00	Helen Wilding		25.10.76	6	London (He)	3	Aug
11.99	Jenny Grimstone		30.04.79	2	London (He)	8	Jun
11.96	Shelley McLellan	U20	21.03.83	1	Bedford	28	Apr
	(50)						
11.92	Jolene Marshall	U20	22.10.83	1	London (CP)	12	May
11.91	Sharon Gibson	V40	31.12.61	1	Nottingham	11	May
11.91	Leah Weatheritt		18.09.74	1	Gateshead	25	Aug
11.89	Shelley Newman		8.08.73	6	Birmingham (Un)	19	Jun
11.85	Maureen Knight		15.11.73	2H	Birmingham	1	Jun
11.85	Navdeep Dhaliwal		30.11.77	3	London (He)	21	Jul
11.82 i	Laura Fox	U20	25.10.84	4	Birmingham	24	Feb
	11.58			1	Eton	23	Jun

11.81	Cathy-Ann Hill		4.05.77	10	Rugby	19	May
11.80 i	Julia Bennett		26.03.70	9P	Zaragoza, ESP	27	Jan
11.80				14H	Desenzano, ITA	11	May
11.78	Natasha Mighty		21.12.70	1	Abingdon	11	May
	(60)						
11.76	Debbie Collinson	U17	23.10.85	1	Cudworth	15	Sep
11.74	Louise Finlay	U20	2.10.83	6	Aberdare	15	Jun
11.70	Laura Chalmers	U17	1.05.86	1	Elgin	8	Sep
11.69	Paula Blank-Collis		13.12.77	1	Welwyn	6	May
11.66	Sue Lawrence		25.11.70	2	Chelmsford	27	Jul
11.64	Sarah Beer	U20	29.04.84	1	Nottingham	13	Jul
11.63	Kerry Jury		19.11.68	21H	Arles, FRA	1	Jun
11.62	Laura Shirley	U17	27.03.87	1	Chelmsford	15	Jun
11.60	Katherine Livesey		15.12.79	9H	Baton Rouge LA, USA	29	May
11.55	Elizabeth Dwan	U23	16.10.82	1	Gateshead	12	May
	(70)						
11.55	Roz Gonse	U23	1.03.82	3	Bedford	27	Jul
11.51	Clova Court	V40	10.02.60	13	Rugby	19	May
11.48	Kerry Elliott	U20	17.05.85	1	Cudworth	21	Apr
11.48	Norma Gregory		10.06.69	4	Abingdon	23	Jun
11.48	Karen Smith		25.12.78	3	Kingston	6	Jul
11.45	Amanda Sheppard		26.02.68	1	Leeds	14	Jul
11.44	Hayley Bryan	U17	4.03.86	2	Exeter	23	Jun
11.41	Claire Parkin	U20	26.02.84	3	Scunthorpe	23	Jun
11.40	Candie Lintern	U23	5.02.82	2	Crawley	27	Jul
11.39	Rebecca Jones	U20	17.01.83	2H	Woodford	27	Apr
	(80)						
11.39	Joanne Holloway		10.05.76	1	Plymouth	8	Jun
11.38	Stephanie Owen	U17	31.12.86	1	Cannock	15	Jun
11.37	Mercedes Foy	U17	9.08.86	1	Ipswich	28	Jul
11.36	Joan Amaa	U23	15.12.81	1	Crawley	27	Apr
11.33 i	Sharon Wray	U23	8.10.82	3	Birmingham	19	Jan
11.29	Lauren Therin	U17	19.01.86	2	Woking	8	Jun
11.29	Clare Mcaleese		15.09.79	5	Bangor	23	Jul
11.26	Liz Edwards	U23	30.04.82	2	Menai	8	May
11.26	Fiona Harrison	U23	30.11.81	1	Cudworth	11	May
11.25	Emma Shaw	U17	19.09.86	1	Cudworth	11	May
	(90)						
11.23	Anne Hollman		18.02.74	4	Eton	27	Apr
11.20	Rebecca Chamberlain		7.09.79	1	Bournemouth	7	Apr
11.19	Kerri Fardoe	U20	22.11.83	4	Nottingham	13	Jul
11.18	Debbie Callaway	V35	15.07.64	8	London (He)	3	Aug
11.18	Jo Smith/White		22.11.78	1	Colchester	26	Aug
11.14	Andrea Jenkins		4.10.75	1	Aldershot	8	Jun
11.08	Katherine Newton	U17	25.10.85	2	Leeds	14	Jul
11.01	Louise Watton	U17	30.10.86	1	Bournemouth	22	Jun

Additional Under 17 (1 - 13 above)

10.96	Phyllis Agbo		16.12.85	1H	Derby	22	Sep
10.89	Hayley Thomas		16.12.86	1	Chelmsford	30	Mar
10.86	Amy Davis		28.01.86	1	Antrim	25	May
10.77	Nichole Martins		21.06.86	1	Leamington	15	Jun
10.74	Naomi Magbadelo		16.04.87	6	Nottingham	13	Jul
10.70	Suzie Dudley		24.02.87	1	Milton Keynes	15	Jun
10.70	Rachel Cork		11.10.86	1	Bournemouth	16	Jul
	(20)						
10.68	Emily Clowes		24.10.86	7	Birmingham	11	Aug
10.65	Kate Butters		25.07.86	1	Crawley	15	Jun
10.54	Gemma Llewelyn		23.04.87	1	Colwyn Bay	30	Mar
10.52 i	Tania Nell		21.05.86	6	Birmingham	23	Feb
10.49	Clare Palmer		30.12.85	2	Milton Keynes	7	Sep

10.48	Clare Robertson		17.08.86	1	Birmingham	22	Jun
10.47	Ashleigh Palmer-Johnson		19.09.86	3	Chelmsford	27	Jul
10.45	Heidi Rogers		27.05.86	1	Tidworth	8	Sep
10.45	Lianne Tucker		18.07.87	2	Cudworth	15	Sep
10.41	Kirsty Law		11.10.86	1	Inverness	11	Jun
	(30)						
10.30	Lucy Fisher		27.09.85	1	Warrington	12	May

Foreign

13.21	*Angeline Gbahy (FRA)*		*16.07.76*	*1*	*Yate*	*7*	*Jul*
12.42	*Silvia Cruz (POR)*	*U23*	*29.12.80*	*1*	*Peterborough*	*26*	*Aug*
11.79	*Sulueti Tagilala (FIJ)*	*U23*	*24.08.80*	*1*	*Tidworth*	*25*	*Jun*
11.67	*Laura Ballotta (ITA)*		*17.08.71*	*8*	*Birmingham*	*6*	*Jul*
11.29	*Alison Moffitt (IRL)*		*6.10.69*	*3*	*Eton*	*27*	*Apr*

Shot - Under 15 - 3.25kg

12.85	Candee Rhule	16.09.87	1	London (BP)	15	Jun
12.48	Kayleigh Southgate	15.01.88	1	Norwich	11	Aug
12.37	Liz Millward	29.10.88	1	Cannock	24	Jul
12.33	Eden Francis	19.10.88	1	Grimsby	7	Sep
12.27	Tolani Agoro	7.09.87	3	Nottingham	12	Jul
11.94 i	Rebecca Hall	15.09.88	P	Gateshead	23	Mar
11.62			1	Grantham	15	Jun
11.57	Laura Gomery	7.08.88	2	Tamworth	26	Aug
11.29	Laura Booth	28.04.88	1	Mansfield	19	May
11.11	April Barter	2.08.88	1	Eton	27	Apr
11.02	Bethany Staniland	10.05.88	1	Hull	8	Sep
	(10)					
10.91	Kate Dickinson	12.02.88	1	Manchester (Str)	8	Jun
10.87	Katrina Mountain	12.01.88	2	London (Elt)	7	Sep
10.85	Anna Griffiths	28.12.87	1	Blackpool	12	May
10.72	Chloe Beckett	10.06.88	1	Wakefield	21	Sep
10.71	Rebecca Saunders	8.02.88	1	London (TB)	30	Jun
10.70	Nicola McSweeney	17.11.87	1	Bedford	18	May
10.68	Katy Wilson	1.09.88	1	Gateshead	23	Jun
10.63	Victoria Thomas	24.09.87	2	Watford	26	May
10.61	Nicola Cunningham	2.10.87	1	Macclesfield	15	Jun
10.53	Nicola Stevenson	8.05.89	1	Newport	9	Jun

Under 13

| 9.26 | Bonnie Francis | 21.12.89 | 1 | Poole | 7 | Sep |
| 9.13 | Shakira Akanwale | 27.11.89 | 2 | Exeter | 7 | Sep |

Shot - Under 13 - 2.72kg

11.53	Finesse Thompson	30.03.90	1	Brighton	30	Jun
10.25	Rachel Wallader	1.09.89	1	Solihull	7	Jul
9.94	Emma Pattison	21.11.89	1	Grimsby	25	Sep
9.85	Rachael Fleary	16.07.90	1	Grangemouth	24	Aug
9.84	Elizabeth Goddard	1.09.89	1	Woking	22	Sep
9.57	Shaunagh Brown	15.03.90	1	Bromley	22	Jun
9.24	Amelia Montagnani	10.03.90	1	London (TB)	27	Apr
9.20	Naomi Hall	26.09.89	1	Manchester (Str)	23	Jul
9.18	Kate Heller	24.03.90	1	Carn Brea	11	Aug
9.17	Ruth Kelly	30.04.90	1	Blackpool	21	Jul
	(10)					
9.17	Shantel Rock	7.11.89	1	Kingston	28	Jul
9.13	Suzy Scott	1.09.89	1	Birmingham	21	Jul
9.12	Imogen Walters	5.05.90	1	Warrington	16	Jun
9.06 i	Stephanie Hopkinson	27.10.89	1	Gateshead	14	Mar
9.02	Lucy Underdown	18.05.90	2	Crawley	26	Aug
9.01	Bethan Mason	25.10.89	2	Yate	19	May

Discus

60.29	Shelley Newman		8.08.73	5	Sheffield	30	Jun
59.62				1	Bedford	4	Jun
58.39				1	Floro, NOR	1	Jun
58.34				1	London (He)	21	Jul
58.13				3	Manchester (C)	30	Jul
58.10				1	Varazdin, CRO	6	Jul
57.99				1	Manchester (C)	16	Jun
57.96				1	Birmingham (Un)	19	Jun
57.89				6	Annecy, FRA	22	Jun
57.38				10	Munich, GER	7	Aug
57.37				2	Loughborough	17	Jul
57.10				1	Manchester (Str)	9	Jul
56.80				7	Pula, CRO	9	Mar
56.57				Q	Munich, GER	6	Aug
56.36				1	Manchester (Str)	23	Jul
56.18				1	Bedford	26	May
55.27				1	Bromley	8	Jun
55.25				1	Eton	27	Apr
55.05				2	Loughborough	18	May
54.67				1	Bedford	17	Aug
54.08				2	Birmingham	13	Jul
53.77				1	Cheltenham	6	May
58.26	Philippa Roles		1.03.78	1	Loughborough	17	Jul
57.65				4	Manchester (C)	30	Jul
56.82				1	Cardiff	8	Jul
56.75				1	Amsterdam, NED	26	May
56.52				3	Manchester (C)	16	Jun
56.32				1	Birmingham	13	Jul
56.13				6	Halle, GER	11	May
56.12				1	London (He)	3	Aug
56.03				1	Loughborough	18	May
55.74				10	Sheffield	30	Jun
55.57				1	Rugby	19	May
54.45				1	Newport	9	Jun
54.31				2	Bedford	17	Aug
53.90				15	Pula, CRO	9	Mar
53.56				1	Birmingham	6	Jul
53.38				1	Stoke-on-Trent	21	Jul
56.63	Emma Carpenter	U23	16.05.82	2	Manchester (C)	16	Jun
53.88				2	Cardiff	8	Jul
53.67				3	Bedford	4	Jun
53.56				1	Bedford	30	Jun
53.28				3	Birmingham	13	Jul
52.71				1	Watford	2	Jun
52.09				1	Aldershot	8	Jun
55.03	Claire Smithson	U20	3.08.83	7	Manchester (C)	30	Jul
54.90				2	Bedford	4	Jun
54.34				4	Manchester (C)	16	Jun
53.91				1	Bedford	30	Jun
53.61				2	Eton	27	Apr
52.57				2	Watford	2	Jun
54.01	Emma Merry		2.07.74	3	Loughborough	18	May
53.38				5	Manchester (C)	16	Jun
53.84	Jackie McKernan	V35	1.07.65	1	Loughborough	12	Jun
52.05	Navdeep Dhaliwal		30.11.77	1B	Birmingham (Un)	12	Jun
	55 performances to 52.00 by 7 athletes						
51.16	Rebecca Roles		14.12.79	14	La Jolla, USA	27	Apr
49.89	Kara Nwidobie	U23	13.04.81	2	Bedford	30	Jun
49.14	Ade Oshinowo	U23	12.02.80	6	Madison, USA	19	May

47.73	Vickie Foster		1.04.71	1	Bath	12 May
47.39	Nicola Talbot		17.02.72	1	Birmingham	2 Jun
47.31	Susan Backhouse		6.12.78	1	Coventry	19 May
47.02	Elaine Cank		5.12.79	1	Cudworth	25 Aug
46.74	Joanna Bradley		23.08.79	1	Ashford	18 May
46.70	Claire Moore	U23	29.03.82	2	Cudworth	25 Aug
46.29	Ellisha Dee	U20	24.10.84	1	Nottingham	12 Jul
46.27	Lorraine Shaw		2.04.68	3	Birmingham	6 Jul
46.25	Susan Freebairn	V35	22.08.65	2	Coventry	19 May
44.44	Carly Burton	U23	14.10.80	4	Coventry	19 May
(20)						
44.25	Rebecca Hardy		11.11.68	1	London (ME)	11 May
44.09	Joan Macpherson	U23	18.09.80	4	Bedford	30 Jun
44.07	Laura Fox	U20	25.10.84	2	Nottingham	12 Jul
43.93	Emma Forrester	U20	2.12.83	2	Coventry	28 Apr
43.85	Eva Massey	U23	22.12.80	2	Belfast	8 Jun
43.69	Tracy Axten	V35	20.07.63	1	Exeter	4 Jul
42.03	Alison Rodger	U20	29.10.84	3	Derby	11 Aug
42.02	Hannah Corneby	U23	22.01.81	4	Derby	11 Aug
41.95	Natalie Hart		25.05.72	1	Great Yarmouth	11 May
41.73	Lydia Morgan	U20	1.09.83	1	Cudworth	15 Sep
(30)						
41.67	Angela Mitchell	V35	17.08.65	1	Aldershot	3 Jul
40.89	Sarah Henton		4.05.73	7	Birmingham	6 Jul
40.85	Claire Cameron	V40	3.10.58	2	Exeter	4 Jul
40.56	Laura Douglas	U20	4.01.83	1	Colwyn Bay	30 Mar
40.46	Christina Bennett		27.02.78	1	Portsmouth	18 May
40.45	Candice Francis	U20	7.02.85	1	Derby	28 Apr
40.44	Tasha Saint-Smith		20.12.75	2	Crawley	27 Jul
40.23	Jo Smith/White		22.11.78	2	Colchester	26 Aug
40.23	Debbie Callaway	V35	15.07.64	3	London (Ha)	7 Sep
40.01	Katie Halford	U23	4.10.82	1	Exeter	9 Jun
(40)						
39.93	Andrea Jenkins		4.10.75	5	London (He)	21 Jul
39.69	Helen Wilding		25.10.76	7	London (He)	3 Aug
39.67	Kate Morris	U20	18.01.83	5	Coventry	19 May
39.62	Carol Parker		22.09.69	6	Coventry	19 May
39.60	Christina Carding	U17	26.02.87	1	Nottingham	12 Jul
39.31	Julie Dunkley		11.09.79	7	Rugby	19 May
39.08	Kirsty Law	U17	11.10.86	1	Inverness	20 Jun
39.07	Amie Hill	U23	9.09.80	6	Bedford	5 May
39.06	Elizabeth Dwan	U23	16.10.82	1	Jarrow	24 Apr
38.94	Lauren Therin	U17	19.01.86	1	Bromley	27 Jul
(50)						
38.88	Lianne Tucker	U17	18.07.87	1	Jarrow	22 Jun
38.83	Alana Smith	U20	18.01.85	2	Scunthorpe	23 Jun
38.74	Alyson Hourihan	V40	17.10.60	1	Tidworth	21 Sep
38.72	Laura Wood		31.10.78	1	Manchester (Str)	7 Jul
38.69	Amy Howard	U17	3.03.87	2	Nottingham	12 Jul
38.65	Candie Lintern	U23	5.02.82	4	Crawley	27 Jul
38.58	Maggie Lynes	V35	19.02.63	7	Coventry	19 May
38.55	Ffion Jones	U20	19.07.83	5	Bedford	30 Jun
38.50	Hollie Redman	U17	12.12.85	1	Great Yarmouth	3 Aug
38.49	Danielle Hall	U20	27.11.84	2	Perivale	8 Jun
(60)						
38.38	Jacqui Loney		17.04.79	1	Aberdeen	29 Aug
38.22	Catherine Lane		18.11.76	2	Exeter	18 May
38.15	Joanne John	U23	12.11.80	2	London (ME)	11 May
38.13	Donna Swatheridge	U20	4.03.85	6	Nottingham	12 Jul
38.09	Myrtle Augee	V35	4.02.65	2	Hoo	7 Sep
38.04	Melanie Harrison	U17	27.11.85	3	Nottingham	12 Jul

38.04	Fallon Harrison	U20	1.05.85	7	Nottingham	12	Jul
38.03	Amanda Sheppard		26.02.68	6	Wakefield	7	Jul
37.95	Jenny Duff	U23	29.07.82	1	Oxford	18	May
37.72	Lucy Sutton	U17	29.08.86	1	Watford	1	Jun
(70)							
37.71	Lorraine Henry		16.09.67	2	Newark	24	Aug
37.65	Sue Lawrence		25.11.70	1	Brighton	6	Jul
37.55	Laura Perry		4.06.75	1	Brierley Hill	25	Aug
37.17	Dominique Lord	U17	8.04.87	1	Abingdon	17	Mar
36.87	Lisa Kenney	U20	17.02.83	2	Stoke-on-Trent	19	May
36.82	Debbie Woolgar	V35	10.03.65	3	Oxford	8	Jun
36.75	Kim Rawling	U20	22.07.83	1	High Wycombe	18	May
36.68	Lesley Bryant	V45	12.04.56	1	Grantham	11	May
36.65	Rebecca Chamberlain		7.09.79	1	Bournemouth	7	Apr
36.56	Jayne Fisher/Hill		2.11.70	2	Aberdare	18	May
(80)							
36.53	Natasha Smith		6.06.77	1	Kingston	17	Mar
36.51	Emily Clowes	U17	24.10.86	1	Blackpool	22	Sep
36.44	Diana Holden		12.02.75	3	Eton	27	Apr
36.42	Gemma Llewelyn	U17	23.04.87	2	Liverpool	14	Jul
36.12	Laura Seaman	U20	12.03.83	2	Eton	23	Jun
36.05	Laura Chalmers	U17	1.05.86	2	Inverness	15	Sep
35.70	Anna Bowyer	U23	29.09.82	1	Exeter	7	Jul
35.69	Mary Anderson		2.09.67	2	Coatbridge	11	Aug
35.55	Caroline Jones	U20	30.04.84	1	Watford	15	Jun
35.54	Laura Evans		28.09.74	2	Peterborough	26	Aug
(90)							
35.53	Hayley Bryan	U17	4.03.86	1	Exeter	15	Jun
35.50	Sarah Davies	U17	13.03.86	5	Nottingham	12	Jul

Additional Under 17 (1 - 14 above)

35.47	Chloe Beckett	U15	10.06.88	1	Nottingham	13	Jul
35.47	Ruth Hay	U15	4.11.87	1	Worcester	25	Aug
35.21	Ami Fawcett	U15	31.10.87	1	Wakefield	11	Aug
35.05	Anita Oliver		28.11.85	2	Bromley	8	Jun
34.79	Rebecca Saunders	U15	8.02.88	1	Erith	5	May
34.64	Lynsey Clark		2.09.86	2	Southend	6	May
(20)							
34.42	Lisa Rigby		12.02.86	3	Bournemouth	22	Jun
34.31	Katherine Newton		25.10.85	1	Scunthorpe	4	Aug
34.24	Monique Buchanon		27.09.86	1	London (WF)	23	Jun
34.19	Eshere Singh		15.07.87	4	Bournemouth	22	Jun
34.14	Samantha Manchester		10.12.86	1	Ashford	30	Jun
34.07	Alex Merrill		12.05.86	1	Manchester (Str)	11	Jun
34.04	Claire Lyne-Ley	U15	14.03.88	1	Exeter	7	Sep
33.57	Sarah Holt		17.04.87	9	Nottingham	12	Jul
33.53	Ella Newington		30.01.87	1	Dudley	18	Aug
33.18	Elizabeth Polson		26.06.86	1	Ipswich	12	May
(30)							
33.11	Hazel Robertson		27.07.87	2	Grangemouth	15	Jun
33.07	Amber Spencer		12.01.87	1	Poole	21	Apr
33.07	Vicky Cooper		10.10.85	1	Cannock	11	May
33.00	Rachel Gray		18.12.86	3	Basingstoke	7	Sep
32.95	Iyesha Tomlinson		19.02.86	1	Basildon	18	Aug
32.84	Rachael Atkinson		20.12.85	3	Birmingham	1	Sep
32.67	Karenate Songhorn		8.01.87	1	London (BP)	15	Jun

Additional Under 15 (1 - 5 above)

31.85	Hannah Cameron		3.03.88	2	Grangemouth	24	Aug
31.68	Kate Grundy		12.12.87	1	Tipton	30	Jun
31.39	Hannah James		28.06.88	1	Horsham	18	Aug

31.11	Jenny Dunford		31.03.89	5	Nottingham	13	Jul
30.90	Catrin Hardy		27.02.88	1	Connah's Quay	18	Aug
(10)							
30.62	Claire Williams		29.09.87	1	Neath	28	Apr
30.48	Rebecca Hall		15.09.88	4	Birmingham	10	Aug
30.43	Eden Francis		19.10.88	5	Birmingham	10	Aug
30.40	Sarah Boreham		13.06.88	6	Nottingham	13	Jul
30.39	Victoria Thomas		24.09.87	1	Watford	2	Jun
29.94	Bethany Staniland		10.05.88	2	Gateshead	24	Aug
29.44	Rachel Blackie		9.12.87	2	Birmingham	31	Aug
29.39	Soko Kauwale		27.01.88		High Wycombe	21	Jul
29.29	Kayleigh Southgate		15.01.88	1	Bury St. Edmunds	22	Sep
29.23	Ashley Maddison		24.05.89	8	Nottingham	13	Jul
(20)							
29.16	Laura Donnelly		2.10.87	2	Corby	22	Jun

Foreign

40.24	*Katharina Heinrich (GER)*		*5.07.72*	*2*	*Darlington*	*14*	*Jul*
39.56	*Sulueti Tagilala (FIJ)*	*U23*	*24.08.80*	*1*	*Tidworth*	*25*	*Jun*
39.39	*Alison Moffitt (IRL)*		*6.10.69*	*1*	*Eton*	*27*	*Apr*
38.80	*Yolande Jacobs (RSA)*		*9.11.76*	*2*	*Bath*	*12*	*May*

Discus - Under 13 - 0.75kg

31.52	Finesse Thompson	30.03.90	1	Woking	1	Sep
26.43	Lucy Underdown	18.05.90	1	Crawley	26	Aug
26.27	Kate Heller	24.03.90	1	Par	22	Sep
25.65	Kashmere Joseph	15.02.90	1	London (Nh)	25	Jun
25.27	Eleanor Probert	23.05.90	1	Southampton	6	Jul
24.63	Elidh Tait	10.02.90	1	Inverness	19	May
24.20	Shaunagh Brown	15.03.90	1	Bromley	22	Jun
24.17	Rachael Beckett	29.05.90	1	Cleckheaton	1	Sep
24.00 (1kg)	Elizabeth Goddard	1.09.89	1	Basingstoke	7	Sep
23.90	Abigail Peters	27.12.89	1	Eton	30	Sep
(10)						
23.76	Emma Hart	13.03.90	1	Southend	18	Aug
23.75	Katherine LeSueur	6.07.90	1	Luton	11	May
23.55	Rebecca Duquemin	7.01.90	1	Guernsey	15	Sep

Hammer

66.83	Lorraine Shaw		2.04.68	1	Manchester (C)	26	Jul
	66.10			Q	Manchester (C)	26	Jul
	65.43			1	Loughborough	17	Jul
	65.34			1	Manchester (C)	16	Jun
	64.97			1	Birmingham	14	Jul
	64.81			3	Pula, CRO	10	Mar
	64.53			1	Port Elizabeth, RSA	1	Mar
	64.38			1	Birmingham	1	Jun
	63.81			1	Birmingham	6	Jul
	63.62			3	Glasgow (S)	18	Aug
	63.61			1	Bedford	17	Aug
	63.09			7	Annecy, FRA	23	Jun
	62.62			1	Stoke-on-Trent	21	Jul
	61.95			1	Bath	11	Aug
	61.50			20QA	Munich, GER	7	Aug
	61.09			1	Perivale	17	Mar
62.27	Zoe Derham	U23	24.11.80	2	Manchester (C)	16	Jun
	61.70			2	Loughborough	17	Jul
	61.43			7	Halle, GER	11	May
	60.65			1	Loughborough	5	Jun
	60.57			1	Bedford	30	Jun
	60.50			2	Bedford	17	Aug

(Derham)	60.38			3	Loughborough	18	May
	60.22			Q	Manchester (C)	26	Jul
	59.96			1	Derby	11	Aug
	59.89			3	Birmingham	14	Jul
	59.87			11	Varazdin, CRO	6	Jul
	59.64			1	Rugby	25	Aug
	59.57			8	Manchester (C)	26	Jul
	59.20			13	Pula, CRO	10	Mar
	58.99			3	Bedford	4	Jun
	58.34			2	Birmingham	1	Jun
62.08	Liz Pidgeon		27.04.77	2	Birmingham	14	Jul
	61.42			1	Watford	1	Jun
	61.39			1	Loughborough	27	Apr
	60.79			8	Halle, GER	11	May
	60.26			1	Bedford	4	Jun
	60.21			1	Chelmsford	27	Jul
	59.91			3	Alfaz del Pi, ESP	30	Mar
	59.69			1	Barking	7	Apr
	59.55			1	Crawley	20	Apr
	59.37			1	Wakefield	7	Jul
	59.33			1	Eton	4	Aug
	59.23			4	Manchester (C)	16	Jun
	59.04			1	London (He)	21	Jul
	58.66			4	Loughborough	17	Jul
	58.51			3	Gothenburg, SWE	27	Aug
	58.49			2	Bedford	25	May
	58.43			1	Ashford	18	Aug
	58.34			1	Watford	1	Sep
61.11	Lyn Sprules		11.09.75	1	Almarar, POR	3	Apr
	60.94			1	Loughborough	18	May
	60.52			2	Watford	1	Jun
	60.39			1	Bedford	25	May
	60.12			1	Guildford	21	Apr
	59.41			1	London (ME)	11	May
	59.23			3	Bedford	17	Aug
	59.22			2	Bedford	4	Jun
	58.94			5	Manchester (C)	16	Jun
	58.00			1	Rugby	19	May
60.38	Suzanne Roberts		19.12.78	2	Loughborough	18	May
	59.75			3	Manchester (C)	16	Jun
	59.72			1	Loughborough	12	Jun
	59.38			12	Varazdin, CRO	6	Jul
	59.16			3	Loughborough	17	Jul
	58.93			4	Birmingham	14	Jul
	58.85			Q	Manchester (C)	26	Jul
	58.66			9	Manchester (C)	26	Jul
	58.38			1	Loughborough	22	May
	58.36			2	Loughborough	27	Apr
	58.04			5	Bedford	4	Jun
59.95	Shirley Webb	U23	28.09.81	1A	Manchester (Str)	8	Sep
	59.88			4	Loughborough	18	May
	59.71			1C	Manchester (Str)	8	Sep
	59.03			1	Edinburgh	12	May
	58.83			1B	Manchester (Str)	8	Sep
	58.08			6	Manchester (C)	16	Jun
58.97	Diana Holden		12.02.75	4	Bedford	4	Jun
	58.17			2	London (ME)	11	May
58.47	Mhairi Walters	U23	19.06.81	2	Edinburgh	12	May
	58 performances to 58.00 by 8 athletes						
57.63	Nicola Dudman	U20	5.10.83	8	Manchester (C)	16	Jun
57.47	Lesley Brannan		13.09.76	1	Manchester (Str)	28	May

56.18	Sarah Moore		15.03.73	1	Neath	1	Jun
55.22	Laura Douglas	U20	4.01.83	7	Loughborough	18	May
54.01	Carys Parry	U23	24.07.81	2	Groningen, NED	30	Mar
52.68	Christina Bennett		27.02.78	1	Kingston	6	Jul
52.31	Vicci Scott	U23	21.09.80	1	Bebington	11	May
52.31	Andrea Jenkins		4.10.75	4	Watford	1	Jun
52.15	Lucy Marshall	U23	28.11.81	3	Watford	1	Sep
51.95	Katy Lamb	U23	21.08.82	1	Eton	27	Apr
51.37	Ade Oshinowo	U23	12.02.80	4	El Paso TX, USA	30	Mar
50.39	Joanne John	U23	12.11.80	5	Watford	1	Jun
(20)							
49.93	Sheena Parry		16.11.77	2	Connah's Quay	1	Jun
49.44	Esther Augee	V35	1.01.64	2	Eton	4	Aug
48.64	Helen Wilding		25.10.76	3	Manchester (Str)	25	Jun
47.90	Janet Smith	V35	7.10.64	9	Bedford	4	Jun
47.64	Joanne Holloway		10.05.76	1	Plymouth	8	Jun
46.88	Julie Lavender		9.11.75	1	Sunderland	12	Jan
46.59	Susan McKelvie	U20	15.06.85	1	Yate	21	Apr
46.39	Jean Clark		5.10.68	1	Cannock	14	Sep
46.20	Bola Ogun		2.09.77	1	Sutton Coldfield	24	Aug
45.70	Laura Chalmers	U17	1.05.86	1	Inverness	15	Sep
(30)							
45.43	Faye Blacktin	U23	5.11.81	1	Basingstoke	7	Sep
45.31	Katie Horne		23.05.79	3	Loughborough	22	May
44.92	Suzanne Last		11.01.70	3	Coventry	19	May
44.82	Vickie Foster		1.04.71	1	Exeter	23	Jun
44.66	Carly Burton	U23	14.10.80	3	London (CP)	11	May
44.07	Natasha Forgie	U20	12.05.84	1	Hoo	18	Aug
44.01	Anna Johnson		17.12.87	2	Birmingham	10	Aug
43.87	Jenny Duff	U23	29.07.82	9	Rugby	19	May
43.58	Emily Oliver	U20	8.02.84	1	Bromley	6	Jul
43.41	Diane Smith	V40	15.11.60	1	Darlington	14	Jul
(40)							
43.37	Helen Ephgrave	U20	29.10.84	1	London (Ha)	7	Sep
43.36	Anna Howard	U20	18.07.83	2	Oxford	8	Jun
43.20	Jacqui Loney		17.04.79	1	Elgin	20	Jul
43.11	Maddy Robinson	U23	13.10.81	1	Wigan	4	Aug
43.07	Cassie Wilson		24.09.77	5	Loughborough	27	Apr
42.97	Lydia Morgan	U20	1.09.83	1	Bebington	28	Jul
42.91	Sarah Deacon	U20	18.03.83	1	Walton	8	Jun
42.65	Sarah Drake	U20	13.08.85	2	Nottingham	13	Jul
42.41	Sarah-Louise Dobriskey	U20	13.08.85	3	Nottingham	13	Jul
42.41	Samantha Hynes	U17	28.01.86	1	Perivale	14	Sep
(50)							
42.35	Bethan Lishman	U20	15.11.83	1	Manchester (C)	26	May
42.27	Joan Macpherson	U23	18.09.80	1	Colchester	18	May
41.97	Jenna Lander	U20	31.08.85	4	Nottingham	13	Jul
41.69	Laura Allan	U20	11.02.85	1	Dunfermline	14	Apr
41.66	Helen Gilbert	U23	1.03.82	2	Stoke-on-Trent	21	Jul
41.66	Catherine Marvin	U17	18.04.87	1	Sandown IOW	18	Sep
41.65	Marina Semenova	V35	12.07.64	2B	Eton	20	Oct
41.50	Sue Lawrence		25.11.70	2	Portsmouth	18	May
41.41	Amy Church	U17	22.04.86	1	Sandown IOW	15	Sep
41.21	Lisa-Marie Shippen	U20	19.10.83	6	Nottingham	13	Jul
(60)							
41.12	Jenny Wood	V45	23.02.57	3	Wakefield	21	Sep
41.06	Sarah Holt	U17	17.04.87	2	Glasgow (S)	20	Jul
40.88	Karen Ainsley/Bailey	U23	24.06.80	2	Wrexham	11	Aug
40.87	Kim Rawling	U20	22.07.83	1	Carn Brea	1	Sep
40.82	Elizabeth Edwards	U20	18.12.84	2	London (WF)	18	Aug
40.81	Laura Perry		4.06.75	1	Brierley Hill	25	Aug

40.69	Emma King	U23	25.07.81	8	Bedford	17	Aug
40.51	Tanya Bilous	U17	7.05.86	1	Gloucester	20	Aug
40.37	Catherine Lane		18.11.76	1	Hemel Hempstead	6	Jul
40.04	Eleanor Gatrell		5.10.76	4	Eton	21	Jul
	(70)						
39.66	Siobhan Hart		15.06.75	2	Hemel Hempstead	6	Jul
39.59	Susan Freebairn	V35	22.08.65	6	Wakefield	7	Jul
39.38	Angela Lockley	U20	7.10.84	3	Wakefield	28	Jul
39.26	Jennifer West		13.09.79	2	Perivale	8	Jun
39.00	Karen Brown		31.08.68	1	Carlisle	11	May
38.97	Sally Hinds	U17	2.02.86	1	Dudley	18	Aug
38.89	Sarah Morgan	U20	9.05.84	9	Nottingham	13	Jul
38.76	Rebecca Hardy		11.11.68	2	London (PH)	27	Apr
38.72	Anna Bowyer	U23	29.09.82	3	Eton	27	Apr
38.71	Melissa Ashley		17.03.77	4	Perivale	27	Jul
	(80)						
38.66	Debra Monds		25.02.78	3	Scunthorpe	7	Jul
38.55	Jenna Wheatman	U20	6.03.84	4	Gateshead	25	Aug
38.39	Emma Murdoch	U20	26.03.84	1	Inverness	11	May
38.34	Emma Kirby	U23	11.11.81	6	Loughborough	22	May
38.14	Alex Merrill	U17	12.05.86	2	Manchester (C)	25	May
38.10	Karen Moody	V35	20.07.67	4	Rugby	25	Aug
37.87	Alana Smetham		14.12.86	1	Tamworth	26	Aug
37.79	Gemma Roach	U20	16.02.83	5	Perivale	27	Jul
37.67	Joanne Harding	V35	12.04.64	2	Manchester (Str)	30	Apr
37.54	Zoe Bridger		4.03.76	3	London (Ha)	7	Sep
	(90)						
37.36	Laura Wood		31.10.78	2	Manchester (Str)	8	Sep
37.32	Carol Parker		22.09.69	8	Wakefield	7	Jul
37.28	Jenny Earle	V40	28.11.58	1	Malta	12	Jan
37.24	Kelly Anderson	U23	17.07.80	2	Portsmouth	12	May
37.08	Vikki Grime	U23	21.08.82	1	Blackpool	14	Sep
36.68	Joanna Bennett	U20	6.08.83	6	Kingston	6	Jul
36.50	Sarah Etherton		19.10.78	1	Tonbridge	21	Apr

Additional Under 17 (1 - 8 above)

34.54	Helen Gibbens		11.02.87	3	Kingston	27	Jul
34.26	Hazel Robertson		27.07.87	5	Glasgow (S)	2	Jun
	(10)						
34.17	Hayley Bryan		4.03.86	1	Exeter	7	Jul
33.82	Melanie Harrison		27.11.85	4	Kingston	4	Aug
33.63	Katherine Newton		25.10.85	1	Mansfield	28	Apr
33.32	Shaeleen Bruce		3.11.86	1	Middlesbrough	23	Jun
33.24	Lorne Tait		16.01.87	1	Elgin	24	Dec
32.70	Lauren Therin		19.01.86	2	Banbury	27	Jul
31.79	Hannah Hogben		4.06.86	5	Kingston	4	Aug
31.69	Stephanie Fuller		8.03.87	1	London (Ha)	7	Sep
31.55	Kate Gillett	U15	5.09.87	9	Birmingham	10	Aug
31.39	Hollie Redman		12.12.85	2	Chelmsford	30	Mar
	(20)						
30.78	Amy Davis		28.01.86	5	Tullamore, IRL	22	Jun
30.44	Kirsty Law		11.10.86	2	Inverness	14	Apr
30.38	Ruth Wilsher		8.02.86	6	Wakefield	28	Jul

Foreign

37.04	*Yolande Jacobs (RSA)*		*9.11.76*	*2*	*Bath*	*12*	*May*

Hammer - Under 15 - 3.25kg

45.15	Anna Johnson		17.12.87	1	Manchester (Str)	15	Sep
37.62	Hannah Cameron		3.03.88	1	Grangemouth	24	Aug
35.70	Natalie Bodiam		30.09.87	1	Inverness	15	Sep

33.30	Kayleigh Brading		22.11.88	1	Sandown IOW	18	Sep
32.47	Nicola Stevenson		8.05.89	1	Newport	28	Aug
31.12	Laura Edwards			1	Watford	28	Aug

3kg

51.00	Anna Johnson		17.12.87	1	Manchester (Str)	3	Sep
33.68	Claire Phillips		27.05.88	1	Perivale	14	Sep
31.54	Kelly Coombs		4.03.88	1	Hastings	11	Aug

Javelin

64.87	Kelly Morgan	U23	17.06.80	1	Birmingham	14	Jul
	63.03			1	Manchester (C)	15	Jun
	58.58			1	Bournemouth	8	Jun
	57.09			3	Manchester (C)	29	Jul
	56.90			QB	Munich, GER	6	Aug
	56.55			6	Annecy, FRA	22	Jun
	56.50			1	Aldershot	10	Jul
	53.89			12	Munich, GER	8	Aug
58.20	Goldie Sayers	U23	16.07.82	1	Bedford	29	Jun
	57.86			4	Pihtipudas, FIN	7	Jul
	56.96			2	Birmingham	14	Jul
	56.85			2	Riga, LAT	31	May
	54.59			3	Manchester (C)	15	Jun
	53.63			1	Bedford	5	May
	53.60			1	Bedford	17	Aug
	52.49			1	Bedford	25	May
	51.69			5	Tartu, EST	2	Jun
	51.32			6	Manchester (C)	29	Jul
56.34	Karen Martin		24.11.74	3	Birmingham	14	Jul
	55.59			1	Loughborough	18	May
	55.02			2	Manchester (C)	15	Jun
55.74	Kirsty Morrison		28.10.75	1	Watford	1	Jun
	55.01			1	London (CP)	11	May
	54.38			1	Watford	1	Sep
	52.81 A			3	Germiston, RSA	5	Apr
	51.55			2	Bedford	17	Aug
	51.15			1	Ashford	18	Aug
	51.12			1	London (He)	21	Jul
54.18	Shelley Holroyd		17.05.73	4	Manchester (C)	15	Jun
	52.08			1	Manchester (Str)	11	May
	51.25			1	Stoke-on-Trent	21	Jul
	31 performances to 51.00 by 5 athletes						
48.73	Sharon Gibson	V40	31.12.61	1	Nottingham	5	May
48.54	Lorna Jackson		9.01.74	1	Edinburgh	12	May
48.39	Katie Amos		13.11.78	2	Watford	1	Jun
47.74	Joanne Bruce		26.10.78	1	Yeovil	7	Sep
47.73	Helen Mounteney	U20	24.09.84	1	Nottingham	12	Jul
	(10)						
47.66	Samantha Redd	U20	16.02.84	1	Bedford	29	Jun
47.61	Chloe Cozens	U23	9.04.80	2	Niort, FRA	3	Aug
47.33	Katy Watts	U23	25.03.81	3	Watford	1	Jun
46.94	Louise Watton	U17	30.10.86	1	Mansfield	12	Jul
46.57	Louise Mathews	U20	27.10.83	1	Bedford	28	Apr
44.72	Suzanne Finnis	U20	12.08.83	2	Bedford	29	Jun
44.59	Rebecca Bartlett	U20	7.03.85	4	Nottingham	12	Jul
44.51	Melanie Burrows		7.08.76	3	Basildon	12	May
44.37	Charlotte Rees	U20	14.06.84	1	Neath	14	May
44.22	Jenny Grimstone		30.04.79	1	Crawley	31	Mar
	(20)						
44.07	Jennifer West		13.09.79	6	Bedford	25	May
43.83	Jenny Kemp	U23	18.02.80	1	Derby	21	Jul

43.81	Hayley Thomas	U17	16.12.86	2	Mansfield	12	Jul
43.79	Jo Chapman	U20	10.01.85	1	Bury St. Edmunds	27	Jul
43.52	Nicola Gautier		21.03.78	5H	Bydgoszcz, POL	30	Jun
43.11	Candace Schofield	U20	3.11.84	2	Crawley	25	May
43.00	Paula Blank-Collis		13.12.77	1	Welwyn	6	May
42.61	Tammie Francis/Conniff		14.11.78	1	Cardiff	4	Aug
41.72	Noelle Bradshaw	V35	18.12.63	2	Eton	21	Jul
41.37	Debbie Collinson	U17	23.10.85	1	Cudworth	21	Apr
	(30)						
41.37	Lauren Therin	U17	19.01.86	1	Guernsey	21	Sep
41.20	Alison Siggery	U20	14.09.83	2	Brecon	6	Jul
41.07	Roz Gonse	U23	1.03.82	12H	Bydgoszcz, POL	30	Jun
41.04	Jo Blair	U17	1.03.86	3	Mansfield	12	Jul
41.01	Rosie Semenytsh	U17	28.05.87	1	Millfield	19	Jun
40.91	Louise Smith		11.07.77	2	London (Ha)	20	Apr
40.71	Paula Hendriks	U20	25.01.83	1	Tallahassee FL, USA	13	Apr
40.71	Gillian Stewart	U23	21.01.80	H	Hexham	16	Jun
40.68	Lianne Clarke	U17	14.01.87	1	Cardiff	26	Aug
40.54	Helen Potter		25.06.74	1	Exeter	4	Jul
	(40)						
39.87	Christine Lawrence	U17	4.04.86	6	Mansfield	12	Jul
39.80	Laura Kerr	U17	3.09.85	1	Tullamore, IRL	3	Aug
39.68	Emily Skucek	U23	24.09.81	5	Bedford	5	May
39.62	Carol Wallbanks	U23	9.12.82	6	Bedford	5	May
39.54	Julie Hollman		16.02.77	5H	Manchester (C)	27	Jul
39.52	Kate Grainger	U20	17.02.84	1	Inverness	14	Apr
39.32	Vicky James	U23	13.05.81	6	Watford	1	Sep
39.30	Georgina Hogsden	U23	23.11.81	1	Aldershot	3	Jul
39.13	Liz Pidgeon		27.04.77	4	Wakefield	7	Jul
38.98	Hayley Boddey	U20	14.02.83	1	Cleckheaton	7	Jul
	(50)						
38.85	Laura Bolton		22.01.79	2	Exeter	23	Jun
38.82	Stacey Mohamed	U23	22.01.80	3	Derby	11	Aug
38.82	Nicola Smith	U23	6.03.82	1	London (Ha)	7	Sep
38.63	Carrie Williams	U17	9.02.87	1	Newport	8	Jun
38.45	Laura Whittingham	U17	6.06.86	2	Cudworth	21	Apr
38.37	Joanne Harding	V35	12.04.64	4	London (He)	3	Aug
38.22	Joanne Davis		24.03.76	2	Stoke-on-Trent	19	May
38.22	Sarah Ellis	U20	27.10.83	1	Southampton	8	Jun
38.12	Claire Bennett	U20	4.02.83	2	Stoke-on-Trent	21	Jul
37.90	Stephanie Novak	U17	20.09.86	1	Lancaster	10	Aug
	(60)						
37.85	Joanna Parry		5.03.78	3	Ware	27	Apr
37.78	Fiona Harrison	U23	30.11.81	2	Jarrow	1	Jun
37.77	Caroline Garrett	V35	14.06.63	1	Sandown IOW	15	Sep
37.58	Sara Siggery	U20	30.06.85	2	Tullamore, IRL	3	Aug
37.46	Jenny Leng	U20	1.02.84	6	Moscow, RUS	21	Sep
37.45	Rebecca Jones	U20	17.01.83	1	Connah's Quay	14	Apr
37.43	Emma Thornton	U23	27.11.82	2	Derby	21	Jul
37.39	Debbie Woolgar	V35	10.03.65	1	London (SP)	7	Sep
37.23	Eloise Manger	U20	6.01.85	1	Blackburn	11	May
37.22	Kylie Clarke	U15	3.03.88	1	Cardiff	26	Aug
	(70)						
37.20	Tania Nell	U17	21.05.86	2	Ashford	18	May
37.03	Caroline Monk		7.09.75	1	Birmingham (Un)	6	May
37.03	Sarah Browne	U20	8.01.85	1	Carlisle	15	Jun
36.96	Amanda Lyons	U17	12.03.87	3	Derby	8	Sep
36.81	Venetia Ellis	U17	15.09.85	6	Watford	26	May
36.75	Lisa Edwards	U17	4.02.87	7	Bedford	17	Aug
36.66	Nightingale Anek		25.01.78	6	Birmingham	6	Jul
36.55	Amy Harvey	U23	23.04.82	2	Coventry	28	Apr
36.53	Laura Redmond	U23	19.04.81	3	Edinburgh	11	May

340

36.41	Lynsey Stevenson	U17	18.11.86	1	Warley	15	May
	(80)						
36.22	Rebecca Roles		14.12.79	5	Rugby	19	May
36.16	Jennifer Wilkie	U20	4.11.83	1	Grangemouth	7	Aug
36.13	Anna Hoyle	U20	12.02.85	2	Blackburn	11	May

Additional Under 17 (1 - 18 above)

35.84	Melissa O'Neil		13.02.87	1	Stevenage	21	Apr
35.72	Katie Bennett		5.10.86	1	Grantham	17	Jun
	(20)						
35.19	Sarah Devoy		12.01.87	4	Derby	8	Sep
34.79	Abby Wildbore		12.09.85	1	Salisbury	15	Jun
34.53	Stephanie Ashmore		11.09.86	2	Nuneaton	21	Jul
34.33	Shani Rainford		6.07.87	1H	Hemel Hempstead	30	Jun

Additional Under 15 (1 above)

34.36	Emma Gray		17.04.88	1	Tullamore, IRL	3	Aug
34.25	Carly Smith		28.04.88	1	Cudworth	15	Sep
33.03	Laura Carr		18.02.89	1	London (He)	25	Aug
32.72	Chloe Beckett		10.06.88	1	Cleckheaton	5	May
32.59	Lucy Boggis		27.01.89	1	Watford	25	May
32.50	Sasha Corbin		23.04.88	1	London (Nh)	7	Sep
32.48	Rebecca Furber		14.10.87	2	Mansfield	12	Jul
32.45	Soko Kauwale		27.01.88		High Wycombe	21	Jul
32.39	Ashley Austin		29.09.87	1	Grangemouth	17	Aug
	(10)						
32.04	Laura Scott		16.09.87	1	Grimsby	7	Sep
31.53	Hannah Cameron		3.03.88	1	Grangemouth	23	Jun
31.00	Jo Wray		29.07.89	1	Watford	21	Aug
30.90	Nicole MacAuley		6.07.88	3	Mansfield	12	Jul
30.86	Hannah Ferson		21.10.87	1	Antrim	25	May
30.56	Rachelle Brace		18.03.89	1	Braintree	7	Sep
30.48	Jade White		1.01.88	1	Bebington	4	Aug
30.44	Maria Williamson		7.09.87	1	Solihull	7	Jul
30.30	Kimberley Eke		10.02.89	2	Exeter	24	Sep
30.23	Alexis Walker		14.02.88	2	Manchester (C)	26	May
	(20)						
30.20	Nikki Cross		11.04.88	1	Portsmouth	15	Jun
30.19	Emma Smith		3.12.87	1	London (Ha)	8	Jun

Foreign

43.51	*Alison Moffitt (IRL)*		*6.10.69*	*1*	*Eton*	*27*	*Apr*
38.00	*Heiline Rademeyer (RSA)*		*10.06.69*	*1*	*London (TB)*	*20*	*Jul*
36.35	*Sonia Martinez-Roura (ESP)*		*21.03.73*	*1*	*Eastbourne*	*11*	*Jun*

Javelin - Under 13 - 400 gm

33.50	Rachael Fleary		16.07.90	1	Carlisle	31	Aug
31.10	Diane Neva		20.10.89	1	Carn Brea	14	Jul
29.54	Hannah Bryan		21.02.90	1	Kingston	28	Jul
28.17	Catrin Vaughan		14.01.90	1	Barry	31	Aug
27.38	Emily Martin		18.09.89	1	Exeter	18	Aug
27.35	Charlotte Kitney		16.10.89	2	Kingston	28	Jul
26.81	Emma Pattison		21.11.89	1	Grimsby	1	Sep
26.72	Jemma Tewkesbury		29.09.90	1	Exeter	24	Sep
26.64	Beckie Slater		20.04.90	1	Portsmouth	11	May
26.38	Emma Mccarthy		3.11.89	1	Guernsey	15	Sep
	(10)						
25.32	Lara Whittaker		13.09.89	1	Crawley	1	Sep
24.77	Natalie Evernden		12.01.90	1	Kingston	28	Jul
24.72	Charlotte Bennington		2.02.90	1	Tamworth	26	Aug
24.54	Danielle Summers		18.05.90	1	Woking	22	Sep
24.00	Jenny Banfield		10.04.90	1	Stoke Mandeville	8	Sep

Decathlon

6145	Kerry Jury				19.11.68	1		Jarrow			29 Sep
	12.5/-1.1	5.31/-1.1	10.55	1.63	58.0	14.3		20.11	2.35	31.05	5:43.5
4767 irr	Clare Ridgley				11.09.77	1		Exeter			29 Sep
	13.6	26.41	3.40	22.81	69.0	17.5	4.81w/3.3	8.7	1.37		6:25.4
4371 irr	Lucy Webber				5.02.72	2		Exeter			29 Sep
	13.7	16.56	3.60	20.93	66.2	19.0	4.10/1.6	7.47	1.34		6:04.4
irr	100	DT	PV	JT	400	100H	LJ		SP	HJ	1500

Heptathlon

6135	Julie Hollman				16.02.77	5		Gotzis, AUT		2 Jun
	14.02/0.2	1.85	12.09	24.36/1.3	6.42/1.3	36.65	2:13.00			
	6093					1		Desenzano, ITA		12 May
	13.88/0.4	1.82	12.64	24.53/-0.2	6.24/-0.5	38.38	2:14.44			
	5825					5		Manchester (C)		27 Jul
	14.26/-0.2	1.77	11.78	24.97/0.7	6.03/-0.9	39.54	2:15.31			
5794	Kelly Sotherton				13.11.76	12		Bydgoszcz, POL		30 Jun
	14.13/-1.0	1.75	12.25	24.12/-0.4	6.17/0.2	32.39	2:18.26			
	5772					12		Arles, FRA		2 Jun
	13.96/-1.6	1.73	12.38	23.93/-0.7	6.06/0.4	29.90	2:15.86			
	5742					8		Talence, FRA		22 Sep
	13.7/0.1	1.70	12.06	23.93/0.0	6.11/0.2	29.16	2:16.58			
	5734					9		Desenzano, ITA		12 May
	13.94/1.0	1.67	12.74	23.99/-0.2	5.93/-0.7	31.76	2:14.55			
	5728					7		Manchester (C)		27 Jul
	13.89/-0.2	1.71	12.03	23.83/0.7	6.07/-0.4	27.69	2:14.29			
5657	Kerry Jury				19.11.68	15		Arles, FRA		2 Jun
	13.86/-0.1	1.76	11.63	24.44/-0.7	5.81/0.7	31.45	2:17.40			
	5631					10		Desenzano, ITA		12 May
	13.98/0.9	1.76	11.09	24.75/-0.2	5.72/-0.1	34.29	2:15.33			
	5554					8		Manchester (C)		27 Jul
	13.82/-0.2	1.77	10.68	24.64/0.7	5.49/-0.5	34.33	2:17.41			
5577	Katherine Livesey				15.12.79	1		Columbia SC, USA		18 May
	13.60/-0.6	1.74	11.36	24.76/0.6	5.80w/2.4	30.98	2:19.85			
	5574					3		College Station, USA		15 Mar
	13.84w/3.6	1.7?	11.21	24.72w/2.2	5.81/0.6	33.02	2:20.10			
5307	Nicola Gautier				21.03.78	23		Bydgoszcz, POL		30 Jun
	14.98/-0.4	1.60	14.07	25.74/-0.6	5.33/-0.2	43.52	2:27.66			
5294	Roz Gonse			U23	1.03.82	1		Birmingham		2 Jun
	14.65/-2.3	1.65	11.28	25.27/-2.0	5.67w/2.6	37.61	2:24.54			
	5275					25		Bydgoszcz, POL		30 Jun
	14.50/-0.6	1.60	10.90	25.31/-2.0	5.55/2.0	41.07	2:23.35			
	5273					6		Pratteln, SUI		4 Aug
	14.28/1.7	1.56	11.46	25.19/0.4	5.57/0.0	40.43	2:25.16			
5254	Rebecca Jones			U20	17.01.83	24		Arles, FRA		2 Jun
	14.83/-2.3	1.88	11.06	26.14/-0.2	5.81/1.7	32.33	2:36.52			
	5140					1		Woodford		28 Apr
	14.53/1.3	1.80	11.39	26.16/1.2	5.56w/3.1	32.25	2:36.25			
5229	Kate Brewington			U23	15.10.81	1		London (He)		11 Aug
	14.02w/2.1	1.65	10.81	25.29/-0.9	5.75/0.3	32.57	2:28.15			
5194	Jessica Ennis			U17	28.01.86	2		Pratteln, SUI		4 Aug
	14.32/0.6	1.74	9.21	24.52w/2.5	5.63/0.0	26.54	2:21.84			
5176	Laura Redmond			U23	19.04.81	4		Hexham		16 Jun
	14.96/0.6	1.61	10.96	25.35w/2.7	5.52w/3.6	35.00	2:17.58			
	5098					27		Bydgoszcz, POL		30 Jun
	14.98/-1.6	1.60	10.48	25.55/-0.6	5.60w/2.2	34.13	2:19.06			
	5050					10		Pratteln, SUI		4 Aug
	15.19/0.7	1.56	12.15	25.81/0.7	5.43/0.9	34.05	2:19.90			

(10)

5108	Caroline Pearce	U23	1.09.80	1	Wrexham	23 Jun
	14.84/-3.9 1.71 10.90	26.17/0.7	5.85/1.9	29.98	2:27.31	
	5017			12	Pratteln, SUI	4 Aug
	14.45/0.6 1.65 11.02	26.14/0.7	5.70/-0.8	26.27	2:24.78	
5043	Gillian Stewart	U23	21.01.80	5	Hexham	16 Jun
	15.13/0.2 1.67 11.72	26.66w/2.7	5.32w/4.0	40.71	2:30.42	

27 performances to 5000 points by 12 athletes

4901	Phyllis Agbo	U17	16.12.85	2	Woodford	28 Apr
	14.85w/4.0 1.62 10.88	25.57/1.2	5.78w/3.5	32.08	2:41.21	
4786 w	Wendy Davidson	U23	14.10.82	6	Hexham	16 Jun
	14.33/0.6 1.64 9.57	25.27w/2.7	5.44W/4.1	24.91	2:33.96	
	4783			*	Hexham	16 Jun
				5.43w/3.1		
4784	Kimberley Goodall	U20	5.10.83	10	Manchester (C)	27 Jul
	16.33/-0.1 1.56 9.06	25.54w/2.1	5.58/-0.8	32.00	2:16.11	
4767	Danielle Parkinson	U23	2.09.81	2	London (He)	11 Aug
	14.94w/2.1 1.62 9.44	25.67/-0.9	5.36w/2.9	30.15	2:29.45	
4736	Louise Hazel	U17	6.10.85	3	Wrexham	23 Jun
	15.31/-4.1 1.53 9.63	24.86/1.7	5.28w/3.6	31.28	2:26.56	
4713	Hannah Stares		13.11.78	4	London (He)	11 Aug
	14.66w/2.1 1.59 9.86	25.54/-0.9	5.12/-1.5	27.27	2:27.31	
4689	Maureen Knight		15.11.73	5	London (He)	11 Aug
	15.09/0.5 1.65 11.76	27.85/0.0	5.47/0.5	34.23	2:44.03	
4607	Charmaine Johnson	V35	4.06.63	4	Woodford	28 Apr
	15.35/1.3 1.53 12.29	27.22/1.2	5.22w/3.6	32.48	2:34.50	
(20)						
4568 w	Kirsty Roger		24.03.78	5	Woodford	28 Apr
	15.32/1.3 1.65 9.70	27.91/1.2	5.38W/4.7	26.92	2:26.17	
	4566			*	Woodford	28 Apr
				5.38w/3.7		
4517	Katy Taylor	U23	18.06.80	1	Aldershot	3 Jul
	15.3 1.56 10.56	26.3	5.24	24.77	2:26.67	
4502	Faith Cripps	U20	23.09.83	1	London (He)	11 Aug
	15.45w/2.1 1.56 9.37	26.25/1.2	5.21/1.9	26.61	2:26.51	
4463	Samantha Backwell	U20	4.02.85	1	Street	26 May
	15.2 1.51 8.46	26.4	5.19	27.29	2:18.9	
4442 w	Tina Thirwell	U23	5.09.81	7	Hexham	16 Jun
	16.04/0.2 1.58 8.46	25.84W/4.2	5.18w/2.5	30.27	2:30.21	
4432	Anna Clayton	U20	20.03.85	2	London (He)	11 Aug
	15.36w/2.1 1.59 8.82	26.16/1.2	5.22/1.7	25.47	2:32.12	
4420	Danielle Fawkes	U20	11.08.85	3	Derby	22 Sep
	15.01/0.5 1.60 8.48	26.10/-2.4	4.86/-1.5	24.84	2:27.49	
4357	Chanelle Garnett	U20	16.08.85	1	Crawley	15 Sep
	14.94/1.1 1.56 8.66	26.7/1.2	5.45	24.65	2:37.9	
4318	Jenny Pacey	U20	5.02.83	2	Birmingham	2 Jun
	16.16/-1.2 1.65 10.57	26.77/-3.4	5.00/0.9	25.17	2:38.89	
4286	Grace Clements	U20	2.05.84	5	Derby	22 Sep
	15.56/0.6 1.57 9.81	28.15/-3.9	4.88/-1.7	31.19	2:33.14	
(30)						
4245	Vicky Consterdine		25.04.75	6	Birmingham	2 Jun
	15.86/-2.3 1.53 8.79	27.19/-2.0	5.07w/2.9	25.95	2:26.82	
4146	Rebecca Hampson	U20	14.07.84	2	Preston	30 Jun
	15.7 1.56 7.30	26.6	5.20	25.48	2:33.4	
4141	Rebecca Reid	U20	9.11.83	3	Preston	30 Jun
	16.1 1.50 9.74	26.6	4.88	24.08	2:28.0	
4083	Melanie Umbleja	U20	14.01.84	5	Wrexham	23 Jun
	17.82/-4.1 1.56 9.99	27.63/1.7	5.10/1.7	26.97	2:30.07	
4074	Jenny Brown	V40	21.05.59	1	Erith	22 Sep
	16.8 1.60 9.92	28.0	4.92	30.00	2:38.1	
4060	Juliet Fullwood	U20	1.07.85	2	Grantham	30 Jun
	16.2 1.59 8.42	28.2	4.97	26.52	2:30.3	

4020	Helen Walker			U23	12.10.80	14		Knoxville TN, USA	11 Apr
	15.66/1.9	1.50	7.71	28.00w/2.3	4.56/0.8	27.56		2:24.93	
3973	Laura Bolton				22.01.79	8		London (He)	11 Aug
	16.43/0.5	1.44	9.26	27.12/0.0	4.94/-0.3	36.26		2:52.93	
3960	Nicola Plews			U20	15.12.83	4		London (He)	11 Aug
	15.01w/2.1	1.53	8.14	27.40/1.6	5.02/0.6	22.67		2:49.02	
3930	Amanda Wale				14.10.70	9		London (He)	11 Aug
	15.87/0.5	1.44	8.11	27.51/0.0	4.66w/2.1	27.06		2:31.08	
	(40)								
3928	Jane Greer			U20	19.07.84	2		Navan	12 May
	16.98/0.8	1.49	8.75	27.38	4.98	28.92		2:39.36	
3924	Claire Everett				25.06.79	23		Azusa, USA	19 Apr
	16.07/1.2	nh	12.38	26.53/1.9	5.33/0.4	23.57		2:23.59	
3886	Sarah-Jane Darrington			U20	25.06.85	10		Derby	22 Sep
	16.14/0.6	1.63	8.13	28.53/-3.9	4.70/-1.0	24.98		2:41.23	
3861	Claire Tranter			U20	28.03.85	11		Derby	22 Sep
	15.99/0.6	1.51	7.68	27.95/-1.7	4.90/-1.2	24.09		2:37.38	
3861	Danny White				1.06.79	1		Rotherham	29 Sep
	17.2	1.51	10.79	27.8	5.05	22.95		2:41.6	
3860	Helen Browne			U20	31.07.85	12		Derby	22 Sep
	15.61/0.6	1.42	7.08	26.47/-1.7	4.87/-1.8	19.56		2:32.57	
3838	Nikki Brady			U20	26.07.85	5		Preston	30 Jun
	17.6	1.50	7.89	27.6	5.12	29.80		2:36.6	
3830	Samantha Brough			U20	22.02.85	2		Hemel Hempstead	30 Jun
	17.7/1.4	1.46	10.27	28.3/-1.4	4.76/-1.2	22.95		2:26.3	
3824	Jade Weekes			U20	15.11.84	14		Derby	22 Sep
	16.39/0.6	1.57	9.31	28.32/-2.5	4.60/-0.7	28.62S		2:50.25	
3801	Fiona Wright			U20	11.05.85	15		Derby	22 Sep
	18.36/0.8	1.51	9.52	28.35/-2.5	4.68/-1.6	32.91		2:36.92	

Heptathlon - Under 17

4725	Phyllis Agbo				16.12.85	1		Derby	22 Sep
	11.49/0.3	1.60	10.96	25.79/-1.5	5.29/-3.0	33.86		2:44.67	
4574	Naida Bromley				27.09.86	1		Stoke-on-Trent	29 Sep
	12.54/0.2	1.59	10.13	26.27/-0.9	5.55/0.2	27.80		2:32.72	
4531	Jenny Christie				28.09.85	2		Stoke-on-Trent	29 Sep
	12.36/-0.1	1.62	8.13	25.64/-0.9	5.22/0.2	30.78		2:31.68	
4432	Catherine Holdsworth				3.01.86	3		Stoke-on-Trent	29 Sep
	11.66/-0.1	1.56	9.53	26.37/-0.9	5.43/0.2	21.40		2:34.44	
4399	Layla Hawkins				3.09.86	1		London (He)	11 Aug
	12.34w/3.7	1.58	9.07	26.14/2.0	5.15/1.3	22.67		2:26.36	
4369	Lucy Rodgers				1.07.87	2		London (He)	11 Aug
	12.87w/3.7	1.58	8.34	26.28/2.0	5.20/1.6	26.09		2:25.09	
4240	Jade Halket				5.05.86	1		Grangemouth	25 Aug
	12.43/1.4	1.59	8.13	27.79/1.1	5.42	22.17		2:28.51	
4218	Emma Morris				21.02.86	1		Jarrow	30 Jun
	12.5	1.72	7.25	27.1	5.09	19.62		2:29.3	
4202	Bridget Tidball				25.02.87	1		Bournemouth	30 Jun
	13.5	1.48	9.51	26.5	5.00	27.81		2:24.9	
4197	Rachel Culshaw				11.08.86	1		Preston	30 Jun
	12.7	1.68	7.30	27.5	4.72	31.21		2:32.1	
	(10)								
4148	Frances Noble				2.05.86	1		Rotherham	29 Sep
	12.4	1.48	8.45	26.8	5.22	26.87		2:35.2	
4068	Katie Renouf				3.06.87	6		Derby	22 Sep
	13.28/-0.8	1.57	8.99	28.60/-3.5	4.74/0.3	29.53		2:28.04	
4064	Shani Rainford				6.07.87	2		Hemel Hempstead	30 Jun
	15.3/-0.1	1.68	8.80	27.2/-0.5	5.04/1.3	34.33		2:46.1	
4052	Katia Lannon				14.09.85	2		Hexham	19 May
	13.44	1.60	8.23	27.3	5.15	23.50		2:33.25	

4037	Cherri Morrison			27.09.86	1	Birmingham	2 Jun
	13.23/-2.4	1.50	8.21	27.15/-2.7	5.15/1.0	20.23 2:24.70	
4001	Nicola Martell			20.09.85	7	Derby	22 Sep
	12.50/-0.6	1.57	9.00	27.99/-1.8	4.93/-2.0	19.49 2:33.38	
3992	Rebecca Long			3.10.86	2	Rotherham	29 Sep
	12.8	1.54	7.19	27.5	4.82	26.85 2:29.3	
3967	Stephanie Owen			31.12.86	6	Stoke-on-Trent	29 Sep
	12.34/-0.1	1.41	10.67	27.51/-1.1	5.19/0.2	19.84 2:42.07	
3956	Nadine Simpson			28.02.86	10	Derby	22 Sep
	12.57/0.3	1.60	8.86	28.94/-2.6	4.97/-0.9	25.93 2:43.93	
3924	Sara Luck			18.11.86	7	Stoke-on-Trent	29 Sep
	12.97/0.2	1.50	6.67	27.26/-1.1	4.37/0.9	24.54 2:18.02	
(20)							
3907	Sarah Fielding Smith			19.11.86	1	Crawley	15 Sep
	12.88w/2.1	1.65	6.84	27.4/1.6	5.01	18.15 2:35.8	
3902	Kate Marsh			15.05.86	2	Preston	30 Jun
	12.3	1.47	9.22	27.4	4.91	31.43 2:58.7	
3894	Sarah Allison			18.11.86	3	Preston	30 Jun
	13.4	1.62	7.68	26.1	4.80	18.88 2:39.0	
3891	Nia Nwidobie			4.01.86	4	Preston	30 Jun
	13.0	1.56	8.96	27.2	4.82	22.45 2:42.6	
3891	Lindsey Nash			7.11.86	1	Watford	29 Sep
	13.0/-2.0	1.51	9.51	27.92/-0.4	4.77/-0.2	20.39 2:33.0	
3877	Deandra Smith			3.12.86	13	Derby	22 Sep
	13.30/0.8	1.60	7.12	25.83/-1.5	5.00/-0.7	24.51 2:55.05	
3862	Rachel Gibbens			31.01.86	1	Derby	30 Jun
	13.5	1.59	7.84	28.1	5.01	20.70 2:32.6	
3860	Tamara Renouf			3.06.87	3	Bournemouth	30 Jun
	13.0	1.51	8.21	27.6	4.88	20.93 2:32.3	
3846	Nadine Okyere			29.11.86	8	Stoke-on-Trent	29 Sep
	13.43/-0.1	1.53	7.41	26.56/-1.1	4.94/1.2	19.32 2:34.75	
3822	Stephanie Sweeney			28.11.86	6	Preston	30 Jun
	12.3	1.50	8.57	26.5	4.27	21.46 2:39.0	

Pentathlon - Under 15

3273	Dominique Blaize			3.10.87	1	Hemel Hempstead	30 Jun
	12.1/-0.9	9.54	1.78	5.21/-1.1	2:42.8 (a)		
3202	Emily Bonnett			22.09.87	1	Derby	22 Sep
	11.83/-1.5	8.97	1.60	4.85/-0.9	2:22.50 (a)		
3126	Jade Surman			27.03.89	1	Stoke-on-Trent	29 Sep
	5.48/1.1	12.39/-1.9	9.21	1.52	2:31.15 (b)		
2945	Lucy Boggis			27.01.89	1	Derby	30 Jun
	11.7	8.18	1.60	4.93	2:42.2 (a)		
2930	Bethany Staniland			10.05.88	1	Rotherham	29 Sep
	4.72	12.6	10.70	1.43	2:28.1 (b)		
2869	Gemma Weetman			4.10.87	2	Stoke-on-Trent	29 Sep
	5.23/0.6	12.75/-1.9	8.27	1.46	2:32.75 (b)		
2806	Alice Simpson			26.02.89	2	Rotherham	29 Sep
	5.22	12.1	9.80	1.52	3:00.2 (b)		
2799	Kirsty Parr			6.04.88	3	Stoke-on-Trent	29 Sep
	4.73/0.2	12.62/-1.9	10.06	1.49	2:40.94 (b)		
2798	Hannah Weekes			14.12.87	1	Watford	29 Sep
	4.89/0.6	11.98/0.6	8.34	1.55	2:47.32 (b)		
2785	Ashley Little			19.01.89	3	Rotherham	29 Sep
	5.00	12.6	8.67	1.58	2:50.2 (b)		
(10)							
2762	Rebecca French			26.09.88	6	Derby	22 Sep
	12.34/1.2	8.51	1.51	4.89/-0.3	2:43.71 (a)		
2735	Emily Noble			28.04.88	4	Rotherham	29 Sep
	4.82	11.6	8.86	1.43	2:46.3 (b)		

2732	Anna Griffiths		28.12.87	1	Hexham	18 May
	11.99/1.6 9.16	1.36	4.73	2:35.6 (a)		
2686	Sasha Corbin		23.04.88	2	Watford	29 Sep
	4.96/0.0 12.46/1.9	9.59	1.49	2:56.24 (b)		
2685	Dani Perks		17.01.89	8	Derby	22 Sep
	13.18/-3.2 5.14	1.57	4.61/-0.6 2:24.79 (a)			
2683	Nimneh Hyde		20.09.87	2	Derby	30 Jun
	13.3 9.67	1.51	4.79	2:46.5 (a)		
2639	Chloe Gale		24.02.88	3	Hemel Hempstead	30 Jun
	12.3/-0.4 9.44	1.36	4.79/2.0 2:43.6 (a)			
2635	Lorna Heaton		9.02.88	4	Stoke-on-Trent	29 Sep
	4.89w/2.2 12.77/-1.9	7.73	1.40	2:35.99 (a)		
2634	Lauren Rowe		29.05.88	1	Macclesfield	15 Sep
	13.2 8.23	1.51	4.78	2:43.0 (a)		
2632	Jenny Johnston		15.04.88	10	Derby	22 Sep
	13.03/-1.0 7.91	1.51	4.69./-0.6 2:40.79 (a)			
	(20)					
2630	Claire Lyne-Ley		14.03.88	1	Exeter	29 Sep
	12.5 9.50	1.34	4.85	2:42.5 (a)		
2614	Katie Sadler		15.01.88	4	Hemel Hempstead	30 Jun
	13.0w/2.3 9.21	1.57	4.19/-0.5 2:45.2 (a)			
2604	Stephanie Lamb		18.11.88	1	Jarrow	1 Jun
	12.9 8.31	1.42	4.81	2:40.7 (a)		
2567	Erin Leggate		6.02.89	5	Stoke-on-Trent	29 Sep
	4.28/1.8 13.24/-3.2	7.53	1.49	2:31.93 (b)		
	a) 75H, SP, HJ, LJ, 800		b) LJ, 75H, SP, HJ, 800			

Pentathlon - Under 13

2390	Amelia Montagnani		10.03.90	1	Crawley	15 Sep
	4.86 12.9	8.93	1.38	2:53.5		
2380	Kirsty Hunter		16.12.89	1	Grangemouth	22 Jun
	4.13 13.55	6.13	1.41	2:27.59		
2213	Rozy Cooper		27.10.89	1	Exeter	28 Sep
	4.13 12.4	6.30	1.31	2:34.6		
2165	Hayley Comer		26.09.89	2	Exeter	28 Sep
	3.98 11.8	7.08	1.25	2:39.8		
2137	Nadine Hinze		19.12.89	3	Exeter	28 Sep
	4.08 12.4	7.80	1.40	2:56.0		
2073	Linzi Herron		18.09.89	1	Antrim	24 Aug
	4.34 13.34	7.78	1.39	3:01.43		
2042	Joanne Rowlands		29.12.89	2	Crawley	15 Sep
	3.89 13.8	6.81	1.32	2:38.3		
2040	Jade Bee		30.12.89	3	Crawley	15 Sep
	3.66 11.7	7.60	1.20	2:44.5		
1946	Stephanie Hopkinson		27.10.89	1	Carlisle	6 Jul
	4.01 13.5	7.20	1.33	3:04.0		
1940	Jasmin Hicks		1.03.90	1	Par	25 May
	3.80 12.8	6.34	1.23	2:42.3		

2000 Metres Walk - Track - Under 13

10:34.0	Lauren Gimson		14.10.90	1	Leicester	21 Nov
11:12.3	Kathryn Granger		9.02.91	1	Dudley	13 Oct
13:39.0	Helen Anstead	U11		1	Douglas IOM	5 Jun

3000 Metres Walk - Track

13:03.76 +	Lisa Kehler	V35	15.03.67	1	Birmingham	13	Jul
13:08.64 i	Niobe Menendez	V35	1.09.66	2	Cardiff	2	Feb
13:52.6	Sara-Jane Cattermole		29.01.77	1	Perth, AUS	1	Mar
	14:00.8 B race			1	Tonbridge	1	Apr
	14:20.31 mx			2	Perth, AUS	16	Mar
13:53.8	Sharon Tonks		18.04.70	1	Stourport	12	May
	13:57.87 i			3	Cardiff	2	Feb
	14:17 +e			2	Birmingham	13	Jul
14:25.66	Katie Stones		22.11.85	1	Derby	22	Sep
14:34.11 i	Sophie Hales	U20	30.03.85	1	Birmingham	24	Feb
	15:03.31 mx			1	Crawley	11	May
14:38.8	Karen Ratcliffe	V40	1.06.61	1	Sutton Coldfield	11	May
14:44.39	Rebecca Mersh		28.01.89	1	Derby	22	Sep
14:53.6	Claire Reeves	U20	31.07.84	2	Ashford	18	Aug
14:58.5	Kate Horwill		26.01.75	1	Dudley	13	Oct
(10)							
15:04.7	Nicola Phillips	U20	23.04.83	3	Ashford	18	Aug
15:08.9	Jo Hesketh		16.06.69	4	Ashford	18	Aug
15:10.28	Jenny Gagg		20.02.88	2	Derby	22	Sep
15:23.25	Bryna Chrismas		18.06.86	2	Derby	22	Sep
15:37.4	Fiona McGorum		10.11.88	1	Loughborough	12	May
16:01.9	Verity Snook		13.11.70	1	Portsmouth	11	May
16:07.8	Sarah Brown	V35	28.09.64	5	Ashford	18	Aug
16:17.58	Ann Wheeler	V45	17.10.55	1	London (He)	27	Jul
16:20.37	Sarah Chetwynd		4.06.74	2	Bedford	26	May
16:29.47	Natasha Fox		21.09.85	2	Glasgow	20	Jul

Additional Under 13

17:35.14	Lauren Gimson	U13	14.10.90	4	Birmingham	11	Aug

Foreign

13:51.73	*Estle Viljoen (RSA)*		*8.07.70*	*1*	*Watford*	*1*	*Sep*

5000 Metres Walk - Track

21:42.51	Lisa Kehler	V35	15.03.67	1	Birmingham	13	Jul
	22:34.1			1	Dartford	29	Sep
24:05.49	Sharon Tonks		18.04.70	2	Birmingham	13	Jul
24:19.06	Sophie Hales	U20	30.03.85	3	Newport	20	Jul
24:44.3	Sara-Jane Cattermole		29.01.77	1	Perth, AUS	6	Jan
25:26.84	Niobe Menendez	V35	1.09.66	1	Potsdam, GER	18	Aug
25:50.83	Claire Reeves	U20	31.07.84	1	Leamington	18	May
25:57.11	Katie Stones		22.11.85	1	Birmingham	11	Aug
26:00.4	Jo Hesketh		16.06.69	2	Dartford	16	Mar
26:22.83	Kim Braznell	V45	28.02.56	1	London (He)	28	Jul
26:45.5	Nicola Phillips	U20	23.04.83	3	Dartford	16	Mar
(10)							
27:06.2	Natalie Geens	U20	27.12.84	4	Dartford	16	Mar
27:13.8	Rebecca Mersh		28.01.89	2	Dartford	29	Sep
27:16.09	Bryna Chrismas		18.06.86	2	Birmingham	11	Aug
27:31.1	Ann Wheeler		17.10.55	2	Dartford	29	Sep
27:49.6	Jenny Gagg		20.02.88	1	Hull	26	Jun
29:13.46	Natasha Fox		21.09.85	4	Birmingham	11	Aug
29:59.4	Nicky Reynolds	U20	24.06.85	3	Dartford	29	Sep

Foreign

24:26.11	*Estle Viljoen (RSA)*		*8.07.70*	*3*	*Birmingham*	*13*	*Jul*

Road

22:20	Lisa Kehler	V35	15.03.67	1	Sutton Coldfield	6	Jul
	23:54 +			m	Turin, ITA	12	Oct
23:44	Sara-Jane Cattermole		29.01.77	1	Perth, AUS	27	Jan
23:53	Sharon Tonks		18.04.70	2	Sutton Coldfield	6	Jul
24:56 B	Wendy Bennett	V35	21.12.65	1	Birmingham	14	Dec
25:11	Jane Gibson		26.01.73	1	Isle of Man	6	Jun
25:27	Karen Ratcliffe	V40	1.06.61	3	Birmingham	6	Jul
25:42	Kate Horwill		26.01.75	2	Leamington	6	Apr
25:55	Catherine Charnock		3.05.75	3	Leamington	6	Apr
26:39	Jenny Gagg		20.02.88	2	Tamworth	1	Dec
27:16	Bryna Chrismas		18.06.86	2	Sheffield	27	Apr
(10)							
27:54	Natasha Fox		21.09.85	1	Bexley	14	Dec
27:58	Bridget Kaneen	V35	15.08.65	1	Birkenhead	2	Nov
28:15	Kelly Mann	U20	8.09.83	1	Birmingham	9	Feb
29:02	Nicky Reynolds	U20	24.06.85	2	Birmingham	14	Dec

short course

23:53	Sophie Hales	U20	30.03.85	1	Steyning	23	Jun
25:22	Jo Hesketh		16.06.69	2	Steyning	23	Jun
26:44	Sarah Brown	V35	28.09.64	3	Steyning	23	Jun

Foreign

23:28	*Estle Viljoen (RSA)*		*8.07.70*	*1*	*Bexley*	*19*	*Oct*

10000 Metres Walk - Track

54:47.0	Claire Reeves	U20	31.07.84	1	London (He)	11	Aug
56:27.1	Nicola Phillips	U20	23.04.83	2	London (He)	11	Aug

Foreign

50:16.7	*Estle Viljoen (RSA)*		*8.07.70*	*1*	*London (BP)*	*24*	*Apr*

10 Kilometres Walk - Road

45:53	Lisa Kehler	V35	15.03.67	1	Dublin, IRL	15	Jun
	48:16 +			2m	Manchester (C)	28	Jul
	48:22 +			3=m	Manchester	21	Apr
	48:29 +			m	Turin, ITA	12	Oct
46:38	Niobe Menendez	V35	1.09.66	2	Dublin, IRL	15	Jun
	47:18			1	Riccione, ITA	24	May
	48:22 +			3=m	Manchester	21	Apr
	49:19 +			m	Naumburg, GER	5	May
	49:26 B			1	Horsham	26	Jan
	B judging						
47:48	Sara-Jane Cattermole		29.01.77	1	Murdoch, AUS	16	Jun
	47:57			1	Murdoch, AUS	17	Mar
	50:19			1	Wembley, AUS	15	Dec
48:40	Sharon Tonks		18.04.70	1	Leamington	23	Mar
	50:29			4	Leamington	14	Sep
51:49	Katie Stones		22.11.85	3	Leamington	14	Sep
52:05	Sophie Hales	U20	30.03.85	4	Leamington	14	Sep
52:08	Nicola Phillips	U20	23.04.83	5	Leamington	14	Sep
52:16 +	Karen Ratcliffe	V40	1.06.61	m	Dublin, IRL	15	Jun
52:25 +	Kim Braznell	V45	28.02.56	8=m	Manchester	21	Apr
52:25 +	Catherine Charnock		3.05.75	8=m	Manchester	21	Apr
(10)							
52:28	Jane Gibson		26.01.73	1	Douglas IOM	30	Mar
52:42	Kate Horwill		26.01.75	5	Leamington	14	Sep
52:58	Claire Reeves	U20	31.07.84	4	Dublin, IRL	15	Jun
52:58	Jo Hesketh		16.06.69	6	Leamington	14	Sep

54:27	Bridget Kaneen		15.08.65	1	Isle of Man	6	Jan
54:57	Bryna Chrismas		18.06.86	7	Leamington	14	Sep
55:27	Sarah Chetwynd		4.06.74	1	Birmingham	16	Nov
56:13	Vicky Lupton/White		17.04.72	3	Sheffield	27	Apr
56:45	Katie Ford	U23	21.10.81	4	Sheffield	27	Apr
56:46	Marie Latham		18.10.60	1	Isle of Man	20	Jan

Foreign

48:50	*Estle Viljoen (RSA)*		*8.07.70*	*3*	*Leamington*	*14*	*Sep*

20 Kilometres Walk Road

1:39:10	Sara-Jane Cattermole		29.01.77	1	Murdoch, AUS	21	Jan
1:39:41				1	Perth, AUS	29	Jul
1:40							
1:36:45	Lisa Kehler	V35	15.03.67	2	Manchester (C)	28	Jul
1:39:13				3	Manchester	21	Apr
1:43:08				1	East Molesey	3	Mar
1:39:59	Niobe Menendez	V35	1.09.66	4	Manchester	21	Apr
1:40:05				1	Douglas IOM	16	Feb
1:41:23				15	Naumburg, GER	5	May
1:46:16				7	Manchester (C)	28	Jul
1:41:51	Sara-Jane Cattermole		29.01.77	1	Cambridge, AUS	17	Feb
1:46:04				7	Manchester	21	Apr
1:43:29	Sharon Tonks		18.04.70	2	East Molesey	3	Mar
1:45:21				6	Manchester	21	Apr
1:48:33				71	Turin, ITA	12	Oct
1:49:21				8	Manchester (C)	28	Jul
1:44:54	Cal Partington	V35	27.06.66	1	York	23	Mar
1:45:07	Kim Braznell	V45	28.02.56	1	Sutton Coldfield	4	May
1:46:53				9	Manchester	21	Apr
1:49:44				3	East Molesey	3	Mar
1:46:35	Karen Ratcliffe	V40	1.06.61	8	Manchester	21	Apr
1:49:54	Kate Horwill		26.01.75	10	Manchester	21	Apr
1:50:45	Jo Hesketh		16.06.69	11	Manchester	21	Apr
1:51:12	Jane Gibson		26.01.73	2	Isle of Man	16	Feb
(10)							
1:58:32	Marie Latham		18.10.60	2	Douglas IOM	9	May
1:59:35	Cath Reader/Duhig		19.10.54	1	Basildon	11	May
1:59:58	Bridget Kaneen	V35	15.08.65	12	Manchester	21	Apr

Foreign

1:44:16	*Estle Viljoen (RSA)*		*8.07.70*	*5*	*Manchester*	*21*	*Apr*

50 Kilometres Walk Road

5:41:15	Cath Reader/Duhig	V45	19.10.54	1	Bradford	3	Jun

100 Miles Walk Road

20:27:27 +	Sandra Brown	V50	1.04.49	1m	Blackpool	11	Aug

24 Hour Walk Road

186.32 km	Sandra Brown	V50	1.04.49	1	Blackpool	11	Aug

4 x 100 METRES

42.84	England		3	Manchester (C)	31	Jul
	(J.Maduaka, S.Anderson, V.James, A.Oyepitan)					
44.22	National Junior Team	U20	3	Kingston, JAM	21	Jul
	(J.Lucas-Read, J.Kwakye, A.Spencer, V.James)					
44.45	National Team		1	Bedford	4	Jun
	(E.Freeman, S.Wilhelmy, S.Anderson, J.Maduaka)					
44.49	National Junior Team	U20	2h1	Kingston, JAM	20	Jul
	(J.Lucas-Read, D.Norville, A.Spencer, V.James)					
44.53	National Under 20 Team	U20	2	Bedford	4	Jun
	(J.Lucas-Reed, M.Douglas, A.Spencer, V.James)					
44.70	England		1	Loughborough	18	May
	(D.Allahgreen, S.Anderson, A.Forrester, J.Maduaka)					
44.96	National Junior Team	U20	2	Loughborough	18	May
	(J.Kwakye, D.Norville, A.Spencer, V.James)					
45.03	Big Entertainers		3	Bedford	4	Jun
	(C.Bloomfield, L.Miller, J.Pratt, D.Norville)					
45.36	National Junior Team	U20	1	Gorizia, ITA	6	Jul
	(J.Kwakye, M.Douglas, A.Spencer, J.Lucas-Read)					
45.63	National Under 23 Team	U23	1	Niort, FRA	3	Aug
	(L.Fairweather, E.Freeman, S.Burnside, K.Endacott)					
46.13	Belgrave Harriers		1	Bedford	17	Aug
	(A.Onuora, A.Spencer, C.Bloomfield, S.Claxton)					
46.51	National Under 23 Team	U23	2	Newport	20	Jul
	(K.Brewington, L.Trotman, L.Turner, K.Endacott)					
46.53	Loughborough University		3	Loughborough	18	May
	(K.Butler, T.Stephens, K.Palmer, K.Thomas)					
46.6	Windsor Slough E & H AC		1	Eton	21	Jul
46.63	Scotland		4	Loughborough	18	May
	(S.Whigham, S.Burnside, N.Beattie, M.Wardrop)					
46.73	Windsor Slough E & H AC		1	Birmingham	6	Jul
	(F.Louisy, M.Richardson, A.Thorne, B.Liston)					
46.83	England Schools	U17	1	Glasgow (S)	20	Jul
	(P.Agbo, S.Johnson, N.Robinson, M.Douglas)					
46.96	Scotland Schools	U17	2	Glasgow (S)	20	Jul
	(G.Nicol anchor)					
47.00	Belgrave Harriers		1	London (He)	21	Jul
47.09	Surrey Schools U19		1	Nottingham	13	Jul

Additional National Teams

47.70	Wales		6	Loughborough	18	May
	(R.King, A.James, S.Lane, K.Jones)					
50.96	Northern Ireland U23 Team	U23	5	Namur, BEL	31	Aug

Additional Club Teams (1- 3 above)

47.4	Birchfield Harriers	1	Birmingham	9	Jun
47.7	Trafford AC	2	Rugby	19	May
47.87	Sale Harriers Manchester	1	Amsterdam, NED	26	May
48.0	Coventry Godiva Harriers	1	Eton	4	Aug
48.04	UWIC	2	Bedford	6	May
48.05	Cambridge University	1	Oxford	18	May
48.2	Wakefield Harriers	1	Wakefield	7	Jul
48.27	Walton AC	1	Bedford	17	Aug
48.28	Edinburgh Woollen Mill	2	London (He)	3	Aug
48.30	Birmingham University	3	Bedford	6	May
48.4	Peterborough AC	1A	London (He)	21	Jul
48.4	Shaftesbury Barnet Harriers	2A	London (He)	21	Jul
48.5	Team Solent	1	Southampton	8	Jun

48.5	Wigan & District H & AC		1	Wigan	4	Aug
48.56	Bath University		4	Bedford	6	May
48.6	Ealing Southall & Middlesex AC		1	Perivale	8	Jun
48.65	Team West		1	Glasgow (S)	2	Jun

Additional Under 20 Teams (1 - 7 above)

47.31	Buckinghamshire Schools	U17	1	Nottingham	13	Jul
47.40	South		1	Watford	1	Sep
47.41	Scotland		1	Grangemouth	25	May

Additional Under 20 National Teams

49.42	Wales	U18	3	Tullamore, IRL	3	Aug
50.81	Northern Ireland	U18	4	Tullamore, IRL	3	Aug

Under 20 Club Teams

48.3	Windsor S E & H AC		1	London (WF)	18	Aug
48.4	Edinburgh Woollen Mill		1	Scunthorpe	23	Jun
48.9	Medway & Maidstone AC	U17	h	Tonbridge	15	Sep
49.07	Birchfield Harriers		2	Derby	8	Sep
49.40	Sale Harriers Manchester		4	Moscow, RUS	21	Sep
49.5	Milton Keynes AC	U17	1	Norwich	2	Jun
49.60	Pitreavie AAC	U17	1	Glasgow (S)	9	Jun
49.60	Shaftesbury Barnet Harriers		5	Derby	8	Sep
49.6	Bromley AC	U17	1	Tonbridge	21	Apr
49.7	Wakefield Harriers		2	Wakefield	28	Jul

Additional Under 17 Teams (1 - 7 above)

47.51	London Schools		2	Nottingham	13	Jul
47.58	Kent Schools		3	Nottingham	13	Jul
48.54	Buckinghamshire AA		1	Kingston	4	Aug

Additional Under 17 Club Teams (1 - 4 above)

49.83	Edinburgh Woollen Mill		1	Birmingham	1	Sep
50.11	Birchfield Harriers		2	Birmingham	1	Sep
50.12	Windsor S E & H AC		3	Birmingham	1	Sep
50.14	Sale Harriers Manchester		4	Birmingham	1	Sep
50.2	Telford AC		1	Birmingham	9	Jun
50.3	Queen Anne HS		1	Glenrothes	12	Jun
50.3	Bristol AC		1	Tipton	30	Jun

Under 15 Teams

48.63	London Schools		1	Nottingham	13	Jul
48.91	Surrey Schools		2	Nottingham	13	Jul
50.03	Hertfordshire Schools		2h2	Nottingham	13	Jul
50.22	Yorkshire AA		1	Cudworth	15	Sep
50.4	Birchfield Harriers		1	Birmingham	9	Jun
50.41	Edinburgh Woollen Mill		1	Birmingham	1	Sep
50.43	Merseyside Schools		2h1	Nottingham	13	Jul
50.5	Northamptonshire Schools		1	Corby	22	Jun
50.8	West Midlands Schools		1	Birmingham	22	Jun
50.8	Gateshead Harriers & AC		1	Wakefield	21	Jul

Additional Under 15 Club Teams (1 - 3 above)

50.9	Milton Keynes AC		1	Bedford	18	May
51.1	Blackheath Harriers		1	Tonbridge	15	Sep
51.27	Lothian AC		2	Glasgow (S)	2	Jun
51.4	Giffnock North AC		1	Grangemouth	17	Aug
51.4	Bromley AC		2	Tonbridge	15	Sep
51.4	Havering Mayesbrook AC		1	Chelmsford	21	Sep
51.6	Chelmsford AC		2	Chelmsford	21	Sep

Under 13 Teams

53.0	Mandale Harriers		1	Middlesbrough	19 May
53.5	Enfield & Haringey AC		1	Norwich	2 Jun
53.7	Blackheath Harriers		1	Tonbridge	15 Sep
54.2	Bromley AC		2	Tonbridge	15 Sep
54.4	Herne Hill Harriers		1	London (TB)	30 Jun
54.46	Giffnock North AC		1	Glasgow (S)	9 Jun
54.72	Liverpool Harriers AC		1	Birmingham	1 Sep
54.9	Woodford Green & Essex Ladies		1	Chelmsford	21 Sep
54.96	Ayr Seaforth AAC		2	Glasgow (S)	9 Jun
55.13	Lothian AC		1	Glasgow (S)	2 Jun
55.2	Birchfield Harriers		1	Tipton	30 Jun

4 x 200 METRES

1:38.11 i	England		2	Cardiff	10 Feb
	(C.Milborough, J.Meadows, R.Harris, E.Ruddock)				
1:40.39 i	Loughborough University		1	Glasgow	24 Feb
1:41.11 i	UWIC		2	Glasgow	24 Feb
1:41.66 i	England	U20	1	Cardiff	10 Feb
	(M.Cooksey, D.Norville, J.Sims, A.Onuara)				
1:42.5	Bromley AC	U17	1	Tonbridge	15 Sep
1:42.9	Blackheath Harriers		1	Tonbridge	15 Sep
1:42.9	Medway & Maidstone AC	U17	1	Tonbridge	15 Sep
1:43.06 i	Wales		3	Cardiff	10 Feb
	(S.Lane, A.Cutler, S.Newman, D.Higgins)				
1:43.26 i	Bath University		3	Glasgow	24 Feb
1:44.00 i	Wales U20	U20	2	Cardiff	10 Feb
	(S.Gamble, F.Harding, D.Carpenter, D.Barker)				

Additional Under 17 Teams (1 - 2 above)

1:45.65 i	Pitreavie AAC		1	Glasgow	9 Mar
1:46.82 i	Edinburgh Woollen Mill		2	Glasgow	9 Mar
1:46.95 i	Shropshire Schools		1	Birmingham	20 Feb
1:47.27 i	City of Glasgow AC		3	Glasgow	9 Mar
1:47.5	Humberside AA	U15	1	Grimsby	7 Sep
1:47.88 i	Warwickshire & Glos Schools		2	Birmingham	20 Feb

Additional Under 15 Teams (1 above)

1:48.4	Derbyshire AA		2	Grimsby	7 Sep
1:48.4	Warwickshire AA		3	Grimsby	7 Sep
1:49.0	Leicestershire AA		4	Grimsby	7 Sep
1:49.6	Bromley AC		1	Tonbridge	15 Sep
1:50.6	Ashford AC		2	Tonbridge	15 Sep
1:51.20 i	Falkirk Victoria H.		1h2	Glasgow	24 Mar

Under 13 Teams

1:58.17 i	Giffnock North AC		1	Glasgow	6 Feb
1:59.83 i	Ayr Seaforth AAC		1h2	Glasgow	24 Mar
2:01.1	North Down AC		1	Bangor	23 Jul
2:01.45 i	Kilbarchan AAC		2	Glasgow	6 Feb
2:02.80 i	Falkirk Victoria Harriers		2h1	Glasgow	24 Mar

4 x 300 METRES

2:40.28	England Schools	U17	1	Glasgow (S)	20 Jul
2:43.31	Scotland	U18	1	Tullamore, IRL	3 Aug
2:45.25	Scotland Schools	U17	2	Glasgow (S)	20 Jul
2:51.05	Wales	U18	3	Tullamore, IRL	3 Aug
2:53.21	Northern Ireland	U18	4	Tullamore, IRL	3 Aug
2:56.53	Wales Schools	U17	2	Glasgow (S)	20 Jul

4 x 400 METRES

3:26.65	National Team	4	Munich	11	Aug
	(H.Karagounis 52.6, H.Frost 52.3, M.Purkiss 51.90, L.McConnell 49.90)				
3:26.73	England	2	Manchester	31	Jul
	(H.Frost 52.3, H.Karagounis 51.1, M.Purkiss 52.03, L.Miller 51.36)				
3:27.87	National Team	1	Annecy, FRA	23	Jun
	(C.Murphy 51.90, H.Frost 52.34, H.Karagounis 52.49, L.McConnell 51.14)				
3:30.46	National Junior Team	U20 2	Kingston, JAM	21	Jul
	(K. Wall 53.9, A.Spencer 53.2, V.James 51.69, L.Miller 51.67)				
3:30.63	England	1h2	Manchester	30	Jul
	(H.Frost 53.1, H.Karagounis 51.3, J.Meadows 52.67, L.Miller 53.67)				
3:31.50	Scotland	4	Manchester	31	Jul
	(C.A.Easton 54.0, S.Dudgeon 52.0, S.Burnside 54.44, L.McConnell 51.06)				
3:33.88	National Team	2h2	Munich	10	Aug
	(H.Karagounis 53.2, H.Frost 54.4, M.Purkiss 54.13, L.McConnell 52.13)				
3:36.41	Scotland	4h2	Manchester	30	Jul
	(G.Nicol 55.2, S.Burnside 54.8, C.A.Easton 53.21, S.Dudgeon 53.32)				
3:37.80 I	National Team	3	Glasgow	9	Mar
	(L.Clarkson, J.Meadows 52.34, M.Purkiss, C.Murphy)				
3:37.86	England	1	Loughborough	18	May
	(K.Gear 54.7, J.Meadows 53.5, T.Duncan 55.2, H.Frost 54.3)				
3:38.49	National Junior Team	U20 2h2	Kingston, JAM	20	Jul
	(K.Wall 54.3, R.Thompson 55.6, V.Griffiths 54.15, L.Miller 54.45)				
3:39.14	National Junior Team	U20 1	Gorizia, ITA	6	Jul
	(G.Nicol, R.Thompson, V.Griffiths, Wall)				
3:39.92	National Under 23 Team	U23 1	Newport	20	Jul
	(D.Halsall, H.Wood, L.Clarkson, J.Meadows)				
3:40.63	British Universities	2	Loughborough	18	May
	(D.Halsall, H.Wood, H.Stares, H.Karagounis)				
3:42.30	Scotland	4	Loughborough	18	May
	(J.McKay, L.Clarkson, C.Easton, Ovens)				
3:43.11	Birchfield Harriers	1	Bedford	17	Aug
	(M.Thomas, R.Harris, H.Frost, K.Sotherton)				
3:43.14	National Under 23 Team	U23 1	Niort, FRA	3	Aug
	(Wood, N.Sanders, R.Lyne, D.Halsall)				
3:43.40	Trafford AC	1	Birmingham	6	Jul
	(E.Fairs, L-D.Trotman, K.Jones, Eagland)				
3:45.15	Shaftesbury Barnet Harriers	2	Birmingham	6	Jul
	(C.Brown, Heath, Pierre, C.Murphy)				
3:46.20	South	1	Watford	1	Sep
	(K.Gear, T.Duncan, N.Bowring, S.Williams)				

Additional National Teams

3:48.44	Wales	6	Loughborough	18	May
	(R.Newcombe, E.Davies, F.Harding, K.Sage)				
4:03.69	Northern Ireland Under 23 Team	U23 1	Antrim	18	Jun

Additional Club Teams (1- 3 above)

3:47.08	Loughborough University	1	Bedford	6	May
3:48.33	Windsor Slough E & H AC	1	London	3	Aug
3:50.04	Sale Harriers Manchester	1	Amsterdam, NED	26	May
3:50.16	Edinburgh Woollen Mill	1	Edinburgh	28	Apr
3:50.59	Lothian AC	1	Glasgow (S)	2	Jun
3:50.71	Liverpool Harriers & AC	U20 1	Derby	8	Sep
3:50.81	Team West	2	Glasgow (S)	2	Jun
3:51.05	Birmingham University	2	Birmingham	19	Jun
3:51.5	Crawley AC	1	Eton	21	Jul
3:51.52	City of Glasgow AC	1	Wakefield	7	Jul
3:52.75	Sales Harriers Manchester	U20 2	Derby	8	Sep
3:52.8	Wakefield Harriers	1	Eton	4	Aug

3:54.1	Wigan & District H & AC		1	Stoke-on-Trent	19 May
3:54.5	Shaftesbury Barnet Harriers	U20	1	London (WF)	18 Aug
3:55.51	City of Norwich AC		2	Wakefield	7 Jul
3:55.86	UWIC		2	Bedford	6 May
3:56.1	Border Harriers		1	Scunthorpe	7 Jul
3:56.6	Ashford AC		2	Eton	4 Aug
3:57.0	Crawley AC	U20	1	Crawley	5 Jun
3:57.5	Coventry Godiva Harriers		3	Eton	4 Aug
3:57.60	Rugby & Northampton AC		4	London (He)	3 Aug
3:57.83	Cambridge University		1	Oxford	18 May
3:57.9	Epsom & Ewell Harriers		2	Eton	21 Jul
3:57.9	Swansea Harriers		2	Eton	21 Jul

Additional Under 20 Teams (1 - 7 above)

3:46.65	National Junior Team		5	Loughborough	18 May
	(G.Nicol, J.Simpson, R.Thompson, L.Singer)				
3:51.00	South		1	Watford	1 Sep
	(K.Wall, C.Best, E.Parker, N.Plateau)				
3:55.63	Scotland		1	Grangemouth	26 May

Additional Under 20 National Team

4:02.67	Wales		2	Grangemouth	26 May

Additional Under 20 Club Teams (1 - 4 above)

3:57.29	Birchfield Harriers		4	Derby	8 Sep
3:57.9	Trafford AC		2	Birmingham	18 Aug
3:59.1	Reading AC		1r1	Woking	23 Jun
4:01.8	Reading AC	U17	1	Eton	28 Jul
4:03.7	Havering Mayesbrook AC		2	Eton	23 Jun
4:04.6	Guildford & Godlaming AC		1	Woking	18 Aug
4:05.0	Woodford Green & Essex Ladies		2	London (He)	15 Sep

Additional Under 17 Club Teams (1 above)

4:24.7	Herts Phoenix		1	Welwyn GC	6 May
4:35.5	OWLS		1	Loughborough	May

With Foreign athletes

3:41.57	Loughborough University		3	Loughborough	18 May
	(*M.Carey IRL*, N.Sanders, *M.Marks USA*, K.Wall)				
3:44.19	Belgrave Harriers		2	Bedford	17 Aug
	(*M.Marks USA*, H.Stares, *M.Carey IRL*, J.Culley)				

3 x 800 METRES

Under 17 Teams

6:58.98	Central AC		1	Grangemouth	26 May
7:07.78	Pitreavie AAC		2	Grangemouth	26 May

Under 15 Teams

7:15.2	Basildon AC		1	Chelmsford	21 Sep
7:15.4	Orion		2	Chelmsford	21 Sep

Under 13 Teams

7:53.2	Blackheath Harriers		1	Tonbridge	15 Sep
7:53.53	Pitreavie AAC		1	Grangemouth	26 May
7:55.7	Medway & Maidstone AC		2	Tonbridge	15 Sep

ASH Ben U15 3.05.88, Lincs Sch :
SPB - 13.09
ASHE Richard 5.10.74, Harrow :
800 - 1:51.47 (1:49.38-96), 1500 - 3:43.42 (3:41.2-96)
ASKEW Richard U20 26.04.84, Derby & Co :
LJ - 6.86
ASPDEN Richard William 15.10.76, Belgrave :
HJ - 2.14 (2.17i-99/2.16-95)
ASTON Edward U15 10.08.88, Cambridge & Col :
800 - 2:05.58
ATKINSON Gary U17 7.01.87, Sale :
100 - 11.11w (11.5/11.59-01),
ATKINSON Jamie U20 12.02.84, Sevenoaks :
1500 - 3:52.12, 3k - 8:30.7
ATKINSON Jason U17 28.10.85, Cwmbran :
800 - 1:58.29 (1:57.44-01)
ATKINSON Mark U13, :
100 - 12.68
ATTON Karl Ronald 14.09.71, Roadhogs :
10kWR - 46:15 (45:40-89), 50kW - 4:23:05 (4:16:30-97)
30kW - 2:34:16+ (2:29:11-93)
ATTWOOD David U17 5.04.87, Bristol :
DTY - 44.35
AUDU Henry 5.03.79, Thames Valley/NGR :
60 - 6.87i, 100 - 10.48w/10.70
AWANAH Mark U23 23.09.82, Blackheath :
LJ - 7.70, TJ - 14.86w/14.63
AWDE Christopher U20 14.02.85, WGreen & Ex L :
Dec - 5894, DecJ - 5529, DECJI - 5835
AWOYINKA Dolapo U15 19.11.87, Newham & E B :
LJ - 6.11, TJ - 12.60

B ABB Jacob U17 7.12.85, Wessex & Bath :
SPY - 15.93
BACKLEY Stephen James 12.02.69, Cambridge H :
JT - 88.54 (91.46-92)
BACON Daniel U15 5.10.87, Mansfield :
80HB - 12.0, PenB - 2560
BADDELEY Andrew James U23 20.06.82, Harrow/CUAC :
800 - 1:51.27, 1500 - 3:45.96
BADERIN Richard AdeKunmi U20 25.03.83, Liv H :
60H - 8.40i, 110HJ - 14.5/14.84,
110H - 14.8w/15.02w/15.21
BAILEY Colin U20 15.11.83, Burnley :
110HJ - 15.2/15.25, 110H - 15.59w?,
HJ - 2.00, DecJ - 5853
BAILEY James U20 1.06.83, Sale/Loughborough :
3kSt - 9:33.4 (9:31.2-00)
BAILEY Mark U15, Southend :
3k - 9:28.1
BAILEY Stuart 6.08.78, Sale :
800 - 1:50.57 (1:49.46-00), 1500 - 3:49.14 (3:45.6-98)
BAILLIE Christopher U23 21.04.81, Birch/V P AAC :
60H - 7.89i, 110H - 13.95 (13.70w/13.82-01)
BAILY Chris U17 1.12.86, Fife AC :
100HY - 13.8w/14.1, LJ - 6.72
BAIRD Lawrence W. 14.12.77, Trafford :
100 - 10.81 (10.62w-98),
200 - 21.66 (21.6w-99/21.64w-00),
400 - 48.14i/48.25 (47.56i-98/47.83-97)
BAKER Craig U20 26.05.85, Worthing :
HJ - 1.98
BAKER Francis U15 22.09.87, City of Norwich :
80HB - 12.0, HJ - 1.75, PV - 2.80, PenB - 2541
BAKER James 21.12.76, Chichester :
3kSt - 9:42.1
BAKER Michael Thomas U13 6.04.90, Med & Maid :
75HC - 12.4, 80HC - 13.54
BALCH Gareth U20 18.05.83, Bath Univ :
800 - 1:51.99, 1500 - 3:54.3
BALDOCK Sean Michael 3.12.76, Belgrave :
200 - 21.9 (21.1w-97/21.43w-01/21.50i/21.50-99,
400 - 45.71 (45.20-00)
BALDWIN Gerraint U15, Pontypridd :
SPB - 13.55

BALL Christopher Steven U20 29.06.83, Trafford :
400H - 56.9
BALL Nicholas Robert U15 29.04.88, Steyning :
3kW - 14:08.26, 3kWR - 13.34
BANGS Neil U23 28.03.80, Thurrock :
1500 - 3:45.60, 3k - 8:19.0 (8:15.90-01)
BANKS Philip U20 8.03.83, AF&D/Brunel Univ :
3k - 8:30.07, 5k - 14:54.8
BANKS Steven U13 4.10.89, :
75HC - 13.1
BANNISTER Dominic 1.04.68, Shaftesbury Barnet :
5MR - 23:58, 10kR - 30:05 (29:39-99),
10MR - 48:59 (48:57-99),
Mar - 2:16:18 (2:14:39-00)
BAPTISTE Leon U20 23.05.85, Enf & Har :
100 - 10.6/10.64w/10.72, 200 - 21.06w/21.34
BARBER Andrew 20.08.74, Peterborough :
Mar - 2:31:35
BARBOUR Jonathan U23 3.11.80, Blackheath :
100 - 10.46 (10.13w-01/10.28-00),
200 - 21.41 (20.78-01)
BARDEN Spencer Christian 31.03.73, Belgrave :
1500 - 3:45.00 (3:39.64-98), 3k - 8:02.39 (7:53.2-97),
5k - 13:48.03 (13:43.84-97), 10k - 30:52.75 (30:14.11-98)
BARGH Andrew 21.08.76, Team Solent :
110H - 15.5/15.60 (15.0w-96/15.13w-97/15.20-96),
400H - 53.7/53.72 (52.4-96/52.47-98)
BARK Thomas U20 18.10.83, Corby :
2kSt - 6:13.1
BARKER Kie U15 1.11.87, Rowheath :
100 - 11.51
BARKER Leo 26.12.78, Havering M :
LJ - 7.02 (7.07-96), Dec - 6184 (6617-96)
BARNES-SMITH Matthew U17 5.10.85, Ipswich :
1500 - 3:59.65, 3k - 8:31.11
BARNETT Leon U17 30.11.85, Luton :
TJ - 13.20
BARNETT Tony U17, :
100 - 11.08w
BARRETT Oliver U20 25.12.84, Ipswich :
800 - 1:53.86
BARTON Matthew U23 22.05.81, IoW/St. Marys Un C :
TJ - 13.97i/13.84 (14.13-01)
BARTON Tim D. 3.10.70, Charnwood :
100 - 10.8/11.12w (10.55w-98/10.67-97)
BARTRAM Daniel U15 1.02.89, Cannock & Stafford :
LJ - 5.96
BARZEY Victor U17 10.01.86, Bexley :
100 - 11.1, 200 - 22.4/22.59, 400 - 48.95
BATCHELOR Perry 11.12.75, Rugby & Nor PH :
60H - 8.49i (8.23i-01),
110H - 15.3/15.34 (14.50w/14.54-01)
BATE Roger U20 16.01.83, Trafford/UMIST :
SPJ - 13.85, DT - 42.83, DTJ - 49.99,
HT - 54.41, HTJ - 60.14, HT6K - 62.43
BATES Neil U20 5.04.84, Manx :
5kW - 24:20.07 (24:15.1-01), 10kWR - 47:42
BATES Robert U15 29.10.87, Sphinx :
400 - 53.6, 800 - 2:04.4
BATY Jonathan U17 1.02.87, Stratford :
400HY - 57.55, OctY - 4443
BAUER David 25.03.66, Harlow :
DT - 41.69
BAULCH James Steven 3.05.73, Cardiff :
100 - 10.65 (10.51-95), 400 - 46.01 (44.57-96)
BAYLEY Tim U23 4.10.81, Belgrave/Brunel Univ :
400 - 47.76 (47.52-01)
BAYLIFFE James U15 11.10.87, Cheltenham :
PV - 3.20, PenB - 2574
BAYLISS Ashley U17 14.01.86, Cwmbran :
400 - 50.95
BAZELL Stephen 1.02.74, City of Stoke :
3kSt - 9:37.5 (9:29.2-00)
BEARD Gregory U23 10.09.82, Belgrave :
SP - 16.80, DT - 45.18 (47.90-00)

356

BEARD Keith Alan V40 8.11.61, Leiden :
JT - 67.65 (76.10r-91/73.88-90)
BEARMAN Donald J. 16.04.66, Steyning :
5kW - 21:55.07, 10kWR - 43:12, 20kW - 1:29:53
BEASLEY Benjamin Roy U15 25.02.88, Banbury :
400 - 52.43
BEASLEY Graham Alexander 24.10.77, Belgrave :
100 - 10.4w/10.6/10.63 (10.54w-99), 200 - 20.76
BEAUCHAMP William Ronald 9.09.70, Newham & E B :
HT - 68.78 (72.63-99)
BEAUFORD Adam U23 24.10.81, Yeovil Olympiads :
HT - 49.99 (53.77-01)
BEDFORD Thomas James U20 12.12.83, Shaft B :
2kSt - 5:44.21
BEECH Alexander 17.04.77, Med & Maid :
110H - 15.2/15.50, 400H - 54.6/55.37
BEEKEN George U17 4.09.86, Corby :
DecY - 5394, OctY - 4392
BEEVOR Luke U20 4.03.84, Vauxhall :
3k - 8:29.26
BEHARRELL Mark U23 10.01.81, Sale/Loughbro :
PV - 5.25
BELL Andrew U20 7.09.84, Milton Keynes :
TJ - 14.35w/14.33w?/14.19
BELL John 10.09.73, Newham & Essex B :
400H - 53.70 (53.70-92)
BELL Martin V40 9.04.61, Cardiff :
3kW - 13:31.10i (11:53.3-95)
BELL Matthew 2.06.78, Corby :
HT - 64.16
BELL Matthew 14.07.76, City of Edinburgh :
3kSt - 9:28.0 (9:23.01-01)
BELL Simon 26.12.66, Cambridge Harriers :
Mar - 2:32:15 (2:25:26-97),
3kSt - 9:38.7 (8:53.39-96)
BELL Stuart 29.07.67, Chester le Street :
5k - 14:40.26 (14:23.1-95),
10k - 31:15.1 (29:24.30-97), 10kR - 30:05 (29:15-98)
BELSHAM Matthew 11.10.71, Sale :
PV - 5.10 (5.40i-96/5.35-93)
BENJAMIN Ekakier U20 4.12.84, Notts :
HJ - 1.98, PV - 4.32, DECJI - 6356
BENJAMIN Timothy U23 2.05.82, Cardiff :
200 - 21.40 (20.60w-99/20.67-01),
300 - 32.61, 400 - 45.73
BENN Andrew 2.09.77, Blackheath/West London HS :
HT - 46.72 (56.86-96)
BENNETT Andrew U23 30.09.82, Belgrave :
400 - 48.33, 400H - 52.6/53.52
BENNETT Andrew U17 19.12.85, Southampton City :
SPY - 14.10
BENNETT Christopher U23 18.10.80, Team Solent :
200 - 22.06 (21.7/21.87-99), 400 - 49.0 (47.80-99)
BENNETT Simon 16.10.72, Team Solent :
SP - 13.72, JT - 64.09 (66.58-96)
BENNETT-GRANT Chris U13, :
75 - 10.1
BENNETT-JACKSON Wade U17 27.02.87, Belgrave :
100 - 10.80w/10.92, 200 - 22.0w/22.08w/22.32
BENSON Stuart U23 12.02.81, Ayr Seaforth/RAF :
LJ - 6.97, TJ - 14.11
BENT Colin 12.04.70, Shaftesbury Barnet/RAF :
HJ - 2.00 (2.20-96)
BENTLEY Robin 17.02.65, Wessex & Bath :
Mar - 2:28:48 (2:28:31-99)
BERGL James U20 23.02.85, Warwicks Sch :
SPJ - 13.72
BERNARD Jermaine U20 1.12.84, Ipswich :
LJ - 7.11 (7.19-01)
BERNARD Martyn U20 15.12.84, Sheffield :
HJ - 2.21
BERRILL Nick 6.10.64, Bedford & County :
Mar - 2:33:56 (2:29:02-93)
BERRY Kris U20 13.11.84, Corstorphine :
1500 - 3:52.11

BERRY Robert 29.07.69, Southport :
3kSt - 9:29.62 (8:51.2-01)
BERWICK Christopher V55 1.05.46, Leics WC :
50kW - 4:56:13 (4:23:22-86)
BEST Jonathan U23 9.11.82, Border :
TJ - 14.19
BETTS Elliot U15 13.11.87, Enf & Har :
DTB - 37.82
BEVAN Nigel Charles 3.01.68, Birchfield :
JT - 61.81 (81.70-92)
BIDWELL Mark U20 4.09.84, Chesterfield :
HJ - 1.95 (1.99i-00/1.95-99)
BIGNALL Douglas 20.10.74, Enf & Har :
100 - 10.29w/10.32
    (10.27wA-00/10.29w-01/10.30A-00/10.30-01)
BILENKYJ Paul U20 9.11.84, Exeter :
SP6K - 13.56
BILTON Darren 9.03.72, Kingston u Hull :
Mar - 2:21:24
BINNS Christopher John U23 7.05.82, Blackpool :
HJ - 2.10
BIRBECK Rory 24.09.73, Hyndburn :
SP - 14.37 (14.75-97)
BIRCH Shane U15 22.10.87, Med & Maid :
SPB - 16.40, DTB - 50.85
BIRCH Simon U13 11.09.89, Lewes :
JTC - 34.36
BIRCHALL Chris 8.03.79, E Cheshire/DePaul Univ :
3k - 8:19.69i# (9:15.03-96), 5k - 14:28.65,
10k - 29:29.85, Mar - 2:18:57
BIRCHALL Robert 14.06.70, Birchfield :
5k - 14:06.44, 10k - 29:56.44 (29:17.65-97),
10kR - 29:37 (29:22-97), HMar - 65:59 (64:30-01)
BISHOP Mark Andrew Paul 12.02.67, Havering M :
Dec - 5515 (7594-89)
BISHOP Sam 17.08.79, City of Stoke :
HJ - 1.95, Dec - 5857
BISSELL Simon Peter U17 25.12.85, Sale :
SPY - 14.75, DTJ - 42.81, DTY - 48.61,
HTJ - 57.82, HTY - 65.26
BIVINS Tom U20 18.11.83, Charnwood :
SPJ - 13.71
BLACK Christopher Francis V50 1.01.50, C of Edinb :
HT - 60.97 (75.40-83)
BLACK Iain Russell 18.09.70, City of Edinburgh :
PV - 4.20 (4.51-97)
BLACKETT Daniel U15 4.10.88, Gateshead :
TJ - 12.48
BLACKLEDGE Jonathan Edward U20 15.09.84, Bel :
5k - 15:0.0
BLACKMAN Gary U23 24.09.80, Harrow/Loughbro :
3kSt - 8:50.3
BLAIR Alexander U13 23.11.89, Giffnock :
400 - 61.63, TJ - 9.56
BLAIR Richard U20 15.09.84, Shaftesbury B/Clyde :
HJ - 1.95, LJ - 7.02, TJ - 13.85
BLAKE Max U15, Thurrock :
JTB - 43.55
BLAKE Stephen U15 29.09.87, AF&D :
3k - 9:31.1
BLUNDELL J. U13, Coventry Godiva :
LJ - 4.96
BODY Steven 6.11.75, Vauxhall :
1500 - 3:47.01, 3k - 8:08.86,
5k - 14:20.58, 10kR - 29:56 (29:48-01)
BOLT Christopher U23 21.09.80, Shaftesbury Barnet :
800 - 1:48.85, 1500 - 3:42.92 (3:42.36-00),
3k - 8:24.86 (8:11.8-00)
BOMBA Michael U17 10.10.86, Liverpool H :
HTY - 52.98
BONNETT Stephen 13.07.78, City of Stoke :
110H - 15.65 (15.3/15.53-99), Dec - 6805 (7146-99),
HJ - 1.95i/1.95 (2.05i-99/2.04-97),
PV - 4.10i/4.10 (4.20i/4.20-99),
LJ - 6.97i/6.96 (7.05w/7.01i-99/6.99-00)

BOOKER Christian U13 29.06.90, Halesowen :
800 - 2:13.1
BOOTH Adam Lee U17 22.10.85, Rotherham :
DecY - 5130, OctY - 4200
BOOTH Wayne U17 12.10.85, Gloucester AC :
400 - 50.44
BORSUMATO Anthony Patrick 13.12.73, Sale :
400 - 48.54i (46.92-98), 300H - 35.46, 400H - 48.90
BOTFIELD Alasdair U13 11.11.89, Halesowen :
1500 - 4:47.4
BOUGH Richard U17 12.12.85, Mansfield :
1500 - 4:01.5
BOUNDY Christopher James 25.12.79, Gateshead :
PV - 4.75
BOUNDY Patrick 19.02.79, R & Twick'ham/Notts Un. :
JT - 62.85
BOURNAT Oliver U20 4.12.84, Tonbridge :
DecJ - 5550
BOVELL Dwayne U17 2.12.85, Blackheath :
100 - 10.9w/11.06w/11.10, 200 - 22.44w
BOWDEN Adam U23 5.08.82, Harrow :
1500 - 3:48.43 (3:48.27-01), 3kSt - 8:56.5
BOWDEN Des U15 13.01.88, Lancashire Sch :
200 - 23.55
BOWDITCH Kristen Robert 14.01.75, Newham & E B :
5MR - 23:54 (23:49-01)
BOWLER James 2.09.79, Brom & R/Un of Nebraska :
800 - 1:52.43 (1:52.4-01),
1500 - 3:42.85 (3:41.75-01), 1M - 4:06.45i
BOWLES Ian U20 6.01.84, Bolton :
2kSt - 5:55.33, 3kSt - 9:22.6
BOWLEY Ian U23 14.11.81, Bedford & Co/Notts Un :
PV - 4.22
BOWN Simon Paul 21.11.74, Newham & Essex B :
HT - 66.77
BOWRON Lee U17 2.10.85, Ealing,Southall & Mx :
800 - 1:52.14, 1500 - 3:52.24, 3k - 8:50.05
BOWSER Matthew U20 3.07.83, Lincoln Well :
800 - 1:52.4, 1500 - 3:48.12,
1M - 4:06.44, 3k - 8:20.38
BOXALL Sam U13 5.12.89, Chelmsford :
100 - 12.4, 200 - 25.7
BRACKSTONE David U23 13.03.82, C of Stoke/Loughbro :
200 - 21.5/22.13i (23.02-98), 400 - 48.1 (49.19i-00),
400H - 52.0/52.66 (52.60-01)
BRADBURY Martin U23 20.10.82, Sheff/Loughbro :
200 - 22.14w (22.1-99/22.40-01), 400 - 48.9 (47.94-00)
BRADLEY Dominic 22.12.76, Birchfield :
60H - 8.19i (7.84i-01)
BRADLEY Samuel Peter U15 2.12.87, Milton Keynes :
800 - 2:02.70
BRADY David V40 5.07.62, North Belfast :
Mar - 2:25:32
BRANCH Kit U20 5.06.85, Basildon :
PV - 4.20
BRANDWOOD Daniel U23 1.10.82, Kingston u Hull :
400 - 49.17, Dec - 6130
BRASIER Samuel Alan Michael U15 5.11.87, Milton K :
800 - 2:03.87
BRAVINGTON Craig U17 9.12.86, Bournemouth :
800 - 1:58.44
BRAY Daniel Paul U20 6.09.83, Havant :
400 - 49.41 (49.38-01), 110HJ - 15.4, 400H - 53.18
BREND Peter A. 2.02.77, Team Solent :
200 - 21.8/21.92w (21.94-01), 400 - 46.9/46.94 (46.8-01)
BREWER James U15 18.06.88, Gloucester AC :
800 - 2:02.00
BREWER Oliver U20 14.09.83, Bingley :
2kSt - 6:08.1, 3kSt - 9:41.1
BRIDGE James U20 28.11.83, Invicta :
100 - 10.91w/11.1, 200 - 21.78w/22.0/22.13 (21.7/21.92-01)
BRIDGEWATER Robert U17 18.04.86, Dudley & St :
DTY - 44.99
BRIERLEY James Richard 31.07.77, Telford :
HJ - 1.95 (2.26-96)

BRIGGS Jason U15 8.10.87, Newham & Essex B :
PenB - 2717
BRINDLEY Sean U15 1.01.88, Notts :
400 - 52.90
BRIODY Jordon U15 17.11.87, Dacorum & Tring :
PV - 3.20
BRISTOW Garry Andrew U17 3.05.87, Salford :
1500 - 4:05.22
BRITTAIN Scott 24.08.75, London Heathside :
Mar - 2:35:19
BRITTAN Andrew John 17.01.67, Cannock & Staff :
DT - 47.94 (49.76-88)
BRIZZEL Paul 3.10.76, Liverpool H/IRL :
60 - 6.99i, 200 - 20.59w/20.72 (20.54A/20.65-00)
100 - 10.32w/10.59A/10.63 (10.28w/10.35-00),
BROADLEY Sam U23 17.05.81, Bingley :
HT - 45.89 (46.55-98)
BROCKLEBANK Robert J. 12.10.76, Sale :
HJ - 2.10 (2.16-95)
BROOKS Jerome T. S. 9.08.73, London I/Oxford Un. :
5k - 14:39.19 (14:22.71-00), 10kR - 30:08
BROOKS Steven 8.06.70, Bingley :
HMar - 66:13 (61:28-97)
BROWN Andrew 20.12.77, Nene Valley H/CUAC :
800 - 1:51.9
BROWN Andrew 17.06.77, WGreen & Ex L/C of Edinb :
800 - 1:50.51 (1:49.74-01)
BROWN Christopher David U15 5.09.87, Mansfield :
1500 - 4:15.80
BROWN David 1.03.78, Bristol :
400H - 56.0 (57.88-96)
BROWN Derek V40 23.01.60, Chiltern :
Mar - 2:29:00
BROWN Gareth 2.09.73, Swindon :
LJ - 6.95 (7.41w-00/7.14-01)
BROWN Gareth James 10.05.68, Steyning :
10kWR - 45:59 (45:29-00), 20kW - 1:32:08 (1:30:15-89),
30kW - 2:34:17+ (2:31:02-89), 50kW - 4:16:45
BROWN Jay U15 27.10.87, Kettering :
100 - 11.4w
BROWN John 2.02.69, Salford :
3kSt - 9:20.17 (8:55.6-98)
BROWN Jonathan Michael 27.02.71, Sheffield :
10k - 27:32.47 (27:18.14-98),
10kR - 28:40 (27:20dh-95/28:05-93),
10MR - 47:33 (46:28+e-97), HMar - 62:32 (61:49-97)
BROWN Kevin Dave 10.09.64, Belgrave :
DT - 60.54 (62.10-00)
BROWN Mark 3.11.76, Newham & Essex B :
200 - 21.7w/22.0
(21.5w-01/21.6-99/21.89i-01/21.91w-00,21.95-99)
400 - 46.86 (46.37-99)
BROWN Mark 1.08.79, Morpeth :
3k - 8:21.40, 5k - 14:26.27
BROWN Michael V40 6.05.62, Enf & Har :
TJ - 13.97 (16.15-89)
BROWN Murray U13 2.01.90, Kilbarchan :
SPC - 10.85, DTC - 25.58
BROWNE Curtis 11.09.75, Birchfield :
60 - 6.95i (6.77i-96), 100 - 10.46 (10.38w/10.42-99),
200 - 21.74 (21.40w-00/21.5/21.54-94)
BROWNE Philip Anthony U17 10.11.85, North Down :
100HY - 13.84
BRUCE Calum 28.02.75, Pitreavie :
HT - 53.19 (54.79-00)
BRUCE Vincent U20 15.04.83, Luton :
100 - 10.76w/10.9, 200 - 22.08w/22.1/22.19
BRUNSDON Daniel U15 18.04.88, Bournemouth :
SPB - 15.33, JTB - 45.77
BRUNT Daniel 23.04.76, Sheffield :
SP - 13.52 (14.49-97), DT - 44.91 (47.94-00)
BRYAN Justin 16.08.69, Cwmbran :
SP - 13.68 (14.54-99), DT - 40.77 (45.29-98)
BRYANT Mark 1.01.72, Harrow :
3kSt - 9:41.94

358

BUCHAN Stuart V40 20.03.60, Kingston u Hull :
24Hr - 230.501km
BUCK Matthew 5.04.74, WGreen & Ex L :
PV - 4.30 (4.60-96)
BUCK Richard Thomas U17 14.11.86, Scarborough :
400 - 49.17
BUCKFIELD Nicholas Jean 5.06.73, Crawley :
PV - 5.81i/5.50 (5.80-98)
BUCKINGHAM Mark John U20 4.05.85, Holmfirth :
2kSt - 6:09.73
BUCKLEY Adam John U23 6.12.80, Sale/Bath Univ :
400 - 49.04i (47.04-00)
BUCKLEY Jamie U17 3.02.86, Sale :
800 - 1:55.61
BUDD David 8.12.79, Sheffield :
TJ - 14.25
BUDDEN Nicholas 17.11.75, City of Norwich :
200 - 21.90 (21.10-96), 300 - 34.14,
400 - 48.35i/48.53 (46.34-96)
BULL Gareth U20 3.03.85, Cardiff :
DT - 42.35, DTJ - 44.85
BULL Michael P. 6.06.70, Notts :
Dec - 5699 (6051-97)
BULMAN Neil Andrew 7.09.77, Rugby & Nor PH :
HT - 48.49 (49.02-98)
BURGESS Louis U20 21.03.83, E & E/Enf & Har :
100 - 10.7w/10.8, 200 - 22.0, 400 - 47.85, LJ - 7.44
BURGESS Mark U15 13.11.87, WGreen & Ex L :
800 - 1:59.9, 1500 - 4:07.77
BURNS Daniel U20 6.09.84, Gateshead :
HJ - 1.95 (1.95-01)
BURNS Ian T. 20.09.77, Gateshead :
JT - 63.53
BURNS William 13.12.69, Salford :
Mar - 2:17:36 (2:15:42-00)
BURRELL Jonathan 24.11.75, Chelmsford :
1500 - 3:51.28 (3:51.11-01)
BURSLEM Michael U23 1.12.80, Arbroath/Dundee U :
200 - 22.20
BURTON Matthew U15 18.12.87, London Schools :
TJ - 12.44w/12.09
BUTLER Matthew Stephen U17 25.02.86, Leamington :
1.5kSt - 4:33.52
BUTTERWORTH Joshua U15 21.04.88, Notts :
200 - 23.11, TJ - 12.03
BYRD B. U13, Cannock & Stafford :
JTC - 38.41

C AINE Andrew 17.06.77, Tynedale :
1500 - 3:49.51, 5MR - 23:36, 10k - 29:27.07,
3k - 8:09.99, 5k - 14:26.7 (14:11.42-01)
CAINES Daniel Stephen 15.05.79, Birchfield :
60 - 6.88i (6.86i-01), 200 - 20.62i (21.05-01),
300 - 32.7i+, 400 - 44.98
CAIRNS Steven Mark 3.11.67, Border/Annadale Str :
5k - 14:30.81, 3kSt - 8:51.06
CALDWELL Benjamin Ian U23 3.03.82, Bolton :
400H - 54.6/56.42 (54.4/54.67-00)
CALLAGHAN James U13 30.12.89, W Cheshire :
DTC - 25.80
CALVER Matthew U13 14.09.89, Wimborne :
TJ - 11.57w?
CAMERON Paul, :
Mar - 2:35:38
CAMERON Rezlimond V40 18.05.60, Thames Valley :
TJ - 13.94 (16.32w-89/16.20-88)
CAMPBELL Christian U20 10.06.85, Ealing,S & Mx :
TJ - 14.21i/12.98w (13.49w-01)
CAMPBELL Christopher U17 13.04.86, Gateshead :
400 - 50.61
CAMPBELL Daniel U17 24.02.86, Croydon :
HJ - 1.90 (1.90-01)
CAMPBELL Darren Andrew 12.09.73, Sale :
60 - 6.89 (6.60i-99), 100 - 10.11 (10.04-98),
200 - 20.21 (20.13-00)

CAMPBELL Darryn U23 14.07.82, Team Solent :
400 - 48.81
CAMPBELL Fraser U17 30.05.86, Elgin :
HTJ - 48.85, HTY - 55.98
CAMPBELL James U15 1.04.88, Cheltenham :
JTB - 52.59
CAMPBELL Kenneth William 30.09.72, C of Edinb :
110H - 14.9 (13.86-94)
CAMPBELL Malcolm 3.01.71, Cambuslang :
5k - 14:19.54 (14:13.30-01), HMar - 66:19 (64:48-97)
10k - 29:46.29 (29:16.47un-96)
CANTY Nick U15 9.02.88, Croydon :
80HB - 11.6w/11.8/12.02
CAPES Lewis 26.05.71, WGreen & Ex L :
SP - 15.03i/14.54 (16.55-91)
CARELESS Robert 7.09.74, Notts :
HT - 59.58 (60.65-01)
CAREY Thomas U20 26.02.84, Huntingdon :
110HJ - 14.81, 400H - 54.57
CARISS Chris 1.03.75, Bingley :
5k - 14:42.8, HMar - 66:08, Mar - 2:20:46
CARLETON Jonathan 4.11.79, Ballymena & A/IRL :
100 - 10.38w/10.65, 200 - 21.81w (21.60?/21.66-00)
CARNE Ben U17 11.06.86, Harrow :
100HY - 14.1, 400H - 58.4, 400HY - 55.68
CARPENTER Stephen John U17 30.12.85, Woking :
PV - 3.95, OctY - 4220
CARPENTER Tom U13 26.03.90, Yate :
1500 - 4:47.6
CARR Gary U23 24.09.82, Ashford :
100 - 10.57w/10.7/10.96 (10.93-00), 200 - 21.6/21.85)
CARSON Sean U20 13.04.84, Shaftesbury Barnet :
JT - 59.66
CARTER Daniel W. U23 15.04.80, WG & E L/Brunel U :
JT - 69.56 (73.56-00)
CARTER Simon 5.03.75, Med & Maid/Reading Univ :
JT - 65.11 (66.37-98)
CARTER Thomas U23 20.08.82, Vale Royal/Loughbro :
800 - 1:50.46, 1500 - 3:43.62
CARTER Tyrone U15 11.08.88, WGreen & Ex L :
80HB - 11.9, TJ - 13.29w/12.88
CASHIN Kyle U15 11.10.87, Notts :
100 - 11.5w, 200 - 23.52
CASTILLO Richard U23 3.12.81, Notts/Notts Trent U :
400H - 53.64
CAUDERY Stuart 19.11.66, Cornwall AC :
Dec - 5683 (6118-97)
CAUTHRON Edwin U13 20.02.90, Exeter :
3k - 10:53.3
CAVANAGH Steven U20 9.07.85, Sparta :
100 - 10.90w (11.6-99)
CAVERS David 9.04.63, Border :
Mar - 2:28:52 (2:16:06-98)
CAWTHORNE Mark U15 7.09.87, Humberside Sch :
TJ - 12.07w
CAYTON Neil 19.03.70, Otley :
Mar - 2:34:05
CHALLENGER Benjamin 7.03.78, Belgrave :
HJ - 2.26 (2.30-99)
CHAMBERS Dwain Anthony 5.04.78, Belgrave :
100 - 9.87, 200 - 20.27
CHAMBERS Roy U17 9.02.86, Woking :
JTY - 50.91, OctY - 4573
CHAMPION Michael 3.01.75, Blackheath :
100 - 10.7 (10.71w/10.81-00)
CHAN Edward U13, Sale :
200 - 25.9
CHANDLEY Adam Michael U17 4.12.85, Southport :
TJ - 13.25w/13.10
CHAPMAN Daniel U15 14.09.88, Southend :
HTB - 42.06
CHAPMAN Keith U23 15.02.81, Salford :
10k - 31:22.80
CHAPMAN Tom U17 29.12.85, Charnwood :
400 - 49.90

CHARION Laurent 24.07.64, Coventry Godiva/FRA :
  Mar - 2:34:13
CHARLTON Adam U20 11.05.84, Huntingdon/Shaft B :
  100 - 10.77 (10.7-01), 200 - 21.06w/21.44,
  300 - 34.5, 400 - 47.24
CHATT James U23 11.02.80, Dartford/Loughbro :
  200 - 22.11i (21.2w/21.53-01), 400 - 47.65i/47.92 (47.1-01)
CHEESEMAN Christopher V40 11.12.58, Surrey WC/
  Thames H & H : 10kWR - 43:16 (42:11-00),
  20kW - 1:31:47 (1:26:53-99),
  30kW - 2:34:09+ (2:27:11-94),
  50kW - 4:18:49 (4:07:49-99)
CHESTER Karim U20 6.11.84, Blackheath :
  HT - 49.97, HTJ - 55.16, HT6K - 57.89
CHEUNG Lewis U20 12.12.83, Liverpool H :
  TJ - 14.53w/14.10 (14.60i-01)
CHILDS Naved U23 12.05.81, Brecon/Cambridge Un :
  TJ - 14.05
CHILDS Richardo U20 9.10.84, Brecon :
  LJ - 6.96
CHIN Darren U23 30.06.81, Belgrave :
  60 - 6.72i, 100 - 10.46, 200 - 21.38
CHISHOLM Neil 26.01.74, St Bern :
  1500 - 3:51.42
CHOUTKA Ondrej 24.11.76, Oxford Univ :
  Dec - 5958
CHRISTIAN Tasham U15 6.10.87, Chelmsford :
  100 - 11.5/11.54, 200 - 23.0/23.18
CHRISTIE Jeffrey U23 24.09.82, WSE&H/Bath Univ :
  400H - 51.33
CHRISTIE Mark U20 11.09.84, Sale :
  PV - 4.70 (4.70-01)
CHURCH Scott U15 17.05.88, Isle of Wight :
  HTB - 43.80
CLAGUE Samuel U17 26.02.86, WSE&H :
  SPY - 15.03, DTY - 43.57
CLARE Julian 13.09.74, Trafford :
  LJ - 7.07un (6.81-94)
CLARK Andrew U17 1.10.85, Aberdeen :
  1.5kSt - 4:32.47
CLARK Dean 20.12.73, Thames Valley :
  800 - 1:52.92 (1:49.20-99)
CLARK Matthew U13 4.06.90, :
  PV - 2.00
CLARKE Chris U13 25.01.90, Milton Keynes :
  200 - 25.7
CLARKE Ian 6.11.72, Enf & Har :
  60 - 6.96i (6.8i/6.88i-98),
  100 - 10.99w (10.6/10.79-00)
CLARKE Jonathan 20.11.67, Swansea :
  JT - 60.70 (68.74-86)
CLARKE Richard U15 27.09.87, Bedford & County :
  HJ - 1.75
CLARKE Simon 31.10.78, Border :
  LJ - 6.93w/6.86 (7.37w/7.10-97)
CLARKE Wayne A. R. 24.12.75, Peterborough :
  HT - 57.68 (60.78-01)
CLAY Matthew U20 9.06.84, Skyrac :
  HJ - 1.96, LJ - 6.96, DecJ - 5984
CLAYTON Isaac U15 12.10.87, Newquay & Par :
  PV - 3.20, TJ - 12.14
CLAYTON Richard U20 12.11.84, Worthing :
  800 - 1:54.6
CLEEVE Andy, Les Croupiers :
  100kR - 8:06:28
CLEGG Sam U17 31.12.85, Bingley :
  3k - 8:56.05
CLEMENT Christian U20 19.07.83, Bournemouth :
  800 - 1:52.63
CLEMENTS Andrew U23 28.11.82, WSE&H/UWIC :
  400H - 54.37
CLUNIE David U13 18.02.90, :
  TJ - 10.36
COATES Peter 21.03.68, Durham City H :
  Dec - 4921 (5226DD-00/5184-99)

COLE David U17 15.04.87, WSE&H :
  HJ - 1.90
COLE Michael David U13 1.12.89, N Devon :
  400 - 62.0, 800 - 2:16.3, 80HC - 14.2,
  HJ - 1.50, PV - 2.05, TJ - 9.65
COLE Robert 13.10.79, Midd AC :
  3kSt - 9:35.0
COLEMAN David U17 14.02.86, Tonbridge :
  DTY - 44.94
COLEMAN Matthew U13 6.03.90, :
  PV - 2.00
COLEMAN Michael 14.05.78, Med & Maid :
  5k - 14:40.6, 10k - 30:31.2, 10MR - 49:10
COLLARD David U20 25.01.85, City of Edinburgh :
  110HJ - 15.11w/15.19, HJ - 1.95i (1.95-01)
COLLINS Liam James O'Neill 23.10.78, Sale/
  Loughborough Studnts : 400 - 47.9 (48.45-99),
  110H - 14.25 (14.05-00), 400H - 50.30
COLLIS Gary U23 3.01.80, Coventry Godiva :
  3kSt - 9:35.9
COLLYMORE Fabian U20 19.10.84, Blackheath :
  60 - 6.98i, 200 - 22.16i (21.9/22.49-01)
COLTHERD Michael U23 28.12.82, Barrow & Furness :
  800 - 1:51.79 (1:50.31-00)
COMBER Gavin U15 28.05.88, Dartford :
  100 - 11.3/11.41, 200 - 23.3
COMISSIONG Jason Kyle U20 7.09.83, Thames V :
  60 - 6.9i/6.94i, 100 - 10.93w/11.2,
  LJ - 7.14i/7.05w/6.84, TJ - 14.68 (14.46w-00)
CONDON Allyn 24.08.74, Sale :
  60 - 6.77i (6.64i-98/6.68-00), 100 - 10.26w/10.32 (10.21-99),
  200 - 20.86w/20.90 (20.53i-98/20.59w-99/20.63-97)
CONDON David Jonathan 11.04.72, Newham & E B :
  SP - 16.34i/16.28 (17.16-00)
CONN Charles U13 9.05.90, Crawley :
  JTC - 38.41
CONNOR James U20 21.03.83, Kent :
  3kSt - 9:48.3
CONNOR Joseph U17 17.12.86, Liverpool H :
  HTY - 47.25
CONROY Paul 24.08.71, WGreen & Ex L/IRL :
  110H - 14.68 (14.50-01)
COOK Austin James Gareth 20.02.69, Kingston & P :
  SP - 13.73 (14.59-90), DT - 42.70 (49.20-90),
  HT - 59.12 (67.32-91)
COOK Gavin 30.03.70, Thames Valley :
  HT - 52.88 (62.58-88)
COOKE Simon U17 3.10.85, Chichester :
  SPY - 15.76, DTY - 49.80, JTY - 50.50
COOKEY Dimean 8.10.79, Kent :
  110H - 15.6 (15.5-99)
COOKSON David U15 15.02.88, Sale :
  PV - 2.80
COOMBES James U23 4.10.81, Cardiff :
  SP - 13.86
COOPER Nicholas 4.02.77, Belgrave :
  110H - 14.93 (14.29-99), 400H - 55.36
COOPER Paul 4.12.76, WGreen & Ex L :
  JT - 55.83 (67.03-99)
CORBETT Peter U17 5.11.85, City of Bath :
  100HY - 13.9w
CORRIGAN J. Paul 19.01.66, North Shields Poly :
  SP - 13.94 (16.04-89)
CORRIGAN Kyle U17 27.09.86, Lagan Valley :
  PV - 3.70
CORRIGAN Matthew U17 1.12.85, Border :
  SPY - 14.22, DTY - 41.18
CORRIGAN Michael 1.12.77, IoW/St. Marys Un./IRL :
  TJ - 14.32 (14.33-01)
COSSINS Daniel U20 22.12.84, Wessex & Bath :
  200 - 22.0 (21.8/22.15-01)
COTTON Steven James 8.02.79, N Devon :
  JT - 59.33
COTTRELL James U23 19.12.80, Derby & Co :
  SP - 13.80

360

COTTRELL Neil U15, Wycombe :
PV - 3.00
COULDRIDGE Paul 9.05.74, WSE&H/Army :
400H - 55.2
COUPLAND Michael U17 5.01.86, Rotherham :
100 - 11.1, 200 - 22.35
COURT Alex U20 27.02.84, Med & Maid :
400H - 56.3/57.35
COURTNEY Marshall U13 12.01.90, Herne Hill :
80HC - 14.0, HJ - 1.50, TJ - 10.67
COVINGTON Mark U17 3.10.85, Guildford & G :
HTY - 53.32
COWARD Adam U15 26.03.88, Border :
PV - 3.20
COX Laurence U15 15.03.88, AF&D :
1500 - 4:09.56, 3k - 9:12.8
COX Michael U17 15.01.86, Harrow :
PV - 3.80
COYLE William V40 3.10.62, Shettleston :
Mar - 2:32:55
CRANFIELD Nick U13 25.06.90, Liverpool H :
DTC - 26.90
CRANFIELD Peter U20 26.09.84, Liverpool H :
SP - 14.73i/14.50, SPJ - 15.72, SP6K - 15.74, DT - 42.63,
DTJ - 45.44, HT - 48.52, HTJ - 54.26, HT6K - 54.80
CRAWFORD Paul U15 4.10.87, Harrow :
100 - 11.30, 200 - 23.34
CRAWLEY Luke U23 5.09.81, Solihull & S H/Bath U :
HJ - 2.14 (2.15-00)
CRAWSHAW Oliver U13 20.03.90, Crawley :
80HC - 14.34
CREAK David U20 30.08.83, Gt Yarmouth/Loughbro :
400 - 49.01
CREAK Jonathon 10.04.74, AF&D/Army :
3kSt - 9:25.2
CREIGHTON James U20 15.09.83, Liverpool H :
HJ - 2.07
CRIMMEN Nicholas Philip 15.07.65, Spenborough :
SP - 13.44i/13.26 (13.43-96)
CRIPPS Damon 9.10.70, Liverpool H :
HT - 51.78 (52.60-01)
CROASDALE Mark J. 10.01.65, Bingley/Royal Navy :
Mar - 2:21:10 (2:16:02-00)
CROFT Dominic, Woodstock R :
Mar - 2:32:04
CROMBIE Iain U15 30.09.88, Devon Sch :
DTB - 38.52
CROSS Gary Andrew U15 26.03.88, Kingston u Hull :
TJ - 12.07
CROSS Stefan U15 27.01.88, Chelmsford :
HJ - 1.77
CROSSLEY Neil U15 15.04.88, Cheltenham :
400 - 53.2/53.36, 80HB - 11.54,
SPB - 13.28, JTB - 45.78, PenB - 3071
CROSSLEY Paul 30.03.79, Luton :
110H - 14.75 (14.3w/14.37w/14.4/14.42-01
CROWLEY Mark U20 15.11.83, Enf & Har :
HJ - 2.16
CRYER Martyn U20 23 16.10.81, Salford/Loughbro :
3k - 8:19.1, 5k - 14:31.3
CUMMINGS Tony V40 18.11.60, Thurrock :
Mar - 2:33:43
CUNNINGHAM Tony U20 20.02.83, Law & Dist :
100 - 10.7w
CURRAN Patrick 15.12.76, Med & Maid :
10k - 31:44.8
CURRAN Paul 3.04.77, North Down :
TJ - 13.98w (15.15-97)
CUTTS Luke Arron U15 13.02.88, Barnsley :
PV - 3.40

DAISH Adam U15 27.10.87, Herts Phoenix :
200 - 23.4/23.45
DAKO Owusu 23.05.73, Sale/Warwick Univ. :
60 - 6.94i (6.83i-96)

DALKINS Mark 9.09.71, Birchfield :
HMar - 65:53
DANIEL Dean U17 12.04.87, Midd AC :
200 - 22.24
DANIELS Darren 2.09.70, Birchfield :
HMar - 66:32
DANILE Leon U15 28.07.88, Nene Valley H :
800 - 1:59.8
DARAMOLA Femi 19.12.71, Belgrave/NGR :
LJ - 6.91 (7.56-01), TJ - 14.44w/14.18 (15.72-99)
DARBY Brian Roy Senfuma 14.10.72, Coventry G :
200 - 21.9 (21.5-00/21.73w-01),
400 - 48.55 (47.40-01)
DASHPER Wayne 19.10.74, Havant/Royal Navy :
3kSt - 9:33.8 (9:17.82-00)
DAVENPORT Richard John U17 12.09.85, Glouc AC :
100 - 10.9w/11.04 (11.0-01), 200 - 21.8w/21.83,
400 - 47.29, 600 - 1:18.42, 800 - 1:52.3,
400HY - 51.7/53.08
DAVEY Ian U23 25.10.82, Shildon/Loughborough :
800 - 1:52.46 (1:52.1-01)
DAVIDSON Christopher 4.12.75, Newham & Essex B :
LJ - 6.96 (7.94w-97/7.90-99)
DAVIES Christopher 19.10.76, Telford/Staffs Univ :
3k - 8:19.6 (7:57.48-00), 5k - 14:35.51 (14:01.97-99),
5MR - 22:49, 10k - 31:44.0, 10kR - 30:05 (29:51-00)
DAVIES Fraser U15 30.01.88, Skyrac :
HJ - 1.75, PenB - 2695
DAVIES James U23 5.12.82, Wakefield :
400 - 48.5 (48.1/48.25-01)
DAVIES James U17 29.09.86, Walton :
LJ - 6.59
DAVIES Kevin 11.01.78, WGreen & Ex L/RAF :
HT - 60.17
DAVIES Kris U23 30.10.81, Cardiff :
LJ - 7.23w/7.04 (7.28w/7.09-01)
DAVIES Mark Howard 10.01.71, Tonbridge :
SP - 14.40 (15.56-92), DT - 46.22 (53.06-92)
DAVIES Raymond U13 11.09.90, Telford :
PV - 2.30
DAVIES Stephen U20 16.02.84, Newport :
800 - 1:54.08 (1:52.47-01)
DAVIES Thomas U17 9.11.86, Telford :
PV - 3.95
DAVIS Adam Gareth 19.11.72, Bedford & Co/RAF :
PV - 4.60 (4.70-92), SP - 15.63, DT - 44.91
DAVIS Andrae Dean U17 27.09.85, WGreen & Ex L :
400 - 49.9/50.18, SPJ - 13.67, SPY - 16.40i/16.18,
DTY - 47.76, DecY - 6264, OctY - 5425
DAVIS Daniel U15 12.12.87, Sutton & District :
100 - 11.5/11.64, 200 - 23.3/23.45, 80HB - 10.75
DAVIS Mark Gavin 1.03.77, Birchfield :
PV - 5.20 (5.20-99)
DAVOLLS Martin U20 2.09.83, Enf & Har :
200 - 22.07w (22.2-00)
DAVOREN Patrick 13.03.72, Phoenix :
2kSt - 5:35.73, 3kSt - 8:41.3
DAWSON David L. U20 3.02.84, Exeter :
SP - 15.22, SPJ - 16.85, SP6K - 16.34,
DT - 41.43, DTJ - 41.81
DE JAGER Christiaan 23.04.74, Hercules Wimb/RSA :
110H - 15.4
DE LEON-PADMORE Juan U13 1.04.90, Tamworth :
100 - 12.3, 200 - 25.0, LJ - 5.35, SPC - 11.50
DEACON Gareth 8.08.66, Coventry Godiva :
10k - 31:46.4 (30:41.3-94)
DEACON Kevin U20 25.02.84, Havering M :
HTJ - 50.17
DEACON Mark Jared 15.10.75, Border :
200 - 21.30 (21.14-96), 300 - 33.7 (32.78-96),
400 - 45.57, 400H - 50.68
DEACON-BROWN James U20 26.05.84, Gateshead :
JT - 55.56 (56.59-01)
DEAN Andrew 30.06.78, Sheffield :
110H - 15.6, 400H - 54.77 (54.52-01)

DEAN Andrew Christopher U20 25.09.83, Havant :
800 - 1:52.09
DEARMAN Geoffrey Clive 4.08.77, Bel/Brunel Univ :
200 - 22.0/22.15 (21.5-98/21.85w-01/22.08i-98,
400 - 47.41 (45.83-00)
DEETH Ian 25.06.79, Belgrave/Falkirk/Brunel Univ :
400 - 48.30 (48.10-01)
DELL Gregory J. 20.11.64, Woodstock R :
Mar - 2:32:39 (2:26:51-98)
DEMPSEY Thomas Christopher U20 15.12.83, Hales :
HT - 55.93 (57.26-01), HTJ - 62.53
DENMARK Robert Neil 23.11.68, Basildon :
3k - 8:08.89 (7:39.55-93),
5k - 13:46.63 (13:10.24-92),
10k - 28:43.42 (28:03.31-00)
DENSLEY Martin Richard U23 1.05.81, E,S & Mx :
PV - 4.80i/4.20 (4.85-01)
DENTON Lewis U13 17.10.89, Crawley :
600 - 1:36.8, 800 - 2:14.8
DEPOVRE Andre U17, Donc & Stain :
800 - 1:57.9
DERRICK R. U17, Devon Sch :
100 - 11.0w
DEVLIN Gareth 2.06.76, Sale/Ballymena & A/IRL :
LJ - 7.46 (7.55w-00)
DEVONISH Marlon 1.06.76, Coventry Godiva :
100 - 10.30w/10.32 (10.13-98),
200 - 20.18w/20.19
DICKENSON Derek Paul V50 4.12.49, Dacorum & T :
HT - 49.17 (73.20-76)
DICKINSON John U20 27.01.83, Haslemere :
LJ - 6.89w (5.02-97),
Dec - 5935 (5986w/5976-01), DECJI - 6325
DICKINSON Timothy 14.10.72, Blackheath :
HMar - 65:41, Mar - 2:23:36
DICKSON Charles U15 25.11.88, Southend :
80HB - 12.0
DICKSON Edward U15 4.09.87, Bucks Sch :
PenB - 2521
DICKSON Marlon 17.11.78, Belgrave :
60 - 6.71i, 100 - 10.50w/10.55 (10.46w-99)
DINGLEY Matthew U20 12.01.83, Birchfield :
JT - 58.34
DINHAM Ryan U20 19.08.85, Belgrave/Tonbridge :
400H - 54.0/55.26
DIRRANE Sean U17 17.10.85, Leeds :
1500 - 4:03.54, 1.5kSt - 4:35.5
DOBBING Thomas F. 5.02.73, Newham & Essex B/
City of Edinburgh/RAF : JT - 68.87
DOCHERTY Ross U13 15.08.90, Milton Keynes :
3k - 10:56.1
DOCHERTY William U20 2.04.85, Belgrave/Kilb :
2kSt - 6:11.5, 3kSt - 9:48.6
DODSWORTH Ian U20 16.12.84, Peterlee :
PV - 4.20
DOHERTY Brian U20 2.06.83, W Dunb :
SPJ - 14.32, SP6K - 14.47i/14.28, DTJ - 46.88
DOHERTY Ciaran 14.01.75, Cardiff/IRL :
JT - 57.73 (58.72-97), Dec - 5695 (6648-97)
DOHNAL James U17 18.09.85, City of Stoke :
100HY - 14.1/14.22, DecY - 5404, OctY - 4604
DON Tim 14.01.78, :
5k - 14:41.34
DONALDSON Alasdair M. 21.06.77, Newham & E B :
800 - 1:48.09 (1:47.32-00)
DONALDSON Andrew U17 23.01.86, Liv.Pemb Seft :
800 - 1:56.70
DONKIN Bradley 6.12.71, Birchfield :
800 - 1:51.26 (1:46.86-98)
DONNAN Iain U20 21.06.85, Aberdeen :
5k - 15:26.8
DONNELLY Dermot 23.09.70, Annadale Striders/IRL :
3k - 8:09.24 (7:58.03-00), 5k - 14:05.23 (13:27.63-98)
DONOGHUE Mark U20 27.09.83, Liv.Pemb Sefton :
2kSt - 6:11.39 (6:10.83-01)

DONOVAN Daniel 8.10.70, Shaftesbury Barnet :
60 - 6.73i, 100 - 10.47w/10.49 (10.4wdt-99),
200 - 21.41 (21.18-97)
DORAN Lee Michael U20 5.03.85, Carlisle/Aspatria :
JT - 57.17
DORRIAN Matthew U20 24.03.84, Giffnock :
PV - 4.70
DOSANJH Nathan Luke 13.02.79, S & SH/ Butler Un,
USA : 800 - 1:52.81 (1:51.88-00),
1500 - 3:50.33 (3:47.77-00)
DOUGAL Neil U23 7.03.80, Thames Val/Motherwell :
800 - 1:49.89 (1:48.71-01)
DOUGLAS Matthew 26.11.76, Belgrave/Brunel Univ :
200 - 21.64, 400 - 47.4 (46.65A-00), 110H - 14.39 (14.00-99),
300H - 35.56 (35.25-00), 400H - 49.38 (49.26-00)
DOUGLAS Nathan James U23 4.12.82, Ox C/Loughbro :
60 - 6.9i, 100 - 10.6w/10.7 (10.96w-01),
LJ - 7.40, TJ - 16.13w/15.69
DOUGLAS Scott U23 10.08.82, W Dunb/Strathclyde U :
LJ - 6.88i
DOWLING Carl U17 9.09.85, Med & Maid :
1.5kSt - 4:39.7
DOWNES John Michael 21.07.67, London Irish/IRL :
3k - 8:22.2 (7:54.53-94),
5k - 14:38.4 (13:29.91-94), 10MR - 49:45
DOWSE Richard U20 3.01.85, Sale :
800 - 1:52.78
DOWSETT Nicholas J.E. 24.11.78, WG & E L/Lond U :
LJ - 7.03w/7.01 (7.15w-96/7.04i-97)
DOYLE Brian 12.03.77, Harrow :
60 - 6.75i, 100 - 10.71 (10.59-98),
200 - 21.1/21.35 (21.15w-00/21.20-01)
DRAKE Andrew Paul 6.02.65, Coventry Godiva :
3kW - 11:58.49i (11:31.0-90), 20kW - 1:24:43
10kWR - 42:16+/43:35 (41:25+/41:26-00)
DRAPER Anthony 23.04.74, Blackheath :
400 - 48.5, 800 - 1:49.6 (1:48.78-00)
DRAPER Mark U20 28.06.84, WSE&H :
1500 - 3:51.14, 3k - 8:33.55 (8:29.53-01), 5k - 15:08.6
DRAYCOTT Adam U20 7.11.84, Notts :
110HJ - 15.08, 400H - 56.7
DRISCOLL Connor U15, :
PV - 2.85
DRZEWIECKI Jacek J. V45 29.11.57, Bracknell :
DT - 40.96 (44.40-91)
DUBLIN Gavin U20 5.10.83, Croydon :
400 - 48.31
DUCK Chris U17 7.06.86, Milton Keynes :
100HY - 13.97w, 400HY - 56.21
DUDMAN Robert U17 9.06.86, Herts Phoenix :
HTY - 52.04
DUDZIK Gavin U17 22.02.86, Ballymena & Antrim :
JTY - 55.10
DULLER Grant U17 20.11.85, Grantham :
SPY - 13.96
DUNFORD Edward James U20 15.09.84, Birchfield :
60H - 8.38i, 110HJ - 14.29, 110H - 14.7w?/14.92,
HJ - 1.95 (1.98-01), LJ - 6.90, SPJ - 14.78,
SP6K - 15.30, DT - 40.92, DTJ - 45.15,
Dec - 6388, DecJ - 7050, DECJI - 6989
DUNFORD James Robert U17 14.01.86, Birchfield :
DecY - 5189, OctY - 4703
DUNLOP Guy U20 28.07.83, Campbell College :
400H - 55.89
DUNN Lee 21.08.70, Sale :
10k - 31:24.32
DUNSON Gregory Ian 2.12.63, Army/Shaftesbury B :
110H - 14.91 (14.23w-89/14.29-86)
DUNWOODY Andrew 6.02.76, Kent :
3kSt - 9:43.14
DURU Ogadima U17 5.09.86, Enf & Har :
400HY - 57.32
DYER Michael U20 27.09.84, Reading :
110HJ - 15.1, 110H - 15.51w/15.6, 400H - 56.7,
Dec - 5941, DecJ - 6298, DECJI - 5860

362

DYSON Joseph U15 2.11.87, Chesterfield :
TJ - 12.65

EARLE James U17 18.05.87, Colchester H :
HTY - 50.04
EARLE Robert Bernard V40 15.09.60, WG & Ex L :
SP - 13.58i/13.29 (14.87i-93/14.80-86),
DT - 43.65 (45.12-90), HT - 58.89 (62.60-95)
EAST Andrew U23 25.07.81, Loughborough Studnts :
Dec - 6092
EAST Michael John 20.01.78, Newham & Essex B :
800 - 1:48.30, 1500 - 3:37.35,
1M - 3:58.40, 3k - 8:18.41i (8:04.27-00)
EASTMAN Gavin U23 28.06.80, Enf & Har/Herts Un :
60 - 6.85i, 100 - 10.65w/10.69 (10.43w-01),
200 - 21.6 (21.4w-01/22.09-00)
EASTON Mark Jonathan 24.05.63, Surrey WC :
10kWR - 45:17 (40:53-89), 20kW - 1:30:10 (1:24:04-89),
30kW - 2:30:22+ (2:13:33-89),
50kW - 4:11:29 (4:03:53-98)
EAVES Max U15 31.05.88, Blackpool :
PV - 3.22
EDGAR Tyrone U23 29.03.82, WGreen & Ex L :
60 - 6.90i (6.86i-01), 200 - 21.04 (20.8w/20.96-01),
100 - 10.20w/10.28 (10.17w-01)
EDIMANN L. U20, Dorset :
110HJ - 15.4
EDMUNDS Gregor 25.04.77, Shettleston :
SP - 15.92 (15.85un-01)
EDWARDS Jonathan 6.11.78, Peterbro/Loughbro :
400 - 47.38
EDWARDS Jonathan David 10.05.66, Gateshead :
TJ - 17.86 (18.43w/18.29-95)
EDWARDS Levi U23 23.11.80, Blackheath :
LJ - 7.14 (7.35w/7.27-00)
EDWARDS Lewis U15 13.09.87, Harrow :
DTB - 37.33, HTB - 45.05
EDWARDS Mark Simon 2.12.74, Belgrave :
SP - 18.41 (19.72-00)
EDWARDS Nicholas U23 22.03.81, Gloucs AC/R Navy :
400H - 54.6 (55.34-99)
EFOBI Nnamdi U17 14.09.86, Enf & Har :
DTY - 45.04, HTY - 50.13
EGGLETON Robert U20 13.02.84, City of Stoke :
JT - 55.30
EL-SADIKI Mohamed 3.11.74, Sheffield :
5k - 14:44.24, 10k - 30:32.9, 3kSt - 9:37.1
ELDIN Darren U23 10.04.82, Goole :
400 - 48.3/48.52
ELIAS Matthew 25.04.79, Cardiff :
100 - 10.74, 200 - 21.46, 300 - 33.13,
400 - 46.59, 400H - 49.11
ELLERSHAW Philip 9.02.76, Blackpool :
100 - 10.7w/11.11 (10.6w/10.7/10.83-99)
ELLINGTON James U17 6.09.85, Belgrave :
60 - 6.93i, 100 - 10.69,
200 - 21.80i/22.1/22.12w/22.25 (21.94w-01)
ELLIOTT Mensah Abraham 29.08.76, Blackheath :
60 - 6.95i, 60H - 7.91i (7.91i-01),
110H - 13.85 (13.69w/13.7/13.82-00),
400H - 54.7 (54.37-01)
ELLIOTT Nathan U15 4.03.88, Wakefield :
800 - 2:05.42
ELLIOTT Neil 10.04.71, Border/Shettleston :
SP - 16.43, DT - 50.44 (51.97-01)
ELLIOTT Ross U20 6.09.83, Peterlee :
DecJ - 5451
ELLIS Benjamin John U23 16.11.81, Winch/Bucks Un :
100 - 10.8 (10.6w-01/10.8-00/10.94w-01)
ELLIS Ieuan T. V40 11.05.60, Elswick :
Mar - 2:29:20 (2:13:21-86)
ELLIS James U17 6.09.85, City of Portsmouth :
1500 - 3:56.23
ELLIS Kevin 18.06.76, Trafford :
60 - 6.76i, 100 - 10.37, 200 - 21.8 (21.7w/21.73-01)

ELLIS S. U13, Stratford :
LJ - 4.95
ELLIS Samuel U23 23.06.82, Barnsley/Hallam Un. :
400 - 47.61, 800 - 1:48.83
ELY Marcus U13, Sale :
1500 - 4:47.0
EMANUEL Lee U20 24.01.85, Hastings :
1500 - 3:50.06
ENGLAND Russell U17 18.11.85, Leeds :
1.5kSt - 4:23.41
ENGLISH Desmond 6.06.67, Havering M/IRL :
800 - 1:50.54 (1:48.4-91), 1500 - 3:46.28 (3:41.13-96)
ENIH-SNELL Chuka U20 2.03.84, Swansea :
HJ - 2.12i (2.18-01)
ERWOOD Paul Stephen U17 26.03.86, Vale of Ayles :
1500 - 3:58.81
ETHERINGTON Glenn U17 10.12.86, Exeter :
100HY - 14.1w
EVANS David 23.01.76, Birchfield :
JT - 58.25
EVANS Gareth 28.05.77, RAF/Sheffield :
110H - 15.6 (15.3-99/15.37-98)
EVANS Jake U17 26.07.86, Carmarthen :
SPY - 14.06
EVANS James U17 7.11.86, Cardiff :
JTY - 50.10
EVANS Matthew U15 9.09.88, Carmarthen :
SPB - 15.63, DTB - 39.42
EVANS Michael, :
Mar - 2:35:49
EVANS Paul William V40 13.04.61, Belgrave :
5k - 14:30.11 (13:25.38-95),
10k - 29:25.55 (27:47.79-93),
10MR - 49:57 (46:10+/46:35-97),
HMar - 64:47 (60:09un-95/61:18-97)
EVERARD James U23 16.05.81, Basildon :
JT - 57.51
EVERETT Daniel U23 30.01.81, City of Norwich :
110H - 15.0, 400H - 55.1/55.71
EVISON Steven U20 29.01.83, Hallamshire :
800 - 1:54.03
EVLING-WHITE Joseph U17 3.12.86, Corby :
DecY - 5319, OctY - 4335
EWULO Ezekiel U17 29.01.86, Herne Hill :
LJ - 6.78
EYONG Onen U20 18.02.85, Belgrave :
LJ - 7.06 (7.47w/7.46-01)

FABEN Stuart 28.02.75, Belgrave :
JT - 76.17 (76.66i-96)
FALCONER William 20.12.78, Clydesdale/Stirling Un :
SP - 14.64 (14.81-01), DT - 41.41
FARAH Mohamed U20 23.03.83, WSE&H :
800 - 1:50.2, 1500 - 3:47.78 (3:46.1-01),
5k - 14:00.5 (13:56.31-01)
FARENDEN Simon U17 6.10.85, Chesterfield :
60 - 6.93i, 200 - 22.1 (21.46-01)
FARLEY Paul Ivor U20 1.12.84, Isle of Wight :
HT - 49.92, HTJ - 53.36
FARMER Lea U23 22.01.80, Swansea/UWIC :
400 - 49.1 (48.50-98), 800 - 1:52.54
FARMER Paul 23.11.77, Luton :
3kSt - 8:50.50
FARQUHARSON Andy 24.08.65, Kent :
Mar - 2:31:40
FARQUHARSON Ruddy Anthony V40 26.03.61,
Telford/RAF : TJ - 14.54 (15.59w/15.57-85)
FARROW Kevin 8.09.75, Derby & Co :
5k - 14:14.2, 10k - 31:07.2
FAUCHER-FOLIE Enrico U13 5.01.90, Cambridge H :
LJ - 5.05
FAULKNER Stewart 19.02.69, Birchfield :
LJ - 7.00 (8.15-90)
FAURE Marcus U15 15.01.88, Surrey Sch :
TJ - 12.06

FAY Christopher U17 1.07.86, Cheltenham :
  TJ - 13.18
FEASEY Terry 5.08.77, Basingstoke & MH :
  800 - 1:50.27
FELCE Alex U17 11.09.86, Gloucester AC :
  800 - 1:57.7, 1500 - 4:05.2, 1.5KSt - 4:21.42,
  2kSt - 6:14.7, 3kSt - 9:38.70
FELL Adam U20 20.04.85, Holmfirth :
  400H - 56.1/57.13
FENNELL Steven U17 4.04.86, Tonbridge :
  800 - 1:56.01, 1500 - 4:01.4
FENNEMORE Dennis U20 19.06.84, Harrow :
  TJ - 14.18
FENTON Malcolm Leonard V45 12.02.56, Ipswich :
  SP - 14.01 (14.62-96), DT - 40.98 (47.40-79),
  HT - 62.13 (62.42-82)
FERDINAND Philip U23 18.11.82, Birchfield/Birm Un :
  TJ - 15.94
FERGUS Jason Robert 11.10.73, Shaftesbury Barnet :
  100 - 10.78w (10.34w-94/10.4-93/10.44-92)
FERGUSON Martin M. 17.09.64, City of Edinburgh :
  Mar - 2:36:20 (2:26:45-95)
FERNANDEZ Andre U23 2.03.80, Thames Valley :
  400 - 47.3/47.65, LJ - 7.54
FERNS Austin U23 12.01.81, Belgrave/Brunel Univ :
  400H - 55.1 (52.74-99)
FEWTRELL James U23 22.12.80, Beds & Co/DMU Un :
  800 - 1:52.9, 1500 - 3:45.10, 3k - 8:04.26,
  5k - 14:13.11
FIELD Grenville 17.11.77, City of Stoke :
  200 - 22.20, 400 - 49.10
FIELD Jack U15 6.11.87, N Devon :
  HJ - 1.75, LJ - 6.48, PenB - 2707
FIELDSEND Brian, Inverness :
  Mar - 2:35:02
FIFTON Rikki U20 17.06.85, Vic Park & Tower H :
  60 - 6.9i/6.95i, 100 - 10.74 (10.56-01),
  200 - 21.53 (21.4w/21.48w/21.5-01)
FILBY Nick U17 17.09.85, Chelmsford :
  LJ - 6.62w
FINCH Lloyd Lewis U20 26.10.83, Leics WC :
  3kW - 12:28.63i/12:40.96 (12:26.0i-01/12:34.98-99),
  5kW - 23:56.8 (20:47.23-01),
  10kW - 43:09.82, 10kWR - 43:14
FINCH Luke U17 21.09.85, Leics WC :
  3kW - 12:30.14, 5kW - 22:15.93 (21:58.8-01),
  5kWR - 22:04, 10kW - 46:55.33,
  10kWR - 43:02, 20KWT - 1:35:20
FINCH Michael David U17 11.01.86, Cleethorpes :
  PV - 4.10
FINCH Rodney 5.08.67, Team Solent/Soton C/Army :
  1500 - 3:47.02 (3:37.97-93), 5k - 13:57.5 (13:27.75-98)
FINDLAY James U17 18.09.86, Shettleston :
  400HY - 58.00
FINILL Chris V40 31.12.58, Harrow :
  100kR - 7:17:06
FINLAYSON Ross U15 26.09.87, Lasswade :
  800 - 2:04.5
FISHER Ian 15.09.70, Otley :
  HMar - 66:46 (66:35-00), Mar - 2:22:08 (2:20:26-00)
FISHER Martin V40 27.09.62, York RWC :
  50kW - 4:56:55, 100MWT - 21:28:09+,
  24HrWT - 177.227km
FITZGERALD Karl U15 4.11.87, Cleethorpes :
  DTB - 39.90, HTB - 42.60
FITZGERALD Richard U20 6.06.84, Med & Maid :
  110HJ - 14.8/15.09
FITZSIMMONS James 20.04.74, Shaftesbury Barnet :
  3kSt - 9:25.99 (8:57.93-01)
FITZSIMONS David John U13 8.09.89, Giffnock :
  800 - 2:14.63
FLADGLEY Nicholas U15 23.11.87, Wimborne :
  HJ - 1.75
FLANNERY Kieran U17 29.04.87, Gateshead :
  400HY - 57.2/57.60

FLEARY Jordan U17 1.12.85, Carlisle/Aspatria :
  100HY - 13.67
FLECKNEY William David Michael U17 19.10.85,
  Bedford & County : LJ - 6.76w/6.70
FLEMING Peter Ross V40 5.01.61, Leslie Deans RC :
  Mar - 2:23:49dh (2:13:33-93)
FLETCHER Dale U17 4.09.85, Grantham :
  SPY - 13.82, DTY - 42.05
FLETCHER John U17 15.07.86, Wakefield :
  LJ - 6.83
FLETCHER Mark U17 4.11.86, Preston :
  OctY - 4225
FLINT Benjamin 16.09.78, Bel/Ripon & York Univ :
  PV - 5.10 (5.40-99)
FLINT Christopher V55 6.12.44, London Vidarians :
  100MWT - 21:39:22+ (20:21:41-97),
  24HrWT - 171.627km (184.208km-97)
FLOOD Aaron U17 7.10.85, :
  OctY - 4270
FLOYD Michael Anthony 26.09.76, Sale :
  HT - 67.74 (69.38-00)
FLYNN Julian T. 3.07.72, Belgrave :
  LJ - 7.32w (7.76w/7.70-99)
FOGG Joshua U13 13.10.89, Wirral :
  200 - 26.0
FOGG Nicholas 24.03.78, Shaftesbury Barnet :
  HT - 50.15 (52.56?-00)
FOOKS Andrew 26.04.75, Thames Valley :
  3kSt - 9:12.5 (8:56.83-95)
FORBES Robert 13.09.75, Glasgow Univ/Perth :
  TJ - 13.92
FORD Antony U20 26.05.83, Blackpool/Un of Montana :
  3k - 8:30.07 (8:25.0-01), 5k - 14:29.28
FORDE James U20 10.04.85, Sparkhill :
  HTJ - 52.23
FORDE Karl U20 15.04.83, Rowheath :
  100 - 10.6w/10.63w/10.7/10.74 (10.70-99), 200 - 21.72
FORDHAM Gavin James 1.02.79, Beds & Co/DMU Un :
  HJ - 1.96 (2.00i-01/1.99-00), PV - 4.22i/4.15,
  LJ - 6.82, Dec - 6183 (6590-01)
FOSTER Darren U13 14.10.89, Carlisle/Aspatria :
  JTC - 33.20
FOSTER Sean U17 10.11.86, Ipswich :
  400 - 51.0
FOWLES Steven James U20 16.05.85, Enf & Har :
  100 - 10.83w/10.9/10.97 (10.78w/10.82-01)
FOX Morris 30.04.63, City of Stoke :
  SP - 16.14, DT - 46.52
FOXWORTHY Nicholas U20 20.05.83, Exeter/UWIC :
  110H - 15.6, Dec - 5537, DECJI - 5635
FRAMPTON Matthew U20 10.04.84, Bournemouth :
  HT - 52.20, HTJ - 57.20, HT6K - 60.88
FRANCE Chris U20 29.01.84, Telford :
  HJ - 2.00i/1.98 (1.98-00)
FRANCE Craig Colin U17 1.01.87, W Cheshire :
  100HY - 13.71
FRANCIS Nick 29.08.71, Shaftesbury Barnet :
  Mar - 2:22:27 (2:20:00-01)
FRANCIS Ricardo U15 26.11.88, Hallamshire :
  100 - 11.5w (12.5-01), 200 - 23.59
FRANKIS Gianni U15 16.04.88, Ashford :
  80HB - 12.0
FRANKLIN Andrew U23 13.09.80, Trafford :
  3kSt - 8:55.54 (8:42.82-01)
FRANKLIN John 1.03.66, WGreen & Ex L :
  110H - 15.66w/16.23 (15.1w-90/15.13-91/15.2-92)
FRANKS Thomas U17 8.11.85, Leics Cor :
  400 - 50.85
FRASER Peter 28.01.78, Aberdeen :
  JT - 57.13 (58.95-98)
FRAZER John U23 10.09.81,
  St Malachy's/Loughbro/IRL : 1500 - 3:49.43
FRAZER Thomas U23 10.09.81, Loughbro/IRL :
  1500 - 3:47.04

FREARY Paul 3.04.68, Belgrave :
5k - 14:43.47 (13:55.34-96),
10k - 31:06.94 (30:55.0-92), Mar - 2:35:28
FREEMAN Kyle U17 12.10.85, :
OctY - 4519
FREMPONG Kenneth U20 17.07.84, Kingston u Hull :
110HJ - 14.76w/14.78 (14.44-01)
FRENCH Jon 11.12.75, City of Norwich/Bucks Univ :
LJ - 6.93w (7.38w/7.22-99)
FRENCH Nathan U13, Chelmsford :
75HC - 13.0
FROGGATT Darren U17, Sale :
800 - 1:57.2
FROST Andrew Derek U23 17.04.81, IoW/St. Marys U :
SP - 14.04, HT - 65.01
FROST Howard U23 9.12.81, Kent :
400H - 53.95 (52.9-01)
FROST Russell U23 23.06.80, Kent :
400H - 55.6
FRY Kevin U17 28.12.85, N Devon :
200 - 22.4
FULFORD Andrew U23 23.06.82, Swindon :
800 - 1:50.7
FULLER Christopher U23 2.02.82, Havant :
110H - 15.4
FULLER Peter John 30.04.78, Epsom & Ewell :
HT - 52.22 (53.23-01)
FULLER William 19.10.76, Epsom & Ewell :
SP - 16.34 (16.36-97), DT - 43.75,
HT - 53.87 (54.20-97)

G ADD Richard U17 30.07.86, Bedford & County :
400 - 50.9
GAINEY James U15 9.10.87, :
PV - 2.80
GALE Howard U17 23.09.85, Dacorum & Tring :
HJ - 1.90
GALLAGHER Andrew U20 15.02.83, Border/B & A :
JT - 63.44 (66.95-01)
GALLAGHER Anthony U20 16.10.84, Liv.Pemb Seft :
DTJ - 41.74
GALLANT Simon U13 7.12.89, Southampton City :
1500 - 4:44.5, 3k - 10:15.82
GALLIE Adam David U20 5.11.84, Derby & Co :
HJ - 2.06
GALLOWAY Dwayne U17 22.01.86, Birchfield :
LJ - 6.94w/6.83, TJ - 13.14
GAMESTER Neil U20 15.02.83, Enf & Har :
3kSt - 9:28.6
GARDENER Jason John 18.09.75, Wessex & Bath :
60 - 6.49i (6.46i-99), 100 - 10.11w/10.13 (9.98-99)
GARDINER Richard 11.06.73, Cardiff :
HMar - 66:49, Mar - 2:23:21
GARDNER Rupert Arthur John U20 9.10.84, Milton K :
110HJ - 15.5, 400H - 52.29
GARENAMOTSE Gable 28.02.77, Cardiff/UWIC/BOT :
LJ - 8.01i/7.91 (8.26w/7.99-01),
TJ - 15.32i (16.05-98)
GARLAND Dale U23 13.10.80, Channel Isl/Bath Univ :
200 - 22.01, 400 - 47.80, 110H - 15.2/15.50, 400H - 52.86,
HJ - 1.95, LJ - 7.23 (7.25-01), TJ - 14.51w/14.36, Dec - 6919
GARLAND Lee 18.12.74, Channel Islands :
3kSt - 9:23.55
GARNER Mark U20 2.11.83, Mansfield :
400H - 55.1/56.88
GASCOIGNE Robert 5.10.74, Sale :
400H - 55.7/56.00 (55.21-97)
GASSON Christopher 28.02.79, Crawley :
JT - 54.98 (55.70-97)
GAUSON Kris U15 29.01.88, City of Edinburgh :
1500 - 4:20.25
GAY Richard V50 26.10.50, Beverley :
Mar - 2:36:21 (2:31:56-00)
GAYLE Nicholas U20 4.01.85, City of Stoke :
110HJ - 14.6/14.88, 110H - 15.5

GAYLE Thomas U20 16.06.83, City of Stoke :
800 - 1:54.19, 1500 - 3:55.56
GEARING Chris U17 30.09.86, Belgrave :
SPJ - 15.41, SPY - 17.41, DTJ - 44.60,
DTY - 48.30, HTY - 49.47
GEBBIE Joel U15 14.09.87, Tonbridge :
JTB - 43.07
GERRARD Keith U17 24.03.86, Manx :
3k - 8:48.04
GHENT Brendon 7.09.76, Birchfield :
60 - 6.78i (6.77i-01), 200 - 21.3w/21.40 (21.0/21.01-99),
100 - 10.52w/10.6/10.66 (10.36w/10.4-00/10.51-99)
GIBBONS Martyn U15 7.09.87, Notts :
400 - 52.56, 800 - 1:59.07
GIBLIN Christopher U23 20.06.81, Liverpool H :
HJ - 2.09i/2.08 (2.12-99)
GIBSON Alex 3.11.77, Chelmsford :
LJ - 6.91, SP - 13.69, JT - 60.99, Dec - 7028
GILDING Paul 2.10.75, Worthing :
110H - 15.1/15.29 (15.0/15.15w-01/15.28-00),
HJ - 1.95 (2.03i/2.01-93), Dec - 6026
GILHOOLY Anthony 26.03.76, Newham & Essex B :
HJ - 2.05 (2.18i-97/2.18-99)
GILL Jamie U17 29.10.85, Cannock & Stafford :
100 - 10.8w/10.95w/11.0/11.03 (11.0-01),
200 - 22.0
GILL Shoaib Waseem U13 14.12.89, Altrincham :
TJ - 9.51
GILLESPIE Ian 18.05.70, Birchfield :
1500 - 3:50.6 (3:39.8-97), 1M - 4:08.82 (3:57.6-98),
3k - 7:51.72i/8:17.3 (7:48.28-97),
5k - 14:06.02 (13:18.06-97)
GILSON Stewart U15 13.09.87, Wellington Sch :
TJ - 12.21
GIRDLER Alexander U20 13.05.84, Tamworth :
HJ - 2.00
GIRDLER Dominic Paul U23 6.03.82, Bel/Loughbro :
100 - 10.95 (10.8w-00/10.95-01), 110H - 13.95,
60H - 7.92i (7.92i-01), HJ - 1.95 (2.03-00), LJ - 7.16
GIRVAN Richard Thomas 26.07.76, Annadale St/Bord :
800 - 1:50.44 (1:49.13-97),
1500 - 3:49.81 (3:46.44-01)
GITTENS Luke U23 4.01.81, Cardiff :
60H - 8.37i (8.36i-00)
GLANCY George U15 3.09.87, WSE&H :
800 - 2:04.28, 1500 - 4:19.68, 3k - 9:34.28
GLANVILLE Craig U17 21.09.86, Gateshead :
400 - 49.95, DecY - 5096, OctY - 4492
GLASSE Peter U15 1.05.88, :
JTB - 44.72
GLOVER Ross Ricki John U17 2.11.85, Rugby & Nor :
400 - 50.6, 800 - 1:57.1
GLYMOND Daniel U15 15.02.88, Barnsley :
LJ - 5.97
GODDARD Samuel John U20 4.01.83, Paddock Wood :
JT - 59.16 (59.37-01)
GOLDING Julian Antonio 17.02.75, Blackheath :
100 - 10.71 (10.28-97),
200 - 20.62w/21.02 (20.18-98)
GOLLEY Julian Quintin Patrick 12.09.71, Thames Val :
TJ - 15.77w/15.66 (17.06-94)
GOODALL Nicholas U23 12.05.82, Holmf/Staffs U :
1500 - 3:49.28 (3:48.29-01), 3k - 8:22.93,
5k - 14:27.7
GOODREM Greg U20 14.09.83, Southend :
HJ - 1.95 (2.00-01)
GOODRIDGE Mark C. 13.04.70, Royal Navy :
Mar - 2:31:41
GOODWIN Jon 22.09.76, T Solent/St. Marys Un Coll :
400H - 54.5/55.65 (52.5/53.14-97)
GOODWIN Robert U20 19.04.84, Sale :
1500 - 3:54.11
GORDON Alastair 16.04.78, Newham & Essex B :
100 - 10.94 (10.8-98/10.92-01),
200 - 21.40w/21.88 (21.73-01), 400 - 47.46

GORDON Malwyn U23 29.04.82, Bristol :
TJ - 14.91 (15.26-99)
GORDON Peter V50 2.07.51, Gateshead :
DT - 49.18 (61.62-91)
GOSS George 28.07.77, Eastbourne GS :
TJ - 14.00
GOUDIE Andrew 4.10.78, Belgrave :
3kW - 13:21.35 (12:37.8-01),
5kW - 23:22.6 (21:49.63-01), 10kWR - 44:59 (44:57-01)
GOULD Robert John 16.01.76, Trafford :
5k - 14:33.59 (14:12.56-01),
10k - 30:39.2 (29:34.10-01)
GOULDBOURNE Marcus U23 12.06.81, Pud & Bram :
SP - 15.28, DT - 49.53
GOW David Allan 9.02.79, Shettleston :
800 - 1:50.73 (1:49.18-99)
GOWELL Chris U17 26.09.85, Cwmbran :
800 - 1:56.13
GRABARZ Robbie U15 3.10.87, Bedford & County :
HJ - 1.75
GRAFFIN Allen Gordon 20.12.77, Belgrave :
800 - 1:52.0 (1:50.1-00), 3k - 8:02.20,
5k - 13:45.77 (13:40.07-01), 5MR - 23:19,
10kR - 29:45 (29:35-00), HMar - 64:09
GRAFFIN Andrew Neill 20.12.77, Belgrave :
800 - 1:49.03 (1:47.5-01), 1500 - 3:35.53,
1M - 3:54.70, 3k - 8:03.2i+ (8:07.58-99),
2M - 8:37.94i, 5k - 13:53.60
GRAHAM Andrew U20 14.11.84, Gosforth :
800 - 1:54.34
GRAHAM Andrew U13 19.12.89, Belgrave :
2kW - 11:44.4 (10:48.0-99)
GRAHAM Ben U15 15.09.87, Chesterfield :
DTB - 37.26
GRAHAM Daniel Alexander 3.08.79, Liverpool H :
HJ - 2.13 (2.22-00)
GRAHAM Douglas 1.01.77, City of Edinburgh :
PV - 4.30i/4.20 (4.26-96)
GRAHAM Martin U23 25.04.81, Shettleston :
3kSt - 9:32.82
GRAHAM Thomas U13 10.09.89, Thurrock :
HJ - 1.49
GRANT Andrew U23 4.10.82, Aberdeen :
110H - 15.6
GRANT Dalton 8.04.66, WGreen & Ex L :
HJ - 2.26 (2.37i-94/2.36-91)
GRANT Dwayne U23 17.07.82, Blackheath :
100 - 10.48w/10.52 (10.22w/10.4/10.47-01),
200 - 20.60w/20.79 (20.4w/20.64-01)
GRANT Mark 17.05.71, Luton :
PV - 5.00 (5.11-01)
GRAY Neil U17 16.03.86, Orkney Islands :
400 - 50.09
GRAY Paul 25.05.69, Cardiff :
110H - 13.85 (13.53-94)
GRAY Richard U17 20.08.86, Aberdeen :
400HY - 57.38
GREAVES Damien David 19.09.77, Newham & E B :
60H - 7.75i (7.68i-00), 110H - 13.54
GREAVES Daniel U23 4.10.82, Charnwood :
DT - 43.08
GREEN Adam U13, Warrington :
800 - 2:18.3
GREEN Ben U17 14.08.86, Warrington :
400 - 51.0, 800 - 1:55.76, 1500 - 4:00.82
GREEN Clifton Paul 10.10.79, Belgrave :
JT - 63.37 (66.73-01)
GREEN Deonte U15 26.01.88, Ipswich :
LJ - 6.34
GREEN James U13 25.04.90, Poole :
80HC - 14.11
GREEN Leighton 10.01.78, Thames Valley :
200 - 22.04 (22.0-99)
GREEN Matthew U13 18.08.90, :
PV - 2.12

GREEN Michael Stephen 12.10.76, Blackburn :
1500 - 3:49.49 (3:48.14-00), 3k - 8:10.67 (8:10.06-01),
5k - 14:25.43 (14:12.56-99), Mar - 2:24:12
GREEN Steven Christopher U20 15.01.83, Corn/CUAC :
400 - 48.32, 110HJ - 14.53,
200H - 24.54, 400H - 50.96
GREENFIELD Luke U23 6.05.81, Thames V/NZL :
HT - 63.11
GREENING Stephen 15.02.68, Birchfield :
JT - 55.23 (63.24r?-91/57.80-87)
GREENLAND Philip U20 10.10.84, Croydon :
LJ - 7.36w/7.19
GREENWOOD Terry 22.08.74, Trafford :
JT - 56.16
GREGG Steven U17 27.06.87, Chesterfield :
400 - 50.9/51.08
GREGORY Jamie U17 24.12.86, Cleethorpes :
HTY - 47.53
GREGORY Philip U15 14.02.88, Harrow :
JTB - 49.92
GREY Edwin U23 23.03.81, Crawley/Loughbro :
60 - 6.96i, 100 - 10.90,
60H - 8.46i, 110H - 15.2/15.25
GRIERSON Gordon U17 12.10.85, WSE&H :
HTY - 62.62
GRIFFIN Colin U23 3.08.82, IRL :
3kW - 11:46.03i
GRIFFIN Neil V50 28.05.48, WSE&H :
SP - 13.90i/13.52 (16.06-77), DT - 44.19 (51.66-80)
GRIFFIN Samuel U17 18.10.85, Sale :
OctY - 4483
GRIFFITH Mark U23 25.11.81, WG & E L/St. Marys U :
3kSt - 9:26.6 (9:22.44-99)
GRIFFITHS Kyle U17 19.09.86, London Schools :
LJ - 6.59
GRIME Ian Stuart 29.09.70, Newham & Essex B :
1500 - 3:49.1 (3:40.1-96), 3k - 8:07.91 (7:55.4-96),
5k - 13:59.45 (13:37.00-97), 5MR - 23:49,
10kR - 29:57 (29:21-00)
GRIME Peter John 8.11.69, N & E B/Durham Univ :
10k - 31:02.0 (30:52.69-01)
GRIPTON Paul 9.11.76, Birchfield :
110H - 15.4/15.62 (14.59-98)
GRISTWOOD William E. V40 20.03.59, E,S & Mx :
Mar - 2:33:18 (2:25:09-94)
GROVES Michael U20 21.03.84, Cwmbran :
200 - 21.9 (21.90-01)
GRUBB Andrew Mark U20 26.12.83, Mansfield :
110HJ - 15.4, 400H - 55.12, DecJ - 5352
GULLIVER Mark 11.02.72, Leeds :
HT - 51.39
GUMBS Lloyd U15 5.10.87, Charnwood :
80HB - 11.7
GUNN Alistair 1.09.79, SGA (Prof) :
SP - 14.24
GUNN Chris U23 13.09.82, Birchfield :
Dec - 5993
GUNN Luke U20 22.03.85, Derby & Co :
1500 - 3:54.02, 2kSt - 5:55.03, 3kSt - 9:21.5

HAGAN Garry U20 21.11.84, Shaft B/Clydesdale :
SP - 13.69i (13.31-01), SPJ - 14.36,
SP6K - 14.49i, DT - 40.39 (42.26-01), DTJ - 46.82
HAINES Alex U23 27.10.82, Cardiff :
3k - 8:18.08, 5k - 14:19.89
HAINES Gareth U20 21.11.84, Carmarthen :
HJ - 1.98
HAINES Paige U13 28.06.90, Newham & Essex B :
800 - 2:17.6
HALCROW Patrick U17 9.01.86, Thurrock :
100HY - 14.03w/14.1, OctY - 4453
HALE Darren V40 2.10.59, Salford :
Mar - 2:33:18 (2:22:09-97)
HALE Steven 20.04.77, Birchfield :
DT - 42.24 (44.53-00)

366

HALES Matthew John MacKenzie 6.10.79, Steyning :
  3kW - 12:38.24 (12:07.54-00),
  5kW - 21:40.3 (20:06.66-00), 20kW - 1:33:11 (1:28:40-01)
HALL Alex U23 2.02.82, Cambridge Harriers :
  100 - 10.7w/10.98, 200 - 21.6, LJ - 7.46
HALL Brendan Russell U15 5.09.87, Cannock & St :
  SPB - 16.04
HALL Brian 24.01.63, Blackpool :
  Mar - 2:34:11
HALL Brian Nigel U23 17.11.82, Bolton/Salford Univ. :
  HJ - 2.10 (2.11-01)
HALL Calvin U20 15.11.83, Birchfield :
  HJ - 2.04
HALL Dominic 21.02.71, Highgate Harriers :
  800 - 1:49.47 (1:49.1-98)
HALL Samuel Thomas U17 15.10.85, Shaftesbury B :
  3k - 8:59.1, 1.5kSt - 4:34.86 (4:30.04-01)
HALL Stuart 21.12.64, Tipton :
  HMar - 66:45 (65:42-01), Mar - 2:16:23
HALLETT Jason U23 29.03.82, Cardiff :
  JT - 59.45 (60.15-01)
HAMBLIN Ben U17 2.11.85, City of Norwich :
  100 - 11.0/11.04w (11.51-00), 200 - 22.13
HAMILTON Aaron U23 7.08.82, Trafford :
  60 - 6.96i
HAMILTON Christopher 14.11.78, Rotherham :
  100 - 10.7w/10.77
HAMPSON Jonathan U13 1.10.89, East Grinstead :
  1k - 3:01.5
HAND Rob V40 17.01.62, Durham City H :
  Mar - 2:31:26
HANSARD Richard U17 5.11.86, Watford :
  100HY - 13.9/14.09w/14.15
HANSFORD Matthew U17 20.02.86, Exeter :
  100HY - 13.7w/13.74 (13.7-01), LJ - 6.61,
  OctY - 4538 (4543-01)
HANSON Mark U23 13.05.81, Enf & Har/Brunel Univ :
  60 - 6.87i, 100 - 10.7/10.71 (10.60w-01)
HAQUE Daniel U15 26.07.88, Bromley :
  TJ - 12.36
HARDING Ben U17 12.12.86, City of Portsmouth :
  800 - 1:54.68, 1500 - 4:01.2
HARDING David John U23 8.11.80, Herts Ph/OUAC :
  JT - 57.73
HARDING Jason U23 24.09.82, Coventry Godiva :
  100 - 10.7w (10.90w-01)
HARGRAVE Christopher 27.02.79, Bedford & County :
  110H - 15.1 (14.6/14.66-98)
HARGREAVES Mark V40 26.08.60, Bournemouth :
  10k - 31:56.1,
  Mar - 2:33:53 (2:23:25-94)
HARLAND Issac U13 9.11.89, Tonbridge :
  400 - 60.1
HARLE Robert Keith 1.06.79, Chelmsford/CUAC :
  200 - 21.9/22.07 (21.8/22.07-00)
HARPER John U20 23.08.85, North Down :
  DTY - 43.64o
HARRIES Kirk 7.08.74, Thames Valley :
  60H - 8.54i (8.3i-94)
HARRIS Daryl U15 23.11.87, Oxford City :
  TJ - 13.28w
HARRIS Richard 16.08.71, Rotherham :
  3kSt - 9:24.2 (9:21.73-01)
HARRIS Ricky U15 8.02.88, Tipton :
  200 - 23.45
HARRISON Chris U17 19.09.85, Lancashire Sch :
  SPY - 14.14
HARRISON Edward U17 10.12.86, Med & Maid :
  100HY - 13.69, 400HY - 56.72, OctY - 4383
HARRISON Julian 4.08.76, Sheffield :
  HJ - 2.03 (2.05-01)
HARRISON Nsa U20 27.11.83, Worcester AC :
  SPJ - 15.94
HARRISON Stephen 19.12.72, Blackheath/London U :
  JT - 63.54 (75.32-95)

HART Christopher James U17 23.05.86, Burnley :
  1500 - 3:57.14, 3k - 8:43.28, 1.5kSt - 4:19.85
HARVEY Chris 1.08.64, Severn :
  Mar - 2:34:34
HARVEY Jonathan U20 12.09.83, Braintree :
  JT - 56.88
HARVEY Lawrence Edward U23 26.08.81, Trafford/
  Loughborough Studnts : TJ - 14.36
HARVEY Mark U20 2.07.84, Neath :
  PV - 4.20
HARVEY Stuart U15 2.09.87, Blackheath :
  JTB - 54.27
HARWOOD Laurence U20 9.03.85, Isle of Wight :
  HT6K - 49.31
HARWOOD Paul 19.07.71, AF&D :
  Mar - 2:35:59 (2:28:44-99)
HASTEY Rhian U17 5.08.86, Rotherham :
  800 - 1:57.50
HATTON Darren 21.03.79, Ashford :
  PV - 4.32i/4.32, LJ - 6.88 (7.01w-97/6.97-98),
  SP - 13.88 (13.89i-01), DT - 40.96 (42.30-01),
  JT - 57.58 (61.86-01), Dec - 6803 (7020-01)
HATTON Felix Edward Libretto U20 9.10.84, Kingst & P :
  DTJ - 42.00, JT - 59.15
HAUGHIAN Samuel 9.07.79, WSE&H :
  3k - 8:01.49 (7:57.24-99), 5k - 13:19.45, 10k - 28:25.87
HAUGHIAN Tim U17 29.11.86, WSE&H :
  800 - 1:58.1, 1500 - 4:03.7
HAWKINS Colin John U20 23.03.84, Derby & Co :
  3k - 8:35.81, 5k - 15:23.8
HAWKINS James 14.12.79, Med & Maid :
  HT - 50.43 (51.34-98)
HAWKINS Malcolm U20 17.12.83, Stratford :
  400H - 56.38
HAWKINS Scott U13 24.03.90, Kilbarchan :
  1500 - 4:47.5
HAWKSWORTH Duncan U17 23.05.86, Derby & Co :
  100HY - 13.8/14.10
HAY Alistair U17 7.09.85, Central :
  800 - 1:58.13 (1:57.8-01), 1500 - 3:59.66,
  3k - 8:55.5
HAY Joss U15 6.06.88, Perth :
  PenB - 2501un
HAYES Martin 31.08.79, Chesterfield :
  HT - 47.00 (48.12-97)
HAYES Scott 4.01.73, Newham & Essex B :
  SP - 15.03 (16.15i-98/15.62-95), DT - 47.43 (54.16-97)
HAYFORD Kenneth Nicholas 10.03.63, Cambridge H :
  JT - 60.25 (69.90-87)
HAYMAN Nigel 25.09.74, Bournemouth :
  110H - 15.6 (15.2-97/15.33w-99/15.39-97)
HAYMAN Rick 11.10.79, Sale :
  5k - 14:43.44
HAYNES Alex John U20 6.09.84, North Shields Poly :
  2kSt - 6:11.91
HAYWARD Andrew 26.10.74, Rowntrees :
  JT - 61.42
HAZELL Benjamin Nicholas Rodney U20 1.10.84,
  Basingstoke & MH : 110HJ - 15.2/15.39,
  400H - 55.2/55.22, Dec - 5880,
  DecJ - 6654, DECJI - 6069
HEAD Paul 1.07.65, Newham & Essex B :
  DT - 43.57 (44.40-00), HT - 69.61 (74.02-90)
HEANLEY John U23 25.09.80, WSE&H/London Univ. :
  100 - 10.97w/11.36, 60H - 8.42i,
  110H - 14.8w/14.92, HJ - 2.00,
  PV - 4.61 (4.62-01), LJ - 7.18w/7.12 (7.23i-01),
  TJ - 14.41 (14.42-01), Dec - 7411
HEDMAN Graham 6.02.79, WGreen & Ex L :
  100 - 10.56w/10.7/10.84, 200 - 21.20w/21.24,
  400 - 46.37
HEMERY Adrian U23 6.08.82, Swindon/Cambridge U :
  110H - 15.3/15.33, PV - 4.20, Dec - 6924
HENDERSON Adam U15 25.09.87, South Shields :
  HJ - 1.75

HENDERSON Shaun U15, Midd AC :
80HB - 11.90
HENDRY Martyn John 10.04.75, City of Edinburgh :
110H - 15.09 (14.16-97)
HENNESSY Andrew D. 24.08.77, Wells/Thames Val/
London Univ. : 1500 - 3:50.9 (3:46.32-99),
3k - 8:16.5, 3kSt - 8:55.23 (8:39.71-99)
HENRY Cori 9.12.76, Notts :
100 - 10.8 (10.5w/10.8-96/10.96-00),
200 - 20.98 (20.8w-96/20.9-99), 400 - 46.46
HENRY James U20 31.07.84, Spenborough :
2kSt - 6:12.33, 3kSt - 9:39.9
HENRY Robert U20 31.05.85, Kingston u Hull :
100 - 10.9w, 110HJ - 14.51, DecJ - 6005
HENTHORN James Brett 20.02.77, Team Solent :
100 - 10.47w/10.64 (10.22w-97/10.39-99),
200 - 21.03 (20.93-99)
HEPPLES Stephen David U23 6.01.80, Loftus/
New Marske/Teeside Univ : 1500 - 3:46.68,
3k - 8:12.43 (8:10.53-01), 5k - 14:09.5 (14:09.41-01),
10kR - 30:10, 10MR - 49:22
HEPPLEWHITE Daniel U17 2.09.86, Bournemouth :
SPY - 15.18, DTY - 42.85
HERBERT Scott 12.02.74, Milton Keynes :
100 - 10.7 (10.6w-93/10.89-96), 200 - 22.0 (21.20-96)
HERMANN Derek 7.04.79, Cardiff :
JT - 60.89 (61.85-00)
HERRING Clint U15 3.10.87, Peterborough :
HJ - 1.75
HERRINGTON Charles 28.09.71, Belgrave :
10k - 31:55.2 (30:50.1-99)
HERRINGTON Gary Hugh V40 31.03.61, Rug & Nor :
DT - 51.18 (56.66-96)
HERRINGTON Samuel Edward U17 2.10.86, Birch :
SPY - 15.36, DTJ - 47.90,
DTY - 52.48, HTY - 47.13
HESLOP Adam U17 15.04.86, Wirral :
HJ - 1.95
HEWITSON Dale U20 11.09.84, Elswick :
SPJ - 13.93
HIBBERT David 31.01.79, Trafford :
1500 - 3:45.82, 3k - 8:19.52 (8:06.34-99), 5k - 14:07.18
HICKEY Adam U15 30.05.88, Southend :
1500 - 4:04.86, 3k - 9:04.7
HICKS Maurice 1.01.70, Team Solent/Junction 10 :
HT - 49.53 (56.14-96)
HIGBEE Tony U20 21.09.83, Weymouth :
HJ - 1.96, DecJ - 5898
HIGGINS Benjamin U17 27.09.86, Ipswich :
100 - 11.1, 200 - 22.22
HIGGINS Marcus U15 3.11.88, Solihull & S Heath :
SPB - 13.22
HIGGS Thomas U15 11.12.87, Brymore Sch :
HTB - 40.08, PenB - 2725
HIGHAM Keith Robert U17 7.11.85, Border :
PV - 4.80
HILL Andrew U15 3.12.87, R Sutton Coldfield :
80HB - 11.6/11.63
HILL Gareth 24.05.79, Ballymena & Antrim :
800 - 1:52.92
HILL Gavin U17 22.12.86, Middlesbro & C :
DTY - 42.82
HILL Liam U13, Victoria Park AAC :
TJ - 9.43
HILL Michael Christopher 22.10.64, Leeds :
JT - 82.90 (86.94-93)
HILL Richard U17 12.02.86, Notts :
800 - 1:57.9
HILL Walter V45 19.06.53, Crawley :
24Hr - 217.663km (216.650km-00)
HILLIER James 3.04.78, Birchfield :
60H - 8.50i (8.36i-01), 110H - 15.20,
400H - 51.02 (50.40-01)
HILTON Jonathan 11.01.74, Sale :
TJ - 15.10 (15.59w/15.42-00)

HILTON Martin 9.05.75, Leeds :
3k - 8:23.81 (8:16.17-01), 5k - 14:33.3,
HMar - 66:48, Mar - 2:20:54
HINES Damien U17 6.09.85, Skyrac :
DTY - 41.82
HINZE Alistair U17 25.09.85, Herne Hill :
LJ - 6.52i (6.72w-01/6.20-00)
HITCHENS Alex U17 12.12.86, Cornwall AC :
DTY - 41.71, HTY - 47.46
HOAD James U15 1.02.88, Enf & Har :
PV - 3.70, LJ - 5.98
HOAD Oliver U23 1.10.81, Cambridge & Colr'dge :
HT - 46.34
HOAD Paul Andrew 29.10.63, Enf & Har :
PV - 4.30 (5.01-86)
HOCKEDY Thomas U15 20.11.87, Somerset Sch :
400 - 52.49, TJ - 12.02w
HOCKIN Peter V40 16.05.61, Bideford :
Mar - 2:29:23
HODGES Robert Adam U15 5.12.87, Kingston u Hull :
800 - 2:03.88, 3k - 9:33.0
HODGKINSON Alex U20 1.12.84, Shaftesbury Barn :
1500 - 3:50.90
HODGSON Jason 21.02.73, Horwich :
10k - 31:52.37
HOEY Michael 29.04.69, Bournemouth :
3kSt - 9:41.2 (9:06.6-95)
HOGARTH Charles U17 11.02.86, Midd AC :
HTY - 53.11
HOLBOROW David U17 27.09.85, Dorset Sch :
LJ - 6.57
HOLDEN Oliver U17 30.05.86, Halesowen :
3k - 8:57.5 (8:56.36-01)
HOLDEN Tom U20 2.02.84, Tipton :
800 - 1:52.38
HOLDER Carlos U17 28.03.86, Trafford :
100 - 10.99, 200 - 22.15
HOLDER Graham Paul 16.01.72, Shaftesbury Barnet :
HT - 60.97 (61.91-99)
HOLGATE Andrew U17 16.08.86, Cwmbran :
100HY - 13.9/14.16
HOLLIDAY Adrian U17 17.01.87, Trafford :
1.5kSt - 4:33.5
HOLLIDAY Ian 9.12.73, Sale :
HJ - 2.14i/2.05 (2.16-98)
HOLLIER Steven 27.02.76, Wolverhampton & B :
2kW - 7:49.30, 3kW - 11:55.7 (11:35.5-97),
5kW - 20:36.0, 10kW - 44:52.0+ (42:57+-00/45:08.97-98),
10kWR - 42:47 (42:18+-00/42:29-95),
20kW - 1:31:09+t/1:33:11 (1:27:04t-00/1:28:34-99),
30kW - 2:28:32+ (2:18:31-01),
35kW - 2:54:24+ (2:52:47-99),
50kW - 4:14:33 (4:07:18-00)
HOLLOWAY Mark U20 6.10.83, Bracknell :
100 - 10.7w/10.75w/10.9/10.95, LJ - 6.80
HOLSGROVE Tim U23 11.12.82, Liv H/Bath Univ :
PV - 4.56
HONEY John U17 6.02.86, Cardiff :
HTY - 49.26
HONOUR Nathan 15.11.77, Woking :
100 - 10.7/10.76w/10.77 (10.7-01), 200 - 21.77 (21.7-99)
HOOSON-OWEN Glyn U20 22.01.85, Manx H :
DTJ - 43.21
HOOTON Robin David 5.05.73, City of Edinburgh :
800 - 1:50.7 (1:47.7-96), 1500 - 3:44.18
HOPE Kevin 18.04.78, Notts :
3kSt - 9:30.1
HOPKINS Joel 24.11.77, Enf & Har :
400H - 54.2/54.45 (54.0-01)
HOPKINSON Andrew U20 20.09.83, Sale :
110HJ - 14.64, 110H - 15.18w (15.6-01)
HOPLEY James Edward U17 28.01.87, Telford :
JTY - 51.60
HORNE Christopher U17 17.05.86, N Devon :
DTY - 42.52

HORSBURGH Ian Joseph 10.01.78, C of Edinburgh :
200 - 22.0 (21.50i/21.5w/21.61-97)
HORSBURGH Steven U15 11.11.87, Gateshead :
LJ - 5.87
HORSMAN James U17 27.09.85, Bedford & County :
1500 - 4:01.01, 3k - 8:54.08
HORTON Sam U15 2.04.88, Hereford :
PV - 3.00
HOUGHTON Ben U23 6.08.80, WSE&H/IRL :
JT - 71.85
HOUSDEN D., :
60 - 6.8i
HOUSLIN Livon V40 2.11.60, Thames Valley :
JT - 57.64 (63.92-92)
HOWARD Alex U13 28.08.90, Isle of Wight :
JTC - 36.79
HOWARD Paul 19.10.66, WGreen & Ex L :
JT - 60.85 (65.10-91)
HOWARTH Paul 30.10.77, Wirral :
3k - 8:22.86i (8:19.53i-01),
5k - 14:34.00i (14:39.64-00)
HOWE Christopher William 17.11.67, WGreen & E L :
HT - 63.58 (66.97-98)
HOWELL Tim U23 6.12.82, City of Stoke :
Dec - 5398 (5462-01)
HOYTE Gavin U13, WGreen & Ex L :
100 - 12.7
HUBBARD Louis U20 31.07.85, City of Norwich :
3kSt - 9:38.1
HUDSPITH Ian 23.09.70, Morpeth :
3k - 8:07.64 (8:03.9-95), 5k - 13:46.90,
10k - 28:46.40 (28:35.11-97),
10kR - 29:42 (28:17sh/29:08RL-96/29:09-97)
HUDSPITH Mark E. 19.01.69, Morpeth :
5k - 14:22.58+ (13:49.37-00),
10kR - 29:42 (29:14-94),
HMar - 64:17 (62:50dh-95/63:19-97)
HUGGINS Sam U17 30.11.85, AF&D :
100 - 11.10, 200 - 22.5
HUGHES Andrew 10.07.67, RAF/Shaftesbury Barnet :
100 - 10.84 (10.53w/10.57-00),
200 - 21.9/22.18 (21.3/21.31-98)
HUGHES Brian C. 6.01.70, Trafford :
Dec - 5578 (6105-00)
HUGHES David U20 31.05.84, Scunthorpe :
60H - 8.44i, 110H - 14.58w/14.77, LJ - 6.81w,
DecJ - 6370, DECJI - 6552
HUGHES David John U17 31.10.85, Leighton Buzz :
LJ - 6.67
HUGHES Ioan 8.10.78, Trafford :
LJ - 7.03 (7.22w/7.14-01)
HUGHES Kevin Michael 30.04.73, Newham & E B :
PV - 5.20 (5.61-99)
HUGHES Peter U20 12.12.83, Eyryi :
DTJ - 42.92
HUGHFF Christopher U23 5.12.81, Trafford/Army :
JT - 67.17
HULL Gregory 16.11.65, Leeds :
Mar - 2:31:57 (2:26:34-95)
HULSE G.Ewart W. V40 21.01.62, Colwyn Bay :
HT - 50.12 (54.62-91)
HULYER Matthew Joseph Thomas U20 20.06.84,
Ashford : LJ - 7.26w
HUMPHREY Peter U13 7.10.89, S London :
800 - 2:18.4
HUMPHRIES Bradley U15 21.09.88, Yeovil Oly :
80HB - 12.0
HUMPHRIES Tom U20 24.09.84, Cannock & Stafford :
3k - 8:33.01, 5k - 15:02.7
HUNT Douglas U13 3.12.89, Harrow :
400 - 61.2
HUNT Toby U17 28.12.86, WSE&H :
DTY - 42.67, OctY - 4620
HUNTER Roger 10.03.76, Skyrac :
DT - 40.74 (41.31-01)

HURREN Richard U20 24.09.83, Harrow/Falkirk/
S Clyde Un : PV - 4.90i/4.71
HURST David U15 25.10.87, Oldham & Royton :
100 - 11.39w/11.48, 200 - 22.93
HURST Lee 29.07.72, Belgrave :
3kSt - 9:10.11 (8:48.34-96)
HUSSAIN Bashir 20.12.64, Stockport/Riverside CC, USA :
5k - 14:42.98 (14:07.89-90),
10k - 31:01.84 (29:16.29-94), 3kSt - 9:17.99
HUTCHESON Peter U17 18.11.86, Crawley :
JTY - 54.50
HUTCHINSON Michael Innes 5.10.65, Trafford :
3kSt - 9:25.3 (8:50.61-92)
HUTTON Paul U20 20.12.84, Gosforth :
3k - 8:35.42
HYDE Timothy 22.02.72, WSE&H :
3kSt - 9:32.8 (9:06.66-96)
HYLTON Mark David 24.09.76, WSE&H :
200 - 21.5 (21.04i-97/21.09-95), 400 - 46.18 (45.24-98)

I BRAHIM Husseyin 13.05.68, Brighton & Hove AC :
Mar - 2:34:32
IDOWU Phillips Olaosebikan 30.12.78, Belgrave :
LJ - 7.79w/7.68 (7.83-00), TJ - 17.68
IGI Abdi U15 15.12.87, Ealing,Southall & Mx :
800 - 1:59.50, 1500 - 4:08.07, 3k - 9:28.88 (9:24.61-01)
ILIFFE Niklas U23 6.03.81, Team Solent :
DT - 48.47
INGHAM C. U17, Surrey Sch :
TJ - 13.18
INGRAM David U23 19.01.80, Brighton & Hove AC :
PV - 4.10 (4.20-98), Dec - 5102
IRVING Peter U20 28.01.83, Channel Islands :
110HJ - 14.75w/14.93,
110H - 15.17w/15.5 (15.31-01), 400H - 54.25
IRWIN Stephen U17 16.05.86, Pitreavie :
1.5kSt - 4:32.74
ISZATT Adrian M. 6.03.66, Rowheath :
Mar - 2:35:09
IVEMY Craig U17 28.03.86, Hailsham :
1500 - 4:01.6, 3k - 8:38.43

J ACKSON Colin Ray 18.02.67, Brecon :
60H - 7.40i (7.30i-94),
110H - 13.11 (12.8w-90/12.91-93)
JACKSON Edward U23 4.01.82, AF&D/Notts Univ :
1500 - 3:48.34
JACKSON Graham U17 11.12.85, Gateshead :
LJ - 6.93w/6.70, TJ - 14.45w/14.40
JACKSON James U15 20.02.88, Halesowen :
LJ - 5.89w
JACOBS Sam U20 19.09.84, Ipswich :
3k - 8:36.12, 5k - 14:54.18
JAMES Alan V40 26.03.62, WSE&H :
HT - 51.88
JAMES Robert U17 1.04.87, Birchfield :
100HY - 13.75
JAMES Ronnie 14.12.64, Cornwall AC :
Mar - 2:29:42 (2:25:33-97)
JAMES Ryan U20 10.05.85, Stratford :
LJ - 6.99
JAMIESON Steven 4.02.79, Shaftesbury B/Loughbro :
JT - 57.04 (60.94-00)
JANES Matt U23 12.12.82, Bedford & Co/Brunel Un :
3k - 8:23.12, 5k - 14:42.0
JANVIER Nick 9.08.70, :
Mar - 2:27:10
JARRETT Anthony Alexander 13.08.68, Enf & Har :
60H - 7.92i (7.42i-95), 110H - 13.40 (13.00-93)
JEAN-THEODORE Oliver 13.11.74, Birchfield/FRA :
400 - 47.28
JEFFERSON Chris U17 9.07.87, Durham Sch :
TJ - 13.66
JEGEDE Samuel U17 3.10.85, Newham & Essex B :
LJ - 6.97w/6.62

JEMI-ALADE Michael 13.10.64, City of Edinburgh :
DT - 45.49 (52.38-87)
JENNINGS Neil A. 18.09.77, Trafford/Newcastle Un :
400 - 48.50 (46.91-01)
JENNS Scott U23 13.12.80, Tipton :
DT - 44.12
JOHN Alwin 7.01.79, Tipton :
100 - 10.8
JOHN Royden 6.09.72, Hercules Wimbledon/RSA :
110H - 15.4
JOHNSON Allandre U17 8.12.85, Herne Hill :
JTY - 57.74
JOHNSON Andrew U17 13.05.86, Blackheath :
400HY - 58.0
JOHNSON Kim Luis Ferreira U13 22.01.90, B'mouth :
80HC - 14.19, SPC - 11.02
JOHNSON Michael U15 19.09.87, Enf & Har :
80HB - 11.59w/12.0 (12.0-01)
JOHNSON Michael U17 25.09.85, Grantham :
PV - 3.80
JOHNSON Nathan U17, Halesowen :
PV - 3.60
JOHNSON Peter 25.09.75, Liverpool H :
JT - 58.36 (62.76-96)
JOHNSON Robert U17 10.07.86, London Schools :
HJ - 1.90
JOHNSON Samuel U15 20.06.88, Reading :
DTB - 39.17
JOHNSON Tyson U17 24.06.87, Halesowen :
JTY - 56.74
JOHNSTON Cameron B. U23 22.10.82, Croy/Surr Un :
PV - 4.80i/4.80
JOHNSTON Ian James 12.02.68, Thames Valley :
Mar - 2:36:08
JONES Andres 3.02.77, Cardiff :
3k - 8:24.08 (7:54.12-00), 5k - 14:03.56 (13:39.43-00),
10k - 28:43.93 (28:00.50-00)
JONES Andrew 10.10.78, Salford :
10kR - 30:06, HMar - 66:48
JONES Ben U23 6.11.82, Milton Keynes :
HT - 46.14
JONES Ben U17 14.01.86, Liv.Pembroke Sefton :
1500 - 4:02.11, 3k - 8:53.32 (8:52.51-01)
JONES David U15 5.11.87, Belfast Sch :
PenB - 2660
JONES Egryn 1.11.71, Cardiff :
PV - 4.80 (4.90-95)
JONES Gary 6.01.72, WSE&H :
60 - 6.91i (6.91i-00), 100 - 10.75 (10.60w-01/10.7-97),
200 - 21.8 (21.59w-01/21.6-00/21.76-01)
JONES J., Bournemouth :
LJ - 6.93
JONES Jamie U13 16.10.89, Barry :
100 - 12.4, LJ - 5.07
JONES Jonathan Garfield 12.09.74, Bournemouth :
LJ - 6.93 (6.95-91)
JONES Kris U20 7.03.83, Newport :
110HJ - 14.77w/15.00, 110H - 14.83w/15.2/15.21
JONES Louis Evling U20 20.07.83, Corby :
HJ - 1.95
JONES Michael David 23.07.63, Belgrave :
HT - 73.99 (76.43-01)
JONES Miles U15 17.12.87, Shaftesbury Barnet :
80HB - 11.44
JONES Nick 10.07.74, Tipton :
10kR - 29:54 (29:27-99), HMar - 63:25 (63:12-00)
JONES Owen U15 2.09.87, Carmarthen :
80HB - 11.79, TJ - 12.50
JONES Paul 11.04.78, Stoke :
PV - 4.18 (4.76i-01/4.75-99),
LJ - 7.03w/6.86 (7.03-01), Dec - 6712 (7071-00)
JONES Rhodri 14.08.66, Westbury/Yate :
Mar - 2:22:54 (2:18:34-00)
JOSEPH Cleophuis 11.09.79, Army :
60 - 6.9i

JOSEPH Jason U17 27.11.85, Enf & Har :
SPY - 15.07, DTY - 46.36,
HT - 45.60, HTJ - 53.97, HTY - 61.08
JOSEPH Rafer Ernest Lewis 21.07.68, Bas & MH :
DT - 42.46 (52.00-96)
JOUSIFFE Warren 27.05.77, WSE&H :
PV - 4.20 (4.70-96)
JUBB Michael 20.06.70, Derby & Co :
Mar - 2:28:09
JUDSON Paul U17 20.06.86, Cannock & Stafford :
100 - 11.09, 200 - 22.1/22.31w/22.34,
400 - 50.67
JUKES Robert U20 18.09.83, Basingstoke & MH :
DTJ - 45.87
JULIEN Christopher U15 14.09.87, Enf & Har :
100 - 11.17, 200 - 23.0/23.10

KACOU Alain U15 25.10.88, Herne Hill :
TJ - 12.49i/12.15
KANEEN Peter V40 12.07.61, Manx H :
3kW - 12:42.2, 10kWR - 45:02 (47:12-01),
20kW - 1:38:27 (1:38:26-99),
30kW - 2:36:50+, 50kW - 4:35:31
KANONIK Nick U15 24.10.87, Cheltenham :
200 - 23.59
KARAGOUNIS Leon 15.10.75, Notts/Notts Univ/GRE :
JT - 58.63 (61.75-01)
KAVANAGH Samuel U15 1.11.87, Sale :
100 - 11.60, 200 - 23.15, 400 - 52.21
KEARNS Martin 6.04.73, Newham & Essex B/IRL :
3kSt - 9:33.30 (9:12.12-00)
KEATING Scott U17 24.10.86, Havering M :
HJ - 1.90
KEATON T., Serpentine :
LJ - 6.88
KEEP Matthew U13 14.07.90, Walton :
JTC - 35.87
KELLEY John U20 6.08.84, Newark :
200 - 21.9/22.14 (21.8w/21.89w-01
KELLIE Peter U20 2.01.84, Gloucester AC :
2kSt - 5:49.10, 3kSt - 9:24.0 (9:22.7-01)
KELLY Andrew U15 15.11.87, Liverpool H :
400 - 51.94
KELLY Bryan 29.12.73, Trafford :
SP - 16.80, DT - 53.72
KELLY Kieran U17 14.02.86, Team Solent :
SPY - 15.93
KELLY Matthew U23 4.12.80, Herne Hill :
Dec - 5169
KELLY Sean Robert 8.11.72, Rown/Kingston & Poly :
800 - 1:51.8 (1:49.9-95)
KELSEY Ben U20 23.09.84, Oxford City :
DTJ - 43.06
KELVEY Sam U17 12.07.86, Notts :
JTY - 60.66
KENNARD Andrew 2.01.66, Walton :
400H - 55.97 (53.1-95/53.58-90)
KENNEDY Ian U20 1.10.83, Ayr Seaforth/Shaft B :
100 - 10.8/10.83w/10.85
KERR Benjamin U17 1.05.86, Shetland :
OctY - 4435
KERR Eric 9.12.64, Luton :
HT - 47.18 (54.58-95)
KERR Glen 27.10.74, Bedford & County :
HT - 60.56 (61.48-01)
KERR Hugh 4.01.76, Ayr Seaforth :
400 - 49.14i (47.69i/47.75-95),
800 - 1:52.94i (1:52.2-01)
KERRY Philip U20 19.03.83, Cov G/Birmingham Un :
60 - 6.96i, 100 - 10.8/10.90w (11.91-97)
KESKA Karl 7.05.72, Birchfield :
5k - 13:20.30, 10k - 28:01.72 (27:44.09-00),
10kR - 29:22 (28:39-99)
KETELEERS Luke U15 8.01.88, Chelmsford :
80HB - 11.80, PenB - 2511

370

KHAN Kamran U20 2.10.83, Sale :
 HT - 49.49 (51.20-01), HTJ - 55.26, HT6K - 57.83
KIDGER Joel U23 16.03.80, Crawley/Loughbro :
 800 - 1:47.82, 1500 - 3:43.30
KILTY Richard U13 2.09.89, Midd AC :
 75 - 9.9
KIMTAI Julius, Tipton/KEN :
 10kR - 28:47, Mar - 2:18:13
KING Andrew U15 19.07.88, Harrow :
 PV - 3.10
KING Daniel U20 30.05.83, Colchester H :
 3kW - 12:20.46, 5kW - 21:46.29, 10kW - 44:06.6,
 10kWR - 44:51, 20kW - 1:37:50
KING Dominic U20 30.05.83, Colchester H :
 3kW - 12:00.99i/12:22.27,
 5kW - 20:48.1+ (21:25.17i-00/21:50.48-01),
 10kW - 42:17.1, 10kWR - 42:21, 20kW - 1:29:48
KINGMAN Robert 21.02.73, Newham & Essex B/RAF :
 PV - 4.20 (5.02-94)
KINGSBERRY Jon U15 19.03.88, Regent House :
 DTB - 38.50, HTB - 42.60
KINGWELL Damien U15 6.07.88, Ashford :
 SPB - 14.24
KIRK Christopher U17 6.09.85, Wakefield :
 PV - 3.60, LJ - 7.06w/6.83,
 DecY - 5761, OctY - 4627
KIRK Neil 14.09.78, Med & Maid/Michigan Univ :
 800 - 1:51.35 (1:49.57-98), 1500 - 3:48.53 (3:46.89-01),
 1M - 4:03.45i (4:02.83iot-01)
KISSI Sam U15 16.02.88, Herne Hill :
 400 - 53.4
KNIGHT Andrew G. 26.10.68, Cambridge Harriers :
 800 - 1:51.20 (1:48.38-94)
KNIGHTS Christopher U17 17.10.85, Peterborough :
 800 - 1:58.3, 1500 - 4:00.2, 3k - 8:49.84
KNOTT Neil 6.02.70, Wolverhampton & B :
 HT - 45.52
KNOX-HOOKE Jacob U20 11.04.85, Enf & Har :
 HJ - 1.95
KRUGER Alexander Eaton 18.11.63, Sheffield :
 PV - 4.20 (4.90-95), SP - 13.34 (14.76-94),
 DT - 41.38 (45.46-96)
KRUSZEWSKI Andrew P. V40 7.04.59, Cambridge H :
 DT - 46.35 (51.26-92)
KYEREME Kojo 23.12.74, Shaftesbury Barnet :
 1500 - 3:50.04i/3:54.0 (3:49.90-01), 5k - 14:10.06

LAING Calum U20 21.08.83, Central :
 110HJ - 15.13w/15.4, 110H - 15.38w/15.63
LAKELAND Kierran U15 10.02.88, Team Solent :
 HJ - 1.76
LAMB Josh U20 14.04.83, Crawley/Bath Univ :
 SPJ - 14.45, DT - 43.10, DTJ - 48.17
LAMBERT Christopher Patrick U23 6.04.81, Bel/Harv :
 60 - 6.73i, 100 - 10.19w/10.28 (10.24-01),
 200 - 20.37
LAMBERT Toby 31.08.79, Alton :
 Mar - 2:34:03
LAMBLEY Matthew U15 18.09.87, Sheffield :
 HTY - 58.07, HTB - 64.70
LAMMIE Graeme U23 3.10.81, S B/Perth/Glasgow U :
 400H - 54.7/55.38
LANCASHIRE Thomas U20 2.07.85, Bolton :
 800 - 1:52.2, 1500 - 3:48.91
LANE Nathaniel G. 10.04.76, Cardiff :
 3k - 8:24.63 (8:13.39i-00/8:19.22-99),
 5k - 14:25.85 (13:58.44-00),
 10k - 30:43.06 (29:01.17-99)
LAPSINS Gareth U17 5.07.87, Blackpool :
 PV - 3.60
LARNER Chris U15 20.01.88, Stroud :
 400 - 53.7
LASHORE Akinola 28.03.73, Blackheath :
 60 - 6.65i/6.7i,
 100 - 10.70 (10.35A-99/10.38r-00/10.4-98/10.44-97)

LASLETT Paul U23 12.05.80, AF&D :
 800 - 1:51.86
LATHAM Mark U20 13.05.85, Liverpool H :
 HJ - 1.95i (1.95-01)
LAU Jordon U20 23.09.83, Chelmsford :
 LJ - 7.08w/6.95 (7.21-00)
LAW Alexander U13 14.10.89, Taunton :
 75HC - 12.7, 80HC - 13.2
LAWRENCE Benjamin Thomas David U17 13.04.86,
 Cann & St : SPJ - 13.77, SPY - 15.66, HTY - 48.51
LAWRENCE Mark 26.01.71, Notts :
 LJ - 6.99 (7.33-93), TJ - 14.17 (14.76w/14.67-01)
LAWRENCE Tim U20 31.03.84, Derby & Co :
 3kSt - 9:37.0
LAWS Oliver U23 18.03.80, Telford/Loughbro :
 1500 - 3:47.09, 3k - 8:11.72, 5k - 14:13.7
LAWS Richard 8.10.75, Hastings :
 HJ - 1.97 (2.10-95)
LAWTON Nathan U17 3.11.86, City of Stoke :
 PV - 3.80
LAY Graham 13.11.75, Scarborough :
 JT - 54.90 (63.14-94)
LEADER Steven 24.11.66, Enf & Har :
 PV - 4.20 (4.90-90)
LEAVEY Nick U17 27.08.86, Ashford :
 200 - 22.3, 400 - 48.96
LECKENBY Sean U17 26.09.86, Midd AC :
 JTY - 51.15
LEDGER Matthew U23 23.11.81, Univ Wales I Card :
 Dec - 4919
LEE Christian U17 19.02.87, Nene Valley H :
 100 - 11.1
LEE Gordon 28.03.67, Nuneaton :
 5k - 14:42.5
LEE James 6.02.79, WSE&H :
 400H - 53.81
LEES Simon 19.11.79, Solihull & S Heath :
 400 - 48.3 (48.87i-01/49.08-00),
 800 - 1:47.60 (1:47.35-01)
LEITCH Ian U20 12.07.84, Pitreavie :
 HJ - 1.95i (1.95-01)
LEITCH Mark 17.11.68, Army/Shaftesbury Barnet :
 SP - 13.84 (15.57i-00/14.72-99)
LEMONCELLO Andrew U23 12.10.82, Fife/Stirling U :
 3kSt - 9:17.1 (9:04.41-01)
LEONARD Daniel Jason U20 3.01.84, Milton Keynes :
 HJ - 2.05
LEVETT William 6.09.75, Vauxhall :
 3k - 8:15.89, 5k - 14:16.61,
 10k - 29:51.64, 10kR - 29:39
LEVY Noel 22.06.75, Belgrave :
 400 - 48.73 (47.8-92/47.82-93),
 110H - 15.16 (14.52w/14.55-00), 400H - 51.04 (50.70-94)
LEWIS Andrew 9.03.68, Harrow :
 110H - 15.48 (14.67w/14.8-94/14.87-01),
 LJ - 7.12 (7.54-97), SP - 13.54 (14.21i-01/14.10-98)
LEWIS Benjamin U23 6.03.81, Birchfield :
 100 - 10.8w/10.98 (10.58-01),
 200 - 21.63i (20.80w/21.32-99)
LEWIS Daniel U20 16.10.83, Shaftesbury Barnet :
 2kSt - 5:58.44, 3kSt - 9:19.15
LEWIS David U13 8.11.89, Shaftesbury Barnet :
 LJ - 5.04
LEWIS Darren U17 12.04.86, Tipton :
 100HY - 13.78, 110HJ - 14.8w, 400HY - 56.45
LEWIS Ieuan U15 27.11.87, Stevenage & NH :
 80HB - 11.79
LEWIS Junior 19.03.66, Herts Phoenix :
 TJ - 14.05 (14.84-96)
LEWIS Marlon U20 7.09.83, Rowheath :
 LJ - 7.47w/7.43
LEWIS Robert 2.09.78, Bedford & County :
 300 - 34.7, 400H - 53.0 (51.29-00)
LEWIS Sean U15 10.09.87, City of Stoke :
 HTB - 53.64

LEWIS Steven U17 20.05.86, City of Stoke :
PV - 4.65
LEWIS-FRANCIS Mark U23 4.09.82, Birchfield :
50 - 5.73i+, 60 - 6.53i (6.51i-01),
100 - 9.97w/10.04 (9.97w?-01), 200 - 20.94
LIGHTFOOT Robert U17 7.09.85, Wrexham :
400 - 49.84, 800 - 1:57.7
LINDLEY Ian V45 3.12.55, Bingley :
SP - 13.38i (17.87i/17.58-81)
LINDSAY Mark Stephen U20 5.11.84, Wakefield :
JT - 54.68
LINGARD Andrew U23 12.09.81, Basildon :
3kSt - 9:40.1 (9:29.14-00)
LINSKEY Christian U23 14.06.80, Shaftesbury B :
PV - 5.00 (5.21i-99/5.20-98)
LIPMAN Paul U17 2.09.85, Shaftesbury Barnet :
800 - 1:56.3
LITTLE David Andrew U23 28.02.81, Border :
HT - 57.26 (59.15-01)
LITTLE John M. V45 14.04.53, Border :
DT - 40.61 (43.70-95)
LIVESEY Christopher James U23 8.08.80, Preston :
1500 - 3:46.58 (3:45.3-99)
LIVINGSTONE Andrew U15 3.05.88, Thurrock :
1500 - 4:10.65, 3k - 8:57.5
LIVINGSTONE Stuart 29.08.79, City of Edinburgh :
HJ - 2.05 (2.08i-97/2.06-98)
LLEWELLYN Anthony U20 21.12.83, Team Solent :
JT - 56.52
LLOYD Joseph 9.04.73, Swansea/Cheltenham :
400H - 53.28
LLOYD Martin Andrew U23 18.06.80, Bexley :
110H - 15.6, HJ - 2.10i/2.10 (2.15i/2.15-98),
Dec - 6008 (6030-01)
LOADER Joe 21.07.73, Bristol Univ./Highgate H :
Mar - 2:25:21
LOBB Huw 29.08.76, Bedford & County :
5k - 14:43.7, Mar - 2:21:16,
3kSt - 9:12.4 (9:05.77-01)
LOBO Jason 18.09.69, Belgrave :
800 - 1:50.97 (1:45.82-99), 1500 - 3:50.14 (3:44.06-99)
LOCKWOOD Bobby U17 1.02.86, Cambridge H :
SPY - 15.02, DTY - 47.90
LOLE Matthew U20 23.01.83, Coventry Godiva :
5k - 14:44.0
LONG Jonathan U17 4.10.86, WGreen & Ex L :
400HY - 58.54
LOUTH Jake U23 20.05.82, Boston TC :
DT - 41.15
LOVE Matthew Alexander Royston U20 28.12.84,
WSE&H : 110HJ - 15.0
LOVETT Anthony U23 20.09.82, Enf & Har :
JT - 63.21
LOVETT David 13.09.78, Portsmouth/St. Marys U Col :
SP - 14.15 (15.06-00), DT - 47.56 (52.97-01)
LOW Charles 9.10.74, Shaftesbury Barnet :
2kSt - 5:48.29, 3kSt - 8:44.4 (8:37.63-00)
LOWE Ricahrd U23 7.07.81, Newton Abbot :
HJ - 1.97
LOWERY James U23 17.10.80, WGreen & Ex L :
110H - 15.22, PV - 4.20, Dec - 6688
LOWNDES William Peter U17 10.10.86, :
SPY - 14.38
LOWTHIAN Ian U23 10.10.80, Sale :
400 - 47.35 (47.11-99)
LUCKWELL Mervyn U20 27.11.84, Milton Keynes :
DTJ - 42.39
LUMM Matthew U13, Basildon :
400 - 61.2
LUND Simon N. 22.12.65, Woodstock R :
Mar - 2:32:52 (2:27:39-94)
LUNDMAN Jonathan U23 7.12.81, Newham & E B :
JT - 65.71
LYNAS Matt, Thames H & H :
100kR - 7:42:08

MACDONALD Daniel Robert U17 12.09.85,
Bournemouth : HJ - 2.00
MACFARLANE Andrew U20 28.03.83, Leeds/
Loughbro : HJ - 2.06
MACHIN Andrew U13, Wolverhampton & B :
80HC - 14.31
MACKAY Allan U13 25.03.90, Shettleston :
DTC - 27.32
MACKAY Craig U20 30.10.84, Perth :
110HJ - 15.4
MACKENZIE Alisdair U17, :
150 - 17.33
MACKIE Ian 27.02.75, Pitreavie :
100 - 10.38 (10.00w-98/10.17-96),
200 - 21.6 (20.68w-00/20.85-01)
MACLEAN Angus U23 20.09.80, Team Solent :
800 - 1:48.82, 1500 - 3:41.61 (3:39.88-01),
3k - 8:04.36, 10kR - 29:53
MADDEN Michael J. 13.09.65, Newquay & Par :
HT - 47.29 (55.92-93)
MADDY Emeka U20 19.12.84, Herne Hill :
HJ - 1.95 (1.95-01)
MADEIRA-COLE Charles H. 29.11.77, Newham & EB :
TJ - 15.43w/15.22 (15.86w-01/15.82i/15.79-98)
MAHONY Olly U20 21.10.83, Liverpool H :
110H - 15.49w, PV - 4.45
MAITLAND Matthew David Robert U20 27.08.83,
Aberdeen : HT6K - 48.83
MAITLAND Peter 21.01.73, Swansea :
SP - 14.45
MAITLAND Tim U17 5.12.86, Harrow :
HJ - 2.00
MAJEKODUNMI Semi U20 29.06.83, Belgrave :
TJ - 14.27 (14.52-01)
MAJOR Stuart 5.05.70, Newham & Essex B :
10k - 31:15.5 (30:51.12-01)
MALCOLM Anthony 15.02.76, Cardiff/Loughbro :
LJ - 6.81i (7.55-00)
MALCOLM Christian Sean 3.06.79, Cardiff :
50 - 5.81i+, 100 - 10.29 (10.09w?/10.11-01),
60 - 6.67i (6.64i-01), 200 - 20.29w/20.30 (20.08-01)
MALEY Gavin 19.05.78, Havering M :
800 - 1:51.6
MALIN Darren U20 19.06.85, Belgrave :
5k - 15:08.65
MALINS Duncan 12.06.78, Newham & Essex B :
110H - 14.25 (14.08w/14.10-00)
MALLOCH Ewan 4.08.76, Shaftesbury Barnet :
3kSt - 9:21.45 (8:54.70-99)
MALONE Ian 17.03.64, Ackw RR. :
Mar - 2:25:10
MALONE-LEE Francis U23 3.03.80, Cambridge Un :
3kSt - 9:35.7 (9:27.9-00)
MAMMANA Matthew U13 20.09.90, AF&D :
LJ - 5.01
MANDY Mark 19.11.72, Birchfield/IRL :
HJ - 2.15i/2.10 (2.26i-97/2.25-95)
MANN Philip U17 25.10.85, Barnsley :
JTY - 56.51
MANVELL Lee U23 11.12.80, Bournemouth :
Dec - 5938
MANVILLE Gerald 21.12.78, Crawley/Army :
400H - 55.7, PV - 4.30, Dec - 5814
MARAR Leith A. 7.11.68, Belgrave :
DT - 42.76 (55.68-96)
MARCHETTA Marco U15 6.10.87, Enf & Har :
SPB - 13.10
MARCHMENT Carl U23 30.12.82, Basingstoke & MH :
Dec - 5924 (6048-01)
MARKHAM Gregory 28.11.78, Rotherham :
JT - 56.17 (60.86-98)
MARLOW Steven U20 13.12.84, Shaftesbury Barnet :
DTJ - 42.39
MARRAUD Matthew U23 15.01.82, Thames Valley :
200 - 22.0

372

MARSH Andrew U13 26.01.90, City of Stoke :
PV - 2.90, JTC - 38.42
MARSH Brett 20.01.76, Newquay & Par :
SP - 13.84, HT - 46.36 (47.98-99)
MARSHALL Guy Richard ¶ 24.09.71, Birchfield :
SP - 15.84 (16.65-98), DT - 41.44 (42.55-99)
MARSHALL James U23 6.02.81, Dudley & Stourb :
200 - 21.98
MARSHALL Miles U15 20.02.88, Herne Hill :
100 - 11.5/11.59, 200 - 23.3/23.32
MARSHALL Stuart U23 2.12.80, Coventry Godiva :
400 - 48.9/49.48 (48.6/48.98-01)
MARTEAU David U17 31.12.86, Liverpool H :
1.5kSt - 4:35.36
MARTIN Daniel U23 9.03.82, Southampton City :
HT - 50.05
MARTIN Gordon 16.07.68, SGA (Prof) :
SP - 13.84
MARTIN Lee 21.05.64, Rossendale :
Mar - 2:34:49 (2:31:34-98)
MARTIN Nathan U20 10.05.84, Shaftesbury Barnet :
100 - 10.8/10.97w (11.59age?-00)
MARTIN Paul 10.07.78, Tonbridge :
3kSt - 9:34.14
MARTIN Wayne Daniel 12.08.76, WGreen & Ex L :
400 - 48.1/48.48 (48.07-99)
MARTYN Nicholas 28.09.63, Highgate Harriers :
Mar - 2:30:18
MASON James U20 12.03.83, Cambridge University :
5k - 15:29.8
MASON Kieran U15 26.11.87, Milton Keynes :
DTB - 38.96, HTB - 41.59
MASSINGHAM Gavin U23 4.10.82, Sunderland :
800 - 1:51.32
MATTHEWS Andrew U20 26.10.84, WSE&H :
60 - 6.88i, 100 - 10.8/10.82w/10.98 (10.93-01), 200 - 22.0
MATTHEWS Gary M. V40 9.04.60, East Cheshire :
Mar - 2:34:27 (2:22:32-92)
MATTHEWS Graeme U17 21.06.86, Wirral :
TJ - 13.13
MATTHEWS Owain U23 4.11.81, Vauxhall/Un of Tulsa :
5k - 14:42.55, 3kSt - 9:02.65
MATTIS Anthony U17 25.03.86, Bristol :
TJ - 13.49w
MAXFIELD Jason U15 28.03.88, Rotherham :
1500 - 4:18.36, 3k - 9:37.2
MAY Curtis U20 28.01.84, Herne Hill :
LJ - 6.82, TJ - 14.40i/14.36w/14.31
MAY Daniel 27.06.71, Epsom & Ewell :
100 - 10.8
MAY Richard U17 10.12.85, Donc & Stain :
SPY - 14.03
MAYNARD Daniel U15 4.12.87, Charnwood :
100 - 11.48, 200 - 23.52, 80HB - 10.87, 100HY - 13.71
MAYNARD Darrell StClair V40 21.08.61, Abertil/Bir :
400 - 48.74 (48.18-00), 800 - 1:52.70 (1:49.5a-88)
MAYNARD Joseph U20 25.07.85, Cwmbran :
800 - 1:54.29, 400H - 55.86
MAYO James 24.02.75, Cannock & Stafford/Army :
800 - 1:49.50 (1:48.2-96), 1M - 4:06.09 (4:05.4-96)
MAYO M., Wessex & Bath :
HT - 48.75
MAYO Thomas 2.05.77, Cannock & Stafford :
800 - 1:48.17, 1500 - 3:40.25 (3:38.3+/3:38.34-01),
1M - 4:03.57 (3:55.57-01),
3k - 8:06.3 (8:00.62-01)
MAYOCK John Paul 26.10.70, Barnsley :
1500 - 3:34.89 (3:31.86-97),
1M - 3:55.85 (3:50.32-96),
3k - 7:41.09i/8:00.50 (7:47.28-95),
2M - 8:17.06i (8:32.54-91), 5k - 13:19.43
MAYS Jermaine U23 23.12.82, Kent :
800 - 1:50.5, 1500 - 3:48.15, 3kSt - 8:46.48
MCADAMS Phil U15 15.09.87, Chelmsford :
3k - 9:35.2

MCADOREY John 16.09.74, Border/B & A/IRL :
100 - 10.34w/10.45 (10.28w-00), 200 - 21.34w (21.21-00)
MCALLISTER Joe U23 23.12.80, Loughbro/IRL :
5k - 14:33.05 (14:19.31-01)
MCCABE Chris U15 25.09.87, Shaftesbury Barnet :
SPB - 13.11
MCCALLA Isacc U23 28.03.82, Harrow :
110H - 15.0w?/15.17
MCCALLUM Jonathan 19.11.75, Croydon :
800 - 1:49.90, 1500 - 3:39.57 (3:37.75-00)
MCCARTHY Alex U15, Devon Sch :
80HB - 11.8
MCCLEERY William U13, :
100 - 12.73
MCCLOSKEY Paul U20 9.05.85, Pitreavie :
3kSt - 9:45.2
MCCLUSKEY Mark U17 19.07.86, Whitemoss :
100HY - 14.1/14.20
MCCONKEY Michael U20 5.12.84, North Down :
DecJ - 5283
MCCONNELL Kieran U15 13.10.87, Milton Keynes :
DTB - 43.77, HTB - 41.85
MCCONVILLE Brendan 3.01.79, Liverpool H :
110H - 15.32, HJ - 2.00 (2.02-98), PV - 4.55,
LJ - 6.82 (6.87w-99), Dec - 7076
MCCORMICK Nicholas U23 11.09.81, WG & EL/
Northumbria Univ : 800 - 1:51.51,
1500 - 3:42.73, 3k - 8:09.01
MCCOURT Colin U20 11.12.84, Bournemouth :
800 - 1:51.40, 1500 - 3:44.67, 3k - 8:28.36
MCCREA Mark U15 17.09.87, Lagan Valley :
HJ - 1.76
MCCULLOCH Jacob U15 21.12.87, WSE&H :
800 - 2:02.4
MCCULLOUGH Alan 9.08.63, North Belfast :
Mar - 2:34:35 (2:29:18-00)
MCDADE Jason U23 3.04.80, WGreen & Ex L :
110H - 15.3/15.39 (14.8w/14.90w/15.01-01),
HJ - 2.05 (2.16i-99/2.15-98),
SP - 13.58, Dec - 6350 (6774-99)
MCDERMID Liam U20 23.11.84, Victoria PAAC/IRL :
200 - 21.92w/22.08i (21.87-01), 400 - 49.38 (48.78-01)
MCDIARMID Alistair U17 16.10.85, Harrogate :
SPY - 14.69i/14.18, DTJ - 44.98,
DTY - 51.45, HTY - 54.13
MCDIARMID Scott U23 15.11.80, Pitreavie/Stirling U :
400 - 48.7/48.80
MCDONALD Callum U17 30.04.86, Mansfield :
JTY - 52.04
MCDONALD Denzil 11.10.65, Newham & Essex B :
SP - 14.31 (16.10-94), DT - 50.98 (55.04-95)
MCDONALD Michael John Joseph 24.08.65,
Ballymena & Antrim/Border/Queen's Univ/IRL :
TJ - 14.44w/14.10 (15.78-94)
MCDONALD Richard U23 11.01.80, Shaft B/Perth :
400 - 48.57 (47.67-01), 110H - 15.53,
400H - 50.83 (50.70-01)
MCDONNELL Stephen U23 24.07.80, Shaft B/IRL :
110H - 14.59, 400H - 51.45
MCEVOY Stephen 23.05.63, Met. Police :
HT - 51.21 (57.14-96)
MCEWAN Alex U15 8.12.87, :
JTB - 45.78
MCEWAN Carl U23 9.04.81, Newport/Un Wales Newp :
400 - 49.05 (48.92-00)
MCFALL David U23 15.10.80, Brecon/UWIC :
PV - 4.25
MCFARLANE Jim 16.06.79, Cambridge University :
JT - 59.27
MCGARRITY Chris U13 7.09.89, Shettleston :
800 - 2:18.0, 1500 - 4:42.7
MCGARVA Adrian 17.12.74, Ealing,S & Mx/AUS :
800 - 1:52.72
MCGAUGHEY James 4.12.73, Kent :
Mar - 2:29:55

373

MCGEOCH Michael I. V45 15.08.55, Les Croupiers :
Mar - 2:36:21 (2:17:58-83)
MCGINLEY Edward U20 29.01.83, Annadale Striders :
3k - 8:37.04, 5k - 14:54.42
MCGLORY Philip U20 2.09.83, Liverpool H :
5k - 15:23.0 (15:18.69-01)
MCGREGOR David V45 12.06.56, Serpentine :
Mar - 2:30:50
MCILROY Benjamin U20 2.09.83, Lisburn :
DecJ - 5490
MCILROY James 30.12.76, WSE&H/Abbey :
400 - 48.35, 800 - 1:45.52 (1:45.32-98),
1500 - 3:42.84
MCILWHAM John 29.02.72, Blackpool :
400H - 54.7 (52.7/52.80-99)
MCINTOSH Leslie U23 25.02.81, Liverpool H :
HT - 47.30 (52.09-00)
MCKAY David U23 22.09.80, W Cheshire :
JT - 60.56 (63.18-00)
MCKEE Paul 15.10.77, Border/IRL :
200 - 20.81, 300 - 34.5, 400 - 45.58
MCKENZIE Alistair U17 15.04.86, East Kilbride :
100 - 11.06w
MCKENZIE Ian U23 3.07.81, Invercl/Bel/Glasgow U :
PV - 4.10i (4.41-01)
MCKEOWN Paul U20 23.01.83, Brighton & Hove AC :
110HJ - 15.09
MCKERNAN Michael 28.11.78, Coventry Godiva :
TJ - 16.01w?/15.12 (15.49-01)
MCKEVITT Scott U15 15.09.87, Peterborough :
PV - 2.85, HTB - 45.96
MCKINNEY Patrick, Lisburn/IRL :
Mar - 2:29:57
MCKOWN David U20 27.02.84, Liverpool H :
JT - 56.81
MCLAGGON Calvin U17 13.11.85, Barry :
100 - 11.08, 200 - 22.25
MCLAUGHLIN John, Springburn :
100kR - 7:54:32
MCLEAN Colm U23 7.06.80, Liverpool H/IRL :
1500 - 3:41.79 (3:40.42-00), 3k - 8:20.9
MCLEAN-FOREMAN Alasdair James U23 10.11.81,
Belgrave/Harvard : 800 - 1:52.15 (1:49.84-01),
1500 - 3:47.53, 1M - 4:06.47i
MCLELLAN Neil 10.09.78, Stevenage & NH :
JT - 66.33 (68.78-01)
MCLENNAN Stephen 17.11.78, WSE&H :
PV - 4.40 (4.70-96)
MCMASTER Colin U23 15.01.80, Shaft B/Law & Dist :
HJ - 2.00 (2.15-97)
MCMILLAN Stewart 12.09.69, Sale/Pitreavie :
JT - 60.01 (64.02-96)
MCMULLAN Iain George 15.06.78, Lisburn/Ulster Un/
Trafford : SP - 17.61
MCNAMARA Ryan U17 17.06.86, Luton :
100HY - 13.55
MCNEILL Andrew 2.12.65, Long Eaton :
Mar - 2:36:15
MCNEILL Mark U23 19.10.82, Bristol :
200 - 21.99
MCNEILLIS Oliver Frederick U15 24.11.87, Hales :
80HB - 11.48, HJ - 1.81, LJ - 6.43, PenB - 3081
MCNIEL Jamie U20 23.11.84, Sparkhill :
100 - 10.8/10.81w/10.92 (10.76w/10.83-01)
MCPHERSON Matthew 1.08.75, Dunfermline & W Fife :
PV - 4.25
MCQUEEN Sean U15 28.02.88, Pitreavie :
400 - 53.08
MCRAE Leon U23 3.11.80, WG & EL/U of Tennessee :
100 - 10.58w/10.70, 200 - 21.46w/22.18 (22.12-01),
400 - 48.86i (48.38-01), 400H - 51.73
MCSORLEY Edward U15, :
SPB - 13.45
MCWILLIAM Ron 20.08.68, Deeside/RAF :
3kSt - 9:30.4 (9:27.87-01)

MCWILLIAMS Anthony U15 14.12.87, Northants Sch :
LJ - 5.90
MCWILLIAMS Timothy James 19.02.79, East Grinstead :
TJ - 13.97 (14.11-00)
MEDCALF Timothy James 19.02.79, East Grinstead :
TJ - 13.97 (14.11-00)
MEEKING Jake U13 15.09.89, Wells/Yeovil Olympiads :
1500 - 4:44.7, LJ - 4.99
MELIN Enrique U17 29.06.87, Newham & Essex B :
1.5kSt - 4:42.1
MELLOR Dean Ashley 25.11.71, Trafford :
PV - 5.00i/4.80 (5.30-95)
MENLOVE Matthew 20.12.79, Ilford :
400 - 49.00
MENSAH Andrew Peter 30.11.71, Enf & Har :
100 - 10.7/10.88 (10.39w/10.49-94)
MEPANDY Farel 27.06.78, Belgrave/CGO :
TJ - 14.85
MERCER James U13 18.11.89, Bournemouth :
75HC - 12.8
MERCHANT Jahmaine U20 3.08.83, Birchfield :
100 - 10.9/10.93w, 200 - 21.92w/22.2
MERRIEN Lee 26.04.79, Channel Islands :
1500 - 3:46.23, 3k - 8:21.3
MIAH Monu U20 10.01.84, WGreen & Ex L :
200 - 22.20i (21.31w/21.45-00)
MICHAELSON Thomas U17 3.01.87, Liverpool H :
1.5kSt - 4:40.0
MIDDLETON Darren U23 14.10.80, Barnsley :
1500 - 3:50.14
MIDDLETON Peter Alan U20 27.01.84, North S Poly :
110HJ - 14.9, 400H - 54.8/55.41
MIELE Felice U23 24.11.81, Harrow/Brunel Univ :
DT - 44.69
MILES Mark Thomas 24.03.77, Belgrave/Birm Univ. :
1500 - 3:45.72, 3k - 8:05.06 (7:57.21-99),
5k - 13:48.60, 10k - 29:38.2
MILES Paul U23 14.09.80, Birchfield/Wolvs Univ :
PV - 4.40
MILL Thomas U17 21.12.85, Birchfield :
HJ - 2.02
MILLAR Stuart U20 9.03.83, Cheltenham :
SP - 14.36, SPJ - 15.50, SP6K - 14.69, JT - 60.79
MILLER David 14.05.71, :
Mar - 2:35:23
MILLER Robert U20 20.01.84, Harrow :
110HJ - 15.5, JT - 57.14, Dec - 5817, DecJ - 5981
MILLER Stephen U17 15.12.85, Aberdeen :
DecY - 5238, OctY - 4327
MILLESOM Kyle U13 18.09.89, :
HJ - 1.48
MILLINGTON John U20 7.09.83, Wolverhampton & B :
3k - 8:36.54, 5k - 15:19.8
MILLINGTON Luke U17 7.11.86, Birchfield :
JTY - 52.32
MILLS Christopher Leslie 12.11.75, Winch/Loughbro :
PV - 4.81
MILLS Joseph 9.07.72, Blackheath :
1500 - 3:49.64i (3:42.23-99)
MILLS Sheldon U15 10.02.88, :
JTB - 44.82
MILLS Simon U17 30.04.86, Sale :
1500 - 4:03.9
MILLWARD Stephen 29.06.79, Wirral/UWIC :
3kSt - 9:35.1 (9:30.75-01)
MINNIKIN Stephen 4.01.72, Sheffield :
HT - 60.63 (62.20-96)
MINTER James Joseph U17 20.08.87, Midd AC :
1.5kSt - 4:31.62
MITCHELL A. U13 5.11.89, :
75HC - 12.5
MITCHELL Adam U17 12.06.86, Preston :
800 - 1:57.24
MITCHELL Andrew U23 30.07.80, Newham & E B :
3kSt - 9:20.5 (9:01.28-01)
MITCHELL Ian 10.03.76, Tipton :
5k - 14:47.7 (14:03.30-00)

374

MITCHELL James U17 11.10.86, Peterborough :
3k - 8:47.56
MITCHELL Mark U15 23.05.88, Forres/Elgin :
800 - 2:00.51, 1500 - 4:19.76
MITCHELL Neil U20 25.09.84, R Sutton Coldfield :
100 - 10.7w, 200 - 21.5w?/21.65
MITCHELL Robert U23 14.09.80, Shaftesbury Barnet :
HJ - 2.15 (2.25-01)
MITCHINSON David 4.09.78, Newham & Essex B :
HMar - 66:43, 3kSt - 9:19.1 (8:45.06-00)
MKANDWIRE Wanangma U23 4.10.80, Rugby & Nor
/Sheffield U/MAW : HJ - 2.00
MOHAMED Mustaffa 11.11.78, Sheffield/SUD :
3k - 8:24.08, 5k - 14:42.7
MOIR Gareth U23 17.12.80, Ipswich :
HJ - 2.00i/1.95 (2.00-00)
MOISEY Louis U17 9.08.86, Notts :
100 - 11.0w/11.02w/11.12
MONAGHAN Ian U23 6.11.81, Harrow/Brunel Univ :
400H - 54.60 (54.2-01)
MONAGHAN Peter U23 25.05.81, Swansea/
Leeds Univ/IRL : 110H - 14.83
MONEY Daniel James 17.10.76, Sale :
60 - 6.74i (6.72i-98), 200 - 21.7 (20.75w/20.92-97),
100 - 10.49w/10.78 (10.16w/10.32-97)
MONYE Ndubuisi U20 10.05.85, WSE&H :
SPJ - 13.82i
MOORE Jonathan U20 31.05.84, Birchfield :
LJ - 8.03
MOORE Louis Calvin U17 8.09.85, City of Stoke :
100 - 10.8w (13.8/14.01-97), 100HY - 14.08,
HJ - 1.90 (1.90i-01), PV - 3.70, LJ - 6.96,
DecY - 6501, OctY - 4975
MOORES Paul U20 3.08.84, Tamworth :
3k - 8:37.79i (8:44.8-00), 2kSt - 6:05.4 (5:59.19-01)
MOORHOUSE Julian 13.11.71, Birchfield :
3k - 8:09.89i (7:53.11-00)
MORAN Anthony U17 8.01.86, Trafford :
800 - 1:56.88, 1500 - 3:49.40, 3k - 8:27.79
MORANT Martyn 26.06.78, WGreen & Ex L :
400 - 47.9/48.67 (48.38-99)
MORELAND John R. V40 13.09.58, Rugby & Nor PH :
DT - 47.00 (51.76-95)
MORGAN Derek N. 4.04.69, Bristol :
100 - 10.7w/10.8dt (10.6-93/10.77-89)
MORGAN Mark 19.08.72, Swansea :
5k - 14:08.05 (13:57.91-99)
MORGAN Nathan 30.06.78, Birchfield :
60 - 6.84i (6.77i-99), 100 - 10.55 (10.38-01),
LJ - 8.17w/8.06 (8.11-98)
MORGAN Tom U13 2.11.89, Dartford :
HJ - 1.62
MORGAN-LEE Andrew 1.03.69, Salford :
5k - 14:45.1 (14:02.43-99), 10MR - 49:45,
3kSt - 9:01.92 (8:43.95-00)
MORGANELLA Alessandro 28.05.77, Border :
DT - 42.83 (44.64-00)
MORLAND Stuart U17 16.05.86, Liverpool H :
800 - 1:56.66
MOSCROP Howard Wilson V45 16.12.57, Swindon :
400H - 55.4 (51.4-84/51.57-82)
MOSELEY Ryan U23 8.10.82, Shaftesbury Barnet :
100 - 10.86, 200 - 22.00
MOSES Alister William 5.07.78, Reigate :
1500 - 3:50.03 (3:44.62-01)
MOSS Christopher Robert 17.06.79, Belgrave :
800 - 1:48.01 (1:47.75-00)
MOSS Damien U23 2.09.82, Rugby & Nor PH :
800 - 1:51.6
MOULTON David U23 7.09.81, Blackheath/Bath Univ :
800 - 1:51.63 (1:50.8-01)
MOUNTFORD David U23 23.06.82, City of Stoke :
LJ - 7.17 (7.33-00)
MOWBRAY Philip 19.03.73, C of Edinb/Hunter's BT :
5k - 14:02.88 (13:49.44-97)

MUIR Andrew Charles 20.06.73, Kilbarchan/Edinb U :
5k - 14:28.65, 10k - 29:57.6
MULHOLAND Danny U15 11.01.88, :
100 - 11.5
MULONSO Jonathan U13 22.04.90, Enf & Har :
SPC - 10.98, DTC - 27.02
MULVANEY Christopher Shaun U23 25.05.81, Border/
Un of Arkansas : 800 - 1:48.14i/1:48.56,
1500 - 3:41.89, 1M - 4:01.63i (4:10.93-00)
MUNGHAM Robert U20 1.12.84, Bracknell :
HTJ - 48.40
MUNRO Ian U20 5.09.83, Cambuslang/Glasgow Univ :
800 - 1:51.31
MUNROE Gary 12.04.69, Shaftesbury B/RAF/CAN :
LJ - 6.94 (7.52w?-99/7.27-96)
MURCH Kevin I. V40 11.11.58, Rugby & Nor PH :
JT - 58.84 (69.02-89)
MURDOCH Iain U23 10.07.80, Law & Dist/Loughbro :
1500 - 3:44.90, 3k - 8:21.67 (8:20.06i-01),
3kSt - 8:54.4 (8:42.79-00)
MURDOCH Steven V40 16.04.61, Border :
10k - 31:39.41 (30:19.1-95)
MURDOCK Andrew U20 16.02.85, Horsham BS :
1500 - 3:55.57
MURPHY Kevin 6.04.74, City of Norwich :
3kSt - 9:24.2 (9:21.56-01)
MURPHY Stephen U23 10.02.82, City of Edinburgh :
400 - 49.18, 400H - 55.01 (53.2/53.37-00)
MURPHY Stephen James U20 6.01.83, Shaftesbury B :
1500 - 3:49.99, 3k - 8:34.38 (8:21.69-00),
5k - 15:21.55, 2kSt - 5:47.81, 3kSt - 8:47.8
MURRAY Declan Robert U13 13.07.90, Macclesfield :
400 - 61.6, 1500 - 4:45.1
MURRAY Michael 8.12.79, WSE&H :
LJ - 6.81 (7.11-01), TJ - 14.20 (15.11-01)
MURRAY Thomas V40 18.05.61, Inverclyde :
HMar - 66:44 (65:34-92)
MUSSETT Adrian 14.04.72, Chelmsford :
5k - 14:39.3 (14:13.7-97), Mar - 2:22:27
MUTAI John 26.05.66, Bromsgrove & R/KEN :
HMar - 63:30 (60:52-99), Mar - 2:13:56 (2:13:20-00)
MWANFE Wolfgang U15 26.08.88, Middlesex Sch :
TJ - 12.37w/12.31
MYERS Richard U20 21.12.83, Gateshead :
110HJ - 15.16
MYERSCOUGH Carl Andrew ¶ 21.10.79, Blackpool/
Univ of Nebraska : SP - 21.26i/20.72, DT - 63.14
MYLES Gary 3.02.63, Cannock & Stafford :
110H - 15.5 (14.55-83)

N AISMITH David 15.12.79, Newham & Essex B :
200 - 22.0 (21.6-99/21.64-01),
400 - 47.12 (46.27-99)
NANCI Pepi U17 7.10.86, Milton Keynes :
OctY - 4437
NASH Kevin 6.02.77, Belgrave :
3kSt - 9:17.33 (8:43.21-96)
NASH Paul U20 13.02.84, Rugby & Nor PH :
HTJ - 50.77
NASH Samuel 22.10.71, Thames Valley :
LJ - 6.82 (7.41wA-00/7.01-97)
NASRAT James Thomas U20 10.01.83, Newport :
400 - 49.1, 800 - 1:49.63, 1500 - 3:54.61i
NAUGHTON Joe 17.10.74, Havering M/IRL :
60H - 8.43i, 110H - 15.3 (15.34-99),
LJ - 7.02i (7.23w-98/7.11-99), SP - 13.97
NAYLOR Donald E. 5.09.71, Swansea/Hunter's BT :
2k - 5:22.53i, 3k - 8:03.17,
5k - 14:09.38 (13:58.88-00), 3kSt - 8:38.68
NAYLOR Tom 9.01.79, Phoenix :
5k - 14:43.3
NEBLETT Gavin 27.12.79, Blackheath :
60 - 6.83i, 100 - 10.87w (10.95-97)
NEELY Ian 29.12.74, Border/Ballymena & Antrim :
400H - 52.8/53.21 (52.34-98)

NEILL Steven 11.08.66, Telford/RAF :
1500 - 3:49.64 (3:46.1-98)
NELSON Alex U15 21.03.88, City of Stoke :
100 - 10.9w/11.17 (11.16w-01), 200 - 22.8w/23.07
NELSON Anthony U20 14.09.84, Croydon :
TJ - 14.57w/14.30
NELSON David U15 18.09.87, Sale :
400 - 52.49
NELSON Peter U15 8.10.87, S Yorks Sch :
HJ - 1.78
NESBETH Michael 1.03.79, Belgrave :
LJ - 7.16 (7.35i-99/7.30-00)
NEVIS John 24.12.69, Kingston u Hull :
HT - 47.99 (56.18-94)
NEWBURY Ian U17 17.09.86, Cardiff :
HJ - 1.90
NEWMAN Lee Jon 1.05.73, Belgrave :
SP - 16.94 (18.85-96), DT - 56.28 (60.48-97)
NEWPORT Spencer John 5.10.66, Blackheath :
5k - 14:36.2 (13:49.74-96)
NEWTON Keith 12.12.68, WGreen & Ex L :
TJ - 14.59 (14.83w/14.79-01)
NEWTON Michael U17 3.04.86, Sale :
400HY - 57.09
NEWTON Richard U17 10.02.87, Preston :
1500 - 4:00.42
NEWTON Robert U23 10.05.81, Sale :
60H - 7.84i, 110H - 13.92
NICELY Jeavon U17 27.11.86, Birchfield :
TJ - 14.03w/13.76
NICHOL Tom U13, :
JTC - 34.57
NICHOLLS Dexter U17 28.05.87, Herne Hill :
TJ - 13.40
NICHOLLS John S. 1.09.65, Sale :
SP - 15.36 (15.98-99)
NICHOLLS Russell U20 8.03.83, Enf & Har :
400 - 48.0/48.06 (47.80-01)
NICHOLSON Andrew U17 25.03.86, Horsham BS :
TJ - 13.70
NICOL James U20 3.06.85, Ilford :
200 - 22.08w
NICOLSON Christian 19.09.73, Team Solent :
5k - 14:07.85 (13:45.26-00), 10k - 28:52.36
NIELAND Nicholas 31.01.72, Shaftesbury Barnet :
JT - 80.05 (85.09-00)
NIFAH Richard 25.08.74, Milton Keynes/GHA :
10MR - 49:44
NIGHTINGALE Tom U13 23.12.89, Milton Keynes :
400 - 60.8, 3k - 10:31.2
NIMMO Thomas 9.05.71, City of Edinburgh :
400 - 48.3 (47.99-92), 800 - 1:50.63 (1:49.0-92)
NIXON Greg U17 2.09.85, City of Stoke :
DTY - 41.91
NNANYERE Bertram U20 26.09.83, Croydon :
110HJ - 15.5, TJ - 13.92w
NOAD Benjamin 6.05.76, Bristol :
5MR - 23:51 (23:20-01), 10kR - 29:40 (29:10-01),
10MR - 48:10, HMar - 64:18
NOBLE Ian 2.04.77, Trafford :
PV - 4.70 (4.80-99)
NORMAN Andrew Richard U23 19.08.80, Altrincham/
University of Tulsa : 3k - 8:15.27i,
5k - 14:15.63, 10k - 31:35.89 (31:08.76-00)
NORMAN Anthony Josephus 5.07.63, Woking :
SP - 13.94 (14.94-88), JT - 56.91 (68.74-87)
NORMAN David 4.11.78, Altrincham :
5k - 14:36.81, 10k - 30:49.77, 10kR - 30:09,
HMar - 65:24, Mar - 2:21:01
NORRISS Paris U20 27.02.85, AF&D :
DTJ - 44.62, DecJ - 5572
NORTH Christian I.R. 2.02.74, WGreen & Ex L :
PV - 5.20 (5.30-99)
NORTH Ewen 13.07.78, Hallamshire/Oklahoma St U :
5k - 14:32.45

NORTHALL Luke U20 30.11.84, Wrexham :
5k - 15:15.62
NORTON Daniel John, Rhondda :
Mar - 2:33:58
NOTMAN Lee 14.10.75, Border :
400 - 49.0 (48.57-01)
NUTTING Chris U17 12.10.85, Notts :
SPY - 13.85i
NWAOLISE Paul Chukwuemeka 31.05.73, Morp/Keele U :
60 - 6.94i (6.9i-98),
100 - 10.85w (10.73w-98/10.74-99)
NYANANYO Suote U20 3.10.84, Midd AC :
110HJ - 14.9/14.95, LJ - 6.93w (6.87-01)

O'BRIEN Barry U17 21.04.86, Dunf & W Fife :
100HY - 13.84
O'CONNOR Alastair Paul 22.06.71, Liverpool H :
1500 - 3:51.15 (3:47.68-00), 5k - 14:45.7,
10kR - 30:04, 3kSt - 8:57.18 (8:42.88-92)
O'DONOVAN Ross U17 12.03.86, Thames Valley :
100 - 10.91w/11.02 (10.87w/11.01-01)
O'DOWD Matthew 15.04.76, Swindon :
5k - 13:43.33 (13:30.56-01), 10kR - 29:23 (28:48-01),
10MR - 47:29, Mar - 2:12:20
O'GRADY Shaun 24.08.75, New Marske :
3kSt - 9:35.1
O'HARA Jason 28.10.76, Shaftesbury Barnet :
PV - 4.10i (4.40-01)
O'KEEFE Kieran U17 19.03.86, Charnwood :
DTY - 45.69, HTY - 49.01
O'LEARY David U23 3.08.80, Liverpool H :
400H - 54.17 (53.3-01/54.03-99)
O'NEILL Mark U23, Bristol :
400 - 48.8/48.93
OAKES Christopher 19.10.70, Army :
Dec - 5772 (5951-97)
OBOH Laurence U20 14.05.84, Belgrave :
60 - 6.85i, 100 - 10.8/10.93 (10.66w/10.70-01),
200 - 21.15w/21.55 (21.30-01)
OCTAVE Philip 12.06.78, WGreen & EL/Reading Un :
200 - 22.0
ODUOZA Uche Francis U17 15.10.86, Exeter :
LJ - 6.61, OctY - 4304
OGUNBOWALE Jeli U15 8.01.88, London Schools :
200 - 23.44
OGUNYEMI Akeem 4.06.74, Enf & Har :
100 - 10.7w/10.79 (10.6-97/10.63-01)
OGUNYSHEYE Segun U17 9.09.85, Shaftesbury B :
100HY - 13.57
OHRLAND Martin 19.11.79, Chelmsford :
110H - 15.1w/15.3/15.66w, HJ - 2.01, Dec - 5705
OHRLAND Stuart 6.09.75, Newham & Essex B :
HJ - 1.95 (2.20i-97/2.18-99)
OJIGHORO Precious U13 27.12.89, :
100 - 12.2, 200 - 24.8w?
OJO Sayo U23 9.05.80, WGreen & Ex L :
TJ - 14.34 (14.62-99)
OKE Tosin U23 1.10.80, Cambridge H/Manchester U :
TJ - 16.65
OKOIGUN Mike U17 1.02.87, Middlesex Sch :
TJ - 13.22
OKOROAFOR Lee 12.09.76, WGrn & EL/Army/NGR :
60H - 8.49i, 110H - 14.8/15.68,
LJ - 7.04 (7.20-01), Dec - 6670
OLDEN Chris, New Forest :
Mar - 2:36:24
OMAR Shugri U20 20.12.84, Ealing,Southall & Mx :
800 - 1:53.12, 1500 - 3:52.66, 3k - 8:38.71
ONI Samson U23 25.06.81, Belgrave/Loughborough :
HJ - 2.00i (2.20i/2.18-01)
ONUOHA Chinedum U17 12.11.86, Trafford :
100 - 11.1/11.12 (11.09w-01)
OPARKA Jonathon U23 29.01.80, Arbroath/Border :
60 - 6.93i (6.74i-01), 200 - 21.73,
100 - 10.67w/10.79 (10.43w-01/10.6-00/10.61-01)

OPENSHAW Michael 8.04.72, Birchfield :
  1500 - 3:50.03 (3:39.7-98), 10kR - 30:00 (29:05-00),
  10MR - 48:35
OPIYO Gilbert U23 19.12.81, Thames Valley/KEN :
  60 - 6.80i, 100 - 10.2w/10.56, 200 - 21.5w/21.70
ORMEROD Martin U15 12.10.87, Tonbridge :
  LJ - 6.09
ORMESHER Andrew J. U20 29.05.85, Wigan :
  JT - 54.24
ORR Christopher James U20 20.06.83, Border :
  DTJ - 45.69
OSAZUWA Osamudieaken John U23 4.05.81,
  Belgrave/Army/NGR : HT - 61.45 (62.87-00)
OSBORNE Patrick 5.06.74, Thames Valley :
  100 - 10.87w (10.6-98)
OSHO Setonsi U17 28.09.86, Brighton & Hove AC :
  200 - 22.5/22.79
OSTRIDGE Matthew U20 23.02.83, Trafford/Leeds U :
  HJ - 2.01i (2.10-01)
OSUIDE Stanley 30.11.74, Thames Valley :
  HJ - 2.05i/2.05 (2.15-91)
OUDNEY Graeme U20 11.04.85, Belgrave/Pitreavie :
  800 - 1:54.03
OUOU Abdel-Karim 18.07.77, Kent/ALG :
  800 - 1:50.49, 1500 - 3:49.7, 3k - 8:21.8,
  5k - 14:48.3
OVERALL Scott U20 9.02.83, WSE&H/Leics Univ :
  800 - 1:53.9 (1:53.89-01), 1500 - 3:48.72,
  3k - 8:38.02 (8:28.0-01), 5k - 14:42.3
OWEN John N. 28.10.64, Swansea :
  HT - 50.83 (52.96-95)
OWEN Neil James 18.10.73, Belgrave :
  60H - 7.97i (7.72i-96),
  110H - 13.90 (13.5w-96/13.60-95)
OWEN Nicolas John Lloyd U23 17.07.80, Kingston & P/
  Brunel Univ : SP - 16.29, DT - 44.20
OWEN Ross U15 16.11.87, Peterborough :
  400 - 53.67
OWENS Andrew U17 5.11.85, Liverpool H :
  TJ - 13.49
OWENS Scott U13 15.06.90, East Grinstead :
  HJ - 1.50
OYEDIRAN Akinbode Ademola V40 27.11.59, Herne H :
  TJ - 14.54 (15.91i/15.78-84)

PAAR David U13 28.09.89, Stevenage & NH :
  75HC - 12.0
PAGE Christopher U23 13.11.80, Card/Cloud Co CC :
  100 - 10.84?, 400 - 49.01 (47.51-00)
PAIN Ashleigh U15 16.10.87, Tipton :
  1500 - 4:15.35
PAINTER John James Thomas ¶ V40 12.06.58, C of Nor :
  SP - 13.43i (16.32i/16.09-89), DT - 40.13 (50.36-88)
PAISLEY Derek 1.12.73, Border/Pitreavie :
  400H - 53.6/53.66 (52.83-94)
PALLISTER Jack U17 22.02.87, Cannock & Stafford :
  HTY - 47.67
PALLOT M. U15, Devon Sch :
  TJ - 12.03w
PALMER Adrian Mark 10.08.69, Cardiff :
  HT - 58.22 (62.56-94)
PALMER Andrew 13.04.77, Team Solent :
  HJ - 2.00 (2.00-95)
PALMER Ian U23 22.11.81, B'mouth/RAF/Brunel U :
  400 - 49.1, 400H - 55.5 (54.3-01/56.62-00)
PALMER Nathan U23 16.06.82, WGrn & EL/Bath Un :
  60H - 7.98i, 110H - 14.24 (14.06-01),
  LJ - 6.86w (6.92w/6.58-98)
PALMER Ryan U20 21.06.83, Sale :
  400 - 48.01
PAPURA Dominic U23 12.02.81, Cardiff/Loughbro :
  100 - 10.5w/10.7/10.85 (10.70w-01), 200 - 21.15
PARK Iain Ross 16.07.74, Harrow/Falkirk/NESH :
  DT - 41.22 (44.96-98), HT - 69.29

PARKER Andrew U20 10.12.83, Wolverhampton & B :
  3kW - 12:49.02i (12:29.90-00), 10kW - 45:32.37,
  5kW - 23:11.7 (22:36.98-01), 10kWR - 45:33
PARKER Andrew 5.08.75, Bolton/Birmingham Univ. :
  5k - 14:45.02, 10k - 31:24.3, HMar - 66:46
PARKER David U23 28.02.80, Shaft B/Loughbro :
  JT - 74.80 (78.33A-01/78.24-00)
PARKER James 28.10.79, Team Solent/Loughbro :
  800 - 1:52.25 (1:49.80-00)
PARKER James U23 29.09.80, E & E/Plymouth Univ :
  110H - 15.2/15.60 (15.1/15.15-01), 400H - 53.9/53.96
PARKER Richard U17 21.11.86, Cannock & Stafford :
  SPY - 15.06
PARPER Michael 20.05.78, Belgrave :
  400 - 49.0 (46.54-97)
PARR Christopher Daniel U20 13.11.84, Gateshead :
  1500 - 3:49.22, 3k - 8:26.17
PARRY Philip John 4.10.65, Harrow :
  JT - 58.74 (70.00-94)
PARRY Richard U17 23.05.86, Halesowen :
  400 - 49.51
PARSONS Dominic Edward U15 8.09.87, Blackheath :
  200 - 23.42, 400 - 52.3/52.46
PARSONS Gary 17.05.71, Cambridge & Colr'dge :
  DT - 41.04 (42.95-98)
PARSONS Geoffrey Peter 14.08.64, :
  HJ - 1.95 (2.31-94)
PARSONS Thomas Martin U20 5.05.84, Solihull & S H :
  HJ - 2.10
PARTINGTON Stephen Wyand 17.09.65, Manx H :
  3kW - 11:58.4 (11:33.4-95),
  5kW - 21:06.3 (20:09.0-92),
  10kWR - 42:18 (40:40hc-92/40:49-94),
  20kW - 1:28:48 (1:24:09sh-94/1:24:18-90)
PARTYKA Scott U15 19.03.88, Kirkintillock :
  400 - 53.50
PASK Freddie U13 9.11.89, Coventry Godiva :
  HJ - 1.59
PATRICK Adrian Leroy John 15.06.73, WSE&H :
  100 - 10.7 (10.3/10.38-96), 400 - 47.61 (45.63-95),
  200 - 21.29w/21.31 (20.62w-95/20.9-96/20.92-99)
PAUL Robert U23 12.11.80, N & EB/St. Marys U Coll :
  HJ - 2.00i (2.10-00)
PAYN Tom 18.10.79, Colchester & T/Birm Univ. :
  3kSt - 9:29.4
PAYNE Garry V45 31.01.57, :
  Mar - 2:29:53
PAYNE Nigel 27.01.67, Nuneaton :
  Mar - 2:36:05 (2:33:53-00)
PAYNE Russell H. V40 11.09.60, Birchfield :
  HT - 48.32 (56.62-86)
PAYNE Stephen J. V45 1.12.55, Royal Navy :
  Mar - 2:30:29 (2:29:36-00)
PAYNE Tim U17 23.09.86, Solihull & S Heath :
  HJ - 1.90
PEACOCK Shane 5.03.63, Birchfield :
  HT - 63.83 (71.60-90)
PEAD Andrew 18.02.66, Stockport :
  Mar - 2:34:17 (2:33:15-00)
PEARCE Curtis U13 1.05.90, Blackburn :
  1500 - 4:45.5
PEARSON John Terry 30.04.66, Charnwood :
  HT - 64.42 (70.33-00)
PENFOLD Tom U20 4.05.84, White Horse :
  1500 - 3:51.06
PENK Andrew 19.09.78, Cardiff/Chester Un :
  HJ - 2.00 (2.16i-00/2.15-97),
  PV - 4.80i/4.70 (5.01-01)
PENN Andrew Shaun 31.03.67, Nuneaton :
  2kW - 7:45.84, 20kW - 1:26:04 (1:23:34-92),
  10kWR - 43:20+ (41:47+-92/42:00-93)
PENNY Sean U17 17.06.86, Cheltenham :
  HTY - 47.83
PEPPER Jonathan Samuel U15 2.06.88, Enf & Har :
  3k - 9:31.28

PERRY Kevin V50 7.12.48, Southend :
100MWT - 20:41:17+, 24HrWT - 182.591km
PERRYMAN Guy St. Denis Mansfield V40 2.11.58,
Reading : SP - 14.03 (16.58-89)
PETERS Craig U15 4.03.88, Bristol :
3k - 9:30.6
PETERSON Garth, RRC :
24Hr - 190.494km
PETTS Chris U23 22.01.80, Ashford :
HJ - 1.95 (2.07-00)
PHELAN Simon U17 26.02.86, Channel Islands :
HJ - 1.95, OctY - 4345
PHILLIPS A. U15, :
PV - 2.85
PHILLIPS Adrian Martin 29.07.75, Ealing,S & M :
LJ - 7.29w/7.27
PHILLIPS Craig U17 29.09.85, Deeside :
TJ - 14.32w/14.14
PHILLIPS Nicolas Kevin U15 12.10.87, Poole Runners :
PenB - 2769
PHILLIPS Steven 17.03.72, Rugby & Nor PH :
LJ - 7.44 (8.07w-99/8.03-98), TJ - 14.34 (15.47w/15.10-98)
PHILLIPSON James U17 18.03.87, Sale :
3k - 8:57.43
PICKERING Craig U17 16.10.86, Milton Keynes :
60 - 6.9i/6.95i, 100 - 10.70, 200 - 21.82w/22.13
PICKERING Lee U20 16.09.83, Chelmsford :
3kSt - 9:43.36
PICKERING Robert U15 3.11.87, Bridlington :
3k - 9:15.33
PILKINGTON James U13 21.10.89, Colchester & T :
100 - 12.1, 200 - 25.6, LJ - 5.02
PILSBOROUGH Matt 10.07.79, Halesowen/USA :
PV - 4.60
PITT David U15 1.09.88, Halesowen :
100 - 11.4w/11.5
PITT Roderick U23 4.03.81, Pitreavie :
100 - 10.80w (11.4/11.80-97), 200 - 21.93 (21.9w-01)
PLANK Daniel U23 27.04.82, Birchfield :
HJ - 1.95 (2.08i/2.07-99)
PLANT Raymond 13.05.68, City of Stoke :
10k - 31:44.6, Mar - 2:23:15 (2:20:23-97)
PLASKETT Simon 9.04.79, Trafford/Loughbro :
300 - 34.69i (34.14-01), 400 - 47.13
PLUMMER Daniel U23 4.01.81, Blackheath :
60 - 6.77i, 100 - 10.33,
200 - 21.3/21.67i (21.66w/22.03-01)
PLUNKETT Gerard Paish U23 30.06.80, Sale/Hallam :
110H - 15.63, HJ - 1.95 (1.98-99), PV - 4.20i/4.10,
SP - 13.82, DT - 40.08, JT - 67.42, Dec - 7112
POBIE William 6.12.78, WGreen & Ex L :
100 - 10.6w/10.85 (10.70w-01), 200 - 22.05 (22.0w-01)
POGUE Steven U17 12.09.85, Midd AC :
1.5kSt - 4:31.09
POPE Daniel U17 24.12.86, Gateshead :
OctY - 4216
POPOWOSKI James U15 9.01.88, :
HTB - 40.31
PORTER Alan 21.10.75, Cambridge Harriers :
DT - 40.33
POTTER Adam Charles U23 12.04.80, WG & EL/Bath U :
100 - 10.8w/11.14 (10.7-01), 400 - 48.39 (46.75-01),
200 - 21.9/22.64 (21.4/21.95-01)
POWELL Joelle U15 2.03.88, Bristol :
100 - 11.5w (12.3-00), 200 - 23.4
POWELL John V40 4.06.62, :
JT - 58.22 (60.30-92)
POWER Gareth U23 5.06.82, Newp/U Wales Newport :
110H - 15.2/15.47
POWER Garry V40 1.09.62, Herne Hill/IRL :
DT - 47.19 (48.98-86)
PRATT David 23.11.75, Bedford & County :
400 - 49.0/49.09 (48.32-01)
PRENDERGAST Grant U15 8.09.87, Leics Cor :
800 - 1:58.79

PRESTON Marc U15 20.09.87, Brymore Sch :
HTB - 47.15
PREVOST Ricardo U17 31.10.85, Harrow :
HJ - 2.00
PRICE Daniel U13 31.10.89, Bournemouth :
800 - 2:16.7
PRICE David U17 12.01.87, Newport :
DTY - 44.84
PRICE Glyn A. 12.09.65, Swansea :
PV - 4.30i/4.20 (4.80-90)
PRICE Stuart U13 16.11.89, Kingston & Poly :
75HC - 13.04, 80HC - 13.7
PRICKETT Edward U20 28.01.83, Crawley :
800 - 1:54.3, 1500 - 3:47.60, 3k - 8:16.43
PRIDE Simon 20.07.67, Swansea/Keith :
Mar - 2:22:21 (2:16:27-01)
PRINCE Warren U20 18.03.85, Luton :
100 - 10.8/10.82, 200 - 21.9/22.16
PRITCHARD Ashley 14.07.79, Macclesfield :
Dec - 5061 (5620-01)
PRITCHARD Jamie U17 25.09.85, Cardiff :
SPY - 13.97, HTY - 48.71
PRITCHARD Nicholas 5.12.72, Swansea :
PV - 4.40 (4.60-95)
PRITCHARD Nick U17 19.01.87, Crawley :
100HY - 14.17
PROCTER David U20 11.11.84, Carmarthen :
HTJ - 50.78
PROCTOR David U17 22.10.85, Rochdale :
400 - 49.70, 800 - 1:54.24
PROCTOR Mark Anthony 15.01.63, N & EB/RAF :
SP - 19.13 (20.85i-98/20.40-99),
DT - 49.77 (57.14-00), HT - 45.44 (53.70-93)
PROSSER Michael U17 11.10.86, Telford :
400 - 50.89
PROSSER Paul, Brighton & Hove AC :
Mar - 2:36:24
PROSSER Stephen U15 24.10.87, Channel Islands :
200 - 23.3w/23.83
PROUDLOVE Michael 26.01.70, City of Stoke :
Mar - 2:30:03 (2:23:17-01)
PROWSE Barrie U20 2.03.85, Cornwall AC :
DecJ - 5071
PUGH David U17 15.08.86, Ballymena & Antrim :
100 - 10.96w
PUGH Jamie U13, :
TJ - 9.43
PULLAN Mathew U23, Epsom & Ewell :
TJ - 13.75
PURCELL Ian U20 20.12.84, Ballymena & Antrim :
400H - 55.9/56.34
PURSGLOVE Lee U17 14.10.86, Chorley :
HJ - 1.90, OctY - 4261

QUARRY Jamie Stephen 15.11.72, Harrow/Falk :
60H - 8.16i (8.07i-01),SP - 14.68,
110H - 14.7/14.83 (14.10-94), PV - 4.70i/4.65 (4.65-98),
LJ - 7.20w/7.18 (7.42w-00/7.29-01), Dec - 7630 (7739-99)
QUINLAN Carl U15 8.09.87, :
JTB - 46.64
QUINN Daniel U17 21.12.86, Southend :
1.5kSt - 4:39.8
QUINN Robert 10.12.65, Kilbarchan :
5k - 14:23.08 (14:00.91-95)
QUIRK James 16.03.78, Yeovil Olympiads :
110H - 15.47

RAESIDE Bruce U23 2.12.81, Notts :
3kSt - 9:14.6
RAGAN David James U20 26.03.83, Bas & MH :
800 - 1:54.5
RAESIDE Bruce U23 2.12.81, Notts :
3kSt - 9:07.85
RALPH Ollie U15 21.02.88, Epsom & Ewell :
800 - 2:04.09

378

RALPH Paul 16.12.67, Trafford :
LJ - 7.03 (7.38w-00/7.29w?-01/7.25-00),
TJ - 15.06 (15.76w-97/15.67-95)
RAMOS Jonathan U23 29.06.80, Enf & Har/Brunel U :
LJ - 7.20w/7.05, TJ - 13.91w (13.09-96)
RANGER Tom 20.11.77, Morpeth :
800 - 1:50.62, 1500 - 3:43.97, 1M - 4:08.45
RATCLIFFE Trevor 9.03.64, Dacorum & Tring :
JT - 62.56 (66.78-96)
RAVEN Gareth 9.05.74, Sale :
1500 - 3:49.96, 5k - 14:12.10, 10kR - 30:10,
HMar - 66:18 (66:05-01)
RAWLINSON Christopher 19.05.72, Traff/Loughbro :
200 - 21.21, 300 - 32.5, 400 - 46.03,
300H - 34.48, 400H - 48.21 (48.14-99)
RAYNER Thomas William U15 26.01.88, Sale :
100 - 11.60, 200 - 23.30
READ Simon 24.06.70, Herne Hill :
DT - 43.09
READLE David U23 10.02.80, Bel/Kansas State Univ :
SP - 17.28i/16.95 (17.69i-01/17.50-00),
DT - 42.04 (45.72-00), HT - 50.17
RECORD Chris U17 12.09.86, WSE&H :
OctY - 4241
REDDYOFF Nick U15 21.04.88, :
TJ - 12.39
REDMOND John V45 15.10.57, Kingston u Hull :
Mar - 2:35:08 (2:27:50-94)
REED Paul V40 2.06.62, Border :
SP - 15.89 (17.04-88), DT - 53.86 (58.36-99)
REEKS Richard Kenneth U17 6.12.85, Poole :
100HY - 14.1w/14.2, OctY - 4335
REES James U20 25.07.83, Torfaen :
HT6K - 49.02
REES Jason U17 17.09.85, Cardiff :
PV - 3.80
REES Martin V45 28.02.53, Swansea :
HMar - 66:44 (66:29-01)
REES Thomas U17 9.03.86, Swansea :
JTY - 54.89
REES-JONES Steve 24.12.74, Sheffield :
800 - 1:50.74 (1:49.92-97), 1500 - 3:48.14 (3:44.09-01)
REESE Ben 29.03.76, Trafford :
1500 - 3:46.30 (3:41.87-97)
REETZ Tim U23 18.11.80, Adams State Univ :
60H - 7.92i, 110H - 13.91wA/13.93w/14.10A/14.1,
110H - 14.18
REID Aidan U13 26.12.89, Mansfield :
1500 - 4:46.4
REID Alan 19.04.66, Peterhead :
100kR - 7:36:09 (7:13:30-01)
REID Edward U23 22.07.81, Charnwood :
DT - 48.77
REID Graeme 14.04.79, Clydesdale/Iona Coll, USA :
1M - 4:06.06i, 10k - 30:22.82,
5k - 13:52.64i/14:32.46 (14:04.46-01)
REID James 6.07.73, Law & Dist :
5k - 14:35.43, 10k - 30:16.66, 10MR - 49:46,
Mar - 2:21:46 (2:21:15-00)
REID Noel U23 19.11.81, Harrow :
HJ - 1.95
REID Stewart 15.11.73, Border/Pitreavie :
1500 - 3:51.26 (3:48.49-00)
REIDY Sean U23 27.01.81, Nene Valley H :
400H - 55.0/55.93 (55.41-00)
REILLY Matthew U15, :
HTB - 41.58
REISS Michael 17.06.63, Highgate Harriers :
HT - 45.49 (50.60-94)
RENFREE Andrew James 18.05.75, Shaftesbury B :
1500 - 3:48.63 (3:44.88-00), 2k - 5:22.37i, 5k - 14:46.13
RENSHAW William V50 7.08.49, Rotherham :
DT - 41.12 (45.16-80)
REVELL Paul U23 18.11.80, Scarborough/Loughbro :
TJ - 14.49 (14.55w-99)

REYNOLDS Christopher U20 23.01.85, WGrn & EL :
800 - 1:50.18, 1500 - 3:49.40
REYNOLDS Tomas James U20 20.12.84, N Down :
110HJ - 15.4, DecJ - 5837
RICE John U23 29.08.81, Liv.Pembroke Sefton :
3kSt - 9:31.5 (9:30.7-00)
RICHARDS Dominique 12.09.79, Harrow :
60 - 6.90i/6.9i (6.83i-99),
LJ - 7.10i (7.66w-00/7.52i-99/7.35-00)
RICHARDS Gregory Roy V45 25.04.56, N Lond & MH :
SP - 13.57 (15.24-94), DT - 43.72 (50.66-91)
RICHARDS Henry U23 15.05.81, Charnwood :
60 - 6.94i (6.89i-99), 100 - 10.7w (10.69w/10.75-98)
RICHARDS Leslie U20 29.03.85, Middlesbro & C :
DT - 42.86, DTJ - 47.87
RICHARDS Matthew U17 10.05.86, Swansea :
HTY - 50.64
RICHARDS Thomas Austin 13.11.78, N & EB/CUAC :
PV - 4.80 (5.25-99)
RICHARDSON Alan Matthew U23 15.01.81, Border/
Leeds Univ : PV - 4.75
RICHARDSON Paul U23 11.02.82, Charnwood :
1M - 4:08.72
RICHARDSON Peter U15 14.07.88, WSE&H :
HJ - 1.80
RICKETTS David 2.12.79, Kingston u Hull/Birm Un :
5k - 14:39.49, 10k - 30:33.2
RIDER Scott Frederick 22.09.77, Harrow :
SP - 17.56, DT - 50.56 (52.81-00)
RIEKSTINS Ben U13 11.09.90, Telford :
100 - 12.6, LJ - 5.22
RILEY Alex U20 17.09.83, Notts :
100 - 10.8, 200 - 22.0 (22.05w/22.36-01)
RILEY David U20 25.10.84, Morpeth :
200 - 21.95 (21.67-01)
RILEY Kassim U20 9.08.84, Enf & Har :
400 - 49.39
RILEY Peter 6.07.79, Trafford/Iona Coll, USA :
1500 - 3:49.57, 1M - 4:06.9r ,5k - 13:52.81,
3k - 8:13.46i (8:15.60-00), 10k - 29:27.05
RIMMER Michael U17 3.02.86, Liv.Pembroke Sefton :
400 - 48.9, 800 - 1:50.55, 1500 - 3:54.07
RITCHIE Darren 14.02.75, Sale/Scottish Borders :
LJ - 7.93
ROBB Bruce 27.07.77, Pitreavie :
SP - 16.00 (16.67-01), DT - 52.22 (54.25-01)
ROBB Curtis Alexander 7.06.72, Liverpool H :
400 - 49.0 (48.9-93), 800 - 1:48.50 (1:44.92-93),
1500 - 3:51.15 (3:38.56-93)
ROBB David U17 25.09.85, North Down :
HJ - 1.90
ROBERSON Mark W. 13.03.67, Newham & Essex B :
JT - 78.80 (85.67-98)
ROBERSON Mark W. 21.03.75, Milton Keynes :
HT - 50.48
ROBERTS Barry U17 24.09.86, Menai :
DTY - 41.03
ROBERTS Ben U23 15.01.80, City of Stoke :
SP - 13.86 (14.05i/13.98-01), DT - 40.90
ROBERTS Colin U23 20.01.81, C of Norw/Loughbro :
110H - 14.8/15.30 (14.58w/14.7/14.95-01)
ROBERTS Dai V40 10.05.61, Havant :
Mar - 2:28:32
ROBERTS Daniel U20 29.11.84, Swindon :
200 - 22.07w/22.1
ROBERTS Euron Lloyd U17 18.11.85, Eryri :
100HY - 14.12 (14.12-01)
ROBERTS Wyn U17, Pontypridd :
TJ - 13.15
ROBERTSON David T. V40 11.09.61, Sunderland :
Mar - 2:27:11 (2:26:09-00)
ROBERTSON Kenneth U15 6.04.88, Falkirk :
JTB - 44.99
ROBERTSON Kris U15 9.09.87, Kirkintillock :
400 - 52.06, PenB - 2780

379

ROBERTSON-ADAMS Charles Lyndon 5.12.77,
N & E B : 110H - 15.0w?, 400H - 50.97 (50.24-01)
ROBINSON Andrew 20.04.78, Newham & Essex B :
1500 - 3:50.55, 2kSt - 5:41.41, 3kSt - 8:53.39
ROBINSON Daniel 4.08.73, Tipton :
10kR - 29:46, 10MR - 48:55, HMar - 65:10, Mar - 2:17:51
ROBINSON Darren U23 20.06.80, Vic Pk & Tower H :
400H - 55.1
ROBINSON David 12.01.78, Gateshead/NESH/
Northumbria Univ : HT - 54.83 (56.07-00)
ROBINSON Emile U23 26.11.81, Grantham :
110H - 15.4/15.67
ROBINSON Warren U15 17.09.87, Durham Sch :
TJ - 12.00
ROBSON Lewis U15 9.01.88, Gateshead :
200 - 23.17, 400 - 50.97, 800 - 1:59.81,
80HB - 11.59, LJ - 6.25, TJ - 12.30, PenB - 3129
RODRIGUEZ Lee 30.01.74, New Forest/Winchester :
10kR - 30:08, 3kSt - 9:43.1
ROE Thomas U23 25.06.82, City of Norwich :
LJ - 7.08 (7.19-01)
ROGERS Adam U20 10.04.83, Jarrow & Hebburn :
200 - 21.89 (21.64-99), 400 - 48.5 (48.11i-01/48.85-99)
ROGERS Craig 14.02.76, Birchfield :
SP - 14.32 (15.88-97)
ROGERS Duncan U20 10.10.84, Horsham BS :
110HJ - 15.16, 110H - 15.27w
ROGERS Jason U20 19.07.84, Ayr Seaforth/Shaft B :
200 - 21.97, 400 - 49.15
ROGERS John 30.07.73, Annadale Striders/Sale :
800 - 1:52.26 (1:49.61-00), 1500 - 3:43.3
ROGERS Stephen A. 1.09.71, Liv.Pembroke Sefton :
JT - 56.99 (61.10-97)
ROLLINS Andrew 20.03.78, Trafford :
SP - 13.52 (15.34-99), DT - 46.71 (48.56-00)
ROPER Peter 25.07.65, Poole :
Mar - 2:29:36
ROPER Simon 20.09.79, Derby & Co :
LJ - 7.19 (7.25w/7.21-00)
ROSCOE Martin Peter 19.09.64, Leeds :
Mar - 2:30:45, 3kSt - 9:18.0 (8:53.2-89)
ROSENBERG Luke U23 29.06.80, Harrow :
SP - 14.27, DT - 50.48 (52.81-01)
ROSSITER Martin R. 4.09.69, Peterborough :
LJ - 6.80 (7.14-99), TJ - 15.43 (15.53w-99)
ROUTLEDGE Joe U15, Mansfield :
PV - 2.90
ROWAN Stuart Ronald U17 16.01.87, Perth :
400HY - 57.27
ROWBERRY Charlie U13 25.02.90, Dorset :
80HC - 14.18
ROYDEN Barry Mark 15.12.66, Med & Maid :
10k - 31:30.6 (28:47.17-94)
ROYE Jordan Peter U15 3.11.87, Croydon :
80HB - 11.24
RUBEN Alan V45 9.03.57, :
Mar - 2:35:43 (2:29:54-98)
RUBENIS Richard 10.11.73, Telford :
60 - 6.93i (6.89i-97), 400 - 48.5 (47.4/47.76-94),
100 - 10.6w/10.94 (10.5w-94/10.75-00),
200 - 22.17i (21.6-94/21.88-00),
RUDKIN Alan 5.11.78, Peterborough :
DT - 40.51 (43.84-99)
RUMBLE Mark John U15 10.07.88, Oxford City :
DTB - 37.71, JTB - 45.55
RUMBLE Robert John U17 18.10.86, Herts Phoenix :
OctY - 4269
RUMBOLD James Lee U23 4.11.81, Bournemouth/
St. Marys Univ Coll : DT - 44.56
RUND Brett 27.07.77, City of Edinburgh/Edinb Univ :
100 - 10.8/10.96, 200 - 21.32
RUSH Martin Gavin Anthony 25.12.64, Bideford :
10kWR - 47:08 (41:08+84/42:39-83)
RUSIUS Ben U15 26.01.88, Pendle :
800 - 2:03.69, 1500 - 4:16.29, 3k - 9:22.57

RUSLING Steven U15 21.02.88, Aberdeen :
800 - 2:00.77, 3k - 9:39.2
RUSSELL Daniel U17 2.04.87, Shaftesbury Barnet :
1.5kSt - 4:27.32, 2kSt - 6:14.49
RUSSELL James U15 19.09.87, :
HJ - 1.78
RUSSELL Jamie U23 1.10.81, Sheffield/Danville CC :
HJ - 2.19
RUSSELL Karl U23 3.11.81, Lagan Valley :
PV - 4.30, Dec - 5011
RUSSELL Matthew U23 20.01.81, Belgrave :
100 - 10.96w (10.6w/10.63w/10.76-98),
200 - 22.0 (21.89w-96/21.9-99/22.20-96)
RUSSELL Tom U17 3.10.85, Cornwall AC :
1500 - 4:01.64
RUTT Martin U23 3.08.81, Rugby & Nor PH :
LJ - 7.22w/6.91
RYAN Charles Peter V45 9.04.54, Sheffield RWC :
50kW - 4:56:55 (4:18:30-82)
RYAN Maurice U17 17.02.86, Enf & Har :
100HY - 14.05

S AGGERS Carl Peter Maurice U20 20.09.83,
Enf & Har : SP - 13.38 (14.07-01),
SPJ - 15.33 (15.46-01), SP6K - 15.19,
DT - 42.16 (43.70-01), DTJ - 49.62,
HT - 58.99, HTJ - 66.17, HT6K - 66.22
SALISBURY Ian 22.11.70, Trafford :
800 - 1:52.14
SALVADOR-AYLOTT Livio 18.07.73, Harrow :
110H - 15.6 (15.1-93/15.58-97),
PV - 4.22 (4.50-94), Dec - 6593 (7024-94)
SAMMUT Steven 3.05.67, WSE&H :
HT - 61.96
SAMPSON Christopher 30.09.75, Morpeth :
3kSt - 9:21.0 (9:13.54-00)
SAMUELS Ben U17, Bromley :
100 - 11.15w, 200 - 22.4/22.55
SAMUYIWA David 4.08.72, Thames Valley :
60 - 6.9i/6.93i (6.86i-98)
SANCHEZ Marien 28.05.77, Wirral/CUB :
HJ - 2.05 (2.18-00)
SANDERSON David 6.05.71, Sale :
TJ - 14.71 (15.72w-93/15.29-92)
SANFORD Mark 19.04.78, Basildon :
800 - 1:52.91, 1500 - 3:51.02 (3:49.87-01), 3kSt - 9:41.9
SANKOFA Moyo U17 12.12.86, Herne Hill :
400 - 50.6/50.86
SAULTERS Alan U20 29.01.83, Border :
TJ - 14.68w/14.14 (14.22-01)
SAUNDERSON Adie U17 14.03.86, Ballymena & A :
TJ - 13.46
SAVAGE David 13.11.72, Sale :
400H - 55.2 (50.97-96)
SAVILLE Ben 10.11.77, Cleethorpes/Hull Univ :
JT - 62.54
SAWHNEY Simon U20 10.06.83, Border/Lagan Valley/
Aberdeen Univ : TJ - 14.05i (14.26w/14.15-01)
SAWREY Michael U17 30.05.86, Barrow & Furness :
800 - 1:56.69, 1500 - 4:04.73
SAWYER Anthony J. U23 29.04.80, WGreen & Ex L :
110H - 14.67w/14.80, HJ - 2.00, PV - 4.30,
LJ - 7.13w/6.87, Dec - 7377
SCAIFE Martin 18.05.72, Chester le Street :
10kR - 29:59, 10MR - 49:10
SCANLON Robert 13.04.74, Coventry Godiva :
1500 - 3:50.86 (3:41.3-96)
SCARR Andy U20 7.05.85, Enf & Har :
HJ - 2.00
SCHOEMAN Pieter 27.02.79, Walthamstow/RSA :
JT - 56.03
SCHULER Jan 29.10.72, Thames Valley :
Dec - 6119
SCOTT Allan U23 27.12.82, Shaft Ba/Glasgow Univ/
Whitemoss : 60Hi - 7.87i, 110H - 14.05

SCOTT Christopher Mark U15 21.03.88, Guildf & G :
HTB - 43.19
SCOTT Darren 7.03.69, Trafford :
100 - 10.7w/10.84 (10.5w?-99/10.61w-98/10.74-95),
200 - 21.5w?/21.62 (21.0w?-99/21.19w-98/21.3/21.35-95)
SCOTT Lawrence U15 17.09.87, Coventry Godiva :
80HB - 11.8
SCOTT Richard 14.09.73, WGreen & Ex L :
110H - 15.3/15.53 (15.03w/15.2-01),
400H - 52.7/52.89 (52.39-99)
SCOTT Ryan U17 20.02.87, Yate :
100 - 10.7w/10.81w/10.95, 200 - 22.1/22.17
SCOTT Sandy 1.09.76, Shett/Glasgow Univ/Border :
400 - 48.10 (47.40-99)
SEAMAN Nat U17 27.11.85, Leics Cor :
SPY - 14.96
SEAR Richard A. 21.08.79, Belgrave/London Univ :
60H - 8.12i, 110H - 14.45 (14.3w/14.34w-01/14.37-97)
SELBY Alan U17 2.07.86, Morpeth :
100 - 11.0w/11.35, 200 - 22.48
SEMPERS Kevin U17 24.11.85, Scunthorpe :
HJ - 1.99, DecY - 5888, OctY - 4897
SEMPLE Stuart U20 3.11.83, Basingstoke & MH :
DTJ - 42.06
SENBANJO Oladipo U23 20.03.82, Notts/Oxford Un :
TJ - 14.45
SENIOR Nat U13 14.11.89, Havering M :
HJ - 1.49
SENIOR Thomas U15 26.01.88, Hallamshire :
SPB - 13.74
SETTLE Tom U17 25.07.86, Chester le Street :
800 - 1:57.06, 1500 - 4:05.97
SHALDERS Steven U23 24.12.81, Cardiff/UWIC :
60 - 6.78i, 100 - 10.73, TJ - 16.41
SHANKEY Mark U20 19.12.84, Serpentine :
1500 - 3:50.22, 3k - 8:22.20
SHARLAND Tom U20 5.10.83, Ipswich :
1500 - 3:52.01, 3k - 8:11.26, 5k - 14:16.01
SHARMAN William U20 12.09.84, Corby :
110HJ - 15.1, HJ - 2.01i/1.95 (1.95-01), DecJ - 6005
SHARP Adam U15 1.04.88, City of Plymouth :
JTB - 51.56
SHARP Alexis 31.10.72, Blackheath :
DT - 43.00 (49.65-99)
SHARP Stephen 31.12.75, Belgrave :
1500 - 3:44.76 (3:43.42-99), 3k - 8:03.17, 5k - 14:12.73
SHARPE Phill U23 6.03.81, Border :
JT - 71.09 (71.79-00)
SHAW Philip U15 18.11.87, Herts Sch :
HJ - 1.75
SHAW Ryan U17 30.12.86, WGreen & Ex L :
100HY - 14.09, DecY - 5204, OctY - 4436
SHEERAN Richard U17 27.11.85, Sale :
400 - 49.36
SHELTON Christopher 19.10.78, Chesterfield :
3kSt - 9:39.9
SHEPHERD Bruce David 20.03.67, Aberdeen :
HT - 49.09 (53.18-96)
SHEPLEY Sebastian 23.11.67, Westbury :
Mar - 2:28:32 (2:27:01-98)
SHEPPARD Kevin 27.01.79, Army/Tipton :
800 - 1:50.06, 1500 - 3:46.85,
1M - 4:09.70, 2kSt - 5:41.78
SHERIDAN Mark D. 17.06.70, Crawley :
HT - 49.73 (56.02-91)
SHERMAN Andrew U23 28.09.81, Swindon/Loughbro :
1500 - 3:47.57
SHIELDS David Andrew U15 18.02.88, :
HJ - 1.90
SHONE Matthew 10.07.75, WGreen & Ex L :
800 - 1:46.72, 1500 - 3:42.08
SHORROCK Andrew U20 28.09.84, Wigan :
SPJ - 14.35, SP6K - 14.54
SHORT O. U13, Leics Sch :
400 - 62.4

SHORTHOUSE Chris U15 23.06.88, :
HTB - 40.62
SHORTMAN Luke U15 14.10.87, Cambridge & C :
HTB - 50.01
SHOWELL Gavin 29.09.72, Tamworth :
PV - 4.60 (4.75-00)
SHURMAN Anthony U13 27.11.89, Chichester :
75 - 10.1
SICHEL William Morley V45 1.10.53, Moray RR :
100kR - 7:51:11 (7:07:49-96)
SILLAH-FRECKLETON Mohammed U23 11.09.80,
Blackheath : 60H - 8.1i (8.09i-00), 110H - 14.05
SIMEY Gregor U15 25.10.88, Corby :
PenB - 2548
SIMMONDS Robert U20 30.08.85, Ryston :
DecJ - 5363
SIMMONS Dedan U20 9.04.83, Harrow :
400 - 48.87
SIMNER Paul U17 13.12.85, Tipton :
1.5kSt - 4:36.56
SIMON Delroy 27.11.78, Harrow :
3kSt - 9:07.51 (9:00.81-00)
SIMONS Daniel 8.06.76, Cornwall AC :
3kSt - 9:36.73
SIMPSON Alexander U23 19.01.82, Med & Maid :
JT - 57.44
SIMPSON D. U13, :
TJ - 9.71
SIMPSON Jason 14.01.67, S London :
10k - 30:33.0, HMar - 66:56
SIMPSON Neil U20 11.09.83, Blackheath :
200 - 22.18w/22.25
SIMPSON Scott E. 21.07.79, Birchfield/UWIC :
PV - 5.31i/5.00 (5.20-01)
SINCLAIR James U15 22.10.87, Gateshead :
100 - 11.38, 200 - 22.99, JTB - 43.17
SINCLAIR Robert 8.11.77, Oxford Univ :
Dec - 5301
SINGH Darsham U17 26.07.86, Basildon :
1500 - 4:01.0
SINGLETON Jack U17 17.12.85, Yeovil Olympiads :
100HY - 13.8w, OctY - 4377
SKETCHLEY David 25.02.76, Team Solent :
JT - 66.40
SKINNARD Joseph U15 14.09.87, City of Plymouth :
LJ - 6.08, PenB - 2500
SKINNER Michael 21.11.79, Blackheath/Brunel Univ :
800 - 1:50.00, 1500 - 3:42.43
SKRIVANOS Yiannis Michael U17 10.10.86, Exeter :
HJ - 1.95
SLEEMAN Christopher J. U23 20.03.80, Ox C/OUAC :
200H - 25.78, 400H - 53.12 (52.6/52.97-01)
SLUE Leroy U23 11.12.81, Harrow :
60 - 6.98i, 100 - 10.72w/10.95 (10.8-01/10.92-99)
SLYTHE Paul J. 5.09.74, Newham & Essex B :
400 - 47.21 (45.94-98)
SMALL Michael V45 31.03.54, Belgrave :
SP - 14.03, DT - 43.91 (45.40-85),
HT - 47.69?/46.10 (49.98-86)
SMALL Steven U17 6.12.85, Bournemouth :
LJ - 6.61
SMART Julius U17 18.11.85, Harrow :
1500 - 3:55.66
SMITH Alex U15 6.03.88, Hull Achilles :
HTB - 45.26
SMITH Alistair U20 22.02.84, AF&D :
2kSt - 6:02.47, 3kSt - 9:33.3
SMITH Andrew U20 2.10.84, Middlesbro & C :
HT - 45.33, HTJ - 52.71
SMITH Andrew U13 15.11.89, Dundee HH :
75HC - 13.1
SMITH Ben U23 12.06.82, Shaftesbury Barnet :
HJ - 2.00 (2.00-98)
SMITH Cameron U20 17.01.84, Cardiff :
3kW - 12:35.60i (13:05.18-00)

SMITH Carl Anthony V40 17.05.58, Shaftesbury B :
 JT - 64.04 (69.94r-91)
SMITH Christopher James 27.11.75, Border :
 JT - 60.58 (62.30-96)
SMITH Christopher James U17 4.12.85, Tamworth :
 800 - 1:57.4
SMITH Dan U15 16.04.88, Wimborne :
 HJ - 1.76
SMITH David V40 21.06.62, NESH/Kingston u Hull :
 HT - 63.40 (77.30-85)
SMITH Francis U23 2.10.81, Border :
 60H - 8.41i, 110H - 14.62
SMITH Gary 20.02.71, Luton :
 110H - 15.4 (14.87w/15.00-91), LJ - 7.06 (7.58w-00/7.49-97)
SMITH Gavin U20 15.02.85, AF&D :
 5k - 15:28.6, 2kSt - 6:08.73, 3kSt - 9:47.9
SMITH Glen Ernest 21.05.72, Birchfield :
 SP - 14.30 (14.71-96), DT - 63.10 (65.11-99)
SMITH Gregory U20 29.01.84, Bournemouth :
 110HJ - 15.27 (15.0/15.25-01)
SMITH James U17 11.12.86, Halesowen :
 HTY - 52.09
SMITH Leigh Matthew U23 24.09.82, Birchfield :
 LJ - 7.37w/7.19 (7.29-00)
SMITH Luke U13 7.11.89, Swindon :
 100 - 12.5, 200 - 26.1
SMITH Matthew 26.12.74, Tipton :
 5k - 13:53.30, 10k - 29:13.60 (28:43.45-01),
 10kR - 29:30, HMar - 65:06
SMITH Michael 3.06.79, Bolton :
 100 - 10.8/10.94w (10.50w-01/10.8/10.85-00),
 200 - 21.6/22.08w (22.10-01)
SMITH Michael John 20.04.63, Coventry RWC :
 30kW - 2:39:14+ (2:24:14+-89/2:26:01.0t+-86/2:37:11-01),
 35kW - 3:11:55 (2:40:37-89),
 50kW - 4:42:58 (4:09:22-89)
SMITH Mike 1.02.68, Cirencester :
 Mar - 2:26:26
SMITH Nicholas U23 6.12.82, Dunfe & W Fife/S B :
 60 - 6.76i, 100 - 10.4w/10.49,
 200 - 21.5w/21.6/21.89 (21.5w/21.58-01)
SMITH Richard Blake U23 12.10.82, Newham & E B :
 400 - 48.1 (49.34-99), 400H - 51.14
SMITH Robert U20 3.03.85, Colchester & T :
 400 - 49.20 (49.19-01)
SMITH Robin Alistair U20 11.09.83, City of Stoke :
 110HJ - 14.5 (14.89w/14.99-01), 110H - 15.38,
 DECJI - 6351
SMITH Steven U15 3.09.87, Herts Phoenix :
 800 - 2:05.4
SMITH Sullivan 16.09.76, Swansea :
 3kSt - 9:21.6
SMITH Wesley 26.02.79, Belgrave :
 JT - 58.25 (60.86-00)
SMITH-GILLESPIE Iain U17 5.02.86, Herne Hill :
 SPY - 13.81
SMYTH Jeremy 11.08.78, City of Edinburgh/Shett :
 JT - 56.85 (59.95-00)
SNODGRASS James, Kilbarchan :
 Mar - 2:36:17
SNOW Shane 31.10.66, Highgate Harriers :
 Mar - 2:31:36 (2:26:51-00)
SNOW Tom U17 7.09.85, WGreen & Ex L :
 800 - 1:54.57, 1500 - 3:59.51
SNOWBALL Oliver U13, Eastbourne AC :
 HJ - 1.48
SOALLA-BELL Anthony 3.10.76, Shaftesbury B/SLE :
 SP - 16.01, DT - 44.75
SOLLITT Gary 13.01.72, Team Solent :
 SP - 17.85
SOOS Ricky Istvan U20 28.06.83, Mansf/Loughbro :
 400 - 48.5/48.68, 800 - 1:47.18,
 1500 - 3:48.32 (3:46.70-01), 3k - 8:37.18
SOUGRIN Neil 14.05.71, Enf & Har :
 DT - 41.80 (47.82-94)

SOUTH James 4.01.75, Southend :
 SP - 14.54, DT - 49.04
SOUTHWARD Anthony 31.01.71, Trafford :
 110H - 15.06w/15.44 (14.6w-98/14.69-96),
 PV - 4.20 (4.45-01), Dec - 5582unf (7425-96)
SPARKS Steven U13 24.04.90, :
 TJ - 9.40
SPEAIGHT Neil Anthony 9.09.78, Belgrave :
 800 - 1:46.92, 1500 - 3:44.89
SPEAKE William J. 24.01.71, Notts :
 Mar - 2:26:48
SPENCER-JONES Ryan U17 14.10.86, Brecon :
 SPY - 14.00
SPRINGER Craig U17, Enf & Har :
 PV - 3.60
SPUFFARD Daniel Gavin U15 6.09.87, WSE&H :
 400 - 53.32
SQUIRE Derrick John Preston U20 7.12.83, Can & St :
 SP - 14.79i/14.67, SPJ - 17.12, SP6K - 16.15,
 HT - 54.35, HTJ - 55.26, HT6K - 57.55
ST.CLAIR Darren U20 6.04.85, Enf & Har :
 400 - 49.2/49.25, 800 - 1:53.88
STACEY John Michael U17 23.11.85, Gateshead :
 TJ - 13.26, OctY - 4515
STAMP Terence 18.02.70, Newham & Essex B :
 60 - 6.85i (6.70i-98), 100 - 10.65 (10.4-97/10.47-95)
STANBURY Luke U13, :
 TJ - 9.52
STANILAND Andrew William U17 21.01.87, Skyrac :
 OctY - 4957
STANISAVIJEVIC Nick U17 10.12.86, Woking/YUG :
 HJ - 1.97
STANISLAUS Sam U15 29.04.88, Richmond & Zet :
 TJ - 12.01
STANNARD Joshua U15 15.10.87, Taunton :
 JTB - 49.16
STAPELY Stephen U20 19.05.84, Dartford :
 DecJ - 5049 (5452-01)
STAPPLETON Ricky U13 8.12.89, Enf & Har :
 SPC - 11.51
STARK Graeme 12.10.63, Rotherham :
 SP - 13.40 (14.88i-94/14.70-85)
STASAITIS Reginaldas 6.04.67, London Heath/LTU :
 HJ - 1.95 (2.08-84), LJ - 6.91 (7.02-00),
 TJ - 14.45 (15.62w/15.53-99)
STATTER Ian V45 11.07.57, Surrey WC :
 100MWT - 21:07:15+, 24HrWT - 179.764km
STEADMAN Darren U17 26.01.87, Colchester H :
 HJ - 1.93
STEELE Andrew U20 19.09.84, Trafford :
 300 - 34.7, 400 - 47.36
STEELE Joe U15 13.02.88, Luton :
 TJ - 12.10w
STEELE Josh U15 14.09.87, Bedford & County :
 HTB - 41.08oa
STEELE Laurence U17 24.04.86, Blackpool :
 PV - 4.00
STEINLE Mark 22.11.74, Blackheath :
 5k - 14:01.81 (13:58.42-99),
 10k - 29:31.64 (28:04.48-00), 10kR - 29:09,
 10MR - 47:53+ (48:25-98),
 HMar - 62:47+/63:02 (62:23-99), Mar - 2:09:17
STEPHENS Gavin James 12.09.77, Enf & H/Brunel U :
 100 - 10.7w (10.8-00), LJ - 6.92 (6.97-99),
 200 - 22.07i/22.20 (21.57w/22.00-00)
STEPHENSON Christian 22.07.74, Cardiff :
 3kSt - 8:41.32 (8:25.37-00)
STEVENS Kyle U20 3.06.85, Kingston & Poly :
 SP - 13.74, SPJ - 15.16, SP6K - 14.82
STEVENS Nathan U17 7.08.86, Channel Islands :
 200 - 22.5, 400 - 50.5/50.94
STEVENS Paul U20 15.11.83, Kingston u Hull :
 PV - 4.80st/4.70 (4.70-01)
STEVENSON James U13 8.12.89, :
 DTC - 29.20

382

STEWART Alaster 5.10.72, Belgrave :
 5k - 14:39.22
STEWART Callum U15 13.01.88, :
 JTB - 45.42
STEWART Camara U20 11.09.83, Notts :
 HJ - 2.00
STEWART Craig U17 24.11.85, Kilbarchan :
 400 - 49.94, 400HY - 58.3/58.64
STEWART Glen 7.12.70, RRC :
 3k - 8:01.42i/8:03.49 (7:55.15-99),
 5k - 13:47.10 (13:37.17-01), 5MR - 23:54 (23:17-99),
 10k - 28:47.52 (28:40.14-01), HMar - 66:25 (65:34-01)
STEWART Jonathan U23 22.05.80, Holmfirth :
 800 - 1:52.71 (1:49.53-00)
STEWART Kris George U23 11.04.80, S B/Stirling Un/
 Scottish Border : 100 - 10.66, 200 - 21.17w/21.24
STIMPSON Alan 25.04.68, New Marske :
 10k - 31:03.5
STIMSON Thomas U17 2.09.86, Nene Valley H :
 100HY - 13.40
STOBART Christopher U23 27.03.82, Manx/Bath Un :
 100 - 10.75 (10.7wdb-98/10.73w-99), 200 - 21.54
STOCKDALE Daniel U17 2.09.85, Trafford :
 TJ - 13.78
STODDART Barry, Army :
 3kSt - 9:34.2
STODDART Dwayne U23 29.12.80, WSE&H :
 200 - 22.0/22.09, 60H - 8.08i, 110H - 14.48
STOKES Stuart 5.12.76, Sale :
 1500 - 3:45.48, 10kR - 29:37, HMar - 66:39, 3kSt - 8:26.45
STONE Darrell Richard 2.02.68, Steyning :
 10kW - 46:24.0+ (41:10.11-95), 10kWR - 42:54 (40:45-89)
STONE Darryl Frank U20 6.06.83, Basildon :
 HJ - 2.09i/2.05 (2.10-00)
STONE David 13.02.70, Exmouth :
 Mar - 2:34:52
STONE Kairnil 21.10.76, Newham & Essex B :
 3k - 8:13.80, 5k - 14:17.61
STOTT Adrian V45 5.08.54, Sri Chinmoy :
 24Hr - 211.056km (230.667km-00)
STOVES Christopher U20 20.02.84, Sale :
 800 - 1:52.69 (1:50.13-01)
STRACHAN Richard U17 18.11.86, Leeds :
 400 - 50.27
STRANGE Alasdair U20 5.04.83, Shettleston :
 PV - 4.30i (4.10-01)
STROUD Guy U15 9.08.88, Newquay & Par :
 80HB - 11.62, PenB - 2758
STUART Allan U23 14.08.81, Shettleston :
 60 - 6.94i, 100 - 10.96 (10.9-00),
 200 - 21.63 (21.54-00), 400 - 47.19
STURLA Michael U13, Exeter :
 JTB - 28.83
STURROCK Craig U20 7.01.85, Gateshead :
 SP6K - 13.64
STYLES Iain Bruce 2.10.75, Chelt/Birmingham Univ. :
 SP - 14.16i/13.99 (15.47un/15.13-01),
 DT - 40.08 (42.72-00)
SUMNER Ben U20 16.08.83, Enf & Har/Man Univ :
 400H - 54.35
SUMNER Richard U23 20.09.80, Basingstoke & MH :
 800 - 1:51.5
SURETY Steven Christopher U23 18.02.80, Basildon/
 Brunel Univ : 100 - 10.6w (10.95-98),
 200 - 21.95i (21.89-98), 300 - 34.58i,
 400 - 47.52, 400H - 50.16
SUTTON Adam Christopher U23 22.03.81, Preston/
 Providence Un : 3k - 8:17.25 (8:12.77i-01),
 5k - 14:01.26, 10k - 28:40.32
SUTTON Matthew U23 8.09.81, Birchfield :
 HT - 52.76 (57.64-00)
SWAIN Anthony Michael 17.01.75, Wakefield/Hudd U :
 HT - 50.09 (62.88-97)
SWAIN Ashley U23 3.10.80, Team Solent/Staffs Un :
 PV - 5.30

SWARAY Tyrone 7.11.77, Blackheath :
 100 - 10.82 (10.56-99)
SWEARMAN Andrew 1.02.74, Kingston u Hull :
 10k - 30:40.80
SWEENEY Conor U23 28.12.81, Loughbros/IRL :
 800 - 1:49.79 (1:49.35-01), 1500 - 3:41.30, 1M - 4:01.58
SWEENEY Mark 26.02.77, Army :
 HJ - 2.00 (2.00i/2.00-97)
SWEENEY Oliver U17 13.07.86, Luton :
 HJ - 2.00
SWINBURN David 4.06.78, Morpeth :
 3kSt - 9:28.2
SYERS Aidan U20 29.06.83, Newham & Essex B :
 100 - 10.5w/10.52w/10.78 (10.31w/10.52-01)
SYMONDS Chris 21.11.73, Enf & Har :
 3kSt - 9:31.1 (9:28.4-01)
SYMONDS David 21.10.68, Gade Valley :
 Mar - 2:33:28
SZADE Richard 15.02.71, Cardiff :
 Mar - 2:28:25

T ABARES Ruben 22.10.78, Blackheath :
 400 - 47.13A/48.02 (48.01-97)
TADESSE Kassa 21.08.74, Belgrave :
 10MR - 48:53 (47:43-93), HMar - 64:43 (62:51-97),
 Mar - 2:34:20 (2:19:14-93)
TALBOT Nicholas P. 14.12.77, Notts/Oxford Univ :
 5k - 14:40.2, 3kSt - 8:49.2
TANNER Alex 29.12.78, Enf & Har :
 800 - 1:52.73
TARRAN Michael U23 10.12.80, Birchfield :
 JT - 71.00
TASKER Bruce U15 2.09.87, Carmarthen :
 400 - 52.51
TATHAM Alasdair 16.09.72, Quakers :
 Mar - 2:36:06
TAWANAEE Alistair U15 31.03.88, Blackheath :
 HTB - 47.97
TAYLOR David U20 21.11.84, Swindon :
 110HJ - 15.1, 110H - 15.6, 400H - 54.7, DecJ - 5838
TAYLOR David William 9.01.64, Blackheath :
 1500 - 3:49.10 (3:47.9-99), 5MR - 23:51 (23:30-99),
 10k - 29:20.02 (29:00.04-99), HMar - 63:47 (63:24-97)
TAYLOR Duncan U13 5.09.89, Milton Keynes :
 3k - 10:30.08
TAYLOR Gary U17 5.07.86, WSE&H :
 3k - 8:59.6
TAYLOR Gregg 1.08.77, Trafford :
 800 - 1:48.93, 1500 - 3:40.70,
 3k - 8:12.28i/8:15.37 (8:10.68-01)
TAYLOR Ian J. 2.07.67, Telford :
 DT - 42.43 (49.44-93)
TAYLOR Jonathan U15 10.10.87, Midd AC :
 800 - 2:04.14, 1500 - 4:12.79
TAYLOR Kurt U13 1.10.89, :
 SPC - 10.67
TAYLOR Martin J.M. U23 31.01.82, S B/Vic Pk & T H :
 LJ - 7.07 (7.47-00), Dec - 6174 (6470-00)
TAYLOR Philip U20 20.03.85, Liv.Pembroke Sefton :
 100 - 10.8, 400 - 48.37
TAYLOR Wayne Richard U15 17.10.87, Grimsby :
 400 - 52.52, 80HB - 11.9 (11.9-01),
 HJ - 1.78, PenB - 2666
TEASDALE Jack U15 14.09.87, Halifax :
 SPB - 13.24
TEASEL Oliver James U20 24.04.84, Birchfield :
 400 - 48.38, 800 - 1:50.56, 400H - 56.0
TEDD Phil J.A. 7.11.76, Bingley :
 1500 - 3:47.13 (3:43.54-00)
TELFORD Craig 1.06.79, Morpeth :
 60 - 6.8i, 200 - 22.0/22.07
TENNY Joe U17 9.06.87, Watford :
 100HY - 13.67
THACKERY Carl Edward V40 14.10.62, Hallamshire :
 10MR - 48:20 (46:21+/46:26-91), HMar - 64:28 (61:04-87)

383

THAKE Andrew 16.11.76, R Sutton Coldfield :
Mar - 2:36:03
THICKPENNY Robert 17.07.76, Peterborough :
PV - 4.60 (4.80-99)
THIE James 27.06.78, Cardiff :
800 - 1:50.00, 1500 - 3:41.06,
1M - 3:58.24, 3k - 8:09.16
THOMAS Andrew U23 29.01.81, Med & M/Brunel Un :
2kSt - 5:49.85, 3kSt - 9:13.52
THOMAS Andrew 9.02.74, Swansea :
LJ - 6.81w (7.16w/7.13-00)
THOMAS Andrew U17 14.06.86, Birchfield :
SPJ - 14.45, SPY - 16.00, DTJ - 45.13,
DTY - 52.84, HTJ - 49.06, HTY - 56.81
THOMAS Barry V.S. 28.04.72, Sheffield :
60H - 8.53i (8.32i-96), HJ - 1.95 (2.05-92),
110H - 15.11 (14.62w-95/14.81-92),
PV - 4.75 (5.00-92), LJ - 7.21w/7.17 (7.44-92),
SP - 13.87 (14.15i-01/14.06-96), DT - 41.86 (42.92-01),
JT - 57.08 (62.40-97), Dec - 7546 (7766-95)
THOMAS Darryl U15 23.11.87, Ealing,Southall & Mx :
100 - 11.53, LJ - 6.48
THOMAS David U15 13.02.88, Grantham :
100 - 11.1w/11.25w/11.5/11.55, SPB - 13.40
THOMAS Iwan Gwyn 5.01.74, Newham & Essex B :
100 - 10.96 (10.67w-01/10.90+-97), 200 - 21.89 (20.87-97),
300 - 33.77 (32.08+-97/32.36-98), 400 - 46.48 (44.36-97)
THOMAS Jamie U17 7.06.86, Solihull & S Heath :
HJ - 2.00
THOMAS Jay U15 5.10.88, Kent :
SPB - 15.65
THOMAS Joselyn 11.07.71, WGreen & EL/Army/SLE :
100 - 10.40 (10.3w/10.36w-98),
200 - 21.9/22.11 (21.10w-98/21.2/21.29-94)
THOMAS Josephus ¶ 11.07.71, WGn & EL/Army/SLE :
100 - 10.6w/10.90w (10.19w-98/10.2-96/10.29-98)
THOMAS Julian U17 28.12.86, Birchfield :
100 - 10.86w/10.87, 200 - 21.65, LJ - 6.97
THOMAS Keston U23 17.04.81, Serpentine/GRN :
LJ - 7.19
THOMAS Luke U15 27.03.89, Enf & Har :
LJ - 6.12
THOMAS Martin 21.09.78, Liverpool H :
400H - 54.1 (53.52-97)
THOMAS Matthew 27.04.76, Newham & Essex B :
60 - 6.95i, 100 - 10.6/10.65, 200 - 21.7/21.87
THOMAS Nicholas 4.04.79, Newham & Essex B :
60 - 6.8i/6.84i (6.8i-00/6.84i-01),
100 - 10.58w/10.80 (10.61-00),
200 - 22.0/22.17 (21.53w-01/21.9-00/22.09-01),
LJ - 6.90 (7.24w-99/7.13-00), TJ - 16.17 (16.31-00)
THOMAS Rhyan U15 9.02.88, Birchfield :
TJ - 12.04, SPB - 13.70
THOMAS Ryan U17 21.03.87, Epsom & Ewell :
400 - 49.70
THOMAS Simon David U23 4.03.81, Southend/CUAC :
HJ - 2.00i/1.95 (2.10-99)
THOMAS Timothy Paul 18.11.73, Cardiff :
PV - 5.30i/5.25 (5.40-97)
THOMASSEN Olau U23 19.02.80, Newham & E B/
Loughbro/DEN : 110H - 15.23, 400H - 52.27
THOMPSON Christopher U23 17.04.81, AF&D/
Loughbro : 1500 - 3:45.56 (3:43.55-01),
3k - 8:00.25, 5k - 13:50.8 (13:45.27-01)
THOMPSON Daniel U20 27.12.84, City of Stoke :
DecJ - 5588
THOMPSON Darren 6.11.79, Belgrave :
LJ - 7.34 (7.84w-01/7.56-98)
THOMPSON Gavin U23 9.04.80, Craw/East Mich Un :
3k - 8:10.30i (8:46.18-97),
5k - 14:07.29, 10k - 30:07.37
THOMPSON Kemel 25.09.74, Loughbro/JAM :
400 - 47.99i/48.1
THOMPSON Kevin U20 24.10.83, Liverpool H :
TJ - 15.30

THOMPSON Kevin U13 29.12.89, Herne Hill :
SPC - 11.96, JTC - 34.47
THOMPSON Matthew U20 29.12.84, Black Isle/NSP :
110HJ - 15.44
THOMPSON Neville Leigh V45 28.03.55, Shaft B :
DT - 50.71 (55.68-93)
THOMPSON Ross U23 7.12.81, Gateshead :
HT - 55.80 (57.38-99)
THOMPSON Scot William U23 10.08.81, Pitr/Bel/
Bath Univ : SP - 15.76, DT - 52.97
THOMPSON Stephen U17 5.09.86, :
100 - 11.1 (11.43w/11.48-01)
THOMSON Fearghas U13 23.09.89, Musselburgh :
400 - 62.5
THOMSON Matthew U23 20.09.81, Yate/
Oklahoma St Un : 800 - 1:50.94
THORNE-LADEJO Du'aine 14.02.71, Birchfield :
100 - 10.5w (10.28w/10.45-98),
200 - 21.3w? (20.96-93), 400 - 46.05 (44.66-96)
THURGOOD Matthew U20 29.12.83, Herts Phoenix :
HJ - 2.00, TJ - 14.69
THURGOOD Stuart Dennis 17.05.76, Harlow :
HT - 55.39 (56.91-00)
TICKNER Ben U23 13.07.81, Wells/Yeovil Oly/Ex U :
1500 - 3:46.60, 3k - 8:18.19, 5k - 14:29.0
TICKNER Frank U20 12.10.83, Wells/Yeovil Oly :
3k - 8:30.62, 2kSt - 5:47.02, 3kSt - 9:08.24
TIDY Stephen U15 14.10.87, Peterborough :
400 - 53.50
TIETZ Michael 14.09.77, Birchfield :
100 - 10.60 (10.39w-97/10.51-98)
TILLEY Grant U13 2.07.91, Milton Keynes :
3k - 10:43.9
TINDAL Lee U23 19.02.80, Team Solent :
110H - 14.64, 400H - 55.87 (55.77-00)
TINSLEY Ian U23 23.01.81, Liverpool H :
800 - 1:52.7 (1:52.7-98)
TIPPET Andrew U17, Oxford City :
400HY - 58.25
TIPPING Tom 29.04.66, Inverclyde :
3kSt - 9:31.37
TITMAN Carl U17 9.09.86, Peterborough :
PV - 3.60
TOAL Thomas U17 23.12.86, Charnwood :
DTY - 41.89
TOBIN Ian U13 2.09.89, Herts Phoenix :
LJ - 5.88
TOBIN Robert John U20 20.12.83, Basingstoke & MH :
100 - 10.9 (10.9-01), 200 - 21.33, 400 - 46.80i/46.80
TODD Stuart U15 4.09.87, Vic Park & Tower H :
80HB - 11.70
TOHILL Paul U23 9.10.82, Bord/M Ulster/Loughbro :
60H - 8.34i, 110H - 14.78, Dec - 6678,
HJ - 2.05i/1.95 (2.01-00), PV - 4.20, LJ - 6.96w
TOMASI Vito U15 17.01.88, Channel Islands :
80HB - 11.51
TOMLINSON Christopher U23 15.09.81, Ne & E B :
100 - 10.69 (10.6w/10.61w-01),
200 - 21.73, LJ - 8.27
TOMPSETT Scott 21.08.77, Hillingdon :
5k - 14:43.5
TOOLE Ross U17 8.10.86, Kilbarchan :
1500 - 4:05.14
TOPHAM Arran U15 25.06.88, Lancashire Sch :
400 - 52.20
TOPLISS Daniel U17 8.10.85, Newark :
100 - 10.9/11.05, 200 - 22.5
TOUGH Mark U13 3.03.90, Montrose :
DTC - 27.82
TOUGH Sean U17 25.12.86, Montrose :
DecY - 4936
TOWARD Andrew U20 29.07.83, Morpeth :
1500 - 3:54.86, 5k - 14:53.7
TOWNSON Daniel U17, City of Stoke :
400HY - 58.19

384

TOYE Simon David U17 24.09.85, Thurrock :
200 - 22.1, 400 - 48.13
TRAVIS Martin Richard U20 10.07.85, Bristol :
JT - 56.82
TREES Mike V40 26.09.62, Belgrave :
10k - 31:52.3, 10kR - 29:58
TREMAYNE Christopher James U20 11.11.84,
Cannock & Stafford : PV - 4.85
TRESSIDER Ross U20 8.01.83, Thurrock :
110HJ - 14.67w/14.7/14.96 (14.88-01),
110H - 15.4, 400H - 54.2/55.31, DecJ - 5620
TROMANS Glynn 17.03.69, Coventry Godiva :
3k - 8:15.13 (7:58.31-99), 5k - 13:57.44 (13:43.40-01),
5MR - 23:26, 10k - 29:26.80 (28:21.07-99)
TROW Rory U13 18.02.90, Dorset :
JTC - 35.58
TUCK Robin U13 19.10.89, Watford :
HJ - 1.50
TUFTON Kevin U23 30.04.80, Havering M/Brunel Un :
PV - 4.20 (4.20-99)
TULLETT Ian Roger 15.08.69, Luton :
PV - 5.00 (5.35-98)
TURNBULL Gareth 14.05.79, Loughbro/IRL :
800 - 1:47.96 (1:55.13un-95), 1M - 3:57.61,
3k - 7:57.90i (8:09.29-99)
TURNBULL Josh U15 3.12.88, Carmarthen :
JTB - 45.52
TURNER Andrew 29.08.63, Bournemouth :
SP - 14.77 (14.86i-96), DT - 48.00, HT - 52.01
TURNER Andrew D. U23 19.09.80, Notts :
100 - 10.7, 60H - 7.89i, 110H - 13.90
TURNER Clive U20 24.11.84, Enf & Har :
100 - 10.75 (10.69w-01), 200 - 21.8 (22.14-01)
TURNER Daniel 27.11.78, Team Solent :
HJ - 2.05 (2.20-01)
TURNER David V45 20.10.57, York RWC :
5kW - 23:58.2, 50kW - 4:53:31 (4:45:56-91)
TURNER David James U20 4.07.84, Blackpool :
JT - 55.02
TURNER Douglas 2.12.66, Cardiff :
60 - 6.69i, 100 - 10.84 (10.26w-96/10.37-01),
200 - 20.59i/20.75 (20.36w-97/20.43-96)
TURNER Stuart U15 25.12.87, Corstorphine :
SPB - 13.10
TURVILL Steven 17.02.75, Basingstoke & MH :
800 - 1:50.75
TWIGG Matthew 18.07.69, Rugby & Nor PH :
SP - 14.90 (15.05-98), DT - 54.53
TWISS Daniel U13, :
SPC - 10.90, DTC - 32.59, JTC - 35.74
TYE-WALKER Christopher U23 20.09.82, WSE&H/
Brunel Univ : 60H - 8.23i, 110H - 14.9w (15.0-01)
TYLER Ben U15 14.03.88, Med & Maid :
3k - 9:31.5
TYPE Christopher U23 5.10.81, Cardiff/UWIC :
PV - 4.70i/4.70 (4.80i-00/4.75-01)

UDECHUKU Emeka 10.07.79, WG & EL/Lough :
SP - 18.69, DT - 58.64 (62.07-00)
UGONO Uvie 8.03.78, WGreen & Ex L :
100 - 10.50w/10.54 (10.32w-98/10.36-00),
200 - 21.41 (20.89w/21.08-00)
URSELL Nangeloum U23 1.10.81, Blackheath :
400H - 51.5/52.55

VAN DER MERWE Alexander U20 5.01.84, Exeter :
JT - 68.85
VANDENBERG Adam Philip U20 2.06.84, AF&D :
800 - 1:53.15
VASS David U17 31.12.85, West Norfolk :
400 - 50.98 (50.91-01)
VAUX-HARVEY Matthew 30.03.76, Kidd & Stourport :
5MR - 23:47
VERNON Steven U23 17.10.80, Stockport/Loughbro :
1500 - 3:48.08

VICKERS Gary 26.02.71, Telford :
800 - 1:49.68 (1:48.85-01)
VICKERS Peter U20 11.06.84, Midd AC :
100 - 10.8/11.12 (10.95w-01/11.04-00), 200 - 21.99
VIERA Adryan U15 4.11.87, :
100 - 11.5
VINCE Nicholas U23 29.01.82, Falkirk/Sale :
SP - 14.46i/13.18 (13.55-00), DT - 44.11
VINCENT Martin U17 12.04.86, Rugby & Nor PH :
PV - 3.80 (3.80-01)
VINT Richard 16.02.79, AF&D/Butler Univ, USA :
1500 - 3:45.31, 1M - 4:07.85i, 3kSt - 8:58.63

WADDINGTON Anthony 30.06.75, Luton :
100 - 10.78w/10.91 (10.6-99/10.61-00),
200 - 21.95 (21.68-00)
WADE Ben U15 9.11.87, Tonbridge :
DTB - 37.24
WADE Tom U13 16.06.90, Tonbridge :
DTC - 27.81
WAHAB Abdi U15 10.02.89, Ealing,Southall & Mx :
1500 - 4:20.21, 3k - 9:35.42
WAIN Andrew 2.06.65, Nene Vallley H :
SP - 14.27 (14.86-99)
WALCOTT Andrew U15 6.01.88, R Sutton Coldfield :
400 - 52.3/53.18
WALDEN Matthew U20 30.11.83, Scunthorpe :
DecJ - 6332
WALES Alan U20 7.08.85, Aberdeen :
800 - 1:53.78, 1500 - 3:50.34
WALKER Adam 16.11.79, Crawley/Loughborough :
PV - 4.20 (4.60-01)
WALKER Leigh 17.08.77, Crawley :
PV - 4.80 (4.90-00)
WALKER Michael U15 22.07.88, Cardiff :
PV - 3.10i/2.80
WALKER Paul James U20 15.08.85, Cardiff :
PV - 4.61
WALKER Stuart 22.09.78, Derby & Co :
JT - 55.78 (58.94-96)
WALL Darren U23 6.04.80, Team Solent/Soton Univ :
100 - 10.92 (10.71w/10.8-98), 200 - 21.76 (21.65w/21.70-98)
WALLER Joe U15 13.11.87, :
JTB - 48.17
WALLIS Tim U20, Wessex & Bath :
400H - 56.61
WALMSLEY Dennis V40 5.09.62, Bourton RR :
Mar - 2:28:18 (2:21:19-95), 100kR - 7:07:39
WALSH Christopher U23 1.10.78, Shaft B/Teeside Univ :
HT - 54.05 (60.53-00)
WALSH Peter U23 5.05.80, Liverpool H :
800 - 1:50.92 (1:50.01-01)
WALTER Bill U17 11.10.85, Bournemouth :
SPY - 15.42
WARBURTON Christopher William U20 23.08.83,
Notts : 800 - 1:53.1, 2kSt - 5:55.72
WARD A. U17, :
DTY - 41.38
WARD Ashley Keith 1.08.64, Crawley :
DT - 41.87 (47.70-82)
WARD J. U13, Pudsey & Bramley :
LJ - 5.13
WARD Jason 15.09.78, Hallamshire :
3kSt - 9:39.4 (9:24.88-98)
WARD Jonathan 25.11.65, Ashford :
DT - 40.10 (44.55-00)
WARD Richard James Stephen U23 5.05.82,
Belgrave/Manchester Univ :
1500 - 3:45.88 (3:44.96-01)
WARD Tim U23 27.05.82, Border/Edge Hill Univ :
100 - 10.73 (10.63w-01), 200 - 22.0 (21.8/21.91-01)
WARDLE Dave 1.10.75, London Irish :
5k - 14:48.8 (14:28.47-00)
WARISO Solomon Christopher 11.11.66, Enf & Har :
100 - 10.86 (10.3-95/10.33-94), 200 - 21.65 (20.50-95)

WARKE Peter U17 22.05.86, Lagan Valley :
400 - 50.21
WARLEY Matthew James U20 1.08.85, Cheltenham :
800 - 1:54.27
WARMBY Mark 12.12.78, Newham & Essex B :
5k - 13:59.68, 3kSt - 8:49.33
WARNES Ben U15 2.01.88, Norfolk Sch :
TJ - 12.10
WARREN Carl 28.09.69, Birchfield :
HMar - 64:36
WATERS Lee U17 1.06.86, Rushcliffe :
400 - 50.07
WATKINS Andrew U15 8.12.87, Pontypridd :
100 - 10.99, 200 - 22.13, 400 - 52.1 (53.27?-01)
WATKINSON Robert 10.03.74, Rotherham :
800 - 1:50.70 (1:49.62-01), 1500 - 3:51.1 (3:48.35-01)
WATSON David U20 29.06.83, Kilbarchan :
TJ - 14.26
WATSON David 23.09.70, Holmfirth :
10k - 31:41.8 (31:31.2-99)
WATSON Derek U20 22.05.83, Bel/Victoria PAAC :
1500 - 3:46.93
WATSON Leon U15 9.07.88, Tipton :
80HB - 11.8
WATSON Matthew U23 23.02.80, Bingley :
3k - 8:19.48, 5k - 14:42.66,
10k - 30:59.7 (30:27.50-99)
WATT Adam U20 29.10.84, Aberdeen :
800 - 1:54.1
WEAVER Matthew 14.11.73, Harrow :
PV - 4.80 (5.00-99)
WEBB David U23 17.03.82, Leeds/Birmingham Univ. :
5k - 14:45.64, 3kSt - 9:41.0
WEBB Nicholas U15 23.09.87, Woking :
DTB - 43.34
WEEKES Michael U13 17.11.89, Watford :
100 - 12.3, 200 - 26.0
WEIR Andrew 22.08.67, Thames H & H :
Mar - 2:26:20
WEIR Robert Boyd V40 4.02.61, Birchfield :
DT - 62.46 (65.08-00), HT - 56.54 (75.08-82)
WEITZ Chris U20 28.04.83, Gateshead :
LJ - 6.85
WELLS Stuart 26.07.79, WGreen & Ex L :
LJ - 7.08 (7.68w-99/7.56-97)
WELLSTEAD David U23 17.12.82, Belgrave :
TJ - 14.47
WELSH Graeme 8.10.75, Border :
60 - 6.99i
WENDEN Stuart U20 21.01.84, Kent :
100 - 10.8w, 400 - 49.3/49.35
WEST Jordan U15 4.11.88, Cornwall AC :
800 - 2:02.23
WESTAWAY Ryan U20 2.03.83, Yeovil Oly/Brunel U :
HJ - 1.97i (1.96-01), Dec - 5708 (5738-01),
DECJI - 6218
WESTLAKE-CANN Samuel Walter U20 14.09.83,
N Devon : SP - 15.16, SPJ - 16.18, SP6K - 16.44,
DT - 46.08, DTJ - 49.65
WESTON Paul 6.10.67, Bristol :
TJ - 14.16 (15.64w-98/15.46-92)
WETHERIDGE Nicholas 11.10.72, Basildon :
HMar - 64:30 (64:03-01), Mar - 2:19:41
WHALLEY Robert Simon 11.02.68, City of Stoke :
1500 - 3:49.03i (3:40.7-96), 3k - 8:10.91i (7:51.4-97)
WHEELER Craig 14.06.76, Trafford :
3k - 8:22.35 (8:13.0-98), 3kSt - 8:52.79 (8:34.67-99)
WHITBY Benedict 6.01.77, WSE&H :
1500 - 3:43.72, 3kSt - 8:38.0 (8:32.68-01)
WHITE Gary U20 16.06.85, Rugby & Nor PH :
TJ - 14.48
WHITE Nathan U13 1.11.89, WSE&H :
3k - 10:23.7
WHITE Steffan David 21.12.72, Coventry Godiva :
5k - 14:41.18 (13:56.56-01)

WHITE Warren U23 23.08.80, Croydon :
PV - 4.10
WHITEFIELD Ian U15 22.12.87, Stroud :
800 - 2:05.1
WHITEHOUSE Michael U17 6.08.86, Guildford & G :
HJ - 1.95
WHITEHOUSE Paul U20 10.03.83, Birchfield :
200 - 21.78i (24.26-97)
WHITEMAN Anthony William 13.11.71, Shaft Barnet :
800 - 1:46.23A/1:47.7 (1:45.81-00),
1k - 2:19.23i (2:18.8i-96/2:18.82-98),
1500 - 3:32.43 (3:32.34-97),
1M - 3:53.21 (3:51.90-98), 3k - 7:52.62 (7:43.61-98)
WHITFIELD Ian U15 22.12.87, Stroud :
1500 - 4:11.36
WHITMORE Andrew U20 8.02.85, Peterborough :
200 - 21.9
WHITTAKER Daniel U17 10.01.86, Burnley :
100 - 10.8w/11.17, 200 - 22.28
WHITTAKER Robert U15 28.02.88, Sale :
800 - 2:03.08
WHITTINGTON James U15 5.01.88, Winchester :
1500 - 4:17.21
WHITTLE Robert U23 14.06.81, Bas & MH/Loughbro :
800 - 1:51.96 (1:51.76-00), 1500 - 3:47.96
WHITWAM Adrian 25.11.75, Tonbridge/Army :
3kSt - 9:39.0
WHYTE Stephen Anthony 14.03.64, Luton/Falkirk :
DT - 40.39 (50.40-94), HT - 54.79 (67.82-89)
WIFFEN Ben U20 30.10.84, Tonbridge :
800 - 1:51.18
WIGGANS John 1.07.71, Blackpool :
TJ - 14.06w (14.34w-91/14.21-93)
WILD James Gary U23 1.10.82, Birchfield/Loughbro :
HJ - 2.00i (2.05-01)
WILD Jonathan D. 30.08.73, Sale :
3k - 8:15.4 (7:53.10i-96/7:55.16-95),
5k - 13:52.59 (13:45.1-96), 5MR - 23:32,
10k - 28:43.82 (28:39.33-01)
WILD Kyle Nicholas U15 28.10.87, :
HTB - 45.29
WILDING Nick U15 11.11.87, Cannock & Stafford :
100 - 11.5/11.59, 200 - 23.5
WILKIN Mitchell U17 6.12.85, Southend :
LJ - 6.96w/6.88 (6.83-01), TJ - 13.96
WILKINS Duaine U20 17.07.85, Birchfield :
TJ - 14.53w/14.31
WILKINS Perris ¶ 12.12.67, Sale :
SP - 15.37 (15.29lght-00), DT - 64.34 (66.64-98)
WILKINSON Andrew 4.01.79, Sale :
200 - 21.7w, 400 - 47.69
WILKINSON Jonathon V40 17.02.62, Telford :
JT - 57.86 (63.88-00)
WILKINSON Neil 12.03.69, Cambuslang/Salford :
5MR - 23:57, 10k - 30:39.75 (29:56.52-96),
10kR - 29:34, HMar - 65:52
WILLIAMS Alex U15 12.01.88, City of Stoke :
PV - 3.70
WILLIAMS Alexander U17 7.11.85, Birchfield :
200 - 22.05
WILLIAMS Allan Peter V45 30.05.53, Blackheath :
PV - 4.50 (5.25-77)
WILLIAMS Conrad U23 20.03.82, Kent/Southbank U :
200 - 22.0, 300 - 34.45, 400 - 47.48,
TJ - 14.16w/14.02
WILLIAMS Daniel U23 26.03.81, Wolverhampton & B :
LJ - 6.80 (6.81-01)
WILLIAMS Edward 1.10.70, Thames Valley :
400 - 48.91i (46.84-94), 800 - 1:51.4 (1:49.41-96)
WILLIAMS Gareth J. 16.08.66, Med & Maid :
10k - 30:58.8, Mar - 2:24:39
WILLIAMS Glenn David U20 24.03.85, Cardiff :
SP6K - 14.67, HT6K - 51.17
WILLIAMS James John U23 17.07.82, Cardiff/UWIC :
3kSt - 9:27.8 (9:26.9-01)

386

WILLIAMS Kevin S. 15.12.71, Cardiff :
  100 - 10.53w/10.62 (10.30w/10.34-97),
  200 - 21.80 (21.30-97)
WILLIAMS Mark 7.09.64, Tamworth :
  3kW - 13:20.37i/13:24.7 (13:12.0-01),20kW - 1:37:30
  5kW - 23:34.4 (23:13.4-01), 10kW - 46:14.61
WILLIAMS Matthew U20 31.01.84, Wolves & B :
  400H - 56.40 (55.73-01)
WILLIAMS Rhys U20 27.02.84, Cardiff :
  400 - 48.3/49.22, 400H - 51.68
WILLIAMS Rhys U23 4.10.81, Swansea :
  JT - 61.41
WILLIAMS Richard U23 22.10.81, Shaftesbury B :
  3kSt - 9:43.0 (9:15.72-00)
WILLIAMS Ryan U13 6.09.89, :
  DTC - 27.42
WILLIAMS Simon U23 3.01.82, Swansea :
  JT - 55.05
WILLIAMS Simon David U23 5.10.80, Bas & MH :
  SP - 13.48 (13.52-01), DT - 45.60 (46.38-00)
WILLIAMSON Lewis U17 7.09.85, Leeds :
  DTJ - 41.58, DTY - 44.12 (44.14-01)
WILLIAMSON Paul Lee 16.06.74, Belgrave :
  PV - 5.20i/5.20 (5.55-00)
WILLIAMSON Simon U17 16.01.86, Highgate H :
  100 - 11.0w/11.1
WILLIAMSON Wilby U23 8.08.81, Notts/Lagan Val:
  400H - 55.16
WILLS Christopher 18.05.76, Birchfield :
  PV - 4.20 (4.80-98)
WILSON Alloy U23 25.01.80, Blackheath :
  100 - 10.8w (10.8w-98),
  400 - 48.0/48.21 (46.64-98)
WILSON Ben U15 1.07.88, AF&D :
  3k - 9:26.0
WILSON Chris U17 23.09.85, Enf & Har :
  PV - 4.01
WILSON Colin 30.10.77, WGreen & Ex L :
  60 - 6.85i (6.8i-01), 100 - 10.7/10.72,
  200 - 21.6w?/21.81
WILSON Gary U17 18.09.85, Belgrave :
  LJ - 6.72 (7.09w/6.87-01), TJ - 13.36 (13.50-01)
WILSON Kelvin U15 7.05.88, Enf & Har :
  400 - 53.52
WILSON Kirk U17 21.12.85, Morpeth :
  800 - 1:58.32, 1500 - 4:01.77
WILSON Simon 30.04.74, Med & Maid :
  400H - 55.2 (54.9-98/55.03-99)
WILSON Vincent 1.04.73, Belgrave :
  800 - 1:50.76 (1:48.68-98)
WILTSHIRE Gareth U17 6.09.85, City of Bath :
  400HY - 57.99
WINFIELD Phillip U20 10.02.84, Milton Keynes :
  800 - 1:51.12
WINSHIP Mark U20 29.09.83, Enf & Har :
  110HJ - 15.00, 110H - 15.6/15.63,
  400H - 54.3/54.48 (54.1-01)
WINWARD Christopher 25.03.75, Barrow & Furness :
  5k - 14:45.05
WISCOMBE Lee U23 12.07.80, Jarrow & Hebburn :
  400H - 54.27 (53.68-01)
WISEMAN Mark 9.02.69, Army/WSE&H :
  SP - 14.63 (15.65-01), DT - 53.57
WOMBWELL Simon U20, Herts Phoenix :
  110HJ - 14.5db/15.48
WOOD Andy V40 27.03.62, Lincoln Well/RAF :
  3kSt - 9:38.3
WOOD Joshua 19.04.74, Harrow :
  100 - 10.95 (10.7-98/10.74w-99/10.79-00)
WOOD Matt U17 14.12.86, Blackburn :
  800 - 1:56.93, 1500 - 4:04.69
WOODS Jordan U13, Sale :
  SPC - 11.09
WOODTHORPE Tim 3.01.79, Notts :
  3kSt - 9:30.2

WOODWARD Lyndon U23 22.11.80, Cannock & St :
  SP - 16.52, DT - 40.43
WOODWARD Nathan U13 17.10.89, Tamworth :
  400 - 60.7, 800 - 2:14.3, HJ - 1.61
WOOLCOTT Nicholas David V40 7.04.61, Enf & Har :
  DT - 47.35 (55.34-88)
WOOLLEY Matthew U17 6.05.86, Mansfield :
  100 - 11.0w, SPY - 13.90, OctY - 4603
WORKMAN Eric Alexander U20 2.03.83, AF&D :
  JT - 58.35
WORKMAN Richard J. 31.05.71, Trafford :
  200 - 22.16 (21.7/21.98-92), 400 - 47.72
WORTHINGTON John 6.02.70, Wigan Phoenix :
  Mar - 2:36:23
WRAY Alan 6.01.71, Harrow :
  3kSt - 9:27.7 (9:13.14-01)
WRIGHT Alex U23 29.06.82, City of Stoke :
  1500 - 3:50.27
WRIGHT Finlay F.H. U23 7.02.81, WSE&H/Oxford U :
  100 - 10.62w, 200 - 21.62
WRIGHT James U23 2.04.82, WGreen & Ex L :
  110H - 15.23, PV - 4.12i (4.20-00),
  LJ - 6.91w, Dec - 6400
WRIGHT Liam U20 26.07.85, West Suffolk :
  DecJ - 5034
WU Yu, Northumbria Univ/CHN :
  JT - 57.29
WURR Simon D. 7.01.77, Herne Hill :
  3kSt - 9:08.5 (8:57.52-97)
WYLLIE William 12.07.73, Halesowen :
  110H - 15.4 (14.91-92),
  LJ - 6.88 (7.33w-92/7.11-94)
WYSS Mark U20 12.07.85, Cheltenham :
  DTJ - 43.42, JT - 53.23

*Y*AMBASU Aiah 10.11.73, Thames Valley/SLE :
  60 - 6.78i
YATES Craig Paul U20 9.02.83, Spenborough :
  100 - 10.96w, 200 - 22.04w (25.0-97), 400 - 47.68
YATES Daniel U23 7.06.81, Matlock :
  3kSt - 9:27.0 (9:17.77-00)
YATES Hugh U17 26.01.86, Dorset Sch :
  TJ - 13.58
YATES Peter Derek V45 15.06.57, Dacorum & Tring :
  JT - 64.79 (77.84-87)
YATES Richard U17 26.01.86, Trafford :
  400 - 49.75, 800 - 1:56.46
YEBOAH Bernard U17 7.01.86, Croydon :
  LJ - 7.47, TJ - 13.65w/13.59
YELLING Martin 7.02.72, Bedford & County :
  5k - 14:36.6 (14:26.01-00)
YEOMANS Charlie U13, Tonbridge :
  SPC - 10.70
YEOMANS Paul Michael U17 9.10.85, Watford :
  PV - 3.60
YIEND Bradley U23 25.10.80, Birchfield/Loughbro :
  400 - 47.90, 400H - 52.44
YOUNG Jason 18.07.69, SGA (Prof) :
  SP - 14.75 (15.05-01)
YOUNG Martin 11.07.72, Roadhogs :
  5kW - 22:15.9, 10kWR - 44:23 (45:22hco-88),
  20kW - 1:35:34 (1:29:48-96),
  30kW - 2:26:47 (2:42.57-98), 35kW - 3:04:30

*Z*AIDMAN Antony Adam V40 18.03.62, Enf & Har :
  SP - 13.44 (17.87i-83/17.22-81)
ZAWADZKI Adam 19.12.74, Belgrave :
  800 - 1:50.54, 1500 - 3:42.32
ZELLER Adam U23 6.06.81, Harrow :
  TJ - 13.91 (15.33-99)
ZOLA Thembelani 14.02.75, /RSA :
  3k - 8:23.5
ZULEWSKI Alex U23 6.06.82, Thames V/Bath Univ :
  60H - 8.43i, 110H - 14.82w/15.1 (15.47-01),
  200H - 25.0, 400H - 54.4 (54.0/54.45-01)

WOMENS INDEX

BACKHOUSE Susan 6.12.78, Wakefield/
  Loughbro : DT - 47.31
BACKWELL Samantha U20 4.02.85, Yeovil Oly :
  Hep - 4463
BAGNALL Susan U17 4.08.86, Deeside :
  100 - 12.53w, TJ - 11.04w/10.98
BAILEY Emma Louise U20 25.07.84, Rugby & Nor :
  100 - 12.06w (12.24-00)
BAILEY Karen U23 24.06.80, Rowheath/Birm Univ. :
  (nee AINSLEY) HT - 40.88
BAILEY Kathryn 25.03.68, Havant :
  10MR - 58:41 (55:48-93), HMar - 78:02 (74:07-95)
BAIRD Kirsty 29.08.71, City of Glasgow :
  800 - 2:11.23, 400H - 64.4
BAIRD Lauren U15 21.09.87, Giffnock :
  800 - 2:17.71
BAKER Claire U20 13.08.84, Kidd & Stourport :
  TJ - 11.00
BAKER Eleanor U20 11.12.83, S London :
  800 - 2:12.87, 1500 - 4:27.84
BAKER Helen 5.02.79, Cardiff :
  TJ - 11.83
BAKER Joanne U15 15.10.87, Wigan :
  75HG - 11.43
BAKER Nicola 8.10.74, Gateshead :
  LJ - 5.57w
BAKER Sally V35 30.11.67, :
  Mar - 3:03:04
BALDWIN Samantha Louise U17 29.04.86, Wimb :
  PV - 2.60
BALLOTTA Laura 17.08.71, Edinburgh WM/ITA :
  PV - 3.95, SP - 11.67 (13.18-01)
BANFIELD Jenny U13 10.04.90, Vale of Aylesbury :
  JTM - 24.00
BANNER Andrea 5.06.70, Elswick :
  Mar - 3:08:55
BARKER Danielle U17 19.01.87, Neath :
  100 - 12.16w/12.48, 200 - 25.24w/25.30
BARLOW Holly U17 4.10.86, R Sutton Coldfield :
  300 - 40.41
BARNES Danielle Claire U17 8.10.85, Newquay & P :
  800 - 2:07.44mx (2:06.51-01), 1500 - 4:24.53,
  3k - 9:24.40mx/9:40.76 (9:35.46+-01)
BARNES-SMITH Natasha U17 21.04.87, Ipswich :
  3k - 10:38.2
BARR Lyndsey U15 19.01.88, Shaftesbury Barnet :
  800 - 2:15.6
BARR Victoria U23 14.04.82, Gateshead/
  Loughbro : 200 - 24.75 (24.34-00)
BARRETT Angela U17 25.12.85, Harrow :
  LJ - 5.40, TJ - 12.02w/11.85i/11.83 (12.03w/11.87-01)
BARRY Sara U20 8.06.83, Yate :
  TJ - 11.92w/11.74
BARTER April U15 2.08.88, Exeter :
  SPG - 11.11
BARTLETT Rebecca U20 7.03.85, Telford :
  JT - 44.59
BAUGH Simone U17 25.02.87, Derby LAC :
  200 - 24.9/25.17
BAYLEY Lorna U20 6.07.85, Sutton :
  PV - 2.70 (2.70-00)
BEARD Hayley Jane U17 2.12.85, Stevenage & NH :
  400 - 58.5, 800 - 2:07.98i/2:08.91 (2:08.02-01),
  1500 - 4:32.23mx/4:40.3
BEATTIE Natalie 30.01.78, Pitreavie :
  100 - 12.00 (11.82w/11.89-99), 200 - 24.70 (24.49-99)
BEATTIE Sharon 26.11.72, Border :
  PV - 2.70 (2.70-00)
BECKETT Charlotte U17 4.01.86, Milton Keynes :
  100 - 12.4, 200 - 25.1w/25.3/25.44 (25.20-00),
  300 - 41.2
BECKETT Chloe U15 10.06.88, Wakefield :
  SPG - 10.72, DT - 35.47, JT - 32.72
BECKETT Rachael U13 29.05.90, Wakefield :
  DTM - 24.17

BEE Jade U13 30.12.89, Herne Hill :
  70HM - 11.55, PenM - 2040
BEER Sarah U20 29.04.84, Exeter :
  SP - 11.64 (11.87-01)
BEESLEY Megan U13 15.11.89, Tamworth :
  75 - 9.95, 100 - 13.1, 150 - 19.6, 200 - 26.9, LJ - 5.08
BEEVERS Sarah 18.11.76, Wakefield :
  2kSt - 7:29.03, 400H - 66.2 (65.4-99/65.63-00)
BEIGHTON Amy U17 6.03.86, Leics Cor :
  60HI - 9.10i, 80HI - 11.8/11.99w, 100H - 15.3, 300H - 45.26
BELL Rebecka U17 1.12.85, City of Norwich :
  HJ - 1.66 (1.73-01)
BELLE Symone U20 12.11.84, Vic Park & Tower H :
  100 - 12.0w (12.18w/12.3-99), 60H - 8.58i,
  100H - 13.96, LJ - 6.05 (6.11-00)
BEMROSE Antonia Marie 3.09.79, AF&D/Coventry U :
  HJ - 1.65i/1.65 (1.76-96)
BENJAMIN Dawn Donita 7.03.72, Trafford/Army :
  60 - 7.42i (7.40i-01), 100 - 11.70 (11.4w/11.43-00),
  LJ - 6.17w/6.12i/6.10 (6.45w/6.26-00)
BENNETT Alison L. U15 12.04.88, Dacorum & Tring :
  75HG - 11.8/11.84, LJ - 5.19w/5.17
BENNETT Christina Jayne 27.02.78, Epsom & Ewell :
  SP - 15.12 (15.55-99), DT - 40.46 (42.88-99),
  HT - 52.68 (53.74-00)
BENNETT Claire U20 4.02.83, Cannock & Stafford :
  JT - 38.12 (41.92-01)
BENNETT Clare Mary U17 21.09.86, Reading :
  400 - 57.7, 800 - 2:15.36
BENNETT Gemma U20 4.01.84, Newham & Essex B :
  100 - 12.16w, 60H - 8.96i,
  100H - 14.03w/14.11, 400H - 64.14
BENNETT Joanna U20 6.08.83, Epsom & Ewell/
  Greenwich Univ : SP - 13.24, HT - 36.68
BENNETT Julia Margaret 26.03.70, Epsom & Ewell :
  60H - 8.84i (8.83i-98), TJ - 11.38w (11.77w-01),
  100H - 15.14 (14.43w-96/14.67-00),
  HJ - 1.84i/1.83 (1.92i-90/1.89-94),
  LJ - 5.89w/5.83i/5.70 (6.13i-98/6.12-94),
  SP - 11.80i/11.80 (12.15i-99/12.07-98)
BENNETT Katie U17 5.10.86, Notts :
  JT - 35.72
BENNETT Wendy V35 21.12.65, Worcester AC :
  5kWR - 24:56 (24:36-01)
BENNEWORTH Katy U20 5.10.84, Blackheath :
  LJ - 5.70
BENNINGTON Charlotte U13 2.02.90, Kidd & Stour :
  JTM - 24.72
BENTLEY Nicola U17 9.10.86, Trafford :
  100 - 12.2w/12.3, 200 - 25.2w/25.46, 300 - 40.21
BERRY Catherine Ann 8.10.75, Belgrave :
  1500 - 4:15.65, 1M - 4:41.95 (4:38.28-01),
  3k - 9:02.79, 5k - 15:31.23, 5KR - 16:02, 10kR - 33:24
BERRY Lizzie U15 15.02.88, Southport :
  LJ - 5.13
BEST Charlotte U20 7.03.85, Crawley :
  400 - 56.2, 800 - 2:09.25, 1500 - 4:29.91
BETTS Laura Nadine U20 6.11.84, Tonbridge :
  TJ - 11.17 (11.27-01)
BETTS Natalie U13 26.12.89, Portsmouth :
  LJ - 4.55
BEVAN Adele U20 26.03.84, Crawley :
  800 - 2:11.10
BICKERSTAFF Laura U17 10.11.85, Dromore :
  1500 - 4:46.43
BILOUS Tanya U17 7.05.86, Gloucester L :
  HT - 40.51
BINGLOW Veronique V35 11.06.65, Sutton Runners :
  Mar - 2:59:39
BINKS Aneska 24.06.77, Charnwood :
  HJ - 1.65 (1.65-94)
BIRD Tara Joy U17 22.07.87, WGreen & Ex L :
  200 - 25.3, 300 - 39.19
BIRKIN Kelly U17 27.04.86, Cwmbran :
  100 - 12.3/12.31w/12.32, 200 - 25.16w/25.27

389

BLACK Gillian Elizabeth 27.10.79, City of Glasgow :
HJ - 1.70i/1.70 (1.83-99)
BLACKIE Rachel Elizabeth U15 9.12.87, Bromley :
DT - 29.44
BLACKTIN Faye U23 5.11.81, Herts Phoenix :
HT - 45.43
BLAIR Joanna Louise U17 1.03.86, Coventry Godiva :
JT - 41.04
BLAIR Patricia U17 18.03.86, Edinburgh WM :
300H - 46.29
BLAIR Saranna U13 4.02.90, Weymouth :
LJ - 4.51
BLAIZE Dominique M. U15 3.10.87, Kingston & Poly :
100 - 12.5/12.51, HJ - 1.78,
LJ - 5.52w/5.51i/5.49, PenG - 3273
BLAKE Tanya-Gee 16.01.71, Trafford/MLT :
800 - 2:01.92 (2:00.10-98), 1500 - 4:22.98
BLAKEMAN Beverley 4.04.74, Sunderland :
800 - 2:09.66 (2:05.33-98),
1500 - 4:32.22 (4:28.56-99)
BLANK-COLLIS Paula 13.12.77, Herts Phoenix :
SP - 11.69, JT - 43.00 (43.75-01)
BLISS Jennifer Anne U17 6.07.86, Brighton & H AC :
400 - 58.4, 80HI - 12.0, 300H - 44.1/44.82, TJ - 11.14
BLOOMER Mandy 3.03.74, Cardiff/IRL :
400H - 61.16
BLOOMFIELD Tracey 13.09.79, Guildford & G :
PV - 4.05
BLOOR Louise U17 21.09.85, Rotherham :
60 - 7.85io, 100 - 12.60, LJ - 5.68w/5.67, TJ - 10.75
BODDEY Hayley U20 14.02.83, Derby LAC :
JT - 38.98
BODEN Veronica Vivienne V40 23.12.58, Radley :
400H - 65.4 (58.8-87/59.53-78)
BODIAM Natalie U15 30.09.87, Elgin :
HTG - 35.70
BODMAN Erica U15, Channel Islands :
HJ - 1.60
BOGGIS Lucy Isobel U15 27.01.89, Radley :
60HG - 9.26i, 75HG - 11.39w/11.52,
HJ - 1.60, JT - 32.59, PenG - 2945
BOINTON Phoebe U17 11.04.87, Devon Sch :
TJ - 10.99
BOLTON Laura Clare 22.01.79, Newquay & Par :
JT - 38.85, Hep - 3973 (4000-01)
BONNETT Emily U15 22.09.87, Yeovil Olympiads :
75HG - 11.3/11.75w/11.83, 80HI - 12.0,
HJ - 1.60, LJ - 5.33, PenG - 3202
BONNY Emma U15 9.09.87, Havering M :
LJ - 5.20 (5.20-01)
BOOTH Laura U15 28.04.88, Rotherham :
SPG - 11.29
BOREHAM Sarah U15 13.06.88, Epsom & Ewell :
DT - 30.40
BOUCHARD Sarah 23.10.74, Salford :
800 - 2:08.98 (2:08.57-01),
1500 - 4:31.05mx (4:23.74mx-00/4:25.6-01)
BOULD Carol V50 8.11.51, :
Mar - 3:08:18
BOWDEN Annie U23 5.06.82, Oxford Univ :
TJ - 11.02
BOWERS Lucy U15 12.01.88, Southampton City :
800 - 2:17.0, 1500 - 4:47.82
BOWRING Nicole 27.01.74, WSE&H :
100 - 12.0, 400 - 54.25,
200 - 24.4/24.64 (24.1w/24.42w/24.60-01
BOWYER Anna U23 29.09.82, Exeter/Worcs Univ :
DT - 35.70, HT - 38.72 (39.23-01)
BOYES Suzanne U17 26.05.87, Scarborough :
800 - 2:14.8, 1500 - 4:38.7, 3k - 9:55.6
BOYLE Anna U20 29.03.83, B & A/Ulster Univ. :
60 - 7.70i, 100 - 11.78w/11.97, 200 - 25.17w (25.21-99)
BRACE Rachelle U15 18.03.89, Dartford :
JT - 30.56
BRACKSTONE Lorraine 15.02.78, Cov G : (see GODBER)

BRADING Kayleigh U15 22.11.88, Isle of Wight :
HTG - 33.30
BRADLEY Joanna 23.08.79, Ashford :
DT - 46.74 (49.10-00)
BRADSHAW Noelle Elizabeth V35 18.12.63, AF&D :
PV - 3.20 (3.50-98), JT - 41.72 (46.81-00)
BRADY Emma Elizabeth 3.01.74, Trafford :
800 - 2:11.5 (2:09.04-01)
BRADY Nicola U20 26.07.85, Stoke :
Hep - 3838
BRAMWELL Monica U13 24.10.89, Luton :
100 - 13.08, 200 - 26.3
BRANNAN Lesley 13.09.76, Birchfield :
SP - 12.63 (12.97-01), HT - 57.47
BRANT Natalie V. U23 11.12.82, Epsom & Ewell/
Roehampton Univ : TJ - 11.82 (11.94w-00)
BRAR Sundeep U20 26.02.85, Basildon :
PV - 3.20i/2.75 (3.20i/3.00-01)
BRASON Claire U20 16.03.83, North Shields P/Sale :
200 - 25.0, 400 - 56.6/57.37, 400H - 60.46
BRAZNELL Kimberley V45 28.02.56, Dudley & Stour :
5kW - 26:22.83 (24:16.4-95), 20kW - 1:45:07 (1:44:29-99)
10kWR - 52:25+/53:18 (48:36-98)
BRENNAN Katie U23 27.04.82, Warrington :
800 - 2:11.68 (2:11.05-01)
BRENTON Rachel U20 18.01.85, Radley :
LJ - 5.72, TJ - 12.03 (12.27w/12.10-01)
BRERETON Ruth U23 26.06.81, Herne H/London Un :
400 - 57.2, 400H - 60.05
BRETHERWICK Samantha 16.04.69, Pembroke H :
Mar - 2:50:35
BRETT Debra U17 9.09.85, City of Norwich :
800 - 2:16.76
BREWINGTON Katherine Ann U23 15.10.81, Hav M :
200 - 25.29, 60H - 8.62i, 100H - 13.85, Hep - 5229,
HJ - 1.65i/1.65 (1.65-01), LJ - 5.84 (5.88w/5.87-01)
BRIDGER Zoe 4.03.76, AF&D :
HT - 37.54
BRINDLEY Tracy 25.08.72, Carnethy :
10kR - 34:32
BRISCOE Frances Annabel U20 12.04.83, Swindon/
Bath Univ : 1500 - 4:33.25
BRITTON Rebecca U20 3.10.83, Tipton :
100 - 12.1, 200 - 25.1
BRITTON Samantha U17 12.09.86, Sheffield :
60HI - 8.82i, 80HI - 11.61
BROADBELT Angelita U17 12.09.85, Thames Valley :
80HI - 11.7 (12.04-01), 100H - 14.9w/15.6, 300H - 44.99
BROMLEY Naida U17 27.09.86, Wakefield :
300H - 45.13, 400H - 65.3, LJ - 5.95w/5.67, Hepl - 4574
BROOKS Hannah U15 25.06.88, Crawley :
800 - 2:18.47
BROOKS Lois U17 10.01.87, Stockport/Trafford :
300 - 41.06, 400 - 58.59mx, 800 - 2:10.95
BROUGH Samantha U20 22.02.85, Stevenage & NH :
Hep - 3830
BROWN Celia 22.01.77, Shaftesbury B/Birm Univ. :
400 - 57.32i (56.09i/56.69-01), 400H - 60.31 (59.49-01)
BROWN Gemma U17 22.06.86, Shildon :
300 - 41.23
BROWN Jennifer Anne V40 21.05.59, Ashford :
HJ - 1.65 (1.73-89), TJ - 11.41 (11.56-97),
Hep - 4074 (4803w-89/4757-90)
BROWN Judy V45 27.10.54, St Albans Striders :
Mar - 2:56:08
BROWN Karen Louise 31.08.68, Border :
HT - 39.00 (48.66-00)
BROWN Kay U13 12.10.89, Biggleswade :
70HM - 11.8
BROWN Kayleigh U13 24.11.89, Carmarthen :
1200 - 4:01.5
BROWN Kimberley U17 1.02.87, Oadby & Wigston :
60HI - 9.29i, 80HI - 11.4/11.75
BROWN Louise Emma 6.05.78, Scarborough :
3kSt - 11:09.64

390

BROWN Melanie 10.12.70, City of Norwich :
400 - 56.1/56.16
BROWN Morgan U13 24.12.89, Vale Royal :
100 - 13.1
BROWN Sandra V50 1.04.49, Surrey WC :
24Hr - 181.272km (194.032km-98),
100MW - 20:27:27+ (18:50:29-92),
24HrW - 186.32km (196.000km+-92)
BROWN Sarah Jean V35 28.09.64, Steyning :
3kW - 16:07.8 (13:48.0-87), 5kWR - 26:44sh (23:57-80)
BROWN Shaunagh U13 15.03.90, Blackheath :
SPM - 9.57, DTM - 24.20
BROWN Tina 22.08.76, Coventry Godiva :
800 - 2:08.62, 1500 - 4:22.25, 3k - 9:49.6,
2kSt - 7:00.09, 3kSt - 10:56.22
BROWN Zoe U20 15.09.83, Shaftesbury B/B & A :
PV - 4.00
BROWNE Helen U20 31.07.85, Blackley :
Hep - 3860
BROWNE Sarah U20 8.01.85, Barrow & Furness :
JT - 37.03
BROWNING Charlotte Lucy U15 8.10.87, AF&D :
800 - 2:12.31, 1500 - 4:30.12
BRUCE Joanne 26.10.78, Woking/Chichester Coll :
JT - 47.74
BRUCE Shaeleen U17 3.11.86, Pitreavie :
HT - 33.32
BRUNNING Natasha Rosina 10.03.73, Dacorum & Tr :
PV - 2.60, TJ - 11.16w (11.59-01)
BRYAN Hannah U13 21.02.90, Banbury :
JTM - 29.54
BRYAN Hayley U17 4.03.86, Exeter :
SP - 11.44, DT - 35.53, HT - 34.17
BRYANT Claire U23 1.02.80, WSE&H :
400H - 65.6
BRYANT Lesley Karen V45 12.04.56, :
DT - 36.68 (55.42-80)
BRYSON Emma U23 5.04.81, C of Glasgow/Glas Un :
60 - 7.69i, 100 - 12.13, 200 - 24.47i/24.51
BUCHANAN Hayley U15 9.11.87, City of Glasgow :
HJ - 1.60
BUCHANON Monique U17 27.09.86, WGreen & Ex L :
DT - 34.24
BUCKINGHAM Penny V35 26.04.67, Guernsey/C I :
Mar - 2:58:40
BULL Sarah 4.06.75, Derby LAC :
800 - 2:06.75, 1500 - 4:12.21, 3k - 9:18.11
BURDON Rhiannon U20 29.10.83, AF&D :
100 - 12.24w
BURGE Kate 15.10.72, Staffs H :
5MR - 27:23, 10MR - 58:07 (57:41-00), HMar - 77:51 (75:35-00)
BURLES Gail V35 14.11.67, Cocoon Runners :
Mar - 3:06:13
BURNSIDE Susan U23 3.02.80, Edinburgh WM :
60 - 7.37i, 100 - 11.61w/11.66 (11.6w/11.61w-01),
200 - 23.90w/24.04 (23.88-01), 400 - 54.85
BURRELL Helen V35 1.07.63, Redhill :
Mar - 2:55:23
BURROWS Melanie 7.08.76, Ashford :
JT - 44.51
BURTON Carly U23 14.10.80, Ashford/Cant Christ CC :
DT - 44.44, HT - 44.66
BUTLER Alice 27.07.73, Wakefield :
400 - 57.33 (55.6/55.81-97),
800 - 2:10.32 (2:04.9mx/2:06.8-98)
BUTLER Katherine 22.10.73, WSE&H :
1500 - 4:18.36i+/4:18.42 (4:07.68-97), 5KR - 15:36,
1M - 4:36.70i (4:27.71-98), 3k - 9:04.51 (8:40.97-01),
5k - 15:17.59 (15:10.69-98), 10kR - 34:14 (33:01-99)
BUTLER Katie U23 16.05.80, Ashford/Loughbro :
200 - 25.14w
BUTLER Keeley 24.03.75, Cov G/City of Edinburgh :
100 - 12.00w/12.03 (12.01-96), 200 - 24.55 (24.4w/24.45-93)
BUTLER Lucy U23 18.11.81, Gateshead/Loughbro :
LJ - 5.83, TJ - 11.50

BUTTERS Kate U17 25.07.86, Hastings :
SP - 10.65
BUTTERWORTH Lisa U13 8.04.90, R S Coldfield :
600 - 1:47.5, 800 - 2:24.3, 1200 - 4:01.5
BUTTLER Jemma U17 17.06.87, Birchfield :
100 - 12.56 (12.21w/12.3/12.52-01)
BUXTON Leanne 27.05.78, Birchfield :
100H - 15.0w (13.96w-00/13.97-99), 400H - 63.19 (61.7/62.02-01)

C ADDICK Leah U17 1.06.86, Southport :
100 - 12.56w (12.4-01),
200 - 25.1/25.42 (24.9/24.96w/25.41-01),
300 - 39.7/39.72, 400 - 58.6
CAFFEL Kelly 10.02.79, Oxford City :
800 - 2:06.95mx (2:03.48mp/2:04.35-00)
CAIRNEY Cheryl U17 27.03.87, Glasgow SOS :
60HI - 9.15i
CALLAGHAN Katherine Jane U23 11.04.80, WSE&H :
PV - 3.40 (3.40-01)
CALLAWAY Deborah Ann V35 15.07.64, T Solent :
SP - 11.18 (14.88-93), DT - 40.23 (58.56-96)
CALLOWAY Victoria U17 22.03.86, R S Coldfield :
1500 - 4:45.5
CAMERON Claire V40 3.10.58, City of Glasgow :
DT - 40.85 (46.34-85)
CAMERON Hannah U15 3.03.88, Edinburgh WM :
DT - 31.85, HTG - 37.62, JT - 31.53
CAMPBELL Sarah 31.10.74, Glasgow Univ :
Mar - 2:51:26
CANDLISH Lauren U17 4.04.86, Pitreavie :
200 - 25.50, 300 - 39.90, 400 - 56.7/56.88
CANEY Eleanor Joanna U20 28.05.84, S & S H :
100 - 12.1 (11.92w/12.0/12.09-01),
200 - 24.9w (24.15w-01/24.29-00)
CANK Elaine 5.12.79, Trafford :
SP - 12.65, DT - 47.02
CANNING Melanie Shivon U20 19.05.85, E,S & Mx :
400 - 56.7, 400H - 61.54
CARDING Christina U17 26.02.87, Basingstoke & MH :
DT - 39.60
*CAREY Michelle U23 20.02.81, Bel/Loughbro/IRL :
200 - 24.7 (24.79w-01), 400 - 54.9/55.25, 400H - 58.57*
CARISS Susan V50 17.11.49, Bingley :
Mar - 3:03:08
CARNEY Treena V40 29.08.61, Dewsbury :
Mar - 3:01:21
CARPENTER Emma U23 16.05.82, Exeter/Bath Univ :
SP - 12.63i (12.53-00), DT - 56.63
CARR Laura U15 18.02.89, Dorchester :
JT - 33.03
CARRINGTON Eve U15 19.04.88, Stornoway :
HJ - 1.60
CARROLL Emma-Lisa U17 23.03.86, Liverpool H :
300 - 40.54, 400 - 58.2, 800 - 2:16.6, 1500 - 4:43.98
CARSON Sara 14.09.68, Cumberland :
10MR - 57:11
CARSON Susanne V35 2.05.67, Gala :
Mar - 3:01:18
CARTER Alexandra U23 1.04.80, V Royal/Loughbro :
400 - 55.7 (55.7-01), 800 - 2:04.72 (2:03.78mp-00),
1500 - 4:28.66i (4:14.44-01)
CARWARDINE Hazel U23 6.11.80, Bolton :
LJ - 5.81, TJ - 12.40
CASE Jessica U17 29.10.85, S London :
300H - 45.7/46.11
CASE Samantha U17 5.01.86, Guildford & G :
HJ - 1.63
CATHRO Anna U13 6.01.90, Dunbar RC :
HJ - 1.46
CATTERMOLE Sara-Jane 29.01.77, Dartford :
3kW - 13:52.6, 5kW - 24:44.3 (24:16.0-97),
5kWR - 23:44 (23:32+-00), 10kWR - 47:48 (47:05-01),
20kW - 1:41:51 (1:35:52sh/1:36:40-00)
CAVACIUTI Rozelle U20 21.05.84, Newport :
100 - 12.26w

391

CAWTHORNE Helen V40 9.07.61, Redhill :
Mar - 2:49:38
CEESAY Nusrat U23 18.03.81, N & E B/Loughbro :
100H - 14.9/15.06 (14.8-99/15.02-01), 400H - 63.36 (60.53-98)
CEESAY Zainab U20 27.10.83, Newham & Essex B :
LJ - 5.61 (6.15-00)
CHADWICK Julie U13 20.05.90, Wigan :
70HM - 11.6
CHADWICK Rachel U17 21.09.85, Bromley :
300H - 46.9
CHALMERS Laura U17 1.05.86, Elgin :
SP - 11.70, DT - 36.05 (36.31-01), HT - 45.70
CHAMBERLAIN Rebecca 7.09.79, B'mouth/Brunel U :
SP - 11.20 (11.46i-98/11.44-01), DT - 36.65
CHAPMAN Joanna U20 10.01.85, West Suffolk :
JT - 43.79
CHARLES Shereen U20 27.10.84, Ealing,S & Mx :
200 - 24.97
CHARLES Stacy U13 12.12.89, Herne Hill :
70HM - 11.8
CHARNOCK Catherine 3.05.75, Dudley & Stourbr :
5kWR - 25:55 (23:09-99), 10kWR - 52:25+ (47:51-99)
CHATTING Donna U20 30.10.83, Team Solent :
400 - 57.41 (57.13-01)
CHETWYND Sarah Joanne 4.06.74, Tamworth :
3kW - 16:20.37, 10kWR - 55:27
CHILAKA Chioma U13 2.09.89, Leics Cor :
LJ - 5.24w/5.14
CHILD Eilidh Shona U17 20.02.87, Pitreavie :
300 - 39.8/40.07, 400 - 58.2, 80HI - 12.0, 300H - 42.21
CHRISMAS Bryna U17 18.06.86, Kingston u Hull :
3kW - 15:23.25, 10kWR - 54:57,
5kW - 27:16.09 (27:04.5-01), 5kWR - 27:16 (26:11-00)
CHRISTIE Catriona Rosanna U20 26.04.85, WSE&H :
HJ - 1.70i/1.65 (1.70-01)
CHRISTIE Erica M. V45 10.03.56, Bellahouston :
Mar - 3:04:53 (2:54:24-86)
CHRISTIE Jade U15 20.11.87, Luton :
LJ - 5.17
CHRISTIE Jenny U17 28.09.85, Leamington :
300 - 39.20, 400 - 57.37, 300H - 46.4 (46.15-01),
400H - 65.54, HJ - 1.62, Hepl - 4531
CHRISTIE Nathalie 28.02.74, City of Edinburgh :
Mar - 3:08:12
CHRISTMAS Danielle U15 21.12.87, Crawley :
800 - 2:16.04, 1500 - 4:40.9
CHRISTMAS Natalie U20 9.04.84, Crawley :
400H - 63.36 (62.4-01)
CHURCH Amy U17 22.04.86, Isle of Wight :
HT - 41.41
CLAFFEY Juliet 30.04.78, Border/IRL :
PV - 3.50
CLAGUE Jennifer 6.08.73, Liverpool H :
5k - 17:11.7 (16:11.61i-92/17:02.53-98),
10kR - 34:47 (34:02-92)
CLANCY Amy U15 26.03.88, Edinburgh WM :
60 - 8.02i, 100 - 12.63, 200 - 25.67
CLARK Jean 5.10.68, Milton Keynes :
HT - 46.33 (50.34-97)
CLARK Juliette V35 22.04.64, Belgrave :
Mar - 2:52:13
CLARK Lynsey U17 2.09.86, Havering M :
DT - 34.64
CLARK Natalie U23 4.09.82, Kingst u Hull/Loughbro :
HJ - 1.78i/1.78, LJ - 5.50w
CLARK Nicola 14.04.77, Kingston u Hull :
TJ - 11.39 (11.66w/11.62-97)
CLARKE Kathy U17 16.10.85, Solihull & S Heath :
300H - 46.7
CLARKE Kylie U15 3.03.88, Carmarthen :
JT - 37.22
CLARKE Lianne Theresa U17 14.01.87, Neath :
JT - 40.68
CLARKE Rhian Clare 19.04.77, WG & EL/U of Houst :
PV - 4.15 (4.20i-01/4.15-00)

CLARKE-GAY Madelaine 16.03.69, Bristol/Bideford :
5k - 17:26.3mx, HMar - 78:27
CLARKSON Lesley U23 18.07.82, Invern/Glasgow U :
400 - 54.85 (54.44-01)
CLAXTON Sarah 23.09.79, Belgrave :
100 - 12.00w (11.7w-96/11.88w-94/11.9-99/12.19-94),
60H - 8.34i (8.28i-01), LJ - 6.30 (6.56-99),
100H - 13.9w/13.92 (13.28w-98/13.36-01), TJ - 11.35
CLAYTON Anna Caroline U20 20.03.85, W Suffolk :
100H - 15.28, LJ - 5.56, Hep - 4432
CLEGG Samantha U17 17.03.87, City of Plymouth :
100 - 12.4
CLEMENTIS Natasha U17 11.09.86, Epsom & Ewell :
60HI - 9.21i, 80HI - 11.9w/12.01, 300H - 44.13
CLEMENTS Grace U20 2.05.84, Dartford :
Hep - 4286
CLEMENTS Ruth 15.05.74, Radley :
TJ - 11.05 (11.14-01)
CLOGGIE Emma U15 10.07.88, Banchory :
800 - 2:17.60i/2:18.51
CLOWES Emily U17 24.10.86, City of Stoke :
SP - 10.68, DT - 36.51
CLUBLEY Christina U17 4.11.85, Kingston u Hull :
60 - 7.84i
CODDINGTON Aliysa U13 20.06.90, Oxford City :
100 - 13.3, 200 - 27.3
COLE Charlotte U13 06.91, Walton :
100 - 13.25, 200 - 27.51
COLEMAN Jeannette V45 3.02.57, Chorley Harriers :
Mar - 3:03:00
COLLIER Gemma U17 25.11.85, Exeter :
400 - 58.5, 300H - 44.34, 400H - 65.71
COLLIER Louise U15 14.02.88, Belgrave :
800 - 2:13.57
COLLINGE Emily U15 27.02.88, Mansfield :
1500 - 4:45.68
COLLINS Jayne U23 27.03.80, Birchfield :
PV - 3.00 (3.10-99)
COLLINS Verity U13 22.01.90, Blackpool :
75 - 9.9, 100 - 13.2, 150 - 19.7, 200 - 27.0
COLLINSON Deborah Joy U17 23.10.85, King u Hull :
SP - 11.76, JT - 41.37
COLLYER Isaura U15 21.10.87, Kettering :
HJ - 1.61
COMER Hayley Frances U13 26.09.89, Hillingdon :
70HM - 11.78, PenM - 2165
CONNEELY Vivienne 4.01.76, Altrincham :
Mar - 2:46:13
CONNELL Hazel U23 8.01.82, VPAAC/Glas Un Cal :
400 - 57.48
CONNIFF Tamara 14.11.78, Bournemouth :
(nee FRANCIS) JT - 42.61 (48.24-00)
CONOLLY Anna R. U17 19.04.86, Telford :
60 - 7.96i, 80HI - 11.6
CONSTERDINE Victoria 25.04.75, Stockport :
Hep - 4245 (4372-01)
CONWAY Catherine U15 30.03.88, Orion :
1500 - 4:43.60
CONWAY Rachel U15 30.09.87, Newport :
60 - 7.87ioa, 100 - 12.32w/12.37,
200 - 25.67w, LJ - 5.15
COOK Samantha U17 6.05.87, Herts Phoenix :
80HI - 12.0
COOKE Alexandra U23 24.06.82, Leighton Buzzard/
Cambridge University : 400 - 57.0
COOKE Gillian U23 3.10.82, Edinburgh WM/Glas Un :
PV - 3.90, LJ - 5.65i/5.64
COOKE Jacqueline 20.06.76, Derby LAC :
400H - 64.0 (63.9-96/65.15-95)
COOMBS Kelly U15 4.03.88, Hastings :
HTG - 31.54
COOPER Clare U15 7.11.87, Blackheath :
60HG - 9.3i, 75HG - 11.17
COOPER Louise J. 25.08.75, Rossendale :
Mar - 3:06:23 (2:58:16-95)

COOPER Rozy Elizabeth U13 27.10.89, Wx & Bath :
PenM - 2213
COOPER Vicky U17 10.10.85, City of Stoke :
DT - 33.07
CORBIN Sasha U15 23.04.88, Newham & Essex B :
JT - 32.50, PenG - 2686
CORFIELD Leila U17 7.02.86, Bristol :
300H - 45.8/46.66
CORK Rachel U17 11.10.86, Wimborne :
SP - 10.70
CORNEBY Hannah E. U23 22.01.81, Cannock & Staff/
Birmingham Univ. : DT - 42.02 (42.85-01)
COSSEY Laurie U23 24.11.81, Havering M :
800 - 2:13.05 (2:11.67-01)
COUNSELL Ursula U23 7.12.82, Bristol/Bath Univ :
1500 - 4:29.10, 2kSt - 6:52.94, 3kSt - 10:47.62
COURT Clova V40 10.02.60, WSE&H :
60H - 8.80i (8.12i-91), 100H - 14.30 (13.04-94),
SP - 11.51 (14.44-97)
COZENS Chloe U23 9.04.80, Sale/Loughbro :
SP - 12.73 (12.75-01), JT - 47.61 (51.79-00)
CRADDOCK Clare Helen U13 20.12.89, Spenborough :
600 - 1:45.6, 800 - 2:25.4
CRAFT Jude 13.08.72, Headington :
10MR - 58:30, HMar - 78:29
CRAIGEN Shauna U13 16.05.91, Nuneaton :
75 - 10.0
CRANE Julie 26.09.76, Sale :
HJ - 1.83 (1.85i-00/1.83-98)
CRAWFORD Catherine Marie U20 17.12.84, Regent H :
60H - 8.98i, 100H - 14.31
CRESSWELL Lois U23 12.01.81, Sale/Loughbro :
400 - 56.7/57.12 (55.45-01)
CRILLY Louise U15 18.01.88, Livingston :
100 - 12.61, 200 - 25.87
CRIPPS Faith Jayne U20 23.09.83, Milton Keynes :
400H - 63.7/64.51 (63.77-01), Hep - 4502
CRIPSEY Susan U23 8.01.81, Bed & Co/U of EAnglia :
800 - 2:13.2, 1500 - 4:26.85,
3k - 9:34.0mx/9:50.3, 5k - 17:10.44
CRITCHLOW Anna V35 4.12.67, London Heathside :
10MR - 58:53
CROAD Alison U23 10.06.82, Poole/UWIC :
TJ - 11.26i/11.20 (11.24-01)
CROCKER Linda 2.04.79, Huntingdon :
400H - 66.4 (65.5/66.64-97)
CROMBIE-HICKS Shona 1.06.71, Mornington :
HMar - 78:12, Mar - 2:40:53
CROOK Alison 19.01.72, Preston :
10MR - 58:47, Mar - 3:00:59
CROSBY Nicole 23.10.76, Wakefield :
200 - 25.07 (24.3w/24.35-98)
CROSKELL Helen 22.11.72, Tonbridge :
PV - 2.70i/2.65 (2.80-01)
CROSS Nikki U15 11.04.88, Guildford & G :
JT - 30.20
CROWE Samantha U17 28.09.86, Elswick :
3k - 10:35.89
CROWLE Revis V40 26.01.62, East Cornwall :
Mar - 3:06:33
CROXFORD Holly U13 6.12.89, Andover :
100 - 12.98, 150 - 19.9, 200 - 27.0, 600 - 1:42.2
CRUMLY Sophie U13 6.07.90, Newbury :
1200 - 4:01.6
CULLEY Jennifer 4.03.75, Belgrave :
200 - 24.68, 400 - 55.39 (54.11-98),
400H - 60.3/60.34
CULSHAW Rachel U17 11.08.86, Wigan :
300H - 46.8, HJ - 1.68, Hepl - 4197
CUNLIFFE Jessica 25.11.77, Rugby & Nor PH :
400H - 63.20
CUNNINGHAM Lauren Kerry U17 22.08.87, S & NH :
800 - 2:15.84
CUNNINGHAM Nicola U15 2.10.87, Cheshire Sch :
SPG - 10.61

CURL Tracey V40 8.07.62, Norwich RR :
Mar - 3:02:44
CURLEY Gemma U15 13.05.88, Mansfield :
1500 - 4:46.55
CURLING Roseanne U23 5.09.80, Bristol/CUAC :
LJ - 5.65 (5.77-01)
CURTIS Laura U23 2.05.81, Kingston u Hull/Birm Un :
400 - 57.4, 100H - 15.2w (15.2-01), 400H - 60.75
CUTHBERTSON Jenny U20 11.06.84, Rotherham :
PV - 2.75
CUTLER Aimee Louise U23 7.10.81, Cardiff/Bath Un :
LJ - 5.60 (5.84w/5.77-98)

D AGNE Birhan 8.04.78, Belgrave :
3k - 9:52.32 (9:10.47-94), 5KR - 16:03
DALE Cathryn 31.05.77, Rugby & Nor PH :
LJ - 5.53 (5.69w/5.66-00),
TJ - 11.36w/11.33 (11.78-00)
DALE Charlotte U20 23.03.84, Invicta :
3k - 9:17.61mx/9:25.04, 5k - 15:58.8mx/16:16.55,
5KR - 16:43 (16:38-01), 10k - 33:10.6, 10kR - 33:05
DALES Ruth Marie U23 29.10.80, Wakef/Bradford U :
100H - 14.3w/14.4/14.51
DAMEN Louise U23 12.10.82, B'mouth/Loughbro :
1500 - 4:29.5 (4:23.38-00), 3k - 9:29.28 (9:28.61-01),
5k - 16:24.13, 5KR - 16:04, 10k - 34:05.1, 10kR - 33:58
DANBY Joy U20 5.09.84, Kingston u Hull :
LJ - 5.53
DANIELS Nikki U23 25.08.82, City of Stoke :
800 - 2:11.16mx/2:12.4 (2:11.1-00), 1500 - 4:33.8
DANSON Ann Elizabeth 4.05.71, Sale :
LJ - 6.38
DANVERS Natasha 19.09.77, Shaftesbury Barnet :
100H - 13.20 (12.8w-99/13.19w-00/13.20-98),
400H - 55.68 (54.94-01)
DARBY Ellie U17 20.12.85, Birchfield :
LJ - 5.57 (5.71w-00/5.59-01)
DARBY Sian 8.11.70, Yate :
(nee ADLAM) 200 - 25.1w (25.1-98)
DARRINGTON Sarah-Jane U20 25.06.85, Beds & Co :
HJ - 1.68, Hep - 3886
DATE Natasha U17 18.11.86, Swansea :
100 - 12.4
DAVEY Sarah 13.10.78, Worthing/Un N Florida :
5k - 17:11.38 (16:50.74i-01/16:52.67-00),
10k - 34:30.20
DAVIDGE Sharon U23 15.09.81, Birchfield :
60 - 7.74i, 60H - 8.95i
DAVIDSON Claire 17.09.68, Tipton :
Mar - 3:01:09
DAVIDSON Wendy U23 14.10.82, C of Stoke/Staffs U :
200 - 25.27w, 100H - 14.3w/14.33, HJ - 1.65 (1.68i-00),
LJ - 5.61 (5.66w-99), Hep - 4786w/4783
DAVIDSON Zoe U17 17.12.85, Banchory :
TJ - 11.09
DAVIES Alison V40 6.04.61, WSE&H :
PV - 3.50 (4.00-00)
DAVIES Carys U13 9.05.90, Sarn Helen :
1500 - 5:02.0
DAVIES Diana Clare V40 7.05.61, Leics Cor :
HJ - 1.65 (1.95-82)
DAVIES Elen U17 24.04.86, City of Norwich :
LJ - 5.46, TJ - 10.88
DAVIES Elizabeth Sian U20 16.02.85, Dudley & St :
400H - 64.8/65.06
DAVIES Emma J. 9.10.78, Belgrave :
400 - 55.03, 800 - 2:03.93 (2:02.39-98)
DAVIES Gael Iona 5.02.79, Sale :
PV - 3.80i/3.40 (3.75-01)
DAVIES Leri 31.01.79, Swansea :
400 - 57.4
DAVIES Sarah U17 13.03.86, Bournemouth :
DT - 35.50
DAVIES Wendy V40 13.06.60, Windle Valley :
Mar - 3:03:13

DAVIS Amy U17 28.01.86, Lagan Valley :
SP - 10.86, HT - 30.78
DAVIS Joanne 24.03.76, Swansea :
JT - 38.22
DAWES Joanne U20 4.10.83, Sale :
800 - 2:12.1
DAY Samantha U17 8.02.86, Tamworth :
60HI - 9.17i, 80HI - 11.8/11.85 (11.76-01),
100H - 14.94, 300H - 46.0/46.03
DEACON Sarah U20 18.03.83, Havering M :
HT - 42.91
DEADMAN Lauren U20 27.03.84, Havering M :
1500 - 4:28.3
DEAN Carly U17 14.10.85, Bournemouth :
80HI - 12.0 (11.9-01), 300H - 44.90
DEBONO Michelle 1.05.72, Herne Hill :
400H - 65.1 (63.96-01)
DEE Ellisha U20 24.10.84, Thames Valley :
DT - 46.29
DENNISON Andrea M. V35 22.04.63, Bradford :
Mar - 3:01:48 (2:59:15-01)
DENNISON Kate U20 7.05.84, Stoke :
PV - 4.00
DERHAM Zoe U23 24.11.80, Birchfield :
HT - 62.27
DERING Joanne 7.02.69, WSE&H :
Mar - 2:55:35
DESAI Nisha U20 5.08.84, Morpeth :
400 - 57.3/57.57, 800 - 2:10.23
DEVINE Andrea V35 18.05.67, London Frontrunners :
Mar - 3:02:03
DEVLIN Mary 14.09.79, Abbey/Ulster Univ. :
LJ - 5.76w/5.75i/5.73 (5.76w-01), TJ - 12.08
DEVOY Sarah U17 12.01.87, Liverpool H :
JT - 35.19
DEWELL Sophie Violet U20 18.09.83, Gateshead :
PV - 2.80 (2.90-01)
DHALIWAL Navdeep 30.11.77, Shaftesbury Barnet :
SP - 11.85 (13.35-98), DT - 52.05
DICKIE Angela 6.01.77, Morpeth :
3k - 9:56.43mx
DICKINSON Kate U15 12.02.88, Bolton :
SPG - 10.91
DICKINSON Louise U17 5.11.86, Park Hill HS :
60 - 7.93i (7.88i-01), 100 - 12.4/12.51mx,
200 - 25.27, 300 - 41.1/41.29
DICKSON Lauren U17 2.04.86, Ayr Seaforth :
60 - 7.91i
DICKSON Louise U17 4.09.86, Edinburgh WM :
100 - 12.47 (12.3/12.37w-01/12.46-00)
DISNEY Glennys V40 11.06.59, Erewash Valley :
Mar - 3:08:55
DIXON Alyson 24.09.78, Sunderland/Sunderland Un :
10k - 36:05.9
DIXON Sharon Jane 22.04.68, Bristol :
HMar - 75:14, Mar - 2:45:05
DOBRISKEY Lisa Jane U20 23.12.83, Ashford :
400 - 56.0, 800 - 2:03.86, 1500 - 4:14.58
DOBRISKEY Sarah-Louise U20 13.08.85, Ashford :
HT - 42.41
DODDS Shadina U17 16.08.86, Telford :
300 - 40.8/40.90, 400 - 57.9
DOHERTY Michelle U20 24.09.84, Sparta :
TJ - 11.63w/11.48 (11.75w-01)
DOHERTY Tamara U17 15.11.85, W DUNB :
60 - 7.89i (7.95i-01),
100 - 12.4/12.47 (12.2w/12.45w-01), 300 - 40.35
DOLAN Sue V40 25.01.61, Harrogate :
Mar - 2:56:35 (2:49:21-97)
DONNELLY Katie U17 12.11.85, Solihull & S Heath :
HJ - 1.62
DONNELLY Laura U15 2.10.87, Hallamshire :
DT - 29.16
DOONEY Gemma U20 12.05.84, Wigan :
400H - 61.8/62.10 (60.07-01)
DORRIAN Eilidh U17 8.10.85, Giffnock :
PV - 3.30
DORSETT Torema U13 15.02.90, Enf & Har :
100 - 12.8, 150 - 19.1, 200 - 27.2
DOUGLAS Laura U20 4.01.83, Sale :
SP - 12.01i/11.61 (11.95-01), DT - 40.56,
HT - 55.22
DOUGLAS Montell U17 24.01.86, Bromley :
60 - 7.59i, 100 - 11.75w/11.77, 200 - 24.33
DOUGLAS Sophie Jane U20 16.01.85, Guildford & G :
400 - 56.7/56.84
DOUGLASS Louise U23 8.12.80, AF&D/Brunel Univ :
400H - 63.0/63.45
DOWDEN Cara U17 11.05.87, Cardiff :
1500 - 4:46.26
DOWSETT Amy U20 30.12.84, Croydon :
100 - 12.21w/12.25, 200 - 25.02 (25.0-01)
DOWSETT Gemma Louise U20 3.02.84, Med & Maid :
PV - 2.90
DOWSING Laura U15 17.06.89, Ipswich :
1500 - 4:39.58
DOYLE Natalie U15 5.01.89, Central :
60 - 8.02i, 60HG - 9.29i, 75HG - 11.57
DRAKE Sarah U20 13.08.85, Wakefield :
HT - 42.65
DRASKAU-PETERSSON Jessica 8.09.77, Manx/DEN :
Mar - 2:53:24
DUBRARID Eloise 25.06.75, Shaftesbury B/AUS :
PV - 3.40?
DUCK Emma U23 9.02.81, Team Solent :
100H - 14.5/14.57 (14.42w-01)
DUCK Jacqueline Sarah "Joey" U15 14.04.89, Milt K :
60 - 8.08i, 100 - 12.29w/12.3/12.40, 200 - 25.29
DUDGEON Sinead Marie 9.07.76, Edinburgh WM :
200 - 23.93 (23.23w-00/23.59-99),
400 - 53.95 (52.05-99),
400H - 56.701hm/56.88 (55.24-99)
DUDLEY Suzie U17 24.02.87, Aylesbury :
SP - 10.70
DUDMAN Nicola Pauline U20 5.10.83, Herts Phoenix :
SP - 12.70, HT - 57.63
DUFF Jennifer U23 29.07.82, R & Nor PH/Ox Univ :
DT - 37.95, HT - 43.87
DUFFY Teresa 6.07.69, WGreen & Ex L/IRL :
(see MCCLUSKEY)
DUGDALE Catherine 29.11.74, Swansea :
1500 - 4:28.07 (4:25.40-01),
3k - 9:27.78mx/9:32.52, 5k - 16:19.62
DUHIG Catherine V45 19.10.54, Colchester H :
(nee READER) 20kW - 1:59:35 (1:48:22-92),
50kW - 5:41:15 (5:22:04-93)
DUNCAN Joanne V35 27.12.66, WGreen & Ex L :
SP - 16.73 (17.08-01)
DUNCAN Lauren U15 21.03.88, WSE&H :
100 - 12.3/12.49, 200 - 25.7/25.96
DUNCAN Tracey Andrea 16.05.79, WGreen & Ex L :
400 - 55.28i/55.60 (55.2-00), 400H - 56.53
DUNFORD Jennifer U15 31.03.89, Birchfield :
DT - 31.11
DUNKLEY Julie 11.09.79, Shaftesbury Barnet :
SP - 16.37 (16.40-00), DT - 39.31 (40.70-00)
DUPONT Celia U17 23.07.87, Norfolk Sch :
HJ - 1.62
DUQUEMIN Rebecca U13 7.01.90, Channel Islands :
DTM - 23.55
DURANT Lisa U17 6.10.85, Somerset Sch :
TJ - 11.00
DURMAN Louise U17 23.11.86, Dursley :
1500 - 4:45.2
DURO-EMMANUEL Temi U13 19.06.90, Shaft Barnet :
100 - 13.0w/13.4
DUTTON Caitlin U17 15.12.86, Newark :
PV - 2.60
DWAN Elizabeth U23 16.10.82, Gateshead :
SP - 11.55, DT - 39.06

394

EAGLAND Anita 29.09.72, Trafford :
400 - 55.20
EARLE Jennifer S. V40 28.11.58, Guildford & G :
HT - 37.28 (42.49-98)
EAST Claire 10.03.70, Havant :
(nee HISCOCK) 800 - 2:12.85 (2:11.99-99)
EASTMAN Gemma U17 1.02.87, Bournemouth :
HJ - 1.65
EASTON Carey Anne 16.11.79, Edinburgh WM :
(see MARSHALL)
EDWARDS Beverley V35 1.09.65, Winchester :
Mar - 2:59:48
EDWARDS Chloe U17 12.05.87, Huntingdon/S B :
SP - 12.24
EDWARDS Elizabeth U20 18.12.84, Huntingdon/S B :
HT - 40.82
EDWARDS Elizabeth U23 30.04.82, Wrex/NE Wales I :
SP - 11.26 (11.45-99)
EDWARDS Laura U15, Harrow :
HTG - 31.12
EDWARDS Lisa U17 4.02.87, Exeter :
JT - 36.75
EDWARDS Megan U13 6.01.90, Oxford City :
100 - 13.39
EDWARDS Megan U13, 11.01.90, Dartford :
1k - 3:15.7
EGAN Elizabeth 3.06.79, Liverpool H/Liv Univ/IRL :
2kSt - 7:10.94
EGAN Laura U13 8.09.89, Giffnock :
150 - 19.8
EGBUNIWE Rachel Onyeoma Nkechi U17 5.07.86,
Braintree : 100 - 12.3, HJ - 1.63, LJ - 5.56
EKE Kimberley U15 10.02.89, City of Plymouth :
JT - 30.30
ELEY Louise U13 11.10.89, AF&D :
600 - 1:47.3
ELLIOTT Kerry U20 17.05.85, Gateshead :
SP - 11.48 (11.67-01)
ELLIOTT Lucy Helen V35 9.03.66, Shaftesbury B :
3k - 9:32.5 (9:19.2-97), 5k - 16:38.90 (15:34.40-97),
5KR - 16:24 (15:54-95),
5MR - 26:55 (25:54sh-97/26:31-01),
10k - 34:51.28 (33:12.8-99), 10kR - 33:53 (33:02-98)
ELLIS Melanie V35 16.04.64, Shaftesbury Barnet :
3k - 9:50.35
ELLIS Rebecca U17 20.12.86, Vale Royal :
1500 - 4:37.60, 3k - 10:13.89
ELLIS Sarah U20 27.10.83, Havant :
JT - 38.22 (41.99-00)
ELLIS Venetia U17 15.09.85, Herne Hill :
JT - 36.81
ELMS Yvonne U15 6.05.88, Edinburgh WM :
75HG - 11.72
ELWISS Hannah U20 8.12.84, Preston :
100H - 14.32
ELY Emma U15 20.01.88, East Grinstead :
PV - 2.55
EMMERSON Annaleah 10.05.70, Bath Univ :
5KR - 16:42
ENDACOTT Katherine U23 29.01.80, C of Plymouth :
60 - 7.55i (7.52i-01), 100 - 11.58w/11.87,
200 - 24.13w/24.3/24.41
ENGLAND Hannah U17 6.03.87, Oxford City :
800 - 2:11.3, 1500 - 4:33.05
ENGLISH Allison 4.03.79, Kingston u Hull :
60H - 8.84i, 100H - 14.7w/14.89 (14.64w/14.76-97)
ENNIS Jessica U17 28.01.86, Sheffield :
60 - 7.88i, 200 - 24.52w/24.72, 60H - 8.76i,
60HI - 8.90i (8.65i-01), 100H - 13.99w/14.01,
HJ - 1.80i/1.80, LJ - 5.63, Hep - 5194
ENNIS Jolene U17 17.03.87, Clydesdale :
3k - 10:37.81
ENTWISTLE Claire 9.12.76, Wigan :
800 - 2:10.2 (2:09.73-97), 1500 - 4:27.54,
2kSt - 6:54.92, 400H - 65.9 (64.4-94)

EPHGRAVE Helen U20 29.10.84, Guildford & G :
HT - 43.37
ERSKINE Joanne U20 28.05.85, Shaftesbury Barnet :
100H - 14.73, 400H - 64.1/64.95
ETHERTON Sarah 19.10.78, Dartford :
HT - 36.50 (36.80-98)
EVANS Kate Victoria 4.02.74, Rugby & Nor PH :
LJ - 5.59w (5.60-90), TJ - 12.33 (13.04w-00/13.03-97)
EVANS Kathryn U20 1.03.84, Elgin :
60 - 7.71i (7.65i-01), 400 - 56.49
EVANS Laura U13 22.12.89, Bury :
800 - 2:38.0, 1200 - 4:01.0 (4:00.1-01)
EVANS Laura Mair 28.09.74, Grantham :
DT - 35.54 (39.54-01)
EVANS Lucy Hannah 2.10.82, Sale/Birm Univ. :
200 - 24.82w/25.29
EVANS Sally 14.05.75, Sale :
800 - 2:08.36 (2:04.97-01), 1500 - 4:26.40
EVANS Susannah U23 19.09.81, Cov G/Coventry Un :
800 - 2:08.36
EVERETT Claire 25.06.79, City of Norwich/Brunel U :
SP - 12.87, Hep - 3924 (4759-96)
EVERITT Amie 1.11.78, Huntingdon :
PV - 2.70 (2.80-98)
EVERNDEN Natalie U13 12.01.90, Kingston & Poly :
JTM - 24.77

FAGAN Collette U23 6.06.82, C of Glas/Abertay Un :
3k - 9:36.03 (9:22.45-01), 5k - 16:33.31 (16:16.39-01)
FAIRLESS Rachel U23 19.03.82, M & C/Luton Univ :
PV - 2.80 (2.80-01)
FAIRS Elizabeth 1.12.77, Trafford :
200 - 24.6/25.07 (24.65w/24.76-00), 400 - 55.89,
60H - 8.47i (8.40i-99), 100H - 13.72 (13.49-00),
400H - 58.48
FAIRWEATHER Kelly Ann U15 5.03.88, Harrow :
60 - 8.06i, 100 - 12.3/12.60, 200 - 25.82i/26.0
FAIRWEATHER Lyndsey Emma U15 5.03.88, Harrow :
100 - 12.5
FAIRWEATHER Lynne U23 15.01.80, Edinburgh WM :
60H - 8.72i, 100H - 13.73w/13.76
FAIRWEATHER Sheila 24.11.77, City of Glasgow :
10kR - 34:17
FARDOE Kerri U20 22.11.83, Shrewsbury :
SP - 11.19 (11.26-01)
FAWCETT Ami U15 31.10.87, Leeds :
DT - 35.21
FAWKES Danielle U20 11.08.85, Barrow & Furness :
100H - 14.85, Hep - 4420
FELTON Rachel 27.06.79, Shaft B/Boston Unviersity :
1500 - 4:30.66 (4:18.72-01)
FENN Joanne 19.10.74, WGreen & Ex L :
400 - 55.3/55.95i (55.0-01/55.72-00),
800 - 1:59.86, 1500 - 4:23.56
FERGUSON Anna U20 30.06.84, Chelmsford :
PV - 2.60
FERGUSON Lisa U17 10.09.86, Ellon :
100 - 12.3/12.50, HJ - 1.67i/1.65, LJ - 5.41
FERGUSON Lucy U17 11.06.87, Bristol :
1500 - 4:46.29
FERGUSON Ni-Kysha U17 8.09.86, Trafford :
100 - 12.3w/12.4, 200 - 25.0w/25.28,
300 - 40.16, TJ - 10.70
FERGUSSON Gemma U20 20.08.84, North Shields P :
100H - 13.64w/13.76
FERSON Hannah U15 21.10.87, :
JT - 30.86
FIDDES Gemma 28.03.75, Sale :
Mar - 3:02:39
FIDGE Danielle U20 19.03.85, Croydon :
HJ - 1.69
FIELDEN Juliet L. U15 9.10.88, Tonbridge :
HJ - 1.60
FIELDING SMITH Sarah U17 19.11.86, Brighton & H :
HJ - 1.71, HepI - 3907

FIELDING Shelley U17 10.11.86, Wessex & Bath :
200 - 25.4?
FINES Helen 11.07.73, Forest of Dean :
Mar - 3:02:59
FINLAY Louise U20 2.10.83, Rhondda :
SP - 11.74 (12.05-00)
FINNIS Suzanne U20 12.08.83, W & EL/
St. Marys Univ Coll : JT - 44.72 (45.84-00)
FINUCANE Laura U17 3.08.86, Pendle :
200 - 24.9, 300 - 39.03, 400 - 55.33, 800 - 2:07.44
FISHER Jayne 2.11.70, Swansea : (see HILL)
FISHER Lucy U17 27.09.85, City of Stoke :
SP - 10.30
FITZGERALD Lyndsay U23 31.01.80, WSE&H :
100H - 15.0, 400H - 63.0/63.07
FLAHERTY Katie U17 1.10.85, Basildon :
100 - 12.4/12.45w (12.3w/12.4/12.49-01,
200 - 24.97w/25.13 (24.8/24.89w-01/24.98-00)
FLEARY Rachael V. U13 16.07.90, Carlisle/Aspatria :
SPM - 9.85, JTM - 33.50
FLEETWOOD Victoria Louise U13 13.04.90, Charn :
70HM - 11.3, LJ - 4.73
FLETCHER Alison Kay V40 8.06.61, Camb H/ Dulw R :
5k - 17:05.76, 10k - 35:10.30, 10kR - 34:59,
10MR - 56:44, HMar - 75:22, Mar - 2:44:42
FLETCHER Amanda U17 18.11.86, Rugby & Nor PH :
LJ - 5.41
FLINT Stacy U17 18.10.85, Kingston u Hull :
60Hi - 9.00i, 80Hi - 11.72w/11.77
FOLEY Megan Elizabeth U15 14.04.88, Havering M :
800 - 2:13.95, 1500 - 4:41.6
FORD Katie U23 21.10.81, Sheffield RWC :
10kWR - 56:45 (52:55-98)
FORD Rebecca U13 19.01.90, W DUNB :
HJ - 1.46
FORGIE Natasha U20 12.05.84, Dartford :
HT - 44.07 (44.65-01)
FORREST Catriona U20 25.08.84, Guildford & G :
HJ - 1.65i (1.65-99)
FORRESTER Amanda 29.09.78, City of Stoke :
60 - 7.48i (7.45i-01), 100 - 11.34,
200 - 23.94 (23.9-00)
FORRESTER Emma U20 2.12.83, Telford :
DT - 43.93
FORSYTH Amy U17 16.10.85, Belgrave :
300H - 45.1/46.11
FOSTER Vickie 1.04.71, Team Solent :
SP - 14.68i/14.39 (15.44-00),
DT - 47.73 (49.25-00), HT - 44.82 (45.46-97)
FOX Laura Elizabeth U20 25.10.84, Ashford :
SP - 11.82i/11.58, DT - 44.07
FOX Natasha U17 21.09.85, Dartford :
3kW - 16:29.47, 5kW - 29:13.46, 5kWR - 27:54
FOY Mercedes U17 9.08.86, Thurrock :
SP - 11.37
FRANCIS Azaria U20 12.04.83, Croy/St. Marys U Col :
TJ - 12.34
FRANCIS Bonnie U13 21.12.89, S London :
SPG - 9.26, JT - 23.49
FRANCIS Candice U20 7.02.85, Birchfield :
DT - 40.45
FRANCIS Eden Cherrelle U15 19.10.88, Leics Cor :
SPG - 12.33, DT - 30.43
FRANCIS Nafalya LeKeziah U15 21.04.89, Leics Cor :
75HG - 11.26
FRANCIS Tamara 14.11.78, Bournemouth :
(see CONNIFF)
FRANCIS-SMITHSON Hannah U13 10.11.89, Leeds :
75 - 9.9i, 70HM - 11.3
FRANKA Magali U13 24.01.90, Herne Hill :
150 - 19.7
FRANKSON Hannah U15 11.01.89, Ilford :
100 - 12.6 (13.21-01), LJ - 5.31
FREEBAIRN Susan V35 22.08.65, City of Glasgow :
DT - 46.25 (46.70-94), HT - 39.59

FREEMAN Amy U23 23.08.82, Spenborough/Bristol U :
400 - 56.3/56.66 (55.75-01)
FREEMAN Danielle U23 11.02.80, Leeds :
HJ - 1.67 (1.72-00), TJ - 12.98
FREEMAN Emily Kaye U23 24.11.80, Wakef/Lond U :
60 - 7.50i, 100 - 11.58, 200 - 23.41w/23.43,
400 - 54.02
FREEMAN Henrietta U20 12.07.83, Invicta :
5k - 17:01.14 (16:37.18-00)
FRENCH Rebecca U15 26.09.88, Chelmsford :
PenG - 2762
FRIDAY Sarah U23 14.11.82, Deeside :
PV - 2.65
FROST Bryony U20 21.02.84, Isle of Wight :
1500 - 4:31.0, 3k - 9:47.53,
5k - 17:22.10, 2kSt - 6:55.83
FROST Helen Paula 12.03.74, Birchfield :
200 - 23.93, 400 - 52.67 (52.40-00)
FROST Kathryn U20 21.02.84, Isle of Wight :
1500 - 4:32.9, 3k - 9:46.09,
5k - 17:17.92, 2kSt - 7:01.32
FULLELOVE Alyssa U23 16.09.81, C of Glas/Glas U :
60H - 8.67i (8.6i-01), 100H - 13.89w/13.93,
400H - 63.7 (63.96-01)
FULLER Amy U17 24.06.87, Basildon :
HJ - 1.65
FULLER Stephanie Anne U17 8.03.87, Harlow :
HT - 31.69
FULLERTON Faye Alexis U20 31.05.84, Havering M :
800 - 2:09.00 (2:08.88-01),
1500 - 4:24.76 (4:22.76-01), 3k - 9:54.5 (9:42.3-00)
FULLWOOD Juliet U20 1.07.85, Grantham :
HJ - 1.66, Hep - 4060
FURBER Rebecca U15 14.10.87, Tamworth :
JT - 32.48

GAGG Jennifer Elizabeth U15 20.02.88, K u Hull :
3kW - 15:10.28, 5kW - 27:49.6, 5kWR - 26:39
GALE Chloe U15 24.02.88, Dartford :
PenG - 2639
GALLAGHER Lynne 21.11.74, Shaftesbury Barnet :
800 - 2:12.70 (2:11.21-98)
GANNON Sharon V35 16.01.64, Ware Joggers :
Mar - 3:05:03
GARAVAND Maria U17 30.06.86, City of Norwich :
300 - 41.1, 60Hi - 9.1i, 80Hi - 11.6,
100H - 14.5/14.74, 300H - 43.15, 400H - 62.44
GARNETT Chanelle U20 16.08.85, Herne Hill :
60H - 8.66i, 100H - 14.27, LJ - 5.65 (5.74-99),
TJ - 11.07, Hep - 4357
GARRAD Victoria U15 22.11.87, Wirral :
60Hi - 9.19i, 60HG - 9.35i, 75HG - 11.3/11.35
GARRETT Caroline Jane V35 14.06.63, Worthing :
JT - 36.88 (37.16-01)
GASPAR Charlie U15 7.09.87, Milton Keynes :
1500 - 4:44.60
GATRELL Eleanor 5.10.76, Woking :
SP - 13.77 (14.68-98), HT - 40.04 (43.57-01)
GAULD Louise U23 24.08.80, Edinburgh WM :
TJ - 11.04i (11.04-98)
GAULD Nicola U23 28.03.82, Aberdeen/Aberdeen U :
400 - 57.0/57.09, 800 - 2:11.53
GAUTIER Nicola Louise 21.03.78, Traff/Hallam Un. :
100H - 14.35 (13.92w-99/14.05-01),
SP - 14.07 (15.09-00), JT - 43.52 (49.25-01),
Hep - 5307 (5784-01)
GAYLE Denise 11.09.79, Barnet :
HJ - 1.70 (1.73-01)
GAYTER Sharon M. V35 30.10.63, New Marske :
100kR - 8:53:17 (8:12:03-95),
24Hr - 217.508km (212.606km-98)
GBAHY Angeline 16.07.76, Newham & Essex B/FRA :
SP - 13.21 (14.35-01)
GEAR Cassie U15 19.04.88, New Forest :
100 - 12.6

396

GEAR Karen 30.09.79, N Devon :
60 - 7.70i, 200 - 24.4/24.45i/24.84 (24.2w-01,
400 - 54.12 (53.31-01)
GEE Michala 8.12.75, Rotherham/Hallam Un. :
LJ - 5.55 (5.74w/5.64-00), TJ - 12.15
GEENS Natalie U20 27.12.84, Solihull & S Heath :
5kW - 27:06.2
GEMMELL Lucy Elisabeth U13 20.10.89, Warrington :
1500 - 5:07.7
GEORGE Lianne U17 25.11.86, Phoenix :
100 - 12.4, 300 - 41.09
GERRARD Adele V40 24.11.59, Fife AC :
Mar - 2:57:06
GIBBENS Helen U17 11.02.87, Milton Keynes :
HT - 34.54
GIBBENS Rachel U17 31.01.86, Milton Keynes :
80HI - 12.0, 300H - 46.5,
PV - 3.20i/3.10 (3.20-01), Hepl - 3862 (3912-01)
GIBBS Amy U15 30.03.89, Bromley :
100 - 12.39, 200 - 25.49w/25.5/25.73
GIBBS Rachel U17 13.10.85, Bedford & County :
3k - 10:37.07
GIBSON Claire U23 25.12.82, Kilbarchan/Glas U Cal :
800 - 2:11.98 (2:09.3-00)
GIBSON Jane 26.01.73, Manx H :
5kWR - 25:11 (24:44-99), 10kWR - 52:28 (51:34-99),
20kW - 1:51:12 (1:47:39-01)
GIBSON Sharon Angelia V40 31.12.61, Notts :
SP - 11.91 (13.50-82), JT - 48.73 (50.85-99)
GILBERT Helen U23 1.03.82, Birchfield :
HT - 41.66 (45.28-01)
GILES Emma U17 26.07.86, Med & Maid :
80HI - 12.0, 300H - 43.7/44.22, 400H - 66.0
GILL Victoria Lesley U23 21.08.80, Chorley/
Florida State Univ : 3k - 9:27.00mx,
5k - 17:04.43, 10k - 33:59.67, 10MR - 56:40
GILLETT Kate U15 5.09.87, Croydon :
HT - 31.55
GILLHAM Michele 8.10.74, Ashford :
400 - 57.5 (56.9-99), 400H - 61.4/62.28 (60.18-97)
GILLIBRAND Kerry 13.09.76, Sale :
800 - 2:07.54, 1500 - 4:11.8, 10kR - 34:21 (34:10-01)
GIMSON Lauren U13 14.10.90, Leics Cor :
2kW - 10:34.0, 3kW - 17:35.14
GLAYSHER Jennifer U20 3.05.83, Preston/Liv Univ :
HJ - 1.69 (1.75-01)
GLOVER Helen U17 17.06.86, Cornwall AC :
800 - 2:15.11, 1500 - 4:37.94, 3k - 10:25.3 (10:10.73-01)
GODBEER Sarah 10.06.77, Exeter :
100H - 15.1w
GODBER Lorraine 15.02.78, Cov G : (nee BRACKSTONE)
100H - 15.0 (14.2w/14.4/14.65-99)
GODDARD Elizabeth Anne U13 1.09.89, Reading :
SPM - 9.84, DT - 24.00
GODDARD Rachel 30.04.73, Swansea :
5k - 17:15.82
GODDING-FELTHAM Lisa 24.11.69, White Horse :
Mar - 3:00:22 (2:56:50-99)
GODLEY Emily U13 22.10.89, Blackheath :
LJ - 4.72
GODSELL Amy U15 31.03.88, Bromley :
60 - 8.05i
GOMERY Laura U15 7.08.88, Cannock & Stafford :
SPG - 11.57
GONSE Rosalyn U23 1.03.82, Beds & Co/U of E Anglia :
200 - 25.19, 60H - 8.96i, 100H - 14.28, HJ - 1.65,
LJ - 5.74w/5.66i/5.60 (5.60-98), SP - 11.55,
JT - 41.07, Hep - 5294
GOODALL Hayley Jane U20 20.09.84, Ashford :
400H - 66.43, HJ - 1.65
GOODALL Kimberley Louise U20 5.10.83, Channel I :
LJ - 5.85w/5.73, Hep - 4784
GOODWIN Kim Louise 16.05.70, Kingston u Hull :
200 - 24.8/24.87i/25.28 (24.25w-96/24.3-99/24.49-96),
400 - 54.69 (54.40-01)

GOSSMAN Nicola U17 4.11.86, City of Glasgow :
60 - 7.72i, 100 - 12.2/12.23 (12.0w/12.09w/12.13-01),
200 - 25.1/25.12i/25.33 (24.81i/24.85-01)
GOURIO Marion U23 9.02.80, Sale/FRA :
PV - 3.30
GOWING Paula E. 31.05.78, Bristol/Oklahoma St Un :
5k - 17:18.86, 3kSt - 10:58.13
GRAHAM Jennifer U20 1.07.84, C of Glas/Glas Univ :
PV - 3.50
GRAHAM Kara U15 13.10.87, Newham & Essex B :
200 - 25.8
GRAINGER Amy Jane U15 7.08.88, Derby LAC :
HJ - 1.62
GRAINGER Kate U20 17.02.84, Inverness :
JT - 39.52
GRANGER Kathryn U13 9.02.91, City of Sheffield :
2kW - 11:12.3
GRAY Alma U15 17.04.88, Shetland :
JT - 34.36
GRAY Jenny V40 21.06.60, Vauxhall :
Mar - 3:07:21 (2:57:06-01)
GRAY Rachel Lilian U17 18.12.86, Portsmouth :
DT - 33.00
GRAY Samantha 11.01.78, Bristol :
3k - 9:50.3, 5k - 17:25.6
GREEN Aisha U13 5.10.89, WSE&H :
600 - 1:45.1
GREEN Andrea 14.12.68, Dartford :
3k - 9:26.61 (9:26.1-00), 5k - 16:25.70,
5KR - 16:46+, 10kR - 33:50 (33:41-00),
10MR - 56:13 (55:41-01), HMar - 75:53 (73:28-00)
GREEN Susannah U23 5.12.81, Liv H/Leeds Met Un :
HJ - 1.65 (1.68-99)
GREER Jane U20 19.07.84, Oxford City :
Hep - 3928
GREGORY Louise 11.05.74, Ipswich :
400 - 57.5
GREGORY Norma Jacqueline 10.06.69, Herne Hill :
SP - 11.48
GREWCOCK Sarah U13 25.06.90, Leics Cor :
100 - 13.3
GRIFFITH Michelle Amanda 6.10.71, WSE&H :
TJ - 13.44 (14.14w-00/14.08-94)
GRIFFITHS Anna Catherine U15 28.12.87, Hyndburn :
SPG - 10.85, PenG - 2732
GRIFFITHS Victoria U20 9.10.84, Liverpool H :
200 - 24.9w (25.3-01/25.49-00), 400 - 55.72,
LJ - 5.52 (5.55-00)
GRIME Victoria Leanne U23 21.08.82, Hyndburn :
HT - 37.08
GRIMSTONE Jenny 30.04.79, Shaftesbury Barnet :
SP - 11.99, JT - 44.22
GRUNDY Catryn U17 25.05.86, Pontypridd :
PV - 2.90
GRUNDY Kate U15 12.12.87, Cheltenham :
DT - 31.68
GUINEY Cheryl U17 24.09.85, Lagan Valley :
3k - 10:36.8 (10:07.93-01)
GUMBS Seemita U23 27.12.81, Charnwood/Birm U :
100H - 14.80
GUTHRIE Rebecca U20 19.03.83, Rugby & Nor PH :
PV - 2.70

H ADLAND India U20 7.01.85, N Devon :
HJ - 1.65 (1.70-00)
HALE Jane 4.01.74, Sale :
100H - 13.84w/14.04 (13.59-96), 400H - 61.82
HALES Sophie Rebecca U20 30.03.85, Steyning :
3kW - 14:34.11i (14:20.70-01), 5kW - 24:19.06,
5kWR - 23:53sh (24:19-01), 10kWR - 52:05
HALEY Emma U15 23.02.88, Thurrock :
800 - 2:18.6mx/2:19.5
HALEY Seandelle U20 19.03.84, Herne Hill :
60 - 7.60i
HALFORD Katie U23 4.10.82, Exeter :
DT - 40.01

397

HALKET Jade U17 5.05.86, Ellon :
LJ - 5.42, Hepl - 4240
HALL Andrea 28.01.77, Bedford & County :
TJ - 11.01i (11.54-98)
HALL Danielle U20 27.11.84, Cambridge Harriers :
DT - 38.49 (41.28-01)
HALL Naomi U13 26.09.89, Bolton :
SPM - 9.20
HALL Rebecca Ann U15 15.09.88, Boston TC :
SPG - 11.94i/11.62, DT - 30.48
HALSALL Danielle U23 27.06.81, Sale/Edge Hill Un :
100 - 12.0w, 200 - 24.12w/24.55, 400 - 53.91
HAMBLIN Nikki U15 20.05.88, Dorchester :
800 - 2:11.29, 1500 - 4:30.45
HAMMOND Cheryl-Leigh U17 13.07.87, AF&D :
3k - 10:21.0
HAMMOND Michelle U20 26.03.85, Kernou :
HJ - 1.66
HAMPSON Rebecca U20 14.07.84, Leigh/UWIC :
LJ - 5.51i, Hep - 4146
HANNAFIN Cathriona 19.09.72, Border/IRL :
TJ - 11.11 (12.08-99)
HANSEN Ashia Nana 5.12.71, Birchfield :
60 - 7.61i (7.51i-98), LJ - 6.18 (6.47A-96/6.27-94),
TJ - 15.00w/14.86 (15.16i-98/15.15-97)
HARDING Faye Marie U17 7.09.85, Wrexham :
100 - 12.4 (12.3-00), 200 - 24.6 (25.37w-01),
300 - 39.75 (39.46-01), 400 - 55.55,
60HI - 9.18i, 300H - 44.69 (43.20-01),
400H - 61.3/61.32 (60.06-01), LJ - 5.30 (5.35i-01)
HARDING Jemma 15.02.79, Beds & Co/DMU (Beds) U :
PV - 3.40mx/3.35i/3.35
HARDING Joanne V35 12.04.64, Trafford :
HT - 37.67 (40.99-00), JT - 38.37 (39.39-99)
HARDY Catrin U15 27.02.88, Menai :
DT - 30.90
HARDY Rebecca Jana 11.11.68, Highgate Harriers :
DT - 44.25 (45.20-97), HT - 38.76 (40.93-98)
HARKNESS Camilla U17 10.01.87, Guildford & G :
200 - 25.4/25.57 (25.4-01)
HARPER Jo U17 11.05.87, Cannock & Stafford :
800 - 2:15.8, 1500 - 4:27.77, 3k - 10:08.85
HARRIS Amy M. U15 14.09.87, Birchfield :
200 - 25.70, LJ - 5.59w/5.48
HARRIS Elizabeth U23 19.12.80, Stevenage & NH :
PV - 2.60 (2.70-01)
HARRIS Frances 1.06.72, Newham & Essex B :
LJ - 5.59 (5.62-01)
HARRIS Jenny 9.01.79, Team Solent :
400 - 56.89
HARRIS Rachel U23 17.07.82, Birchfield :
200 - 24.47 (24.4w-01), 400 - 56.5/57.32i (56.87-01)
HARRISON Deborah 13.11.78, Birchfield/Birm Univ. :
LJ - 5.79 (6.02w-00/5.89-99)
HARRISON Fallon U20 1.05.85, Chesterfield :
DT - 38.04
HARRISON Fiona Jane U23 30.11.81, Barnsley :
100H - 14.9w (14.01-01), HJ - 1.74,
LJ - 5.55 (5.91w-99/5.88-01), SP - 11.26, JT - 37.78
HARRISON Katie U17 22.10.86, City of Stoke :
800 - 2:14.79mx/2:16.0
HARRISON Melanie U17 27.11.85, Havering M :
DT - 38.04, HT - 33.82
HARRISON Susan 6.08.71, Leamington :
10MR - 56:15, HMar - 73:43, Mar - 2:38:52
HARRISON Susanna J. V35 25.01.63, Woking :
Mar - 3:02:24 (3:02:22-01)
HARRISON-BLOOMFIELD Christine Beverley 12.02.68,
Belgrave : 60 - 7.60i (7.32i-99),
100 - 11.70 (11.32-99),
200 - 23.94w/23.97 (22.85-99)
HART Emma U13 13.03.90, Southend :
DTM - 23.76
HART Louise U20 27.05.83, Beds & Co/DMU (Beds)U/
Shaftesbury Barnet : PV - 3.20

HART Natalie 25.05.72, Diss :
SP - 12.50 (13.94i/13.46-89), DT - 41.95 (48.02-90)
HART Siobhan 15.06.75, Enf & Har :
HT - 39.66 (39.75-01)
HARTIGAN Beverley Marie V35 10.06.67, Birchfield :
5k - 16:53+e, 5KR - 16:21 (15:49-95),
5MR - 27:07, 10k - 34:41.30 (34:21.91-98),
10kR - 34:43 (33:02-95),
Mar - 2:41:27 (2:36:02-01)
HARVEY Amy Charlotte Elizabeth U23 23.04.82,
Rugby & Nor PH : JT - 36.55 (47.57-00)
HARVEY Dana U23 7.08.81, Newbury :
400H - 66.3
HASLER Suzanne U23 7.04.82, R Sutton Coldfield/
Loughbro : 800 - 2:09.53
HATCH Ruth Louise U17 4.07.87, Epsom & Ewell :
TJ - 11.26 (11.48w/11.47-01)
HATCH Sharon V35 5.09.64, Sparta :
3k - 9:39.2 (9:37.42-01), 5k - 16:18.71
HAWKINS Layla U17 3.09.86, Bromley :
LJ - 5.37, TJ - 10.71, Hepl - 4399
HAWKINS Victoria U20 12.06.84, Halesowen :
HJ - 1.66
HAY Ruth Marion U15 4.11.87, Corby :
DT - 35.47
HAYWARD Melanie 14.07.71, Beverley :
HMar - 77:35 (77:17-01)
HAZEL Louise U17 6.10.85, Peterborough :
100 - 12.05 (12.01w-01), 200 - 24.86, 100H - 14.75,
LJ - 5.50 (5.53-01), Hep - 4736
HEAFFORD Claire U23 9.07.81, Epsom & Ewell :
400H - 62.4/63.05
HEATH Emma U17 1.10.86, Bristol :
LJ - 5.54
HEATH Jennifer 22.12.77, Sale :
3k - 9:38.16mx/9:45.5, 5k - 16:35.38, 5KR - 16:29,
5MR - 27:30, 10kR - 34:02
HEATH Sarah V40 4.01.62, Shaftesbury Barnet :
800 - 2:12.74 (2:07.3-80)
HEATON Lorna U15 9.02.88, Liverpool H :
PenG - 2635
HEATON Mathilde 2.09.74, London Irish :
Mar - 3:05:24
HECKFORD Jennifer U13 24.12.89, WSE&H :
70HM - 11.6
HEFFERNAN Kim S. V35 20.12.66, Med & Maid :
400H - 62.7/64.91 (61.30-01)
HEINRICH Katharina 5.07.72, Rowntrees/GER :
DT - 40.24
HELLER Kate U13 24.03.90, Cornwall AC :
SPM - 9.18, DTM - 26.27
HELSBY Ashley U13 1.07.90, Liverpool H :
70HM - 11.58
HENAGHAN Dianne V35 6.08.65, Chester le Street :
3k - 9:14.27, 5KR - 16:17, 5MR - 27:04, 10kR - 34:39
HENDRIKS Paula U20 25.01.83, Wolves & B/Birm U :
SP - 12.85i/12.79, JT - 40.71
HENRY Lorraine V35 16.09.67, City of Norwich :
DT - 37.71 (43.88-90)
HENRY Yvette 8.06.73, Wigan/Sheffield Univ :
60 - 7.69i, 100 - 11.98w/12.07 (12.04-00),
200 - 24.93
HENTON Sarah 4.05.73, Birchfield :
DT - 40.89 (50.98-97)
HERBERT Caroline 30.06.70, Arena : (see HOYTE)
HERRON Linzi U13 18.09.89, Craigavon :
PenM - 2073
HESKETH Joanne 16.06.69, Steyning :
3kW - 15:08.9, 5kW - 26:00.4, 5kWR - 25:22sh (25:35-01),
10kWR - 52:58, 20kW - 1:50:45 (1:50:35-01)
HEWITT Karrie U17 19.03.86, Warrington :
3k - 10:26.5mx
HEYES Lisa 5.06.71, Salford :
5KR - 16:47, 5MR - 27:39,
10k - 35:21.57, 10MR - 57:37

398

HIBBERT Ashia U17 30.03.86, Rowntrees :
  TJ - 10.72
HICKS Jasmin U13 1.03.90, Newquay & Par :
  PV - 2.40, PenM - 1940
HIGGINS Allison 8.04.72, Kilmarnock :
  3k - 9:28.55mx/9:38.56, 5k - 16:09.0,
  10k - 33:21.1, HMar - 78:25
HIGGINS Dawn 10.12.75, Belgrave :
  400 - 56.79i (53.24-00)
HIGHAM Stephanie Anne U20 26.12.83, Border :
  HJ - 1.85
HIGMAN Jessica U13 4.06.90, Derby LAC :
  HJ - 1.44
HIGNETT Susie U17 26.02.86, Bournemouth :
  1500 - 4:39.83
HILL Amie U23 9.09.80, Oxford City/Birmingham Un :
  DT - 39.07 (40.72-96)
HILL Cathy-Ann 4.05.77, Team Solent :
  SP - 11.81 (13.10-96)
HILL Clare 14.12.76, Border/Sparta :
  400 - 55.6/56.13
HILL Irie Heidi Alexa 16.01.69, WSE&H :
  PV - 4.15 (4.20-00), TJ - 11.29
HILL Jayne 2.11.70, Swansea :
  (nee FISHER) DT - 36.56 (45.52-96)
HILL Jenna U17 16.10.85, Sale :
  800 - 2:15.38 (2:13.86-01), 1500 - 4:40.27 (4:34.49-01),
  3k - 10:19.82 (9:58.9mx/10:06.2-01)
HILL Karen 6.11.72, Trafford :
  800 - 2:08.35mx/2:09.78 (2:06.3-91),
  1500 - 4:29.91 (4:24.8-97)
HILTON Tracey 9.03.78, Wakefield :
  400H - 65.2/66.27
HINDS Sally U17 2.02.86, Swansea :
  SP - 12.54, HT - 38.97
HINDS Tanya U15 19.05.88, Leics Cor :
  60 - 7.98i, 100 - 12.37w/12.39
HINES Olivia U20 19.10.83, Herne Hill :
  400 - 56.54i (54.97-01)
HINZE Nadine U13 19.12.89, Hillingdon :
  HJ - 1.43, LJ - 4.54, PenM - 2137
HIRD Jocelyn U20 3.12.83, Wimborne :
  PV - 3.06
HIRD Leyna U20 4.02.84, Exeter :
  100H - 14.1w/14.16
HISCOCK Claire 10.03.70, Havant :
  (see EAST)
HOBAN Aine U20 13.07.84, Wakefield :
  3k - 9:48.97
HODGES Lindsay U23 21.09.82, WSE&H :
  PV - 3.40i (3.66i-01/3.55-99)
HODGKINSON Sonia U17 2.12.86, Wigan :
  300 - 40.85
HOGAN Sally R. 16.11.79, Oxford Univ :
  100H - 14.94w/15.38
HOGBEN Hannah U17 4.06.86, Ashford :
  HT - 31.79
HOGSDEN Georgina U23 23.11.81, Sutton & District :
  JT - 39.30 (41.62-00)
HOLDEN Diana 12.02.75, Belgrave :
  DT - 36.44 (41.68-93), HT - 58.97
HOLDSWORTH Catherine U17 3.01.86, Colch H :
  60HI - 9.06io/9.1i, 80HI - 11.42w/11.47,
  300H - 44.21, LJ - 5.83w/5.76, Hepl - 4432
HOLLAND Vicky U17 12.01.86, Cheltenham :
  800 - 2:15.3, 1500 - 4:26.25, 3k - 9:57.5
HOLLINGS Kirsty U15 4.10.87, City of Norwich :
  100 - 12.6
HOLLINSHEAD Monique Gabrielle V35 31.12.67,
  Dewsbury : Mar - 3:01:58
HOLLIS Claire U13 8.11.89, Tipton :
  1200 - 3:58.06
HOLLMAN Anne Marie 18.02.74, Belgrave :
  SP - 11.23 (12.07-01)

HOLLMAN Julie Caroline 16.02.77, Belgrave :
  200 - 24.36, 800 - 2:13.00, JT - 39.54, Hep - 6135,
  60H - 8.7i/8.79i (8.78i-01), 100H - 13.81, HJ - 1.85,
  LJ - 6.42 (6.51-00), SP - 12.72 (12.98i-01),
HOLLOWAY Carys U23 23.07.82, Brecon/Notts Univ :
  PV - 2.80i/2.80 (2.90-00)
HOLLOWAY Joanne 10.05.76, WSE&H :
  SP - 11.39 (12.02i-96/12.00-98), HT - 47.64 (51.04-01)
HOLLYFIELD Marchessa U17 7.11.85, Reading :
  80HI - 11.8, 100H - 15.2, 300H - 44.71, 400H - 66.7
HOLMES Claire U20 11.08.85, Wigan :
  400H - 62.45, PV - 3.30
HOLMES Kelly 19.04.70, Ealing,Southall & Mx :
  600 - 1:28.8+ (1:26.0+-95), 800 - 1:59.83 (1:56.21-95),
  1500 - 4:01.91 (3:58.07-97), 1M - 4:32.83 (4:28.04-98)
HOLMES Sarah Jane U17 21.11.85, Woking :
  60 - 7.83i, 100 - 12.44, 200 - 25.37w
HOLROYD Shelley Ann 17.05.73, Sale :
  JT - 54.18
HOLT Emily U13 10.07.90, :
  PV - 2.00
HOLT Gemma 20.12.72, AF&D :
  LJ - 5.93w/5.58 (6.03A-99/5.99-98),
  TJ - 11.24 (11.40-01)
HOLT Sarah Joanne U17 17.04.87, Spenborough :
  DT - 33.57, HT - 41.06
HOOPER Natalie U17 10.08.86, Tipton :
  300H - 46.3/46.34
HOPESON Joscelynn U15 18.05.88, Surrey Sch :
  100 - 12.39
HOPKINS Emma Clare U17 16.09.86, Leics Cor :
  800 - 2:16.63 (2:11.1-01)
HOPKINSON Sarah U13 11.08.91, Gloucester AC :
  1k - 3:15.5, 1200 - 3:59.8, 1500 - 5:01.2
HOPKINSON Stephanie U13 27.10.89, Birtley :
  SPM - 9.06i, PenM - 1946
HORLER Jessica U15 9.06.88, Barnsley :
  HJ - 1.64
HORNBY Emma 12.12.73, Birchfield :
  PV - 3.75 (3.91-98)
HORNE Katherine Ann 23.05.79, C of Glas/Loughbro :
  HT - 45.31
HOROVITZ Gillian P. V45 7.06.55, AF&D :
  Mar - 2:54:29 (2:36:52-92)
HORTON Maddie 7.06.78, Headington :
  Mar - 3:06:35
HORWILL Katherine 26.01.75, Dudley & Stourbridge :
  3kW - 14:58.5 (13:59.89-99), 5kWR - 25:42 (24:37-99),
  10kWR - 52:42 (49:38-99), 20kW - 1:49:54
HOUNSLOW Anastasia U23 13.12.82, Guildford & G :
  400H - 63.56
HOURIHAN Alyson J. V40 17.10.60, Cardiff :
  DT - 38.74 (43.58-92)
HOWARD Amy U17 3.03.87, Skyrac :
  DT - 38.69
HOWARD Anna U20 18.07.83, Oxford City :
  HT - 43.36
HOWARD Christine 9.11.70, Matlock :
  5k - 17:17.17, Mar - 3:01:26
HOWARD Rachel U17 5.08.87, Chesterfield :
  HJ - 1.70
HOWARTH Lucie U15 15.12.87, Exeter :
  800 - 2:18.68
HOWARTH-BROWN Ellen U17 26.04.87, Portsmouth :
  80HI - 11.9, 300H - 44.2/44.21
HOWCROFT Lucy U23 23.04.82, Hillingdon/Staffs U :
  PV - 2.60 (2.60-00)
HOWES Lucy U17 27.06.86, Thurrock :
  HJ - 1.63 (1.66-01)
HOYLE Anna U20 12.02.85, Preston :
  JT - 36.13 (36.94-01)
HOYTE Caroline 30.06.70, Arena :
  (nee HERBERT) 5k - 17:06.19 (16:52.5-98)
HUBBARD Vikki U15 13.07.89, Grantham :
  HJ - 1.63

HUCK Claire U17 11.10.86, Kendal :
HJ - 1.66i (1.64-01)
HUDSON Helen U17 10.01.86, Sale :
800 - 2:15.9, 1500 - 4:43.65mx/4:43.68
HUGHES Elizabeth 9.06.77, Bromley :
PV - 4.16
HUGHES Emma L. U23 15.09.80, Luton/Bath Univ :
LJ - 5.68i (6.14w-99/5.97-98)
HUGHES Johanne 7.02.71, Med & Maid :
PV - 2.80 (3.13-99)
HUGHES Rebecca U13 4.04.90, Oadby & Wigston :
70HM - 11.79
HUGHES Sally U15 17.02.88, Neath :
75HG - 11.75
HUGHES Shona 18.02.70, Giffnock :
3k - 9:57.28
HULSE Natalie U23 2.12.82, City of Stoke :
HJ - 1.68 (1.70-98)
HUMBLE Amanda 15.08.79, Liverpool H :
PV - 2.70 (2.90-01)
HUME Carin 25.03.75, Sevenoaks AC/RSA :
Mar - 2:50:22
HUMPHREYS Danielle U20 16.05.84, Mansfield :
LJ - 5.72 (5.80-01)
HUMPHRIES Katherine U17 28.11.85, Exeter :
3k - 10:25.43mx/10:40.41 (10:28.15-01)
HUNT Emma U17 25.04.86, Shaftesbury Barnet :
1500 - 4:45.18mx (4:34.12-01),
3k - 10:25.50 (10:00.65-01)
HUNT Jane U15 8.09.87, West Norfolk :
LJ - 5.14
HUNTER Kirsty U13 16.12.89, Livingston :
100 - 13.39, 200 - 27.30i, 800 - 2:27.59, PenM - 2380
HUNTER Sarah 19.05.78, Shaftesbury Barnet :
TJ - 11.13 (11.41w/11.25-00)
HURST Jodie 21.06.77, Sale :
TJ - 11.70 (12.64-00)
HUTCHISON Ann-Marie 21.08.77, Neath :
3k - 9:35.39mx/9:45.4 (9:20.93mx-01/9:42.52-00)
HUTT Donna-Louise 6.06.72, Coventry Godiva :
100H - 14.6 (14.4-91/14.63-01)
HYDE Nimneh U15 20.09.87, Birchfield :
60 - 7.94i, 100 - 12.3/12.62, 200 - 25.53i/25.7,
HJ - 1.60, PenG - 2683
HYNES Samantha U17 28.01.86, Ealing,S & Mx :
HT - 42.41

IANNONE Rosanna 15.06.79, Vale of Aylesbury :
1500 - 4:29.70
IMPEY Teresa U23 6.05.81, Huntingdon :
400H - 63.0/64.04
INGMAN Jilly 17.08.78, Barnsley :
1500 - 4:33.1 (4:19.3-99), 5k - 16:41.72 (15:59.00-99)
INNES Stephanie U15 26.12.88, Edinburgh WM :
75HG - 11.9
IRVING Ruth 20.07.74, Edinburgh WM :
LJ - 6.25 (6.33-01), TJ - 12.64i/12.00
IRWIN Sally U17 12.10.85, Reading :
100 - 12.38
ITURBE Veronica V40 30.11.61, WSE&H :
Mar - 2:58:54

JACKSON Emma Frances U15 7.06.88, C of Stoke :
800 - 2:15.13mx/2:16.63, 1500 - 4:42.0
JACKSON Lorna J. 9.01.74, Edinburgh WM :
JT - 48.54 (57.19-00)
JACOBS Yolande 9.11.76, Bristol/RSA :
DT - 38.80 (42.93-99), HT - 37.04 (40.91-99)
JAMES Angharad 7.04.79, Swansea/UWIC :
60 - 7.61i (7.61i-00),
100 - 12.18w/12.23 (11.87w/11.90-00),
200 - 25.00w/25.09 (24.37-01), 400 - 57.08
JAMES Christina V45 1.06.55, Watford :
PV - 2.60i
JAMES Hannah U15 28.06.88, Horsham BS :
DT - 31.39

JAMES Stephanie U13 27.09.90, Southport :
600 - 1:45.7, 1200 - 3:59.9
JAMES Vernicha U20 6.06.84, Belgrave :
100 - 11.39w/11.40, 200 - 22.93 (22.93-01), 400 - 53.84
JAMES Vicky U23 13.05.81, Cheltenham :
JT - 39.32 (40.37-00)
JAMISON Victoria Anne 19.05.77, WSE&H :
400 - 54.07 (52.87R/52.97-98), 800 - 2:11.80
JELBERT Zoe U20 21.01.84, Newquay & Par :
1500 - 4:31.94 (4:20.56-01)
JENKINS Andrea Louise 4.10.75, Bedford & County :
SP - 11.14 (11.64-01), DT - 39.93 (41.02-01), HT - 52.31
JENKINS Beverley 6.02.70, Salford :
5MR - 27:39 (27:27-01), HMar - 78:05 (76:21-98),
Mar - 2:44:32
JENKINS Kate 26.03.74, Carnethy :
Mar - 3:01:26 (2:56:09-99)
JENNER Jackie 25.10.76, Tonbridge :
100H - 15.1 (14.84w/15.0/15.12-95),
LJ - 5.61 (5.62-99), TJ - 11.36
JENNINGS Joanne Loraine 20.09.69, Rugby & Nor PH :
HJ - 1.81i/1.70 (1.94i-93/1.91-98)
JOHN Joanne E. U23 12.11.80, E,S & M/St. Marys UC :
DT - 38.15 (40.92-00), HT - 50.39
JOHNS Karen Lesley U23 18.08.80, Shildon :
800 - 2:07.10
JOHNSON Abbie U13 29.03.90, Scarborough :
800 - 2:25.2
JOHNSON Anna U15 17.12.87, Trafford :
HT - 44.01, HTG - 51.003Kg/45.15
JOHNSON Charmaine Rachael V35 4.06.63, E & E/
Southampton Univ : 100H - 15.1/15.11 (14.36-94),
SP - 12.90 (14.29-93), Hep - 4607 (5495-92)
JOHNSON Jade U23 7.06.80, Herne Hill :
LJ - 6.73
JOHNSON Lindsay U23 3.12.81, Trafford/Sheff UN :
PV - 3.10
JOHNSON Sinead U17 24.12.86, Telford :
60 - 7.64i, 100 - 11.89, 200 - 24.66
JOHNSON Stacey U17 15.04.87, Cannock & Stafford :
800 - 2:11.53, 1500 - 4:40.9
JOHNSTON Jenny U15 15.04.88, Thurrock :
PenG - 2632
JONES Caroline U20 30.04.84, Herts Phoenix :
DT - 35.55
JONES Claire U17 8.11.86, Pembroke :
60HI - 9.04i, 80HI - 11.75w/12.0
JONES Davina 12.12.69, Coventry Godiva :
Mar - 2:52:05
JONES Debbie 6.01.78, Cardiff :
800 - 2:11.97, 1500 - 4:31.19
JONES Ffion U20 19.07.83, Deeside :
DT - 38.55
JONES Hannah U15 9.06.88, AF&D :
1500 - 4:41.74
JONES Heather U17 10.09.86, Carmarthen :
60HI - 8.75, 80HI - 11.3w/11.39
JONES Jillian Avril 23.12.69, AF&D :
800 - 2:09.19i/2:09.90 (2:04.97-93)
JONES Katherine U20 21.01.85, Cannock & Stafford :
100 - 12.0, 200 - 24.73
JONES Katie 4.01.77, Trafford :
100 - 12.29, 400 - 55.60,
100H - 14.33 (14.2w-00), 400H - 57.69
JONES Lyndsey U13 27.11.89, Carmarthen :
150 - 20.0
JONES Rachel U17 25.09.85, Forres :
800 - 2:13.13, 1500 - 4:31.30, 3k - 10:20.9
JONES Rebecca U20 17.01.83, Wrexham :
60H - 8.67i, 100H - 14.53, HJ - 1.88, LJ - 5.81,
SP - 11.39, JT - 37.45, Hep - 5254
JONES Samantha U15 2.12.87, Carmarthen :
75HG - 11.6/11.73w/11.85
JONES Sian U20 20.01.83, Swansea/Coventry Un :
TJ - 11.66w/11.46 (11.47i-01)

400

JONES Susan Eva 8.06.78, Trafford :
100H - 14.05 (13.95-97), HJ - 1.92i/1.92 (1.95-01)
JONES Thalia U15 16.09.87, Holmfirth :
800 - 2:18.8
JOSEPH Kashmere U13 15.02.90, :
DTM - 25.65
JOSEPH Tracy Carol 29.11.69, Basingstoke & MH :
LJ - 6.05 (6.44w-97/6.39-98)
JOWETT Natalie U17 18.09.86, Milton Keynes :
100 - 12.3/12.31, LJ - 5.33
JURY Kerry 19.11.68, Wakefield :
60 - 7.71i, 200 - 24.44 (23.80w-98/24.12-99),
60H - 8.55i (8.51i-00), 100H - 13.82 (13.71-01),
HJ - 1.77 (1.81-97), LJ - 6.14, SP - 11.63 (12.00-98),
Hep - 5657 (6005w-98/5908-99), Dec - 6145

KAISER Kathryn Mary V50 24.08.51, Valley Str :
Mar - 3:08:21 (2:55:03-94)
KALMEIJER Saskia U15 10.08.88, Radley :
LJ - 5.21
KANEEN Bridget V35 15.08.65, Manx H :
5kWR - 27:58 (26:57-00), 10kWR - 54:27 (54:27-01),
20kW - 1:59:58 (1:54:21-00)
KARAGOUNIS Helen U23 28.09.81, Birch/Notts Univ :
(nee THIEME)
200 - 24.4/24.78 (23.9/24.32w/24.37-01), 400 - 51.97
KAUWALE Soko M. U15 27.01.88, New Forest :
DT - 29.39, JT - 32.45
KAY Judith U15 29.06.88, Wimborne :
PV - 2.60
KAY Rachael U23 8.09.80, Wigan :
400 - 56.71i (55.79i/56.2-01), 100H - 15.0/15.30
KEDDIE Gill 1.02.69, Leeds :
3k - 9:55.27mx, 5k - 17:31.10
KEENLEYSIDE Julie U13 22.12.89, Elswick :
75 - 10.1
KEHLER Lisa Martine V35 15.03.67, Wolves& B :
3kW - 13:03.76+ (12:50.61-00) 5kW - 21:42.51,
5kWR - 22:20 (21:55-98), 10kWR - 45:53 (45:03-98),
20kW - 1:36:45 (1:33:57-00)
KELLY Anna U17 18.05.87, Shrewsbury :
TJ - 11.33
KELLY Jennifer Angela 20.06.70, Peterborough :
100H - 14.6w/15.2 (13.80-98), LJ - 5.59 (6.09-93),
SP - 13.21 (14.88i-90/14.73-91)
KELLY Ruth U13 30.04.90, Liverpool H :
SPM - 9.17
KELSEY Jo 20.05.77, Woking/Army :
3k - 9:57.10, 5k - 17:06.21, 10k - 35:09.70, 10MR - 58:03
KEMP Jennifer U23 18.02.80, Traff/DMU (Beds) Un :
JT - 43.83 (52.76-01)
KENNEDY Laura U13 10.09.89, Kilbarchan :
800 - 2:27.62
KENNEY Laura U20 27.06.85, R Sutton Coldfield :
3k - 9:49.07
KENNEY Lisa Helen U20 17.02.83, Kingston u Hull :
DT - 36.87
KENWRIGHT Dawn L. V45 30.08.55, Sarn Helen :
Mar - 3:06:01 (3:03:36-89)
KERR Gillian U20 10.11.83, Edinburgh WM/Glas U :
PV - 2.60i, TJ - 11.07w
KERR Laura U17 3.09.85, Lagan Valley :
JT - 39.80
KEYS Alison U23 11.07.81, Cannock & Stafford :
100H - 15.0 (14.9w-01/15.0-99/15.01w-01)
KING Bacardi U17 13.05.86, Grimsby :
300H - 46.9
KING Emma U23 25.07.81, Channel Islands :
HT - 40.69 (42.02-00)
KING Joanne 6.08.69, London Heathside :
2kSt - 7:18.51, 3kSt - 11:40.24
KING Rachel 11.05.76, Belgrave :
60 - 7.55i, 60H - 8.17i, 100H - 13.19
KINNEAR Erin U20 26.10.84, Lagan Valley/IRL :
PV - 3.70

KINNER Kate U23 28.05.81, Basingstoke & MH/
Brunel Univ : TJ - 11.62
KINNEY Jordan U13 15.05.90, R Sutton Coldfield :
800 - 2:26.3
KINNEY Justine U15 6.04.88, R Sutton Coldfield :
800 - 2:18.0
KIRBY Emma U23 11.11.81, Bracknell/Loughbro :
HT - 38.34
KIRBY Joanna U15 26.10.87, Wirral :
60HG - 9.27i, 75HG - 11.41
KIRK Laura U17 20.02.87, Skyrac :
800 - 2:15.9
KIRTLEY Anne V35 12.02.66, Hallamshire :
Mar - 3:04:29 (2:54:39-01)
KITNEY Charlotte U13 16.10.89, Belgrave :
JTM - 27.35
KNIGHT Maureen 15.11.73, Belgrave :
100H - 15.09, HJ - 1.68 (1.73i-01), LJ - 5.57,
SP - 11.85, Hep - 4689
KNOWLES Katie Rebecca U13 6.06.90, Cornwall AC :
600 - 1:44.4, 800 - 2:25.92, 1500 - 4:59.9
KOTAI Sarolta 22.02.79, Barnet/HUN :
PV - 2.70
KRZYWICKI Tara 9.03.74, Charnwood :
1500 - 4:27.85 (4:21.67-00),
5k - 16:38.61 (15:48.1mx/15:53.28-98), 5KR - 16:56,
10kR - 34:15, 2kSt - 6:31.77,
3kSt - 10:23.21 (10:08.11-00)
KUZ Lynne V40 14.07.61, :
100kR - 10:46:08
KWAKYE Jeanette U20 20.03.83, WGreen & Ex L :
60 - 7.52i, 100 - 11.70, 200 - 25.1 (24.4w/25.00-98)
KYDD Natalie U20 27.06.84, Motherwell :
400H - 63.23 (60.6/62.51-01)

LACEY Kiera U17 13.08.86, Cleethorpes :
PV - 2.60 (2.60-01)
LAING Nicola U15 5.05.88, Central :
PV - 2.60
LAING Wendy Jean V40 29.12.62, N Veterans :
100H - 14.9/14.99 (14.14w-93/14.2-81/14.35-86),
HJ - 1.66 (1.75-93), LJ - 5.58 (5.77w-93/5.65-92)
LAMB Katy U23 21.08.82, WSE&H :
HT - 51.95 (53.13-01)
LAMB Stephanie U15 18.11.88, Solihull & S Heath :
PenG - 2604
LAMBERT Vicky U20 20.11.84, Wakefield :
TJ - 11.54
LAMONT Sharon U17 12.08.86, Pitreavie :
800 - 2:16.5, 1500 - 4:41.5 (4:40.92-01),
3k - 10:27.5 (10:15.86-01)
LAMPKIN Fiona Amanda 4.10.69, Montrose :
2kSt - 7:33.03
LANDER Jenna U20 31.08.85, Tamworth :
HT - 41.97
LANE Catherine 18.11.76, Dacorum & Tring :
DT - 38.22 (40.72-98), HT - 40.37 (42.95-01)
LANE Sarah U23 4.06.81, Cardiff/UWIC :
60H - 8.92i, 100H - 14.7 (14.7-01)
LANNON Katia U17 14.09.85, Manchester/Sale :
HJ - 1.65, Hepl - 4052
LASHLEY Charlene U17 1.09.85, WSE&H :
60 - 7.93i (7.91i-01)
LAST Suzanne F. 11.01.70, Med & Maid :
HT - 44.92 (49.68-00)
LATHAM Marie V40 18.10.60, Manx H :
10kWR - 56:46, 20kW - 1:58:32
LATTO Emma J. 16.01.69, Herne Hill :
Mar - 3:03:55 (2:52:18-01)
LAVENDER Julie 9.11.75, Sunderland :
HT - 46.88 (51.62-94)
LAW Kirsty U15 20.01.88, Worcester AC :
1500 - 4:31.89
LAW Kirsty U17 11.10.86, Inverness :
SP - 10.41, DT - 39.08, HT - 30.44

LAWRENCE Christine U17 4.04.86, Invicta :
JT - 39.87
LAWRENCE Helen 3.12.76, Wirral/Liverpool Univ :
3k - 9:52.1, HMar - 77:50
LAWRENCE Sonia U23 19.01.80, Cardiff/UWIC :
PV - 4.00i/3.90 (3.90-01)
LAWRENCE Susan 25.11.70, Thurrock :
SP - 11.66, DT - 37.65 (37.73-01), HT - 41.50
LAWRENCE Victoria 9.06.73, Blackpool :
400 - 57.4 (56.63i/56.9-01), 800 - 2:06.58 (2:03.52-96),
1500 - 4:20.85mx/4:22.85 (4:19.77-96)
LAWSON Abbie U15 1.03.88, Dorchester :
3k - 11:07.7
LEACH Hannah V35 7.02.66, Blackheath :
10k - 36:36.2mx
LEADBETTER Helen U23 24.06.82, Ealing,S & Mx :
PV - 2.70 (2.70-01)
LEE Dorothea 28.07.77, Bristol :
800 - 2:11.1 (2:06.67-94), 1500 - 4:25.18,
3k - 9:46.3, HMar - 78:41
LEE India Alice U15 31.05.88, AF&D :
1500 - 4:47.47, 3k - 10:47.61
LEE Michelle 11.09.72, St Albans Striders :
Mar - 2:53:05
LEGGATE Ellen Jane 4.02.78, Cirenc/Fife AC/CUAC :
800 - 2:10.46 (2:06.59-96), 1500 - 4:21.18 (4:14.46-01)
LEGGATE Erin U15 6.02.89, Whitemoss :
HJ - 1.60, PenG - 2567
LENG Jennifer U20 1.02.84, Sale :
JT - 37.46 (38.51-01)
LENNON Leigh Katie U13 22.05.91, Hyndburn :
600 - 1:48.3, 800 - 2:27.74
LENNON Stacey U13 15.01.90, Leeds :
150 - 19.9
LESTRANGE Katy 17.09.79, Sale :
100H - 14.7/14.78 (14.36w-97/14.4-98/14.52-97)
LESUEUR Katherine U13 6.07.90, Bedford & County :
DTM - 23.75
LEWIS Annabelle U15 20.03.89, Kingston u Hull :
100 - 12.60w/12.68
LEWIS Emma U13, Lagan Valley :
LJ - 4.79
LEWIS Natalie U23 25.05.82, Cardiff/UWIC :
800 - 2:07.35, 1500 - 4:19.47
LEWIS Rosalind 16.02.76, Shaftesbury Barnet :
3k - 9:53.4
LEYSHON Anna Sian U23 19.01.80, Swansea/UWIC :
PV - 3.50i/3.50
LIDSTER Claire U23 26.10.81, Channel Islands :
100H - 15.19 (15.09w-01), 400H - 65.3 (63.20-01)
LILLEY Rebecca Anne Louise U15 4.03.88, Hales :
PV - 2.90
LINKILL Claire Marie U15 12.01.88, N Devon :
LJ - 5.35
LINTERN Candie U23 5.02.82, Crawley :
SP - 11.40 (11.82-99), DT - 38.65 (44.49-99)
LISHMAN Bethan U20 15.11.83, Border :
HT - 42.35
LISTON Bianca 28.05.78, WSE&H :
100H - 13.78 (13.4/13.52-00)
LITTLE Ashley Louise U15 19.01.89, Leeds :
HJ - 1.61i/1.60, LJ - 5.12, PenG - 2785
LITTLE Ruth U20 24.05.84, :
800 - 2:08.10
LITTLEJOHN Holly U15 15.02.88, Rugby & Nor PH :
200 - 25.7/25.84w
LIVESEY Katherine Dawn 15.12.79, Blackp/U of Neb :
200 - 24.40 (24.33w-01), 60H - 8.57i, 100H - 13.60,
HJ - 1.74 (1.75-96), LJ - 5.81 (5.91w/5.83-01),
SP - 11.60, Hep - 5577
LIVINGS Jane 13.08.70, Wells :
5MR - 27:49 (27:17-01), HMar - 77:02
LLEWELYN Gemma U17 23.04.87, Wigan :
SP - 10.54, DT - 36.42

LLOYD Jacqui-Ann U20 16.06.84, Carmarthen :
PV - 3.00
LLOYD Vicky U17 5.03.86, Pembroke :
TJ - 10.86w/10.84
LOCKLEY Angela U20 7.10.84, Trafford :
HT - 39.38 (45.15-01)
LODGE Joanna 6.01.68, WSE&H :
3k - 9:37.9, 5k - 16:05.23, 10kR - 34:37,
10MR - 55:51, HMar - 74:01, Mar - 2:34:17
LOMAS Claire U23 18.04.80, C of Edinb/Edinb Univ :
60H - 8.98i, 100H - 15.16 (14.62-01)
LONEY Jacqui 17.04.79, Elgin :
DT - 38.38 (40.78-01), HT - 43.20
LONG Rebecca U17 3.10.86, Bingley :
300H - 45.79, Hepl - 3992
LONGMORE Hannah U23 12.11.80, Rotherham :
100H - 15.0/15.26
LORD Dominique U17 8.04.87, Radley :
DT - 37.17
LOUISY Felicia 17.05.74, WSE&H :
100 - 12.1/12.17 (11.74-00), 200 - 24.97 (24.06w/24.37-00)
LOWE Larissa V35 19.08.63, WSE&H/Bournemouth :
PV - 3.54 (3.60i/3.60-01)
LUCAS-READ Jade U20 17.01.84, Team Solent :
100 - 11.70w/11.88 (11.64w/11.82-01)
LUCK Sara U17 18.11.86, Havering M :
800 - 2:14.53 (2:14.52-01), Hepl - 3924
LUKE Hayley U13 3.01.90, Oxford City :
1200 - 4:01.7
LUMB Rebecca 3.09.77, Trafford :
PV - 3.50i (3.60i/3.60-01)
LUPTON Victoria Anne 17.04.72, Sheff RWC : (see WHITE)
LYNE Rebecca Louise U23 4.07.82, Hallam/Loughbro :
800 - 2:02.45, 1500 - 4:25.18
LYNE-LEY Claire U15 14.03.88, Exeter :
DT - 34.04, PenG - 2630
LYNES Margaret Tracey V35 19.02.63, WGrn & Ex L :
SP - 15.38 (16.57-94), DT - 38.58 (44.76-93)
LYON Janet A. V40 12.03.62, Aberdeen :
PV - 2.70i/2.65 (2.70-00)
LYONS Amanda U17 12.03.87, Edinburgh WM :
JT - 36.96
LYONS Emma Jane U17 14.06.87, Notts :
TJ - 10.95

MABBETT Sophie U17 27.10.86, Reading :
400 - 58.0, LJ - 5.40, TJ - 11.00
MACALISTER-HALL Emma U15 19.02.89, Rowntrees :
800 - 2:16.4
MACAULEY Nicole U15 6.07.88, Liverpool H :
JT - 30.90
MACDERMOTT Nicole U17 15.08.86, WSE&H :
60 - 7.88i, 100 - 12.2/12.21, 200 - 25.40
MACDONALD Mhari U20 10.02.83, Corstorphine :
400 - 57.40
MACDOUGALL Lynne V35 18.02.65, City of Glasgow :
10kR - 34:19 (33:22-00), HMar - 76:24 (74:24-01),
Mar - 2:36:29
MACKENZIE Rachael U15 23.12.87, Inverness :
HJ - 1.62
MACLARTY Morag U17 10.02.86, Central :
800 - 2:08.9 (2:07.25-01), 1500 - 4:30.00
MACPHAIL Ann 3.05.70, City of Glasgow :
5k - 17:05.52 (16:32.41-99), HMar - 78:39 (76:26-00)
MACPHERSON Joan U23 18.09.80, B & MH/Brunel U :
SP - 12.93i/12.71 (12.82-01), DT - 44.09 (46.08-01),
HT - 42.27 (44.45-01)
MACPHERSON Shona U23 31.08.80, C of Glasgow :
400H - 61.8/61.88 (61.47-99)
MACRAE Catherine 1.01.79, WSE&H :
PV - 3.60 (3.60-01)
MADDICK Nicola U17 6.08.87, Kingston u Hull :
800 - 2:16.23 (2:14.32-01), 1500 - 4:41.58
MADDISON Ashley U15 24.05.89, Gateshead :
DT - 29.23

402

MADGETT Stephanie U17 22.02.87, WSE&H :
  60HI - 8.85i, 80HI - 11.9/11.91, LJ - 5.63w (5.66w/5.52-01)
MADUAKA Joice 30.09.73, WGreen & Ex L :
  60 - 7.27i, 100 - 11.29w/11.31 (11.24-99),
  200 - 23.00 (22.83-99)
MAGBADELO Naomi U17 16.04.87, Cambridge H :
  SP - 10.74
MAGUIRE Kirsty U20 5.07.83, EWM/Glasgow Univ :
  PV - 3.71i/3.60 (3.60-01)
MAJOR Pippa V35 23.04.65, S London :
  Mar - 3:06:31 (3:01:48-01)
MAKIN Emma U17 12.10.85, Warrington :
  300H - 44.85, 400H - 67.0 (66.5-01)
MALE Samantha Kate 11.04.76, AF&D :
  100H - 15.2 (14.25w/14.38-99)
MALLON Samantha U13 13.11.90, Liverpool H :
  600 - 1:48.2
MANCHESTER Samantha U17 10.12.86, Med & Maid :
  DT - 34.14
MANGER Eloise U20 6.01.85, Chorley :
  JT - 37.23 (38.51-01)
MANN Kelly U20 8.09.83, Birchfield :
  5kWR - 28:15 (25:10-99)
MARCHANT Zina D. V50 30.09.50, City of Bath :
  Mar - 3:02:09 (2:39:26-91)
MARKENDALE Eleanor U13 9.10.89, Pendle :
  LJ - 4.78
MARKS Maiteland 19.09.76, Belgrave/Loughbro/USA :
  200 - 24.52i/24.8 (23.97-99), 400 - 54.40 (53.65-01),
  100H - 13.97 (13.82w/13.88-98), 400H - 58.10 (57.81-01)
MARQUIS Shelley U13 26.12.89, Ilford :
  75 - 10.0, 150 - 19.9
MARSH Danielle U17 22.04.86, Tipton :
  300 - 41.2
MARSH Kate U17 15.05.86, City of Stoke :
  Hepl - 3902
MARSHALL Carey Anne 16.11.79, Edinburgh WM :
  (nee EASTON) 200 - 25.0 (24.56-99),
  300 - 38.86, 400 - 52.91
MARSHALL Jolene U20 22.10.83, Ashford :
  SP - 11.92
MARSHALL Lucy A. U23 28.11.81, Rugby & Nor PH :
  HT - 52.15
MARTELL Nicola U17 20.09.85, Colchester H :
  TJ - 11.24, Hepl - 4001
MARTI Debora Jane 14.05.68, Bromley :
  HJ - 1.85 (1.95i/97/1.94-96)
MARTIN Clare 18.05.76, Newport :
  1500 - 4:21.69, 3k - 9:51.14i (9:45.50-01)
MARTIN Emily U15 7.10.88, Hercules Wimbledon :
  LJ - 5.15
MARTIN Emily U13 18.09.89, Newton Abbot :
  JTM - 27.38
MARTIN Karen Lesley 24.11.74, Derby LAC/WRAF :
  JT - 56.34 (59.50-99)
MARTIN Kirsten 24.04.76, Newport :
  400 - 56.9/56.91
MARTIN Rachel 9.09.78, Sale :
  HJ - 1.65i/1.65 (1.76-97)
MARTINEZ-ROURA Sonia 21.03.73, N Lond & MH/ESP :
  JT - 36.35
MARTINS Nichole U17 21.06.86, Rugby & Nor PH :
  SP - 10.77
MARVIN Catherine Price U17 18.04.87, Isle of Wight :
  HT - 41.66
MASALIN Niina 3.01.77, Sale/FIN :
  HJ - 1.70 (1.76-01)
MASON Bethan U13 25.10.89, Swansea :
  SPM - 9.01
MASON Emily U20 28.04.85, Wakefield :
  HJ - 1.65 (1.65-01)
MASSEY Eva Maria U23 22.12.80, Belgrave/Ulster U :
  SP - 15.57, DT - 43.85 (47.72-00)
MASSEY Jacqueline Ann V35 24.01.64, Mansfield :
  Mar - 2:53:06

MASSINGHAM Louise U17 28.02.87, Walton :
  60HI - 9.2i
MATHESON Patricia V45 7.01.54, Stourbridge RC :
  Mar - 3:03:41
MATHEWS Louise U20 27.10.83, Thurrock :
  JT - 46.57
MATTHEW Denae U17 3.04.87, Leics Cor :
  60 - 7.94i, 100 - 12.51 (12.29w/12.31-01),
  LJ - 5.47 (5.56-01)
MAUND Lyndsey U17 27.02.86, Pontypridd :
  TJ - 10.71w
MAWER Lisa 22.05.68, Bingley :
  3k - 9:56.9 (9:44.36-94), 5MR - 27:55, 10kR - 34:31
MAWER Rebecca U20 31.01.84, Great Yarmouth :
  HJ - 1.65 (1.73-99)
MAWHINNY Rachel U17 28.09.86, Ballymena & A :
  TJ - 11.25
MAY Natasha U23 21.02.80, Sale/Hallam Un. :
  60 - 7.75i, LJ - 6.26
MAYLOR Donna U23 20.05.82, Birchfield :
  100 - 11.84w/12.03 (11.62w-98/11.72-00)
MCALEESE Clare 15.09.79, Ballymena & Antrim :
  SP - 11.29
MCALLISTER Alison U20 26.02.85, Sale :
  TJ - 12.04w/11.90
MCCALLUM Michaela Jane V35 2.06.66, Winchester :
  HMar - 78:39 (76:07-00), Mar - 2:41:41 (2:38:28-99)
MCCANN Danielle U15 22.09.87, Preston :
  800 - 2:16.0
MCCARTHY Emma U13 3.11.89, Channel Islands :
  JTM - 26.38
MCCARTHY Lorraine P. V35 30.12.63, :
  Mar - 2:59:20
MCCLUNG Mary 19.12.71, Edinburgh WM :
  400 - 55.56 (54.06-00), 800 - 2:06.60 (2:03.92-00)
MCCLUSKEY Teresa 6.07.69, WG & EL/IRL : (nee DUFFY)
  10MR - 58:48 (55:56-00), Mar - 2:40:29 (2:35:27-01)
MCCOLGAN Elizabeth V35 24.05.64, Dundee HH :
  10kR - 33:03sh (30:39-89)
MCCONNELL Anouska 13.04.76, Peterborough :
  800 - 2:11.3
MCCONNELL Lee 9.10.78, Shaftesbury Barnet :
  200 - 23.48w/23.79 (23.66-01), 400 - 50.82
MCCREESH Laura U23 18.12.80, Sale :
  5k - 16:57.26
MCCUTCHEON Anna 3.03.68, Highgate H/CAN :
  Mar - 2:54:32
MCDIARMID Kirsteen U17 28.04.86, Pitreavie :
  100 - 12.1/12.15 (12.0w/12.15-01),
  200 - 25.17 (25.16-01), 300 - 41.2
MCDONNELL Lindsey-Ann 13.08.79, N Devon :
  100 - 12.1w, HJ - 1.80 (1.80-01)
MCDONNELL Morag 27.08.73, Chester le Street :
  3k - 9:58.3 (9:54.32mx-01), 5k - 16:44.67, 5KR - 16:40,
  10kR - 34:53, 10MR - 57:41 (57:18-01), HMar - 77:19
MCGHEE Abbey U13 2.03.90, Victoria Park AAC :
  800 - 2:26.68
MCGING Kate U17 12.04.86, Liverpool H :
  300 - 41.29
MCGORUM Fiona U15 10.11.88, Leics Cor :
  3kW - 15:37.4
MCGOWAN Suzanne 13.04.78, City of Glasgow :
  400 - 56.5/56.78 (56.50-01)
MCGREAVY Sara U23 13.12.82, Leamington/Bath U :
  60H - 8.49i, 100H - 13.96 (13.77w/13.94-01)
MCKAY Jane 22.04.77, C of Glasgow/Strathclyde U :
  400 - 55.30, 800 - 2:06.77
MCKELVIE Susan U20 15.06.85, Edinburgh WM :
  HT - 46.59
MCKENNA Carolyn U20 4.05.84, Edinburgh WM :
  60 - 7.74i, 100 - 12.03w (12.29-01)
MCKERNAN Jacqueline Lena V35 1.07.65, Lisburn :
  DT - 53.84 (60.72-93)
MCKIRDY Frances U17 9.07.87, Stevenage & NH :
  HJ - 1.70i/1.68

403

MCLELLAN Shelley U20 21.03.83, Stevenage & NH :
  SP - 11.96 (12.56-01)
MCLOUGHLIN Eleanor Rachael U15 9.02.89,
  Stockport : 800 - 2:18.0
MCLOUGHLIN Lauren U23 8.09.82, Shaftesbury B :
  100H - 14.55 (14.14w-00/14.20-01)
MCLOUGHLIN Lucy U13 17.06.91, Stockport :
  600 - 1:44.7, 800 - 2:28.08, 1200 - 3:53.7, 1500 - 4:59.7
MCMANUS Lisa U17 3.01.86, Oadby & Wigston :
  60HI - 9.07i, 80HI - 11.4/11.61
MCMANUS Lucy U17 2.03.87, Guildford & G :
  HJ - 1.65
MCNEICE Kelly Alana 17.06.78, Lisburn/IRL :
  400 - 57.31 (57.0-97), 800 - 2:04.55, 1500 - 4:16.46
MCSWEENEY Nicola U15 17.11.87, Milton Keynes :
  SPG - 10.70
MCWILLIAMS Elizabeth Marion U17 2.06.87, B & A :
  800 - 2:12.30
MEADOWS Jennifer U23 17.04.81, Wigan :
  100 - 11.9 (11.8w/11.94-01),
  200 - 23.99w/24.0 (23.90w-01/24.32-00),
  400 - 53.25i/53.67 (53.32-01), 800 - 2:03.35i/2:04.46
MEADOWS-SMITH Wendy U15 15.07.88, W Suffolk :
  HJ - 1.64
MELIA Kelly-Ann U13 8.01.90, Solihull & S Heath :
  75 - 10.1
MELLOWDEW Anita 1.12.70, Epsom & Ewell/Bath U :
  Mar - 2:56:44 (2:46:17-98)
MELVIN Hazel 19.11.73, City of Glasgow :
  HJ - 1.70 (1.85-97)
MENENDEZ Niobe J. V35 1.09.66, Steyning :
  3kW - 13:08.64i (13:14.73-01), 10kWR - 46:38,
  5kW - 25:26.84 (23:46.30-01), 20kW - 1:39:59
MERRILL Alexandra U17 12.05.86, Skyrac :
  DT - 34.07, HT - 38.14 (40.93-01)
MERRY Emma Louise 2.07.74, Rugby & Nor PH :
  SP - 12.99 (13.77-00), DT - 54.01 (57.75-99)
MERSH Rebecca Jane U15 28.01.89, Sheffield RWC :
  3kW - 14:44.39, 5kW - 27:13.8
MIGHTY A. D. Natasha 21.12.70, Radley/Wolvs Univ :
  SP - 11.78 (11.87-01)
MIKNEVICIUTE Dalia 5.09.70, Shaftesbury Barnet :
  HJ - 1.78i (1.89-97)
MILBORROW Clare 10.01.77, Horsham BS :
  100 - 12.18 (12.16w-00/12.18-01),
  200 - 25.1 (25.00-99), 50H - 7.2i (7.2i-00),
  60H - 8.40i, 100H - 13.71w/14.09 (13.61w-00/13.89-99)
MILES Imogen U17 7.08.86, Radley :
  LJ - 5.62, TJ - 11.60
MILLER Clare 30.06.76, Aberdeen :
  3k - 9:59.22mx, 5k - 17:09.94
MILLER Kara U20 6.04.85, S London :
  TJ - 11.30
MILLER Lisa U20 13.01.83, Cambridge Harriers :
  100 - 11.79, 200 - 23.89w/24.05 (24.0-01),
  400 - 53.18
MILLWARD Elizabeth U15 29.10.88, Cannock & St :
  SPG - 12.37
MILNE Vicky U23 12.07.80, Wirral :
  HJ - 1.67
MITCHELL Angela V35 17.08.65, Harrow :
  DT - 41.67 (42.05-98)
MITCHELL Emily U13 19.12.90, Carmarthen :
  75 - 10.1
MITCHELL Jeina Sophia 21.01.75, Croydon :
  800 - 2:07.25 (2:03.36-97)
MITCHELL Julie 3.10.74, Belgrave :
  1500 - 4:21.76
MITCHELL Rebecca U20 10.12.83, Regent House :
  100H - 15.05w/15.37 (15.24-00)
MITCHELL Virginia C. V35 29.01.63, Woking :
  400 - 57.34 (56.36-99), 400H - 62.93 (61.85-99)
MOFFITT Alison J. 6.10.69, WSE&H/IRL :
  SP - 11.29 (11.96-96), DT - 39.39 (47.22-91),
  JT - 43.51 (47.72-99)

MOHAMED Stacey U23 22.01.80, Jarrow & Hebburn :
  JT - 38.82
MOLLOY Jennifer U20 23.09.83, Bournemouth :
  60H - 8.97i
MONDS Debra 25.02.78, Wigan :
  HT - 38.66
MONK Caroline 7.09.75, Halesowen :
  JT - 37.03 (37.44-99)
MONKS Kamela U17 6.05.87, Channel Islands :
  TJ - 10.85
MONTADOR Karen 14.05.79, Edinburgh WM :
  800 - 2:12.13 (2:10.99-01), 1500 - 4:32.83i (4:25.6-01)
MONTAGNANI Amelia U13 10.03.90, Herne Hill :
  75 - 9.9, 100 - 13.0, 150 - 19.8, 200 - 27.4, HJ - 1.55,
  LJ - 4.86, SPM - 9.24, PenM - 2390
MONYE Chinedu U13 29.12.89, WSE&H :
  75 - 9.9, 100 - 13.1, 150 - 19.8, 200 - 27.4
MOODY Karen V35 20.07.67, Cannock & Stafford :
  HT - 38.10 (39.02-00)
MOONEY Rosanna U17 14.07.86, Livingston :
  800 - 2:15.45, 1500 - 4:41.5mx
MOORCROFT Karen U17 12.12.86, Wigan :
  300H - 46.85
MOORE Charlotte U20 4.01.85, Bournemouth :
  400 - 56.93mx/57.0/57.45 (57.0-01), 800 - 1:59.75,
  1500 - 4:13.94, 5KR - 16:38
MOORE Claire U23 29.03.82, Gateshead :
  DT - 46.70
MOORE Sarah Louise 15.03.73, Bristol :
  HT - 56.18 (57.40-01)
MORGAN Kelly U23 17.06.80, WSE&H/Army :
  JT - 64.87
MORGAN Louise U17 8.09.85, Ipswich :
  100 - 12.3/12.52
MORGAN Lydia U20 1.09.83, Vale Royal :
  SP - 13.09, DT - 41.73, HT - 42.97
MORGAN Sarah U20 9.05.84, Midd AC :
  HT - 38.89 (42.25-01)
MORGAN Stephanie 4.03.75, Cannock & Stafford :
  LJ - 5.90w/5.89 (5.97-93), TJ - 12.20
MORRIS Emily U23 30.09.82, Kingst u H/Leeds M U :
  PV - 2.70 (3.00-99)
MORRIS Emma U17 21.02.86, South Shields/Gates :
  60HI - 9.20i, 300H - 46.0/46.71 (45.4/46.50-01),
  400H - 67.0, HJ - 1.72 (1.72-01), Hepl - 4218 (4224-01)
MORRIS Kate U20 18.01.83, Med & Maid :
  SP - 12.23 (12.49i/12.49-01), DT - 39.67
MORRIS Sharon 5.07.68, Bedford & County :
  1500 - 4:22.13 (4:20.35-00), 3k - 9:22.15,
  5k - 15:51+e/16:52.1, 5MR - 26:56,
  10k - 33:36.8, 10kR - 33:50 (33:39-01),
  10MR - 56:56, HMar - 74:24 (74:04-01)
MORRIS Tracy 25.12.69, Coventry Godiva :
  PV - 3.00
MORRISEY Natalie U15 22.08.88, Derby LAC :
  100 - 12.40w/12.5/12.58, 200 - 25.3w/25.36
MORRISON Cherri A. U17 27.09.86, Sale :
  300H - 45.59, 400H - 66.09,
  LJ - 5.30i/5.30, Hepl - 4037
MORRISON Kirsty 28.10.75, Shaftesbury Barnet :
  JT - 55.74 (55.91-99)
MORTIMER Rowenna Mari U17 4.07.86, Bristol :
  200 - 25.2w, 300 - 39.73, 400 - 57.3
MOSS Gillian U15 6.10.88, West Norfolk :
  1500 - 4:42.18
MOULD Jayne U20 7.11.83, Birchfield :
  400H - 66.26
MOUNTAIN Katrina U15 12.01.88, Worthing :
  SPG - 10.87
MOUNTENEY Helen U20 24.09.84, Birchfield :
  JT - 47.73
MUDGE Angela 8.07.70, Carnethy :
  5MR - 27:04, Mar - 2:43:05
MULHOLLAND Lisa U17 19.12.85, Basingstoke & MH :
  TJ - 10.73

404

MULLAN Stacy U17 15.09.86, Regent House :
80HI - 11.71w/11.8, 300H - 45.1/45.76
MULLEN Natasha U13 25.05.90, Yate :
150 - 20.0
MURDOCH Emma U20 26.03.84, Elgin :
HT - 38.39
MURPHY Catherine Ann 21.09.75, Shaftesbury B :
100 - 11.98 (11.48-01), 200 - 23.42i/23.84 (23.28-99),
300 - 37.1i+ (37.48-00), 400 - 51.36
MURPHY Laura U13 10.12.89, Liverpool H :
1200 - 4:00.3
MURPHY Tara U20 16.05.85, Team Solent :
LJ - 5.52
MURRAY Freya U20 20.09.83, Edinburgh WM :
1500 - 4:19.98, 3k - 9:56.5 (9:54.1-01)
MURRAY Seonaid U20 16.03.85, Macclesfield :
400H - 64.8/65.51
MURRAY-JESSEE Alison V35 13.01.67, C of Glasgow :
PV - 3.90Aun/3.75un/3.20A/3.20 (3.95A-99/3.60-98)
MURTAGH Sarah U15 18.11.88, AVON S :
PV - 2.57
MUSCROFT Leanne U17 2.12.85, Rotherham :
800 - 2:16.64i/2:17.00
MYATT Julia V35 3.08.63, North Staffs RRA :
Mar - 3:07:04 (3:01:38-01)
MYTON Aisha U20 3.01.84, Herne Hill :
TJ - 11.82i/11.71

NAKANGU Vanessa U13 3.12.89, S London :
150 - 19.4
NASH Lindsey U17 7.11.86, Basildon :
Hepl - 3891
NASH-ODEI Michelle U17 19.03.87, Herne Hill :
100 - 12.4/12.45w/12.48, 200 - 25.18w/25.28,
LJ - 5.38i
NATHAN Rachael U17 27.04.86, Lincoln Well :
800 - 2:13.1 (2:12.8-01), 1500 - 4:23.30mx/4:26.9,
3k - 9:24.38mx/9:31.93 (9:31.69-01)
NAYLOR Paula U17 13.09.86, Rockingham :
HJ - 1.68
NELL Tania U17 21.05.86, WSE&H :
SP - 10.52i (10.46-01), JT - 37.20
NELSON Caroline U17 1.07.86, Trafford :
800 - 2:13.21
NEVA Diane U13 20.10.89, City of Plymouth :
JTM - 31.10
NEVE Clare U17 11.06.86, Trafford :
PV - 3.40
NEWCOMBE Rachel V35 25.02.67, Liverpool H :
400 - 57.4 (55.19-92), 800 - 2:04.69 (2:03.28-98),
1500 - 4:11.24
NEWINGTON Ella U17 30.01.87, Swansea :
DT - 33.53
NEWINGTON Sophie U17 15.09.85, Swansea :
LJ - 5.64
NEWMAN Lauren U17 17.01.87, WGreen & Ex L :
HJ - 1.62
NEWMAN Sarah 7.10.79, Newport/UWIC :
400H - 65.7 (64.48-01)
NEWMAN Shelley Jean 8.08.73, Belgrave :
SP - 11.89 (12.34-96), DT - 60.29 (60.82-98)
NEWTON Caroline U17 26.10.85, Leics Sch :
HJ - 1.62
NEWTON Katherine U17 25.10.85, Chesterfield :
SP - 11.08, DT - 34.31, HT - 33.63
NEWTON Maria Angela V35 22.07.66, Med & M/JAM :
PV - 3.00 (3.40-98)
NICCOLLS Janette 7.09.76, Thames Valley :
60 - 7.64i, 100 - 11.8/11.94 (11.84w-96),
200 - 24.4/24.56
NICHOLAS Samantha U17 3.09.85, Carmarthen :
TJ - 11.01w
NICHOLS Angela U20 22.09.84, Wycombe :
PV - 3.10 (3.10-01)
NICHOLS Sara U20 9.06.83, Wycombe/Bath Univ :
PV - 3.00

NICOL Abbey U13 1.01.90, Vale of Aylesbury :
75 - 10.0
NICOL Gemma U17 27.07.86, Dunf & W Fife/S B :
60 - 7.62i, 100 - 12.26, 200 - 24.8/24.89,
300 - 38.49, 400 - 55.00
NICOLL Joanne U20 27.12.84, Motherwell :
LJ - 5.59w
NOBLE Emily U15 28.04.88, Bingley :
75HG - 11.4/11.47, PenG - 2735
NOBLE Frances U17 2.05.86, Bingley :
80HI - 12.08, LJ - 5.51 (5.53-01), Hepl - 4148
NORFORD Natalia U23 29.09.82, Beds & Co/
Loughbro : HJ - 1.65 (1.73-99)
NORMAN Katrina 1.01.76, Walton :
400H - 64.5/64.63 (60.15-95)
NORRISTON Cherelle U15 29.11.88, Thames Valley :
60 - 8.00i, 100 - 12.48w/12.5/12.61
NORVILLE Danielle U20 18.01.83, Telford :
60 - 7.60i (7.52i-01), 200 - 24.35 (23.61-01),
100 - 11.75w/11.87 (11.69w/11.75-01)
NOVAK Stephanie U17 20.09.86, Preston :
JT - 37.90
NUGENT Jessica Natalie Rosemary U20 27.08.84,
Shaftesbury B : 3k - 9:54.93
NUTT Caroline U20 17.06.83, Wakefield :
PV - 3.50i/3.40 (3.50-01)
NWIDOBIE Kara U23 13.04.81, Blackpool :
SP - 14.28, DT - 49.89
NWIDOBIE NiaBari Zoey U17 4.01.86, Blackpool :
TJ - 11.46, Hepl - 3891

O'CALLAGHAN Leanne 15.07.74, Wycombe/IRL :
60 - 7.72i (7.60i-00),
100 - 12.00w/12.09 (11.88w-01/11.96-00),
200 - 24.94 (24.50w/24.8/24.87i-00)
O'CONNOR Gayle 24.08.79, Liverpool H :
HJ - 1.65 (1.75-99)
O'CONNOR Gillian V40 24.09.61, S London :
Mar - 2:55:07 (2:53:01-00)
O'NEIL Melissa U17 13.02.87, West Suffolk :
JT - 35.84 (36.37-01)
O'SULLIVAN Katie U17 16.02.87, Havering M :
HJ - 1.62
OATES Joanne 21.02.78, Sale :
400H - 61.58 (61.19-01)
OBERN Kirsty U23 7.03.81, Rugby & Nor PH :
PV - 2.80
OGDEN Katherine U13 25.01.90, :
PV - 2.20
OGDEN Rachael 23.07.79, Worthing :
1500 - 4:34.16 (4:30.51-97)
OGUN Bolanle 2.09.77, Exeter/Wolvs Univ :
HT - 46.20
OKORO Marilyn U20 23.09.84, Shaftesbury Barnet :
400 - 56.14
OKWUE Maurine Inkeira 13.05.78, Thames Valley :
TJ - 11.88
OKYERE Nadine U17 29.11.86, Birchfield :
Hepl - 3846
OLDFIELD Sally Grace U20 25.06.84, Kettering :
800 - 2:11.9, 1500 - 4:25.3, 3k - 9:31.12
OLIVER Anita U17 28.11.85, Blackheath :
DT - 35.05
OLIVER Emily Jane U20 8.02.84, Blackheath :
HT - 43.58
OLSON Hannah Astrid U15 29.01.88, Ashford :
PV - 3.80
OLSON Natalie Victoria U17 9.05.86, Ashford :
PV - 3.75
ONUORA Amalachukwu U17 16.03.86, Belgrave :
60 - 7.8i, 100 - 12.0/12.01 (11.97w/12.01-01),
200 - 24.67w/24.7/24.96i/24.98 (24.96-01)
ONUORA Anyika U20 28.10.84, Liverpool H :
60 - 7.56i, 100 - 11.83w/12.05 (11.86-01),
200 - 24.29

ORROW Amy U17 4.06.87, Lincs Sch :
DT - 32.33
OSAGEDE Diana U20 18.01.85, WGreen & Ex L :
100H - 15.2, TJ - 11.13 (11.30-01)
OSHINOWO Adeoti Efundademu U23 12.02.80, U of Ill :
SP - 15.50, DT - 49.14, HT - 51.37,
OSIFODUNRIN Nike U17 21.11.86, Edinburgh WM :
LJ - 5.44
OUGHTON Dominique U23 2.01.81, Team Solent :
800 - 2:13.1 (2:12.90-01)
OUGHTON Karen U20 26.01.83, Cov G/Cov Univ :
60 - 7.73i (7.64i-01), 200 - 24.75,
100 - 11.9/12.05w/12.09 (11.96w/12.05-01)
OVENS Hayley 5.12.75, Edinburgh WM :
800 - 2:06.06, 1500 - 4:12.47, 3k - 9:28.45
OWEN Hollie U13 16.06.90, Nuneaton :
150 - 20.1
OWEN Judith 20.06.71, S London :
400H - 65.70 (63.14-00)
OWEN Stephanie U17 31.12.86, Cannock & Stafford :
SP - 11.38, HepI - 3967
OWEN Suzanne 5.05.79, City of Stoke/Staffs Univ :
1500 - 4:27.68mx (4:26.78-00), 5MR - 27:59,
3k - 9:26.53mx/9:36.7, 5k - 16:52.1+/16:56.00
OWENS Jenni U17 15.05.87, Liverpool H :
400H - 67.05
OWUSU Lesley D. 21.12.78, WSE&H/U of Nebraska :
100 - 11.93w/12.05A (11.7w-98/11.93w/11.99-01),
200 - 23.94 (23.73i/23.75w/23.86-01),
400 - 52.39 (52.15i/52.27-01), 800 - 2:09.59
OYEPITAN Abiodun 30.12.79, Shaftesbury Barnet :
60 - 7.32i, 100 - 11.33rs/11.36 (11.17w/11.29-01),
200 - 23.52

P ACEY Jenny U20 5.02.83, Lincoln W/Loughbro :
HJ - 1.65i/1.65 (1.65-01), LJ - 5.54, Hep - 4318
PALLANT Emma U15 4.06.89, AF&D :
1500 - 4:40.34
PALMER Aimee U17 7.11.86, Birchfield :
LJ - 5.61
PALMER Carly U20 21.12.84, Milton Keynes :
TJ - 11.41
PALMER Clare U17 30.12.85, Crawley :
SP - 10.49
PALMER Gillian U23 30.12.80, Edinburgh Univ :
1500 - 4:25.88 (4:22.93-00), 3k - 9:12.47,
5k - 15:53.96, 5KR - 16:15, 10k - 33:09.70
PALMER Karlene J. U23 23.10.80, WSE&H/Loughbro :
100 - 12.07w/12.1 (11.96w/12.12-97),
200 - 24.9/25.12 (24.41w/24.42-97)
PALMER-JOHNSON Ashleigh U17 19.09.86, WSE&H :
100 - 12.3w, 200 - 25.58w, SP - 10.47
PANGBOURNE Laura U17 10.11.85, Wimborne :
PV - 2.60
PANNETT Meredith 13.06.71, Cambridge H/Dulwich R :
1500 - 4:30.7, 3k - 9:42.4, 5k - 16:44.0mx/16:46.94,
5KR - 16:36, 5MR - 27:31, 10kR - 34:49
PAPURA Lisa U15 21.04.88, Barry :
100 - 12.60, 200 - 25.63w
PARKER Barbara U23 8.11.82, City of Norwich :
800 - 2:12.10 (2:10.00-01)
PARKER Carol Ann 22.09.69, Coventry Godiva :
SP - 13.94 (14.76i-91/14.71-90),
DT - 39.62 (44.70-89), HT - 37.32 (39.08-95)
PARKER Emily Jane U20 7.11.84, Epsom & Ewell :
100H - 15.0w/15.1 (14.2w/14.58-01), TJ - 12.52,
400H - 62.98 (62.0-01), LJ - 5.80w/5.68 (5.76-01)
PARKER Fern U15 20.02.88, Andover :
100 - 12.5, 200 - 26.0
PARKER-SIMPSON Rhianna U20 20.07.83, Hales/
Bath Univ : 400 - 57.30
PARKIN Claire U20 26.02.84, Edinburgh WM :
SP - 11.41
PARKINSON Danielle U23 2.09.81, Sale/Leeds Met U :
100H - 14.94w/15.29 (15.07-01),
HJ - 1.65 (1.67-98), Hep - 4767

PARLETT Alyson V35 12.02.64, Bexley :
Mar - 3:08:36
PARR Kirsty U15 6.04.88, Leeds :
LJ - 5.17, PenG - 2799
PARRY Carys L. U23 24.07.81, Rhondda/Loughbro :
HT - 54.01 (54.12-01)
PARRY Joanna 5.03.78, Southampton City :
JT - 37.85
PARRY Sheena 16.11.77, Rhondda :
HT - 49.93
PARSONS Lucy 10.02.79, Cardiff/Univ Wales Inst C :
200 - 25.1, 400 - 55.9/56.42
PARTINGTON Carolyn V35 27.06.66, Manx :
20kW - 1:44:54
PARTRIDGE Susan U23 4.01.80, City of Glasgow :
5k - 16:32.31, 5KR - 16:54, 5MR - 27:31,
10k - 34:48.86, 10kR - 34:19, HMar - 76:11
PASSLEY Rebekah U17 9.03.87, Herne Hill :
LJ - 5.93w/5.86i/5.83 (5.86-01), TJ - 11.36
PATERSON Pamela U17 26.10.85, Edinburgh WM :
60 - 7.79i (7.75i-01), 100 - 12.39,
60HI - 9.03i (8.94i-01),
80HI - 12.03 (11.71w/11.8/11.87-01)
PATERSON Sarah U17 22.06.87, Birchfield :
800 - 2:16.70
PATERSON Sarah U23 7.09.80, Pitreavie :
3k - 9:57.56mx
PATRICK Elizabeth Sian 29.08.77, Birchfield :
TJ - 12.06w/11.83 (12.92-00)
PATTERSON Laura Joanne U23 31.01.81, Wycombe /
Staffs Univ : PV - 3.50 (3.60i/3.60-01)
PATTINSON Helen Teresa 2.01.74, Preston :
800 - 2:03.20mx (2:03.75-00), 1500 - 4:01.10,
3k - 8:58.33, 5k - 15:50.16
PATTISON Emma U13 21.11.89, Grantham :
SPM - 9.94, JTM - 26.81
PATTON Channah 22.02.72, Hallamshire :
HMar - 78:43 (78:30-00)
PAUZERS Clare E. V40 2.08.62, Herne Hill :
Mar - 2:49:26 (2:43:27-97)
PAVEY Joanne 20.09.73, Exeter :
1500 - 4:11.16 (4:07.28-97), 2k - 5:42.5+,
3k - 8:31.27, 5k - 14:48.66
PAXTON Henrietta U20 19.09.83, Birchfield :
LJ - 5.52 (5.75-99)
PAYNE Judith A. U23 7.07.80, Wakefield/CUAC :
HJ - 1.70i/1.70 (1.76-98)
PEACOCK Rachel Eleanor U23 18.05.82, B'mouth/
Bath Univ : LJ - 5.61 (5.69w-01/5.66-97),
TJ - 12.35w/12.12
PEAKE Rebecca Louise U20 22.06.83, Derby LAC/
Loughbro : SP - 14.23 (14.34-01)
PEAKE Sally U17 8.02.86, Wirral :
LJ - 5.76w/5.66, TJ - 11.89w/11.77
PEARCE Caroline U23 1.09.80, Huntingdon/Loughbro :
60H - 8.68i, 100H - 14.20, HJ - 1.71i/1.71,
LJ - 6.01, Hep - 5108
PEARSON Claire 23.09.78, Leics Cor/Loughbro :
60H - 8.65i, 100H - 14.3/14.32 (14.18w-00)
PEARSON Natalie Grace U15 7.06.88, Sheffield :
100 - 12.51
PEASTON Stephanie U15 28.10.87, Edinburgh WM :
75HG - 11.87
PECKHAM Rachel U17 14.02.87, Epsom & Ewell :
60HI - 9.2i, 80HI - 11.8, 300H - 46.4, LJ - 5.34
PELLING Amy U15 10.12.88, Kettering :
HJ - 1.60
PENNET Catriona U20 10.10.83, EWM/Aberdeen Un :
100H - 14.36, 400H - 65.90
PEREIRA Jennifer U20 8.08.85, Med & Maid :
1500 - 4:32.60, 3k - 9:46.6
PERKINS Emma U17 4.09.85, Worthing :
HJ - 1.80, LJ - 5.72
PERKS Dani U15 17.01.89, Cornwall AC :
PenG - 2685

406

PERRY Kathryn U17 2.10.85, Mansfield :
  300H - 45.7/46.43, 400H - 66.8
PERRY Laura Helen Susan 4.06.75, Dudley & Stour :
  DT - 37.55 (39.56-91), HT - 40.81 (42.62-00)
PERRY Victoria A. V45 25.11.57, Altrincham :
  Mar - 3:00:22 (2:59:00-01)
PETERS Abigail U13 27.12.89, WSE&H :
  DTM - 23.90
PETERS Emma U20 12.01.84, Yate :
  400H - 65.97
PHILLIPS Claire U15 27.05.88, Ealing,Southall & Mx :
  HTG - 33.683Kg
PHILLIPS Emma 10.06.74, Tipton :
  5MR - 27:36
PHILLIPS Gemma U23 27.10.80, Kendal/Birm Univ. :
  1500 - 4:29.66mx, 3k - 9:54.35, 10k - 36:17.9
PHILLIPS Nicola U20 23.04.83, Dartford :
  3kW - 15:04.7 (14:29.37i-00/14:49.59-99),
  5kW - 26:45.5 (25:11.46-99), 10kW - 56:27.1,
  10kWR - 52:08 (51:36-00)
PICKETT Sarah-Jane U20 24.10.84, AF&D :
  400H - 63.39
PICKVANCE Ruth V40 29.09.61, Swansea :
  10MR - 58:40, HMar - 77:19, Mar - 2:45:17
PIDGEON Elizabeth Sarah 27.04.77, WGreen & Ex L :
  HT - 62.08 (63.61-00), JT - 39.13 (42.94-99)
PIDGEON Emily Claire U15 1.06.89, Gloucester L :
  800 - 2:17.96, 1500 - 4:32.58,
  3k - 9:44.39mx (9:55.71i-01)
PIDGEON Jane V35 23.01.64, Notts :
  2kSt - 7:11.67, 3kSt - 11:23.69
PIERRE Cherie U20 15.05.84, Shaftesbury Barnet :
  100 - 12.1 (12.08-99), 200 - 24.80
PIERRE Michelle 30.09.73, Shaftesbury Barnet :
  200 - 25.1/25.19 (24.4w-96/24.8-95/25.08-99),
  400 - 54.31 (52.77-97)
PIKE Zoe 17.11.71, :
  Mar - 3:07:10
PINCOMBE Victoria 19.06.73, Bideford :
  5KR - 16:42+, 5MR - 27:35 (26:43-99),
  10kR - 34:02, HMar - 75:28 (74:59-01)
PINEL Syreena 13.01.79, Birchfield :
  100 - 12.0/12.06, 200 - 25.1 (24.32w/24.46-00)
PITTS Laura U17 9.01.86, Exeter :
  HJ - 1.71
PITTWOOD Eloise Adele U17 4.12.85, N Devon :
  1500 - 4:40.30, 3k - 10:39.5
PLATEAU Carolyn Rose U15 22.08.88, Radley :
  800 - 2:12.81, 1500 - 4:46.3
PLATEAU Natalie Jane U20 19.10.84, Radley :
  400 - 56.30
PLATT Joedy U15 27.11.87, N Devon :
  100 - 12.67, 200 - 25.8
PLEWS Nicola U20 15.12.83, Invicta :
  100H - 15.01w, Hep - 3960
POCOCK Nicola 9.05.79, AF&D :
  400H - 62.8/62.92
POLIUS Ann-Margaret U17 17.06.86, Newham & E B :
  TJ - 11.01
POLIUS Leandra U23 14.05.80, Newham & Essex B :
  LJ - 5.67w, TJ - 12.45 (12.52-00)
POLSON Elizabeth U17 26.06.86, Suffolk Sch :
  DT - 33.18
PONSFORD Sarah U17 15.05.87, Salisbury :
  1500 - 4:39.55, 3k - 10:18.9mx/10:19.93
PORAZINSKI Donna-Marie U23 28.01.81, Newport :
  400H - 62.75 (60.42-01)
PORTER Katherine U23 19.08.82, Blackheath :
  60H - 8.8i (8.77i-01), 400H - 62.8/65.74,
  100H - 14.5w/14.79 (14.4/14.41-99)
POTTER Helen 25.06.74, Trafford :
  JT - 40.54 (40.74-01)
POTTER Jane U23 24.10.81, Charn/Notts Trent Univ :
  1500 - 4:30.2 (4:26.63-00),
  3k - 9:43.14 (9:30.13-00), 5k - 17:05.24

POTTER Susan 11.08.79, Team Solent :
  100H - 15.1/15.31 (15.0/15.05w-01),
  400H - 63.0/64.78 (63.14-01)
POWELL Pauline 17.05.73, Blackburn :
  5k - 17:00.37 (16:40.04-01), 5MR - 27:36,
  10k - 34:23.9, 10MR - 57:59, HMar - 77:37,
  Mar - 2:46:28
POWELL Xanine 21.05.79, Cambridge Harriers :
  100 - 12.1/12.11w/12.21 (11.96w/12.1-01),
  200 - 24.87 (24.61w?-00/24.74i/24.76-01)
POWER Anne V35 20.03.63, Reading RR :
  Mar - 2:58:54
PRATT Julie 20.03.79, WGreen & Ex L :
  200 - 25.10 (24.5w-01/24.8-99), 100H - 13.08
PRINGLE Lucy 3.08.78, WSE&H :
  800 - 2:12.56
PROBERT Eleanor U13 23.05.90, Southampton City :
  DTM - 25.27
PROCTOR Amanda 25.07.71, Basingstoke & MH :
  15kR - 54:22, Mar - 3:06:38 (3:04:27-01)
PROCTOR Elizabeth 31.10.72, Bolton :
  1500 - 4:28.78mx (4:28.28mx-00/4:29.1-99)
PROCTOR Ruth U20 4.05.84, City of Norwich :
  1500 - 4:33.48, 3k - 9:40.59, 5k - 17:30.3
PRYCE Janice V40 2.09.59, R Sutton Coldfield :
  TJ - 11.42
PRYER Helen 21.01.79, Bracknell :
  100 - 12.1w, 200 - 24.4/24.47
PULLINGER Stefanie U20 3.04.83, Brack/Loughbro :
  100H - 13.95 (13.9-01)
PUNTER Sheryl U17 17.06.87, Leeds :
  LJ - 5.32
PURDY Helen 5.10.75, Bideford :
  5MR - 27:52
PURKISS Melanie 11.03.79, Team Solent :
  100 - 11.9 (11.55w/11.76-99),
  200 - 23.81 (23.64w/23.80-99), 400 - 52.99
PYWELL Stephanie U17 12.06.87, Mansfield :
  HJ - 1.73i/1.73 (1.75-01)

QUINE Laura U15 16.02.88, Liverpool H :
  1500 - 4:46.88

RADCLIFFE Paula Jane 17.12.73, Bedford & Co :
  1500 - 4:12c (4:05.37-01), 2k - 5:37.01+,
  3k - 8:22.20, 5k - 14:31.42, 5kR - 15:02+ (14:57-01),
  5MR - 24:38+8k/26:17+ (24:47-99), 10k - 30:01.09,
  10kR - 30:38, 15kR - 49:05+, 10MR - 52:40+ (51:41+-00),
  HMar - 69:01+ (66:47-01), Mar - 2:17:18
RADEMEYER Heiline 10.06.69, Herne Hill/RSA :
  JT - 38.00
RADON Christina Maria 12.07.79, Shaft B/Birm Univ. :
  5k - 16:51.94, 10k - 35:15.4
RAINFORD Shani U17 6.07.87, Herne Hill :
  HJ - 1.77, JT - 34.33, HepI - 4064
RANDALL Charlotte U23 10.05.80, Sutton & D/Lond U :
  400H - 63.4/64.44 (63.18-00)
RATCLIFFE Karen V40 1.06.61, Coventry RWC :
  3kW - 14:38.8 (14:02.29-93), 5kWR - 25:27 (24:03-94),
  10kWR - 52:16+ (48:30-94), 20kW - 1:46:35
RAWLING Kimberley U20 22.07.83, Newquay & Par :
  DT - 36.75 (38.43-01), HT - 40.87 (40.98-01)
READ Katey U17 20.03.86, Stockport :
  60HI - 8.93i, 80HI - 11.62
READ-CAYTON Sally V35 1.04.65, Woking :
  800 - 2:12.93 (2:09.1-92)
READE Joanne Lesley U20 28.11.84, Rushcliffe :
  TJ - 11.03
READER Catherine V45 19.10.54, Colchester H :
  (see DUHIG)
REAL Natalie U15 14.11.87, Bournemouth :
  1500 - 4:42.3
REDD Samantha U20 16.02.84, Brighton & Hove AC :
  JT - 47.66
REDMAN Hollie U17 12.12.85, Braintree :
  DT - 38.50, HT - 31.39 (31.67-01)

REDMOND Laura Ann U23 19.04.81, Edinburgh WM :
100H - 14.96 (14.86w-01),
HJ - 1.65i (1.70-00/1.70i-01), LJ - 5.67 (5.69-01),
SP - 12.15 (12.22-01), JT - 36.53, Hep - 5176
REED Kate U23 28.09.82, Bristol :
1500 - 4:26.38, 3k - 9:34.88
REES Charlotte U20 14.06.84, Swansea :
JT - 44.37
REEVES Claire U20 31.07.84, Dartford :
3kW - 14:53.6, 5kW - 25:50.83,
10kW - 54:47.0, 10kWR - 52:58
REGENT Odette U15 27.11.87, Ashford :
HJ - 1.60
REGIS Yasmin U17 12.12.86, WSE&H :
TJ - 10.74
REID Emma U23 5.01.81, Edinburgh WM/Pitreavie :
100H - 14.83, 400H - 62.53
REID Rebecca U20 9.11.83, Barrow & Furness :
400H - 65.47, Hep - 4141
REILLY Sarah E. 3.07.73, Birchfield/IRL :
60 - 7.43i, 100 - 12.00 (11.45w/11.49-00),
200 - 23.30i/23.90 (23.02-01)
RENNISON Amy U20 15.06.83, Sale/Loughbro :
PV - 3.10 (3.10-99)
RENOUF Elaine U17 2.07.87, Pitreavie :
800 - 2:17.0, 1500 - 4:33.76, 3k - 9:33.0
RENOUF Katie U17 3.06.87, Exeter :
Hepl - 4068
RENOUF Tamara U17 3.06.87, Exeter :
Hepl - 3860
RETCHAKAN Selva Gowry V40 21.06.60, Highgate H :
400H - 59.6 (54.63-92)
REVITT Shelley U17 28.11.85, Doncaster :
LJ - 5.34
REYNOLDS Kay Suzzanne V35 15.09.67, Radley :
100 - 12.1w (12.1-01), 100H - 13.9w/13.96 (13.9-99)
REYNOLDS Nicky U20 24.06.85, Birchfield :
5kW - 29:59.4 (27:57.3-01), 5kWR - 29:02 (26:32-01)
REYNOLDS Stephanie U17 15.06.86, Elgin :
800 - 2:14.98
RHODES Josephine U17 22.03.86, Swindon :
800 - 2:16.02, 1500 - 4:36.4mx/4:37.42,
3k - 10:17.54
RHODES Sarah U17 4.01.86, Coventry Godiva :
300 - 41.17i/41.3
RHULE Candee U15 16.09.87, S London :
SPG - 12.85
RICHARDS Lara Elesia U20 7.03.83, Newp/Bath Un :
LJ - 6.01, TJ - 11.22 (11.62i-00/11.60w-99/11.53-00)
RICHARDSON Marcia Maureen 10.02.72, WSE&H :
100 - 11.67 (11.29w/11.35-00)
RICHOLD Faye Helen U15 24.10.87, Milton Keynes :
60HG - 9.29i, 75HG - 11.5/11.54w/11.74
RIDDIOUGH Georgina U17 28.11.86, Crawley :
800 - 2:16.07
RIDGLEY Clare Louise 11.09.77, Team Solent :
PV - 3.70, Dec - 4767
RIDGLEY Rebecca Jane U23 26.02.80, Team Solent/
Loughbro : PV - 3.51
RIDING Donna U20 28.11.83, Sale :
800 - 2:06.97, 1500 - 4:32.19mx/4:32.86
RIDLEY Elysia U17 3.12.86, Witney :
800 - 2:16.8
RIDLEY Laura U17 20.03.86, Preston :
LJ - 5.63w/5.60
RIGBY Lisa Marie U17 12.02.86, N Devon :
DT - 34.42
RILEY Catherine U23 4.06.82, Trafford/Manchester U :
400 - 56.23, 800 - 2:06.14
ROACH Elizabeth U13 12.09.90, Barrow & Furness :
LJ - 4.57
ROACH Gemma U20 16.02.83, WSE&H :
HT - 37.79 (39.22-01)
ROACH Justine U20 21.12.84, Leics Cor :
60H - 8.81i, 100H - 14.4, 400H - 60.30

ROBERTS Cara U20 24.05.85, Bournemouth :
100 - 12.24w, LJ - 5.55 (5.56-00)
ROBERTS Lowri U23 9.10.81, Newport/Birm Univ. :
100H - 14.41w/14.62 (14.40w/14.47-00)
ROBERTS Melanie 2.03.78, Liverpool H :
60 - 7.61i (7.60i-01), 100 - 11.69,
200 - 24.44 (24.4-01)
ROBERTS Sarah Jane 25.06.78, Forest of Dean :
LJ - 5.73w/5.65 (5.73-01), TJ - 11.66
ROBERTS Suzanne 19.12.78, Wakefield/Loughbro :
HT - 60.38
ROBERTSON Clare U17 17.08.86, Cannock & Staff :
SP - 10.48
ROBERTSON Hayley U17 29.10.86, Humberside Sch :
100 - 12.38
ROBERTSON Hazel U17 27.07.87, Falkirk :
DT - 33.11, HT - 34.26
ROBILLIARD Kylie U15 11.06.88, Channel Islands :
75HG - 11.2/11.24
ROBINSON Claire 18.01.78, Bas & MH/Birm Univ. :
400 - 56.19 (55.75-01)
ROBINSON Debra 31.01.68, Tipton :
5MR - 27:27, 10kR - 33:42,
HMar - 76:56 (75:07-01), Mar - 2:39:42 (2:35:40-01)
ROBINSON Harriet U17 21.04.87, Blackheath :
80HI - 11.56, 300H - 45.7/46.78, LJ - 5.30
ROBINSON Laura U17 11.10.85, Wakefield :
60 - 7.99i, 200 - 25.5w (25.31w/25.4-01),
300 - 40.55, 400 - 58.3
ROBINSON Linsi U20 9.01.84, Birchfield :
TJ - 12.10
ROBINSON Madeleine U23 13.10.81, Bord/Glasgow U :
HT - 43.11
ROBINSON Nicola Jane U17 16.04.86, Nuneaton :
100 - 12.0, 200 - 25.1/25.54 (25.36-01),
60HI - 8.86i, 80HI - 11.2/11.33
ROBINSON Sian Louise U23 31.03.82, Nuneaton :
100 - 11.92w/12.0/12.29 (11.83w/12.00-01),
200 - 25.24 (24.95-01)
ROBINSON-SCANLON Taneisha 19.11.77, S B/IRL :
LJ - 5.87 (5.93-98), TJ - 13.00i/12.98
ROBSON Carly U20 5.12.83, WSE&H :
LJ - 5.52, TJ - 12.16
ROCK Shantel U13 7.11.89, Thames Valley :
SPM - 9.17
RODGER Alison U20 29.10.84, Sale/Victoria P AAC :
SP - 12.86i/12.58 (12.67-01), DT - 42.03
RODGERS Heather U17 12.09.86, North Shields P :
300H - 46.7
RODGERS Lauren U13 13.03.90, Cambridge & Col :
70HM - 11.8
RODGERS Lucy Christine U17 1.07.87, Thurrock :
300 - 41.2/41.29, Hepl - 4369
RODMELL Kelly U17 26.11.85, Kingston u Hull :
800 - 2:16.9
ROGER Faye U13 21.12.89, Liverpool H :
LJ - 4.95
ROGER Kirsty 24.03.78, City of Glasgow :
100H - 15.32 (14.6w-97/14.76-00),
HJ - 1.65i/1.65 (1.72i-99/1.70-97),
Hep - 4568w/4566 (4921-00)
ROGERS Heidi U17 27.05.86, City of Bath :
SP - 10.45
ROGERS Lorna Jane 10.01.74, S Barnet/Dundee HH :
60H - 8.75i
ROLES Philippa 1.03.78, Sale :
SP - 15.88i/14.91 (15.95i-99/15.19-01),
DT - 58.26 (60.00-99)
ROLES Rebecca 14.12.79, Rugby & Nor PH :
SP - 12.70 (13.23-01), DT - 51.16 (51.79-99),
JT - 36.22
ROOMES Kelly U17 19.01.87, Med & Maid :
60 - 7.94i, 100 - 12.35, 200 - 25.14w/25.37
ROONEY Claire U20 23.08.83, C of Glas/Strath Univ :
60 - 7.54i, 100 - 12.19 (12.02-01)

408

ROSCOE Helen 4.12.79, Sale/Loughbro :
  60 - 7.70i (7.59i-01), PV - 3.50i (3.50-00),
  200 - 24.75i/25.26 (23.4w/23.80-01)
ROSS Joanna U23 18.02.81, Victoria Park AAC :
  800 - 2:05.56, 1500 - 4:31.5mx
ROTHMAN Kimberly V35 6.09.64, WSE&H :
  LJ - 6.13i/6.08w?/6.01 (6.19-00)
ROUGH Alison U20 1.06.83, C of Glas/Glas Univ Cal :
  TJ - 11.60
ROWE Deborah 8.09.72, Birchfield :
  TJ - 12.84 (13.14w/12.97-00)
ROWE Jasmine U13 14.09.89, City of Stoke :
  75 - 9.8, 100 - 12.8, 200 - 26.8
ROWE Lauren U15 29.05.88, Warrington :
  PenG - 2634
ROWLANDS Joanne U13 29.12.89, Crawley :
  PenM - 2042
RUDDOCK Ellena 23.02.76, Rugby & Nor PH :
  60 - 7.63i (7.54i-98), 200 - 23.41w/23.78 (23.71-97)
  100 - 11.76w/11.9/11.91 (11.49w-00/11.63A-99/11.67-98),
  200 - 23.41w/23.78 (23.71-97)
RULE Hayley U17 11.10.86, Cambridge & Colr'dge :
  800 - 2:16.67
RUSSELL Molly U17 3.08.86, Radley :
  100 - 12.1/12.19w/12.20, 200 - 25.5 (25.3-01)
RUTHERFORD Susannah Rose 26.02.79, Darl/N Ariz U :
  3k - 9:36.23, 5k - 16:40.67i/17:13.84 (16:31.73-01)
RYDE Gemma U20 23.06.83, Pitreavie :
  100 - 12.09 (11.89-00), 200 - 24.59 (24.35w/24.59-00)

S ADLER Angela V40 25.07.59, Cheltenham :
  Mar - 3:08:46
SADLER Katie U15 15.01.88, Reading :
  HJ - 1.63, PenG - 2614
SADLER Nicole U15 10.11.88, Ipswich :
  100 - 12.50w/12.5, 200 - 25.6/25.77
SAGE Kathryn 27.03.76, Newport :
  400 - 55.6/55.65 (54.81i-01/55.58-00),
  800 - 2:11.7 (2:10.70-01)
SAINT-SMITH Tasha 20.12.75, Enf & Har :
  DT - 40.44 (44.68-94)
SAKA Lydia 20.01.79, WSE&H/SWE :
  TJ - 11.48 (11.92-01)
SALMON Sarah 9.09.74, Newquay & Par :
  800 - 2:09.17, 1500 - 4:20.21,
  3k - 9:24.17mx (9:27.75i-00/9:40.87-96),
  5k - 16:52.83, 10k - 34:11.78
SAMUELS Belinda 29.11.78, Birchfield :
  100H - 14.86 (14.50w-00),
  LJ - 5.71w/5.70 (5.81-01)
SAMUELS Debby U13 8.02.90, Stevenage & NH :
  800 - 2:25.6
SANDERS Nicola U23 23.06.82, Wycombe/Loughbro :
  100 - 12.28mx (11.89w/12.15-98),
  200 - 24.94mx (24.6/24.64w-98/25.11-97,
  400 - 56.54 (55.66-99), 100H - 15.0, 400H - 58.72
SANDERSON Charlotte Elizabeth 18.03.79, Bingley/
  University of Tulsa : 10k - 36:40.32 (34:25.78-01)
SANDERSON Danielle V40 26.10.62, Watford :
  100kR - 7:47:29
SARGENT Claire Lucy U17 11.03.86, Havering M :
  80HI - 11.7/11.85w (12.06-01)
SAUNDERS Kerry 28.03.77, Derby LAC :
  TJ - 11.20 (11.47w/11.45-97)
SAUNDERS Rebecca U15 8.02.88, Dartford :
  SPG - 10.71, DT - 34.79
SAVUNDRA Cecilia U15 29.12.87, AF&D :
  800 - 2:17.81
SAYERS Goldie Katherine D. U23 16.07.82, Belgrave/
  Loughbro : JT - 58.20
SCALES Kath 28.06.77, Tipton :
  3k - 9:53.11
SCARAMALGA Hatty U13 31.05.90, Wells :
  HJ - 1.45
SCHOFIELD Candace U20 3.11.84, Horsham BS :
  JT - 43.11

SCHOFIELD Nicola U17 13.09.86, Havering M :
  300H - 45.8/46.90
SCOTT Jackie U20 31.01.85, Pitreavie :
  200 - 25.10w/25.24
SCOTT Jemma U20 14.03.83, Edinburgh WM :
  HJ - 1.65 (1.70i/1.70-99)
SCOTT Laura U15 16.09.87, Chesterfield :
  JT - 32.04
SCOTT Sabrina 2.06.79, WGreen & Ex L :
  100 - 11.58 (11.50w-01), 200 - 23.73
SCOTT Sian U20 20.03.84, Bournemouth :
  400 - 57.0 (57.69-99), 400H - 60.48
SCOTT Susan 26.09.77, City of Glasgow :
  800 - 1:59.30, 1500 - 4:09.79
SCOTT Suzy U13 1.09.89, Coventry Godiva :
  SPM - 9.13
SCOTT Victoria Rosemary U23 21.09.80, Trafford/
  Liv Univ : HT - 52.31 (55.42-01)
SCOUGALL Laura U15 21.01.89, Birchfield :
  200 - 25.99, 800 - 2:18.0
SEAMAN Laura Mary Elizabeth U20 12.03.83, C of Norw/
  DMU (Beds) Univ : DT - 36.12
SEARLE Jenny 7.06.76, Belgrave :
  PV - 2.60i
SEARLE Kim U20 27.12.83, Kingston u Hull :
  400 - 56.75
SELLARS Caroline U15 26.09.87, Cleveland :
  HJ - 1.60
SEMENOVA Marina V35 12.07.64, Birchfield :
  HT - 41.65 (50.04-99)
SEMENYTSH Rosanna Marie U17 28.05.87, WSE&H :
  JT - 41.01
SEPHTON Deborah U17 9.01.87, Liv.Pembroke Seft :
  TJ - 10.70
SHARP Carly U15 7.09.87, Edinburgh WM :
  HJ - 1.70, LJ - 5.13w
SHARP Lyndsey U13 11.07.90, Edinburgh WM :
  800 - 2:25.97, 70HM - 11.61
SHARROCK Michelle U23 8.09.82, Wigan :
  PV - 3.20
SHAW Amanda U20 28.09.84, Barnsley :
  200 - 25.21
SHAW Emma U17 19.09.86, Skipton :
  SP - 11.25
SHAW Georgina U17 13.03.86, Sale :
  LJ - 5.38 (5.43w/5.41-01)
SHAW Lorraine A. 2.04.68, Sale :
  SP - 12.00 (14.21-94), DT - 46.27 (55.04-94),
  HT - 66.83 (68.15-01)
SHEARER Angela U20 18.01.85, Aberdeen :
  400H - 65.48
SHENTON Fiona V40 19.04.59, Elvet Striders :
  Mar - 3:07:09
SHEPPARD Amanda 26.02.68, Wakefield :
  SP - 11.45 (12.05-92), DT - 38.03 (42.81-98)
SHERLIKER Kessia U17 9.11.85, Southampton City :
  100 - 12.2/12.47, 200 - 25.14 (25.01w/25.10-00)
SHIELD Rebecca U13 1.10.89, Durham City H :
  800 - 2:25.2
SHIPPEN Lisa-Marie U20 19.10.83, Gateshead :
  HT - 41.21
SHIRLEY Laura U17 27.03.87, Basildon :
  SP - 11.62
SHURLEY Harriet U15 30.06.88, WSE&H :
  75HG - 11.5/11.56
SHUTTLEWORTH Sarah U17 16.08.86, Sale :
  300 - 40.42, 400 - 57.62
SIGGERY Alison U20 14.09.83, Carmarthen :
  JT - 41.20
SIGGERY Sara U20 30.06.85, Carmarthen :
  JT - 37.58
SILTO Katherine U20 12.08.83, Swindon/Bath Univ :
  TJ - 11.22 (11.25w-00)
SIMCOX Aimee U17 5.07.86, City of Stoke :
  800 - 2:14.65mx

SIMMONDS Anna U17 22.09.86, Worcester AC :
    800 - 2:09.74
SIMPSON Alice U15 26.02.89, Spenborough :
    LJ - 5.31w/5.28, PenG - 2806
SIMPSON Jemma Louise U20 10.02.84, Newquay & P :
    400 - 56.3/56.43i (55.8-01), 800 - 2:04.11, 1500 - 4:26.43
SIMPSON Nadine U17 28.02.86, Stevenage & NH :
    HJ - 1.68, PV - 2.60 (2.70-01), Hepl - 3956
SIMPSON Sarah U13 22.11.89, Luton :
    1500 - 4:53.78
SIMS Jemma U20 2.05.85, Notts :
    60 - 7.65i, 200 - 24.81i/25.09 (24.2-01/24.63-00)
SINDALL Karen U23 17.01.81, Ilford :
    10kR - 34:44, HMar - 78:08
SINGER Lindsey U20 4.06.83, Birchfield :
    400 - 55.81i/56.82 (56.6-01)
SINGER Samantha U23 8.05.82, Blackheath :
    400 - 56.4/56.52 (55.31-00)
SINGH Eshere U17 15.07.87, Exeter :
    DT - 34.19
SINGLETON Laura U20 6.04.85, Wolverhampton & B :
    LJ - 5.98w/5.69
SINGLETON Sarah V35 18.12.65, Liverpool H :
    3k - 9:47.32mx/9:57.6 (9:34.0-97),
    5k - 17:23.32 (17:15.8-97), 10k - 35:29.6
SKELTON Maria U23 18.05.80, Lagan Valley :
    1500 - 4:27.11, 3k - 9:34.20, 5k - 16:26.24
SKELTON Vicky V35 4.11.67, North Devon RR :
    Mar - 3:08:52, 100kR - 8:55:06
SKETCHLEY Katy 9.07.73, Team Solent :
    100 - 12.13 (12.1w-98),
    100H - 13.82 (13.57w/13.78-98), 400H - 64.1
SKINNER Kimberly U15 21.09.87, Falkirk :
    60 - 7.83i, 200 - 25.75, 60HG - 9.18i,
    PV - 3.50i/3.40 (3.50i/3.40-01)
SKORUPSKA Katharine Wanda Taylor 3.11.78, EWM/
    Oxford Univ : 5k - 17:30.1 (15:55.64-99)
SKUCEK Emily U23 24.09.81, Newport/Birm Univ. :
    JT - 39.68 (40.89-00)
SLATER Beckie U13 20.04.90, Channel Islands :
    JTM - 26.64
SLY Helen V35 13.12.67, Horsforth :
    Mar - 3:00:45 (2:58:40-00)
SMALE Dorothy V40 26.05.60, WSE&H :
    Mar - 3:03:30 (2:59:59-97)
SMALL Natasha U13 9.09.89, Birchfield :
    70HM - 11.77
SMALLWOOD Claire 15.03.77, Jarrow & Hebburn :
    1500 - 4:29.1, 3k - 9:35.04, 5k - 16:49.60,
    5KR - 16:50, 10kR - 34:52
SMALLWOOD Nicole 9.10.77, Belgrave :
    HJ - 1.65i/1.65 (1.80i/1.78-96)
SMETHAM Alana U17 14.12.86, Tamworth :
    HT - 30.97
SMETHURST Helen V35 6.10.64, London Frontr :
    Mar - 3:07:02
SMITH Alana U20 18.01.85, Edinburgh WM :
    SP - 13.15, DT - 38.83 (39.32-01)
SMITH Carly U15 28.04.88, Macclesfield :
    JT - 34.25
SMITH Caroline Jane U20 31.07.83, Radley/Bucks U :
    PV - 3.00i/2.90 (3.20-01)
SMITH Deandra U17 3.12.86, Stevenage & NH :
    100 - 12.4/12.48, 200 - 25.5,
    LJ - 5.43, Hepl - 3877
SMITH Dennise U23 29.10.82, Kilbarchan/Glas Un C :
    3k - 9:53.83
SMITH Diane V40 15.11.60, Hull Achilles :
    HT - 43.41 (46.10-01)
SMITH Elaine U20 16.05.83, Sale/Teeside Univ :
    LJ - 5.97w/5.84 (5.97-01)
SMITH Emma U15 3.12.87, Braintree :
    JT - 30.19
SMITH Emma Marie U17 14.09.85, City of Norwich :
    300H - 46.27, 400H - 68.0

SMITH Grace U23 30.01.82, Sale/Bath Univ :
    60H - 8.95i (8.93i-00), 100H - 14.58w (14.39w-00/14.47-01)
SMITH Helen Nicola U20 9.10.84, Basildon :
    HJ - 1.69i/1.65 (1.68-01)
SMITH Hilary 28.02.76, Birchfield :
    PV - 3.50i/3.50 (3.83-01)
SMITH Hollie U20 9.12.84, Chelmsford :
    800 - 2:12.98
SMITH Janet Carole V35 7.10.64, WSE&H :
    HT - 47.90 (50.62-97)
SMITH Joanne 22.11.78, Thurrock :
    (see WHITE)
SMITH Karen 25.12.78, Ashford :
    PV - 2.60 (2.70-01), SP - 11.48 (11.92-97)
SMITH Kimberley U17 18.01.87, Tipton :
    PV - 3.20
SMITH Kimberley U13 11.11.89, Radley :
    70HM - 11.8, LJ - 4.52
SMITH Kirsty U17 25.04.87, Havering M :
    TJ - 10.93
SMITH Leonie M.E. U17 20.12.86, AF&D :
    800 - 2:16.82, 1500 - 4:35.49, 3k - 9:57.32
SMITH Louise 11.07.77, Stevenage & NH :
    JT - 40.91 (42.62-00)
SMITH Natasha 6.06.77, WSE&H :
    DT - 36.53
SMITH Nicola U23 6.03.82, AF&D :
    JT - 38.82
SMITH Rowan 25.10.68, Scarborough :
    10kR - 33:37
SMITH Yasmin U13 19.10.89, Swindon :
    1500 - 5:06.0
SMITHSON Claire U20 3.08.83, Brighton & Hove AC :
    SP - 14.16 (14.68-01), DT - 55.03
SMY Catherine U17 7.04.87, Banchory :
    HJ - 1.67i/1.65, TJ - 11.13w
SNELGROVE Charlene U23 6.05.82, Wakef/Leeds M U :
    800 - 2:09.16
SNOOK Verity Beatrice 13.11.70, AF&D :
    3kW - 16:01.9 (13:16.23-96)
SNOW Linzi U17 8.06.87, WGreen & Ex L :
    800 - 2:14.07, 1500 - 4:45.73mx
SONGHORN Karenate U17 8.01.87, Vic Park & Tower H :
    DT - 32.67
SOTHERTON Kelly Jade 13.11.76, Birchfield :
    60 - 7.70i, 100 - 11.8/11.95 (11.80w/11.85-97),
    200 - 23.83, 60H - 8.57i, 100H - 13.71,
    400H - 58.30, HJ - 1.75 (1.75-97),
    LJ - 6.22i/6.22 (6.28w/6.23-01), TJ - 11.95w/11.88,
    SP - 12.77, Hep - 5794
SOUTHGATE Kayleigh U15 15.01.88, C of Norwich :
    SPG - 12.48, DT - 29.29
SPAIN Elizabeth U23 23.08.82, Shaftesbury Barnet :
    PV - 3.85 (3.90-00)
SPARGO Jacqueline 12.01.71, Coventry Godiva :
    LJ - 6.07w/6.02 (6.11w-95/6.08-96)
SPEIGHT Natasha U15 9.09.87, Mansfield :
    HJ - 1.67i/1.61
SPELZINI Charlotte U20 7.01.83, Camb & C/Birm Un :
    SP - 13.72 (13.99-01)
SPENCE Natasha 8.11.74, Oxford City :
    100H - 14.8 (14.23w/14.4-93/15.28-92)
SPENCER Amber U17 12.01.87, Southampton City :
    DT - 33.07
SPENCER Amy U17 19.09.85, Belgrave :
    60 - 7.55i (7.54i-01), 100 - 11.51w/11.68 (11.66-01),
    200 - 23.44i/23.46 (23.3w/23.45-01), 300 - 37.72i
SPENCER-CUSICK Susan V35 8.07.63, S London :
    Mar - 2:58:33
SPRULES Lyn 11.09.75, Shaftesbury Barnet :
    HT - 61.11 (63.96-00)
SPURLING Tania U17 20.08.87, West Suffolk :
    HJ - 1.63, TJ - 11.19
SPURWAY Claire 4.04.78, Cannock & Stafford :
    200 - 25.1 (25.1/25.16-93)

410

STAMMAS Hannah U13 16.01.90, Bournemouth :
  800 - 2:27.0
STAMP Melissa U23 5.07.81, Gateshead :
  PV - 3.00 (3.00-01)
STANFORD Non R. U15 8.01.89, Swansea :
  1500 - 4:39.20
STANILAND Bethany May U15 10.05.88, Kingst u Hull :
  SPG - 11.02, DT - 29.94, PenG - 2930
STANLEY Joanne Marie 30.03.77, Edinburgh WM :
  TJ - 11.55 (11.90i/11.82w?-99/11.81-00)
STANTON Linda Mary 22.06.73, Sale :
  PV - 3.40i/3.40 (3.72-95)
STARES Hannah 13.11.78, Belgrave/DMU (Beds) Un :
  400 - 56.38i/57.2, 60H - 8.99i, 100H - 14.22w/14.61,
  400H - 59.7/60.45 (60.28-01), Hep - 4713
STEAD Caroline 14.09.71, Belgrave :
  TJ - 12.24 (12.67-96)
STEEL Kerry U13 13.10.89, Ayr Seaforth :
  LJ - 4.80
STEPHENS Tamsin Anne U23 2.08.80, Bir/Loughbro :
  200 - 24.95w (25.1-99), 60H - 8.59i, 100H - 13.52
STEVENSON Lynsey U17 18.11.86, Tipton :
  JT - 36.41
STEVENSON Nicola J. U15 8.05.89, Bridgend :
  SPG - 10.53, HTG - 32.47
STEVENSON Sara Ann U23 12.11.82, Giff/Glas Univ :
  800 - 2:13.10
STEWART Gillian U23 21.01.80, EWM/Napier Univ :
  100H - 14.94 (14.7-00/14.71w-98/14.73-99),
  HJ - 1.67 (1.69-97), SP - 12.13,
  JT - 40.71 (40.78-99), Hep - 5043
STEWART Staci U17 20.09.85, City of Glasgow :
  60HI - 8.94i, 80HI - 11.69
STILES Amy 6.02.75, Westbury :
  10kR - 34:43, 10MR - 58:43 (57:42-98),
  Mar - 2:44:11
STILL Sarah 24.09.75, Aberdeen :
  LJ - 5.52 (5.85-99)
STOATE Isabelle U17 16.07.86, N Devon :
  800 - 2:15.2 (2:14.35-01), 1500 - 4:41.14 (4:39.26-01)
STOKES Jacqui V35 1.04.67, Border/IRL :
  LJ - 5.71
STOKOE Ceri U23 19.04.82, Swansea :
  HJ - 1.70 (1.73-00)
STONES Katie U17 22.11.85, Kingston u Hull :
  3kW - 14:25.66 (14:21.90-01),
  5kW - 25:57.11, 10kWR - 51:49
STRACHAN Emma U17 10.04.87, Leamington :
  60 - 7.90i, 100 - 12.2 (12.43w/12.50-01), 200 - 24.93
STRAKER Julia U23 25.11.82, Morpeth/Edinburgh U :
  TJ - 11.69 (11.77-01)
STREATFIELD Katharine U20 28.07.83, Soton City/
  Cambridge Univ : TJ - 11.02i (12.17-01)
STREET Natalie U20 8.11.83, Harlow/Havering M :
  400 - 55.04
STREVENS Sarah U23 7.10.81, Newham & Essex B :
  TJ - 11.04i/11.01 (11.26-00)
SUDDES Joanne 27.01.77, Edinburgh WM :
  100H - 14.79 (14.29w/14.4/14.53-99), 400H - 61.25
SULLIVAN Deborah 13.02.72, Havering M :
  1500 - 4:21.92 (4:21.12-99), 5k - 16:28.27 (16:07.51-00),
  5KR - 16:23, 10k - 34:55.76 (34:30.16-99), 10kR - 34:24
SUMMERS Danielle U13 18.05.90, Reading :
  JTM - 24.54
SURMAN Jade U15 27.03.89, Birchfield :
  LJ - 5.74w/5.64, PenG - 3126
SUTTON Lucy U17 29.08.86, Oxford City :
  SP - 12.12, DT - 37.72
SUTTON Marian R. V35 7.10.63, Westbury :
  10kR - 33:50 (32:38-97), HMar - 73:08 (69:41-97),
  Mar - 2:31:44dh/2:45:55 (2:28:42-99)
SWANSON Bryony U13 18.10.89, Inverness :
  800 - 2:22.02, 1200 - 3:53.40, 1500 - 4:59.9
SWATHERIDGE Donna Louise U20 4.03.85,
  Bas & MH : DT - 38.13

SWEENEY Elizabeth U17 13.01.86, Southport :
  HJ - 1.73i/1.65
SWEENEY Rebecca U20 9.02.85, Sale :
  400 - 56.01
SWEENEY Stephanie U17 28.11.86, Crewe & Nant :
  Hepl - 3822
SYKES Nicola U17 30.06.87, Leighton Buzzard :
  1500 - 4:42.42 (4:41.06-01)
SYMONDS Lora Catherine U15 7.06.88, Cannock & St :
  800 - 2:16.36

*T*AGILALA Sulueti U23 24.08.80, Army/FIJ :
  SP - 11.79 (12.13-01), DT - 39.56
TAIT Elidh U13 10.02.90, Elgin :
  DTM - 24.63
TAIT Jillian 4.02.76, Eyemouth/Carnethy :
  Mar - 3:08:44
TAIT Lorne U17 16.01.87, Elgin :
  HT - 33.24
TAKER Jennifer U13 16.03.90, Trafford :
  70HM - 11.7, LJ - 4.58
TALBOT Nicola 17.02.72, Birchfield :
  DT - 47.39 (54.24-93)
TAPPIN Lia Adina U17 9.01.87, Enf & Har :
  60 - 7.85i
TAPPIN Philippa U13 19.03.91, Enf & Har :
  75 - 10.1
TARPLEE Claire U15 22.09.88, Solihull & S Heath :
  1500 - 4:43.40
TAS Meliha U15 25.05.89, Enf & Har :
  75HG - 11.90
TAYLOR Helen U20 29.01.84, Southport :
  100 - 12.10, TJ - 11.32w/11.09
TAYLOR Kate U13 4.05.90, Bournemouth :
  75 - 10.1
TAYLOR Katy U23 18.06.80, Cambridge U/Army :
  400H - 64.0/64.59, Hep - 4517
TAYLOR Lauren U17 29.10.86, Radley :
  LJ - 5.36 (5.37w-01)
TAYLOR Rebecca U13 17.11.89, Blackheath :
  800 - 2:22.3, 1k - 3:07.5, 1200 - 3:56.0, 1500 - 5:02.9
TEALE Amy U23 30.12.82, North Shields P/Bath Un :
  100H - 15.34w/15.39 (14.63w/14.9/14.93-01)
TEASDALE Amy U17 3.09.86, Spenborough :
  PV - 2.80i/2.70
TEASDALE Ella U17 8.09.85, Spenborough :
  PV - 2.70
TELFORD Rebekah 4.11.76, Wigan :
  PV - 3.60
TERJESEN Siri 29.06.75, /USA :
  Mar - 3:05:31
TEWKESBURY Jemma U13 29.09.90, Dorchester :
  JTM - 26.72
THACKRAY Penny D. 18.08.74, Wakefield :
  1500 - 4:29.59 (4:22.4-97), HMar - 78:44,
  3k - 9:34.9 (9:23.5mx-96/9:31.2-01),
  5k - 16:25.01 (16:16.01-97), 5MR - 27:44 (27:10-01),
  10k - 35:49.98 (33:25.74-01), 10kR - 34:49 (33:07-01)
THAKE Jemma U17 17.12.85, West Suffolk :
  200 - 25.37w/25.57i (25.06-00), 300 - 40.18 (39.84-01)
THERIN Lauren U17 10.01.86, Channel Islands :
  SP - 11.29, DT - 38.94, HT - 32.70, JT - 41.37
THEVENT-SMITH Ramona V40 20.12.59, RRC :
  100kR - 9:06:22
THIEME Helen U23 28.09.81, Bir/Notts U (see KARAGOUNIS)
THIRWELL Tina M. U23 5.09.81, Sale/Staffs Univ :
  Hep - 4442w (4205-99)
THOMAS Hayley U17 16.12.86, Thurrock :
  SP - 10.89, DT - 32.38, JT - 43.81
THOMAS Kadi-Ann U17 10.02.86, Milton Keynes :
  60 - 7.7i/7.74i, 100 - 11.92, 200 - 25.4
THOMAS Katalin 20.12.78, Coventry Godiva :
  1500 - 4:28.56, 3k - 9:41.77
THOMAS Kelly U23 9.01.81, Sale/Loughbro :
  60 - 7.51i, 100 - 11.74 (11.71w-01),
  200 - 24.8/24.89 (24.32-00)

THOMAS Kirsty U15 2.10.87, Gateshead :
100 - 12.6
THOMAS Michelle 16.10.71, Birchfield :
200 - 24.6w/24.86 (23.98-97),
400 - 56.08 (52.47-99), 400H - 64.7
THOMAS Sonia 16.05.79, Sale/Loughbro :
1500 - 4:30.8 (4:28.60-99), 3k - 9:36.1
THOMAS Victoria U15 24.09.87, Bournemouth :
SPG - 10.63, DT - 30.39
THOMPSON Finesse U13 30.03.90, WGreen & Ex L :
SPM - 11.53, DTM - 31.52
THOMPSON Gemma U17 17.01.86, Sparta :
100 - 12.26w/12.4 (12.2/12.52-01),
200 - 25.2
THOMPSON Nicola 10.02.68, Charnwood :
Mar - 3:06:56 (3:06:24-01)
THOMPSON Rachael U17 15.11.85, Liverpool H :
200 - 25.4, 300 - 39.8, 400 - 55.68,
800 - 2:06.82, 1500 - 4:37.84mx
THOMSON Trudi V40 18.01.59, Pitreavie :
10kR - 34:49 (34:46-99), 10MR - 58:16 (56:22-00),
HMar - 76:21 (74:34-96), Mar - 2:42:30 (2:38:23-95)
THORNAL Danielle 9.08.75, :
800 - 2:10.31 (2:06.55-01), 1500 - 4:28.04 (4:24.63i+-01)
THORNE Louretta 6.05.77, WSE&H :
200 - 24.8w/25.0/25.02 (24.2/24.35i/24.38-99),
400 - 56.5/57.37 (54.23-99)
THORNTON Emma U23 27.11.82, Bolton :
JT - 37.43
THORPE Anna-Maria 15.07.71, Thames Valley/BAR :
TJ - 12.14 (12.84-99)
TIDBALL Bridget U17 25.02.87, Exeter :
HepI - 4202
TINN Hollie U23 14.04.81, Rugby & Nor PH/UWIC :
PV - 2.90 (3.00i-01)
TODD Sara L. 3.11.79, Border/Ripon & York Univ :
200 - 24.72, 60H - 8.84i,
100H - 14.3/14.36w/14.57 (14.55-00), 400H - 60.65
TOMLINS Sarah U23 5.04.82, Horsham BS/U West Eng :
200 - 24.8/25.11 (24.67w/24.71-00), 400 - 55.5/55.81
TOMLINSON Iyesha U17 19.02.86, WGreen & Ex L :
DT - 32.95 (34.48-01)
TONKS Sharon Jayne 18.04.70, Bromsgrove & R :
3kW - 13:53.8, 5kW - 24:05.49, 5kWR - 23:53,
10kWR - 48:40, 20kW - 1:43:29 (1:42:10sh-00)
TOWNSEND Lucy 26.03.72, Bourton RR :
Mar - 3:06:25
TRANTER Claire U20 28.03.85, Leamington :
Hep - 3861
TROLLOPE Kellie 28.12.74, Exmouth :
Mar - 3:08:54
TROTMAN Joanna U23 5.10.80, T Solent/Grnwich U :
LJ - 5.84 (6.02?-00/6.02-01)
TROTMAN Lisa-Deane U23 6.12.82, Trafford :
100 - 11.88w/12.16, 200 - 24.23w/24.44
TUCKER Jessica U17 3.06.87, Brecon :
60 - 7.92i, 100 - 12.55 (12.49w-01)
TUCKER Lianne U17 18.07.87, Blaydon :
SP - 10.45, DT - 38.88
TUCKER Lynette U17 18.07.87, Blaydon :
DT - 32.35
TULLETT Hayley 17.02.73, Swansea :
800 - 2:03.76i/2:06.39 (2:01.25-00),
1500 - 4:07.52 (4:01.23-00),
3k - 9:07.98 (8:45.36i-01/8:45.39-00)
TURNER Charmaine U23 5.12.81, T Solent/Brunel U :
LJ - 5.66, TJ - 12.44w/12.43
TURNER Karlene U20 9.01.85, WSE&H :
LJ - 5.93w/5.90, TJ - 12.39w/11.95
TURNER Laura Kate U23 12.08.82, Harrow/Brunel U :
60 - 7.65i, 100 - 11.9/11.91w/12.19,
200 - 25.0/25.16mx,
100H - 14.4w/14.7/14.74w/14.83 (14.35w/14.5/14.61-01)
TURNER Michelle 25.12.77, Harrow :
100 - 12.0/12.18 (11.9w-99/11.92-00)

TURTLE Gemma Anne U17 15.05.86, Chiltern/S B :
800 - 2:15.82, 1500 - 4:33.8mx/4:34.2,
3k - 9:49.89mx/9:51.94
TURTON Judy U20 26.05.84, Wycombe :
PV - 2.90 (3.20-01)
TYLER Megan U13 2.05.90, Warrington :
HJ - 1.43
TYSON Abbi U15 5.07.89, Cannock & Stafford :
100 - 12.58

UMBLEJA Melanie U20 14.01.84, Cardiff :
Hep - 4083
UNDERDOWN Lucy U13 18.05.90, Paddock Wood :
SPM - 9.02, DTM - 26.43

VAN GRAAN Stephanie 4.02.77, Shaft B/RSA :
1500 - 4:30.97, 3k - 9:55.4mx (9:31.9-00)
VAN KEMPA Helen U13 28.10.90, Herts Phoenix :
70HM - 11.73
VAN WULVEN Chloe U15 10.09.87, Havering M :
60HI - 9.2i, 75HG - 11.70w/11.7, HJ - 1.60
VAUGHAN Catrin Ffion U13 14.01.90, Carmarthen :
JTM - 28.17
VAUGHAN Lucy 20.04.69, AF&D :
400 - 56.7 (56.6-01), 800 - 2:03.70
VELDMAN Margaret 7.06.74, Sale/NED :
LJ - 5.76 (6.03w-00/5.94i-98/5.94-00)
VICKERS Lauren U13 11.05.90, Dartford :
HJ - 1.48
VILJOEN Estle 8.07.70, Hercules Wimbledon/RSA :
3kW - 13:51.73, 5kW - 24:26.11, 5kWR - 23:28,
10kW - 50:16.7, 10kWR - 48:50, 20kW - 1:44:16
VOGEL Kiera U17 31.05.86, Liv.Pembroke Sefton :
3k - 10:19.57
VUAGNIAUX Alison V40 31.05.60, City of Bath :
Mar - 2:58:25

WAINWRIGHT Anne V45 26.10.54, Cann & Staff :
PV - 2.70 (2.70-01)
WAINWRIGHT Kimberley U17 18.01.86, Doncaster :
100 - 12.3, 300 - 40.36
WAIT Claire U17 7.11.86, Shrewsbury :
TJ - 10.71i
WALBY Roxanne U13 8.02.90, Blackpool :
LJ - 4.52
WALDRON Sarah U15 11.02.88, Shaftesbury Barnet :
800 - 2:18.5, 1500 - 4:44.09
WALE Amanda 14.10.70, Wrexham :
Hep - 3930 (4546-98)
WALKER Alexis U15 14.02.88, Burnley :
JT - 30.23
WALKER Carly U17 30.08.87, Bournemouth :
LJ - 5.46
WALKER Donna Marie U15 10.07.88, S London :
100 - 12.5, 200 - 25.01
WALKER Helen Charlotte U23 12.10.80, M & C/
Pennsylvania S Univ : 400H - 63.54 (62.92-98),
Hep - 4020 (4106w/4096-98)
WALKER Hilary C. V45 9.11.53, Serpentine :
100kR - 8:54:41 (7:50:09-93)
WALKER Marcia 27.05.70, WSE&H :
TJ - 12.10 (12.11-01)
WALL Kimberly Jaclyn U20 21.04.83, Bas/Loughbro :
200 - 24.11w/24.70 (24.04-00), 400 - 54.05 (53.52-01)
WALLACE Ailsa 12.03.77, Cardiff :
HJ - 1.70 (1.73i/1.70-94)
WALLADER Rachel U13 1.09.89, Halesowen :
150 - 19.9, HJ - 1.45, SPM - 10.25
WALLBANKS Carol U23 9.12.82, Border/Staffs Univ :
JT - 39.62 (42.73-00)
WALLER Ruth U20 6.03.84, Sale :
2kSt - 7:21.84, 400H - 65.24 (65.21-01)
WALLS Sharon-Louise U20 9.10.84, Wigan :
100H - 14.8w/14.89
WALTERS Imogen Alice U13 5.05.90, Hyndburn :
SPM - 9.12

412

WALTERS Mhairi Lee U23 19.06.81, :
SP - 13.13i/13.05 (13.62-01), HT - 58.47
WARD Emma U23 2.01.82, City of Stoke/Staffs Univ :
3k - 9:45.5 (9:27.63-00)
WARD Jennifer 22.09.78, City of Glasgow :
800 - 2:06.23 (2:05.10-00)
WARD Vanessa U15 19.09.88, Guildford & G :
75HG - 11.9
WARD Victoria 19.06.72, WGreen & Ex L :
200 - 25.1/25.11 (23.84w/24.07-98), 400 - 55.71 (53.58-00)
WARDROP Malgorzata 25.03.77, City of Glasgow :
60 - 7.6i/7.61i (7.52i-96), 100 - 11.75 (11.63-98),
200 - 24.47w/24.53 (24.17-99)
WARNER Laura U15 8.03.88, Harrow :
800 - 2:17.7
WATERS Christina U17 4.06.87, Wirral :
60HI - 8.95i, 80HI - 11.61, 300H - 46.0/46.38
WATERS Elizabeth 19.02.77, Corby :
400H - 66.2 (62.69-98)
WATSON Anna U23 30.04.82, C of Glas/Glas Univ :
PV - 2.90i/2.60 (3.03-98)
WATSON Louise Carole 13.12.71, Med & Maid :
5k - 17:12.3 (15:57.06-95), HMar - 77:12 (75:45-00)
WATTON Louise U17 30.10.86, Wimborne :
SP - 11.01, JT - 46.94
WATTS Katy Louise U23 25.03.81, Bas & MH/
Brunel U : JT - 47.33
WATTS Samantha Louise U23 13.10.81, Sale/OUAC :
400H - 62.92
WAUGH Kathryn 20.02.73, Chester le Street :
5k - 17:17.89
WEATHERITT Leah J. 18.09.74, Gateshead :
SP - 11.91
WEBB Helen Julie U23 14.04.80, Halesowen :
PV - 2.90 (3.20-00)
WEBB Lauren U17 17.11.85, Sutton & District :
300 - 40.24, 400 - 57.6
WEBB Shirley Catherine U23 28.09.81, C of Edinb/
Edinburgh U : HT - 59.95
WEBBER Lucy Kate 5.02.72, Belgrave :
PV - 4.00 (4.04-00), Dec - 4371
WEBSTER Victoria U20 14.08.84, Shaftesbury B :
1500 - 4:32.2, 3k - 9:44.89
WEEKES Hannah U15 14.12.87, Stevenage & NH :
75HG - 11.80w, HJ - 1.60, LJ - 5.16, PenG - 2798
WEEKES Jade U20 15.11.84, Dartford :
Hep - 3824
WEETMAN Anji Holly Gemma U15 4.10.87, Oswestry :
LJ - 5.29w/5.24, PenG - 2869
WELLINGTON Christina 18.02.77, Serpentine :
Mar - 3:08:17
WELLS Elaine 30.05.78, Crawley/Chichester Coll :
400 - 57.15
WELLS Louisa U20 30.12.84, W Suffolk/C of Norwich :
100 - 12.18w (12.2/12.40-01)
WELLSTEAD Sarah 22.10.79, Sutton & District :
HJ - 1.65, LJ - 6.29w/6.14, TJ - 11.81 (11.84w-01)
WENHAM Carley Ann U15 14.03.88, Crawley :
100 - 11.9/12.06w/12.08 (12.03w-01), 200 - 24.5/25.81
WERRETT Gemma Elizabeth Harvie U17 15.03.86,
Cann & St : 60HI - 9.25i, 80HI - 11.78w/11.8/12.01
WEST Jennifer 13.09.79, Ealing,Southall & Mx :
HT - 39.26 (39.63-01), JT - 44.07 (45.81-01)
WESTER Victoria U17 24.12.85, Gateshead :
300 - 40.30, 400 - 58.99
WESTLEY Abby U17 15.07.87, Hallamshire :
800 - 2:11.4, 1500 - 4:35.01
WESTWOOD Fiona U23 27.02.81, Wakef/Loughbro :
LJ - 5.79 (6.02-00)
WHEATLAND Vicky U13 13.12.89, Colchester H :
HJ - 1.45
WHEATMAN Jenna U20 6.03.84, Scarborough :
HT - 38.55
WHEELER Ann V45 17.10.55, Nuneaton :
3kW - 16:17.58, 5kW - 27:31.1

WHIGHAM Lisa U23 14.08.80, C of Glas/Strath Univ :
400 - 55.64, 800 - 2:11.38
WHIGHAM Sara U20 7.10.83, EWM/Strathclyde Univ :
60 - 7.58i, 100 - 11.82w/11.95,
200 - 24.4w/24.60w/24.85
WHILEY Lesley V40 14.05.60, Reading RR :
Mar - 2:55:59
WHITE Danielle Louise 1.06.79, Skyrac :
Hep - 3861
WHITE Jade U15 1.01.88, Southport :
JT - 30.48
WHITE Joanne 22.11.78, Thurrock :
(nee SMITH) SP - 11.18, DT - 40.23
WHITE Kendra 8.04.68, Quakers :
100kR - 10:18:13 (9:27:15-01)
WHITE Natasha U13 8.12.89, Havering M :
75 - 9.9w/10.04, 100 - 13.3, 150 - 19.6w,
200 - 27.3
WHITE Rebecca U23 5.06.80, Sale/Bath Univ :
60 - 7.73i (7.55i-98),LJ - 6.01, TJ - 13.15w/12.97,
100 - 12.16 (11.45w-98/11.9/11.98-01)
WHITE Victoria Anne 17.04.72, Sheffield RWC :
(nee LUPTON) 10kWR - 56:13 (45:28sh-93/45:48-94)
WHITESIDE Leigh U17 6.08.86, Abbey :
100 - 12.56
WHITLOCK Janine ¶ 11.08.73, Trafford :
60 - 7.52i (7.36i/7.5mx-00),
PV - 4.44i/4.41drg (4.40-01)
WHITMORE Hannah U20 24.02.84, Charnwood :
800 - 2:13.0
WHITTAKER Emma U17 31.10.85, Bristol :
1500 - 4:45.54i (4:37.74-01),
3k - 10:19.14mx/10:34.33
WHITTAKER Lara U13 13.09.89, Hastings :
JTM - 25.32
WHITTAKER Louise U23 29.11.82, Sale :
800 - 2:08.45mx/2:09.15, 1500 - 4:21.93,
3k - 9:35.00mx (9:58.86-01)
WHITTINGHAM Laura U17 6.06.86, Wakefield :
JT - 38.45
WICKHAM Charlotte U20 21.06.85, Gateshead :
1500 - 4:31.17
WILDBORE Abby U17 12.09.85, Wilts Sch :
JT - 34.79
WILDER Kelley E. 30.07.71, City of Glasgow/USA :
3k - 9:47.70i (9:36.51-00), 5k - 16:46.64 (16:36.7-00)
WILDING Helen 25.10.76, Trafford :
SP - 12.00 (13.88-95), DT - 39.69 (42.90-95),
HT - 48.64 (50.27-01)
WILHELMY Sarah U23 2.02.80, Southend :
100 - 11.63w/11.72 (11.24w/11.44-01),
200 - 24.06 (22.84w-01/23.23-98)
WILKIE Jennifer U20 4.11.83, Edinburgh WM/Glas U :
JT - 36.16
WILKINS Emily Louise May U13 10.10.89, WSE&H :
600 - 1:46.3, 800 - 2:25.6, 1k - 3:13.4, 1200 - 3:57.3
WILKINS Melani Dawn 18.01.73, WSE&H :
60H - 8.20i (8.15i-01), 100H - 13.12 (13.08w-01)
WILKINSON Joanne 2.05.73, Bedford & County :
1500 - 4:21.15, 3k - 9:38.7 (9:37.0mx-00),
5k - 15:59.54, 10k - 33:36.60, 10kR - 33:48
WILKINSON Sarah 2.01.70, Salford :
3k - 9:28.49mx (8:57.75mx-00/9:04.27-98),
5KR - 16:57 (15:53-00)
WILLEY Laura U17 22.10.86, Wigan :
100 - 12.54w/12.56
WILLI Roisin U15 29.10.87, Gateshead :
100 - 12.5/12.55
WILLIAMS Carrie U17 9.02.87, Carmarthen :
JT - 38.63
WILLIAMS Claire U15 29.09.87, Carmarthen :
DT - 30.62
WILLIAMS Elizabeth 2.06.77, Walton :
100 - 12.1/12.26, 200 - 24.61 (24.1-99/24.19w-01),
300 - 39.09, 400 - 54.76 (54.53-99)

WILLIAMS Helen 2.06.77, Walton :
60 - 7.7i, 100 - 11.8w/12.12 (11.99w-98/12.0/12.10-01),
200 - 25.1/25.25 (24.49w/24.8-98/25.07-95)
WILLIAMS Sarah U13 23.03.91, Nuneaton :
LJ - 4.54
WILLIAMS Susan 2.06.77, Walton :
60 - 7.63i (7.60i-98),
100 - 11.7/12.12w/12.25 (11.61w-98/11.79-00),
200 - 24.18w/24.34 (23.59-99),
400 - 55.42i (56.6-00), 400H - 59.89
WILLIAMS Victoria U23 11.04.81, Yate/UWIC :
60H - 8.75i, 100H - 14.2/14.40w/14.56
WILLIAMSON Maria U15 7.09.87, Leamington :
JT - 30.44
WILSHER Ruth U17 8.02.86, Wakefield :
HT - 30.38
WILSON Aileen J. U20 30.03.84, Peterborough :
60H - 8.81i, 100H - 14.55 (14.20-01),
HJ - 1.83i/1.75 (1.87-01), LJ - 5.68i
WILSON Amy U23 31.12.80, Ipswich :
SP - 12.29 (13.03-99)
WILSON Bernice U20 21.04.84, Birchfield :
200 - 24.90
WILSON Beverley V35 26.03.67, Cleethorpes :
Mar - 2:59:44 (2:55:58-01)
WILSON Cassie 24.09.77, Bingley/Loughbro :
HT - 43.07 (43.18-01)
WILSON Claire U17 7.11.85, Channel Islands :
800 - 2:16.57
WILSON Donna U17 1.10.86, Erme Valley :
HJ - 1.62
WILSON Emma U17 15.07.87, Harrow :
100 - 12.4
WILSON Katy U15 1.09.88, Birtley :
SPG - 10.68
WILSON Sharon 27.10.74, Edinburgh WM :
100 - 12.17 (11.96-01), 200 - 24.98
WILSON Stephanie U17 18.10.86, WSE&H :
1500 - 4:37.51, 3k - 10:29.9
WILSON Zoe 28.08.76, Birchfield :
60 - 7.61i (7.39i-00),
100 - 12.0/12.14 (11.52w/11.66-00),
200 - 24.67 (23.74w-00/23.91-99)
WITRYLAK Julia U17 25.08.87, Blackpool :
PV - 2.60
WITTON Nikki 30.09.72, Newport :
PV - 2.80 (2.85-00)
WOOD Hannah U23 17.11.81, Solihull & S H/Sheff U :
400 - 55.04, 400H - 58.8/59.06
WOOD Jennifer V45 23.02.57, Spenborough :
PV - 2.90 (3.20-97), HT - 41.12 (44.93-98)
WOOD Laura 31.10.78, Trafford :
DT - 38.72 (41.28-98), HT - 37.36 (42.06-01)
WOOD Louisa U23 31.10.80, Beds & Co/DMU (Beds) U :
800 - 2:12.40 (2:11.7-01), 1500 - 4:31.79
WOOD Louise U20 13.05.83, Braintree :
TJ - 11.17 (11.19-01)
WOODCOCK Sally U23 14.03.80, Cleethorpes :
PV - 3.00

WOODMAN Amy U20 1.11.84, Bristol/Birchfield :
HJ - 1.65, LJ - 5.72i/5.66 (5.71w/5.67-01)
WOODS Danielle U20 2.10.84, Trafford :
800 - 2:11.83, 1500 - 4:29.4
WOODS Suzanne 29.12.76, Charnwood :
PV - 3.20 (3.20i/3.20-98)
WOOFF Emma U20 21.05.85, Wigan :
TJ - 11.59
WOOLGAR Deborah Caroline V35 10.03.65, Worthing :
SP - 13.28 (14.18-89), DT - 36.82 (40.92-91),
JT - 37.39 (38.78-99)
WOOTTON Katrina U17 2.09.85, Bedford & County :
400 - 58.9 (57.5-01), 800 - 2:05.87,
1500 - 4:19.93, 3k - 9:20.2mx/9:37.00
WORSEY Helen U23 29.08.82, Birchfield/Loughbro :
60H - 8.43i, 100H - 13.46w/13.6/13.62
WRAY Josephine Anne U15 29.07.89, West Suffolk :
JT - 31.00
WRAY Sharon U23 8.10.82, Oswestry/Lancaster Un :
SP - 11.33i (11.71-00)
WRIGHT Claire U20 9.09.83, Liverpool H :
HJ - 1.73 (1.77-00)
WRIGHT Dawn-Alice 20.01.76, Cov G/Brunel Univ :
PV - 3.20
WRIGHT Fiona-Lisa U20 11.05.85, Rugby & Nor PH :
Hep - 3801
WRIGHT Laura Marie U13 11.10.89, Bas & MH :
600 - 1:44.6
WRIGHT Lucy 17.11.69, Leeds :
1500 - 4:24.4 (4:19.71-00), 5k - 16:10.32 (15:59.51-98),
5KR - 16:13, 5MR - 26:43, 10kR - 33:56
WRIGHT Rebecca 20.12.77, WSE&H :
400H - 63.2 (61.38-00)
WYATT Jenna U17 3.12.86, Reading :
300H - 46.6
WYLIE Alison U13 12.09.89, Aberdeen :
100 - 13.2, 200 - 27.7

YARNOLD Elizabeth U15 31.10.88, Tonbridge :
PV - 2.60
YELLING Elizabeth 5.12.74, Bedford & County :
3k - 9:19.43 (8:57.3mx-01/9:15.25-98),
5k - 15:45.08, 5KR - 16:21+, 10k - 32:29.73,
5MR - 26:46 (26:09-00), 10k - 31:58.39,
10kR - 33:18 (33:10-00), 10MR - 54.00+/54:34,
HMar - 71:42 (71:29-01)
YELLING Hayley 3.01.74, WSE&H :
1500 - 4:30.6 (4:23.8-01),
3k - 9:19.50+/9:28.3 (8:58.98mx/9:03.5+-01),
5k - 15:38.30 (15:19.12-01), 5KR - 16:35 (16:20-99)
YEOMANS Susan V45 16.03.53, Watford :
PV - 2.82
YORWERTH Amanda E. V35 18.05.67, St Albans Str :
Mar - 3:02:11 (2:54:56-97)
YOUNG Sula 2.01.79, Highgate Harriers/Bristol Un :
10k - 36:53.2, HMar - 78:18
YULE Helen V35 10.09.65, Lliswerry :
Mar - 3:06:27 (3:04:32-01)

ZENNER Helen U23 15.08.82, Team Solent/Oxf U :
1500 - 4:32.32i/4:47.01 (4:31.55-00)

Obituary 2002 *Information provided by Peter Matthews*

Sir **Arthur** Abraham **GOLD** (GBR) (b. 10 Jan 1917) on 25 May in London. He made a huge contribution to his beloved sport. He competed for Britain in two internationals at high jump in 1937 (pb 1.90 that year) and was among the pioneers of British coaching from his early twenties; his most notable coaching success was with Dorothy Tyler.
He succeeded Jack Crump as honorary secretary of the BAAB in 1965 and engineered many vital changes during his 12 years in office, his policy being "evolution not revolution". During that period he was athletics team leader at the three Olympics of 1968-76. He was chairman of the British Olympic Association 1988-92 and commandant of the entire team at the Albertville and Barcelona Olympics in 1992. His crowning achievement was presiding over the European AA 1976-87. In that post his diplomatic skills, encyclopaedic knowledge and a mission to protect the sport from the dangers of drug use and over commercialisation made him one of the most respected figures in world sport. He was elected president of the AAA in 1995.
He was awarded the CBE in 1974 and knighted in 1984 for his services to athletics.

Karl ANDREWS (GBR) (b. 21 Mar 1975) on 10 January from injuries sustained in an attack outside a Tenerife nightclub. He placed ninth in the hammer at the 1994 World Junior Champs and had a personal best of 65.30 from that year, not competing after his junior days.

Sheila FAIRWEATHER (GBR) (b. 24 Nov 1977) on 31 May. Scottish 5000m champion at the age of 19 in 1997. She ran for Britain in the World Junior CC in 1996 and was 10th in the European U23 10,000m in 1999. pbs: 3000m 9:21.19 (2001), 5000m 16:07.34 (1998), 10000m 34:23.55 (2001).

Steve GOWER (GBR) (b. 7 Oct 1950) on 21 August. He competed in four internationals for Britain 1971-8, setting a pb for 20km walk with 1:30:27.8t against the GDR in 1978. Other bests: 3000mW 13:02.6 (1976), 10000mW 46:38.0 (1975).

Mike MAYNARD (GBR) (b. 30 Oct 1930 Sydenham) in Hove on 8 October. His highest placing in the English National Cross Country championship was 3rd in 1959 and he ran four times in the International CC Championships, finishing 8th in 1955. Track pbs: 1M 4:11.4 (1955), 2M 8:48.8 (1959), 3M 13:42.2 (1956) 5000m 14:20.8 (1955), 6M 29:20.6 (1958), 10000m 30:09.8 (1956).

David Lionel PUGH (GBR/Canada) (b. 1 Apr 1922 Barry, Wales) on 10 July in Vancouver. After war service as a fighter pilot in the RAF and with an economics degree from the University of Wales in Cardiff, he won the Welsh javelin title in 1949 and became national coach for the Midlands. He coached several world-class British athletes including Mike Rawson and Carole Quinton. He resigned in 1964 and moved to Canada to become track and field coach at the University of British Columbia in Vancouver where he stayed until his retirement in 1987. He was best known as the coach of the great high jumper Debbie Brill and was also a TV commentator.

Kenneth SMITH (GBR) (b. 3 Dec 1935) in August. Starting as a middle-distance runner, he progressed to marathons (pb 2:29:35 in 1964) and to walking, with a 50km walk pb of 4:28:54 (1977). He became at various times president, championships secretary and chairman of the Race Walking Association. His son Michael was RWA 50km champion in 2001 and daughter Karen walked for England at the 1990 Commonwealth Games.

Crew STONELEY (GBR) (b. 9 May 1911 Leeds) on 27 August. A member of Britain's 1932 Olympic 4x400m relay team that finished second in Los Angeles, he was AAA 440y champion in 1932 and placed fifth in his Olympic 400m semi in 48.6. At the 1934 Empire Games in London he completed an English clean sweep in the 440y, finishing third in an estimated 48.7 behind Godfrey Rampling and Bill Roberts, and ran on the winning relay team. He retired from the Army in 1964 with the rank of Brigadier, having been Colonel Commandant of the Royal Signals. He organised the World Championships at modern pentathlon in 1957.

Henry **Stuart TOWNEND** (GBR) (b. 24 Sep 1909) on 26 October. An idiosyncratic and charming man who became a notable educationalist, he was a Cambridge Blue 1929-31 and won a gold medal at 4x440y relay and was 6th in the 880y at the Empire Games in 1930. He also ran that year for Britain against France. He was commissioned into the Royal Artillery and retired from the army in 1947 with the rank of Lieutenant Colonel. He took charge of the housing committee for the Olympic Games in London in 1948 and for this work was awarded the OBE in 1949. In 1951 he founded Hill House International Junior School, London (Prince Charles was one of his pupils) and at Glion, Switzerland, devoting the rest of his working life into his 90s to what became a series of six schools with up to 1100 boys and girls from 3 to 13. pbs: 440y 49.9e (1931), 880y 1:55.6e (1930), 1M 4:22.6e (1929).

John WALSH (b. 27 Apr 1940) on 29 September at his home in Carmarthen after returning from a training run. He was a runner's runner and never dropped out of a race in his entire career; he ran 58 marathons and completed every one in under 3 hours (pb 2:32). He was an excellent team manager and compiled marathon rankings for both Wales and the UK for over 30 years for the NUTS and for Welsh Athletics. He was for many years the official scrutineer for the Championship Section of the London Marathon.

Joseph Nicholas Neville **'Nick' WHITEHEAD** (GBR) (b. 29 May 1933) died of cancer on 6 October at Newport, Pembrokeshire. He was a fine sprinter, who won sprint relay bronze medals at the 1960 Olympic Games and on the Welsh team at the 1962 Commonwealth Games, and later a most successful British team manager 1978-84. A member of Birchfield Harriers, he was Welsh champion at 100y and 220y in 1957, 1958 and 1960 and set seven Welsh records at 100y from 9.8 in 1958 to 9.7 in 1960 and one at 220y, 21.6 in 1958. He represented Britain in seven internationals 1957-60 and for Wales was a quarter-finalist at both 110y and 220y at the Commonwealth Games of 1958 and 1962. Other pbs: 100y 9.6dh (1962), 100m 10.5 (1960) Educated at Loughborough University, Nick became Head of Department at Leeds Polytechnic, the first director of the National Coaching Foundation in 1983 and director of development for the Sports Council for Wales until his retirement in 1996. For his many services to sport he was awarded the OBE in 1985.

Peter Martin a long standing NUTS member and contibutor to the Annual died just before this Annual went to press, Tony Miller contributes the following.

PETER V MARTIN

One of the UK's foremost and long-standing statisticians, Peter Martin, has died. Following a massive stroke, he was taken to the North Hampshire Hospital in Basingstoke on March 10, but he never regained consciousness and passed away four days later.

The death of his beloved wife Marion a few years ago hit him very badly and he never fully recovered. Indeed, he had been under treatment ever since.

A member of the National Union of Track Statisticians (NUTS), Peter took over the compilation of the Under 20 and Under 17 Women and Under 15 Girls rankings and all-time lists in 1963. I took over the two younger age groups in 1973, but Peter retained the Under 20's and his final lists appeared in Athletics Weekly on October 23 2002. He was also a member of the international body of statisticians (ATFS).

Peter served on the UK Junior Commission as statistician and compiled regular lists throughout the season for the selectors. In the early years, he was also part of the management team 'on the day'.

His enthusiasm showed in the quality and accuracy of his lists. In fact, he was so attached to them, he was almost 'sad' when the athletes no longer qualified as they had moved on to the next age group.

I first corresponded with Peter in 1968 in relation to a project I was undertaking, and I can honestly say that it was his enthusiasm that was largely instrumental in me joining the NUTS.

Despite his long-term illness, he continued to keep his statistical work going and provided information to the National and regional selectors. He looked upon it as therapy.

One of the kindest and helpful people you could ever hope to meet, he will be sorely missed and a hard act to follow. Nothing was ever too much trouble to him.

Peter was 71. He leaves a son Graham and daughter in law Caroline.

AMENDMENTS TO BRITISH ATHLETICS 2002
From Peter Matthews, Martin Rix and others

MEN 2001

60m:	delete 6.65 and 6.67 Chris Lambert (these were by Lambert of GRN)
100m:	10.71/10.6w Cleophus Joseph 11.9.79 (& 200m 22.05),
	11.08 Danny Whittaker 10.1.86 (club: Burnley), 11.17w Wedderburn 7 Exeter 7 Jul
200m:	add 21.25w/+2.5 Laurence Oboh 2J Rieti, ITA 2 Sep; 21.72 Baptiste 21 Jul;
	22.89/+0.8 Bennett-Jackson 2 London (He) 26 Aug; 25.8 (hand) Baxter
300m:	add 35.1 Richard Davenport 12.09.85 1 Cheltenham 4 Jul
400m:	48.59 Davenport 24 Jul
800m:	1:52.69 Sheppard (27.1.79, also for 1500m 3:48.91);
	add 1:52.70 Matt Thomson 5h4 College Station TX, USA 18 May
1000m:	UK U15 best: 2:35.4 Alex Felce 11.9.86 4 Cheltenham 25 Jul
1500m:	3:48.06 Body 6.11.75 (also in1M, 3k, 5MR, 10kR lists)
3000m:	8:31.22 Shankey 14r1 Duffel 27 May
10kR:	29:08 de Jonge RSA (note for index ran 8:28.79 3000SC in 1996)
Mar:	2:29:02 Reid 6.7.73
1500mSt:	4:40.2 Darsham Singh 26.7.86
80mH:	11.3 Harrison 1P1 15 Sep. 11.87 France 1.1.87 (& Pen 2592)
110HJ:	14.16 Anthony etc. 27 May; 14.7 Lishman - U17 100H race
400H:	51.8 McRae London (Ha) 10 Jun
HJ:	2.01 Macfarlane
PV:	4.13 Coats and Fordham at Sheffield, 3.60 Rees 17.9.85, Allen 9.7.85
LJ:	7.46 0.0 Eyong, 7.18 Wells at Southend, Lau 1J, 6.85 Burgess 21.3.83, 6.81 Daniel Williams U23 26.3.81
TJ:	14.53 Farquharson 10 Jul, 14.12w Bell 7.9.84
HT:	delete 48.29 Melluish (6kg hammer), 46.66 Alex Bailey .81 Saint-Dizier, FRA 2 Jun
JT:	68.78 McLellan - venue Carquefou
JTY:	Note: van der Merwe U20 68.78 1 Murcia, ESP 25 Jul
JTB:	51.34 Hutcheson 27 Aug, 49.04 Johnson 8 Sep
JTC:	35.03 Batten 10.3.89
Pent:	2974 Nanci LJ -5.37, 2641 Yao 15 Sep
3000mW:	12:56.52 Daniel King (2) London (WF) 19 Aug (12:40.8 was by Dominic King), 12:37.8 Goudie
10kW:	45:16 Daniel King U20 30.5.83 2 Leicester 2 Sep
4x400:	3:00.96 (Hylton 46.1, Thomas 44.9...)

WOMEN 2001

200m:	25.1 Wardrop
300m:	41.0 Victoria Wester
1500m:	4:44.94 Emma-Lisa Carroll, 4:45.7i Pidgeon U15 at time of race
3000m:	9:55.71i Pidgeon U15 at time of race
5000m:	16:18.62 Sullivan d.o.b 13.2.72 (and correct in other events)
5kR:	16:41 Damen @ Boscombe
8kR:	25:25 Butler was in 8km race and not a split time
2000mSt:	7:11.2 B. Frost
400mH	59.5 Hodge - St. Ives
PV:	3.10 Nichols position 3, 2.90 Dorrian pos 3
SP:	12.77i Rodger was U20 by time of event, 10.84 Francis U13
HT:	32.30 Katherine Newton
JT:	41.71 Chrissie Head, 31.16 Carr U13
3000W:	15:06.0 Véronique Lauer FRA 27.2.74 1 Enfield 23 May
5kWR:	24:19 Hales was U20 by time of race, best as U17 25:10 4 Budapest, HUN 9 Sep;
	delete 26:11 Chrismas (2000 mark)
20kWR:	1:39:41 Cattermole - at Murdoch
100kWR:	add 11:59:16+ Sandra Brown m Roubaix, FRA 16 Sep 2001
4x100:	49.83 JER 13 Jul
4x400:	3:26,94 (McConnell 52.2...), 3:27.25 (McConnell 52.4, Owusu 51.8...),
	3:35:55 SCO - all athletes member of Edinburgh WM; 3:59.78 JER & 4:04.55 IOM 13 Jul